The Fontana
English
Dictionary

The Fontana English Dictionary

Edited under the direction of
A. H. Irvine, M.A. (Hons.)
Officier d' Académie

Collins
FONTANA BOOKS

General Editor: J. B. Foreman
First Published 1967
Second Impression August 1970
Third Impression October 1974

© 1967
William Collins Sons & Co. Ltd.
Printed in Great Britain by
William Collins Sons & Co Ltd, Glasgow

Contents

key to pronunciation

(a) Apart from "g" (always hard as in *get*) the consonants retain their name-sounds.

(b) All unmarked vowels are sounded as in *pat, pet, pit, pot, nut*.

(c) Special symbols used are:—

(i)	ā	as in	late		ō	as in	vote
	å	,,	far		ôò	,,	moon
	ạ	,,	ado		oo	,,	wood
	ē	,,	me		ū	,,	tune
	ẹ	,,	her		aw	,,	awl
	ī	,,	mite		ou	,,	foul

(ii)	th	,,	thin		hw	,,	when
	TH	,,	then		ch	,,	church
	H	,,	loch		j	,,	jam
	zh	,,	leisure		y	,,	yet

(d) The French nasal vowels (*an, on, in, un*), so difficult to interpret accurately, have been reduced to the following simple approximations:—

an, am, en, em	=	ong
on, om	=	ōng
in	=	ang
un	=	ung

For example, embonpoint=ong-bōng-pwang

abbreviations used in this dictionary

a. adjective
Abbrev. abbreviation
adv. adverb
Anat. Anatomy
Anglo-Ind. Anglo-Indian
Anthropol. Anthropology
Arch. Archaic
Archit. Architecture
Astrol. Astrology
Astron. Astronomy
Austral. Australia
aux. auxiliary
Aviat. Aviation

B.C. before Christ
Bib. Biblical
Biol. Biology
Bot. Botany

Ch. Church
Chem. Chemistry
Class. Hist. Classical
  History
Colloq. Colloquial
Comm. Commerce
compar. comparative
conj. conjunction
contr. contraction

demons. demonstrative

E. East
Eccl. Ecclesiastical
e.g. for example
Elect. Electricity
esp. especially

fem. feminine
Fig. Figuratively
form. formerly
fr. from

Geog. Geography

Geolog. Geology
Geom. Geometry
GK. Greek
Gram. Grammar

Her. Heraldry
Hist. History, Historical
Hort. Horticulture

i. intransitive
inc. including
indic. indicative
interj. interjection

L. Latin
Lit. literally

Math. Mathematics
Med. Medicine
Meteor. Meteorology
Mil. Military
MS(S) Manuscript(s)
Mus. Music
Myth. Mythology

n. noun
N. North
Naut. Nautical
n. pl. noun plural
n. sing. noun singular
N.T. New Testament

obs. obsolete
opp. opposite, opposed
Opt. Optics
orig. originally
O.T. Old Testament

Paint. Painting
pa. p. past participle
pa. t. past tense
Path. Pathology
pers. personal

pert. pertaining (to)
Phil. Philology
Philos. Philosophy
Phon. Phonetics
Photog. Photography
Phys. Physics
Physiol. Physiology
pl. plural
Poet. poetic
poss. possessive
prep. preposition
pres. present
Print. Printing
pron. pronoun
pr. p. present participle
Psych. Psychology

R.C. Roman Catholic
reflex. reflexive
Rev. Revelation

S. South
S. Afr. South Africa
Scot. Scottish
sing. singular
superl. superlative
Surg. surgery

t. transitive
Theat. Theatre
Theol. Theology

U.S. United States (of
  America)
usu. usually

v. verb
v.i. verb intransitive
viz. namely
v.t. verb transitive

W. West
Zool. Zoology

A

A (ā, ạ) *a*, indefinite article, meaning *one*. It is a contraction of *an*.

A1 (ā wun) denotes a ship listed as "first-class" in Lloyd's Register of Shipping; hence, first-rate, excellent; physically fit.

ab- (ab) L. prefix meaning from, away, off.

aback (ạ-bak') *adv.* backward; on the back; (*Naut.*) against the masts, of sails pressed back by the wind.—**taken aback**, taken by surprise; disconcerted.

abacus (ab'-ạ-kus) *n.* instrument with parallel wires on which calculations are made with sliding balls or beads; a counting-frame; (*Archit.*) tablet crowning a column and its capital.

abaft (ạ-baft) *adv.* and *prep.* (*Naut.*) at or towards the stern; behind.

abandon (ạ-ban'-don) *v.t.* give up wholly and finally; relinquish; surrender; *n.* careless freedom; a yielding to unrestrained impulse; dash.—**aban'doned** *a.* deserted; forsaken; unrestrained; given up entirely to, esp. wickedness.—**aban'donedly** *adv.*—**aban'donment** *n.* act of abandoning, or state of being abandoned; (*Law*) the relinquishing of a claim.

abase (ạ-bās') *v.t.* bring low; cast down; humble.—**abase'ment** *n.* humiliation.

abash (ạ-bash') *v.t.* strike with shame or fear; excite a consciousness of guilt, inferiority, etc.—**abash'ment** *n.* confusion from shame, etc.

abate (ạ-bāt') *v.t.* beat down, lessen; (*Law*) put an end to, as a nuisance; annul, as a writ;—*v.i.* decrease, subside, decline.—**abat'able** *a.*—**abate'ment** *n.*—**abat'er** *n.*

abattoir (a-ba-twär') *n.* slaughter-house, esp. one under a local government authority.

abbacy (ab'-ạ-si) *n.* office or dignity of an abbot; building under control of an abbot; abbey.—**abbatial** (ạ-bā'-shạl) *a.* pert. to an abbot, or abbey.—**abbé** (ab'-ā) *n.* designation of an R.C. priest in France; abbot.—**abb'ey** *n.* church establishment forming dwelling-place of a community of monks or nuns.—**abb'ot** (*fem.* abb'ess) *n.* head of an abbey or monastery.—**abb'otship** *n.*

abbreviate (a-brē'-vi-āt) *v.t.* shorten, reduce by contraction or omission.—**abbrevia'tion** *n.* act of abbreviating; a shortened form.—**abbre'viator** *n.*—**abbre'viatory** *a.*

abdicate (ab'-di-kāt) *v.t.* and *i.* formally give up power or office.—**abdica'tion** *n.*

abdomen (ab-dō'-men, ab'-dō-men) *n.* the lower part of the trunk of the body; the belly.—**abdom'inal** *a.* pert. to abdomen.—**abdom'inous** *a.* having a big belly; paunchy.

abduct (ab-dukt') *v.t.* take away by fraud or force; kidnap; (*Anat.*) draw e.g. a limb, away from its natural position.—**abducent** (ab-dū'-sent) *a.* (*Anat.*) abducting.—**abduc'tion** *n.*

abeam (ạ-bēm') *adv.* (*Naut.*) at right angles to ship's length; hence, straight across a ship; abreast.

abed (ạ-bed') *adv.* in bed.

aberrate (ab'-er-āt) *v.i.* deviate from the right path or normal course.—**aber'rant** *a.* deviating from normal.—**aberra'tion** *n.* a wandering, esp. mental disorder, forgetfulness; moral lapse; defect in optical system.

abet (ạ-bet') *v.t.* encourage or aid, esp. in doing wrong.—*pr.p.* abet'ting.—*pa.p.* and *pa.t.* abet'ted.—**abet'ment** *n.*—**abet'ter**, **abet'tor** *n.*

abeyance (ạ-bā'-ạns) *n.* state of suspension or temporary inactivity; condition of not being in use or action. Also **abey'ancy.**

abhor (ab-hor') *v.t.* hate extremely.—*pr.p.* abhor'ring.—*pa.p.* and *pa.t.* abhorred'.—**abhor'rence** *n.* detestation.—**abhor'rent** *a.* detestable; abominable; repugnant.—**abhor'rer** *n.*

abide (ạ-bīd') *v.i.* stay; reside; continue firm or stable;—*v.t.* tolerate; bear; wait for.—*pa.p.* and *pa.t.* abode'.—**abid'ance** *n.*—**abid'ing** *a.* lasting; enduring.

Abigail (ab'-i-gāl) *n.* (*Bib.*) wife of David (See I Sam. 25); also name of a sister of David.—**ab'igail** *n.* waiting-maid; lady's maid.

ability (ạ-bil'-i-ti) *n.* quality, state, or condition of being able; power to act; skill; capacity; competence.

abject (ab'-jekt) *a.* base; degraded; mean and worthless; contemptible; miserable.—**ab'jectly** *adv.*—**abjec'tion**, **ab'jectness** *n.* degradation; abasement; servility.

abjure (ab-jōōr') *v.t.* renounce upon oath; abandon allegiance to a cause, doctrine, or principle; repudiate; forswear.—**abjura'tion** *n.*

ablative (ab'-lạ-tiv) *a.* (used as *n.*) sixth case of Latin nouns and pronouns expressing *time when*; originally implied *separation from.*—**ablati'val** *a.*

ablaze (a-blāz') *a.* on fire; aglow; gleaming.

able (ā'-bl) *a.* (*comp.* a'bler; *superl.*

a'blest) having skill, strength to perform a task; competent; talented; vigorous.—**a'ble-bod'ied** *a.* of sound body; robust; (of a seaman, *abbrev.* **A.B.**) having all-round knowledge of seamanship.—**a'bleness, abil'ity** *n.*—**a'bly** *adv.* competently.

ablution (ab-lōō'-shun) *n.* cleansing or washing (usually pl.); ritual purification; (pl.) wash-place.—**ablu'tionary** *a.*

abnegate (ab'-ne-gāt) *v.t.* deny; surrender; relinquish.—**abnega'tion** *n.* denying; renunciation.

abnormal (ab-nor'-mạl) *a.* contrary to rule or system; deviating from a recognised standard; exceptional; psychologically maladjusted. Also **abnor'mous.**—**abnor'malism** *n.*—**abnormal'ity** *n.* the state of being abnormal; deformity; idiosyncrasy.—**abnor'mally** *adv.*—**abnor'mity** *n.* abnormality; monstrosity.

aboard (ạ-bōrd') *adv.* and *prep.* (*Naut.*) on board; within a vessel, train or aircraft.

abode (ạ-bōd') *n.* residence, permanent or temporary; a dwelling-place.

abolish (ạ-bol'-ish) *v.t.* do away with; repeal; obliterate.—**abol'ishment** *n.*—**aboli'tion** *n.* act of abolishing, as of laws, taxes, etc.—**aboli'tional** *a.*—**aboli'tionism** *n.* policy of abolition, esp. of slavery.—*n.* **abolit'ionist.**

abominate (ạ-bom'-i-nāt) *v.t.* loathe; detest extremely; abhor.—**abom'inable** *a.* loathsome; morally detestable; odious.—**abom'inableness** *n.*—**abom'inably** *adv.*—**abomina'tion** *n.* act or object of loathing; a despicable practice.

aborigines (ab-o-rij'-i-nēz) *n.pl.* the original inhabitants of a country, e.g. "black-fellows" of Australia or Maoris of New Zealand.—**aborig'inal** *n. sing.* and *a.*

abort (ab-ort') *v.i.* miscarry in giving birth; (*Fig.*) fail to come to fruition.—**abortifac'ient** *n.* drug causing abortion;—*a.* capable of producing abortion.—**abor'tion** *n.* termination of pregnancy before 28th week.—**abor'tionist** *n.*—**abor'tive** *a.* prematurely produced; undeveloped; imperfect.—**abor'tively** *adv.*

abound (ạ-bound') *v.i.* be in great plenty (used with preps. *with* and *in*).—**abound'ing** *a.* plentiful.

about (ạ-bout') *adv.* and *prep.* on every side; concerning; approximately; (before an infin.) on the point of.—**to bring about,** to effect.

above (ạ-buv') *adv.* and *prep.* and *a.* higher than; more in number, quantity, or degree.—*a.* previously mentioned.—**above board,** open or openly; honourably.

abracadabra (ab'-rạ-kạ-dab'-rạ) *n.* corrupt. of ancient Egyptian magi-cal formula; catchword; gibberish.

abrade (ab-rād') *v.t.* rub or wear off; scrape or grate off; graze (of skin).—**abra'dant** *n.* substance, e.g. emery powder, for polishing.—**abra'ding** *n.* soil-erosion.—**abra'sion** *n.* rubbing or scraping off; grazing of the skin.—**abra'sive** *a.* tending to abrade; scouring.—*n.* something used for scouring.

abreast (ạ-brest') *adv.* side by side; on a line with.

abridge (ạ-brij') *v.t.* shorten; curtail; reduce; diminish.—**abridg'ment, abridge'ment** *n.* a cutting-off; summary; précis; abstract of evidence.—**abridg'er** *n.*

abroad (ạ-brawd') *adv.* and *a.* at large, over a wide space; beyond or out of house, camp, or enclosure; in foreign countries; overseas; (*obs.*) perplexed, quite wrong.

abrogate (ab'-rō-gāt) *v.t.* annul; repeal (a law).—**abroga'tion** *n.*

abrupt (ạ-brupt') *a.* broken off; steep; precipitous; describing sudden change of subject, etc., in speech or writing; curt; brusque; (*Bot.*) without a terminal leaf.—**abrup'tion** *n.* a breaking off; wrenching asunder.—**abrupt'ly** *adv.*—**abrupt'ness** *n.*

abscess (ab'-ses) *n.* gathering of pus in any infected organ or tissue of the body.

abscind (ab-sind') *v.t.* cut off; pare away; separate; rend apart.—**ab'sciss, absciss'sa** *n.* (*Geom.*) the distance of a point from a fixed line measured horizontally;—*pl.* **absciss'ses, absciss'-ae.**—**abscis'sion** *n.* act or process of cutting off.

abscond (ab-skond') *v.i.* take oneself off; flee from justice.—**abscon'dence** *n.*—**abscon'der** *n.*

absence (ab'-sens) *n.* being absent; failure to appear.—**ab'sent** *a.* not present; inattentive.—**absent'** *v.t.* withdraw(oneself); deliberately fail to appear.—**absentee'** *n.* one who is not present.—**absentee'ism** *n.* habitual absence from work or duty.—**ab'sently** *adv.* casually; forgetfully.—**ab'sent-minded** *a.* abstracted; absorbed; preoccupied.

absinth, absinthe (ab'-sinth) *n.* green-coloured liqueur flavoured with wormwood and other aromatics.

absolute (ab'-sō-lōōt, (-lūt)) *a.* uncontrolled; unconditional; without restraint; pure.—**ab'solutely** *adv.* positively; very; entirely.—**ab'soluteness** *n.*—**absolu'tion** *n.* remission of sin after confession; acquittal.—**absol'utory,** *a.*—**absolutism** *n.* dictatorship.—**ab'solutist** *n.*

absolve (ab-solv') *v.t.* set free from obligation, guilt, debt, penalty; pardon; acquit.—**absolv'er** *n.*—**absol-v'atory** *a.*

absorb (ab-sorb') *v.t.* swallow up; drink in; suck up; engage one's whole attention.—**absorbabil'ity** *n.*—**absorb'-able** *a.*—**absorbefac'ient** *n.* that which causes absorption; a drying up;—*a.* absorbing rapidly.—**absorb'ent** *a.* absorbing;—*n.* anything which absorbs.

absorption (ab-sorp'-shun) *n.* the act of absorbing.—**absorp'tive** *a.* able to absorb.—**absorptiv'ity** *n.* the power of absorbing.

abstain (ab-stān') *v.i.* refrain.—**abstain'er** *n.* one who abstains, esp. from alcohol.

abstemious (ab-stēm'-i-us) *a.* showing moderation in the use of food and drink.—**abstem'-iously** *adv.*—**abstem'iousness** *n.*

abstention (ab-sten'-shun) *n.* act of abstaining or refraining from.—**absten'tionist** *n.*

abstinence (abs'-tin-ens) *n.* voluntary forbearance from using or doing something. Also **abs'tinency**.—**abs'-tinent** *a.* temperate; refraining from.—**abs'tinently** *adv.*

abstract (ab-strakt') *v.t.* separate from; remove, esp. secretly, for one's own use; summarise; reduce.—**ab'stract** *a.* not concrete; theoretical;—*n.* that which comprises in itself the essential qualities of a larger thing, or of several things; summary.—**abstrac'tion** *n.* abstracting or separating; theoretical idea;—**in the abstract**, without reference to particular cases.

abstruse (ab-strōōs') *a.* hidden; difficult or hard to be understood.—**abstruse'ly** *adv.*—**abstruse'ness** *n.*

absurd (ab-surd') *a.* contrary to reason; ridiculous; silly.—**absurd'ly** *adv.*—**absurd'ity** *n.* that which is absurd. Also **absurd'ness**.

abundance (a-bun'-dans) *n.* ample sufficiency; great plenty.—**abun'dant** *a.*—**abun'dantly** *adv.*

abuse (a-būz') *v.t.* make a wrong use of; ill-treat; violate; revile; malign.—**abuse** (a-būs') *n.* ill-usage; improper treatment; a corrupt practice; rude language.—**abu'sive** *a.* practising abuse; insulting.—**abu'siveness** *n.*

abut (a-but') *v.i.* end; touch with one end; border on; adjoin.—*pr.p.* **abut'ting**—*pa.p.* **abut'ted.**—**abut'ment** *n.* (*Archit.*) support at end of arch or bridge.

abyss (a-bis') *n.* any deep chasm; gulf.—**aby'smal** *a.* bottomless; vast; profound.—**abys'mally** *adv.*—**abyss'al** *a.* inhabiting, or characteristic of, the depths of the ocean; abysmal.

acacia (a-kā'-shi-a) *n.* genus of leguminous wattle; mimosa.

academy (a-kad'-e-mi) *n.* garden or grove near Athens, where Plato taught philosophy; place of education or specialised training; society for the promotion of the arts and sciences.—**academ'ic, academ'ical** *a.* pert. to an institution of learning; pert. to Platonic philosophy; scholarly; pedantic.—**academician** *n.* (a-kad-e-mish'-an).

acanthus (a-kan'-thus) *n.* prickly plant, also called "bear's breech" or "brank-ursine"; (*Archit.*) an ornament like this leaf, esp. on the capitals of Corinthian pillars.

acarus (ak'-ar-us) *n.* (*Zool.*) group of animal parasites; mites, ticks, etc.

accede (ak-sēd') *v.i.* assent; consent; arrive at a certain state; succeed as heir.—**acced'er** *n.*

accelerate (ak-sel'-e-rāt) *v.t.* and *i.* cause to move faster; become swifter.—**accelera'tion** *n.* increase in speed, etc.; rate of increase in the velocity of a moving body.—**accel'erative** *a.* quickening.—**accel'erator** *n.* mechanism for increasing speed; machine for accelerating charged atomic particles e.g. cyclotron; substance which speeds chemical reaction.—**accel'-eratory** *a.*

accent (ak'-sent) *n.* stress on a syllable or syllables of a word; mark to show this; inflection of the voice; manner of speech; pronunciation and inflection of the voice peculiar to a country, town, or individual.—**accent** (ak-sent') *v.t.* utter, pronounce, or mark with accent; emphasise; stress.—**accent'ual** *a.*—**accent'uate** *v.t.* accent; stress; make more prominent.—**accentua'tion** *n.*

accept (ak-sept') *v.t.* take; receive; admit; believe; agree to; (*Comm.*) agree to meet a bill.—**accept'able** *a.* welcome; pleasing; agreeable.—**accept'ably** *adv.*—**accept'ance** *n.* act of accepting.—**accepta'tion** *n.* usual meaning of a word, statement, etc.—**accept'ed** *a.*—**accept'er, accept'or** *n.*

access (ak'-ses) *n.* a coming to the means or way of approach; admission; entrance; attack; fit.—**access'ary** *a.* (See accessory).—**access'ible** *a.* easy of access or approach; approachable.—**accessibil'ity** *n.*—**acces'sion** *n.* increase; a coming to, esp. to throne, office, or dignity.—**accessory** (ak-ses'-o-ri, ak'-ses-or-i), *a.* aiding; contributing; additional;—*n.* additional, secondary piece of equipment.—**access'ary** *n.* and *a.* (*Law*) one implicated in a felony (though not as a principal).

accident (ak'-si-dent) *n.* chance; mishap; casualty; contingency;—**accidental** *a.* occurring by chance.—(*Mus.*) *n.* sharp, flat or natural not implicit in key signature.—**accident'ally** *adv.*—**accident-prone** *a.* having abnormal predisposition to accidents.

acclaim (a-klām') *v.t.* and *i.* receive with applause, etc.; cheer; hail as;—**acclama'tion** *n.* general applause.—**acclam'atory** *a.*

acclimatise (ạ-klī'-mạ-tīz) *v.t.* accustom to a new climate. Also **accli'mate.—acclimatisa'tion** *n.* Also **acclima'tion, acclimatisa'tion** *n.*

accolade (ak'-ō-lād) *n.* ceremony used in conferring knighthood.

accommodate (ạ-kom'-ō-dāt) *v.t.* render fit or suitable; adapt; adjust; reconcile; provide room for.—**accom'modating** *a.* obliging.—**accommoda'tion** *n.* convenience; room or space for; lodgings; loan of money.—**accom'modative** *a.*

accompany (ạ-kum'-pạ-ni) *v.t.* go with; (*Mus.*) play the accompaniment.—**accom'paniment** *n.* that which goes with; (*Mus.*) the instrumental parts played with vocal or solo instrumental part.—**accom'panist** *n.*

accomplice (ạ-kom'-plis) *n.* companion in evil deeds; an associate in crime.

accomplish (ạ-kom'-plish) *v.t.* carry out; finish; complete; perform.—**accom'plished** *a.* complete; skilled.

accord (ạ-kord') *n.* agreement; harmony;—*v.t.* grant; settle; compose; *v.i.* agree; agree in pitch and tone.—**accord'ance** *n.*—**accord'ant** *a.*—**accord'ing** *a.*—**accord'ingly** *adv.*—of one's own accord, of one's own free will.

accordion (ạ-kor'-di-on) *n.* wind instrument fitted with bellows and button keyboards; in the piano-accordion the right-hand keyboard is like that of a piano.—**accor'dion-pleat'ed** *a.* having narrow folds like those of the bellows of an accordion.

accost (ạ-kost') *v.t.* speak first to; address.

account (ạ-kount') *n.* reckoning; record; report; description; statement of debts and credits; value; advantage; profit;—*v.t.* reckon, judge;—*v.i.* give a reason; give a financial reckoning.—**account'able** *a.* liable to be held responsible; able to be explained.—**account'ably** *adv.*—**accountabil'ity** *n.*—**account'ancy** *n.* profession of an accountant.—**account'ant** *n.* one trained in recording financial transactions.

accoutre (ạ-kōō'-tẹr) *v.t.* furnish with dress or equipment, esp. military; equip.—**accou'trements** *n.pl.* dress; military dress and equipment.

accredit (ạ-kred'-it) *v.t.* give trust or confidence to; vouch for; recommend; furnish with credentials, as an ambassador.

accretion (ạ-krē'-shun) *n.* increase in growth, esp. by addition of parts externally.—**accret'ive** *a.*

accrue (ạ-krōō') increase; result naturally; come as an addition, e.g. interest, profit, etc.

accumulate (ạ-kū'-mū-lāt) *v.t.* heap up; collect;—*v.i.* grow into a mass; increase.—**accumula'tion** *n.* collection; mass; pile.—**accu'mulative** *a.*—**accu'-**

mulatively *adv.*—**accu'mulator** *n.* collector; apparatus for storage of electricity; cumulative bet on four or more races.

accurate (ak'-ū-rāt) *a.* correct.—**ac'curately** *adv.*—**ac'curacy** *n.* correctness; exactness; precision.

accurse (ạ-kurs') *v.t.* doom to destruction; curse.—**accurs'ed** *a.* under a curse.

accuse (ạ-kūz') *v.t.* charge with a crime or fault; blame.—**accused'** *a.* charged with a crime;—*n.* one so charged.—**accus'er** *n.*—**accusa'tion** *n.* a charge.—**accus'ative** *a.* producing or containing accusations; (*Gram.*) of the case which forms the direct object of a transitive verb;—*n.* the accusative case.—**accus'atory** *a.*

accustom (ạ-kus'-tom) *v.t.* make familiar by use; familiarise; habituate.—**accus'tomed** *a.*

ace (ās) *n.* card, domino, etc. with only one spot; single point; particle; the best, highest; outstanding performer in any field.

acerbate (ạ-ser'-bāt, as'-ẹr-bāt) *v.t.* make bitter; exasperate;—*a.* embittered; severe; exasperated.—**acer'bitude** *n.*—**acer'bity** *n.*

acetic (ạ-set'-ik, ạ-sē'-tik) *a.* pert. to acetic acid, the acid in vinegar.—**a'cetate** *n.* (*Chem.*) a salt formed by acetic acid.—**acet'ify** *v.t.* and *v.i.* turn into vinegar.—**acetifica'tion** *n.*—**acetous** (ạ-sē'-tus) *a.* sour.—**acetylene** (ạ-set'-i-lēn) *n.* highly inflammable gas used as an illuminant.

ache (āk) *n.* a continuous pain; dull, heavy pain;—*v.i.* be in pain.—**ach'ing** *a.* and *n.*

achieve (ạ-chēv') *v.t.* bring to a successful end; accomplish.—**achiev'able** *a.*—**achieve'ment** *n.* performance; feat; attainment; commemorative armorial shield.

achromatic (ak-rō-mat'-ik) *a.* (*Opt.*) free from colour; transmitting light without decomposing it.—**achromaticity, achro'matism** *n.*—**achro'matise** *v.t.* deprive of colour.

acid (as'-id) *a.* sour; sharp to the taste; having properties of an acid;—*n.* (*Chem.*) substance which dissolves in water and forms hydrogen ions, or which contains hydrogen replaceable by metals in reactions which form salts.—**acid'ify** *v.t.* and *i.* make or become sour; turn into an acid.—**acid'ity** *n.* state or quality of being acid; sourness; sharpness.—**acid'ulate** *v.t.* make slightly acid or sour; (*Fig.*) embitter.—**acid'ulated, acid'ulous** *a.*—**acid test** (*Fig.*) conclusive proof of genuineness.

acknowledge (ak-nol'-ej) *v.t.* admit as true; give a receipt for; give thanks for; reward.—**acknowl'edgment, acknowl'edgement** *n.*

acme (ak'-mē) *n.* the highest point,

top; perfection; (*Med.*) crisis of an illness.

acolyte (ak'-ō-līt) *n.* candidate for priesthood; lesser church officer; assistant; novice.

aconite (ak'-o-nīt) *n.* (*Bot.*) wolf's-bane or monk's-hood; poisonous drug extracted from it.—**acon'itine** *n.* poisonous substance in aconite.

acorn (ā'-korn) *n.* seed or fruit of the oak.

acoustic (a-koŏ'-stik a-kou'-stik) *a.* pert. to sense of hearing.—**acou'stics** *n.pl.* science of sounds; estimation of audibility in a theatre, etc.

acquaint (a-kwānt') *v.t.* make fully known or familiar; inform.—**ac-quaint'ance** *n.* familiar knowledge; person known slightly.—**acquaint'-anceship** *n.*

acquiesce (ak-wi-es') *v.i.* agree in silence; assent.—**acquies'cence** *n.* silent assent.—**acquies'cent** *a.* sub-missive; consenting.

acquire (a-kwīr') *v.t.* gain; obtain; get.—**acquir'able** *a.*—**acquire'ment** *n.*—**acquisi'tion** *n.* act of acquiring; thing acquired.—**acquisitive** (a-kwiz'-i-tiv) *a.* grasping; greedy for gain.—**acquis'itiveness** *n.*

acquit (a-kwit') *v.t.* set free; release; declare innocent; conduct oneself; discharge a debt.—*pr.p.* **acquitt'ing.**—*pa.p.* and *pa.t.* **acquitt'ed.**—**acquitt'al** *n.* judicial release; declaration of "not guilty."—**acquitt'ance** *n.*

acre (ā'-ker) *n.* measure of land con-taining 4840 square yards.—**a'creage** *n.* extent of a piece of land in acres.

acrid (ak'-rid) *a.* bitter; sharp; pungent; harsh; ill-tempered.—**ac'-ridly** *adv.*—**acrid'ity, ac'ridness** *n.*

acrimony (ak'-ri-mon-i) *n.* bitter-ness of temper or language.—**acrimonious** (ak-ri-mō'-ni-us) *a.* sharp; bitter; stinging; sarcastic.—**acrimo'-niously** *adv.*

acrobat (ak'-rō-bat) *n.* one skilled in gymnastic feats; rope-dancer; tumbler.—**acrobat'ic** *a.*—**acrobatics** *n.*

acronym (ak'ro-nim) *n.* word formed from initial letters of other words, e.g. NATO.

across (a-kros') *adv.* and *prep.* from side to side; transversely; athwart; at an angle with.

acrostic (a-kros'-tik) *n.* composition in verse, in which the first, and sometimes last, letters of the lines read in order form a name, a sentence or title.

act (akt) *v.t.* perform, esp. upon stage; behave as;—*v.i.* exert energy; fulfil a function; operate; dissemble.—*n.* deed; performance; decree; principal division of a play.—**act'ing** *a.* per-forming a duty; performing on the stage; deputising for, as *Acting Captain.*—*n.* action.—**act'or** *n.* one who performs on a stage.—**act'ress** *n.*

female actor.—**Act of Parliament,** written law of a country.

action (ak'-shun) *n.* thing done; be-haviour; physical movement; func-tion; battle; development of events in a play, etc.; legal proceedings; (*Chem.*) effect.—**ac'tionable** *a.* afford-ing grounds for legal proceedings.—**ac'tionably** *adv.*—**ac'tive** *a.* having power to act; agile; busy; alert.—**ac'tively** *adv.*—**activ'ity, ac'tiveness** *n.*

actual (ak'-tū-al) *a.* existing now or as a fact; real; effectual.—**act'ualise** *v.t.* make real in fact or by vivid description.—**act'ualist** *n.* realist.—**actual'ity** *n.* reality, existence.—**act'ually** *adv.*

actuary (ak'-tū-ar-i) *n.* registrar or clerk; official who calculates for insurance companies.—**actua'rial** *a.*—**actua'rially** *adv.*

actuate (ak'-tū-āt) *v.t.* put into action; incite; motivate; influence.—**actua'tion** *n.*

acumen (a-kū'-men) *n.* quickness of perception or discernment; sharp-ness; penetration.—**acu'minous** *a.*

acute (a-kūt) *a.* sharp; pointed; subtle; penetrating; shrill; (*Med.*) of disease with severe symptoms and sharp crisis, (*Geom.*) less than a right angle.—**acute'ly** *adv.*—**acute'ness,** acuity *n.*—**acute accent,** mark (') over a letter, as in French, to indicate pronunciation.

adage (ad'-āj) *n.* saying or maxim that has obtained credit by long use; proverb; byword.—**adag'ial** *a.*

adagio (a-dä'-jō) *adv.* (*Mus.*) slowly. —*n.* slow movement.

adamant (ad'-a-mant) *n.* a stone of impenetrable hardness; the diamond. —*a.* very hard; unyielding.—**adaman'-tine** *a.*

adapt (a-dapt') *v.t.* make fit or suitable; make to correspond.—**adaptabil'ity, adapt'ableness** *n.* quality of being adaptable.—**adapt'able** *a.* may be adapted; versatile.—**adapta'-tion** *n.* gradual process of adjustment to new physical conditions exhibited by living organisms.—**adap'ter, -or** *n.* any appliance which makes possible a union of two different parts of an apparatus.—**adap'tive** *a.*—**adap'tively** *adv.*—**adap'tiveness** *n.*

add (ad) *v.t.* join, unite to form one sum or whole; annex; increase; say further.—**add'able, add'ible** *a.*—**add'er** *n.* one who adds; machine which adds:—**addibil'ity** *n.*—**addi'tion** *n.*—**addi'tional** *a.* supplementary; extra.—**addi'tionally** *adv.*—**add'itive** *a.* to be added; of the nature of an addition.

addendum (a-den'-dum) *n.* thing to be added; appendix esp. to a written work.—*pl.* **adden'da.**

adder (ad'-er) *n.* venomous serpent.

addict (a-dikt') *v.t.* apply habitually; habituate.—**ad'dict** *n.* one who has acquired compulsive habit.—**addict'-ed** *a.*—**addic'tion** *n.*

addle (ad'-l) *v.t.* corrupt; putrefy; confuse.—**add'le, add'led** *a.*—**add'le-brained, -head'ed, -pa'ted** *a.* muddle-headed.

address (ą-dres') *v.t.* direct in writing, as a letter; apply (oneself); make a speech; accost; —*n.* formal speech; manner of speaking; direction of letter; skill.—**address'es** *n. pl.* attentions in courtship.—**addressee'** *n.* person to whom communication is sent.—**address'er** *n.*

adduce (ą-dūs') *v.t.* bring forward as proof; cite; quote.—**adduc'er** *n.*—**adduc'ible** *a.*—**adduc'tion** *n.* drawing together or bringing forward.—**adduc'tive** *a.* tending to bring together —**adduc'tor** *n.* adducent muscle.

aden(o)- (ą'-den-(o)-) combining form (fr. Gk. *aden*, gland).—**ad'-enoid, ad'enoidal** *a.* glandular; gland-shaped.—**ad'enoids** *n.pl.* swelling of tissue between nose and throat.

adept (ą-dept', ad'ept) *n.* one skilled in any art; expert;—*a.*; (ą-dept') expert.

adequate (ad'-e-kwăt) *a.* equal to; sufficient.—**ad'equacy, ad'equateness** *n.*—**ad'equately** *adv.*

adhere (ąd-hēr') *v.i.* stick fast; be devoted to; hold to (an opinion).—**adher'ence** *n.* state of adhering; steady attachment.—**adher'ent** *a.* united with or to;—*n.* supporter of person or cause.—**adhe'sion** *n.* act of adhering.—**adhes'ive** *a.* sticky; tenacious;—*n.* agent which sticks things together.—**adhes'ively** *adv.*—**adhes'iveness** *n.*

adieu (ą-dū') *interj.* good-bye; farewell.—*n.* a farewell; a leave-taking.—*pl.* adieus, adieux (ą-dūz').

adipose (adi-'-pōs) *a.* pert. to animal fat; fatty.—**adiposity** (ad-i-pos'-i-ti) *n.* fatness.

adjacent (ą-jā'-sent) *a.* lying close to; adjoining; bordering on.—**adja'-cently** *adv.*—**adja'cency** *n.*

adjective (ad'-jek-tiv) *n.* word used with noun to qualify, limit, or define it;—*a.* pert. to adjective.—**adjecti'val** *a.*—**adjecti'vally** *adv.*

adjoin (ą-join') *v.t.* join or unite to; be next or contiguous to;—*v.i.* be next to.—**adjoin'ing** *a.*

adjourn (ą-jurn') *v.t.* put off to another day.—**adjourn'ment** *n.* post-poning; deferring of business.

adjudge (ą-juj') *v.t.* settle judicially; pronounce judgment; award; regard or deem.—**adjudg'ment** *n.*—**adjudicate** (ą-jŏŏ'-di-kāt) *v.t.* settle judicially; —*v.i.* pronounce judgment.—**adjudica'tion** *n.*—**adju'dicator** *n.* judge.

adjunct (ad'-jungkt) *n.* something joined to another thing, but not essential to it; (*Gram.*) word or phrase added to modify meaning;

—*a.* added to; united with.—**adjunc'-tive**—**adjunc'tively** *adv.*

adjure (ąd-jŏŏr') *v.t.* charge or bind, under oath; entreat earnestly.—**adjura'tion** *n.* solemn command on oath; earnest appeal.—**adjur'atory** *a.*

adjust (ą-just') *v.t.* adapt; put in order; alter.—*v.i.* accommodate oneself.—**adjust'able** *a.*—**adjust'ment** *n.* arrangement; settlement; adaptation.

adjutant (ad'-jŏŏ-tant) *n.* assistant; executive officer to unit commander.

admass (ad'-mas) *n.* body of the public at which advertising in general is aimed.

admeasure (ąd-mezh'-ūr) *v.t.* take the dimensions of; (*Law*) apportion. —**admeas'urement** *n.*, **admensura'tion** *n.*

administer (ąd-min'-is-ter) *v.t.* manage public affairs or estate; dispense, as justice or relief; give, as medicine; apply, as punishment or reproof; (*Law*) settle estate of one who has died intestate;—*v.i.* give aid (to).—**admin'istrable** *a.*—**administra'tion** *n.*—**admin'istrative** *a.*—**administra'tor** *n.* (*fem.* **administra'trix**).

admiral (ad'-mi-rąl) *n.* naval officer of the highest rank (graded as-admiral, vice-admiral, or rear-admiral).—**Admiral of the Fleet,** title corresponding to field-marshal in the army.—**Admiralty** *n.* Lords Commissioners appointed for management of naval affairs; their offices.

admire (ąd-mīr') *v.t.* regard with wonder and approval, esteem, or affection; prize highly.—*v.i.* wonder; marvel.—**admir'er** *n.*—**admir'ing** *a.*—**admir'ingly** *adv.*—**ad'mirable** *a.* excellent; praiseworthy.—**ad'mirably** *adv.*—**admira'tion** *n.*

admissible (ąd-mis'-i-bl) *a.* allowable.—**admis'sibly** *adv.*—**admissibil'ity** *n.*—**admis'sion** *n.* permission to enter; price paid for this.

admit (ąd-mit') *v.t.* grant entrance; concede as true; acknowledge.—**admit'tance** *n.* permission to enter.

admix (ąd-miks') *v.t.* mingle with something else.—**admix'ture** *n.*

admonish (ąd-mon'-ish) *v.t.* reprove gently; instruct or direct.—**admon'-isher** *n.*—**admoni'tion** *n.* rebuke.—**admon'itory** *a.*

ado (ą-dŏŏ') *n.* fuss; bustle; trouble.

adobe (a-dō'-bi) *n.* sun-dried brick.

adolescence (ad-ō-les'-ens) *n.* stage between childhood and manhood; youth.—**adoles'cent** *a.* growing up; advancing towards maturity.—*n.* young man or woman.

adopt (ą-dopt') *v.t.* receive the child of another and treat it as one's own; select and accept as one's own, e.g. a view.—**adopt'er** *n.*—**adop'table** *a.*—**adop'tion** *n.*—**adop'tive** *a.* that adopts or is adopted.

adore (ą-dōr') *v.t.* worship; love deeply; idolise; venerate.—**ador'er** *n.*

a lover.—**ador'able** *a.*—**ador'ably** *adv.*
—**ador'ableness** *n.* **adora'tion** *n.*

adorn (ạ-dorn') *v.t.* decorate; deck or ornament; dignify; set off to advantage.—**adorn'ing** *a.*—**adorn'ment** *n.*

adrenal (ạd-rē'-nạl) *n.* small, ductless gland situated close to upper end of each kidney (same as *supra-renal*).—**adre'nalin** *n.* hormone of the adrenal glands.

adrift (ạ-drift') *adv.* and *a.* floating at random; unfixed; (*Fig.*) at a loss.

adroit (ạ-droit') *a.* dexterous; skilful; ingenious; resourceful; adept.—**adroit'ly** *adv.*—**adroit'ness** *n.*

adsorb (ad-sorb') *v.t.* said of solids, take up a gas on the surface.—**adsorb'ent** *a.*; **adsorb'tion** *n.*

adulate (ad'-ū-lāt) *v.t.* praise or flatter in a servile manner; fawn; cringe.—**adula'tion** *n.*—**adula'tor** *n.*—**ad'ulatory** *a.* excessively.

adult (a-dult', a'-dult) *a.* grown to maturity, or to full size and strength; appropriate for a grown-up.—*n.* grown-up person.—**adult'ness** *n.*

adulterate (ạ-dul'-tẹr-āt) *v.t.* debase by addition of inferior materials; vitiate; corrupt.—*a.* debased.—**adult'erant** *n.* person or thing that adulterates.—**adultera'tion** *n.*

adultery (ạ-dul'-tẹr-i) *n.* violation of the marriage vows; sexual intercourse between married person and one who is not the legal wife or husband.—**adult'erer** *n.* (*fem.* **adult'eress**)—**adult'erous** *a.*—**adult'erously** *adv.*

adumbrate (ạd-um'-brāt) *v.t.* shadow forth; give faint outline of; forecast; typify.

advance (ạd-vans') *v.t.* bring or push forward; raise in status, price, or value; propose as a claim; supply beforehand, esp. money;—*v.i.* go forward; improve; rise in rank, etc.—*a.* before the time, as in *advance-booking*.—*n.* forward movement; gradual approach; paying out of money before due; increase in price; expansion of knowledge.—**advanced'** *a.* in the front rank; progressive; well on in years; beyond elementary stage (in education).—**advance'ment** *n.* promotion; improvement; success; loan of money.—**advanc'er** *n.* promoter.—**make advances**, solicit friendship (of another).

advantage (ạd-van'-tāj) *n.* state or means favourable to desired end; upperhand; profit; in tennis, point gained after deuce;—*v.t.* benefit, promote the interests of; profit.—**advan'tageable** *a.* able to be turned to advantage.—**advanta'geous** *a.* beneficial; opportune; convenient.—**advanta'geously** *adv.*—**to advantage**, with good results; most effectively.

advent (ad'-vent) *n.* arrival; approach; anticipated coming of Christ; four weeks from the Sunday nearest to St. Andrew's Day (30th Nov.) to Christmas.

adventitious (ad-ven-tish'-us) *a.* accidental; out of the proper place; extraneous.—**adventi'tiously** *adv.*

adventure (ạd-ven'-tūr) *n.* risk; bold undertaking; chance; trading enterprise of a speculative nature;—*v.t.* risk;—*v.i.* venture; dare.—**adven'turer** *n.* (*fem.* **adven'turess**).—(**ad)vent'uresome** *a.*—**advent'uresomeness** *n.*—**advent'urous** *a.*—**advent'urously** *adv.*

adverb (ad'-vẹrb) *n.* word used to modify the sense of verb, adjective, or other adverb.—**adverb'ial** *a.*—**adverb'ially** *adv.*

adversary (ad'-vẹr-sar-i) *n.* an opponent; one who strives against us; an enemy.

adverse (ad'-vẹrs) *a.* contrary; opposite in position; unfortunate; opposed.—**ad'versely** *adv.*—**ad'verseness** *n.*—**advers'ity** *n.* adverse circumstances; misfortune; distress; calamity.

advertise (ad'-vẹr-tīz) *v.t.* and *v.i.* give public notice of; inform; publicise through mass media.—**adver'tisement** *n.* act of advertising public intimation in the press TV etc.; legal notification.—**adverti'ser** *n.* one who advertises; advertising sheet or newspaper.—**adverti'sing** *n.* and *a.*

advice (ạd-vīs') *n.* opinion offered as to what one should do; counsel; information;—*pl.* notification regarding mercantile transactions, especially despatch of goods.

advise (ạd-vīz') *v.t.* give advice to; counsel; give information to; consult (with).—*v.i.* deliberate.—**advisabil'ity**, **advis'ableness** *n.* expediency.—**advis'able** *a.* prudent; expedient.—**advis'ably** *adv.*—**advised'** *a.* acting with due deliberation; cautious; prudent; judicious.—**advis'edly** *adv.* purposely; deliberately.—**advis'edness** *n.* deliberate consideration; expediency.—**advis'er** *n.*—**advis'ory** *a.* having power to advise; containing advice.

advocate (ad'-vō-kāt) *n.* vocal supporter of any cause; one who pleads or speaks for another; (*Law*) in Scotland and France, a barrister.—*v.t.* plead in favour of; recommend; maintain by argument.—**ad'vocacy** *n.* a pleading for; judicial pleading.

adze, (adz) *n.* carpenter's tool for chipping, having a thin arching blade set at right angles to the handle.

aegis (ē'-jis) *n.* originally the shield of Jupiter; (*Fig.*) protection.

aeon, eon (ē'-on) *n.* infinitely long period of time; a kalpa or age.

aerate (ā'-ẹ-rāt) *v.t.* charge with carbonic acid or other gas; supply with air.—**aera'tion** *n.*

aerial (ā'-ẹr-i-ạl) *a.* pert. to, consisting of, air;—*n.* and *a.* (*Radio*) exposed wire, rod, etc., capable of receiving or radiating electromagnetic waves.—ae'rially adv.

aero- (ā'-ẹr-ō) a combining form from Gk. aēr, air, used in many derivatives.

aerobatics (ā-ẹr-ō-ba'-tiks) n.pl. aerial acrobatics, performed by an aeroplane.

aerodrome (ā'-ẹr-ō-drōm) n. stretch of ground or water, prepared for ascents and descents of aircraft.

aerodynamics (ā-ẹr-ō-dī-nam'-iks) n. science that treats of gases in motion.—aerodyne (ā'-ẹr-ō-dīn) n. aircraft deriving its lifting power from aerodynamic forces.

aerofoil (ā'-ẹr-ō-foil) n. body, e.g. aircraft wing, so shaped as to produce lift when in motion.

aerolite (ā'-ẹr-ō-līt) n. stoney meteorite. Also a'erolith.—aerolith'ic a.—aerolithol'ogy n. study of meteorites.

aerology n. science which treats of air and its phenomena.

aeronaut (ā'-ẹr-ō-nawt) n. airman; balloonist.—aeronaut'ic a. pert. to aeronautics.—aeronaut'ics n. science of air-navigation.

aeroplane (ā'-ẹr-ō-plān) n. powered heavier-than-air flying-machine. Also air'plane, esp. in America.

aerosol (ā'-ẹr-ō-sol) n. a suspension of fine particles of liquid or solid in a gas; spray container for such mixture.

aerostat (ā'-ẹr-ō-stat) n. generic term for lighter-than-air flying-machines.—aerostat'ics n. science that treats of the equilibrium of gases; science of ballooning.

aesthetics (ēs-, es-thet'-iks) n. laws and principles determining the beautiful in nature, art, taste, etc.—aesthet'ic, aesthet'ical a.—aesthet'ically adv.—aesthete (ēs'-, es'-thēt) n. lover of the beautiful.—aesthet'icism n. cult of the beautiful.

aestival (es'-ti-vạl) a. pert. to, or produced in, summer.—Also es'tival.—aes'tivate v.t. pass the summer.

aetiology (ē-ti-ol'-o-ji) n. doctrine of causation; science of the causes of a disease.—aetiolog'ical a.

afar (ạ-far') adv. from, at, or to a distance; far away.

affable (af'-ạ-bl) a. ready to converse; easy to speak to; courteous; friendly.—a'ffably adv.—affabil'ity n.

affair (ạ-fār') what is to be done; business or matter; concern; thing; amorous intrigue.—affairs' n.pl. public or private business; finances.—affair of honour, duel.

affect (ạ-fekt') v.t. act upon; produce a change in; put on a pretence of; influence.—affect'ed a. inclined or disposed; not natural.—affect'edly adv.—affect'edness n.—affect'ing a. moving; pathetic.—affect'ingly adv.—affecta'tion n. striving after artificial appearance or manners.—affec'tion n. disposition of mind; good-will; tender attachment; disease.—affec'tionate a. loving; proceeding from love.—affec'tionately adv.—affec'tionateness n.—affec'tive a. pert. to the affections.—affec'tively adv.

afferent (af'-ẹr-ent) a. conveying to, esp. of nerves carrying sensations to the centres.

affiance (ạ-fī'-ạns) n. plighted faith; betrothal; marriage contract; reliance; confidence;—v.t. betroth.—affi'anced a. and n.

affidavit (af-i-dā'-vit) n. (Law) written statement of evidence on oath.

affiliate (ạ-fil'-i-āt) v.t. adopt as son; receive into fellowship; unite a society, firm, or political party with another, but without loss of identity.—affilia'tion n. (Law) establishment of paternal responsibility for illegitimate child.

affinity (ạ-fin'-i-ti) n. relationship by marriage; close agreement; resemblance; attraction; likeness of nature or disposition; similarity.

affirm (ạ-fẹrm') v.t. assert positively; confirm; aver; strengthen; ratify a judgment; confirm;—v.i. (Law) make a solemn promise to tell the truth without oath; ratify a law.—affirm'able a.—affirma'tion n.—affirm'ative a. affirming; dogmatic; ratifying; positive.—n. affirmative word or answer.—in the affirmative, yes.—affirm'atively adv.

affix (ạ-fiks') v.t. fasten to; attach; append to.—af'fix n. addition to either end of word to modify meaning or use (includes prefix and suffix).

afflation (ạ-flā'-shun) n. act of blowing or breathing on.—affla'ted a. inspired.—affla'tus n. inspiration.

afflict (ạ-flikt') v.t. give continued pain to; cause distress or grief to.—afflict'ed a. distressed in mind; diseased.—afflict'ing a. distressing.—afflict'ingly adv.—afflic'tion n. cause of continued pain of body or mind.

affluence (af'-lōō-ens) n. abundance, esp. riches.—af'fluent a. wealthy; flowing to;—n. tributary of river.—af'fluently adv.

afford (ạ-fōrd') v.t. yield, supply, or produce; be able to bear expense.

afforest (a-for'est) v.t. plant out as forest.—afforesta'tion n.

affray (ạ-frā') n. noisy quarrel or fight in public;—v.t. frighten; startle.

affront (ạ-frunt') v.t. confront; meet face to face; insult one to the face; abash.—affront'ed a. insulted.

afield (ạ-fēld') adv. to or in the field; abroad; off the beaten track; astray.

afire (ạ-fīr') adv. and a. on fire.

aflame (ạ-flām') adv. and a. flaming;

in or into flame; on fire; glowing.

afloat (a-flōt') *adv.* and *a.* borne on the water; not aground or anchored.

afoot (a-foot') *adv.* on foot; astir.

afore (a-fōr') *adv.* and *prep.* before.—**afore'hand** *adv.* beforehand; before;—*a.* provided; prepared.—**afore'mentioned** *a.* spoken of, or named, before.—**afore'said** *a.* said or mentioned before.—**afore'thought** *a.* thought of beforehand; premeditated.—**afore'time** *adv.* in times past; at a former time; previously.

afraid (a-frād') *a.* filled with fear; frightened.

afresh (a-fresh') *adv.* anew; over again.

African (af'-ri-kan) *a.* (*Geog.*) pert. or belonging to Africa;—*n.* a native of Africa.—**African'er** *n.* a native of S. Africa, born of white parents, esp. of Dutch descent. Also **Afrikan'der**.—**Afrikaans** (af-ri-kăns') *n.* S. African Dutch; Taal.

aft (aft) *adv.* or *a.* (*Naut.*) toward, or at, the stern.—**fore and aft**, lengthwise.

after (af'-ter) *prep.* behind; later; in pursuit of; in imitation of; according to;—*adv.* behind;—*a.* in the rear; succeeding.—**af'terbirth** *n.* (*Med.*) the placenta, etc., expelled from uterus after childbirth.—**af'ter-damp** *n.* gas formed in mine after explosion of fire-damp; choke-damp.—**af'ter-glow** *n.* glow in sky after sunset.—**af'termath** *n.* second crop of grass after first mowing; (*Fig.*) result; consequence.—**af'termost** *a.* hindmost; nearest to stern.—**af'ternoon** *n.* time from noon to evening.—**af'ter-pains** *n.pl.* pains succeeding childbirth.—**af'terthought** *n.* reflection after an act; idea occurring later.—**af'terward(s)** *adv.* later; subsequently.

again (a-gen') *adv.* another time; once more; in return; moreover.

against (a-genst') *prep.* in contact with; opposite to; in opposition to; in preparation for; in exchange for.

agape (a-gāp') *a.* or *adv.* open-mouthed, as in wonder, expectation, etc.; gaping.

agate (ag'-āt) *n.* precious stone, composed of layers of quartz of different colours.

age (āj) *n.* length of time person or thing has existed; period of time; periods of history; maturity; (*Colloq.*) a long time;—*v.t.* cause to grow old; —*v.i.* grow old;—*pr.p.* aging—*pa.p.* and *pa.t.* aged; also *a.* of the age of.—**aged** (āj'-ed) *a.* old; having lived long.—**ag'edness** *n.*—**age'less** *a.*—**age'long** *a.*—**to come of age**, attain one's 21st birthday.

agenda (a-jen'-da) *n.* literally, things to be done; items of business to be discussed at a meeting.

agent (ā'-jent) *n.* person or thing that

exerts power or has power to act; one entrusted with business of another; deputy or substitute.—**a'gency** *n.* instrumentality; mode of exerting power; office or duties of agent.

agglomerate (a-glom'-e-rāt) *v.t.* and *i.* collect into a mass;—*a.* heaped up;—*n.* (*Geol.*) mass of compacted volcanic debris.—**agglomera'tion** *n.*—**agglom'erative** *a.*

agglutinate (a-glōō'-ti-nāt) *v.t.* unite with glue;—*a.* united, as with glue; —**agglutina'tion** *n.* coalescing of small particles or organisms to form clumps;—**agglut'inative** *a.* having tendency to cause adhesion; (*Phil.*) applied to languages which are non-inflectional.

aggrandise (ag'-ran-dīz) *v.t.* make greater in size, power, rank, wealth, etc.; promote; increase; exalt.—**aggran'disement** *n.*

aggravate (ag'-ra-vāt) *v.t.* make more grave, worse; (*Colloq.*) irritate.—**ag'gravating** *a.* making worse; provoking.—**ag'gravatingly** *adv.*—**aggrava'tion** *n.*

aggregate (ag'-re-gāt) *v.t.* collect into a total; accumulate into heap;—*n.* assemblage; sum total; coarse material mixed with cement to make concrete;—*a.* collected together.—**aggrega'tion** *n.* act of aggregating; combined whole.—**ag'gregative** *a.* collective; accumulative.

aggress (a-gres') *v.i.* attack; start a quarrel.—**aggres'sion** *n.* first act of hostility; unprovoked attack.—**aggres'sive** *a.*—**aggres'sively** *adv.*—**aggres'siveness** *n.*—**aggres'sor** *n.* one who first attacks, who provokes quarrel.

aggrieve (a-grēv') *v.t.* give pain or sorrow to; vex.—**aggrieved'** *a.*

aghast (a-gást') *a.* struck with amazement, horror, terror; transfixed with fright.

agile (aj-īl, aj'-il) *a.* having power of quick motion; nimble.—**ag'ilely** *adv.* —**ag'ileness**, **agil'ity** *n.*

agitate (aj'-i-tāt) *v.t.* throw into violent motion; stir up; disturb, excite, upset; debate earnestly;—*v.i.* cause a disturbance.—**agita'tion** *n.* violent and irregular motion; perturbation; inciting to public disturbance.—**ag'itator** *n.*

agnate (ag'-nāt) *n.* any male relation on father's side.—*a.* related on father's side; akin; allied.

agnomen (ag-nō'-men) *n.* additional name given by Romans, generally because of some famous exploit.

agnostic (ag-nos'-tik) *n.* one who believes that God, life hereafter, etc., can neither be proved nor disproved, and who accepts material phenomena only.—**agnos'ticism** *n.*

ago, agone (a-gō', a-gon') *adv.* and *a.* past; gone; in time past.

agog (a-gog') *a.* and *adv.* eagerly excited; expectantly.

agonic (a-gon'-ik) *a.* not forming an angle.

agony (ag'-o-ni) *n.* extreme physical or mental pain; death struggle; pang.—**ag'onise** *v.t.* distress with great pain; torture.—*v.i.* suffer torment.—**ag'onising** *a.*—**ag'onisingly** *adv.*—**agony column**, personal column of newspaper.

agoraphobia (ag-or-a-fō'-bi-a) *n.* fear of open spaces.

agouti (a-gōō'-ti) *n.* genus of rodents, natives of S. America, allied to guinea-pig.

agrarian (a-grā'-ri-an) *a.* relating to lands, their management and distribution; (*Bot.*) growing in field.—*n.* advocate of equal division of property.—**agra'rianise** *v.t.*—**agra'rianism** *n.*

agree (a-grē') *v.i.* be of one mind; acquiesce; resemble; (*Gram.*) correspond in gender, case, or number.—*pr.p.* **agree'ing.**—*pa.p.* **agreed'.**—**agree'able** *a.* favourable; suitable; pleasant; congenial.—**agree'ably** *adv.*—**agree'ableness** *n.*—**agree'ment** *n.* agreeing; bargain; written statement accepting certain conditions.

agriculture (ag'-ri-kul-tūr) *n.* science and practice of cultivating the soil.—**agricul'tural** *a.*—**agricul'turist** or **agricul'turalist** *n.*

agronomy (a-gron'-om-i) *n.* rural economy; husbandry.—**agronom'ial, agronom'ic** *a.*

aground (a-ground') *adv.* and *a.* on ground; stranded; run ashore; beached.

ague (ā'-gū) *n.* (*Med.*) intermittent malarial fever, marked by fits of shivering, burning, sweating.—**a'gued, a'guish** *a.*

ahead (a-hed') *adv.* farther forward; in advance; in front; head foremost.

ahoy (a-hoi') *interj.* used in hailing, as in *ship ahoy* [form of interj. *hoy*].

aid (ād) *v.t.* and *v.i.* help; relieve.—*n.* help; assistance; person or thing which aids; auxiliary; assistant.—**aids** *n.pl.* subsidies or moneys granted to a king.

aide-de-camp (ād-de-kong') *n.* officer attached to personal staff of general to assist him.—*pl.* **aides-de-camp'.**

ail (āl) *v.t.* trouble; disturb; pain; afflict.—*v.i.* feel pain; be ill.—**ail'ing** *pr.p.*—**ail'ment** *n.* illness; morbid disease; sickness.

aileron (ā'-le-ron) *n.* adjustable flaps on trailing edge of wings of aeroplane for lateral control.

aim (ām) *v.t.* point at; direct; endeavour after; intend;—*n.* direction; end; purpose; intention.—**aim'less** *a.* without aim or purpose.—**aim'lessly** *adv.*—**aim'lessness** *n.*

air (ār) *n.* the atmosphere; a gas;

light breeze; tune; manner, bearing of a person; carriage; appearance; mien.—*v.t.* expose to air or heat, for drying or warming; parade before the public.—**airs** *n.pl.* affected manner.—**air'ing** *n.* ride or walk in open air.—**air'y** *a.* of air; exposed to air; light-hearted; unsubstantial.—**air'ily** *adv.*—**air'iness** *n.*—**air'-base** *n.* place for housing, or directing operations of, aircraft.—**air'borne** *a.* carried by aircraft; supported by air (of aircraft). —**air'-brake** *n.* brake worked by compressed air; device for slowing down an aircraft.—**air'-chief-marsh'al** *n.* R.A.F. rank corresponding to admiral or general.—**air'-comm'odore** *n.* R.A.F. rank equivalent to commodore in navy or brigadier in army.—**air'-condi'tioning** *n.* control of purity, temperature and humidity of air in a building or enclosure.—**air'craft** *n.* all kinds of flying-machines. —**air'craft(s)man** *n.* rank in the R.A.F.—**air'craft-carrier** *n.* armed vessel built to carry aircraft.—**air'-cush'ion** *n.* rubber or plastic cushion which can be inflated.—**air'field** *n.* tract of land, used for accommodation and maintenance of aircraft.—**air force** *n.* branch of armed services organised for air warfare.—**air'-gun** *n.* gun discharged by elastic force of air.—**air'-lift** *n.* large-scale transport operation by aircraft.—**air'-line** *n.* service of aircraft plying regularly.—**air'li'ner** *n.* large passenger aeroplane flying on an air-line.—**air'-load** *n.* cargo carr'ed by aircraft.—**air'-lock** *n.* stoppage of flow of liquid in a pipe caused by presence of air; small chamber to allow passage of men or materials at top of a caisson.—**air'-mail** *n.* transport of letters, parcels, etc., by aeroplane.—**air'-man** *n.* aviator.—**air'plane** *n.* (*U.S.*) aeroplane.—**air'port** *n.* station for commercial aircraft.—**air'-pump** *n.* machine for exhausting air from closed vessel.—**air'-raid** *n.* attack by hostile aircraft.—**air'-sacs** *n. pl.* air-cells in the bodies of birds.—**air'-screw** *n.* aircraft propeller.—**air'ship** *n.* mechanically propelled lighter-than-air machine.—**air'-strip** *n.* concrete runway on airfield; aerodrome.—**air terminal** *n.* place of assembly for air-line passengers.—**air'-tight** *a.* admitting no air.—**air'-trap** *n.* contriv nce to prevent or facilitate escape of foul air from sewers, etc.—**air-vice-marshal**, rank in R.A.F. equivalent to rear-admiral.—**air'way** *n.* prepared route for travel by aeroplane; ventilating passage.

airedale (ār'-dāl) *n.* kind of large terrier, with close, wiry coat of tan and black.

aisle (īl) *n.* wing of building; any lateral division of church; (incorrectly) passage-ways between pews.

aitchbone (āch'-bōn) n. rump bone of ox; cut of beef surrounding it.

ajar (a-jär') adv. partly open, as a door.

akimbo (a-kim'-bō) adv. with crook; bent.—**with arms akimbo**, with hands on hips and elbows turned outward.

akin (a-kin') a. related by blood; allied by nature; having same properties.

alabaster (al'-a-bas-ter) n. gypsum; semi-transparent kind of soft marble-like mineral;—a. made of, or white as, alabaster.—**alabas'trian**, **alabas'trine** a.

alacrity (a-lak'-ri-ti) n. cheerful readiness; eagerness; briskness.

alar (ā'-lár) a. wing-like; pert. to wings; having wings.

alarm (a-lärm') n. sound giving notice of danger; mechanical contrivance to rouse from sleep; summons to arms; sudden fear or apprehension; dismay; trepidation.—v.t. fill with apprehension; call to arms.—**alarm clock**, clock made to ring loudly at set time.—**alarm'ingly** adv.—**alarm'ist** n. one given to exciting alarm, esp. needlessly;—**alar'um** n. old spelling of "alarm."

alas (a-las') interj. exclamation of sorrow, pity, etc.

alate (al'-āt) a. having wings; winged. Also **al'ated** a.

alb (alb) n. vestment of white linen, reaching to feet, worn by R.C. clergy officiating at Eucharist.

albatross (al'-ba-tros) n. large web-footed sea-bird commonest in South Seas.

albeit (awl-bē'-it) conj. although; even though; notwithstanding that.

albert (al'-bert) n. kind of short watch-chain [after Prince Albert].

albino (al-bī'-no, bē'-no) n. person, or animal, with abnormal whiteness of skin and hair, and pink colour in eyes.—**al'binism** n.

Albion (al'-bi-on) n. old and poetic name for Britain.

album (al'-bum) n. book for autographs, photographs, stamps, etc.; of selection of writings, music, etc.

albumen (al-bū'-men) n. white of egg; similar substance found in tissues of animals and plants.—**albu'min** n. any of a class of proteins, necessary for growth in body.—**albu'minise** v.t. convert into albumen.—**albu'minoid** n. substance resembling albumen.—**albu'minous** a.

alburnum (al-bur'-num) n. sapwood, part of tree under bark and outside heart up which sap rises.

alchemy (al'-ke-mi) n. forerunner of modern chemistry. Chief aims were (a) transmuting baser metals into gold, (b) discovery of elixir of life.—**alchem'ic** a.—**al'chemist** n.

alcohol (al'-kō-hol) n. pure spirit; liquid of strong pungent taste, intoxicating element in fermented or distilled liquor.—**al'coholism** n. uncontrollable addiction to alcoholic liquor.—**alcoholic** a. pert. to alcohol;—n. one suffering from alcoholism; habitual drunkard.—**absolute alcohol**, alcohol entirely free from water.

alcove (al'-kōv) n. recess in room; covered seat in garden.

alder (awl'-der) n. tree of birch family.

alderman (awl'-der-man) n. civic dignitary, next in rank to mayor.—**alderman'ic** a.

ale (āl) n. liquor made from malt by fermentation; a festivity (from amount of ale drunk at it).

alembic (a-lem'-bik) n. vessel of glass or metal formerly used in distillation; (Fig.) refining medium, as in alembic of the mind.

alert (a-lert') a. watchful; vigilant; brisk; nimble; active;—n. signal by sirens of air attack; period of air-raid.—**alert'ly** adv.—**alert'ness** n.

alexandrine (al-eg-zan'-drin) n. a verse of six iambic feet.

alfa (al'-fa) n. N. African name for esparto grass.

alfalfa (al-fal'-fa) n. plant of pea family, valued as fodder, esp. in U.S.

alfresco (al-fres'-kō) a. and adv. in fresh air, as an alfresco meal.

algae (al'-jē) n.pl. (Bot.) large group of simple plants, mainly aquatic, including seaweeds.—**al'gal**, **al'goid**, **al'gous** a.—**algol'ogy** n. scientific study of marine plants.

algebra (al'-je-bra) n. branch of mathematics in which calculations are made by using letters to represent numbers or quantities.—**algebra'ic(al)** a.—**algebra'ically** adv.

alias (ā'-li-as) adv. otherwise named;—n. assumed name;—n.pl. a'liases.

alibi (al'-i-bī) n. (Law) plea that prisoner was elsewhere when crime was committed. (Colloq.) excuse.

alien (āl'-yen) a. foreign; different in nature; estranged;—n. non-naturalised foreigner.—**al'ienable** a. (of property) capable of being sold or handed over.—**alienabil'ity** n.—**al'ienate** v.t. transfer to another; estrange.—**aliena'tion** n. (Med.) insanity.—**al'ienator** n.—**al'ienism** n. study of mental diseases.—**al'ienist** n. specialist in treatment of mental diseases, a psychiatrist.

alight (a-līt') adv. or a. on fire; illuminated; kindled.

alight (a-līt') v.i. dismount; finish one's journey; fall; descend; land.

align (a-līn') v.t. adjust by line; line up; range;—v.i. form in line; fall in, as troops. Also **aline'**.—**align'ment** n.

alike (a-līk') a. having likeness; similar;—adv. similarly; equally.

aliment (al'-i-ment) n. nourishment, nutriment; (*Law*) provision for maintenance.—*v.t.* maintain.—aliment'al *a.*—aliment'ally *adv.*—aliment'ary *a.* pert. to food; nutritive.—alimenta'tion *n.* process of introducing nutriment into body.— alimentary canal *n.* digestive system.

alimony (al'-i-mon-i) n. means of living, esp. allowance made to wife out of her husband's income, after legal separation.

alive (a-liv') *a.* having life; existent; active; alert; thronged with.

alkali (al'-ka-li) *n.* one of a class of chemical compounds which combine with acids to form salts—used with fats to form soap.—*pl.* al'kalis, sl'kalies.—alkalify *v.t.* render alkaline;—*v.i.* become alkaline;—*pa.p.* al'kalified.—alkalifi'able *a.*—alkalim'etry *n.* quantitative estimation of strength of alkalies.—al'kaline *a.* pert. to alkali; with qualities of alkali.—alkalin'ity *n.*—al'kaloid *n.* nitrogenous organic compound which acts chemically like an alkali;—*a.* resembling an alkali in properties.

all (awl) *a.* whole of; every one of;—*n.* whole amount; whole duration of;—*adv.* wholly; entirely.—all-fours' *n.* hands and feet; a card-game.—all-hail'! *interj.* welcome! good health!—all'-in *a.* (of wrestling) no style debarred.—all'-pow'erful *a.* omnipotent.—all but, nearly; almost.—all in all, in all respects.

Allah (al'-a) *n.* Mohammedan God.

allay (a-lā') *v.t.* lighten; make quiet; lessen grief or pain.—allay'er *n.*—allay'ment *n.*

allegation (al-e-gā'-shun) *n.* affirmation; that which is positively asserted; the act of alleging.

allege (a-lej') *v.t.* bring forward with positiveness; assert as argument, plea, or excuse; declare; affirm; cite.

allegiance (a-lē'-jans) *n.* duty of subject to his liege, sovereign, or government; loyalty; oath of homage.—alle'giant *a.* loyal;—*n.* one who owes allegiance.

allegory (al'-e-gor-i) *n.* narrative in which abstract ideas are personified.—allegor'ic, -al *a.*—allegor'ically *adv.*—al'legorise *v.t.*—al'legorist *n.*

allegretto (al-le-gret'-tō) *adv.* (*Mus.*) livelier than *andante* but not so quick as *allegro.*—*n.* fairly quick movement.

allegro (al-lē-grō) *adv.* (*Mus.*) brisk, gay, sprightly.—*n.* quick movement.

alleluiah (al-e-lōō'-ya) *interj.* hallelujah;—*n.* song of praise to God.

allergy (al'-er-ji) *n.* hyper-sensitivity to certain substances.—al'lergen *n.* a substance which induces allergy.—aller'gic *a.*

alleviate (a-lēv'-i-āt) *v.t.* make light; lighten; ease; afford relief; mitigate.—allevia'tion *n.*—alle'viator *n.*

alley (al'-i) *n.* narrow passage between buildings; garden path; long, narrow passage adapted for playing bowls or skittles.—*pl.* al'eys.

alliance (a-lī'-ans) *n.* persons, parties, or states allied together for common purpose; union by marriage.

alligator (al'-i-gā-tor) *n.* reptile of America and China, distinguished from crocodile by broad flat head, depressed muzzle and unequal teeth.

alliteration (al-it-er-ā'-shun) *n.* recurrence of a letter or sound at the beginning of words in close succession; head rhyme.—*v.i.* alliterate.

allocate (al'-ō-kāt) *v.t.* distribute; assign to each his share; place.—alloca'tion *n.*—allocs'tur *n.* (*Law*) certificate that costs have been allowed.

allocution (al-ō-kū'-shun) *n.* formal address, esp. of the Pope to his clergy.

allot (a-lot') *v.t.* divide by lot; distribute as shares.—allot'ment *n.* allotting; what is allotted; distribution; share; portion of a field divided among many holders for vegetable gardens, etc.

allotropy (a-lot'-rō-pi) *n.* property of some chemical substances found in two or more different forms.—allotrop'ic *a.*—allot'ropism *n.*

allow (a-lou') *v.t.* acknowledge; permit; give; set apart;—*v.i.* provide.—allow'able *a.* permissible; lawful; acceptable.—allow'ance *n.* what is allowed; permission; stated quantity to be added or deducted; rebate; grant.—allow'edly *adv.*—to make allowance for, take into consideration.

alloy (a-loi') *v.t.* melt together two or more metals; reduce purity of a metal by mixing with less valuable one; debase.—alloy (a-loi', al'-oi) *n.* mixture of metals, e.g. copper and zinc to form brass; combination; amalgam; (*Fig.*) evil mixed with good.

allspice (awl'-spis) *n.* berry of the pimento, or Jamaica pepper; spice made from it.

allude (a-lūd') *v.i.* refer indirectly to; hint at; suggest; mention lightly.

allure (a-lur') *v.t.* tempt by a lure, offer, or promise.—allure'ment *n.* that which allures.—allur'ing *a.* enticing; attractive; fascinating.—allur'ingly *adv.*

allusion (a-lū'-zhun) *n.* passing or indirect reference; hint; suggestion.—allus'ive *a.* referring to indirectly; marked by allusions; symbolical.—allus'ively *adv.*

alluvium (a-lū'-vi-um) *n.* waterborne matter deposited on low-lying lands.—*pl.* allu'viums, or allu'via.—allu'vial *a.*

ally (a-lī') *v.t.* join by treaty, marriage, or friendship;—*pr.p.* ally'ing;—*pa.p.* and *pa.t.* allied.—ally (a-lī' or a'-li) n. person, family, country, etc., bound to another, esp. of nations in war-time; partner.—pl. **allies** (a-liz', or a'-liz).

almanac (awl'-ma-nak) n. calendar of days, weeks, and months, giving astronomical and other information.

almighty (awl-mīt'-i) a. all-powerful; omnipotent.—**The Almighty**, God; the Supreme Being. **almight'iness** n.

almond (á'-mend) n. kernel of nut of almond-tree; tonsil, from its resemblance in shape to an almond.

almoner (á'-, al'-mon-er) n. one who distributes alms or bounty; medical social worker.—**al'monry** n. place for distributing alms.

almost (awl'-mōst) adv. very nearly; all but.

alms (ámz) n. gifts offered to relieve the poor; charitable donation.—**alms'-house** n. building, usually erected and endowed by private charity, for housing the aged poor.

aloe (al'-ō) n. bitter plant used in medicine.—pl. **al'oes**, purgative drug, made from juice of species of aloe.—**aloes wood**, heart of Asiatic tree *Aquilaria Agallocha.*

aloft (a-loft') adv. on high; (*Naut.*) on yards or rigging.

alone (a-lōn') a. solitary; single;—adv. by oneself; singly.

along (a-long') adv. in a line with; throughout the length of; lengthwise; onward; in the company of (followed by *with*);—prep. by the side of.—**along'side** adv. by the side of, esp. of ship.

aloof (a-loof') a. reserved in manner, almost unsociable;—adv. at a distance; apart.—**aloof'ness** n.

aloud (a-loud') adv. with loud voice or noise; loudly; audibly.

alp (alp) n. high mountain; mountain pasture-land.—**Alps** n.pl. mountains of Switzerland.—**al'pine** a. pert. to Alps;—n. plant that grows on high ground.—**alpinist** (al'-pin-ist) n.

alpaca (al-pak'-a) n. sheeplike animal of Peru; species of llama; thin kind of cloth made of wool of alpaca.

alpenstock (al'-pen-stok) n. long, stout staff, shod with iron, used by mountaineers.

alpha (al'-fa) n. first letter of Greek alphabet; symbol ∝ for this.—**alpha and omega**, the first and the last.—**alpha particle**, helium nucleus travelling at high speed, given off when radioactive substances disintegrate.

alphabet (al'-fa-bet) n. letters of a language arranged in order; first principles.—**alphabet'ic, -al** a.—**alphabet'ically** adv.

already (awl-red'-i) adv. before this; even now; even then; previously to time specified.

alright (awl-rīt) common spelling of all right.

also (awl'-sō) adv. and conj. in like manner; likewise; further.

altar (awl'-tar) n. table or raised structure in place of worship, on which gifts and sacrifices are offered to a deity; communion table.

alter (awl'-ter) v.t. to change;—v.i. become different.—**al'terably** adv.—**alterabil'ity** n.—**altera'tion** n. act of altering; change; modification.

altercate (awl'-ter-kāt) v.i. contend in words; wrangle.—**alterca'tion** n. dispute; controversy.

alternate (a(w)l-ter'-nāt) a. occurring by turns; one following the other in succession.—**al'ternately** adv. by turns.—**alternate** (a(w)l'ter-nāt) v.t cause to follow by turns;—v.i. happen by turns.—**alternation** (a(w)l-ter-nā'-shun) n.—**alter'native** a. offering choice of two things.—n. choice of two things.—**alter'natively** adv. **al'ternator** n. (*Elect.*) dynamo for producing alternating current.—**alternating current** (*Elect.*) current which reverses its direction of flow at fixed periods, *Abbrev.* a.c.

although (awl-thō') conj. admitting that; notwithstanding that.

altimeter (al-tim'-e-ter) n. instrument for taking altitudes; in aviation, instrument indicating height.

altitude (al'-ti-tūd) n. height; perpendicular elevation above given level.

alto (al'-tō) n. (*Mus.*) part sung by lowest female voice or by male counter-tenor; singer with voice higher than tenor, lower than soprano; contralto.

altogether (awl-too-geTH'-er) adv. wholly, entirely, quite.

altruism (al'-troo-izm) n. principle of living for good of others (opp. to *egoism*).—**al'truist** n.—**altruis'tic** a. unselfish.—**altruis'tically** adv.

alum (al'-um) n. a double sulphate of alumina and potash; a mineral salt used as a styptic, astringent, etc., as a mordant in dyeing, and in tanning.

aluminium (al-ū-min'-i-um) n. whitish metal produced largely from bauxite, strong, light, malleable.—**alu'mina, al'umine** n. oxide of aluminium; the clay, loam, etc., from which alum is obtained.

alway, always (awl'-wā, -wāz) adv. at all times; perpetually; invariably; regularly.

alyssum (a-li'-sum) n. genus of cruciferous rock plant with white or yellow flowers; madwort.

amalgam (a-mal'-gam) n. compound of mercury with another metal; mixture of different substances.—**amal'gamate** v.t. mix metal with quicksilver; compound; consolidate; combine (esp. of business firms);—v.i. coalesce.—**amalgama'tion** n.

amanuensis (a-man-ū-en'-sis) *n.* one who writes what another dictates, or copies what another has written; secretary.—*pl.* amanuen'ses.

amass (a-mas') *v.t.* heap up; collect; accumulate.

amateur (am'-a-ter) *n.* one who cultivates any study, art, or sport for love of it, and not for money;—*a.* like an amateur.—amateur'ish *a* unskilled; clumsy.—am'ateurism, amateur'ishness *n.*

amative (am'-a-tiv) *a.* pert. to love; amorous.

amatory (am'-a-tor-i) *a.* pert. to or causing love.—amato'rial *a.* amorous; affectionate.—amato'rially *adv.*

amaze (a-māz') *v.t.* fill with astonishment or wonder; confound; perplex.—amaze'ment *n.* astonishment, surprise.—amaz'ing *a.* causing amazement, wonder, or surprise.—amaz'ingly *adv.*

Amazon (am'-az-on) *n.* one of a mythical race of female warriors of Scythia; masculine woman.—Amazo'nian *a.*

ambassador (am-bas'-a-dor) *n.* envoy of highest rank sent to foreign country; (*Fig.*) intermediary; messenger;—ambass'adress *n. fem.*—ambassado'rial *a.*—ambass'adorship *n.*—am'bassage *n.* now embassage (cf. embassy), business of an ambassador or diplomatic mission.

amber (am'-ber) *n.* yellowish, brittle fossil resin of vegetable origin, used in making beads, brooches, mouthpieces of pipes, etc.;—*a.* of, or like, amber.

ambergris (am'-ber-grēs) *n.* fragrant, ash-coloured, waxy substance, derived from a biliary secretion of the spermaceti whale.

ambidexter (am-bi-deks'-ter) *n.* one able to use either hand with equal dexterity; double-dealer.—ambidexter'ity *n.*—ambidex'trous *a.*

ambient (am'-bi-ent) *a.* encompassing on all sides.—am'bience *n.* environmental atmosphere.

ambiguity (am-bi-gū'-i-ti) *n.* statement that may be interpreted in more than one way.—ambig'uous *a.* doubtful, uncertain; equivocal; susceptible of two or more meanings.—ambig'uously *adv.*—ambig'uousness *n.*

ambit (am'-bit) *n.* circuit or compass; sphere of action; scope.

ambition (am-bish'-un) *n.* eager desire for attainment of honour, fame, or power; aim; aspiration.—ambi'tious *a.* ardently desirous of acquiring power, rank, office, etc.—ambi'tiously *adv.*

ambivalence, ambivalency (am-biv'-a-lens, -i) *n.* simultaneous presence in the mind of contradictory emotions towards same object. ambiv'alent *a.*

amble (am'-bl) *v.i.* move along,

easily and gently;—*n.* peculiar gait of a horse; stroll.—am'bler *n.*—am'bling *a.*—am'blingly *adv.*

ambrosia (am-brō'-zi-a) *n.* (*Myth.*) food of the Greek gods which conferred immortality; exquisite dish.—ambro'sial *a.*—ambro'sially *adv.*

ambulance (am'-bū-lans) *n.* covered vehicle for transport of injured or sick; hospital unit in the field.

ambulant (am'-bū-lant) *a.* walking.—am'bulate *v.i.* walk backwards and forwards.—ambula'tion *n.* walking.—ambula'tor *n.* instrument for measuring distances.—am'bulatory *a.* having power of walking; used for walking; moving from place to place;—*n.* cloister for walking.

ambuscade (am-bus-kād') *n.* surprise attack by assailant(s) lying in wait; place of lying in wait; the force concealed.—*v.i.* lie in wait;—*v.t.* attack from a concealed position.

ambush (am'-boosh) *n.* and *v.t.* same as ambuscade.

ameliorate (a-mēl'-yur-āt) *v.t.* and *i.* make better; improve.—ameliora'tion *n.*—amelio'rative *a.*

Amen (ā-men', ä'-men) *adv.* or *interj.* so be it; truly; verily (uttered at the end of a prayer).

amenable (a-men'-a-bl, a-mē'-na-bl) *a.* liable to be brought to account; easily led; willing to yield or obey.—amenabil'ity, amen'ableness *n.* state of being amenable.—amen'ably *adv.*

amend (a-mend') *v.t.* change for the better; improve; alter in detail as a bill in parliament, etc.;—*v.i.* grow better.—amend'able *a.*—amend'atory *a.*—amend'ment *n.* act of amending; change for the better.—amends' *n.pl.* reparation for loss or injury; compensation.

amenity (a-men'-i-ti, a-mē'-ni-ti) *n.* pleasantness in situation, climate, manners, or disposition; agreeable or convenient feature. *n.pl.* pleasant ways or manners; agreeable surroundings or conditions.

American (a-mer'-i-kan) *a.* pert. to America;—*n.* native or citizen of America.—Amer'icanise *v.t.* and *i.* make American in manners, customs, etc.—Amer'icanism *n.* imported American idiom or usage.

amethyst (am'-e-thist) *n.* kind of quartz, of violet, purple, or blue colour, formerly supposed to prevent intoxication.—amethys'tine *a.* pert. to amethyst; bluish-violet.

amiable (ā'-mi-a-bl) *a.* worthy of love or affection; sweet-tempered.—a'miably *adv.*—amiabil'ity *n.* Also a'miableness.

amicable (am'-i-ka-bl) *a.* friendly; peaceable.—am'icably *adv.*—amicabil'ity *n.* Also am'icableness.

amid, amidst (a-mid', a-mid'-st) *prep.* in the middle of; among.

amiss (ạ-mis') *a.* wrong; faulty; improper;—*adv.* in a faulty manner.—**amiss'ing** *a.* missing; lost; wanting.

amity (am'-i-ti) *n.* friendship.

ammeter (am'-e-tẹr) *n.* instrument used to measure strength of electric current in amperes.

ammonia (a-mō'-ni-ạ) *n.* pungent, alkaline gas, compound of nitrogen and hydrogen, very soluble in water; solution of this gas in water, for household use.—**ammo'niac, ammon'iacal** *a.*—**ammo'niated** *a.*—**ammo'nium** *n.* the ammonia radical NH₄, which behaves like an alkali metal.

ammunition (am-ū-nish'-un) *n.* military projectiles and missiles of all kinds; originally, military stores; often used adjectively, e.g. *ammunition dump.*

amnesia (am-nē'-zi-ạ) *n.* loss of memory.

amnesty (am'-nes-ti) *n.* act of oblivion; general pardon of political offenders.

amoeba (ạ-mē'-bạ) *n.* minute animalcule of the simplest structure constantly changing in shape.—*pl.* **amoe'bae, amoe'bas.**—**amoe'boid, amoe'bic** *a.*

amok (ạ-mok'). See amuck.

among, amongst (ạ-mung', ạ-mungst') *prep.* mixed with; making part of; amidst.

amoral (ā'-mor-ạl) *a.* non-moral; heedless of morals.

amorous (am'-or-us) *a.* having a propensity for love and sexual enjoyment; in love; pert. to love.—**am'orously** *adv.*—**am'orousness** *n.*—**am'orist** *n.*

amorphous (ạ-mor'-fus) *a.* without regular shape; shapeless; irregular; uncrystallised, as glass.

amount (ạ-mount') *v.i.* rise to; result in; come to (in value or meaning); be equal to;—*n.* sum total; whole, or aggregate.

ampere (am-per') *n.* unit of electric current; (*Abbrev.*) A or amp [named after André *Ampère,* a French physicist, 1775-1836].

ampersand (am'-per-sand) *n.* name given to the sign &.

amphibia (am-fib'-i-ạ) *n.pl.* animals that can live either on land or in water, as frogs, toads, newts, etc.—**amphib'ian** *a.* pert. to Amphibia; —*n.* animal of the class Amphibia; vehicle or aircraft which can operate on land or water.—**amphib'ious** *a.*

amphitheatre (am-fi-thē'-ạ-tẹr) *n.* edifice, having tiers of seats, encircling arena, used for sports or spectacles; rising gallery in theatre, concert-hall, etc.

ample (am'-pl) *a.* of full dimensions; of adequate size; of sufficient quantity; abundant; copious.—**am'ply** *adv.*—**am'pleness** *n.*

amplify (am'-pli-fī) *v.t.* make larger; extend; enlarge;—*v.i.* dilate; expatiate upon.—**amplifica'tion** *n.*—**am'plifier** *n.* device for increasing the ratio of output to input from any source.

amplitude (am'-pli-tūd) *n.* largeness; extent; abundance; (*Radio*) (of a wave) vertical distance between highest and lowest levels; (*Elect.*) maximum value of alternating current.

ampoule (am'-pōōl) *n.* small sealed glass container holding measured quantity.

amputate (am'-pū-tāt) *v.t.* cut off, as limb of the body, or bough of tree.—**amputa'tion** *n.*

amuck, amok (ạ-muck', ạ-mok') *adv.* as in phrase, *to run amuck,* rush about frantically attacking and committing murder indiscriminately.

amulet (am'-ū-let) *n.* talisman; charm worn to ward off disease or evil spells.—**amulet'ic** *a.*

amuse (ạ-mūz') *v.t.* entertain agreeably; occupy pleasantly; divert.—**amuse'ment** *n.* anything which entertains or pleases; pastime.—**amus'ing** *a.* pleasing; diverting.—**amus'ingly** *adv.*

anabolism (an-ab'-ol-izm) *n.* (*Physiol.*) constructive process in living organisms, involving the formation of complex from simple substances and the storage of chemical energy.

anachronism (an-ak'-ron-ism) *n.* a chronological error; post- or antedating of an event or thing.—**anachronist'ic** *a.*—**ana'chronous** *a.*—**anachronist'ically** *adv.*

anaconda (an-a-kon'-da) *n.* gigantic, non-venomous snake of S. America, allied to boa species; orig. name given to python of Ceylon.

anaemia, anemia (a-nē'-mi-ạ) *n.* disease characterised by deficiency of blood or of haemoglobin, leading to pallor of skin and mucous membranes.—**anae'mic** *a.*

anaesthesia, anesthesia (an-es-thē'-zi-ạ) *n.* absence of sensibility to external impressions, particularly touch. Also **anaesthe'sis.**—**anaesthet'ic, anesthet'ic** *n.* drug which induces insensibility to pain;—*a.* producing loss of feeling and sensation.—**anaesthet'ically, anesthet'ically** *adv.*—**anaes'thetise, anes'thetise** *v.t.*—**anaesthet'ist** *n.*

anagram (an'-ạ-gram) *n.* a transposition of letters of word or phrase to form new word or phrase.—**anagrammat'ic, -al** *a.*

anal (ā'-nạl) *a.* pert. to or near the anus.

analgesia (an-al-jē'-zi-ạ) *n.* (*Med.*) absence of pain while retaining tactile sense; painlessness.—**analge'sic** *a.* insensible to or alleviating pain;—n. drug which relieves pain; anodyne.

analogy (a-nal'-o-ji) n. resemblance in essentials between things or statements otherwise different; relationship; likeness; parallelism; correspondence.—**analog'ic, -al** a.—**analog'ically** adv.—**anal'ogise** v.t. explain by analogy.—**anal'ogous** a. having analogy.—**anal'ogously** adv.—**an'alogue** n. word or thing resembling another.—**an'alogue computer**, one in which variables are represented by proportional measurable physical quantities.

analysis (a-nal'i-sis) n. resolution, separating, or breaking up of anything into its constituent elements; synopsis; (Chem.) determination of elements comprising a compound or mixture; (Gram.) logical arrangement of sentence into component parts; (Math.) theory of real and complex numbers.—pl. anal'yses.—**an'alyse** v.t. take to pieces; examine critically part by part.—**an'alyst** n. one skilled in analysis; analytical chemist.—**analyti'c, -al** a.—**analyt'ically** adv.

anarchy (an'-ar-ki) n. want of government in society; lawless disorder in a country.—**an'archism** n. political theory, which would dispense with all laws, founding authority on the individual conscience.—**anaroh'ic** a.—**anaroh'ically** adv.—**an'archise** v.t.—**an'archist** n.

anathema (a-nath'-e-ma) n. word used in the R.C. church as part of the formula in excommunication; something highly distasteful; accursed thing.—**anath'ematise** v.t. pronounce a curse against; to excommunicate (See 1 Cor. 16).

anatomy (a-nat'-o-mi) n. art of dissecting animal or plant; study of form or structure of animal; the body; skeleton.—**anatom'ic** (al) a.—**anatom'ically** adv.—**anat'omise** v.t.—**anat'omist** n.

ancestor (an'-ses-tor) n. (fem. an'cestress) forefather; progenitor; forebear.—**ances'tral** a.—**an'cestry** n. lineage.

anchor (ang'-kor) n. heavy iron instrument by which ship is held fast to sea-bottom; moulder's chaplet;—v.t. place at anchor, fix;—v.i. cast anchor; stop.—**anch'orage** n. sheltered place where ship may anchor; dues paid for anchoring.—**anch'ored** a. at anchor; firmly fixed.—**to cast anchor**, let down anchor.—**to weigh anchor**, raise anchor preparatory to sailing.

anchorite, anchoret (ang'-ko-rīt, -ret) n. one who lives apart, renouncing the world for religious reasons; hermit.—**anch'oress, anch'oritess** n. female hermit.—**anch'orage** n. home of anchorite.

anchovy (an-chō'-vi, an'-chō-vi) n. small sea-fish of herring family, caught in Mediterranean, and eaten pickled or prepared as a sauce.

ancient (ān'shent) a. very old; antique; venerable; former;—n. aged or venerable person; one who lived in olden times.—**an'ciently** adv.—**an'cientness** n.—**an'cientry** n. ancientness; ancestry; seniority;—**the Ancient of Days**, biblical title for God.

ancillary (an-sil'-ar-i) a. giving help to; attending upon; auxiliary; subordinate.

andante (an-dan'-te) a. or adv. (Mus.) moving rather slowly, but in a steady, flowing manner.

andiron (and'-ī-ern) n. utensil for supporting logs or fire-irons in fireplace; fire-dog.

anecdote (an'-ek-dōt) n. biographical incident; brief account of any fact or happening (often amusing).—**an'ecdotage** n. anecdotes collectively.—**an'ecdotal** a.—**an'ecdotist** n.

anemograph (a-nem'-ō-graf) n. instrument for recording force and direction of wind.—**anemom'eter** n. wind-gauge.

anemone (a-nem'-ō-nē) n. plant of crow-foot family; wind-flower.—**sea'-anem'one** n. name given to certain plant-like marine animals.

anent (a-nent') prep. concerning; about; in respect of; as to.

aneroid (an'-e-roid) a. denoting barometer depending for its action on pressure of atmosphere on lid of metallic box almost exhausted of air.

aneurism (an'-u-rizm) n. abnormal dilation, e.g. of an artery.

anew (a-nū') adv. in new form or manner; newly; over again; afresh.

angel (ān'-jel) n. heavenly messenger; spirit who conveys God's will to man; guardian spirit; old English coin worth about 10s. bearing figure of archangel Michael; (Colloq.) lovable person; a dear.—**angelic(al)** (an-jel'-ic, -i-kal) a. like an angel.—**angel'ically** adv.

angelica (an-jel'-i-ka) n. (Bot.) genus of umbelliferous plants having white flowers tinged with pink; candied confection prepared from its stem.

angelus (an'-je-lus) n. short devotional service in R.C. Church held morning, noon, and sunset. Opening words are 'Angelus Domini nuntiavit Mariae'; bell rung to remind the faithful to recite the prayer.

anger (ang'-ger) n. strong passion or emotion excited by injury; rage;—v.t. excite to wrath; enrage.—**angry** (ang'-gri) a. roused to anger; displeased; enraged; inflamed.—**ang'rily** adv.—**ang'riness** n.

angina (an-jī'-na, an'-ji-na) n. (Med.) inflammation of the throat, e.g. quinsy.—**angina pectoris**, a heart disease characterised by attacks of agonising pain.

angle (ang'-gl) *n.* fish-hook; rod and line for fishing;—*v.i.* fish with rod, line, and hook; (*Fig.*) use artifice.—**ang'ler** *n.* one who angles.—**ang'ling** *n.*

angle (ang'-gl) *n.* corner; point at which two lines meet; (*Geom.*) amount of turning made by revolving a straight line in a plane, round a point in itself, from one direction to another; (*Fig.*) a point of view.—**angular** *a.* having or forming angles.—**ang'ularly** *adv.*;—**angular'ity** *n.*

Angle (ang'-gl) *n.* member of a Teutonic tribe which, along with the Jutes and Saxons, invaded England in the 5th cent. and gave their name to the country.

Anglican (ang'-gli-can) *a.* English; of, or belonging to, Church of England;—*n.* member of Church of England.—**Ang'licanism** *n.*—**ang'licise** *v.t.* make or express in English idiom.—**ang'licism** *n.*

Anglo- (ang'-glo) *prefix* fr. L. Anglus, an Angle; English.—**Ang'lo-Cath'olic** *a.* belonging or pert. to very ritualistic section of Church of England; —*n.* High-Churchman.—**Ang'lo-In'dian** *n.* one of mixed Indian-European descent; native of Britain resident in India; Eurasian.—**Ang'lo-Sax'on** *a.* pert. Anglo-Saxons or their language; —*n.* one of nations formed by union of Angles, Saxons, and other early Teutonic settlers in Britain; one of English race; earliest form of English language, now more correctly named Old English.—**angloma'nia** *n.* excessive fondness for, or imitation of, everything English.—**anglophile** (ang'-glō-fīl) *a.* favouring anything English;—*n.* supporter of English customs, manners, or policy.—**anglophobia** (ang-glō-fō'-bi-a) *n.* intense dislike or fear of England, or of what is English.—**ang'lophobe** *n.*

Angora (ang-gō'-ra) *n.* former name of Ankara, cap. of Turkey.—**ango'ra** *n.* breed of goat from that area; its long silky wool; mohair cloth; cat or rabbit with long silky fur.

angostura (ang-gos-tōō'-ra) *n.* aromatic bark used as febrifuge and tonic, and in preparation of 'bitters.' Also angustu'ra.

anguish (ang'-gwish) *n.* acute pain of body or of mind; grief; anxiety; moral torment.—**ang'uishment** *n.*

angular (ang'-gū-lar) *a.* having angles; sharp-cornered; (of people) not plump; gawky; irascible.—**angular'ity** *n.*—**ang'ularly** *adv.*

anhydrous (an-hī'-drus) *a.* entirely without water.

aniline (an'-il-īn) *n.* product, orig. obtained from indigo, now got mainly from coal-tar, and used in manufacture of brilliant dyes, coloured inks, soaps, explosives, etc.;—*a.* pert. to aniline.

animadvert (an-i-mad-vert') *v.t.* turn the mind to; consider disparagingly; comment on censoriously; reprove. —**animadver'sion** *n.*

animal (an'-i-mal) *n.* living creature having sensation and power of voluntary motion; living organism, distinct from plants;—*a.* pert. to or got from animals.—**animal'cule** *n.* very minute animal (*pl.* animal'cules. or **animal'cula**).—**animal spirits**, natural buoyancy.

animate (an'-i-māt) *v.t.* give natural life to; endow with spirit or vigour; energise; inspire;—*a.* living or organic.—**an'imated** *a.* alive; spirited.—**an'imatedly** *adv.*—**an'imating** *a.* inspiring.—**an'imatingly** *adv.*—**anima'tion** *n.* state of possessing life or spirit; vivacity.—**an'imator** *n.* one who or that which animates; cinema cartoonist.

animism (an'-i-mizm) *n.* belief that all forms of organic life have their origin in the soul.—**an'imist** *n.*—**animis'tic** *a.*

animosity (an-i-mos'-i-ti) *n.* violent hatred; active enmity; acrimony.

animus (an'-i-mus) *n.* animosity; temper; grudge; (*Law*) intention, purpose.

anise (an'-is) *n.* umbelliferous plant with pungent smell, and bearing aromatic seeds.—**an'iseed** *n.* seed of anise used for flavouring and in manufacture of liqueurs.

ankle (ang'-kl) *n.* joint connecting foot with the leg.—**ank'let** *n.* ornament, support, or fetter for ankle.

anna (an-'a) *n.* former coin of India and Pakistan.

annals (an'-alz) *n.pl.* history of events recorded each year; yearly chronicle.—**ann'alise** *v.t.* write annals; record chronologically.—**ann'alist** *n.*

anneal (a-nēl') *v.t.* heat, and then cool slowly, for purpose of rendering less brittle; heat in order to fix colours.—**anneal'ing** *n.*

annex (a-neks') *v.t.* unite at the end; subjoin; bind to; take additional territory under control.—**annexa'tion** *n.* taking over power of territory by one without consent of other state; what is annexed.—**annexe** (an'-eks) *n.* something joined on; building attached to, or sufficiently near, main building to be considered part of it.

annihilate (a-nī'-hil-āt) *v.t.* reduce to nothing; destroy; make null and void.—**anni'hilable** *a.*—**annihila'tion** *n.*—**annihila'tor** *n.*

anniversary (an-i-ver'-sa-ri) *a.* yearly; annual;—*n.* day on which event is yearly celebrated.

annotate (an'-ō-tāt) *v.t.* mark in writing; write explanatory notes, esp. upon literary text.—**annota'tion** *n.* written commentary.—**an'notator** *n.*—**annota'tory** *a.*

announce (a-nouns') *v.t.* give first public notice of; proclaim; promulgate; publish.—**announce'ment** *n.* giving public notice; proclamation; declaration.—**announc'er** *n.* broadcaster who gives the news, etc.

annoy (a-noi') *v.t.* injure, disturb continually; torment; tease; vex; pester; molest; trouble.—**annoy'ance** *n.*—**annoy'ingly** *adv.*

annual (an'-ū-al) *a.* returning or happening every year; to be renewed each year; performed in course of a year;—*n.* periodical published once a year; plants which complete life-cycle within a year.—**ann'ually** *adv.*

annuity (a-nū'-i-ti) *n.* fixed sum of money payable each year for number of years, or for life.—**annu'itant** *n.* one in receipt of annuity.

annul (a-nul') *v.t.* make void; nullify; repeal; cancel;—*pr.p.* annul'ling; *pa.t.* and *pa.p.* annull'ed.—**annul'ment** *n.*

annular (an'-ū-lar) *a.* ring-shaped; like a ring.—ann'ulated, *a.* having rings or belts.—**ann'ulet** *n.* little ring. —**ann'ularly** *adv.* ann'ulose *a.* ringed. —annula'tion *n.* ring-like formation.

annunciate (a-nun'-si-āt) *v.t.* announce; make known; proclaim.—**annuncia'tion** *n.* an announcing; festival (25th March) in memory of angel's announcement to Virgin Mary; Lady Day.—**annunciat'or** *n.*—**annuncia'tory** *a.*

anode (an'-ōd) *n.* positive electrode; (*Electronics*) electrode in valve or tube which is principal collector of electrons.

anodyne (an'-ō-dīn) *n.* drug or measures to procure relief from pain. —**anod'ynous** *a.*

anoint (a-noint') *v.t.* pour oil upon; rub over with ointment or oil; consecrate by unction.—**anoin'ted** *a.* consecrated; *n.*consecrated person. —**anoint'ment** *n.* consecration; salve. —**the Lord's anointed,** Christ.

anomaly (a-nom'-a-li) *n.* deviation from common rule or type; irregularity;—*pl.* anom'alies.—**anom'-alism** *n.* anomaly; irregularity.—**anomalis'tic** *a.* irregular.—**anom'alous** *a.* irregular; abnormal; incongruous. —anom'alously *adv.*

anon (a-non') *adv.* quickly; at once; forthwith.—**ever and anon,** every now and then.

anonymous (a-non'-i-mus) *a.* applied to writing or work of which author is not named.—**an'onym** *n.* one who remains anonymous.—**anon'ymously** *adv.*—**anonym'ity** *n.*

anorak, anarak (an'-e-rak) *n.* waterproof jacket with hood.

another (a-nuTH'-er) *a.* not the same; different; one more;—*pron.* any one else.

answer (an'-ser) *v.t.* speak or write in return; vindicate; witness for;—*v.i.* reply; suit; suffer consequence of;—*n.* something said or written in return to question, etc.; solution of problem; response.—**an'swerable** *a.* capable of being answered; responsible.—**an'swerer** *n.*—**to answer for,** be responsible for.

ant (ant) *n.* small insect of the same order as bees and wasps; applied also to white ant or termite; emmet.—**ant'bear** *n.* great ant-eater of S. America.—**ant'-eat'er** *n.* one of several edentate quadrupeds, e.g. ant-bear, aardvark, that feed chiefly on ants.—**ant'-hill** *n.* mound raised by colony of ants or termites.

antacid (ant-as'-id) *a.* counteracting acidity;—*n.* remedy for acidity of stomach.

antagonise (an-tag'-o-nīz) *v.t.* contend violently against; act in opposition; oppose; make hostile.—**antag'onism** *n.* opposition; hostility; hatred; dislike.—**antag'onist** *n.*—**antagonist'ic** *a.*—antagonist'ically *adv.*

antarctic (ant-árk'-tic) *a.* opposite to arctic pole; relating to south pole or region near it.

ante- (an'-te) *prefix* fr. L. *ante*, meaning *before* (place, time, or order), combining to form derivatives.

antecedent (an-te-sēd'-ent) *a.* going before in time, place, ránk, etc.; preceding; prior;—*n.* that which goes before; (*Gram.*) noun or pronoun to which relative refers.

antechamber (an'-te-cham-ber) *n.* chamber leading to chief apartment.

antedate (an'-te-dāt) *v.t.* to date before the true time.

antediluvian (an-te-di-lū'-vi-an) *a.* pert. to before the Flood; ancient; antiquated.

antelope (an'-te-lōp) *n.* hoofed ruminant, notable for its graceful and agile movement.

antemeridian (an-te-mer-id'-i-an) *a.* before noon (*Abbrev.*) a.m. [L. before midday, period of time between midnight and noon].

antenatal (an-te-nā'-tal) *a.* pertaining to period before birth.

antenna (an-ten'-a) *n.* feeler of insect, crustacean, etc.; (*Radio, TV,* etc.) aerial.—*pl.* antennae, (*Radio*) antennas.

anterior (an-tē'-ri-or) *a.* before; occurring earlier.—anterior'ity *n.*

ante-room (an'-te-róom) *n.* room giving entry to another.

anthem (an'-them) *n.* hymn sung in alternate parts; Church music adapted to passages from Scriptures; song of praise.

anther (an'-ther) *n.* little sac in a

flower, containing the pollen or fertilising dust.

anthology (an-thol'-o-ji) *n.* orig. collection of flowers; collection of literary passages or poetry.—anthol'ogist *n.*

anthracite (an'-thra-sīt) *n.* type of coal, nearly pure carbon, burning without smoke or flame.

anthrax (an'-thrax) *n.* carbuncle; malignant disease in cattle and sheep, communicable to man; malignant pustule.

anthropo- (an'-thrō-pō) *prefix* fr. Gk. *anthropos*, meaning *man*, combining to form derivatives.

anthropoid (an'-thrō-poid) *a.* manlike.

anthropology (an-thrō-pol'-ō-ji) *n.* study of man, including all aspects of his evolution, physical and social. anthropolog'ical *a.*—anthropolog'ically *adv.*—anthropol'ogist *n.*

anthropomorphism (an-thrō-pō-mor'-fizm) *n.* conception of God as a human being with human attributes; attribution of human qualities to animals etc.—anthropomor'phic *a.*

anti- (an'-ti) *prefix* fr. Gk. *anti*, meaning *against*, *opposite*. instead of, combining to form derivatives; contracted to ant- before a vowel.

antibiotic (an-ti-bī-ot'-ik) *n.* substance (e.g. penicillin) elaborated by micro-organisms and acting as an antibacterial agent.—antibio'sis *n.* an association between organisms which is injurious to one of them.

antibody (an'-ti-bod-i) *n.* substance in blood which counteracts growth and harmful action of bacteria; anti-toxin.

antic (an'-tik) *a.* odd; fanciful; fantastic; grotesque;—*n.* buffoon; comical trick or action.

Antichrist (an'-ti-krīst) *n.* name given in the Bible to various incarnations of opposition to Christ.

anticipate (an-tis'-i-pāt) *v.t.* be before another; be beforehand in thought or action; enjoy prematurely; forestall.—antic'ipant *a.* anticipating; (*Med.*) occurring before the regular time.—anticipa'tion *n.* the act of anticipating.—antic'ipative *a.* full of expectation.—antic'ipatively, antic'ipatorily *adv.*—antic'ipatory *a.* happening in advance.

anticlimax (an-ti-klī'-maks) *n.* sentence or figure of speech in which ideas are arranged in descending order of importance; opp. of *climax*; sudden drop from the dignified to the trivial.

anticyclone (an'-ti-sī'-klōn) *n.* outward flow of air in spiral movement (clockwise in N. Hemisphere, anticlockwise in S. Hemisphere) from atmospheric area of high pressure, tending to produce steady weather,

frosty in winter and hot in summer.

antidote (an'-ti-dōt) *n.* remedy which counteracts the effects of poison; anything which counteracts evil.—an'tidotal *a.*

antifreeze (an-ti-frēz') *n.* substance added to water in motor car radiators to prevent freezing in very cold weather.

antigen (an'-ti-jen) *n.* substance, such as an anti-toxin, which can produce formation of antibodies in blood-stream.

antilogarithm (an-ti-log'-a-rithm) *n.* the number corresponding to a logarithm. (*Abbrev.*) antilog.

antimacassar (an-ti-ma-kas'-ar) *n.* ornamental covering for chair backs, etc., to keep them from being soiled (by hair oil, *i.e. Macassar oil* from Celebes).

antimony (an'-ti-mon-i) *n.* whitish, brittle metallic element; constituent of alloys used for type metal, bearings etc.—antimon'ial *a.*—antimon'iate *n.* salt of antimonic acid.—an'timonite *n.* stibnite.

antipathy (an-tip'-a-thi) *n.* aversion; dislike; enmity; hatred.—antipathet'ical *a.*—antipath'ic *a.* hostile to; having an opposite nature.—antip'athist *n.*

antiphon, antiphony (an'-ti-fōn, -fon) (anti-f'-ō-ni) *n.* the chant, or alternate singing, in choirs; anthem; response.—antiph'onal *a.*—*n.* book of antiphons.—antiph'onally *adv.*—antiphon'ic, antiphon'ical *a.*—antiphon'ically *adv.*

antipodes (an-tip'-ō-dēz) *n.pl.* those living on opposite side of globe; regions directly opposite any given point on globe; (*Fig.*) anything diametrically opposed to anything else.—antipodal, antipodean (an-tip'-ō-dal, an-tip-ō-dē'-an) *a.*

antipyretic (an-ti-pī-ret'-ik) *n.* agent which lowers temperature in fevers; febrifuge;—*a.* counteracting fever.

antique (an-tēk') *a.* ancient; old-fashioned; obsolete; aged;—*n.* relic of bygone times; ancient work of art; style of ancient art.—antiqua'rian *n.* student of antiquity or antiquities; collector of relics of former times;—*a.* pert. to old times or objects; out-of-date; obsolete.—antiquar'ianism *n.* study of antiquities.—an'tiquary *n.* antiquarian.—an'tiquate *v.t.* render obsolete.—an'tiquated *a.* very old; out of date.—antique'ly *adv.*—antique'ness *n.* condition of being antique.—antiq'uity *n.* ancient times; former ages; great age; people of ancient times.—antiq'uities, *n.pl.* remains and relics of ancient times; manners and customs of ancient times.

antirrhinum (an-tir-rī'-num) *n.* common flowering plant; snap-dragon.

antiscorbutic (an-ti-skor-bū'-tik) *n.* agent which prevents or cures scurvy, e.g. lime juice, lemons;—*a.* opposed to scurvy.

anti-semitism (an-ti-sem'-i-tizm) *n.* hatred for the Jewish race.—**anti-sem'ite** *n.*—**anti-semit'ic** *a.*

antisepsis (an-ti-sep'-sis) *n.* prevention of sepsis; destruction or arresting of growth of bacteria.—**antisep'tic** *a. and n.*

antisocial (an-ti-sō'-shạl) *a.* averse to social intercourse; opposed to social order.

antithesis (an-tith'-e-sis) *n.* direct opposition of words or ideas; figure in rhetoric in which words or thoughts are set in contrast.—*pl.* **antith'eses.**—**antithet'ic, antithet'ical** *a.* —**antithet'ically** *adv.*

antitoxin (an-ti-tox'-in) *n.* toxin which neutralises another toxin in the blood serum.—**antitox'ic** *a.*

antivivisection (an-ti-vi-vi-sek'-shun) *n.* opposition to vivisection.

antler (ant'-lẹr) *n.* annual horny outgrowth of frontal bone found in male animals of deer family and in female reindeer.—**ant'lered** *a.*

antonym (an'-tō-nim) *n.* word of contrary meaning.—opposite of *synonym.*

anus (ā'-nus) *n.* lower orifice of the alimentary canal.

anvil (an'-vil) *n.* iron block, usually steel-faced, upon which blacksmith's forgings are hammered and shaped.

anxiety (ang-zī'-et-i) *n.* distress of mind; disquietude; uneasiness; eagerness (to serve, etc.).—**anxious** (angk'-shus) *a.* uneasy; eager.—**an'xiously** *adv.*—**an'xiousness** *n.*

any (en'-i) *a.* one out of many; some; —*adv.* to any extent; at all.—**an'ybody** *n.* any person; ordinary person.—**an'yhow** *adv.* at any rate; in a careless manner; in any case.—**an'ything** *n.* any one thing, no matter what.—**an'ywhere** *adv.* in any place.

Anzac (an'-zak) *a.* (*World War* 1) pert. to Australian and New Zealand expeditionary force;—*n.* soldier of that army [fr. the initials of *A*ustralian and *N*ew *Z*ealand *A*rmy *C*orps].

aorta (ā-or'-tạ) *n.* artery leading from left ventricle of heart.—*pl.* **aortas** (ā-or'-tē)—**aor'tal, aor'tic** *a.*

apace (ạ-pā's) *adv.* at a quick pace; hastily; swiftly; fast.

Apache (ạ-pá'-chi) *n.* one of tribe of N. American Indians.—**apache** (ạ-pásh') *n.* bandit of Paris underworld; street hooligan.

apart (ạ-párt') *adv.* separately; aside; asunder; at a distance.

apartheid (a-párt'-hāt) *n.* segregation of races, esp. in S. Africa.

apartment (ạ-part'-ment) *n.* room in house;—*pl.* suite of rooms; lodgings.

apathy (ap'-ath-i) *n.* want of feeling; indifference.—**apathet'ic** *a.* void of feeling; indifferent; insensible; passionless.—**apathet'ically** *adv.*

ape (āp) *n.* monkey, esp. one without tail; one of the larger species, e.g. chimpanzee, gorilla, etc.; mimic;—*v.t.* imitate; mimic.—**a'pish** *a.*

aperient (a-pē'-ri-ent) *a.* opening;—*n.* laxative.

aperitif (a-pā'-rē-tēf) *n.* alcoholic drink taken before meals as an appetiser.

aperture (a'-pẹr-tūr) *n.* an opening; hole.

apex (ā'-peks) *n.* top, peak, or summit of anything.—*pl.* **a'pexes** or **a'pices.**

aphis (a'-fis) *n.* any plant-louse of the family Aphididae, esp. green-fly.—*pl.* **aphides** (af'-i-dēz).—**aphid'ian** *a.* and *n.*

aphorism (af'-or-izm) *n.* pithy saying; maxim.—**aphoris'tic** *a.*—**aphoris'tically** *adv.*—**aph'orise** *v.t.* and *i.* make or use aphorisms.—**aph'oriser, aph'orist** *n.*

Aphrodite (af-rō-dī-tē) *n.* (*Myth.*) Greek goddess of love and beauty.—**aphrodisiac** (af-rō-diz'-i-ak) *a.* exciting sexual desire;—*n.* anything which so excites, e.g. cantharidin.

apiary (ā'-pi-ạr-i) *n.* place where bees are kept.—**apiarian** (ā-pi-ā'-ri-ạn) *a.* pert. to bees or to bee-keeping.—**a'piarist** *n.* one who keeps or studies bees.—**a'piculture** *n.* bee-keeping.

apiece (ạ-pēs') *adv.* for each one; to each one.

aplomb (a-plom') *n.* perpendicularity; uprightness; (*Fig.*) self-assurance; coolness.

apocalypse (ạ-pok'-ạ-lips) *n.* unveiling of hidden things; revelation; disclosure.—**Apoc'alypse** *n.* (*Bib.*) last book of New Testament, the Revelation of St. John.—**apocalypt'ic(al)** *a.* pert. revelation; of style, allegorical; obscure.—**apocalypt'ically** *adv.*

apocrypha (ạ-pok'-ri-fạ) *n.pl.* originally, hidden or secret things—. **Apoc'rypha** *n.pl.* (*Bib.*) collective name for the fourteen books originally included in the Old Testament, and still incorporated in the Vulgate of the R.C. Church.—**apoc'ryphal** *a.* spurious; unauthentic; pert. to the Apocrypha.

apology (ạ-pol'-o-ji) *n.* something spoken in defence; expression of regret at offence; excuse; poor substitute (with *for*).—**apol'ogise** *v.i.* make an apology, or excuse; express regret.—**apol'ogist** *n.* one who makes an apology; defender of a cause.—**apologet'ic** *a.*—**apologet'ics** *n.* branch of theology charged with defence of Christianity.—**apolo'gia** *n.* defence in writing of author's principles, etc.

apophthegm, apothegm (a'-pō-them) *n.* short, pithy saying; maxim;

proverb.—**apophthegmatic** (a-pŏ-theg-mat'-ik), **apophthegmat'ical** a.

apoplexy (ap'-ō-plek-si) n. stroke due to cerebral haemorrhage or thrombosis.—**apoplec'tic** a.

apostasy, apostacy (a-pos-'ta-si) n. act of renouncing one's faith, principles, or party; desertion of a cause.—**apost'ate** n. renegade; traitor; deserter;—a. false; traitorous.—**apostat'ic(al)** a.—**apost'atise** v.i. abandon one's faith.

apostle (a-pos'-l) n. one sent out to preach or advocate a cause; one of the twelve disciples of Christ sent to preach the Gospel.—**apost'olate** n. office or dignity or mission of apostle.—**apostol'ic, apostol'ical** a.—**apostol'ically** adv.—**apostol'icism** n.—Apostles' Creed, creed supposedly used by apostles, summarising Christian faith.—Apostolic Church, church derived from, and incorporating spirit of, the apostles.—Apostolic See, jurisdiction of the Pope.—Apostolic succession, derivation of spiritual authority in unbroken line from the Apostles, through bishops.

apostrophe (a-pos'-trō-fe) n. address delivered to the absent or dead, or to inanimate thing, as if present; a mark (') indicating possessive case, or omission of one or more letters of a word.—**apostroph'ic** a.—**apos'trophise** v.t. and i. address by, or use, apostrophe.

apothecary (a-poth'-e-kar-i) n. one who prepares or sells drugs for medicines.

apothegm See apophthegm.

apotheosis (a-po-thē'-ō-sis, or a-po-the-ō'-sis) n. act of raising a mortal to rank of the gods; deification.

appal (a-pawl') v.t. shock; scare; horrify;—pr.p. appal'ling;—pa.p. appalled'.—appal'ling a.—appal'lingly adv.

appanage, apanage (ap'-a-näj) n. allowance for food; perquisite; allowance for younger sons of kings.

apparatus (ap-a-rā'-tus) n. collection of implements or materials for effecting experiment, or given work.

apparel (a-par'-el) n. clothing; dress; garments;—v.t. to dress;—pr.p. apparelling, apparel'ing—pa.p. apparel(l)ed.

apparent (a-par'-ent) a. visible; evident; obvious.—appar'ently adv.—appar'entness n.

apparition (ap-a-rish'-un) n. appearance (esp. inexplicable); spectre.—appari'tional a.

appeal (a-pēl') v.i. invoke; call to witness; solicit aid; (Law) reopen case before a higher court; to be pleasing to mind or senses.—n. urgent call for sympathy or aid; personal attraction.

appear (a-pēr') v.i. come in sight; become visible; seem; be obvious or manifest.—appear'ance n. a coming in sight; semblance; outward look or show; likeness; personal presence.

appease (a-pēz') v.t. quiet; calm; pacify; satisfy (hunger, etc.); dispel anger or hatred.—appeas'able a.—appease'ment n. pacifying; policy of making substantial concessions in order to preserve peace.

appellant (a-pel'-ant) n. (Law) one who appeals to higher court against verdict of lower tribunal; one who makes any appeal.—appell'ate a. (Law) pert. to appeals.—appella'tion n. name; title; designation.

append (a-pend') v.t. hang or attach to; add.—append'age n. something added.—append'ant n. adjunct or unessential thing;—a. hanging to; annexed.

appendicitis (a-pen-di-sī'-tis) n. (Path.) inflammation of the appendix vermiformis.

appendix (a-pen'-diks) n. thing added; adjunct; supplement at end of book; (Med.) blind tube extending from caecum into pelvis.—pl. appen'dixes, appen'dices.

apperception (ap-er-sep'-shun) n. (Philos.) act of voluntary consciousness; mental perception of self as conscious agent; spontaneous thought.

appertain (ap-er-tān') v.i. belong by nature; relate.—appertain'ing a.—appertain'ment n.—apper'tinent a. belonging to.

appetite (ap'-e-tīt) n. desire as for food, drink, rest, etc.—appet'itive a.—ap'petise v.t. create an appetite.—appetis'er n. food taken before meal to create appetite.—appetis'ing a.

applaud (a-plawd') v.t. and v.i. praise by clapping; acclaim; commend; extol.—applaud'er n.—applause' n. approval publicly expressed.

apple (ap'-l) n. fruit of apple-tree; apple-tree.

applicant (ap'-li-kant) n. one who applies; candidate; petitioner.—applicabil'ity n. quality of being suitable.—ap'plicable a. suitable; adapted.—ap'plicableness n.—ap'plicably adv.—ap'plicate a. put to some use.—applica'tion n. act of applying; thing applied; close attention.—ap'plicative a. may be applied; useful.—ap'plicatory a.

apply (a-plī') v.t. place one thing upon another; employ for particular purpose; fix attention upon; administer a remedy;—v.i. agree with; be relevant; have recourse to; become a candidate.—appli'ance n. act of applying; thing applied; instrument or tool.—applied' a. of sciences, put to practical use (opp. of pure.)

appoint (ạ-point') v.t. set apart; assign; ordain; decree; designate for office; fix (a date); equip.—**appoint'ed** a. established, furnished.—**appoint'ee** n. person appointed.—**appoint'ment** n. act of appointing; new situation or post.—**appoint'ments** n.pl. equipments; furnishings; fittings.

apportion (ạ-pôr'-shun) v.t. divide and share in just proportion.—**apport'ionment** n.

apposite (ap'-ō-zit) a. appropriate; well adapted.—**ap'positely** adv.—**ap'positeness** n.—**apposition** (ap-ō-zish'-un) n. act of placing beside.—**apposit'ional** a.

appraise (ạ-prāz') v.t. put a price upon; fix the value of.—**apprais'al** n. act of appraising; valuation.—**apprais'ment** n.—**apprais'er** n.

appreciate (ạ-prē'-shi-āt) v.t. value justly—v.i. rise in value.—**appreciation** (ạ-prē-shi-ā'-shun) n. setting of a value on; just estimate; rise in value.—**appre'ciative**, **appre'ciatory** a.—**appre'ciatively** adv.—**appre'ciable** a. measurable.—**appre'ciably** adv.

apprehend (ap-re-hend') v.t. seize; arrest; understand; fear.—**apprehens'ible** a.—**apprehen'sion** n.—**apprehen'sive** a. filled with dread; suspicious.—**apprehen'sively** adv.—**apprehen'siveness** n.

apprentice (ạ-pren'-tis) n. one bound to another to learn a trade or art; beginner;—v.t. bind as apprentice.—**appren'ticeship** n.

apprise (ạ-prīz') v.t. inform; tell; give notice.

approach (ạ-prōch') v.t. come near; —v.t. come near to; enter into negotiations with; resemble; (Golf) play a shot intended to reach the green;—n. act of drawing near; access; road; approximation; negotiation.—**approach'able** a. accessible.—**approachabil'ity** n.

approbation (ap-rō-bā'-shun) n. approval; sanction.—**ap'probate** v.t. approve of.—**ap'probative**, **ap'probatory** a. approving.

appropriate (ạ-prō'-pri-āt) v.t. take as one's own; set apart for particular purpose;—a. suitable; fitting.—**appro'priately** adv.—**appro'priateness** n.—**appropria'tion** n. act of setting apart or appropriating.—**appro'priative** a.—**appro'priator** n.

approve (ạ-proov') v.t. be pleased with; commend; accept; sanction officially.—**approv'al** n.

approximate (ạ-prok'-si-māt) v.t. come near to; bring near;—a. near to; nearly correct; not quite exact.—**approx'imately** adv.—**approxima'tion** n. close estimate.

appurtenance (ạ-pur'-te-nạns) n. that which appertains or is annexed to another thing; adjunct; accessory.—**appur'tenant** a.

apricot (ā'-pri-kot) n. oval, orange-yellow peach-flavoured fruit.

April (ā'-pril) n. fourth month of the year.—**April fool**, one who is victim of playful hoax on 1st April (All Fools' Day).

apron (ā'-pron) n. covering or protection worn in front to protect the clothes; hard-surfaced area outside airport buildings.—**apron stage**, theatre stage, juttng out into auditorium.

apse (aps) n. semi-circular recess as at east end of church.—**ap'sidal** a.

apt (apt) a. fit; suitable; quick-witted.—**apt'ly** adv.—**ap'titude** n. natural capacity for; faculty for learning; talent.—**apt'ness** n. fitness; appropriateness.

aqua (ā'-kwạ, ak'-wạ) n. L.=water.—**aqua fortis** n. 'strong water', nitric acid, esp. as used by etchers and engravers.—**aqua pura** n. pure water.—**aqua vitae** n. 'water of life', any distilled alcoholic liquor, esp. brandy or whisky.

aqualung (ak'-wa-lung) n. light underwater breathing apparatus.

aquamarine (ak-wạ-mạ-rēn') n. semi-precious stone, sea-green coloured beryl;—a. of sea-green colour.

aquarium (ạ-kwā'-ri-um) n. glass tank for living specimens of water animals and plants; building containing such tanks.—pl. **aqua'riums**, or **aqua'ria**.

aquatic (ạ-kwat'-ik) a. growing or living in water; of sports, practised on, or in, water.

aquatint (ak'-wạ-tint) n. etching process by which engravings resembling wash-drawings, are produced;—v.i. engrave thus.

aqueduct (ak'-we-dukt) n. course, channel, or bridge for conveying water either under or above ground.

aqueous (ā'-kwe-us) a. watery; made of, or from, water.—**a'queously** adv.—**aquiferous** (ạ-kwif'-e-rus) a. conveying water, as canals of sponges.

aquiline (ak'-wi-lin, -līn) a. belonging to the eagle; curving; hooked like eagle's beak.

Arab (ar'-ab) n. native of Arabia; Arab horse.—**street arab**, homeless urchin of the streets.—**Arab'ian** n.;—**Ar'abic** n. language of the Arabians.—**gum arabic**, resinous gum from kind of acacia plant.

arabesque (ar-a-besk') n. design in Arabian style; position in ballet dancing.

arable (ar'-ạ-bl) a. fit for ploughing or tillage; cultivable.

arbiter (ar'-bi-tẹr) n. (fem. **ar'bitress**) umpire; judge in a dispute; one who has supreme control.—**ar'bitrable** a. capable of settlement by discussion.—**ar'bitrary** a. guided by will only; high-handed; capricious; absolute.—**ar'bitrarily** adv.—**ar'bitrariness** n.—**ar'bitrate** v.t. and i. hear and give authoritative decision in a dispute.—arbitra'tion n.—ar'bitrator n. (fem. ar'bitratrix) a referee; an umpire.

arbor (ar'-bor) n. tree; spindle.—arbora'ceous a. tree-like; wooded.—arbor'eal a. living in trees.—arbor'eous a. wooded.

arbour (ár'-bur) n. garden seat sheltered or enclosed by trees; bower; shady retreat.

arbutus, arbute (ár-bū'-tus, ár'-būt) n. evergreen shrub with scarlet berries of strawberry type.

arc (ark) n. curved line forming segment of a circle; luminous electric discharge between two points.—arc'-lamp n.

arcade (ár-kād') n. series of arches, supported by pillars; walk, arched above; covered street, usually with shops on both sides.

arch (árch) a. sly; mischievous; roguish.—arch'ly adv.—arch'ness n.

arch (árch, árk) prefix used as a. chief; first of a class, as in arch-bishop, etc.—arohan'gel n. angel of supreme order.—arohbish'op n. chief bishop in a Church province.—archdea'con n. Church dignitary next below bishop.—archdea'conate n. jurisdiction of archdeacon.—archdea'conship n. office of archdeacon.—archduke' n. grand duke; son of Emperor of Austria.—archduch'ess n. —arch'duch'y n. territory of arch-duke.—archdu'cal a.

arch (árch) n. arc of a circle; structure of stone, brickwork, or steel ribs in the form of arc, over open space or river, whereby a load is supported equally at all points and designed to sustain a super-incumbent load;—v.t. or i. form an arch; bend into an arch.—arched a. in the form of an arch; containing arches.—arch'way n. arched passage.

archaeology (ár-kē-ol'-o-ji) n. study of human antiquities.

archaic, archaical (ár-kā'-ik, -al) a. antiquated; ancient; antique; obsolete; primitive.—archa'ically adv.—ar'chaism n. word, expression or idiom out of date.

archer (árch'-er) n. one who shoots with a bow; a bowman.

archetype (ár'-kē-tīp) n. original pattern or model from which thing is made or copied; prototype.—archetyp'al a.

archidiaconal (ark-i-dī-ak'-on-al) a. pert. to an archdeacon.

archiepiscopacy (árk-i-e-pis'-ko-pas-i) n. the office or jurisdiction of an archbishop. Also archiepis'copate n. —archiepis'copal a.

Archimedean (árk-i-mē'-dē-an) a. pert. to the celebrated mathematician of antiquity, Archimedes of Syracuse.

archipelago (ár-ki-pel'-a-gō) n. name originally of Aegean Sea; group of islands; stretch of water scattered with isles.—pl. archipel'agoes.—archipelag'ic (-aj'-ik) a.

architect (ár'-ki-tekt) n. one skilled in the art of building; designer or contriver.—architecton'ics n.pl. science or art of architecture.—architect'ural a.—architect'urally adv.—architect'ure n. art of building; distinct style of designing buildings.

architrave (ár'-ki-trāv) n. (Archit.) epistyle; the lower division of an entablature, which rests the chief beam of a building on the column; the ornamental band of mouldings running round a door or window.

archives (ár'-kīvz) n.pl. place in which public or historical records, charters and documents are stored and preserved; public records.—archi'val a.—ar'chivist n. a keeper of archives.

arctic (árk'-tik) a. pert. to the regions near the N. Pole; northern; extremely cold; frigid.

ardent (ár-dent) a. burning; passionate; eager.—ar'dently adv.—ar'dency n.—ardour (ár'-der) n. heat; warmth of affection; eagerness; enthusiasm; zeal.

arduous (ár'-dū-us) a. high and lofty; steep; difficult to overcome; laborious; strenuous.—ar'duously adv.

area (ā'-re-a) n. open space; tract of land; region; scope; sunken yard round basement of building; superficial extent.

arena (a-rē'-na) n. sand-strewn central space of a Roman amphitheatre, in which the gladiators fought; any place of public contest; battlefield.—arenaceous a. like sand; sandy.

argent (ár'-jent) a. made of, or like, silver; silvery;—n. white or silver colour in heraldry.—argentif'erous a. bearing silver.—ar'gentite n. natural silver sulphide, an ore of silver.

argil (ár'-jil) n. pure clay; potters' earth.—argillaceous (ár-ji-lā'-shus) a. like clay; clayey.—argillif'erous a. producing clay.

argosy (ár'-go-si) n. a large, richly-laden merchant ship.

argot (ár'-gō, ár'-got) n. orig. the slang used as kind of secret language by thieves in France; slang; cant.

argue (ár'-gū) v.t. prove by reasoning; discuss; persuade by debate;—v.i. prove; offer reasons; dispute.—arg'uable a. capable of being argued. —arg'uer n. one who argues.—arg'ument n. reason offered in proof for or against a thing; subject of a speech, etc.—argumenta'tion n. arguing.—argument'ative a. given to arguing; contentious.—argument'atively adv.—argument'ativeness n.

aria (ä'-ri-ạ) n. (Mus.) melody; solo part in cantata, opera, oratorio, etc.; lyrical instrumental movement.—**ariet'ta, ariette'** n. short air.

arid (ar'-id) a. dry; parched; barren; (Fig.) uninteresting.—**arid'ity** n.

aright (ạ-rīt') adv. rightly.

arise (ạ-rīz') v.i. come up; stand up; get up; come into view; spring up; occur;—pr.p. aris'ing.—pa.p. arisen (ạ-rizn').—pa.t. arose'.

aristocracy (ar-is-tok'-rạ-si) n. originally rule of the best; later, rule of hereditary upper class; privileged class in state; nobility; upper classes.—**aristocrat** (a-ris'-to-krat, or ar'-ist-ō-krat) n. member of aristocracy.—**aristocrat'ic** a.—**aristocrat'ically** adv.—**aristoc'ratism** n.

arithmetic (ạ-rith'-met-ik) n. science of numbers; art of reckoning by figures; a work on this subject.—**arithmet'ical** a.—**arithmet'ically** adv.—**arithmetician** (ạ-rith-mẹ-tish'-ạn) n. one skilled in arithmetic.—**arithmetical progression**, a series of numbers which increase or decrease by a common difference, e.g. 2, 4, 6, 8, or 21, 18, 15, 12.

ark (ärk) n. large floating vessel in which Noah lived during the Flood (Genesis 6-8); vessel of bulrushes in which infant Moses was placed (Exodus 2)—**Ark of the Covenant**, chest containing the two Tables of the Law, pot of manna, and Aaron's rod (Exodus 25); a chest; a coffer.

arm (ärm) n. the limb extending from shoulders to hand; anything projecting from main body, as a branch;—v.t. give an arm to for support.—**arm'less** a. without arms.—**arm'ful** n. as much as arms can hold of anything.—**arm'chair** n. chair with arms.—**arm'let** n. bracelet; band round the arm, often as official badge.—**arm'-pit** n. cavity under the shoulder.—**at arm's length**, at a safe distance.—**with open arms**, cordially.

arm (ärm) n. weapon; branch of the army, e.g. infantry, artillery, etc.;—pl. all weapons; war; warlike; exploits; military profession; armour; heraldic bearings;—v.t. equip with weapons;—v.t. take up arms.—**armed** (ärmd, or arm'-ed) a. equipped with, or supported by, arms; fortified, strengthened.—**armed neutrality**, condition of holding aloof from a contest, while ready to repel attack.—**small arms**, weapons that can be carried by hand, e.g. pistols, revolvers, shotguns, rifles, etc.—**under arms**, enlisted for military service; fully equipped for battle.—**up in arms**, eager to give battle; roused to anger.—**to lay down arms**, surrender.

armada (är-mā'-dạ, är-mä'-dạ) n. fleet of armed ships.

armadillo (är-mạ-dil'-ō) n. animal, having the body encased in armour-like covering of small, bony shell plates.

Armageddon (ar-ma-ged'-on) n. scene of last battle between powers of good and evil, before Day of Judgment; final decisive battle between great nations.

armament (är'-ma-ment) n. land, naval, or air forces equipped for war; munitions of ship of war, esp. guns, torpedoes, etc.; process of equipping forces in time of war.

armature (är'-ma-tūr) n. armour; protective covering (of plants); 'keeper' of horse-shoe magnet; rotating part of electrical generator; coil of wire in electric motor which breaks magnetic field.

armistice (är'-mis-tis) n. temporary or lasting cessation of hostilities; truce.

armlet (ärm'-let) n. small arm, as of sea; band worn round arm.

armory (är'-mor-i) n. science of heraldry.—**armor'ial** a. pert. to heraldic bearings.

armour (är'-mor) n. defensive covering for the body in battle; orig. chain-mail etc.; steel plates used to protect ships of war, tanks, cars, etc.; armoured fighting vehicles.—**arm'our-bear'er** n. one who carried arms of a superior.—**arm'ourer** n. maker or repairer of weapons; one in charge of small arms.—**arm'our-plat'ed** a. protected by steel plates.—**arm'oury** n. place where weapons are stored.

army (är'-mi) n. body of men trained and equipped for war; military force commanded by a general; organised body for some special purpose, e.g. Salvation Army; large number of people.—**army corps**, a division comprising various branches of the service commanded by lieutenant-general.—**standing army**, the regular army in peacetime.

aroma (ạ-rō'-mạ) n. fragrance in plants; perfume or flavour; charm; atmosphere.—**aromat'ic** a. fragrant; spicy;—n. plant, drug with fragrant smell.

around (ạ-round') adv. in a circle; near;—prep. on all sides of; about.

arouse (ạ-rouz') v.t. excite to action; awaken;—v.i. wake; become active.

arpeggio (är-ped'-jē-ō) n. (Mus.) the sounding of notes of a chord in quick succession.

arrack (är'-ak) n. spirit distilled in E. Indies from rice or juice of coconut tree.

arraign (ạ-rān') v.t. call or set a prisoner at the bar; call to account; accuse publicly.—**arraign'er** n.—**arraign'ment** n.

arrange (ạ-rānj') v.t. put into order;

settle terms; prepare; adapt; adjust; —*v.i.* make agreement; take steps. —**arrange'ment** *n.* act of arranging; way or manner in which things are placed; needful preparation; (*Mus.*) transcription or adaptation of piece of music to instrument other than that for which it was originally composed.—**arrang'er** *n.*

arrant (ar'-ant) *a.* notorious; unmitigated; utter.—**ar'rantly** *adv.* (doublet of *errant*).

arras (ar'-as) *n.* tapestry.

array (ar-rā') *v.t.* set in order; draw up, as troops for battle; dress; equip;—*n.* order; equipment; fine apparel; raiment.

arrear (a-rēr') *n.* state of being behind.—**arrears** *n.pl.* moneys still owing; work still to be overtaken.

arrest (a-rest') *v.t.* stop; check; hinder; seize by authority of law; engage the attention;—*n.* apprehending of a person by authority of law; any seizure, physical or moral; stoppage.—**arresta'tion** *n.* act of arresting.—**arrest'er, arrest'or** *n.* one who, or that which, arrests.— **arrest'ing** *a.* impressive; striking.— **arrest'ment** *n.* arrest of criminal; seizure of person's wages, etc. in debt claims.

arrive (a-rīv') *v.i.* reach a point; come to; attain to any aim or object. —**arriv'al** *n.* act of arriving.

arrogance (ar'-o-gans) *n.* insolent pride; intolerable presumption; overbearing manner.—**ar'rogant** *a.*—**ar'- rogantly** *adv.*—**ar'rogate** *v.t.* claim unduly; take upon one's self without authority.—**arroga'tion** *n.*

arrow (ar'-ō) *n.* pointed barbed missile shot from a bow; sign → to show direction.—**ar'rowy** *a.* of, like an arrow.—**ar'rowhead** *n.* pointed end of arrow; plant with arrow-shaped leaves.

arrowroot (ar'-ō-rōōt) *n.* highly nutritious, farinaceous starch obtained from roots and tubers of various West Indian plants [so-called because used to counteract the poison of arrows].

arsenal (ar'-sen-al) *n.* factory for military and naval arms and stores; armoury.

arsenic (ar'-se-nik) *n.* semi-metallic element; poisonous, whitish, or steel-grey powder of white oxide of arsenic.—**ar'senic, arsen'ical** *a.* pert. to arsenic.—**ar'senate, arsen'iate** *n.* salt of arsenic acid.—**arsen'icate** *v.t.* combine with arsenic; treat with arsenic.

arson (ar'-son) *n.* crime of intentionally setting buildings, etc., on fire.

art (art) second person singular, present indicative, of the verb *to be*.

art (art) *n.* skill; human skill as opposed to nature; skill applied to

music, painting, poetry, etc.; any of the subjects of this skill; system of rules; profession or craft; cunning; trick.—**arts** *n.pl.* certain branches of learning, languages, history, etc. as distinct from natural science.— **art'ful** *a.* exhibiting art or skill; crafty; cunning.—**art'fully** *adv.*—**art'fulness** *n.*—**art'less** *a.* free from art; guileless.—**art'lessly** *adv.*—**art'lessness** *n.*—**art'y** *a.* (*Colloq.*) affectedly artistic.—**art and part** (*Scots Law*) participation.—**black art**, magic.—**fine arts**, painting, sculpture, architecture, music.

artefact (ar'-ti-fakt) See **artifast**.

artery (ar'-te-ri) *n.* vessel carrying blood from the heart; (*Fig.*) any essential channel of communication. —**arterial** (ar-tē'-ri-al) *a.* pert. to an artery; pert. to first-class road.— **arte'rio-sclero'sis** *n.* (*Med.*) hardening of the arteries.

arthritis (ar-thrī'-tis) *n.* inflammation of a joint; gout.—**arthritic** (ar-thrit'-ik) *a.*

arthropod (ar'-thro-pod) *n.* animal with segmented body and jointed limbs, e.g. a spider, crustacean, etc. —**arthrop'odal** *a.*

artichoke (ar'-ti-chōk) *n.* plant with thistle-like head, which can be cooked and fleshy base eaten.—**Jerusalem artichoke** *n.* entirely different plant, bearing edible tubers.

article (ar'-ti-kl) *n.* clause or term in contract, treaty, etc.; literary composition in a journal, etc.; paragraph or section; point of faith; rule or condition; item; commodity or object; (*Gram.*) one of the words *a*, *an* (the indefinite article) and *the* (the definite article);—*v.t.* bind as an apprentice.

articular (ar-tik'-ū-lar) *a.* pert. to the joints.

articulate (ar-tik'-ū-lāt) *v.t.* connect by a joint; utter clearly-defined sounds;—*v.i.* to be connected by joints; speak in distinct syllables or words;—*a.* jointed; of speech, clear, distinct.—**articulated** *a.* of a vehicle, having a detachable, swivelling driving-cab.—**artic'ulately** *adv.*—**artic'ulateness** *n.*—**articula'tion** *n.* act of articulating; consonant; joint between two or more bones.

artifact (ar'-ti-fakt) *n.* something shaped by the art of man and not by nature.

artifice (ar'-ti-fis) *n.* artful or skilful contrivance; ruse; trick; cunning.— **artif'icer** *n.* skilled workman; inventor; (*Navy*) term denoting ranks in the engine-room.—**artific'ial** (ar-ti-fish'-al) *a.* synthetic; imitation; affected in manners.—**artific'ially** *adv.*—**artificial'ity** *n.*

artillery (ar-til'-e-ri) *n.* cannon; troops trained in use of guns, missiles, etc.—artill'eryman n. soldier serving in the artillery.

artisan (ár'-ti-zan) n. craftsman; mechanic.

artist (ár'-tist) n. one who practises one of the fine arts, e.g. painting, sculpture, etc.—artis'tic, artis'tical a.—artis'tically adv.—artistry (ár'-tis-tri) n. artistic ability or effect; beauty of work.

artiste (ar-tēst') n. expert in some art, not one of the fine arts; often applied to member of theatrical profession, esp. music-hall performer.

arum (ā'-rum) n. genus of plants, including the wake-robin or cuckoo-pint.—arum lily, a kind of large white lily.

Aryan (ā'-ri-an) n. early race of pure Hindu stock, thought to have originated in plains of Northern India, progenitors of Indo-European group, i.e. Celtic, Teutonic, etc.

as (az) adv. like; in like manner; similar to; for example:—conj. since; because; when; while;—pron. that.

asbestos (as-bes'-tos) n. fibrous non-inflammable mineral, used in manufacture of fire-proof materials.

ascend (a-send') v.t. climb, mount; walk up;—v.i. rise; arise; soar; climb; mount; go back in time.—ascen'dable, ascen'dible a.—ascen'dancy, ascen'dency n. controlling influence; authority; domination.—ascen'dant, ascen'dent a. rising; just above the horizon; predominant; surpassing;—n. ascendancy; superiority.

ascension (a-sen'-shun) n. act of ascending or rising;—(Bib.) visible rising of Christ to heaven.—ascent (a-sent') n. act of rising; way by which one rises; slope; way up.

ascertain (as-er-tān') v.t. get to know; find out for a certainty.—ascertain'able a.—ascertain'ment n.

ascetic (a-set'-ik) a. sternly self-denying; austere; strict;—n. one who practises rigorous self-denial; hermit.—ascet'icism n.

ascribe (as-krīb') v.t. attribute; impute; assign.—ascrib'able a.—ascrip'tion n.

asepsis (a-sep'-sis) n. freedom from putrefaction; freeing from bacteria by use of antiseptics.—asep'tic a. not liable to putrefaction; sterilised.—asep'ticise v.t. make surgically clean.—asep'ticism n. process of sterilising a wound, etc.

asexual (a-sek'-sū-al) a. without sex; lacking sexual instinct or reproductive organs.—asexual'ity n.

ash (ash) n. tree of the olive family having tough, hard, elastic wood.—mountain ash, rowan tree.—ash'en a.

ash (ash) n. dry white or greyish dust

left after substance has been burned.—ash'es n.pl. remains of human body after cremation or disintegration; (Fig.) a dead body; (Chem.) potash.—ash'en a. of the colour of ashes; pale.—ash'-pan n. removable receptacle for ashes under grate.—ash'tray n. receptacle for cigarette ash.—ash'y a.—sackcloth and ashes, symbols of abject humiliation.—Ash Wednesday, first day of Lent.

ashamed (a-shāmd') a. affected by shame; covered with confusion, caused by awareness of guilt.—asham'edly adv.

ashore (a-shōr') adv. on or to shore; on land, opp. to aboard.

Asian, Asiatic (ā'-shi-an, ā'-shi-at'-ik) a. pert. to Asia or its people.

aside (a-sīd') n. something said in an undertone, esp. on stage by actor and supposed not to be heard by other actors.—adv. on or to one side; apart; dismissed from use.

asinine (as'-in-īn) a. pert. to an ass; stupid.—asinin'ity n.

ask (ask) v.t. seek information; interrogate;—v.i. (for, about) request; inquire.—ask'er n.

askance, askant (a-skans', a-skant') adv. towards one corner of the eye; awry; with disdain or suspicious; not straightforward; sideways.

askew (a-skū') adv. askant; aside; awry; obliquely; off the straight [See skew].

aslant (a-slant') adv. in a slanting direction.

asleep (a-slēp') adv. and a. in a state of sleep; at rest; benumbed; dormant; dead.

aslope (a-slōp') a. sloping; tilted; oblique. adv. with a slope.

asp, aspic (asp, asp'ik) n. poisonous serpent.

asparagus (as-par'-a-gus) n. succulent vegetable with tender shoots.

aspect (as'-pekt) n. look; appearance; position or situation; view.

aspen (as'-pen) n. British tree known also as the trembling poplar because of its quivering leaves.

asperity (as-per'-i-ti) n. roughness of surface, taste, or speech; harshness; bitterness; tartness; crabbedness; sharpness; acrimony.

asperse (as-pers') v.t. slander; defame; vilify; calumniate.—asper'ser n.—asper'sion n. slander.—aspers'ive, aspers'ory a.

asphalt (as'-falt, as-falt') n. black, hard, tar-like substance, used for paving, roofing, etc.;—asphalt' v.t. cover with asphalt.—asphal'tic a. bituminous.

asphodel (as'-fō-del) n. any plant of genus Asphodelus; kind of lily; daffodil; (Myth.) immortal flower that grew in Elysian fields.

asphyxia, asphyxy (as-fik'-si-a, -si)

n. suspended animation due to lack of oxygen in the blood; it is caused by obstructed breathing, as in drowning, inhalation of gases, etc.— **asphyx'ial** *a.*—**asphyx'iant** *n.* substance that produces asphyxia.—**asphyx'iate** *v.t.* produce asphyxia; suffocate.— **asphyxia'tion** *n.*

aspic (as'-pik) *n.* the asp; (*Bot.*) the great lavender.

aspic (as'-pik) *n.* savoury meat jelly containing fish, fowl, egg, etc.

aspidistra (as-pi-dis'-tra) *n.* genus of broad-leaved house-plants.

aspirate (as'-pi-rāt) *v.t.* to pronounce with full breathing sound; to prefix the sound *h* to word or letter;—*n.* letter marked with note of breathing; breathed sound;—*a.* pronounced with rough breathing.

aspire (as-pīr') *v.i.* desire with eagerness; strive towards something higher (usually followed by *to* or *after*).—**as'pirant** *a.* ambitious;—*n.* one who aspires; candidate.—**aspiration** (as-pi-rā'-shun) *n.*

ass (as) *n.* quadruped of horse family but smaller and with longer ears; donkey; (*Fig.*) stupid person.

assail (a-sāl') *v.t.* leap or fall on; attack; assault; ply with arguments, reproaches, etc.—**assail'able** *a.*—**assail'ant** *a.* and *n.*

assassin (a-sas'-in) *n.* one who murders by secret or treacherous assault, esp. hired murderer.— **assas'sinate** *v.t.* to murder by guile or by sudden violence.—**assassina'tion** *n.* —**assas'sinator** *n.*—**the Assassins,** fanatical Moslem sect (11th cent.), who murdered enemies of the Moslem faith. They served themselves with *hashish*, an intoxicating drug, hence their name.

assault (a-sawlt') *n.* violent onset or attack;—*v.t.* attack violently, both physically and with words or arguments; storm.—**assault'able** *a.*—**assault'er** *n.*—**assault and battery** (*Law*) crime of violently attacking and beating a person.

assay (a-sā') *n.* trial; test; examination; analysis of amount of metal in ores or coins, or of ingredients in drugs;—*v.t.* test, esp. with a view to determining presence or amount of metals in ores.—**assay'er** *n.*

assegai (as'-e-gī) *n.* light, slender spear used by S. African natives.

assemble (a-sem'-bl) *v.t.* bring or call together; collect; fit together the parts, e.g. of machine;—*v.i.* meet together.—**assem'blage** *n.* act of assembling.—**assem'bly** *n.* meeting; company gathered; putting together of component parts; group of assembled parts.—**assem'bly-line** *n.* line of machines and workers handling product to be assembled.

assent (a-sent') *v.i.* agree; admit;

concur;—*n.* acquiescence; approval. —**assenta'tion** *n.* servile assent; obsequiousness.—**assent'er, assent'or** *n.* one who assents.—**assentient** (a-sen'-shent) *a.* giving assent;—*n.* one who assents.

assert (a-sert') *v.t.* declare strongly; maintain or defend by argument.— **assert'er, assert'or** *n.*—**asser'tion** *n.*— **assert'ive** *a.* positive; self-confident. —**assert'ively** *adv.*—**assert'iveness** *n.*— **assert'ory** *a.* affirmative.

assess (a-ses') *v.t.* fix the amount (of a tax or fine); tax or fine; estimate for damage, taxation, etc.; rate; appraise.—**assess'able** *a.*—**assess'ment** *n.*—**assess'or** *n.* legal adviser to a lay magistrate; official who assesses taxes; one appointed as associate by the holder of an office.—**assesso'rial** *a.*—**assess'orship** *n.* office of assessor.

assets (as'-ets) *n.pl.* funds or property available for payment of debts, etc.; estate of insolvent or deceased person; entire property of business company, association, society, etc.;—*n.sing.* item of such property; thing of value.

assiduous (a-sid'-ū-us) *a.* constant in application or attention; diligent; hard-working.—**assid'uously** *adv.*—**assid'uousness, assiduity** (as-i-dū'-i-ti) *n.*

assign (a-sīn') *v.t.* allot; apportion; give out; fix; transfer; ascribe.— **assign'able** *a.*—**assignation** (a-sig-nā'-shun) *n.* act of assigning; appointment; tryst; (*Law*) assignment, or the deed by which it is made.— **assignee** (a-sī-nē') *n.* one to whom something is assigned; trustee.— **assign'ment** *n.* allotting to particular person or use; transfer of legal title or interest; alloted task or mission. —**assign'er, assign'or** *n.*

assimilate (a-sim'-i-lāt) *v.t.* make similar; change into a like substance; absorb into the system; digest;— *v.i.* become similar; be absorbed.— **assim'ilable** *a.*—**assimilabil'ity** *n.* the quality of being assimilable.—**assimila'tion** *n.* act of assimilating; (*Fig.*) full comprehension of anything.— **assim'ilative** *a.* capable of assimilating.—**assim'ilatory** *a.* tending to assimilate.

assist (a-sist') *v.t.* help; aid; give support to;—*v.i.* lend aid; be present.—**assist'ance** *n.* help; aid.— **assist'ant** *a.* helping; acting under direction of a superior;—*n.* one who assists; helper; subordinate.

assize (a-sīz') *v.t.* fix the rate of; assess;—*n.* orig. the regulation of a court fixing selling price of bread, ale, etc.; sitting of a court of justice; (*Scot.*) trial before a jury; the jury. —**assiz'es** *n.pl.* courts held periodically in counties of England and Wales by judges on circuit.

associate (a-sō'-shi-āt) *v.t.* join with

as a friend, colleague, confederate, or partner; class together; (*reflex.*) express agreement with;—*v.i.* (foll. by *with*) keep company; combine;—*n.* companion; coadjutor; member of a group; junior member of an academy or society;—*a.* affiliated.—**asso'ciateship** *n.*—**associa'tion** *n.* act of associating; connection; bond; union of persons for some special cause or purpose.—**asso'ciative** *a.*

assonance (as'-ō-nans) *n.* resemblance of sounds; imperfect rhyme in which vowel sounds only are same. —**as'sonant(al)** *a.*

assort (a-sort') *v.t.* classify; arrange;—*v.i.* suit or agree or match (foll. by *with*).—**assort'ed** *a.* classified; varied.—**assort'edness**, **assort'ment** *n.* act of arranging in groups; miscellaneous collection.

assuage (a-swāj') *v.t.* soften; allay; mitigate.—**assuage'ment** *n.*

assume (a-sūm') *v.t.* take upon oneself; take for granted; appropriate; usurp;—*v.i.* claim unduly; be pretentious or arrogant.—**assum'able** *a.* —**assumed'** *a.* supposed; feigned; hypothetical.—**assum'edly** *adv.*—**assum'ing** *a.* arrogant.—**assum'ingly** *adv.*—**assum'ption** *n.* act of taking to or upon oneself by force or right; act of taking for granted; thing supposed to be true, or to have happened.—**assump'tive** *a.* capable of being assumed or taken for granted. —**assump'tively** *adv.*—**Feast of the Assumption**, festival in honour of translation to heaven of the Virgin Mary—celebrated annually on 15th August.

assure (a-shŏŏr') *v.t.* make sure or certain; affirm; insure; convince.—**assur'able** *a.*—**assur'ance** *n.* act of assuring; promise; self-confidence; presumption; insurance, in sense of life assurance.—**assured'** *a.* certain; safe; confident.—**assur'edly** *adv.*—**assur'edness** *n.* certainty.—**assur'er** *n.* —**assur'ingly** *adv.*

aster (as'-ter) *n.* genus of plants of the order of Compositae, so called because the expanded flowers of various hues are like stars.

asterisk (as'-te-risk) *n.* mark (*) used in printing to indicate words for reference or words omitted.

astern (a-stern') *adv.* in, at, or toward the hinder part of a ship; behind.

asteroid (as'-ter-oid) *a.* star-shaped; —*n.* one of the smaller planets; (*Zool.*) star-fish.—**asteroid'al** *a.*

asthma (ast'-ma, as'-ma, asth'-ma) *n.* chronic disorder of respiratory organs.—**asthmat'ic(al)** *a.*—**asthmat'ically** *adv.*

astigmatism (a-stig'-ma-tizm) *n.* defect of eye, lens or mirror causing blurred image.—**astigmat'ic** *a.*

astir (a-ster') *adv.* or *a.* on the move; alert; stirring.

astonish (as-ton'-ish) *v.t.* impress with sudden surprise, wonder, or admiration; strike with sudden terror; amaze; astound.—**aston'ished** *a.* greatly surprised; dazed; stunned; dismayed.—**aston'ishing** *a.* amazing; remarkable.—**aston'ishingly** *adv.*—**aston'ishment** *n.* amazement; surprise.

astound (as-tound') *v.t.* strike dumb with terror or amazement; astonish greatly; stun.—**astound'ing** *a.*

astrakhan (as'-tra-kan) *n.* the skin of the young Persian lamb with soft, curling ringlets of wool; a cheap fabric, made in imitation.

astral (as'-tral) *a.* pert. to stars.

astray (a-strā') *adv.* out of the right way; in the wrong direction.

astride (a-strīd') *adv.* straddling; with legs apart;—*prep.* with one foot on each side of an object.

astringe (as-trinj') *v.t.* bind together; draw together; constipate.—**astrin'gency** *n.*—**astrin'gent** *a.* binding; strengthening; constricting; contracting;—*n.* drug causing contraction of tissues.—**astrin'gently** *adv.*

astro- (as'-trō) *prefix* used in compound words having some reference to stars.

astrology (as-trol'-o-ji) *n.* the science, originally identical with astronomy, which interprets celestial phenomena as having a bearing upon mundane affairs, thus affording a means of predicting the course of future events.—**astrol'oger** *n.*—**astrolog'ic, astrolog'ical** *a.*—**astrolog'ically** *adv.*

astronaut (as'trō-nawt) *n.* one who flies in space; pilot of space vehicle.—**astronautics** *n.* science of space travel.

astronomy (as-tron'-ō-mi) *n.* the science which treats of the heavenly bodies, describing their magnitudes, positions, motions, etc.—**astron'omer** *n.* one versed in astronomy.—**astrono'mic, -al** *a.* pert. to astronomy; boundless; countless; prodigious.—**astronom'ically** *adv.*—**astron'omise** *v.i.*

astrophysics (as-trō-fiz'-iks) *n.* (*Astron.*) study of physical properties of stars and of interstellar space.

astute (as-tūt') *a.* cunning; shrewd; sagacious; crafty; wily; sly; subtle; keen.—**astute'ly** *adv.*—**astute'ness** *n.*

asunder (a-sun'-der) *adv.* apart; into different pieces; in a divided state.

asylum (a-sī'-lum) *n.* sanctuary; refuge for criminals, debtors and others liable to be pursued; place of refuge; institution for the deaf and dumb, the blind, or the insane; protection afforded by such places.

asymmetry (a-sim'-e-tri) *n.* want of symmetry—**asymmet'ric, -al** *a.*

at (at) *prep.* denoting rest in a place, presence, or nearness; near to, by, in; engaged on; in the direction of.

atavism (at'-ạ-vizm) n. recurrence in human beings, animals, or plants of hereditary characteristics, diseases, etc. which have skipped one or more generations; reversion to type.—**atavist'ic** a.

ate (et) past tense of the verb **eat**.

atelier (at-ẹl-yā') n. a workshop, esp. of an artist; hence, a studio.

atheism (ā'-thē-izm) n. disbelief in existence of God.—**a'theist** n.—**atheis'tic, atheis'tical** a.—**atheis'tically** adv.

Athena, Athene (a-thē'-na, -nē) n. (Myth.) Greek goddess of wisdom, etc.—**athenaeum, atheneum** (ath-ẹ-nē'-um) n. originally, her temple at Athens, the meeting-place of philosophers, orators, and poets; name often given to literary institutions. —**Athe'nian** a. pert. to Athens—n. native of Athens.

athirst (ạ-thẹrst') a. thirsty.

athlete (ath'-lēt) n. one trained to physical exercises, sports, etc.; man strong and active by training.—**athletic** (athlet'-ik) a. pert. to physical exercises, contests, etc.; strong; vigorous; muscular.—**athlet'ics** n.pl. athletic sports.—**athlete's foot** n. fungal infection of the foot.

athwart (ạ-thwort') prep. across; from side to side;—adv. crosswise.

Atlantic (at-lan'tik) a. pert. to the ocean separating Europe and Africa from America;—n. the ocean itself.

Atlas (at'-las) n. (Myth.) a Titan, condemned by Zeus to carry the world on his shoulders.—**at'las** n. book of maps, so called because the figure of Atlas often embellished the title-page of old atlases.

atmosphere (at'-mos-fēr) n. mass of air, clouds, gases, and vapour, surrounding the earth or other heavenly body; any similar mass; atmospheric pressure; air in any place, esp. if enclosed, e.g. in a theatre; (Fig.) any surrounding influence.—**atmospher'ic, atmospher'ical** a. pert. to, or depending on, the atmosphere.—**atmospher'ically** adv.—**atmospher'ics** n.pl. radio interference of atmospheric origin.

atoll (at'-ol, ạ-tol') n. ring-shaped coral reef surrounding lagoon.

atom (at'-om) n. smallest unit of an element which can take part in a chemical reaction; (Fig.) anything very small; a tiny bit.—**atom'ic, atom'ical** a. pert. to the atom.—**atomi'city** n. number of atoms in molecule of an element.—**atomisa'tion** n. changing of any liquid into form of fine spray.—**at'omiser** n. instrument for reducing a liquid to form of spray.—**atom (atomic) bomb,** bomb in which great heat and explosive power is generated by nuclear fission.—**atomic energy,** energy derived from nuclear fission or fusion.—**atomic fission, nuclear fission.—atomic pile,** nuclear reactor.—**atomic weight,** weight of an atom of an element, taking weight of hydrogen atom as 1.

atonal (ā'-tō-nạl) a. (Mus.) without tone; unreferred to any scale or tonic.—**atonal'ity** n.—**atonic** (ā'-tonik) a. without tone; unaccented; (Med.) lacking tone or energy.—**atony** (at'-ō-ni) n. lack of tone or accent.

atone (ạ-tōn') v.t. appease; expiate (rare);—v.i. make amends or reparation for an offence; satisfy by giving; an equivalent (with for).—**atone'ment** n. amends; reconciliation, esp. reconciliation of God and man by sufferings and death of Christ.

atrocious (ạ-trō-shus) a. savagely brutal; extremely cruel; very wicked; grievous; (Colloq.) of work, etc., of very poor quality.—**atro'ciously** adv.—**atro'ciousness** n.—**atrocity** (ạ-tros'-i-ti) n. extreme wickedness; cruel and brutal act.

atrophy (at'-rō-fi) n. a wasting away through lack of nutrition or use; emaciation; Also v.t. and i. waste away; cause to waste away.—**atroph'ic, at'rophied** a.

atropin, atropine (at'-rō-pin) n. poisonous alkaloid obtained from the deadly nightshade, used as drug to dilate pupil of the eye.

attach (ạ-tach') v.t. bind, fasten, or tie; take by legal authority; bind by affection; assign, e.g. an officer to a regiment;—v.i. adhere; be ascribed to.—**attach'able** a.—**attached'** a.—**attach'ment** n.

attaché (a-ta'-shā) n. one attached to the suite of an ambassador.—**attaché-case,** n. small hand-case.

attack (ạ-tak') v.t. fall on with force; assail with hostile criticism in words or writing; set to work on; begin to affect (of illness);—n. violent onset or assault.

attain (ạ-tān') reach by exertion; obtain by effort; accomplish; achieve;—v.i. arrive at (generally foll. by to). —**attain'able** a.—**attainabil'ity, attain'ableness** n.—**attain'ment** n. act of attaining; that which is attained.

attaint (ạ-tānt') v.t. stain or disgrace; accuse of; find guilty; deprive of civil rights for treason;—n. a taint or disgrace.—**attain'der** n. loss of civil rights after conviction for treason or felony.— **attaint'ment** n.

attar (at'-ạr) n. fragrant volatile oil from rose-petals. Also **ot'to, ot'tar.**

attempt (ạ-temt') v.t. try; endeavour to do; attack; tempt;—n. trial; effort, esp. unsuccessful; assault.—**attempt'able** a.

attend (a-tend') v.t. take part in; accompany as companion or servant; be present with or at; give medical care to;—*v.i.* pay attention; take care of; wait or be in waiting.— **attend'ance** *n.* act of attending; persons present.—**attend'ant** *a.* being present; consequent;—*n.* one who accompanies as friend or servant; caretaker.—**atten'tion** *n.* careful observation; watching; act of civility; command issued, as in military sense, to ensure readiness to act.— **atten'tions** *n. pl.* courtship.—**attent'ive** *a.* full of attention.—**attent'ively** *adv.* —**attent'iveness** *n.*

attenuate (a-ten'-ū-āt) *v.t.* make thin or fine; make slender; weaken power of;—*a.* slender; thin; (*Bot.*) tapering. —**atten'uated** *a.*—**attenua'tion** *n.*— **atten'uator** *n.*

attest (a-test') *v.t.* and *i.* bear witness to; vouch for; certify; (*Law*) witness officially (a signature).— **attest'able, attest'ative** *a.*—**attesta'tion** *n.* —**attested'** *a.* of cows or milk certified free of T.B. bacilli.

attic (a'tik) *n.* room under roof of house where ceiling follows line of roof (common in Greek archit.);—a garret.

attire (a-tīr') *v.t.* dress; array in splendid garments;—*n.* apparel; dress.—**attire'ment, attir'ing** *n.*

attitude (at'-i-tūd) *n.* posture of a person; pose (in portrait); (*Fig.*) mental or moral disposition.

attorney (a-ter'-ni) *n.* one put in the *turn* or place of another; one legally authorised by another to transact business; solicitor.—**attor'neyship** *n.* —**attor'neydom** *n.*—**power, letter or warrant of attorney**, legal authorisation by which one person may act for another.

attract (a-trakt') *v.t.* and *i.* draw toward; cause to approach; (*Fig.*) allure; provoke notice.—**attractabil'ity** *n.* quality of being attractable.— **attract'able** *a.*—**attract'ile** *a.* attractive. —**attrac'tion** *n.* act of drawing to; force which draws together bodies or particles; affinity existing between one chemical body and another; (*Fig.*) that which allures, or fascinates.—**attract'ive** *a.* having the power to attract.—**attract'ively** *adv.*—**attract'iveness** *n.*

attribute (a-trib'-ūt) *v.t.* consider as belonging to; ascribe to.—**attribute** (at'-ri-būt) *n.* something inherent in person or thing; inseparable property.—**attrib'utable** *a.* that may be ascribed to.—**attribu'tion** *n.* act of ascribing to; quality attributed.— **attrib'utive** *a.*

attrition (a-trish'-un) *n.* act of wearing away by friction; state of being worn; (*Mil.*) deliberate exhaustion of enemy's men and resources.—**attrite'** *a.* worn by rubbing or friction; (*Theol.*) penitent through fear.

attune (a-tūn') *v.t.* put in tune; make musical; make one instrument accord with another; (*Fig.*) bring into spiritual harmony; fit for a purpose. —**attune'ment** *n.*

aubergine (ō'-ber-zhēn) *n.* edible, white, egg-shaped fruit of egg-plant, used as vegetable.

Aubrietia (aw-bri-ē'-sha) *n.* or *Purple Rock Cress*, genus of hardy, evergreen trailing plant.

auburn (aw'-burn) *a.* reddish brown. —*n.* rich chestnut colour.

auction (awk'-shun) *n.* method of public sale whereby object for sale is secured by highest bidder.—*v.t.* sell by auction.—**auc'tionary** *a.*—**auctioneer'** *n.* one licensed to sell by auction;—*v.i.* sell by auction.—**Dutch auction**, auction at which the upset price is very high, and is gradually lowered.—**auction bridge** *n.* card game for four players.

audacious (aw-dā'-shus) *a.* bold, fearless; impudent; insolent.—**auda'ciously** *adv.*—**audac'iousness** *n.*—**audac'ity** *n.* boldness, effrontery.

audible (aw'-di-bl) *a.* capable of being heard.—**aud'ibly** *adv.*—**audibil'ity, aud'ibleness** *n.*

audience (aw'-di-ens) *n.* act of hearing; assembly of hearers; ceremonial reception or interview; judicial hearing.—**aud'ient** *a.*

audio (aw'di-ō) *a.* pert. to sound.

audit (aw'-dit) *n.* examination, by qualified persons, of accounts of business, public office, or undertaking;—*v.t.* test and vouch for accuracy of accounts.—**audi'tion** *n.* act, or sense, of hearing; hearing given to performer as test.—**aud'itor** *n.* hearer; one authorised to investigate the financial condition of company or society.—**auditor'ium** *n.* body of concert hall or theatre where audience are seated; nave of church. —**aud'itorship** *n.*—**aud'itory** *a.* pert. to sense of hearing.

auger (aw'-ger) *n.* boring tool for woodwork, like a large gimlet.

aught (awt) *n.* anything; any part; a whit;—*adv.* to any extent.

augment (awg-ment') *v.t.* increase; add to; enlarge;—*v.i.* grow larger.— **aug'ment** *n.* increase.—**augment'able** *a.*—**augmenta'tion** *n.* act of enlarging; increase.—**augmen'tative** *a.* increasing, etc.—**augment'er** *n.*

augur (aw'-gur) *n.* soothsayer; diviner;—*v.t.* foretell; presage.— **au'gural** *a.*—**au'gurship** *n.*—**au'gury** *n.* art of augur; omen.

august (aw-gust') *a.* majestic; imposing; sublime; grand; magnificent.

August (aw'-gust) *n.* eighth month of the year.

auk (awk) *n.* marine bird, of Arctic regions, with short wings, webbed feet and heavy body.

aunt (ånt) *n.* father's or mother's sister; also applied to uncle's wife.—Aunt Sally, game at fairs, which consists in throwing balls or sticks at a woman's head or other effigy.

aura (aw'-ra) *n.* subtle invisible essence said to emanate from human and animal bodies: (*Fig.*) the atmosphere surrounding a person; character; personality; (*Path.*) premonitory symptom of epilepsy and hysteria, as of cold air rising to the head.—aur'al *a.* pert. to the air, or to an aura.

aural (aw'-ral) *a.* pert. to the ear, or sense of hearing.—aur'ally *adv.*

auric (aw'-rik) *a.* pert. to gold; (*Chem.*) applied to compounds in which gold is trivalent.

auricle (aw'-ri-kl) *n.* external ear; each of two upper cavities of the heart.—auric'ula *n.* (*Bot.*) kind of primula, 'dusty miller' or' bear's ear.'—auric'ular *a.* pert. to ear, or to hearing; told in the ear (of confession).—auric'ulate, aur'iform *a.* earshaped.

auriferous (aw-rif'-e-rus) *a.* yielding gold.

Aurora (aw-ro'-ra) *n.* (*Myth.*) Roman goddess of the dawn.—auro'ra dawn; rosy tint in sky before sun rises: an orange-red colour.—aurora borealis (bō-rē-ā'-lis), luminous phenomenon seen in the far northern sky, caused by high-speed particles emanating from the sun. Also called 'northern lights.'—aurora australis, corresponding phenomenon in southern sky.

auspice (aw'-spis) *n.* omen based on observing birds; augury; divination; *n.pl.*—au'spices, patronage.—auspi'cious (aw-spi'-shus) *a.* giving promise of success; favourable; propitious.—auspi'ciously *adv.*—auspi'ciousness *n.*

austere (aws-tēr') *a.* harsh; severe; strict; simple and without luxury.—austere'ly *adv.*—austere'ness, austerity *n.* severity; extreme simplicity; asceticism.

austral (aws'-tral) *a.* southern.—Australasian (aws-tral-ā'-shan) *a.* pert. to Australia and neighbouring islands:—*n.* a native there.—Australian (aws-trāl'-yan) *a.* pert. to Australia:—*n.* native of Australia.

authentic (aw-thent'-ik) *a.* genuine; real; not of doubtful origin; trustworthy; of attested authority. Also authent'ical.—authent'ically *adv.*—authent'icate *v.t.* prove to be genuine; confirm.—authentica'tion *n.*—authenticity *n.* (aw-then-tis'-i-ti) quality of genuineness.

author (aw'-thor) *n.* (*fem.* au'thoress) beginner or originator of anything; writer of a book, article, etc.—au'thorship *n.* quality or function of being an author; source; origin.

authorise (aw'-thor-iz) *v.t.* clothe with authority; empower; sanction; make legal; justify.—authoris'able *a.*—authorisa'tion *n.*

authority (aw-thor'-i-ti) *n.* legal power or right; influence exercised by virtue of character, office, or mental or moral qualities; one who is appealed to in support of actions or measures; writing by expert on particular subject; writer himself; justification; permission; body or group of persons in control (often *pl.*).—authorita'rian *a.* advocating obedience to authority as opposed to individual liberty:—*n.*—author'itative *a.* having the weight of authority; justified.—author'itatively *adv.*—author'itativeness *n.*

auto- (aw'-tō) a combining form used in many derivatives and meaning *self, oneself,* etc.

auto (aw'-tō) *n.* (*Colloq.*) abbrev. for automobile.—au'tocar *n.* motor-car.

autobiography (aw-tō-bi-og'-ra-fi) *n.* story of a person's life, written by himself.—autobiog'rapher *n.*—autobiograph'ic, *a.*—autobiograph'ically *adv.*

autocrat (aw'-tō-krat) *n.* one who rules by his own absolute right; despot.—autocrat'ic *a.*—autocrat'ically *adv.*—autocracy (aw-tok'-ra-si) *n.* uncontrolled power; a state, the ruler of which has absolute power.

autograph (aw'-tō-graf) *n.* person's own handwriting or signature; original manuscript:—*a.* written in one's own handwriting;—*v.t.* write one's own hand signature.

autogyro (aw-tō-ji'-rō) *n.* aeroplane obtaining its lift from freely revolving rotors.

automatic (aw-to-mat'-ik) *a.* self-acting; mechanical; not voluntary; done unconsciously:—*n.* automatic pistol—automat'ical *a.*—automat'ically *adv.* mechanically.—automa'tion *n.* automatic control of production processes by electronic apparatus.—autom'atism *n.* involuntary action; power of self-movement without external stimulus.—autom'aton *n.* mechanical contrivance, having motive power within itself; robot.—*pl.* autom'ata.

automobile (aw-tō-mō'-bil, aw'-tō-mō-bēl) *n.* road vehicle driven by mechanical power; motor-car;—*a.* pert. to motor-cars.

autonomy (aw-ton'-ō-mi) *n.* the right of self-government; independence.—auton'omous, autonom'ic *a.* self-governing; independent.

autopsy (aw'-top-si) *n.* the dissection and examination of a dead body; a post-mortem examination; personal observation.—autop'tic(al) *a.* self-observed.—autop'tically *adv.*

auto-suggestion (aw'-tō-su-jest'-yun) *n.* a mental process similar to hypnotism but applied by the subject to himself.

autumn (aw'-tum) *n.* third season of year, generally applied to August, September, October; season of decay; time of declining powers.—**autum'nal** *a.* pert. to autumn; past the prime.

auxiliary (awg-zil'-ya-ri) *a.* helping; assisting; subsidiary;—*n.* helper; (*Gram.*) verb which helps to form moods, tenses, or voice of another verb, e.g. *be, have, shall, will, may.*

avail (a-vāl') *v.i.* profit by; take advantage of;—*v.t.* benefit; profit;—*n.* advantage; profit; benefit; utility.—**avail'able** *a.* capable of being used to advantage; procurable.—**avail'-ableness, availabil'ity** *n.*

avalanche (av'-a-lansh) *n.* mass of snow and ice moving down from a height and gathering momentum; (*Fig.*) tremendous downpour.

avant-garde (a-vong gard') *a.* pert. to extreme modernism in the arts.

avarice (av'-a-ris) *n.* excessive love of money; greed; miserliness; cupidity.—**avari'cious** *a.* covetous; grasping.—**avari'ciously** *adv.*—**avari'ciousness** *n.*

avast (a-vast') *interj.* hold! stop!

ave (ā'-vā, ā'-vē) *interj.* hail! farewell! **Ave Maria** *n.* a Hail Mary, invocation to the Virgin Mary, from first two words of angel Gabriel's salutation (Luke 1).

avenge (a-venj') *v.t.* and *i.* take satisfaction for an injury; punish a wrong-doer; seek retribution.—**a-venge'ful** *a.* desiring retribution.—**avenge'ment** *n.*—**aveng'er** *n.* (*fem.* **aveng'eress**) one who avenges.

avenue (av'-e-nū) *n.* principal approach bordered with trees to a mansion; road in park bordered with trees; wide street; (*Fig.*) means of approach.

aver (a-ver') *v.t.* declare positively; assert; allege.—*pr.p.* **aver'ring;**—*pa.p.* **averred'.**—**aver'ment** *n.* act of averring; positive assertion; (*Law*) proof of a plea.

average (av'-e-rāj) *a.* containing a mean proportion; ordinary; normal;—*n.* medial estimate obtained by dividing sum of a number of quantities by number of quantities.—*v.t.* reduce to a mean.

averse (a-vers') *a.* reluctant (to do) or disinclined for; unwilling; set against (foll. by *to*).—**averse'ly** *adv.* with repugnance.—**averse'ness** *n.*—**aver'sion** *n.* strong dislike, antipathy.

avert (a-vert') *v.t.* turn away from or aside; ward off.—**avert'ed** *a.*—**avert'edly** *adv.*—**avert'ible** *a.* capable of being avoided.

avian (ā'-vi-an) *a.* pert. to birds.—**av'iary** *n.* enclosed space for breeding, rearing and keeping of birds.—**av'iculture** *n.* scientific breeding of birds.

aviation (ā-vi-ā'-shun) *n.* art of flying aircraft.—**a'viate** *v.i.* fly.—**a'viator** *n.* pilot of aircraft.

avid (av'-id) *a.* eager; greedy; desirous (foll. by *of* or *for*).—**avid'ity** *n.* greediness; eagerness; hunger; (*Fig.*) zest; burning desire.

avocation (av-ō-kā'-shun) *n.* originally the business which diverted or distracted one from pleasures of life, now used for one's primary vocation in life; distraction.

avoid (a-void') *v.t.* shun; elude; keep clear of; eschew; abstain from; escape; (*Law*) invalidate; annul.—**avoid'able** *a.*—**avoid'ance** *n.* act of shunning.

avoirdupois (av-ur-dū-poiz') *n.* common system of weights.

avow (a-vou') *v.t.* declare openly; own; confess freely; acknowledge.—**avow'able** *a.*—**avow'sal** *n.* open declaration or admission.—**avow'ance** *n.* evidence; testimony.—**avow'edly** *adv.*

avuncular (a-vung'-kū-lar) *a.* pert. to an uncle.

await (a-wāt') *v.t.* wait for; be in store for; attend; be ready for.

awake (a-wāk') *v.t.* rouse from sleep; stir up;—*v.i.* cease from sleep; bestir oneself;—*pa.t.* **awake'**; *pa.p.* **awoke', awaked';**—*a.* not asleep; alert; vigilant; alive.—**awak'en** *v.t.* and *v.i.* rouse from sleep; awake; excite.—**awak'enment, awak(en)'ing** *n.* art of awaking; revival of interest or conscience.

award (a-wawrd') *v.t.* adjudge; determine (a point submitted); decide authoritatively; assign judicially;—*n.* judgment; recorded decision of arbitrator in court of law; thing awarded; prize.

aware (a-wār') *a.* watchful; mindful; conscious of; possessing knowledge of; sensible.—**aware'ness** *n.*

awash (a-wosh') *adv.* (*Naut.*) level with the surface of the water; washed by waves.

away (a-wā) *adv.* absent; distant; on the way; apart; (*interj.*) go!

awe (aw) *n.* great fear mingled with veneration and apprehension of danger; dread; terror;—*v.t.* inspire with awe.—**awe'some** *a.* inspiring awe.—**awestruck', awe'stricken** *a.* overwhelmed with awe.—**aw'ful** *a.* full of awe; filling with fear and admiration; impressive; venerable; majestic; dreadful; terrible; horrible; ugly; unsightly.—**aw'fulness** *n.*

aweigh (awā') *adv.* (*Naut.*) when a ship's anchor is just broken out of the ground by the initial strain on the cable; atrip.

awful See under **awe**.

awhile (a-whīl') *adv.* for a while.

awkward (awk'-ward) *a.* unskilful; ungainly; clumsy; difficult to manage; inconvenient; embarrassing;

perverted; sinister.—**awk'wardly** *adv.*
—**awk'wardness** *n.*

awl (awl) *n.* small pointed instrument for boring holes.

awn (awn) *n.* bristle-like growth, popularly known as the beard, of cereals (oats, barley) and grasses; scale or husk.—**awned'**, **awn'y** *a.*

awning (aw'-ning) *n.* covering of canvas, etc. to shelter from the sun.

awoke See **awake**.

awry (a-ri') *adv.* and *a.* twisted to one side; cooked [See **wry**].

axe, ax (aks) *n.* cutting instrument with blade in line with handle, used for hewing down trees or chopping wood.—*v.t.* reduce or remove for reasons of economy.—**an axe to grind**, private end or purpose to serve.

axes (ak'-ses) plural form of **axe** and **axis**.

axil (ak'-sil) *n.* (*Bot.*) upper angle between leaf and stem.

axiom (ak'-si-om) *n.* self-evident proposition, requiring no proof.—**axiomat'ic, -al** *a.* self-evident.—**axiomat'ically** *adv.*

axis (ak'-sis) *n.* imaginary line round which a body or figure is symmetrically disposed.—*pl.* **ax'es.—ax'ial** *a.* forming the axis; disposed around an axis.—**ax'ially** *adv.*

axle, axle-tree (ak'-sl-trē) *n.* bar of wood or iron rod on which wheel, or system of wheels, turns.—**ax'le-arm** *n.* portion of axle passing through hub of the wheel.—**ax'le-bed**, *n.* portion of axle between wheels.—**ax'led** *a.* having an axle.—**ax'le-pin** *n.* pin or bolt securing axle to body of vehicle.

ay, aye (ī) *adv.* yes; yea.—**ayes** (īz) *n.pl.* affirmative votes or voters.

aye, ay (ā) *adv.* always; ever.

Azalea (a-zā'-le-ạ) *n.* genus of plants allied to rhododendron.

azimuth (az'-i-muth) *n.* of a heavenly body, arc of the horizon comprehended between meridian of observer and vertical circle passing through centre of the body; bearing, as opp. to elevation.—**az'imuthal** *a.*

azure (azh'-ūr) *n.* sky-blue; the sky; —*a.* sky-blue.

B

babble (ba'-bl) *v.t.* and *i.* chatter senselessly; prate; reveal secrets;—*n.* prattling; idle talk; noise of running water.—**bab'bler** *n.*—**bab'bling** *a.*

babel (bā-bel) *n.* confusion of unintelligible sounds; noisy babble of many people talking at one time; uproar, at public meeting.—**ba'beldom** *n.* uproar.

baboon (bạ-bŏŏn') *n.* species of monkey with large body, big canine teeth and capacious cheek-pouches.

baby (bā'-bi) *n.* infant; young child; —*a.* pert. to a baby; small.—**ba'by-farm'er** *n.* one who, for a fee, accepts care of infants.—**ba'byhood** *n.* period of infancy.—**ba'byish** *a.* infantile; behaving like a young child.—**ba'byishness** *n.*—**ba'byism** *n.* characteristics or qualities of a baby.—**ba'by-sitt'er** *n.* one who takes over duties of parents for an evening.

Bacchus (bak'-us) *n.* (*Myth.*) the god of wine.—**bacch'anal** *n.* worshipper of Bacchus; drunken reveller; orgy in honour of Bacchus;—*a.* pert. to Bacchus; riotous; drunken.—**bacchana'lia** *n.pl.* feasts in honour of Bacchus; drunken revels.—**bacchana'lian** *n.* and *a.*—**bacch'ant** *n.* priest or worshipper of Bacchus; reveller.—(**bacchan'te** *n. fem.*).—**bacc'hic** *a.*

bachelor (bach'-e-lor) *n.* unmarried man; celibate; formerly, young knight who fought under aegis of another; one who has taken first degree at university; monk who performed menial duties.—**bach'elorhood**, *n.* state of being a bachelor; celibacy.—**bach'elordom** *n.* bachelors collectively.—**bachelor's buttons**, small yellow double flowers of buttercups or red double flowers of daisy.

bacillus (bạ-sil'-us) *n.* microscopic, rod-like organisms capable of causing certain diseases.—*pl.* **bacil'li.—bacil'lar, bacil'lary** *a.*—**bacil'licide** *n.* a substance used to destroy bacilli; a disinfectant.—**bacil'liform** *a.* of a rod-like shape.

back (bak) *n.* upper or hinder part of trunk of animal; hinder part of object; footballer whose position is in front of goal-keeper;—*a.* of the back; at rear of; not current (as a magazine); reversed; remote;—*adv.* to or toward former place, state, condition, or time; away from the front; in return;—*v.t.* get, or ride, upon back of; provide with a back; move backward; place a bet on; support; endorse (cheque, etc.);—*v.i.* move back; of wind, to change direction counter-clockwise.—**back'-ache** *n.* continuous pain in the back. —**back'ben'cher** *n.* member of parliament not entitled to sit on front benches.—**back'bite** *v.t.* speak evil of someone in his absence.—**back'biter** *n.*—**back'-bone** *n.* spine or vertebral column; (*Fig.*) firmness.—**to the back'-bone**, wholly.—**back'-chat** *n.* perky reply; insolence; impertinence.—**back'er** *n.* supporter; one who bets on a horse, greyhound, etc.; punter.—**back'-fire** *n.* in internal combustion engines, explosion in cylinder occurring before piston has reached top of the stroke;—*v.i.* to do this.—**back'-ground** *n.* ground at the back; situation not readily noticed; part behind foreground; past history; environment; knowledge gained by experience.—**back'-hand** n. writing sloped from left to right; stroke in tennis with hand turned backwards.—**back'-hand'ed** a. with back of the hand; deceitful; indirect; sarcastic; doubtful.—**back'hander** n. blow with back of the hand; bribe.—**back'ing** n. support; sympathy; providing anything with a support; wind-change in counter-clockwise direction; musical accompaniment.—**back'lash** n. lost motion between two elements of a mechanism; **back'log** n. arrears of work, etc.—**back'-num'ber** n. copy of out-of-date publication; one behind the times or unprogressive.—**back'-side** n. back or hinder part; rear side; buttocks; rump.—**back'slide** v.i. slide backwards; lapse from a high moral standard.—**back'slider** n.—**back'sliding** n.—**back'-stays** n.pl. ropes supporting upper mast.—**back'ward** adv. with the back in advance; towards, or on, the back; to a worse state; in reverse direction;—a. directed to back or rear; dull; behind in one's education; shy; unwilling; late.—**back'wardness** n.—**back'wards** adv.—**back'wash** n. backward current; (Slang) dire consequences.—**back'.water** n. water held back by dam; water thrown back by paddle-wheel; by-way in river or creek.—**back'woods** n.pl. outlying forest districts or remote undeveloped country.—**backwoods'man** n.—**to back out**, retract; recede from a promise.—**to back up** support.—**to break the back of**, lay too onerous a burden on; perform successfully most difficult part of.—**to put one's back into**, work with a will.—**to put one's back up**, annoy or irritate.

bacon (bā'-kn) n. finished product of flesh of pigs and hogs after being salted and smoked; rustic, or chawbacon.—**to save one's bacon** (Colloq.) escape bodily injury or loss.

bacterium (bak-tē'-ri-um) n. minute unicellular or filamentous living organisms causing fermentation, putrefaction and diseases.—pl. **bacte'ria**.—**bacteriaem'ia** n. presence of bacteria in the blood.—**bacte'rial** a.—**bacte'ricide** n. agent capable of destroying bacteria.—**bactericid'al** a.—**bacteriol'ogy** n. study of bacteria.—**bacteriolog'ical** a.—**bacteriol'ogist** n.

bad (bad) a. ill or evil; wicked.—**bad'ly** adv.—**bad'ness** n.—**bad blood**, ill feeling.—**to go bad**, rot or decay.

bade (bad) past tense of the verb bid.

badge (baj) n. emblem, usually symbolic, worn to distinguish members of societies, regiments, etc.; token; mark; symbol.

badger (baj'-ẹr) n. greyish-brown hibernating animal;—v.t. follow hotly as dogs the badger; tease, by persistent questioning; pester.

badminton (bad'-min-tun) n. game similar to tennis with substitution of shuttlecocks for tennis balls.

baffle (baf'-l) v.t. frustrate; bewilder.—**baf'fler** n.—**baf'fling** a.

baffle (baf'-l) n. plate for regulating the flow of a liquid or gas; rigid mounting holding reproducing diaphragm of loudspeaker.

bag (bag) n. sack or pouch; content of sack; results of one's fishing or hunting;—v.t. put into a bag; seize;—v.i. hang loosely; bulge or swell out.—pr.p. **bag'ging**.—pa.p. **bagged**.—**bag'gage** n. tents and stores of an army; luggage; dissolute woman.—**bag and baggage**, with all one's belongings.—**bag'ging** n. cloth or material for bags.—**bag'giness** n. state of being baggy (as trousers).—**bag'gy** a. hanging loosely; puffy.—**bags** n.pl. trousers;—(Colloq.) plenty.—**to let the cat out of the bag**, reveal a secret unwittingly.

bagatelle (bag-ạ-tel') n. a trifle; thing of little worth or importance; game played with balls and cue on a board; short piece of light music.

bagpipe (bag'-pīp) n. musical instrument, fitted with wind-bag, chanter on which the melody is played, and drones which furnish the ground bass.—**bag'-pip'er** n.

bail (bāl) n. (Law) security taken by the court that person charged will attend at future date to answer to charge; one who furnishes this security;—v.t. obtain release of person from custody by giving bail.—**bail out** v.i. see **bale**.—**to admit to bail**, release upon security.

bail, bale (bāl) n. scoop; shallow vessel for clearing water out of boat;—v.t. empty of water with some kind of scoop.—**bail'er** n.

bail (bāl) n. little cross-piece bar laid on tops of stumps in cricket; pole separating horses in stable.

bailie, baillie (bāl'-i) n. magistrate of Scottish burgh with certain judicial and administrative authority within the burgh.

bailiff (bā'-lif) n. under-officer of sheriff; land-owner's agent.

bairn (bārn) n. (Scot.) child.

bait (bāt) n. food, set to entice fish or animal; food taken on journey for refreshment; lure; snare;—v.t. put food on hook or in trap as lure; give refreshment on journey; set dogs on an animal, such as badger, bear, etc.; harass; tease.—**bait'er** n.—**bait'ing** a. and n.

baize (bāz) n. woollen or cotton cloth with long nap, usually dyed in plain colours and used for curtains, table-coverings and linings.

bake (bāk) v.t. harden by heat; cook in oven or over fire;—v.i. work at baking; to be baked.—**bake'house** n.—**bak'er** n.—**bak'ery** n. bakehouse.—**bak'ing** n. batch of bread, etc.—a baker's dozen, thirteen.—**baking powder**, mixture of tartaric acid and bicarbonate of soda as substitute for yeast.

balalaika (bal-a-lī'ikạ) n. old Slavic musical instrument, having triangular base with two or three strings.

balance (bal'-ạns) n. apparatus for determining weight, or comparing masses, of bodies; poised beam with two opposite scales; any condition of equilibrium; part of watch or clock which regulates the beats; sense of proportion and discretion; poise; payment still due, or cash in hand;—v.t. weigh, as in a balance; equal in proportion, etc.; adjust, as an account;—v.i. be of same weight; be in equipoise; hesitate.—**balance sheet**, statement of assets and liabilities.—**bal'ance-wheel** n. wheel regulating the beat in watches.

balcony (bal'-kọ-ni) n. platform or gallery projecting from building; lower gallery in theatre or concert hall.

bald (bawld) a. destitute of hair or feathers on crown of head; bare; unadorned; undisguised; without literary style; monotonous.—**bald'head, bald'pate** n. one destitute of hair.—**bald'ly** adv.—**bald'ness** n.

balderdash (bawl'-dẹr-dash) n. jargon of meaningless words jumbled together; senseless talk; nonsense.

bale (bāl) n. that which causes sorrow or ruin; evil; misery; mischief; injury; woe.—**bale'ful** a. full of grief and misery, hurtful.—**bale'fully** adv.—**bale'fulness** n. perniciousness.

bale (bāl) n. package, compactly compressed, and wrapped in protecting cover;—v.t. pack in bales.—**bal'er** n. one employed in baling goods.

bale (bāl) v.t. See **bail**.—**to bale out**, to jump from an aeroplane by parachute.

balk, baulk (bawk) n. great beam or rafter of squared timber, stretching from wall to wall; unploughed ridge of land; barrier or check; disappointment; part of a billiard table;—v.t. frustrate; bar the way;—v.i. stop abruptly; jib.—**balk'y** a.

ball (bawl) n. any round body; sphere; globe; the earth; bullet or shot; delivery by bowler in cricket; heavy piece of a pendulum;—v.t. and i. form into a ball.—**ball'bear'ings** n. hardened steel balls interposed in channels between rotating and stationary surfaces of a bearing.—**ball'-cock** n. automatic cistern tap operated by lever attached to floating ball.—**ball-point pen** n. fountain pen with tiny ball point leaving fine trace of ink on paper.—**ball'-race** n. grooves in which ball-bearings run.—**ball and socket**, joint formed by ball partly enclosed in a cup and so adjusted that it can move freely in all directions.

ball (bawl) n. social gathering for purpose of dancing; an assembly.—**ball'-room** n.

ballad (bal'-ạd) n. story in verse, of popular origin; concert-room melody, usually sentimental.—**bal'lad-mon'ger**, n. ballad-writer.

ballast (bal'-ạst) n. heavy material taken on board ship to increase vessel's draft and steadiness; sandy material dredged from river; crushed stone, etc. that which renders anything steady;—v.t. load with ballast; to steady.

ballerina (ba-lẹr-ē'-nạ) n. principal female ballet dancer.

ballet (bal'-ā) n. spectacular representation, consisting of dancing and miming, aiming to express an idea or tell a story, to accompaniment of music.—**ball'etomane** n. enthusiast for ballet.

ballistic (bạ-lis'-tic) a. pert. to projectile and its flight.—**ballis'tics** n.pl. scientific study of motion of projectiles.

balloon (bạ-lōōn') n. aerostat consisting of gas-filled envelope, not equipped for mechanical propulsion; line enclosing spoken words in cartoon.—**balloon'ing** n.—**balloon'ist** n.

ballot (bal'-ọt) n. secret voting, usually by marking a ballot-paper and inserting it in ballot-box; little ball or slip of paper used in secret voting;—v.t. draw lots.

balm (bám) n. fragrant plant; any fragrant or healing ointment; anything which soothes pain.—**balm'iness** n.—**balm'y** a. fragrant.

balmoral (bạl-mor'-ạl) n. round cap like a beret; long laced boot; petticoat.

balsa (bawl'-sạ) n. extremely light wood of the W. Indian cork tree; raft made of this wood.

balsam (bawl'-sạm) n. name applied to many aromatic resins and oils with stimulant and tonic properties; soothing ointment; healing agent.—**balsam'ic** n. soothing, oily medicine;—a. having fragrance of balsam.—**balsamif'erous**, a. yielding balsam.—**bal'samous** a. soothing.—**bal'samy** a.

baluster (bal'-us-tẹr) n. short stone shaft turned and moulded, used to support hand-rail or coping.—**bal'ustered** a.—**bal'ustrade** n. row of balusters with continuous base and coping, forming ornamental parapet to bridge or balcony.

bamboo (bam-bōō') n. genus of immense grasses in the tropics, stems hollow and partitioned at the nodes.

ban (ban) n. proclamation; sentence of outlawry; excommunication; curse; prohibition; v.t. prohibit; curse;—pr.p. ban'ning.—pa.t. and pa.p. banned.

banal (bǎn'-al, ban-al') a. trite, trivial, petty, vulgar, commonplace.—**banal'ity** n. triteness, triviality.

banana (bạ-ná'-na) n. large herbaceous plant; edible fruit.

band (band) n. cord, tie, or fillet; flat strip of material for binding; stripe on a building or dividing a wall space; endless belt used for driving wheels or rollers; group of radio wavelengths.—**band'box** n. light cardboard box for millinery.—**band'-saw** n. saw in form of mechanically driven endless steel belt.

band (band) n. players of musical instruments in combined performance; company united for common purpose; number of armed men;—v.t. bind together;—v.i. associate; join together.—**band'master** n. director of military or brass band.—**bands'man** n. member of brass band.—**band'stand** n. open-air structure suitable for musical performances.—**to join the band-wagon**, participate in movement when its success is assured.

bandage (band'-āj) n. swathe of cloth, used for binding up wounds, etc.—v.t. bind with bandage.—**ban'daging** n. material for bandages.

bandied, bandiness See bandy.

bandit (ban'-dit) n. desperate robber; brigand; outlaw; highwayman;—pl. ban'dits, bandit'ti n.

bandoleer, bandolier (band-dō-lēr') n. broad leather belt fitted with pockets to hold cartridges.

bandolero (band-o-lār'-ō) n. robber; bandit; highwayman.

bandy (ban'-di) a. crooked; bent; bandied; bandy-legged;—v.t. beat to and fro; toss from one to another, as 'to bandy words.'—**ban'died** a. bandy.—**ban'diness** n.—**ban'dy-leg'ged** a. having legs, which bend outwards.

bane (bān) n. any cause of ruin; destruction; mischief; noxious substance; poison.—**bane'ful** a. having poisonous qualities.—**bane'fully** adv.—**bane'fulness** n.

bang (bang) v.t. beat, as with club; handle roughly; make a loud noise;—n. blow with club or fist; loud noise; explosion.—**bang'ing** n.

bangle (bang'-gl) n. ornamental ring worn round arm or ankle; bracelet.

banish (ban'-ish) v.t. condemn to exile; drive away; expel; cast from the mind.—**ban'ishment** n. exile.

banister (ban'-is-tẹr) n. Same as baluster.

banjo (ban'-jō) n. stringed instrument with long neck and drum-like body.

bank (bangk) n. ridge of earth; shoal; sandbank; edge of stream or lake; raised edge of road, etc.; mass of heavy clouds or fog;—v.t. raise a mound; dike; make sloping; cover a fire with small coal to procure slow combustion; tilt an aeroplane about the longitudinal axis when turning.—**bank'ing** n. portion of road or track sloped to minimise effect of curve.—**to bank on** v.t. depend on.

bank (bangk) n. bench on which rowers sit; tier of oars; bench on which judges sat.

bank (bangk) n. establishment where money is received for custody and repaid on demand; money-box; money at stake in card games of hazard; pool;—v.t. deposit money in bank.—**bank'er** n. one employed in banking; in games of chance proprietor against whom the other players stake; card game; safe bet.—**bank'-note** n. promissory note on bank of issue promising to pay its face value to bearer on demand.—**bank'-rate** n. rate of discount, fixed weekly, at the Bank of England.

bankrupt (bangk'-rupt) n. insolvent person compelled to place his affairs in hands of creditors;—v.t. cause to go bankrupt;—a. insolvent; lacking in (ideas, etc.).—**bank'ruptcy** n.

banner (ban'-ẹr) n. flag.—**ban'nered** a. provided with banners.—**ban'neret** n. small banner, or streamer. Also **ban'nerette**.—**banner headline**, prominent headline in newspaper, extending the whole width of paper.

bannock (ban'-ok) n. (Scot.) flat cake of oatmeal or pease-meal, baked on a griddle.

banns (banz) n.pl. proclamation of intended marriage.

banquet (bang'-kwet) n. feast; rich repast; something specially delicious;—v.t. entertain to a banquet.—**banq'ueting** n.

banshee (ban'-shē) n. in Ireland and W. Highlands of Scotland, fairy-elf who, by shrieks and wailing, foretells approaching death in family.

bantam (ban'-tam) n. variety of the small common domestic fowl;—a. of very light weight; plucky.—**bantamweight**, boxer weighing less than 8 stones, 6 lbs.

banter (ban'-tẹr) v.i. make good-natured fun of someone; joke; jest;—n. wit at expense of another; chaff; pleasantry.—**bant'erer** n.—**ban'tering** n.—**ban'teringly** adv.

Bantu (ban'-tōō) n. generic name applied to the native languages and natives of S. half of Africa.

banyan, banian (ban'-yan) n. Indian fig tree; Hindu trader; loose Indian garment.

baptise (bap'-tīz') *v.t.* administer sacrament of baptism to; christen; give a name to.—**bap'tism** *n.* sacrament by which person is initiated into membership of Christian Church, either by sprinkling of water or by immersion.—**baptis'mal** *a.*—**bap'tist** *n.* one who baptises; Baptist *n.* one who insists that rite of initiation is duly administered only by immersion and only to adults.—**bap'tistery**, **bap'tistry** *n.* ancient circular building in which baptisms took place.

bar (bár) *n.* long piece of solid material, used especially for preventing ingress or egress; bolt of a door; boom across a river; sandbank; counter for dispensing liquor, etc.; room in which it is situated; public-house; rail before the judge's seat where prisoners appear; members of legal profession allowed to plead in court; (*Her.*) horizontal band crossing shield; (*Mus.*) perpendicular line on stave between each measure;—*v.t.* fasten or mark with bar; obstruct; prevent; exclude;—*prep.* except.—**bar'maid**, **bar'man**, **bar'tender** *n.* bar attendant.—**bar'ring** *prep.* excepting.—*n.* exclusion of any kind.—**to call to the Bar**, admit as barrister.

barb (bárb) *n.* spike of arrow, fish-hook, etc.; horse of great speed and endurance, originally from Barbary.—*v.t.* furnish with barbs or prongs, as an arrow; trim the beard.—**barbed** *a.* bearded; furnished with barb or barbs.—**barbed'-wire** *n.* wire armed with sharp points.

barbarian (bar-bā'-ri-ạn) *n.* orig. one who could not speak Greek, now an uncivilised being without culture; cruel, brutal man;—*a.* savage; rude.—**barbar'ic** *a.*—**bar'barise** *v.t.*—**bar'barism** *n.* incorrect use of idiom or word; want of civilisation.—**barbar'ity** *n.* cruelty; savagery.—**bar'barous** *a.*—**bar'barously** *adv.*—**bar'barousness** *n.*

barbecue (bár'-be-kū) *n.* grid-iron on which an animal is roasted whole; animal so roasted; upper storey of house where grain or coffee is stored; open-air feast.—*v.t.* roast whole.

barbel (bár'-bel) *n.* small, beard-like process, appended to mouth of certain fishes; large fresh-water fish.

barber (bárb'-ẹr) *n.* one who shaves or trims and dresses the hair; hairdresser.

barberry (bár'-ber-i) *n.* (*Bot.*) spiny shrub with red berries, used for hedging.

barbican (bár'-bi-kạn) *n.* outwork to protect approaches to castle or fortified town.

barbiturates (bar-bit'-ū-rāts) *n.* (*Med.*) derivatives of barbituric acid, non-habit forming, sedative drugs.

barcarolle, barcarole (bár'-kạ-rōl) *n.* musical composition written in imitation of gondoliers' songs of Venice.

bard (bárd) *n.* Celtic minstrel who celebrated in song the great deeds of heroes; poet.—**bard'ic** *a.* pert. to bards or their poetry.

bare (bár) *a.* without covering; naked; empty; open to view; paltry;—*v.t.* strip off or uncover.—**bare'ly** *adv.* openly; poorly; scarcely.—**bare'ness** *n.*—**bare'backed** *a.* with bare back; having no saddle.—**bare'faced** *a.* shameless.—**bare'facedness** *n.* sheer impudence.—**bare'footed** *a.* and *adv.* unshod.—**bare'headed** *a.*

bargain (bár'-gin) *n.* agreement between parties in buying and selling; profitable transaction; something purchased cheaply.—*v.i.* make a contract; haggle.—**bar'gainer** *n.*—**into the bargain**, over and above what is agreed upon.

barge (barj) *n.* flat-bottomed boat, designed for transporting merchandise on rivers, canals; naval commander's boat;—*v.i.* push forward roughly.—**bar'gee**, **barge'man** *n.* one who is employed working a barge.

baritone, (bar'-i-tōn) *n.* the male human voice between tenor and bass.

barium (bā'-ri-um) *n.* metallic element (symbol *Ba.*).—**ba'ric** *a.* pert. to barium.

bark (bárk) *n.* outer covering of tree; rind; waste tan used in manufacturing white-lead;—*v.t.* strip off bark; graze the skin.—**bark'en** *v.i.* become dry like bark.

bark (bárk) *v.t.* utter a cry like dog; yelp; snarl (at);—*n.* sound emitted by dog; coughing; sound of gun.—**to bark up the wrong tree**, be on wrong trail.

bark, (bárk) *n.* (*Poet.*) ship or boat.

barley (bár'-li) *n.* important cereal of very ancient culture, the grain being used for malt-making, bread, and food for cattle.—**bar'ley-corn** *n.* grain of barley; third part of an inch.—**John Barleycorn** (*Fig.*) whisky.—**bar'ley-su'gar** *n.* confection made from sugar boiled till brittle in barley water.—**bar'ley-wat'er** *n.* infusion of pearl barley.—**pearl'-barley** *n.* grain of barley.

barn (bárn) *n.* covered farm-building for storing grain, hay, etc.;—*v.t.* store in a barn.—**barn'-dance** *n.* lively dance resembling the schottische.—**barn'-yard** *a.* pert. to domestic fowls.—*n.* open enclosure attached to barn.—**barn'-owl** *n.* bird of prey which takes up permanent residence in steeples, barns, etc.—**barn'-storm'er** *n.* strolling-player.

barnacle (bár'-nạ-kl) *n.* shell-fish which attaches itself to bottoms of ships and to rocks.—**bar'nacles** n.pl. spectacles.

barograph (bar'-ō-graf) n. self-recording barometer.

barometer (ba-rom'-e-ter) n. instrument for measuring atmospheric pressure.—**baromet'ric, baromet'rical** a.—**baromet'rically** adv.—**barom'etry** n.

baron (bar'-on) n. title of nobility, lowest of the British peerage to sit in the House of Lords; judge of the Court of Exchequer; commercial magnate.—**bar'onage** n. whole body of barons.—**bar'oness** n. baron's wife; woman holding a barony.—**baron'ial** a. pert. to a barony.—**bar'ony** n. the lordship of a baron; domain of a baron; in Ireland, division of county; in Scotland, large freehold estate.—**baron of beef,** joint consisting of both sides of the back; double sirloin.

baronet (bar'-ō-net) n. hereditary title ranking below baron and above knight but without privilege of peerage.—**bar'onetcy** n. rank of a baronet.

baroque (ba-rok') n. orig. jeweller's trade term for ill-shaped pearls; florid style of late Renaissance art, architecture and music;—a. over-lavish; bizarre.

barque (bärk) n. sailing-ship with not less than three masts, having fore and main masts rigged square, and the last (the mizzen in three-masted vessel) fore-and-aft rigged.

barrack (bar'-ak) n. building for accommodation of soldiers (generally used in plural).

barracking (bar'-ak-ing) n. shouting and cheering in chorus with view to encouraging or discouraging one of the participants in a game.

barrage (bár'-äj) n. artificial bar erected across stream to regulate its flow; screen of continuous military fire produced to protect advance of troops or to stop hostile attacks.

barrel (bar'-el) n. cylindrical wooden container consisting of staves bound by hoops; measure of capacity, of ale, 36 gall., of wine, 31½ gall.; anything cylindrical, as gun-barrel;—v.t. stow in barrels.—**bar'rel-or'gan** n. street-organ actuated by pins on rotating drum.

barren (bar'-en) a. incapable of producing offspring or fruit, infertile.—**bar'renly** adv.—**bar'renness** n

barricade (bar'-i-kād) n. make-shift fortification, built as obstruction; any erection which hinders free passage;—v.t. build this.

barrier (bar'-i-er) n. chain of military posts to protect frontiers; railing, fence, or wall; any obstruction; line of separation.—**barrier cream** n. substance rubbed on the

hands for protection when working.

barrister (bar'-is-ter) n. member of highest branch of legal profession, with exclusive right of practising in superior courts of England.—**barris-ter'ial** a.—**bar'ristership** n.

barrow (bar'-ō) n. small wheeled cart for carrying loads.—**bar'row-boy,** n. street trader.

barrow (bar'-ō) n. artificial mound of stone, wood, or earth, piled up in prehistoric times over remains of the dead.

barter (bár'-ter) v.t. exchange or give in exchange;—v.i. traffic by exchange of one kind of goods for another;—n. direct exchange of commodities.

basal See base.

basalt (ba'-sawlt) n. igneous rock of greenish-black colour.—**basalt'ic** a.—**basal'tiform** a. columnar, having form of basalt.

bascule (bas'-kūl) n. balancing lever.—**bas'cule-bridge** n. counterpoise bridge.

base (bās) a. of humble birth or of low degree; morally low.—**base'ly** adv.—**base'born** a. illegitimate.—**base metal** n. non-precious metal.

base (bās) n. bottom; part of thing on which it rests; foundation; support; starting-place; fixed point; supply point of an army; station at base-ball; main ingredient; (Chem.) substance capable of combining with an acid to form a salt;—v.t. put on a base; found.—**bas'al** a. situated at the base.—**base'less** a. having no foundation.—**base'lessness** n.—**base'ly** adv.—**base'ment** n. lowest storey of building.—**bas'ic** a.

base (bās) (Mus.). See bass.

baseball (bās'-bawl) n. American ball game, bearing resemblance to rounders; the ball used.

bash (bash) v.t. (Colloq.) smash in; beat in; knock out of shape; beat;—n. severe blow; dent.—**bash'ing** n. thrashing.

bashful (bash'-fool) a. easily confused; not desiring to attract notice.—**bash'fully** adv.—**bash'fulness** n.

basic (bā'-sik) a. relating to or serving as base; primary; containing small amount of silica.—**basic dyes,** colour bases with hydrochloric acid.—**basic English,** simplification of English for foreigners by reducing number of essential key-words.—**bas'ic-slag** n. by-product in manufacture of steel, used as fertiliser.

basil (baz'-il) n. aromatic culinary herb; sweet basil.

basilica (ba-sil'-i-ka) n. public building or hall of the Romans, later often converted into a church by early Christians; spacious church built on model of original basilicas.—**basil'ican** a.

basin (bā´-sn) n. wide, hollow, bowl-shaped vessel; land-locked bay with good anchorage; whole tract of country drained by river.

basis (bā´-sis) n. that on which a thing rests; foundation.—pl. ba´ses.

bask v.i. sun oneself; lie in warmth or sunshine.

basket (bas´-ket) n. vessel made of willow, cane, rushes, or other flexible materials, interwoven.—bas´ket-ball n. game where ball has to be propelled into basket.—bas´ketful n.—bas´ket-hilt n. steel, basket-shaped hilt of sword or fencing-stick.—bas´ketry, bas´ket-work n. wickerwork.

Basque (bàsk) n. native or language of Basque country (W. Pyrenees); part of lady's dress, resembling jacket with short skirt;—a.

bas-relief, bass-relief (bás or bá-re-lēf´) n. or a. low relief, sculpture in which figures or objects are raised slightly upon a flat surface, like embossed work.

bass, base (bās) n. (Mus.) lowest part of harmony, whether vocal or instrumental; deepest quality of human voice or stringed instrument; —a. low.—bass´-clef n. sign on fourth line of bass stave.—doub´le-bass´ n. largest of the stringed instruments.

basset (bas´-et) n. hound formerly used in badger hunting.—bass´et-horn n. rich-toned single-reed wood-wind instrument.

bassoon (bạ-sōōn´) n. low-pitched double-reed wood-wind instrument; organ reed stop of that name.—double bassoon, one which sounds octave lower.—bassoon´ist n.

bastard (bas´-tard) n. child born out of wedlock; impure, coarse brown refuse product of sugar-refining, used to colour beer;—a. illegitimate; false; counterfeit;—bas´tardy n.—bas´tardise v.t. render illegitimate.

baste (bāst) v.t. beat with a cudgel; drop fat on meat when roasting.

baste (bāst) v.t. sew loosely with long stitches.

bastille (bas-tēl´) n. originally tower or bastion; state prison.—The Bastille, famous state prison of Paris, demolished by revolutionary mob on 14th July, 1789.

bastion (bast´-yun) n. stronghold of defence.

bat (bat) n. club or stick; shaped club used in cricket, baseball, etc.; batsman; piece of brick larger than a closer;—v.i. face the bowling in cricket;—pr.p. bat´ting; pa.p. bat´ted. —bat´ter, bats´man n. one who is batting at cricket.—bat´ting n.—off one's own bat, alone, without any assistance.

bat (bat) n. animal, related to the hedgehog and shrew and able to fly as long fingers are united by a membrane to hind legs and tail.—bat´ty a. (Slang) crazy. Also bats.—to have bats in the belfry, be crazy or eccentric.

batch (bach) n. quantity of bread baked at one time; number of articles received or despatched at one time; set of similar articles.

bate (bāt) v.t. lessen; abate.

bath (bàth) n. vessel or place to bathe in; water in which to bathe; solution or receptacle in which anything is immersed;—v.t. wash oneself.—bath´-chair n. wheeled chair for invalids, first used at Bath.—bath´-house n.—bath´room n.—bath´-stone n. soft, easily worked limestone quarried near Bath.—blood´-bath n. massacre.

bathe (bāTH) v.t. wash by immersion; —v.i. be immersed; enter sea or fresh-water for recreation;—pr.p. bath´ing.—bath´er n.—bath´ing n.—bath´ing-pool n.

bathos (bā´-thos) n. term indicating ludicrous descent from sublime to ridiculous in speech or writing; anti-climax.—bathet´ic a.

bathy- (bath-i) prefix used in the construction of compound terms relating to sea-depths.—bathyal zone, floor of the sea at a depth of 600-3000 feet.—bathym´etry n. science of deep-sea sounding (cf. bathom´eter).—bath´y-orograph´ical a. term applied to maps which by suitable colouring indicate both the land altitudes and sea depths.—bath´ysphere n. form of deep-sea diving-bell.

batman (bàt´-man) n. officer's servant.

baton (ba´-ton) n. short staff or club; truncheon, symbolic of authority or used as offensive weapon; in music, wand used by conductor in beating time; marshal's staff.—v.t. strike with a baton.—bat´on-sin´ister n. (Her.) diagonal bar on shield indicating illegitimacy.

battalion (bạ-tal´-yun) n. military tactical and administrative unit of command.—battal´ions n.pl. great numbers, swarms.

batten (bat´-n) v.t. fatten;—v.i. grow fat in luxury.

batten (bat´-n) n. piece of wood nailed on a surface to give it strength; a cleat; row of lamps used for stage-lighting; board used on ships to fasten down hatch-covers in stormy weather;—v.t. fasten or form with battens.

batter (bat´-ẹr) v.t. strike or beat continuously; assault; wear by hard use;—n. mixture moistened to a paste and briskly beaten up.—batt´ering ram, n. suspended beam, with head like a ram's, formerly used to breach walls.

battery (bat´-ẹr-i) n. act of battering;

place where cannon are mounted; unit of artillery; electric cells which store electric current; tier of coops for poultry.

battle (bat'-l) n. encounter between enemies; struggle of any kind;—v.i. fight on large scale.—**bat'tle-axe** n. primitive weapon of warfare; (Colloq.) formidable female **bat'tlecrui'ser** n. large warship combining heavy armament of a battleship and speed of a cruiser.—**bat'tle-cry** n. war-shout; slogan.—**bat'tle-dress** n. standardised uniform in the Army.—**bat'tle-field**, **bat'tle-ground** n.—**bat'tler** n.—**bat'tle-ship** n.largest and most heavily armed of fast warships.

battlement (bat'-l-ment) n. protective parapet on wall with embrasures or crenelles at regular intervals for discharge of fire-arms.

bauble (baw'-bl) n. trifling piece of finery; gew-gaw; stick with a fool's head attached carried by jesters of former times.

baulk (bawk) See balk.

bauxite (bo'-zīt, bok-sīt) n. hydrated oxide of aluminium and ferric oxide valuable as an ore of aluminium.

bawd (bawd) n. procurer or procuress of women for immoral purposes.—**bawd'ily** adv.—**bawd'iness** n.—**bawd'ry** n.—**bawd'y** a. obscene; filthy; unchaste.—**bawd'y-house**, n. brothel.

bawl (bawl) v.t. shout, proclaim;—v.i. shout out with a loud voice;—n. loud, prolonged cry.

bay (bā) a. reddish-brown;—n. chestnut horse.

bay (bā) n. inlet of the sea, wider at mouth than a gulf.

bay (bā) n. subdivision longitudinally of a building by piers, arches, girders, etc.—**bay'-win'dow** n. window projecting beyond the wall.—**sick'-bay**, ship's hospital.

bay (bā) n. laurel tree.—**bays** n.pl. victor's garland or crown.—**bay'-rum** n. aromatic liquid used as perfume and cosmetic for the hair.

bay (bā) n. barking, esp. of hounds in pursuit of prey;—v.t. bark at; v.i. bark.—**at bay**, said of hunted animal, when all escape is cut off.

bayonet (bā'-ō-net) n. dagger-like weapon for fixing to muzzle of rifle;—v.t. stab with bayonet.

bazaar, **bazar** (ba-zár') n. Oriental market-place; sale of work where articles given are sold for charity; shop selling miscellaneous goods.

be (bē) v.i. and aux. (pres. indic. am; past indic. was; past part. been), exist; live; have a state, existence, or quality; remain.—**let be**, leave alone.

beach (bēch) n. shore of sea or lake, esp. where sandy or pebbly; shore;—v.t. run or haul boat up on to beach.—**beach'-comb'er** n. long, rolling wave; lounger who frequents wharves of seaports; scrounger.—**beach'head** n. footing gained on hostile shores by opposing army.

beacon (bē'-kn) n. fire lit on high eminence, usually as warning; warning; floating buoy; traffic sign indicating pedestrian crossing; beamed radio transmitter acting as guide to aircraft or shipping;—v.t. mark a channel by beacons.

bead (bēd) n. little ball pierced for stringing; any small spherical object.—v.t. furnish with beads;—v.i. string beads.—**beads** n.pl. rosary, necklace; astragal; flange of tyre;—**bead'ed** a. in bead form.—**bead'ing** n. small rounded moulding; rosary.—**bead'y** a.—**to draw a bead on**, aim gun at.—**to tell one's beads**, recite the rosary.

beadle (bē'-dl) n. mace-bearer; in Scotland, an attendant on the minister.—**bead'ledom** n. stupid officiousness.

beagle (bē'-gl) n. small hound used in hunting hares.

beak (bēk) n. horny bill of bird, turtle, etc.; anything shaped like a beak; (Slang) magistrate or schoolmaster.

beaker (bē'-ker) n. large drinking-cup or vessel; tumbler-shaped vessel of thin glass used by chemists.

beam (bēm) n. strong, horizontal piece of timber or reinforced concrete for spanning and supporting weights; part of balance from which the scales hang; cross-timber of ship; extreme width, measured athwartships, of a ship; wooden cylinder on which the warp is wound in a loom; pole of a carriage; shaft of an anchor; sharply defined ray of light; directional radio wave; sparkle in a person's eyes manifesting extreme pleasure or interest;—v.t. transmit by beams;—v.i. send forth beams; shine; smile benignly.—**beam'-ends** n. position when ship lies on her side with cross-beams upright; (Fig.) last of a person's resources.—**beam'ing** a. radiantly happy; shining;—n. rays of light; manifestation of pleasure by smiling.—**beam'less** a.

bean (bēn) n. flat, kidney-shaped seed of various plants, chiefly of the order Leguminosae.—**bean'-feast** n. feast where food is abundant; a jollification.—**bean'o** n. (Slang) jollification; festivity.—**full of beans**, in good fettle; energetic.—**without a bean**, penniless.

bear (bār) v.t. support or carry; endure; suffer; behave; give birth to;—v.i. produce (as fruit); endure; press;—pa.t. bore; pa.p. borne or born.—**bear'able** a. able to be borne; tolerable.—**bear'ably** adv.—**bear'er** n. carrier or messenger; person who helps to carry coffin; presenter of cheque; body-servant.—bear'ing n. manner in which a person acts or behaves; direction in which one thing lies from another; relation to or connection with;—bear'ings n.pl. machine surfaces carrying a moving part and bearing friction.—to bear out, corroborate.—to bear one's cross, endure suffering.—to bear with, endure patiently.—to bring to bear, apply pressure.—to lose one's bearings, lose all sense of direction.

bear (bār) n. carnivorous mammal of the Ursidae order; rough, boorish person; one who sells stocks before he has bought them in the hope of a fall in price before settlement.—bear'ish a.—bear'skin n. skin of bear; tall fur cap worn by Guards on ceremonial occasions.

beard (bērd) n. hair that grows on chin and cheeks; awns or prickles of ear of corn; gills of oysters; barb of an arrow;—v.t. confront or defy someone.—beard'ed a.—beard'less a.

beast (bēst) n. any inferior animal as opposed to man; four-footed animal especially if wild; cattle; person of brutal nature or of dirty habits.—beast'ly a. like a beast; filthy; displeasing.—beast'-liness n.

beat (bēt) v.t. strike or hit repeatedly; pommel; crush; defeat; be too difficult for; spread flat and thin with a tool, as gold leaf; drive game out of cover; mark time in music;—v.i. throb; dash against, as waves, wind, etc.—pa.t. beat; pa.p. beat'en;—n. recurrent stroke; pulse throb; (Mus.) the divisions in bar; movement of conductor's baton; zig-zag sailing of ship working up against wind; round or course followed repeatedly by someone, e.g. policeman; place of resort.—beat'en a. hammered into shape by a tool; worn by continual use.—beat'er n.—beat'ing n. act of giving blows; thrashing; throbbing; driving out game.—to beat about the bush, approach a subject in a roundabout way.—to beat hollow, surpass someone completely.—dead beat, absolutely exhausted.

beatify (bē-at'-i-fī) v.t. render supremely blessed or happy; bless with celestial enjoyment (preliminary to canonisation in R.C Church).—beati'-ie(si) a. having power of making happy or blessed.—beatif'-ically adv.—beatifica'tion n. act of the Pope in permitting one, after death, to be declared blessed.

beatitude (bē-at'-i-tūd) n. highest form of heavenly happiness; supreme blessedness.—**The Beatitudes,** blessings spoken by our Saviour in regard to particular virtues (Matt. 5).

beatnik (beet'-nik) n. young person who eschews the conventional social pattern in dress, mode of living etc.

beau (bō) n. fop; dandy; lady's man; suitor.—pl. beaux (bōz).

beauty (bū'-ti) n. inherent quality in object pleasing to the eye, ear, or mind; particular grace or excellence; beautiful woman; fine specimen.—beau'teous a. full of beauty; very handsome.—beau'teously adv.—beau'teousness n.—beautic'ian n. expert in use of cosmetics.—beau'tifier n.—beau'tiful a. highly pleasing to eye, ear, or mind; handsome; lovely; fine; excellent.—beau'tifully adv.—beau'tify v.t.—beau'tiless a.—beauty parlour, establishment of beautician.—beau'ty-spot n. place noted for its scenery; a patch placed on the face to heighten beauty.

beaver (bēv'-er) n. amphibious, four-footed rodent valued for its fur and for castoreum, an extract from its glands used in medicine; fur of the beaver; beaver hat;—a. made of beaver fur.

becalm (bē-kàm') v.t. make calm or quiet.—becalmed' a.

because (be-kawz') adv. and conj. for the reason that; since.

beck (bek) n. sign or gesture of head or hand; nod;—v.i. make such a gesture;—v.t. call by nod or sign; beckon.—at one's beck and call, entirely at someone's disposal.

beckon (bek'-n) v.t. and i. make sign with hand or head; summon with hand or finger.

become (bē-kum') v.t. pass from one state to another; suit or be suitable to;—pa.t. became'; pa.p. become'.—becom'ing a. appropriate or fit.—becom'ingly adv.—becom'ingness n.

bed (bed) n. couch on which to sleep or take rest; plot of ground in which plants are cultivated; channel of a stream; bearing surface of anything; thin layer of mortar between two surfaces; layer of rock; stratum;—v.t. place in bed; plant out; arrange in layers;—pr.p. bed'ding pa.p. bed'ded.—bed'-bug n. brown, wingless insect which sucks blood of human beings.—bed'-cham'ber n. bedroom.—bed'der n. plant for the garden bed.—bed'ding n. materials of bed—bed'-fel'low n. one who sleeps in same bed with another.—bed'-pan n.—pan for warming bed; chamber-pot.—bed'rid, bed'ridden a. permanently confined to bed by age or infirmity.—bed'-rock n. solid rock beneath loose material; fundamentals.—bed'room n.—bed'-sore n. ulcer caused by constant pressure on part of body of bed-ridden patient.—bed'spread n. covering of fine material for a bed.—bed'stead n. framework, of iron or wood, of bed.—bed'-tick n. cloth case for holding stuffing of mattress.

bedazzle (bĕ-daz'-l) *v.t.* overpower by employing too strong a light or by a magnificent show.

bedeck (bĕ-dek') *v.t.* deck, adorn, ornament.

bedevil (bĕ-dev'-l) *v.t.* treat with devilish malignity; torment; throw into confusion; confound; bewitch.

bedew (bĕ-dū') *v.t.* moisten with dew.

bedlam (bed'-lạm) *n.* mad-house; lunatic asylum; mental institution; scene of uproar; pandemonium.

Bedlington (bed'-ling-tun) *n.* rough-coated terrier.

bedraggle (bĕ-drag'-l) *v.t.* soil by trailing in wet or mud. Also **bedagg'le.**

bee (bē) *n.* highest form of insect belonging to order Hymenoptera, having two pairs of membranous wings; social gathering for amusement or mutual help.—**bee'-hive** *n.* case or box where bees are housed;—*a.* shaped like bee-hive.—**bee'-keep'er, bee'-mas'ter** *n.* one who keeps bees.—**bee'-line** *n.* shortest route from one place to another.—**bees'wax** *n.* wax secreted by bees; floor-polish;—*v.t.* polish with beeswax.—**to have a bee in one's bonnet,** be hare-brained; be cranky on some subject.

beech (bēch) *n.* tree of temperate and sub-frigid zones, greatly valued for its wood.—**beech'en** *a.* made of beech.—**beech'mast** *n.* nuts of beech-tree.—**beech'nut** *n.* triangular, edible nut of the beech.

beef (bēf) *n.* flesh of ox, bull, or cow; flesh and muscle; muscular strength; vigour;—*a.* consisting of beef;—*v.t.* (*Slang*) make finicky complaints.—**beeves** (bēvz) *n.pl.* oxen.—**beef'eater** *n.* one of the Yeomen of the Guard; Warder of Tower of London.—**beef'iness** *n.* tendency to put on flesh.—**beef'steak** *n.* thick slice of beef for grilling.—**beef'-tea** *n.* extract of beef used as stimulating drink.—**beef'y** *a.* stolid; fat; stout.

beer (bēr) *n.* alcoholic beverage made by fermentation from malted barley, hops, sugar and water with yeast.—**beer'y** *a.*—**not all beer and skittles,** not all pleasure and easy living.—**small beer,** beer of poor quality, hence person of little or no importance in the scheme of things.

beet (bēt) *n.* garden or field plant having succulent tap root, the red variety being used as a salad, the white yielding sugar.—**beet'root** *n.* root of beet plant.—**beet'-sugar** *n.* sugar extracted from beetroot.

beetle (bē'-tl) *n.* name of a large order of insects, Coleoptera.

beetle (bē'-tl) *v.i.* be prominent; jut out; overhang.—**beet'ling** *a.* overhanging.—**beet'le-browed** *a.* with overhanging brows; scowling.

befall (bĕ-fawl') *v.t.* happen to;—*v.i.* come to pass; happen;—*pr.p.* be-

falling; *pa.t.* befell'; *pa.p.* befall'en.

befit (bĕ-fit') *v.t.* fit or be suitable to; become; be right for;—*pr.p.* befit'ting; *pa.t. pa.p.* be fit'ted.—befit'ting *a.*—be fit'tingly *adv.*

befog (bĕ-fog') *v.t.* envelop in fog; perplex.

before (bĕ-fōr') *prep.* in front of; preceding; in presence of; prior to; previous to; superior to;—*adv.* in front; in advance; short time ago; already.—*conj.* sooner than; rather than.—**before'hand** *adv.* previously.—**before'time** *adv.* of old; formerly.

befoul (bĕ-foul') *v.t.* foul, soil.

befriend (bĕ-frend') *v.t.* act as a friend to; favour; help a stranger.

beg (beg) *v.t.* ask earnestly and humbly; ask for alms; practise begging; beseech;—*pr.p.* beg'ging; *pa.t.* and *pa.p.* begged.—**beg'gar** *n.* one who solicits alms; mendicant;—*v.t.* reduce to beggary; ruin financially.—**beg'garliness** *n.*—**beg'garly** *a.*—**beg'gary** *n.* extreme poverty.—**beg'gingly** *adv.*—**to beg of,** solicit pardon or a favour.—**to beg the question,** assume truth of thing to be proved.—**to go a-begging,** not to be in demand.

began (bĕ-gan') *pa.t.* of begin.

beget (bĕ-get') *v.t.* generate; procreate; produce or cause; get; give rise to.—*pr.p.* beget'ting; *pa.t.* begot', begat'; *pa.p.* begot', begot'ten.

begin (bĕ-gin') *v.t.* enter on; set on foot;—*v.i.* set about;—*pr.p.* begin'ning; *pa.t.* began'; *pa.p.* begun'.—**begin'ner** *n.* one who begins; novice.—**begin'ning** *n.* what comes first.

begone (bĕ-gon') *interj.* go away! depart!—**woe'begone** *a.* gloomy and miserable.

begonia (bĕ-gōn'-yạ) *n.* genus of tropical plants.

begrime (bĕ-grīm') *v.t.* soil with grime.

begrudge (bĕ-gruj') *v.t.* grudge; allow reluctantly.

beguile (bĕ-gīl') *v.t.* cheat or deceive by trickery; ensnare; delude; while away (time); amuse or divert.—**beguile'ment** *n.*—**beguil'er** *n.*—**beguil'ingly** *adv.*

beguine (bā-gēn') *n.* dance tune in common time with broken chord accompaniments.

begum (bē'-gum) *n.* Hindustani name given to Moslem princess.

behalf (bĕ-häf') *n.* favour; advantage; benefit; support; defence.

behave (bĕ-hāv') *v.t.* and *i.* conduct oneself; act.—**behav'iour** *n.* bearing or conduct; deportment.—**behav'iourism** *n.* theory that man's actions are automatic responses to stimuli and not dictated by consciousness.—**behav'iourist** *n.*—**behaviouris'tic** *a.*

behead (bĕ-hed') *v.t.* sever head from body.—**behead'al, behead'ing** *n.*

beheld (bē-held') *pa.p.* of **behold**.

behest (bē-hest') *n.* that which is willed or ordered.

behind (bē-hīnd') *prep.* at the back of; in the rear (of); after; late; farther back than; in an inferior position;—*n.* rump; buttocks; posterior.—**behind'hand** *adv.* and *a.* late; backward; in arrears; clandestine.

behold (bē-hōld') *v.t.* look at; fix the eyes upon; observe carefully;—*v.i.* look; fix the attention;—*pa.t.* and *pa.p.* **beheld'**.—**be'hold'en** *a.* obliged (to).—**behold'er** *n.* onlooker; spectator.

behoof (bē-hōōf') *n.* need; necessity; advantage; benefit; profit; use.—**behove'**, **behoove'** *v.t.* be necessary; convenient for; befit.

beige (bezh, bāzh) *n.* woollen cloth made of undyed wool; hence, the greyish colour of unbleached wool.

being (bē'-ing) *n.* existence; that which exists; an animal.

belabour (bē-lā'-bur) *v.t.* beat soundly; cudgel; exert much labour upon.

belay (bē-lā') *v.t.* make fast a rope, by winding it round pin, cleat, or rock.—**belay'ing-pin** *n.* pin or cleat, to which running rigging may be belayed.

belch (belsh, belch) *v.t.* emit wind from the stomach by way of the mouth; cast forth;—*n.* eructation.

beleaguer (bē-lē'-ger) *v.t.* surround with army to preclude escape.—**beleag'uerment** *n.*

belfry (bel'-fri) *n.* bell-tower, or part of steeple, where bells are hung. Orig. watch-tower.—**bel'fried** *a.*

belie (bē-lī') *v.t.* give the lie to; falsify; speak falsely of; misrepresent;—*pr.p.* **bely'ing**.

believe (bē-lēv') *v.t.* regard as true; trust;—*v.i.* have faith (in); think; suppose.—**belief** *n.* that which is believed; full acceptance of a thing as true; faith.—**believ'able** *a.* credible.—**believ'er** *n.*—**to make believe**, pretend; fancy.

belittle (bē-lit'-l) *v.t.* make small; think lightly of; disparage.—**belit'tlement** *n.*—**belit'tling** *a.*

bell (bel) *n.* hollow, cup-shaped metal vessel which gives forth clear, musical note when struck; anything shaped like bell;—*v.t.* provide with bell.—**bells** *n.pl.* (*Naut.*) half hours of a watch at sea, struck on ship's bell.—**bell'-boy** *n.* page-boy in hotel.—**bell'-buoy** *n.* buoy which by its swaying rings bell with tongue attached.—**bell'man** *n.* town crier.

belladonna (bel-a-don'-a) *n.* deadly nightshade; its poisonous extract, source of atropine.

belle (bel) *n.* very beautiful woman.

bellicose (bel'-i-kōs) *a.* pugnacious; contentious; war-like; quarrelsome.—**bel'licosely** *adv.*—**bellicos'ity** *n.*

belligerence (bel-ij'-er-ens) *n.* state of being at war.—**bellig'erency** *n.* state of war.—**bellig'erent** *n.* nation, party, or person taking part in war; contending party;—*a.* carrying on legalised war; pugnacious; bellicose.

bellow (bel'-ō) *v.i.* roar like bull; shout loudly; make an outcry;—*n.* loud hollow roar, as of a bull, cannon, etc.; any deep cry.—**bell'ower** *n.*

bellows (bel'-ōz) *n.pl.* instrument for producing strong blast of air.

belly (bel'-i) *n.* part of the body which contains bowels; abdomen; stomach; part of anything bulging like paunch;—*a.* ventral; abdominal;—*v.i.* swell out; bulge.—**bellyache** *n.* stomach pains; *v.i.* (*Colloq.*) complain unreasonably.—**bel'lied** *a.* swelled out; bulging; pot-bellied.

belong (bē-long') *v.i.* pertain to; be connected with; be property or attribute of; be resident or native of.—**belong'ings** *n.pl.* what belongs to one; possessions.

beloved (bē-luv'-ed, bē-luvd') *a.* greatly loved;—*n.* one very dear to others.

below (bē-lō') *prep.* under; beneath; of inferior rank or status; on lower level than; unworthy of;—*adv.* in a lower place; beneath; on earth or hell, as opposed to heaven.

belt (belt) *n.* band, girdle, or zone, used for encircling; zone given over to raising of one plant, e.g. wheat;—*v.t.* encircle, as with belt; thrash with belt.—**belt'ed** *a.* wearing a belt, esp. as mark of honour, as in 'a belted knight'; thrashed with belt.—**belt'-conveyor** *n.* endless belt used for conveying material from one place to another.—**belt'ing** *n.* material for skirt or bodice bands; thrashing.

bemoan (bē-mōn') *v.t.* express deep grief for, by moaning; lament; mourn for.

bemuse (bē-mūz') *v.t.* put into a state of confusion; stupefy; daze.—**bemused'** *a.*

ben (ben) *n.* (*Scot.*) mountain peak.

bench (bensh) *n.* long seat or form; table on which work is done; seat in court of judge or magistrate; collective name for body of judges sitting in judgment;—*v.t.* furnish with benches.—**bench'er** *n.* (*Law*) senior member of Inns of Court.—**bench'ing** *n.* row of benches.—**Front Bench**, in parliament, the leaders of party in power.

bend (bend) *n.* type of knot; (*Her.*) type of band on shield.—**curve**; crook, curvature; turn;—*v.t.* curve; arch; turn out of direct course; incline; sway; apply earnestly; subdue; tie, make fast—of ropes and sails;—*v.i.* be moved out of a straight line;

stoop; lean; incline; bow; yield;—*pa.t.* **bent,** *pa.p.* **bent** or **bend'ed.**—**round the bend** (*Colloq.*) mentally unbalanced, crazy.—**bend'er** *n.* instrument for bending; drinking bout.—**to be bent upon,** be determined upon.

beneath (bē-nēth') *prep.* under; below; lower than; unworthy of; below level of;—*adv.* below.

benediction (ben-e-dik'-shun) *n.* blessing of formal character; blessing uttered by priest at end of religious service.—**benedict'ory** *a.* imparting a blessing.

benefaction (ben-e-fak'-shun) *n.* act of doing good; benefit conferred; donation.—**benefac'tor** *n.* (*fem.* **benefac'tress**) one who helps others; donor; patron.—**benefac'tory** *a.*

benefice (ben'-e-fis) *n.* ecclesiastical living or preferment in Church of England, generally held by vicars and perpetual curates.—**beneficed'** *a.* in enjoyment of benefice.

beneficence (be-nef'-i-sens) *n.* habitual practice of doing good; charity.—**benef'icent** *a.*—**benef'icently** *adv.*

beneficial (ben-e-fish'-al) *a.* conferring benefits; receiving or entitled to receive advantages; advantageous; helpful.—**benefic'ially** *adv.*—**benefic'ialness** *n.*—**benefic'iary** *n.* one who benefits from act of another; holder of ecclesiastical benefice.

benefit (ben'-e-fit) *n.* act of kindness; ~~favour; advantage; profit~~ ~~proceeds~~ ~~charity or an i~~ ~~allowance~~ under national sch~~ ~~of insurance,~~ etc.;—*v.t.* do good ~~be useful to;~~ profit;—*v.i.* gain ~~tage (from).~~

benevolence (ben-ev'-o-lens) *n.* disposition to do good; love of mankind; act of kindness; generosity.—**benev'olent** *a.* of a kindly nature; beneficent.—**benev'olently** *adv.*

benighted (bē-nīt'-ed) *a.* overtaken by night; enveloped in moral or mental darkness; ignorant; unenlightened; lost.

benign (bē-nīn') *a.* of kindly disposition; not malignant (of disease); propitious (of climate).—**benignancy** (be-nig'-nan-si) *n.*—**benig'nity** *n.*—**benig'nant** *a.*—**benign'ly** *adv.*

benison (ben'-i-zn) *n.* benediction; blessing.

bent (bent) *pa.t.* and *pa.p.* of **bend**.

bent (bent) *n.* (of mind), leaning, bias, inclination for; tendency.

bent (bent) *n.* bent grass; any stiff, wiry, coarse grass.

benumb (bē-num') *v.t.* make numb, through cold or fear; deprive of all sensation; deaden.—**benumbed'** *a.*

benzene (ben'-zēn) *n.* colourless, volatile, inflammable liquid derived from coal-tar and coke-oven gas, solvent for fats and grease.

benzine (ben'-zēn) *n.* mixture of petroleum hydrocarbons.

benzoin (ben'-zō-in) *n.* aromatic gum used in medicine and perfumery and as an incense. On heating it yields **benzoic acid.**

bequeath (bē-kwēTH') *v.t.* leave by will, said of personal property; leave to those who follow on, as problem, trouble, etc.—**bequest'** *n.* that which is devised by will, esp. to public body or institute.

berate (bē-rāt') *v.t.* rate or chide vehemently; scold vigorously.

berceuse (ber-sgz') *n.* lullaby or cradle song; slumber song.

bereave (bē-rēv') *v.t.* make destitute; deprive of;—*pa.p.* **bereaved'** or **bereft'**.—**bereaved'** *a.* robbed by death, esp. of a relative.—**bereave'ment** *n.* loss, esp. by death.

beret (ber'-ā, ber'-et) *n.* soft, round tight-fitting cap without any peak.

berg (berg) *n.* large mass of ice; an iceberg; hill or mountain, as in S. Africa.

beri-beri (ber'-i-ber'-i) *n.* nervous disease due to deficiency of vitamin B, prevalent in tropical countries.

berry (ber'-i) *n.* small, pulpy, juicy fruit; strictly, simple fruit with succulent pericarp.—**ber'ried** *a.*

berserk, berserker (ber'-serk, -ker) *n.* battle-frenzied Norse warrior;—frenzied.—**to go berserk,** go mad with ~~fury.~~

berth (berth) ~~*n.* place where ship is~~ ~~anchored~~ ~~moored; sleeping-place~~ on ship, ~~situation or job;—~~ *v.t.* bring to anchorage.—**berth'age** *n.* dock or harbour dues.—**to give a wide berth to,** steer clear of; shun; avoid.

beryl (ber'-il) *n.* group of greenish precious stones; **ber'ylline** *a.*

beseech (bē-sēch') *v.t.* ask or entreat earnestly; solicit; beg; implore;—*pa.t.* and *pa.p.* **besought'**.—**beseech'er** *n.*—**beseech'ing** *a.* imploring.—**beseech'ingly** *adv.*—**beseech'ment** *n.*

beseem (bē-sēm') *v.t.* be fit for; befit; suit; become.—**beseem'ing** *a.*

beset (bē-set') *v.t.* place on, in, or around; hem in on all sides; surround; enclose; assail;—*pr.p.* **beset'ting** *pa.t.* and *pa.p.* **beset'.**—**beset'ment** *n.*—**beset'ter** *n.*—**beset'ting** *a.* customary; habitual, as in 'besetting sin.'

beshrew (bē-shrōō') *v.t.* wish some slight evil to befall one; curse; rate.

beside (bē-sīd') *prep.* and *adv.* at the side of; over and above; in addition to; apart from; distinct from.—**besides'** *adv.* moreover;—*prep.* over and above.—**beside oneself,** out of one's wits.

besiege (bē-sēj') *v.t.* lay siege to; surround with armed forces; beleaguer.—**besiege'ment** *n.*—**besieg'er** *n.* —**besieg'ing** *a.*—**besieg'ingly** *adv.*

besmear (bē-smēr') *v.t.* smear over

with any sticky, gluey matter; soil; bedaub.

besmirch (bě-smẹrch') *v.t.* soil; sully; tarnish one's reputation, etc.

besom (bē'-zum, bez'-um) *n.* brush of twigs for sweeping; broom; troublesome woman or girl; hussy.

besot (bě-sot') *v.t.* make sottish by drink; make stupid.—**besot'ted** *a.*

besought (bě-sawt') *pa.t.* and *pa.p.* of beseech.

bespatter (bě-spat'-ẹr) *v.t.* sprinkle or splash with mud, ink, etc.; defame.

bespeak (bě-spēk') *v.t.* order, speak for, or engage beforehand; betoken; —*pa.t.* **bespoke'**.—*pa.p.* **bespoke'** and **bespok'en**.—**bespoke'**, **bespok'en** *a.* ordered beforehand; of goods, made to measure, esp. shoes and clothes.

best (best) *a. superl.* good in highest degree; excellent beyond all others; most suitable, advantageous, advisable, or appropriate;—*adv.* in the most excellent manner;—*n.* utmost; highest endeavour; perfection.—**best man**, groomsman at wedding.—**best seller**, current popular book with enormous sale.—**to make the best of**, resign oneself to conditions, etc.

bestial (bes'-ti-ạl) *a.* pert. to a beast; having instincts of beast; like repulsive beast.—**bestial'ity** *n.* depravity.—**bes'tially** *adv.*

bestir (bě-stẹr') *v.t.* rouse into vigorous action; exert (oneself); stimulate.

bestow (bě-stō') *v.t.* lay up in store; expend, as energy; give ceremoniously; confer; award; grant; present; impart.—**bestow'al** *n.*—**bestow'er** *n.*—**bestow'ment** *n.* bestowing; what is bestowed.

bestrew (bě-strōō') *v.t.* scatter over; besprinkle; — *pa.p.* **bestrewed'**, **bestrewn'**.

bestride (bě-strīd') *v.t.* stride over; stand or sit with legs extended across;—*pr.p.* **bestrid'ing**; *pa.t.* **bestrode'**, **bestrid'**; *pa.p.* **bestrid'**.

bet (bet) *n.* stake or wager on problematical event;—*v.t.* stake money upon a contingency;—*pr.p.* **bet'ting**; *pa.t.* and *pa.p.* **bet** or **bet'ted**.—**bet'ter**, **bet'tor** *n.* one who lays bet.

beta (bě'-tạ, bā-tạ) *n.* second letter of Greek alphabet; symbol β for this.

betake (bě-tāk') *v.t.* have recourse to; apply; (with reflexive) go, repair to; make one's way;—*pr.p.* **betak'ing**; *pa.t.* **betook**; *pa.p.* **betak'en**.

betel (bě'-tl) *n.* species of pepper, leaves of which are prepared as stimulant, and chewed by inhabitants of India, staining the saliva brilliant red.—**be'tel-nut**, *n.* nut of areca palm.

betide (bě-tīd') *v.t.* happen to;—*v.i.* occur; happen.

betimes (bě-tīmz') *adv.* in good time;

seasonably; soon; early; forward.

betoken (bě-tō'-kn) *v.t.* show by some visible sign; foreshow.

betony (bet'-o-ni) *n.* herb used for dyeing wool.

betray (bě-trā') *v.t.* give up treacherously; be disloyal to; disclose (a secret); seduce; show signs of; deceive.—**betray'al** *n.* act of betraying.—**betray'er** *n.* traitor; seducer.

betroth (bě-trōTH') *v.t.* promise to give or take in marriage; affiance.—**betroth'al** *n.* agreement with view to marriage.—**betrothed'** *n.* person engaged to be married; fiancé, (fem.) fiancée.—**betroth'ment** *n.* state of being betrothed.

better (bet'-ẹr) *a.* (compar. of good), showing greater degree of excellence; improved in health;—*adv.* (compar. of well), in more excellent or superior manner; more fully;—*v.t.* and *i.* make better; amend; raise one's worldly position.—**bet'terment** *n.* improvement; enhanced value of property due to local improvements.—**bet'ters** *n.pl.* one's superiors in rank or wealth.—**better half**, jocular for wife.—**better off**, in more prosperous circumstances.—**to get the better of**, gain an advantage over.—**to think better of**, reconsider.

between (bě-twēn') *prep.* in the middle of two (of space, time, etc.); in middle or intermediate space; shared by two;—*adv.* midway.—**betwixt'** *prep.* between; midway.—**go'-between'** *n.* intermediary.

bevel (bev'-l) *n.* angle, not being a right angle, formed by two surfaces; adjustable instrument used in building, etc. for testing angles;—*a.* having form of bevel; slanting;—*v.t.* cut to bevel angle;—*pr.p.* **bev'elling**;—*pa.t.* and *pa.p.* **bev'elled**.—**bev'elled** *a.* cut to a slope or bevel.—**bev'elling**, **bev'elment** *n.*

beverage (bev'-e-rāj) *n.* refreshing liquid suitable for drinking.

bevy (bev'-i) *n.* flock of birds, esp. quails or larks; assembly, esp. of young ladies; collection or group.

bewail (bě-wāl') *v.t.* express grief for; lament; deplore; mourn over.

beware (bě-wār') *v.i.* be wary of; be on one's guard; be alive to impending danger; take care (lest).

bewilder (bě-wil'-dẹr) *v.t.* lead astray or into confusion; confound; perplex; puzzle.—**bewil'dered** *a.* bewil'dering *a.* confusing.—**bewil'derment** *n.*

bewitch (bě-wich') *v.t.* gain power over, by sorcery; charm; captivate; entrance.—**bewitch'er** *n.*—**bewitch'ery**, **bewitch'ment** *n.* power to bewitch; enchantment.—**bewitch'ing** *a.* charming; alluring.—**bewitch'ingly** *adv.*

beyond (bě-yond') *prep.* on farther side of; out of reach of; above; past in time; later than; superior to;—

adv. farther off; at a distance;—*n.* the future life.

bi-, bis- (bī, bis) *prefix*, used in compound nouns to indicate two, twice, or double.

bias (bī'-as) *n.* weight on one side of a bowl (in game of *Bowls*), which gives a tendency to diverge from straight line when running; prejudice;—*v.t.* influence; prejudice;—*pa.t.* and *pa.p.* bi'assed or bi'ased.

bib (bib) *n.* piece of cloth worn mainly by children over the breast when eating; part of workman's overalls to protect chest;—*v.t.* and *v.i.* sip; tipple; drink frequently;—*pr.p.* bib'bing;—*pa.t.* and *pa.p.* bibbed.—biba'cious *a.* addicted to tippling.—bib'ber *n.* person given to frequent and excessive imbibing of liquor or wines; tippler.

Bible (bī'-bl) *n.* volume which contains the Scriptures of Old and New Testaments; authoritative book on specific subject.—bib'lical *a.* pert. to the Bible; scriptural.

biblio- (bib'-li-ō) *prefix* from Gk. *biblion*, a book, used to form compound words referring to books.—bibliog'raphy *n.* expert knowledge of history of books; list of books on specific subject.—biblio'grapher *n.*—bibliograph'ic(al) *a.*—biblioma'nia *n.* mania for possessing rare books.—biblioman'iac *n.*—bib'liophile *n.* lover of books.

bibulous (bib'-ū-lus) *a.* given to excessive or frequent drinking; absorbent; spongy.—bib'ulously *adv.*

bicameral (bī-kam'-e-ral) *a.* pert.to or containing two legislative or other chambers.

bicarbonate (bī-kár'-bo-nāt) *n.* a salt or compound containing two equivalents of carbonic acid to one of a base—usually applied loosely for 'bicarbonate of soda.'

bicentenary (bī-sen'-te-na-ri, bī-sen-tē'-na-ri) *a.* pert. to the two hundredth year;—*n.* two hundredth anniversary. Also **bicentennial** *a.*

biceps (bī-seps) *n.* two-headed muscle of arm or leg; a flexor muscle.

bicker (bik'-er) *v.i.* bandy words; wrangle; move quickly and lightly.—bick'ering *n.*—bick'erment *n.*

bicuspid (bī-kus'-pid) *n.* tooth with two fangs;—*a.* having two cusps or fangs. Also **bicus'pidate**.

bicycle (bī'-si-kl) *n.* vehicle with two wheels, one in front of the other, propelled by pedals; *v.i.* cycle.—bi'cyclist *n.*—bike *n.* (*Colloq.*).

bid (bid) *v.t.* ask; invite; order or direct; offer price; give, as goodbye;—*pr.p.* bid'ding; *pa.t.* bid or bade; *pa.p.* bid, bid'den;—*n.* offer price, esp. at auctions; attempt.—bid'dable *a.* compliant; docile; obedient; submissive; willing; (*Cards*) that may be bid without undue risk.—bid'der *n.*—bid'ding *n.* invitation; command; offer at auction; series of bids at cards.

bide (bīd) *v.i.* dwell permanently; abide; remain; continue; tarry; sojourn; reside;—*v.t.* endure; put up with; suffer; tolerate; bear.

biennial (bī-en'-i-al) *a.* happening once in two years; lasting for only two years;—*n.* plant which requires two seasons to produce its flowers and fruit.—bienn'ially *adv.*

bier (bēr) *n.* frame or carriage for conveying dead to the grave; coffin; grave; tomb.

bifocal (bī-fō'-kal) *a.* having two foci;—*n.pl.* spectacles with small lens for reading, set into larger lens for distant vision.

bifurcate (bī-fur'-kāt) *v.t.* divide into two branches;—*v.i.* fork.—bifur'cate, bifur'cated *a.* divided into two prongs, forks, or branches.—bifurca'tion *n.*

big (big) *a.* bulky; massive; huge; great; pregnant; generous; important.—big'-bug *n.* (*Slang*) important person.—big'-end *n.* crankpin end of connecting rod.—big'ness *n.*—big'-noise *n.* (*Colloq.*) person of much authority.—big'wig *n.* (*Colloq.*) person of great influence.

bigamy (big'-a-mi) *n.* crime of having two wives or husbands at one time.—big'amist *n.*—big'amous *a.*—big'amously *adv.*

bight (bīt) *n.* curve; loop of rope when folded; bend in the sea-coast; open bay.

bigot (big'-ot) *n.* one obstinately and unreasonably wedded to particular belief or creed; dogmatist.—big'oted *a.*—big'otedly *adv.*—big'otry *n.*

bijou (bē-zhōō') *n.* gem; trinket of precious material or workmanship.—*pl.* bijoux (bēzhōō').—bijou'terie.

bike (bīk) *n.* (*Colloq.*) bicycle.

bikini (bi-kē'-ni) *n.* scanty two-piece bathing suit.

bilateral (bī-lat'-e-ral) *a.* having two sides; affecting two parties.—bilat'erally *adv.*

bilberry (bil'-ber-i) *n.* whortleberry; in Scotland, blaeberry (=blueberry).

bile (bīl) *n.* greenish, viscous, bitter fluid secreted by the liver; gall; general disorder of health due to faulty secretion of bile; bad temper.—biliary (bil'i-ar-i) *a.* pert. to the bile.—bil'ious. *a.* pert. to bile; affected by bile; peevish; ill-humoured.—bil'iousness *n.* disturbance of digestive system associated with excess of bile.

bilge (bilj) *n.* swelling part of cask; broadest part of ship's bottom nearest keel, acting as a sump; (*Colloq.*) nonsense;—*v.i.* spring a leak.—bilge'-wa'ter *n.* water which gathers in ship's bottom.

bilingual (bi-ling'-gwạl) a. speaking, or written in, two languages. Also **biling'uar.—biling'uist** n. person who can speak fluently in two languages.

bilious, biliousness. See **bile.**

bilk (bilk) v.t. defraud, swindle.—**bilk'er** n.

bill (bil) n. beak of bird; promontory;—v.i. stroke bills, as birds; caress; fondle.

bill (bil) n. kind of axe with two sharp pointed spikes mounted on long staff; hook-shaped pruning instrument.—**bill'-hook** n. small bill with hooked end for lopping branches.

bill (bil) n. printed notice for public display; account of money; written engagement to pay money under the hand of the granter; declaration of certain facts in legal proceedings; draft of proposed law;—v.t. announce by posters; cover with posters; placard.—**bill'head** n. printed matter at top of stationery; invoice form.—**bill'ing** n. advertising by use of posters.—**bill'post'er, bill'-stick'er** n. one who posts up bills. —**bill of fare,** menu.—**to fill the bill,** be satisfactory in all respects.

billet (bil'-et) n. short note; order requisitioning accommodation for soldiers; quarters occupied by soldiers in private houses, etc.; situation, job, or post;—v.t. quarter or lodge troops.—**billet-doux** (bil-e-dóó') n. love-letter.

billet (bil'-et) n. small log used as fuel.

billiard (bil'-yard) a. pert. to billiards.—**bill'iards** n. table game played with three balls which are hit by leather-tipped cue.

billion (bil'-yun) n. a million millions (10^{12}); in U.S. a thousand millions (10^9).—**bill'ionnaire** n. fabulously rich person.—**bill'ionth** a. and n.

billow (bil'-ō) n. great, swelling wave of the sea; surge of flame, smoke, cloud, etc.; breaker;—v.i. swell or roll, as waves.—**bill'owed, bill'owy** a.

billygoat (bil'-i-gōt) n. he-goat; tufted beard.

bimetallism (bi-met'-ạl-izm) n. in currency, use of both gold and silver coins at a fixed relative value. —**bimet'allist** n. one who advocates the policy of bimetallism.

bimonthly (bi-munth'-li) a. properly once in two months, but often means, erroneously, twice a month;—n. periodical which appears once in two months.

bin (bin) n. box or enclosed place with lid, for corn, bread, etc.; receptacle for bottles of wine;—v.t. store in bin.

binary (bi'-nạ-ri) a. composed of two; twofold; double; dual;—n.

double star.—**binary scale** n. scale of counting with radix 2, used in computers.

bind (bind) v.t. tie together as with band, cord, etc.; constrain by moral influence; secure together and enclose in cover; place under legal obligation; be obligatory; apprentice; constipate;—v.i. stick; seize up;—pa.t. and pa.p. **bound.**—**bind'er** n. person who binds; machine for binding, as sheaves, books, etc.; transfer case in filing and loose-leaf systems; bandage.—**bind'ery** n. bookbinding establishment.—**bind'ing** a. obligatory; constipating;—n. act of fastening; anything which binds; cover of book.—**bind'weed** n. plant with twining stems; convolvulus.

bing (bing) n. heap of grain; bin; weight of lead ore, 8 cwt.; slag heap.

binge (binj) n. concerted eating and especially drinking, to celebrate an occasion; spree.

binnacle (bin'-ạ-kl) n. box containing the compass of ship.

binocular (bin-ok'-ū-lạr) a. adapted for use of both eyes;—n. binocular telescope.—**binoc'ulars** n.pl. fieldglasses.

binomial (bi-nō'-mi-ạl) n. algebraic expression involving two terms connected by the sign plus (+) or minus (−), e.g. a + b, or c−d;—a. pert. to binomials.—**binomial theorem,** algebraic formula for expressing any power of a binomial by a converging infinite series.

bio- (bi'-ō) prefix used in compound terms, to express having organic life.

biochemistry (bi-ō-kem'-is-tri) n. chemistry of living things.

biography (bi-og'-rạ-fi) n. detailed story of person's life and achievements; section of literature devoted to the writing of life-stories of individuals.—**biograph'ic, biograph'ical** a.—**biograph'ically** adv.

biology (bi-ol'-o-ji) n. science of life, whether animal or vegetable.—**biolog'ic, biolog'ical** a.—**biolog'ically** adv.—**biol'ogist** n.—**biological warfare,** method of fighting in which disease bacteria would be used.

bipartisan (bi-par'-ti-zạn) a. pert. to, representing, or composed of, members of two parties.

bipartite (bi-par'-tit) a. divided or split into two parts as far as the base, as a leaf; consisting of two corresponding parts; shared by two parties concerned.—**biparti'tion** n.

biped (bi'-ped) n. animal with two feet.—**bi'ped, biped'al** a.

biplane (bi'-plān) n. aeroplane or glider having two main planes.

bipod (bi'-pod) n. two-legged stand.

bipolar (bi-pōl'-ạr) a. having two poles.

birch (bẹrch) n. tree with slim

branches and silvery bark-scales; hard, close-grained wood of birch;—v.t. flog with birch-rod.—**birch, birch'en** a. of birch.—**birch'rod** n. rod of birch twigs for inflicting corporal punishment.

bird (berd) n. feathered animal.—**bird'-eyed** a. keen of vision.—**bird'-fan'cier** n. one who breeds birds for show or sale.—**bird'-lime** n. sticky substance used to catch birds.—**bird's-eye** n. kind of tobacco; speedwell.—**bird's eye view**, comprehensive view as seen by a bird.—**to get the bird**, be hissed off the stage.

birdie (berd'-i) n. (Golf) holing ball in one stroke below par.

birth (berth) n. act of coming into life or of being born; delivery of newly born child alive; descent; origin.—**birth'-control'** n. restriction of conception.—**birth'day** n. day on which one is born; anniversary of that day.—**birth'day suit** n. state of nudity.—**birth'mark** n. peculiar mark on body at birth.—**birth'-place** n. place where person is born.—**birth'-rate** n. ratio of births to total population.—**birth'right** n. anything to which one is entitled by birth.

bis (bis) adv. twice; (Mus.) shows that bar or passage is to be performed twice;—n. form of applause in France.

biscuit (bis'-kit) n. small thin cake; pottery etc. after firing but before glazing;—a. half-coloured.

bisect (bi-sekt') v.t. divide into two equal parts.—**bisec'tion** n. one of two equal parts.—**bisec'tor** n. bisecting line.—**biseg'ment** n. one of two segments of bisected line.

bisexual (bi-seks'-ū-al) a. having organs of both sexes in one individual; hermaphroditic.

bishop (bish'-op) n. clergyman of highest rank, head of diocese, himself under archbishop; chess man moving diagonally.—**bish'opric** n. diocese, jurisdiction, or office of bishop.—**bish'opweed** n. grab-weed, hedge plant. Also **bishop's weed**.

bismuth (biz'-muth) n. reddish-white metallic element, salts of which are used in medicine.—**bis'muthal, bis'-muthic** a.

bison (bi'-son, bis'-on) n. large wild ox or buffalo of Rocky Mountains.

bisulphate (bi-sul'-fāt) n. salt of sulphuric acid in which one-half of the hydrogen in the acid is replaced by metal.

bit (bit) n. mouthful; morsel; small piece of anything; fragment; small coin, as threepenny bit; (Slang) woman; boring tool generally for use in brace; part of bridle which is placed in horse's mouth; binary digit used in computers;—v.t. put bit in mouth of horse.—**to take the** bit between the teeth, become unmanageable.

bitch (bich) n. female of dog, wolf, or fox; (Colloq.) opprobrious term for woman.

bite (bit) v.t. cut, crush, seize, or wound with teeth; pinch with cold; eat into, as acid; corrode; gnaw; champ; nip; grip; cheat;—v.i. be given to biting; be pungent;—pr.p. bit'ing; pa.t. bit; pa.p. bit or bit'ten;—n. act of biting; portion bitten off; food; morsel; sharp, pungent taste; nibble of fish at hook; grip of edged tool on metal.—**bi'ter** n.—**bi'ting** a. sharp; severe; sarcastic; caustic; pungent; chilling.

bitter (bit'-er) a. biting or acrid to taste; causing pain or smart to feelings;—n. bitter beer.—**bitt'erly** adv.—**bitt'erness** n. quality of being bitter to taste; animosity.—**bitt'ers** n. alcoholic liquor containing bitter flavourings, e.g. angostura.—**bitt'ersweet** n. woody nightshade; meadowsweet.

bittern (bit'-ern) n. wading marshbird of heron family.

bitumen (bi-tū'-men, bit'-ū-men) n. inflammable, mineral pitch, as asphalt, etc.—**bitu'minise** v.t. cover roads, etc. with bitumen preparations.—**bitu'minous** a.

bivalve (bi'valv) a. having two valves;—n. animal with shell of two parts opening like hinge; seed case of this kind.—**bival'vous** a. having bivalve shells.—**bivalv'ular** a. having two valves; bivalved.

bivouac (biv'-ōō-ak) n. encampment in open air, without cover.—v.i. encamp without covering.—pr.p. biv'ouacking; pa.t. and pa.p. biv'ouacked.

bi-weekly (bi'-wēk'-li) a. occurring once in every two weeks, occurring twice in each week;—n. periodical issued twice a week or once in two weeks.

bizarre (bi-zár') a. odd; eccentric; grotesque.

blab (blab) v.t. reveal imprudently secrets entrusted to one;—v.i. tell tales;—pr.p. blab'bing; pa.t. and pa.p. blabbed.—n. chatterer; gossip; tell-tale. Also **blab'ber**.

black (blak) a. of darkest colour; dark; night-like; destitute of light; funereal; ominous; — n. darkest colour; Negro; mourning;—v.t. make black.—**blacks** n.pl. black clothes;—**black'en** v.t. make black; polish with blacking; defame;—v.i. grow or turn black.—**black'ly** adv.—**black'ness** n.—**black'amoor** n. Negro or Moor.—**black art**, magic; necromancy.—**black and tan** (Manchester) terrier; drink made of beer and stout.—**Black and Tans**, semi-military police force raised in 1920 for suppression of I.R.A. in Ireland, uniform being khaki with black hat.—**black'-ball** v.t. reject candidate for admission to club by putting black ball in ballot box.—**black'-beet'le** n. cockroach found indoors.—**black'berry** n. fruit-bearing shrub, bramble.—**black'-bird** n. song-bird of thrush family.—**black'-board** n. board painted black for writing on.—**black'-book** n. record of offenders.—**black'-bread** n. rye bread.—**black'-cap** n. small British song-bird, allied to thrush, male of which has jet-black head; cap assumed by judges when sentence of death is being imposed. —**black'-cock** n. male bird of the common black grouse.—**black'-currant** n. fruit of garden bush or bush itself.—**black'-damp** n. suffocating mixture, in mines, of carbon dioxide and air; choke damp.—**black diamonds** (*Colloq.*) coal.—**black'-eye** n. discolouration due to blow.—**black'-faced** n. breed of sheep.—**black'-fel'low** n. Australian aborigine.—**black'-flag** n. flag popularly associated with pirates.—**black'-fri'ar** n. Dominican friar, from his black mantle.—**black'-frost** n. frost without rime.—**blackguard** (blag'-árd) n. orig. menial of scullery; low scoundrel;—a. low; vile;—v.t. treat as blackguard; revile;—v.i. act in vile manner.—**black'guardism** n.—**black'-guardly** a.—**black'head** n. small black-topped mass which plugs mouths of follicles of the skin.—**black'ing** n. old form of boot-polish.—**black'jack** n. can, originally of leather, now of tin, for liquids; flag of pirate; miner's name for zinc-blende; black bituminous mixtures used for roof repairs.—**black'-lead** n. graphite.—**black'-leg** n. one who works during industrial dispute.—**black'-list** n. list of undesirable persons;—v.t. place on such list.—**black'mail** n. extortion of money by threats of exposure or denunciation; hush-money; orig. moneys paid over to robbers to obviate constant pillaging.—**Black Maria**, prison-van used for conveyance of prisoners between court and prison.—**black'-mar'ket** n. clandestine market for sale of essential goods whose distribution is regulated, and which are not on free sale.—**black'-out** n. temporary loss of vision or memory; total cutting off of all lights.—**black'-pud'ding** n. mixture of ox-blood, oatmeal, suet and seasoning enclosed in sausage-skin.—**Black Rod**, usher of Order of the Garter and of House of Lords.—**black'-sheep** n. loose, dissolute member of respectable family.—**black'smith** n. smith who works in iron.—**black'thorn** n. sloe; stout cudgel cut from tree.—**black velvet** n.

stout mixed with cider.—**Black Watch**, Highland Regiment, so called from dark colour of the tartan.—**blackwater fever**, intermittent fever of malarial origin, characterised by dark coloured urine.—**black widow** n. venomous American spider.—**black and blue**, to describe bruise.

bladder (blad'-ẹr) n. thin musculo-membranous bag, in pelvis, serving as reservoir for urine; windbag of bagpipe; any membranous sac.—**bladd'ered** a. swollen like bladder.—**bladd'erwort** n. water-plant with floating leaves.

blade (blād) n. leaf, or flat part of leaf, of plant; cutting part of knife or tool; broad part of oar; sword; (*Colloq.*) dashing fellow.—**blade'-bone** n. upper bone in shoulder; scapula. —**blad'ed** a.

blae (blā) a. bluish-black in colour; livid (of skin); bleak.—**blae'ber'ry** n. (*Scot.*) bilberry; whortleberry.

blain (blān) n. inflamed eruption on skin.

blame (blām) v.t. express disapprobation of; censure;—n. fault.—**blam'able** a.—**blam'ableness** n.—**blam'ably** adv.—**blame'ful** a.—**blame'fully** adv.—**blame'fulness** n.—**blame'less** a.—**blame'lessness** n.—**blame'worthy** a.—**blame'worthiness** n.

blanch (blansh) v.t. whiten; bleach; strip (the husk);—v.i. become white; turn pale; gloss over.—**blanch'ing** n.

blanc-mange (blạ-mawngzh') n. pudding of cornflour, milk, etc.

bland (bland) a. mild; gentle; affable.—**bland'ly** adv.—**bland'ness** n.

blandish (blan'-dish) v.t. flatter and coax; wheedle; caress.—**bland'isher** n.—**bland'ishing, bland'ishment** n.

blank (blangk) a. without writing or any marks; empty; confused.—n. empty space; lottery ticket not drawing prize; white disc of target. —**blank'ly** adv.—**blank verse**, unrhymed verse often in iambic pentameters.—**pointblank**, a. direct aim at close range; downright.

blanket (blang'-ket) n. loosely woven woollen bedcover; horse-covering; thick canopy of cloud.—a. all-embracing;—v.t. cover with blanket; toss in blanket.—**blank'eting** n. thick material for blankets; tossing in blanket.—**wet blanket**, one who depresses others; kill-joy.

blare (blār) v.t. and v.i. sound loudly; trumpet;—n. long, prolonged noise.

blarney (blár'-ni) coaxing, cajoling talk; outrageous flattery.

blasé (blạ-zā) a. surfeited with everything; absolutely bored; sophisticated.

blaspheme (blas-fēm') v.t. speak irreverently of God; desecrate by impious talk;—v.i. take God's name in vain; curse and swear.—**blasphem'-er** n.—**blasphem'ing** n. impious talk. — **blas'phemous** a. — **blas'phemously** adv.—**blas'phemy** n. irreverence in speaking of sacred matters; profane talk.

blast (blast) n. gust or puff of air; forced stream of air; blowing of wind instrument; explosion of gunpowder in rending rocks; blight, affecting plants or cattle.—v.t. injure, as by noxious wind; blight; split, as by gunpowder; abuse vehemently.—**blast off** v.i. and n. of rockets or space vehicles, take off from launching pad.—**blast'ed** a. blighted; accursed; struck by lightning; (Colloq.) confounded; infernal. —**blast'er** n.—**blast'-fur'nace** n. smelting-furnace in which hot draught is furnished by bellows or other apparatus.—**blast'ing** n. blast; explosion; withering effect; blaring of loud trumpets; (Radio) distortion due to over-loading.

blatant (blā'-tant) a. offensively noisy; loud-(voiced); brawling; obtrusive.—**blat'ancy** n.—**blat'antly** adv.

blaze (blāz) n. bright flame; big conflagration; outburst of activity or zeal; display; white mark upon horse's forehead; mark on tree made by pathfinders;—v.t. mark tree by chipping off pieces of bark;—v.i. burn brightly; glow with anger.—**blaz'er** n. sporting jacket of bright colour.—**blaz'es** pl. hell, as in 'Go to blazes.'

blaze (blāz) n. wide publicity;—v.t. proclaim; spread abroad.

blazon (blā'-zn) v.t. make known to everybody; display armorial bearings in their proper colours; embellish;—n. art of drawing or explaining coats of arms.—**blaz'oner** n. —**blaz'onment** n.—**blaz'onry** n. art of describing or explaining coats of arms in heraldic terms.

bleach (blēch) v.t. whiten by exposure to sunlight and air, or by chemical action;—v.i. become whiter or paler. —n. decolourising, chemical agent. —**bleach'er** n. one who, or that which, bleaches.

bleak (blēk) a. without colour; pale; desolate and exposed.—**bleak'ly** adv. —**bleak'ness** n.

blear (blēr) a. dim or watery, due to inflammation of eye;—v.t. dim or blur.—**blear'edness** n.—**blear'y** a. dim.

bleat (blēt) v.i. cry as sheep; talk in complaining, whining fashion; —n. sound made by sheep.

bleed (blēd) v.t. draw blood surgically; extort money from someone;—v.i. lose blood; die in battle;—pa.t. and pa.p. bled.—**bleed'er** n. person who is afflicted by haemophilia, excessive bleeding (confined to males).—**bleed'ing** n.

blemish (blem'-ish) n. deformity, physical or moral; flaw; disfigurement;—v.t. mark with flaw; mar or disfigure.—**blem'ishment** n.

blench (blensh) v.i. start back from lack of courage; flinch.

blend (blend) v.t. mix two allied articles together to improve quality or change colour shade;—v.i. intermix (as in marriage); mingle well;— pa.p. blend'ed or blent;—n. mixture. —**blend'er** n.—**blend'ing** n.

blende (blend) n. ore of zinc, consisting of zinc and sulphur; name given to certain lustrous minerals.

bless (bles) v.t. consecrate; glorify; sanctify; praise; give thanks to; invoke happiness on; magnify;— pa.p. blessed or blest.—**blessed** (bles'-id), **blest** a. happy; favoured with blessings; hallowed; heavenly; (Colloq.) confounded.—**bless'edly** adv.— **bless'edness** n. happiness; heavenly joy; bliss; felicity.—**bless'ing** n. source of happiness or gratitude; benefaction; boon; benediction.

blight (blīt) n. disease of plants caused by certain fungi or parasitic bacteria; anything which has adverse effect, injures, or destroys; v.t. affect with blight; arrest growth of.—**blight'ing** n. and a.

blind (blīnd) a. destitute of sight; ignorant; undiscerning; reckless; unaware of; heedless; at random; invisible; concealed; closed at one end; (Slang) drunk;—v.t. deprive of sight; dazzle; darken or obscure; hide; deceive;—n. window-covering or screen; something intended to mislead; pretext; (sl.) drinking bout.—**blind alley**, cul-de-sac;—a. employment, esp. juvenile, without prospects.—**blind'ed** a.—**blind'fold** a. —v.t. cover the eyes with something; mislead.—**blind'ing** a.—**blind'-lan'ding** n. one made by aircraft using instruments only.—**blind'ly** adv.— **blind'ness** n. lacking power of sight; ignorance; obstinacy.—**col'our-blind'-ness** n. inability to distinguish certain colours.—**night'-blind'ness** n. vision subnormal at night.—**snow'-blind'ness** n. defective vision, due to glare of sunlight upon snow.— **blind'worm** n. slow worm, legless lizard with very tiny eyes.— **blindman's buff**, game where blindfolded person tries to catch others.

blink (blingk) v.i. wink; look with eyes half-shut; glimmer as candle; —v.t. ignore;—n. glimpse; glance. —**blink'ard** n. one who blinks; that which twinkles, as dim star.— **blink'ers** n.pl. pieces of leather preventing horse from seeing to either side.

bliss (blis) n. acme of happiness; perfect felicity; heavenly rapture.— **bliss'ful** a. supremely happy; enjoyable.—**bliss′fully** *adv.*—**bliss′fulness** *n.* —**bliss′less** *a.*

blister (blis′-ter) *n.* vesicle of the skin filled with clear or blood-stained serum; pustule; any swelling as on plants, paint or steel;—*v.t.* raise blisters upon; wither up with scorn and sarcasm;—*v.i.* rise in blisters.

blithe (blīth) *a.* gay; happy; gladsome; jolly; merry; sprightly.— **blithe′ly** *adv.*—**blithe′ness** *n.*—**blithe′-some** *a.* merry; cheerful.—**blithe′-someness** *n.*

blitz (blits) *n.* heavy, sudden attack; —*v.t.* bomb from air.—**blitzed** *a.* wrecked or demolished by bombs or gunfire.

blizzard (bliz′-ard) *n.* blinding snowstorm.

bloat (blōt) *v.t.* cause to have unsound, swollen appearance; swell or puff out; cure fish by salting and smoking.—**bloat′ed** *a.* swollen with self-indulgence; pampered and insolent.—**bloat′edness** *n.*—**bloat′er** *n.* Yarmouth smoked herring.

blob (blob) *n.* anything small and globular (*Colloq.*) mistake.

bloc (blok) *n.* combination of two or more countries or political parties.

block (blok) *n.* solid mass of matter; roughly squared piece of wood, stone, etc.; large piece of wood on which persons were beheaded; wheel of pulley with its case of wood; number of buildings forming one compact mass; obstruction, esp. on roads; mounted plate for printing;—*v.t.* shut in, enclose; obstruct; shape (a hat); sketch out roughly.— **block′ing** *n.* process of stamping book-covers with decorative pattern.—**block′-head** *n.* stupid dolt; dullard.—**block′house** *n.* improvised fort made of logs; fortified place.— **block′letters** *n.* form of script where letters are printed instead of in usual cursive style.

blockade (blo-kād′) *n.* prevention of imports into enemy countries during war;—*v.t.* shut up hostile troops in town by surrounding it; prevent trade with hostile country.—**block-ade′-runn′er** *n.* vessel employed to slip through with goods to blockaded country.—**blockade′-runn′ing** *n.*

blond (blond) *n.* (*fem.* blonde) person of fair complexion and, generally, blue eyes;—*a.* fair; light golden-brown.

blood (blud) *n.* red, viscid fluid which circulates in the body of men and animals; relationship, consanguinity, kindred; honourable birth; descent; rake, man about town; sensational tale;—*v.t.* (*Med.*) let blood, bleed; (*Fig.*) initiate.— **blood′-bank** *n.* store of blood for use in transfusion.—**blood′-corpus′cle** *n.* cell normally contained in suspen-

sion in blood.—**blood′-curd′ling** *a.* terrifying to extent of making blood appear to curdle.—**blood donor** *n.* one who gives blood for transfusion.—**blood′ed** *a.* initiated; of good stock; pedigreed.—**blood′-feud** *n.* vendetta, involving shedding of blood. —**blood′-group** *n.* one of four groups in which human blood is classified.— **blood′-heat** *n.* heat approximating to 98° F.—**blood′-hound** *n.* large hound, prized for keen scent and perseverance.—**blood′ily** *adv.*—**blood′less** *a.* without blood; anaemic; spiritless. —**blood′lessness** *n.*—**blood′-mon′ey** *n.* money paid for betraying another on capital charge.—**blood plasma**, fluid part of blood.—**blood′-pois′oning** *n.* morbid condition due to circulation of bacteria in blood stream; pyaemia; septicaemia.—**blood′-press′-ure** *n.* pressure exerted by blood on walls of arteries.—**blood′-pud′ding** *n.* black pudding, mixture of blood, suet and other materials.—**blood′-red** *a.* crimson, red as blood.—**blood′-se′rum** *n.* fluid part of blood after fibrin and corpuscles have been eliminated.—**blood′shed** *n.* shedding of blood; slaughter.—**blood′shot** *a.* of eyes, red or congested with blood.— **blood′-sports** *n.pl.* fox-hunting and similar sports where animal is hunted.—**blood′-stain** *n.* dried and darkened stain left on clothing, floors, etc. after contact with blood. — **blood′-stock** *n.* thoroughbred horses. — **blood′-suck′er** *n.* animal which sucks blood, esp. leech; extortioner.—**blood′-thirst′y** *a.* eager to shed blood.—**blood′-transfu′sion** *n.* transference of blood from one person to another.—**blood′-ves′sel** *n.* artery or vein through which blood flows.—**blood′y** *a.* pert. to blood; stained with or containing blood; ruthless in shedding blood; vulgarly used as expletive to add intensive force;—**bloody minded** (*Colloq.*) *a.* obstructive.—*v.t.* make bloody.—**bad blood**, state of ill-feeling and enmity. —**flesh and blood**, human frame or nature.—**his blood is up**, he is in state of rage.—**in cold blood**, coolly and deliberately.

bloom (blōōm) *n.* flower; blossom; state of freshness and vigour; flush of youth; velvety bluish colour of grapes and plums; coating on photographic lens.—**bloom′ing** *a.*

blossom (blos′-um) *n.* flower of plant, esp. tree;—*v.i.* put forth blossoms; flourish.—**bloss′omed** *pa.p.* —**bloss′omy** *a.* rich in blossoms.

blot (blot) *v.t.* spot or bespatter, esp. with ink; stain with infamy; obliterate; dry with blotting paper; —*pr.p.* **blot′ting**; *pa.p.* **blot′ted**;—*n.* spot or stain, as of ink; blemish; disgrace.—**blot′ter** *n.* blotting-pad.—

blot'ting-pa'per n. kind of unsized paper for drying ink.

blotch (bloch) n. irregular, coloured spot; eruption upon skin; pustule; pimple;—v.t. mark with blotches; make spotted.—blotch'y a.

blouse (blouz, blous) n. light, loose upper garment with belt.

blow (blō) n. stroke; knock; thump; smack; rap; sudden misfortune.

blow (blō) v.i. produce current of air; move, as air; breathe hard or quickly; puff; pant; (Slang) squander; spout (of whales);—v.t. direct current of air on; sound wind instrument; put out of breath;—pa.t. blew; pa.p. blown;—n. high wind; short walk in open air.—blow'er n. supercharger; (Slang) telephone.—blow'-fly n. flesh-fly; bluebottle.—blow'-lamp n. portable lamp for applying intense local heat.—blown' a. swelled; tired; out of breath; tainted.—blow'-out n. (Slang) feast or big meal; burst tyre.—blow'y a.—to blow hot and cold, be inconsistent.—to blow off steam, get rid of superfluous energy.—to blow one's horn or trumpet, praise oneself; brag.

blowzy (blouz'i) a. coarse and ruddy-faced; slovenly; dishevelled.

blubber (blub'-er) n. fat of whales and other marine animals;—v.i. weep unrestrainedly.

bludgeon (bluj'-un) n. short cudgel with one end loaded;—v.t. knock out with club.

blue (blōō) n. colour of clear sky; one of seven primary colours; dye or pigment; indigo powder used in laundering; sea; one who has represented his university in major sport.—blues n.pl. (Slang) fit of depression; slow sad music of Negro origin.—The Blues, Royal Horse Guards.—blue a. of colour blue; livid; learned; pedantic; melancholy; aristocratic; indecent.—v.t. make or dye blue; dip linen in blue solution; (Slang) squander.—blu'ish a. slightly blue.—blue'bell n. wild hyacinth; in Scotland, harebell.—blue'berry n. heath plant, with small berries.—blue'bird n. migratory bird of N. America of the thrush family.—blue'-blood n. aristocrat.—blue'-bottle n. corn-flower; large fly which lays its eggs in meat.—blue chip reliable industrial shares.—blue ensign, blue flag of Royal Naval Reserve.—blue'-jack'et n. sailor, as distinguished from marine, in Royal Navy.—blue'-pet'er n. flag with blue ground and white square in centre, hoisted when ship is about to sail.—blue'-print n. simple white on blue reproduction of technical drawings; (Fig.) preliminary plan of any project.—blue'-stock'ing n. female pedant, especially if she airs her knowledge.—blue'-tit n. bird with blue wings and tail.—true blue, faithful staunch; unwavering; supporter of Conservative party.—once in a blue moon, rare occurrence.

bluff (bluf) a. steep and broad; rough and ready; frank and hearty in manner;—n. high bank or cliff presenting steep front; headland;—bluff'ness n. steepness; frank, blunt manner of speech.

bluff (bluf) n. attempt to mislead in regard to one's real purpose;—v.t. mislead by giving wrong impression.—bluff'er n. one who bluffs.

blunder (blun'-der) v.i. make gross mistake; err through thoughtlessness;—n. gross mistake.—blun'derer n.—blun'derhead n. one continually blundering.—blun'dering n. and a. continually making mistakes; bungling; clumsy.—blun'deringly adv.

blunderbuss (blun'-der-bus) n. obsolete short gun with bell-shaped muzzle and wide bore.

blunt (blunt) a. having dull edge or point; dull; brusque in speech;—v.t. render less sharp; dull appetite or desire.—blunt'ly adv.—blunt'ness. n.

blur (blur) n. spot; stain; smudge; whatever dims without effacing;—v.t. smear; make indistinct;—pr.p. blur'ring; pa.t. and pa.p. blurred.

blurb (blerb) n. fulsome praise and synopsis of book printed on its outside wrapper.

blurt (blurt) n. sudden outburst.—to blurt out v.t. give information suddenly, indiscreetly, or tactlessly.

blush (blush) v.i. redden in face, from shame, modesty, or confusion;—n. rosy tint; red colour suffusing face.—blush'ing n. and a.

bluster (blus'-ter) v.i. blow in boisterous gusts, of wind; talk with violence and noise; bully or swagger;—n. fitful noise and violence.—blus'terer n.—blus'tering n. noisy, menacing language;—a. boisterous; roaring; bullying; bragging.—blus'teringly adv.—blus'tery a.

boa (bō'-a) n. genus of constricting, non-venomous serpents; long round coil of fur or feathers for neck.—bo'a-constrict'or n. serpent which crushes its victims by compression.

boar (bōr) n. male of swine.—boa'r-hound n. great mastiff used in hunting boars.

board (bōrd) n. long, narrow strip of timber; table, hence food or diet; council-table; council itself; directors of a company collectively; thick paper made by pasting together several layers (card-board, pasteboard, etc.);—v.t. cover with boards; supply with meals and lodging for payment; embark on ship;—v.i. be a lodger.—boards n.pl. stage in theatre; covers of book.—board'er n.

one who boards ship; one receiving food and lodging.—**board'ing** n. wooden fence, floor, etc.; entering ship; obtaining food and lodging.—**board'ing-house** n. house in which boarders are accommodated.—**board'ing-out** n. system by which Local Authorities send children under their charge to be cared for in private houses for payment.—**board'ing-school** n. school in which scholars are in residence.—**board'-room** n. room in which company meetings are held.—**to go by the board**, be abandoned.—**to sweep the board**, take all stakes or prizes.

boast (bōst) v.t. speak with vanity of; be unduly proud of;—v.i. brag; vaunt; praise extravagantly oneself; —n. statement, expressive of pride or vain glory; that which is boasted of.—**boast'er** n.—**boast'ful** a.—**boast'fully** adv.—**boast'fulness, boast'ing** n.—**boast'ingly** adv.

boat (bōt) n. small vessel, generally undecked, moved by oars or sails or small motor; ship; anything resembling boat, e.g. sauce-boat;—v.t. carry in boat;—v.i. row or sail about in boat.—**boat'er** n. one who boats; straw hat.—**boatswain** (bō'-sun) n. warrant officer in navy who had particular charge of boats, sails, rigging, cables and anchors.—**to burn one's boats**, commit oneself irrevocably to course of action.

bob (bob) n. short, jerking motion; anything which swings when suspended; jerk; pendant; weight of pendulum; hair cut short and square across; docked tail;—v.t. move with jerk; cut hair semi-short;—v.i. dangle; move up and down or in and out;—pr.p. **bob'bing**; pa.p. **bobbed.**

bob (bob) n. (Slang) shilling.

bobbin (bob'-in) n. small wooden cylinder on which thread is wound.

bobby (bob'-i) n. (Slang) policeman.

bobsleigh, bobsled (bob'-slā, -sled), n. four-runner steerable sleigh;—v.i. use bobsleigh.

bode (bōd) v.t. and v.i. portend; presage; foretell; foreshadow; be omen of.—**bod'ing** a. ominous;—n. omen; presentiment.

bodge n. Same as **botch.**

bodice (bod'-is) n. that part of woman's dress above waist, with or without sleeves, and close-fitting.

bodkin (bod'-kin) n. short, sharp dagger or stiletto; instrument for piercing holes in material; large blunt needle; pin for dressing hair.

body (bod'-i) n. frame of human being or of animal; main part of anything; coachwork, seating and upholstery of car; assemblage of things or persons; solid substance; strength or consistency of liquid;—v.t. produce in definite shape;—pa.t.

and pa.p. **bod'ied.**—**bod'ied** a. used in compounds, e.g. able-bodied.—**bod'iless** a.—**bod'ily** a. of body;—adv. physically, in the body, in the flesh; completely; in mass.—**bod'yguard** n. protector; escort.

Boer (bōōr) n. Dutch farmer of S. Africa; person of Dutch descent.

boffin (bof'in) n. (Slang) scientist.

bog (bog) n. wet soft ground; deep soft marsh;—v.t. engulf in bog.—**bogg'y** a.—**bog'-land** n.—**bog'-moss** n. sphagnum.

bogey (bō'-gi) n. (Golf) standard score for hole or course expected of good player.

boggle (bog'-l) v.i. stop at; make difficulties; shrink back through fear; equivocate.—**bogg'ler** n. See **bogle.**

bogie, bogey (bō'-gi) n. small low truck; pivoted undercarriage of locomotive, etc.

bogle (bō'-gl) n. ghost or demon; fearsome apparition, imp, or hobgoblin.—**bog'ey, bog'y** n. devil; bugbear; goblin.—**bogey'man** n.

bogus (bō'-gus) a. sham; counterfeit; false.

boil (boil) v.t. bring to seething condition, by heating; cook, by boiling; —v.i. be agitated by action of heat; seethe; reach boiling-point.—**boil'er** n. one who boils; vessel for boiling; steam generator.—**boiling point**, temperature at which liquid boils.

boil (boil) n. local inflammation of skin round hair follicle.

boisterous (bois'-ter-us) a. wild; noisy; hearty; turbulent; windy.—**bois'terously** adv.—**bois'terousness** n.

bold (bōld) a. daring; ready to meet danger; brave; cheeky; prominent; standing out.—**bold'ly** adv.—**bold'ness** n.

bole (bōl) n. trunk of tree.

bolero (bo-lā'-rō) n. national Spanish dance, in triple time; music for this dance; lady's short jacket, usually without sleeves, worn over blouse.

boll (bōl) n. seed capsule of cotton, flax, etc.

bollard (bol'-ard) n. short post on wharf, traffic island, etc.

Bolshevik (bol'-she-vik) n. member of Russian Majority, or Extreme, Communist Party; violent revolutionary.—a. pert. to Bolsheviks or Bolshevism.—**bol'shevism** n.—**bol'shevist** n. and a.—**bolshevis'tic** a.—**bol'shevise** v.t.

bolster (bōl'-ster) n. long round bedpillow; anything designated as support.—v.t. sustain; support; prop. —**bol'sterer** n.—**to bolster up**, support weak case or person.

bolt (bōlt) n. bar for fastening door, window, etc.; part of lock which engages with keeper; pin for holding objects together; narrow roll of cloth; thunder-bolt; arrow; shackle for prisoners; sudden rush;—*v.t.* fasten with bolt; swallow food hurriedly;—*v.i.* rush away; start suddenly forward, as of horse.—**bolt'-hole** *n.* underground shelter; emergency exit.—**bolt'-up'right** *adv.* straight up, as bolt or arrow.

bomb (bom) *n.* container filled with high explosives, etc. exploding by percussion or by timing mechanism; —*v.t.* attack with bombs.—**bomb'er** *n.* one who bombs; aeroplane for bombs.—**bomb'shell** *n.* bomb; something devastating and unexpected.

bombard (bom'-bard) *n.* early mortar with wide bore, using stone-shot; large vat for liquor; powerful organ stop.—**bombard** (bom-bard') *v.t.* subject to sustained artillery fire; ply with many questions.—**bombardier** *n.* artillery N.C.O. equivalent to corporal.—**bombard'ment** *n.* sustained attack with guns, bombs, etc.

bombast (bom'-, bum'-bast) *n.* cotton-wool; wadding; padding; inflated, high-sounding language.—**bombas'tic** *a.*—**bombas'tically** *adv.*

bon (bong) *a.* Fr. *bon*, good, used in words and phrases not yet Anglicised.—**bon'-bon** *n.* sweetmeat.

bonanza (bō-nan'-zạ) *n.* exceptionally rich vein of ore; profitable enterprise; large shop or store.

bond (bond) *n.* that which binds, band, link, tie; oath or promise; obligation; duty; arrangement of bricks or stones in wall so that successive courses interlock;—**bonds** *n.pl.* fetters; chains; captivity.—**bond'age** *n.* state of being bound; **slavery.**—**bond'maid, bond'man, bonds'man, bond'ser'vant, bond'wom'an, bonds'wom'an** *n.* serf.

bond (bond) *n.* legal engagement in writing to fulfil certain conditions; certificate of ownership of capital lent to government, municipality, etc.; mortgage on house, etc.;—*v.t.* put dutiable articles in customs store till duties are paid.—**bond'ed** *a.* placed in bond; mortgaged.—**bonded ware-house,** customs store for bonded goods.—**in bond,** in bonded store.

bone (bōn) *n.* hard tissue which forms skeleton of mammals, birds, reptiles and fishes;—*v.t.* remove bones; fillet (fish); stiffen corsets with whale-bone, etc.—**bones** *n.pl.* human remains; corpse; dice; castanets.—**bone'-dry** *a.* absolutely dry.—**bone'less** *a.*—**bone'-meal** *n.* fertiliser, made from ground bones.—**bone'-set'ter** *n.* one skilled in manipulation of dislocated bones of limbs.—**bone'-shak'er** *n.* early form of bicycle with solid tyres.—**bon'iness** *n.*—**bon'y** *a.* —**bone of contention,** subject in dispute.

bonfire (bon'-fir) *n.* orig. fire for

burning bones; large fire specially built and lit to express public joy.

bongo (bong'gō) *n.* small W. Indian drum; African bush buck.

bonhomie (bon'-o-mē) *n.* frank and simple good-nature; geniality.

bonnet (bon'-et) *n.* flat cap; woman's head-gear, of various shapes; movable protecting cover, as of valve-box, motor-engine, etc.;—*v.t.* put on bonnet.—**bonn'eted** *a.*—**bonn'et-laird** *n.* one who farms his own property.

bonny (bon'-i) *a.* pretty; beautiful; handsome; comely; considerable.—**bonn'ily** *adv.*—**bonn'iness** *n.*

bonus (bō'-nus) *n.* extra dividend given to shareholders in public company; extra gratuity paid to employees.

boo (bóó) *interj.* exclamation of disapproval or contempt.—**booes** *n.pl.*—**boo** *v.t.* and *v.i.* hoot; show disapproval.—*pr.t.* (he) **booes;** *pa.t.* **booed.**

booby (bóó'-bi) *n.* sea-bird of gannet type, said to be easily caught; dunce; numskull; blockhead.—**boob** *n.* (*Slang*) simpleton; stupid fellow;—*v.i.* to make a blunder.—**boo'by-prize** *n.* prize to worst performer.—**boo'by-trap** *n.* practical joke set in motion by the victim; apparently innocent object which explodes when handled.

book (book) *n.* number of sheets of paper, etc. bound together; literary composition or treatise, written or printed; record of betting transactions; words of play, libretto;—*v.t.* put into book; obtain or give, business order, ticket, etc.; engage in advance; take name of, for alleged offence.—**books** *n.pl.* records of business transactions; ledgers.—**book'-bin'der** *n.* one who binds books.—**book'-bin'ding** *n.*—**book'-case** *n.* case with shelving for books.—**book'-club** *n.* club to distribute specially chosen books to subscribers.—**book'-ends** *n.pl.* heavy props to keep books upright on shelf.—**book'ing** *n.*—**book'ing-clerk** *n.* clerk who issues railway, etc., tickets or registers orders.—**book'ing-hall, book'ing-off'ice** *n.* place where tickets are issued.—**book'ish** *a.* fond of books and study.—**book'ishness** *n.*—**book'-jack'et** *n.* outer paper wrapper of book.—**book'-keep'er** *n.*—**book'-keep'ing** *n.* art of keeping systematic account of financial transactions.—**book'let** *n.* small book; pamphlet.—**book'-mak'er** *n.* professional betting-man who accepts bets; turf accountant.—**book'-mark** *n.* something placed in book to mark particular page.—**book'-plate** *n.* label, often illustrated, pasted on front end-papers of book to denote ownership.—**book'work** *n.* theory as opposed to practice.—

book'worm n. one who reads intensively; larvae of insects which bore holes through pages and bindings.—**to bring to book**, call to account.—**to take a leaf out of his book**, follow his example.

boom (bóóm) n. light spar for stretching bottom of sail; obstruction across harbour, etc.; long beam, esp. one for holding microphones, lighting equipment, etc.

boom (bóóm) v.i. make deep hollow sound; be extremely popular and successful; be in great demand;—n. hollow roar; cry of the bittern; sudden advance in popular favour; sudden demand for an article.—**boom'er** n.—**boom'ing** a.

boomerang (bóó'-me-rang) n. curved wooden missile used by natives of Australia which returns towards thrower; (Fig.) action or attack which has reverse effect;—v.i. recoil.

boon (bóón) n. some good thing given or asked for; benefaction.

boor (bóór) n. peasant; lout.—**boor'ish** a.—**boor'ishly** adv.—**boor'ishness** n.

boost (bóóst) v.t. hoist; give lift to; help forward; advertise on big scale; increase output or power of machine; —n. shove; increase in power.—**boost'er** n. supercharger, subsidiary rocket of space vehicle.

boot (bóót) n. covering for foot and ankle; luggage compartment in coach, motor-car, etc.;—v.t. put on boots; kick.—**boot'ee** n. knitted boot for infant.—**boot'lace** n. lace or thong for fastening boots.—**boot'-last, boot'-tree** n. instrument to stretch, or preserve shape of, boot.—**boot'leg** v.t. import or sell illicitly alcoholic liquor; smuggle.—**boot'legger** n.—**boot'legging** n.—**boots** n. male servant in hotel who cleans boots and acts as handy-man.

boot (bóót) v.t. profit or advantage; —n. profit; avail; advantage; (Law) compensation paid for injuries.—**boot'less** a. useless; without profit.—**boot'lessly** adv.—**boot'lessness** n.—**to boot**, in addition.

booth (bóóth) n. temporary hut of boards or other slight materials; covered stall at market or fair.—**poll'ing-booth** n. place for voting.

booty (bóó'-ti) n. spoil taken in war; plunder; pillage.

booze, boose (bóóz) n. alcoholic liquor; drinking-bout;—v.i. drink excessively.—**boo'zer, boo'ser** n. one who drinks to excess; tippler.—**boo'zy, boo'sy** a. a little intoxicated.

boracic See under borax.

borax (bō'-raks) n. hydrated sodium borate.—**borac'ic** a.—**boracic acid**, n. mildly antiseptic white powder.—**bo'rate** n. salt of boracic acid.

border (bord'-er) n. outer part or edge; frontier; ornamental design round outside edge; flower-bed;—v.t. adorn with border; adjoin;—v.i. touch at edge; come near.—**bord'erer** n. one who lives near frontier.—**bord'ering** n. material for border.—**bor'derland** n. land contiguous to frontier; indeterminate state or condition.

bore (bōr) v.t. make hole in; pierce; drill; weary by uninteresting talk; fatigue;—n. hole made by boring; inside diameter measurement of cylinder; hollow interior part of gun barrel; thing or person that wearies one.—**bore'dom** n.—**bor'er** n.

bore (bōr) n. tidal wave of great force in some rivers; eagre.

bore (bōr) pa.t. of bear.

boric (bōr'-ik) a. pert. to boron.

born (born) pa.p. of bear, bring forth;—a. natural; innate; perfect.

borne (bōrn) pa.p. of bear, carry.

boron (bō'-ron) n. non-metallic element.

borough (bur'-ō) n. incorporated town; town represented in Parliament.

borrow (bor'-ō) v.t. obtain on loan or trust.—**borr'owed** a.—**borr'ower** n.—**borr'owing** n.

Borstal (bors'-tal) n. system of reformatory schools for youthful offenders.

borzoi (bor'-zoi) n. Russian wolf-hound.

bosom (bóó'-zum) n. breast of human being; part of dress over breast; the heart; embrace; enclosure; expanse; shirt-front;—v.t. press to bosom;—a. intimate.

boss (bos) n. prominent circular projection on any article; stud; knob; round, slightly raised ornament.—v.t. emboss; provide with bosses.—**bossed** a. embossed.

boss (bos) n. (Colloq.) master; employer; one in charge;—v.t. manage; supervise; (Colloq.) browbeat.—**boss'iness** n.—**boss'y** a.

bo'sun See boatswain (under boat).

botany (bot'-a-ni) n. study of plants.—**botan'ic, botan'ical** a.—**botan'ically** adv.—**bot'anist** n.—**bot'anise** v.i. study or collect plants.

botch (boch) n. large ulcerous affection; clumsy patch of garment; bungled work;—v.t. bungle; patch clumsily. Also **bodge**.—**botch'er** n.—**botch'ery, botch'work** n.—**botch'ily** adv.—**botch'y** a.

both (bōth) a. and pron. the one and the other;—conj. (foll. by and) as well.

bother (boTH'-er) v.t. annoy; worry; trouble; perplex;—v.i. fuss; worry;—n. trouble; annoyance; fuss; worry;—interj. exclamation of annoyance.—**bothera'tion** n. trouble and worry; mild imprecation.—**both'ersome** a. troublesome; annoying

bothie, bothy (both'-i) n. hut: hovel.

bottle (bot'-l) n. vessel with narrow neck for holding liquids; its contents; hard drinking;—v.t. put into bottles; restrain; curb.—**bott'led** a. enclosed in bottles; of bottle shape. —**bott'led-up** a. confined; not allowed to speak; repressed.—**bott'le-green** a. of dark-green colour.—**bott'ling** n. and a.—**bott'le-neck** n. narrow outlet which impedes smooth flow of traffic or production of goods.— **bott'le-par'ty,** n. one where guests provide the drinks.—**bott'ler** n.

bottom (bot'-um) n. lowest part of anything; posterior of human body; base; bed of sea, river or lake; foundation or groundwork; stamina; origin;—v.i. put bottom on article; lay foundation for road, etc.— **bott'omed** a.—**bott'omless** a.

botulism (bot'-ū-lizm) n. form of food poisoning.

boudoir (bōō'-dwār) n. lady's small private room.

bougainvillea (bōō'-gān-vil'-e-a) n. S. American plant with great masses of red or lilac bracts.

bough (bou) n. arm or large branch of tree.

bought (bawt) pa.t. and pa.p. of buy.

boulder (bōl'-der) n. rock torn from its bed, and rounded by water.— **boul'der-clay** n. stiff clay of glacial or ice-drift age.

boulevard (bōōl'-e-var) n. street or promenade planted with trees.

bounce (bouns) v.i. leap or spring suddenly; come or go suddenly; (of a cheque) be returned; boast; —v.t. cause to rebound, as ball; eject;—n. sudden fall; rebound; boast; boaster;—**bounc'ing** a. lusty; boastful.—**bounc'ingly** adv.

bound (bound) pa.t. and pa.p. of bind.—**bound, boun'den** a. imposed as duty.

bound (bound) v.i. leap; jump; spring; skip; frisk.—n. leap; jump.

bound (bound) a. prepared for going; intending to go, etc.; direction, as in homeward bound.

bound (bound) n. usually in pl. limit or boundary; confines; precincts;— v.t. restrain; form boundary of; set bounds to.—**bound'ed** a. restricted; bordered.—**bound'er** n. (Slang) objectionable, vulgar person.—**bound'less** a. without limits; vast; infinite. —**bound'lessness** n.—**out of bounds,** not allowed to enter.

boundary (bound'-ar-i) n. border or limit; dividing line; barrier; precincts; termination; perimeter of cricket pitch.

bounty (boun'-ti) n. liberality; generosity; gratuity; payment made to volunteers for the army or navy; grant to assist certain branches of industry, agriculture, etc.—**boun'-**

teous, boun'tiful a.—**boun'teously, boun'tifully** adv. **boun'teousness, boun'-tifulness** n.—**King's (Queen's) bounty,** grant of money made to parents of triplets.

bouquet (bōō'-kā) n. nosegay; bunch of flowers; perfume; aromatic flavour and aroma of wine; compliment.

bourg (bōōrg) n. See **borough, burgh.**

bourgeois (boor-zhwaw') n. member of the middle-class;—a. middle-class; conventional.—**bour'geoisie** n.

bourn, bourne (bōrn, bōōrn) n. boundary; limit; realm; domain, goal.—**last bourne,** the grave.

bout (bout) n. turn; conflict; contest; continuous drinking.

bovine (bō'-vīn) a. pert. to cattle; ox-like; dull; stupid; stolid; obtuse.

bow (bou) v.i. bend body in respect, assent, etc.; submit;—v.t. bend downwards; crush; subdue;—n. inclination of head or body; rounded forward part of ship; stem or prow. —**bowsprit** (bō'-sprit) n. large spar projecting over stem of vessel.

bow (bō) n. anything bent or curved; weapon from which arrow is discharged; fiddle-stick; lace or ribbon tied in slip-knot; rainbow; metal ring used as attachment;—v.t. manipulate bow of violin, etc.—**bowed** a. bent like bow, crooked.—**bow'-legged** a. having crooked legs.—**bow'-man** n. archer.—**bow'-saw** n. thin-bladed saw kept taut by bow-shaped frame.—**bow'-win'dow** n. curved, bay window.—**to draw the long bow,** exaggerate.

bowdlerise (bōd-, boud'-ler'īz) v.t. leave out indelicate words or passages in book in alleged interest of moral purity.—**bowd'lerism** n.

bowel (bou'-el) n. inside part; the large intestine; (Fig.) seat of pity, tenderness, etc.—**bowels** n.pl. intestines.

bower (bou'-er) n. boudoir; shady recess; arbour; small country dwelling.—**bow'ery** a. shady.

bowl (bōl) n. round vessel; deep basin; drinking-cup; hollow part of anything.

bowl (bōl) n. ball rolled along the ground in certain games; large ball with bias;—pl. game played on bowling-green with bowls;—v.t. roll, as a bowl;—v.i. play with bowls; move rapidly and smoothly; deliver ball.—**bowl'er** n.—**bowl'ing** n.— **bowl'ing-all'ey** n. covered place for playing at bowls.—**bowl'ing-green** n. pitch for bowling.

bowler (bōl'-er) n. hard, felt hat.

bowsprit (bō'-sprit) n. See **bow.**

box (boks) n. small case or chest, generally with lid; its contents; compartment in law-court for witnesses; small wooden hut for sentry; compartment in auditorium

box 63 brand

of theatre, etc.; driver's seat on carriage; gratuity at Christmas time;—*v.t.* enclose in box.—**box′-car** *n.* closed railway-car used for transporting perishable goods.— **Boxing Day,** day after Christmas. **box′-kite** *n.* kite with square frame. —**box′-off′ice** *n.* ticket office at theatre.—**box′-pleat** *n.* double fold in dress-cloth with knife edge.—**box spanner** *n.* hollow tubular spanner turned with metal bar.

box (boks) *n.* small evergreen shrub. —**box′-tree** *n.* tree variety of box.— **box′-wood** *n.*

box (boks) *n.* buffet on head or ears; —*v.t.* buffet; mix up playing-cards; —*v.i.* fight in arena with fists.— **box′er** *n.*—**box′ing** *n.*—**box′ing-glove** *n.* padded glove worn by boxers.

boy (boi) *n.* male child; lad; native servant or labourer.—**boy′hood** *n.* state of being a boy.—**boy′ish** *a.* boy-like; puerile.—**boy′ishly** *adv.*—**boy′ish-ness** *n.* natural actions of boy.

boycott (boi′-kot) *n.* method of coercion by conspiracy, whereby all dealings cease with undesirable individual;—*v.t.* act as above; ost-racise.—**boy′cotter** *n.*—**boy′cotting** *n.*

bra (bra) *n.* short for brassière.

brace (brās) *n.* rod or bar crossing space diagonally to connect two structural parts; carpenter's tool for boring;—*v.t.* furnish with braces; ~~support; tighten; nerve or strength-~~ ~~... ... ... which sup-~~ ~~... ...~~ — brac′ing *a.* ~~strengthening~~ ~~... ...~~ ting.

bracelet (brās-~~...~~) ornament for wrist.—**brace′lets** *n. ~~...~~* (*Colloq.*) hand-cuffs.

bracken (brak′-e~~...~~) large coarse species of fern.

bracket (brak′-et) *n.* projecting support fastened to wall; one of two signs, [ ], ⟨ ⟩ or ( ), used to enclose explanatory words;—*v.t.* place within brackets; couple names together as of equal merit, etc.

brackish (brak′-ish) *a.* somewhat salty; of fresh water which has been mixed with salt water.—**brack′ish-ness** *n.*

bract (brakt) *n.* leaf in axil of which a flower or inflorescence arises.— **brac′teal** *a.*

brad (brad) *n.* cut nail tapering in width with small head projecting on one side.—**brad′-awl** *n.* small hand-boring tool.

brae (brā) *n.* (*Scot.*) side of hill; stretch of sloping ground.

brag (brag) *v.i.* boast; praise oneself or one's belongings;—*pr.p.* brag ging; *pa.t.* and *pa.p.* bragged;—*n.* boast; card game resembling poker.— **bragg′art** *a.* boastful;—*n.* boaster.— **bragg′ing** *a.* boastful;—*n.* boastful language.—**bragg′ingly** *adv.*

Brahmin (brā′-min) *n.* person of highest or priestly caste among Hindus.—**brah′minism** *n.*

braid (brād) *v.t.* plait, entwine, or interweave; bind with braid;—*n.* narrow ribbon or tape used as dress or upholstery trimming; tress of hair.—**braid′ed** *a.*;—**braid′ing** *n.*

Braille (brāl) *n.* system of printing books in relief for the blind; letters (groups of dots) used.

brain (brān) *n.* whitish, soft mass in skull in which are the nerve centres; intellect; mental capacity; under-standing; intelligence;—*v.t.* dash out brains of.—**brained** *a.* having brains beaten out; used in compound terms as *feather-brained,* etc.—**brain′child** *n.* inspiration or idea of particular person.—**brain′-fev′er** *n.* inflamma-tion of brain; meningitis.—**brain′less** *a.*—**brain′lessness** *n.*—**brain′-storm** *n.* sudden attack of insanity.—**brain-wash** *v.t.* subject to psychological stress in order to change views or extract confession.—**brain′-wave** *n.* (*Colloq.*) unexpected, spontaneous bright idea.—**brain′y** *a.* highly intel-lectual; clever.

braise (brāz) *v.t.* stew with vege-tables, etc., and then bake;—*n.* the roach.—**brais′er** *n.* covered pot used in braising.

brake (brāk) *n.* place overgrown with ferns, etc.; thicket; brushwood.

brake (brāk) *n.* instrument for ~~... ... ...~~ ap; harrow; large wagonette; motor car designed to carry people and goods; device for retarding motion of a body; re-straining influence or curb;—*v.t.* pound or crush flax, hemp, etc., by beating; check by applying brake.— **brak′ing** *n.*—**brake′-horse′power** *a.* that developed by a motor, as measured by braking the output shaft.—**brake′-shoe** *n.* rubbing surface of brake.— **brake′-van** *n.* railway carriage contain-ing brake.

bramble (bram′-bl) *n.* prickly hedge-plant; wild blackberry; small, dark purple fruit of bramble.

bran (bran) *n.* husk of wheat and other grain, separated in milling from flour.—**bran′-tub** *n.* lucky dip in which parcels are concealed in bran.

branch (bransh) *n.* limb of tree or shrub; bough; department of busi-ness, etc.; line of family descent; off-shoot; ramification; section; part; sub-division;—*v.t.* divide, as into branches;—*v.i.* spread, in branches; diverge.—**branched** *a.*—**branch′ing** *a.* —**root and branch,** thoroughly.

brand (brand) *n.* burning, or partly burnt, piece of wood; iron used for burning marks on; mark made by hot iron; article with trade-mark; grade; sword; mark of infamy; stigma;—*v.t.* burn mark on; fix stamp on; designate commodity by special name or trade-mark; stigmatise; reproach.—**brand′ed** *a.*—**brand′er** *n.* gridiron;—*v.t.* broil on gridiron; grill.—**brand′-new, bran′-new** *a.* quite new.

brandish (bran′-dish) *v.t.* flourish or wave, as weapon.

brandy (bran′-di) *n.* ardent spirit distilled from wine.—**bran′dy-ball** *n.* sweet in the shape of ball.—**bran′dy-snap,** *n.* thin, round, gingerbread.

brash (brash) *n.* slight indisposition; rash on skin; clear watery eructation from stomach due to acidity; sudden downpour of rain;—*a.* sudden; hasty; insolent.

brass (bras) *n.* yellow alloy of two parts of copper to one of zinc; (*Colloq.*) money; effrontery: impudence; obstinacy;—*a.* brazen; made of brass.—**brass′es** *n.pl.* monumental plates in church to commemorate deceased persons; brass instruments of orchestra.—**brass′-band** *n.* musicians who perform on brass instruments; (*Colloq.*) military band.—**brass′founder** *n.* one who casts articles of brass.—**brass′-hat** *n.* (*Colloq.*) staff-officer (from gold braid on hat).—**brass′iness** *n.*—**brass′y** *a.*—**brass′y, brass′ie** *n.* wooden golf-club with brass sole.—**to get down to brass tacks** (*Colloq.*) return to essentials, fundamentals.

brassiere (bras-i-er′) *n.* woman's undergarment supporting the breasts.

brat (brat) *n.* apron of coarse cloth; child (used contemptuously); offspring.

bravado (bra-vá′-dō) *n.* swaggerer; showy bravery; **brava′does.**

brave (brāv) *a.* courageous; noble; finely-dressed;—*n.* Red Indian warrior;—*v.t.* encounter with courage.—**brave′ly** *adv.*—**brav′ery** *n.*

brawl (brawl) *v.i.* flow noisily, as water; squabble noisily;—*n.* noisy quarrel.—**brawl′er** *n.*

brawn (brawn) *n.* thick flesh; muscular strength, esp. of arms and legs; muscles; flesh of boar; preparation made from pigs' head, salted, boiled, and allowed to settle in its own jelly.—**brawn′iness** *n.*—**brawn′y** *a.* muscular; athletic.

bray (brā) *n.* harsh noise of ass; any harsh, strident noise; continual complaining;—*v.i.* utter harsh noise, like ass.

braze (brāz) *v.t.* join metal surfaces with hard solder.—**braz′ing** *n.*

brazen (brā′-zn) *a.* pert. to, or made of, brass; impudent; shameless; sounding like brass instrument;—*v.t.* face situation in bold, impudent manner when in the wrong, as in 'to brazen it out.'—**bra′zenly** *adv.*

brazier (brāzh′-yer) *n.* portable iron container to hold burning coke; worker in brass.

brazil nut (bra-zil′ nut) *n.* hard shelled edible seed of S. American fruit-tree.

breach (brēch) *n.* break or opening, esp. in wall; hole or gap; non-fulfilment of contract, promise, etc.; infringement of rule, duty, etc.; quarrel;—*v.t.* make breach or gap in something.—**breach of promise,** non-fulfilment of promise of marriage.

bread (bred) *n.* form of food prepared by baking from dough made from cereal; food in general.—**bread′-bas′ket** *n.* (*Slang*) stomach.—**bread′less** *a.* starving.—**to break bread,** partake of Holy Communion.

breadth (bredth) *n.* distance from side to side; width; freedom from narrowness of mind.

break (brāk) *v.t.* shatter by force; divide into two; mitigate (blow, fall); tame (horse, etc.); wean (from habit); dismiss from office; bankrupt; weaken or impair (health); subdue person's temper); violate (promises, etc.); interrupt friendship, silence, etc.);—*v.i.* divide into several parts; open (as abscess); curl over (as waves); burst forth (as storm); dawn (as idea, day, etc.); crack or falter (as voice); change direction (as cricket ball); make first stroke at billiards; change pace (as horse); —*pa:t.* broke; *pa.p.* brok′en.—**break through** *n.* major advance in science, negotiations, etc.—**to break down,** crush opposition, etc.; lose control of feelings; go out of action.—**to break new ground,** change activities.

break (brāk) *n.* act or state of being broken; fracture; gap; opening; dawn; separation; interruption; breathing space; (*Slang*) a chance; sudden fall in price; scoring sequence at billiards.—**break′able** *a.* fragile.—**break′age** *n.* act of breaking; allowance for articles broken.—**break′-away** *n.* animal which darts away from the herd; panic rush; leaving parent body to start new movement.—**break′down** *n.* loss of health; failure of machinery; suspension of negotiations;—*v.t.* divide into small categories.—**break′er** *n.* one who breaks; long wave or crest as it breaks into foam.—**break′fast** *n.* first meal of day.—**break′neck** *a.* dangerous to life and limb.—**break′-wat′er** *n.* strong structure to break force of waves.—**break′-of-day** *n.* dawn.—**a bad break,** period of misfortune.

bream (brēm) *n.* fresh-water fish of the carp family.

breast (brest) *n.* external part of thorax or chest between neck and abdomen; bosom; seat of affections and passions;—*v.t.* bare the breast against; oppose, face, or meet boldly (a wave); mount (a hill, etc.).—**breasts** *n.pl.* milk glands of women and female animals.—**breast'-bone** *n.* sternum, flat narrow bone to which first seven ribs are attached.—**breast'-plate** *n.* metal plate or piece of armour for protecting chest.—**breast'-stroke** *n.* swimming stroke made with breast facing forward.—**breast'work** *n.* parapet on building; hastily constructed defensive earthwork.—**to make a clean breast**, confess.

breath (breth) *n.* air respired by lungs; life; respite; single respiration; very slight breeze; whisper; fragrance.—**breath'less** *a.* out of breath; panting; expectant.—**breath'lessness** *n.*—**to catch the breath**, stop breathing momentarily from excitement.—**with bated breath**, breath held from fear or excitement.

breathe (brēTH) *v.t.* draw in and give out air from lungs; infuse or inspire, as life, courage, etc.;—*v.i.* inhale and emit air—hence to live; take breath.—**breath'able** *a.*—**breath'er** *n.* short spell of rest.—**breath'ing** *n.* respiration.—**breath'ing-space, breath'ing time,** *n.* pause; short respite.

bred *pa.t.* and *pa.p.* of **breed**.

breech (brēch) *n.* buttocks; hinder part, esp. of gun-barrel.—**breech'es** *n.pl.* trousers, esp. those which fit tightly round knees.

breed (brēd) *v.t.* beget; generate; propagate; hatch; train or bring up;—*v.i.* be produced; be with young; increase in number;—*pa.t.* and *pa.p.* **bred**;—*n.* race of animals from same stock; kind; sort.—**breed'er** *n.*—**breed'ing** *n.* producing; rearing of live stock; manners; deportment; courtesy.—**breeder reactor** (*Phys.*) one which produces, by neutron capture, more fissile material than it consumes.

breeze (brēz) *n.* wind of moderate strength; quarrel; disturbance.—**breez'y** *a.* windy; gusty; of person, with animation and bluffness.

breeze (brēz) *n.* finely broken coke; furnace ashes; clinkers.

brethren (breTH'-ren) *n.pl.* brothers; members of same society or profession.—**Plymouth Brethren,** Christian sect [See **brother**].

breviary (brēv'-i-ạ-ri) *n.* abridgment; book containing daily service of R.C. Church.

brevity (brev'-i-ti) *n.* shortness; conciseness; briefness; terseness.

brew (brōō) *v.t.* prepare fermented liquor, from malt, hops, etc.; infuse (tea); plot; concoct;—*v.i.* perform operations of brewing; be impending;—*n.* something brewed; particular brand or quality of beer.—**brew'er** *n.*—**brew'ery** *n.*

briar (brī'-ạr) *n.* common heath-plant of Mediterranean region; pipe made from root of this; wild rose; any prickly bush; thorn.—**sweet-bri'ar, sweet-bri'er** *n.* wild rose.

bribe (brīb) *n.* anything bestowed with view to influence judgment and conduct;—*v.t.* influence by gifts;—*v.i.* practise bribery.—**brib'able** *a.*—**brib'ery** *n.*

brick (brik) *n.* special clay moulded into rectangular block and hardened by burning; wooden block used in kindergarten instruction; (*Colloq.*) dependable friend;—*v.t.* lay, or pave, with bricks.—**brick'bat** *n.* fragment of brick.—**brick'bats** *n.pl.* angry comments. — **brick'-field** *n.* place where bricks are made.—**brick'layer** *n.* one skilled in building with bricks.—**brick'-laying** *n.*—**brick'work** *n.* structure built of bricks as distinguished from other materials.—**brick'yard** *n.* place where bricks are made.—**to drop a brick** (*Slang*) to be tactless.

bride (brīd) *n.* woman about to be, or just, married.—**bri'dal** *n.* wedding, orig. bride-ale, ale-drinking at wedding;—*a.* pert. to bride or wedding; nuptial; connubial; conjugal.—**bride'groom** *n.* man newly-married, or about to be married.—**brides'maid** *n.* unmarried woman who acts as attendant on bride; best maid.—**brides'man** *n.* man who attends bridegroom; best man.

bridge (brij) *n.* roadway over arches spanning river or valley; support for strings of violin; control deck of vessel; bone of nose, etc.;—*v.t.* build bridge or bridges over.—**bridge'-head** *n.* work protecting end of bridge nearest enemy; footing gained by attacking force on far bank of river.—**pontoon bridge**, bridge made across stream upon boats or metal pontoons.—**suspension bridge**, bridge hung on chains or cables stretched over piers.—**swing bridge**, bridge which moves on pivot and opens for vessels to pass.

bridge (brij) *n.* card game for four players, development of whist; **auction bridge, contract bridge,** variant forms of this.

bridle (brī'-dl) *n.* headgear of beast of burden, or horse; curb;—*v.t.* put a bridle upon; subdue; curb; control.—**bri'dle-path,** *n.* narrow track for riders on horseback.

brief (brēf) *a.* short in duration; using few words;—*n.* abridged statement of client's case, prepared by solicitor for instruction of counsel;—*v.t.* instruct or retain counsel by giving him a brief; inform personnel of details of impending action.—**brief'ly** *adv.*—**brief'ness** *n.*—**in brief,** in a few words.

brier *n.* See **briar**.

F.D.

C

brig (brig) *n.* sailing-ship with two masts, both square-rigged.

brigade (bri-gād') *n.* sub-division of army under the command of a general officer.—**armoured brigade,** brigade with mobile guns and tanks.—**brigade'-maj'or** *n.* staff officer attached to a general.—**brigadier',** **brigadier'-gen'eral** *n.* officer in command of brigade.

brigand (brig'-and) *n.* one who lives by plunder; bandit; freebooter; highwayman.—**brig'andage** *n.*

brigantine (brig'-an-tēn) *n.* light, two-masted vessel, with square rigged foremast and schooner rigged mainmast.

bright (brīt) *a.* shining; full of light or splendour; cheerful; vivacious; sparkling; luminous; radiant; clear; clever; intelligent.—**bright'en** *v.t.* make bright;—*v.i.* grow bright.—**bright'ly** *adv.*—**bright'ness** *n.*—**bright'some** *a.* brilliant.

brilliant (bril'-yant) *a.* glittering; sparkling; radiant; shining; illustrious; distinguished; splendid; very clever;—*n.* polished cut diamond—**brill'iantly** *adv.*—**brill'iantness** *n.*—**brill'iance** *n.*—**brill'iancy** *n.*

brilliantine (bril'-yon-tēn) *n.* oily hair dressing.

brim (brim) *n.* rim or border; rim of hat;—*v.i.* be full to the brim.—**brim'ful** *a.* full to the brim.—**brimmed** *a.* brimful.

brimstone (brim'-stōn) *n.* sulphur; hellfire;—*a.* lemon-coloured (of butterfly).

brinded, brindled (brin'-ded, -dld) *a.* streaked with coloured stripes; spotted.

brine (brīn) *n.* water containing admixture of salt; sea-water; the sea; tears.—**brin'ish** *a.* salty, like brine.—**brin'y** *a.* pert. to brine or the sea; saltish.—**the briny** (*Colloq.*) the sea.

bring (bring) *v.t.* carry; fetch; convey from one person or place to another; transfer; transport; draw; lead; prevail on;—*pa.t.* and *pa.p.* brought (brawt).—**to bring about,** effect; cause to happen.—**to bring down the house,** earn great applause.—**to bring forth,** produce, give birth to.—**to bring home to,** prove, make realise.—**to bring round,** restore to consciousness.—**to bring to,** resuscitate; check the course of ship.—**to bring to bear,** apply pressure.—**to bring up,** rear; educate; raise in discussion; vomit.

brink (bringk) *n.* edge, margin of steep slope; verge.—**brink'manship** *n.* policy which exploits a calculated risk to its limit.

briquette (bri-ket') *n.* brick of compressed coal dust.

brisk (brisk) *a.* full of activity;—*v.t.* and *i.* enliven; cheer up.—**brisk'ly** *adv.*—**brisk'ness** *n.*

brisket (bris'-ket) *a.* part of animal's breast which lies next to ribs.

brisling (bris'-ling) *n.* Norwegian sprat.

bristle (bris'-l) *n.* very stiff, erect, coarse hair, as of swine; quill;—*v.t.* erect the bristles of;—*v.i.* stand up erect, like bristles; show anger; be surrounded with.—**bristled** (bris'-ld) *a.* provided with bristles.—**brist'liness** *n.*—**brist'ly** *a.* thick set with bristles.—**to bristle up,** flare up in temper.—**to bristle with,** abound in.

brittle (brit'-l) *a.* easily broken; apt to break; frail; frangible; fragile;—**britt'leness** *n.*

broach (brōch) *n.* roasting-spit; tapered, hardened-steel bit for enlarging holes in metal; guiding-pin of lock into which barrel of key fits;—*v.t.* pierce; tap, as cask; open; approach subject.—**to broach to** (*Naut.*) turn to windward.

broad (brawd) *a.* wide, open; unrestrained; indelicate; tolerant; with marked local dialect; unmistakable (hint); full (daylight).—**broad, broad'ly** *adv.*—**broad'-bean** *n.* common bean of Europe.—**broad'cast** *v.t.* scatter seed; transmit radio or television programmes for public reception;—*n.* that which is broadcast.—**broadcaster** *n.*—**broad'cloth** *n.* finely woven woollen cloth for men's wear.—**broad'en** *v.t.* and *v.i.* make or grow broad.—**broad'-mind'ed** *a.* tolerant.—**broad'ness** *n.*—**broad'-sheet** *n.* sheet of paper printed on one side of paper only; ballad, political squib.—**broad'side** *n.* whole side of ship above water-line; volley from guns on one side of naval craft.—**broad'sword** *n.* cutting sword with short, flat blade.

brocade (brō-kād') *n.* fabric of silk, rayon, cotton, etc., variegated with gold and silver thread or raised ornamentations;—*v.t.* ornament fabric with raised designs.—**broca'ded** *a.*

broccoli (brok'-o-li) *n.* variety of cauliflower.

brochure (bro-shōōr') *n.* booklet; pamphlet.

brock (brok) *n.* badger.

broderie anglaise (bro-drē' ongglez') *n.* open embroidery on white linen.

brogue (brōg) *n.* stout, coarse kind of shoe.

brogue (brōg) *n.* accent, esp. Irish.

broil (broil) *v.t.* cook by roasting over hot fire, or on gridiron; grill;—*v.i.* suffer discomfort through heat; be overheated.—**broil'er** *n.* battery-reared fowl.

broke (brōk) *pa.t.* and old *pa.p.* of break;—*a.* (*Colloq.*) penniless; ruined; bankrupt.—**brok'en** *pa.p.* of break; *a.* shattered; fractured; severed; separated; parted; abrupt; rough; impaired; exhausted, spent.—**broken**

English, imperfect English, as spoken by non-native.—**brok'en-heart'ed** *a.* crushed with grief; inconsolable.—**brok'enly** *adv.* intermittently.—**brok'enness** *n.*

broke (brōk) *v.i.* act for another on commission basis.—**brok'er** *n.* person employed in negotiating commercial transactions between parties in the interests of one of the principals; pawnbroker; dealer in second-hand goods; agent.—**brok'erage, brok'age,** *n.* business of broker; commission charged by broker.—**brok'ery** *n.* business of broker.—**brok'ing** *a.*

bromide (brō'-mīd) *n.* compound of bromine with some other elements; sedative drug, employed to induce sleep [See bromine].

bromine (brō'-min, -mīn) *n.* non-metallic element, related to chlorine, iodine, and fluorine.—**brom'ic** *a.*

bronchi, bronchia (brong'-kī, -iȧ) *n.pl.* two tubes forming lower end of the trachea.—**bron'chial** *a.* pert. to bronchi.—**bronchi'tis** *n.* inflammation of bronchial tubes.

bronco (brong'-kō) *n.* half-broken native horse in America.

brontosaurus (bron-tō-saw'-rus) *n.* large prehistoric dinosaur, giant lizard;—*pl.* **brontosau'ri.**

bronze (bronz) *n.* alloy of copper, tin and zinc; work of art cast in bronze; colour of bronze;—*a.* made of or coloured like bronze;—*v.t.* give appearance of bronze to; sunburn.—**Bronze Age,** prehistoric period between the Stone and Iron Ages.

brooch (brōch) *n.* ornamental clasp with pin for attaching to garment.

brood (brōōd) *v.t.* sit upon, as hen on eggs; brood over;—*v.i.* sit upon to hatch; meditate moodily.—*n.* offspring; family of young, esp. of birds; tribe; race.—**brood'y** *a.* wishing to sit, as hen; moody; sullen.

brook (brook) *n.* small stream.—**brook'let** *n.* streamlet.

brook (brook) *v.t.* bear; endure; support.

broom (brōōm) *n.* wild evergreen shrub producing yellow flowers and pods; besom; broom of broom.—**broom'stick** *n.* handle of broom.

broth (broth) *n.* water in which flesh has been boiled with vegetables.

brothel (broth'-el) *n.* house of prostitution.

brother (bruTH'-ẹr) *n.* male born of same parents; one closely resembling another in manner or character; associate or fellow-member of corporate body;—*pl.* **broth'ers, breth'ren.**—**broth'er-ger'man,** *n.* full brother as distinguished from half-brother.—**broth'erhood** *n.* state of being a brother; association of men of same religious order, profession, or society;—**broth'er-in-law** *n.* brother of one's

husband or wife; sister's husband.—**broth'erly** *a.*—**broth'erliness** *n.*

brought (brawt) *pa.t.* and *pa.p.* of bring.

brow (brou) *n.* ridge over the eyes; eyebrow; forehead; rounded top of hill.—**brow'-beat** *v.t.* bully a person by over-bearing speech.

brown (broun) *n.* dark colour inclining to red or yellow; mixture of black, red and yellow;—*a.* of brown colour; swarthy; sunburnt;—*v.t.* make or give brown colour to; sunbathe; grill or roast brown.—**brown'ish** *a.*—**brown'ness** *n.*—**brown study,** absent-minded reverie. —**browned off** (*Slang*) depressed; bored.

brownie (broun'-i) *n.* good-natured household elf; member of junior section of Girl Guides.

browse (brouz) *v.t.* and *i.* nibble the shoots and leaves of plants; graze; pore over book.—**brows'ing** *n.*

bruise (brōōz) *v.t.* injure or crush by contact with solid body; contuse; pound or pulverise; fight with the fists;—*n.* contusion, caused by blow or pressure, accompanied by discolouration of skin.—**bruis'er** *n.* prize-fighter; rough.

bruit (brōōt) *n.* report; rumour; fame; noise;—*v.t.* report; noise abroad.

brunette (brōō-net') *n.* woman with dark brown hair or brown complexion.

brunt (brunt) *n.* main shock of onset. —**to bear the brunt.** endure consequences, main impact, or stress.

brush (brush) *n.* implement made of bristles, twigs, feathers, etc., bound together and used for removing dust, dressing the hair, applying paint, etc.; smaller trees of forest, brushwood; sharp skirmish; bushy tail of fox or squirrel; (*Elec.*) contact for current between a stationary and a moving surface.—*v.t.* remove dust, etc., from; touch lightly in passing; —*v.i.* touch with light contact.—**brush'wood** *n.* low scrubby bushes; thicket or coppice; undergrowth.—**brush—off** *n.* rebuff.—**to brush up,** brighten or revive; recall what has been partly forgotten.

brusque (brusk, broosk') *a.* blunt; abrupt in speech.—**brusque'ness** *n.*—**brusquerie** (brōōs'-ker-ē) *n.* brusque expression or act.

Brussels sprouts cultivated variety of cabbage with small clustering heads like miniature cabbages.

brute (brōōt) *a.* irrational; ferocious; brutal;—*n.* beast; one of lower animals; low-bred, unfeeling person.—**brut'al** *a.* savage; inhuman.—**brut'alism** *n.* brutality.—**brutal'ity** *n.* inhumanity; savagery.—**brut'alise** *v.t.* —**brut'ally** *adv.*—**brut'ish** *a.*—**brut'ishly** *adv.*—**brut'ishness** *n.*

bryony (brī'-ō-ni) *n.* wild climbing plant with red poisonous berries.

bubble (bub'-l) *n.* hollow globe of water or other liquid blown out with air or gas; small bladder-like excrescence on surface of paint, metals, etc.; anything fragile or empty; swindle;—*a.* deceptive; not solid; unsubstantial;—*v.i.* rise in bubbles; effervesce; make noise like bubbles; gurgle; boil; (*Colloq.*) weep noisily.—**bubble and squeak**, cold potatoes, cabbage and meat fried together.—**bubb'ly** *a.* abounding in bubbles;—*n.* (*Slang*) champagne.—**bubb'ly-jock** *n.* (*Scot.*) turkey.

buccaneer, buccanier (buk-a-nēr') *n.* pirate, esp. in Caribbean.—*v.i.* play the buccaneer.

buck (buk) *n.* he-goat; male of rabbit, hare and deer; gay, spirited young dandy;—*v.i.* attempt to unseat rider by jumping vertically with arched back and head down; foil all attempts at improvement.—**buck'ish** *a.* gay; frivolous; lively.—**buck'-shot** *n.* large leaden shot.—**buck'-skin** *n.* soft leather made of deerskin or sheepskin; twilled fabric of fine quality wool, with nap cropped off very finely.—**buck'-tooth** *n.* protruding tooth.—**buck up!** (*Colloq.*) hurry up! cheer up!

buck (buk) *n.* U.S. (*Slang*) dollar.

bucket (buk'-et) *n.* vessel for carrying water, etc.; pail; holder for whip; piston of reciprocating pump;—*v.t.* ride horse almost beyond endurance; splash much water by hurrying the stroke in rowing.—**bucket'ful** *n.*—**to kick the bucket** (*Slang*) die.

buckle (buk'-l) *n.* metal clasp with rim and tongue, for fastening straps, bands, etc.; distortion of shape;—*v.t.* and *v.i.* fasten or clasp with buckle; twist out of shape; bend.—**buck'ler** *n.* small, round shield, with boss, for parrying a stroke.

buckram (buk'-ram) *n.* coarse linen cloth stiffened with glue;—*a.* made of buckram.

buckshee (buk'-shē) *n.* extra allowance; windfall;—*a.* free of charge; unexpected but welcome.

buckthorn (buk'-thorn) *n.* genus of shrubs yielding sap-green pigment.

buckwheat (buk'-hwēt) *n.* plant, allied to rhubarb, yielding grain like beechnuts.

bucolic (bū-kol'-ik) *a.* rustic; countrified;—*n.* pastoral poem.

bud (bud) *n.* shoot or sprout on plant containing unexpanded leaf, branch, or flower;—*v.i.* put forth buds; begin to grow;—*v.t.* graft by budding.—**bud'ding** *n.* act of inserting the bud of one tree under bark of another, for propagation.—**to nip in the bud**, destroy at beginning.

Buddhism (bóó'-dizm) *n.* religious system of Gautama, named *Buddha*, 'The Enlightened' (6th cent. B.C.); chief religion of E. Asia.—**Bud'dhist** *n.* worshipper of Buddha.

budge (buj) *v.t.* and *i.* move; stir.

budgerigar (buj-er-e-gar') *n.* small Australian parrakeet.

budget (buj'-et) *n.* bag with its contents; store; annual financial estimates of Chancellor of the Exchequer;—*n.* and *v.* plan for systematic spending.

buff (buf) *n.* soft, yellow leather prepared from skin of buffalo, elk, and other animals; rough strong felt; revolving wooden disc covered with layers of leather or cloth used with abrasive for polishing; buff-wheel; polishing pad or stick; light yellow colour;—*a.* made of, or coloured like, buff leather;—*v.t.* polish with a buff.

buff (buf) *n.* blow as in blind-man's-*buff*.

buffalo (buf'-a-lō) *n.* ruminating horned animal, resembling an ox, but larger; in America, the bison.

buffer (buf'-er) *n.* resilient cushion or apparatus to deaden the concussion between moving body and one on which it strikes. — **buffer-state**, country lying between two powerful and rival nations.

buffet (buf'-et, buf'-ā, bóóf-ā') *n.* cupboard for displaying fine china, plate, etc.; refreshment (bóóf-ā') bar; low three-legged stool.

buffet (buf'-et) *n.* blow with fist; slap; cuff on the ears;—*v.t.* strike with fist; contend against.—**buff'ets** *n.pl.* hardships.

buffoon (bu-fóón') *n.* person who acts the clown by clumsy attempts at humour; fool.—**buffoon'ery** *n.* silly, vulgar antics or jokes of buffoon.—**buffoon'ish** *a.*

bug (bug) *n.* parasitic insect that feeds on juice of plants or blood of animals, e.g. **bed'-bug**.—*v.t.* (*Colloq.*) install hidden microphones.—**bugbear** (bug'bār) *n.* anything which frightens or annoys.—**a big bug** (*Slang*) someone of importance.

buggy (bug'-i) *n.* word applied to various types of carriages.

bugle (bū'-gl) *n.* wind instrument, bell-mouthed, of copper with brass mouthpiece, used for conveying orders by certain calls;—*v.i.* sound a call.—**bu'gler** *n.*

bugloss (bū'-glos) *n.* popular name for many common English plants which have rough, bristly leaves.

build (bild) *v.t.* erect structure; construct public work, etc.; fabricate; establish (reputation, etc.); raise (hopes);—*v.i.* exercise art or work of building; depend (with *on*, *upon*);—*pa.t.* and *pa.p.* **built**;—*n.* form, construction; physique; style of construction.—**build'er** n. one who builds or supervises erection of building.—**build'ing** n. act of constructing; any substantial structure; edifice.—**built'-in** a. forming integral part of.—**built up area**, piece of land occupied by streets and buildings.

bulb (bulb) n. modified leaf-bud emitting roots from its base and formed of fleshy leaf scales containing reserve supply of food; any globular form, shaped like bulb; dilated glass tube containing filament for electric lighting;—v.i. form bulbs; bulge.—**bulbos'ity** n. state of being bulbous.—**bul'bous** a. having appearance of bulb; growing from bulbs.

bulge (bulj) n. anything rounded which juts out; part of cask which swells out; outer protective hull, below water-line;—v.i. swell out. —**bul'gy** a. swollen out.

bulk (bulk) n. size; main body; majority; largest portion; cargo stowed in ship's hold;—v.t. pile up; —v.i. be of some importance.— **bulk'iness** n.—**bulk'y** a. voluminous and clumsy in shape.—**bulk-buying** n. large-scale purchase.

bulkhead (bulk'-hed) n. partition in ship made with boards, etc., to form separate compartments.

bull (bŏŏl) n. male of any bovine, esp. ox; male of numerous animals as elephant, whale, seal, deer; sign of the zodiac, constellation Taurus; speculator who buys stocks or shares to make a profit by selling at higher rate before time of settlement arrives; score gained by hitting target in centre ring; (*Milit. Slang*) spit and polish; nonsense—a. denoting male animal.—**bull'-calf** n. male calf; —**bull'dog** n. breed of dog formerly used for bull-baiting; person who displays obstinate courage.—**bull'dozer** n. tractor, with attachments for moving, levelling, or spreading earth, etc.—**bulldoze** v.t. level by bulldozer; brush aside all obstacles; intimidate.—**bull'-finch** n. common red-breasted finch.—**bull-frog** n. large, dusky-brown N. American frog.— **bull'ish** a.—**bull'-mas'tiff** n. large size, fawn-coated dog of English breed.— **bull'ock** n. ox or castrated bull.— **bull's-eye** n. small circular or elliptical window; boss or lump of glass in centre of plate of glass; ball-shaped sweet with coloured stripes; centre of target or hit therein.—**bull'-ter'rier** n. cross between bulldog and terrier.—**bull'-trout** n. fish allied to salmon.—**to take the bull by the horns**, face difficulty resolutely.

bull (bŏŏl) n. seal appended to edicts of the pope; papal edict.—**bull'ery** n. collection of papal bulls.

bullet (bŏŏl'-et) n. projectile fired from small-arms.—**bullet head'ed** a. round-headed; stubborn.

bulletin (bŏŏl'-e-tin) n. daily report; official medical report; brief statement of facts issued by authority.

bullion (bŏŏl'-yun) n. uncoined, refined gold or silver, generally in ingots.

bully (bŏŏl'-i) n. noisy, over-bearing person who tyrannises over the weak; man who lives on immoral earnings of woman; hired ruffian; —v.t. domineer; intimidate; overawe; ill-treat;—v.i. bluster;—*interj.* (*Slang*) fine! well-done!

bully (bŏŏl'-i) n. canned or corned meat. Also **bull'y-beef**.

bulrush (bŏŏl'-rush) n. name applied to several species of marsh plants.

bulwark (bŏŏl'-wark) n. outwork for defence; sea defence wall;—pl. railing round deck of ship; any defence of a ship.—v.t. fortify with rampart; protect

bum (bum) n. (*Vulgar*) buttocks.

bum (bum) n. in N. America, lazy, dissolute person, loafer;—v.i. loaf, cadge.

bumblebee (bum'-bl-bee) n. large kind of bee.

bump (bump) n. dull, heavy blow; thump; swelling resulting from bump or blow; protuberance on skull;—v.t. strike against;—v.i. rise abruptly (of cricket ball).—**bump off** v.t. (*Colloq.*) murder; get rid of. —**bump'y** a. covered with bumps.

bumper (bum'-per) n. cup or glass filled to brim; anything large and satisfying; in motoring, bar carried in front and rear of car to minimise damage to mudguards, etc., in collisions;—a. very large; excellent, as 'a bumper crop.'

bumpkin (bump'-kin) n. awkward, stupid person; country lout; yokel.

bumptious (bump'-shus) a. rudely self-assertive; quarrelsome; self-important.—**bump'tiousness** n.

bun (bun) n. kind of small cake, light in texture and well sweetened; hair twisted into knot at back of head.

bunch (bunsh) n. cluster of similar things, tied or growing together; tuft or knot; bouquet of flowers; (*Slang*) group, gang, or party;—v.t. tie up or gather together; crowd;— v.i. swell out like bunch.—**bunched** a. crowded together.—**bunch'y** a. growing in bunches.

bundle (bun'-dl) n. number of things bound together; package; definite number of things;—v.t. make up into bundle or roll; push roughly, hustle;—v.i. hurry off.

bung (bung) n. stopper for opening in cask; large cork; pick-pocket;— v.t. close or stop up with bung.

bungalow (bung'-gạ-lō) n. small detached, one-storied house.

bungle (bung'-gl) v.t. make or mend clumsily; manage clumsily; botch; —v.i. act awkwardly;—n. blundering performance. — bung'ler n. — bung'ling a.

bunion (bun'-yun) n. inflamed swelling on foot, esp. on large toe joint.

bunk (bungk) n. box-like structure used as seat by day and bed at night; sleeping-berth on board ship, in camp, etc.;—v.i. lodge or sleep with person in small, confined space containing bunks.—**to do a bunk** (Slang) vanish rapidly from sight.

bunk (bungk) n. (Colloq.) humbug; nonsense.

bunker (bung'-kẹr) n. large hopper or bin for holding coal, etc.; storage room on board ship for coal or oil fuel; sand-pit placed as obstacle on golf course; underground shelter;—v.t. load up ship with coal.

bunny (bun'-i) n. pet name for rabbit.

bunting (bun'-ting) n. group of birds of finch family, including yellow-, reed-, and snow-buntings; coarse woollen fabric of which flags are made; flags in general.

buoy (boi) n. any floating body of wood or iron employed to point out particular situation of ship's anchor, shoal, navigable channel, etc.; life-buoy;—v.t. fix buoys.—**to buoy up**, keep afloat; sustain (hopes, etc.). —buoy'age n. series of buoys in position; providing of buoys.—buoy'ancy n. capacity for floating in water or air; cheerfulness.—buoy'ant a. floating lightly; lighthearted; hopeful.—buoy'antly adv.

bur n. See burr.

burble (bur'-bl) v.i. bubble up; froth up; gurgle, as of running water; (Colloq.) talk idly.—bur'ling n.

burden (bur'-dn) n. that which is borne or carried; anything difficult to bear, as care, etc.; capacity of vessel stated in tons; (Scots Law) encumbrance or restriction on property;—v.t. load; oppress; encumber. Also burth'en.—bur'denous, bur'densome, burth'ensome a. heavy, onerous; felt as burden.—bur'densomeness n.

burden (bur'-dn) n. refrain of song; chorus; main theme; drone of bagpipe.

burdock (bur'-dok) n. roadside plant, of the Compositae order, with hooked leaves.

bureau (bū-rō', bū'-rō) n. writing-desk; small chest of drawers; display-cabinet; office, esp. for public business; government department in U.S.;—pl. bureaux (bū'-rō), bureaus (bū'-ōz).

bureaucracy (bū-ro'-kra-si) n. highly centralised form of administration in which officials control every detail of public and private life; identified with officialism and 'red tape.'—bu'reaucrat n. one who advocates or takes part in such system. —bureaucrat'ic a.

burette (bū-ret') n. graduated glass tube provided with stop-cock at lower end, used for delivering measured quantities of liquid.

burg (burg') n. (U.S.) town or village; common ending of names of continental cities; borough.—burgess (bur'-jes) n. inhabitant, citizen, or freeman of borough.—burg'omas'ter n. chief magistrate of town in Holland or Germany.

burgee (bur-jē') n. pennant of yacht club, ending in two points; small coal for furnaces.

burgess See under **burg**.

burgh (bur'-ạ) n. Scots word corresponding to 'borough'; town with certain privileges resting upon charter.—burgh'al a.—burgher (bur'-gẹr) n. citizen or freeman.

burglar (burg'-lar) n. one guilty of house-breaking by night.—burg'lary n. breaking and entering into dwelling-house between 9 p.m. and 6 a.m. with intent to commit felony. —burglar'ious a.—bur'gle v.t.

burgomaster See under **burg**.

burial (ber'-i-ạl) n. act of burying; interment; sepulture; funeral; entombment.—bu'rial-mound n. barrow. [See bury].

burlesque (bur-lesk') n. distorting, exaggerating, and ridiculing a work of art; travesty; parody;—a. comical; ludicrous; jocular;—v.t. turn into burlesque.

burly (bur'-li) a. of stout build; big and sturdy; boisterous; lusty.—bur'liness n.

burn (burn) n. small stream; brook.

burn (burn) v.t. consume with fire; subject to action of fire; char; scorch;—v.i. be on fire; flame; flare; blaze; glow; be excited or inflamed with passion;—pa.t. and pa.p. burned or burnt;—n. injury or damage caused by heat; lesion of skin caused by burning.—burn'er n. part of lamp or gas jet from which flame issues.—burn'ing n. act of consuming by fire; inflammation;—a. flaming; scorching; parching; ardent; excessive.—burn'ing-glass n. convex lens causing great heat by bending rays of sun and concentrating them upon single point.—burning question, topic of universal discussion.—burnt'-off'ering n. sacrifice of living person or animal by burning.—to burn one's boats, act so that there can be no retreat.

burnish (bur'-nish) v.t. polish by continual rubbing;—n. polish; gloss; lustre.

burr, bur (bur) *n.* rough, sticky seed-case of certain plants with hooked spines; rough edge left on metal by cutting tool.

burr (bur) *n.* trilled guttural sound of *r*, as heard in Northumberland and Scotland;—*v.t.* and *i.* roll the 'r' sound.

burrow (bur'-ō) *n.* hole dug in ground by certain small animals to serve as abode or for concealment; —*v.i.* tunnel through earth; search assiduously; live in a burrow.

bursar (bur'-sar) *n.* one who holds the purse; treasurer of college; registrar; in Scotland, holder of scholarship at school or university. —**bur'sary** *n.* scholarship gained in open competition or by presentation.

burst (burst) *v.t.* fly asunder; break into pieces; break open violently; break suddenly into expression of feeling; split;—*v.i.* shatter; break violently;—*pa.t.* and *pa.p.* **burst;**—*n.* bursting; explosion; outbreak; spurt; (*Slang*) drunken spree.

bury (ber'-i) *v.t.* inter in grave; put underground; hide or conceal by covering;—*pa.p.* **bur'ied.**—**bur'ying** *n.* burial; interment.—**to bury the hatchet,** cease from strife; restore friendly relations.

bus, 'bus (bus) *n.* popular contraction for *omnibus*; vehicle for public conveyance of passengers on the roads; (*Slang*) motor car or aeroplane;—*pl.* **bus'es.**—**a busman's holiday,** one spent in similar environment to regular vocation.

busby (buz'-bi) *n.* bearskin cap, part of dress uniform of hussars and horse artillery of British Army.

bush (boosh) *n.* shrub; low woody plant with branches near ground-level; thicket of small trees and shrubs; interior of a country; backwoods;—*v.i.* grow thick or bushy; —*v.t.* plant bushes about.—**bush' craft** *n.* skilled knowledge of conditions of life in the bush.—**bush'iness** *n.* quality of being bushy.—**bush'man** *n.* member of aboriginal, Negroid race of S.W. Africa; settler in the backwoods of the colonies; woodsman.—**bush'-rang'er** *n.* in Australia, desperado, usually escaped convict who lived the life of highwayman. —**bush telegraph,** information by unofficial channels—**bush'y** *a.* full of bushes; thick and spreading.—**to beat about the bush,** approach a matter in roundabout way; unwilling to come to the point.

bush (boosh) *n.* internal lining of a bearing, to form plain bearing surface for pin or shaft.

bushel (boosh'-el) *n.* dry measure of 8 gallons, for corn, fruit, etc.—**to hide one's light under a bushel,** be unduly modest.

business (biz'-nes) *n.* employment; profession; vocation; trade; firm; concern.—**bus'iness-like** *a.* practical; systematic; methodical.

busk (busk) *v.i.* hurry; hasten; cruise along shore; seek.—**busk'er** *n.* entertainer who depends on voluntary contributions from audiences; itinerant musician.

buskin (busk'-in) *n.* kind of half-boot, part of costume of actors in tragic drama on Greek stage; synonym for 'tragedy.'—**busk'ined** *a.* dressed in buskins; tragic.

bust (bust) *n.* sculptured representation of person from waist upwards; upper part of human body; woman's bosom.—**bust'ed** *a.* breasted.

bust (bust) *v.i.* and *v.t.* (*Slang*) burst; break;—*n.* drinking bout.

bustle (bus'-l) *v.i.* busy oneself with stir and movement; be ostentatiously active;—*n.* great stir and hurried activity.—**bust'ler** *n.*

bustle (bus'-l) *n.* stuffed pad worn by ladies to support and elevate back of skirt just below waist.

busy (biz'-i) *a.* having plenty to do; active and earnest in work; engaged; industrious; officious;—*n.* (*Slang*) detective.—*v.t.* make or keep busy; occupy (oneself);—*pr.p.* **bus'ying;** *pa.p.* **bus'ied.**—**bus'ily** *adv.*—**bus'y-bod'y** *n.* person who meddles in other people's business.—**bus'yness** *n.* state of being busy.

but (but) *conj.* yet; unless; nevertheless; notwithstanding;—*prep.* except; without;—*adv.* only.—**all but,** nearly; almost.

but (but) *a.* (*Scot.*) outside.—**but and ben,** two-roomed cottage, with outer and inner room.

butane (bū'-tān) *n.* paraffin hydrocarbon used as domestic gas.

butcher (booch'-er) *n.* one who slaughters animals for food or retails the flesh; one who recklessly destroys human life;—*v.t.* slaughter animals for food; murder in cold blood; spoil work.—**butch'ering** *n.*— **butcher meat, butcher's meat,** flesh of domestic animals exposed for sale.— **butch'ery** *n.* wanton slaughter.

butler (but'-ler) *n.* male servant in charge of the liquors, plate, etc. who exercises supervision over house-staff.—**but'lery** *n.* butler's pantry.

butt (but) *n.* lower end of tree-trunk providing the strongest timber; type of sunken hinge; one continually subject to ridicule; joint between the square ends of two pieces of wood;—*v.t.* strike by thrusting head downwards.—**butts** *n.pl.* mound with targets where shooting is practised. —**butt'-end** *n.* thick or large end, as of rifle; cigarette stub.—**to butt in** (*Colloq.*) intervene without permission.

butt (but) *n.* large cask.

butter (but'-er) *n.* fatty ingredients of milk, emulsified by churning; gross flattery;—*v.t.* spread with butter; flatter; fail to accept catch at cricket.—**butt'er-bean** *n.* large, dried haricot bean.—**butt'ercup** *n.* plant of Ranunculus family with cup-shaped yellow flowers.—**butt'er-fin'gers** *n.* (*Colloq.*) one who has failed to hold catch at cricket.—**butt'er-milk** *n.* fluid residue after butter has been churned from cream.—**butt'er-mus'lin** *n.* thin, loosely woven cotton fabric.—**butt'er-scotch** *n.* kind of toffee with butter as ingredient.—**butt'ery** *a.* like butter.

butterfly (but'-er-flī) *n.* common name of all diurnal, lepidopterous insects; gay, flighty woman; fast type of breast-stroke in swimming.—**butterfly nut**, nut with wings designed to be turned by hand.

buttery (but'-er-i) *n.* pantry for storage of food and wine.—**butt'ery-bar** *n.* ledge for holding tankards.

buttock (but'-ok) *n.* rump; rounded prominence at lower posterior part of body; hip; haunch (usually in *pl.*).

button (but'-n) *n.* knob or stud for fastening clothing; bud; safety knob at end of fencing foil; small round protuberance, e.g. that of electric bell;—*v.t.* fasten with buttons;—*v.i.* be fastened by button.—**butt'ons** *n.pl.* jocular term for page-boy.—**butt'on-hole** *n.* hole or loop in which button is fastened; flower or spray worn in button-hole;—*v.t.* detain person in talk against his will.—**butt'on-hook** *n.* hook for pulling button through button-hole.—**butt'-on-stick** *n.* strip of brass with slit used for polishing metal buttons.

buttress (but'-res) *n.* projecting support to wall; prop or support;—*v.t.* support.

buxom (buks'-um) *a.* lively; plump; comely; winsome.—**bux'omness** *n.*

buy (bī) *v.t.* obtain by payment; purchase; pay price for; bribe;—*pa.t.* and *pa.p.* bought.—**buy'er** *n.* purchaser; one who buys.

buzz (buz) *v.i.* make humming or hissing sound;—*v.t.* spread news abroad secretly; tap out signals by means of buzzer.—**buzz'er** *n.* one who buzzes; apparatus used for Morse signalling;—**buzz'ingly** *adv.*

buzzard (buz'-ard) *n.* genus of birds of hawk family; dunce or block-head.

by (bī) *prep.* near; beside; in neighbourhood of; past; through agency of; according to;—*adv.* near; in neighbourhood; close; out of the way; beyond.—**by** and **by**, soon; in near future.—**by'-elec'tion** *n.* parliamentary election at any time except general election.—**by'-pass** *n.* road

for diversion of traffic from crowded centres;—*v.t.* avoid place by going round it.—**by'-path** *n.* side path. —**by'-play** *n.* action carried on apart from main part of play; diversion.—**by'-pro'duct** *n.* secondary product obtained during manufacture of principal commodity.—**by'-road** *n.* less frequented side road.— **by'stander** *n.* onlooker.—**by'-street** *n.* less important street.—**by'way** *n.* secluded path or road.—**by'word** *n.* common saying; proverb; name become notorious.

bye (bī) *n.* anything subordinate; walk-over in round of competition due to odd number of competitors; holes still to be played at golf after game has been won; run made at cricket without ball having been hit by batsman; goal in lacrosse.— **bye-bye** (*Colloq.*) good-bye; bed; sleep.

bylaw, **bye-law** (bī'-law) *n.* local law made by subordinate authority.

byre (bīr) *n.* cow-house or -shed.

C

cab (kab) *n.* light carriage drawn by one horse; public carriage; covered part of locomotive; driver's accommodation on motor-lorry or 'bus.— **cab'man** *n.* driver of cab.—**cab'-rank** *n.* official stance for taxis.—**cabb'y** *n.* (*Colloq.*) cabman.

cabaret (ka'-ba-rā, -ret) *n.* restaurant providing entertainment; the entertainment itself.

cabbage (kab'-āj) *n.* garden vegetable of Brassica family.—**cabbage-butterfly**, large white butterfly whose larvae are injurious to cabbage.

caber (kā'-ber) *n.* stout pole or stem of tree, used in Highland game of 'tossing the caber.'

cabin (kab'-in) *n.* small room; hut; apartment in ship;—*v.t.* confine in cabin;—*v.i.* live in cabin; lodge.— **cabin boy**, boy who waits on officers of ship.

cabinet (kab'-i-net) *n.* small room; closet; council of ministers; chest, box, or case.—**the Cabinet**, the centre of executive power, the Prime Minister and his Ministers.

cable (kā'-bl) *n.* large, strong rope or chain, to retain vessel at anchor, etc.; submarine telegraph line; message sent by such line;—*v.t.* fasten with cable; send message by cable.—**ca'blegram** *n.* telegram sent by cable; cable.—**cable's length**, measure equal to 100 fathoms.— **cable stitch**, knitting pattern resembling twisted rope.

cabriolet (kàb-ri-ō-lā') *n.* light one-horse carriage with hood; cab; type of motor-car body with folding hood.

cacao (ka-kâ'-ō) n. tropical tree from the seeds of which cocoa and chocolate are prepared.

cache (kash) n. orig. hole in ground for storing or hiding provisions, etc.; any hiding-place.

cachet (ka'-shā) n. seal, as on a letter; distinctive mark or character. —**lettre de cachet** (i.e. sealed letter) warrant ordering imprisonment of individual without trial, issued by former kings of France.

cachou (ka-shōō') n. aromatic preparation in form of tablet or pellet.

cackle (kak'-l) v.i. make noise like hen or goose; gossip noisily;—n. noise of hen; prattle; silly talk.

cacophony (ka-kof'-ō-ni) n. harsh or disagreeable sound; discord; use of ill-sounding words.—**cacoph'onous** a.

cactus (kak'-tus) n. plant with thick, fleshy, prickly stems, found in dry climates.—pl. **cac'tuses**, or **cac'ti**.—**cacta'ceous, cac'tal** a. allied to cactus.

cad (kad) n. low, mean fellow. —**cadd'ish** a. ill-bred, mean.

cadaver (ka-dā'-ver) n. (Med.) corpse. —**cada'verous** a. corpse-like; gaunt; sickly-looking.

caddie, caddy (kad'-i) n. attendant who carries golfer's clubs;—v.i. carry clubs.—**caddy-car** n. two-wheeled carrier for golf bag.

caddis, caddice (kad'-is) n. worm-like aquatic larva of caddis-fly.

caddy (kad'-i) n. small box for holding tea.

cadence (kā'-dens) n. fall of voice in reading or speaking; modulation; rhythmical beat of any rhythmical action; (Mus.) subsiding of melody or harmony towards a close.— **ca'denced** a. rhythmical.—**ca'dency** n. rhythmical flow.

cadenza (ka-den'-za) n. (Mus.) ornamental passage for voice or solo instrument in an aria or concerto.

cadet (ka-det') n. younger, or youngest son of noble family; (Mil.) youth in training for commissioned rank; member of Cadet Corps.—**cadet'ship** n.—**Cadet Corps,** organisation for training of boys on military lines.

cadge (kaj) v.t. and i. hawk goods; beg.—**cadg'er** n. hawker; beggar; loafer; sponger.

cadmium (kad'-mi-um) n. (Chem.) soft, bluish-white metal of zinc group.—**cad'mia** n. oxide of zinc.

cadre (kā'-dr) n. framework of a regiment or corps.

caecum (sē'-kum) n. (Med.) first part of large intestine, opening into colon; blind gut.—pl. **cae'ca.**— **cae'cal** a.

Caesarean operation (sē-zār'-i-an) n. (Med.) delivery of child through opening cut in abdominal wall.

caesura, cesura (sē-zū'-ra) n. break or division in line of poetry; in English prosody, natural pause of the voice in mid line.—**caesu'ral** a.

café (ka-fā, kaf'-e) n. coffee-house; restaurant, usually licensed for sale of light refreshments only.

cafeteria (kaf-i-tēr'-i-a) n. restaurant where customers help themselves.

caffeine (kaf'-e-in, -ē'-in, -ēn) n. stimulating alkaloid found in coffee and tea.—**caffe'ic** a. pert. to coffee or caffeine.

cage (kāj) n. place of confinement; box-like enclosure, with bars of iron or wire, for keeping animals or birds; moveable enclosure of lift, mine shaft, etc.—v.t. confine in cage; imprison.—**ca'gey** a. cautious, wary.

cairn (kârn) n. rounded or conical pile of stones.—**cairngorm'** n. yellowish-brown variety of rock-crystal from Cairngorm Mts., Scotland.— **Cairn** terrier, type of short-haired Scottish terrier.

caisson (kā'-son) n. ammunition chest or waggon; (Engineering) water-tight chamber of sheet-iron or wood, used in laying foundations of piers or bridges, quay-walls, etc.; apparatus for raising sunken vessels.

caitiff (kā'-tif) n. (Arch.) captive; mean, despicable person;—a. base; vile; mean.

cajole (ka-jōl') v.t. delude by flattery; coax; deceive.—**cajol'er** n.—**cajol'ery** n. act of cajoling.

cake (kāk) n. piece of dough baked; fancy bread; flattish mass of matter, esp. soap, tobacco, etc.; v.t. make into cake;—v.i. become flat, doughy mass.—**cak'y** a.

calabash (kal'-a-bash) n. bottle-gourd tree of India and W. Africa; fruit of this tree; vessel made from the gourd, or gourd itself; species of pear.

calamine (kal'-a-mīn) n. zinc carbonate; native silicate of zinc.

calamity (ka-lam'-i-ti) n. great misfortune; disaster; affliction; mischance.—**calam'itous** a. producing distress and misery.—**calam'itously** adv.—**calam'itousness** n.

calcareous (kal-kā'-rē-us) a. having nature of limestone; containing chalk or lime.

calceolaria (kal-sē-ō-lā'-ri-a) n. kinds of plants producing slipper-shaped flower.

calcify (kal'-si-fī) v.t. and i. turn into lime; harden or petrify, by deposit of lime.—**calcifica'tion** n.

calcine (kal'-sin, -sīn, kal-sīn') v.t. reduce to powder by heat; expel water and other volatile substances by heat;—v.i. be turned into powder.—**cal'cinable** a.—**calcina'tion** n.—**calcin'atory** n. vessel used in calcination.

calcium (kal'-si-um) *n.* metallic base of lime.—**cal'cic** *a.* containing calcium.—**cal'cite** *n.* native carbonate of lime.

calculate (kal'-kū-lāt) *v.t.* count; estimate; compute; (*U.S.*) plan; expect;—*v.i.* make a calculation.—**cal'culable** *a.*—**cal'culated** *a.* adapted to a purpose; intended to produce certain effect.—**cal'culating** *a.* capable of performing calculations; shrewd in matters of self-interest; scheming.—**calcula'tion** *n.*—**cal'culative** *a.* tending to calculate.—**cal'culator** *n.*

calculus (kal'-kū-lus) *n.* (*Med.*) hard concretion which forms, esp. in kidney, bladder, etc. usually called stone or gravel;—*pl.* **cal'culi.**—**cal'culose, cal'culous** *a.* hard like stone; gritty.

calculus (kal'-kū-lus) *n.* higher branch of mathematics concerned with properties of continuously varying quantities.

caldron, cauldron (kawl'-dron) *n.* large metal kettle or boiler.

Caledonia (kal-e-dō'-ni-ą) *n.* Roman name for Scotland.—**Caledo'nian** *a.*

calefaction (kal-e-fak'-shun) *n.* act of heating, state of being heated.—**calefacient** *a.* making warm;—*n.* heat-giving remedy.—**calefac'tor** *n.* that which gives heat.—**calefac'tory** *a.*

calendar (kal'-en-dąr) *n.* table of days, months, or seasons; almanack; list of criminal cases; list of saints.—*v.t.* enter in list; index documents.

calender (kal'-en-dęr) *n.* hot press with rollers, used to make cloth, etc. smooth and glossy.

calends (kal'-endz) *n.pl.* first day of each month, among Romans.—**at the Greek calends,** never (because the Greeks had no calends). Also **kal'ends.**

calf (kāf) *n.* young of cow, and some other mammals, such as elephant, whale, etc.; fine, light-coloured leather used for binding books;—*pl.* **calves** (kāvz).—**calf-love,** youthful, transitory attachment to one of opposite sex.—**calf's-foot jelly,** palatable jelly made from calves' feet.—**calve** *v.i.* bring forth calf.

calf (kāf) *n.* thick, fleshy part of leg below knee;—*pl.* **calves.**

calibre (kal'-i-bęr) *n.* diameter of bore of cannon, gun, etc.; internal diameter of tube or cylinder; (*Fig.*) capacity; quality of mind; character.—**cal'ibrate** *v.t.* determine calibre of; determine correct scale of readings on an instrument.—**calibra'tion** *n.*

calico (kal'-i-kō) *n.* white cotton cloth, first made in *Calicut* in India; coarse printed cotton cloth;—*a.* made of calico.

caliph, calif (kal'-if, kā'-lif) *n.* title given to successors of Mahomet in the high priesthood.—**cal'iphate, cal'-ifate** *n.* office of caliph.

call (kawl) *v.t.* announce; name; summon; name, as for office; utter in loud voice; ring up on the telephone;—*v.i.* speak in loud voice; cry out; make brief visit;—*v.t.* and *v.i.* (in game of Bridge, etc.) bid;—*n.* vocal address of summons or invitation; short visit; public claim; requisition; communication on telephone; authorised command; invitation, as to be minister of a church; note blown on horn, bugle, etc, in game of Bridge, etc. bid.—**call'er** *n.* one who calls.—**call'ing** *n.* person's usual occupation.—**at call,** on demand.—**on call,** of person, ready if summoned.—**within call,** within hearing; close at hand.—**call'-bird,** *n.* decoy-bird.—**call'-boy** *n.* (*Theatre*) boy who calls actors to go on stage.—**call'-box** *n.* telephone kiosk.—**call'-girl** *n.* prostitute on call by telephone.—**to call down,** rebuke sharply.—**to call in question,** impugn; challenge statement.—**to call to account,** demand explanation of.—**to call to the bar,** admit as barrister.—**to call up** (*Mil.*) summon to military service.

calligraphy (ka-lig'-rą-fi) *n.* art of beautiful writing; penmanship.—**callig'rapher, callig'raphist** *n.*—**calligraph'ic** *a.*

callipers (kal'-i-pęrz) *n.* two-legged instrument for measuring diameters.—**walking callipers** (*Med.*) surgical appliance, with steel supports, fitted to boot and strapped to knee or thigh, to take weight of the body off injured leg. Also **calipers.**

callous (kal'-us) *a.* hardened; hardened in mind; unfeeling.—**call'ously** *adv.*—**call'ousness** *n.*—**callos'ity** *n.* horny hardness of the skin.

callow (kal'-ō) *a.* pert. to condition of young bird; unfledged; (*Fig.*) inexperienced; raw.—**cal'lowness** *n.*

calm (kām) *a.* still; quiet; at rest;—*n.* state of being calm;—*v.t.* make calm; pacify; quiet;—*v.i.* become calm.—**calm'ly** *adv.*—**calm'ness** *n.*

calomel (kal'-ō-mel) *n.* (*Med.*) subchloride of mercury, used as purgative.

caloric (ką-lor'-ik) (*Arch.*) *n.* heat;—*a.* heat-producing.—**caloric'ity** *n.* power of animals to develop heat.—**calorifacient** *a.* heat-producing.—**calorif'ic** *a.* pert. to heat; heat-producing.—**calorifica'tion** *n.* production of heat.

calorie, calory (kal'-or-i) *n.* (*Phys.*) unit of heat; unit of heat or energy produced by any food substance.—**calorim'eter** *n.* scientific instrument for determining amount of heat produced by any substance.—**calorim'etry** *n.*

calumniate (ką-lum'-ni-āt) *v.t.* accuse falsely; slander;—*v.i.* utter slanders.—**calumnia'tion** *n.* false and slanderous representations.—**calum'-niator** *n.*—**calum'niatory, calum'nious** *a.* slanderous.—**calum'niously** *adv.*—**cal'umny** *n.* false accusation; malicious slander; libel.

calve (käv) See **calf.**

calypso (kalip'-sō) *n.* improvised song in native rhythm from W. Indies.

calyx, calix (kā'-liks) *n.* cup-shaped cavity; outer covering or leaf-like envelope of flower, segments being called *sepals.*

cam (kam) *n.* projecting part of wheel, or moving piece, so shaped as to give alternating or variable motion to another wheel or piece.—**cam'shaft** *n.* shaft on which cams are fixed or formed.

camaraderie (kam-a-rad'-e-rē) *n.* good-fellowship; comradeship; loyalty to one's fellows.

camber (kam'-ber) *n.* slight convexity of upper surface, as of ship's deck, bridge, road surface.

cambric (kām'-brik) *n.* fine white linen fabric first made at *Cambrai,* in N. France.

camel (kam'-el) *n.* large ruminant animal of Asia and Africa, with one or two humps, used as beast of burden.—**cam'eleer** *n.* camel driver.

camellia (ka-mēl'-ya) *a.* species of Asiatic shrub with showy flowers and dark-green, laurel-like leaves.

cameo (kam'-ē-ō) *n.* stone of two layers cut in ornamental relief;—*pl.* **cam'eos.**

camera (kam'-e-ra) *n.* apparatus in which light-sensitive material is exposed for the purpose of taking photographs; (*TV*) apparatus for converting visual scene into electrical impulses for transmission.—**cam'eraman** *n.* professional photographer.—**camera obscura,** optical contrivance by means of which images of external objects are made to appear on light-coloured surface in darkened room.

camera (kam'-e-ra) *n.* vaulted room; judge's private room; hence (*Law*) 'to hear a case' in **camera,** hear evidence in private.

camisole (kam'-i-sōl) *n.* lady's under-bodice; lady's light dressing-jacket.

camomile, chamomile (kam'-ō-mīl) *n.* aromatic creeping plant whose flowers are used medicinally for making infusions.

camouflage (ká'-moo-flazh) *n.* (*Mil.*) method of visual deception of enemy by disguising; any form of disguise;—*v.t.* cover with camouflage material; disguise.

camp (kamp) *n.* area of ground where soldiers, holiday-makers, workers etc., are lodged in huts or tents; permanent barracks near suitable exercise ground; encampment;—*v.t.* and *i.* encamp; pitch tents.—**camp'er** *n.*—**camp'ing** *n.*—**camp'-bed** *n.* light, portable bed with folding legs.—**camp'-foll'ower** *n.* non-combatant attached to body of troops, usually for provisioning purposes.

camp (kamp) *a.* (*slang*) perverse.

campaign (kam-pān') *n.* extensive tract of level country; large plain; (*Mil.*) series of operations in particular theatre of war; organised series of operations in politics, advertising, etc.;—*v.i.* serve in war; conduct, or assist in political, etc. operations.—**campaign'er** *n.*

campanile (kam-pa-nē'-le, kam'-pa-nīl) *n.* bell-tower constructed beside church, but not attached to it;—*pl.* **campani'les.**—**campanol'ogy** *n.* art of bell-ringing, or of bell-founding; bell-lore.—**campanol'ogist** *n.*

campanula (kam-pan'-ū-la) *n.* genus of plants bearing bell-shaped flowers, common species being the harebell.—**campan'iform, campan'ular, campan'ulate** *a.* bell-shaped.

camphor (kam'-for) *n.* whitish substance with aromatic taste and smell, obtained from camphor laurel-tree.

can (kan) *pres. indic.* of defective, intransitive verb meaning, to be able, to have the power, to be allowed.

can (kan) *n.* metal container for holding liquids, etc.;—*v.t.* put into tin or can for purpose of preserving; —*pr.p.* **can'ning.**—*pa.p.* and *pa.t.* **canned.**—**can'nery** *n.* factory where foods are preserved by **canning.**

canal (ka-nal') *n.* artificial water-course for transport, drainage or irrigation purposes; duct in the body; groove.—**can'alise** *v.t.* convert a canal; direct along a particular course.

canary (ka-nā'-ri) *n.* yellow singing bird, species of finch; bright yellow colour; light wine made in Canary Islands.—*a.*

cancel (kan'-sel) *v.t.* cross out; blot out; annul; suppress; (*Math.*) strike out common factor; balance; offset; —*pr.p.* **can'celling.**—*pa.p.* and *pa.t.* **can'celled.**—**can'cellate, can'cellated** *a.* marked with cross-lines.—**cancella'-tion** *n.* act of cancelling.

cancer (kan'-ser) *n.* (*Med.*) malignant growth or tumour; (*Fig.*) any form of spreading evil.—**can'cerate** *v.i.* grow into a cancer.—**cancera'tion** *n.*—**can'cerous** *a.*—**can'croid** *a.*—**cancer-opho'bia** *n.* morbid dread of cancer.

candelabrum (kan-de-lā'-brum) *n.* tall stand for lamp; branched and highly ornamented candle-stick; chandelier.—*pl.* **candela'bra.** Also **candela'bra** *n.sing.* and **candela'bras** *n.pl.*

candid (kan'-did) *a.* fair; open; frank.—**can'didly** *adv.*—**can'didness** *n.* frankness; ingenuousness.

candidate (kan'-di-dāt) *n.* one who seeks appointment, office, honour, etc.—**can'didature** (*U.S.* **can'didacy**) *n.* position of being candidate.

candle (kan'-dl) *n.* stick of tallow, wax, etc. with wick inside, used for giving light.—**candle power**, unit of luminosity.—**can'dlestick** *n.* object for holding candle.—**not fit to hold a candle to (a person)**, very inferior to.—**not worth the candle**, not worth the trouble, risk or expense.

Candlemas (kan'-dl-mas) *n.* religious festival, held on 2nd Feb. in Catholic and Anglican churches, to commemorate the Purification of the Blessed Virgin.

candour (kan'-dur) *n.* candidness; sincerity; frankness.

candy (kan'-di) *n.* kind of sweetmeat made of sugar;—*v.t.* preserve in sugar; form into crystals, as sugar; —*v.i.* become candied. — **candied** (kan'-did) *a.* preserved or coated with sugar; (*Fig.*) flattering.

cane (kān) *n.* stem of small palm or long, strong reed; bamboo, etc.; sugar-cane; walking-stick;—*v.t.* beat with cane; fix cane bottom to, e.g. chair.—**cane'-su'gar** *n.* sugar obtained from sugar-cane.

canine (kā'-nīn) *a.* of, or pert. to, dog. —**canine teeth**, two pointed teeth in each jaw, one on each side, between incisors and molars.

canister (kan'-is-ter) *n.* small case or box usually of metal.

canker (kang'-ker) *n.* eating sore; ulceration of mouth; fungus; disease of trees, disease of the ear of dogs, cats etc.; (*Fig.*) anything that eats away, corrupts, etc.;—*v.t.* consume; gnaw at; corrupt;—*v.i.* decay, become cankered.—**can'kered** *a.*—**can'kerous** *a.*—**can'ker-worm** *n.* destructive caterpillar.

cannibal (kan'-i-bal) *n.* one who eats human flesh;—*a.* relating to this practice.—**cann'ibalism** *n.* practice of eating human flesh.—**cannibalist'ic** *a.*—**cann'ibalise** *v.t.* dismantle apparatus or vehicle to obtain spare parts.

cannon (kan'-on) *n. Sing.* or *Pl.* large gun; guns which fire small shells from aircraft;—*v.i.* cannonade.—**cannonade'** *n.* attack with cannon; firing of cannon; — *v.t.* bombard. — **cann'on-ball,** *n.* ball fired by early cannon.

cannon (kan'-on) *n.* billiard stroke, hitting both object balls in succession with one's own;—*v.t.* make this stroke;—*v.i.* collide; rebound.

cannot (kan'-ot) combination of *can* and *not,* therefore=not to be able.

canny (kan'-i) *a.* (*Scot.*) cautious; thrifty.

canoe (ka-nōō') *n.* boat propelled by hand paddle; skiff; light boat.—**canoe'ist** *n.*

canon (kan'-on) *n.* law or rule, esp. of the church; list of saints; church dignitary, esp. one connected with cathedral; (*Mus.*) form of composition in which the melody is repeated at set intervals by the other parts.—**canon'ic, canon'ical** *a.*—**canon'ically** *adv.*—**canonisa'tion** *n.*—**can'onise** *v.t.* place in list of saints.—**can'onry** *n.*—**canon law,** ecclesiastical laws.

canopy (kan'-ō-pi) *n.* covering fixed above bed, or dais, or carried on poles above head; overhanging shelter; hood or fitted cover.—*v.t.* cover with canopy.

cant (kant) *n.* inclination from the level; tilted position;—*v.t.* tilt; jerk; toss;—*v.i.* have, or take, leaning position.

cant (kant) *n.* insincere or conventional utterance; expression peculiar to a class, as *thieves' cant*; slang;—*v.i.* speak hypocritically.

cantabile (kan-ta'-bē-lā) *adv.* (*Mus.*) in flowing, lyrical style.

cantaloup, cantaloupe (kan'-ta-loop) *n.* variety of musk-melon, having furrowed rind.

cantankerous (kan-tang'-ke-rus) *a.* perverse; ill-natured; cross-grained; quarrelsome.—**cantan'kerously** *adv.*—**cantan'kerousness** *n.*

cantata (kan-ta'-ta) *n.* choral work resembling a short oratorio or lyric drama.

canteen (kan-tēn') *n.* store and refreshment-room in camps and barracks for soldiers, sailors, etc.; similar place in social or institutional club; mess-tin; case of cutlery.

canter (kan'-ter) *v.i.* move at easy gallop;—*n.* easy gallop or gait.

cantilever (kan'-ti-lēv-er) *n.* bracket for supporting cornice or balcony.—**cantilever bridge,** bridge built on same principle with two long arms or brackets projecting towards each other from opposite banks or piers.

canto (kan'-tō) *n.* division or part of poem.—**can'tor** *n.* precentor; leader of singing, in church or synagogue.—**canto'rial** *a.*

canton (kan'-ton) *n.* administrative district.—**canton'ment** *n.* quarters for troops.

canvas (kan'-vas) *n.* coarse cloth made of hemp, for sails, tents, etc.; sails of vessel; specially prepared material for painting on; hence, oil-painting.

canvass (kan'-vas) *v.t.* sift; examine thoroughly; solicit support, or votes, or contributions;—*v.i.* solicit votes; —*n.* close examination (by discussion); scrutiny; solicitation; seeking to obtain votes.—**can'vasser** *n.*

canyon (kan'-yon) *n.* ravine; deep gorge. Also **cañon.**

cap (kap) *n.* brimless covering, for the head; top or highest point; small lid used as cover; small capsule of explosive for detonation by percussion;—*v.t.* cover top or end of; raise one's cap in salutation or out of respect; surpass; (*University, etc.*) confer degree on;—confer membership of team; *pr.p.* **cap′ping.**—*pa.p.* and *pa.t.* **capped.**—to set one's cap at, said of woman who tries to attract suitor.—if the cap fits, if the remark applies.

capable (kā′-pǝ-bl) *a.* competent; gifted; skilful.—**ca′pably** *adv.*—**ca′pableness** *n.*—**capabil′ity** *n.* power.

capacious (kǝ-pā′-shus) *a.* roomy; spacious.—**capa′ciously** *adv.*—**capa′ciousness** *n.*

capacity (ka-pas′-i-ti) *n.* power of holding or grasping; room; volume; power of mind; character; ability; cubic content.—**capac′itate** *v.t.* render capable.—**capac′itor** *n.* (*Elec.*) device for collecting and storing intermittently applied current.

cape (kāp) *n.* covering for shoulders.

cape (kāp) *n.* point of land running out into the sea; headland.

caper (kā′-pǝr) *v.i.* leap about like goat, in sprightly manner; skip; dance; frolic;—*n.* frolicsome skip.

caper (kā′-pǝr) *n.* herb or shrub whose flower-buds when pickled in vinegar are used in sauces.

capercailzie (ka-pǝr-kāl′-i) *n.* large game-bird, wood-grouse.

capillary (kap′-i-lǝr-i, ka-pil′-ǝ-ri) *a.* resembling a hair; as fine as hair; descriptive of very fine bore of tube or similar passage;—*n.* one of microscopic blood-vessels connecting arteries and veins.

capital (kap′-i-tǝl) *a.* pert. to the head; involving forfeiture of life; first in importance; principal; excellent;—*n.* (*Archit.*) head of column, pilaster, etc.; chief city; metropolis; (*Print.*) type larger than that used in body of page; estimated total value of business, property, stock, etc.; ready money.—**cap′itally** *adv.* in capital manner; splendidly.

capitalism (kap′-i-tǝl-ism) *n.* form of economic, industrial, and social organisation of society involving ownership, control, and direction of production by privately owned business organisations.—**cap′italist** *n.* one who has capital.—**cap′italise** *v.t.* convert into capital or ready money. —**cap′italisation** *n.*

capitation (kap-i-tā′-shun) *n.* census; tax or grant per head.—**capitation fee,** under National Health Service, sum paid to doctor for each patient under his care.

capon (kā′-pon) *n.* young castrated cock fed for the table.—**ca′ponise** *v.t.*

Capitol (kap′-i-tol) *n.* temple of Jupiter in Rome; buildings of U.S. Congress in Washington.

capitulate (kǝ-pit′-ū-lāt) *v.i.* surrender on conditions; draw up terms of agreement.—**capitula′tion** *n.*—**capit′ulator** *n.*

caprice (kǝ-prēs′) *n.* illogical change of feeling or opinion; whim; fancy.—**capricious** (kǝ-pri′-shus) *a.*—**capri′ciously** *adv.*—**capric′iousness** *n.*

capsize (kap-sīz′) *v.t.* and *i.* upset; overturn.

capstan (kap′-stǝn) *n.* heavy cable-holder revolving on upright spindle.

capsule (kap′-sūl) *n.* seed-vessel of plant; small gelatinous case containing medicine; enclosed space vehicle, manned or unmanned.—**cap′sular** *a.* hollow like capsule.

captain (kap′-tin) *n.* in army, officer next in rank below major; in navy, officer equivalent in rank to colonel in army; master of merchant ship or aircraft; in sport, leader of team; in school, head boy or girl;—*v.t.* command; lead.—**cap′taincy** *n.* rank or commission of captain.

caption (kap′-shun) *n.* heading of newspaper, chapter, page, etc.; title of illustration; subtitle of film scene.

captious (kap′-shus) *a.* apt to find fault; difficult to please.—**cap′tiously** *adv.*—**cap′tiousness** *n.* fault-finding.

captivate (kap′-ti-vāt) *v.t.* capture fancy of.—**cap′tivating** *a.* winning, charming.—**captiva′tion** *n.*

captive (kap′-tiv) *n.* one taken prisoner by force, surprise, or stratagem; one held in captivity;—*a.* made prisoner.—**captiv′ity** *n.* imprisonment; bondage; servitude. —**cap′tor** *n.* (fem. **cap′tress**) one who takes prisoner or prize.—**cap′ture** *n.* act of seizing by force or stratagem; arrest; thing seized; prize;—*v.t.* take captive; take possession of by force.

car (kär) *n.* any kind of vehicle on wheels; abbrev. for motor-car; part of balloon in which aeronauts sit.

carabine, carabineer See **carbine.**

carafe (kǝ-räf′) *n.* glass water-bottle or decanter.

caramel (kar′-ǝ-mel) *n.* burnt sugar, used for colouring spirits, wines, etc. and in cooking; kind of sweetmeat.

carat (kar′-ǝt) *n.* measure of weight for gold and precious stones.

caravan (kar′-a-van, kar-a-van′) *n.* parties of merchants or pilgrims travelling together for greater security, esp. across deserts; mobile dwelling.—**caravan′serai** *n.* large unfurnished Eastern inn, with court in middle for accommodation of caravans.

caraway (kar′-ǝ-wā) *n.* biennial aromatic plant; its seed, used as flavouring for bread, cakes, etc.

carbide (kär′-bīd) *n.* compound of

carbon with certain elements; calcium carbide.

carbine, carabine (kár'-(a)-bīn) n. short cavalry rifle.—**carabineer'** n.

carbohydrate (kár-bō-hī'-drāt) n. substance, such as sugar, starch, cellulose, etc. composed of carbon, hydrogen, and oxygen.

carbolic (kár-bol'-ik) a. derived from carbon;—n. carbolic acid.—**carbolic acid**, poisonous acid distilled from coal-tar and used as antiseptic and disinfectant.

carbon (kár'-bon) n. non-metallic element existing pure in nature as diamond, graphite, charcoal, etc. and as compound of animal and vegetable substances; thin rod of hard carbon used in electric arc-lamp; copy made by using carbon paper. — **carbonaceous** (kar-bon-ā-shus) a. pert. to, or composed of, coal.—**car'bonate** n. salt of carbonic acid.—**carbon'ic** a. pert. to, or coming from, carbon.—**carbonif'erous** a. producing carbon or coal.—**car'bonise** v.t. make into carbon; coat with carbon.—**carbonisa'tion** n.—**carbon paper**, thin paper coated with colouring-matter on one side, used for making copies of written or typewritten work.

carbuncle (kár'-bung-kl) n. gem of deep red colour; variety of garnet; inflamed bunion or boil.—**carbun'cular** a.

carburettor (kár'-bū-ret-or) n. apparatus in internal-combustion engine for producing mixture of air and vaporised fuel.—**carbura'tion** n.

carcase, carcass (kár'-kas) n. dead body of man or animal, esp. of latter; framework or shell.

card (kárd) n. pasteboard; small piece of pasteboard often with figures, pictures, etc. on it for playing games; piece of paste-board having on it person's name and address; (*Slang*) queer or humorous fellow.—**card'board** n. finely finished pasteboard.—**card'-in'dex** n. index in which each entry is made on separate card.—**card'sharper** n. one who cheats at cards.—**on the cards**, possible; likely to happen.

card (kárd) n. toothed instrument for combing wool, flax, etc.;—v.t. comb, as wool, flax, etc.—**card'er** n. one who cards.

cardiac see cardio-.

cardigan (kár'-dig-an) n. kind of knitted jacket.

cardinal (kár'-di-nal) a. chief; main; of great importance; fundamental; (*Colour*) deep scarlet.—**car'dinally** adv.—**cardinal numbers**, 1, 2, 3, 4, 5, etc.—**cardinal points** (of compass), north, south, east, west.

cardinal (kár'-di-nal) n. highest rank next to the Pope, in R.C. Church.

—**car'dinalate, car'dinalship** n. office of cardinal.

cardio- (kár'-di-ō) *prefix* from Gk. *kardia*, heart.—**car'diac** a. pert. to heart.—n. heart stimulant.—**cardiol'ogy** n. (*Med.*) branch of medicine which deals with functions and diseases of heart.

care (kār) n. concern or anxiety; object of anxiety; pains or heed; caution; charge or oversight; trouble; —v.i. be anxious, concerned; be affected with solicitude; have fondness (with *for*).—**care'ful** a. full of care or solicitude; cautious or watchful; painstaking.—**care'fully** adv.—**care'fulness** n.—**care'less** a. heedless; thoughtless; regard less.—**care'lessly** adv.—**care'lessness** n.—**care'worn** a.—**care'taker** n. one who takes care of unoccupied premises.

career (ka-rēr) n. rapid motion; course of action; profession; conduct in life, or progress through life;—v.i. speed along; rush wildly.—**career'ist** n. one who makes his personal advancement his one aim in life.

caress (ka-res') v.t. treat with affection; fondle; kiss;—n. loving touch; embrace.—**caress'ing** a.

caret (kar'-et, kā'-ret) n. mark (∧) which shows where something that has been omitted is to be inserted.

cargo (kár'-gō) n. freight of ship; goods or merchandise carried in vessel.—*pl.* **car'goes**.

caribou (kar'-i-bōō) n. N. American reindeer. Also **car'iboo**.

caricature (kar'-i-ka-tūr) n. ludicrous exaggeration (usually in picture form) of peculiar personal characteristics;—v.t. exaggerate or distort, in words or in pictorial form.—**caricatur'ist** n.

carillon (kar'-i-lon, ka-ril'-yon) n. set or peal of bells of different tones; melody played on such bells.

carmine (kár'-mīn) n. and a. brilliant crimson colouring matter.

carnage (kár'-nāj) n. slaughter; massacre.

carnal (kár'-nal) a. pert. to flesh; sensual; animal; sexual; material, as opposed to spiritual.—**car'nalise** v.t. make carnal.—**carna'lity** n. fleshly lust; sensuality.—**car'nally** adv.—**carnal knowledge**, sexual intercourse.

carnation (kár-nā'-shun) n. flesh-colour; variety of clove-pink, noted for its beauty and sweet scent.

carnival (kár'-ni-val) n. in R.C. countries season of feasting and revelry preceding Lent; any feasting or merrymaking.

carnivora (kár-niv'-ō-ra) n.pl. animals that feed on flesh.—**carnivore** (kar'-ni-vŏr) n. flesh-eating animal.—**carniv'orous** a. flesh-eating.—**carniv'orously** adv.—**carniv'orousness** n.

carol (kar'-ol) *n.* song of joy, esp. Christmas hymn;—*v.i.* sing carol; sing joyfully.

carotid (ka-rot'-id) *n.* each of two main arteries in neck conveying blood to head;—*a.* pert. to these.

carouse (ka-rouz') *v.i.* revel; drink deep; hold drinking-party.—**carou'sal** *n.* noisy drinking-party.—**carou'ser** *n.* reveller.

carousel (kar'-ōō-zel) *n.* merry-go-round; roundabout.

carp (karp) *v.i.* catch at small faults or errors; find fault petulantly.

carp (karp) *n.* fresh-water fish.

carpel (kar'-pel) *n.* (*Bot.*) seed-bearing part of plant; part of compound ovary.—**car'pellary** *a.*

carpenter (kar'-pen-ter) *n.* worker in timber as used in building of houses, ships, etc.—**car'pentry** *n.* carpenter's trade or his work.

carpet (kar'-pet) *n.* woven or felted covering for floors, etc.;—*v.t.* cover with carpet; (*Fig.*) strew.—**on the carpet,** under consideration; (*Slang*) awaiting probable reprimand from superior.

carraway See **caraway**.

carriage (kar'-ij) *n.* act of carrying passengers or goods; cost of carrying; vehicle for passengers; railway coach; bearing; demeanour; conduct.—**carriageable** *a.*—**carriage forward,** cost of transport to be paid by receiver.—**carriage paid,** cost of transport paid by sender.

carrier (kar'-i-er) *n.* one who carries, esp. for hire; receptacle or rack for carrying objects; pigeon used for carrying messages; modulated radio waves; (*Med.*) one who, without showing symptoms of disease, can convey infection to others.

carrion (kar'-i-on) *n.* dead, rotting flesh; anything putrid.—**carr'ion-crow** *n.* crow which feeds on carrion.

carrot (kar'-ot) *n.* plant cultivated for edible root.—**carr'oty** *a.* reddish-yellow; red-haired.

carry (kar'-i) *v.t.* convey; transport; impel; transfer, as from one column, page, or book to another; accomplish; obtain possession of by force; behave;—*v.i.* reach, of projectile;—*n.* range.—**to carry all before one,** overcome all difficulties; win triumphantly.—**to carry off,** win; gain.—**a carry-on** (*Colloq.*) unusual conduct; unnecessary fuss.—**to carry one's bat** (*Cricket*) not to be out at end of innings.—**to carry weight,** exert influence; impress; have power.—**to be carried away,** be very greatly excited.

carse (kars) *n.* in Scotland stretch of low fertile land along banks of river.

cart (kart) *n.* two-wheeled vehicle used for transport of heavy goods;—*v.t.* convey in cart.—**car'tage** *n.*

carting; price paid for carting.—**car'ter** *n.*—**to be in the cart** (*Slang*) be in a fix.

cartilage (kar'-ti-lāj) *n.* (*Anat.*) gristle; strong, transparent tissue in body, very elastic, softer than bone.—**cartilaginous** (kar-ti-la'-ji-nus) *a.*

cartography (kar-tog'-ra-fi) *n.* art of making charts or maps.—**cartog'rapher** *n.*

carton (kar'-ton) *n.* thin pasteboard; pasteboard box.

cartoon (kar-tōōn') *n.* design drawn for transference to murals, tapestries, etc.; humorous or satirical drawings or series of drawings; pictorial caricature; comic strip; cine film of animated drawings.—**cartoon'ist** *n.*

cartridge (kar'-trij) *n.* case to contain charge for gun; any small cylindrical container.—**blank cartridge,** one without missile.—**ball cartridge,** live cartridge, i.e. one with bullet not extracted.—**cartridge paper,** soft, thick paper.

carve (karv) *v.t.* and *i.* fashion artistically by cutting; hew out, as path, career, etc.; cut in pieces or slices, as meat, etc.; divide.—**car'ver** *n.* one who carves; large knife for carving.

cascade (kas'-kād) *n.* waterfall, or series of waterfalls; anything resembling this;—*v.i.* fall in cascades.

cascara (kas-ka'-ra) *n.* **cascara sagrada,** fluid extracted from dried Californian bark and used as laxative.

case (kās) *n.* receptacle; covering; sheath; anything which encloses or contains; box and its contents; set; (*Print.*) frame for holding type;—*v.t.* put in case.—**cas'ing** *n.* case or covering.

case (kās) *n.* event, occurrence, or circumstance; state or condition of things or persons; question of facts or principles requiring investigation; (*Med.*) patient under treatment; (*Gram.*) inflection or terminal change in nouns, pronouns, etc.—**in case,** lest.—**to make out a good case,** give good reasons for.

casein (kā'-sē-in) *n.* calcium salt form-albuminous constituent of milk.

casement (kās'-ment)- *n.* window-frame; window, or part of window, opening on hinges.

cash (kash) *n.* money, esp. ready money; coin; paper-money, bank-notes, etc.;—*v.t.* turn into, or exchange for, money.—**cash-reg'ister** *n.* automatic money-till which registers and indicates amount paid for goods sold.

cashew (ka-shōō') *n.* tropical American tree whose fruit, the cashew-nut, is eaten raw or roasted.

cashier (kash-ēr') *n.* one who has charge of cash.

cashier (kash-ēr') *v.t.* dismiss from

office in disgrace; discard; annul.

cashmere (kash'-mēr) n. fabric made from hair of Kashmir goat; woollen material similar to this.—a.

casino (ka-sē'-nō) n. public assembly-room or building for dancing, gambling, etc.

cask (kàsk) n. large wooden vessel for holding liquor; barrel;—v.t. put in cask.

casket (kàs'-ket) n. small cask or case; small box for jewels, etc.; container for ashes of cremated person; (U.S.) coffin.

casserole (kas'-e-rōl) n. stew-pan; vessel in which food is cooked and served; kind of stew.

cassette (ka-set') n. lightproof holder for photographic film; holder for reels of magnetic tape.

cassock (kas'-ok) n. long, close-fitting robe worn by clergymen and choristers under gown or surplice.

cast (kàst) v.t. fling; hurl; direct or bestow, as glance; project, as shadow; shed, as skin; reckon or compute (with up); shape in mould (as metal); distribute parts of play among actors; throw line in angling; forecast (cast horoscope); let down (anchor); give (vote); bring to birth prematurely;—n. act of casting; throw; distance thing is thrown; mould or form; change of direction; that which is shed or ejected (skin of insect, excrement of earthworm); reckoning; forecast; assignment of parts in play; actors appearing in play; expression (of face); squint (of eye).—**cast'ing** n. piece of metal cast in mould; act of founding and moulding metal.—**cast'ing-vote** n. vote of chairman, which decides question when votes are equally divided.—**cast-i'ron** a. made of cast iron; rigid; indefatigable; unshakable; (Slang) irrefutable.—**cast'-steel** n. steel melted, cast, and rolled out into bars.—**cast'-off** a. discarded;—n. thing discarded.—**to cast up**, cast ashore; add; bring up as reproach against person.

castanets (kas'-ta-nets) n.pl. two small concave shells of ivory or hard wood, fastened to thumb and clicked in time to dances and music of Spanish type.

castaway (kàst'-a-wā) n. shipwrecked person; outcast.

caste (kàst) n. one of hereditary classes into which society in India was divided; any exclusive social order in other countries.—**to lose caste**, lose social standing.

castellated (kas'-te-lā-ted) a. adorned with turrets and battlements like castle.

caster, castor (kas'-ter, -tor) n. small bottle with perforated top for sugar, pepper, etc.; small swivelled wheel on foot of chair-leg, etc.—**cas'ter-, cas'tor- su'gar** n. finely-powdered sugar.

castigate (kas'-ti-gāt) v.t. correct; rebuke severely; chastise; punish.—**castiga'tion** n. severe chastisement; discipline.—**cas'tigator** n.

castle (kas'-l) n. fortified residence; stronghold, esp. of nobleman; any imposing mansion; piece (also called 'rook') in chess.—**cas'tled** a. having castle; built like castle.

castor-oil (kas'-tor-oil) n. oil extracted from seeds of castor-oil plant.

castrate (kas'-trāt) v.t. deprive of testicles; emasculate.—**castra'tion** n.

casual (kazh'-ū-al) a. accidental; incidental; occasional; offhand or careless;—n. casual or occasional worker, etc.; flat-heeled shoe.—**cas'ually** adv.—**cas'ualty** n. accident, mishap.—**cas'ualties** n. pl. (Mil.) losses caused by death, wounds, capture, etc.

casuistry (kaz'-ū-is-tri) n. resolving of conflicting moral issues by reference to conscience; superficial, unsound reasoning.—**cas'uist** n.—**casuis'tic** a.

cat (kat) n. small domestic feline; undomesticated cat, usually called wild-cat; spiteful woman; whip;—v.t. and i. (Colloq.) vomit.—**cat'ty**, **cat'tish** a. spiteful.—**cat burglar**, burglar who makes his entry by climbing to windows, roofs, etc.—**cat'-call** n. cat-like cry, used by audiences to express disapproval.—**cat'gut** n. string made from animal intestines.—**cat'-nap** n. short, light sleep.—**cat's'-eye** n. gem with light-reflections like those from cat's eye; reflector set in road surface.—**cat's'-paw** n. dupe of another; (Naut.) light breeze.—**cat-o'-nine-tails** n. whip with nine thongs.—**tabby cat**, female cat; striped cat.—**tom cat**, male cat.

cataclysm (kat'-a-klizm) n. deluge; catastrophe; sudden and violent alteration in earth's surface.—**cataclys'mal** a.

catacombs (kat'-a-kōmz) n.pl. underground galleries with niches for tombs.

catafalque (kat'-a-falk) n. structure on which coffin is placed for lying-in-state.

catalepsy (kat'-a-lep-si) n. (Med.) suspension of senses and bodily powers, with muscular rigidity; trance.—**catalep'tic** a.

catalogue (kat'-a-log) n. list, usually alphabetical, of names, books, goods, etc.; descriptive price; list;—v.t. make such list.—**cat'aloguer** n.

catalysis (ka-tal'-i-sis) n. (Chem.) chemical change effected in one substance by aid of another which itself undergoes no change.—**cat'-**

alyst n. substance producing such change.—**catalyt'ic** a.

catamaran (kat-ạ-mạ-ran') n. raft consisting of pieces of wood lashed together; sailing craft with twin hulls.

catapult (kat'-ạ-pult) n. siege engine for hurling stones, etc.; forked piece of wood, with elastic attached to the two points, for propelling small stones, etc. through air;—v.t. hurl by means of catapult.

cataract (kat'-ạ-rakt) n. waterfall; flow of large body of water over precipice; torrent; (Med.) disease of eye, characterised by opaque state of lens.

catarrh (kạ-tár') n. (Med.) inflammation of mucous membranes of the body; particularly applied to inflammation of nose (nasal catarrh). —**catarrh'al, catarrh'ous** a.

catastrophe (kạ-tas'-trō-fe) n. disaster; calamity; decisive event in drama; denouement; culmination.— **catastroph'ic** a.

catch (kach) v.t. seize; grasp; arrest; trap; take disease by infection or contagion; detect; understand; come upon unexpectedly;—v.i. become entangled or hooked; be spread e.g. infection;—n. seizure; anything that holds, stops, etc.; that which is caught; sudden advantage.—**catch'able** a.—**catch'er** n.—**catch'y** a. containing hidden difficulty; (Mus.) attractive.—**to catch it** (Colloq.) be scolded or punished.—**catch-as-catch-can,** Lancashire style of wrestling.

catchment (kach'-ment) n. area in which water, from rainfall or otherwise, collects, to form supply of river, stream, or drainage area.

catchpenny (kach'-pen-i) n. something of little value and usually showy, made to sell quickly;—a. cheap and showy.

catchup, catsup, ketchup (kach'-up, kat'-sup, kech'-up) n. bottled sauce made from tomatoes, mushrooms, walnuts, etc.

catchword (kach'-wurd) n. word or short phrase that takes popular fancy; slogan; (Theat.) actor's cue; first word in column of dictionary, etc., repeated above column as reference.

catechise (kat'-e-kīz) v.t. instruct by question and answer, esp. in Christian doctrine; question; examine orally.—**catechism** (kat'-e-kizm) n. set form of question and answer to teach tenets of religion.

category (kat'-e-gor-i) n. class, group, or order; in logic, any fundamental conception.—**categor'ical** a. pert. to category; admitting no conditions; absolute; precise.—**categor'ically** adv.—**cat'egorise** v.t. place in category.

cater (kā'-tẹr) v.i. buy or procure food; provide food, entertainment, etc.; purvey.—**cat'erer** n.

caterpillar (kat'-ẹr-pil-ạr) n. larva of butterflies and moths; tracked vehicle.

caterwaul (kat'-ẹr-wawl) v.i. cry like cats in heat.

catfish (kat'-fish) n. species of fish, with barbels beside mouth like cat's whiskers.

cathartic (kạ-thár'-tik) a. (Med.) purgative; cleansing the bowels;— n. purging medicine.—**cath'arise** v.t. cleanse; purify.—**cathar'sis** n. purging; purification; Aristotelian concept of purging of the emotions.

cathedral (kạ-thē'-drạl) n. principal church in diocese, which contains bishop's throne.

Catherine-wheel (kath'-e-rin-hwēl) n. rose-window; firework which rotates in burning.

cathode (kath'-ōd) n. conductor by which electric current leaves electrolytic cell.—**cathode rays,** electrons emitted by cathode.—**cathode ray tube** device in which stream of electrons impinges on fluorescent glass screen, e.g. in TV.

catholic (kath'-o-lik) a. universal; embracing all Christians; pert. to Roman Catholics;—n. member of Church Universal, or of R.C. Church. — **catholicism** (kạ-thol'-i-sizm) n.—**catholi'city** n.

catkin (kat'-kin) n. spike of downy flowers of willow, etc.

catmint, catnip (kat'-mint, kat'-nip) n. aromatic plant with blue flowers, attractive to cats.

cattle (kat'-l) n.pl. domestic livestock, esp. cows and bulls.—**catt'le-grid'** n., parallel bars placed across road or pit to prevent cattle from straying.—**catt'le-rust'ler** n. cattle-thief.

caucus (kaw'-kus) n. small but powerful committee, esp. one connected with political party.

caudal (kaw'-dal) a. pert. to tail.— **caudate** a. having tail.

caudle (kaw'-dl) n. warm drink for invalids.

caught (kawt) pa.p. and pa.t. of catch.

caul (kawl) n. net, etc. worn on the head; membrane covering head of some babies at birth.

cauldron (kawl'-dron) n. large kettle or boiler.

cauliflower (kaw'-li-flou-ẹr)n. variety of cabbage with white flowering head.

caulk, calk (kawk) v.t. press tarred oakum between planks of boat to prevent leaks.—**caulk'er** n.

causal (kaw'-zạl) a. relating to cause or causes.—**causal'ity** n. manner in which cause works; relation of cause and effect.—**causa'tion** n. agency by which effect is produced. —**caus'ative** a. expressing cause or reason.

cause (kawz) n. that which produces result or effect; origin or motive of action; action or lawsuit in court; principle supported by person or party;—v.t. produce; be occasion of; induce.—**cause'less** a. without reason or motive.

causerie (kō'-zẹ-rē) n. chat; informal newspaper article or broadcast.

causeway, causey (kawz'-wā, kaw'-ze) n. raised paved road.

caustic (kaws'-tik) a. burning; (Fig.) biting, satirical;—n. substance that corrodes and destroys animal tissue. —**caus'tically** adv.—**causti'city** n.

cauterise (kaw'-tẹr-īz) v.t. burn or sear animal tissue to destroy diseased tissue, or promote healing. —**cauterisa'tion** n.

caution (kaw'-shun) n. carefulness; wariness; warning; guarantee; (Colloq.) odd or droll person;—v.t. advise to take care; warn or admonish.—**cau'tious** a.—**cau'tiously** adv.—**cau'tionary** a. containing warning.

cavalcade (kav-al-kād') n. procession on horseback; parade; pageant.

cavalier (kav-ạ-lēr') n. horseman; a knight; a gallant; attendant escort to a lady;—a. gay and offhand; inconsiderate.—**Cavalier'** n. partisan of Charles I—**cavalier'ly** adv.

cavalry (kav'-al-ri) n. horse-soldiery.

cave (kāv) n. small chamber hollowed out of the earth horizontally, either by nature or by man; den.—**to cave in,** of ground, fall in, subside; (Fig.) yield; admit defeat.

caveat (kā'-vē-at) n. warning; legal notice to stop proceedings.

cavern (kav'-ẹrn) n. deep, hollow place under the earth; large dark cave.—**cav'erned** a. full of caverns.—**cav'ernous** a. hollow; deep-set.

caviare, caviar (kav-i-är') n. delicacy made from roes of sturgeon.

cavil (kav'-il) v.i. (with 'at') find fault unreasonably;—n. frivolous objection.

cavity (kav'-i-ti) n. hole; hollow place of any size.

cavort (kạ-vort') v.i. (Colloq.) prance; curvet; frisk about.

caw (kaw) v.i. cry like crow or raven; —n. sound made by crow, rook, or raven.—**caw'ing** n.

cayenne (kā-yen') n. pungent red pepper, from dried and ground fruit of capsicum plant.

cayman (kā'-mạn) n. S. American alligator. Also **cai'man.**

cease (sēs) v.t. put stop to;—v.i. stop; discontinue; give over.—**cease'less** a. without stopping.—**cease'lessly** adv.

cedar (sē'-dạr) n. species of conifer-

ous, evergreen trees yielding durable, fragrant wood.

cede (sēd) v.t. yield; surrender; give up, esp. of territory.

ceiling (sē'-ling) n. interior part of roof of room; maximum height to which particular aeroplane can ascend; (Fig.) upper limit of production, wages, prices, etc.

celandine (sel'-an-dīn) n. wild plant bearing star-shaped yellow flowers, popularly known as swallow-wort. Also **lesser celandine,** pilewort, variety of ranunculus.

celebrate (sel'-e-brāt) v.t. make famous; mark by ceremony, as an event or festival; observe with solemn rites.—**cel'ebrated** a. renowned; famous.—**celebra'tion** n. act of celebrating.—**cel'ebrant** n. one who celebrates.—**celeb'rity** (sel-eb'-ri-ti) n. renown; fame; person of distinction.

celerity (sel-er'-i-ti) n. rapidity of motion; speed; swiftness.

celery (sel'-e-ri) n. umbelliferous plant with edible leaf-stalks.

celestial (sel-est'-yạl) a. heavenly; divine; blessed;—n. inhabitant of heaven.—**celest'ially** adv.—**celestial body** n. sun, star or planet.

celibacy (sel'-i-bạ-si) n. single life; unmarried state.—**cel'ibate** n. one unmarried;—a. unmarried.

cell (sel) n. small room, as in prison or monastery; small cavity; simplest unit in structure of living matter; small group of members of political party; division of electric battery.—**cell'ular** a. consisting of, or containing, cells; open-textured.

cellar (sel'-ạr) n. underground storeroom, esp. for wines, liquors.—**cell'arage** n. space for cellars; charge for storage in cellars.—**cell'arer** n. monk in charge of stores, wines, etc.; spirit merchant.

cello, 'cello (chel'-ō) n. (Mus.) contraction for violoncello.—**cell'ist, 'cell'ist** n. player on violoncello.

cellulose (sel'-ū-lōs) n. chemical substance, one of the carbohydrates, forming chief constituent of walls of plant cells; varnish made from compounds of cellulose.

Celt, Kelt (selt, kelt) n. one of race, including Highlanders of Scotland, the Irish, Welsh, Bretons, Manx, and Cornish.—**Cel'tic, Kel'tic** n. language spoken by Celts.—a. pert. to Celts.

cement (sẹ-ment') n. plastic mixture that can unite two bodies; mortar; bond of union;—v.t. unite by using cement; join closely.—**cementa'tion** n. act of cementing; conversion of iron into steel.

cemetery (sem'-e-ter-i) n. graveyard; burying-ground, unattached to church.

cenotaph (sen'-ō-taf) n. monument

erected to one buried elsewhere; empty sepulchre.

censer (sen'-ser) n. metal vessel in which incense is burned.—**cense** v.t. perfume with incense.

censor (sen'-sor) n. Roman official who looked after property, taxes, and people's morals; one appointed to examine books, plays, letters, etc., before publication or delivery, and delete or ban any objectionable contents; one who blames or finds fault;—v.t. blame or reprove; subject to examination by censor.—**censo'rial** a. pert. to correction of morals; pert. to censor.—**censo'rious** a. apt to find fault.—**censo'riously** adv.—**censo'riousness** n.—**cen'sorship** n. office of censor; act of censoring.

censure (sen'-shūr) n. act of finding fault; disapproval;—v.t. reprove; express disapproval of; criticise adversely.—**censurable** a.—**censurably** adv.—**cen'surableness** n.

census (sen'-sus) n. official numbering of inhabitants of country.—**cen'sual** a.

cent (sent) n. hundred, as 10 per cent; American coin worth hundredth part of dollar.—**cent'al** n. 100 lb. avoirdupois.

centaur (sen'-tawr) n. (Myth.) fabulous being, half man and half horse.

centenary (sen-ten'-ar-i, sen-tēn'-ar-i, sen'-ten-a-ri) n. period of hundred years; century; commemoration of hundredth anniversary; centennial.—**centenarian** (sen-te-nā'-ri-an) n. person a hundred years old.

centennial (sen-ten'-i-al) a. pert. to period of 100 years; happening once in hundred years;—n. hundredth anniversary.

centesimal (sen-tes'-i-mal) a. hundredth; counted or counting by hundredths;—n. hundredth part.

centi- (sen'-ti) prefix L. centum, a hundred.—**cen'tigrade** a. divided into 100 degrees.—**centimetre** (sen'-ti-mē-ter) n. 100th part of metre = ·394 inch.

centipede (sen'-ti-pēd) n. arthropod with segmented body, each segment having a pair of legs.

central (sen'-tral) a. relating to, or placed in, centre; chief; important.—**cen'trally** adv.—**cen'tralise** v.t. draw to central point; concentrate; put under one control.—**centralisa'tion** n.—**cen'tralism** n. centralisation, esp. of government.—**central'ity** n. state of being central.

centre, center (sen'-ter) n. mid-point of anything; pivot; axis; point to which things move or are drawn; point of concentration;—v.t. and i. place in centre; collect round point; be fixed; (Sport) propel from wing to centre.—**cen'tric(al)** a. placed in centre

or middle.—**cen'trically** adv.—**centricity** (sen-tris'-i-ti) n. state of being centric.—**centre of gravity**, point in a body about which it will balance.

centrifugal (sen-trif'-ū-gal) a. tending to move away from centre of revolving body.

centripetal (sen-trip'-e-tal) a. tending to move towards centre.

centurion (sen-tū'-ri-on) n. officer in command of company of hundred men in Roman legion.

century (sen'-tū-ri) n. period of hundred years; set of hundred; in cricket, score of hundred runs; company of Roman legion numbering hundred soldiers under command of a centurion.

ceramic (ser-am'-ik) a. pert. to pottery.—**ceram'ics** n.pl. art of moulding, modelling, and baking clay; study of pottery as an art.

cereal (sē'-re-al) a. pert. to edible grain;—n. any edible grain (wheat, barley, oats, etc.).

cerebrum (ser'-e-brum) n. upper and larger division of brain.—**cerebell'um** n. part of brain behind and below cerebrum.—**cer'ebral** a. pert. to brain.—**cerebral haemorrhage**, rupture of artery of brain with consequent escape of blood.—**cer'ebrate** v.i. have brain in action.—**cerebra'tion** n.—**cerebro-spinal** (ser'-e-brō-spī'nal) a. pert. to both brain and spinal cord.—**cerebro-spinal fever** (Med.) epidemic form of meningitis.

ceremony (ser'-e-mo-ni) n. sacred rite; formal observance; formality; usage of courtesy; prescribed rule; public or private function.—**ceremo'nial** a. pert. to ceremony; formal.—n. outward observance; usage followed in performing rites.—**ceremo'nially** adv.—**ceremo'nious** a. full of ceremony; particular in observing forms.—**ceremo'niously** adv.—**ceremo'niousness** n.—**master of ceremonies**, at public functions, etc. one who sees that formal courtesies are observed.

cerise (ser-ēz') n. and a. of colour, light clear red; cherry-coloured.

certain (ser'-tin) a. sure; settled; undoubted; inevitable; some; one; regular; constant; of moderate quantity, degree, etc.—**cer'tainly** adv.—**cer'tainty** n. quality of being certain.—**cer'titude** n.

certificate (ser-tif'-i-kāt) n. written testimony to truth of a fact; testimonial or written statement of qualifications;—v.t. attest by certificate; furnish with certificate.—**certify** (ser'-ti-fī) v.t. testify to in writing; vouch for truth of; officially declare insane.—**cert'ifiable** a.—**certifica'tion** n. act of certifying.

cervical (ser'-vi-kal) a. pert. to the neck.

cessation (se-sā'-shun) *n.* stoppage; discontinuance.

cesspool (ses'-pool) *n.* pit or hollow for collection of filthy drainage water or sewage.

chafe (chāf) *v.t.* warm by rubbing; wear away by rubbing; irritate; vex;—*v.i.* be worn by rubbing or friction; rage or fret;—*n.* friction; injury caused by rubbing.—**chaf'er** *n.* one who chafes; dish for heating water.—**chaf'ing-dish** *n.* vessel for cooking or keeping food warm on table.

chafer (chā-fer) *n.* any of various beetles; cockchafer.

chaff (chaf) *n.* husk of grains; straw cut small for cattle-feeding; worthless matter; refuse.—**chaff'y** *a.*

chaff (chaf) *n.* banter; jesting talk;—*v.t.* tease.

chaffer (chaf'-er) *v.t.* buy and sell; haggle about price.—**chaff'erer** *n.*

chaffinch (chaf'-insh) *n.* small songbird of finch family.

chagrin (sha-grēn') *n.* ill-humour; vexation;—*v.t.* vex deeply.

chain (chān) *n.* series of metal rings or links connected and forming flexible cable; fetter; succession of things or events; mountain range; anything that connects; measure equal to 22 yards;—*v.t.* fasten or connect with chain; fetter; restrain.—**chain'-gang** *n.* number of convicts chained together.—**chain'mail, -arm'our** *n.* flexible metal shirt made of rings closely linked.—**chain'-reac'tion** *n.* process in which one reaction stimulates another similar to it.—**chain-store** one of many similar shops under same ownership.

chair (chār) *n.* movable seat with back; portable covered vehicle for carrying one person, e.g. sedan; official seat occupied by president of meeting, university professor, bishop, etc.; one of the iron blocks supporting rails on railway;—*v.t.* carry in triumph.—**chair'man** *n.* presiding officer at meeting; one who carries a sedan.—**chair'woman** *n.*

chaise (shāz) *n.* light, one-horse carriage.—**chaise'-longue** (löng) *n.* couch with back-rest at one end.

chalcedony (kal-sed'-ō-ni) *n.* whitish or bluish-white variety of quartz; white agate.

chalet (sha'-lā) *n.* timber-built Alpine house; holiday hut.

chalice (chal'-is) *n.* wine-cup; goblet; communion-cup.

chalk (chawk) *n.* soft, white, carbonate of lime;—*v.t.* rub or mark with chalk.—**chalk'y** *a.* containing or like chalk.—**chalk'iness** *n.*—**French chalk**, soft, impure variety of talc used by tailors, etc. for marking cloth; soapstone.

challenge (chal'-enj) *n.* invitation to contest, esp. to duel; defiance; warning call of sentry; call for great effort. —*v.t.* call upon person to settle dispute by fighting; defy; summon to answer; call in question.—**chall'engeable** *a.*—**chall'enger** *n.*

chamber (chām'-ber) *n.* room; place where assembly meets, and the assembly itself; cavity; cavity at rear end of bore of gun; vessel for urine.—**cham'bers** *n.pl.* room or rooms where professional men, esp. barristers, conduct business; lodgings.—**cham'ber-maid** *n.* woman servant who has care of bedrooms, esp. in hotels, etc.—**cham'ber-mus'ic** *n.* music suitable for performance in house or small hall.

chamberlain (chām'-ber-lin) *n.* official at court of monarch having charge of domestic and ceremonial affairs; treasurer of public money, esp. of city.—**cham'berlainship** *n.*

chameleon (ka-mēl'-yun) *n.* small lizard, which changes colour with its surroundings; (*Fig.*) inconstant person.

chamois (sham'-wä) *n.* goat-like species of mountain antelope; with pronunciation (sha'-mi), kind of soft leather. — popularly written **sham'my.**

champ (champ) *v.t.* and *i.* bite, chew, or munch noisily.—**to champ at the bit** (*Fig.*) be impatient at delay.

champagne (sham-pān') *n.* light effervescent white wine.

champion (cham'-pi-on) *n.* one who fought in single combat to defend honour of another; defender of any cause; one capable of defeating his competitors in any form of sport;—*a.* first-class;—*v.t.* defend; maintain or support.—**cham'pionship** *n.* position of champion; defence; advocacy.

chance (chäns) *n.* unforeseen occurrence; accident; risk; opportunity; possibility;—*a.* accidental;—*v.t.* venture upon; risk;—*v.i.* happen.—**chan'cy** *a.* lucky; uncertain.—**main chance**, money-making.

chancel (chan'-sel) *n.* east part of church, where altar is placed, orig. shut off by screen of lattice-work from nave.

chancellor (chan'-sel-or) *n.* title of various high officials in state, and in the law; head of university.—**chan'cellorship** *n.* office of chancellor.—**chan'cellory, -ery** *n.* premises of chancellor.—**Chancellor of the Exchequer**, British minister of finance.

chancery (chan'-ser-i) *n.* formerly, chief English court of justice next to Parliament; now division of High Court of Justice.—**in Chancery** (*Law*) under superintendence of the Lord Chancellor.

chancre (shang'-ker) *n.* venereal ulcer.—**chan'crous** *a.* ulcerous.

chandelier (shan-de-lēr') n. branched framework for holding lights, esp. one hanging from ceiling; orig. for holding candles.

chandler (chānd'-lẹr) n. orig. candlemaker; now dealer in candles, soap, oil, etc.; dealer in goods for specific purposes.—**chand'lery** n.

change (chānj) v.t. alter; put one thing for another; shift; exchange, as pence for a shilling; convert;—v.i. become different; change one's clothes;—n. act of changing; alteration; money of small denomination given in exchange for money of larger; balance of money returned after payment; fresh clothing; exchange.—**change'able** a. variable; fickle; unsteady.— **change'ful** a. changeable; fickle.—**change'fully** adv. —**change'fulness** n.—**change'less** a. unchanging; constant.—**change'ling** n. child left in place of another taken by fairies.

channel (chan'-el) n. watercourse; deeper part of river, harbour, etc.; strait; groove or furrow; means of communication;—v.t. form a channel; groove or furrow.

chant (chànt) v.t. and i. sing; celebrate in song; intone;—n. song; melody; sacred words recited in singing manner.—**chant'er** n. (fem. **chant'ress**) one who chants; tube with finger-holes, in bagpipe.—**chant'ry** n. endowed chapel where masses for the dead are sung.—**chan'ty** (shan'-ti) n. sailor's song.

chanticleer (chant-i-klēr') n. cock.

chaos (kā'-os) n. empty, infinite space; complete confusion; state of universe before the Creation.—**chaotic** (kā-ot'-ik) a.

chap (chap) n. crack in the skin, esp. in hands, caused by exposure to cold.

chap (chap) n. (Colloq.) fellow.—**chap'man** n. pedlar; hawker.—**chap'book** n. book or pamphlet, hawked by chapmen.

chapel (chap'-el) n. private church; subordinate place of worship, as one attached to school, prison, etc.; division of church with its own altar; in England Dissenters' or Nonconformists' place of worship; in Scotland and Ireland, Roman Catholic church; association of journeymen printers.

chaperon (shap'-e-rŏn) n. kind of hood; lady who escorts unmarried lady in public as protector;—v.t. escort as chaperon.

chaplain (chap'-lin) n. clergyman attached to ship of war, army, or family.—**chap'laincy** n.

chaplet (chap'-let) n. garland or wreath for the head; string of beads; division of the rosary.

chapter (chap'-tẹr) n. division of book; bishop's council in diocese; organised assembly of society, or military order.—v.t. divide into chapters.

char (chàr) v.t. reduce to charcoal; burn to black cinder;—pr.p. **char'ring**.—pa.p. and pa.t. **charred**.—**char'coal** n. residue of partially burnt animal or vegetable matter, esp. wood.—**char'coal-burn'er** n. one who makes charcoal.

char (chàr) n. (Slang) tea.

char, chare (chàr, chār) n. job; work done by the day;—v.i. work by the day; do small jobs.—**char'woman** n. woman who does cleaning by the day—(Colloq.) a **char**.

character (kar'-ak-tẹr) n. mark, letter, figure, sign, stamp; distinctive mark; essential feature; nature; total of qualities making up individuality; testimonial; person noted for eccentricity; personage in play or novel.—v.t. characterise; portray; represent.—**char'acterise** v.t. depict peculiar qualities of; distinguish; give character to.—**characteris'tic** a. serving to mark the character of; peculiar; distinctive; —n. that which distinguishes person or thing from another;—**characteris'tically** adv.—**characterisa'tion** n. act of characterising; literary or dramatic portrayal of character.

charade (shạr-rãd') n. sort of puzzle-game, consisting of the interpretation (usually dramatic) of a word.

charge (chàrj) n. load or burden; price or cost; care or trust; earnest exhortation, as of judge or bishop; accusation or allegation; clergyman's parish or parishioners; amount of powder, etc., that gun is fitted to hold; attack, or signal for it; custody; quantity of electricity in a cell or on a body.—v.t. lay task, command, trust upon; ask as payment; accuse; fill; load, as gun;—v.i. make an onset.—**charge'able** a.—**charg'er** n. large flat dish; war-horse.

chariot (char'-i-ot) n. in ancient times, two-wheeled car used in warfare; four-wheeled state carriage. —**charioteer** n.

charity (char'-i-ti) n. (Bib.) love and goodwill to men; liberality to the poor; leniency in judging others; act of kindness; alms; charitable cause or institution.—**char'itable** a. pert. to charity; liberal to the poor; generous-minded.—**char'itably** adv.

charlatan (shár'-lạ-tạn) n. quack medicine vendor; mountebank or imposter.

charm (chàrm) n. magic spell; anything supposed to possess magic power; talisman; attractiveness;—v.t. subjugate by magic; attract irresistibly;—v.i. please greatly; be fascinating.—**charm'ing** a. attractive;

alluring; delightful.—**charm'ingly** adv.

charnel (chär'-nel) a. containing dead bodies.—**char'nel-house** n. place where bodies or bones of dead are deposited; sepulchre.

chart (chärt) n. map of part of sea, showing currents, depths, islands, coasts, etc.; diagram giving information in tabular form; graph;—v.t. represent on chart; map; delineate.—**chart'less** a.

charter (chär'-ter) n. formal document confirming privileges, titles, or rights; act of incorporation; patent; hiring of vessel;—v.t. establish by charter; grant privileges to; hire, as ship, aircraft etc.—**char'tered** a.

chary (chār'-i) a. careful.—**char'ily** adv.

chase (chās) v.t. pursue; run after; hunt; drive away;—v.i. hasten; hurry;—n. pursuit; hunting of enemy, game, etc.; what is pursued or hunted; land maintained as game preserve.—**chas'er** n.—**a wild-goose chase**, pursuit of something unattainable.

chase (chās) v.t. enchase; engrave metal.

chasm (kazm) n. deep opening in the earth.

chassis (sha'-sĕ) n. under-carriage of motor-car; framework of aeroplane gun, radio, etc.

chaste (chāst) a. pure; virtuous; undefiled; pure and simple in taste and style.—**chaste'ly** adv.—**chaste'ness** n.—**chas'tity** n. purity; virginity.

chasten (chā'-sn) v.t. correct by punishment; (Fig.) subdue.

chastise (chas'tīz') v.t. inflict pain in order to reform; punish.—**chastisement** (chas'-tiz-ment) n. punishment; correction.

chat (chat) v.i. talk idly or familiarly; n. light, familiar talk; louse;—pr.p. **chatt'ing**;—pa.p. and pa.t. **chatt'ed**.—**chatt'er** v.i. talk idly or rapidly; rattle together, of teeth.—**chatt'erer** n.—**chatt'iness** n.—**chatt'y** a.

chateau (shȧ-tō') n. castle; country-seat, esp. in France; mansion;—pl. **chateaux** (shȧtōz').

chattel (chat'-l) n., usually in pl. **chattels**, any kind of property, except freehold.—**goods and chattels**, goods, possessions, and property.

chatter See chat.

chauffeur (shō-fer', shō'-fer) n. (fem. **chauffeuse'**) paid driver of private motor-car.

chauvinism (shō'-vi-nizm) n. absurdly exaggerated patriotism; jingoism.—**chau'vinist** n.—**chauvinis'ic** a.

chaw (chaw) n. chew or quid of tobacco; piece suitable for chewing;—v.t. chew; champ (of horses).

cheap (chēp) a. low in price; of low cost, as compared with value, or usual cost; dealing in low-priced articles; inferior, vulgar.—**cheap'ly** adv. — **cheap'ness** n. — **cheap'en** v.t. bring down price; lessen value; render less estimable.—**cheap'-jack,** n. travelling hawker, selling inferior goods.

cheat (chēt) v.t. deceive; defraud; trick;—v.i. practise trickery;—n. fraud; imposture; one who cheats; impostor.—**cheat'er** n.

check (chek) n. stop; restraint; interruption in progress; obstacle, obstruction; control or supervision, or one employed to carry out such; mark placed against items in list; cheque, or order to bank to pay money; term in chess to indicate that opponent's king must be moved or guarded; criss-cross pattern in cloth, etc.—v.t. restrain; hinder; chide or reprove; verify; mark against, in list; in chess, to put in check;—v.i. come to sudden stop; pause. — **checkers** n.pl. game of draughts.—**check'-key** n. latch-key.—**check'mate** n. final movement in chess, when king can be neither moved nor protected; complete defeat.—**luggage check,** ticket given to passenger depositing luggage.

checker (chek'-er) v.t. variegate with cross lines; diversify;—v.i. produce checkered effect, esp. of alternate light and shade;—n. square; pattern like chess-board; piece in game of checkers.

Cheddar (ched'-ar) n. kind of cheese.

cheek (chēk) n. fleshy wall or side of mouth; each side of face below eyes; insolence or impudence; side-post of door, window, etc.;—v.t. (Slang) speak saucily to.—**cheek'y** a. pert; insolent.

cheer (chēr) n. spirits; disposition; state of mind; gaiety; expression of approval, or encouragement, by shouting; rich food; welcome;—v.t. render cheerful; comfort; hearten; salute with cheers;—v.i. shout hurrah. — **cheer'er** n. — **cheer'ful** a. having good spirits.—**cheer'fully** adv.—**cheer'fulness** n.—**cheer'ily** adv. with cheerfulness.—**cheer'iness** n.—**cheer-io!** interj. informal salutation at parting.—**cheer'less** a.—**cheer'lessness** n.—**cheer'y** a.

cheese (chēz) n. curd of milk, separated from the whey, and pressed into solid mass; ball used in skittles.—**cheese'-cloth** n. thin loosely woven cotton cloth, for wrapping cheese in.—**cheese'-par'ing** a. parsimonious; scrimping.

cheetah (chē'-ta) n. hunting leopard of India.

chef (shef) n. head-cook.—**chef-d'oeuvre** (shā-devr') n. masterpiece, esp. in art or literature.

chemical (kem'-i-kal) a. pert. to, or made by, chemistry;—n. substance used in chemistry, or produced by chemical processes.—**chem'ically** adv.

chemise (shem-ēz') n. woman's shirt.—**chemisette** (shem-ē-zet') n. kind of bodice.

chemist (kem'-ist) n. person versed in chemistry; one permitted by law to sell medicines, drugs and poisons; druggist; apothecary.—**chem'istry** n.

chenille (she-nēl') n. soft plush-like cord of silk, wool, worsted, etc. used for ornamental trimmings, fringes, etc.; soft, velvety fabric used for hangings, curtains, covers, etc.

cheque, check (chek) n. specially printed form for use as money order on a banker.—**cheque-book** n. book of such forms.

chequer, chequered See **checker**.

cherish (cher'-ish) v.t. hold dear; treat tenderly; foster.

cheroot (sher-óót') n. kind of cigar, open at both ends.

cherry (cher'-i) n. bright red fruit of tree akin to plum; cherry-tree;—a. pert. to cherry; red.—**cherr'y-brand'y** n. liqueur made by steeping cherries in brandy.

cherub (cher'-ub) n. winged creature with human face; angel; celestial spirit; beautiful child;—pl. **cherubim** (cher'-óò-bim) or **cherubs** (cher'-ubz). —**cherubic** (cher-óò'-bik) a.

chess (ches) n. game of Eastern origin played by two persons on board containing sixty-four squares, with two differently coloured sets of pieces or 'men'.—**chess'man** n. piece used in game.

chest (chest) n. large box; coffer; trunk; trunk of human body; part enclosed by ribs and breast-bone; v.t. place in chest.—**chest'note** n. in singing, very low note.—**chest of drawers,** piece of furniture fitted with drawers.

chestnut (ches'-nut) n. fruit, seed, or nut of tree belonging to genus Castanea; tree itself, or its timber; reddish-brown colour; horse of this colour; (Colloq.) stale joke or story; —a. reddish-brown.

chevron (shev'-ron) n. rafter; (Her.) representation on shield of two bands meeting rafter-like; (Mil.) V-shaped band of braid or lace worn on sleeve to designate rank.

chew (chóò) v.t. bite and crush with the teeth; masticate; ruminate; champ;—n. action of chewing; quid of tobacco.—**chew'ing-gum** n. sweetmeat (usually flavoured with mint) prepared from chicle, gum of Mexican rubber-tree.—**to chew the cud,** chew regurgitated food; meditate.

Chianti (kē-an'-ti) n. Italian red or white wine.

chiaroscuro (kyà-ros-kóò'-rō) n. reproduction in art of effects of light and shade in nature.

chic (shēk) n. style and elegance; effectiveness;—a. stylish; modish.

chicane (shi-kān') n. trick or artifice; sharp practice, esp. in legal proceedings; (Cards) bridge hand with no trumps in it;—v.i. use shifts and trickery.—**chica'nery** n.

chick, chicken (chik, chikēn) n. young of fowls, esp. of hen; young child.—**chick'en-heart'ed** a. timid.—**chick'en-pox** n. mild, contagious, eruptive disease.—**chick'weed** n. weed with small white blossoms used for feeding cage-birds.

chicory (chik'-o-ri) n. plant whose taproot when roasted and ground is used to mix with coffee.

chide (chīd) v.t. scold; rebuke;—v.i. find fault;—pr.p. **chid'ing**.—pa.p. **chid,** **chid'den**.—pa.t. **chid**.

chief (chēf) a. foremost in importance; principal; main; at head; most influential;—n. head or leader; principal person or thing.—**chief'ly** adv. principally; for the most part. —**chief'tain** n. (fem. **chief'tainess**) head of clan; commander.—**chief'ship** n. **chief'taincy, chief'tainship** n. government over clan.

chiffon (shif'-on) n. thin, soft, gauzy material.—**chiffonier** (shif-on-ēr') n. ornamental cabinet, with drawers or shelves.

Chihuahua (chi-wa'-wa) n. small Mexican breed of dog.

chilblain (chil'-blān) n. blain, or inflammatory swelling caused by cold and bad circulation.

child (chīld) n. very young person of either sex; offspring; descendant;— pl. **chil'dren,** offspring, descendants. —**child'birth** n. act of bearing child; labour.—**child'bed** n. childbirth.—**child'hood** n. state of being child; time during which one is child.—**child'ish** a. pert. to child; silly; trifling.—**child'ishly** adv.— **child'ishness** n.—**child'less** a.—**child'lessness** n.—**child'like** a.

chill (chil) a. cold; tending to cause shivering; cool in manner or feeling; discouraging;—n. feeling of coldness, attended with shivering; illness caused by cold; discouragement;— v.t. cool; cause to shiver; benumb; keep meat cold;—v.i. grow cold.— **chill'y** a. cold; creating cold; depressing; ungenial.—**chill'iness** n.

chime (chīm) n. musical sound of bells; set of bells tuned to musical scale (generally used in the plural); —v.t. and i. sound harmoniously; be in harmony; agree with.

chimera, chimaera (ki-mē'-ra) n. fabulous, fire-breathing monster; creature of imagination.—**chimer'ic(al)** a.

chimney (chim'-ni) n. passage through which smoke of fireplace, etc., is carried off; deep, narrow cleft in rock.—**chim'ney-cor'ner** n. corner of fireplace; fireside.—**chim'ney-piece** n. mantelpiece.—**chim'ney-pot** n. pipe placed at top of chimney to create greater draught.—**chim'ney-stack** n. group of chimneys.

chimpanzee (chim'-pan-zē') n. large African anthropoid ape.

chin (chin) n. part of face below mouth.

china (chī'na) n. chinaware.—**chi'na-clay** n. finer kinds of pottery and porcelain clay, called kaolin.—**chi'naware** n. porcelain.—**Chi'nese-white** n. pigment composed of white oxide of zinc.

chinchilla (chin-chil'-a) n. small animal, with fine, soft fur; the fur; soft furred breed of rabbit.

chine (chīn) n. backbone; deep ravine; mountain ridge.

chink (chingk) n. small cleft, rent, or fissure; gap or crack;—v.t. open;—v.i. crack.

chink (chingk) n. sound of piece of metal when struck; ring of coin;—v.i. jingle; ring.

chintz (chintz) n. calico cloth, printed in different colours.

chip (chip) v.t. chop off into small pieces; break little pieces from; shape by cutting off pieces;—v.i. break or fly off in small pieces;—pr.p. **chip'-ping**;—pa.p. and pa.t. **chipped**;—n. piece of wood, etc. separated from larger body by axe, etc.; fragment; counter, instead of money, used in gambling, esp. at poker.—**chips** n.pl. fried slices of potato; (Naut.) ship's carpenter.—**chip'board** n. board made from compressed mixture of wood-waste and resin.—**chip'-shot** n. (Golf) short, lofted shot on to the green.

chipmunk (chip'-mungk) n. American burrowing ground-squirrel or striped gopher. Also **chip'muck**.

chippendale (chip'-pen-dāl) n. style of furniture introduced by 18th cent. cabinet-maker, Thomas Chip-pendale.

chiro- (kī'-ro) prefix Gk. cheir, the hand, forming derivatives.

chiropodist (kī-rop'-ō-dist) n. one skilled in treatment of disease of hands and feet.—**chirop'ody** n.

chirp, chirrup (cherp, chir'-up) n. short, sharp note, as of bird or cricket;—v.i. make such sound; twitter; talk gaily.—**chirp'er** n.—**chirp'ingly** adv. gaily.—**chirp'y** a. lively; cheerful.

chisel (chiz'-el) n. tool sharpened to cutting edge at the end, used in carpentry, sculpture, etc.;—v.t. cut or carve with this tool;—pr.p. **chis'-elling**;—pa.p. and pa.t. **chis'elled**.

chit (chit) n. informal note; voucher; permit or pass. Also **chit'ty**.

chit-chat (chit'-chat) n. prattle; trivial talk; gossip.

chitterlings (chit'-er-lings) n.pl. smaller intestines of swine, etc., used as food.

chivalry (shiv'-al-ri) n. system of knighthood in medieval times; body of knights; qualities of knight, viz. dignity, courtesy, bravery, generosity, gallantry.—**chival'ric, chiv'alrous** a.—**chiv'alrously** adv.

chive (chīv) n. herb of onion kind.

chivvy, chivy (chiv'-i) v.t. chase; harass; worry; tease.

chlor-, chloro- (klōr-, klō'-rō) combining forms fr. Gk. chloros, green.

chlorine (klō'-rēn) n. heavy gas of yellowish-green colour used in disinfecting, bleaching, and poison-gas warfare.—**chlo'ral** n. sleep-producing drug.—**chlo'rate** n. salt of chloric acid.—**chlo'ric** a. pert. to chlorine.—**chlo'ride** n. compound of chlorine with another element.—**chlo'rinate** v.t. disinfect or bleach, with chlorine.—**chlorina'tion** n.—**chlo'rite** n. mineral of green colour, soft and friable.—**chlo'roform** n. colourless, volatile liquid used as anaesthetic;—v.t. make insensible by using chloroform.

chlorodyne (klōr-ō-din) n. proprietary medicine used as narcotic and anodyne.

chlorophyll (klō'-rō-fil) n. (Bot.) green colouring matter of plants.

chock (chok) n. wedge to steady cask lying on its side;—v.t. make fast, with block or wedge.—**chock'-full, choke'full, chock'-a-block** a. packed full; jammed together.

chocolate (chok'-ō-lāt) n. paste made from powdered seeds of cacao plant, mixed with sugar, etc.; beverage made from this.—a. dark-brown.

choice (chois) n. act of choosing; power or opportunity of choosing; selection; thing chosen; alternative.—a. worthy of being chosen; rare.

choir (kwīr) n. company of singers, esp. belonging to church; part of church set aside for them; chancel.—**choir'-screen** n. screen dividing chancel from nave.

choke (chōk) v.t. stop the breath as by compression of windpipe; stifle or smother;—v.i. have wind-pipe stopped; be suffocated.—**chok'er** n. one who chokes; (Colloq.) high collar or cravat.

choke (chōk) n. act of choking; obstructing piece in mechanism.

choler (kol'-er) n. bile; anger; wrath.—**chol'eric** a.—**cho'lera** n. deadly, epidemic, bilious disease.

choose (chōōz) v.t. pick out; select; take one thing in preference to another;—v.i. decide; think fit.—pa.p. **cho'sen**; pa.t. **chose**.—**choo'sey** a. (Slang) fastidious.

chop (chop) v.t. cut into pieces;—v.i. make quick stroke or repeated strokes with sharp instrument, as axe;—n. act of chopping; piece chopped off; thick slice of meat attached to rib or other bone; cutlet.—pr.p. chop'ping.—pa.p. and pa.t. chopped.—chop'per n.,—chop'py a. of the sea, having small broken waves.—chop'-stick n. one of two small sticks of wood, ivory, etc. used by Chinese in taking food.

chop (chop) v.t. barter; exchange;—v.i. shift suddenly, as wind.—to chop and change, be inconstant.

chop (chop) n. jaw or chap, esp. of beasts.

choral (ko'-ral) a. pert or belonging to choir or chorus.—cho'rally adv.—chorister (kor'-ist-er) n. member of choir.

chorale (ko-räl') n. simple, dignified melody sung to religious words.

chord (kord) n. (Mus.) series of tones having harmonic relation to each other, and sounded simultaneously; (Geom.) straight line between two points in circumference of circle.

chore (chōr) n. any odd job, or occasional piece of house-work.

chorea (ko-rē'-a) n. (Med.) uncontrollable spasms of limbs, body and facial muscles; St. Vitus's dance.

choreographer (ko'-rē-o-graf-er) n. designer of ballet.—choreograph'ic a.—choreog'raphy n.

chortle (chor'-tl) v.i. chuckle gleefully.—chort'ling n.

chorus (kō'-rus) n. orig. band of singers and dancers; combination of voices singing together; what is sung or spoken by the chorus; in Greek play, certain performers who witness the action, and at intervals express their feelings regarding it; refrain;—v.t. join in refrain; call out or sing together.—cho'ric a. pert. to chorus.

chose (chōz) pa.t. of choose.—chosen (chō'-zn) pa.p. of same verb.—the Chosen People, Jews.

Christ (krist) n. the Anointed—name given to the Saviour, and synonymous with the Hebrew Messiah.—Christ'hood n. condition of being the Christ.—Christ'liness n.—Christ'like a.

christen (kris'-n) v.t. baptise in name of Christ; give name to.—Chris'tendom n. all Christian countries; whole body of Christians.—chris'tening n. baptism.

Christian (krist'-yan) n. follower or disciple of Christ; professed adherent of Church of Christ;—a. pert. to Christ or his religion.—chris'tianise v.t. make Christian; convert to Christianity.—Christian'ity n. religion of followers of Christ.—Chris'tianlike, Chris'tianly a. in Christian manner.—Christian era, era counting from birth of Christ.—Christian name, name given at baptism; individual name, as opposed to surname or family name.—Christian Science, religious doctrine of faith-healing founded in America by Mrs. Mary Eddy.

Christmas (kris'-mas) annual festival in celebration of birth of Christ, observed on Dec. 25; Christmasday;—a. belonging to Christmas or its festivities.—Christ'mas-box n. box for Christmas presents; Christmas gift.—Christ'mas-card n. card, sent to friends at Christmas as token of remembrance.—Christmas carol, religious hymn of joy in praise of Christ's Nativity.—Christ'mas-Eve n. evening of 24th December.—Christ'-mas rose n. Black Hellebore.

chroma-, chromo- (krō'-ma-, krō'-mō-), combining forms fr. Gk. chroma, colour.

chromatic (krō-mat'-ik) a. pert. to colour; (Mus.) proceeding by semitones.

chrome, chromium (krōm, krō'-mi-um) n. metal, very resistant to corrosion, used generally for plating other metals.—chro'mate n. salt of chromic acid.—chro'mite n. mineral, chief source of chromium.—chrome colour, yellow prepared from chromium salt.

chromosome (krō'-mo-sōm) n. (Biol.) one of the gene-carrying bodies in the tissue of a cell.

chronic (kron'-ik) a. continuing for long time; of disease, deep-seated and lasting; inveterate; (Slang) bad; terrible.—chron'ically adv.

chronicle (kron'-i-kl) n. register of events in order of time; history or accounts;—v.t. record in order of time.—chron'icler n.

chrono- (kron'-o) Gk. chronos, time.—chron'ograph n. instrument for measuring and recording time very exactly.—chronol'ogy n. science that treats of historical dates and arranges them in order; table of events and dates.—chronol'oger, chronol'ogist n.—chron-olog'ical a. arranged in order of time.—chronolog'ically adv.—chronom'eter n. very accurate watch or time-keeper.—chronomet'ric, chronomet'rical a.—chronom'etry n.

chrysalis (kris'-a-lis) n. inactive pupal stage of insect, esp. butterfly or moth.—pl. chrysalides (kris-al'-i-dēz).—chrys'alid n. chrysalis.

chrysanthemum (kris-an'-the-mum) n. large, mop-headed, garden flower.

chryso- (kris'-o) combining form fr. Gk. chrusos, gold.

chub (chub) n. fresh-water fish of carp family, small and fat.—chub'by a. round and plump.—chub'biness n.

chuck (chuk) v.i. cluck, as hen calling her chickens; tap under chin;—n. call of hen; term of endearment.

chuck (chuk) v.t. (Colloq.) throw; toss;

pitch; stop;—*n.* act of tossing.—
chuck it! (*Slang*) stop! leave me in
peace.—**chuck'er-out** *n.* one employed
to eject obstreperous people.

chuck (chuk) *n.* in machinery, part
of lathe for holding piece of work.

chuckle (chuk'-l) *v.i.* laugh in
suppressed manner;—*n.* short, quiet
laugh; call of hen.

chug (chug) *n.* pull or tug; explosive
sound made by car exhaust or railway engine;—*v.i.* pull or tug; make
explosive sound as above.

chum (chum) *n.* intimate friend;
pal; room-mate;—*v.i.* be friendly
(with); share room with;—*pr.p.*
chum'ming;—*pa.p.* and *pa.t.* **chum-
med.**—**chum'my** *a.* friendly.

chump (chump) *n.* lump of wood;
thick end of loin of mutton; (*Slang*)
head; blockhead.

chunk (chungk) *n.* short, thick piece
of wood, etc.—**chunk'y** *a.*

church (church) *n.* building for
Christian worship; collective body
of Christians; denomination or sect
of Christian religion; clergy; church
service.—**churchwar'den** *n.* officer
entrusted with interests of church or
parish; long clay-pipe.—**church'yard**
n. ground adjoining church, generally
used as burial ground.

churl (churl) *n.* countryman; surly
clown.—**churl'ish** *a.*—**churl'ishly** *adv.*
—**churl'ishness** *n.*

churn (churn) *n.* vessel in which
cream is violently stirred to produce
butter; large milk-can;—*v.i.* agitate
cream so as to produce butter; stir
up violently;—*v.i.* produce butter.

chute (shoot) *n.* rapid descent in a
river; rapid; sloping contrivance for
transferring coal, rubbish, etc. to
lower level.

chutney (chut'-ne) *n.* E. Indian condiment, generally made with man-
goes, peppers and spices.

cicada, cicala (si-ka'-da, si-ka'-la)
n. insect, male of which emits
shrill, chirping sound.

cicatrice, cicatrix (sik'-a-tris, sik-
a'-triks) *n.* scar left after healed
wound; — *pl.* **cicatri'ces.** — **cicatrise**
(sik'-a-triz) *v.t.* heal.

cider, cyder (si'-der) *n.* drink made
from fermented juice of apples.

cigar (si-gar') *n.* tobacco-leaf made
up in roll for smoking.—**cigarette'** *n.*
finely cut tobacco rolled in thin
paper.

cinch (sinch) *n.* saddle-girth; (*Slang*)
certainty;—*v.t.* fasten cinch round;
tighten (girth).

cinder (sin'-der) *n.* remains of
burned coal; partially burned combustible substance.

cinema (sin'-e-ma) *n.* hall or theatre
where moving pictures are screened;
picture house.—**cinemat'ograph** *n.*
instrument by which moving pic-

tures are projected.—**cinematograph'-
ic** *a.*—**cinematog'raphy** *n.* art of
filming.—**cin'e-cam'era** *n.* camera for
taking successive pictures of scenes
involving movement.

cinerary (sin'-e-ra-ri) *a.* pert. to
ashes; made to hold ashes.—
cinera'tion *n.* reducing to ashes;
incineration.

cinnabar (sin'-a-bar) *n.* red sulphide
of mercury used as pigment; vermilion;—*a.* vermilion coloured.

cinnamon (sin'-a-mon) *n.* inner bark
of laurel tree of Ceylon; aromatic
substance obtained from bark;—*n.*
and *a.* light-brown colour.

cinque (singk) *n.* representation, by
five spots, of figure 5 upon dice or
cards. — **cinque'foil** *n.* five-bladed
clover. — **Cinque ports**, Hastings, Rom-
ney, Hythe, Dover, Sandwich.

cipher, cypher (si'-fer) *n.* arithmetical symbol 0; any figure; person of no
account; secret writing; code; key
to code;—*v.i.* write in cipher; work
at arithmetic.

circa (sir'-ka) *prep.* about; around;
approximately;—(*abbrev.*)**circ., ca., c.**

circle (ser'-kl) *n.* plane figure bounded by single curved line called its
circumference, every point of which
is equally distant from point within
called the centre; curved line that
bounds such figure; circumference;
round body; sphere; orb; ring;
company associated with person;
society group; club or group, esp.
literary; never-ending series;—*v.t.*
move or revolve round; encompass,
as by circle; surround;—*v.i.* move in
circle.—**dress circle**, first gallery in
theatre (formerly reserved for those
in evening dress).

circuit (ser'-kit) *n.* act of moving
round; space enclosed within fixed
limit; area; (*Law*) round made by
judges, holding assizes; district thus
visited; path of electric current.—
circuitous (ser-ku'-i-tus) *a.* round
about.—**circu'itously** *adv.*

circular (ser'-ku-lar) *a.* in form
of circle; round; moving in circle;
roundabout; addressed to circle of
people;—*n.* notice sent out in
quantities. — **cir'cularly** *adv.* — **circular'ity** *n.*—**cir'cularise** *v.t.* send
circulars to.

circulate (ser'-ku-lat) *v.t.* cause to
pass round as in circle; spread
abroad;—*v.i.* move round and
return to same point; be spread
abroad.—**circula'tion** *n.* act of moving
round; flow of blood from, and back
to, the heart; extent of sale of
newspaper, etc.; money circulating
in country; currency.—**cir'culative,
cir'culatory** *a.* circulating.—**cir'culator**
n.—**circulating library**, library from
which books are lent out to the
public, or to subscribers.

circum- (sẽr'-kum) *prefix* fr. Latin meaning *round, about,* combining to form derivatives.—**circumam'bient** *a.* surrounding; enclosing.—**circumam'biency** *n.* environment.—**circumam'bulate** *v.t.* and *i.* walk round or about.

circumcise (sẽr'-kum-sīz) *v.t.* cut off the foreskin.—**circumcision** (sẽr-kum-sizh'-un) *n.*

circumference (sẽr-kum'-fer-ens) *n.* line that bounds circle; distance round; area.—**circumferen'tial** *a.*

circumflex (sẽr'-kum-fleks) *n.* accent mark (∧) placed over French vowel to denote length, contraction, etc.

circumlocution (sẽr-kum-lō-kū'-shun) *n.* roundabout way of speaking.—**circumloc'utory** *a.*

circumnavigate (sẽr-kum-nav'-i-gāt) *v.t.* sail round.—**circumnav'igable** *a.* capable of being sailed round.—**circumnaviga'tion** *n.*—**circumnav'igator** *n.* one who sails round, esp. the world.

circumscribe (sẽr-kum-skrīb') *v.t.* draw circle round; enclose within limits; confine; define.—**circumscription** (sẽr-kum-skrip'-shun) *n.* limitation.—**circumscrip'tive** *a.* confined or limited in space.

circumspect (sẽr-kum-spekt) *a.* watchful on all sides; prudent; discreet.—**cir'cumspectly** *adv.*—**circumspec'tion** *n.* caution; prudence; discretion; tact.—**circumspec'tive** *a.* cautious.

circumstance (sẽr'-kum-stans) *n.* particular fact, event, or case;—*v.t.* place in particular situation.—**cir'cumstances** *n.pl.* condition as to pecuniary resources; situation; details.—**circumstantial** (sẽr-kum-stan'-shal) *a.* accidental; not essential; full of details.—**circumstan'tially** *adv.* —**circumstan'tiate** *v.t.* detail exactly.—**circumstantial evidence,** evidence inferred from circumstances.

circumvent (sẽr-kum-vent') *v.t.* get around by stratagem; outwit; cheat.—**circumven'tion** *n.*—**circumven'tive** *a.*

circus (sẽr'-kus) *n.* circular enclosure for games, feats of horsemanship, etc.; the performance itself; ring or arena; circular area at intersection of streets.

cirrhosis (si-rō'-sis) *n.* (*Med.*) hardening and tawny-coloured enlargement of liver.—**cirrhot'ic** *a.*

cirrus (sir'-us) *n.* tendril; curled filament; lofty, fleecy cloud;—*pl.* **cirri** (sir'-ī).

cis- (sis) *prefix.* L. meaning 'on this side.'—**cisalp'ine** *a.* on this (Roman) side of Alps.

cistern (sis'-tẽrn) *n.* large tank for holding water; reservoir.

citadel (sit'-a-del) *n.* fortress or castle in or near city.

cite (sīt) *v.t.* summon; quote; name; bring forward as proof.—**cit'al** *n.*

summons.—**cita'tion** *n.* official notice to appear; act of quoting; passage or words quoted.—**cita'tor** *n.* one who cites.—**cit'atory** *a.*

citizen (sit'-i-zn) *n.* inhabitant of city; freeman; townsman; member of state;—*a.* having character of citizen.—**cit'izenship** *n.* state of being citizen; rights and duties of citizen.

citron (sit'-ron) *n.* acidulous fruit of citron-tree, resembling lemon; tree itself.—**cit'rate** *n.* salt of citric acid. —**cit'ric** *a.* extracted from citron, lemon, etc.—**cit'rus** *n.* citron-tree.—**citrus fruits,** citrons, lemons, limes, oranges, etc.

city (sit'-i) *n.* large town; corporate town; business or shopping centre of town; town that is, or has been, seat of bishop;—*a.* pert. to city.

civet (siv'-et) *n.* perfume, with strong musk-like smell.—**civ'et-cat** *n.* animal, yielding this perfume.

civic (siv'-ik) *a.* pert. to city or citizen.—**civ'ics** *n.pl.* study of good citizenship.

civil (siv'-il) *a.* pert. to city, state, or citizen; lay, as opposed to military, etc.; polite.—**civ'illy** *adv.*—**civilian** (si-vil'-yan) *n.* orig. one versed in Civil Law; one whose employment is non-military;—*a.* pert. to civilian life (e.g. civilian dress).—**civil'ity** *n.* courtesy; politeness;—*pl.* acts of politeness.—**civ'ism** *n.* good citizenship.—**civil engineer,** one who plans railways, canals, roads, etc.—**Civil Service,** collective name for non-military servants of the Crown.—**civil war,** war between citizens of same country.

civilise (siv'-il-īz) *v.t.* reclaim from savage state; refine; enlighten.—**civilisa'tion** *n.* act of civilising, or state of being civilised.

clad (klad) *pa.p.* and *pa.t.* of **clothe**; —*a.* clothed.

claim (klām) *v.t.* demand as right, or as due; call for; need;—*n.* demand of right or supposed right; title; thing claimed.—**claim'ant** *n.* one who claims.—**claim'-jump'er** *n.* one who seizes piece of land marked out by settler or miner.

clairvoyance (klār-voi'-ans) *n.* power of seeing things not normally perceptible to senses; second sight. —**clairvoy'ant** *n.* one who claims power of clairvoyance. Also *a.*

clam (klam) *n.* edible bivalve shell-fish having faculty of closing its shell like vice.

clam (klam) *v.t.* clog with sticky matter;—*v.i.* be moist or sticky.—**clam'my** *a.* sticky; moist and adhesive; cold and damp.—**clam'miness** *n.*

clamant (klam'-ant) *a.* crying insistently; calling loudly; demanding notice; urgent.—**clam'ancy** *n.*

clamber (klam'-ber) v.i. climb with difficulty, holding on with hands.

clamour (klam'-ur) n. loud shouting; tumult; outcry; uproar;—v.i. shout loudly; utter loud complaints or demands.—**clam'orous** a. vociferous; turbulent.

clamp (klamp) n. appliance with parts brought together by screw for holding anything; brace;—v.t. render firm by a clamp.

clan (klan) n. tribe bearing same surname, united under chieftain; set or clique of persons having common interest.—**clan'nish** a. disposed to associate only with members of same sect or clique.—**clan'nishly** adv.—**clan'nishness** n.

clandestine (klan-des'-tin) a. hidden; secret, and contrary to law, morals, etc.—**clandes'tinely** adv.—**clandes'tineness** n.

clang (klang) v.t. strike with ringing, metallic sound;—v.i. give forth ringing, metallic sound;—n. sharp, ringing sound.—**clang'ing** n. clang.

clangour (klang'-gur, klang'-ur) n. loud, harsh, ringing sound.—**clang'orous** a.—**clang'orously** adv.

clank (klangk) n. brief, ringing sound;—v.t. and i. produce sharp, ringing sound.

clap (klap) v.t. bring together with clap; strike hands together in approval; slap;—v.i. strike hands together in applause;—n. sudden, sharp noise caused by impact; applause; slap or pat;—pr.p. **clap'ping**.—pa.p. and pat.t. **clapped**.—**clap'per** n. one who claps; tongue of bell.—**clap'-trap** n. in speech-making, tricks to win applause.

claque (klak) n. section of audience hired to applaud.

claret (klar'-et) n. any red Bordeaux wine.—a. purplish-red.—**clar'et-cup** n. drink composed of claret, lemon, ice and flavourings.

clarify (klar'-i-fī) v.t. make clear or pure; explain or clear up; remove possibility of error;—v.i. become clear.—**clarifica'tion** n.—**clar'ity** n. clearness; lucidity of mind.

clarion (klar'-i-on) n. trumpet with shrill piercing note; its sound.—**clar'inet**, **clar'ionet** n. wood-wind instrument.—**clar'inet'tist** n.

clash (klash) v.t. strike noisily together;—v.i. dash noisily together; collide; conflict; disagree.

clasp (klasp, klȧsp) v.t. shut or fasten together with catch or hook; embrace; grasp; surround and cling to;—n. catch or hook for fastening; close embrace; grasping of hand; (Mil.) bar on medal-ribbon.—**clasp'-knife** n. knife whose blade folds into handle.

class (klas) n. order or division or grouping of persons or things, possessing same characteristics or status; group of pupils or students taught together; grouping of plants or animals; rank or standing in society;—v.t. arrange in classes; rank together;—v.i. rank.—**class'-able**, **class'ible** a.—**class'y** a. (Colloq.) high-class.—**class war**, hostility between classes of society.

classic (klas'-ik) n. work, writer of recognised worth; ancient Latin or Greek writer or book;—a. of model excellence in music, literature or art.—**class'ics** n.pl. study of ancient Latin or Greek.—**class'ical** a. pert. to classics; not Romantic in style; conforming with tradition.—**class'ically** adv.—**classical'ity**, **class'icalness** n.—**classicism** (klas'-i-sizm) n.—**class'icist** n.

classify (klas'-i-fī) v.t. arrange in classes; put into class.—**classifi'able** a.—**classifica'tion** n.

clatter (klat'-er) v.t. strike and so make rattling noise;—v.i. make rattling sounds; prattle; talk rapidly and idly;—n. repeated rattling noise; noisy and idle talk.

clause (klawz) n. (Gram.) sentence; subordinate part of sentence; (Law) article or distinct portion of document, contract, etc.; paragraph; subdivision.

claustrophobia (klaws-trō-fō'-bi-ạ) n. (Med.) morbid dread of confined spaces.

clave (klāv) pa.t. of **cleave**.

clavichord (kla'-vi-kord) n. (Mus.) early keyboard instrument on which strings were struck by metal tangents.

clavier (kla'-vēr) n. (Mus.) stringed musical instrument with keyboard.

claw (klaw) n. sharp, hooked nail, as of beast or bird; foot of animal armed with hooked nails; anything like this;—v.t. pull, tear, or scratch with claws or nails; grasp.

clay (klā) n. soft earth, consisting of alumina and silica, with water; earth in general; human body; corpse; tobacco-pipe, made of baked clay.—**clayey** (klā'-i) a. consisting of clay; like clay.

claymore (klā'-mōr) n. large, two-handed sword, formerly used by Scottish Highlanders; basket-hilted broadsword.

clean (klēn) a. free from dirt, stain, or any defilement; pure; guiltless;—v.t. free from dirt; purify;—adv. so as to leave no dirt; quite; entirely.—**clean'er** n. one who, or that which, cleans.—**cleanliness** (klen'-li-nes) n. freedom from dirt; purity.—**cleanly** (klen'-li) a. habitually clean in person and habits; pure.—**cleanly** (klĕn'-li) adv. in clean manner; neatly.—**cleanness** (klĕn-nes) n.—**clean'-cut** a. well-shaped; definite.—

to make a clean breast of (*Fig.*) make full confession; reveal everything.— **to make a clean sweep** (*Fig.*) get rid of completely.

cleanse (klenz) *v.t.* make clean; make pure; purify; wash away; purge.— **cleans'er** *n.* one who, or that which, cleanses.

clear (klēr) *a.* bright; free from cloud; undimmed; pure; free from obstruction; plain; distinct; manifest; without defect or drawback; transparent;—*adv.* clearly; wholly; —*v.t.* make bright or clear; make evident; free from accusation; acquit; pass over or through; cleanse; empty; make as profit; free by payment of dues; settle debt; free fom difficulty, obstruction, suspicion, etc.;—*v.i.* become clear, bright, transparent, free; (*Naut.*) leave port.—**clear'age** *n.* clearance.— **clear'ance** *n.* act of clearing; certificate that ship has been cleared at custom-house; in machinery, distance by which one part is clear of another.—**clear'ing** *n.* tract of land cleared of wood for cultivation.— **clear'ly** *adv.*—**clear'ness** *n.*—**clear'-cut** *a.* sharply defined.—**clear'eyed, clear'-see'ing, clear'-sight'ed** *a.* having acuteness of sight or intellect.—**clear'head'ed** *a.* sagacious.—**clear'ing-sta'tion** *n.* (*War*) place from which wounded are removed.—**clear'way** *n.* section of road on which vehicles are forbidden to stop.—**to clear off,** depart.—**to clear out,** remove encumbrances; (*Colloq.*) depart without further ado.

cleat (klēt) *n.* wedge; (*Naut.*) piece of wood or iron with two projecting ends, round which ropes are belayed or fastened; porcelain insulator.

cleave (klēv) *v.t.* split asunder; cut in two;—*v.i.* fall apart; split; open; crack asunder;—*pa.p.* clov'en or cleft.—*pa.t.* clove or cleft.—**cleav'age** *n.* of rocks, quality of splitting naturally; (*Fig.*) separation due to difference of opinions, etc.; rupture. —**cleav'er** *n.* one who, or that which, cleaves; butcher's chopper.

cleave (klēv) *v.i.* adhere closely; stick; agree; be faithful to;—*pa.p.* and *pa.t.* cleaved or clave.

clef (klef) *n.* (*Mus.*) sign used to indicate pitch.

cleft (kleft) *pa.p.* and *pa.t.* of verb cleave;—*n.* fissure or split; chasm; chink of notes on stave.

clematis (klem'-a-tis) *n.* climbing-plant; also called Traveller's Joy, and Virgin's Bower.

clemency (klem'-en-si) *n.* leniency; mildness; gentleness; mercy;—**clem'ent** *a.* mild; compassionate.

clench, clinch (klensh, klinsh) *v.t.* grasp firmly; close together tightly (hands, teeth); confirm (bargain);—

n. firm closing; decisive proof; firm grip.—**clench'er** *n.* unanswerable argument.

clerestory (klēr'-stō-ri) *n.* upper part of central nave of churches, which rises clear of other buildings and has its own row of windows. Also **clear'story.**

clergy (klēr'-ji) *n.* body of men ordained for the services of the Christian Church; clerical order. —**cler'gyman** *n.* one of the clergy; minister.

cleric (kler'-ik) *n.* clerk or clergyman; —*a.* clerical.—**cler'ical** *a.* belonging to clergy; pert. to clerk or copyist.

clerk (klárk, klerk) *n.* one employed to do correspondence, keep accounts, etc. in office; clergyman; scholar; (*U.S.*) shop assistant;—*v.i.* act as clerk or secretary.—**clerk'ess** *n.* woman-clerk or secretary.—**clerk'ly** *a.* scholar-like.

clever (klev'-er) *a.* able; skilful; ingenious; intelligent.—**clev'erly** *adv.* —**clev'erness** *n.* intelligence.

cliché (klē'-shā) *n.* electrotype or stereotype plate; photographic negative; stereotyped or hackneyed phrase.

click (klik) *n.* slight, short sound, as of latch in door;—*v.i.* make such sound; (*Slang*) to be successful, esp. in striking up acquaintance with one of opposite sex.

client (klī'-ent) *n.* one who employs another (esp. lawyer) professionally as his agent; customer; in ancient times dependent.—**clientele** (klī'-entel, klē-ong-tel') *n.* clients or customers collectively.

cliff (klif) *n.* high rock-face; sheer side of mountain.—**clift** *n.* cleft or break in cliff.

climacteric (klī-mak'-te-rik) *n.* period in human life in which change takes place in the constitution; menopause; critical period;—*a.* pert. to climacteric; critical.

climate (klī'-māt) *n.* general atmospherical conditions (temperature, moisture, etc.) of country or region; (*Fig.*) prevailing trend or condition.—**climat'ic** *a.*—**climat'ical** *a.* climatic.

climax (klī'-maks) *n.* arrangement of words, phrases, etc. such that they rise in rhetorical force and impressiveness; acme; point of greatest tension in play, story, etc.— **climac'tic** *a.* pert. to climax.

climb (klīm) *v.t.* and *i.* go up, ascend (as hill, tree, etc.); grow upward as plant by tendrils; rise in social scale; slope upward;—*n.* going up; ascent.—**climb'er** *n.*

clime (klīm) *n.* region or country; (*Poet.*) climate.

clinch (klinsh) *v.t.* and *i.* grapple or struggle at close quarters in wrestling or boxing; fasten with rivet; (*Fig.*) settle or conclude, as agreement;—*n.* close holding in wrestling or boxing; rivet.

cling (kling) *v.i.* adhere or stick close to; be attached firmly to;—*pa.p.* and *pa.t.* **clung.**

clinic, (klin'-ik) *n.* teaching of medical subjects at the bedside; institution where patients attend for treatment, which is also teaching centre.—**clin'ical** *a.* pert. to clinic; objective.

clink (klingk) *n.* sharp, tinkling sound.

clink (klingk) *n.* (*Slang*) prison.

clinker (kling'-ker) *n.* mass of fused cinders from furnaces; kind of brick.

clinker-built (kling'-ker) *a.* of boats, made of overlapping planks.

clip (klip) *v.t.* clutch tightly;—*n.* device for grasping or holding thing firmly.

clip (klip) *v.t.* cut with scissors or shears; prune or cut short; shear sheep; pare edge of a coin; shorten or slur words;—*v.i.* move quickly,— *n.* act of clipping; season's shearing of wool; rapid pace; (*Colloq.*) sharp blow;—*pr.p.* **clip'ping.**—*pa.p.* and *pa.t.* **clipped.**—**clip'per** *n.* one who clips; fast sailing-vessel, with long sharp bow.—**clip'pers** *n.* two-bladed instrument for cutting hair, shearing sheep, etc.—**clip'pie** *n.* (*Colloq.*) conductress of bus or tram.

clique (klēk) *n.* narrow circle of persons with common interests; coterie.—**cliqu'ish** *a.*—**cliqu'ishness** *n.*

cloak (klōk) *n.* long, loose, outer garment; something that conceals; pretext;—*v.t.* cover with cloak; hide; mask or dissemble.—**cloak'-room** *n.* room where coats, hats, etc. may be temporarily left; lavatory.

cloche (klosh) *n.* glass covering used for intensive cultivation of vegetables, etc.; close-fitting bell-shaped hat worn by women.

clock (klok) *n.* device which measures time.—**clock'-wise** *adv.* in direction of hands of clock; circling to right.—**an'ti-clock'wise,** *adv.* circling to left.—**clock'work** *n.* movements or machinery of clock; regular movement as of clock;—*a.* mechanically regular.—**o'clock,** by the clock.— **to clock in, to clock out,** in factory, office, etc., register time of arrival and departure.

clod (klod) *n.* lump of earth, clay, or turf; sod; earth; dull, stupid fellow. —**clod'hopper** *n.* rustic; boor.

clog (klog) *n.* strong, clumsy shoe with thick wooden sole; block of wood attached to animal's leg to prevent it from straying; impediment; obstruction;—*v.t.* hinder; encumber; choke up;—*v.i.* become choked, encumbered; adhere.

cloister (klois'-ter) *n.* covered arcade running along one or more walls of inner court of monastery or college; monastery or nunnery; secluded spot;—*v.t.* confine in cloister or within walls.—**clois'teral, clois'tral** *a.*

close (klōz) *v.t.* shut; stop up; finish; conclude; complete (electric circuit); —*v.i.* come together; unite; end.— **clos'ing** *a.* ending;—*n.* act of shutting; end; conclusion.—**closure** (klōz'-ūr) *n.* act of shutting; closing; close of debate.—**closed circuit** (*T.V.*) installation in which camera is connected directly with receivers for operation within restricted area.— **closed shop,** establishment in which all employees have to be members of trade union.

close (klōs) *a.* shut up; confined; tight; stifling; unventilated; near at hand; secret; niggardly; familiar; intimate; compact; crowded; searching;—*adv.* in close manner or state; nearly; tightly;—*n.* enclosed place; precinct of cathedral; narrow passage leading from street; small field or paddock; courtyard.—**close'ly** *adv.* —**close'ness** *n.*—**close by,** little distant. —**close call,** very narrow escape.— **close'-fist'ed** or **close'-hand'ed** *a.* miserly; niggardly; penurious.—**close'-hauled** *a.* (*Naut.*) kept as near as possible to point from which wind blows.—**a close shave,** very narrow escape.—**close'-up** *n.* close view of anything.—**(to sail) close to the wind,** keep as near against wind as it is possible to sail; court disaster, esp. financially.

closet (klo'-zet) *n.* small private room; lavatory; water-closet;—*v.t.* take into private room for consultation.

clot (klot) *n.* soft mass or lump; (*Med.*) coagulated mass of blood; (*Colloq.*) stupid person;—*v.t.* form into clots; —*v.i.* coagulate;—*pr.p.* **clot'ting.**— *pa.p.* and *pa.t.* **clot'ted.**

cloth (kloth) *n.* woven fabric, esp. of wool or hair; dress of profession, e.g. clerical; cover for table; duster.

clothe (klōTH) *v.t.* put garments on; cover as with garment; furnish with raiment; (*Fig.*) surround with; wrap up in;—*pr.p.* **cloth'ing.**—*pa.p.* and *pa.t.* **clothed** or **clad.**—**clothes** *n.pl.* garments; wearing apparel; short for bedclothes, i.e. sheets, blankets, etc.—**clothier** *n.* one who makes, or sells, clothes; tailor; outfitter.— **cloth'ing** *n.* garments in general; dress.—**clothes'-horse** *n.* frame for hanging clothes on to dry indoors.— **clothes'-peg** or **-pin** *n.* forked wooden peg for fastening clothes on line to dry.

cloud (kloud) *n.* body of visible vapour floating in atmosphere; mass of smoke, flying dust, etc.; that which has dark, threatening aspect; state of obscurity or impending trouble; great multitude;—v.t. overspread with clouds; darken; sadden; defame;—v.i. grow cloudy; be blurred.—cloud'y a. darkened with clouds; overcast; hazy; dim; blurred; indistinct; gloomy.—cloud'ily adv.—cloud'iness n.—cloud'burst n. violent downpour of rain; deluge.—in the clouds (Fig.) unreal; absent-minded; dreamy.—to be under a cloud, be under suspicion; be in temporary disgrace.

clout (klout) n. piece of cloth used for patch; rag; piece of old cloth used for cleaning, scouring, etc.; centre of butt at which archers shoot; slap or blow; short nail with large head (used for studding boots);—v.t. patch; join in clumsy manner; to strike with open hand.

clove (klōv) n. flower-bud of clove-tree, used as spice; also yields oil.

clove (klōv) pa.t. of cleave.

clove-hitch (klōv'-hich) n. (Naut.) hitch used to secure rope round a spar.

cloven (klōv'-n) pa.p. of cleave. Also a. split; divided into two parts.—clov'en-foot'ed (-hoofed) a. having foot (hoof) divided into two parts.

clover (klō'-ver) n. common field plant of trefoil family, used for fodder.—to be in clover, live in luxury.

clown (kloun) n. peasant or rustic; ill-bred man; boor; fool or buffoon in play or circus;—v.i. play fool; behave like a fool.—clown'ish a. like a clown; loutish; awkward.—clown'ishly adv.—clown'ishness n.

cloy (kloi) v.t. induce sensation of loathing by overmuch of anything, esp. of sweetness, sentimentality, or flattery; satiate, glut, or surfeit.—cloy'ing a. satiating; disgusting.

club (klub) n. heavy stick, thickening towards one end, used as weapon; cudgel; stick used in game of golf; association of people united in pursuance of common interest; premises in which such association meets;—v.t. beat with club; gather into club;—v.i. form club; unite for common end; pay shares in common expense;—pr.p. club'bing.—pa.p. and pa.t. clubbed.—club'-foot n. congenitally deformed or crooked foot; talipes.

cluck (kluk) n. call of hen.

clue (klōō) also clew n. ball of thread or cord used as guide through maze, hence anything that serves as guide or helps to solve mystery.—clue'less a. stupid.

clump (klump) n. shapeless mass of any substance; cluster of trees or shrubs; heavy extra sole on shoe; tramping sound;—v.t. put in clump or group;—v.i. tramp heavily.

clumsy (klum'-zi) a. ill-made; awkward; ungainly.—clum'sily adv.—clum'siness n.

clung (klung) pa.p. and pa.t. of cling.

cluster (klus'-ter) n. bunch; number of things growing together, as grapes; collection;—v.t. collect into bunch;—v.i. grow, or be, in clusters.

clutch (kluch) v.t. and i. seize or grip with hand; grasp;—n. grasp; tight grip; set of eggs hatched at one time; brood of chicks; device for disconnecting or taking up the drive between two shafts or rotating members.—clutch'es n. pl. claws; hands; (Fig.) power (esp. ruthless).

clutter (klut'-er) n. crowded confusion; disorder; noise;—v.t. crowd together in disorder; make untidy.

co- (kō) prefix meaning together, joint, etc.

coach (kōch) n. large four-wheeled travelling carriage; tutor who prepares students for examination; trainer in athletics;—v.i. travel in coach;—v.t. tutor or train.—coach'box n. driver's seat on coach.—coach'man n. driver of coach or carriage.

coadjutant (kō-ad'-jōō-tant) a. assisting.—n. assistant.—coadjutor (kō-ad-jōō'-tur) n. assistant; associate and destined successor.—coadju'trix n. female helper.

coagulate (kō-ag'-ū-lāt) v.t. cause to curdle or congeal; solidify;—v.i. curdle; clot.—coag'ulant n. substance that causes coagulation.—coagula'tion n.—coag'ulative a. causing coagulation.

coal (kōl) n. black substance used for fuel, composed of mineralised vegetable matter; piece of this substance;—v.t. supply with coal;—v.i. take in coal.—coal'-bed n. seam or stratum of coal.—coal'-bunk'er n. recess for storing coal.—coal'-field n. district where coal abounds.—coal'-gas n. gas produced from distillation of coal.—coal'-mine, coal'-pit n. excavation from which coal is dug.—coal'-tar n. thick, sticky substance, produced during distilling of coal.—coal'y a. like coal.—to haul over the coals, take to task.

coalesce (kō-a-les') v.t. grow together; unite into one body or mass; fuse.—coales'cent a. coalescing.—coales'cence n.

coalition (kō-a-lish'-un) n. union or combination of persons, parties, or states into one body; league.

coarse (kōrs) a. rough, rude; not refined; without grace or elegance; ill-mannered; vulgar.—coarse'ly adv.—coars'en v.t. and i. make or become coarse.—coarse'ness n.

coast (kōst) n. country bordering sea; sea-shore; country near shore;—v.t. and i. sail near or along coast; run downhill without application of power; free-wheel.—**coast'al** *a.*—**coast'er** *n.* vessel trading between towns along coast.—**coast'guard** *n.* one employed in prevention of smuggling and in watching for wrecks, etc.—**coast'line** *n.* outline of coast.—**coast'-wards** *adv.* toward coast.—**coast'wise** *adv.* along coast.

coat (kōt) *n.* outer garment; jacket; overcoat; fur or skin of animal; covering; layer spread over another, as paint;—*v.t.* cover with coat; clothe.—**coat'ing** *n.* covering; layer; cloth for making coats.—**coat of arms**, armorial bearings;—**coat of mail**, soldier's jacket, quilted with small plates or rings of iron.

coax (kōks) *v.t.* win over by fond pleading or flattery.—**coax'ingly** *adv.*

co-axial (kō-ak'-si-al) *a.* having common axis; (*Elec.*) of cable, having central wire surrounded by flexible tubular conductor.

cob (kob) *n.* head of maize; corn-cob; lump or ball of anything; short-legged sturdy horse; male swan.—**cob'-nut** *n.* large hazel-nut.

cobalt (kō'-bawlt) *n.* chemical metallic element classified with iron and nickel, and used as ingredient of many alloys.—**co'balt-blue** *n.* pigment of alumina and cobalt;—*a.* dark-blue colour.—**cobalt'ic** *a.*

cobble (kob'-l) *v.t.* mend or patch coarsely; mend boots or shoes.—**cobb'ler** *n.*

cobble (kob'-l) *n.* stone rounded by action of water;—*v.t.* pave with cobbles.

cobra (kō'-bra, kob'-ra) *n.* venomous 'hooded' snake of Africa and India.

cobweb (kob'-web) *n.* spider's web; anything flimsy, transparent, and fragile; trap or entanglement.

cochineal (koch'-i-nēl) *n.* scarlet dye-stuff, made from dried bodies of insects.

cock (kok) *n.* male of birds, esp. of domestic fowl; weather-cock; tap to regulate flow of fluids; hammer of firearm; cocked position of hammer (of firearm); chief or leader;—*v.t.* draw back hammer of gun; set up; set erect, set at angle, as hat;—*v.i.* swagger.—**cock'-crow** *n.* early morning.—**cock'erel** *n.* young cock.—**cock'-eyed** *a.* squinting.—**cocks'comb** *n.* comb of cock.—**cock'sure** *a.* quite sure.—**cock'tail** *n.* drink concocted of spirits, bitters, vermouth and flavourings used as appetiser.—**cock'y** *a.* vain and confident.—**cock'ily** *adv.*—**cock'iness** *n.*—**cock'-a-hoop** *a.* exultant.—**cock'-a-leek'ie** *n.* soup made of boiled fowl and leeks.—**cocked hat**, brimless hat with point in front and behind. —a **cock-and-bull story**, preposterous story.

cockade (ko-kād') *n.* knot of ribbons,

rosette or badge, often worn on hat.

cockatoo (kok-a-tóo') *n.* kind of parrot with crested head.

cockatrice (kok'-a-tris) *n.* fabulous animal represented as cock with dragon's tail; fabulous serpent.

cockchafer (kok'-chā-fer) *n.* large winged beetle.

cocker (kok'-er) *n.* cocker spaniel, small variety of spaniel, used for retrieving game.

cockle (kok'-l) *n.* bivalve shell-fish, with thick ribbed shell.—**cock'le-shell** *n.* shell of cockle; shallow boat. —to warm the cockles of the heart, cheer and hearten.

cockle (kok'-l) *v.t.* cause to pucker; wrinkle.

Cockney (kok'-ni) *n.* native of London, esp. one born within sound of Bow Bells.

cockpit (kok'-pit) *n.* pit or ring in which game-cocks fought, hence arena of frequent strife; pilot's compartment in aircraft; driver's seat in racing car.

cockroach (kok'-rōch) *n.* orthopterous insect infesting houses.

cockswain (kok'-swān, kok'-sn) *n.* cox'swain.—Abbrev. **cox**.

coconut, cocoanut (kō'-kō-nut) *n.* fruit of coco palm.

cocoa (kō'-kō) *n.* powder made from kernels of cacao or chocolate plant; beverage from this.

cocoon (ko-kóon') *n.* silky envelope which silkworm and other larvae spin for themselves before passing into pupa stage.

cod, codfish (kod, kod'-fish) *n.* large fish from northern seas, much used as food.—**cod'ling** *n.* young cod.

coddle (kod'-l) *v.t.* parboil; roast; pamper or spoil.

code (kōd) *n.* orderly collection of laws; system of words, or symbols, or numbers adopted for secrecy or economy; cipher;—*v.t.* put into form of code.—**codify** (kō'-di-fī) *v.t.* collect laws, etc. into digest.

codicil (kod'-i-sil) *n.* supplement or appendix to will.

codling (kod'-ling) *n.* kind of cooking-apple. Also **cod'lin**.

codling (kod'-ling) *n.* young cod.

co-education (kō-ed-ū-kā'-shun) *n.* education of boys and girls together in mixed classes—**co-educa'tional** *a.*

coefficient (kō-e-fish'-ent) *a.* co-operating; combining; — *n.* that which unites with something else to produce result; (*Math.*) number or other factor placed before another as multiplier; (*Phys.*) constant number or factor measuring some specified property of substance.—**coeffi'ciency** *n.*

coequal (kō-ē'-kwal) *a.* equal; of same rank or power as another;—*n.* person having equality with another.

coerce (kŏ-ẹrs') v.t. compel by force; constrain; restrain.—**coer'cible** a.—**coer'cive** a. having power to compel.—**coer'cively** adv.—**coercion** (kŏ-er'-shun) n.

coeval (kŏ-ē'-vạl) a. of same age;—n. contemporary.

co-exist (kŏ-eg-zist') v.i. exist at same time or together.—**co-exist'ent** a.—**co-existe'nce** n.

co-extend (kŏ-eks-tend') v.t. extend equally with.—**co-exten'sive** a.

coffee (kof'-e) n. evergreen shrub, valuable for its berries; seeds of berries, esp. when ground and roasted; drink from this.

coffer (kof'-ẹr) n. chest for holding valuables; large money-box; canal-lock;—v.t. put in coffer; hoard (money, etc.).

coffin (kof'-in) n. box or casket in which dead are enclosed before burial or cremation; v.t. place in coffin.

cog (kog) n. one of series of teeth on wheel; support to roof of mine;—**cog'-wheel** n.

cogent (kŏ'-jent) a. having great force; powerful; convincing.—**co'gently** adv.—**co'gence**, **co'gency** n. urgency; force; convincing power.

cogitate (koj'-i-tāt) v.i. reflect deeply; meditate.—**cog'itable** a.—**cogita'tion** n.

cognac (kon'-yak) n. French brandy, so called from town of *Cognac*; brandy in general.

cognate (kog'-nāt) a. allied by blood or birth; of same stock; from same origin, formation, etc.

cognisance (kog'-ni-zạns, kon'-i-zạns) n. knowledge.—**cog'nisant** a. aware of.

cognition (kog-ni'-shun) n. apprehension; awareness; state of being able to perceive objects or remember ideas.—**cog'nitive** a.

cognomen (kog-nŏ'-men) n. surname; nickname.

cohabit (kŏ-hab'-it) v.i. live together as husband and wife (usually of unmarried persons).—**cohabita'tion** n.

cohere (kŏ-hēr') v.i. stick together; be connected; follow regularly in natural order; be consistent; coalesce; adhere.—**cohe'rence**, **cohe'rency** n.—**cohe'rent** a.—**cohe'rently** adv.—**cohe'sible** a. capable of cohesion.—**cohe'sion** n. act of sticking together.—**cohe'sive** a.—**cohe'siveness**, **cohe'sibility** n.

cohort (kŏ'-hort) n. division of Roman legion, from 300 to 600 soldiers; company of persons.

coif (koif) n. close-fitting cap; head-dress.—**coiffeur** (kwạ-fẹr') (fem. **coiffeuse'**) n. hairdresser.—**coiffure** (kwạ-fŏŏr') n. style of dressing hair.

coign (koin) n. corner; corner-stone; wedge.

coil (koil) v.t. wind in rings, as rope;

twist into spiral shape;—v.i. take up spiral shape;—n. spiral of rings into which a thing is wound; one of the rings of spiral.

coin (koin) n. wedge or corner-stone; piece of stamped metal issued by government authority used as money; money.—v.t. make into money; mint; invent or fabricate, as word or phrase.—**coin'age** n. money coined; currency.—**coin'er** n. one who makes coins, esp. counterfeit coins; inventor.

coincide (kŏ-in-sīd') v.i. correspond in detail; happen at same time; agree (in opinion).—**coincidence** (kŏ-in'-sid-ens) n. correspondence in nature, circumstances, etc.—**coin'cident**, **coincident'al** a. occupying same space; agreeing; simultaneous.—**coin'cidently** adv.

coir (koir) n. fibre from husk of coconut, for ropes, matting, etc.

coition (kŏ-i'-shun) n. sexual intercourse; copulation.

coke (kŏk) n. fuel remaining after distillation of volatile parts of coal.—v.t. turn into coke.

colander (kul'-ạn-dẹr) n. strainer for vegetables, etc. Also **cull'ender**.

cold (kŏld) a. wanting in heat; chill; deficient in emotions; spiritless;—n. absence of warmth; cold weather; virus infection causing catarrh of nose, throat and chest.—**cold'ly** adv.—**cold'ness** n.—**cold front** (*Meteor.*) boundary between advancing cold air and mass of warmer air—**cold'blood'ed** a. having cold blood, like fish; callous.—**to cold-shoulder**, rebuff; be unfriendly.

colic (kol'-ik) n. severe paroxysmal pain in abdomen.

collage (kol-azh') n. picture composed wholly or partly of scraps and oddments stuck on to the surface.

collaborate (ko-lab'-ō-rāt) v.t. work or labour together; act jointly, esp. in works of literature, art, science.—**collabora'tion** n. joint labour; willing co-operation with enemy.—**collab'orator** n.

collapse (kol-aps') v.i. fall in together; break down; fail suddenly; lose strength; give way under strain; become discouraged;—v.t. cause to collapse;—n. falling in or down; sudden and complete failure; breakdown.—**collaps'able**, **collaps'ible** a.

collar (kol'-ạr) n. something worn round neck; part of garment that fits round neck; ring; band;—v.t. seize by collar; hence, arrest; capture; grab; put collar on.—**coll'ar-bone** n. bone from shoulder to breast-bone; clavicle.

collate (ko-lāt') v.t. compare critically; arrange in order, as sheets of book for binding; appoint to benefice.—**colla'tion** n. act of collat-

ing; lunch or repast.—**colla'tive** a.—
colla'tor n.

collateral (kol-at'-e-rạl) a. side by
side; running parallel; descended
from same ancestor but through
different line; additional (of security).
—**collat'erally** adv.

colleague (kol'-ēg) n. associate or
companion in office or employment.

collect (ko'lekt) v.t. bring together;
gather; assemble; muster; deduce;
—v.i. be assembled; come together.
—**collect** (kol'-ekt) n. short prayer,
containing only one petition.—
collect'able, collect'ible a.—**collect'ed** a.
cool; self-possessed.—**collect'edly** adv.
—**collect'edness** n.—**collec'tion** n. act
of collecting; sum of money gathered
for a cause; assemblage.—**collec'tive**
a. formed by gathering; gathered
into mass, sum, or body.—**collect'ively**
adv.—**collect'ivism** n. term embracing
all systems based on state, municipal, co-operative, etc. control of the
economy.—**collect'ivist** n.—**collect'or** n.

college (kol'-ej) n. institution for
higher education; buildings, etc. of
such institution; association of professional men, e.g. of physicians;
assembly, as of electors or cardinals.
—**colle'giate** a.

collet (kol'-et) n. collar; neckband;
rim in which stone of ring is set.

collide (ko-līd') v.i. strike or dash
together; clash; come into conflict.
—**collision** n. (ko'lizh'-un) n. act of
striking together; violent impact;
encounter; conflict.

collie (kol'-i) n. breed of sheep-dog.

collier (kol'-yẹr) n. coal-miner; ship
whose usual cargo is coal.—**coll'iery**
n. coal-mine.

collinear (kōl'in'-ẹ-ạr) a. in same
straight line; aligned.

colloid (kol'-oid) a. like glue; gelatinous;—n. viscous, non-crystalline substance, not soluble in water and
unable to pass through animal
membranes.—**colloid'al** a.

collop (kol'-op) n. small slice or piece
of meat.

colloquy (kol'-ō-kwi) n. conversation;
dialogue; discussion; conference,
esp. political; debate.—**collo'quial** a.
pert. to, or used in, familiar conversation.—**collo'quially** adv.—**collo'-
quialism** n. expression used in
ordinary conversation.

collusion (ko-lū'-zhun) n. secret
agreement between two or more
persons for fraudulent purpose.—
collu'sive a.

colon (kō'-lon) n. punctuation mark
(:), separating parts of sentence that
are almost independent; (Anat.)
part of large intestine extending
from caecum to rectum.

colonel (kur'-nel) n. officer commanding regiment or battalion.—
colon'elcy, colon'elship n.

colonnade (kol-o-nād') n. series of
columns arranged symmetrically.

colony (kol'-on-i) n. body of people
who settle in new country; country
thus occupied; overseas dependency
of a state; communal group of plant
or animal organisms.—**colo'nial** a.
pert. to colony;—n. colonist.—
colonial'ism n. policy of exploitation
of overseas colonies.—**col'onise** v.t.—
col'onist n.—**colonisa'tion** n.

coloration (kul-u-rā'-shun) n. colouring; arrangement or disposition of
colours in art. Also **coloura'tion**.

coloratura (kol-or-a-tū'-rạ) n. (Mus.)
ornamental runs and trills in vocal
music.

colossal (ko-los'-ạl) a. of enormous
size; gigantic.

colour (kul'-ur) n. hue or tint; paint;
complexion; flush; false show; pretext; show of reason; kind or
species; vividness in writing; in
music, variety of timbre;—v.t. paint
or tinge with colour;—v.i. blush.—
colours n. pl. flag or standard; coloured
badge, device, rosette, etc. used as
distinguishing mark.—**col'ourable** a.
—**col'ourful** a. (Fig.) picturesque—
col'ouring n.—**col'ourist** n. artist to
whom colouring is of supreme importance.—**col'our-blind** a. unable to
distinguish between colours.—**to join
the colours**, enlist in the army.—**to
nail one's colours to the mast**, to
commit oneself irrevocably.—**colour
bar**, discrimination between white
and coloured races.—**off colour**, indisposed.

colt (kōlt) n. young horse, esp. male;
inexperienced youth.—**colt'ish** a.

coltsfoot (kōlts'-foot) n. wild plant,
with heart-shaped leaves and yellow
flowers.

columbine (kol'-um-bīn) a. of, or
like, a dove; dove-coloured;—**Columbine** n. in pantomime, Harlequin's
mistress; (Bot.) Aquilegia, flower
with five spurred petals.

column (kol'-um) n. round pillar;
support; body of troops drawn up in
deep files; division of a page;
perpendicular line of figures.—
columnar (ko-lum'-nạr) a.—**col'umn-
ist** n. writer who contributes column
to newspaper.

coma (kō'-mạ) n. (Med.) deep sleep
or stupor generally resulting from
injury to brain, alcoholic or narcotic
poisoning; (Fig.) lethargy; drowsiness.—**com'atose** a. lethargic.

comb (kōm) n. toothed instrument
for separating, cleansing, adjusting,
or fastening hair, dressing wool, etc.;
also decoration for lady's hair;
cock's crest; crest of a wave; cell
structure in which bees store their
honey;—v.t. separate, cleanse, dress,
etc. with a comb;—v.i. roll over or
break with white foam (said of

waves).—**comb'er** n. one who, or that which, combs; long, curling wave; kind of fish, the sea-perch.—**comb'ing** n.—**comb'ings** n.pl. hair, wool, etc. removed by combing.

combat (kum'-bat, kom'-bat) v.t. fight against; oppose by force; contend with;—v.i. struggle; contend;—n. fight; struggle; contest;—pr.p. **com'bating.**—pa.p. and pa.t. **com'bated.**—**com'batant** a. contending;—n. one engaged in fight or combat.—**com'bative** a.

combe (kóom) n. deep valley; hollow among hills.

combine (kom-bīn') v.t. join together; unite; connect;—v.i. form a union; co-operate; (*Chem.*) unite and form new compound.—**combine** (kom'-bīn) n. association formed to control trade; trust; syndicate.—**com'bine-har'vester** n. agricultural machine that reaps, threshes and bags grain in one operation.—**combi'nable** a.—**combina'tion** (kom-bi-nā'-shun) n. union or connection; association of persons; alliance; chemical union; arrangement of code letters and figures used to open a **combination lock.**—**combina'tions** n.pl. undergarment combining vest and drawers.—**combined operations** operations in which combined military, naval, and air forces are used.

combustion (kom-bust'-yun) n. act of fire on inflammable substances; act of burning; chemical action accompanied by heat and light.—**combust'ible** a. liable to take fire; inflammable;—n. substance that burns readily.—**combustability** n.

come (kum) v.i. approach; arrive; arrive at some state or condition; move towards; reach; happen (to); originate (from); occur; turn out to be;—pr.p. **com'ing.**—pa.p. **come.**—pa.t. **came.**—a **come'-back,** n. return to former activity.—a **come'-down,** n. set-back; descent in social status. —**to come by,** pass; obtain possession of.—**to come in for,** obtain.—**to come of age,** reach one's twenty-first birthday.—**to come to,** recover consciousness; (*Naut.*) anchor.

comedy (kom'-e-di) n. stage play dealing with the lighter side of life, ending happily, or treating subject humorously.—**comedian** (ko-mē'-di-an) n. actor in comedy; humorous entertainer; (*Colloq.*) funny person; comic.—**comedienne** (kom-ē-di-en') n. fem.

comely (kum'-li) a. good-looking; graceful.—**come'liness** n.

comestible (ko-mes'-ti-bl) a. fit for eating. — **comes'tibles** n.pl. edible foodstuffs; eatables.

comet (kom'-et) n. heavenly body consisting of diffuse, nebulous head, nucleus, and tail.

comfit (kum'-fit) n. dry sweetmeat; fruit, or fruit kernel, preserved with sugar and dried.

comfort (kum'-fort) v.t. allay grief or trouble; console, cheer, gladden; —n. consolation; ease of body or mind, or whatever causes it.— **com'forts** n.pl. circumstances which give greater ease to life.—**com'fortable** a. promoting or enjoying comfort.—**com'fortably** adv.—**com'forter** n. one who comforts; knitted woollen scarf; rubber teat for comforting a baby.—**com'fortless** a. lacking comfort.—**Job's comforter,** one who, in seeking to comfort, achieves the opposite.

comic (kom'-ik) a. pert. to comedy; mirth-provoking; funny;—n. that which induces amusement or laughter; (*Colloq.*) comedian; (*Colloq.*) comic paper.—**com'ical** a. droll; ludicrous.—**com'ically** adv.—**comical'ity** n. quality of being comical.

comity (kom'-i-ti) n. courtesy; civility.—**comity of nations** traditional respect by nations for the laws of other nations.

comma (kom'-a) n. punctuation mark (,), used to mark shortest pauses in division of a sentence.— **inverted commas,** quotation marks (' ', or " ").

command (ko-mánd') v.t. order or demand with authority; govern or control; have at one's disposal; overlook or have a view over;— v.i. be at the head;—n. order; body of troops under an officer; district or region under a commander; word of command; disposal; mastery or facility.—**command'ing** a.—**commandant'** n. officer in charge of military station or body of troops.— **commandeer** (kom-an-dēr') v.t. seize for military purposes; take forcible possession of.—**commander** (ko-mán'-der) n. leader; commanding officer; in navy, officer ranking between lieutenant and captain.—**command'ment** n. command; precept.—**comman'do** n. body of specially trained troops; member of such body.

commemorate (ko-mem'-o-rāt) v.t. call to remembrance; celebrate memory of someone or something by solemn act of devotion.—**commemora'tion** n.—**commem'orative, commem'oratory** a.

commence (ko-mens') v.t. begin, start, originate;—v.i. originate; begin. —**commence'ment** n. beginning.

commend (ko-mend') v.t. praise; speak favourably of; present as worthy; entrust to.—**commend'able** a. — **commend'ably** adv. — **commend'ableness** n.—**commenda'tion** n. act of commending; praise; approval.— **commend'atory** a.

commensurate (ko-men'-sū-rāt) a.

equal in extent; proportionate; adequate.—**commen'surately** *adv.*—**commen'surateness** *n.*—**commensura'tion** *n.*—**commen'surable** *a.* having common measure; suitably proportioned.—**commen'surably** *adv.*—**commensurabil'ity** *n.*

comment (ko-ment', kom'-ent) *v.t.* and *i.* make remarks, notes, criticisms;—**comm'ent** *n.* note; collection of notes; explanation; critical remark; observation.—**commentary** (kom'-en-tar-i) *n.* exposition of a book; historical narrative.—running **commentary** description (by eye-witness) of an event while in actual progress.—**comm'entate** *v.t.* annotate; interpret.—**comm'entator** *n.*

commerce (kom'-ers) *n.* buying and selling; trade or intercourse between individuals; social or personal intercourse.—**commercial** (ko-mer'-shal) *a.* pert. to commerce; mercantile. —*n.* Short advertising sequence on TV or radio.—**commercial traveller**, travelling agent for business firm.—**commer'cialism** *n.* business principles, methods, or viewpoint.—**commer'cially** *adv.*

commiserate (ko-miz'-e-rāt) *v.t.* and *i.* have compassion for; condole with; pity.—**commisera'tion** *n.*

commissar (kom'-i-sár) *n.* one of the heads of Soviet government department or commissariat.—**commissariat** *n.* department which supplies food, stores, equipment, transport as for army.

commissary (kom'-i-sar-i) *n.* one to whom a duty is assigned; deputy; commissioner; (*Mil.*) one who supervises supply of food and stores to army.—**commissa'rial** *a.*

commission (ko-mish'-un) *n.* act of committing; something entrusted to be done; payment by percentage for doing something; legal warrant to execute some office, trust, or duty; power under such warrant; document that contains it; thing to be done as agent for another; (*Mil., Naval, etc.*) warrant of appointment to rank of officer;—*v.t.* give power to; authorise; give an order for; appoint to rank of officer.—**commis'sioner** *n.* one holding commission to act; member of body of enquiry. —**royal commission**, body appointed by royal warrant to conduct impartial inquiry into matter of public interest.

commissionaire (ko-mish-un-ār') *n.* uniformed messenger in offices, theatres, hotels, etc.; door-keeper.

commit (ko-mit') *v.t.* entrust; give in charge; perform; be guilty of; pledge or bind; send for trial or confinement;—*pr.p.* **commit'ting.**—*pa.p.* and *pa.t.* **commit'ted.**—**commit'tal, commit'ment** *n.*—**to commit one-**

self, compromise or entangle oneself.

committee (ko-mit'-i) *n.* number of persons appointed to attend to particular business by legislative body, court, society, etc.

commode (ko-mōd') *n.* chest of drawers; small piece of furniture containing chamber-pot.

commodious (ko-mō'-di-us) *a.* convenient; roomy; spacious.—**commo'diously** *adv.*—**commo'diousness** *n.*—**commod'ity** *n.* any useful thing; article of trade.—**commod'ities** *n.pl.* goods.

commodore (kom'-o-dōr) *n.* (*Naval*) rank between rear-admiral and captain; senior captain (or leading ship) of convoy of merchantmen.

common (kom'-un) *a.* shared by all, or several; public; ordinary; usual; frequent; vulgar; of little value; of low social status;—*n.* unenclosed land not belonging to private owner.—**comm'ons** *n.pl.* ordinary people; House of Commons; rations. —**comm'onalty** *n.* general body of the people.—**comm'oner** *n.* one of the common people.—**comm'only** *adv.* in common manner; usually; jointly; meanly.—**comm'onness** *n.*—**comm'onplace** *a.* ordinary; trite;—*n.* common topic; trite remark.—**comm'on-sense** *n.* well-balanced judgment.—**common law**, law based on usage and custom.

commonweal (kom'-un-wēl) *n.* public welfare; common good.—**comm'onwealth** (welth) *n.* whole body of people; form of government in which power resides with the people; association of states tenuously linked by mutual interest.

commotion (ko-mō'-shun) *n.* violent motion; agitation; tumult; public disorder.

commune (ko-mūn') *v.i.* converse together intimately; have spiritual intercourse (with); (*Eccl.*) receive communion.—**communion** (kom-ūn'-yun) *n.* act of communing; celebration of Lord's Supper.

commune (kom'-ūn) *n.* people having common rights; small administrative district (esp. in France) governed by mayor.—**comm'unal** *a.* pert. to commune or community; for common use.—**comm'unalise** *v.t.* —**comm'unism** *n.* theory of social system in which private property is abolished.—**comm'unist** *n.*—**communis'tic** *a.*

communicate (ko-mū'-ni-kāt) *v.t.* impart information; reveal; convey; —*v.i.* have connection with; have dealings, correspondence, with; partake of the Lord's Supper.—**commu'nicable** *a.*—**communica'tion** *n.* intercourse by speech, correspondence, etc.; information; means of passing from one place to another; connecting passage.—**commun'icant** n. one who imparts information; one who receives communion.—**commun'icative** a. ready to converse, or impart information; talkative.—**commu'nicatory** a. imparting information.

communiqué (kom-ū'-ni-kā) n. official announcement.

community (ko-mū'-ni-ti) n. people having common interests; public or people in general.

commute (ko-mūt') v.t. exchange; substitute; mitigate a sentence; use season-ticket for travelling daily to one's work in town.—**commut'able** a. exchangeable.—**commutabil'ity** n.—**commuta'tion** n.—**comm'utator** n. (Elect.) device for collecting current from winding of electric motor or generator; rotating contact.—**commut'er** n. suburban dweller who travels to and from work in town.

compact (kom-pakt') a. firm; solid; closely packed; condensed; terse;—v.t. press closely together; make firm.—**compact'ly** adv.—**compact'ness** n.—**compact'ed** a. firmly united.

compact (kom-pakt) n. agreement or contract.—**com'pact** n. case to hold face-powder; pocket vanity-case.

companion (kom-pan'-yun) n. one who is in another's company; comrade; member of order of knighthood. — **compan'ionable** a.—**compan'ionably** adv—**companionabil'ity, compan'ionableness** n.—**compan'ionship** n.

companion (kom-pan'-yun) n. (Naut.) skylight on upper deck, to let light into cabin below.—**companion-ladder**, one between deck and cabin or quarter-deck.—**companion-way**, cabin staircase.

company (kum'-pa-ni) n. gathering of persons; assembly; group; association of persons in trade; social circle; visitors; part of regiment.

compare (kom-pār') v.t. notice or point out likeness and differences of two or more things; liken or contrast;—v.i. be like; compete with.—**comparable** (kom'-par-a-bl) a. capable of being compared; of equal regard or value.—**com'parably** adv.—**comparative** (kom-par'-a-tiv) a. estimated by comparison; (Gram.) expressing 'more'. — **compar'atively** adv.—**compar'ison** n.

compartment (kom-pàrt'-ment) n. part divided off; section; division of railway carriage.

compass (kum'-pas) n. instrument for showing the north, and so, directions; (Mus.) range of voice or instrument; circuit; circumference; measurement round; space; area; scope; reach;—v.t. go round; surround; contrive; attain.—**com'passes** n.pl. mathematical instrument for describing circles, measuring, etc.

compassion (kom-pash'-un) n. sympathy with distress or suffering of another; pity.—**compas'sionate** a. full of sympathy; showing pity; merciful.—v.t. pity.—**compas'sionately** adv.—**compas'sionateness** n.

compatible (kom-pat'-i-bl) a. consistent; agreeing with; capable of harmonious union.—**compat'ibly** adv.—**compatibil'ity** n.

compatriot (kom-pā'-tri-ot, kom-pat'-ri-ot) n. fellow-countryman.

compel (kom-pel') v.t. force; oblige; bring about by force;—pr.p. **compel'ling**.—pa.p. and pa.t. **compelled'**.—**compel'lable** a.

compendium (kom-pend'-i-um) n. comprehensive abridgement or summary.—**compend'ious** a. comprehensive; abridged.—**compend'iously** adv.

compensate (kom'-pen-sāt) v.t. recompense suitably; reward; pay;—v.i. make amends; make up for.—**compensa'tion** n.—**compensa'tive, compensa'tory** a.

compère (kom'-per) n. (fem. **commère**) one who introduces a variety or other performance.

compete (kom-pēt') v.i. strive against others to win something; vie with; contend; rival.—**competition** (kom-pe-tish'-un) n. act of competing; trial of skill.—**compet'itive** a.—**compet'itively** adv. — **compet'itor** n. rival.

competent (kom'-pe-tent) a. able; skilful; properly qualified; legitimate; suitable; sufficient.—**com'petently** adv.—**com'petence, com'petency** n. state of being fit or capable; sufficiency, esp. of means of subsistence.

compile (kom-pīl') v.t. put together literary materials from works of others; collect.—**compil'er** n.—**compila'tion** n.

complacent (kom-plā'-sent) a. self-satisfied; pleased or gratified.—**compla'cently** adv.—**compla'cence, compla'cency** n. self-satisfaction.

complain (kom-plān') v.i. express distress, grief, dissatisfaction; lament; grumble; be ailing.—**complain'ant** n. complainer; (Law) plaintiff.—**complaint'** n. expression of distress, dissatisfaction, etc.; ailment.

complement (kom'-ple-ment) n. that which supplies a deficiency; something making up a whole; full quantity or number.—**complement'** v.t. to supplement; to supply a deficiency.—**complement'al, complement'ary** a. completing.

complete (kom-plēt') a. entire; finished; with no part lacking;—v.t. to bring to state of entirety; perfect.—**complete'ly** adv.—**complete'ness** n.—**completion** (kom-plē'-shun) n.

complex (kom'-pleks) a. consisting of two or more parts; not simple; involved or intricate.—n. complicated whole; (*Psych.*) group of repressed emotional ideas.—**complexity** *n.*

complexion (kom-plek'-shun) *n.* colour of skin, esp. of face; aspect or appearance; quality or texture; character or disposition.

compliance (kom-pli'-ans) *n.* submission; yielding; consent;—**compli'ant** *a.* yielding; obedient.—**compli'antly** *adv.*—**compli'able** *a.*

complicate (kom'-pli-kāt) *v.t.* fold or twist together; entangle; embarrass; make intricate. — **com'plicated** *a.* tangled; involved.—**complica'tion** *n.* state of being complicated.

complicity (kom-plis'-i-ti) *n.* state of being an accomplice, of having share in the guilt.

compliment (kom'-pli-ment) *n.* expression of regard or admiration; flattering speech; formal greeting (usually *pl.*).—**compliment** (kom-pli-ment') *v.t.* congratulate.—**compliment'ary** *a.* expressing praise; gratis (tickets, etc.).

comply (kom-pli') *v.i.* yield to; agree; consent; conform; adapt oneself to.—**compli'er** *n.*

component (kom-pō'-nent) *a.* constituting; composing; making up; helping to form a compound;—*n.* part helping to make a whole.

comport (kom-pōrt') *v.t.* behave; conduct oneself;—*v.i.* agree; accord.

compose (kom-pōz') *v.t.* form by uniting parts; arrange; put in order; write; invent; adjust; calm; soothe; set up types in proper order for printing;—*v.i.* practise composition.—**composed'** *a.* sedate; quiet; calm.—**compos'edly** *adv.*—**compos'edness** *n.*—**compos'er** *n.* one who composes; author, esp. musical author.—**composite** (kom'-poz-it) *a.* made up of distinct parts or elements.—**composition** (kom-pō-zish'-un) *n.* act of composing; thing formed by composing; in schools, pupil's essay; literary, musical, artistic, etc. work.—**compositor** (kom-poz'-i-tor) *n.* typesetter.—**composure** (kom-pō-zhūr) *n.* calmness; tranquillity.

compost (kom'-post) *n.* fertilising mixture; composition for plaster-work, etc.

compound (kom-pound') *v.t.* put together, as elements or parts, to form a whole; combine; mix; compromise; condone; make settlement of debt by partial payment.

compound (kom'-pound) *a.* composed of various parts; not simple; mixed; composite; — *n.* mixture; joining; substance to which something has been added; word, etc. made up of parts; (*Chem.*) substance composed of two or more elements, always present in same fixed proportions.

compound (kom'-pound) *n.* in the East, enclosure about house; S. Africa, enclosed area in which native labourers reside.

comprehend (kom-pre-hend') *v.t.* understand; take in; include; comprise; contain.—**comprehensible** (kom-pre-hen'-si-bl) *a.* understandable; conceivable.—**comprehen'sibly** *adv.*—**comprehensibil'ity, comprehen'sibleness** *n.*—**comprehen'sion** *n.*—**comprehen'sive** *a.* including much within narrow limits; inclusive. — **comprehen'sively** *adv.*—**comprehen'siveness** *n.*—**comprehensive school** one which covers all types of secondary education.

compress (kom-pres') *v.t.* press together; reduce volume by pressure; condense.—**compres'sible** *a.*—**compressibil'ity** *n.*—**compression** (kom-presh'-un) *n.* act or effect of compressing.—**compres'sive** *a.* tending to compress.—**compres'sor** *n.*

compress (kom'-pres) *n.* (*Med.*) pad to make pressure on a wound; wet pad to reduce inflammation.

comprise (kom-priz') *v.t.* include; comprehend or embrace; consist of.—**compris'able** *a.*—**compris'al** *n.* act of comprising.

compromise (kom'-prō-miz) *n.* settling of matters by mutual adjustment, each side making concessions; middle course.—*v.t.* and *i.* settle by making concessions; commit oneself; expose to risk of scandal or disgrace.

comptroller *n.* same as controller. See control.

compulsion (kom-pul'-shun) *n.* act or effect of compelling; force; constraint; violence; (*Psych.*) irresistible impulse.—**compul'sive** *a.*—**compul'sory** *a.* obligatory; enforced.—**compul'sorily** *adv.*

compunction (kom-pungk'-shun) *n.* remorse of conscience; pity; scruple.

compute (kom-pūt') *v.t.* count; calculate; estimate.—**comput'able** *a.*—**computa'tion** *n.*—**comput'er** *n.* calculating machine.

comrade (kum'-rād) *n.* close friend or companion; mate; associate.—**com'radeship** *n.* close friendship; fellowship; affectionate association.

con (kon) *adv.* (*abbrev.* of *contra*) against.

con- (kon) *prefix* fr. L. *cum*, with, together.

concatenation (kon-kat-e-nā'-shun) *n.* series of things depending on each other.

concave (kon'-kāv) *a.* hollow and curved inwards, as inner surface of vault.—**concavity** (kon-kav'-i-ti) *n.* hollowness.

conceal (kon-sēl') *v.t.* hide or secrete; mask or disguise; withhold from knowledge.—**conceal'ment** *n.*

concede (kon-sēd') *v.t.* yield; admit to be true; grant; surrender:—*v.i.* admit.

conceit (kon-sēt') n. over-estimation of self; vanity; opinion; fanciful thought.—**conceit'ed** a. vain.—**conceit'edly** adv.

conceive (kon-sēv') v.t. form idea in the mind; think; imagine; understand; realise;—v.i. become pregnant; have a notion.—**conceiv'able** a. that may be believed, imagined, or understood.—**conceiv'ably** adv.

concentrate (kon'sen-trāt) v.t. bring to common centre; reduce to small space; increase in strength; condense;—v.i. come together; devote all attention.—**concentra'tion** n. act of concentrating; condensation; increased strength; fixation of mind on something.

concentric (kon-sen'-trĭk) a. having same centre.

concept (kon'-sept) n. abstract notion; mental impression of an object.—**conception** (kon-sep'-shun) n. act of conceiving; thing conceived; mental picture; idea; (Med.) beginning of pregnancy.—**concep'tive** a.—**concep'tual** a.

concern (kon-sern') v.t. relate or belong to; be of importance to; be the business of; make uneasy;—n. that which relates or belongs to one; interest in, or care for, any person or thing; worry; a business establishment.—**concerned'** a. connected with; interested; worried; anxious; troubled; involved.—**concern'ing** prep. regarding; with respect to.

concert (kon-sert') v.t. plan together; arrange; design.—**concert'ed** a. mutually planned; (Mus.) arranged in parts.—**concert** (kon'-sert) n. agreement in a plan; harmony; musical entertainment.—**concertina** (kon-ser-tē'-na) n. small musical wind instrument with hexagonal ends, fitted with bellows and keys.—**concerto** (kon-cher'-tō) n. musical composition for solo instrument with orchestral accompaniment.

concession (kon-sesh'-un) n. act of conceding; special privilege; grant; admission.—**concessionaire** (kon-sesh-un-ār') n. one who holds concession.—**conces'sionary** a.

conciliate (kon-sil'-i-āt) v.t. win over to goodwill; appease; make peace; pacify.—**concilia'tion** n.—**concil'iatory** a. tending to pacify.

concise (kon-sīs') a. brief; shortened; condensed.—**concise'ly** adv.—**concise'ness** n.

conclave (kon'-klāv) n. private meeting of cardinals for election of pope; where they meet; secret meeting.

conclude (kon-klōōd') v.t. bring to an end; close; finish; complete; make a final judgment of; infer;—v.i. come to an end.

conclusion (kon-klōō'-shun) n. end; last part of anything; final judg-

ment; inference; result from experiment.—**conclu'sive** a. final; decisive; convincing.

concoct (kon-kokt') v.t. (Arch.) digest in the mind; make a mixture; make up, esp. a story.—**concoc'tion** n. act of concocting; thing concocted.

concomitant (kon-kom'-i-tant) a. accompanying; attending; going along with.

concord (kong'-kord, kon'-kord) n. agreement; union between persons, as in opinions, etc.; harmony; unison; consonance;—v.i. agree.—**concord'ance** n. agreement; index to words of a book (esp. of Bible) with references to places of their occurrence.—**concord'ant** a. agreeing; harmonious.

concourse (kon'-kōrs) n. gathering together; assembly; meeting; crowd.

concrete (kon'-krēt) a. made of concrete; consisting of matter, facts, etc.; solid; not abstract; specific;—n. mixture of sand, cement, etc., used in building; anything real or specific, as opposed to abstract or general; v.t. form into solid mass;—v.i. unite into mass; harden.—**concretely** (kon-krēt'-li) adv.

concubine (kong'-kū-bĭn) n. woman who lives with a man without being his lawful wife.—**concubinage** (kon-kū'-bi-nāj) n.

concupiscence (kon-kū'-pis-ens) n. violent sexual desire; lust.—**concu'piscent**.

concur (kon-kur') v.i. agree; express agreement; meet in the same point; coincide.—pr.p. **concur'ring**.—pa.p. and pa.t. **concurred'**.—**concur'rence** n. coming together; agreement.—**concur'rent** a.—**concur'rently** adv.

concussion (kon-kush'-un) n. act of shaking by sudden striking; shock; (Med.) violent disturbance of the brain caused by blow or fall.

condemn (kon-dem') v.t. blame; censure; pronounce guilty; sentence; reprove; declare unfit for use.—**condemna'tion** n.—**condem'natory** a.

condense (kon-dens') v.t. make more dense, close, or compact; to make more solid; concentrate; change vapour into liquid; pack into few words;—v.i. become more dense or compact; pass from vapour to liquid.—**condensa'tion** n.—**condensed'** a. compressed; concise; (of milk) evaporated and preserved in tins.—**condens'er** n. one who, or that which, condenses; apparatus for changing vapour into liquid during distillation; (Elec.) former term for capacitor.

condescend (kon-de-send') v.i. come down from one's position, rank, or dignity; stoop; deign; be gracious or affable to inferiors; patronise.—**condescend'ing** a.—**condescen'sion** n. act of condescending.

condign (kon-dīn') a. deserved; well-merited; adequate; sufficient.—**condign'ly** adv.—**condign'ness** n.

condiment (kon'-di-ment) n. relish; seasoning for food.

condition (kon-dish'-un) n. thing on which statement, happening, or existing depends; state or circumstances of anything; position as to worldly circumstances; rank; disposition; pre-requisite; stipulation;—v.t. stipulate; impose conditions on; render fit and in good health.—**condi'tional** a. depending on conditions; not absolute.—**condi'tionally** adv.—**condi'tioned** a.

condole (kon-dōl') v.i. grieve with; offer sympathy.—**condol'ence, condole'ment** n. expression of grief for sorrow of another.

condone (kon-dōn') v.t. pardon; forgive; overlook.—**condonation** (kon-dō-nā'-shun) n.

condor (kon'-dor) n. large species of vulture.

conduce (kon-dūs') v.i. lead to some end or result; help; promote.—**conduc'ive** a. having tendency to promote, help, or forward; inducing.—**conduc'iveness** n.

conduct (kon'-dukt) n. act of guiding; guidance; management; behaviour.—**conduct'** v.t. guide; lead; convey; manage; behave.—**conduc'tion** n. act of conducting; transmission or flow of heat from one body to another.—**conduc'tive** a.—**conductiv'ity** n.—**conduc'tor** n. guide; director of choir or orchestra; one in charge of bus, etc. who collects fares; substance capable of transmitting heat, electricity, etc.—**conduc'tress** n. fem.

conduit (kon'-, kun'-dit) n. pipe or channel for conveying water.

cone (kōn) n. solid body tapering to a point from circular base; anything of this shape; fruit of pine, fir, etc.—**conic, conical** (kon'-ik, -al) a. having form of, or pert. to, a cone.—**con'ically** adv.

confection (kon-fek'-shun) n. act of compounding different substances into one compound; sweetmeat; ready-made millinery, dresses, etc.—**confec'tionary** a.—**confec'tioner** n. one who makes or sells sweet meats.—**confec'tionery** n. sweetmeats.

confederate (kon-fed'-er-āt) a. united in league; bound by treaty; allied;—n. ally; accomplice;—v.t. and i. unite in league.—**confed'eracy** n. union; alliance.—**confedera'tion** n. act of forming confederacy; alliance.

confer (kon-fer') v.t. bestow upon; grant; award;—v.i. consult together; take advice; discuss.—pr.p. **confer'ring**.—pa.p. and pa.t. **conferred'**.—**con'ference** n. meeting for discussion of problems, policy, etc.

confess (kon-fes') v.t. admit; own; acknowledge; grant; (of a priest) hear sins of;—v.i. acknowledge; declare sins orally to priest.—**confes'sedly** adv. admittedly.—**confession** (kon-fesh'-un) n. admission; avowal of sins.—**confes'sional** n. stall where priest sits to hear confessions;—a. pert. to confession.—**confes'sor** n. priest who hears confessions.

confetti (kon-fet'-i) n.pl. small discs of coloured paper, for throwing at weddings, carnivals, etc.

confide (kon-fīd') v.t. hand over to charge of; entrust to; tell secret to;—v.i. put faith in; rely on.—**confidant** n. (fem. **confidante**) person to whom one can tell one's private affairs.

confidence (kon'-fi-dens) n. that in which faith is put; belief; trust; feeling of security; self-reliance; presumption; intimacy; secret.—**con'fident** a. trustful; having assurance; bold.—**con'fidently** adv.—**confidential** (kon-fi-den'-shal) a. enjoying, or treated with, confidence; private; secret.—**confiden'tially** adv.

configuration (kon'-fig-ū-rā'-shun) n. outward shape, form, or figure; grouping; outline.

confine (kon-fīn') v.t. keep within bounds; limit; enclose; imprison;—v.i. have common boundary.—**con'fine** n. usually in pl. con'fines, boundary; limit.—**confine'ment** n. imprisonment; restraint; detention; child-birth.

confirm (kon-ferm') v.t. make strong; settle; make valid by formal assent; ratify; make certain; verify.—**confirma'tion** n. act of making strong, valid, certain, etc.; proof; in certain churches, rite administered by bishop to confirm baptised persons in vows made for them at baptism.—**confirm'ative** a. tending to confirm or establish.—**confirm'atory** a. serving to confirm.—**confirmed'** pa.p.

confiscate (kon'-fis-kāt) v.t. seize by authority; take possession of without compensation;—a. forfeited.—**confisca'tion** n.—**con'fiscator** n.—**confis'catory** a.

conflagration (kon-fla-grā'-shun) n. destructive fire.

conflict (kon-flikt') v.i. dash together; clash; be at odds with; be inconsistent with; differ.—**con'flict** n. violent clashing; trial of strength; strong disagreement; battle.—**conflic'ting** a. differing; contradictory.

confluence (kon'-flōō-ens) n. flowing together; meeting of two or more rivers, streams, etc.—**con'fluent** a.

conform (con-form') v.t. make like; bring into agreement; adapt to rule, pattern, custom, etc.;—v.i. comply; agree;—a. in accord.—**conform'able** a. corresponding in form; similar;

submissive.—conform'ably adv.—conforma'tion n. manner in which a body is formed or shaped; structure.—conform'ist n.—conform'ity n.

confound (kon-found') v.t. mix up; bring to confusion; bewilder; defeat.—confound'ed a. confused; baffled; perplexed.

confront (kon-frunt') v.t. face boldly; oppose; bring face to face; compare.—confronta'tion n.

confuse (kon-fūz') v.t. mix up; jumble together; muddle; perplex; hence, mistake one thing for another.—confused' a. mixed up; perplexed.—confus'edly adv.—confu'sion n. state of being confused.

confute (kon-fūt') v.t. prove to be wrong; disprove.—confut'able a.

congeal (kon-gēl') v.t. and i. freeze, as a fluid; stiffen; solidify; curdle; coagulate;—v.i. become stiff or solidified, from cold.—congeal'able a.—congeal'ment n. thing congealed; clot.—congela'tion n.

congenial (kon-jēn'-yal) a. allied in disposition and tastes; kindred; agreeable; suited sympathetic.—congen'ially adv.—congenial'ity n.

congenital (kon-jen'-i-tal) a. existing at time of birth.

conger (kong'-ger) n. large species of sea-eel. Also con'ger-eel.

congest (kon-jest') v.t. collect into a mass; produce hampering accumulation; overcrowd.—congest'ed a. overcrowded; clogged.—congest'ion n. overcrowding.

conglomerate (kon-glom'-e-rāt) a. gathered into a mass; concentrated;—v.t. bring together into united mass.—conglomera'tion n.

congratulate (kon-grat'-ū-lāt) v.t. wish joy to; compliment.—congratulation (kon-grat-ū-lā'-shun) n. expression of pleasure at good fortune of someone.—congrat'ulatory a.

congregate (kong'-gre-gāt) v.t. gather into crowd or assembly;—v.i. meet together, in a large body.—congregation (kong-gre-gā'-shun) n. act of assembling; assemblage; gathering of persons for worship.—congrega'tional a.

congress (kong'-gres) n. meeting together of persons; formal assembly.—Con'gress n. legislative body of United States of America.—congressional (kon-gresh'-un-al) a.

congruent (kong'-grōō-ent) a. suitable; agreeing together; corresponding.—cong'ruence, cong'ruency n. suitableness.—congruity (kong-grōō-i-ti) n. harmony; conformity.—cong'ruous a. accordant; suitable.

coniferous (kō-nif'-e-rus) a. bearing cones.

conjecture (kon-jek'-tūr) n. guess; opinion founded on insufficient proof; surmise; inference; — v.t.

guess; surmise; infer on insufficient grounds.—conjec'turable a.—conjec'tural a.—conjec'turally adv.

conjoin (kon-join') v.t. join together.—conjoint' a. united; concerted; associated.

conjugal (kon'-jōō-gal) a. pert. to marriage; connubial; matrimonial.—con'jugally adv.

conjugate (kon'-jōō-gāt) v.t. (Gram.) recite or write all different parts of a verb.—conjuga'tion n. act of uniting; (Gram.) class of verbs inflected in same manner.

conjunct (kon-jungkt') a. joined together; united; associated.—conjunct'ly adv.—conjunc'tion n. union; concurrence of events; (Gram.) word used to join clauses.—conjunc'tive a.

conjure (kon-jōōr') v.t. call on by a sacred name; solemnly implore.—conjure (kun'jer) v.i. practise magic; practise the arts of a conjurer; (Fig.) to imagine.—conjura'tion n. act of calling upon or summoning by a sacred name.—con'jurer, con'juror n. magician; juggler.—conjur'or n. one bound by oath with others.—con'jury n. tricks of conjurer; magic; jugglery.

connect (ko-nekt') v.t. fasten together; associate; relate; attach; join;—v.i. unite; have a close relation.—connec'ted a.—connec'tedly adv.—connec'tion, connex'ion n.—connec'tive a. well connected, of good family.

connive (ko-nīv') v.i. wink at; pretend not to see; co-operate secretly (with at).—conni'vance n. consent in wrong-doing.

connoisseur (kon-i-ser', sur') n. competent judge, esp. in fine arts; expert.

connote (ko-nōt') v.t. mean; imply; signify; have meaning in addition to primary meaning.—connota'tion n. sum of qualities forming significance of a term.—con'notative a.

connubial (ko-nū'-bi-al) a. pert. to marriage.—connubial'ity n.

conquer (kong'-ker) v.t. overcome; subjugate; vanquish; surmount;—v.i. be victorious; prevail.—con'querable a.—con'queror n.—conquest (kong'-kwest) n. act of conquering or gaining by force; that which is conquered.

consanguineous (kon-sang-gwin'-ē-us) a. of same blood; related by birth.—consanguin'ity n.

conscience (kon'-shens) n. faculty by which we know right from wrong.—conscientious (kon-shi-en'-shus) a. governed by conscience.—conscien'tiously adv.—conscien'tiousness n.

conscious (kon'-shus) a. having inward knowledge (of); aware (of); having use of one's faculties.—con'sciously adv.—con'sciousness n.

the state of being mentally aware.

conscribe (kon-skrīb') v.t. conscript.

conscript (kon-skript') v.t. enrol compulsorily for state service in armed forces.—**con'script** n. one compelled to serve in armed forces.—**conscrip'tion** n.

consecrate (kon'-se-krāt) v.t. declare to be sacred; set apart for sacred uses; dedicate.—**consecra'tion** n.

consecutive (kon-sek'-ū-tiv) a. following one another in unbroken order; successive; resulting; (Gram.) expressing consequence.—**consec'utively** adv.—**consec'utiveness** n.

consensus (kon-sen'-sus) n. general agreement; unanimity.

consent (kon-sent') n. oneness of mind; agreement; assent; permission;—v.i. agree.—**consentient** (konsen'-shi-ent) a. united in opinion; agreeing in mind.

consequent (kon'-se-kwent) a. following as result.—n. effect.—**con'sequently** adv. therefore; as a result; by logical sequence.—**con'sequence** n. that which naturally follows; result; importance; value. — **consequential** (kon-se-kwen'-shal) a.

conserve (kon-serv') v.t. keep safe; preserve; maintain;—n. anything conserved; fruit, etc. prepared with sugar.—**conser'vancy** n. official safeguarding of trees, rivers, ports, etc.—**conserva'tion** n. preservation.—**conser'vative** a. tending to conserve; hostile to changes;—n. one opposed to hasty changes.—**conser'vatory** a. preservative;—n. green-house.

consider (kon-sid'-er) v.t. reflect upon carefully; examine carefully; be of opinion; regard as;—v.i. deliberate seriously.—**consid'erable** a. worthy of attention; moderately large.—**consid'erably** adv.—**consid'erate** a. thoughtful for others; circumspect.—**consid'erately** adv.—**consid'erateness** n.—**considera'tion** n. act of considering; deliberation; fee or recompense.—**consid'ered** a. carefully thought out.—**consid'ering** prep. in view of; taking into account.

consign (kon-sīn') v.t. give, transfer, or deliver in formal manner.—**consignee** (con-sī-nē) n. person to whom goods are consigned.—**consigner** (konsī'-ner) n. person who consigns goods.—**consign'ment** n. act of consigning; that which is consigned.

consist (kon-sist') v.i. be composed of; be in fixed or permanent state; subsist; exist; be compatible with.—**consistence, consistency** (kon-sis'-tens, -ten-si) n. degree of firmness or density; agreement.—**consis'tent** a.

console (kon-sōl') v.t. comfort in distress; solace.—**consol'able** a. able to be consoled.—**consola'tion** n. act of comforting; that which comforts; solace.—**consol'atory** a.

console (kon'-sōl) n. section of organ at which organist sits, control panel of computer, power station, etc.

consolidate (kon-sol'-i-dāt) v.t. and i. make solid; make firm; combine into connected whole; strengthen;—a. compact; united.—**consolida'tion** n. act of making or becoming compact and firm.

consonant (kon'-son-ant) a. agreeing with; harmonising with; in accord;—n. sound making a syllable only if with vowel; non-vowel.—**consonant'al** a. pert. to consonant.—**con'sonantly** adv.—**con'sonance, con'sonancy** n. quality of being consonant.

consort (kon'-sort) n. companion or partner; wife or husband.—**consort'** v.t. join;—v.i. keep company; associate; agree.

conspectus (kon-spek'-tus) n. general sketch or outline of subject; synopsis; epitome.

conspicuous (kon-spik'-ū-us) a. easy to be seen; very noticeable.—**conspic'uously** adv.—**conspic'uousness, conspicu'ity** n.

conspire (kon-spīr') v.i. unite for evil purpose; plot together.—**conspiracy** (kon-spir'-a-si) n. combination of persons for evil purpose.—**conspir'ator** n. (fem. conspir'atress).—**conspirato'rial** a.

constable (kun'-sta-bl, kon'-sta-bl) n. high officer in State establishments of the Middle Ages; policeman.—**con'stableship** n. office of constable. — **constabulary** (kun-stab'-ū-lar-i) a. pert. to constables;—n. police force.

constant (kon'-stant) a. fixed; steadfast; invariable; faithful;—n. that which is not subject to change.—**con'stantly** adv.—**con'stancy** n.

constellation (kon-ste-lā'-shun) n. group of fixed stars; assemblage of notable persons or things.

consternation (kon-ster-nā'-shun) n. amazement; terror; dismay.

constipate (kon'-sti-pāt) v.t. clog; make costive.—**constipa'tion** n. insufficient and irregular evacuation of the bowels.

constitute (kon'-sti-tūt) v.t. appoint to office or function; establish; set up; form; compose.—**constitu'tion** n. act of constituting; natural state of body or mind; composition; system or body of laws under which state exists.—**constitu'tional** a.;—n. short walk.—**constitu'tionally** adv.—**constit'uent** a. serving to compose or make up; component;—n. elector; component part; element.—**constit'uency** n. parliamentary district.

constrain (kon-strān') v.t. force or compel; confine; compress; restrain; limit.—**constraint'** n. compelling force; restraining force; unnaturalness or embarrassment of manner.

constrict (konstrikt') v.t. draw together; cramp; cause to shrink or contract; squeeze.—**constric'tion** n.—**constric'tive** a.—**constric'tor** n. that which constricts; boa-constrictor.

construct (kon-strukt') v.t. build; fabricate; devise or invent; compile.—**construc'tion** n. act of building; erection; structure; interpretation or meaning.—**construc'tive** a. opposite of destructive; of criticism, making positive suggestions.

construe (kon-ströö', kon'-ströö) v.t. explain structure of sentence and connection of words in it; translate; interpret; infer.

consubstantiate (kon-sub-stan'-shi-āt) v.t. and i. unite in one substance or nature.—**consubstan'tial** a.

consul (kon'-sul) n. officer appointed by government to represent it in foreign country.—**con'sular** a.—**con'sulate** n. official residence of consul.

consult (kon-sult') v.t. ask advice of; seek opinion of; refer to;—v.i. deliberate.—**consult'ant** n. one who consults; specialist.—**consulta'tion** n.—**consult'ative** a. advisory.

consume (kon-sūm') v.t. waste; destroy; use up; eat or drink up;—v.i. waste away.—**consum'able** a.—**consum'er** n.—**consumer goods**, goods used or consumed in everyday life.

consummate (kon'-sum-āt) v.t. complete; finish; perfect.—**consumm'ate** a. complete; perfect.

consumption (kon-sum'-shun) n. act of consuming; amount consumed; (Med.) pulmonary tuberculosis;—**consump'tive** a. wasting, affected with pulmonary tuberculosis.

contact (kon'-takt) n. touching; close union; meeting;—v.t. get in touch with a person.—**contact lens**, invisible eye-glass fitting exactly over the eyeball or cornea.

contagion (kon-tā'-jun) n. transmission of disease by direct contact; pestilence.—**conta'gious** a.

contain (kon-tān') v.t. hold; have room for; comprise; include; restrain.—**contain'er** n. one who, or that which, contains; vessel; holder.

contaminate (kon-tam'-i-nāt) v.t. soil; taint; corrupt; infect.—**contam'inable** a.—**contamina'tion** n.

contemplate (kon'-tem-plāt, kon-tem'-plāt) v.t. look at with attention; meditate on; have in view; intend; —v.i. think studiously; reflect.—**contempla'tion** n. act of contemplating.—**contem'plative** a. studious; thoughtful.—**contem'platively** adv.

contemporaneous (kon-tem-po-rā'-ne-us) a. having or happening at same time.—**contempora'neously** adv. at same time.—**contem'porary** a. contemporaneous; present-day.—n. one who lives at same time as another.

contempt (kon-temt') n. scorn; disgrace; disregard; disobedience of the rules and orders of a court of justice.—**contempt'ible** a. worthy of contempt.—**contempt'uous** a. expressing contempt or disdain.—**contempt'uously** adv.

contend (kon-tend') v.i. fight or struggle with; strive for; endeavour; dispute; assert strongly.

content (kon-tent') a. satisfied; pleased; willing;—v.t. satisfy the mind of; please; appease;—n. satisfaction; freedom from anxiety.—**content'edly** adv.—**content'edness** n.—**content'ment** n. satisfaction; pleasure; ease of mind.

content (kon'-tent) n. that which is contained; extent or area; volume.—**con'tents** n.pl. index of topics treated in a book.

contention (kon-ten'-shun) n. strife; debate; subject matter of argument or discussion.—**conten'tious** a. quarrelsome.

conterminous (kon-ter'-min-us) a. having same boundary; bordering; touching.

contest (kon-test') v.t. strive for; question or resist, as claim; to dispute; oppose;—v.i. contend or vie (with).—**contest** (kon'-test) n. struggle; competition; dispute.—**contest'able** a.—**contest'ant** n. disputant; competitor.

context (kon'-tekst) n. that which comes immediately before or after passage or word quoted; setting.—**context'ual** a.—**context'ually** adv.

contiguity (kon-ti-gū'-i-ti) n. nearness.—**contiguous** (kon-tig'-ū-us) a. touching; near; adjacent; neighbouring.

continent (kon'-tin-ent) n. one of larger divisions of unbroken land.—**continent'al** a.—**the Continent**, mainland of Europe.

continent (kon'-tin-ent) a. exercising self-restraint.—**con'tinence, con'tinency** n. moderation; chastity.

contingent (kon-tin'-jent) a. liable to happen, but not sure to do so; possible; conditional;—n. contingency; quota, esp. of troops.—**contin'gently** adv.—**contin'gence, contin'gency** n.

continue (kon-tin'-ū) v.t. prolong; go on with; persist in; resume;—v.i. remain in a state or place; persevere; last.—**contin'ual** a. lasting; without interruption.—**contin'ually** adv.—**contin'uance** n. a remaining in existence; duration; uninterrupted succession.—**continua'tion** n. act of continuing.—**continuity** (kon-tin-ū'-i-ti) n. state of being continuous; uninterrupted succession; close union.—**contin'uous** a. united without break; uninterrupted; constant.—**contin'uously** adv.

contort (kon-tört') v.t. twist violent-

ly; writhe; bend out of shape.—
contor'tion n. twisting; writhing.—
contor'tionist n. acrobat who bends
his body into extraordinary and
unnatural postures.—**contor'tive** a.

contour (kon'-tŏŏr, kon-tŏŏr') n.
bounding line; outline;—v.t. draw
the contour of.—**con'tour-line** n. line
on map connecting points of same
elevation.

contra- (kon'-tra) Latin *prefix* meaning against; contrary; in opposition
to; used to form many compounds.

contraband (kon'-tra-band) a. prohibited by law or treaty;—n. goods,
exportation or importation of which
is forbidden; smuggled goods.

contraception (kon-tra-sep'-shun) n.
prevention of conception; birth control.—**contraceptive** a. preventing
conception.—n. device so doing.

contract (kon-trakt') v.t. draw together; shorten; reduce; incur or
bring on;—v.i. become smaller;
agree upon; become involved in.—
contract (kon'-trakt) n. bargain;
agreement.—**contract'ed** a. drawn
together; narrow; mean.—**contract'-
ible** a.—**contrac'tion** n.—**contract'or** n.
one who undertakes to execute work
for fixed sum.—**contract'ual** a. implying, or connected with, contract.

contradict (kon-tra-dikt') v.t. speak
against; assert the contrary of;
deny.—**contradic'tion** n.—**contradict'-
ory** a. implying a denial; diametrically opposed; inconsistent.

contradistinction (kon-tra-dis-
tingk'-shun) n. direct contrast.

contrail (kon'-trāl) n. vapour trail
made by high-flying aircraft.

contralto (kon-tral'-tō) n. lowest of
the three ranges of female voices;
singer of that voice.

contraption (kon-trap'-shun) n. device; gadget.

contrapuntal (kon-tra-pun'-tal) a.
pert. to counterpoint [See **counterpoint**].

contrary (kon'-tra-ri) a. opposite;
different; adverse; (*Colloq.*) (kon-
trā'-r-i) perverse; obstinate.—n.
exact opposite of.—**con'trarily** adv.—
contrariwise (kon-trā'-ri-wīz) adv. on
the contrary.

contrast (kon-trast') v.t. bring out
differences; set in opposition for
purpose of comparing;—v.i. be or
stand in opposition.—**contrast** (kon'-
trast) n. striking difference; comparison of objects, qualities, etc. to
show the difference.

contravene (kon-tra-vēn') v.t. oppose; break or infringe, as a law.—
contraven'tion n.

contribute (kon-trib'-ūt) v.t. give or
pay to common fund; help to a
common result; write for newspaper,
magazine, etc.;—v.i. lend assistance.
—**contribution** (kon-tri-bū'-shun) n.

that which is contributed.—**contrib'-
utive** a. tending to contribute;
lending aid or influence; helping.—
contrib'utor n.—**contrib'utory** a.

contrite (kon'-trīt) a. humbly penitent; full of remorse.—**con'tritely** adv.
—**con'triteness** n.—**contrition** (kon-
trish'-un) n. remorse.

contrive (kon-trīv') v.t. and i. plan;
effect or bring about; invent.—
contriv'ance n. act of planning;
artifice or device; mechanical invention.—**contrived** a. artificial.

control (kon-trōl) v.t. have under
command; regulate; check; restrain;
direct;—n. authority or power;
government; — pr.p. **control'ling**. —
pa.p. and pa.t. **controlled'**.—**control'-
lable** a.—**control'ler** n.

controvert (kon'-trō-vert) v.t. oppose or dispute by argument; deny
or refute.—**controvert'ible** a.—**controvert'ibly** adv.—**controversy** (kon'-trō-
ver-si) n. disputation; argument.—
controversial (kon-trō-ver'-shal) a.
likely to provoke argument.—
controver'sially adv.—**controver'sialist** n.

contumacy (kon'-tū-ma-si) n. contempt of orders or authority; stubborn disobedience. — **contumacious**
(kon-tū-mā'-shus) a. rebellious.—
contuma'ciously adv.—**contuma'ciousness** n.

contumely (kon'-tūm-li) n. insult;
indignity; disdainful insolence; reproach.—**contume'liousness** n.

contuse (kon-tūz') v.t. bruise or
injure by beating, without breaking
skin.—**contu'sion** n. bruise.

conundrum (kon-un'-drum) n. riddle;
anything that puzzles.

conurbation (kon-ur-bā'-shun) n.
built-up area formed by aggregation
of several towns.

convalesce (kon-va-les') v.i. recover
from illness.—**convales'cent** a. recovering health;—n. one recovering
from sickness.—**convales'cence** n.

convection (kon-vek'-shun) n. transmission, esp. of heat, by means of
currents in liquids or gases.—**convec-
to'r** n. heating appliance which sets
up convection currents.

convene (kon-vēn') v.t. call together;
—v.i. come together or assemble.—
conven'er n. chairman of committee.
—**conven'able** a.

convenient (kon-vēn-'yent) a. fit;
suitable; handy or easy of access.—
conven'iently adv.—**conven'ience** n.
that which is convenient; appliance
which makes for comfort; lavatory.
—**conven'iency** n.

convent (kon'-vent) n. community,
esp. of nuns, devoted to religious
life; nunnery.

conventicle (kon-ven'-ti-kl) n.
gathering, esp. for worship; clandestine meeting of the Covenanters.

convention (kon-ven'-shun) n. act of

coming together; formal assembly of representatives; provisional treaty; accepted usage, custom, or rule.—**conven'tional** a. formed by agreement or compact; sanctioned by usage; customary. — **conven'tionally** adv. — **conven'tionalism** n. that which is established by usage.—**conventional'ity** n. adherence to social usages and formalities.

converge (kon-verj') v.i. tend to one point; tend to meet; approach.—**conver'gent** a. tending to one point.—**conver'gence, conver'gency** n. coming together.

converse (kon-vers') v.i. talk with.—**convers'able** a. disposed to talk; affable; sociable.—**convers'ably** adv.—**convers'ance, convers'ancy** n. state of being acquainted with.—**convers'ant** a. familiar with by use or study.—**conversa'tion** n. talk.—**conversa'tional** a.—**conversa'tion(al)ist** n. one who excels in conversation.—**convers'ative** a. inclined to talk.

converse (kon'-vers) a. opposite; turned round; reversed in order or relation;—n. opposite; contrary.—**con'versely** adv.

convert (kon-vert') v.t. apply to another purpose; change; cause to adopt a religion, opinion, etc.; in Rugby football, complete (a try) by kicking a goal.—**convert** (kon'-vert) n. converted person.—**conver'sion** n. change from one state to another.—**convert'er** n.—**convert'ible** a. capable of change;—n. car which can be converted at will from saloon to open tourer.—**convert'ibly** adv.—**convertibility** n.

convex (kon'-veks, kon-veks') a. curving outwards; opposite of concave; bulging.—**convex'ity** n.

convey (kon-vā') v.t. carry; transport; transfer; make over by deed; impart; communicate; steal;—v.i. steal.—**convey'able** a.—**convey'ance** n. act of conveying; means of transit; vehicle; transference of property.—**convey'ancer** n. one skilled in legal transfer of property.—**convey'ancing** n.—**convey'er, convey'or** n.

convict (kon-vikt') v.t. prove guilty; pronounce guilty.—**con'vict** n. person undergoing penal servitude.—**convic'tion** n. act of convicting; verdict of guilty; firm belief.

convince (kon-vins') v.t. persuade by argument; satisfy by proof.—**convin'cible** a.—**convin'cing** a. capable of compelling belief.—**convin'cingly** adv.

convivial (kon-viv'-i-al) a. festive; jovial; social; mirthful; merry.—**conviv'ially** adv.—**convivial'ity** n.

convoke (kon-vōk') v.t. call together; convene; assemble.—**convoca'tion** n. act of calling together; assembly.

convolve (kon-volv') v.t. and i. roll or wind together; twist; coil.—**con-**

volute (kon'-vō-lūt), **convolu'ted** a.—**convolution** (kon-vō-lū'-shun) n.

convolvulus (kon-vol'-vū-lus) n. (Bot.) genus of climbing plants, including bindweed.

convoy (kon-voi') v.t. accompany or escort for protection, by land, sea, or air.—**convoy** (kon'-voi) n. act of convoying; escort; column (of lorries, etc.).

convulse (kon-vuls') v.t. shake violently; affect with violent and irregular spasms. — **convul'sion** n. violent agitation;—pl. (Med.) violent and involuntary contractions of the muscles; spasms; fits of laughter.—**convul'sive** a.

cony, coney (kō'-ni) n. rabbit.

coo (kōō) v.i. make low, melodious sound like note of dove; act in loving manner.

cook (kook) v.t. prepare food by boiling, roasting, baking, etc.; concoct; tamper with; falsify;—v.i. prepare food; undergo cooking;—n. one who cooks food.—**cook'ery** n. art or process of cooking.—**cook'er** n. stove for cooking.

cool (kōōl) a. slightly cold; self-possessed; frigid in manner; impudent;—n. moderate state of cold; —v.t. cause to cool; moderate or calm;—v.i. become cool; lose one's ardour or affection.—**cool'ant** n. substance used for cooling.—**cool'ly** adv.—**cool'ness** n.

coolie (kōō'-li) n. Asiatic labourer.

coop (kōōp) n. basket placed over sitting fowls; fowl-run;—v.t. put in coop (coop up); confine.

cooper (kōōp'-er) n. maker of casks or barrels.—**coop'erage** n. cooper's work or workshop.

co-operate (kō-op'-e-rāt) v.i. act jointly with others; unite for common effort.—**co-operation** (kō-op-e-rā'-shun) n. joint action; union of persons for same end.—**co-operative** (kō-op'-e-rā-tiv) a. working jointly for same end.—**co-op'erator** n.—**co-operative store**, shop of co-operative society, where members make purchases and share profits.

co-opt (kō-opt') v.t. choose or elect into a body or committee by votes of its members.—**co-op'tion** n.

co-ordinate (kō-or'-di-nāt) a. equal in degree, rank, importance, etc.; v.t. bring into order as parts of whole; adjust;—n. person or thing of same rank, etc. as another.—**co-or'dinately** adv. in same order.—**co-ordina'tion** n.—**co-or'dinative** a.

coot (kōōt) n. small black waterfowl of rail family.

copartner (kō-pàrt'-ner) n. joint partner; sharer; associate.—**copart'nership** n.

cope (kōp) n. covering; cap or hood; long, sleeveless vestment.—**coping**

(kōp'-ing) n. highest course of masonry in a wall.—**cop'ing-stone** n. stone that crowns a wall.

cope (kōp) v.t. match oneself against; —v.i. deal successfully (with).

copious (kō'-pi-us) a. abundant; plentiful; of style, not concise.—**co'piously** adv.—**co'piousness** n.

copper (kop'-er) n. red-coloured metal; bronze money; bronze coin (1d. or ½d.); large vessel for boiling clothes;—a. copper-coloured; made of copper.—**copp'ery** a. made of copper; like copper.—**copp'er-plate** n. plate of copper for engraving or etching; print from such plate; copybook writing.

coppice, copse (kop'-is, kops) n. a wood of small trees.

copra (kop'-ra) n. dried kernel of coconut.

copse (kops) n. See **coppice**.

copulate (kop'-ū-lāt) v.i. unite sexually; have sexual intercourse.—**copula'tion** n.—**cop'ulative** a.

copy (kop'-i) n. imitation; reproduction; matter for printing;—v.t. imitate.—**cop'ier** n.—**cop'y-writer** n. writer of advertisements.—**cop'y-right** n. exclusive right to reproduce literary or musical work or illustration;—a. protected by law of copyright.

coquet, coquette (ko-ket') v.i. attempt to attract notice, admiration, or love of; flirt with.—**pr.p. coquet'ting.**—**pa.p.** and **pa.t. coquet'ted.**—**coquetry** (ko'-ket-ri) n.—**coquette'** n. a flirt.—**coquet'tish** a.

coracle (kor'-a-kl) n. boat used by ancient Britons, consisting of wicker frame covered with hide, oilskin, etc.

coral (kor'-al) n. hard limy substance composed of skeletons of marine polyps;—a. coral-coloured; made of coral.—**cor'alline** a. coral-red; consisting of coral.

cor anglais (kor-ong'-lā) n. (Mus.) instrument of oboe family, also called 'English horn.'

corbel (kor'-bel) n. stone or timber projection from wall to act as support for something superimposed.—**cor'belling** n.

corbie (kor'-bi) n. (Scot.) raven or crow.

cord (kord) n. thick string or thin rope of several strands; anything like cord;—v.t. bind with cord.—**cord'age** n. assemblage of ropes esp. rigging of ship.—**cord'ed** a.

cordial (kord'-yal) a. of, or proceeding from, the heart; sincere;—n. anything that comforts or strengthens; refreshing drink or medicine.—**cor'dially** adv.—**cordial'ity** n.

cordite (kord'-īt) n. smokeless explosive.

cordon (kor'-don) n. circle of guards round place or thing to prevent access.

cordon (kor'-don) n. tasselled cord or ribbon worn as badge of honour.

corduroy (kor-'dū-roi) n. thick cotton fabric, corded or ribbed on surface.—**cord'uroys** n.pl. trousers made of this fabric.

core (kōr) n. heart or inner part of, esp. of fruit;—v.t. take out core.

co-respondent (kō-re-spon'-dent) n. in divorce suit man or woman charged along with the respondent as guilty of adultery.

corgi (kor'-gi) n. Welsh breed of dog.

cork (kork) n. outer bark of cork-tree; stopper for bottle, cask, etc. cut out of cork;—a. made of cork;—v.t. stop up with a cork; stop up generally.—**cork'screw** n. tool for drawing corks from bottles.

corm (korm) n. underground stem resembling a bulb, but more solid.

cormorant (kor'-mō-rant) n. voracious sea-bird, allied to the gannet and pelican.

corn (korn) n. single seed of oats, wheat, rye, barley, maize, etc.; inclusive term for grain of all kinds; plants that produce corn; (U.S.) maize; (Scot.) oats;—v.t. preserve meat by salting.—**corn'cake** n. cake made from maize.—**corn'chand'ler** n. dealer in corn.—**corn'cob** n. head or seed-pod in which are encased the grains of maize-plant.—**corn'crake** n. landrail, migratory bird which nests in cornfields.—**corn'flour** n. foodstuff consisting of finely ground starch granules of Indian corn (maize).—**corn-flow'er** n. annual weed growing in cornfields and bearing blue flowers.—**corn'y** a. (Slang) out of date.

corn (korn) n. horny growth of the skin, usually on toes and feet.

cornea (kor'-nē-a) n. transparent membrane which forms part of outer coat of eyeball.

cornelian (kor-nēl'-yan) n. precious stone of light-red or flesh colour, variety of chalcedony.

corner (kor'-ner) n. point where two lines meet; part of room where two sides meet; angle; nook; embarrassing position; (Football, Hockey) free kick (from corner of field);—v.t. drive into a corner; cut off escape; establish monopoly.—**corn'er-stone** n. stone which lies at corner of two walls, and unites them; thing of fundamental importance.—**corn'er-wise** adv. diagonally; with corner in front.

cornet (kor'-net) n. kind of trumpet with valves; formerly lowest rank of cavalry officer, now second-lieutenant; cone-shaped holder for ice-cream.—**cor'netist** n. cornet-player.

cornice (kor'-nis) n. (Archit.) upper part of an entablature; moulded projection which crowns capital or column; ornamental moulding round top of walls of a room.

cornucopia (kor-nū-kō'-pi-ą) n. horn of plenty, emblem of abundance.

corollary (kor-ol'-ą-ri) n. inference from preceding statement; deduction; consequence.

corona (ko-rō'-ną) n. flat projecting part of cornice; top or crown; halo around heavenly body.—**cor'onary** a. resembling crown or circlet; (Anat.) encircling, as of vessel or nerve.—**coronary thrombosis** (Med.) disease of heart.—**cor'onate** v.t. crown.—**corona'tion** n. crowning of sovereign.—**cor'onet** n. small crown.

coroner (kor'-o-nęr) n. legal officer appointed to hold inquest on cases of unnatural death.

corporal (kor'-po-rąl) n. non-commissioned officer next in rank below a sergeant.

corporal (kor'-po-rąl) a. belonging or relating to the body; material, not spiritual.—**cor'porally** adv.—**corporality** (kor-pō-ral'-i-ti) n. state of having a body; bodily substance.—**corporate** (kor'-po-rāt) a. united legally in a body, and acting as individual.—**corporately** adv.—**corporation** (kor-pō-rā'-shun) n. association authorised to act as individual; (U.S.) company; (Colloq.) protuberant stomach.—**cor'porative** a.—**corporeal** (kor-pō'-rē-ąl) a. pert. to the body; having a body; bodily; physical.—**corpo'really** adv.—**corporal punishment,** punishment inflicted on body.

corps (kōr) n. largest tactical army unit; organised body of persons.—pl. **corps** (kōrz).

corpse (korps) n. dead body, esp. of human being.

corpulence (kor'-pū-lens) n. excessive fatness; fleshiness; stoutness.—**cor'pulency** n.—**cor'pulent** a.

corpus (kor'-pus) n. a body; main substance of anything.

corpuscle (kor'-pus-l, kor-pus'-l) n. little body; minute particle; (Anat.) organic cell, either moving freely, as in blood, or intimately connected with others, as bone-corpuscles.—**corpuscular** (kor-pus'-kū-lęr) a.

corral (ko-rål') n. enclosure for cattle, or for defence.—v.t. drive into a corral.

correct (ko-rekt') a. right; free from faults; accurate;—v.t. make right; bring to the standard of truth; punish; counteract.—**correct'ly** adv.—**correc'tion** n. amendment; change to remedy a fault; punishment.—**correc'tional** a.—**correct'ive** a. having power to correct;—n. that which corrects or counteracts.—**correct'ness** n.—**correct'or** n.

correlate (kor'-e-lāt) v.i. be mutually related;—v.t. place in reciprocal relation.—**correla'tion** n. reciprocal

relation.—**correl'ative** a. reciprocally related;—n. one who, or that which is correspondingly related to another person or thing.—**correl'atively** adv.—**correlativ'ity** n.

correspond (kor-e-spond') v.i. exchange letters; answer or agree with in some respect; be congruous.—**correspond'ence** n. exchange of letters; the letters themselves; mutual adaptation of one thing to another; suitability.—**correspond'ent** a. suitable; conformable; congruous;—n. one with whom intercourse is maintained by exchange of letters.

corridor (kor'-i-dor) n. gallery or passage in building; side-passage in railway-train.

corrigendum (kor-i-jen'-dum) n. something to be corrected, esp. misprint in book;—pl. **corrigen'da.**

corrival (ko-ri'-vąl) n. fellow rival.

corroborate (ko-rob'-ō-rāt) v.t. add strength to; confirm; support statement, etc.—**corrobora'tion** n.—**corroborative** a. confirming; strengthening.

corrode (ko-rōd') v.t. eat away by degrees (by chemical action, disease, etc.); rust.—**corrod'ible, corros'ible** a. capable of being corroded.—**corrosion** n.—**corros'ive** a.

corrugate (kor'-ū-gāt) v.t. form into wrinkles or folds.—**corruga'tion** n. act of wrinkling; wrinkle.—**corrugated iron,** sheet-iron, corrugated to increase rigidity.

corrupt (ko-rupt') v.t. and i. make rotten; rot; defile; contaminate; make evil; bribe;—a. putrid; depraved; tainted with vice or sin; influenced by bribery; spoilt, by mistakes, or altered for the worse (of words, literary passages, etc.).—**corrup'ter** n.—**corrupt'ible** a.—**corruption** n.—**corrup'tive** a. having quality of corrupting.—**corrupt'ly** adv.—**corrupt'ness** n.

corsage (kor'-sāj) n. bodice of lady's dress; posy worn on dress.

corsair (kor'-sār) n. Moorish seamarauder; pirate; pirate's vessel.

corset (kor'-set) n. under-garment, fitting close to body to give support to the figure.

cortège (kor-tezh') n. train of attendants or procession; funeral procession.

coruscate (kor'-us-kāt) v.i. flash; glitter; gleam.—**corusca'tion** n.

corvette (kor-vet') n. orig. fast full-rigged warship (small frigate) of not more than 20 guns; small warship fitted with anti-submarine devices.

cosh (kosh) n. (Slang) small bludgeon—v.t. fell with bludgeon.

co-signatory (kō-sig'-ną-tor-i) a. signing jointly;—n. joint signer of document.

cosmetic (koz-met'-ik) a. making for beauty, esp. of skin;—n. substance helping to improve or enhance the appearance.

cosmic (koz'-mik) *a*. See **cosmos**.

cosmo- (koz'-mō) combining form from Gk. *kosmos*, the universe.

cosmopolitan (koz-mo-pol'-i-tan) *a*. relating to all parts of the world; free from national prejudice;—*n*. cosmopolitan person; citizen of the world.

cosmos (koz'-mos) *n*. ordered universe; order (as opposed to 'chaos'). —**cos'mic**, **cos'mical** *a*. pert. to universe, or to earth as part of universe; orderly.—**cos'mically** *adv*. —**cosmic rays**, radiations of great penetrating power, coming to earth from outer space.—**cos'monaut** *n*. space-traveller.

Cossack (kos'-ak) *n*. one of a tribe, skilled in horsemanship, inhabiting southern steppes of Russia.

cosset (kos'-et) *n*. pet lamb; pet;— *v.t.* pamper.

cost (kost) *v.t.* entail payment, loss, or sacrifice of;—*n*. price; amount paid, or to be paid, for anything; suffering undergone for any end.— **costs** *n.pl.* (*Law*) expenses of lawsuit. —**cost'ing** *n*. system of calculating cost of production.—**cost'liness** *n*. expensiveness.—**cost'ly** *a*. expensive.

costal (kos'-tal) *a*. pert. to ribs or to side of the body.

costermonger (kos'-ter-mung-ger) *n*. itinerant seller of fruit, vegetables, fish, etc.—(*Abbrev.*) **cos'ter**.

costive (kos'-tiv) *a*. having sluggish motion of bowels; constipated.— **cos'tiveness** *n*.

costume (kos'-tūm, kos-tūm') *n*. dress peculiar or appropriate, as to a country, period, office, or character; woman's dress or gown.—**costumier** (kos-tūm'-i-er) *n*. one who makes or deals in costumes.—**costume jewellery** *n*. imitation jewellery worn as dress ornament.

cosy (kō'-zi) *a*. snug; comfortable;— *n*. covering to keep teapot hot (tea cosy).—**co'sily** *adv*.

cot (kot) *n*. cottage.

cot (kot) *n*. small bed or crib, esp. for child; (*Naut.*) swinging bed on board ship.

cote (kōt) *n*. shelter or enclosure for animals or birds; sheep-fold.

coterie (kō'-te-rē) *n*. set or circle of persons usually with common interests.

cotoneaster (kot-ō-ni-as'-ter) *n*. genus of shrubs of order Rosaceae bearing red berries.

cottage (kot'-āj) *n*. small dwelling house, esp. in country.—**cott'ager** *n*. one who inhabits cottage.

cottar, **cotter** (kot-er, -er) *n*. in Scotland, a farm-worker who occupies rent-free cottage.

cotter (kot'-er) *n*. pin or wedge used

for tightening or fastening, esp. parts of machine; split-pin.

cotton (kot'-n) *n*. soft, downy substance, resembling fine wool, got from pods of cotton-plant; cloth made of cotton; thread made of this;—*a*. made of cotton;—*v.i.* become friendly; take to.—**cott'on wool** *n*. hairs of cotton plant, cleaned and prepared in masses, forming fleecy wool.

cotyledon (kot-i-lē'-don) *n*. (*Bot.*) one of the seed-lobes or primary leaves of the embryo plant.

couch (kouch) *v.t.* cause to lie down, esp. on a bed; phrase; express; lower a lance, spear, etc. for action; —*v.i.* lie down; crouch;—*n*. sofa; bed.—**couchant** (kouch'-ant) *a*. lying down.

couch-grass (kouch'-grås) *n*. (*Bot.*) popular name for *Triticum repens*, troublesome creeping weed.

cougar (kōō'-gar) *n*. puma or American panther.

cough (kof) *n*. noisy, violent, explosive effort to expel irritating matter from lungs;—*v.i.* make such effort;—*v.t.* expel by cough.

could (kood) *pa.t.* of verb **can**.

coulter (kōl'-ter, kōōl'-ter) *n*. sharp blade of iron placed at front end of plough to act as cutter.

council (koun'-sil) *n*. assembly summoned for consultation or advice; municipal body; deliberation carried on in such assembly.— **coun'cillor** *n*. member of council.

counsel (koun'-sel) *n*. advice; opinion; deliberation together; one who gives advice, esp. legal; barrister; advocate;—*v.t.* advise; admonish; recommend; — *pr.p.* **coun'selling**. — *pa.p.* and *pa.t.* **coun'selled**.—**coun'sellor** *n*. one who counsels; adviser.— **coun'sellorship** *n*. office of a counsellor.

count (kount) *n*. title of foreign nobility equal to that of earl.— **countess** *n*. wife of count or earl.

count (kount) *v.t.* number; reckon; sum up; consider or esteem; include; recite numerals in succession;—*v.i.* depend or rely (*with* on).—*n*. act of reckoning; number ascertained by counting; (*Law*) charge in an indictment.—**count'able** *a*.—**count'less** *a*. innumerable.—**count'er** *n*. one who counts; token or disc used in reckoning; table on which goods are laid out or money counted.—**countdown** *n*. backward count from a set time to zero for initiation of operation, e.g. for launching of rocket.

countenance (koun'-te-nans) *n*. face; aspect; appearance; favour; encouragement;—*v.t.* favour; support.

counter (koun'-ter) *a*. contrary; opposite; reciprocal;—*adv*. in opposition; opposite way;—*n*. that which is opposite; return blow **or parry**;—

v.t. and *i.* parry; oppose; make a counter-move.—**coun'ter-attack'** *n.* attack launched to recapture position recently lost.—**count'er-attrac'tion** *n.* rival attraction.—**coun'ter-claim** *n.* claim set up by someone to counter another claim.—**coun'ter-ten'or** *n.* man's voice singing alto.

counteract (koun-ter-akt') *v.t.* act in opposition to; hinder; defeat.

counterbalance (koun'-ter-bal-ans) *v.t.* act against with equal power or effect; neutralise.—**counterbal'ance** *n.* equal opposing weight, power, or agency. — **counterblast** (koun'-ter-blåst) *n.* retaliatory answer to statement or accusation.

countercharge (koun'-ter-chárj) *n.* charge brought in opposition to another.

counterfeit (koun'-ter-fēt) *v.t.* copy without authority; imitate with intent to deceive; forge; feign;—*a.* sham; forged; false;—*n.* imitation; forgery; impostor.—**coun'terfeiter** *n.*

counterfoil (koun'-ter-foil) *n.* that part of cheque, receipt, etc. retained by issuer for record purposes.

countermand (koun-ter-mand') *v.t.* cancel order;—*n.* contrary order.

countermarch (koun'-ter-march) *v.i.* march back;—*n.* marching back.

counterpane (koun'-ter-pān) *n.* coverlet for bed; stitched quilt.

counterpart (koun'-ter-párt) *n.* duplicate; something complementary to another.

counterplot (koun-ter-plot') *v.t.* oppose one plot by another.—**coun'-terplot** *n.*

counterpoint (koun'-ter-point) *n.* (*Mus.*) art of combining melodies; addition of subsidiary melody to another.—**contrapuntal** *a.*

counterpoise (koun'-ter-poiz) *v.t.* act against with equal weight or power;—*n.* weight sufficient to balance another.

countersign (koun-ter-sīn') *v.t.* sign document already signed by another; ratify; attest authenticity.—**coun'tersign** *n.* password, military watchword.

country (kun'-tri) *n.* region; district; tract of land; territory of a nation; nation itself; land of birth, residence, etc.; rural districts as opposed to town;—*a.* rural; rustic.—**countrified** (kun'-tri-fîd) *a.* rural in manner or appearance. — **coun'trify** *v.t.* — **coun'try-dance** *n.* dance in which the couples line up in rows, facing each other.—**coun'tryman**, *n.* one who lives in the country; rustic; one born in same country; compatriot.—**coun'-try-seat** *n.* country mansion.—**coun'-tryside** *n.* any rural district.—**to go to the country**, have a general election.

county (koun'-ti) *n.* originally lands of count or earl; shire; administra-

tive division of country; inhabitants of a county.

coup (kóó) *n.* lit. stroke or blow; then, successful stroke or move.

coup d'état (kóó-dā-ta') *n.* sudden and revolutionary change of government achieved by force.

coupé (kóó-pā') *n.* two-seater motor-car with enclosed body.

couple (kup'-l) *n.* two things of same kind taken together; two; pair; brace; husband and wife; leash for two hounds; that which joins two things together;—*v.t.* join together; marry;—*v.i.* copulate.—**coup'let** *n.* pair of lines of verse, esp. if rhyming and of equal length.—**coup'ling** *n.* connection.

coupon (kóó'-pon) *n.* negotiable ticket or voucher; (*Betting*) printed form on which to mark forecasts of racing or football results.

courage (kur'-āj) *n.* bravery; fearlessness; daring; boldness.—**courageous** (ku-rā'-jus) *a.*—**coura'geously** *adv.*—**coura'geousness** *n.*—**Dutch courage**, courage that is not genuine, but consequent on drinking.

courier (kóó'-ri-er) *n.* runner or messenger; state messenger; tourist guide who accompanies travellers.

course (kōrs) *n.* act of passing from one point to another; progress or movement, both in space and in time; ground traversed; way or direction; line of conduct; track or ground on which race is run; career; series (of lessons, lectures, etc.); each of successive divisions of a meal; continuous line of masonry at one level in a building;—*v.t.* hunt; pursue; chase;—*v.i.* run swiftly; gallop.—**cours'er** *n.* one who courses or hunts; swift horse.—**cours'ing** *n.* hunting hares with greyhounds.

court (kōrt) *n.* uncovered area enclosed by buildings; yard; residence of sovereign; retinue of sovereign; homage or attention; legal tribunal; judge or judges, as distinguished from counsel; hall where justice is administered; (*Sport*) space, usually rectangular, laid out for certain sports, as tennis, etc.—**courteous** (kurt'-yus) *a.* polite; well-bred; of courtlike manners.—**court'eously** *adv.*—**court'eousness** *n.*—**courtier** (kōrt'-yer) one who frequents courts of princes.—**court'ly** *a.* elegant; flattering.—**court'liness** *n.*—**court'-card** *n.* corrupt. of **coat'-card**; a playing-card with coated figure, i.e. king, queen, or knave.—**court'-mar'tial** *n.* court of military or naval or air force officers for trial of service personnel —*pl.* **courts-mar'tial**.

court (kōrt) *v.t.* seek favour of; try to gain affections of; seek in marriage;—*v.i.* woo; play the lover.—**court'ship** *n.*

courtesan (kŏr'-te-zan) *n.* court mistress; prostitute.

courtesy (kur'-te-si) *n.* politeness of manners.

cousin (kuz'-n) *n.* formerly any kinsman; now, son or daughter of uncle or aunt.

couture (koo-tūr) *n.* fashion designing; dress-making.—**coutur'ier** *n.*

cove (kōv) *n.* small inlet or creek; small bay;—*v.t.* arch over.

covenant (kuv'-e-nant) *n.* mutual and solemn agreement; contract; compact; written agreement;—*v.t.* agree to by covenant;—*v.i.* enter into agreement.—**cov'enanter** *n.* one who makes covenant or agreement.—**Covenan'ters** *n.pl.* (*Scot.*) those who supported the Scottish National Covenant of 1638.

cover (kuv'-er) *v.t.* be over whole top of; overspread; enclose; include; protect; put hat on; point revolver, gun, etc. at; wager equal sum of money;—*n.* anything that covers; lid; wrapper; envelope; binding; cloak; disguise; concealment; shelter; defence.—**cov'ering** *n.* anything that covers.—**cov'erlet** *n.* bed-cover.—**cov'ert** *a.* concealed; secret; veiled; —*n.* place sheltering game.—**cov'ertly** *adv.* secretly; in private.

covet (kuv'-et) *v.t.* long to possess, esp. what belongs to another.—**cov'etable** *a.* that may be coveted.—**cov'etous** *a.* very desirous; excessively eager; avaricious for gain.—**cov'etously** *adv.*—**cov'etousness** *n.*

covey (kuv'-i) *n.* brood of partridges or quail; (*Fig.*) company; set.

cow (kou) *n.* female ox; female elephant, whale, etc.—**cow'-boy** *n.* herdsman employed on ranch.—**cow'herd** *n.* one who herds cows.—**cow'-pars'ley, cow'pars'nip** *n.* umbelliferous plants bearing white or pink flowers and used as fodder.—**cow'-punch'er** *n.* cowboy.

cow (kou) *v.t.* frighten into submission; overawe.

coward (kou'-ard) *n.* one given to fear; one who lacks courage.—**cow'ard, cow'ardly** *a.* lacking in courage; afraid; mean.—**cowardice** (kou'-ar-dis) *n.* want of courage; fear.—**cow'ardliness** *n.*—**cow'ardly** *adv.* in cowardly manner; basely; meanly.

cower (kou'-er) *v.i.* crouch down through fear, shame, cold.

cowl (koul) *n.* monk's hooded cloak; hood itself; hooded top for chimney;—**cowled** (kould) *a.* wearing a cowl; hooded.—**cow'ling** *n.* (*Aviation*) metal cover which encloses aero-engine.

cowry, cowrie (kou'-ri) *n.* small shell, used as ornament, or as money in parts of India and Africa.

cowslip (kou'-slip) *n.* common British meadow flower.

coxcomb (koks'-kōm) *n.* one given to showing off; fool; fop.

coxswain (kok'-sn), **cox** (koks) *n.* steersman of boat; (*Naval*) petty officer in charge of boat.—to **cox** *v.t.* and *i.* to act as coxswain. Also **cockswain.**

coy (koi) *a.* shy; bashful; modest; pretending to be shy.—**coy'ly** *adv.*—**coy'ness** *n.*

coyote (koi-ōt', -ō'-te) *n.* prairie wolf.

crab (krab) *n.* short-tailed crustacean with ten legs, of which front pair are armed with strong pincers.—to **catch a crab,** miss stroke in rowing, and fall backwards.

crab (krab) *n.* wild apple of sour taste; the tree; one of sour temper; —*a.* sour. Also **crab'-app'le.**

crabbed (krab'-ed) *a.* harsh; rough; austere; perverse; bad-tempered; of writing, hard to read.—**crabb'edly** *adv.*—**crabb'edness** *n.*

crack (krak) *v.t.* break with sharp noise, either wholly or partially; split or break; produce sudden sharp sound; snap;—*v.i.* break partially; burst open in chinks; give forth sudden sharp sound; *n.* partial break; fissure; sharp noise; flaw; break in the voice; mental flaw;—*a.* superior; special; smart; expert.—**crack'er** *n.* one who cracks, that which cracks; boaster; small zig-zag firework; paper cylinder which explodes when pulled asunder; thin crisp biscuit.—**cracks'man** *n.* burglar.—to **crack a crib** (*Slang*) burgle.

crackle (krak'-l) *v.i.* produce slight but repeated cracking sounds;—*n.* noise composed of frequent, slight crackling sounds.—**crack'ling** *n.* succession of small sharp reports; rind of roasted pork.—**crack'ly** *a.* crisp.

cracknel (krak'-nel) *n.* dry, brittle kind of biscuit.

cradle (krā'-dl) *n.* cot for infants that can be rocked; infancy; place of origin; frame- work used as support; —*v.t.* place or rock in a cradle; tend or train in infancy.

craft (kräft) *n.* skill; skilled trade; cunning; vessel; vessels collectively.—**craft'y** *a.* cunning; artful.—**craft'ily** *adv.*—**crafts'man** *n.* one engaged in a craft or trade.—**crafts'manship** *n.*

crag (krag) *n.* steep, rugged rock or peak.—**cragged** (krag'-ed) *a.*—**crag'gy** *a.*—**crag'gedness** *n.*—**crag'giness** *n.*

cram (kram) *v.t.* and *i.* stuff; pack tightly; prepare a person hastily for an examination;—*n.* cramming; crush or crowd of people.

cramp (kramp) *n.* painful contraction of muscles of the body; that which restrains; clamp for holding masonry, timbers, etc. together;—*v.t.* affect with cramp; restrict or hamper; hold with a cramp;—*a.* narrow; restricted.

cran (kran) *n.* measure of catch of herrings, holding roughly 750 fish; hence, basket, esp. for fish or fruit.

cranberry (kran'-ber-i) *n.* red, sour, berry.

crane (krān) *n.* tall wading-bird with long legs, neck, and bill; machine for lifting and lowering heavy weights;—*v.t.* stretch out neck to look at something.—**crane'-fly** *n.* genus of long-legged insects, commonly called 'daddy-long-legs.'—**crane's'-bill** *n.* geranium.

cranium (krā'-ni-um) *n.* skull;—*pl.* **cra'nia.**—**cra'nial** *a.* pert. to skull;—**craniol'ogy** *n.* study of skulls.

crank (krangk) *n.* bend; handle attached to shaft for turning it; bent portion of an axis, used to change horizontal or vertical into rotatory motion, etc.; fanciful twist or whimsy in speech; faddist; eccentric or crotchety persons;—*v.t.* provide with a crank; shape like a crank; operate by a crank.—**crank'y** *a.* shaky or in bad condition, of machinery; (*Fig.*) irritable; eccentric.—**crank'iness** *n.*

cranny (kran'-i) *n.* open crack; small opening; crevice.—**crannied** (kran'-id) *a.*

crape (krāp) *n.* semi-transparent silk fabric of light weight, unglossed and finely crimped, often dyed black.

crash (krash) *n.* violent fall or impact accompanied by loud noise; burst of mixed, loud sound; bankruptcy; sudden collapse or downfall;—*v.i.* make a crash; fall, come with, strike with, a crash; collapse;—*v.t.* break into pieces.—**crash'-hel'met** *n.* padded helmet worn by aviators, racing motorists and motorcyclists.

crass (kras) *a.* thick; gross; dense; stupid.—**crass'itude** *n.*—**crass'ly** *adv.* —**crassness** *n.*

crate (krāt) *n.* wicker-work hamper, or open-work packing-case.

crater (krā'-ter) *n.* cup-shaped mouth of volcano; cavity resulting from explosion of large shell, bomb, mine, etc.

cravat (kra-vat') *n.* man's neckcloth; necktie.

crave (krāv) *v.t.* and *i.* have very strong desire for; ask with earnestness or humility; beg.—**cra'ver** *n.*—**cra'ving** *n.*

craven (krāv'-n) *a.* cowardly; spiritless.—*n.* coward.

crawl (krawl) *v.i.* move along the ground on belly or on hands and knees; move very slowly; move abjectly; swim with the crawlstroke;—*n.* a crawling motion.

crayfish, crawfish (krā'-, kraw'-fish) *n.* fresh-water crustacean, resembling lobster but smaller.

crayon (krā'-on) *n.* stick, or pencilshaped piece of coloured chalk; drawing made with crayons;—*v.t.* draw with crayons.

craze (krāz) *n.* strong, habitual desire or passion; general mania; individual mania; very common fashion;—*v.t.* make crazy.—**crazed** *a.* weak in mind; covered with fine cracks.—**craz'iness** *n.*—**craz'y** *a.* insane; extremely foolish; madly eager (*with* for); rickety; falling to pieces; full of cracks.—**craz'ily** *adv.*

creak (krēk) *n.* harsh, grating sound;—*v.i.* make harsh, grating sound.—**creak'y** *a.*

cream (krēm) *n.* fatty substance that rises to surface of milk; best part of anything; anything resembling cream;—*v.t.* take off cream; add cream to; whip or beat to a cream-like consistency;—*v.i.* become like cream.—**cream'y** *a.*—**cream'ery** *n.* butter and cheese factory; dairy.—**cream'iness** *n.*

crease (krēs) *n.* line or mark made by folding anything; (*Cricket*) area within which batsman stands and bowler bowls;—*v.t.* make a crease or mark on;—*v.i.* become creased.

create (krē-āt') *v.t.* bring into existence out of nothing; originate; make; (*Slang*) cause a commotion.—**creation** (krē-ā'-shun) *n.* act of creating; world; anything created; any original production of the human mind.—**crea'tive** *a.*—**crea'tor** *n.* (*fem.* crea'trix, crea'tress).—**Creator** *n.* God.—**creature** (krē'-tūr) *n.* anything created; any living being.

crèche (krāsh) *n.* public nursery for young children.

credence (krē'-dens) *n.* trust; belief.—**credentials** (krē-den'-shals) *n.pl.* testimonials, showing that person is entitled to belief or credit.—**credible** (kred'-i-bl) *a.* worthy of belief, trustworthy; likely.—**cred'ibly** *adv.*—**credibil'ity** *n.*

credit (kred'-it) *n.* belief; trust; trustworthiness; honour or reputation; anything that procures esteem or honour; amount at person's disposal in bank; side of an account used for recording incoming sums;—*v.t.* believe; put trust in.—**cred'itable** *a.* reliable; meriting credit.—**cred'itably** *adv.*—**cred'itableness** *n.*—**cred'itor** *n.* one to whom money is due.

credulous (kred'-ū-lus) *a.* too prone to believe; easily imposed on.—**cred'ulously** *adv.*—**cred'ulousness** *n.*—**credulity** (kre-dū'-li-ti) *n.* gullibility.

creed (krēd) *n.* system of religious faith; statement of principles.

creek (krēk) *n.* small inlet; branch or small tributary of river.

creel (krēl) *n.* osier basket; angler's basket.

creep (krēp) *v.i.* move along with body close to ground, like worm or reptile; spread, like certain plants, by clinging to supports.—**creep'er** n. esp. creeping plant; genus of small birds.—**creep'y** a. causing creeping sensation on the skin.

cremate (kre-māt') v.t. burn; consume by burning, esp. the dead; reduce to ashes.—**cremation** (kre-mā'-shun) n.—**cremato'rium** n. establishment for cremation of bodies.

crenellated (kren'-el-lā-ted) a. battlemented.

creosote (krē'-ō-sōt) n. oily liquid obtained from distillation of coal tar, extensively used to preserve wood from decay.

crêpe (krep) n. fine, coloured silk crape material, also called **crêpe de chine** (shēn).—**crêpe rubber**, raw, unprocessed sheet rubber. rough surfaced rubber used for soles of shoes, etc.

crept (krept) pa.p. and pa.t. of **creep**.

crescendo (kre-shen'-dō) n. (Mus.) gradual increase in loudness;—adv. with increase in loudness. (Abbrev.) **cresc.**

crescent (kres'-ent) a. like the young moon in shape; increasing;— n. moon in her first quarter; semicircular street of buildings.

cress (kres) n. name of various edible cruciferous plants.

crest (krest) n. comb or tuft on bird's head; plume or top, of helmet; top of mountain, ridge, etc.; highest part of wave; badge above shield of coat of arms;—v.t. reach the top of.—**crest'fallen** a. cast down by defeat or failure; dispirited; dejected.

cretinism (kret'-in-izm) n. arrested physical and mental development, caused by deficient thyroid secretion; form of idiocy.—**cret'in** n. one suffering from cretinism.—**cret'inous** a.

cretonne (kret-on') n. strong, unglazed printed cotton cloth.

crevasse (kre-vas') n. deep open chasm in a glacier; fissure; cleft.

crevice (krev'-is) n. cleft; rent; narrow fissure; crack.

crew (króó) n. ship's or boat's company; **crew-cut** n. very short hair-cut.

crib (krib) n. barred rack for fodder; manger; stall for cattle; child's cot; hut or small dwelling; key or translation (used by schoolboys or students); plagiarism;—v.t. shut or confine in narrow place; at examinations, copy unfairly.

cribbage (krib'-āj) n. (Cards) game played by two or four players.

crick (krik) n. spasm or cramp, esp. of neck or back.

cricket (krik'-et) n. small, brown, chirping insect, belonging to family of grasshoppers, locusts, etc.

cricket (krik'-et) n. open-air game played with bats, ball, and wickets by teams of eleven a side.

crier (krī'-er) n. public official who makes proclamations.

crime (krīm) n. violation of the law (usually of serious nature); offence. —**criminal** (krim'-i-nal) a. guilty of, or pert. to, crime; wicked;—n. one guilty of crime.—**criminal'ity** n. guiltiness.—**crim'inally** adv.—**criminol'ogist** n.—**criminol'ogy** n. branch of sociology which deals with study of crime and criminals.

crimp (krimp) v.t. form into tiny parallel pleats; wrinkle; decoy or press into military or naval service.

crimson (krim'-zn) a. of rich deep red colour;—n. colour itself.

cringe (krinj) v.t. shrink; cower; behave obsequiously.

crinkle (kring'-kl) v.t. wrinkle; make a series of bends, windings, or twists in line or surface.

crinoline (krin'-ō-lin, -lin, -lēn) n. structure used by women in middle of 19th cent. for expanding their skirts; hoop skirt.

cripple (krip'-l) n. person without use of limb or limbs; lame person;— a. lame;—v.t. lame.

crisis (krī'-sis) n. decisive moment; turning-point, esp. in illness; emergency; time of difficulty or danger; —pl. **crises** (krī'-sēz).

crisp (krisp) a. brittle; breaking with short snap; of hair, curly or wavy;— v.t. make crisp;—n. thin slice of potato fried hard.—**crisp'ly** adv.— **crisp'ness** n.

criss-cross (kris'-kros) a. crossing; arranged in crossing lines;—adv. crossing one another in different directions; contrarily;—v.t. and i. intersect; mark or be marked with cross lines;—n. cross-shaped mark.

criterion (krī-tē'-ri-on) n. standard of judging; rule by which opinions may be judged.—pl. **crite'ria**.

critic (krit'-ik) n. one who expresses reasoned judgment, esp. on art or literature; one whose profession it is to write reviews; one given to expressing adverse judgment or finding fault.—**crit'ical** a. pert. to criticism; captious; crucial; decisive.—**crit'ically** adv.—**crit'icism** n. art of making a reasoned judgment, critical appreciation.—**crit'icise** v.t. and i. pass judgment; censure; review.—**critique** (kri-tēk') n. criticism; review.

croak (krōk) v.t. and i. make a low, hoarse noise in throat; (Slang) die;— n. hoarse, harsh sound made by frog or crow.—**croak'y** a.

crochet (krō'-shā) n. kind of netting or lace consisting of loops;—v.t. and i. work in crochet.

crock (krok) n. earthenware pot or pitcher; piece of broken earthenware; (Slang) person broken-down, or crippled by ill-health.—**crock'ery** n. earthenware vessels and dishes.

crocodile (krok'-ō-dīl) n. large, amphibious reptile of lizard kind; school-children walking in long double file.—**crocodil'ian** a.—**crocodile tears**, hypocritical tears; sham grief.

crocus (krō'-kus) n. bulbous plant of iris kind, with white, yellow, or purple flowers; saffron.

croft (kroft) n. small area of cultivable land attached to a dwelling; small farm.—**croft'er** n. one who works a croft.

cromlech (krom'-lek) n. circle of upright stones, sometimes enclosing dolmens, each two or three being topped by large, flat stone.

crone (krōn) n. wizened old woman.

crony (krō'-ni) n. intimate friend.

crook (krook) n. hooked staff; hook, bend, or sharp turn; shepherd's or bishop's staff; thief; swindler;—v.t. bend into crook; curve; pervert;—v.i. be bent or curved.—**crook'ed** a. bent; twisted; (Fig.) not straightforward.—**crook'edly** adv.—**crook'edness** n.—**by hook or by crook**, by any means by fair means or foul.

croon (krōon) v.t. and i. sing or hum softly; sing in monotonous undertone.—**croon'er** n.—**croon'ing** n.

crop (krop) n. year's produce of cultivation of any plant or plants, in farm, field, country, etc.; harvest; best ore; pouch in bird's gullet; craw; hunting-whip; closely-cut head of hair;—v.t. reap produce of a field.—pr.p. **crop'ping**.—pa.p. and pa.t. **cropped**.—**crop'-eared** a. with clipped ears; with hair short to show the ears.—**crop'per** n. one who, or that which, crops; (Colloq.) heavy fall.—**to crop up**, appear unexpectedly.

croquet (krō'-kā) n. outdoor game played with balls, mallets and hoops.

croquette (krō-ket') n. (Cookery) ball of finely minced meat, fish, etc. seasoned and fried; rissole.

crosier, crozier (krō'-zhyer) n. pastoral staff of bishop.

cross (kros) n. stake used for crucifixion, consisting of two pieces of timber placed one upon another in shape of † or ×; anything of this shape, e.g. medal; (Fig.) affliction; tribulation; misfortune;—v.t. mark with cross; make sign of the cross.—**cross'let** n. small cross.—**cross'-stitch** n. in embroidery, stitch, in form of a cross.—**cross'wise** adv. in form of a cross.

cross (kros) a. transverse; intersecting; interchanged; contrary, adverse; out of temper; dishonest;—n. intermixture of breeds;—v.t. place so as to intersect; pass from one side to the other of; pass over; thwart; oppose; interbreed, of animals, plants, etc.;—v.i. intersect; move or pass from one side to other;—adv. across.—**cross'ing** n. act of passing across; intersection, esp. of roads, rails, etc.; place of crossing; intermixture of breeds.—**cross'ly** adv. in ill-tempered manner.—**cross'ness** n. state of being cross; ill-humour; peevishness.—**cross'-bones** n.pl. two thigh bones crossed and surmounted by a skull, used as symbol of death, sign of deadly danger, or flag of pirate ship.—**cross'-breed** n. breed produced from parents of different breeds; hybrid.—**cross'breed'ing** n.—**cross'-bred** a.—**cross'-coun'try** a. across fields, avoiding roads.—**cross'-cut** v.t. cut across;—n. short road between two points or places.—**cross'-examina'tion** n. examination of a witness by counsel on the other side;—**cross'-eyed** a. squinting.—**cross'-fertilisa'tion** n. fertilisation of one plant by pollen of another.—**cross'-fire** n. (Mil.) intersecting lines of fire from two or more positions.—**cross'-grained** a. of wood, having grain running across, or irregularly; of person, ill-natured.—**cross'-hatch'ing** n. in drawing, etching, etc. art of shading by parallel intersecting lines.—**cross'-pur'pose** n. contradictory purpose.—**cross'-question** v.t. question person, e.g. a witness, in order to verify statements already made.—**cross'-ref'erence** n. in book, e.g. dictionary, directing of reader to another part for related information.—**cross'-roads,** n. point of intersection of two roads.—**cross'-sec'tion** n. transversal cutting of object to expose inner layers; surface so exposed; representative group.—**cross-word** (puzz'le) n. puzzle in which a chequered square has to be filled in with words to which clues are given.

crossbill (kros'-bil) n. bird of Finch family, whose mandibles cross.

crossbow (kros'-bō) n. medieval weapon in form of strongly made bow attached to grooved, musket-like stock and propelling arrow or bolt; arbalest.

crosse (kros) n. long-handled racquet used in the game of lacrosse.

crotch (kroch) n. fork or bifurcation; angle where the legs branch off from the human body.—**crotched** a.

crotchet (kroch'-et) n. small hook; bracket in printing; whim or fancy; (Mus.) note equal in duration to half a minim.—**crotch'ety** a. full of whims, or fads.

crouch (krouch) v.i. huddle down close to ground; stoop low; cringe or fawn servilely.

croup (krōop) n. rump or hindquarters of horse; hence, place or seat behind saddle.

croup (krōop) n. (Med.) acute inflammation of wind-pipe, accompanied by hoarse ringing cough and difficulty in breathing.—**croup'y** a.

croupier (króó'-pi-ęr) *n.* one who assists chairman at public banquet; official who sits at gaming table to observe the cards and collect stakes.

crow (krō) *n.* large bird, of genus Corvus; cry of cock; name of tribe of American Indians; crowbar;—*v.i.* give the shrill cry of cock; utter sound of pleasure.—**crow'bar** *n.* (bar with a beak) bar of iron bent at one end, used as lever.—**crow's-foot** *n.* wrinkle about the outer corners of eyes in old age.—**crow's-nest** *n.* box or perch for look-out man near top of ship's mast.

crowd (kroud) *v.t.* press or drive together; fill or occupy by crushing together;—*v.i.* be numerous; gather in numbers;—*n.* number of things or persons collected into a close body; dense multitude or throng; (*Colloq.*) set or clique.

crowfoot (krō'-fóót) *n.* (*Bot.*) Ranunculus or buttercup.

crown (kroun) *n.* diadem or state head-dress worn by sovereign; sovereign; royalty; anything resembling a crown; something achieved or consummated; topmost part of head; upper part of hat; summit; five-shilling piece (stamped with a crown);—*v.t.* invest with crown or with royal dignity; bestow upon as mark of honour; top or surmount; complete.—**crown'-col'ony** *n.* one directly administered by home government. — **crown'-impe'rial** *n.* plant of the lily family, with cluster of bell-shaped flowers.—**crown'-lands** *n.pl.* lands belonging to the sovereign. —**crown'-prince** *n.* heir apparent to throne.—**crown'-wheel** *n.* wheel with cogs at right angles to its plane.—**crown and anchor**, gambling game.

crucial (króósh'-ygl) *a.* decisive; critical; (*Anat.*) cross-shaped.

crucible (króó'-si-bl) *n.* earthenware melting-pot, capable of withstanding great heat, used for melting metals, etc.; (*Fig.*) severe test.

crucify (króó'-si-fī) *v.t.* put to death by nailing to a cross; torture; mortify.—**cru'cifer** *n.* cross-bearer.—**cru'cifix** *n.* image of Christ on the Cross.—**crucifixion** (króó-si-fik'-shun) *n.* death by nailing to a cross; Christ's death upon the cross; intense suffering or affliction.—**cru'ciform** *a.* cross-shaped.

crude (króód) *a.* in natural or raw state; unripe; rough; unfinished.—**crude'ly** *adv.*—**crude'ness** *n.*—**crud'ity** *n.*

cruel (króó'-el) *a.* delighting in, or callous to, others' pain; merciless; hard-hearted; inhuman. — **cru'elly** *adv.*—**cru'elty** *n.*

cruet (króó'-et) *n.* small stoppered bottle for holding vinegar, oil, condiments, etc.; stand for these.

cruise (króóz) *v.i.* sail about without precise destination; in motoring and aviation, go at normal operating speed;—*n.* organised pleasure-sail. —**cruis'er** *n.* (*Naval*) fast warship of medium displacement and fighting power.

crumb (krum) *n.* small particle; bit, esp. of bread; soft part of bread; —*v.t.* reduce to crumbs; cover with crumbs.—**crumb'y, crum'my** *a.*

crumble (krum'-bl) *v.t.* break into crumbs or fragments;—*v.t.* fall into crumbs.—**crum'bly** *a.*

crumpet (krum'-pet) *n.* flat, soft pancake.

crumple (krum'-pl) *v.t.* wrinkle; crease; rumple;—*v.i.* become wrinkled or creased; shrink irregularly.

crunch (krunsh) *n.* sound made by chewing crisp food, treading on gravel, hard snow, etc.;—*v.t.* and *i.* chew, tread, etc. with this sound.

crupper (krup'-ęr) *n.* strap of leather buckled to saddle, and passing under horse's tail; rump or croup of horse.—*v.t.* to fit with a crupper.

crusade (króó-sād') *n.* medieval Christian war to recover the Holy Land from Saracens; campaign against evil or vice.—*v.i.* join in a crusade.

cruse (króós, króóz) *n.* small earthen pot for holding water, oil, etc.

crush (krush) *v.t.* press between two hard bodies so as to break, bruise, or crumple; break into fragments; squeeze out by pressure; defeat utterly;—*v.i.* be broken or compressed by weight or force;—*n.* violent pressure; closely packed crowd of people.—**crush'-hat** *n.* collapsible hat; opera-hat.—**to have a crush on** (*Slang*) be infatuated with.

crust (krust) *n.* hard outer coat or covering of anything; outer part of baked bread; pastry, etc. forming covering of a pie; deposit from wine collected on interior of bottles;—*v.t.* cover with a crust;—*v.t.* gather into a crust; form a crust.—**crust'ily** *adv.* in crusty manner; peevishly; morosely.—**crust'iness** *n.*—**crust'y** *a.* having a crust; hard; surly.

crustacean (krus-tā'-shi-ąn) *a.* and *n.* pert. to, or one of, Crustacea, a class of mainly aquatic animals including lobsters, crabs, shrimps, etc.—**crusta'ceous** *a.* having hard shell.

crutch (kruch) *n.* staff with a cross-piece to go under the armpit for the use of cripples; support;—*v.t.* support; aid.

crux (kruks) *n.* perplexing problem; knotty point; real issue.

cry (krī) *v.t.* call out; shout; proclaim or advertise by crier;—*v.i.* call loudly; exclaim vehemently; weep. —*n.* loud utterance, esp. sound of child or animal; prayer; shedding of tears; sound of pack of hounds on the scent, hence the pack itself.—*pa.p.* and *pa.t.* **cried** (krīd);—*pl.* **cries.**—**cri'er** *n.*—**cry'ing** *a.* calling for notice or attention.—**a far cry**, great distance.—**to cry off**, withdraw from an agreement.—**to cry wolf**, give false alarm.

crypt (kript) *n.* cell or chapel under a church, or underground, used for burial.—**cryp'tic(al)** *a.* hidden; secret; mysterious.—**cryp'tically** *adv.*

crypto- (krip'-tō) *prefix fr.* Gk. *kruptos*, secret, combining to form compounds.

cryptogam (krip'-tō-gam) *n.* (*Bot.*) plant that has no apparent or true flower, as fern, moss, etc.

crystal (kris'-tal) *n.* transparent colourless quartz; ornament made from it; ball cut from it for crystal-gazing; superior sort of glass; (*Chem.*) mineral body which has assumed regular geometrical form; —*a.* consisting of, or like, crystal; clear; transparent.—**crys'talline** *a.* resembling crystal; transparent; pellucid.—**crys'tallise** *v.t.* cause to form crystals; (*Fig.*) cause to assume a definite shape;—*v.i.* be formed into crystals; (*Fig.*) become definite in shape.—**crystallis'able** *a.*—**crystallisa'tion** *n.*—**crystallog'raphy** *n.* science that deals with origin and structure of crystals.—**crys'talloid** *a.* crystal-like.

cub (kub) *n.* young of bear, fox, wolf, etc.; (*Colloq.*) ill-mannered youth; —*v.i.* bring forth young (of animals). —**cub'bing** *n.* hunting fox-cubs.— **Wolf Cub** junior Boy Scout.

cubby-hole (kub'-i-hōl) *n.* small secret place for storing things, or for hiding in.

cube (kūb) *n.* (*Geom.*) solid body with six equal square sides; (*Math.*) product of a number multiplied twice by itself;—*v.t.* raise to the third power.—**cu'bic(al)** *a.* having form of cube; of three dimensions, e.g. **cubic foot.**—**cu'boid** *a.* resembling cube in shape.—**cube'-root** *n.* number which gives the stated number if raised to third power.—**cubic content**, volume.

cubicle (kū'-bi-kl) *n.* one of small compartments into which dormitory, hairdressing saloon etc., is divided.

cubit (kū'-bit) *n.* measure of length, about 18 inches, orig. length of forearm, from elbow to tip of middle finger.—**cu'bital** *a.*

cuckold (kuk'-ōld) *n.* man whose wife is unfaithful to him;—*v.t.* make a cuckold of; be unfaithful to a husband.—**cuck'oldry** *n.* adultery.

cuckoo (koo'-kóò) *n.* migratory bird named from its call and remarkable for laying its eggs in other birds' nests; call of the bird; fool.—**cuck'-oo-flow'er** *n.* lady's smock.—**cuck'oo-pint** *n.* plant, wild arum, popularly known as wake-robin or lords-and-ladies.—**cuck'oo-spit** *n.* frothy secretion deposited on leaves of plants by certain insects.

cucumber (kū'-kum-ber) *n.* edible plant of gourd family and its fruit, used as salad and for pickling.

cud (kud) *n.* food brought up by ruminating animals, from their first stomach, and chewed again. —**to chew the cud** (*Fig.*) meditate.

cuddle (kud'-l) *v.t.* caress; hug; fondle;—*v.i.* lie close or snug; nestle; —*n.* close embrace.

cudgel (kud'-jel) *n.* short thick stick; —*v.t.* beat with cudgel.—*pr.p.***cud'-gelling;**—*pa.p.* and *pa.t.* **cud'-gelled.**

cue (kū) *n.* long tapering stick used by billiard player; pigtail.—**cue'ist** *n.* billiard player.

cue (kū) *n.* last words of actor's speech as signal to next actor to speak; hint.

cuff (kuf) *n.* blow with open hand;— *v.t.* strike with open hand.

cuff (kuf) *n.* ending of a sleeve; wrist-band of sleeve.

cuirass (kwi-ras') *n.* metal or leather armour, consisting of breastplate and backplate.

cuisine (kwē-zēn') *n.* literally kitchen; style of cooking.

cul-de-sac (kool'-de-sak') *n.* street or lane open only at one end; blind alley.

culinary (kū'-lin-ar-i) *a.* pert. to kitchen or cookery.

cull (kul) *v.t.* select, or pick out; gather.

cullender See **colander.**

culminate (kul'-mi-nāt) *v.i.* reach the highest point (*with* in); reach a climax.—**culmina'tion** *n.* attainment of highest point; climax.

culpable (kul'-pa-bl) *a.* deserving blame or censure; criminal.—**cul'-pably** *adv.*—**culpabil'ity**, **cul'pableness** *n.* state of being culpable; guilt; blame.

culprit (kul'-prit) *n.* one accused of crime; criminal; offender.

cult (kult) *n.* system of religious belief, esp. rites and ceremonies attendant on it.

cultivate (kul'-ti-vāt) *v.t.* prepare for raising of crops; till; produce by tillage, labour, or care; civilise.— **cul'tivable** *a.*—**cultiva'tion** *n.* practice of cultivating.—**cul'tivator** *n.*

culture (kul'-tūr) *n.* tillage or cultivation; mental training and development; refinement; civilisation; propagation of bacteria and other micro-organisms in artificial media; —*v.t.* cultivate.—**cul'tural** *a.* pert. to culture.—**cul'tured** *a.* educated and refined.

culvert (kul'-vert) *n.* arched drain or conduit for passage of water under road, railway, or canal.

cumber (kum'-ber) *v.t.* burden or hinder with useless load; lumber.—**cum'bersome** *a.* burdensome; clumsy.—**cum'brous** *a.* bulky; unwieldy.

cumulate (kūm'-ū-lāt) *v.t.* heap together;—*a.* heaped up.—**cumula'tion** *n.*—**cum'ulative** *a.* increasing or gaining force by successive additions.

cumulus (kū'-mū-lus) *n.* heap; piled-up cloud mass with rounded outlines.

cunning (kun'-ing) *a.* wily; sly; artful;—*n.* craft or skill; guile; deceit.—**cunn'ingly** *adv.*

cup (kup) *n.* small, round drinking-vessel; cup-shaped object; mixed drink made with wine, etc., contents of cup; ornamental vessel given as prize for sport, etc.; *v.t.*—hold, as in a cup; form into cup-shape.—**cup-board** (kub'-ard) *n.* small closet with shelves for cups, plates, etc.—**cup'-tie** *n.* in association football, game determining or contributing to determination of winners of a cup.—**lov'ing-cup** *n.* large cup with several handles which is drunk from by each guest in turn.—**cupboard-love**, pretended affection, assumed in hope of gain.—**in one's cups**, drunk.

cupidity (kū-pid'-i-ti) *n.* eager desire for possession; greed of gain.

cupola (kū'-pō-la̱) *n.* spherical vault on top of building; dome.

cupreous (kū'-prē-us) *a.* of, pert. to, or containing copper.—**cu'pric** *a.* (*Chem.*) containing copper (with valency of one).—**cu'prous** *a.* (*Chem.*) containing copper (with valency of two).—**cuprif'erous** *a.* bearing or producing copper.

cupro-nickel (kū'-prō-nik-el) *n.* alloy of copper and nickel.

curate (kū'-rāt) *n.* one who has the cure of souls; assistant to vicar or rector.—**cu'racy**, **cu'rateship** *n.*

curator (kū-rā'-tor) *n.* superintendent, as of museum, library, etc.; trustee; guardian.—**cura'torship** *n.*

curb (kurb) *n.* chain or strap attached to bit of bridle and passing under horse's lower jaw; check or means of restraint; stone edging to pavement or sidewalk (also **kerb**); hearth fender;—*v.t.* apply curb to (a horse); restrain; confine.—**curb'-stone** *n.* stone placed against earth or stonework to prevent its giving way.

curd (kurd) *n.* cheesy part of milk; coagulated milk; coagulated part of any liquid.—**curd'le** *v.t.* and *i.* turn into curd; coagulate.

cure (kūr) *v.t.* heal; restore to health; remedy; preserve fish, skins, etc. by salting, drying, etc.;—*n.* act of healing; that which heals;

remedy.—**cure of souls**, care of parish or congregation by clergyman.—**cu'rable** *a.*—**cu'rative** *a.*

curfew (kur'-fū) *n.* time after which persons may not be out of doors.

curio (kū'-ri-ō) *n.* rare or curious object, of kind sought for by collectors; curiosity.

curious (kū'-ri-us) *a.* eager to know; inquisitive; puzzling; strange; (of books) indecent.—**cu'riously** *adv.*—**curios'ity** *n.* eagerness to know; inquisitiveness; strange or rare object; novelty.

curl (kurl) *v.t.* twist into ringlets; coil; bend into spiral or curved shape;—*v.i.* take a spiral or curved shape or path; turn into ringlets; ripple; play at the game of curling; —*n.* ringlet of hair; anything of similar shape.—**curl'y** *a.*—**curl'iness** *n.*—**curl'ing** *n.* game like bowls played on ice with large, rounded stones.

curlew (kurlū) *n.* long-billed wading bird.

curmudgeon (kur-muj'-un) *n.* grasping ill-natured fellow; miser; churl.—**curmud'geonly** *a.* churlish.

currant (kur'-ant) *n.* fruit of various plants allied to gooseberry; small dried grapes.

current (kur'-ent) *a.* running; flowing; fluent; in circulation or general use;—*n.* running; flowing; body of water or air in motion; flow of river, etc.; tendency; drift; flow of electricity through conductor.—**curr'ently** *adv.* in current manner; commonly.—**curr'ency** *n.* time during which anything is current; money in use or circulation.

curriculum (ku-rik'-ū-lum) *n.* specified course of study;—*pl.* **curric'ula**.

curry (kur'-i) *n.* (*Cookery*) highly-flavoured and pungent dish.—*v.t.* cook or season with curry-powder.

curry (kur'-i) *v.t.* dress leather; comb, rub down, and clean a horse; beat or thrash.—**curr'ier** *n.* one who dresses tanned leather.—**to curry favour**, try to win favour by flattery.

curse (kurs) *v.t.* utter wish of evil against; invoke evil upon; swear at; torment;—*v.i.* utter blasphemous words; swear;—*n.* invocation of evil or injury upon person; profane words or oaths.—**cursed** (kurs'-ed, kurst) *a.* hateful; abominable.—**cur'sedly** *adv.*—**cur'sedness** *n.*—**curst** *a.* (*Arch.*) crabbed; shrewish.

cursory (kur'-so-ri) *a.* characterised by haste; careless; superficial; fleeting.—**cur'sorily** *adv.*—**cur'soriness** *n.*

curt (kurt) *a.* short; concise to point of rudeness; abrupt; terse.—**curt'ly** *adv.*—**curt'ness** *n.*

curtail (kur-tāl') *v.t.* cut short; abridge; diminish.—**curtail'ment** *n.* decrease.

curtain (kur'-tin) n. hanging drapery at windows, round beds, or at doors; screen in front of stage of theatre; —v.t. enclose or furnish with curtains.—**cur'tain-rais'er** n. short play preceding main piece in theatre.—**iron curtain** (*Fig.*) government restriction to prevent outsiders from obtaining information about conditions in a country.

curtsy, curtsey (kurt'-si) n. gesture of civility or respect made by women or girls;—v.i. make a curtsey.

curve (kurv) n. bending without angles; that which is bent; arch;— a. bent;—v.t. and i. bend.—**curva'ceous** a. shapely; buxom.—**cur'vature** n. curve or amount of bending of a line.—**curvilin'ear** a. having, or bound by, curved lines.

cushion (koosh'-un) n. bag or case filled with soft stuffing or air, to support or ease the body; anything which softens a blow or forms a soft support;—v.t. seat on a cushion; provide or protect with a cushion.

cusp (kusp) n. point or horn of crescent; prominence on molar tooth; point at which two branches of curve have common tangent.

custard (kus'-tard) n. sweet dish made with milk and eggs.

custody (kus'-to-di) n. keeping or guarding; safe-keeping; guardianship; imprisonment.—**custodial** (kus-tō'-di-al) a.—**custo'dian, custo'dier** n. keeper; caretaker.

custom (kus'-tum) n. fashion; usage; habit; business patronage; toll, tax, or tribute.—**cus'toms** n.pl. duties levied on imports.—**cus'tomable** a. common; customary; liable to duty. —**cus'tomary** a. according to custom. —**cus'tomarily** adv.—**cus'tomer** n. one who enters a shop to buy.

cut (kut) v.t. sever, penetrate, or wound with edged instrument; divide; separate; intersect; cross; mow; hew; carve; trim; shape; reduce; abridge; intentionally ignore a person; (*Tennis, Golf, etc.*) hit the ball obliquely;—v.i. (*Slang*) run rapidly.—pr.p. **cut'ting.**—pa.p. and pa.t. cut;—n. act of cutting; opening made with edged instrument; gash; wound; piece cut off, as e.g. joint of meat; notch; reduction, esp. in salary or wages.—**cut'ter** n. he who, or that which, cuts; warship's rowing and sailing boat.—**cut'ting** n. incision; excavation (for road, canal, etc.) through high ground; clipping from newspaper; small branch, slip, etc. cut from plant, bush, etc. for propagation;— a. sarcastic. — **cut'-throat** n. murderer; assassin;—a. merciless.—**to be cut up** (*Fig.*) (*colloq.*) be deeply affected; be downcast.

cutaneous (kū-tā'-nē-us) a. belonging to, or affecting, the skin.

cute (kūt) a. clever; sharp; shrewd; (*Colloq.*) attractive.

cuticle (kū'-ti-kl) n. outer skin or epidermis.—**cutic'ular** a.

cutlass (kut'-las) n. short, broad-bladed, curving sword formerly used in navy.

cutler (kut'-ler) n. one who makes, repairs, or deals in knives and cutting implements.—**cut'lery** n. business of a cutler; cutlers' wares.

cutlet (kut'-let) n. piece of meat or chop from rib-bones, for broiling or frying.

cuttle, cuttle-fish (kut'-l, -fish) n. sea mollusc with long tentacles, which evades pursuit by ejecting inky fluid.—**cut'tle-bone** n.

cybernetics (si-ber-net'-iks) n. study of communications and control mechanisms, esp. those stimulating human activities.

cyclamen (sik'-la-men) n. bulbous plant of primula family.

cycle (sī'-kl) n. regularly recurring succession of events or phenomena, or period of time occupied by such succession; body of myths or legends, relating to period, person, or event; series of songs dealing with phases of same subject; bicycle or tricycle;—v.i. pass through cycle of changes; ride bicycle or tricycle.—**cy'clic(al)** a. pert. to or moving in cycles; alternating.—**cy'clist** n. one who rides bicycle or tricycle.

cyclone (sī'-klōn) n. violent storm characterised by strong winds rotating about centre of low barometric pressure.—**cyclon'ic** a.

cyclopedia See encyclopedia.

cyclotron (sī'-klō-tron) n. device for accelerating sub-atomic particles spirally in a magnetic field to speeds at which nuclear transformations can take place.

cygnet (sig'-net) n. young swan.

cylinder (sil'-in-der) n. roller-like body with straight sides, ends being equal, parallel circles; object of similar shape.—**cylin'dric, cylin'drical** a. having form of a cylinder.—**cylin'driform** a. shaped like a cylinder.

cymbal (sim'-bal) n. one of pair of saucer-shaped pieces of brass, used as musical instrument of percussion.

cynic (sin'-ik) n. one who believes man's conduct is based on self-interest; misanthrope.—**cyn'ic(al)** a. —**cyn'ically** adv.—**cyn'icalness** n.—**cynicism** (sin'-i-sizm) n.

cynosure (sī'-nō-, sin'-ō-shŏor) n. something to which all eyes are turned; guiding star.

cypher See cipher.

cypress (sī'-pres) n. coniferous tree formerly regarded as symbol of mourning.

cyst (sist) n. (*Med.*) bladder or membranous sac containing liquid

secretion or morbid matter; tumour.
—cys'tic a.

Czar (zär) n. title used by various Slavonic rulers, esp. by Emperors of Russia.—**Czarina** (zä-rē'-nạ) n. wife of a Czar. (Other forms are **Tsar, Tzar, Tsari'na, Tzari'na,** etc.)

D

dab (dab) n. small flat fish of the flounder variety.

dab (dab) v.t. touch gently and intermittently, as with some soft or moist substance.—pr.p. **dabb'ing**;—pa.p. **dabb'ed**;—n. gentle blow with soft substance; small lump of anything soft, as butter.—pl. (Slang) fingerprints.

dabble (dab'-l) v.t. wet by little dips; moisten.—v.i. play in water; pursue subject superficially.

dabchick (dab'-chik) n. small grebe or water-fowl.

dace (dās) n. small fresh-water river fish of the carp family. Also **dart, dare.**

dachshund (daks'-hóónt, dash'-hund) n. dog with long body, short legs, and drooping ears.

daddy-long-legs (dad'-i-long'-legz) n. flying insect with long body, legs, antennae, and gossamer wings; the crane-fly.

dado (dā'-dō) n. (Archit.) part of pedestal between base and cornice; lower part or wide skirting of walls of room painted differently from the rest of room.

daffodil (daf'-ō-dil) n. spring plant of genus Narcissus; its yellow colour.

daft (daft) a. insane; stupid; foolish; giddy.—daft'ness n.

dagger (dag'-ẹr) n. short, two-edged sword; dirk; stiletto; mark of reference in typography (†) or (‡).

dago (dā'-gō) n. U.S. term of contempt for Spaniard, Portuguese, or Italian.

dahlia (dāl'-ya) n. genus of plants with large, brightly coloured flowers.

daily (dā'-li) a. or adv. happening each day;—n. newspaper published each day; charwoman or non-resident servant.

dainty (dān'-ti) a. pleasing to the taste; elegant; refined; pretty and slender; scrupulous;—n. a delicacy.—dain'tily adv.—dain'tiness n.

dairy (dā'-ri) n. place where milk and cream are kept cool, butter is churned, and cheese is made; shop where milk and its products are sold.—dai'rying n.—dai'ry-maid, dai'ryman n.—dai'ry-farm n.

dais (dā'-is) n. raised platform at upper end of room, esp. of dining-hall.

daisy (dā'-zi) n. common wild flower growing chiefly in grass.—dai'sied a.—dai'sy-chain n. chain of daisies made by inserting one stem through another.—dai'sy-cut'ter n. (Slang) cricket ball that barely clears the grass (or daisies).

dale (dāl) n. low place between hills; valley or vale; glen.—dales'man n. one living in a dale, esp. used in N. England in Lake District.

dally (dal'-i) v.i. waste time; act in futile manner; fondle or interchange caresses. — pr.p. **dall'ying.** — pa.p. **dall'ied.**—dall'iance n. act of trifling and wasting time; love-making.

dalmatian (dal-mā'-shun) n. breed of large white dog with black or liver-coloured spots.

dam (dam) n. female parent (used only of animals).

dam (dam) n. barrier of earth, stones, etc. to obstruct the flow of water; water confined by dam;—v.t. confine water by dam.

damage (dam'-āj) n. injury or harm to person, property, or reputation;—v.t. harm; hurt.—dam'ages n.pl. legal compensation paid to injured party.—dam'ageable a.

damask (dam'-ask) n. figured silk or linen fabric, orig. made at Damascus; steel ornamented with wavy pattern; rose-pink colour, like that of damask rose;—a. woven with figured pattern like damask.—damask rose, pink rose brought orig. from Damascus,.

dame (dām) n. noble lady; mistress of a household; (Colloq.) managing woman.—**Dame** n. title of wife of knight or baronet; title awarded to women members of the Order of the British Empire (Abbrev.) **D.B.E.**

damn (dam) v.t. consign to everlasting punishment; give over to death; (Colloq.) condemn irritably (used as interjection); destroy reputation of;—n. oath; curse; (Colloq.) a trifle.—dam'nable a.—dam'nably adv.—damna'tion n. punishment in future state.—dam'natory a. containing sentence of condemnation.—damned a. odious; horrible.

damp (damp) n. moist air; humidity; fog; vapour; noxious gases in coal mines, wells, etc. (as fire-damp, choke-damp);—a. slightly moist;—v.t. moisten slightly; retard combustion (damp down a fire).—damp'en v.t. moisten; (Fig.) depress.—damp'er n. one who or that which damps; contrivance in flue of kitchen range to regulate draught; device to minimise vibration.—damp'ish a. rather moist.—damp'ness n. state of being moist; humidity.—damp'-proof a. impervious to damp.

damsel (dam'-sel) n. young unmarried woman.

damson (dam'-zon) n. small black plum used for jam or jelly.

dance (dàns) v.t. and v.i. move with measured steps; move rhythmically; caper;—n. lively and rhythmical movement with certain steps and gestures; social gathering for purposes of dancing.—**danc'er** n. one who dances.—**danseuse'** n. female dancer, esp. in ballet.—**to lead someone a dance**, to lead someone in vain pursuit.—**St. Vitus's dance** (Med.) nervous disorder accompanied by twitching of muscles; chorea.—**danc'ing der'vish**, n. one of fanatical Mohammedan priests who practised wild, ritual dances.—**danc'ing-girl** n. professional dancer.

dandelion (dan-de-lī'-on) n. plant with yellow flowers, and tooth-edged leaves.

dander (dan'-der) n. anger; passion; temper.

Dandie Dinmont (dan'-di-din-mont) n. breed of small terrier, named after character in Scott's Guy Mannering.

dandle (dan'-dl) v.t. move up and down in affectionate play, as an infant; pet; caress.

dandruff (dan'-druf) n. disease affecting scalp and producing scurf or small scales of skin under the hair.

dandy (dan'-di) n. one who affects special finery in dress; a fop;—a. (Colloq.) fine; first-rate.—**dan'dify** v.t. make like a dandy.—**dan'dified** a. foppish.—**dandi'acal** a. dandified.

danger (dān'-jer) n. exposure to injury or evil; peril; hazard; insecurity; jeopardy.—**dan'gerous** a. attended with danger; involving risk.—**dan'gerously** adv.—**dan'gerousness** n.

dangle (dang'-l) v.t. swing loosely or carelessly; (Fig.) use as bait;—v.i. hang loosely.

dank (dangk) a. unpleasantly damp or moist.—**dank'ness** n.

daphne (daph'-ne) n. genus of garden shrubs, producing red berries.

dapper (dap'-er) a. little and active; neat; trim; smart.

dapple (dap'-l) n. spotted, applied to horses and deer.—**dapp'led** a. spotted, esp. of chequered pattern made by sunlight through trees.

dare (dār) v.i. have courage for; venture (to); be audacious enough;—v.t. defy; challenge; terrify.—**dar'ing** n. audacity; bold action;—a. bold; courageous; audacious.—**dar'ingly** adv.—**dare'-dev'il** n. foolhardy, reckless fellow.

dark (dàrk) a. lacking light; black; sombre; evil; unenlightened;—n. absence of light; gloom; obscurity; evil.—**dark'en** v.t. obstruct light; render dim; cloud; (Fig.) sully;—v.i. grow dark.—**dark'ish** a. rather dark.—**dark'ly** adv.—**dark'ness** n.—**dark'y, dar'key** n. a negro.—**dark'-horse** n.

a person of unknown capabilities.

darling (dàr'-ling) n. beloved or lovable one;—a. cherished.

darn (dàrn) v.t. mend; repair a hole by weaving threads at right angles to one another to imitate original material;—n. place darned.

dart (dàrt) n. pointed weapon thrown by hand; anything which pierces or wounds; small seam or intake in garment to make it fit more closely; sharp, forward movement.—v.t. send forward quickly; throw suddenly;—v.i. run forward swiftly; move like a dart.—**darts** n.pl. a popular game using darts and dartboard.

dash (dash) v.t. throw violently; cast down; shatter;—v.i. rush forward; strike violently against;—n. rapid movement; mark of punctuation (—) to denote parenthesis; small amount; showy display; a mild oath.—**dash'-board** n. orig. screen to protect occupants of carriage from mud-splashes; in motor-vehicles, aircraft, etc. panel in front of driver or pilot.—**dash'ing** a. daring; spirited; showy.—**dash'y** a. showy.

data (dā'-ta) n.pl. (sing. datum) things known and from which inferences may be deduced; punched cards or tape for feeding into computer.

date (dāt) n. time of event; epoch; duration; (Slang) appointment or engagement;—v.t. note or fix time of; refer to as starting-point.—v.i. reckon back a given time (foll. by from or back to).

date (dāt) n. stone fruit of date-palm.

dative (dā'-tiv) n. case of noun which is indirect object of verb, or which is preceded by certain prepositions.

datum See da'ta.

daub (dawb) v.t. smear with mud or plaster; paint crudely;—n. crude painting; smudge. — **daub'er** n.—**daub'ing** n. daub; rough cast for exterior of houses.

daughter (daw'-ter) n. female child;—a. like a daughter. —**daugh'ter-in-law** n. the wife of one's son.

daunt (dawnt, dànt) v.t. subdue courage of; dismay; dishearten; disconcert.—**daunt'less** a. fearless; intrepid.

davits (da'-vits) n. apparatus for lowering ship's life-boats.

Davy Jones (dā'-vi-jōnz) n. sailor's name for the Devil.—**Davy Jones's Locker**, the sea, as sailor's grave.

Davy-lamp (dā'-vi-lamp) n. safety lamp for miners.

dawdle (daw'-dl) v.i. loiter; move very slowly.

dawn (dawn) v.i. grow towards daylight; begin to be visible; (Fig.) come to mind;—n. daybreak; morning half-light; beginning.

day (dā) n. period from sunrise to sunset; period of sun's revolution on its axis; 24 hrs.; time of life; epoch.—**day'break** n. dawn.—**day'-dream** n. reverie;—v.i. indulge in reveries.—**day'-light** n. natural light of sun.—**day'-nur'sery** n. crèche.—**day'-school** n. school attended in daytime by pupils who live at home.—**day'time** n. time between sunrise and sunset.

daze (dāz) v.t. confuse; stupefy; bewilder; stun;—n. state of being bewildered; stupefaction. — **dazz'le** v.t. daze with sudden light; make temporarily blind; confuse mentally;—n. brilliancy.—**dazz'ling** a.

deacon (dē'-kon) n. assistant to regular minister; one who superintends Church property and funds; (Scot.) chairman of an incorporated trade.—**dea'coness** n.—**dea'conhood** n. the office of deacon.—**dea'conry** n. body of deacons.—**dea'conship** n. office of deacon.

dead (ded) a. without life; (Colloq.) exact.—adv. wholly.—**dead'en** v.t. impair in vigour, force, or feeling; benumb.—**dead'ness** n.—**dead'-beat** a. exhausted;—a. a down-and-out.—**dead'-end** n. street with one entrance.—**dead'-heat** n. race where two or more competitors reach the winning post at exactly the same time.—**dead** language, language no longer spoken.—**dead'-lett'er** n. obsolete law; undelivered or unclaimed letter.—**dead'-line** n. last available date.—**dead'-lock** n. state of affairs which renders further progress impossible; impasse.—**dead'-loss** n. loss for which no compensation is payable.—**dead'ly** a. causing death; lethal.—**dead'liness** n.—**deadly nightshade**, poisonous plant, the belladonna.—**dead'-nett'le**, n. non-stinging plant resembling nettle.—**dead-pan** a. (Colloq.) expressionless.—**dead'reck'oning** n. (Naut.) steering of vessel by compass and not by stars.—**dead'-weight** n. heavy burden.

deaf (def) a. lacking partially or wholly sense of hearing; heedless; unwilling to listen.—**deaf'en** v.t. make deaf; render the walls of house impervious to sound.—**deaf'ening** a. very loud; thunderous, as applause;—n. material used to make rooms sound-proof.—**deaf'ly** adv.—**deaf'-mute** n. one who is deaf and dumb.—**deaf'-mutism** n.—**deaf'ness** n. state of being deaf.

deal (dēl) v.t. divide; dole out; distribute, as in card games;—v.i. traffic; act; give one's custom to; behave towards;—n. part or portion; distribution of playing cards; a business transaction; bargain.—**deal'er** n.—**deal'ing** n. buying and selling; traffic; treatment;—pl. intercourse or relations with others.—a **raw deal**, iniquitously unfair treatment.—a **square deal**, fair treatment.

deal (dēl) n. plank of fir tree; pine or fir tree timber;—a. made of deal.

dean (dēn) n. dignitary in cathedral or collegiate churches; university office-holder; chairman of guild.—**dean'ery** n. office or residence of a dean.

dear (dēr) a. precious; much loved; highly esteemed or valued; costly; expensive; scarce;—interj. expressing sorrow, pity or wonder.—**dear'ly** adv.—**dearth** (derth) n. deficiency; scarcity; want; famine.

death (deth) n. extinction of life; manner of dying; state of being dead; decease; dissolution; (Fig.) termination.—**death-du'ties** n.pl. duties payable to State on property left at death.—**death'less** a. immortal.—**death'lessness** n.—**death'like** a.—**death'ly** adv.—a. like death.—**death'-mask** n. plaster-cast of person's face taken immediately after death.—**death'-rate** n. mortality rate per thousand of population at given time.—**death's'-head** n. skull of human skeleton.—**death's-head** moth, species of moth with markings resembling skull and cross-bones.—**death'-warr'ant** n. official document authorising execution of criminal.—**death'-watch** n. vigil; beetle which makes a ticking sound.

debacle, débâcle (dā-bak'-l) n. sudden breaking up of ice in river; (Fig.) rout; collapse; disaster.

debar (de-bàr') v.t. cut off from entrance; hinder; prohibit; exclude; preclude;—pr.p. debar'ring.—pa.p. debarred'.

debark (de-bàrk') v.t. and v.i. disembark, oppos. of embark.—**debarka'tion, debark'ment** n.

debase (de-bās') v.t. reduce to a lower state; disgrace; degrade; adulterate.—**debas'ing** a. corrupting, esp. in moral sense.

debate (de-bāt') n. controversy; wrangle; argument; dispute; discussion;—v.t. discuss; dispute; contend; argue in detail;—v.i. take part in discussion; reflect;—pr.p. debat'ing.—pa.p. debat'ed.—debat'able a. open to debate; questionable.—debat'er n.

debauch (de-bawch') v.t. corrupt; vitiate; make depraved; seduce; pervert;—n. excess in eating and drinking; orgy; licentious indulgence; dissipation.—**debauched'** a. dissipated.—**debauch'ee** n. dissipated person.—**debauch'ery** n. moral corruption; intemperate indulgence.

debenture (de-ben'-tūr) n. certificate acknowledging debt and guaranteeing repayment of loan with interest.

debilitate (de-bil'-i-tāt) v.t. weaken; make infirm; enervate.—**debilita'tion, debil'ity** n. enervation; languor.

debit (deb'-it) *n.* item entered on debtor side of account (oppos. of *credit*);—*v.t.* charge with debt.

debonair (deb-ō-nēr) *a.* bearing oneself cheerfully and well; of good air or mien; spruce.

debouch (de-bóósh', de-bouch') *v.i.* march from narrow valley into the open; (of rivers) flow out from confined area into more open spaces.

débris (dā'-brē, deb'-rē) *n.* fragments (taken collectively) of demolished buildings; rubble; ruins.

debt (det) *n.* something owed to another; liability; obligation.—**debt'-or** *n.* one who owes a debt; in book-keeping (abbrev. **Dr.**) debit side of account.—**bad debt**, one unlikely to be repaid.

début, debut (dā-bōō') *n.* first appearance in public, socially or as artiste.—**debutant'** *n.* (*fem.* debutante') one, esp. girl, making first appearance in society, or being presented at Court; abbrev. **deb**.

deca- (dek'-a) *prefix* fr. Gk. *deka*, ten, found in many scientific and technical terms.

decade (dek'-ād) *n.* group of ten things; period of ten years.

decadence (dek'-a-dens or de-kā'-dens) *n.* deterioration; degeneration; decay; falling off in moral or aesthetic standards.—**dec'adent** *n.* writer or artist whose work expresses ideas and ideals of lowered moral value;—*a.* deteriorating; decaying.

decamp (de-kamp') *v.i.* move away from camping ground; move off suddenly or secretly.

decant (de-kant') *v.t.* pour off liquid without disturbing sediment, esp. used of wines.—**decant'er** *n.* slender necked glass bottle into which wine is decanted.

decapitate (de-kap'-i-tāt) *v.t.* cut off head; behead.—**decapita'tion** *n.*

decarbonise (de-kär'-bō-nīz) *v.t.* remove deposit of carbon, as from motor cylinder.—**decarbonisa'tion**.

decay (de-kā') *v.i.* rot away; become decomposed; waste away; wither.—*v.t.* impair;—*n.* gradual wasting or corruption; deterioration; disintegration of radioactive substance.—**decayed'** *a.* rotting.

decease (de-sēs') *n.* death;—*v.i.* die.—**deceased'** *a.* dead;—*n.* dead person.

deceit (de-sēt') *n.* fraud; duplicity; wile.—**deceit'ful** *a.* crafty; fraudulent; illusory.—**deceit'fulness** *n.*—**deceive'** *v.t.* delude; cheat.—**deceiv'able** *a.*—**deceiv'er** *n.*

decelerate (de-sel'-er-āt) *v.t.* and *v.i.* reduce speed.

December (de-sem'-ber) *n.* orig. tenth month of Roman calendar; twelfth month of the year.

decennial (de-sen'-i-al) *a.* lasting for ten years or happening every ten years.—**decenn'ially** *adv.*

decent (dē'-sent) *a.* fitting or becoming; not immodest; suitable; sufficient; (of persons) kindly; (*Colloq.*) pleasant.—**de'cency** *n.* state or quality of being decent.—**de'cently** *adv.*

decentralise (dē-sen'-tral-īz) *v.t.* remove from centre or point of concentration and distribute among smaller areas.

deception (de-sep'-shun) *n.* act of deceiving; fraud; illusion.—**decept'ible** *a.*—**deceptibil'ity** *n.*—**decep'tive** *a.* causing false impression.—**decep'tively** *adv.*

decibel (des'-i-bel) *n.* unit for expressing loudness of sounds.

decide (dē-sīd') *v.t.* determine; make up one's mind about; settle an issue;—*v.t.* give a decision; come to a conclusion.—**decid'ed** *a.* clear; determined.—**decid'edly** *adv.*—**decision** (de-sizh'-un) *n.* act of settling; determination; settlement; judgment.—**decis'ive** *a.* conclusive; resolute.—**decis'ively** *adv.*—**decis'iveness** *n.*

deciduous (de-sid'-ū-us) *a.* (of trees) shedding leaves in autumn; not lasting; liable to fall; (used also of deer's horns).

decimal (des'-i-mal) *a.* pert. to tens; numbered or proceeding by tens;—*n.* fraction with denominator (unexpressed) 10, or some power of 10.—**decimalisa'tion** *n.*—**dec'imalise** *v.t.* reduce to decimal system.—**decimal fraction**, fraction the (unexpressed) denominator of which is 10 or a power of 10.—**decimal system** *n.* system in which each unit is ten times that next below it.

decimate (des'-i-māt) *v.t.* kill (as in Ancient Rome) every tenth man, chosen by lot, as punishment; reduce numbers of, very considerably;—**decima'tion** *n.*

decipher (de-sī'-fer) *v.t.* read cipher; make out what is illegible, unintelligible, or badly written.

decision See **decide**.

deck (dek) *v.t.* adorn; cover; dress up; cover with a deck (of ship).—*n.* covering; horizontal platform extending from one side of ship to the other; pack of cards.—**deck'-chair** *n.* light-weight, collapsible, and easily portable chair.—**deck'-hand** *n.* person employed on deck of ship.—**deck'-house** *n.* small shelter on deck.—**deck'ing** *n.* adornment. **to sweep the deck**, win every game.—**doub'le-deck'er** *n.* vehicle with upper and lower decks.

declaim (de-klām') *v.t.* recite in rhetorical manner;—*v.i.* make formal speech.—**declama'tion** *n.* set speech; rhetorical and dramatic address.—**declam'atory** *a.* pert. to declamation; ostentatiously rhetorical.

declare (dē-klār') *v.t.* proclaim; make clear; state publicly; state in presence of witness;—*v.i.* make a declaration; express favourable attitude towards; (*Cricket*) announce innings closed; (*at Customs*) admit possession of dutiable goods.—**declar'able** *a.*—**declara'tion** *n.*

decline (dē-klīn') *v.t.* bend downward; refuse; avoid; (*Gram.*) give inflections of a word in oblique cases;—*v.i.* slope; hang down; fall in value or quantity; pine away; languish;—*n.* falling off; wasting disease.—**declina'tion** *n.* a sloping away.

declivity (de-kliv'-i-ti) *n.* downward slope; gradual descent.

declutch (dē-kluch') *v.t.* disengage clutch which connects engine and wheels of motor car.

decode (dē-kōd') *v.t.* translate message in code into ordinary language.

décolleté (dā-kol'-tā) *a.* low-necked.

decompose (dē-kom-pōz') *v.t.* break up into elements; separate the constituent parts of; analyse;—*v.i.* decay; become rotten.—**decomposi'tion** *n.* act of decomposing; decay; putrefaction.

decontaminate (dē-kon-tam'-in-āt) *v.t.* cleanse from, esp. from effects of poison-gas.—**decontamina'tion** *n.*

decontrol (dē-kon-trōl') *v.t.* release from government or state control.

decor (dā-kor') *n.* decoration, or setting of theatre, stage, or room.

decorate (dek'-o-rāt) *v.t.* beautify; embellish;. honour person by giving medal or badge of honour.—**dec'orated** *a.*;—**decora'tion** *n.* ornament; badge of honour; insignia.—**dec'orative** *a.* ornamental.—**dec'orativeness** *n.*—**dec'orator** *n.* one who papers and paints houses, shops, etc.

decorous (de-kō'-rus or dek'-o-rus) *a.* becoming seemly; decent; staid.—**decor'ously** *adv.*—**decor'ousness** *n.*—**deco'rum** *n.* decency; behaviour in keeping with social conventions.

decoy (dē-koi') *v.t.* lead into a snare; (*Fig.*) allure; entice by specially tempting means;—*n.* device for leading wild birds into a snare; enticement.

decrease (dē-krēs') *v.t.* lessen; make smaller; reduce gradually;—*v.i.* become less; wane; abate;—*n.* diminution; lessening.—**decreas'ingly** *adv.*

decree (dē-krē') *n.* order made by competent authority; edict; decision in law court; established law; (*Theol.*) divine purpose.—*v.t.* determine judicially; order.—**decre'tal** *a.* pert. to decree;—*n.* order given by high authority, esp. the Pope.—**decree nisi**, decree which becomes absolute after fixed period, unless cause to contrary be proved (as in divorce cases).

decrepit (dē-krep'-it) *a.* worn out or enfeebled by old age; infirm; broken down; (of things) ramshackle.—**decrep'itude** *n.*

decretal See **decree**.

decry (dē-krī') *v.t.* cry down; bring into disrepute; abuse.—**decri'al** *n.* act of decrying.

decuple (dek'-ū-pl) *a.* tenfold.

dedicate (ded'-i-kāt) *v.t.* set apart and consecrate to holy purpose; give oneself wholly to worthy purpose; inscribe book to someone as mark of appreciation or admiration.—**ded'icated** *a.* devoted.—**dedica'tion** *n.*—**ded'icatory** *a.* containing dedication; complimentary.

deduce (dē-dūs') *v.t.* draw from; reach a conclusion by deductive reasoning;. infer; trace down.—**deduce'ment** *n.* that which is inferred.—**dedu'cible** *a.* inferred.—**deduct'** *v.t.* remove; subtract.—**deduct'ible** *a.*—**deduc'tion** *n.* act or process of deducting; amount subtracted; inference or conclusion arrived at.—**deduct'ive** *a.* capable of being deduced.—**deduct'ively** *adv.*

deed (dēd) *n.* that which is done; act; exploit; achievement; legal document or contract.

deem (dēm) *v.t.* believe on consideration; judge.

deep (dēp) *a.* extending far below the surface; having considerable breadth; low in situation; dark; intense; abstruse; low in pitch; sagacious;—*adv.* to a great depth;—*n.* that which is deep; sea.—**deep'en** *v.t.* make deeper;—*v.i.* become deeper.—**deep'ness** *n.*—**deep'-root'ed** *a.* firmly established.—**deep'-seat'ed** *a.* (of disease) not superficial.—**depth** *n.* quality of being deep.

deer (dēr) *n.* ruminant quadruped, such as stag, roebuck, fallow deer, etc.—**deer'-hound** *n.* dog for hunting deer; stag-hound.—**deerstalker** *cap.* one with peaks in front and behind.

deface (dē-fās') *v.t.* destroy or mar the external appearance of; disfigure.—**deface'able** *a.*—**deface'ment** *n.* act or result of defacing; thing which defaces; blemish.

defalcate (dē-fal'-kāt) *v.t.* deduct part of, esp. money, by misappropriation; embezzle.—**defalca'tion** *n.*—**def'alcator** *n.*

defame (dē-fām') *v.t.* harm or destroy good name or reputation of; slander.—**defama'tion** *n.* act of defaming.—**defam'atory** *a.* tending to defame or slander.

default (dē-fawlt') *n.* fault; neglect; defect; failure to appear in law-court when summoned; failure to account for money held in trust.—**default'er** *n.*

defeat (de-fēt') *v.t.* overcome; subdue; conquer;—*n.* act of defeating; overthrow; conquest.—**defeat'ism** *n.* attitude of mind of those who accept their country's defeat as inevitable.—**defeat'ist** *n.*—*a.* pert. to defeatism.

defecate (def'-e-kāt) *v.t.* clear or strain impurities from, as lees, dregs, etc.;—*v.i.* void excrement from the bowels.—**defeca'tion** *n.*

defect (dē-fekt') *n.* want; imperfection; absence of something necessary for completeness.—*v.i.* fail in duty; abandon allegiance to a cause.—**defection** *n.*—**defect'ive** *a.* incomplete; imperfect.—**defect'ively** *adv.*—**defect'iveness** *n.*—**mental defective**, one who is sub-normal in intelligence.

defence (dē-fens') *n.* act of defending; that which shields or protects; vindication; justification; (*Law*) plea or reply to charge.—**defence'less** *a.* open to attack.—**defence'lessly** *adv.*—**defence'lessness** *n.*

defend (dē-fend') *v.t.* protect; ward off attack; maintain; justify; vindicate; (*Law*) state the case of accused person (by counsel).—**defend'able** *a.*—**defend'ant** *n.* one who defends; the accused in criminal case; the one prosecuted in civil case.—**defend'er** *n.*—**defens'ible** *a.*—**defensibil'ity** *n.*—**defens'ive** *a.* serving to defend; resisting attack;—*n.* position of defending against attack.—**defens'ively** *adv.*

defer (dē-fer') *v.t.* submit; yield to opinion of another;—*v.t.* bring or lay before.—**def'erence** *n.* act of deferring.—**deferen'tial** *a.* showing deference.—**deferen'tially** *adv.*

defer (dē-fer') *v.t.* put off; postpone;—*v.i.* delay.—*pr.p.* **defer'ring**; *pa.p.* **deferred'**.—**defer'able**, **defer'rable** *a.*—**defer'ment** *n.* delay; postponement.

defiance (dē-fī'-ans) *n.* act of defying; challenge to combat; contempt; opposition.—**defi'ant** *a.* aggressively hostile; insolent.—**defi'antly** *adv.*—**defi'antness** *n.*

deficient (dē-fish'-ent) *a.* wanting; failing; lacking full supply; incomplete.—**defic'iency** *n.* shortcoming, shortage. — **defic'iently** *adv.* — **deficit** (def'-i-sit) *n.* shortage or deficiency of revenue.—**mentally deficient**, sub-normal in intelligence.

defile (dē'-fīl) *n.* narrow pass in which troops can march only in single or narrow files;—*v.i.* (dē-fīl') march off file by file.

defile (dē-fīl') *v.t.* make unclean; soil; dirty; desecrate.—**defile'ment** *n.*

define (dē-fīn') *v.t.* determine the boundaries of; state exact meaning of; designate; specify.—**defin'able** *a.*—**definite** (def'-i-nit) *a.* fixed or defined; exact; precise; unambiguous; clear; specific; restricted.—**def'initely** *adv.* — **def'initeness** *n.* — **defini'tion** *n.* description of a thing by its properties; explanation of exact meaning of word or term; distinctness.—**defin'itive** *a.* limiting; determining; final; positive.

deflate (dē-flāt') *v.t.* empty of air or gas (as in tyre, balloon, etc.); reduce inflated currency.—**defla'tion** *n.*

deflect (dē-flekt') *v.t.* turn aside; divert from right direction;—*v.i.* swerve; deviate.—**deflect'ed** *a.*—**deflec'tion**, **deflex'ion** *n.*—**deflect'or** *n.* that which causes deflection.

deform (dē-form') *v.t.* mar or alter the form of; disfigure.—**deformed'** *a.*—**deforma'tion**—**deform'ity** *n.* state of being disfigured; malformation.

defraud (dē-frawd') *v.t.* deprive of, by fraud; cheat.

defray (dē-frā') *v.t.* bear cost of; provide money for, as in to *defray the expenses*.—**defray'al**, **defray'ment** *n.*

deft (deft) *a.* dexterous; adroit; handy.—**deft'ly** *adv.*—**deft'ness** *n.*

defunct (dē-fungkt') *a.* dead; deceased; (of things) obsolete.

defy (dē-fī') *v.t.* challenge; dare; set authority at naught.—*pr.p.* **defy'ing**; *pa.p.* **defied'**.

degenerate (dē-jen'-er-āt) *v.i.* decline from noble to lower state of development; become worse physically and morally;—*n.* person of low moral standards;—*a.* having become less than one's kind.—**degen'eracy** *n.*—**degen'erately** *adv.*—**degen'erateness** *n.*—**degenera'tion** *n.* process of degenerating.—**degen'erative** *a.* tending to make degenerate.

degrade (dē-grād') *v.t.* reduce in status; lower the moral reputation of; disgrace.—**degradation** (deg-ra-dā'-shun) *n.* act of degrading; state or process of becoming degraded; degeneration; abasement.

degree (dē-grē') *n.* step or grade; station or status; extent; rank to which one is admitted by a university; 360th part of a revolution; measured space on thermometer, protractor, etc.—**third degree** (*U.S.*) long, searching cross-examination by police of a suspect.

dehumanise (dē-hūm'-an-īz) *v.t.* deprive of human qualities, or of tenderness of feeling.

dehydrate (dē-hī'-drāt) *v.t.* remove water from;—*v.i.* lose water.—**dehydra'tion** *n.*

deify (dē'-i-fī) *v.t.* make a god of; exalt to rank of divinity; worship.—**deif'ic**, **-al** *a.* making godlike.—**deifica'tion** *n.*—**de'iform** *a.* of godlike form.

deign (dān) *v.i.* condescend; stoop;—*v.t.* condescend to do; grant.

deism (dē'-izm) *n.* belief, on purely rational grounds, in existence of God.—**de'ist** *n.*—**deis'tic**, **-al** *a.*—**de'ity** *n.* God; pagan god or goddess.

deject (dē-jekt') *v.t.* cast down; dishearten; depress; dispirit.—**deject'-ed** a. downcast; moody; in low spirits. — **deject'edly** adv. — **deject'-edness** n.—**dejec'tion,** lowness of spirits.

delay (dē-lā') v.t. put off; postpone; stop temporarily; — v.i. linger; dawdle; procrastinate;—n. stoppage; tardiness.—**delay'er** n.

delectable (de-lek'-ta-bl) a. highly pleasing; delightful; enjoyable.—**delect'ableness** n.—**delect'ably** adv.—**delecta'tion** n.

delegate (del'-e-gāt) v.t. entrust authority to deputy.—n. deputy; representative.—**delega'tion** n. act of delegating; body of delegates.—**del'egacy** n.

delete (dē-lēt') v.t. erase; strike out (word or passage).—**dele'tion** n.

deleterious (del-e-tē'-ri-us) a. capable of harming or destroying health; pernicious. — **delete'riously** adv.—**delete'riousness** n.

delf(t) (delf(t)) n. glazed earthenware, orig. made at *Delft* in Holland.

deliberate (dē-lib'-e-rāt) v.t. weigh in the mind; discuss.—v.i. consider carefully; take counsel; hesitate;—a. carefully considered; slow.—**delib'erately** adv.—**delib'erateness** n.—**delibera'tion** n. act of carefully considering; coolness and slowness of action or speech.—**delib'erative** a. showing deliberation.

delicate (del-i-kāt) a. dainty; frail; slender; exquisitely wrought; nicely adjusted; highly sensitive; requiring tact.—**del'icacy** n. fineness of shape, colour, texture, or feeling; something which pleases the palate; dainty; tact.—**del'icately** adv.—**del'-icateness** n.—**del'icates** n.pl. dainties.

delicatessen (del-i-ka-tes'-en) n.pl. table delicacies, esp. cold cooked meats, hors d'oeuvres, etc.; shop selling these.

delicious (dē-lish'-us) a. exquisite; charming (to senses or mind); delightful.—**deli'ciously** adv.

delight (dē-līt') v.t. give great pleasure to; charm;—v.i. take delight;—n. source of pleasure; great satisfaction; joy.—**delight'ful** a.—**delight'fully** adv.

delimit (dē-lim'-it) v.t. fix limit or boundaries of.—**delimita'tion** n.

delineate (dē-lin'-ē-āt) v.t. draw an outline; sketch; portray; (*Fig.*) describe clearly.—**deline'ation** n.

delinquent (dē-lin'-kwent) n. one who fails in duty; offender or criminal, esp. of a young person;—a. failing in duty.—**delin'quency** n.

deliquesce (del-i-kwes') v.i. liquefy by absorbing moisture from air.—**deliques'cence** n. — **deliques'cent** a. liquefying in air.

delirious (de-lir'-i-us) a. wandering in the mind; light-headed; raving; incoherent.—**delira'tion** n. madness. —**delir'iously** adv.—**delir'iousness** n. **delir'ium** n. fever of the brain; strong excitement.—**delirium tremens** (*abbrev.* D.T.) violent delirium resulting from excessive alcoholism.

deliver (dē-liv'-er) v.t. liberate (from danger, captivity, restraint); save from sin; distribute or hand over; pronounce (as a speech); execute (as an attack); give birth to a child (used passively).—**deliv'erable** a.—**deliv'erance** n.—**deliv'erer** n.—**deliv'ery** n. act of delivering; style of utterance of public speech or sermon; (*Cricket*) manner of bowling the ball; (*Med.*) act of giving birth.

dell (del) n. small, deep valley; hollow.

delphinium (del-fin'-i-um) n. genus of annual, biennial, and perennial herbaceous flowering plants.

delta (del'-ta) n. the fourth letter of the Greek alphabet, its form as a capital being $\triangle$ (small letter= δ); (*Geog.*) triangular-shaped tract of alluvium at mouth of large river.—**delta-wing** a. of aircraft, having triangular swept-back wings.

delude (dē-lūd') v.t. lead into error; mislead; deceive.—**delu'sion** n. act of deluding; that which deludes; mistaken belief; (*Med.*) hallucination.—**delu'sive** a.—**delu'sory** a.

deluge (del'-ūj) n. great flow of water; torrential rain; flood, esp. Biblical flood in time of Noah;—v.t. flood; inundate; drench.

de luxe (de lóoks') a. sumptuous; of superlative quality.

delve (delv) v.t. and v.i. dig with spade; to burrow.

demagnetise (dē-mag-net-īz) v.t. deprive of magnetic polarity.—**demag'netisation** n.

demagogue (dem'-a-gog) n. leader of the masses; political agitator who sways people by appealing to emotions more than to reason.—**demagogio, -al** (dem-a-goj'(gog')-ik-al) a. **demagogy** (dem'-a-goj(g)-i) n. Also **dem'agoguery**.

demand (de-mand') v.t. ask authoritatively or peremptorily; question; require;—n. act of demanding; urgent claim; earnest inquiry; (*Econ.*) requirement of purchaser or consumer, oppos. of *supply*.

demarcation, demarkation (dē-mār-kā-shun) n. act of marking line or boundary; boundary; line of distinction between respective fields of operation of two trade unions.—**demarcate'** v.t.

demean (dē-mēn') v.t. conduct or comport oneself; behave.—**demean'-our** n. behaviour; manner of conducting oneself.

demean (dē-mēn') v.t. make mean; debase; degrade (used reflexively).

demented (de-men'-ted) *a.* insane; crazy; suffering from dementia.—**dement'** *v.t.* drive mad.

demerara (dem'-er-ár-a) *n.* kind of brown sugar, orig. from *Demerara* in Guyana.

demerit (de-mer'-it) *n.* fault; bad feature; vice.

demesne, demain (de-mēn', de-mān') *n.* manor-house and estate adjacent to it; private ownership of land.—Also **domain'**.—**demesn'ial** *a.*

demi- (dem'-i) *prefix* signifying *half*.

demise (de-mīz') *n.* transmission by will to successor; conveyance of property; death;—*v.t.* bequeath; transmit to successor.

demobilise (de-mob'-i-līz) *v.t.* dismiss (troops); disband.—**demobilisa'tion** *n.*—(*Abbrev.*) **demob'**.

democracy (de-mok'-ra-si) *n.* form of government for the people by will of majority of the people (based on conception of equality of man); state having this form of government.—**democrat** (dem'-ō-krat) *n.* one who adheres to democracy; (*U.S.*) member of Democratic party.—**democrat'ic, democrat'ical** *a.*—**democrat'ically** *adv.*

demolish (de-mol'-ish) *v.t.* destroy; pull down (of a building); ruin; (*Colloq.*) consume.—**demol'isher** *n.*—**demoli'tion** *n.* act or process of pulling down; destruction.

demon (de'-mon) *n.* spirit (esp. evil); devil.—**demo'nias** *a.* also **demo'niacal**.

demonstrate (dem'-on-strāt, de-mon'-strāt) *v.t.* prove by pointing out; exhibit; explain by specimens or experiment.—**demon'strable** *a.* capable of being demonstrated.—**demon'strably** *adv.*—**demonstra'tion** *n.* act of making clear, esp. by practical exposition; proof beyond doubt; display of emotion.—**demon'strative** *a.*—**dem'onstrator** *n.*

demoralise (de-mor'-al-īz) *v.t.* injure morals of; corrupt; weaken courage or morale of; throw into confusion.

demote (de-mōt') *v.t.* reduce in rank.—**demot'ion** *n.*

demur (de-mur') *v.i.* hesitate because of doubt, difficulty, or scruples; object.—*pr.p.* **demur'ring**; *pa.p.* **demurred'**; *n.* hesitation; pause; statement of objections.

demure (de-mūr') *a.* grave; staid; shy; seemingly modest.—**demure'ly** *adv.*—**demure'ness** *n.*

den (den) *n.* cave or hollow place; lair or cage of wild beast; disreputable haunt; (*Colloq.*) private sanctum, study, or workshop.

denationalise (de-nash'-un-al-īz) *v.t.* deprive of national rights, character, or status; to change from state control to private control.—**denationalisa'tion** *n.*

denature (de-nā'-tūr) *v.t.* make unfit

for eating or drinking by adulteration.—**dena'turant** *n.* that which changes nature of a thing.—**denatura'tion** *n.*

denial (de-nī'-al) *n.* act of denying; contradiction; refusal.—**den'iable** *a.*

denigration (den-i-grā'-shun) *n.* blackening of; (*Fig.*) defamation of person's character.—**den'igrate** *v.t.*

denim (den'-im) *n.* stout cotton twill cloth for making overalls, etc.

denizen (den'-i-zn) *n.* dweller (human being or animal); citizen; naturalised alien with rights of a citizen; *v.t.* to make a denizen of.—**den'izenship** *n.*

denominate (de-nom'-i'nāt) *v.t.* give a name to; designate; style.—**denom'inable** *a.*—**denomina'tion** *n.* act of naming; title; class of people; religious sect; (*Arith.*) unit of measure (money, length, etc.).—**denomina'tional** *a.*—**denom'inative** *a.* conferring or having distinctive name.—**denom'inatively** *adv.*—**denom'inator** *n.* one who, or that which, designates a class; divisor; number below line in vulgar fraction.

denote (de-nōt') *v.t.* signify or imply; express by a sign; mean; be the symbol of; (*Logic*) indicate the objects to which a term refers.—**deno'table** *a.*—**denota'tion** *n.*

dénouement (dā-nōō'-mong) *n.* unravelling of the complication of dramatic plot; issue or outcome of a situation.

denounce (de-nouns') *v.t.* inform against; accuse in public; threaten; repudiate, as a treaty.—**denounce'ment** *n.*—**denounc'er** *n.*

dense (dens) *a.* compact; thick; crowded; (of vegetation) impenetrable, luxuriant; (*Fig.*) stupid.—**dense'ly** *adv.*—**dense'ness** *n.*—**den'sity** *n.* quality of being dense; (*Chem.*) mass per unit volume of a substance.

dent (dent) *n.* small depression made (by a blow) in a surface;—*v.t.* mark by a blow or pressure.

dental (dent'-al) *a.* pert. to teeth or to dentistry;—*n.* and *a.* a consonant sound (e.g. *d* or *t*) made by tip of tongue behind the upper front teeth.—**den'tifrice** *n.* powder, paste, or liquid used to clean and whiten teeth.—**den'tist** *n.* a medically trained specialist in care of teeth (also *dental surgeon*).—**den'tistry** *n.*—**denti'tion** *n.* cutting of teeth.—**den'ture** *n.* set or part set of teeth, esp. artificial teeth.

denude (de-nūd') *v.t.* lay bare; strip; deprive of a quality.—**denuda'tion** *n.*

denunciate (de-nun'-si-āt) *v.t.* Same as **denounce**.—**denuncia'tion** *n.*—**denun'ciator** *n.* one who denounces.—**denun'ciatory** *a.*

deny (de-nī') *v.t.* declare to be untrue; refuse a request; disavow; disown; withhold; (*reflex.*) abstain from.—*pr.p.* **deny'ing**.—*pa.p.* **denied'**.

E

deodorise (dē-ō'-dor-īz) v.t. deprive of odour.—**deo'dorant, deodoris'er** n. something which removes unpleasant smell; disinfectant.

depart (dē-pàrt') v.i. go away; quit; leave; die; abandon; deviate (as from a policy);—v.t. leave (e.g. to depart this life).—**depart'ed** n. (sing. and plur.) the dead.—**depart'ment** n. self-contained section of business or administration; special branch of the arts or science; administrative district of country, as in France.—**department'al** a.—**depart'ure** n. act of going away; divergence from rule.

depend (dē-pend') v.i. hang; be sustained by; rely on; be contingent on; (Law) be awaiting final judgment.—**depen'dable** a. trustworthy.—**depen'dably** adv.—**depen'dant** n. one who is supported, esp. financially by another; retainer; subordinate.—**depen'dent** a. hanging down; relying on for support or favour; varying according to; (spellings -ant, -ent are interchangeable in noun and adjective, but -ant is more common in noun, and -ent in adjective).—**depen'dence** (less common—ance) n. state of depending, relying on.—**depen'dency** n. state of being dependent on; esp. used of colonies.—**depen'dently, depen'dantly** adv.

depict (dē-pikt') v.t. portray; paint carefully; present a visual image of; describe in words.—**depic'tive** a.

depilate (dep'-i-lāt) v.t. remove hair from;—a. hairless.—**depila'tion** n.—**depil'atory** n. agent for removing superfluous hair from body.—a. having property of removing hair.

deplete (dē-plēt') v.t. empty; diminish; exhaust; reduce in numbers.—**deple'tive, deple'tory** a.

deplore (dē-plōr') v.t. weep over; suffer remorse for; lament; regret; deprecate; express disapproval of.—**deplor'able** a.—**deplor'ably** adv.

deploy (dē-ploi') v.t. spread out; extend troops in line; diminish in depth (of troops).—v.i. extend from column into line.—**deploy'ment** n.

depopulate (dē-pop'-ū-lāt) v.t. reduce number of inhabitants of area by any means.—v.i. become depleted in population.—**depopula'tion** n.

deport (dē-pōrt') v.t. carry away; expel; banish into exile (of undesirable aliens); (reflex.) behave; bear oneself.—**deporta'tion** n. compulsory removal of people from a country.—**deport'ment** n. carriage or bearing or posture of a person.

depose (dē-pōz') v.t. remove from throne; oust from high position; degrade; (Law) state upon oath.—**depos'able** a.—**depos'al** n.—**deposi'tion** n. removal of someone from high position; written declaration by witness.

deposit (dē-poz'-it) v.t. lay down; entrust; let fall (as sediment); lodge (in bank); store;—n. that which is deposited or laid down; sediment falling to bottom of a fluid; money placed in safe-keeping of bank (usually with interest); security; pledge.—**depos'itary** n. one with whom anything is left in trust.—**depos'itor** n.—**depos'itory** n. place where things are deposited; storehouse, esp. for furniture.

depot (dep'-ō, dē'-pō) n. depository; store-house; (Mil.) regimental headquarters; training centre for recruits; (U.S.) a railway station.

deprave (dē-prāv') v.t. make bad or worse; corrupt; vitiate; pervert.—**deprava'tion** n. act of corrupting; moral perversion; degeneration.—**deprav'ed** a. immoral; vicious.—**deprav'edly** adv.

deprecate (dep'-re-kāt) v.t. seek to avert by prayer; express disapproval of.—**dep'recable** a.—**dep'recative, dep'recatory** a.—**dep'recator** n.

depreciate (dē-prē'-shi-āt) v.t. lower in value; (Fig.) disparage; underrate;—v.i. lose quality; diminish in market value.—**deprecia'tion** n. decline in value.—**depre'ciative, depre'ciatory** a.—**depre'ciator** n.

depredate (dep'-re-dāt) v.t. plunder; lay waste.—**depreda'tion** n. act of laying waste; pillaging; theft.—**dep'redator** n.

depress (dē-pres') v.t. press down; lower; diminish vigour of; deject or cast gloom over.—**depressed'** a. pressed down; unfortunate; dejected; languid.—**depress'ible** a.—**depres'sion** n. hollow; dip; a sinking; (Fig.) dejection; despondency; slump (in trade); (Meteor.) cyclone, area of low barometric pressure.—**depress'or** n.

deprive (dē-prīv') v.t. take away; dispossess; debar person from; divest clergyman of ecclesiastical office.—**depriva'tion** n. act of depriving; state of being deprived or dispossessed.

depth (depth) n. deepness; distance measured downwards from surface; breadth, as of hem, shelf, etc.; profundity or penetration, as of mind.—**depth'-charge** n. large canister type of bomb fired over side of ship, and detonating at predetermined depth.

depute (dē-pūt') v.t. send to act for another; delegate duties to another.—**depute** (dep'-ūt) a. Scotland, appointed deputy—**deputa'tion** n. act of deputing; persons authorised to transact business for others.—**dep'utise** v.i. act as substitute or deputy for others.—**deputy** n. (dep'-ū-ti) one appointed to act for another.

derail (dē-rāl') v.t. cause to run off rails.—**derail'ment** n. state of being derailed.

derange (dē-rānj') v.t. put out of order or place; upset; make insane. —**deranged'** a. mentally unstable; insane.—**derange'ment** n.

derate (dē-rāt') v.t. relieve from burden of local rates.

derelict (der'-e-likt) a. forsaken; abandoned by owner, esp. used of ships;—n. ship abandoned by captain and crew.—**derelic'tion** n. act of abandoning; failure in duty.

deride (dē-rīd') v.t. ridicule; mock; laugh at with scorn; belittle.—**derid'er** n.—**derid'ingly** adv.—**derision** (dē-rizh'-un) n. mockery; ridicule; ironical contempt.—**deri'sive** a. mocking; ridiculing.—**deri'sively** adv. **deri'siveness** n.—**deris'ory** a. futile; contemptible.

derive (dē-rīv') v.t. obtain or draw from a source; trace etymology (of word); trace descent or origin; (of person);—v.i. have as origin; proceed (foll. by from).—**derivation** (der-i-vā'-shun) n. act of deriving or process of being derived; tracing of word back to its roots; etymology. —**deriv'ative** n. that which is derived or traceable back to something else; word derived from another;—a. obtained by derivation; secondary. —**deriv'atively** adv.

dermal (der'-mal) a. pert. to the skin.—**dermati'tis** n. inflammation of the skin by localised irritation.—**dermatol'ogy** n. branch of medical science concerned with skin and skin diseases.—**dermatol'ogist** n. skin specialist.

derogate (der'-ō-gāt) v.t. remove or detract from; discredit; disparage; —v.i. lessen (as reputation).—**deroga'tion** n.—**derog'atory** a. (with to). —**derog'atorily** adv.

derrick (der'-ik) n. apparatus like a crane for hoisting heavy weights.

derris (der-is) n. powder obtained from root of tropical plant, derris, used as insecticide.

descant (des'-kant) n. variation harmonising with and sung or played as accompaniment to melody; discourse or expatiation on a theme; —v.i. discourse fully; sing a descant. —**descant'er** n.

descend (dē-send') v.t. go down into; traverse downwards; flow down;—v.i. sink; lower oneself or stoop to something; fall (upon an enemy).—**descend'ant** n. one descended from ancestor; offspring.—**descend'ent** a. descending.—**descend'ing** a. and pr.p. —**descent'** n. act of coming down; slope or declivity; inheritance.

describe (dē-skrīb') v.t. represent features of; portray in speech or writing.—**describ'able** a.—**descrip'tion** n. act of describing; representation, in words, of qualities of person or thing; class or order of things; sort;

kind.—**descrip'tive** a. containing description. — **descrip'tively** adv. — **descrip'tiveness** n.

descry (dē-skrī') v.t. discover by the eye; perceive from a distance; make out.—**descri'er** n.

desecrate (des'-e-krāt) v.t. violate the sanctity of; profane.—**des'ecrater, -or** n.—**desecra'tion** n.

desegregate (dē-seg'-re-gāt) v.t. abolish racial segregation.

desert (dē-zert') n. that which is deserved; reward (for merit); punishment (for demerit).

desert (dez'-ert) n. waste region where little or no vegetation is found;—a. uncultivated; solitary.

desert (dē-zert') v.t. abandon; leave; fail;—v.i. quit without permission the Army, Navy, or Air Force.—**desert'ed** a. abandoned.—**desert'er** n. —**deser'tion** n. act of deserting; state of being abandoned.

deserve (dē-zerv') v.t. earn by service; merit; be entitled to; warrant;—v.i. be worthy of reward. —**deserv'edly** adv. justly.—**deserv'ing** a. worthy; meritorious.

desiccate (de-sik'-āt, des'-i-kāt) v.t. extract all moisture from; dry up; dehydrate;—v.i. become dry.—**des'iccant** a. drying;—n. (Chem.) substance capable of absorbing moisture. —**desicca'tion** n. process of extracting moisture from something; state of being dehydrated.—**des'iccator** n. (Chem.) apparatus for dehydration.

desideratum (de-sid-e-ra'-tum) n. that which is earnestly desired; admitted need;—pl. **desidera'ta.**

design (dē-zīn') v.t. draw the outline of; plan;—v.i. purpose;—n. sketch in outline (esp. in architecture); pattern; scheme or plan; purpose.—**design'able** a.—**designate** (des'-ig-nāt) v.t. mark out and make known; to nominate.—**designa'tion** n. distinctive name or title.—**design'edly** adv. intentionally.—**design'er** n. one who designs or makes plans or patterns; schemer or plotter.—**design'ful** a.—**design'ing** a. artful; crafty; selfishly interested.

desire (dē-zīr') v.t. yearn for possession of; request; entreat;—n. anything desired; a longing; object of longing; lust.—**desir'able** a. worth possessing. — **desir'ably** adv. — **desir'ableness, desirabil'ity** n.— **desir'ous** a. wishful; eager.—**desir'ously** adv.

desist (dē-zist') v.i. cease; discontinue; forbear.—**desist'ance, -ence** n.

desk (desk) n. table (or table with moveable sloping flap), for reading or writing; lectern.

desolate (des'-o-lāt) v.t. devastate; depopulate; make lonely or forlorn; —a. waste; deserted; unfrequented; dismal.—**des'olately** adv.—**des'olateness** n.—**des'olater** n.—**desola'tion** n.

despair (de-spâr') v.i. be without hope; lose heart; have no expectation of improvement;—n. despondency; hopelessness.—**despair'ing** a.—**despair'ingly** adv.

despatch, dispatch (des-, dis-pach') v.t. send away, esp. in haste; execute promptly (as an order); dispose of; kill;—n. something which is despatched; speed; promptitude; official message or document sent by special messenger; sending out of mails.—**despatch'es** n.pl. official papers or military reports.

desperado (des-per-a'-dō) n. desperate fellow; unscrupulous ruffian;—pl. **despera'do(e)s**.

desperate (des'-per-ăt) a. beyond hope; critically serious; heedless of danger; furious; frantic; in dire straits.—**des'perately** adv.—**des'perateness** n. state of being desperate.

despicable (des'-pik-a-bl) a. contemptible; mean; vile.—**des'picably** adv. vilely.—**des'picableness** n.—**despicabil'ity** n.

despise (de-spīz') v.t. look down upon; hold in contempt; disdain; scorn.—**despis'able** a. contemptible.—**despis'al** n. contempt.

despite (de-spīt') n. malice; contemptuous defiance; scorn; spite;—prep. in spite of; notwithstanding.—**despite'ful** a.—**despite'fully** adv.

despoil (de-spoil') v.t. take away by force; deprive; rob; strip.—**despoil'er** n. plunderer.—**despolia'tion** n.

despond (de-spond') v.i. be cast down in spirit.—**despond'ence, despond'ency** n. dejection of mind; depression.—**despond'ent** a. depressed.—**despond'ently** adv.—**despond'ingly** adv.

despot (des'-pot) n. one who rules with absolute power; tyrant.—**despot'ic** a.—**despot'ically** adv.—**des'potism** n. absolute power of one man.

dessert (de-zert') n. course, usually fruit or sweets, served at end of dinner.

destine (des'-tin) v.t. determine future condition of; fore-ordain; doom; decree.—**destina'tion** n. purpose for which anything is destined; place to which one is travelling.—**des'tiny** n. fore-ordained lot; fate.

destitute (des'-ti-tūt) a. in want; needy; deprived of means of sustenance;—v.t. forsake.—**destitution** n. state of abject poverty.

destroy (de-stroi') v.t. pull down; put an end to; annihilate.—pa.p. **destroyed'**.—**destroy'able** a.—**destroy'er** n. type of fast warship armed with guns and torpedoes.

destruction (de-struk'-shun) n. act of destroying; state of being destroyed; ruin; death.—**destruc'tible** a. capable of being destroyed.—**destruc'tibleness, destructibil'ity** n.—**destruc'tive** a. causing destruction; fatal.—**destruc'tively** adv.

desultory (des'-ul-tor-i) a. unmethodical; aimless; rambling.—**des'ultorily** adv.—**des'ultoriness** n.

detach (de-tach') v.t. separate; disunite; withdraw; detail for special service (as troops).—**detach'able** a.—**detached'** a. standing alone (e.g. of a house); impersonal; disinterested;—**detach'edly** adv.—**detach'edness, detach'ment** n. state of being detached; that which is detached; small body of troops.

detail (de-tāl') v.t. relate minutely; record every item; appoint for special duty (e.g. troops).—detail (dē'-tāl or de-tāl') n. minute part; item; particular fact; (Mil.) squad assigned to special duty.—**de'tailed** a. giving every particular fact.

detain (de-tān') v.t. keep back or from; prevent someone proceeding; maintain possession of; (Law) keep in custody.—**detain'er** n.—**detain'ment** n.—**deten'tion** n. act of detaining; state of being detained.

detect (de-tekt') v.t. uncover; discover; expose; bring to light (esp. a crime); perceive.—**detect'able, detect'ible** a.—**detect'er, detect'or** n. one who or that which detects.—**detec'tion** n. discovery of something hidden; state of being detected.—**detect'ive** a. employed in detecting;—n. member of police force, not in uniform, who apprehends criminals and investigates cases.

deter (de-ter') v.t. frighten from; discourage; prevent; hinder.—pr.p. **deter'ring**; pa.p. **deterred'**.—**deter'ment** n. hindrance.—**deter'rent** a. having power to deter;—n. that which deters; nuclear weapon.—**deter'rence** n. act of deterring.

deterge (de-terj') v.t. cleanse (wound); wipe off; to purge.—**deter'gence, deter'gency** n.—**deter'gent** a. cleansing (by rubbing or wiping);—n. cleansing, purifying substance.

deteriorate (de-tē'-ri-o-rāt) v.t. and i. make or become worse; degenerate.—**deteriora'tion** n.

determine (de-ter'-min) v.t. fix limits of; define; regulate the form, scope, or character of; influence; ascertain with precision;—v.i. make decision or resolution; (Law) terminate.—**deter'minable** a.—**deter'minant** a. serving to determine, fix, or limit;—n. that which determines.—**deter'minate** a. having fixed limits; decisive; established.—**deter'minately** adv.—**determina'tion** n. act of determining fixed purpose; resolution.—**deter'mined** a. resolute; purposeful.—**deter'minedly** adv.

detest (de-test') v.t. dislike intensely; hate; abhor; abominate.—**detest'able** a. abhorrent; hateful.—**detest'able-**

ness, detest'abil'ity n.—detesta'tion n.

dethrone (dē-thrōn') v.t. remove from throne; depose.—**dethrone'ment** n.

detonate (det'-o-nāt) v.t. cause to explode;—v.t. explode with loud report.—**detona'tion** n. sudden and violent explosion.—**detona'tor** n. detonating substance; percussion cap or fulminating powder used to fire charge of explosive; fog-signal.

detour (dē-tōōr') n. roundabout way, circuitous route; digression.

detract (dē-trakt') v.t. take away part from; defame;—v.i. (with from) diminish.—**detrac'tion** n. disparagement; depreciation; slander.

detrain (dē-trān') v.i. get off train.

detriment (det'-ri-ment) n. injury; harm; loss; mischief.—**detriment'al** a. injurious.—**detriment'ally** adv.

detritus (de-trī'-tus) n. powdery substance accumulated by rubbing down a solid.—**detri'tion** n. wearing away by friction.

devaluate (dē-val'-ū-āt) v.t. reduce value of (esp. the currency). Also **deval'ue.**—**devalua'tion** n.

devastate (dev'-as-tāt) v.t. lay waste; plunder.—**devasta'tion** n. act of laying waste; state of being devastated; destruction; havoc.

develop (de-vel'-op) v.t. unroll; unfold gradually; increase resources of; exploit natural resources; build on; render visible latent image on sensitised surface of photographic negative or positive.—v.i. evolve by natural processes; expand; open out; assume definite character.—**devel'oper** n.

deviate (dē'-vi-āt) v.i. diverge; turn away from direct line; swerve; err; —v.t. cause to swerve.—**devia'tion** n. turning aside from right way; divergence; error.

device (dē-vīs') n. that which is planned out or designed; contrivance; stratagem; (Her.) emblem on shield.

devil (dev'-l) v.t. (Cookery) season with mustard and then broil;—v.i. do the drudgery esp. legal or literary.

devil (dev'-l) n. spirit of evil; in Scripture, tempter; Satan; fiend; any very wicked person; (Colloq.) a fellow.—**dev'ilish** a.—**dev'ilishly** adv. —**dev'il-may-care** a. reckless; happy-go-lucky.—**dev'ilment** n. mischief; prank.—**dev'ilry** n. devilish conduct; collection of devils.—**printer's devil,** printer's youngest apprentice or message boy.—**Tasmanian devil,** carnivorous marsupial, the dasyure.— **give the devil his due,** give even worst person credit for something.

devious (dē'-vi-us) a. not direct; roundabout; circuitous; intricate; erring; not straightforward.—**de'viously.**—**de'viousness** n.

devise (dē-vīz') v.t. invent; contrive; scheme; plan; (Law) leave as a legacy;—v.i. consider;—n. (Law) act of bequeathing real estate by will; clause in will to this effect.— **devis'able** a.—**devis'al** n.—**devis'er** n. one who schemes or contrives.— **devis'or** n. one who bequeaths by will.

devitalise (dē-vī'-tạ-līz) v.t. deprive of life or vitality.—**devitalisa'tion** n.

devoid (dē-void') a. empty; free from.

devolute (de-vol-ūt') v.t. delegate work to others.—**devolu'tion** n. delegation of powers to subsidiary or local bodies; decentralisation. See **devolve.**

devolve (dē-volv') v.t. roll down; transmit; transfer; delegate;—v.i. (with upon) fall to the lot of; cause to be performed by; (Law) pass, by inheritance, from one to another.—**devolve'ment** n.

devote (dē-vōt') v.t. vow; dedicate; consecrate; give oneself wholly to. —**devo'ted** a. zealous; strongly attached to or engrossed by.—**devot'edly** adv.—**devot'edness** n.—**devotee'** n. one devoted to a cause; votary; zealous supporter.—**devo'tion** n.—**devo'tions** n.pl. prayers.—**devo'tional** a. pert. to devotions; religious.

devour (dē-vour') v.t. swallow ravenously; consume completely; destroy; (Fig.) to read avidly.

devout (dē-vout') a. pious; passionately religious; solemn; intense.— **devout'ly** adv.—**devout'ness** n.

dew (dū) n. moisture in the atmosphere or in the soil, condensed on exposed surfaces, esp. at night;— v.t. moisten; bedew; condense.— **dew'iness** n.—**dew'y** a.

dewlap (dū'-lap) n. hanging fold of skin under the throat of oxen, dogs, etc.; fleshy wattle of turkey.

dexter (deks'-tẹr) a. pert. to right hand; on right hand side;—**dexter'ity** n. right-handedness; manual skill; mental adroitness; cleverness; deftness; quickness.—**dex'terous, dex'trous** a. right-handed; deft.—**dex'terously** adv.—**dex'terousness** n.

dextrose (dex'-trōz) n. form of glucose or grape sugar.

dhow (dou) n. Arab coasting vessel.

diabetes (dī-ạ-bē'-tēz) n. disease marked by excessive flow of sugar-urine due to failure of pancreas to produce insulin.

diabolic, diabolical (dī-ạ-bol'-ik, -i-kạl) a. devilish; fiendish; pert. to the devil.—**diabol'ically** adv.

diadem (dī'-ạ-dem) n. fillet or head band worn as symbol of royal power; head-dress or crown significant of royalty; (Fig.) sovereignty.— **di'ademed** a. wearing a crown.

diagnosis (dī-ag-nō'-sis) n. scientific discrimination of any kind; (Med.)

identification of a disease from signs and symptoms;—*pl.* **diagno'ses**.—**di'agnose** *v.t.* (*Med.*) ascertain from signs and symptoms nature of a disease; identify the root-cause of any social or other problem.—**diagnos'tic** *a.*—**diagnosti'cian** *n.*

diagonal (dī-ag'-o-nal) *n.* (*Geom.*) straight line joining two opposite angles in rectilinear figure; (*Print.*) stroke (/) dividing shillings and pence;—*a.* from corner to corner; oblique.—**diag'onally** *adv.*

diagram (dī'-a-gram) *n.* figure drawn to demonstrate theorem; drawing or plan in outline to illustrate something.—**diagrammat'ically** *adv.*

dial (dī'-al) *n.* instrument for showing the time of day from sun's shadow; face of sundial, clock, watch, etc.; any plate or face on which pointer moves; circular device for calling numbers on automatic telephone; (*Slang*) human face;—*v.t.* measure on a dial; call a number on automatic telephone; —*pr.p.* **di'alling.** — *pa.p.* **di'alled.**

dialect (dī-a-lekt) *n.* group variation of language; speech peculiar to district or social group; vernacular.

dialectic, -al (dī-a-lek'-tik, -al) *a.* pert. to dialectics;—*n.* (usually *pl.*) art of discussion, disputation, or debate; science of reasoning.—**dialec'tically** *adv.*—**dialecti'cian** *n.* one skilled in debate.

dialogue (dī'-a-log) *n.* conversation between two (or more) persons.—**dialog'ic, dialogist'ic** *a.* pert. to dialogue.—**dial'ogise** *v.i.* speak in dialogue.—**dial'ogist** *n.*

diameter (dī-am'-e-ter) *n.* (*Geom.*) straight line passing through centre of circle or other curvi-linear figure, and terminated by circumference; transverse measurement; unit of magnifying power of lens.—**diam'etrical, diamet'ric,** *a.* pert. to diameter; directly opposite; contrary. — **diamet'rically** *adv.*

diamond (dī'-a-mond) *n.* one of the crystalline forms of carbon and hardest substance known; popular gem-stone; four-sided figure with two acute and two obtuse angles; rhombus; one of the four suits of playing-cards;—*a.* resembling, set with, consisting of, shaped like diamonds.—**diamond wedding,** sixtieth anniversary of marriage.—**diamond cut diamond,** used of two people well-matched in cunning.—**black diamonds** (*Colloq.*) coal.—**rough diamond** (*Colloq.*) a worthy but uncultured person.

Dianthus (dī-an'-thus) *n.* (*Bot.*) genus of plants to which belong carnations, pinks, and sweet-william.

diapason (dī-a-pā'-zon) *n.* in Greek music, the octave or interval which includes all tones of diatonic scale; concord in which all notes are an octave apart; correct pitch; harmony; passage of swelling, mingled sound; entire compass of voice or instrument; the two foundation stops of an organ.

diaper (dī'-a-per) *n.* an unbleached linen or cotton cloth with diamond pattern used for table linen and towels; baby's napkin; (*Archit.*) geometric pattern (usually diamond shaped, sometimes floral) in low relief on flat surface;—*v.t.* to ornament with diaper pattern.

diaphanous (dī-af'-a-nus) *a.* transparent; translucent; pellucid.—**diaph'anously** *adv.*

diaphragm (dī'-a-fram) *n.* (*Anat.*) dividing membrane; dome-shaped muscular partition between chest and abdomen; the midriff; vibrating disc in microphone. loudspeaker or telephone; disc or iris with circular hole used in telescope or camera to cut off part of ray of light.—**diaphragmat'ic, diaphrag'mal** *a.*

diarrhoea, diarrhea (dī-a-rē'-a) *n.* excessive and frequent looseness of the bowels.—**diarrhoe'al, diarrhoe'ic, diarrhoet'ic** *a.*

diary (dī'-a-ri) *n.* daily record of events; journal; book in which a personal record of thoughts, action, etc. is kept.—**di'arist** *n.*

diathermal (dī-a-therm'-al) *a.* permeable by heat.—**diather'manous, diather'mous, diather'mic** *a.* having property of transmitting radiant heat.—**diather'my** *n.* form of high frequency electrical treatment for generating heat in body tissues.

diatom (dī'-a-tom) *n.* one of an order of microscopic unicellular marine or vegetable organisms.—**diatom earth,** popularly 'infusorial earth' (fossil diatoms) used in manufacture of fireproof cement explosives, etc.—**diatoma'ceous** *a.*—**diat'omite** *n.* diatom earth.

diatonic (dī-a-ton'-ik) *a.* (*Mus.*) pert. to major or minor scales; proceeding by tones, intervals, and harmonies of natural scale.—**diaton'ically** *adv.*

diatribe (dī'-a-trīb) *n.* continued disputation; vituperative harangue; wordy denunciation.—**di'atribist** *n.*

dibble (dib'-l) *n.* a pointed instrument used in gardening for making holes. Also **dibb'er**—*v.t.* plant with a dibble;—*v.i.* make holes.—**dibb'ler** *n.*

dice (dīs) *n.pl.* small cubes on each of six faces of which are spots representing numbers 1-6; used from Egyptian times in games of chance (*pl.* form of **die**);—*v.t.* cut into small squares;—*v.i.* play with dice.—**die'er** *n.* a gambler.—**die'ey** *a.* (*Colloq.*) risky.

dichotomy (dī-kot'-om-i) *n.* cutting

in two; clearage; (*Logic*) division of ideas into two classes positive and negative.—**dichot'omise** *v.t.* and *i.*—**dichot'omous** *a.*

dicker (dik'-ẽr) *v.t.* and *i.* barter; haggle; quibble;—*n.* bargain; deal.

dickey, dicky (dik'-i) *n.* driver's seat in a carriage; seat for servants at back of old-fashioned horse-carriage; extra seat at back of two-seater motor-car; (*Slang*) false shirt front;—*a.* (*Colloq.*) weak, as a *dickey* heart.

dicotyledon (dī-kot-i-lē'-don) *n.* (*Bot.*) plant with two cotyledons, or seed-leaves.—**dicotyle'donous** *a.*

dicta See **dictum**.

dictate (dik-tāt') *v.t.* read aloud passage for another to transcribe; give orders;—*v.i.* speak with authority; prescribe; deliver commands.—**dictate** (dik'-tāt) *n.* order; command; direction that must be obeyed (usually *pl.*).—**dicta'tion** *n.* art or practice of dictating; that which is read aloud for another to write down, esp. as spelling test for children.—**dicta'tor** *n.* (*fem.* **dicta'tress, dicta'trix**) one who holds absolute power.—**dictator'ial** *a.* pert. to or like a dictator; tending to force one's opinions on another.—**dictator'ially** *adv.*—**dicta'torship** *n.*

diction (dik'-shun) *n.* choice of words in speaking and writing; verbal style; phraseology.

dictionary (dik'-shun-a-ri) *n.* book containing, alphabetically arranged, the words of a language, meanings and possibly, etymology; lexicon.

dictum (dik'-tum) *n.* positive assertion; authoritative statement or opinion; apothegm; maxim;—*pl.* **dic'ta**.

did (did) *pa.t.* of verb do.

didactic (di-dak'-tik) *a.* designed to instruct, esp. morally; containing precepts or doctrines; (of people) opinionative.—**didac'tically** *adv.*—**didac'tics** *n.* science of teaching.

diddle (did'-l) *v.t.* (*Colloq.*) cheat; swindle;—*v.i.* toddle; dandle.

die (dī) *n.* small cube of wood, bone, or ivory used in games of chance, each face marked with numbers from one to six;—*pl.* **dice** (dīs).—**the die is cast**, one's fate is irrevocably settled.

die (dī) *v.i.* cease to live; become extinct or extinguished; wither; decline.—*pr.p.* **dy'ing**.—*pa.p.* **died**.—**dy'ing** *a.* pert. to person at point of death; fading; languishing; — *n.* death.—**to die for** (*Colloq.*) want desperately.—**to die hard**, resist stubbornly; be long in dying.—**a die-hard**, one who refuses to accept innovations.

die (dī) *n.* engraved metal block used for stamping design as on a coin; cubical part of pedestal; steel block

used for cutting screws;—*pl.* **dies**.—**die-cas'ting** *n.* method of making castings in permanent moulds.—**die'-sink'er** *n.* engraver of dies.—**die'sink'ing** *n.*

dielectric (dī-e-lek'-trik) *a.* non-conducting; insulating;—*n.* insulator; non-conductor.

Diesel engine (dē'-zl en'-jin) *n.* compression ignition engine using heavy oil as fuel.

diet (dī'-et) *n.* system of food; what one habitually eats and drinks; food specially prescribed by doctor; regulated allowance of provisions;—*v.t.* prescribe a special course of foods;—*v.i.* (*Colloq.*) slim.—**dietar'ian** *n.* one who follows prescribed diet.—**di'etary** *n.* special course of feeding; daily allowance of food;—*a.* pert. to diet.—**dietet'ic** *a.* pert. to diet.—**dietet'ics** *n.* science and study of food values, and their effect on health.—**dieti'cian, dieti'tian** *n.*

diet (dī'-et) *n.* legislative assembly in certain countries of Europe (e.g. *Denmark*) sitting from day to day; international conference; (*Scots Law*) sitting of law court.

differ (dif'-ẽr) *v.i.* be unlike; have distinctive characteristics; disagree (*with* from or with); be at variance;—*pr.p.* **diff'ering**.—*pa.p.* **diff'ered**.—**diff'erence** *n.* unlikeness; dissimilarity; distinguishing characteristic; disagreement; contention; amount by which one thing exceeds another in weight or number.—**diff'erent** *a.* unlike; distinct; various; diverse; not the same (*used with* from).—**differen'tial** *a.* characteristic; special; discriminating; (*Math.*) pert. to infinitely small quantitative differences; proceeding by increments infinitely small.—**differen'tially** *adv.*—**differen'tiate** *v.t.* make different; distinguish; classify as different;—*v.i.* acquire different characteristics.—**differentia'tion** *n.*—**differently** *adv.*—**differential calculus** (*Math.*) method of calculating relative rate of change for continuously varying quantities.—**differential gear**, mechanism by which two sets of wheels are made to rotate at different speeds, as wheels of a car, to facilitate rounding of corners, etc.

difficult (dif'-i-kult) *a.* hard to do or understand; not easy; laborious; awkward; (of persons) exacting; hard to please; not amenable.—**diff'icultly** *adv.*—**diff'iculty** *n.* laboriousness; obstacle; objection; demur; that which is not easy to do or understand.—**diff'iculties** *n.pl.* financial embarrassment.

diffident (dif'-i-dent) *a.* wanting confidence; not self-assertive; modest; timid; shy.—**diff'idence** *n.* lack of confidence.—**diff'idently** *adv.*

diffract (di-frakt') v.t. break or separate into parts, esp. of rays of light and sound waves.—**diffrac'tion** n. name given to effect produced by slight bending or deflection of ray of light or by curvature of electro-magnetic wave around edge of an obstacle; phenomenon caused by light passing through narrow slit.

diffuse (dif-ūz') v.t. pour out in every direction; spread; scatter; cause gases or liquid by diffusion;—v.i. mix; spread, as liquid.—**diffuse** (dif-ūs') a. widely spread; prolix; rambling; wordy.—**diffusely** (di-fūs'-li) adv. widely; in a wordy style.—**diffuse'-ness** n. quality of being diffuse.—**diffus'ible** a. capable of being diffused.—**diffu'sion** n. act or process of scattering abroad; (Chem.) term applied to the intermixture of two gases or fluids without chemical combination.—**diffus'ive** a.—**diffus'-ively** adv.—**diffus'iveness** n.—**diffused lighting**, a form of lighting in which hard brilliance is toned down by diffused transmission.

dig (dig) v.t. break and turn up earth, as with spade; excavate; delve; (Colloq.) poke or nudge someone; (Slang) understand; like; take notice of;—v.i. till the soil; to use spade, trowel, etc.—pr.p. dig'ging.—pa.p. dug.—n. archaeological excavation; thrust; poke; jibe or taunt.—**dig'ger** n. one who digs; excavator; machine which digs; (Austral.) a gold miner; soldier.—**dig'gings** n.pl. areas where mining is carried on (esp. gold); (Slang) lodgings, usually abbrev. to digs.

digest (di-jest') v.t. convert, as food in stomach, into substance which can be readily absorbed into the blood; assimilate in the mind; classify; think over;—v.i. undergo digestion.—**digest** (di'-jest) n. concise summary.—**diges'ter** n.—**diges'tible** a. capable of being digested; easily assimilated.—**digestibil'ity** n.—**diges'-tion** n. act of digesting.—**diges'tive** a. promoting, or pert. to, digestion;—n. medicine that aids digestion.

digit (dij'-it) n. finger; finger's breadth, or three-quarters of an inch; (Arith.) single figure representing a number; (Astron.) twelfth part of the diameter of the sun or moon.—**dig'ital** a. pert. to fingers;—n.—**digita'lin, digita'line** n. drug obtained from leaves of digitalis.—**digita'lis** n. genus of plants including foxglove; strong drug obtained from foxglove.—**dig'itate, dig'itated** a. having separate fingers and toes.—**digita'tion** n.—**dig'itigrade** n. animal which walks on its toes (e.g. dog);—a. walking on the toes.—**digital computer** electronic calculating machine using arithmetical digits.

dignify (dig'-ni-fī) v.t. invest with dignity or honour; exalt; elevate; ennoble;—pr.p. dig'nifying.—pa.p. dig'nified.—dig'nified a. having nobility of bearing.

dignity (dig'-ni-ti) n. state of being dignified in mind, character, or bearing; loftiness; high office or rank.—**dig'nitary** n. one who holds position of exalted rank, esp. ecclesiastical.

digress (dī-gres', di-gres') v.i. turn aside; stray; wander from main theme, topic, or argument; be diffuse.—**digres'sion** n. act of digressing.—**digres'sional, digress'ive** a.

dihedral (dī-hē'-dral) a. having two plane faces.—n. (Aero.) angle by which wings deviate from horizontal.—**dihe'dron** n. figure with two plane surfaces.

dike, dyke (dīk) n. ditch; channel for running water; artificial embankment to prevent inundation of low lying ground; (Scot.) stone wall without mortar.

dilapidate (di-lap'-i-dāt) v.t. suffer to fall into ruin; despoil;—v.i. be in condition of disrepair.—**dilapida'ted** a. in ruins; decayed; tumbled down; (of persons) shabby; unkempt.—**dilapida'tion** n. state of being dilapidated; decay.—**dilap'idator** n.

dilate (di-lāt') v.t. swell out; expand in all directions; distend;—v.t. widen; (Fig.) expatiate; descant; speak at length.—**dilat'able** a. capable of dilation; elastic.—**dila'tancy, dilata'tion, dila'tion** n.

dilatory (dil'-ą-tor-i) a. tardy; inclined to procrastination; loitering.—**dil'atorily** adv.—**dil'atoriness** n. tardiness; procrastination.

dilemma (di-lem'-ą, dī-lem'-ą) n. choice between alternatives equally undesirable; predicament; (Logic) argument which presents antagonist with alternatives equally conclusive against him, whichever he chooses.—**on the horns of a dilemma**, confronted with a perplexity.

dilettante (dil-e-tan'-te) n. lover of the fine arts, esp. in superficial way; dabbler;—pl. dilettan'ti.

diligent (dil'-i-jent) a. steady and constant in application; industrious; assiduous.—**dil'igence** n. willing and painstaking effort; type of stage-coach (18th cent.).—**dil'igently** adv.

dill (dil) n. perennial yellow-flowered herb, aromatic seeds of which are used in medicines, and leaves in flavouring for sauces, etc.—**dill'-wat'er** n. medecine prepared from dill seeds.

dilly-dally (dil'-i-dal'-i) v.i. (Colloq.) loiter; delay.

dilute (di-lūt', dī-lūt') v.t. make thinner or more liquid; reduce the strength of by addition of something, esp. water; (*Fig.*) weaken the force of;—*v.i.* become thin;—*a.* reduced in strength; attenuated; thinned down.—dil'uent *a.* diluting; making weaker;—*n.* that which thins or weakens, strength, colour, etc. of something, such as turpentine for thinning down paint.—dilu'tion *n.* act or process of diluting; state of being diluted.

dim (dim) *a.* not bright or distinct; faint; partially obscure; shadowy; (*Fig.*) dull of apprehension; vague;—*v.i.* cloud; cause to grow dim;—*v.i.* become dull or indistinct;—*pr.p.* dim'ming.—*pa.p.* dimmed.—dim'ly *adv.*—dim'mer *n.* in motoring, a device to diminish power of headlights.—dim'ness *n.* state of being dim.

dime (dīm) *n.* American silver coin equal to 10 cents.

dimension (dī-, di-men'-shun) *n.* measurement of extent in single direction (length, breadth, height, or thickness); usually *pl.* measurement in three directions (e.g. of a room); extent; capacity; (*Fig.*) importance.—dimen'sional *a.*

diminish (di-min'-ish) *v.t.* cause to grow less; weaken; reduce; impair; (*Mus.*) lower note by semi-tone;—*v.i.* become smaller.—dimin'ished *a.*

diminuendo (dim-in-ū-en'-dō) *n.* (*Mus.*) gradual decrease in volume of sound and marked >, opposite of *crescendo*;—*adv.* in gradually diminishing manner.

diminution (dim-in-ū'-shun) *n.* act or process of diminishing; state of being reduced in size, quality, or amount; degradation.—dimin'utive *a.* of small size; minute; miniature; (*Gram.*) applied to suffix expressing smallness, e.g. *-let*, *-ock*;—*n.* word formed from another by addition of such suffix, as *hamlet*, *hillock*.—dimin'utively *adv.*—dimin'utiveness *n.*

dimity (dim'-i-ti) *n.* stout white cotton cloth ribbed or figured.

dimorphic (dī-mor'-fik) *a.* existing in two forms; (*Chem.*) capable of crystallising in two forms under different degrees of temperature.—dimor'phism *n.* state of having two different forms.—dimor'phous *a.*

dimple (dim'-pl) *n.* slight natural depression or hollow on cheek, chin, arm, etc.; slight indentation in any surface;—*v.t.* mark with dimples;—*v.i.* become dimpled.

din (din) *n.* loud, continuous noise; racket; clamour;—*v.t.* strike, stun with noise; harass with insistent repetition.

dine (dīn) *v.t.* entertain to dinner; give accommodation for dining;—*v.i.* take dinner.—din'er *n.* one who dines; restaurant car on railway train. Also din'ing-car.—dinette (din-

et') *n.* alcove in a living-room used for meals.—dinner (din'-er) *n.* principal meal of the day.—dinner-jacket, black coat (without tails) worn as informal evening dress.

dinghy, dingy, dingey (ding'-gi) *n.* small rowing or sailing boat; inflatable life-raft for airmen.

dingle (ding'-gl) *n.* small wooded valley.

dingo (ding'-gō) *n.* type of wild dog found only in Australia.

dingy (din'-ji) *a.* soiled; sullied; of darkish colour.—din'giness *n.*

dinosaur (dī'-nō-sawr) *n.* gigantic Mesozoic four-footed reptile.

dint (dint) *n.* blow; stroke; mark or depression made by a blow; force or energy exerted;—*v.t.* make mark or dent by a blow.—by dint of, by means of.

diocese (dī'-ō-sēs) *n.* district in which a bishop exercises ecclesiastical jurisdiction.—diocesan (dī-os'-es-an or dī'-o-sē-zan) *a.* pert. to diocese;—*n.* holder of diocese.

diopter, dioptre (dī-op'-ter) *n.* unit for measuring power of a lens.

diorama (dī-ō-rä'-ma) *n.* painting viewed through opening in wall of darkened room, illusion of reality being achieved by lighting effects.

dioxide (dī-ok'-sīd) *n.* oxide whose molecules comprise two oxygen atoms.

dip (dip) *v.t.* immerse momentarily in liquid; dye; lower and raise again, as flag; wash, as a sheep; baptise by immersion; lower headlights of car; —*v.i.* sink below certain level; glance cursorily at; short downwards slope; (*Geol.*) incline downwards.—*pr.p.* dip'ping.—*pa.p.* dipped.—*n.* liquid into which something is dipped; immersion; (*Geol.*) inclination downward of rock-strata; candle made by dipping wick in melted tallow; (*Colloq.*) bathe.—dip'per *n.* something used for dipping; anti-dazzle device for motor-car head lamps; semi-aquatic diving bird, water-ouzel, resembling thrush; (*Colloq.*) Great Bear.—dip'ping-nee'dle *n.* magnetic needle indicating on graduated circle, the magnetic dip.—dip'-stick *n.* rod for calculating depth of oil, etc. in tank.

diphtheria (dif-thēr'-i-a) *n.* epidemic disease affecting mainly throat and air passages.—diphthe'rial, diphther'ic, diphtherit'ic, *a.*

diphthong (dif'-thong) *n.* union of two vowel sounds pronounced as one, as in *poise*, *mouth*.—diphthong'al *a.*—diphthong'ally *adv.*—diph'thongise *v.t.* develop diphthong from single vowel.—diphthongisa'tion *n.*

diplex (dī'-pleks) *a.* (*Radio*) pert. to reception or transmission of two messages simultaneously.

diploma (di-plō'-ma) *n.* document or certificate conferring honour, privilege, or degree, as that granted to graduates of university;—*v.t.* furnish with diploma.

diplomacy (di-plō'-ma-si) *n.* art of conducting international negotiations; political dexterity; tact in dealing with people.—**dip'lomat, diplo'matist** *n.* one skilled in art of handling difficult international or personal relations; one engaged in administering international law.—**diplomat'ic, -al** *a.* pert. to diplomacy.—**diplomat'ically** *adv.*—**diplomat'ic** *n.* envoy at foreign court.

dipper (dip'-er) *n.* See dip.

dipsomania (dip-sō-mā'-ni-a) *n.* uncontrollable craving for alcoholic stimulants; confirmed drunkenness.—**dipsoman'iac** *n.* one who suffers from dipsomania.—**dipsoman'iacal** *a.*

diptych (dip'-tik) *n.* ancient writing tablet hinged in the middle and folding together like a book; pair of carvings or pictures similarly hinged.

dire (dīr) *a.* dreadful; horrible; calamitous; disastrous. Also dire'ful.—**dire'ly, dire'fully** *adv.*—**dire'fulness** *n.*

direct (di-rect', dī'-rect) *a.* straight; straight-forward; immediate; in line of descent; sincere;—*v.t.* aim at; guide; point out the way; manage (a business); prescribe a line of procedure; write the name and address on a missive, etc.;—*v.i.* give direction; act as a guide;—*adv.* in a straight line.—**direc'tion** *n.* act of directing; instruction; guidance; management; order; superscription; prescription; address (on a letter); line taken by moving body.—**direc'tional, direct'ing, direct'ive** *a.* tending to guide or to advise.—**direct'ive** *n.* general orders from supreme authority outlining procedure to be taken in directing a new plan or policy.—**direct'ly** *adv.* in a straight line; straightway; immediately after;—*conj.* (*Colloq.*) as soon as.—**direct'ness** *n.* quality of being direct, frank, or unimpeded by extraneous details.—**direct'or** *n.* (*fem.* **direct'ress, direct'rix**) one who directs, esp. producer of a film; member of board of managers in large commercial firm, hospital, etc.; counsellor; that which regulates a machine; in gunnery, optical instrument for calculating line of firing.—**direct'orate** *n.* board of directors.—**direct'orship** *n.* office or period of office of director.—**director'ial** *a.*—**direct'ory** *a.* containing directions; guiding;—*n.* book containing alphabetically arranged names and addresses of residents of town or district.—**direct current** (*abbrev.* d.c.) (*Elect.*) current flowing in one direction. — **direct speech** (*Gram.*)

spoken words which, written down, are within inverted commas.—**direct tax**, tax levied directly on taxpayer, as income tax.—**direction finder** (*Radio*) aerial which determines direction of incoming wireless signals (*abbrev.* D/F).

dirge (derj) *n.* funeral chant; lament.—**dirge'ful** *a.* funereal.

dirigible (dir'-i-ji-bl) *a.* capable of being directed or steered;—*n.* navigable airship.—**dir'igent** *a.* directing.

dirk (derk) *n.* short dagger orig. carried by Scottish clansmen;—*v.t.* to stab with a dirk.

dirndl (dirn'-dl) *n.* type of skirt gathered into broad belt at waist.

dirt (dert) *n.* any filthy substance, as mud, dust, excrement; loose soil; rubbish; squalor; (*Fig.*) obscenity;—*v.t.* make foul; besmirch.—**dirt'-cheap** *a.* (*Colloq.*) uncommonly cheap.—**dirt'ily** *adv.* in a dirty manner; meanly.—**dirt'iness** *n.*—**dirt'y** *a.* foul; unclean; muddy; base; (of weather) stormy; rainy.—*v.t.* befoul.

dis- *pref.* implying *separation*, as in *dis*miss; *negation*, as in *dis*band; *deprivation*, as in *dis*animate; *thoroughness*, as in *dis*annul.

disable (dis-ā'-bl) *v.t.* make incapable or physically unfit; disqualify.—**disable'ment** *n.* disability.—**disabil'ity** *n.* state of being disabled.

disabuse (dis-a-būz') *v.t.* free from misapprehension or error.

disadvantage (dis-ad-van'-tāj) *n.* want of advantage; drawback; hindrance; handicap; detriment; hurt.—**disadvanta'geous** *a.* attended with disadvantage. — **disadvanta'geously** *adv.*

disaffect (dis-a-fekt') *v.t.* alienate the affection of; estrange; fill with discontent.—**disaffect'ed** *a.* discontented; disloyal (esp. to government).—**disaffect'edly** *adv.*—**disaffect'edness, disaffec'tion** *n.*

disagree (dis'-a-grē) *v.i.* be at variance; differ in opinion; be incompatible; be detrimental to health (of food, climate, etc.).—**disagree'able** *a.* not agreeable; unpleasant; repellent. — **disagree'ableness, disagreeabil'ity** *n.*—**disagree'ably** *adv.*—**disagree'ment** *n.* difference of opinion; discord; discrepancy; unsuitableness.

disallow (dis-a-lou') *v.t.* refuse to allow, permit, authorise, or sanction; reject as illegal.—**disallow'able** *a.*—**disallow'ance** *n.*

disappear (dis-a-pēr') *v.i.* vanish; become invisible; cease to exist.—**disappear'ance** *n.* state of being invisible; act of disappearing.

disappoint (dis-a-point') *v.t.* fail to realise the hopes of; frustrate; baffle; foil.—**disappoint'ed** *a.* frustrated; baffled; cheated.—**disappoint'ing**

a. causing disappointment.—**disappoint'ment** *n.* state of being disappointed; frustration of hopes.

disapprobation (dis-ap-rō-bā'-shun) *n.* act of disapproving; censure; mental condemnation of what is considered wrong.

disapprove (dis-a-prōōv') *v.t.* form an unfavourable judgment of; censure; refuse to sanction; dislike;—*v.i.* (*with* of).—**disapprov'al** *n.*—**disapprov'ingly** *adv.*

disarm (dis-ârm') *v.t.* deprive of arms; render unable to attack; (*Fig.*) conciliate; allay;—*v.i.* lay down arms, esp. national armaments.—**disarm'ament** *n.* act of reducing, in peace-time, output of military and naval weapons as prevention of war; state of being disarmed.

disarrange (dis-a-rānj') *v.t.* disturb order or arrangement of; disorganise; throw into confusion.—**disarrange'ment** *n.*

disarray (dis-a-rā') *v.t.* break the array of; throw into disorder; undress;—*n.* disorder; confusion; state of undress.

disassemble (dis-as-em'bl) *v.t.* dismantle; take apart.

disassociate (dis-a-sō'-shi-āt) *v.t.* disunite; dissociate.

disaster (diz-as'-tẹr) *n.* adverse happening; mishap; sudden misfortune; catastrophe.—**disas'trous** *a.* unlucky; inauspicious.—**disas'trously** *adv.*—**disas'trousness** *n.*

disavow (dis-a-vou') *v.t.* refuse to acknowledge; repudiate.—**disavow'al, disavow'ment** *n.*

disband (dis-band') *v.t.* disperse (troops); break up an organisation; dismiss;—*v.i.* break up; disperse.—**disband'ment** *n.*

disbelieve (dis-be-lēv') *v.t.* maintain to be untrue; refuse to believe;—*v.i.* place no reliance or belief (*with* on *or* in).—**dis'belief** *n.*—**disbeliev'er** *n.*

disbud (dis-bud') *v.t.* remove superfluous buds from.—*pr.p.* **disbud'ding**.—*pa.p.* **disbud'ded**.

disburse (dis-burs') *v.t.* pay out money; expend.—**disburse'ment** *n.* expenditure.—**disburse'ments** *n.pl.* expenses.—**disburs'er** *n.*

disc, disk (disk) *n.* flat, circular plate or surface; face of sun or moon; gramophone record; cartilaginous layer between vertebrae.—**disc'al** *a.* pert. to or resembling disc.—**disc'-jock'ey** *n.* (*Colloq.*) announcer of radio programme of recorded music.

discard (dis-kârd') *v.t. and v.i.* throw away cards as useless in the game; put aside; cast off;—*n.* act of discarding; card thrown out as useless.

discern (di-sẹrn') *v.t.* distinguish clearly esp. by sight; perceive by the mind; behold as separate.—**discern'er** *n.*—**discern'ible** *a.* capable of being discerned.—**discern'ibly** *adv.*—**discern'ing** *a.* discriminating; judging with insight.—**discern'ment** *n.* power or faculty of judging.

discharge (dis-chârj') *v.t.* free from load or weight; unload cargo; fire off charge with which gun is loaded; emit, as smoke; perform, as duty; pay, as account or debt; demobilise, as soldiers, etc.; dismiss, as for failure in service or duty;—*n.* act of discharging; end of military or naval service; performance; matter which exudes, as from abscess; that which is discharged; rate of flow of liquid or waste matter through pipe.

disciple (di-sī'-pl) *n.* one who receives instruction from another; one who adheres to particular school of philosophy, religious thought, or art; follower, esp. one of Twelve Apostles of Christ.—**disci'pleship** *n.*

discipline (dis'-i-plin) *n.* instruction; training of mind, or body, or moral faculties; subjection to authority; self-control;—*v.t.* train; improve behaviour by judicious penal methods.—**dis'ciplinable, dis'ciplinal** *a.*—**disciplina'rian** *n.* one who enforces rigid discipline; martinet.—**dis'ciplinary** *a.* pert. to discipline.

disclaim (dis-klām') *v.t.* renounce claim to, or responsibility for; disown; repudiate;—*v.i.* give up all claim (foll. by *in*).—**disclaim'ant** *n.*—**disclaim'er** *n.* denial; disavowal; repudiation.

disclose (dis-klōz') *v.t.* unclose; reveal; divulge; bring to light.—**disclo'ser** *n.*—**disclo'sure** *n.* act of disclosing or state of being disclosed; revelation.

discolour (dis-kul'-ur) *v.t.* spoil the colour of; stain;—*v.i.* become discoloured or stained.—**discolo(u)ra'tion, discol'ourment** *n.*—**discol'oured** *a.* stained.

discomfit (dis-kum'-fit) *v.t.* defeat; disconcert; foil; baffle.—**discom'fiture** *n.*

discomfort (dis-kum'-fort) *n.* want of comfort; uneasiness; pain;—*v.t.* impair comfort of; make uneasy.

discompose (dis-kom-pōz') *v.t.* upset self-possession of; disturb; disarrange.—**discompo'sure** *n.* state of being discomposed; agitation.

disconcert (dis-konsẹrt') *v.t.* discompose; embarrass; break up harmony of; frustrate.—**discon'cert** *n.* state of disagreement.

disconnect (dis-kon-ekt') *v.t.* separate; sever; disjoint.—**disconnect'ed** *a.* —**disconne'xion, disconnec'tion** *n.*

disconsolate (dis-kon'-sō-lāt) *a.* destitute of comfort or consolation; forlorn; utterly dejected.—**discon'solately** *adv.*—**discon'solateness** *n.*

discontent (dis-kon-tent') a. not content; dissatisfied;—n. want of contentment; dissatisfaction; state of being aggrieved;—v.t. cause to be ill-pleased; dissatisfy.—discontent'ed a.—discontent'edly adv.—discontent'edness, discontent'ment n.

discontinue (dis-kon-tin'-ū) v.t. interrupt; break off; stop;—v.i. cease; become intermittent. — discontin'uance, discontinua'tion n.—discontinu'ity n.—discontin'uous a.

discord (dis'-kord) n. want of concord or agreement; lack of harmony; strife; (Mus.) combination of inharmonious sounds.—discord (dis-kord') v.i. disagree; to be out of tune.—discor'dantly adv.

discount (dis-kount') v.t. pay in advance (bill of exchange not yet due); deduct sum or rate per cent from account for prompt payment; depreciate;—v.i. lend money with discount.—discount (dis'-kount) n. sum of money refunded on prompt payment of bill; allowance made on retail price by wholesaler to retailer.

discountenance (dis-koun'-ten-ₐns) v.t. refuse to countenance or give approval to.

discourage (dis-kur'-āj) v.t. deprive of courage; dishearten; deter.—discour'agement n. act of discouraging; state of being discouraged; dissuasion; dejection.—discour'aging a. disheartening.

discourse (dis'-kōrs) n. formal speech; sermon; dissertation; reasoning from premises; conversation. — discourse (dis-kōrs') v.t. utter;—v.i. lecture; converse; hold forth (foll. usually by upon).

discourteous (dis-kur'-tyus) a. lacking in courtesy; ill-bred; rude.—discourt'eously adv.—discourt'eousness, discourt'esy n.

discover (dis-kuv'-er) v.t. expose to view; find out (esp. something hitherto unknown); bring to light.—discov'erable a.—discov'erer n.—discov'ery n. act of finding out; that which is discovered.

discredit (dis-kred'-it) v.t. refuse credit to; bring into disrepute; disgrace; disbelieve;—n. loss of credit or of reputation; doubt.—discred'itable a. disgraceful; damaging; injurious to reputation.

discreet (dis-krēt') a. prudent; circumspect; judicious; cautious (in action or speech).—discreet'ly adv.—discreet'ness n. discretion.

discrepancy (dis-krep'-ₐn-si, dis'-krep-ₐn-si) n. inconsistency; variance; difference.—discrep'ant a. not tallying; inconsistent; discordant; contrary.

discrete (dis-krēt') a. separate; distinct; disjunctive; unrelated.—discrete'ly adv.—discrete'ness n.

discretion (dis-kresh'-un) n. quality of being discreet; prudence; discernment; liberty to act according to one's judgment.—discre'tional, discre'tionary a.—discre'tionally, discre'tionarily adv.

discriminate (dis-krim'-i-nāt) v.t. detect as different; distinguish; select;—v.i. make a distinction in.—discrim'inately adv.—discrim'inating a.—discrim'inatingly adv.—discrimina'tion n.

discursive (dis-kur'-siv) a. passing from one topic to another; rambling; digressive. — discur'sively adv. — discur'siveness n.—discur'sory a.

discus (dis'-kus) n. quoit of stone or metal, used in athletic contests.

discuss (dis-kus') v.t. examine critically; exchange ideas on.—discuss'able (or -ible) a.—discuss'ion n. debate; act of exchanging opinions.

disdain (dis-dān') v.t. look down upon, as unworthy or despicable; scorn;—n. scorn; arrogance; contempt.—disdain'ful a.—disdain'fully adv.—disdain'fulness n.

disease (di-zēz') n. absence of ease; unhealthy condition of mind or body; malady.—diseased' a.

disembark (dis-em-bárk') v.t. put on shore; land passengers, goods, etc.;—v.i. land.—disembarka'tion, disembark'ment n.

disembody (dis-em-bod'-i) v.t. free from the body or flesh; discharge from military organisation.—disembod'iment n.

disembowel (dis-em-bou'-el) v.t. take out the bowels; gut; eviscerate.

disenchant (dis-en-chant') v.t. free from enchantment; disillusion; undeceive.—disenchant'ment n.

disengage (dis-en-gāj') v.t. unfasten; separate from attachment; release.—disengaged' a. vacant; available (for interview); at leisure.—disengage'ment n.

disentail (dis-en-tāl') v.t. break entail of (an estate);—n. act of disentailing.

disentangle (dis-en-tang'-gl) v.t. unravel; untwist; put in order what is entangled.—disentang'lement n.

disentwine (dis-en-twīn') v.t. untwine.

disestablish (dis-es-tab'-lish) v.t. deprive of established position; deprive (the Church) of State aid and recognition.—disestab'lishment n.

diseur (dēz-er) n. (fem. diseuse) (dēz-ez') entertainer; one who recites monologues.

disfavour (dis-fā'-vur) n. disesteem; disapproval; dislike; state of being out of favour;—v.t. regard unfavourably.

disfigure (dis-fig'-ur) v.t. mar appearance of; deface; deform.—disfig'urement n. defect; blemish.

disfranchise (dis-fran'-chīz) v.t. deprive right of voting at elections.—disfran'chisement n.

disgorge (dis-gorj') v.t. eject from the throat; to pour out (as river into sea); hand over.—disgorge'ment n.

disgrace (dis-grās') n. dishonour; discredit; shameful conduct;—v.t. bring dishonour to; degrade.—disgrace'ful a. shameful; infamous; discreditable.—disgrace'fully adv.

disgruntled (dis-grun'-tld) a. vexed; sulky; disappointed; aggrieved.

disguise (dis-gīz') v.t. change the outward appearance of; misrepresent;—n. dress, manner, voice, etc. assumed to hide a person's real identity.—disguis'edly adv.

disgust (dis-gust') n. loathing; nausea; aversion; repugnance;—v.t. provoke disgust in.—disgust'edly adv.—disgust'ing a.—disgust'ingly adv.

dish (dish) n. plate or shallow concave vessel for serving food; food in such vessel; concave object, like a dish;—v.t. put in a dish; (Colloq.) frustrate; outwit.

disharmony (dis-har'-mo-ni) n. lack of harmony; discord.

dishearten (dis-hár'-tn) v.t. deprive of courage, confidence, or hope; depress.

dishevel (di-shev'-el) v.t. ruffle the hair; cause hair or clothes to be untidy or unkempt;—v.i. spread in disorder.—pr.p. dishev'elling.—pa.p. and a. dishev'elled.—dishev'elment n.

dishonest (dis-on'-est) a. lacking in honesty; fraudulent; inclined to cheat; unprincipled. — dishon'estly adv.—dishon'esty n.

dishonour (dis-on'-ur) n. loss of honour; disgrace; shame; indignity;—v.t. disgrace; seduce; refuse payment of (as a cheque).—dishon'ourable a. shameful; void of integrity; discreditable.—dishon'ourableness n.—dishon'ourably adv.

disillusion (dis-i-lōō'-zhun) v.t. free from illusion; make the truth apparent;—n. state of being disillusioned.—disillu'sionment n. disenchantment.—disillu'sive a.

disincentive (dis-in-sent'-iv) something which discourages effort.

disincline (dis-in-klīn') v.t. make unwilling; excite dislike.—disinclina'tion n. unwillingness; reluctance; dislike.—disinclined' a.

disinfect (dis-in-fekt') v.t. free from infection; destroy disease germs.—disinfec'tant n. germicide.—disinfec'tion n.—disinfec'tor n.

disinfestation (dis-in-fes-tā'-shun) n. destruction of insects (e.g. lice).

disingenuous (dis-in-jen'-ū-us) a. not ingenuous; actuated by ulterior motives; insincere.—disingen'uously adv.—disingen'uousness n.

disinherit (dis-in-her'-it) v.t. deprive of rights and privileges of an heir.—disinheri'tance n.

disintegrate (dis-in'-te-grāt) v.t. separate into component parts; break up;—v.i. crumble; be resolved into elements.—disintegra'tion n.

disinter (dis-in-ter') v.t. disentomb; to exhume; (Fig.) to unearth.

disinterested (dis-in'-ter-es-ted) a. free from self-interest; unprejudiced.

disjoin (dis-join') v.t. sever; disunite.—disjoint' v.t. separate at joints; put out of joint; make incoherent;—v.i. fall to pieces.—disjoint'ed a. unconnected; (of speech) rambling; incoherent; illogical. — disjoint'edly adv.—disjoint'edness n.

disk See disc.

dislike (dis-līk') v.t. have aversion to; disapprove of;—n. distaste; antipathy.

dislocate (dis-lō-kāt') v.t. put out of place or out of joint; upset normal working of.—disloca'tedly adv.—disloca'tion n. (Med.) displacement of a bone.

dislodge (dis-loj') v.t. remove from position of rest, hiding, or defence;—v.i. depart.—dislodg(e)'ment n.

disloyal (dis-loi'-al) a. failing in duty or allegiance to the Crown; faithless; treacherous.—disloy'ally adv.—disloy'alty n.

dismal (diz'-mal) a. gloomy; dreary; depressing; bleak.—dis'mally adv.—dis'malness n.

dismantle (dis-man'-tl) v.t. strip of furnishings; remove apparatus, equipment from; destroy defences of (fortified town).

dismay (dis-mā') v.t. alarm; deprive of courage; fill with apprehension; appal;—n. consternation; loss of courage.

dismember (dis-mem'-ber) v.t. tear limb from limb; mutilate; disjoint.—dismem'berment n. taking to pieces.

dismiss (dis-mis') v.t. send away; disperse; discharge from employment; banish (from the mind).—dismiss'al n. discharge; release.

dismount (dis-mount') v.i. alight from horse, bicycle, etc.;—v.t. bring down from place of elevation.

disobey (dis-ō-bā') v.t. disregard orders; refuse to do what is commanded.—disobe'dient a.—disobe'diently adv.—disobe'dience n.

disoblige (dis-ō-blīj') v.t. offend by act of incivility; refuse to grant request to.—disoblig'ing a.

disorder (dis-or'-der) n. want of order; muddle; confusion; discomposure; ailment of body or mind;—v.t. throw out of order; upset.—disor'dered a.—disor'derly a.

disorganise (dis-or'-gan-īz) v.t. upset regular system of; throw into disorder.—disorgan'ic a.—disorganisa'tion n. confusion.

disorientate (dis-or'-i-en-tāt) *v.t.* cause to lose sense of direction.

disown (dis-ōn') *v.t.* repudiate ownership of; disclaim; renounce.

disparage (dis-par'-ãj) *v.t.* decry; belittle; lower in rank or reputation; depreciate.—**dispar'agement** *n.*—**dis-par'agingly** *adv.*

disparity (dis-par'-i-ti) *n.* inequality in form, character, or degree; incongruity.

dispassion (dis-pash'-un) *n.* lack of feeling; serenity.—**dispas'sionate** *a.*; impartial; cool; unruffled.

dispatch See **despatch**.

dispel (dis-pel') *v.t.* drive away; scatter; cause to disappear.—*pr.p.* **dispel'ling.**—*pa.p.* **dispelled'.**

dispense (dis-pens') *v.t.* divide out in parts; administer, as laws; make up medicines;—*v.i.* excuse from.—**dispens'able** *a.* that may be dispensed with or dispensed.—**dispens'ary** *n.* place where medicines are made up. —**dispensa'tion** *n.* act of distributing; licence to do what is normally prohibited.—**dispens'ative, dispensa'tory** *a.* —**dispen'ser** *n.* one who dispenses; one qualified to make up medical prescriptions; container which dispenses measured doses or quantities. —**to dispense with,** do without.

disperse (dis-pers') *v.t.* scatter here and there; spread; distribute; place at intervals (as troops).—*v.i.* separate; vanish.—**dispers'al** *n.*—**dispers'edly** *adv.*—**dispers'edness** *n.*—**disper'sion** *n.*—**disper'sive** *a.* tending to disperse.

dispirit (dis-pir'-it) *v.t.* deject; depress; cast down; discourage.—**dispir'ited** *a.*

displace (dis-plãs') *v.t.* put out of position; oust from situation or office.—**displace'able** *a.*—**displace'ment** *n.* act of putting out of place or removing from office; weight of water, measured in tons, displaced by floating ship.

display (dis-plã') *v.t.* unfold; exhibit; set out conspicuously;—*n.* exhibition; parade; ostentation.

displease (dis-plēs') *v.t.* and *v.i.* offend; cause dissatisfaction to; cause to be angry; annoy.—**displeasure** (dis-plezh'-ŭr) *n.* slight anger or irritation; dislike.

disport (dis-pōrt') *v.t.* and *r.* play; amuse oneself; gambol; frolic.

dispose (dis-pōz') *v.t.* distribute; arrange; regulate; adjust; bestow for an object or purpose; induce tendency or inclination;—*v.i.* settle; determine.—**dispos'able** *a.* liable, free, to be disposed of or employed.— **dispos'al** *n.* act of disposing or disposing of; control; regulation; management; transference (of property by a will).—**dispos'ed** *a.* inclined; minded; arranged.—**dispos'edly** *adv.*

—**disposi'tion** *n.* act of disposing; arrangement; guidance; temperament.—**to dispose of,** get rid of.

dispossess (dis-po-zes') *v.t.* put out of possession; deprive of property; eject.—**dispossess'ion** *n.*

disproportion (dis-prō-pōr'-shun) *n.* want of proportion, or adequacy; inequality; disparity.—**dispropor'tional, dispropor'tionate** *a.* out of proportion.

disprove (dis-próōv') *v.t.* prove to be false; refute; prove the opposite of.

dispute (dis-pūt') *v.t.* consider for and against; debate; question validity of; oppose;—*v.i.* argue; discuss; contend;—*n.* argument; debate.— **dis'putable** *a.* open to argument.— **dis'putably** *adv.*—**disputabil'ity** *n.*— **disputa'tion** *n.* controversy in words; academic discussion.—**disputa'tious, disputa'tive** *a.* inclined to dispute.

disqualify (dis-kwol'-i-fī) *v.t.* make unfit for some special purpose; incapacitate; make ineligible; deprive of legal right.—**disqualifica'tion** *n.*

disquiet (dis-kwī'-et) *v.t.* render uneasy in mind; disturb; make restless;—*n.* apprehensiveness.—**disqui'etude** *n.*

disquisition (dis-kwi-zish'-un) *n.* formal enquiry into subject by argument or discussion; systematic treatise; research.—**disquisi'tional,** *a.*

disregard (dis-re-gãrd') *v.t.* take no notice of; ignore;—*n.* indifference; lack of attention.—**disregard'ful** *a.*— **disregard'fully** *adv.*

disrepair (dis-re-pãr') *n.* state of being out of repair; dilapidation.

disrepute (dis-re-pūt') *n.* discredit; disfavour; state of being unpopular. —**disrep'utable** *a.* disgraceful; degraded; discreditable in character.— **disrep'utableness** *n.*

disrespect (dis-re-spekt') *n.* want of respect; rudeness.—**disrespect'able** *a.* —**disrespect'ful** *a.* uncivil.—**disrespect'fully** *adv.*

disrobe (dis-rōb') *v.t.* undress; discard official dress.

disrupt (dis-rupt') *v.t.* break or burst asunder; create a schism (as in a Party).—**disrup'tion** *n.*—**disrup'tive** *a.*

dissatisfy (dis-sat'-is-fī) *v.t.* fail to satisfy; make discontented.—**dissatisfac'tion** *n.*

dissect (dis-sekt') *v.t.* cut up; divide plant or dead body into parts; (*Fig.*) criticise in detail.—**dissec'tion** *n.*— **dissect'or** *n.*

dissemble (dis-sem'-bl) *v.t.* hide under false semblance; disguise; conceal; mask;—*v.i.* give erroneous impression; assume a false appearance; deceive.—**dissem'bler** *n.*— **dissem'bling** *a.* feigned; deceiving.

disseminate (dis-sem'-i-nāt) *v.t.* sow, as seed; (*Fig.*) broadcast; propagate; circulate.—**dissemina'tion** *n.* scattering; circulation.—**dissem'inative** *a.*—**dissem'inator** *n.*

dissent (dis-sent') *v.i.* differ in opinion; disagree; hold views differing from those of established church; —*n.* disagreement; nonconformity.—**dissen'sion** *n.* open disagreement; discord.—**dissent'er** *n.* one who dissents.—**dissen'tient** *n.* one who differs in opinion.—*a.* disagreeing.

dissertate (dis'-er-tāt) *v.i.* discourse.—**disserta'tion** *n.* treatise, esp. written thesis.

disserve (dis-serv') *v.t.* serve badly another's interests.—**disser'vice** *n.* harm; bad turn.

dissident (dis'-i-dent) *a.* dissentient; disagreeing;—*n.* dissenter; non-conformist.—**diss'idence** *n.*

dissimilar (dis-sim'-i-lar) *a.* unlike; not similar;—**dissimilar'ity, dissimil'itude** *n.*—**dissim'ilarly** *adv.*

dissimulate (dis-sim'-ū-lāt) *v.t.* dissemble; feign;—*v.i.* conceal one's true feelings; be hypocritical.—**dissimula'tion** *n.*

dissipate (dis'-i-pāt) *v.t.* scatter; squander; dispel;—*v.i.* disappear; waste away; (*Colloq.*) lead dissolute life.—**diss'ipated** *a.* dissolute; debauched.—**dissipa'tion** *n.*

dissociate (dis-sō-shi-āt) *v.t.* separate; disunite; (*reflex.*) disclaim connexion with.—**dissociabil'ity** *n.*—**disso'ciable** *a.*—**dissocia'tion** *n.*—**disso'ciative** *a.*

dissoluble (dis'-ol-ū-bl, di-sol'-ū-bl) *a.* capable of being dissolved, liquefied, melted, or decomposed.—**dissolubil'ity** *n.*

dissolute (dis'-o-lūt) *a.* lax in morals; dissipated.—**diss'olutely** *adv.*—**diss'-oluteness** *n.*—**dissolu'tion** *n.* act of dissolving; disintegration; dismissal of an assembly; termination (of marriage, partnership, etc.).

dissolve (di-zolv') *v.t.* break up, esp. solid by action of liquid; terminate (as Parliament); annul (as marriage); —*v.i.* melt; waste away; fade out; be dismissed.—**dissolvabil'ity, dissolv'-ableness** *n.*—**dissolv'able** *a.* capable of being turned into liquid, or melted.—**dissolv'ent** *a.* having power of dissolving substances.

dissonant (dis'-o-nant) *a.* discordant; harsh; (*Fig.*) incompatible.—**diss'-onance** *n.* Also **diss'onancy.**

dissuade (di-swād') *v.t.* advise against.—**dissua'der** *n.*—**dissua'sion** *n.* act of dissuading.—**dissua'sive** *a.*

distaff (dis'-taf) *n.* cleft stick for holding fibre (wool, flax, etc.) from which thread is made in hand-spinning.—**the distaff side,** maternal side; female line.

distance (dis'-tans) *n.* space between two objects; interval between two events; remoteness; aloofness; reserve;—*v.t.* place at a distance;

outstrip; surpass.—**dis'tant** *a.* far off; remote in time, place, or blood-relationship; aloof.—**dis'tantly** *adv.*

distaste (dis-tāst') *n.* dislike, esp. of food; disgust; repugnance; aversion.—**distaste'ful** *a.* unpleasant; repellent; nauseous.

distemper (dis-tem'-per) *n.* flat, water-based paint used on walls, etc.—*v.t.* paint in distemper.

distemper (dis-tem'-per) *n.* disordered state of mind or body; highly infectious disease in young dogs; bad temper.

distend (dis-tend') *v.t.* stretch out; swell; inflate;—*v.i.* become swollen.—**disten'sible** *a.* capable of being distended.—**disten'sion, disten'tion** *n.*

distil (dis-til') *v.t.* cause to fall in drops; cause to trickle; vaporise and recondense liquid;—*v.i.* trickle; ooze; use a still.—*pr.p.* distil'ling.—*pa.p.* distilled'.—**dis'tillate** *n.* essence produced by distilling.—**distilla'tion** *n.* act of distilling.—**distil'ler** *n.*—**distil'lery** *n.* place where distilling is carried on, esp. of alcohol.

distinct (dis-tingkt') *a.* of marked difference; separate; clear; well-defined; obvious; precise.—**distinc'tion** *n.* separation; that which indicates individuality; eminence; repute; mark of honour.—**distinc'tive** *a.* characteristic; exhibiting difference.—**distinc'tively** *adv.*—**distinctly** *adv.* clearly; decidedly.—**distinc'tiveness** *n.*—**distinct'ness** *n.*

distinguish (dis-ting'-gwish) *v.t.* observe the difference between; keep apart; give individuality to; separate by mark of honour; discern;—*v.i.* make distinctions.—**disting'uishable** *adv.*—**disting'uished** *a.* eminent; dignified.—**disting'uishing** *a.* peculiar; characteristic.

distort (dis-tort') *v.t.* twist out of shape; misrepresent; pervert; falsify.—**distort'ed** *a.* altered; perverted.—**distort'edly** *adv.*—**distor'tion** *n.* misrepresentation; irregularity of shape; lack of clarity (*radio*, etc.).

distract (dis-trakt') *v.t.* draw away (the mind); divert; bewilder; unbalance mentally.—**distract'ed** *a.* deranged; frantic.—**distract'edly** *adv.*—**distract'edness** *n.* state of being distracted; madness.—**distrac'tion** *n.*—**distract'ive** *a.*—**distraught** (dis-trawt') *a.* perplexed; bewildered; frantic.

distrain (dis-trān') *v.t.* seize goods, esp. for payment of debt.—**distrain'-ment, distraint'** *n.*—**distrain'or, -'er** *n.*

distress (dis-tres') *n.* extreme pain, mental or physical; misfortune; extreme poverty;—*v.t.* cause pain or anguish to; harass.—**distress'ful** *a.* causing suffering.—**distress'fully** *adv.*—**distressed area,** part of the country where unemployment is rife.

distribute (dis-trib'-ūt) *v.t.* divide

among several; allot or hand out; spread out; classify.—**distrib'utable** *a.* —**distribu'tion** *n.* act of distributing; separation.—**distrib'utive** *a.* involving distribution.—**distrib'utor** (-er) *n.*

district (dis'-trikt) *n.* defined tract of land; administrative division of country; region;—*a.* local; regional.

distrust (dis-trust') *v.t.* have no faith in; suspect; doubt;—*n.* want of trust; doubt; suspicion; lack of confidence.—**distrust'ful** *a.* suspicious. —**distrust'fully** *adv.*

disturb (dis-turb') *v.t.* upset the normal condition of; disquiet; agitate; ruffle.—**disturb'ance** *n.* uproar; derangement.

disunion (dis-ūn'-yun) *n.* separation; discord; dissension.—**disunite'** *v.t.* cause separation; cause breach between.—**disu'nity** *n.* state of being disunited.

disuse (dis-ūs') *n.* cessation of practice or custom.—**disuse** (dis-ūz') *v.t.* cease to use.—**disu'sage** *n.* gradual cessation of use or custom.

disyllable See dissyllable.

ditch (dich) *n.* trench dug esp. for drainage or defence;—*v.t.* cut a ditch in; drain by a ditch; (*Colloq.*) drive into a ditch;—*v.i.* make or mend ditches; make forced landing on sea.

dither (diTH'-er) *n.* (*Colloq.*) state of nervous agitation or confusion;— *v.i.* shake; be confused.

ditto (dit'-ō) *n.* (contracted usually to do.) that which has been said; the same;—*adv.* as aforesaid.

ditty (dit'-i) *n.* song; short poem to be sung.

diuretic (di-ū-ret'-ik) *a.* promoting discharge of urine.—*n.* medicine which tends to increase flow of urine.—**diures'is** *n.* excessive urinary excretion.

diurnal (di-ur'-nal) *a.* belonging to day (opp. of *nocturnal*); during day; lasting one day.—**diur'nally** *adv.*

divalent (div'-a-lent or di-vā'-lent) *a.* (*Chem.*) capable of combining with two hydrogen atoms or their equivalent; bivalent.

divan (di-van') *n.* Turkish council of state; low, cushioned couch or bed.

dive (div) *v.i.* plunge into water head first; remain under water, as diver; penetrate deeply into; plunge the hand into;—*n.* plunge head-first; (*Slang*) cheap restaurant of ill-repute.—**div'er** *n.*—**dive'-bomb'er** *n.* bomber-aircraft which dives low over target.—**div'ing-bell** *n.* apparatus, originally bell-shaped, by which deep-sea divers can work under water.—**diving dress**, water-proof suit, weighted boots and air-supplied water-tight helmet worn by divers.

diverge (di-verj') *v.i.* divide; turn in different directions; deviate from a

course; vary; differ.—**diver'gence**, **diver'gency** *n.*—**diver'gent** *a.*—**diver'gently** *adv.*

divers (di'-verz) *a.* several; sundry; various.—**diverse'** *a.* of different kinds; dissimilar.—**diverse'ly** *adv.*— **diver'sity** *n.* state of being unlike; variety.

diversify (di-ver'-si-fi) *v.t.* make diverse or various; give variety to; break the monotony of; *v.i.* branch out into lines of business other than that for which originally established.— *pr.p.* **diver'sifying**.—*pa.p.* **diver'sified**. —**di-versifica'tion** *n.* act of diversifying; state of being diversified; variegation.

divert (di-vert') *v.t.* turn aside; alter direction of; draw off; amuse or entertain.—**diver'sion** *n.* act of diverting; that which diverts; detour. —**divert'ing** *a.* entertaining.

divest (di-vest') *v.t.* strip, as of clothes, equipment, etc.; to dispossess; (*Reflex.*) to undress.—**divest'-iture**, **divest'ment** *n.*

divide (di-vid') *v.t.* separate into parts; share; keep apart; antagonise; (*Math.*) find how many times one number is contained in another;— *v.i.* be separated; part; in Parliament, vote for or against a motion; —*n.* act of dividing; a water-shed.— **divid'ers** *n.pl.* compasses for measuring or dividing lines.

dividend (div'-i-dend) *n.* (*Arith.*) sum to be divided by divisor to obtain the quotient; interest payable on loans, invested money, etc.; share of profits payable to members of co-operative society; amount of winnings for standard stake in football pool.

divine (di-vin') *a.* belonging to or having the nature of God, or a god; devoted to worship of God; holy; sacred; heavenly; superhuman;—*n.* priest; clergyman; theologian;—*v.t.* and *v.i.* forecast by supernatural means; practise divination.—**divina'-tion** *n.* art of foretelling the future by non-rational methods; intuitive prevision; augury.—**divina'tor**, **divin'-er** *n.* (*fem.* **divin'eress**) one who divines, esp. dowser, one who professes to locate underground water by aid of divining rod.—**divine'ly** *adv.*—**divine'-ness** *n.*—**divining rod**, forked twig, usually of hazel, used by professional dowsers to locate underground water.—**divin'ity** *n.* state of being divine; God; pagan deity; study of theology.

division (di-vizh'-un) *n.* act of dividing; part of whole; section; partition; difference in opinion; (*Mil.*) army unit, the normal command of a *Major-General*.—**divisibil'-ity** *n.*—**divis'ible** *a.* capable of being divided.—**divi'sional**, **divi'sionary** *a.*—

divisor (di-vī'-zor) n. (*Math.*) number by which another is divided.

divorce (di-vŏrs') n. legal dissolution of marriage contract; separation;— v.t. obtain legal dissolution of marriage; separate; sever; disunite.—divorcee' n. divorced person.—divorce'ment n. act of dissolving marriage bond.

divot (div'-ot) n. (*Scot.*) piece of turf; sod; (*Golf*) piece of turf cut out by golf stroke.

divulge (di-vulj') v.t. make known or public; disclose; communicate to others.—divul'gate v.t. publish.—divulga'tion, divul'gence n.

dizzy (diz'-i) a. giddy; light-headed; causing giddiness; bewildered;—v.t. make dizzy; perplex.—dizz'ily adv.—dizzi'ness n. giddiness.

do (dŏŏ) v.t. perform; execute; effect; finish; prepare; suit; confer; offer; (*Colloq.*) swindle;—v.i. act; be;—pr.p. do'ing.—pa.t. did.—pa.p. done.—n. fuss; activity; special entertainment or party.—to do away with, destroy.—do'er n. agent.—to do for; suit; overwhelm; kill; (*Colloq.*) work for someone as charwoman.—to do in, murder.—do'ings n.pl. things done; conduct; activities; (*Slang*) substitute word for another, as in *pass me the doings.*—done'-out a. exhausted.—to do with, concern; need; tolerate.

docile (dŏ'-sīl or dos'-il) a. easily instructed or managed; tractable; amenable to discipline.—docile'ly adv.—docil'ity n.

dock (dok) n. common tap-rooted weed.

dock (dok) v.t. cut short; curtail; clip (as an animal's tail);—n. the part of tail left after clipping.

dock (dok) n. artificial enclosure near harbour or river where ships are berthed, loaded, etc.; enclosed space in law court where accused stands.—dock'er n. one who works at docks.—dock'yard, n. yard or magazine near harbour esp. for naval equipment and repairs.—dry'dock, grav'ing-dock, n. dock from which water can be pumped out.—floating dock, mobile repairing dock.—in dock, of cars etc., under repair.

docket (dok'-et) n. summary of written document; memorandum; bill or label affixed to goods giving instructions for delivery;—v.t. summarise; mark contents of papers.

doctor (dok'-tor) n. one who holds highest degree granted by any faculty of a university; medical practitioner;—v.t. treat medically; adulterate; falsify; repair temporarily;—v.i. practise medicine; take physic.—doc'torate n. degree or status of a university doctor.—doc'torship n.—docto'rial a. pert. to a doctor.

doctrine (dok'-trin) n. instruction; that which is taught; principle of belief; creed; any special truth.—doc'trinal or doctri'nal a. pert. to doctrine, esp. Christian Church.—doc'trinally adv.—doctrinaire (dok-tri-nār') n. political theorist who tends to urge application of doctrine beyond practical considerations;—a. urging impracticable doctrines.

document (dok'-ū-ment) n. written or printed source of information, instructions, or facts; any item which furnishes evidence.—v.t. furnish with written evidence of.—documen'tal, documen'tary a.—documenta'tion n. use of documentary evidence; furnishing of such evidence in book-form.—doc'umented a. furnished with documentary evidence.—documentary film, film which uses characters, objects and scenes of real life.

dodder (dod'-er) v.t. or v.i. totter or tremble, as with age; ramble in speech.—dodd'ering a. trembling.—dodderer n.—dodd'ery a.

dodge (doj) v.t. evade or escape by sudden turning; baffle;—v.i. twist aside; play fast and loose; avoid issue by quibbling;—n. trick; artifice; (*Colloq.*) ingenious device.—dod'ger n.—dod'gy a. (*Slang*) tricky.

dodo (dŏ'-dŏ) n. extinct flightless bird.—pl. do'do(e)s.

doe (dŏ) n. female of fallow deer; also female of antelope, rabbit, hare, goat, rat, mouse, ferret.—doe'skin n. skin of doe; fine close-woven cloth.

doff (dof) v.t. do or take off, esp. hat; rid oneself of.

dog (dog) n. common quadruped of same genus as wolf, mainly domesticated; metal hook for holding logs of wood; support for fire-irons;—a. male, as in *dog-wolf*;—v.t. follow closely; to keep at heels of; pursue relentlessly; importune.—pr.p. dog'ging.—pa.p. dogged.—dog'-cart n. high, usually two-wheeled carriage with two seats back-to-back.—dog'-col'lar n. leather strap with name plate fastened round dog's neck; (*Colloq.*) the collar worn by clergymen.—dog'-days n.pl. hottest period of northern summer, generally from 3rd July-11th August, when dog-star, Sirius, rises and sets with the sun.—dog'eared a. (of a book) having corners of pages turned down.—dog'ged a. stubborn; persistent.—dog'gedly adv.—dog'gedness n.—dog'fan'cier n. one who breeds dogs, esp. for sale.—dog'-fish, n. species of fish of shark order, found in British waters, and sold as rock salmon.—dog'go adv. (*Slang*) hidden, as in *to lie doggo*.—dog'gy a. pert. to dogs; fond of dogs.—dog'like a. faithful.—dog'-rose n. wild-rose.—dog'-star n. alternative name for Sirius, principal

star in constellation *Canis Major*.—
dog'-tired *a.* dead-beat; completely
exhausted. — **dog'-tooth** *n.* canine
tooth; eye-tooth (of human being).
—**dog'-vi'olet** *n.* scentless, wild violet.
—**dog'-watch** *n.* one of two-hour
watches on board ship from 4-6 or
6-8 p.m.—**a dog in the manger**, spoil-
sport; one who refuses to let another
enjoy what he himself has no use for.
—**a hot-dog** a sandwich made with
hot sausage inside a roll.—**to go to
the dogs**, be ruined.—**to let sleeping
dogs lie**, not to stir up trouble unnecessarily.

doge (dōj) *n.* title of chief magistrates
in ancient republics of Venice and
Genoa.

doggerel (dog'-ẹr-ẹl) *n.* irregular,
unpoetical burlesque verse;—*a.* halting; unrhythmic.

dogma (dog'-mạ) *n.* philosophical
tenet; theological doctrine; principle
or belief.—**dogmat'ic, -al,** *a.* pert. to
dogma; opinionative; bigoted; authoritative.—**dogmat'ically** *adv.*—**dog'-
matise** *v.i.* formulate dogma; express
opinion positively or arrogantly.—
dog'matism *n.* positive assertion.

doily (doi'-li) *n.* small table mat
placed under dishes; small, round
linen or paper mat put on plate
holding cakes, etc. Also **doy'ley.**

doldrums (dol'-drums) *n.pl.* belt of
calms at Equator; (*Colloq.*) state of
depression; the dumps.

dole (dōl) *v.t.* distribute in small
portions;—*n.* something given or
paid out; share; alms; (*Colloq.*) unemployment pay.

dole (dōl) *n.* pain; sorrow.—**dole'ful**
a. grievous; dismal.—**dole'fully** *adv.*
—**dole'fulness** *n.*—**dole'some** *a.* dismal;
doleful.

doll (dol) *n.* puppet; toy-baby as
child's plaything; (*Colloq.*) pretty,
rather brainless girl.—**to doll up**,
(*Colloq.*) to dress up smartly.

dollar (dol'-ạr) *n.* silver coin, monetary unit of U.S.A., Canada and
Australia, etc.

dolly (dol'-i) *n.* wooden shaft attached to disc with projecting arms, used
in mining, pile-driving, etc.; wooden
stick for stirring clothes in wash-
tub; mobile platform or carrier.

dolmen (dol'-men) *n.* prehistoric
megalithic monument formed by
large unhewn stone resting on two
or more unhewn uprights.

dolomite (dol'-o-mīt) *n.* natural
double carbonate of magnesium and
calcium.—**the Dolomites**, mountains
of this rock in the Tyrol.

dolour (dō'-lur) *n.* pain; distress;
anguish.—**doloro'so** *adv.* (*Mus.*) in a
mournful manner.—**dol'orous** *a.* full
of grief.—**dol'orously** *adv.*—**dol'ourous-
ness** *n.*

dolphin (dol'-fin) *n.* sea mammal of
whale kind, closely resembling porpoise; mooring buoy.

dolt (dōlt) heavy, stupid fellow;
blockhead.—**dolt'ish** *a.* dull; slow-
witted.—**dolt'ishly** *adv.*

domain (do-mān') *n.* that which one
has dominion over; landed property;
estate, esp. round mansion house;
(*Fig.*) scope of any branch of human
knowledge.—**domain'al, doma'nial** *a.*

dome (dōm) *n.* hemispherical vault
reared above roof of a building;
cupola.—**domed', dom'ical** *a.* possessing a dome.

domestic (do-mes'-tik) *a.* pert. to
house or home; devoted to home and
household affairs; tame (of animals);
not foreign (of a country's policy);
—*n.* household servant.—**domes'tically** *adv.*—**domes'ticate** *v.t.* make fond
of domestic life; tame.—**domestic'ity**
n. life in a household.—**domestic
science**, science of housecraft.

domicile (dom'-i-sīl) *n.* abode;
dwelling-house; (*Law*) person's permanent residence;—*v.t.* establish in
a fixed residence.—**domicil'iary** *a.*
pert. to a domicile.

dominant (dom'-i-nạnt) *a.* ruling;
prevailing.—*n.* (*Mus.*) fifth note of
diatonic scale.—**dom'inance** *n.* authority; ascendancy.—**dom'inancy** *n.*—
dom'inantly *adv.*—**dom'inate** *v.t.* and
v.i.—**domina'tion** *n.*—**domineer'** *v.i.*
rule with arbitrary sway; be over-
bearing.—**domineer'ing** *a.*—**domin'ion**
n. lordship; sovereignty; territory
under one government.

dominical (do-min'-i-kạl) *a.* belonging to our Lord or Lord's Day.

domino (dom'-in-ō) *n.* long cloak
with hood and/or mask; mask; one
of 28 oblong pieces marked each
with certain number of spots, used
in the game of *dominoes*.

dominus (dom'-i-nus) *n.* title given
to clergymen, teachers, etc.—**dom'-
inie** *n.* (*Scot.*) schoolmaster.

don (don) *n.* Fellow or tutor of
Oxford or Cambridge University;
master at Winchester.—**donn'ish** *a.*
pedantic.

don (don) *v.t.* put on; assume.—*pr.p.*
don'ning.—*pa.p.* **donned.**

donation (do-nā'-shun) *n.* act of
giving; gift, esp. money given to
charity.—**donate'** *v.t.* present a gift.
—**don'ative** *n.* official gift; gratuity;
benefice bestowed by patron without
reference to bishop;—*a.* of the nature
of donative.—**do'nor** *n.* one who
gives donation; benefactor.—**blood'-
do'nor** *n.* one who voluntarily gives
blood for transfusion.

done (dun) *pa.p.* of verb do.

donkey (dong'-ki) *n.* ass; (*Colloq.*)
foolish person.—**don'key-en'gine** *n.*
small auxiliary type of steam engine
for working, e.g. crane or pump.

don't (dōnt) (*Colloq.*) contr. of do not.

doodle (dŏŏ'-dl) n. trifler; simple fellow;—v.i. to scribble aimlessly; (Scot.) to drone, as a bagpipe.

doom (dŏŏm) n. judgment; legal decree; ruin; fate; evil destiny;—v.t. pass sentence on; condemn; destine.—**doom'ful** a.—**dooms'day** n. Day of Judgment.—**Doomsday or Domesday Book**, census compiled by order of William the Conqueror, containing assessment of population, property, stock, etc. of England, for purposes of taxation.

door (dōr) n. wooden or metal structure, hinged or sliding, giving access to house, room, passage, or cupboard; (Fig.) means of approach.—**door'-nail**, n. large-headed nail with which doors used to be studded.—**dead as a door-nail** (Colloq.) quite dead.

dope (dōp) n. any thick liquid, or semi-liquid lubricant; varnish; preparation for coating the fabric surfaces of aircraft; drug; any narcotic; (Slang) inside information (esp. about racehorses);—v.t. apply or administer dope to; (Fig.) hoodwink.—**dop'y** a. stupefied with drugs; slow-witted.

dormant (dor'-mant) a. sleeping; hibernating; quiescent; not in action; unclaimed (as title).—**dor'mancy** n. state of being quiescent.—**dor'mer window** n. small vertical window projecting from roof slope.—**dor'mitory**, n. large common bedroom.

dormouse n. (dor'mous) small, hibernating rodent.

dormy, dormie (dor'-mi) n. (Golf) term applied in a match to one player who is leading by as many holes as still remain to be played.

dorsal (dor'-sal) a. pert. to, near, or belonging to, the back.

dory (dō'-ri) n. flat-bottomed fishing-boat used in Newfoundland waters.

dose (dōs) n. prescribed quantity of medicine to be taken at one time; portion; anything disagreeable that must be taken or done;—v.t. administer or order in doses; (Colloq.) adulterate.—**dos'age** n. practice of dosing; amount of a dose.

doss (dos) n. (Slang) bed;—v.i. go to bed.—**doss'-house** n. cheap lodging-house.

dossier (dos'-i-ā) n. set of documents.

dot (dot) n. small point or spot made with pen, pencil, or sharp instrument; speck; (Mus.) point placed after a note or rest to lengthen sound or pause by one-half;—v.t. mark with dots; diversity as with small objects;—v.i. make dots.—pr.p. **dot'ting**.—pa.p. **dot'ted**.—**dot'ty** a. marked with or consisting of dots; (Colloq.) weak in mind; crazy.

dote (dōt) v.i. be in one's dotage; be foolishly sentimental; be over-fond of.—**dot'age** n. childishness of old people; senility; excessive fondness.—**dot'ard** n. one whose intellect is impaired by old age.

dotterel, dottrel (dot'-e-rel, dot'-rel) n. bird of plover family; (Fig.) stupid person; dupe.

double (dub'-l) a. denoting two things of same kind; existing in pairs; twice as much (quantity); twice as good (quality); serving for two; acting two parts; deceitful; ambiguous;—adv. twice; two-fold;—v.t. multiply by two; make twice as great; fold in two;—v.i. increase to twice as much; return upon one's track; run (after marching);—n. twice as much; that which is doubled over; fold; duplicate; actor's substitute or understudy; cumulative bet on two races; running pace, twice as quick as marching.—**doub'le-bass** n. largest and lowest pitched of stringed instruments, played with a bow.—**doub'le-breast'ed** a. (of a coat) able to fasten over on either side.—**doub'le-cross** v.t. (Slang) cheat a swindler.—**doub'le-deal'ing** n. duplicity.—**doub'le-Dutch** n. jargon.—**doub'le-dyed** a. twice immersed in dye; thoroughly infamous.—**doub'le-edged**, a. having two edges; (Fig.) cutting both ways; effective for and against.—**double entendre** (dŏŏbl'-ong-tong'-dr) word or phrase with two meanings, one of which is more or less improper.—**doub'le-en'try** n. in book-keeping, system by which every entry is made both on debit and credit side of an account.—**doub'le-faced** a. hypocritical.—**doub'leness** n.—**doub'ler** n.—**double stop** v.i. play on two strings of instrument at once.—**doub'let** n. one of pair; close-fitting garment for upper part of body as worn by Elizabethan men; one of two words derived orig. from same root but varying in spelling and meaning.—**doub'le-take** compulsive second look.—**doub'le talk** meaningless patter; deliberate use of ambiguous words.—**doub'le-tongued** a. deceitful; spiteful.—**doub'ly** adv. twice as much.

doubt (dout) v.t. disbelieve; hold questionable;—v.i. be in state of uncertainty; hesitate; be apprehensive; suspect;—n. uncertainty of mind; misgiving; distrust of others.—**doubt'able** a.—**doubt'er** n.—**doubt'ful** a. dubious; uncertain in opinion; ambiguous; suspicious; disreputable; obscure.—**doubt'fully** adv.—**doubt'fulness** n.—**doubt'ing** a.—**doubt'ingly** adv.—**doubt'less** adv.—**doubt'lessly** adv.

douche (dŏŏsh) n. jet of water directed upon or into the body; apparatus for douching.

dough (dō) n. mass of flour moistened

and kneaded, afterwards to be baked; (*U.S. Slang*) money.—dough'-nuts *n.* sweetened dough in shape of balls or rings, fried in fat and finally dipped in sugar.—dough'y *a.*

doughty (dou'-ti) *a.* brave; valiant. —dought'ily *adv.*

dour (dóór) *a.* (*Scot.*) obstinate; forbidding in manner.—dour'ly *adv.*

douse, dowse (dous) *v.t.* dip or plunge into water; (*Naut.*) lower a sail; put out a light.

dove (duv) *n.* pigeon; term of endearment; symbol of peace or of Holy Ghost.—dove'-cot(e) *n.* nesting box for pigeons, usually on top of pole.—dove'tail *n.* joint made by fitting one piece toothed with wedgelike projections (tenons) (shaped like dove's tail) into cavities of corresponding shape (mortises) in another piece of timber;—*v.t.* join together by this method; (*Fig.*) link together.

dowager (dou-a-jer) *n.* title given to widow to distinguish her from wife of her husband's heir.

dowdy (dou'-di) *a.* unfashionably dressed; untidy; lacking style.—*n.* dowdy woman.—dow'dily *adv.*—dow'diness *n.*

dowel (dou'-el) *n.* wooden or iron pin for joining two adjacent boards or stones.

dower (dou'-er) *n.* widow's share of her husband's property; portion woman brings in marriage; gift; talent.—dow'ered *a.*—dow'erless *a.*—dow'ry *n.* dower; woman's marriage-portion; any endowment.

down (doun) *n.* fine, soft feathers of birds.—down'y *a.* resembling or covered with down.

down (doun) *n.* hillock of sand by the sea (same as *dune*); treeless upland.

down (doun) *prep.* along a descent; towards lower place, situation, etc.; towards mouth of river; in same direction as; passing from the past to less remote times;—*adv.* in downward direction; on the ground; to the bottom; below the horizon; —*a.* descending;—*v.t.* knock down; baffle; dispirit—used also as an *interjection* with verb get, kneel, etc. understood;—*n.* grudge against; reversal of fortune (as in the *ups and downs* of life).—down'cast *a.* depressed; (of eyes) lowered.—down'fall *n.* ruin; heavy fall of rain, snow.—down'fallen *a.* ruined.—down'heart'ed *a.* despondent.—down'hill *a.* sloping, —*adv.* on a slope.—down'pour *n.* heavy fall of water, esp. rain.—down'right *adv.* straight down; in plain terms;—*a.* straightforward; blunt; unqualified.—down'stairs *adv.* in or to lower floor of house;—*a.* pert. to ground floor;—*n.* ground

floor.—down'-stream *adv.* with the current.—down'trodden *a.* trampled underfoot; oppressed.—down'ward *a.* descending from head or source; descending from higher to lower level;—*adv.* in descending course; from source.—down'wards *adv.*

doze (dōz) *v.i.* sleep lightly; be half asleep;—*n.* nap.

dozen (duz'-n) *n.* collection or set of twelve things of same kind;—*a.* twelve.—baker's dozen, devil's dozen, thirteen.

drab (dráb) *n.* thick woollen cloth; dingy brownish-grey colour;—*a.* (*Fig.*) dull; monotonous.

drachm (dram) See dram.

draft (draft) *n.* act of drawing; that which is drawn; men detached from a force for special work; order directing payment of money by bank; sketch or rough copy; depth of water necessary to float ship.—drafts *n.pl.* (usually draughts) game played on checkered board;—*v.t.* draw outline of; compose and write; draw from military force, etc.

drag (drag) *v.t.* draw with main force; trail slowly; pull violently; trawl with drag or net; harrow (fields);—*v.i.* move heavily or slowly; pass tediously.—*pr.p.* drag'ging.—*pa.p.* dragged.—*n.* net or hook to bring up submerged things; heavy harrow; four-in-hand; device acting as brake on wheel; sledge.

draggle (drag'-l) *v.t.* and *v.i.* make or become wet and dirty by trailing on the ground.—drag'gled *a.* dirty; soiled.—dragg'le-tail *n.* slut.

dragon (drag'-on) *n.* fabulous winged reptile represented as breathing out fire and smoke; constellation *Draco*; giant lizard of Malaya; (*Fig.*) overvigilant chaperone.—drag'onet *n.* little dragon.—drag'on-fish *n.* dragonet. —drag'on-fly *n.* insect of brilliant colouring, with long slender body and two pairs of wings.

dragoon (dra-góón) *n.* orig. mounted infantryman armed with a 'dragon,' or musket; cavalryman; (*Fig.*) harsh disciplinarian;—*v.t.* enforce harsh disciplinary measures.

dragster (drag'-ster) *n.* stripped-down high-powered car chassis for short sprint racing.

drain (drān) *v.t.* filter; draw off by degrees; make dry; swallow down; exhaust; impoverish;—*v.i.* flow off or drip away gradually;—*n.* watercourse; sewer or ditch; gradual exhaustion of means, health, etc.—drain'able *a.*—drain'age *n.* act of draining; system of carrying away surplus water from area by rivers, canals, etc.; water or sewage carried away.—drain'er *n.* kitchen utensil like rack, on which plates, etc. are placed to dry; colander or sieve

drake (drāk) n. male of duck.

dram (dram) n. (contr. of *drachm*) unit of weight; (*avoirdupois*) ⅟₁₆ of an ounce; (*apothecary*) ⅛ of an ounce; (*liquid*) ⅛ of an ounce or 60 minims; small drink of alcoholic liquor.

drama (drä'-ma) n. composition to be acted on stage; series of real emotional events.—**dramat'ic** a. pert. to drama; striking; tense.—**dramat'ically** adv.—**dramatisa'tion**—**dram'atise** v.t. adapt novel, etc. for acting. —**dram'atist** n. writer of plays.—**dramatis personae**, characters of a drama.

drank (drangk) pa.t. of drink.

drape (drāp) v.t. hang something loosely in folds; adorn with drapery. —**drap'er** n. (*fem.* drap'eress) formerly maker, now retail dealer in cloth and articles made from cloth.— **drap'eried** a. draped.—**drap'ery** n. cloth stuffs in general; hangings; shop, or department of shop, where cloth is sold.

drastic (dras'-tik) very powerful; harsh; thorough.

draught (draft) n. act of drawing; quantity of liquid drawn or quaffed off; dose of medicine; depth of water necessary to float ship; catch (of fish) contained in drag-net; sketch; detachment; current of air. — **draughts** n.pl. game played with black and white counters on checkered board;—a. drawn from barrel, as beer;—v.t. (more commonly **draft**) draw out.—**draught'-horse** n. strong trace-horse capable of drawing heavy loads.—**draught'iness** n.— **draughts'man**, n. one who plans and designs, esp. of buildings and engineering projects.—**draughts'manship** n. —**draught'y** a. full of air-currents.

draw (draw) v.t. pull along; haul towards oneself; entice; extract (as tooth); receive (as money, salary, etc.); inhale; sketch; describe; cast lots; bring game, such as fox, out of hiding; take out entrails;—v.i. pull, attract, move towards; be equal in a match; sketch; cast lots; have free passage of air (as chimney). —*pr.p.* draw'ing.—*pa.t.* drew.—*pa.p.* drawn.—n. act of drawing; lottery; game ending with same score for both sides; attraction.—**draw'able** a. —**draw'back** n. disadvantage.—**draw'bridge** n. bridge that can be raised or let down at will, orig. bridge across moat.—**draw'er** n. one who or that which draws; one who draws a cheque; lidless, sliding box in table, chest, etc.—**draw'ers** n.pl. close fitting undergarment for lower limbs.—**draw'ing** n. art of pulling or attracting; art of representing objects by line or colour on paper, canvas, etc.—**draw'ings** n.pl. gross takings of shop.—**draw'ing-pin** n. flat headed pin for fixing paper on

drawing-board. — **draw'ing-room** n. orig. withdrawing room; room in which guests are entertained, esp. after dinner.—a. (of game) equal scoring for both sides.—**to draw the line**, stop.—**at daggers drawn**, openly hostile.

drawl (drawl) v.i. speak with slow and lengthened tone;—v.t. utter (words) in this way;—n. manner of speech, slow and drawn out.

dray (drā) n. low cart for heavy goods.—**dray'-horse** n. horse for pulling dray.—**dray'-man** n.

dread (dred) n. overwhelming apprehension; awe; terror;—a. dreadful; awful;—v.t. regard with fear;—v.i. have fear of future.—**dread'ed** a. feared.—**dread'ful** a. orig. full of dread; terrifying; terrible.—**dread'fully** adv.—**dread'fulness** n.—**dread'nought** n. one who fears nothing; large-sized battleship mounting heavy guns of one calibre.

dream (drēm) n. series of images or thoughts in mind of person asleep; idle fancy; vision; aspiration;—v.i. imagine things during sleep; have yearnings;—v.t. see in dream.—*pa.t.* and *p.p.* dreamed or dreamt (dremt). —**dream'er** n. one who dreams.— **dream'ily** adv.—**dream'iness** n.—**dream'land** n. imaginary land seen in dreams. —**dream'less** a.—**dream'like** a. visionary; shadowy; unreal.—**dream'y** a. given to dreams; abstracted.

drear, dreary (drēr, '-i) a. dismal; gloomy; bleak. — **drear'ily** adv.— **drear'iness** n. cheerlessness.

dredge (drej) v.t. sprinkle.—**dredg'er**, n. container with sprinkler top.

dredge (drej) n. machine for taking up mud from river-bed, harbour, etc.; drag-net for oysters or zoological specimens.—**dredg'er** n. boat fitted with dredge;—v.t. scoop up or deepen with dredge.

dregs (dregz) n.pl. sediment in liquid that falls to bottom; lees; grounds; (*Fig.*) anything worthless esp. disreputable people.

drench (drensh) v.t. wet thoroughly; soak; administer medicine to animal.

dress (dres) v.t. arrange in order; put clothes on; provide with clothes; adorn; treat (a wound)—v.i. come into line; put on one's clothes;— n. clothes; frock; adornment.— **dress'-cir'cle** n. lowest gallery in theatre, orig. for people in evening-dress.—**dress'er** n. one who dresses; surgeon's assistant; kitchen sideboard.—**dress'ing** n. clothes; application of sterile substance to wound; manure; substance used to stiffen fabrics; sauce or stuffing used to add piquancy to a dish (as salad-dressing). — **dress'ing-down** n. (*Colloq.*) scolding or thrashing.—**dress'ing-ta'ble** n. table with mirror used while dressing.—**dress′y** a. fond of dress fashionable.

drew (dróó) pa.t. of **draw**.

dribble (drib′-l) v.i. trickle down, esp. of saliva of babies and idiots; drop quickly;—v.t. cause to fall in drops; (Football) propel the ball forward by short kicks.—**drib** v.t. dribble.—**drib′let** n. small drop.

dried (drīd) pa.t. and pa.p. of verb **dry**.

drift (drift) n. state or process of being driven; that which is driven; accumulation of substance driven by wind, as snow; slow surface current in the sea caused usually by prevailing wind; deviation or tendency; —v.t. drive into heaps; cause to float in certain direction;—v.i. be floated along; be piled in heaps.— **drift′er** n. small fishing vessel using drift nets.—**drift′ing** n.—**drift′-net** n. large fishing net allowed to drift with tide.

drill (dril) v.t. pierce; bore hole through; sow, as seeds, in a row; train in military tactics; instruct (in mental or physical exercises);—n. revolving tool for boring holes in metal, stone, etc.; implement for making holes for seed; row of seeds or root crops; physical exercise or military training; instruction.

drill (dril) n. strong type of twill cloth.

drink (dringk) v.t. swallow, as liquid; empty, as a glass; breathe in, as air;—v.i. swallow liquid; consume intoxicating liquor, esp. in excess.— pr.p. **drink′ing**. — pa.p. **drunk**.—n. liquid for drinking; intoxicating liquor; (Colloq) the sea.— **drink′able** a. fit for drinking.—**drink′er** n. tippler.—**drink′ing-bout** n. prolonged period of excessive drinking.—to **drink in**, absorb rain; (Fig.) absorb through the senses.

drip (drip) v.t. let fall, drop by drop; —v.i. ooze; trickle.—pr.p. **drip′ping**. —pa.p. **dripped**.—n. falling in drops; sound made by water dripping.— **drip′ping** a. thoroughly wet;—n. that which falls in drops, esp. fat from meat when roasting.

drive (drīv) v.t. urge on; keep in motion; guide course of; cause (machine) to work; strike in, as a nail; compel; hurry; conclude, as bargain; to hit ball with force, as in golf, tennis; chase game towards sportsmen;—v.i. be forced along; ride in vehicle.— pr.p. **driv′ing**.— pa.t. **drove**.—pa.p. **driv′en**.—n. excursion in carriage, motor, etc.; private carriage-road or avenue; driving game towards sportsmen; capacity for getting things done; part of mechanism which exerts propelling force.—**driv′er** n. one who or that which drives; golf-club for hitting ball from tee; drover (of cattle).—to **drive at**, hint at.

drivel (driv′-l) v.i. dribble like a child; talk nonsense; be weak or foolish.—n. nonsense.—**driv′eller** n.

drizzle (driz′-l) v.t. and v.i. rain gently;—n. fine rain.

droll (drōl) a. laughable; funny; queer;—n. buffoon; jester; odd character.—**droll′ery** n.

dromedary (drum′-e-dar-i) n. breed of one-humped Arabian camel.

drone (drōn) n. male of honey-bee; (Fig.) idler who lives on work of others, like drone-bee; deep, humming sound; largest pipe of bag-pipes; its sound;—v.t. and v.i. hum; speak or sing in monotonous voice.

droop (dróóp) v.i. hang down; grow weak; pine; sag; wilt (as flowers);— v.t. lower.

drop (drop) n. globular particle of fluid that falls or is allowed to fall; minute quantity of fluid in medical dose; anything hanging like a drop, or resembling a drop in size; fall; —v.t. let fall drop by drop; dismiss or break off (as acquaintance); to set down from vehicle; write letter or pass remark, in casual manner;— v.i. fall in drops; fall down suddenly; sink to lower level (as prices);— pr.p. **drop′ping**—pa.t. and pa.p. **dropped**.—**drop′-cur′tain** n. painted curtain lowered in front of theatre stage between scenes in play.— **drop′-kick** n. (Rugby) kick effected by letting ball fall from hands to ground to be kicked immediately on rebound.—**drop′let** n. tiny drop.— **drop′per** n. small glass tube from which liquid is measured out in drops.—**drop′pings** n.pl. dung.—to **drop a brick** (Slang) make tactless remark.—to **drop in**, make informal visit.—a **drop in the bucket**, very small contribution.

dropsy (drop′-si) n. morbid collection of fluid in part of body.—**drop′sical** a.

dross (dros) n. scum of metals thrown off in smelting; small coal of inferior quality; slag; refuse; (Fig.) anything of little value; money.

drought, drouth (drout, drouth) n. dryness; want or absence of rain over prolonged period; thirst.— **drought′iness**, **drouth′iness** n.— **drought′y**, **drouth′y** a. very dry.

drove (drōv) n. herd or flock, esp. on the move.—**drov′er** n. one who drives cattle or sheep, esp. to market.

drown (droun) v.t. suffocate by submerging in water; deluge; render inaudible; overpower;—v.i. be suffocated in water.

drowse (drouz) v.t. make sleepy; make stupid;—v.i. doze; be heavy with sleep;—n. half-sleep; doze.— **drows′y** a. heavy with sleep.— **drows′ily** adv.—**drows′iness** n.

drub (drub) *v.t.* beat; cudgel;—*v.i.* stamp.—**drub'bing** *n.* thrashing.

drudge (druj) *v.i.* toil hard; labour at menial tasks;—*n.* one made to do menial work; slave.—**drudg'ery** *n.* monotonous toil.—**drudg'ingly** *adv.*

drug (drug) *n.* substance used in composition of a medicine; narcotic; —*v.t.* mix with drugs; administer drug to someone; dose to excess;— *pr.p.* **drug'ging.**—*pa.p.* **drugged.**— **drug'gist** *n.* pharmaceutical chemist.

Druid (dróó'id) *n.* priest of ancient Celtic peoples of Britain, Gaul, etc. **druid'ical** *a.*—**Drui'idism** *n.*

drum (drum) *n.* (*Mus.*) percussion instrument comprising a hollow, parchment-covered cylinder beaten with drumstick; anything drum-shaped; (*Anat.*) middle portion of ear.—*v.t.* play on drum; teach by constant repetition;—*v.i.* beat on drum; beat rhythmically.—*pr.p.* **drum'ming.**—*pa.p.* **drummed.**—**drum'-mer** *n.*

drunk (drungk) *pa.p.* of **drink**;—*a.* overcome by alcohol intoxicated.— *n.* drunk person.—**drunk'ard** *n.* one who habitually drinks to excess.— **drunk'en** *a.* given to excessive drinking; intoxicated.—**drunk'enness** *n.*

dry (drī) *a.* free from moisture; empty of liquid; not giving milk; thirsty; unsweetened; uninteresting; sarcastic; subject to Prohibition Laws; —*v.t.* free from moisture; drain;— *v.i.* grow dry; evaporate;—*pr.p.* **dry'ing.**—*pa.p.* **dried.**—**dri'er** *n.*—to **dry clean,** clean garments with a solvent other than water.—**dry'-goods** *n.pl.* drapery goods.—**dry'ly,** **dri'ly** *adv.*—**dry measure,** measure of bulk, used for grain, etc.—**dry'ness** *n.*—**dry'-rot** *n.* decay of timber caused by fungoid disease.—**dry'-salter** *n.* orig. dealer in salted meats, pickles, etc.; dealer in paints, dyes, and chemicals generally.—**dry'-shod** *a.* with dry feet; without wetting one's feet.—**dry'-stone** *a.* built of stone without mortar.

dryad (drī'ad) *n.* wood-nymph.

dual (dū'al) *a.* consisting of two; twofold.—**dual'ity** *n.* state of being double or having double nature.

dub (dub) *v.t.* knight; give a nick-name to; make smooth; dress a fly for fishing; add one sound track to another or replace one by another on sound film or tape.—*pr.p.* **dub'bing.** —*pa.p.* **dubbed.**—**dub'bin,** or **dub'bing** *n.* oily composition for softening leather.—**dub'ber** *n.*

dubious (dū'-bi-us) *a.* doubtful; liable to turn out well or ill; (of a character) shady.—**du'biously** *adv.*—**du'biousness** *n.*—**dubi'ety** *n.* hesitancy; uncertainty.—**du'bitable** *a.* doubt-ful.—**du'bitancy, dubita'tion** *n.* act of doubting; uncertainty.

ducal (dūk'-al) *a.* pert. to duke.— **du'cally** *adv.* in ducal manner.—

ducat (duk'-at) *n.* coin formerly used in several European countries.—

duch'ess *n.* wife or widow of duke; woman who holds duchy in her own right.—**duch'y** *n.* dominions of duke.

duchess (duch'-es) *n.* See **ducal.**

duck (duk) *n.* coarse cloth or light canvas used for small sails and for men's tropical clothing.—**ducks** *n.pl.* trousers made of this.

duck (duk) *n.* broad-beaked, web-footed, short-legged water bird; female duck as distinct from male *drake;* (*Colloq.*) darling; sudden dip; sudden lowering of head; (*Cricket*) no score.—*v.t.* dip suddenly in water;—*v.i.* bend (head) suddenly; cringe.—**duck'board** *n.* planking to cross swampy areas.—**duck'ling** *n.* young duck.—**duck'-weed** *n.* minute, floating, green plants growing on standing waters.

duct (dukt) *n.* canal or tube for conveying fluids, esp. in animal bodies, plants, etc.

ductile (duk'-til) *a.* (of metals) capable of being drawn out in fine threads; (*Fig.*) tractable; easily influenced.—**ductil'ity** *n.*

dud (dud) *n.* anything defective;—*a.* worthless; defective; futile.

dude (dūd, dóód) *n.* (*Slang*) a fop; a brainless dandy.—**dude ranch** *n.* one run for paying guests.

dudgeon (duj'-un) *n.* haft of a dagger.

dudgeon (duj'-un) *n.* anger; resent-ment, as in phrase *in high dudgeon.*

due (dū) *a.* owing; fitting to be paid or done to another; adequate; appointed to arrive (as train); attributable:—*adv.* exactly; duly; directly;—*n.* that which is owed in money or service; right; tribute; tax. —**du'ly** *adv.* properly; at the right time.

duel (dū'-el) *n.* combat between two persons; two-sided contest;—*v.i.* fight a duel.—*pr.p.* **du'elling.**—*pa.p.* **du'elled.**—**du'ellist** *n.*

duet (dū-et') *n.* musical composition for two performers, vocal or instru-mental.—**duet'tist** *n.*

duffel, duffle (duf'-l) *n.* coarse woollen cloth with thick nap; camping kit.

duffer (duf'-er) *n.* clumsy or stupid person.

dug (dug) *pa.t.* and *pa.p.* of **dig.**— **dug'-out** *n.* canoe hollowed out of tree trunk; hole in ground roughly roofed over to protect in trench warfare.

duke (dūk) *n.* (*fem.* **duch'ess**) highest order of nobility in British peerage; (on the Continent) sovereign prince. —**duke'dom** *n.* status or possessions of a duke.

dulcet (dul'-set) *a.* sweet to the taste or ear.

dulcimer (dul'-si-mer) *n.* a medieval stringed instrument struck by hammers; old Jewish musical instrument.

dull (dul) *a.* stupid; slow of hearing or seeing; tedious; uninspired; sleepy; dim or cloudy; obtuse; blunt; heavy;—*v.t.* stupefy; blunt; mitigate;—*v.i.* become dull.—**dull'ard** *n.* slow-witted person.—**dull'ness** *n.*

dumb (dum) *a.* lacking permanently power of speech; mute; temporarily silent; mimed; inarticulate; stupid; unresponsive.—**dumb'bell** *n.* weights connected by a bar, used in gymnastic exercises; (*U.S. Slang*) a nitwit.—**dumb'ly** *adv.* mutely; in silence. —**dumb'ness** *n.*—**dumb'show** *n.* expressive gesture without words; short play in mime.—**dumb'-wait'er** *n.* dinner-wagon or trolley.—**dum(b)found'** *v.t.* strike dumb; amaze. Also **dum(b)found'er.—dum'my** *a.* dumb; sham;—*n.* dumb person; lay figure, as tailor's dummy; baby's rubber comforter; sham package in shop window; (*Cards*) exposed hand in bridge or whist.

dum-dum (dum'-dum) *n.* soft-nosed bullet.

dump (dump) *v.t.* throw down heavily; deposit; unload; export surplus goods at low price;—*n.* thud; refuse or scrap heap; temporary store for munitions, etc.—**dump'ling** *n.* ball of dough boiled in water, stock, etc.; suet pudding, boiled or steamed.— **dump'y** *a.* short; thick; squat;—*n.* hassock used as a seat; pouffe. Also **dump'ty.—dump'iness** *n.*

dun (dun) *a.* a greyish-brown colour; dark;—*n.* this colour; horse of this colour.

dun (dun) *v.t.* importune for payment of debt.—*pr.p.* **dun'ning.**—*pa.p.* **dunned**—*n.* insistent creditor.

dunce (duns) *n.* one who is slow at learning; dullard; backward child.

dune (dūn) *n.* low hill of sand.

dung (dung) *n.* excrement of animals; manure;—*v.t.* treat with manure;— *v.i.* drop excrement.—**dung'hill** *n.* mound of dung; (*Fig.*) mean condition; vile abode.

dungaree (dung'-ga-rē) *n.* coarse hard-wearing Indian calico.—**dung'arees** *n.pl.* trousers or overalls of this material.

dungeon (dun'-jun) *n.* orig. tower or keep of a castle; subterranean prison-cell;—*v.t.* confine in a dungeon.

duo (dū'-ō) *n.* duet; pair of stage artistes.

duodecimal (dū-o-des'-i-mal) *a.* counted by twelves.—**duodeci'mals** *n.* method of calculation based on units of twelve.

duodenum (dū-o-dē'-num) *n.* upper part of intestines so called as it is about 12 finger-breadths long;—*pl.* **duode'na.—duode'nal** *a.*

dupe (dūp) *n.* one easily cheated or gulled;—*v.t.* cheat; mislead.

duplex (dū'-pleks) *a.* twofold; double.—**du'ple** *a.* double.—**du'plicate** *a.* double; exactly resembling something else.—*n.* exact copy; transcript.—*v.t.* double; make a copy of.—**duplica'tion** *n.*—**du'plicative** *a.*— **du'plicator** *n.* machine for making copies of a document.—**duplic'ity** *n.* doubleness; double dealing; deceitfulness.

durable (dū'-ra-bl) *a.* lasting; able to resist wear and tear; not perishable. —**dur'ableness, durabil'ity** *n.*—**dur'ably** *adv.*—**dur'ance** *n.* continuation; confinement.—**dura'tion** *n.* durability; period anything lasts.

duress (dū-res') *n.* hardship; imprisonment; constraint; compulsion.

during (dū'-ring) *prep.* in the time of; in course of.

durst (durst) *pa.t.* of **dare.**

dusk (dusk) *a.* tending to darkness; darkish;—*n.* twilight; gloaming.— **dusk'y** *a.* partially dark; dim; darkskinned.

dust (dust) *n.* very fine particles of matter deposited on ground or suspended in air; minute particles of gold in river bed; powder; ashes of the dead; grave.—*v.t.* remove dust from; sprinkle with powder.—**dust'-bin** *n.* bucket for holding dust, rubbish, etc.—**dust'cart** *n.* cart for removing rubbish, etc.—**dust'-coat** *n.* overall; light travelling coat.—**dust'-cov'er** *n.* bookjacket.—**dust'er** *n.* one who dusts; cloth for dusting; (*Naut. slang*) flag. —**dust'ily** *adv.*—**dust'iness** *n.*—**dust'man** *n.* scavenger.—**dust'y** *a.* covered with dust; powdery.—**dust'y-mill'er** *n.* the plant, auricula.—**to lick the dust,** grovel.—**not so dusty** (*Colloq.*) not bad or badly.

Dutch (duch) *a.* pert. to Holland, its inhabitants, or their language;—*n.* language of Holland;—*pl.* people of Holland.—**Dutch'man** *n.* (*fem.* **Dutch'woman**) native of Holland.—**Dutch auction,** prices start at high figure and are gradually lowered to meet the bidder.—**Dutch courage,** false courage inspired by intoxicants; bravado.—**Dutch treat,** entertainment for which each person pays his own share.—**to talk like a Dutch uncle,** rebuke a person kindly.

duty (dū'-ty) *n.* that which is due; that which is demanded by law, morality, social conscience, etc.; military service; one's proper employment; period of work set down for each person on roster; customs or excise dues.—**du'teous** *a.* dutiful;

obedient.—du'teously *adv.*—du'tiable *a.* subject to customs duties. Also du'tied.—du'tiful *a.* attentive to duty; submissive; proceeding from sense of duty.—du'tifully *adv.*—du'tifulness *n.* —du'ty-free *a.* exempt from Customs duty.

dux (duks) *n.* leader; head or top pupil of class or school.

dwarf (dwawrf) *n.* animal, plant, or man abnormally small; mannikin;— *v.t.* hinder the growth of; make diminutive by comparison.—dwarf'-ish, dwarf *a.* undersized.

dwell (dwel) *v.i.* abide; be domiciled. —dwell'er *n.*—dwell'ing *n.* habitation; abode.

dwindle (dwin-dl) *v.i.* grow less; shrink; waste away;—*v.t.* lessen;— *n.* decline; pining away.

dye (dī) *v.t.* give new colour to; stain;—*v.i.* undergo change of colour.—*pr.p.* dye'ing.—*pa.p.* dyed.—*n.* colouring matter.—dy'er *n.* one employed in dyeing.—dye'-stuff *n.* substance used for dyeing.

dying (dī'-ing) *pr.p.* of die.

dyke (dīk) *n.* See dike.

dynamic (dī- (or di-) nam'-ik) *a.* pert. to force in motion; pert. to dynamics; (*Med.*) functional; (*Fig.*) possessing energy and forcefulness (of character). Also **dynam'ical.**— **dynam'ics** *n.* branch of mechanics which deals with *force in motion.*— **dy'namite** *n.* powerful high explosive, with great disruptive force;—*v.t.* blow up with dynamite.—dyn'amit-ard, dyn'amiter *n.* one who uses dynamite, esp. for criminal purposes.—dyn'amo *n.* generator for transforming mechanical energy into electrical energy;—*pl.* dyn'amos.

dynasty (din'-as-ti, dī'-nas-ti) *n.* line of kings of same family.—dy'nast *n.* ruler; member of dynasty.—dynas'tic *a.*

dyne (dīn') *n.* centimetre-gramme-second unit of force.

dysentery (dis'-en-ter-i) *n.* inflammation of mucous membrane of large intestine, accompanied by excessive discharge of bowels, pain and fever.—dysenter'ic, -al *a.*

dyspepsia (dis-pep'-si-ạ) *n.* indigestion. Also dyspep'sy.—dyspep'tic *a.* suffering from indigestion; morbid— *n.* one who suffers from dyspepsia.— dyspep'tically *adv.*

E

each (ēch) *a.* and *pron.* denoting every one of a number, separately considered.

eager (ē'-gẹr) *a.* ardent; longing; yearning; impatient; earnest; anxious; keen.—ea'gerly *adv.*—ea'ger-ness *n.*—eager beaver *n.* (U.S.) enthusiastic person; busybody.

eagle (ē'-gl) *n.* large bird of prey; gold 10 dollar piece of the U.S.; military standard in form of the bird; (*Golf*) hole played in two under par.—ea'gle-eyed *a.* sharp-sighted.—ea'glet *n.* young eagle.

ear (ēr) *n.* fruiting spike or head of corn;—*v.i.* to form ears, as corn.

ear (ēr) *n.* organ of hearing, esp. external part of it; sensitiveness to musical sounds; attention; ear-shaped projection.—eared *a.* having ears.—ea'cute pain in ear.—ear'drum *n.* middle ear or tympanum.—eared *a.* having ears. —ear'ing *n.* rope for fastening upper corner of square sail to the yard.— ear'mark *v.t.* mark ears of animal with owner's mark; reserve for particular purpose.—ear'phone *n.* head-phone for receiving wireless broadcasts, etc.—ear'ring *n.* ornament suspended from lobe of ear.—ear'shot *n.* distance at which sounds can be heard.—ear'-splitting *a.* exceedingly loud and piercing.— ear'-trum'pet *n.* instrument for improving hearing.—ear'wax *n.* cerumen, waxy secretion of glands of ear.—ear'wig *n.* insect with body terminating in pair of horny forceps.

earl (ẹrl) *n.* nobleman ranking between marquis and viscount.— earl'dom *n.* territory or dignity of earl.—Earl Mar'shal *n.* officer of state in England, head of College of Heralds.

early (ẹr'-li) *a.* appearing soon; in the beginning of the day; in near future;—*adv.* in good season.— ear'lier, ear'liest.—ear'liness *n.*

earn (ẹrn) *v.t.* gain money by labour; merit by service; get.—earn'ings *n.pl.* wages; savings.

earnest (ẹr'-nest) *a.* eager to obtain; zealous;—*n.* pledge; sum paid as binding an engagement.—ear'nestly *adv.*—ear'nestness *n.*

earth (ẹrth) *n.* planet on which we live; soil, mould, dry land, on surface of the earth; mineral; world; globe; fox's hole; leakage of electric current to earth; wire which connects electrical apparatus with earth.—earths *n.pl.* term in chemistry for certain metallic oxides.—*v.t.* hide in earth; provide path to earth for electrical currents; run to earth;— *v.i.* burrow; take refuge in the ground.—earth'-bound *a.* worldly; sordid.—earth'-clos'et *n.* privy in which earth is applied to excreta.— earth'en *a.* made of earth, clay and the like.—earth'enware *n.* crockery and wares made of earth or clay, and baked or burnt with fire.—earth'iness *n.*—earth'ling *n.* dweller on earth.— earth'ly *a.* belonging to the earth; terrestrial; worldly.—earth'-nut *n.*

name of certain plants whose tubers are edible.—**earth'quake** n. disturbance of earth's surface due to contraction of section of crust of the earth.—**earth'-trem'or** n. slight vibration of surface of the earth.—**earth'ward** adv. toward the earth.—**earth'-work** n. mounds of earth for defence or to form embankments for railways and canals.—**earth'-worm** n. the common worm.—**earth'y** a. like or pertaining to earth; gross.

ease (ēz) n. leisure; quiet; freedom from anxiety, bodily effort, or pain; facility; natural grace of manner.—v.t. free from pain, disquiet, or oppression.—**ease'ful** a. restful; comfortable; quiet.—**eas'ily** adv.—**eas'iness** n.—**eas'ing** n. act of alleviating or slackening; easement; relief; assistance.—**eas'y** a. at ease; free from pain, care, anxiety, or constraint; quiet; not difficult or burdensome; graceful; moderate; comfortable.—**stand at ease!** military term to relax after 'attention'.—**eas'y-chair** n. armchair.

easel (ō'-zl) n. wooden frame to support pictures, blackboard, etc.

easement (ēz'-ment) n. (Law) a right over the land of another, e.g. right of way, right to divert water, etc.

east (ēst) n. one of four cardinal points; part of horizon where sun rises; regions towards that.—a. on, in, or near east.—adv. from or to east.—**east'ern** a. toward east; oriental.—**east'erly** a. from or toward east.—adv. to or on east.—**east'ernmost, east'most** a. furthest to east.—**east'ing** n. distance eastward from given meridian.—**east'ward** adv. or a. toward east.—**east'wards** adv.—**Far East,** China, Japan, etc.—**Middle East,** Iran, Iraq, etc.—**Near East,** Turkey, Syria, Israel, etc.

Easter (ēs'-ter) n. festival commemorating Christ's resurrection, falling on Sunday after Good Friday.

easy See under **ease.**

eat (ēt) v.t. chew and swallow, as food; consume; destroy; gnaw; corrode; wear away;—v.i. take food; be eatable.—pa.t. **ate** (āt or et).—pa.p. **eat'en.—eat'able** a. or n. anything that may be eaten.—**eat'ing-house** n. cheap restaurant.—**eats** n.pl. (Slang) food.

eaves (ēvz) n.pl. lower edges of sloping roof overhanging walls of building.—**eaves'drop** v.i. listen furtively to conversation.—**eaves'drop'per** n.

ebb (eb) n. reflux of tide-water to sea; decline; growing less; diminution;—v.i. flow back; sink; decline.—**ebb'-tide** n. ebbing or retiring tide.

ebon (eb'-on) a. black as ebony;—n. ebony.—**eb'ony** n. valuable cabinet

wood, heart-wood of which is jet-black and takes a fine polish.—**eb'onite** n. hard rubber or form of vulcanite.

ebullient (ē-bul'-yent) a. boiling over; overflowing; exuberant.—**ebull'ience** n.—**ebulli'tion** n. act of boiling; outburst of feeling.

eccentric (ek-sen'-trik) a. departing from centre; not placed, or not having axis placed, centrally; not circular (in orbit); irregular; odd; of whimsical temperament;—n. circular piece of metal mounted out of its centre upon shaft; modification of the crank contrived to change rotary movement of a shaft into up and down or reciprocating motion; whimsical person; one who defies social conventions. — **eccen'trically** adv.—**eccentric'ity** n. departure from normal conduct.

ecclesiastic (e-klē'-zi-as-tik) n. person in orders; clergyman; priest;—a. pertaining to church.—**ecclesias'tical** a.—**ecclesias'ticism** n. adherence to ecclesiastical principles.

echelon (esh'-e-lon) n. arrangement of troops in parallel lines, each a little to left or right of another; (Flying) formation of aeroplanes in which each plane flies slightly above and to right or left of one in front.

echo (ek'-ō) n. repetition of sound produced by sound waves reflected from object denser than aerial medium; close imitation of another's remarks or ideas; reverberation; repetition; answer.—pl. **ech'oes.**—v.t. send back the sound of; repeat with approval; imitate closely;—v.i. resound; be repeated.

éclair (ā-klār') n. long, narrow, sweet cake, filled with cream, and iced.

éclat (ā-klá') n. splendour; renown; show; brilliancy; lustre; applause.

eclectic (ek-lek'-tik) a. selecting at will;—n. thinker who selects and reconciles principles, opinions, belonging to different schools of thought.

eclipse (e-klips') n. interception of light of one heavenly body by another; temporary effacement;—v.t. obscure or hide.

eclogue (ek'-log) n. short poem of pastoral nature.

ecology (ē-kol'-o-ji) n. study of relations between organisms and their environment. Also **oecol'ogy.**

economy (ē-kon'-o-mi) n. management of household and its affairs; wise expenditure of money; careful use of materials; harmonious organisation.—**econom'ic(al)** a.—**econom'ically** adv.—**econom'ics** n.pl.—**political economy,** science which deals with rules governing production, distribution, consumption, and finance.—**econ'omise** v.t. expend with care and prudence;—*v.t.* use with frugality.—**econ'omist** *n.* student of economics; economiser.

ecstasy (ek'-sta-si) *n.* abnormal mental excitement when mind is ruled by one idea, object, or emotion; sense of uplift and joyfulness and increased well-being; excessive joy.—Also **ex'tasy.**—**ec'stasise** *v.t.* or *v.i.* throw or go into state of ecstasy.—**ecstat'ic** *a.*—**ecstat'ically** *adv.*

ecumenic, ecumenical (ek-ū-men'-ik, -i-kạl) *a.* universal; representative, or accepted as representative, of the Church, universal or catholic; general; catholic; concerning unity of Christian churches.

eczema (ek'-ze-mạ) *n.* (*Med.*) non-contagious disease of the epidermis, characterised by redness, itchiness and inflammatory eruption of the skin.

eddy (ed'-i) *n.* current of air, smoke, or water, swirling back contrary to main current; vortex; small whirlpool; whirlwind;—*v.i.* move in a circle.—*pr.p.* **edd'ying**—*pa.p.* **edd'ied.**

edelweiss (ā'-dl-vīs) *n.* small white flowering plant found in the Swiss Alps.

edema (ē-dē'-mạ) *n.* See **oedema.**

edge (ej) *n.* thin cutting side of blade of instrument; part adjacent to line of division; brink; rim; keenness;—*v.t.* put an edge on; sharpen; move almost imperceptibly;—*v.i.* move sideways.—**edged** *a.* sharp; bordered.—**edge'less** *a.*—**edge'(d)-tool** *n.* cutting tool with sharp edge.—**edge'ways, edge'wise** *adv.* in direction of edge; sideways.—**edg'ing** *n.* border or fringe; narrow lace.—**edg'y** *a.* having an edge; angular; irritable.—**to be on edge,** to be irritable.

edible (ed'-i-bl) *a.* fit for eating;—*n.* eatable.—**edibil'ity** *n.*—**ed'ibleness** *n.* quality of being edible.

edict (ē'-dikt) *n.* law or decree; order proclaimed by government or king; statute; ordinance.

edify (ed'-i-fī) *v.t.* build up, esp. in character or faith; instruct in moral and religious knowledge.—*pa.t.* and *pa.p.* **ed'ified.**—**edifica'tion** *n.*—**ed'ifice** *n.* building.—**ed'ifying** *a.*

edit (ed'-it) *v.t.* prepare for publication; compile; conduct a newspaper or periodical; revise and alter or omit.—**edi'tion** *n.* form in which book is published; number of copies of book, newspaper, etc. printed at one time; issue; copy or prototype.—**ed'itor** *n.* (*fem.* **ed'itress**) one who edits; one who conducts newspaper or periodical.—**edito'rial** *n.* leading article in newspaper;—*a.* pert. to work of editor.

educate (ed'-ū-kāt) *v.t.* bring up, as a child; cultivate and discipline, as the mind.—**ed'ucable** *a.* able to absorb education.—**educabil'ity** *n.*—**educa'tion** *n.* process of educating; upbringing; training.—**educa'tional** *a.*—**educa'tionally** *adv.*—**educa'tionist, educa'tionalist** *n.* one versed in theory or practice of education.—**ed'ucative** *a.* tending to educate.—**educa'tor** *n.*

educe (ē-dūs') *v.t.* draw out that which is latent; elicit; evoke.—**educ'ible** *a.*—**e'duct** *n.* that which is educed.—**educ'tion** *n.* process of educing.

eel (ēl) *n.* group of fishes of order Apodes, with elongated bodies and no ventral fins.

e'en, e'er (ēn, er) *contr.* for *even, ever.*

eerie, eery (ē'-ri) *a.* weird; frightening;—**ee'rily** *adv.*—**ee'riness** *n.*

efface (e-fās') *v.t.* erase or scratch out; rub out; wear away; obliterate; delete; destroy.—**efface'able** *a.*—**efface'ment** *n.* act of effacing.

effect (e-fekt') *n.* that which is produced by agent or cause; consequence; impression left on mind; reality;—*v.t.* produce, as cause or agent; bring about; achieve.—**effects'** *n.pl.* property; goods and chattels; devices used in plays to assist realism.—**effec'tible** *a.* practicable.—**effec'tive** *a.* efficient; powerful.—**effec'tively** *adv.*—**effec'tiveness** *n.*—**effec'tual** *a.* producing intended result.—**effectual'ity** *n.*—**effec'tually** *adv.*—**effec'tuate** *v.t.* bring to pass; accomplish.—**to give effect to,** carry out; accomplish.—**in effect,** really; for practical purposes.—**to take effect,** become operative.

effeminate (e-fem'-i-nạt) *n.* effeminate person;—*a.* unmanly; womanish; feeble; weak.—**effem'inacy** *n.*—**effem'inately** *adv.*—**effem'inateness** *n.*

effervesce (ef-er-ves') *v.i.* bubble, seethe, as liquid giving off gas; boil over—hence, be in state of excitement; froth up.—**efferves'cence** *n.*—**efferves'cent** *a.* seething or bubbling.

effete (e-fēt') *a.* no longer capable of bearing young; barren; sterile; unfruitful; worn-out.

efficacious (ef-i-kā'-shus) *a.* producing desired effect.—**effica'ciously** *adv.*—**effica'ciousness, efficac'ity, eff'-icacy** *n.*

efficient (e-fish'-ent) *a.* producing results; actively operative; capable; able; effective.—**effi'ciency** *n.*—**effi'ciently** *adv.*

effigy (ef'-i-ji) *n.* image of person; likeness in bas-relief, etc. on coins and medals; likeness; statue; figure.—*pl.* **eff'igies.**

effloresce (ef-lo-res') *v.t.* burst into bloom; blossom; (*Chem.*) lose water of crystallisation on exposure to air, so that crystals fall into powder.—**efflores'cence** *n.*—**efflores'cent** *a.*

effluent (ef'-lōō-ent) *a.* flowing out;—*n.* stream which flows out from another river or lake; liquid sewage in course of purification; industrial or radio-active waste discharged into rivers or sea.—ef'fluence *n.* flowing out; issue.

effluvium (e-flŏŏ'-vi-um) *n.* foul smell.—*pl.* efflu'via.—efflu'vial *a.*

effort (ef'-ort) *n.* putting forth exertion of strength or power, bodily or mental; attempt; endeavour.—eff'ortless *a.* without effort.

effrontery (e-frun'-tẹr-i) *n.* brazen impudence; excessive assurance; audacity.

effulge (e-fulj') *v.i.* shine brightly; become famous.—efful'gence *n.* great brightness, splendour, or lustre.—efful'gent *a.* diffusing flood of light; splendid.

effuse (e-fūz') *v.t.* pour out or forth; shed (blood);—*n.* effusion; shedding;—*a.* profuse; not compact.—effu'sion *n.* act of pouring out; that which is poured out; verbose piece of writing.—effu'sive *a.* pouring out profusely.—effu'sively *adv.*—effu'siveness *n.*

egalitarian (e-gal-it-ā'-ri-ạn) *n.* and *a.* believing in principle of equality.

egg (on) (eg) *v.t.* urge on; encourage one to take action.

egg (eg) *n.* oval body laid by birds, fish, reptiles, etc., in which the embryo continues development apart from parent body; matured female germ cell or ovum; anything eggshaped; (*Slang*) a bomb.—egg'-cell *n.* ovum, as distinct from any other cells associated with it.—egg'-flip or -nog *n.* drink compounded of ale, spirits, with beaten eggs, sugar and spice.—egg'-head *n.* (U.S.) intellectual.

eglantine (eg'-lan-tīn) *n.* sweet brier; honeysuckle.

ego (ē'-gō, eg'-ō) *n.* I; the whole person; self; personal identity.—e'gocentric *a.* self-centred; egoistic.—e'gocentricism, e'gocentricity *n.*—e'goism *n.* selfishness; self-interest.—e'goist *n.*—egoist'ic, egoist'ical *a.*—e'gotism *n.*—e'gotist *n.*—egotist'ic, -al *a.*—egotist'ically *adv.*

egregious (e-grē'-jus) *a.* remarkable; prominent; notable; notorious.—egre'giously *adv.*

egress (ē'-gres) *n.* act of leaving an enclosed place; exit; right of departure.—egres'sion *n.*

eider (I'-dẹr) *n.* the eider duck, species of sea-ducks yielding the commercial eiderdown. — ei'der-down *n.* breast-down with which female eider-duck lines its nest, used for stuffing quilts and cushions; quilt stuffed with this down.

eight (āt) *n.* and *a.* one more than seven, written as 8 or VIII.—eight'een *n.* and *a.* eight more than ten, written 18 or XVIII.—eight-eenth *n.* and *a.* eighth after tenth, written 18th.—eight'fold *a.* eight times any quantity.—eighth *n.* and *a.* first after seventh;—*n.* one of eight equal parts of a whole, written ⅛.—eight'ieth *a.* ordinal corresponding to eighty, coming after seventyninth; written 80th;—*n.* one of eighty equal parts of a whole, written ⅟₈₀.—eight'y *n.* and *a.* eight times ten; four-score.—eight'some *n.* Scottish reel for eight dancers.—one over the eight, (*Colloq.*) intoxicated.

eisteddfod (I-stedh'-vod) *n.* annual assembly of Welsh bards and musicians.

either (I'-, ē'-THẹr) *a.* or *pron.* one or the other; one of two; each;—*adv.* or *conj.* bringing in the first of alternatives or strengthening an added negation.

ejaculate (ē-jak'-ū-lāt) *v.t.* utter suddenly and briefly; eject;—*v.i.* utter ejaculations.—ejac'ulation *n.* short, sudden exclamation; sudden emission.—ejac'ulatory *a.*

eject (ē-jekt') *v.t.* throw out; cast forth; turn out; dispossess of house or estate.—ejec'tion *n.* act of casting out.—eject'ment *n.* expulsion; dispossession; (*Law*) forcible removal of defaulting tenant by legal process from land or house.—ejec'tor *n.*

eke (ēk) *v.t.* add to or augment; lengthen.—to eke out, supplement; prolong.

elaborate (e-lab'-o-rāt) *v.t.* put much work and skill on; work out in detail; take pains with;—*a.* worked out in details; highly finished; complicated. — elab'orately *adv.* — elab'orateness, elabora'tion *n.* act of elaborating; progressive improvement.

elapse (e-laps') *v.i.* of *time*, pass silently by; slip away.

elastic (e-las'-tik) *a.* possessing property of recovering original form, when distorting or constraining force has been removed; not inflexible; resilient; springy;—*n.* fabric whose threads are interwoven with strands of rubber.—elastic'ity *n.*

elate (e-lāt') *a.* in high spirits;—*v.t.* raise or exalt spirit of; make proud; elevate (as with success).—elat'edly *adv.*—ela'tion *n.* pride; exultation due to success.

elbow (el'-bō) *n.* joint between arm and forearm; right angle bend for joining two pipes; any sharp bend or turn;—*v.t.* and *i.* push with the elbows; jostle.—el'bow-grease *n.* (*Colloq.*) hard work, as in rubbing vigorously.—el'bow-room *n.* ample room for free movement.

elder (el'-dẹr) *a.* older; senior; prior;—*n.* one who is older; senior; senator; office-bearer in the Church of Scotland.—eld'erliness *n.*—eld'erly *a.* somewhat old.—**eld'est** *a.* oldest of a family.

elder (el'-der) *n.* a deciduous shrub which has white clustered flowers, and yields berries used for making wine.

elect (e-lekt') *v.t.* choose; choose by vote; appoint to office; select;—*v.i.* determine on any course of action;—*a.* chosen; selected from a number; (after a noun), appointed but not yet in office;—*n.* those predestined to eternal life.—**elec'tion** *n.* act of electing or choosing; public voting for office.—**electioneer'** *v.i.* canvass for votes.—**elec'tive** *a.* appointed by; dependent on choice.—**elect'ively** *adv.*—**elect'or** *n.* one with right to vote at election; title of German princes with privilege of choosing the Holy Roman Emperor;—*fem.* **elect'ress.**—**elect'oral** *a.*—**elect'orate** *n.* whole body of electors

electric (e-lek'-trik) *a.* pert. to, charged with, worked by, producing, electricity.—**electric arc,** incandescent vapour occurring between two points of gap in electric circuit.—**electric battery,** apparatus for generating electricity by chemical action.—**electric chair,** used in U.S.A. for electrocuting criminals.—**electric circuit,** path followed by electricity.—**electric current,** flow of electricity.—**electric eel,** fresh-water fish of the S. American llanos capable of inflicting shocks.

electrical (e-lek'-tri-kal) *a.* pert. to electricity esp. in a non-functional sense.—**elec'trically** *adv.*

electrician (e-lek-trish'-an) *n.* one who studies the science of electricity; who makes or repairs electrical apparatus or attends to electrical installations.

electricity (e-lek-tris'-i-ti) *n.* form of energy resulting from movement or separation of electrons.

electrify (e-lek'-tri-fi) *v.t.* charge with electricity; install electric system of light, power, etc.; thrill, startle, excite by unexpected statement or action;—*pa.t.* and *pa.p.* **elec'trified.**

electrocute (e-lek'-tro-kūt) *v.t.* cause death by electric shock.—**electrocu'tion** *n.*

electrode (e-lek'-trōd) *n.* metallic conductor of open electric circuit in contact with some other kind of conductor such as electrolyte, gas, etc.; wire used in electric arc welding; plate of vacuum tube, X-ray bulb, or radio valve.

electrolier (e-lek'-tro-lē'-er) *n.* ornamental pendant or stand fitted to carry several electric lamps.

electrolysis (e-lek-trol'-is-is) *n.* resolution of dissolved or fused chemical compounds into elements by passing current of electricity through them.

—**elec'trolyse** *v.t.* subject to electrolysis.—**elec'trolyte** *n.* liquid which carries electric current between two electrodes.

electro-magnet (e-lek'-tro-mag'net) *n.* mass of soft iron temporarily magnetised by being placed within coil of insulated copper wire through which current of electricity is passing.—**elec'tro-magnet'ic** *a.*—**elec'tro-mag'netism** *n.*

electron (e-lek'-tron) *n.* electrically charged particle, constituent of all atoms, around whose nuclei they revolve in orbits.—**electron'ics** *n.* branch of physics which deals with the behaviour of free electrons.—**electron microscope,** instrument of immense magnifying power in which controlled rays of electrons are used instead of light rays.—**electronic brain,** computer.

electro-negative (e-lek'-tro-neg'-a-tiv) *a.* carrying negative charge of electricity; having tendency to form negative ions.

electro-plate (e-lek'-tro-plāt) *v.t.* cover a metal with coating of silver, by means of electrolysis;—*n.* article so covered.

electro-positive (e-lek'-tro-poz'-i-tiv) *a.* carrying positive charge of electricity; having tendency to form positive ions.

electro-statics (e-lek'-tro-stat'-iks) *n.* branch of electrical science which treats of behaviour of electricity in equilibrium or at rest.

electrotype (e-lek'-tro-tīp) *n.* a facsimile printing plate of type or illustrations.

eleemosynary (el-ē-mos'-i-na-ri) *a.* by way of charity; given in charity.

elegant (el'-e-gant) *a.* graceful; tasteful; refined; polished; comely.—**el'egantly** *adv.*—**el'egance** *n.* grace; beauty; propriety; gentility.

elegy (el'-e-ji) *n.* song of mourning after loss; funeral song.—**elegi'ac** *a.* pertaining to elegy; written in elegiacs;—**elegi'acs** *n.pl.* elegiac verse or couplets, each made up of hexameter or pentameter.—**el'egiacal** *a.*—**ele'giast** or **el'egist** *n.* writer of elegies.

element (el'-e-ment) *n.* first principle or rule; component part; ingredient; constituent; essential point; habitation most suited to particular animal; (*Chem.*) substance which cannot be separated into two or more substances; resistance wire of electric heater.—**el'ements** *n.pl.* bread and wine used in the Lord's Supper; fire, air, water and earth, supposed to be foundation of all things; physical forces of nature, as rain.—**element'al** *a.* of powers of nature; not compounded; basic; fundamental; tremendous.—**element'ary** *a.* pertaining to elements or first principles of anything; rudimentary; simple.

elephant (el'-e-fant) *n.* sub-order of ungulates (hoofed mammals) of which there are two species, Indian and African; largest four-footed animal, having long flexible trunk, two ivory tusks and exceedingly thick skin.—**elephant'ine** *a.* huge; unwieldy; ungainly.—**a white elephant,** usless gift.

elephantiasis (el-e-fan-tī'-a-sis) *n.* tropical disease in which there is gross enlargement of lower limbs and scrotum.

elevate (el'-e-vāt) *v.t.* lift up; raise to higher rank or station; elate; exhilarate; make louder or raise the pitch of (the voice); augment.—**el'evated** *a.* raised; promoted; dignified; exhilarated; (*Colloq.*) intoxicated.—**eleva'tion** *n.* act of elevating or state of being raised; elevated place, hill, height; (*Archit.*) geometrical projection, drawn to scale, of vertical face of part of building or object.—**el'evator** *n.* person or thing which lifts up; lift or hoist; in U.S. huge silo where grain is stored; rudder-like movable control surfaces hinged to edge of tail-plane of aeroplane.—**el'evatory** *a.* tending or having power to elevate.

eleven (e-lev'-n) *n.* and *a.* one more than ten, written as 11 or XI; full team at cricket, association football, or hockey.—**elev'enth** *a.* ordinal number corresponding to eleven, next after tenth;—*n.* one of 11 equal parts of a whole.

elf (elf) *n.* supernatural, diminutive being of folk-lore with mischievous traits; hobgoblin; dwarf;—*pl.* **elves.** —**el'fin** *n.* little elf; child;—*a.* dainty, like an elf.—**elf'ish, elv'an, elv'ish** *a.* elf-like; roguish.

elicit (e-lis'-it) *v.t.* draw out; extract; bring to light facts by questioning or reasoning; deduce.

elide (e-līd') *v.t.* cut off or suppress final vowel or syllable.—**eli'sion** *n.* suppression of vowel or syllable.

eligible (el'-i-ji-bl) *a.* legally qualified; fit to be chosen; desirable; suitable.—**el'igibleness, eligibil'ity** *n.*

eliminate (ē-lim'-i-nāt) *v.t.* remove; get rid of; set aside; separate; leave out of consideration; expel; obliterate.—**elim'inable** *a.* capable of being eliminated.—**elimina'tion** *n.*—**elim'-inator** *n.*

elision See **elide.**

élite (ā-lēt') *n.* choice or select body; pick or best part of society [*Fr.*].

elixir (e-liks'-ẹr) *n.* sovereign remedy; essence, vainly sought by alchemists, which would have power to transmute base metals into gold.—**elixir vitae,** elixir of life, cordial believed to bestow perpetual youth.

elk (elk) *n.* largest member of deer family, found in N. Europe and America where it is more commonly called the moose.

ell (el) *n.* measure of length in cloth, formerly taken from the forearm but now 1¼ yds.

ellipse (e-lips') *n.* regular oval, formed by line traced out by a point moving so that the sum of its distance from two fixed points always remains same; plane section across a cone not taken at right angles to the axis; deliberate omission of words within sentence.—**ellip'soid** *n.* closed solid figure of which every plane section is an ellipse.—**ellip'tic(al)** *a.* oval; pertaining to ellipse.

elm (elm) *n.* genus of trees, including common elm and wych elm.

elocution (el-o-kū'-shun) *n.* art of effective public speaking from point of view of enunciation, voice-production, delivery.—**elocu'tionary** *a.*—**elocu'tionist** *n.* teacher of elocution; one who specialises in verse-speaking.

elongate (ē'-long-gāt) *v.t.* make longer; lengthen; prolongate; extend; draw out; stretch out;—*a.* (*Bot.*) tapering.—**elonga'tion** *n.* act of stretching out; part extended.

elope (e-lōp') *v.i.* run away clandestinely, especially of woman who abandons home to run away with lover; abscond unexpectedly.

eloquence (el'-ō-kwens) *n.* art of expressing thought in fluent, impressive and graceful language; oratory; rhetoric; fluency.—**el'oquent** *a.*—**el'oquently** *adv.*

else (els) *adv.* besides; other; otherwise; instead.—**else'where** *adv.* in or to some other place.

elucidate (e-lū'-si-dāt) *v.t.* make clear or manifest; throw light upon; explain; illustrate.—**elucida'tion** *n.* act of throwing light upon or explaining.—**elu'cidative, elu'cidatory** *a.*—**elu'cidator** *n.*

elude (e-lūd') *v.t.* keep out of sight; escape by stratagem; evade; avoid; disappoint; baffle.—**elu'sion** *n.* .act of eluding; evasion.—**elu'sive** *a.* evasive; difficult to catch; deceptive.—**elu'sory** *a.* evasive.

elvan, elves, elvish See **elf.**

elver (el'-vẹr) *n.* young of the eel.

Elysium (e-lizh'-i-um) *n.* (*Myth.*) according to the Greeks, abode of the shades of virtuous dead in nether world where they lived a life of blessedness.—**Elys'ian** *a.*

emaciate (e-mā'-shi-āt) *v.t.* make lean; reduce to flesh and bones; —*v.i.* waste away with loss of strength; become extremely thin;— *a.* in a lean condition.—**ema'ciated** *a.* —**emacia'tion** *n.*

emanate (em'-a-nāt) *v.i.* issue from; originate; proceed from; arise (of intangible things).—**em′anant** *a.* flowing from.—**emana′tion** *n.* flowing out from; that which issues from a source; inert gas produced by radioactive decay.—**em′anative, em′anatory** *a.*

emancipate (e-man′-si-pāt) *v.t.* set free from slavery or servitude; set free from any restraint or restriction.—**emancipa′tion** *n.* state of being set free.—**emancipa′tionist** *n.* advocate of emancipation of slaves.—**eman′cipator** *n.*

emasculate (e-mas′-kū-lāt) *v.t.* castrate; deprive of masculine qualities; render effeminate.—**emascula′tion** *n.*—**emas′culatory** *a.*

embalm (em-bâm′) *v.t.* preserve a corpse from decay by means of balm, aromatic oils and spices; perfume; cherish tenderly memory of.—**embalm′er** *n.*—**embalm′ing, embalm′ment** *n.*

embank (em-bangk′) *v.t.* enclose or defend with bank, mound, or earthwork.—**embank′ment** *n.* act of embanking; earthwork built in low-lying ground, designed to carry road or railway; raised mound or dyke to prevent flooding.

embargo (em-bâr′-gō) *n.* in international law, order by which government prevents foreign ship from leaving port; order forbidding despatch of certain class of goods, usually munitions, to another country; general prohibition;—*pl.* **embar′goes;**—*v.t.* to lay an embargo upon.

embark (em-bârk′) *v.t.* put on board ship; enter on some business or enterprise;—*v.i.* go on board ship.—**embarka′tion** *n.*

embarrass (em-bar′-ás) *v.t.* disconcert; to perplex; to impede; to involve one in difficulties, esp. regarding money matters.—**embarr′assed** *a.*—**embarr′assing** *a.* disconcerting.—**embarr′assment** *n.* state of perplexity; confusion; money difficulties.

embassy (em′-ba-si) *n.* person sent abroad as ambassador along with staff; one entrusted with message to foreign state; residence of ambassador.

embattle (em-bat′-l) *v.t.* furnish with battlements.—**embatt′lement** *n.*

embed (em-bed′) *v.t.* lay as in bed; bed in soil. Also **imbed′.**

embellish (em-bel′-ish) *v.t.* make beautiful or elegant with ornaments; add fanciful details to report or story.—**embell′isher,** *n.*—**embell′ishingly** *adv.*—**embell′ishment** *n.*

ember (em′-bėr) *n.* live piece of coal or wood;—*pl.* red-hot ashes.

embezzle (em-bez′-l) *v.t.* misappropriate fraudulently; purloin.—**embezz′lement** *n.*—**embezz′ler** *n.*

embitter (em-bit′-ėr) *v.t.* make bitter.

—**embitt′ered** *a.* exasperated; soured.

emblazon (em-blā′-zon) *v.t.* adorn with heraldic figures; deck in blazing colours.—**emblaze′** *v.t.* illuminate.—**embla′zonment** *n.*—**embla′zonry** *n.* art of emblazoning; heraldic devices on shield.

emblem (em′-blem) *n.* object, or representation of object, symbolising and suggesting to the mind something different from itself; sign; badge; symbol; device;—*v.t.* symbolise.—**em′blemise** *v.t.* represent by means of an emblem.—**emblemat′ic, -al** *a.*—**emblemat′ically** *adv.*

embody, imbody (em-, im-bod′-i) *v.t.* form into a body; incorporate; give concrete expression to; represent, be an expression of;—*pa.t.* and *pa.p.* **embod′ied.**—**embod′iment** *n.* act of embodying; bodily representation.

embolden (em-bōld′-n) *v.t.* give boldness or courage to; encourage; animate.

embolism (em′-bo-lizm) *n.* insertion of days between other days to adjust reckoning of time; (*Med.*) result of presence in blood-stream of a solid foreign substance, as a clot.—**embolis′mal** *a.*

emboss (em-bos′) *v.t.* raise or form design above surrounding surface, by pressure of a die on metal, leather, card-board or similar substances.—**embossed′** *a.*—**emboss′ment** *n.* boss or protuberance.

embouchure (om-bŏŏ-shŏŏr′) *n.* mouth of river, gun, etc.; mouthpiece of a wind instrument; different positions of the lip, etc. in playing wind instruments.

embower (em-bou′-ėr) *v.t.* lodge, or set in a bower; surround (with flowers).

embrace (em-brās) *v.t.* clasp in the arms; press to the bosom; avail oneself of; accept;—*n.* clasping in the arms; hug.

embrasure (em-brā′-zhur) *n.* bevel of door or window where sides slant on inside; indents or crenelles of a battlement; opening in parapet of fort to allow cannon-fire.

embrocate (em′-brō-kāt) *v.t.* moisten and rub with lotion, etc.—**embroca′tion** *n.* act of embrocating; lotion for rubbing on body.

embroglio See imbroglio.

embroider (em-broi′-dėr) *v.t.* ornament fabrics with threads of silk, linen, etc.; exaggerate a story.—**embroid′erer** *n.*—**embroid′ery** *n.* ornamental needlework.

embroil (em-broil′) *v.t.* involve in quarrel or strife; perplex; entangle; confound.—**embroil′ment** *n.*

embryo (em′-bri-ō) **embryon** (em′-bri-on) *n.* foetus during first months of pre-natal development; plant in rudimentary stage of development within seed; initial or rudimentary stage of anything;—*pl.* em'bryos;—*a.* rudimentary; in early stage.—embryol'ogy *n.* study of embryos.—embryon'ic *a.*

embus (em-bus') *v.t.* and *i.* put into, mount, bus, esp. of troops.

emend (e-mend') *v.t.* remove faults from; amend, esp. of correcting a text; alter for the better.—em'endate *v.t.*—emenda'tion *n.* correction.—em'endator *n.*—emen'datory *a.*

emerald (em'-er-ald) *n.* precious stone of beryl species, transparent and bright-green in colour.—Emerald Isle, Ireland.

emerge (e-merj') *v.i.* rise out of fluid; come forth; come into view.—emer'gence *n.* coming into view.—emer'gency *n.* state of pressing necessity; difficult situation; urgent need. —emer'gent *a.* emerging; rising into view.

emeritus (ē-mer'-i-tus) *n.* and *a.* one who has honourably resigned office to go into retirement.

emery (em'-er-i) *n.* naturally occurring mixture of corundum (impure aluminium oxide) and iron oxide, exceedingly hard and used as abrasive for polishing;—*v.t.* rub with emery.—emery paper, stiff paper coated with emery-powder for polishing.

emetic (e-met'-ik) *a.* inducing vomiting;—*n.* agent causing vomiting.

emigrate (em'-i-grāt) *v.i.* leave one's country to settle in another.—em'igrant *a.* pert. to emigration;—*n.* one who emigrates.—emigra'tion *n.*—émigré (ā'-mē-grā) *n.* emigrant, especially political refugee.

eminent (em'-i-nent) *a.* exalted in rank, office, or public estimation.—em'inence *n.* elevation; rising ground; height; rank; official dignity; fame; title of honour enjoyed by cardinals. —em'inently *adv.*

emir (e-mēr' or em'-ēr) *n.* title bestowed on chieftains in Moslem countries.

emissary (em'-i-sar-i) *n.* agent charged with secret mission; one sent on a mission.

emit (e-mit') *v.t.* send forth.—*pr.p.* emit'ting.—*pa.p.* emit'ted.—emis'sion *n.* the act of emitting; that which is emitted.—emis'sive *a.* emitting; emitted; radiating.

emmet (em'-et) *n.* an ant.

emollient (e-mol'-i-ent) *a.* softening; relaxing;—*n.* outward application of poultices, etc. to inflamed part of body.

emolument (e-mol'-ū-ment) *n.* profit arising from employment; pay; salary; wages; fee.

emotion (e-mō'-shun) *n.* pleasurable or painful condition of mind which may accompany sensations,

memories, or judgments; state of excited feeling or agitation.—emo'tional *a.* easily excited or upset; appealing to the emotions.—emo'tionalism *n.* tendency to emotional excitement. — emo'tionally *adv.* —emo'tionless *a.* emo'tive *a.* appealing to the emotions.

empanel, impanel (em-, im-pan'-el) *v.t.* place name on panel or list; enter names of jury on a panel; to form jury by roll-call.

empathy (em'-pa-thi) *n.* emotional effect of imagination which impels person to assume identity of another and experience the latter's reactions.

emperor (em'-per-or) *n.* ruler of an empire.

emphasis (em'-fa-sis) *n.* stress of utterance or force of voice given to words or syllables to draw attention to them; vigour of speech; intensity of expression; accent.—*pl.* em'phases. —em'phasise *v.t.* utter with emphasis; draw attention to importance of.—emphat'ic, emphat'ical *a.*

empire (em'-pīr) *n.* imperial power; dominion; country with its satellite states under rule of an emperor.

empiric, empirical (em-pir'-ik, -al) *a.* based on results of experiment, observation, or experience, and not from reasoning; having reference to actual facts; experimental.—empir'ic *n.* one who depends for his knowledge entirely on experience.—empir'ically *adv.*—empir'icism *n.* philosophical doctrine that assumes that all our knowledge and mental possessions are product of purely sensuous experience; formulation of scientific laws by process of observation and experiment; quackery.—empir'icist *n.*

emplacement (em-plās'-ment) *n.* place or site of building; fortified platform, pit, or shelter for gun; placing in position.

employ (em-ploi') *v.t.* give occupation to; make use of; hire or engage; exercise; occupy.—employ'able *a.* fit for employment; capable of being employed.—employee' *n.* one employed at wage or salary.—employ'er *n.*—employ'ment *n.* act of employing or using; state of being employed.

emporium (em-pō'-ri-um) *n.* place of extensive commerce or trade; mart; market; big shop; commercial city;—*pl.* empo'ria.

empower (em-pou'-er) *v.t.* give legal or moral power or authority to; authorise.

empress (em'-pres) *n.* wife of emperor; female having similar power to that of an emperor.

empty (emp'-ti) *a.* containing nothing; void; vacant; unoccupied; destitute; hollow; unreal; senseless; inane;—*v.t.* make empty; pour out;

drain;—*v.i.* become empty; discharge;—*pa.t.* and *pa.p.* **emp'tied;**—*n.* empty container.—*pl.* **emp'ties.**—**emp'tiness** *n.* state of being empty.

emu (ē'-mū) *n.* large flightless bird, native of Australia.

emulate (em'-ū-lāt) *v.t.* strive to equal or excel in qualities or actions; vie with; rival; compete with; imitate.—**emula'tion** *n.* act of attempting to equal or excel.—**em'ulative** *a.* imitating with idea of excelling another.

emulsion (e-mul'-shun) *n.* colloidal suspension of one liquid in another; coating of silver salts on photographic film or plate.—**emul'sic** *a.*—**emulsifica'tion** *n.* process of making an emulsion.—**emul'sify** *v.t.*—**emul'sive** *a.*

enable (en-ā'-bl) *v.t.* make able; authorise; empower; fit; qualify.

enact (en-akt') *v.t.* make into a law; act part of.—**enact'ing** *a.*—**enact'ive** *a.*—**enact'ment** *n.* passing of bill into law; decree; law.

enamel (en-am'-el) *n.* vitreous compound fused into surface of metal, pottery, or glass; hard, glossy surface of tooth; paint with glossy finish;—*v.t.* coat or paint with enamel;—*pr.p.* **enam'elling;**—*pa.t.* and *pa.p.* **enam'elled.**

enamour (en-am'-ur) *v.t.* inflame with love; captivate; charm; fascinate.—**enam'oured** *a.*

encage (en-kāj') *v.t.* shut up in cage.

encamp (en-kamp') *v.t.* form into camp;—*v.i.* settle in or pitch camp; settle down temporarily.—**encamp'ment** *n.* place where troops or others have pitched a camp; act of encamping.

encapsulate (en-kap'-su-lāt) *v.t.* enclose in capsule.

encase, incase (en-, in-kās') *v.t.* enclose in case or linings.—**encase'ment** *n.*

enchain (en-chān') *v.t.* fasten with chain; link together; hold fast.—**enchain'ment** *n.*

enchant (en-chant') *v.t.* charm by sorcery; hold, as by a spell.—**enchant'ed** *a.* delighted; held by a spell.—**enchant'er** *n.* (*fem.* **enchant'ress**) one who enchants; sorcerer.—**enchant'ingly** *adv.*—**enchant'ment** *n.* act of enchanting; incantation; magic; delight; fascination; rapture.

encircle (en-serk'-l) *v.t.* enclose in a circle; surround; gird in; embrace; circumscribe.—**encir'clement** *n.*

enclave (en-klāv') *n.* territory entirely surrounded by territories of another power or local authority; anything entirely enclosed into something else.

encloister (en-klois'-ter) *v.t.* shut up in a cloister; immure.

enclose, inclose (en-, in-klōz') *v.t.*

shut in; surround; envelope; wrap up.—**enclos'ure** *n.* act of enclosing; ground fenced in; part of sports ground for spectators; something enclosed in letter or package; container.

encomium (en-kō'-mi-um) *n.* high commendation; formal praise;—*pl.* **enco'miums.**

encompass (en-kum'-pas) *v.t.* describe a circle round; encircle.—**encom'passment** *n.* investment; state of being encircled.

encore (ong-kōr') *interj.* again! once more!—*n.* recall awarded by audience to performer, etc.; the item repeated;—*v.t.* applaud with encore.

encounter (en-kount-er) *v.t.* meet face to face; meet unexpectedly; meet in a hostile manner; contend against; confront;—*n.* unexpected meeting; fight or combat.

encourage (en-kur'-āj) *v.t.* give courage to; inspire with hope; embolden. — **encour'agement** *n.* that which gives courage; act of encouraging.—**encour'aging** *a.* inspiring with hope of ultimate success.—**encour'agingly** *adv.*

encroach (en-krōch') *v.i.* invade rights or possessions of another; intrude on other's property.—**encroach'er** *n.*—**encroach'ingly** *adv.*—**encroach'ment** *n.*

encrust, encrustation See **incrust.**

encumber (en-kum'-ber) *v.t.* load; impede movements of; burden; saddle with debts.—**encum'brance** *n.* burden; legal claim on an estate.

encyclical (en-sīk'-lik-al) *a.* intended to circulate among many people and in many places.

encyclopedia, encyclopaedia (en-sī-klō-pē'-di-a) *n.* works which give detailed account of whole field of human knowledge, or of some particular section in it.—**encyclope'dian** *a.*—**encyclope'dic** *a.*—**encyclope'dist** *n.*

encyst (en-sist') *v.t.* or *i.* enclose or become enclosed in sac or cyst.

end (end) *n.* extreme point of line; last part in general; termination; ending; limit; extremity; issue; result; object; purpose; death;—*v.t.* bring to end or conclusion; destroy; put to death;—*v.i.* come to ultimate point; finish; be finished; cease.—**end'ed** *a.*—**end'ing** *n.*—**end'less** *a.* without end; everlasting; incessant; fruitless.—**end'lessly** *adv.*—**end'lessness** *n.*—**end'long** *a.* lengthwise; continuously; on end.—**end'most** *a.* at the end; farthest.—**at a loose end,** bored.—**at one's wits' end,** perplexed; unable to proceed.—**to make both ends meet,** balance income and expenditure.

endanger (en-dān'-jer) *v.t.* place in

jeopardy; expose to loss or injury.—endan'germent n.

endear (en-dēr') v.t. render dear or more beloved.—**endeared'** a. beloved.—**endear'ing** a.—**endear'ingly** adv.—**endear'ment** n. state of being, or act of, endearing; tender affection; loving word; caress.

endeavour (en-dev'-ur) v.i. exert strength for accomplishment of object; attempt; try; strive; aim;—n. attempt; trial; effort; struggle; essay.—**endeav'ourer** n.

endemic, endemical (en-dem'-ik, -al), **endemial** (en-dē'-mi-al) a. used of a disease constantly recurring in a particular area.—**endem'ic** n. disease peculiar to one district or people, in contrast with epidemic.—**endem'ically** adv.

endiron See andiron.

endive (en'-div) n. annual plant resembling chicory, used for salads after blanching.

endocrine (en'-dō-krin) a. (Zool.) describing tissues and organs giving rise to internal secretion.—**endocrine glands**, ductless glands manufacturing secretions passed directly into blood stream.—**endocrinol'ogy** n. study of internal secretions of ductless glands.

endogamy (en-dog'-am-i) n. custom of compulsory marriage within the limits of tribe or clan or between members of same race.—**endog'amous** a.

endoparasite (en-dō-par'-a-sīt) n. parasite living inside body of its host.

endorse, indorse (en-, in-dors') v.t. write (esp. to sign one's name) on back of, as cheque; back (bill, etc.); sanction; confirm; ratify; enter, on back of licence, convictions for infringements; load or burden.—**endors'able** a.—**endorse'ment** n. act of endorsing.—**endors'er** n.

endoscope (en'-dō-skōp) n. (Med.) instrument for inspecting cavities of internal parts of the body.

endoskeleton (en-dō-skel'-e-ton) n. (Biol.) internal hard supporting structures, as bones, of the body.—**endoskel'etal** a.

endosperm (en'-dō-sperm) n. (Bot.) nutritive starchy tissue which surrounds the embryo in many seeds.—**endosper'mic** a.

endow (en-dou') v.t. give a dowry or marriage-portion to; settle, by deed or will, permanent income on; enrich or furnish.—**endow'er** n.—**endow'ment** n. act of settling fund or permanent provision for institution or individual; grant; bequest; natural capacity.

endure (en-dūr') v.t. remain firm under; bear with patience; put up with; sustain; suffer; tolerate;—v.i. continue; last.—**endur'able** a. can be endured, borne, or suffered.—**endurableness** n.—**endur'ably** adv.—**endurance** n. power of enduring; act of bearing pain or distress; continuance; patience; fortitude; stamina.—**endur'er** n.—**endur'ing** a. and n.—**endur'ingly** adv.—**endur'ingness** n. durability; permanence.

enema (en'-e-ma, e-nē'-ma) n. liquid solution injected into intestine through rectum.

enemy (en'-em-i) n. one actuated by hostile feelings; armed foe; opposing army;—a. of an enemy; due to enemy.

energy (en'-er-ji) n. vigour; force; activity; (Mech.) power of doing mechanical work; (Phys.) equivalent of mass.—**energet'ic**(al) a. exerting force; vigorous; active; forcible.—**energet'ically** adv.—**ener'gic** a. exhibiting energy.—**en'ergise** v.t. give energy to;—v.i. act energetically.

enervate (en'-er-vāt) v.t. deprive of nerve, strength, or courage;—a. spiritless.—**en'ervating, ener'vative** a.—**enerva'tion** n. lack of spirit or courage.

enfeeble (en-fē'-bl) v.t. render feeble; deprive of strength; weaken; debilitate; enervate.—**enfee'blement** n.

enfeoff (enfef') v.t. give a fief to; (Law) bestow or convey the fee-simple of an estate.—**enfeoff'ment** n.

enfilade (en-fi-lād') n. line or straight passage; narrow line, as of troops in marching; fire from artillery or small arms which sweeps line from end to end;—v.t. direct enfilading fire.

enfold See infold.

enforce (en-fōrs') v.t. give strength to; put in force; impress on mind; compel; impose (action) upon; execute.—**enforce'able** a.—**enforce'edly** adv. under threat or compulsion.—**enforce'ment** n.

enfranchise (en-fran'-chīz) v.t. set free from slavery; extend political rights to; grant privilege of voting in parliamentary elections.—**enfran'chisement** n.

engage (en-gāj') v.t. bind by contract, pledge, or promise; hire; order; employ; undertake; occupy; attract; bring into conflict; interlock;—v.i. begin to fight; employ oneself (in); promise.—**engaged'** a.—**engage'ment** n. act of engaging; state of being engaged; obligation; pledge; betrothal; occupation; battle; encounter.—**engag'ing** a. attractive.

engender (en-jen'-der) v.t. beget; cause to exist; sow seeds of; breed; occasion or cause (strife).

engine (en'-jin) n. mechanical contrivance for producing and conveying motive power; machine; locomotive; instrument of war; agency;

means;—*a.* pert. to engines;—*v.t.* furnish with engines.—**engineer'** *n.* one who constructs, designs, or is in charge of engines, machines, military works, or works of public utility (roads, docks, etc.);—*v.t.* contrive; bring about; arrange.—**engineer'ing** *n.* art of constructing and using machines or engines; profession of engineer.—**civil engineering**, business of constructing railways, bridges, etc.

English (ing'-glish) *a.* belonging to England or its inhabitants:—*n.* the people or the language of England;—*v.t.* render into English.

engraft, ingraft (en-, in-graft') *v.t.* graft on; plant deeply; incorporate; add to—**engraft'ment** *n.*

engrain See ingrain.

engrave (en-grāv') *v.t.* draw on metal plate design or picture by means of incised line or on wood by leaving raised surface; imprint; make a deep impression;—*v.i.* practise art of engraving.—**engrav'er** *n.*—**engrav'ing** *n.* art of cutting designs, etc. on wood, metal, or stone; impression taken from an engraved block or plate; a print.

engross (en-grōs') *v.t.* occupy wholly; absorb; increase in bulk; enlarge; copy in a large fair hand or in legal form; monopolise.—**engross'er** *n.*—**engross'ing** *n.* **engross'ment** *n.*

engulf, ingulf (en-, in-gulf') *v.t.* swallow up or absorb as in a gulf; overwhelm; encompass wholly.—**engulf'ment** *n.*

enhance (en-hans') *v.t.* heighten; intensify; increase in value or worth; add to the effect.—**enhance'-ment** *n.*

enigma (en-ig'-ma) *n.* obscure question or saying difficult of explanation; anything or anybody puzzling; riddle.—**enigmat'ic(al)** *a.* obscure and ambiguous.—**enigmat'ically** *adv.*

enjoin (en-join') *v.t.* direct with authority; command; order; impose; (*Law*) prohibit by judicial order; put an injunction on.—**enjoin'ment** *n.*

enjoy (en-joi') *v.t.* delight in; take pleasure in; have use or benefit of.—**enjoy'able** *a.* affording pleasure.—**enjoy'ably** *adv.*—**enjoy'ment** *n.* condition of enjoying; cause of joy or gratification.

enlarge (en-lärj') *v.t.* and *i.* make or become larger; increase; be diffuse in speaking or writing; set free.—**enlarged'** *a.*—**enlar'gedly** *adv.*—**enlar'gedness** *n.*—**enlarge'ment** *n.* act of enlarging; state of being enlarged; increase; expansion; photograph which has been enlarged.

enlighten (en-līt'-en) *v.t.* shed light on; give information to; instruct; make clear.—**enlight'enment** *n.* act of enlightening; state of being enlightened.

enlist (en-list') *v.t.* enter on a list; enrol; secure support of;—*v.i.* engage in public service, as soldiers; enter heartily into a cause.—**enlist'ment** *n.*

enliven (en-līv'-n) *v.t.* give life, action, or motion to; quicken; excite; make gay.—**enliv'ener** *n.*

enmesh (en-, em-mesh') *v.t.* catch in mesh or net; entangle; trap.—**enmesh'ment** *n.*

enmity (en'-mi-ti) *n.* quality of being an enemy; hostile or unfriendly disposition; hatred; hostility.

ennoble (en-nō'-bl) *v.t.* make noble; raise to peerage; raise; exalt; elevate; dignify.—**enno'blement** *n.*

ennui (ong'-nwē) *n.* boredom; feeling of intense weariness; listlessness due to satiety or lack of interest.—**ennuyé** (ong-nwē'-yā) *a.* bored; in state of ennui.

enormous (e-nor'-mus) *a.* huge; vast; excessive; prodigious; immense; colossal; gross; atrocious.—**enor'mity** *n.* quality of being enormous; gross offence; great wickedness; atrocity.—**enor'mously** *adv.*—**enor'mousness** *n.*

enough (e-nuf') *a.* as much or as many as need be; sufficient; adequate;—*n.* sufficiency;—*adv.* sufficiently; fully.

enquire, enquiry See inquire, inquiry.

enrage (en-rāj') *v.t.* fill with rage; provoke to frenzy or madness; anger immoderately.—**enraged'** *a.* angry; furious.

enrapture (en-rap'-chūr) *v.t.* delight excessively; charm.—**enrap'tured, enrapt'** *a.* delighted beyond measure; enchanted; entranced.

enrich (en-rich') *v.t.* make rich; add to; adorn; enhance.—**enrich'ment** *n.*

enrobe (en-rōb') *v.t.* robe; dress; clothe; invest.—**enrobe'ment** *n.*

enrol, enroll (en-rōl') *v.t.* enter name in roll or register; engage; enlist;—*pr.p.* **enroll'ing**;—*pa.t.* and *pa.p.* **enrolled'**—**enrol'ment** *n.* act of enrolling; register.

ensanguine (en-sang'-gwin) *v.t.* smear with blood; make of crimson colour.

ensconce (en-skons') *v.t.* shelter, as with a sconce or fort; protect; hide securely; screen.

ensemble (ong-som'-bl) *n.* all parts taken together; general effect; combined effort by all performers; (*Mus.*) concerted playing by number of musicians.

enshrine (en-shrīn') *v.t.* enclose in shrine; consecrate; treasure with affection.—**enshrine'ment** *n.*

enshroud (en-shroud') *v.t.* cover with shroud; hide from view.

ensiform (en'-si-form) *a.* sword-shaped.

ensign (en'-sīn, -in) *n.* badge of rank or insignia of office; colours of a regiment; national flag displayed on board ship; commissioned officer entrusted with safe-keeping of regiment's ensign (rank abolished in 1871); (*U.S.*) lowest commissioned Navy rank.—**en'signcy**, **en'signship** *n.* rank of ensign.

ensilage (en'-sil-āj) *n.* process of storing crops such as hay, etc. while green, to serve as winter food for cattle; fodder so stored.

enslave (en-slāv') *v.t.* reduce to slavery or bondage.—**enslaved'** *a.*—**enslave'ment** *n.*

ensnare, **insnare** (en-, in-snār') *v.t.* catch in snare; entrap; entangle.

ensue (en-sū') *v.i.* follow; happen after; to be consequence of.—**ensu'ing** *a.*

ensure (en-shoōr') *v.t.* make sure, safe, or certain; bring about; insure.

entablature (en-tab'-la-tūr) *n.* in classic architecture, ornamental, horizontal portion of building resting upon supporting columns and consisting of architrave, frieze and cornice; erection for machinery, mounted on pillars.—Also **entab'lement.**

entail (en-tāl') *n.* law restricting inheritance of land to particular heir or class of heirs;—*v.t.* settle land on persons in succession, none of whom can then dispose of it; bring about or cause.—**entail'ment** *n.*

entangle (en-tang'-gl) *v.t.* twist or interweave so as not to be easily separated; ravel; knot; perplex; ensnare.—**entang'lement** *n.* confusion; barbed wire fence.

entente (ong-tongt') *n.* cordial agreement between nations, but not alliance.

enter (en'-tẹr) *v.i.* go or come into; pass within; pierce; penetrate; join (a society, etc.); put down one's name; share in.—**to enter on, upon,** begin; take possession of.

enter- (en'-ter) *Gk. prefix* used in construction of compound words relating to intestine.—**en'tera** *n.pl.* (*Med.*) intestines.—**en'teral** *a.* by way of the intestine.—**enter'ic** *a.* of or pertaining to intestine;—*n.* typhoid fever.—**enteri'tis** *n.* inflammation of intestines.

enterprise (en'-tẹr-prīz) *n.* that which is undertaken or attempted; force of character in launching out; daring spirit; bold attempt; venture; energy;—*v.t.* undertake.—**en'terprising** *a.* adventurous; go-ahead; energetic.—**en'terprisingly** *adv.*

entertain (en-tẹr-tān') *v.t.* receive a guest; show hospitality to; lodge; amuse; consider favourably; hold in mind.—**entertain'er** *n.*—**entertain'ing** *a.* amusing; diverting.—**entertain'ment** *n.* hospitality; amusement; public performance.

enthral, **enthrall** (en-thrawl') *v.t.* reduce to state of slavery or bondage; enslave; thrill; captivate; hold spellbound; — *pr.p.* **enthrall'ing.** — *pa.t.* and *pa.p.* **enthralled'.**—**enthral'ment** act of enthralling; state of being enthralled; bondage; slavery.

enthrone (en-thrōn') *v.t.* place on throne; raise to sovereignty; install, as bishop; exalt.—**enthrone'ment** *n.*

enthusiasm (en-thū'-zi-azm) *n.* passionate zeal for person or object; religious fervour; intense ardour; fanaticism; keen interest.—**enthusiast** *n.*—**enthusias'tic(al)** *a.*—**enthusias'tically** *adv.*—**enthuse'** *v.i.* (*Colloq.*) become enthusiastic over.

entice (en'tīs') *v.t.* draw on by arousing hope or desire; lead astray.—**entice'able** *a.* possible to be enticed or led astray.—**entice'ment** *n.* act of enticing; that which incites to evil; allurement; blandishment; inducement.—**entic'ing** *a.*—**entic'ingly** *adv.*

entire (en'tīr) *a.* complete in all parts; whole; unimpaired; chief; unmingled; not castrated.—**entire'ly** *adv.*—**entire'ness**, **entire'ty** *n.*

entitle (en-tī'-tl) *v.t.* give title to; name; qualify; fit for; give claim to.

entity (en'-ti-ti) *n.* real being; reality; existence; material substance.

entomb (en-tōōm') *v.t.* deposit in a tomb; inter; bury.—**entomb'ment.** *n.*

entomology (en-to-mol'-o-ji) *n.* scientific study, classification and collection of insects.—**entomolog'ical** *a.*—**entomolog'ically** *adv.*—**entomol'ogise** *v.t.* pursue study of insects;—**entomol'ogist** *n.*

entourage (ong-tōō-räzh') *n.* surroundings; one's habitual associates; retinue.

entr'acte (ong-trakt') *n.* interval or musical interlude between two acts of play.

entrails (en'-trālz) *n.pl.* bowels; intestines; guts; internal parts of anything.

entrain (en-trān') *v.t.* enter or put into railway train.

entrance (en'-trans) *n.* act of entering; right of access; door, gateway, or passage to enter by; beginning.—**en'trant** *a.* entering;—*n.* one who enters; competitor.

entrance (en-trans') *v.t.* put into a trance; fill with delight and wonder.—**entrance'ment** *n.*—**entranc'ing** *a.*

entrap (en-trap') *v.t.* catch, as in a trap; ensnare; entangle.—**entrap'ment** *n.*

entreat (en-trēt') *v.t.* ask earnestly; treat with;—*v.i.* pray.—**entreat'y** *n.* act of entreating; supplication; prayer.

entrée (ong'-trā) *n.* right of access; dish served between main courses; formal entry.

entrench, intrench (en-, in-trensh') v.t. dig a trench; surround, fortify with a trench;—v.i. encroach.—**entrench'ment** n. ditch or trench with parapet for defence; moat; rampart; encroachment.—**entren'ched** a. firmly established.

entrepreneur (ong'-tr-prĕ-nẹr) n. contractor; organiser of business, trade, or entertainment.

entropy (en'-trop-i) n. (Phys.) general tendency in natural processes for a certain quantity of energy to be dissipated and become unavailable for useful work.

entrust, intrust (en-, in-trust') v.t. deliver in trust; confide to care of.

entry (en'-tri) n. act of entering; narrow passage into court-yard; item noted down in ledger, catalogue, notebook.

entwine, intwine (en-, in-twīn') v.t. twist together; plait; embrace; encircle.

entwist (en-twist') v.t. twist round.

enumerate (e'nŭ'-mẹr-āt) v.t. count, one by one; name individually; give in detail.—**enu'meration** n. act of counting singly; detailed account; recapitulation.—**enu'merator** n.

enunciate (e-nun'-si-āt, e-nun'-shi-āt) v.t. state clearly; proclaim formally; announce officially; pronounce each syllable distinctly.—**enun'ciable** a.—**enuncia'tion** n. act of enunciating; articulation or manner of pronunciation; declaration or announcement.—**enun'ciator** n.

enure See **inure**.

enuresis (en-ū-rē'-sis) n. (Med.) inability to control discharge of urine; bed-wetting.

envelop (en-vel'-up) v.t. cover by folding or wrapping; surround; hide or conceal.—**envelope** (en'-vel-ōp) n. cover or wrapper, esp. cover of a letter.—**envel'opment** n. act of enveloping; wrapping.

envenom (en-ven'-um) v.t. impregnate with venom; poison; enrage; exasperate; embitter.

enviable, envious See **envy**.

environ (en-vī'-run) v.t. surround; encircle; envelop; hem in; invest.—**envi'ronment** n. external surroundings and conditions. — **envi'rons** n. pl. adjacent districts; neighbourhood; suburbs.

envisage (en-viz'-āj) v.t. look in the face of; face; imagine; conjure up mental picture of; visualise.

envoy (en'-voi) n. one dispatched upon errand or mission; diplomatic agent of country below rank of ambassador; messenger; courier.

envy (en'-vi) v.t. grudge another person's good fortune; feel jealous of;—pr.p. en'vying;—pa.p. en'vied.—n. pain or vexation excited by sight of another's superiority or success;

jealousy.—**en'viable** a.—**en'viably** adv.—**en'vious** a.—**en'viously** adv.

enzyme, enzym (en'-zim) n. complex organic substance which in solution produces fermentation and chemical change in other substances apparently without undergoing any change itself; form of catalyst; digestive ferment.—**enzymot'ic** a.

eocene (ĕ'-ō-sēn) a. (Geol.) term applied to the geological strata laid down at the beginning of the Tertiary Period.

eolith (ĕ'-ō-lith) n. oldest known flint implement used by prehistoric man.

eon See **aeon**.

epact (ĕ'-pakt) n. excess of solar over lunar month or year in number of days; moon's age in days on 1st Jan. of any particular year, used for fixing days of Easter and other movable feasts of the church.

epaulet, epaulette (ep'-ol-et) n. ornamental shoulder-piece or badge of rank.

ephedrine (ef'-e-drīn) n. an alkaloid drug from plant genus Ephedra.

ephemera (ef-em'-ẹr-a) n. pamphlets and cuttings of temporary interest and value; genus of insects, better known as may-flies, which live only for one day in the adult stage;—pl. **ephem'erae**.—**ephem'eral** a. transitory; fleeting; momentary.—**ephemeral'ity** n. transient glory.—**ephem'erous** a. short-lived; ephemeral.

epic (ep'-ik) n. long narrative poem, usually dealing with part of history of a nation; story or film of this nature;—a. in grand style; memorable; heroic.

epicene (ep'-i-sēn) a. common to both sexes;—n. person having characteristics of both sexes; hermaphrodite.

epicure (ep'-i-kūr) n. one who delights in food and drink; voluptuary; sensualist; gourmand; Sybarite.—**epicure'an** a. pert. to Epicurus (342-270 B.C.), Greek philosopher; voluptuous;—n. follower of Epicurus; sensualist.—**epicure'anism** n. doctrine that chief end of man was physical and mental happiness.

epicycle (ep'-i-sī-kl) n. circle whose centre moves round in circumference of a greater circle.—**epicy'clic** a.

epidemic, epidemical (ep-dem'-ik, -al) a. common to, or affecting, a whole people or community; prevalent; general.—**epidem'ic** n. appearance of infectious disease attacking whole communities within certain area and within certain period (cf. endemic).—**epidem'ically** adv.

epidermis (ep-i-dẹr'-mis) n. (Anat.) outer protective layer of skin which covers the dermis or true skin underneath; (Bot.) sheath, usually one cell in thickness, which forms layer over surface of leaves.— epider'matoid, epider'mic, epider'mal, epider'midal a.

epidiascope (ep-i-dī'-a-skōp) n. projector for throwing images of either opaque or transparent objects on to a screen.

epiglottis (ep-i-glot'-is) n. covering of elastic, cartilaginous tissue, which closes opening leading into larynx during act of swallowing.— epiglott'ic a.

epigram (ep'-i-gram) n. neat, witty, pointed, or sarcastic utterance.— epigrammat'ic, epigrammat'ical a.— epigrammat'ically adv.—epigram'matise v.t. compose an epigram on.— epigram'matist n.

epigraph (ep'-i-graf) n. inscription, esp. on a building; quotation from an author; appropriate motto or popular saying placed at beginning of book or chapter.

epilepsy (ep'-i-lep-si) n. violent, nervous affection, characterised by sudden convulsions, followed by temporary stoppage of breath and rigidity of the body.—epilep'tic n. one subject to epilepsy.

epilogue (ep'-i-log) n. short speech or poem recited at end of a play; conclusion of a literary work.

Epiphany (e-pif'-an-i) n. Church festival held on twelfth day after Christmas (6th Jan.) to commemorate manifestation of Christ to the Magi, the Wise Men of the East.

epiphyte (ep'-i-fīt) n. plant which grows on but does not draw nourishment from another plant.

episcopacy (e-pis'-ko-pas-i) n. government of church by bishops; office of bishop; prelacy; the body of bishops.—epis'copal a. belonging to or vested in bishops; governed by bishops.—episcopa'lian a. of episcopal system or church;—n. member or adherent of episcopal church.— episcopa'lianism n. system of church government by bishops.—epis'copally adv.—epis'copate n. bishopric; office of bishop.

episcope (ep'-i-skōp) n. optical lantern which projects image of opaque object on a screen (cf. epidiascope).

episode (ep'-i-sōd) n. incident; incidental narrative or series of events; (Mus.) intermediate passage between various parts of a fugue.— ep'isodal, episo'dial, episod'ic, episod'ical a.—episod'ically adv.

epistle (e-pis'-l) n. letter, written for instruction, as the epistles of St. Paul, St. Peter, etc. in the New Testament.—epis'tolary a. pert. to epistles or letters; transacted by letter.

epitaph (ep'-i-taf) n. inscription placed on tombstone or cenotaph in commemoration of the dead.

epithalamium (ep-i-tha-lā'-mi-um) n. nuptial song.—epithala'mial, epithalam'ic a.

epithelium (ep-i-thē'-li-um) n. cellular tissue covering cutaneous, mucous, and serous surfaces.—epithe'lial a.—epithelio'matous a.

epithet (ep'-i-thet) n. phrase or word used adjectivally to express quality or attribute of its object; a designation; appellation.—epithet'ic, -al a.

epitome (e-pit'-o-mē) n. brief summary; abridgement of book; abstract; synopsis; digest.—epit'omise v.t. comprise in brief; summarise; condense.—epit'omist n.

epoch (ep'-ok, ē'-pok) n. fixed point or duration of time from which succeeding years are reckoned; era; date; period; age.—e'pochal a.

equable (ek'-wa-bl, ē'-kwa-bl) a. uniform in action or intensity; not variable; of unruffled temperament. —equabil'ity, e'quableness n.—e'quably adv.

equal (ē'-kwal) a. having same magnitude, dimensions, value, degree, or the like; identical; capable; equable; fair or just;—n. a person of same rank, age, etc.;—v.t. be or make equal; become equal to;— pr.p. e'qualling;—pa.p. e'qualled.— equalisa'tion n.—e'qualise v.t. make or become equal.—equalitar'ian n. one who holds that all men are equal in status.—equal'ity n. state of being equal.—e'qually adv.—e'qualness n.

equanimity (ē-kwa-nim'-i-ti) n. evenness of mind or temper; composure; calmness.

equate (ē-kwāt') v.t. make equal; state or assume the equality of; reduce to an average; bring to common standard of comparison.— equa'tion n. act of making equal; allowance for inaccuracies; (Math.) expression of the equality of two like algebraic functions by using the sign of equality (=).—equa'tional a. —equa'tionally adv.

equator (ē-kwā'-tor) n. great circle supposed to be drawn round the earth 90° from each pole and dividing the globe into the N. & S. hemispheres; (Astron.) celestial equator, another name for the equinoctial.—equato'rial a. of or pertaining to equator;—n. astronomical telescope, so mounted that it automatically follows diurnal course taken by heavenly body under observation.—equato'rially adv.

equerry (ek'-we-ri) n. officer whose duty it is to accompany sovereign or royal prince when riding in state.

equestrian (e-kwes'-tri-an) a. pert. to horses or horsemanship; mounted on a horse.—n. (fem. eques'trienne) rider or circus-performer on a horse. —eques'trianism n.

equi- (ē'-kwi) *prefix* fr. L. *aequus*, equal, used in the construction of compound words.

equiangular (ē-kwi-ang'-gū-lạr) *a.* having equal angles.

equibalance (ē-kwi-bál'-ạns) *n.* equal weight; equilibrium;—*v.t.* counterbalance; counterpoise.—**equibal'anced** *a.*

equidistance (ē-kwi-dis'-tạns) *n.* equal distance from some point.—**equidis'tant** *a.*

equilateral (ē-kwi-lat'-ē-rạl) *a.* having all sides equal.

equilibrium (ē-kwi-lib'-ri-um) *n.* (*Mech.*) state of rest of a body produced by action and reaction, of a system of forces; equipoise; state of balance; poise.—**equilib'rate** *v.t.* balance exactly; counterpoise.—**equilib'rial** *a.* pert. to equilibrium.—**equilib'rist** *n.* rope-walker; acrobat.—**equilib'rity** *n.* state of being equally balanced; equilibrium.

equine, equinal (e'-kwīn, -ạl) *a.* pert. to a horse.—*n.* horse.

equinox (ē'-kwi-noks) *n.* time at which sun crosses equator, approx. 21st March and 22nd Sept., and day and night are equal;—*pl.* points at which sun crosses equator.—**equinoc'tial** *a.* pert. to equinoxes.—*n.* (*Astron.*) great circle in heavens corresponding to plane of equator when extended.

equip (e-kwip') *v.t.* fit out; supply with all requisites for service; furnish; provide; arm; to dress;—*pr.p.* **equip'ping.**—*pa.p.* **equipped'.**—**e'quipage** *n.* carriage, horses and attendants; accoutrements.—**equip'ment** *n.* act of equipping; state of being equipped; outfit, especially soldier's; apparatus.

equipment See equip.

equipoise (ē'-kwi-poiz) *n.* state of equality of weight or force; even balance; equilibrium; something used as a counterpoise.—*v.t.* counterbalance.

equitable (ek'-wit-ạ-bl) *a.* giving, or disposed to give, each his due; just.—**eq'uitableness** *n.*—**eq'uitably** *adv.* fairly; justly.

equitation (ek-wi-tā'-shun) *n.* skill in horsemanship; ride on horseback.

equity (ek'-wi-ti) *n.* fairness; equal adjustment or distribution; giving to each his due according to sense of natural right; body of law existing alongside Common and Statute Law.

equivalent (ē-kwiv'-ạ-lent) *a.* equal in value, power, import, etc.; commensurate; tantamount; synonymous; (*Chem.*) of equal valency;—*n.* something of equal value, etc.; word of equal meaning.—**equiv'alence** *n.* identical value; state or condition of being equivalent.—**equiv'alency** *n.* power in elements of combining with

or displacing one another in certain definite proportions.

equivocal (ē-kwiv'-ō-kạl) *a.* of double or doubtful meaning; questionable; ambiguous; doubtful; dubious.—**equiv'ocally** *adv.*—**equiv'ocalness** *n.*—**equiv'ocate** *v.i.* mislead; quibble; prevaricate. — **equivoca'tion** *n.* — **equiv'ocator** *n.*

era (ē'-ra) *n.* fixed point of time from which series of years is reckoned; epoch; time; age; memorable date or period.

eradicate (ē-rad'-i-kāt) *v.t.* pull up by roots; extirpate; exterminate; destroy.—**erad'icable** *a.*—**eradica'tion** *n.* act of eradicating; state of being eradicated; extirpation.

erase (e-rāz') *v.t.* rub or scrape out; efface; obliterate; cancel.—**era'sable** *a.*—**erased'** *a.*—**era'ser** *n.* one who or that which erases.—**era'sion, erase'ment** *n.* act of erasing; that which is erased; traces left by erasing.—**era'sure** *n.* erasion.

ere (ār) *adv.* before; sooner;—*prep.* before;—*conj.* sooner than.

erect (e-rekt') *v.t.* set upright; raise, as a building, etc.; elevate; construct;—*a.* upright; pointing upwards.—**erec'tion** *n.* act of erecting; anything erected; elevation; building.—**erect'or** *n.*

eremite (er'-e-mīt) *n.* religious zealot who lives apart; hermit.—**ere'mic** *a.* inhabiting deserts.

erg (erg) *n.* the absolute unit of measurement of work and energy in metric system; work done by a force which produces a velocity of a centimetre per second in a mass of one gram—1000 ergs equal one joule, the unit used in practice.—**ergatoc'racy** *n.* government by workers.

ergo (er'-gō) *adv.* therefore; consequently.

ergonomics (er-gon-om'-iks) *n.* study of fitting environment to human needs.

Erica (e-rī'-ka, er'-i-ka) *n.* genus of evergreen shrubs, popularly known as heath.

ermine (er'-min) *n.* member of weasel family, stoat, with slender body, about a foot long, and short legs; white winter coat of the stoat, prized as a fur; robe of judge in England.

erode (e-rōd') *v.t.* eat into; wear away; corrode.—**ero'dent** *n.* caustic.—**ero'sion** *n.* act or operation of eating away; corrosion.—**ero'sive** *a.*

Eros (ē'-ros, er'-os) *n.* (*Myth.*) Greek god of love.—**erot'ic** *a.* pert. to love; amatory;—*n.* love poem.—**erot'ics** *n.pl.* art of love.—**erot'ica** *n.* literature dealing with sexual love.—**erot'icism, er'otism** *n.* (*Psych.*) love in all its manifestations.

erotic etc. See Eros.

err (ẽr) v.i. commit a mistake; be mistaken; deviate; go astray; offend; sin; misjudge.—**errat'ic(al)** a. roving; eccentric; changeable; uncertain; capricious; not dependable.—**errat'ic** n. wanderer.—**errat'ically** adv.—**erra'tum** n. error in writing or printing; noted for correction;—pl. **erra'ta.**

errand (er'-and) n. commission; message.

errant (er'-ant) a. wandering; roving; wild; abandoned; vile;—n. knight-errant.—**err'antly** adv.—**err'antry** n. condition of knight-errant.

erratic, erratum etc. See **err.**

error (er'-or) n. deviation from right or truth; mistake; blunder; sin.—**erro'neous** a. wrong; incorrect; inaccurate; false.—**erro'neously** adv.—**erro'neousness** n. falsity.

ersatz (er-zats') a. substituted for articles in everyday use; artificial; makeshift.

erst (ẽrst) adv. formerly; of old; at first; till now; hitherto.—**erst'while** adv. formerly.

erubescent (er-ũ-bes'-ẽnt) a. reddish; rubicund; blushing. — **erubes'cence, erubes'cency** n.

eruct, eructate (ẽ-rukt', -tāt) v.i. belch.—**eructa'tion** n. belching.

erudite (er'-ũ-dīt) a. learned; deeply read; scholarly.—**er'uditely** adv.—**erudi'tion** n. learning; scholarship.

erupt (ẽ-rupt') v.i. throw out; break through; break out in eruptions.—**erup'tion** n. act of bursting forth; sudden sally; outburst of lava, ashes, gas, etc. from crater of volcano; rash on the skin.—**erup'tive** a. breaking forth or out.

erysipelas (er-i-sip'-e-las) n. contagious disease causing acute inflammation of the skin, generally in the face. Also known as 'St. Anthony's Fire' and 'Rose.'

escalade (es-ka-lād') n. mounting walls of a fortress by ladders;—v.t. scale.

escalate (esk'-a-lāt) v.i. grow, increase; rise; intensify, as war.—**escalation** n.

escalator (es'-ka-lā-tur) n. continuous, moving stairway.

escape (es-kāp') v.t. flee; evade; elude;—v.i. hasten away; avoid capture; become free from danger. —n. flight from danger; evasion; leakage (of gas, etc.); outlet for purposes of safety; garden-plant growing wild; conscious effort to forget mental troubles by taking up some other interest.—**escap'able** a.—**escapade'** n. wild prank or exploit.—**escape'ment** n. act or means of escaping; contrivance in a time-piece which connects wheel-work with pendulum, allowing a tooth to escape at each vibration.—**escap'ism** n. desire to escape from realities of life by concentrating on other interest. —**escap'ist** n.

escarp (es-kárp') v.t. cut into steep slope;—n. steep, sloping bank under rampart; sloping bank generally.—**escarp'ment** n. steep face of cliff with other side gradually sloping; escarp.

eschatology (es-ka-tol'-o-ji) n. department of theology which treats of so-called last things, such as death, return of Christ, resurrection and end of the world.

eschew (es-chōó') v.t. shun; avoid; abstain from.

escort (es'-kort) n. armed guard for a traveller, etc.; person or persons accompanying another on a journey for protection or as act of courtesy. —**escort'** v.t. accompany; convoy; conduct.

escritoire (es-krē-twár') n. writing-desk provided with drawers.

esculent (es'-kū-lent) a. suitable as food for man; edible; eatable;—n. something which is eatable.

escutcheon (es-kuch'-un) n. in heraldry, shield bearing armorial bearings; family shield; part of a vessel's stern on which her name is inscribed; ornamental plate or shield placed round keyhole opening.—**escutch'eoned** a.—**a blot on the escutcheon**, stain on good name of the family.

Eskimo, Esquimau (es'-ki-mō) n and a. one of an aboriginal people of Mongolian-Indian stock, thinly scattered along the northern seaboard of America and Asia and in many Arctic islands;—pl. **Es'kimos, Es'quimaux.**

esophagus (ē-sof'-a-gus) n. gullet See **oesophagus.**

esoteric (es-ō-ter'-ik) a. arising from within; applied to doctrines intended only for inner circle of initiates; secret; mysterious.

espalier (es-pal'-yẽr) n. lattice work or wired frame on which plants, especially fruit trees, are trained to grow.

esparto (es-pár'-tō) n. coarse grass of N. Africa and Spain, used in paper manufacture.

especial (es-pesh'-al) a. distinguished; pre-eminent; more than ordinary.—**espe'cially** adv.

Esperanto (es-pe-ran'-tō) n. universal auxiliary language.

espionage (es'-pi-on-āj or -āzh) n. practice of employing secret agents; spying.

esplanade (es-pla-nād) n. level space separating a citadel from the town; sloping parapet leading from fortress; promenade, esp. along seafront of a town.

espouse (es-pouz') v.t. marry; betroth; support, attach oneself to (a cause, etc.).—espous'al n. act of espousing; betrothing; adoption; support.—espous'als n.pl. promise of marriage; nuptials.—espous'er n.

esprit (es-prē') n. spirit; wit; liveliness; animation.—esprit de corps (es-prēd'-kor), loyalty and attachment to the body or corps of which one is a member.

espy (es-pī') v.t. catch sight of; see at a distance; discern; perceive;—v.i. look narrowly.—espi'al n. spying; observation; spy.

Esquimau See Eskimo.

esquire (es-kwīr') n. originally, squire or shield-bearer, one of two attendants on a knight; now courtesy title.

essay (es'-ā) n. trial; attempt; literary composition, shorter than a treatise.—essay' v.t. try; make experiment or trial of; endeavour.—es'sayist n. writer of essays.

essence (es'-ens) n. the very being or power of a thing; formal cause of being; peculiar nature or quality; being; essential part; concentration of active ingredients of substance in smaller mass; (Med.) solution of essential oils in rectified alcohol; perfume.—essen'tial a. belonging to essence; necessary to existence of a thing; inherent;—n. something indispensable; chief point; leading principle.—essential'ity n. quality of being essential; essential part.—essen'tially adv.—essen'tialness n.

establish (es-tab'-lish) v.t. make stable or firm; set up; found; decree by authority; confirm; prove; verify; substantiate; set up and endow state church by law.—estab'lished a. fixed; settled; on permanent staff, supported by the State.—estab'lisher n.—estab'lishment n. act of establishing; that which is established; institution; settlement; full number of a regiment; place of business, residence, etc.; church established by the State.—establishmentar'ian a. and n. supporting church establishment.—The Establishment n. derogatory term for entrenched authority.

estate (es-tāt') n. condition of life; rank; position; quality; property, real or personal; the total assets and liabilities of a bankrupt; total assets of deceased person at time of death; social or political group and class.—estate duties, taxes levied on property on death of owner.—Estates of the Realm, Lords Spiritual, Lords Temporal, and Commons.—the Three Estates, in France, nobles, clergy and middle class.—the Fourth Estate, satirical term for the press.—real estate, property in land.

esteem (es-tēm') v.t. regard with respect or affection; set value on; rate highly; estimate; consider;—

n. high regard; favourable opinion.

ester (es'-ter) n. (Chem.) a salt formed by interaction between ethers or alcohols and an acid.

esthetic See aesthetic.

estimable (es'-tim-abl) a. able to be estimated; worthy of regard.—es'timably adv.

estimate (es'-ti-māt) v.t. judge and form opinion of value of; compute; calculate; offer to complete certain work at stated cost;—n. appraisement; computed cost of anything; valuation.—es'timator n. one who calculates costs of material, labour, etc. for doing certain piece of work.—the estimates, official statement to parliament of probable expenses of government departments.

estivation, aestivation (es-ti-vā'-shun) n. state of torpor, affecting some insects, during dry summer months.—es'tival a. pertaining to or continuing throughout summer; aestival.—es'tivate v.i. (cf. hibernate).

estrange (es-trānj') v.t. alienate, as the affections; make unfriendly; divert from its original use, purpose, or possessor.—estranged' a.—estrange'ment n.

estuary (es'-tū-ar-i) n. narrow arm of sea at mouth of river, up which the tides penetrate.—es'tuarine a. pert. to estuary.

et cetera (et-set'-er-a) phrase meaning "and the others"; and so on; (abbrev.) etc., &c.—etcet'eras n.pl. small extras.

etch (ech) v.t. trace design on metal, glass, etc., by dissolving selected portions with a reagent;—v.i. practise this art.—etch'er n.—etch'ing n. act or art of etching; printed impression taken from etched plate.

eternal (ē-ter'-nal) a. without beginning or end in relation to time; everlasting; timeless; ceaseless; immortal; imperishable; (Colloq.) always recurring.—eter'nalise, eter'nise v.t. make eternal or immortal; perpetuate.—eter'nally adv.—eter'nity n. infinity of time; future state after death.

ether (ē'-ther) n. hypothetical nonmaterial medium supposed to permeate whole of space.—ethe'real a. celestial; airy; heavenly.—ethe-realisa'tion n.—ethe'realise v.t.—ethe'reality n. ethe'really adv.

ether (ē'-ther) n. volatile liquid, prepared by action of sulphuric acid on ethyl alcohol, used as solvent and as anaesthetic.

ethic, ethical (eth'-ik, -al) a. relating to morals or moral principles.—eth'ically adv.—eth'ics n.pl. philosophy which treats of human character and conduct, of distinction between right and wrong, and moral duty and social obligations.

ethnic, ethnical (eth'-nik, -al) *a.* pert. to races or peoples; ethnological.—**eth'nic** *n.* heathen; pagan.—**eth'nicism** *n.* paganism.—**ethnog'raphy** *n.* detailed study of physical characteristics and social customs of racial groups.—**ethnog'rapher** *n.*—**ethnograph'ic** *a.*—**ethnol'ogy** *n.* science of origin and distribution of races.—**ethnolog'ical** *a.*—**ethnol'ogist** *n.*

ethos (ē'-thos) *n.* character, customs and habits which distinguish a people or community from others.

ethyl (e'-thil) *n.* (*Chem.*) monovalent radical C_2H_2 with numerous compounds, e.g. **ethyl-acetate**, used as stimulant and solvent; **ethyl-chloride**, local anaesthetic used by dentists.

etiolate (ē'-ti-o-lāt) *v.t.* render pale by denying light and fresh air; blanch (celery, etc.);—*v.i.* become pale by being deprived of light, etc.—**etiola'tion** *n.*

etiology See **aetiology**.

etiquette (et'-i-ket) *n.* conventional code of good manners which governs behaviour in society; formal ceremonies prescribed by authority; decorum.

étude (ā-tóód') *n.* (*Mus.*) study; a short musical composition.

etymology (et-i-mol'-o-ji) *n.* investigation of origins and meanings of words and word-forms.—**etymolog'ical** *a.*—**etymolog'ically** *adv.*—**etymol'ogist** *n.* one versed in etymology.

eucalypt (ū'-ka-lipt) *n.* any member of the genus Eucalyptus.—**eucalyptus** *n.* gum tree of Australasia.—**eucalyp'tol** *n.* eucalyptus oil, colourless, aromatic, oily liquid distilled from leaves of the eucalyptus.

Eucharist (ū-ka-rist) *n.* offering of praise and thanksgiving in Christian Church; Holy Communion; partaking of consecrated elements at sacrament of the Lord's Supper.—**eucharis'tic, eucharis'tical** *a.*

euchre (ū'-ker) *n.* game of cards for two to four players.

Euclidean (ū-klid'-e-an) *a.* pert. to Euclid who founded school of mathematics about 300 B.C.; geometric; three-dimensional.

eugenic (ū-jen'-ik) *a.* pertaining to eugenics; relating to, or tending towards, production of fine offspring.—**eugen'ics** *n.pl.* scientific application of study of heredity to improve human race.—**eu'genist** *n.*

eulogy, eulogium (ū'-lo-ji, ū-lō'-ji-um) *n.* speech or writing in praise.—**eulog'ic, -al** *a.* commendatory; laudatory.—**eu'logise** *v.t.* speak in flattering terms.—**eu'logist** *n.*—**eulogist'ic** *a.* commendatory; laudatory; encomiastic; panegyrical. — **eulogist'ically** *adv.*

eunuch (ū'-nuk) *n.* human male from whom the testes have been removed;

castrated male, especially in Near East, in charge of women of the harem.

eupepsy, eupepsia (ū-pep'-si, -a) *n.* healthy normal digestion—opposed to *dyspepsia*.—**eupep'tic** *a.* having good digestion; being easy of digestion.

euphemism (ū'-fem-izm) *n.* figure of speech where less disagreeable word or phrase is substituted for a more offensive one.—**eu'phemise** *v.t.* or *v.i.* soften down an expression.—**euphemist'ic** *a.*

euphonium (ū-fō'-ni-um) *n.* brass instrument of saxhorn type.

euphony (ū'-fo-ni) *n.* pleasantness or smoothness of sound; assonance.—**euphon'ic, eupho'nious** *a.*—**eupho'niously** *adv.*

euphoria, euphory (ū-fōr'-i-a, ū'-for-i) *n.* sense of health and well-being; state of irrational happiness.—**euphor'ic** *a.*

euphuism (ū'-fū-izm) *n.* affected, elaborate, bombastic prose style of language, so called from *Euphues*, a work by John Lyly (1553-1606), in that style; a stilted expression.—**eu'phuist** *n.*—**euphuist'ic** *a.*

Eurasian (ūr-ā'-zi-an) *n.* offspring of mixed European and Asiatic parentage;—*a.* pert. to Europe and Asia considered as one land-mass or continent.

eurhythmics (ū-rith'-miks) *n.pl.* art of rhythmical free movement to music.

Eustachian (ū-stā'-ki-an) *a.* derived from Bartolommeo Eustachio (c. 1500-1574), an Italian anatomist.—**Eustachian tube**, open duct extending from throat near tonsils to middle ear.

eutectic (ū-tek'-tik) *a.* easily melted or fused.

euthanasia (ū-than-ā'-zi-a) *n.* easy, gentle, painless death, esp. if deliberately induced.—Also **euthan'asy**.

evacuate (e-vak'-ū-āt) *v.t.* make empty; withdraw from; excrete; discharge; quit.—**evacua'tion** *n.* act of evacuating, emptying out, withdrawing from; system by which noncombatants, in time of war, are sent to safe areas; (*Med.*) discharge of faecal matter from rectum.—**evac'uative** *a.*—**evac'uator** *n.*—**evac'uee** *n.* person, esp. child temporarily removed from dangerous area in time of war.

evade (e'vād') *v.t.* avoid by dexterity, artifice, or stratagem; elude; escape; avoid; shun.—**evad'ible** *a.*

evaluate (e-val'-ū-āt) *v.t.* determine value of.—**evalua'tion** *n.* estimation of worth; quantitative comparison of values.

evanesce (ev-a-nes') *v.i.* vanish; fade away.—**evanes'cence** *n.*—**evanes'cent** *a.* vanishing; fleeting; transitory;

transient; passing.—**evanes'cently** adv

evangel (e-van'-jel) n. good tidings; the Gospel; one of first four books of New Testament.—**evangel'ic, evangel'ical** a. consonant with the Gospel; applied to forms of Christianity which regard the atonement of Christ as central principle of Christian faith; orthodox.—**evangel'ical** n. one who holds views of evangelical school. — **evangel'ically** adv.—**evangel'icism, evangel'icalism, evan'gelism** n. religious movement to spread actively tenets of evangelical school.—**evangelisa'tion** n. preaching of the Gospel; conversion.—**evan'gelise** v.t. and i. convert, by preaching the Gospel.—**evan'gelist** n.—**evangelist'ic** a.

evaporate (e-vap'-or-āt) v.t. and i. pass off in vapour, as fluid; disperse; disappear; vaporise.—**evapora'tion** n.

evasion (e-vā'-zhun) n. act of evading or eluding; subterfuge to escape the force of an accusation; excuse; dodge.—**eva'sive** a.—**eva'sively** adv.—**evas'iveness** n.

eve (ēv) n. evening; evening before some particular day; period immediately preceding an event.—**ev'en** n. evening (poetical).—**ev'ensong** n. evening prayer in Anglican church.—**ev'en-tide** n. evening.

even (ēv'-n) a. level; equal in surface; uniform; flat; smooth; equal in amount; balanced; horizontal; equable; calm; impartial; exactly divisable by two;—v.t. make even; smooth; equalise;—adv. likewise; just; simply; so much as.—**ev'enly** adv.—**ev'enness** n.—**ev'en-tem'pered** a. not irascible.—**even date**, same date.

evening (ēv'-ning) n. close of day; decline or end of life.—**evening dress**, formal dress worn at evening functions.

event (e-vent') n. that which happens; notable occurrence; affair; end; issue; result; effect; item at sports meeting.—**event'ful** a. full of exciting events; momentous.—**event'ual** a. happening as consequence; resulting in the end; ultimate.—**eventual'ity** n. contingency.—**event'ually** adv.—**even'tuate** v.i. happen.

ever (ev'-er) adv. at any time; at all times; perpetually; constantly; unceasingly. — **ev'ergreen** a. always green;—n. non-deciduous tree or shrub which remains green throughout the year.—**evermore'** adv. unceasingly; eternally.

everlasting (ev-er-last'-ing) a. enduring for ever; eternal;—n. eternity; flower which when dried, keeps shape or colour for indefinite time.—**everlast'ingly** adv.

evert (ē-vert') v.t. turn inside out.—**ever'sible** a. capable of being turned inside out.—**ever'sion** n.

every (ev'-ri) a. each of all; all possible.—**ev'erybody** n. every person. —**ev'ryday** a. usual; ordinary; common-place; daily.—**ev'erything** n. all things; all.—**ev'eryway** adv. in every way or respect.—**ev'erywhere** adv. in every place; universally. — **every other**, every second; alternately.

evict (e-vikt') v.t. dispossess by a judicial process; expel; turn out.—**evic'tion** n. ejectment.—**evic'tor** n.

evident (ev'-i-dent) a. visible; clear to the vision; obvious.—**ev'idence** n. that which makes evident; information in law case; a witness; sign; indication; ground for belief; testimony; proof; attestation; corroboration;—v.t. render evident; prove; evince.—**ev'idently** adv. apparently; plainly.—**to turn King's (Queen's) evidence**, give evidence against an accomplice.

evil (ē'-vl) a. having bad natural qualities; bad; ill; harmful; hurtful; disagreeable; vicious; corrupt; wicked; calamitous; unfortunate;—n. harm; misfortune; wickedness; depravity; sinfulness; wrong; injury;—adv. in evil manner; unjustly.—**ev'il-eye** n. power of bewitching others by glance of the eyes.—**e'vilfa'voured** a. ugly in appearance.—**e'villy** adv.—**e'vilness** n. depravity.

evince (e-vins') v.t. prove beyond any reasonable doubt; show clearly; make evident.—**evin'cible** a.—**evin'cibly** adv.—**evin'cive** a. tending to prove.

eviscerate (e-vis'-er-āt) v.t. disembowel; gut; take out entrails or viscera.—**eviscera'tion** n.

evoke (ē-vōk') v.t. call up; summon forth; draw out; bring about.—**ev'ocate** v.t. evoke; call up a materialisation from the spirit world.—**evoca'tion** n.

evolution (ev-ol-ū'-shun, ē-vo-lū'-shun) n. gradual unrolling or unfolding; development of organisation; change; evolving; scientific theory according to which higher forms of life have gradually developed from simple and rudimentary forms; Darwinism; manoeuvre to change position, order, and direction carried out by body of troops.—**evolu'tional, evolu'tionary** a.

evolve (ē-volv') v.t. unroll; throw out; disclose; develop; unfold;—v.i. develop, esp. by natural process; open out.

ewe (ū) n. female sheep.—**ewe'-lamb** n. female lamb; one's most cherished possession.

ewer (ū'-er) n. large water-jug.

exacerbate (eks- egz-as'-er-bāt) v.t. render more bitter; increase the violence of; exasperate; irritate; aggravate.—**exacerba'tion,** n.

exact (egz-akt') a. accurate; correct;

precise; careful;—*v.t.* demand in full extort; enforce; insist upon.—**exact'ing** *a.* making severe demands on; demanding extreme care.—**exac'tion** *n.* authoritative demand; unjust demand.—**exact'itude** *n.* extreme accuracy; correctness; exactness.—**exact'ly** *adv.* precisely; just so!—**exact'ness** *n.*—**exact'or, exact'er** *n.* (*fem.* **exact'ress**) one who exacts.

exaggerate (egz-aj'-er-āt) *v.t.* represent as greater than truth will warrant; magnify in the telling, describing, etc.—**exaggerat'edly** *adv.*—**exaggera'tion** *n.* statement going beyond the facts.—**exagg'erative** *a.*—**exagg'erator** *n.*—**exagg'eratory** *a.*

exalt (egz-awlt') *v.t.* raise high; elevate, as in rank; lift up; elate with joy.—**exalta'tion** *n.* elevation in rank; highly dignified position; elation.—**exalt'ed** *a.*

examine (egz-am'-in) *v.t.* inquire into and determine; inspect; scrutinise; explore; investigate; overhaul; interrogate.—**exam'** *n.* (*Colloq.*) examination.—**exam'en** *n.* investigation; disquisition; scrutiny.—**exam'inate, exam'inee** *n.* one who undergoes examination test.—**examin'ation** *n* act of examining; interrogation; test of knowledge or ability; judicial inquiry.—**exam'iner** *n.*

example (egz-am'-pl) *n.* pattern or copy; something illustrating general rule; specimen.

exasperate (egz-as'-per-āt) *v.t.* irritate in a high degree; rouse angry feelings; provoke beyond endurance.—**exas'perating** *a.* extremely trying; provoking.—**exaspera'tion** *n.* state of one who is exasperated; state of anger and rage.—**exas'perator** *n.* one who exasperates.

excavate (eks'-ka-vāt) *v.t.* hollow out; form a cavity or hole in; dig out.—**excava'tion** *n.* removal of earth from site.—**ex'cavator** *n.*

exceed (ek-sēd') *v.t.* pass or go beyond the limit of; be greater than; surpass; excel.—**exceed'ing** *a.* surpassing; excessive.—**exceed'ingly** *adv.* very; very high degree.

excel (ek-sel') *v.t.* surpass; be better than; exceed; outstrip; outdo;—*v.i.* be very good; be pre-eminent;—*pr.p.* **excel'ling.**—*pa.t.* and *pa.p.* **excelled'.**—**ex'cellence** *n.* state or quality of being excellent; title of honour.—**ex'cellency** *n.* complimentary title borne by viceroys, ambassadors, etc.—**ex'cellent** *a.* surpassing others worthy; choice; superior.—**ex'cellently** *adv.*

except (ek-sept') *v.t.* leave out; take out; exclude; reject;—*v.i.* take exception to; object;—*prep.*with exclusion of; leaving out; excepting; all but; save;—*conj.* unless.—**except'ing** *prep.* with exception of; excluding.—**excep'-tion** *n.* an excepting; that which is not included in a rule; objection.—**excep'tionable** *a.* objectionable.—**excep'tionably** *adv.*—**excep'tional** *a.* outstanding; superior.—**excep'tionally** *adv.*

excerpt (ek-serpt') *v.t.* extract, quote (a passage from a book, etc.); select.—**ex'cerpt** *n.* passage, quoted from a book, speech, etc.

excess (ek-ses') *n.* that which goes beyond definite limit; increase; surplus; remainder; extravagance; intemperance.—**exces'sive** *a.* more than enough; superfluous; extravagant.—**exces'sively** *adv.*

exchange (eks-chānj') *v.t.* give or take in return for; change; barter;—*n.* act of giving or taking one thing in return for another; method of settling debts between two countries; association of merchants or brokers for transaction of business; building where such transactions take place; bourse; method of finding equivalent of a given sum in money of another country; office for interconnecting telephone lines. — **exchange'able** *a.*

Exchequer (eks-chek'-er) *n.* court of law, once responsible for revenues, now a division of High Court of Justice; public treasury.

excise (ek-sīz') *n.* tax or duty upon certain articles of home production and consumption; also includes all licences with exception of those for motor vehicles.

excise (ek-sīz') *v.t.* cut out; cut off.—**excision** (ek-sizh'-un) *n.* act of cutting out or off; surgical removal of any organ of the body; extirpation.

excite (ek-sīt') *v.t.* rouse; call into action; stir up; move to strong emotion; stimulate.—**excitabil'ity** *n.*—**excit'able** *a.* capable of being easily excited; sensitive; passionate; hasty; hot-tempered; violent.—**excitant** (ek'-si-tant) *n.* agent which increases immediately the functional activity of the body or of some particular organs; stimulant.—**excita'tion** *n.*—**exci'tative** *a.*—**exci'tatory** *a.*—**excit'ed** *a.*—**excit'edly** *adv.*—**excite'ment** *n.*—**excit'ing** *a.*—**excit'ingly** *adv.*

exclaim (eks-klām') *v.i.* and *t.* utter loudly; vociferate; declare suddenly;—*n.* clamour; outcry.—**exclamation** (eks-kla-mā'-shun) *n.* loud remark or cry, expressing joy, surprise, etc. — **exclamation mark,** mark (!) used to suggest sudden emotion.—**exclam'atory** *a.* of the nature of an exclamation.

exclude (eks-klóód') *v.t.* thrust out; shut out; debar from; eject.—**exclu'sion** *n.* act of excluding or debarring.—**exclu'sive** *a.* excluding; limited to a special favoured few.—**exclu'sively** *adv.*—**exclu'siveness** *n.*

excogitate (eks-koj'-i-tāt) *v.t.* find out by thinking; think out.—**excogita'tion** *n.*

excommunicate (eks-kom-ūn'-i-kāt) *v.t.* expel from communion of the Church by ecclesiastical sentence; deprive of spiritual privileges.

excoriate (eks-kō'-ri-āt) *v.t.* strip, wear, or rub skin off; flay.—**excoria'tion** *n.*

excrement (eks'-kre-ment) *n.* matter excreted; faeces; ordure; dung.—**excrement'al** *a.*

excrement (eks'-kre-ment) *n.* that which grows on living body, as hair, nails, feathers, etc.; natural excrescence.

excrescence (eks-kres'-ens) *n.* abnormal protuberance which grows out of anything; unnatural outgrowth of tissue, as a wart.—**excres'cent** *a.* growing out unnaturally; superfluous.

excrete (eks-krēt') *v.t.* eject waste matter from the body; expel.—**excre'ta** *n.pl.* normal discharges from the animal body as urine, faeces and sweat.—**excre'tion** *n.* that which is excreted; act of excreting.—**excre'tive, excre'tory** *a.*

excruciate (eks-kroō'-shi-āt) *v.t.* inflict severest pain on; torture, in body or mind.—**excru'ciating** *a.*

exculpate (eks-kul'-pāt) *v.t.* clear from charge of fault or guilt.—**exculpa'tion** *n.*—**excul'patory** *a.*

excursion (eks-kur'-shun) *n.* setting out for place of interest; trip for pleasure.—**excurse'** *v.i.* go on an excursion; digress.—**excur'sionist** *n.* one who makes journey for pleasure.

excuse (eks-kūz') *v.t.* free from blame; free from obligation or duty; pardon; justify; exempt; let off.—**excuse** (eks-kūs') *n.* plea offered in extenuation of a fault; apology.—**excus'able** *a.*

execrate (eks'-e-krāt) *v.t.* feel or express hatred for; curse; abominate loathe.—**ex'ecrable** *a.*—**ex'ecrably** *adv.*—**execra'tion** *n.*

execute (eks'-e-kūt) *v.t.* carry out task to end; accomplish; give effect to; perform, esp. music; complete; enforce judgment of court of law; sign a deed; put to death by sentence of court.—**exec'utable** *a.* can be carried out.—**exec'utant** *n.* performer, esp. of music.—**ex'ecuter** *n.* one who executes; executioner.—**execu'tion** *n.* act of executing or performing; death penalty inflicted by law; accomplishment; mode of performance; workmanship; capital punishment.—**execu'tioner** *n.* one who executes; hangman.—**exec'utive** *a.* capable of executing or performing; administrative;—*n.* body appointed to administer affairs of a company, etc.; high official of such a body.—

exec'utively *adv.*—**exec'utor** *n.* (*fem.* **exec'utrix,** (eks'-e-ū'tress) one who executes or performs; person appointed under a will to fulfil its terms and administer estate.—**execu'to'rial** *a.*

exegesis (eks-e-jē'-sis) *n.* literary commentary; interpretation and elucidation of Holy Scriptures.

exemplar (egz-em'-plar) *n.* person or thing to be imitated; original or pattern; model.—**exem'plarily** *adv.* in manner to be imitated; by way of warning or example.—**exem'plariness** *n.*—**exem'plary** *a.*

exemplify (egz-em'-pli-fī) *v.t.* show by example; illustrate;—*pr.p.* **exem'plifying;**—*pa.p.* **exem'plified.**—**exemplifica'tion** *n.*

exempt (egz-emt') *v.t.* free from; grant immunity from;—*a.* not included; not liable for some duty; privileged; freed from; released from.—**exemp'tible** *a.* able to be exempted.—**exemp'tion** *n.* act of exempting; state of being exempt; immunity; privilege; dispensation.

exercise (eks'-er-sīz) *n.* act of exercising; use (of limbs, faculty, etc.); use of limbs for health; practice for sake of training;—*pl.* military drill;—*v.t.* put in motion; use; exert; apply; engage; practise; —*v.i.* take exercise.

exert (egz-ert') *v.t.* put forth, as strength, force, or ability; exercise; employ; strain; strive; labour.—**exer'tion** *n.* act of exerting; effort; attempt.—**exer'tive** *a.*

exfoliate (eks-fō'-li-āt) *v.t.* free the surface of splinters or small scales; —*v.i.* fall away in flakes, layers, or scales.—**exfolia'tion** *n.*

exhale (eks-hāl') *v.t.* breathe out; give off as vapour or odour; discharge; evaporate;—*v.i.* rise or be given off as vapour.—**exhal'able** *a.*—**exhal'ant** *a.* having property of exhalation.—**exhala'tion** *n.* act or process of exhaling; that which is exhaled; effluvium; mist; damp vapour.

exhaust (egz-awst') *v.t.* draw out or drain off completely; empty; weaken; tire; use up; squander;—*n.* conduit through which steam, waste gases and the like, pass from cylinders to outer air; steam or burnt gases themselves.—**exhaust'ed** *a.* tired out; fatigued; emptied; drawn out; consumed.—**exhaust'ible** *a.*—**exhaust'ion** *n.*—**exhaust'ive** *a.* comprehensive; thorough.—**exhaust'ively** *adv.*

exhibit (egz-ib'-it) *v.t.* hold forth or expose to view; present; show; display; express;—*n.* anything displayed at exhibition.—**exhib'iter, exhib'itor** *n.* one who sends articles to exhibition for display.—**exhibi'tion** *n.* act of exhibiting; show; display; public show (of works of art, etc.);

bursary; scholarship.—**exhibi'tioner** n. one who holds university exhibition.—**exhibi'tionism** n. tendency to show off before people.—**exhibi'tionist** n.—**exhib'itory** a.

exhilarate (egz-il'-a-rāt) v.t. make cheerful; animate.—**exhil'arant** a. exhilarating; exciting joy, mirth, or pleasure;—n. anything which exhilarates.—**exhil'arating** a. enlivening; cheering.—**exhilara'tion** n.

exhort (egz-ort') v.t. incite by words of advice; advise strongly; admonish earnestly; urge.—**exhorta'tion** n.—**exhort'ative**, **exhort'atory** a. tending to exhort.

exhume (eks-hūm') v.t. dig up, as from a grave; unearth; disinter.—**exhuma'tion** n.—**exhum'er** n.

exigent (eks'-i-jent) a. calling for immediate action; pressing; urgent; critical.—**ex'igence**, **ex'igency** n. urgent want; emergency.—**ex'igible** a. capable of being exacted or demanded.—**exigu'ity**, **exig'uousness** n. smallness; slenderness.—**exig'uous** a. small; slender; scanty.

exile (eks'-īl, egz'-īl) n. enforced banishment from one's native country; a banished person; one living away from his native country.—v.t. banish from one's native country.

exist (egz-ist') v.t. be; live; subsist; continue.—**exist'ence** n. condition of objectivity; being; state of being actual; entity; life; reality.—**exist'ent** a. still existing; current; living; extant.—**existen'tial** a. consisting in existence.—**existibil'ity** n.

exit (eks'-it) n. departure; way out of a place; stage direction to indicate when actor is to leave stage;—pl. ex'eunt.—v.t. make an exit.

exodus (eks'-o-dus) n. departure, esp. of a crowd.—**Ex'odus** n. (Bib.) second book of the Old Testament.

exonerate (eg-zon'-ẽr-āt) v.t. declare free from blame.—**exonera'tion** n.—**exon'erator** n.—**exon'erative** a. tending to exonerate.

exorable (eks'-or-a-bl) a. capable of being moved by entreaty.

exorbitant (egz-or'-bi-tant) a. very excessive; extravagant. — **exor'bitance**, **exor'bitancy** n. enormity; extravagance.—**exor'bitantly** adv.

exorcise (eks'-or-sīz, eks-or'-sīz) v.t. cast out (evil spirits) by invocation; free a person of evil spirits.—**ex'orcism** n. conjuration by God or Christ or some holy name, of an evil-possessing spirit to come out of a person.—**ex'orcist** n.

exoskeleton (ek-sō-skel'-e-tun) n. (Zool.) external hard supporting structure such as scales, nails, feathers in vertebrates and carapace, in invertebrates.—**exo-skel'etal** a.

exotic (egz-ot'-ik) a. introduced from a foreign country; not indigenous; foreign;—n. plant, custom, etc. of foreign origin.—**exot'icism** n.

expand (eks-pand') v.t. spread out; enlarge; increase in volume or bulk; extend; widen; stretch; distend; swell; develop.—**expanse'** n. wide extent of surface; open country; arch of the sky.—**expansibil'ity** n.—**expans'ible**, **expans'ile** a. capable of being expanded.—**expans'ibly** adv.—**expan'sion** n. act of expanding; condition of being expanded; spreading; distension; enlargement.—**expans'ive** a. widely extended; effusive; diffusive.—**expans'ively** adv.—**expans'iveness**, **expansiv'ity** n.

expatiate (eks-pā'-shi-āt) v.i. speak or write at great length (on); dilate; ramble.—**expatia'tion** n.—**expa'tiative**, **expa'tiatory** a.

expatriate (eks-pā'-tri-āt, eks-pa'-tri-āt) v.t. banish from one's native land; exile;—n. one who has been forcibly removed from his home country.—**expatria'tion** n.

expect (eks-pekt') v.t. wait for; look forward to; look on as likely to happen; look for as one's due; await; hope; anticipate.—**expect'ance**, **expect'ancy** n. act or state of expecting; that which is expected.—**expect'ant** a.—**expect'antly** adv.—**expecta'tion** n.—**expecta'tions** n.pl. prospects in life; probable gain.

expectorate (eks-pek'-to-rāt) v.t. or v.i. spit; cough up.—**expec'torant** a. aiding expectoration;—n. drug or agent which promotes expectoration.—**expectora'tion** n. act of expectorating; sputum; spittle.

expedient (eks-pē'-di-ent) a. suitable; fitting; advisable; politic; desirable; convenient; useful;—n. suitable means to accomplish an end; shift; contrivance.—**expe'diency** n. fitness; advisability; self-interest.—**expe'diently** adv. quickly; suitably.

expedite (eks'-pe-dīt) v.t. free from hindrance; hurry forward;—a. free from hindrance; easy; quick.—**ex'peditely** adv.—**expedi'tion** n. efficient promptness; speed; despatch of, as army or fleet; exploring party.—**expedi'tionary** a.—**expedi'tious** a. prompt; speedy.

expel (eks-pel') v.t. drive or force out; cast out; eject; exclude; discharge;—pr.p. **expel'ling**;—pa.t. and pa.p. **expelled'**.

expend (eks-pend') v.t. lay out; consume by use; spend; use up; employ; exhaust; dissipate; waste.—**expend'able** a. that may be expended.—**expend'iture** n. act of expending; that which is expended; expense; cost.—**expense'** n. outlay; cost; expenditure. — **expens'ive** a. costly; dear.

experience (eks-pē'-ri-ens) n. practical knowledge gained by trial or practice; personal proof or trial; continuous practice; evidence; unusual event;—*v.t.* know by trial or practice; undergo; feel; endure; encounter.—**expe'rienced** *a.* skilled; expert; wise; capable.—**experien'tial** *a.* relating to or having experience; empirical.

experiment (eks-per'-i-ment) *n.* action of trying anything; putting to proof or test; practical test; trial to find out what happens;—*v.i.* make an experiment. — **experiment'al** *a.* founded on or known by experiment; pert. to experiment.—**experiment'alist** *n.*—**experiment'ally** *adv.*—**experimenta'tion** *n.*—**experiment'ative** *a.*—**experimen'ter, exper'imentist** *n.* one who makes experiments.

expert (eks-pert') *a.* taught by use, practice, or experience; adroit; dexterous; skilful.—**ex'pert** *n.* an authority; specialist.—**expert'ly** *adv.*—**expert'ness, expert'ise** *n.*

expiate (eks'-pi-āt) *v.t.* make satisfaction for; atone for; make amends for; pay penalty for.—**ex'piable** *a.* able to be atoned for.—**expia'tion** *n.*

expire (eks-pīr') *v.t.* breathe out; emit; exhale;—*v.i.* die; come to an end; become invalid or void.—**expira'tion** *n.* exhalation of air from lungs; death; end of limited period of time; close; termination.—**expi'ring** *a.*—**expi'ry** *n.* end; termination; conclusion.

explain (eks-plān') *v.t.* make plain or intelligible; account for; elucidate; define.—**explain'able** *a.*—**explana'tion** *n.*—**explan'atory** *a.*

expletive (eks'-ple-tiv, eks-plē'-tiv) *a.* serving only to fill out sentence, etc.; added for ornamentation;—*n.* word inserted to fill up or to add force to phrase; exclamation; oath.

explicate (eks'-pli-kāt) *v.t.* unfold meaning of; explain; interpret; elucidate.—**ex'plicable** *a.* able to be explained.—**explica'tion** *n.* explanation; elucidation; exposition.—**ex'plicative, ex'plicatory** *a.* serving to explain or elucidate.

explicit (eks-plis'-it) *a.* stated in detail; unambiguous; clear; plain; unequivocal.—**explic'itly** *adv.* definitely.—**explic'itness** *n.*

explode (eks-plōd') *v.t.* cause to blow up; discredit; refute; expose (a theory, etc.); *v.i.* burst with loud report; become furious with rage; burst into laughter.—**explo'ded** *a.* rejected; debunked.—**explo'sion** *n.* act of exploding; sudden release of gases, accompanied by noise and violence; manifestation of rage.—**explo'sive** *a.* liable to explode;—*n.* chemical compound or mixture intended to explode.

exploit (eks-ploit') *n.* brilliant feat; heroic deed; remarkable action, often in bad sense;—*v.t.* make most of; utilise for personal gain; boost.—**exploit'able** *a.*—**exploit'age, exploita'tion** *n.* making full use of industrial plant and materials; underpaying grossly to make excessive profit.—**exploi'ter** *n.*

explore (eks-plōr') *v.t.* search through with view to making discovery; investigate; examine.—**explora'tion** *n.*—**explor'atory** *a.*—**explor'er** *n.*

explosive See explode.

exponent (eks-pō'-nent) *n.* one who expounds, demonstrates, or explains; executant.

export (eks-pōrt') *v.t.* send goods or produce out of a country.—**ex'port** *n.* act of exporting; that which is exported.—**export'able** *a.*—**exporta'tion** *n.*—**export'er** *n.*

expose (eks-pōz') *v.t.* lay open; leave unprotected; put up for sale; submit to light.—**exposé** (eks-pō-zā') *n.* explanatory statement; disclosure.—**exposi'tion** *n.* act of exhibiting or expounding; exhibition; display; illustration; explanation.—**expos'itor** *n.*—**expos'itory** *a.*—**expo'sure** *n.* act of exposing, laying bare shady or doubtful transactions; state of being laid bare; aspect of a building relative to cardinal points of the compass.

expostulate (eks-post'-ū-lāt) *v.i.* remonstrate with; reason in kindly manner with a person.—**expostula'tion** *n.* remonstrance.—**expost'ulative, expost'ulatory** *a.*

expound (eks-pound') *v.t.* explain; set forth; clear of obscurity; interpret; make plain.

express (eks-pres') *v.t.* press or squeeze out; make known one's opinions or feelings; put into words; declare; denote; send by express;—*a.* definitely stated; closely resembling; specially designed; explicit; clear; plain; speedy;—*adv.* plainly; post-haste; by express messenger or train; specially; on purpose;—*n.* messenger sent on special errand; fast train making few stops en route; message.—**express'ible** *a.*—**expres'sion** *n.* act of expressing; lively or vivid representation of meaning, sentiment, or feeling; reflection of character or mood in the countenance; utterance; declaration; phrase; term; remark; aspect; look.—**expres'sionless** *a.*—**expres'sive** *a.* serving to express, utter, or represent; full of expression.—**expres'sively** *adv.*—**expres'siveness** *n.*—**express'ly** *adv.* plainly; specially.

expropriate (eks-prō'-pri-āt) *v.t.* dispossess; deprive of one's property.—**expropria'tion** *n.*

expulsion (eks-pul'-shun) *n.* act of expelling or casting out; ejection; bashishment. **expul'sive** *a.*

expunge (eks-punj') v.t. strike out, as with a pen; erase; obliterate; cancel.

expurgate (eks'-pur-găt, eks-pur'-găt) v.t. remove objectionable parts (from book, etc.); cleanse; purify; purge.—**expurga'tion** n.—**expur'gator** n.—**expurgato'rial, expur'gatory** a. serving to purify or cleanse.

exquisite (eks'-kwi-zit) a. of extreme beauty or delicacy; of surpassing excellence; extreme, as pleasure;—n. one over-nice in dress; fop.—**ex'-quisitely** adv.

extant (eks-tant', eks'-tant) a. still existing.

extasy, extatic See **ecstasy, ecstatic**.

extempore (eks-tem'-po-re) a. or adv. without previous study; off-hand.—**extem'poral, extempora'neous, extem'porary** a. impromptu.—**extem'poriness, extemporisa'tion** n. act of speaking extempore. — **extem'porise** v.i. speak extempore; create music on inspiration of the moment.

extend (eks-tend') v.t. prolong in a single direction, as a line; stretch out; prolong in duration; accord; offer; expand; enlarge;—v.i. be continued in length or breadth; stretch.—**extend'ible, extens'ible, extens'ile** a.—**extensibil'ity** n.—**exten'sion** n. the act of extending; the state of being extended; further period of time.—**exten'sional** a.—**exten'sive** a. having wide extent; comprehensive.—**extens'ively** adv.—**extens'iveness** n.—**extent'** n. space or degree to which thing is extended; size.

extenuate (eks-ten'-ū-āt) v.t. draw out, as a line; make thin; mitigate; make less blameworthy.—**exten'uating** a. palliating; mitigating.—**extenua'tion** n.—**exten'uative, exten'uatory** a.

exterior (eks-tē'-ri-or) a. outer; outward; external; coming from without;—n. outside; outer surface; outward appearance.

exterminate (eks-ter'-mi-nāt) v.t. root out; destroy utterly.—**extermina'tion** n. complete destruction.—**exter'minative, exter'minatory** a.—**exter'minator** n.

external (eks-ter'-nal) a. not inherent or essential; outward; exterior; superficial; apparent.—**externals** n.pl. outward appearances; non-essentials.—**exter'nally** adv.

extinct (eks-tingkt') a. extinguished; put out; no longer existing; dead.—**extinc'tion** n. act of extinguishing; ˌstate of being extinguished.

extinguish (eks-ting'-gwish) v.t. put out; put an end to; quench; destroy.—**exting'uishable** a.—**exting'uisher** n.

extirpate (eks'-ter-pāt) v.t. pull up by roots; destroy utterly.—**extirp'able** a.—**extirpa'tion** n.—**ex'tirpator** n.

extol (eks-tōl') v.t. praise highly.—

pr.p. extoll'ing.—pa.t. and pa.p. extolled'.

extort (eks-tort') v.t. obtain by force or threats; exact.—**extors'ive** a.—**extor'tion** n.—**extor'tionary, extor'tionate** a.—**extor'tioner, extor'tionist** n.

extra (eks'-tra) a. extraordinary; additional;—adv. unusually; especially;—n. something extra; over and above usual charges; additional item; special edition of newspaper; run scored in cricket not directly due to either batsman; person employed casually by film producers to play minor role in production.—**ex'tra-currie'ular** a. pert. to studies or activities not included in curriculum.—**ex'tra-mu'ral** a. beyond the walls; pert. to instruction outside a university.—**extra-sensory** (eks-tra-sen'-sor-i) a. beyond the senses.—**ex'tra-territo'rial** a. outside limits of a country or its jurisdiction.

extract (eks-trakt') v.t. take out, esp. by force; obtain against person's will; get by pressure, distillation, etc.; copy out; quote; elicit; (Math.) calculate.—**ex'tract** n. matter obtained by distillation; concentrated drug, solution, etc.; passage reproduced from book, speech, etc.—**extract'able, extract'ible** a. able to be extracted.—**extrac'tion** n. act of extracting; that which is extracted; ancestry; lineage; descent.—**extract'ive** a.—**extract'or** n.

extradite (eks'-tra-dīt) v.t. deliver up a fugitive to foreign nation in conformity with terms of extradition treaty.

extraneous (eks-trān'-ne-us) a. not naturally belonging to or dependent on a thing; not essential; foreign.—**extran'eously** adv.

extraordinary (eks-tra-or'-di-nar-i, or eks-tror'-) a. beyond or out of common order or method; exceeding common degree or measure; out of usual course; employed on special errand or duty.—**extraor'dinarily** adv.—**extraor'dinariness** n.

extrapolate (eks-tra'-po-lāt) v.t. and i. (Math.) and (Fig.) to estimate or infer on basis of known factors.

extravagant (eks-trav'-a-gant) a. wandering beyond bounds; excessive; prodigal; wasteful; unrestrained.—**extrav'agance** n. excess; prodigality; profusion.

extravaganza (eks-trav-a-gan'-za) n. extravagant, farcical, or fantastic composition, literary or musical.

extravert See extrovert.

extreme (eks-trēm') a. at utmost point, edge, or border; outermost; of high or highest degree; severe; excessive; last; most urgent;—n. utmost point or degree; thing at one end or other; first and last of series; great necessity.—**extreme'ly** adv.—

extre'mism n. holding extreme views or doctrines.—**extre'mist** n.—**extrem'ity** n. most distant point or side, as of place or country; end; greatest difficulty.—**extrem'ities** n.pl. hands and feet; arms and legs; utmost distress or peril; extreme measures.

extricate (eks'-tri-kāt) v.t. free from difficulties or perplexities.—**ex'tricable** a.—**extrica'tion** n. act of extricating or setting free; disentanglement.

extrovert (eks-trō-vert') n. in psychology, person emotionally involved in external actions and events, as opposed to *introvert*.—**extrover'sion** n.

extrude (eks-trōōd') v.t. thrust out; press out; expel.—**extru'sion** n. act of extruding; expulsion; ejection.—**extru'sive, extru'sory** a.

exuberant (eks-ū'-ber-ant) a. overfruitful; over abundant; prolific; luxurious; excessive; effusive; vivacious; very happy.—**exu'berance, exu'berancy** n. state of being exuberant.—**exu'berantly** adv.

exude (eks-ūd') v.t. discharge through the pores; discharge sap by incision.—v.i. ooze out; escape slowly, as a liquid.—**exuda'tion** n.

exult (egz-ult') v.i. rejoice exceedingly; leap for joy; triumph; gloat.—**exult'ance, exult'ancy** n. exultation.—**exult'ant** a. exulting; triumphant.—**exulta'tion** n. triumph.

eye (I) n. organ of sight or vision; the power of seeing; sight; perforation; bud; view; keen sense of value; anything resembling an eye; small staple or ring to receive a hook; aperture for observing;—v.t. observe closely or fixedly; look at; view; *pr.p.* **ey'ing** or **eye'ing**.—*pa.t.* and *pa.p.* **eyed** (id).—**eye'brow** n. arch of hairs above eye.—**eyed** a. having eyes; spotted as if with eyes.—**eye'glass** n. glass to assist sight; monocle; eyepiece of optical instrument.—*pl.* spectacles.—**eye'lash** n. one of the hairs which edge the eyelid.—**eye'let** n. small eye or hole for a lace or cord, as in garments, sails, etc.;—v.i. make eyeholes.—**eye'lid** n. folds of skin which may be drawn at will over the eye.—**eye'o'pener** n. surprising news; revealing statement.—**eye'piece** n. lens in optical instrument by means of which the observer views image.—**eye'shot** n. within range of vision; glance.—**eye'sight** n. power of vision; view; observation.—**eye'sore** n. object offensive to the eye.—**eye'tooth** n. either of the two canine teeth of upper jaw.—**eye'wash** n. humbug; pretence; deception.—**eye'wit'ness** n. one who gives testimony as to what he actually saw.—**to see eye to eye,** agree; think alike.

eyot (āt) n. small island esp. in middle of river or lake.

eyrie, eyry (ē'-ri) n. nest of bird of pray, esp. eagle or hawk.

F

fable (fā'-bl) n. short tale or prolonged personification, often with animal characters, intended to convey moral truth; myth; fiction; falsehood;—v.t. and i. feign; romance.—**fa'bled** a. mythical; legendary.—**fab'ular** a.—**fab'ulise** v.i. compose fables.—**fab'ulist** n.—**fab'ulous** a. feigned or fabled; amazing; exaggerated; immense.

fabric (fab'-rik) n. structure; framework; maintenance of a building; woven material; outer covering of aircraft; texture. — **fab'ricate** v.t. frame; construct mechanically; build according to standard specifications; assemble from standardised components; fake; concoct.—**fabrica'tion** n. that which is constructed; lie, false statement.—**fab'ricator** n.

façade (fa-sād') n. front view or elevation of a building.

face (fās) n. front of the head; outer appearance; cast of countenance; outer or upper surface of anything; dial of a clock, etc.; (*Fig.*) audacity; effrontery.—v.t. confront; stand opposite; admit existence of (as facts); oppose with courage; put a layer of different material on to, or trim an outer surface;—v.i. turn.—**face'cloth** n. square of towelling for washing the face.—**face'-lift'ing** n. operation performed to remove wrinkles from face.—**face'-val'ue** n. apparent worth.—**fa'cial** a. pert. to face.—**fac'ing** n. covering in front for ornament or defence; collar, cuffs, etc. of uniform.—**to face the music,** stand for trail; meet emergency boldly.—**to lose face,** be humiliated.—**to save one's face,** avoid being humiliated.

facet (fas'-et) n. small surface, as of a precious stone.—**fac'eted** a. having facets.

facetious (fa-sē'-shus) a. witty; jocular.—**facetiae** (fa-sē'-shi-ē) n.pl. witty or humorous writings or sayings; improper books.—**face'tiously** adv.—**face'tiousness** n.

facia, fascia (fash'-i-a) n. See fascia.

facile (fas'-il) a. easy; fluent; easily approached or influenced; courteous; glib.—**fac'ilely** adv.—**fac'ileness** n.—**facil'itate** v.t. make easy; expedite.—**facilita'tion** n.—**facil'ity** n. ease; deftness; helpful provision esp. pl.

facsimile (fak-sim'-i-li) n. exact copy;—a. identical;—v.t. make facsimile.—**facsim'ilist** n.—**in facsimile,** accurately.

fact (takt) n. anything done; anything actually true; that which has happened.—**fac'tual** a. pert. to facts; actual.—**mat'ter-of-fact** a. prosaic; unimaginative.

faction (fak'-shun) n. group of people working together, esp. for subversive purposes; dissension; party clique.—**fac'tious** a. seditious.—**fac'tiously** adv.—**fac'tiousness** n.

factitious (fak-tish'-us) a. made or imitated by art, oppos. of natural; unreal; conventional.

factor (fak'-tor) n. agent; one who transacts business for another on commission; (Scot.) steward of an estate; (Math.) one of numbers which, multiplied together, give a given number; contributory element or determining cause;—v.t. (Scot.) manage (an estate).—**fac'torial** a. pert. to factor.—**fac'torise** v.t. (Math.) find the factors of a given number.—**fac'torship** n.

factory (fak'-tor-i) n. building where things are manufactured.

faculty (fa'-kul-ti) n. ability or power to act; mental aptitude; talent; natural physical function; university department; members of a profession, esp. medical; authorisation.—**facul'tative** a. optional.

fad (fad) n. pet whim; fancy or notion.—**fad'dish** a.—**fad'dy** a.—**fad'dist** n. one given to fads.

fade (fād) v.i. lose freshness, brightness, or strength gradually; disappear slowly.—**fade'less** a. not liable to fade; fast (of dye).

faeces, **feces** (fē'-sēz) n.pl. dregs; solid waste matter from the bowels.—**faecal** (fē'-kal) a.

fag (fag) n. toil; fatigue; at public schools, lower form boy who does menial offices for senior; tedious task; (Slang) a cigarette;—v.t. exhaust; employ as a fag;—v.i. become worn out; be a fag.—**fag'-end** n. tail end of anything; remnant.

faggot, fagot (fag'-ot) n. bundle of sticks for fuel; bundle of steel rods cut for welding; contemptuous name for an old woman; savoury pork rissole;—v.t. tie together; gather haphazardly.—**fagg'oting, fag'oting** n. kind of embroidery.

Fahrenheit (fär'-en-hīt) n. term applied to type of thermometer graduated so that freezing point of water is fixed at 32°, and boiling point at 212°.

fail (fāl) v.i. be lacking; diminish; deteriorate; miss; be unsuccessful in; go bankrupt;—v.t. disappoint or desert; omit; (Colloq.) refuse to pass candidate under examination.—pr.p. **fail'ing**.—pa.t. **failed**.—**fail'ing** n. fault; weakness; a short-coming;—prep. in default of.—**fail'ure** n. bankruptcy; lack of success.

fain (fān) a. glad; inclined to; forced;—adv. gladly.—**fain'ness** n.

faint (fānt) a. lacking strength; indistinct; giddy; unenterprising;—v.i. become weak; grow discouraged; swoon;—n. swoon.—**faint'-heart** n. and a.—**faint'-heart'ed** a. cowardly; timorous.—**faint'ly** adv. indistinctly.

fair (fār) a. clear; free from fault or stain; light-coloured; blond; beautiful; not cloudy; hopeful; just; plausible; middling;—adv. in fair or courteous manner; according to what is just.—**fair'-copy** n. rewritten, corrected copy.—**fair game**, open to banter.—**fair'ly** adv. justly; tolerably; wholly.—**fair'ness** n.—**fair'-play** n. straightforward justice.—**fair'-spo'ken** n. polite; plausible.—**fair'-way** n. navigable channel or river; (Golf) stretch of ground between the tee and the green, free from rough grass.—**fair and square**, honest; honestly.

fair (fār) n. periodical market held in certain places, for selling produce of district; usually occasion for holidays and entertainments as circus, shows, etc.—**fair'ing** n. gift purchased at fair.

fairy (fār'-i) n. imaginary creature in form of diminutive human being; a. fairy-like; dainty.—**fair'yland** n. land of the fairies; wonderland.—**fair'y-tale** n. story about fairies and magic; (Colloq.) improbable tale.

faith (fāth) n. belief, esp. in revealed religion; trust or reliance; system of religious doctrines believed in; honesty; pledged word.—**faith'ful** a.—**faith'fully** adv.—**faith'fulness** n.—**faith'less** a.

fake (fāk) v.t. conceal defects of, by artifice; copy, as an antique, and pass it off as genuine;—n. fraud; dodge; deception; forgery; faker.—**fak'er** n.

fakir (fa-kēr', fā'-kẹr) n. member of sect of religious mendicants in India.

falcon (faw'-kn, fal'-kon) n. subfamily of birds of prey, allied to hawk, with strong curved beak and long sickle-shaped claws; one of these birds, trained to hunt game.—**fal'coner** n. one who breeds and trains falcons or hawks for hunting wild-fowl.—**fal'conry** n. sport of flying hawks in pursuit of game.

fall (fawl) v.i. descend from higher to lower position; drop; collapse; abate; decline in value; become degraded; happen;—pr.p. **fall'ing**.—pa.t. **fell**.—pa.p. **fall'en**;—n. act of falling; drop; capitulation; amount (of rain, snow, etc.) deposited in specified time; cascade; cadence; wrestling bout; moral lapse, esp. that of Adam and Eve; lace jabot; diminution in value, amount, or volume; loose end of tackle; (U.S.) the autumn.—**fall'en** a. prostrate; degraded; of loose morals.—**to fall back on**, have recourse to.—**to fall behind**, be outdistanced; be in arrears.—**to fall for** (*Colloq.*) be attracted or taken in by.—**to fall in** (*Mil.*) form ranks; join; give way.—**to fall in with**, meet casually; agree to (a plan).—**to fall off**, decrease; deteriorate.—**to fall out**, quarrel; happen; (*Mil.*) leave the ranks;—**fall-out** *n.* air-borne radioactive particles or dust resulting from nuclear explosion.

fallacy (fal'-a-si) *n.* deceptive appearance; delusion; apparently forcible argument really illogical; sophistry.—**falla'cious** *a.* misleading; illogical.—**falla'ciously** *adv.*

fallible (fal'-i-bl) *a.* liable to error; not reliable.—**fallibil'ity** *n.* quality of being fallible.—**fall'ibly** *adv.*

fallow (fal'-ō) *a.* left untilled for a season;—*n.* land which has lain untilled and unsown for year or more;—*v.t.* plough without sowing.

false (fawls) *a.* untrue; inaccurate; dishonest; deceptive; artificial; forged.—**false'hood** *n.* untruth; lie.—**false'ly** *adv.*—**false'ness** *n.*—**falsifi'able** *a.*—**falsifica'tion** *n.*—**fal'sifier** *n.*—**fal'sify** *v.t.* distort truth; forge.—**fal'sity** *n.* untrue statement; deception.

falsetto (fawl-set'-ō) *n.* forced high notes of male voice.

falter (fawl-ter) *v.i.* stumble; hesitate; lack resolution; stammer.

fame (fām) *n.* public report or rumour, esp. good repute.—**famed** *a.* celebrated.—**fa'mous** *a.* celebrated; eminent; excellent.—**fa'mously** *adv.*

familiar (fa-mil'-yar) *a.* intimate; domestic; informal; free; unconstrained; well-known; current; conversant with;—*n.* close acquaintance.—**famil'iarise** *v.t.* make familiar; (*Reflex.*) get to know thoroughly (foll. by *with*).—**famil'iarism** *n.* colloquialism.—**familiar'ity** *n.* intimacy; forwardness.—**famil'iarly** *adv.*

family (fam'-i-li) *n.* parents, children and servants as making a household; children of same parents; descendants of one common ancestor; (*Biol.*) group of individuals within order or sub-division of order; group of languages derived from common parent tongue.—**family tree**, diagram representing, step by step, genealogy of a family.

famine (fam'-in) *n.* large-scale scarcity of food; extreme shortage; starvation.—**fam'ish** *v.t.* starve;—*v.i.* feel acute hunger.

fan (fan) *n.* instrument to produce currents of air or assist ventilation;—*v.t.* cool with fan; ventilate; winnow; cause to flame (as fire); (*Fig.*) aggravate; spread out.—**fan'ning**.—*pa.p.* fanned.—**fan'light** *n.* window, usually semi-circular, over doorway.—**fan'-tail** *n.* variety of domestic pigeon.—**fan'-tailed** *a.*

fan (fan) *n.* (*Slang*) devoted admirer; wildly enthusiastic follower.

fanatic (fa-nat'-ik) *n.* person inspired with excessive and bigoted enthusiasm, esp. religious zealot; devotee.—*a.* over-enthusiastic; immoderately zealous.—**fanat'ical** *a.*—**fanat'ically** *adv.*—**fanat'icism** *n.* violent enthusiasm.

fancy (fan'-si) *n.* faculty of creating within mind images of outward things; image thus conceived; whim; notion; partiality;—*a.* pleasing to the taste; guided by whim; elaborate; fantastic;—*v.t.* imagine; have a liking for; desire; breed (as dogs);—*pr.p.* fan'cying.—*pa.p.* fan'cied.—**fan'cier** *n.* one who has specialised knowledge, esp. of breeding of animals or birds.—**fan'ciful** *a.* capricious; un-real; fantastic.—**fan'cifully** *adv.*— **fan'cifulness** *n.*—**fan'cy-dress** *n.* dress made according to wearer's fancy, to represent some character.—**fan'cy-free** *a.* heart-free.—**the fancy**, sporting characters generally, esp. pugilists.

fanfare (fan'-fār) *n.* flourish of trumpets.

fang (fang) *n.* canine tooth of carnivorous animal, esp. wolf; long perforated tooth of poisonous serpent.—**fanged** *a.*

fantasy (fan'-ta-si) *n.* fancy; mental image; caprice; hallucination. Also **phan'tasy**.—**fantasia** (fan-tā'-zi-a) *n.* (*Mus.*) composition not written in any prescribed form.—**fan'tasied** *a.* fanciful.—**fan'tasm** *n.* same as phantasm.—**fantas'tic**, -al *a.* fanciful; wild; irregular; capricious.—**fantas'tically** *adv.*

far (får) *a.* distant; remote; more distant of two;—*adv.* to great extent or distance; to great height; considerably; very much;—*n.* distant place.—**farther** (får'-THer) *a.* (*comp.* of far) more remote; tending to a greater distance;—*adv.* at, or to, greater distance; moreover; in addition (variant of further).—**far'thest** *a.* (superlative of far) most remote in space or time;—*adv.* to greatest distance.—**far away**, distant; abstracted in mind.—**far'-fetched** *a.* (*Fig.*) incredible; strained.—**far gone**, in last stages of disease, drunkenness, etc.—**far'-off** *a.* distant.—**far'-see'ing**, or **-sight'ed** *a.* seeing to great distance; (*Fig.*) taking long view; prudent.—**far and away**, very considerably.

farce (fårs) *n.* orig. dramatic interlude; style of comedy marked by boisterous humour and extravagant gesture; absurd or empty show; pretence; stuffing for fowls, meat, fish, etc.; forcemeat;—*v.t.* cram; fill with stuffing.—**farceur** (får-ser') *n.*

joker; wag.—**far'cical** *a.* pert. to farce; absurdly ludicrous; sham.—**far'cically** *adv.*

fare (fār) *v.i.* go; travel; succeed; be in any state, bad or good; be entertained at table;—*n.* sum paid by passenger on vehicle; passenger; food and drink at table.—**farewell'** *interj.* (*Lit.*) may it go well with you; good-bye;—*n.* parting wish for someone's welfare; act of taking leave;—*a.* parting; last.—**farewell to**, no more of.

farm (farm) *n.* tract of land set apart for cultivation, pasturage, poultry breeding etc.; buildings on this.—*v.t.* lease or let out land for agricultural purposes; collect (taxes, etc.) on condition of receiving percentage of what is yielded;—*v.t.* and *i.* till; cultivate.—**farm'er** *n.* (*fem.* **farm'eress**).—**farm'house** *n.* dwelling-house attached to farm.—**farm'ing** *n.*—**farm'stead** *n.* farm with all outbuildings attached to it.—**farm'yard** *n.* enclosure surrounded by farm buildings.

farrier (far'-i-er) *n.* one who shoes horses; horse doctor.—**farr'iery** *n.*

farrow (far'-ō) *n.* litter of pigs;—*v.t.* give birth to (pigs);—*v.i.* bring forth pigs.

farther (får'-THer) *a.* more far; more remote;—*adv.* to a greater distance.—**far'thermost** *a.* most remote; farthest.

farthing (får'-THing) *n.* fourth of a penny.

farthingale (får'-THing-gāl) *n.* hoop petticoat for distending women's dress; kind of crinoline.

fasces (fas'-ēz) *n.pl.* bundle of rods with axe, carried by Roman magistrates as symbol of their authority.

fascia (fash'-i-a) *n.* band, fillet, or bandage; (*Archit.*) a strip of flat stone between two mouldings; instrument board of motor car; flat band above a shop front with owner's name, etc.

fascinate (fas'-i-nāt) *v.t.* deprive of power of movement, by a look; bewitch; enchant.—**fas'cinating** *a.*—**fascina'tion** *n.* act of fascinating; irresistible attraction; state of being bewitched.—**fas'cinator** *n.*

Fascism (fash'-izm) *n.* Italian Nationalist movement organised in 1919 by Benito Mussolini on military lines, hence any extremely right wing political system.—**Fasc'ist** *n.*

fash (fash) *v.t.* (*Scot.*) vex; annoy; trouble;—*v.i.* be anxious;—*n.* trouble; care.

fashion (fash'-un) *n.* style in which thing is made or done; pattern; mode or cut, esp. of a dress; custom; appearance;—*v.t.* form; contrive; shape.—**fash'ionable** *a.* made according to prevailing mode; stylish.—**fash'ionably** *adv.*

fast (fast) *v.i.* abstain from food; go hungry; deny oneself certain foods as form of religious discipline;—*n.* abstinence from food; day of fasting.

fast (fast) *a.* securely fixed; firm; tight shut; immovable; permanent, as a dye; stable; in advance of correct time, as a clock; loyal, as friends; rapid; dissipated;—*adv.* firmly; soundly; securely; dissipatedly; rapidly; near.—**fast'ness** *n.* security; stronghold.—**to play fast and loose with**, be unreliable or irresponsible.

fasten (fås'-n) *v.t.* fix firmly; hold together;—*v.i.* fix itself; catch (of a lock).—**fas'tener** *n.* contrivance for fixing things firmly together; clip.—**fas'tening** *n.* that by which anything fastens.

fastidious (fas-tid'-i-us) *a.* difficult to please.—**fastid'iously** *adv.*—**fastid'iousness** *n.*

fat (fat) *a.* fleshy; plump; corpulent; oily; yielding rich supply; productive; profitable;—*n.* oily substance found in various parts of animal bodies; solid animal or vegetable oil; best or richest part of anything;—*v.t.* make fat;—*v.i.* grow fat.—*pr.p.* **fat'ting**.—*pa.p.* **fat'ted**.—**fat'head** *n.* stupid person.—**fat'-head'ed** *a.*—**fat'ly** *adv.* grossly; clumsily.—**fat'ness** *n.* quality or state of being fat; corpulence; fertility.—**fat'ted** *a.*—**fat'ten** *v.t.* and *i.*—*pr.p.* **fattening**—**fat'tener** *n.*—**fat'tiness** *n.*—**fat'ty** *a.*

fate (fāt) *n.* inevitable and irresistible power supposedly controlling human destiny; appointed lot; death; doom.—**the Fates**, three goddesses supposed to preside over the course of human life.—**fat'al** *a.* appointed by fate; mortal; calamitous; deadly.—**fat'alism** *n.* doctrine that all events are pre-determined and inevitable.—**fat'alist** *n.*—**fatalist'ic** *a.*—**fatal'ity** *n.* state of being fatal; inevitable necessity; accident causing death.—**fat'ed** *a.* preordained.—**fate'ful** *a.* momentous; irrevocable.—**fate'fully** *adv.*—**fate'fulness** *n.*

father (få'-THer) *n.* male parent; male ancestor more remote than parent; title of respect paid to one of seniority or rank, esp. to Church dignitaries; oldest member of a community; producer, author or contriver;—*v.t.* make oneself father of; adopt; admit responsibility for.—**fa'therhood** *n.* state of being a father; paternity.—**fa'ther-in-law** *n.* (*pl.* **fa'thers-in-law**) father of one's wife or husband.—**fa'therland** *n.* land of one's fathers.—**fa'therless** *a.* without a father living.—**fa'therliness** *n.*—**fa'therly** *a.* and *adv.* like a father in affection and care; paternal; bene-volent.—**fa'thership** n.

fathom (faTH'-om) n. nautical measure of depth, 6 ft.; a timber measure, 6 ft. by 6 ft. by 6 ft.;—v.t. ascertain the depth of; sound; (*Fig.*) get to bottom of; understand. —**fath'omable** n.—**fath'omless** a. incapable of being fathomed; un-plumbed.—**fath'omlessly** adv.

fatigue (fa-tēg') n. weariness from bodily or mental exertion; toil; non-military routine work of soldiers; —v.t. weary by toil; exhaust strength of; tire out.—pr.p. **fatigu'-ing**.—pa.p. **fatigued'**.—**metal fatigue** n. weakening of metal due to stress.

fatuous (fat'-ū-us) a. feeble in mind; weak; silly; inane: idiotic.—**fatu'ity** n. weakness of mind; inanity; foolishness.—**fat'uousness** n.

fault (fawlt) n. failing; blunder; mistake; defect; flaw; (*Geol.*) dislocation of rock-strata; v.t. find fault with.—**fault'ily** adv.—**fault'iness** n.—**fault'less** a. without flaws; perfect.—**fault'lessly** adv.—**fault'lessness** n.—**faul'ty** a. imperfect; wrong.

fauna (fawn'-a) n. collective term for animals of any given geographical region or geological epoch;—pl. **faun'ae** (fawn'-ē), **faunas** (fawn'-az).—**faun** n. Roman deity supposed to protect shepherds.

favour (fā'-vor) n. kind regard; good-will; a gracious act; partiality; a rosette or ornament worn at wedding or as badge;—v.t. regard with kindness; show unfair bias towards; tend to promote.—**fa'vourable** a. friendly; advantageous; satisfactory.—**fa'vourableness** n.—**fa'vourably** adv.—**fa'voured** a. fortunate; lucky.—**fa'vourite** n. person or thing regarded with special favour; person unduly praised; likely winner;—a. regarded with particular affection. —**fa'vouritism** n. undue partiality.

fawn (fawn) n. young deer; fallow deer; its colour;—a. delicate greyish-brown.

fawn (fawn) v.i. flatter unctuously; grovel; curry favour.—**fawn'er** n.—**fawn'ing** n. servile flattery;—a. over-demonstrative.—**fawn'ingly** adv. —**fawn'ingness** n.

fear (fēr) n. emotion aroused by sense of impending danger; alarm; dread; anxiety;—v.t. regard with dread; anticipate (as a disaster); hold in awe;—v.i. be afraid; be anxious.—**fear'ful** a. afraid; apprehensive; dreadful.—**fear'fully** adv.—**fear'fulness** n.—**fear'less** a.—**fear'lessly** adv.—**fear'lessness** n.—**fear'some** a. causing fear; terrifying.

feasible (fēz'-i-bl) a. capable of being done.—**feas'ibleness**, **feasibil'ity** n.—**feas'ibly** adv.

feast (fēst) n. festival; day of joyful or solemn commemoration; banquet; —v.t. feed sumptuously;—v.i. eat sumptuously.—**feast'-day** n. festival; religious commemoration.

feat (fēt) n. action of great strength, courage, skill, or endurance.

feather (feTH'-er) n. body-covering of a bird; plume; feathered end of arrow;—v.t. cover with feathers; supply with feathers.—**feath'er-bed** n. mattress stuffed with feathers; v.t. (*Colloq.*) pamper.—**feath'er-brained**, **feath'er-head'ed**, a. silly; frivolous; inane.—**feather-weight**, lightest weight that may be carried by race-horse; boxer weighing not more than 9 st.; any very light person or thing.—**feath'ery** a. pert. to feathers.—**to feather one's nest**, accumulate wealth for oneself.—**a feather in one's cap**, honour or distinction.—**to show the white feather**, be a coward.

feature (fēt'-ūr) n. appearance of the body, esp. any part of the face; distinctive characteristic; newspaper article on specialised subject.—pl. the face;—v.t. portray; outline; in cinema, present as leading actor or actress in a film.—**feat'ureless** a. void of striking features.—**feature film**, film forming main part of cinema programme.

February (feb'-róō-a-ri) n. second month of year.

feces See **faeces**.

fecund (fē'-kund) a. fruitful; fertile.—**fecundate** (fē'-kun'-dāt, fek'-un-dāt) v.t. make fruitful; impregnate.—**fecunda'tion** n.—**fecund'ity** n. the quality or power of reproduction; fertility; productiveness.

fed (fed) pa.t. and pa.p. of the verb **feed**.—**fed' up** a. (*Slang*) bored; dissatisfied.

federal (fed'-e-ral) a. pert. to treaty, esp. between states; of association of states which, autonomous in home affairs, combine for matters of wider national and international policy; pert. to Northern States of America in Civil War.—**fed'eracy** n.—**fed'eralise** v.t. form a union under a federal government.—**fed'eralism** n. —**fed'eralist** n. supporter of such a union.—**fed'erate** v.t. unite states into a federation.—a. united; allied.—**federa'tion** n. a federal union.

fee (fē) n. orig. land held from a lord on condition of certain feudal services; fief; homage; remuneration for professional services; payment for special privilege;—v.t. pay a fee to; to hire.

feeble (fē'-bl) a. weak; frail; futile.—**fee'ble-mind'ed** a. mentally subnormal. **fee'bleness** n.—**fee'bly** adv.

feed (fēd) v.t. give food to; supply with nourishment; supply with material (as a machine);—v.i. eat; graze.—pr.p. **feed'ing**.—pa.p. and *pa.t.* **fed.**—*n.* that which is consumed, esp. by animals; milk in a baby's bottle; material supplied to a machine or channel by which it is fed.—**feed'er** *n.* one who feeds; device for supplying a machine with material; channel taking water to reservoir; branch railway-line connected with main line; baby's feeding-bottle; baby's bib.—**feed'ing** *n.* act of eating; grazing.—**feed'ing-bot'tle** *n.* specially shaped bottle for supplying liquid food to babies.

feel (fēl) *v.t.* perceive by touch; handle; be sensitive to; experience emotionally; have intuitive awareness of;—*v.i.* know by touch; be conscious of being; give rise to definite sensation; be moved emotionally. — *pr.p.* **feel'ing.** — *pa.p.* **felt.**—*n.* sensation of touch; quality of anything touched.—**feel'er** *n.* (*Zool.*) one of the tactile organs (antennae, tentacles, etc.) of certain insects and animals; tentative remark, proposal, etc.—**feel'ing** *n.* sense of touch; awareness by touch; intuition; sensibility; sympathy.—**feel'ings** *n.pl.* emotions;—*a.* kindly; responsive; possessing great sensibility.—**feel'ingly** *adv.*

feet (fēt) *n.pl.* of **foot.**

feign (fān) *v.t.* invent; pretend; counterfeit.—**feigned** *a.* pretended.—**feign'edly** *adv.*—**feign'edness** *n.*—**feign'ing** *n.* pretence; invention.—**feint** *n.* assumed appearance; semblance; misleading move in boxing, military operations, etc.—*v.i.* make deceptive move.

feldspar (feld'-spär) *n.* crystalline mineral comprising silicates of aluminium with varying proportions of potash, lime, or soda. Also **fel'spar.**

felicity (fe-lis'-i-ti) *n.* happiness; contentment.—**felic'itate** *v.t.* express pleasure to; congratulate.—**felicita'tion** *n.* congratulation; act of expressing good wishes.—**felic'itous** *a.* happy; prosperous; aptly expressed.—**felic'itously** *adv.*—**felic'itousness** *n.*

feline (fē'-līn) *a.* pert. to cats; catlike; (*Fig.*) treacherous.

fell (fel) *a.* cruel; ruthless; inhuman; bloody; keen; spirited.

fell (fel) *n.* animal's skin or hide.

fell (fel) *pa.t.* of the verb **fall.**

fell (fel) *v.t.* cause to fall; cut down; throw to the ground.—**fell'er** *n.*

fell (fel) *n.* tract of high moorland, as in the Lake District.

fellow (fel'-ō) *n.* orig. one who laid down money in common enterprise; partner; associate; equal; person; member of governing body of certain university colleges; member of literary or scientific society.—**fell'ow-coun'try-man** *n.* one of the same nationality.—**fell'ow-crea'ture** *n.* one of same race or kind.—**fell'ow-feel'ing**

n. feeling common to different people; sympathetic understanding.—**fell'ow-ship** *n.* state of being an associate; social intercourse; companionship; foundation for maintenance of resident university graduate; status of a Fellow of College or Society.

felon (fel'-on) *n.* one who has committed felony;—*a.* fierce; traitorous.—**felo'nious** *a.* wicked.—**felo'niously** *adv.* — **felo'niousness** *n.* — **fel'ony** *n.* (*Law*) orig. crime punishable by forfeiture of all land, property, etc.; crime more serious than *misdemeanour* (as murder, manslaughter, rape, arson, etc.).

felspar See **feldspar.**

felt (felt) *pa.t.* and *pa.p.* of **feel.**

felt (felt) *n.* closely matted fabric of wool, hair, etc. not made by weaving, but by pressure of heavy steam-heated rollers;—*v.t.* make into felt; cover with felt;—*v.i.* become matted like felt.—**felt'ing** *n.* art or process of making felt; the fabric.

female (fē'-māl) *n.* one of sex that bears young; (*Bot.*) plant which produces fruit;—*a.* pert. to childbearing sex; feminine.—**femine'ity** *n.* quality of being a woman.

feminine *a.* pert. to or associated with women; womanly; tender; (of males) effeminate.—**fem'ininely** *adv.* —**fem'inineness, feminin'ity** *n.* nature of female sex; womanliness.—**fem'inism** *n.* doctrine that maintains equality of the sexes; advocacy of women's rights.—**fem'inist** *n.*

femur (fē'-mur) *n.* thigh-bone.—**fem'oral** *a.*

fen (fen) *n.* low-lying marshy land; bog.—**fen'nish, fen'ny** *a.* boggy; swampy.—**fen'berry** *n.* cranberry.—**fen'-fire** *n.* will-o'-the-wisp.

fence (fens) *n.* means of defence; wall or hedge for enclosing; art of fencing; receiver of stolen goods;—*v.t.* enclose with fence; fend off danger from; guard;—*v.i.* make a fence; practise the art of swordplay; (*Fig.*) evade direct answer to opponent's challenge.—**fenc'er** *n.* one skilled in fencing; (*Fig.*) clever debater.—**fenc'ing** *n.* art or practise of self-defence with the sword; act of enclosing by fence; materials of which fence is made.

fend (fend) *v.t.* keep off; ward off; defend;—*v.i.* resist; parry; (*Scot.*) provide for; support.—**fend'er** *n.* that which acts as protection; kerb to prevent coals falling beyond hearth; device, usually a bundle of rope, to break impact of ship drawing alongside wharf or other vessel.

fennel (fen'-el) *n.* perennial umbelliferous plant with yellow flowers.

feoff (fěf) *v.t.* invest with fee or landed property; to enfeoff.

feral (fēr'-al) *a.* wild; untamed.

ferment (fẹr'-ment) *n.* substance which causes fermentation, as yeast; fermentation; (*Fig.*) tumult; agitation; commotion.—**ferment'** *v.t.* induce fermentation in; arouse commotion;—*v.i.* undergo fermentation; cure (of tobacco); (*Fig.*) become excited; be in state of agitation.—**fermentabil'ity** *n.*—**ferment'able** *a.*—**fermenta'tion** *n.* decomposition of organic substances produced by the action of a living organism, or of certain chemical agents.—**ferment'-ative** *a.* producing fermentation; caused by fermentation.

fern (fẹrn) *n.* plant characterised by fibrous roots, and leaves called fronds.—**fern'y** *a.*

ferocity (fe-ros'-i-ti) *n.* cruelty; savage fierceness; barbarity.—**fero'-cious** *a.* fierce; violent; wild.—**fero'ciously** *adv.*—**fero'ciousness** *n.*

ferret (fer'-et) *n.* small, partially domesticated variety of polecat used for driving out rabbits and rats from their holes;—*v.t.* hunt out with ferrets; (*Fig.*) search out by simple examination. — *pr.p.* **ferr'eting.** — *pa.p.* **ferr'eted.**

ferric (fer'-ik) *a.* pert. to or extracted from iron; applied to compounds of trivalent iron.—**ferric acid**, acid containing iron and oxygen.—**ferrif'erous** *a.* yielding iron.—**ferr'ite** *n.* form of iron oxide.—**ferruginous** *a.* containing iron; of the colour of iron-rust.—**ferru'go** *n.* plant disease caused by fungus.

ferro- (fer'-ō) *prefix fr.* L. *ferrum*, containing or made of iron, occurring in compound words.—**ferr'o-con'crete** *n.* reinforced concrete; concrete with inner skeleton of iron or steel.—**ferr'ous** *a.* pert. to iron; (*Chem.*) applied to compounds in which iron exists in its lower valency.

ferrule (fer'-il, fer'-ōōl) *n.* metal tip or ring on cane, etc. to prevent splitting.—Also **ferr'el.**

ferry (fer'-i) *v.t.* transport over stretch of water by boat or aircraft.—*pr.p.* **ferr'ying.**—*pa.p.* **ferr'ied.**—*n.* place where one is conveyed across river, etc. by boat; ferry-boat.

fertile (fer'-til, fer'-til) *a.* producing or bearing abundantly; prolific; fruitful; (*Fig.*) inventive.—**fer'tilely** *adv.*—**fer'tileness, fertilisa'tion** *n.* act of fertilising; enrichment of soil, by natural or artificial means; (*Biol.*) union of female and male cells.—**fer'tilise** *v.t.* make fruitful; (*Biol.*) fecundate; (*Bot.*) pollinate.—**fertilis'-er,** *n.* one who, or that which, fertilises; material (e.g. manure, nitrates) to enrich soil.—**fertil'ity** *n.*

fervent (fer'-vent) *a.* glowing; ardent; zealous; enthusiastic.—**fer'vency** *n.* ardour; intensity of devotion.—**fer'vently** *adv.*—**fer'vid** *a.* burning; vehement; intense.—**fervid'ity** *n.*—**fer'vidly** *adv.*—**fer'vidness** *n.* zeal; enthusiasm.—**fer'vour** *n.* heat; ardour; passion.

festal (fes'-tal) *a.* pert. to feast or festival; joyous; gay.—**fest'ally** *adv.*

fester (fes'-tẹr) *v.t.* cause to putrefy; —*v.i.* become inflamed; suppurate; (*Fig.*) become embittered.—*n.* ulcer; suppuration; putrefaction.

festive (fes'-tiv) *a.* festal; joyous; convivial.—**fes'tival** *n.* feast or celebration; annual gathering of musical or dramatic societies; special season of musical or dramatic performances.—**fes'tively** *adv.*—**festiv'ity** *n.* merriment; merrymaking; festival.

festoon (fes-tóòn') *n.* garland hanging in a curve;—*v.t.* adorn with garlands.

fetch (fech) *v.t.* go for and bring; summon; bring or yield (a price);—*v.i.* turn;—*n.* act of bringing; trick or artifice.—**fetch'ing** *a.* attractive; alluring.

fete (fet or fāt) *n.* festival; holiday; —*v.t.* honour with celebrations.—**fet'ed** *a.* honoured.

fetid (fē-tid) *a.* having strong offensive smell.—Also **foetid.**

fetish, fetich (fē'-tish, fet'-ish) *n.* object or image superstitiously invested with divine or demoniac power; anything regarded with exaggerated reverence.—**fet'ishism, fet'ich-ism** *n.*—**fetishist'ic, fetichist'ic** *a.*

fetlock (fet'-lok) *n.* tuft of hair behind the pastern joint in horse's leg; the part where this tuft grows.

fetter (fet'-ẹr) *n.* chain or shackle for the feet (usually pl.); impediment or restriction;—*v.t.* shackle; restrain.

fettle (fet'-l) *n.* readiness or fitness for work;—*v.t.* put in order; arrange;—*v.i.* potter about.

fetus, foetus (fē'-tus) *n.* the young of vertebrate animals between embryonic and independent states.—**fe'tal, foe'tal** *a.*—**feta'tion, foeta'tion** *n.*

feud (fūd) *n.* lasting, hereditary strife between families or clans; deadly hatred.

feud (fūd) *n.* estate or land held on condition of service; fief.—**feud'al** *a.* pert. to feuds or to feudalism.—**feud'alism** *n.* medieval system by which vassals held land from overlords in return for military service.—Also **feudal system.**—**feud'ary, feud'a-tory** *a.* holding land by feudal tenure; —*n.* vassal holding land in fee.

fever (fē'-vẹr) *n.* bodily disease marked by unusual rise of temperature; violent mental or emotional excitement; frenzy;—*v.t.* put into a fever;—*v.i.* become fevered.—**fe'-vered** *a.* affected with fever; frenzied.

—fe′verish a. slightly fevered; agitated.—fe′verishly adv.

few (fū) a. not many;—n. and pron. small number.—few′ness n.

fey (fā) a. doomed; fated to die, esp. having abnormal gaiety of spirit, supposed to portend death.

fez (fez) n. red, brimless felt hat with tassel, worn in Egypt, Turkey, etc.; —pl. fezz′es.

fiancé (fē-ong′-sā) n. (fem. fiancée) a betrothed man.

fiasco (fē-ás′-kō) n. failure in musical performance; any ignominious failure.

fibre (fī′-ber) n. one of the bundles of thread-like tissue constituting muscles, etc.; any thread-like substance, animal, mineral, or vegetable, used for weaving fabric; (Fig.) character, as in moral fibre.— fibr′oid a. of fibrous nature;—n. fibrous tumour.—fibrosi′tis n. rheumatic condition caused by inflammation of fibrous tissues.—fi′brous a. composed of fibres.—fi′brousness n.

fickle (fik′-l) a. inconstant; capricious; unreliable.—fick′leness n.

fiction (fik′-shun) n. story dealing with imaginary characters and situations; something invented, or imagined.—fic′tional a.—ficti′tious a. imaginary; feigned; false; (Law) assumed as true.—ficti′tiously adv.

fiddle (fid′-l) n. stringed musical instrument; violin; (Slang) swindle; —v.i. and i. play on fiddle; potter with things; (Slang) act or treat unscrupulously.—fidd′le-stick n. bow for playing on strings of violin.— fidd′ling a. trifling; futile.—to play second fiddle, take a subordinate position.

fidelity (fi-del′-i-ti) n. faithfulness; loyalty; devotion to duty; adherence to marriage vows; accuracy.

fidget (fij′-et) v.i. move restlessly; be inattentive;—pr.p. fidg′eting.—pa.p. fidg′eted. — n. uneasiness. — fidg′ets n.pl. nervous restlessness.—fidg′ety a. restless; nervous; fussy; overparticular.

fief (fēf) n. estate held on condition of military service.

field (fēld) n. cleared land; division of farm land; open country; scene of battle; battle itself; any wide expanse; area of observation; locality of operations, as in surveying; sphere of influence within which magnetic, electrostatic, or gravitational forces are perceptible; surface of escutcheon; background of flag, coin, etc. on which design is drawn; people following a hunt; (Cricket) side not batting; collective term for all competitors in an athletic contest or all horses in a race; area rich in some natural product (e.g. coalfield, oil-field);—v.t. (Cricket) stop

the ball and return it to bowler;— v.i. act as fielder at cricket.— field′-artillery n. light guns for active operations.—field′-battery n. battery of field-guns.—field′er n. one who fields at cricket, base-ball, etc.— field-event n. athletic contest other than a race.—field′-glass n. binocular telescope.—field′-gun n. small cannon on a carriage.—field′-mar′shal n. highest rank in the British, French, or German army.—field′-mouse n. small variety of mouse living in the fields.—field′-offi′cer n. commissioned officer in rank between captain and general.—field′-sports n.pl. outof-door sports such as hunting, racing, etc.—field′-works n.pl. temporary earthworks thrown up for defence.

fiend (fēnd) n. demon; devil; malicious foe; (Colloq.) an addict, as a fresh-air fiend.—fiend′ish a.

fierce (fērs) a. ferocious; violent; savage; intense.—fierce′ly adv.— fierce′ness n. ferocity.

fiery (fīr′-i) a. flaming; (Fig.) ardent; fierce; vehement; irritable.—fier′ily adv.—fier′iness n.

fife (fīf) n. small type of flute.— fif′er n. one who plays the fife.

fifteen (fif′tēn) a. and n. five and ten; team of fifteen players, esp. rugby fifteen.—fifteenth′ a. fifth after tenth; making one of fifteen equal parts.—The Fifteen, Jacobite Rebellion of 1715.

fifth (fifth) a. next after fourth;—n. one of five equal parts of a whole.— fifth′ly adv.

fifty (fif′-ti) a. and n. five times ten. —fif′tieth a. next in a series of forty-nine others; making one of fifty equal parts of a whole;—n. fiftieth part.—to go fifty-fifty (Colloq.) share and share alike.

fig (fig) n. small bag-shaped Mediterranean fruit; tree bearing this fruit; (Colloq.) insignificant thing.

fight (fīt) v.t. wage war against; contend against in single combat or in battle; oppose as in argument;— v.i. take part in single combat or battle; resist.—pr.p. fight′ing.—pa.p. fought (fawt).—n. combat; battle; struggle.—fight′er n. one who fights; (Aero.) aircraft designed for fighting —fight′ing a. able to, or inclined to, fight; pert. to fight.

figment (fig′ment) n. invention, fiction.

figure (fig′-ur) n. outward form of anything; form of a person; diagram, drawing, etc.; design; appearance; steps in a dance; sign of a numeral; price;—v.t. shape; cover with patterns; note by numeral characters; calculate; symbolise;—v.i. make a figure.—figured a. esp. adorned with patterns.—fig′urative a. representing

by a figure; not literal.—**fig'uratively**
adv.—**fig'urativeness** *n.*—**fig'urehead** *n.*
ornamental figure under the bow-
sprit of ship.

filament (fĭl'-ạ-ment) *n.* slender
thread; fibre; (*Elect.*) fine wire,
which glows by passage of electric
current.—**filament'ary** *a.*—**filament'-**
ous *a.* thread-like.

filbert (fĭl'-bert) *n.* nut of the cultivated hazel; the hazel-tree.

filch (fĭlch) *v.t.* steal.—**filch'er** *n.*
thief.

file (fīl) *n.* line, as of soldiers one
behind other; portfolio for keeping
papers in order; papers thus kept;—
v.t. set on a file;—*v.i.* to march in a
file.—**rank and file**, non-commissioned soldiers; general mass of people.

file (fīl) *n.* instrument for smoothing
rough surfaces, or cutting through
metal;—*v.t.* cut with a file.—*pr.p.*
fi'ling.—*pa.p.* **filed.**—**fi'ling** *n.* particle
of metal rubbed off by a file; action
of abrading stone or cutting metal.

filial (fĭl'ĭyạl) *a.* pert. to son or
daughter.—**fil'ially** *adv.*

filibuster (fĭl'-i-bus-tẹr) *n.* lawless
adventurer; pirate; buccaneer;
(*U.S.*) one who deliberately obstructs legislation;—*v.i.* act as
filibuster.

filigree (fĭl'-i-grē) *n.* ornamental
open-work of gold or silver wire.—
fil'igreed *a.*

fill (fĭl) *v.t.* make full; occupy as a
position; supply as vacant office;
stop (a tooth);—*v.i.* become full;—
n. full supply; as much as satisfies,
or fills up a space.—**fill'er** *n.* a funnel-
shaped vessel for filling bottles;
substance for filling cracks or holes.
—**fill'ing** *n.* that which is used by
dentists for stopping a tooth; mixture
put into sandwiches, cakes, etc.;—
a. ample.—**filling station**, depot for
supplying petrol, oil, etc., to
motorists.

fillet (fĭl'-et) *n.* narrow band, esp.
round the head; piece of meat cut
from the thigh; piece of meat boned
and rolled; fish after bones are
removed;—*v.t.* bind with a fillet;
bone (meat or fish, etc.);—*pr.p.*
fill'eting.—*pa.p.* **fill'eted.**

fillip (fĭl'-ip) *v.t.* strike with nail of
finger, first placed against the ball of
thumb then released with sudden
jerk; incite; spur on.—*pr.p.* **fill'iping.**
—*pa.p.* **fill'iped.**—*n.* jerk of finger;
incentive.

filly (fĭl'-i) *n.* young mare; lively
young woman.

film (fĭlm) *n.* thin coating or membrane; delicate filament; dimness
over the eyes; (*Photog.*) flexible,
sensitised material used for photography;—*pl.* (*Colloq.*) cinema show;
—*v.t.* cover with film; take moving
picture of; reproduce on film.—

film'y *a.* covered with film; membranous.

filter (fĭl'-tẹr) *n.* device for separating
liquids from solids, or straining
impurities from liquids; porous
material such as filter-paper, charcoal, etc.; percolator; (*Photog.*) piece
of tinted glass or gelatin for altering
relative intensity of component
wavelengths of light entering lens;
—*v.t.* purify by passing through a
filter;—*v.i.* pass through a filter;
percolate; join, as at road junction,
another line of traffic.—**fil'trate** *v.t.*
purify; filter;—*n.* clear liquid left
after filtering.—**filtra'tion** *n.*

filth (fĭlth) *n.* dirt; pollution; (*Fig.*)
immorality; obscenity.—**filth'ily** *adv.*
—**filth'iness** *n.*—**filth'y** *a.* unclean;
foul; corrupt.

fin (fĭn) *n.* paddle-like organ of fishes
serving to balance and propel;
(*Aero.*) vertical surface, fixed on
tail of aircraft to aid lateral and
directional stability.

final (fī'-nạl) *a.* pert. to the end; last;
decisive; ultimate;—*n.* last stage of
anything;—*pl.* last examination or
contest in a series.—**fi'nalist** *n.*
competitor who reaches the finals of
contest.—**final'ity** *n.* conclusiveness.
—**fi'nalise** *v.t.* give final form to.—
fi'nally *adv.*

finale (fĭ-nä'-lā) *n.* end; (*Mus.*) last
movement of musical composition;
final scene of an opera.

finance (fĭ-nans' or fī'-nans) *n.*
science of controlling public revenue
and expenditure; management of
money affairs;—*pl.* resources; funds;
—*v.t.* provide funds for; supply
capital for.—*pr.p.* **finan'cing.**—*pa.p.*
finan'ced.—**finan'cial** *a.* pert. to
finance; fiscal.—**finan'cially** *adv.*—
finan'cier (*U.S.* fin-an-sēr') *n.* officer
who administers the public revenue;
one who deals in large-scale money
transactions.

finch (fĭnch) *n.* name of small, seed-
eating birds including the *chaf-*
finch, *bullfinch*.

find (fīnd) *v.t.* come to by searching;
discover; perceive; supply (as
funds); (*Law*) give a verdict;—
pr.p. **find'ing.**—*pa.p.* **found.**—*n.* discovery.—**find'er** *n.*—**find'ing** *n.* act of
one who finds; legal decision arrived
at by jury.—**all found**, everything
provided.

fine (fīn) *a.* thin; slender; delicate;
beautiful; polished; excellent; showy;
refined (as *fine gold*); appealing
aesthetically (as the *Fine Arts*);
perceptive;—*v.t.* make fine; refine or
purify;—*v.i.* become fine, pure, or
slender;—*adv.*—**fine'ly** *adv.*—**fine'ness**
n. state of being fine; amount of gold
in an alloy.—**fin'er** *n.* refiner.—
fin'ery *n.* ornament; gay clothes;
—**fine'-spun** *a.* (*Fig.*) subtle; in-

genious. — **finesse'** n. stratagem; (*Whist, Bridge, etc.*) attempt to take trick with low card while holding higher card;—*v.t.* and *i.* use artifice; try to take trick by finesse.

fine (fīn) n. sum of money as penalty for an offence;—*v.t.* impose fine on.

finesse See fine.

finger (fing'-ger) n. digit; any one of the extremities of the hand, excluding thumb; width of a finger;—*v.t.* touch with fingers; handle; meddle with;—*v.i.* use the fingers.—**fing'er-board** n. part of violin, etc., on which fingers are placed.—**fing'ering** n. the act of touching lightly with fingers; manner of manipulating the fingers in playing musical instruments.—**fing'er-plate** n. ornamental plate fixed above handle of door to prevent soiling with finger-marks.—**fing'er-post** n. sign-post.—**fing'er-print** n. impression of markings on the ball of the finger serving as means of identification.—**fing'er-stall** n. protective covering for injured finger.

finicky (fin'-i-ki) a. over-particular about trivialities.

fining (fīn'-ing) n. the process of refining.

finish (fin'-ish) v.t. bring to an end; destroy; complete;—*v.i.* conclude;—n. that which finishes, or perfects; last stage; final coat of paint, etc.—**fin'ished** a. terminated; perfect; polished; (*Colloq.*) exhausted.

finite (fī'-nīt) a. limited in quantity, degree, or capacity; bounded.—**fi'nitely** adv.—**fin'iteness** n.

fiord, fjord (fyord) n. long narrow inlet of the sea, with very steep sides.

fir (fer) n. cone-bearing, evergreen tree.—**fir'-cone** n. fruit of the fir.

fire (fīr) n. heat and light caused by combustion; burning; conflagration; flame; discharge of fire-arms; ardour; spiritual or mental energy; eloquence;—*v.t.* set on fire; kindle; supply with fuel; bake as pottery, cakes, etc.; discharge (fire-arms, etc.); inflame; incite; (*Colloq.*) dismiss;—*v.i.* be ignited; be stimulated; discharge fire-arms.—**fire'-arm** n. weapon discharged by explosive substance.—**fire'-ball** n. meteor.—**fire'-brand** n. piece of flaming wood; torch; (*Fig.*) one who incites others; —**fire-break** n. cleared strips in forest land to prevent spread of fire; —**fire'-brick** n. brick capable of withstanding great heat, used in furnaces, etc.—**fire'-brigade'** n. men specially trained to deal with fire.—**fire'-clay** n. variety of clay used for fire-bricks, furnace-linings, etc.—**fire'-damp** n. combustible marsh-gas generated in coal-mines.—**fire'-dog** n. andiron.—**fire'-drill** n. training in rapid dispersal in event of fire.—

fire'-eat'er n. juggler who pretends to eat fire; bully.—**fire'-fly** n. type of beetle which is phosphorescent (e.g. glow-worm).—**fire'-guard** n. protective grating in front of fire. —**fire'-i'rons** n.pl. poker, tongs, shovel, etc.; a companion set.—**fire'man** n. member of fire-brigade; man who tends furnace; stoker.—**fire'-plug** (*abbrev.* F.P.) n. plug for drawing water by hose from main to extinguish fire; hydrant.—**fire'-rais'ing** n. arson.—**fire'-screen** n. movable screen to intercept the direct rays of a fire; fireguard; ornamental screen used in summer time to cover grate.—**fire'-war'den** n. (*U.S.*) forest fire-fighter; member of fire-fighting squad during enemy air-attacks.—**fire'-wat'er** n. term used by Red Indians for whisky, brandy, etc.—**fire'-wood** n. wood for fuel; kindling.—**fire'-work** n. a preparation containing gunpowder, sulphur, etc. for making spectacular explosions in air;—*pl.* pyrotechnics; (*Fig.*) brilliant display of wit, or eloquence.—**fir'ing** n. act of lighting fire, stoking furnace, or discharging gun; fuel; baking of bread, etc. in oven.—**fir'ing-line** n. battle zone within firing range of enemy.—**baptism of fire**, first time in battle.—**cross'-fire** n. fire from different directions.—**fire away** (*Colloq.*) begin.

firm (ferm) a. fixed; solid; steady; stern.—**firm'ly** adv.—**firm'ness** n.

firm (ferm) n. name, title, or style under which company transacts business.

firmament (fer'-ma-ment) n. region of the air; expanse of the sky; heavens.

first (ferst) a. preceding all others in series or in kind; foremost (in place); earliest (in time); most eminent; most excellent; highest; chief;—adv. before anything else in time, place, degree, or preference;—n. beginning.—**first'-aid** n. treatment given to injured person before arrival of doctor.—**first'-begott'en**, **-born** n. eldest child;—a. born first; eldest.—**first'-class** a. first-rate; of highest worth; of superior accommodation;—adv. in the first-class (of train, boat, etc.);—n. highest honours in examination. — **first'-floor** n. storey immediately above ground-floor; (*U.S.*) ground floor.—**first'-foot** n. (*Scot.*) first visitor to cross threshold on New-Year's Day. —**first'-fruits** n.pl. earliest gathered fruits, orig. dedicated to God; (*Fig.*) earliest results or profits.—**first'-hand** a. obtained direct from source.—**first'ly** adv.—**first'-rate** a. pre-eminent in quality, size, etc.; of highest excellence.—**of the first water**, of the highest quality.

firth (ferth) n. (*Scot.*) long narrow inlet of sea or estuary of river.

fiscal (fis'-kǝl) a. pert. to public treasury or revenue;—n. treasurer; (*Scot.*) one who prosecutes for the Crown in minor criminal cases; procurator-fiscal.

fish (fish) n. a cold-blooded, aquatic animal, with fins, and breathing through gills;—pl. fish, fish'es.—v.t. catch by fishing;—v.i. follow occupation of fisherman, for business or pleasure.—fish'-cu'rer n. one engaged in salting and smoking of fish.— fish'er n.—fish'erman n.—fish'ery n. business of fishing; legal right to fish in certain area.—fish'-hook n. barbed hook for catching fish by line. —fish'ily adv.—fish'ing n. act of fishing; legal right to fish in certain waters; particular stretch of water reserved for anglers.—fish'ing-tack'le n. angler's gear comprising rod, lines, hooks, etc.—fish'-meal n. dried fish ground into meal.—fish'mong'er n. retail dealer in fish.—fish'-slice n. fish-carver.—fish'-tail a. shaped like tail of fish.—fish'wife n. woman selling fish in streets.—fish'y a. abounding in fish; pert. to fish (of smell); expressionless; glazed (of eye); dubious (of a story).

fish (fish) n. strip of wood fixed longitudinally to strengthen mast, or clamp two pieces together;—v.t. splice; join together.—fish'-plate, -joint n. metal clamp used to join lengths of train rails together.

fissile (fis'-il) a. capable of being split or cleft.

fission (fish'-un) n. process of splitting or breaking up into two parts; (*Biol.*) cell-cleavage; in nuclear physics, splitting of atomic nucleus into two approx. equal fragments and number of neutrons, with the liberation of large amount of energy;—v.t. and i. split into two parts.—fiss'ionable a.

fissure (fish'-ūr) n. cleft, crack, or slit.

fist (fist) n. hand clenched with fingers doubled into palm; (*Colloq.*) handwriting.—fist'icuff n. blow with fist; —fisti'cuffs n.pl. boxing.

fistula (fis'-tū-la) n. a narrow duct; old name for water-pipe; (*Med.*) an infected channel in the body leading from an internal abscess to the surface.—fis'tular, fis'tulose a.

fit (fit) a. adapted to end or purpose; suitable; qualified; proper; vigorous (of bodily health);—v.t. make suitable; qualify; adapt; adjust;—v.i. be proper or becoming;—pr.p. fit'ting. —pa.p. fit'ted.—fit'ly adv.—fit'ment n. equipment;—fit'ments n.pl. furnishings.—fit'ness n. state of being fit; appropriateness; sound bodily health.—fit'ter n. one who makes

fit; tailor or dressmaker who fits clothes on a person; mechanic who assembles separate parts of machine. —fit'ting a. appropriate; suitable;— n. anything used in fitting up.— fit'tings n.pl. fixtures; equipment.— fit'tingly adv.—to fit in, insert neatly; to adapt oneself to one's company. —to fit out, equip with stores;—n. equipment.

fit (fit) n. sudden and violent attack of a disorder; a paroxysm; a seizure; a momentary impulse.— fit'ful a. spasmodic; intermittent.— fit'fully adv.

fitchet (fich'-et) n. polecat; its fur.

five (fīv) n. four and one;—a. one more than four.—fives n.pl. game of handball played against a wall.— five'fold a. five times repeated.— fiv'er n. (*Slang*) five-pound note.

fix (fiks) v.t. make firm; secure; make permanent, as photograph; make fast, as dye; determine; gaze at; put in order;—v.i. settle permanently; become hard;—n. calculated flight position of aircraft; (*Colloq.*) dilemma; predicament.—fixa'tion n. act of fixing; state of being fixed; steadiness; in psycho-analysis, emotional arrest of part of psychosexual development.—fix'ative n. fixing agent;—a. capable of fixing. —fixed a. settled; motionless; steady. —fix'edly adv.—fix'edness n.—fix'er n.—fixid'ity, fix'ity n. immobility.— fix'ture n. that which is fixed or attached; anything of accessory nature annexed to house or lands; sporting event, fixed for certain date.

fizz (fiz) v.i. make hissing sound; effervesce;—n. hissing sound; effervescent liquid, esp. champagne or lemonade; (*Slang*) bustle.—fiz'zle v.i. fizz or splutter.—fizzle out, go out like damp squib; (*Fig.*) come to ignominious end.—fiz'zy a.

fjord See fiord.

flabbergast (flab'-ǝr-gàst) v.t. overcome with amazement; confound; disconcert.

flabby (flab'-i) a. soft; yielding to touch; drooping; (*Fig.*) weak.— flab'bily adv.—flab'biness n.

flaccid (flak'-sid) a. soft; flabby; spineless; lax.—flac'cidly adv.—flac'cidness, flac'cidity n.

flag (flag) v.i. hang loosely; grow spiritless or dejected; become languid; lose vigour.—pr.p. flag'ging.— pa.p. flagged.

flag (flag) n. flat, oblong paving-stone.—Also flag'stone;—v.t. pave with flag-stones.

flag (flag) n. (*Bot.*) popular name of certain British plants, belonging to genus *Iris*, with long sword-shaped leaves.—flag'gy a. abounding in flags.

flag (flag) n. ensign or colours;

standard; banner as mark of distinction, rank, or nationality; bushy tail of setter dog;—*v.t.* decorate with flags or bunting; convey a message by flag-signals.—**flag'-cap'tain** *n.* captain of admiral's flag-ship.—**flag'-day** *n.* a day on which miniature flags are given in return for donation to some charity-fund.—**flag-lieuten'ant** *n.* officer in flag-ship.—**flag of convenience** *n.* foreign flag under which ships are registered in order to evade taxes etc. in their country of origin.—**flag'-officer** *n.* naval officer entitled to fly his own flag, i.e. commodore, rear-admiral and above.—**flag'-ship** *n.* ship flying the admiral's flag.—**flag'-staff** *n.* pole on which flag is flown.—**white flag**, symbol of truce or surrender.—**to strike one's flag**, surrender.

flagellate (flaj'-e-lāt) *v.t.* whip; scourge; flog;—*a.*—**flagel'lantism, flagella'tion** *n.*—**flagel'lant or flag'ellant** *n.* ascetic who scourges himself as punishment for sin.

flageolet (flaj'-ō-let) *n.* small whistle-flute with mouthpiece and (usually) six holes.

flagitious (fla-jish'-us) *a.* shamefully criminal; guilty of heinous crimes; atrocious.

flagon (flag'-on) *n.* narrow-necked vessel for holding liquids, usually with handle and spout.

flagrant (flā'-grant) *a.* glaring; notorious; scandalous.—**fla'grance, fla'grancy** *n.* notoriety; enormity; heinousness.—**fla'grantly** *adv.*

flail (flāl) *n.* implement for threshing grain by hand, consisting of stout stick attached to handle so that it swings freely.

flair (flār) *n.* instinctive discernment; keen scent.

flake (flāk) *n.* film; scale-like particle; carnation with two-coloured striped petals;—*v.t.* form into flakes; cover with flakes;—*v.i.* scale.—**flak'y** *a.*

flambeau (flam'-bō) *n.* flaming torch; ornamental candlestick;—*pl.* **flam'beaux.**

flamboyant (flam-boi'-ant) *a.* (*Archit.*) characterised by florid ornamentation; showy; ostentatious.—**flamboy'ance, flamboy'ancy** *n.*

flame (flām) *n.* mass of burning vapour or gas; blaze of light; fire in general; (*Fig.*) ardour; (*Colloq.*) sweetheart;—*v.i.* blaze; blush; become violently excited, fervent, or angry.—**flame'-col'oured** *a.* of colour of flame; bright red or yellow.—**flam'ing** *a.* blazing; gaudy;—**flam'ingly** *adv.*—**flamm'able** *a.* catching fire easily.—**flammabil'ity** *n.*

flamingo (fla-ming'-gō) *n.* tropical wading bird with long neck and legs, and deep pink plumage;—*pl.* **flaming'o(e)s.**

flan (flan) *n.* pastry shell or case filled, after baking, with savoury or fruit filling.

flange (flanj) *n.* projecting edge, as of railway-carriage wheel to keep it on the rails;—*v.t.* furnish with a flange.

flank (flangk) *n.* fleshy part of side of animal between ribs and hip; right or left side of army; part of bastion;—*v.t.* stand at the side of; border;—*v.i.* be posted on the side or flank.

flannel (flan'-el) *n.* soft-textured, loosely woven woollen cloth.—**flann'els** *n.pl.* clothes made of this, esp. sports garments;—*a.* made of flannel.—**flannelette'** *n.* a cotton material imitating flannel.

flap (flap) *n.* stroke; the motion or noise of anything broad and hanging loose; piece of material attached on one side only and usually covering an opening, as of envelope; anything hinged and hanging loose; (*Colloq.*) a state of excitement.—*v.t.* strike with something broad and flexible, such as duster; move rapidly up and down;—*v.i.* flutter; move, as wings.—*pr.p.* **flap'ping.**—*pa.p.* **flap'ped.**—**flap'doodle** *n.* (*Colloq.*) humbug; sheer nonsense.—**flap'jack** *n.* kind of broad, flat pancake; apple-puff; a biscuit made of rolled oats, usually circular; powder compact.—**flap'per** *n.* one who or that which flaps.

flare (flār) *v.i.* burn with glaring, unsteady flame; exhibit showy colours;—*n.* unsteady, blazing light; brilliant light used as a signal.—**flared** *a.* (of a skirt) cut on the cross of the material, hence, spreading or fluting out.—**flare'-path** *n.* line of lights along runway of airfield.—**flar'ing** *a.* blazing; garish; (*Fig.*) furious.—**flar'ingly** *adv.*

flash (flash) *n.* brief burst of light; instant or moment; a badge, as on soldier's uniform;—*a.* showy; tawdry;—*v.i.* blaze suddenly and die out; give out a bright but fitful gleam; shine out, as a sudden idea; pass swiftly;—*v.t.* cause to flash; transmit instantaneously, as news by radio, telephone, etc.—**flash'-back** *n.* (*Cinema*) momentary reproduction on screen of earlier episode in film-story.—**flash'-bulb** *n.* (*Photog.*) electric bulb giving brilliant flash for night picture.—**flash'ily** *adv.*—**flash'iness** *n.*—**flash'light** *n.* light which flashes intermittently; electric torch; brilliant momentary light used by photographers.—**flash'-point** *n.* lowest temperature at which vapour of volatile oils ignite when small flame is applied.—**flash'y** *a.* showy; tawdry; cheap.—**a flash in the pan**, abortive attempt; sensational but momentary success.

flask (flask) *n.* narrow-necked, usually flat, bottle easily carried in pocket; wicker-covered bottle; powder-horn.

flat (flat) *a.* level; even; tasteless; monotonous; dull; matt; uniform; downright; (*Mus.*) below true pitch (opp. of *sharp*);—*n.* level surface; low-lying tract of land; shoal; (part of) storey of house; (*Mus.*) note, semitone below the natural; symbol (♭) for this; piece of canvas mounted on frame used as stage scenery.—*adv.* prone; abruptly; (*Mus.*) below true pitch.—**flat'-fish** *n.* type of fish with flattened bodies, e.g. plaice, sole, etc.—**flat'-foot'ed** *a.* having fallen arches in the feet.—**flat'-i'ron** *n.* an iron for smoothing linen, etc. —**flat'let** *n.* small flat.—**flat'ly** *adv.* peremptorily.—**flat'ness** *n.*—**flat out**, of motor car, etc. at full speed.—**flat'-race** *n.* race over open ground.—**flat rate,** uniform rate.—**flat'-spin** *n.* (*Aero.*) spiral dive where aircraft rotates in a plane more horizontal than vertical; skid.—**flat'ten** *v.t.* make flat; lower the true musical pitch of; (*Fig.*) dismay; depress.

flatter (flat'-ẽr) *v.t.* praise insincerely; pay fulsome compliments to.—**flatt'erer** *n.* one who praises; a sycophant.—**flatt'ering** *a.* over-complimentary;—**flatt'eringly** *adv.*—**flatt'ery** *n.* undue praise; adulation.

flatulent (flat'-ū-lent) *a.* pert. to or affected with wind or gas in stomach and intestines; (*Fig.*) empty; vapid. —**flat'ulence, flat'ulency** distension of stomach or intestines by accumulation of wind or gas.—**flat'ulently** *adv.*

flaunt (flawnt) *v.t.* display ostentatiously;—*v.i.* wave or move in the wind; parade showily;—*n.* a vulgar display.

flautist (flaw'-tist) *n.* a flute-player.

flavour (flā'-vur) *n.* relish; savour; quality affecting taste or smell; (*Fig.*) distinctive quality affecting senses;—*v.t.* season; (*Fig.*) give zest to.—**fla'vorous** *a.*—**fla'vouring** *n.* substance to add flavour to a dish.

flaw (flaw) *n.* crack; defect; weak point as in argument.—**flaw'less** *a.* perfect.

flax (flaks) *n.* fibres of annual purple-flowered plant, *Linum,* used for making linen; the plant.—**flax'en** *a.* pert. to or resembling flax; of the colour of unbleached flax, hence yellowish or golden (esp. of hair).

flay (flā) *v.t.* skin; (*Fig.*) criticise bitterly.

flea (flē) *n.* small wingless insect with irritating bite.

fleck (flek) *n.* spot; streak;—*v.t.* spot.

flection See **flexion.**

fled (fled) *pa.t.* and *pa.p.* of **flee.**

fledge (flej) *v.t.* supply with feathers, as an arrow; rear young bird;—*v.i.* acquire feathers; become able to fly (of birds).—**fledge'ling** *n.* young bird just fledged; (*Fig.*) young untried person.

flee (flē) *v.t.* shun; hasten from;—*v.i.* fly or retreat from danger.

fleece (flēs) *n.* coat of wool covering a sheep or shorn from it; anything resembling wool;—*v.t.* shear wool (from sheep); (*Fig.*) rob; swindle.—**fleec'y** *a.* woolly; resembling wool in appearance or softness.

fleet (flēt) *n.* group of ships; force of naval vessels; (*Fig.*) number of motor-vehicles, etc. working as unit. —**fleet** (flēt) *n.* creek, inlet, or small stream.

fleet (flēt) *a.* swift; nimble.—**fleet'ing** *a.* transient; ephemeral; passing.—**fleet'ingly** *adv.*—**fleet'ness** *n.* swiftness.—**fleet'-footed** *a.*

Fleming (flem'-ing) *n.* native of Flanders.—**Flem'ish** *a.* pert. to Flanders or to the people of Flanders;—*n.* inhabitants of Flanders; language of Flanders.

flesh (flesh) *n.* body tissue; muscles, fat, etc. covering bones of animal; meat of animals or birds; animal nature; body as distinct from soul; mankind; kindred; sensuality; pulpy part of fruit;—*v.t.* glut; thrust into flesh, as a sword; remove flesh from. —**flesh'-eat'er** *n.* a carnivore.—**flesh'er** *n.* (*Scot.*) butcher.—**flesh'iness** *n.* state of being fleshy; plumpness. —**flesh'less** *a.*—**flesh'ly** *a.* corporeal; corpulent; sensual.—**flesh'-pot** *n.* vessel in which meat is cooked; (*Fig.*) luxurious living.—**flesh'y** *a.* pert. to flesh; corpulent; gross.—**proud flesh** (*Med.*) growth of granular tissue over wound.—**in the flesh,** alive.

fletch (flech) *v.t.* feather (as an arrow). —**fletch'er** *n.* a maker of arrows.

fleur-de-lis (fler-dẹ-lē') *n.* flower of the lily; royal insignia of France.

flew (flōō) *pa.t.* of verb **fly.**

flex (fleks) *v.t.* and *i.* bend (as joints of the body);—*n.* (*Elect.*) flexible insulated wire or cable.—**flexibil'ity** *n.* quality of being pliable; (*Fig.*) adaptability; versatility.—**flex'ible, flex'ile** *a.* capable of being bent; pliant.—**flex'ibly** *adv.*—**flex'ion, flec'tion** *n.* bend; fold; inflection.—**flex'or** *n.* a muscle which by contracting allows a joint to bend (opp. of *extensor*).—**flex'ure** *n.* act of bending, esp. under pressure.

flibbertigibbet (flib'-ẹr-ti-jib'-et) *n.* gossip; flighty person.

flick (flik) *v.t.* strike lightly, as with whip;—*n.* light, smart stroke.

flicker (flik'-ẹr) *v.i.* flutter; waver; burn unsteadily.—*n.* act of wavering; quivering (as of leaves, flames, etc.).—**the flicks** (*Slang*) cinema programme.

flight (flīt) *n.* act or power of flying;

distance covered in flying; journey by aeroplane; formation of planes forming unit of command in R.A.F.; flock of birds; soaring, as of the imagination; discharge of arrows; trajectory; series of steps.—flight'-deck n. deck of aircraft carrier for planes to land or take off.—flight'-lieuten'ant n. rank in R.A.F. equivalent to army captain.—flight'y a. capricious; volatile.

flight (flīt) n. act of fleeing; retreat. —to put to flight, to rout.

flimsy (flim'-zi) a. thin; fragile; unsubstantial; — n. thin, transfer-paper; (Slang) banknote.—flim'sily adv.—flim'siness n.

flinch (flinsh) v.i. shrink from pain; wince; fail.—flinch'ing n.

fling (fling) v.t. throw from the hand; hurl; send out; plunge;—v.i. flounce; throw oneself violently.—pr.p. fling'-ing.—pa.p. flung.—n. cast or throw; gibe; abandonment to pleasure; lively dance, as Highland fling.—fling'er n.

flint (flint) n. hard variety of quartz, which produces fire when struck with steel; anything hard; prehistoric stone weapon;—a. made of flint.—flint'-lock n. gun-lock with flint fixed on hammer for firing the priming.—flint'y a. (Fig.) hard-hearted; cruel.

flip (flip) n. hot drink composed of beer and spirits sweetened; drink of hot milk, eggs, sugar and spirits.

flip (flip) v.t. flick; toss by striking fingertip with thumb; fillip; jerk.—pr.p. flip'ping.—pa.p. flipped.—n. flick; snap; (Colloq.) short trip, or pleasure flight, in aeroplane.—flip'per n. limb of an animal which facilitates swimming.

flippant (flip'-ant) a. pert; lacking seriousness; shallow.—flipp'ancy n. frivolity; pertness.—flipp'antly adv.

flirt (flėrt) v.i. move playfully to and fro, as a fan;—v.t. move about briskly; play the coquette; dally;—n. philanderer; flighty girl.—flirta'-tion n.—flirta'tious a.

flit (flit) v.i. fly away; dart along; move unobtrusively; (Scot.) remove from one house to another.—pr.p. flit'ting.—pa.p. flit'ted.

flitch (flich) n. side of hog, salted and cured; steak of halibut; plank of wood.

flite, flyte (flīt) v.i. wrangle; quarrel; (Scot.) scold.

flitter (flit'-ėr) v.i. flutter.—flitt'er-mouse n. bat.—Also flick'ermouse, flind'ermouse.

float (flōt) v.i. rest or drift on surface of liquid; be buoyed up; be suspended in air; (Fig.) wander aimlessly;—v.t. cause to stay on surface of a liquid; set going, as business company; put into circulation;—n.

anything buoyant; raft; cork or quill on fishing line, or net; hollow floating ball of metal indicating depth of liquid in cistern; plasterer's trowel; low, flat lorry; (Aero.) streamlined attachment to sea-plane enabling it to float; theatre footlights.—float'able a. capable of being floated.—float'age n. floating capacity of anything; anything afloat; flotsam.—floata'tion See flotation.—float'er n.—float'ing a. buoyant on surface of liquid or in air; movable; fluctuating; in circulation; unfunded.—floating anchor, sea anchor.—floating ribs, lower ribs not connected to breast-bone.

floccus (flok'-us) n. long tuft of wool or hair;—pl. flocci (flok'-sī).—floc'-cular, floc'culate, floc'culent, floc'-culose, floc'culous a. woolly; having tufts; flaky.

flock (flok) n. small tuft of wool; refuse of wool, used for stuffing cushions, etc.

flock (flok) n. collection of animals (esp. sheep and goats) or birds; crowd of people; Christian congregation;—v.i. come together in crowds.

floe (flō) n. extensive field of ice floating in sea.

flog (flog) v.t. beat or strike, as with whip; thrash; (Slang) sell;—pr.p. flog'ging.—pa.p. flog'ged.

flood (flud) n. overflow of water; inundation deluge; flowing in of tide; (Lit. and Fig.) torrent.—v.t. overflow; drench; (Fig.) overwhelm; —v.i. spill over; rise (as tide).—pr.p. flood'ing.—pa.p. flood'ed.—flood'-gate n. gate to stop or let out flood-water; sluice.—flood'-light'ing n. artificial lighting of building exterior.—flood'-tide n. rising tide; (Fig.) peak of prosperity.

floor (flōr) n. horizontal surface of room; storey; level area; bottom (of sea); minimum level, esp. of prices. —v.t. cover with a floor; strike down; (Fig.) perplex; stump (in argument).—floor'er n. knock-out blow; baffling examination question or situation.—floor'ing n. materials for floors.—first'-floor n. storey immediately above ground-floor; (U.S.) ground-floor.

flop (flop) v.t. flap; set down heavily. —v.i. drop down suddenly or clumsily. — pr.p. flop'ping. — pa.p. flopped.—n. fall, as of soft body; (Slang) fiasco.—flop'py a. slack.

flora (flō'-ra) n. plants native to certain geographical region or geological period.—flor'al a. pert. to flowers.— flor'ally adv.— flor'eated, flor'iated a. decorated with a floral motif.—flor'et n. single flower in cluster of flowers; small compact flower-head.—flor'ist n. grower or seller of flowers.

florescence (flō-res'-ens) n. bursting into flower.—flores'cent a.

floriculture (flo'-ri-kul'-tūr) n. cultivation of flowering plants.—floricul'tural a.—floricul'turist n.

florid (flor'-id) a. orig. flowery; bright in colour; over-elaborate; (of writing) ornate; (of complexion) highly coloured; (Archit.) flamboyant.—flor'idly adv.

florin (flor'-in) n. orig. Florentine gold coin of 11th cent.; silver two-shilling piece; Dutch guilder.

floruit (flō'-rōō-it) n. period of person's life or fame.

floss (flos) n. untwisted threads of very fine silk; outer fibres of silkworm's cocoon.

flotation (flō-tā'-shun) n. act of floating; science of floating bodies; (Fig.) act of launching, esp. limited liability company. Also floata'tion.

flotilla (flō-til'-a) n. fleet of small vessels; esp. of destroyers.

flotsam (flot'-sam) n. goods or wreckage found floating on the sea.

flounce (flouns) v.i. turn abruptly;—n. sudden, jerky movement.

flounce (flouns) n. plaited border or frill on hem of dress;—v.t. trim with flounce.

flounder (floun'-der) n. small, edible flat-fish, allied to plaice.

flounder (floun'-der) v.i. struggle helplessly, as in marshy ground; (Fig.) stumble hesitatingly, as in a speech.

flour (flour) n. finely-ground meal of wheat, etc.; finely powdered substance;—v.t. turn into flour; sprinkle with flour;—flour'y a.

flourish (flur'-ish) v.i. use flowery language; brandish;—v.i. grow luxuriantly; prosper;—n. ornament; fanciful stroke of the pen; rhetorical display; fanfare; brandishing (of a weapon);—flour'ishing a. thriving.

flout (flout) v.t. mock; disregard with contempt;—v.i. jeer.

flow (flō) v.i. run, as liquid; rise, as tide; circulate, as blood; issue forth; glide along; proceed from;—v.t. overflow;—n. stream; current; rise of tide; easy expression of thought, etc.; output.—flow'ing a. moving; running; curving gracefully, as lines; falling in folds, as drapery.

flower (flou'-er) n. (Bot.) reproductive organ in plants; blossom; choicest part of anything; finest type;—v.t. adorn with flowers;—v.i. produce flowers; come to prime condition.—flow'ered a. decorated with flower-pattern. — flow'eret n. small flower; floret.—flow'ering a. having flowers.—flow'ery a. abounding in, or decorated with, flowers; (of style) highly ornate.

flown (flōn) pa.p. of fly.

'flu (flōō) n. (Colloq.) influenza.

fluctuate (fluk'-tū-āt) v.i. move up and down, as wave; be unstable;—v.t. cause to move.—fluc'tuant a.—fluctua'tion n. a rising and falling.

flue (flōō) n. small shaft or duct in chimney; pipe for conveying air through boiler; opening in pipe of an organ.

fluent (flōō'-ent) a. flowing; voluble.—flu'ency n.—flu'ently adv.

fluff (fluf) n. light, floating down; downy growth of hair on skin;—v.i. become downy; (Slang) make errors in speaking of stage part; bungle.—fluff'y a.

fluid (flōō'-id) n. substance which flows (liquid, gas, etc.);—a. capable of flowing; liquid; gaseous; unstable;—fluid'ify v.t.—fluid'ity, flu'idness n.

fluke (flōōk) n. the flounder; kinds of parasitic flat-worm causing liver-rot in sheep, etc.; flattened barb at extremity of either arm of anchor; (Colloq.) any lucky chance.

flummox (flum'-oks) v.t. (Slang) disconcert; confound. Also flum'mux.

flung (flung) pa.t. and pa.p. of fling.

flunkey (flung'-ki) n. liveried man-servant; footman; (Fig.) toady; cringing, obsequious person.—flun'keydom n. flunkeys collectively.—flun'keyism n.

fluor (flōō'-or) n. mineral, fluoride of calcium, usually called fluorspar, also called Blue John.—fluoresce' v.i. exhibit fluorescence; emit radiation.—fluores'cence n. property of absorbing radiation and emitting it as light of a greater wavelength.—fluores'-cent a.—flu'oride n. compound of fluorine with another element.—flu'ordise v.t.—flu'orine n. gaseous very active element, obtained from fluorspar and cryolite.—flu'orite n. fluorspar.—flu'orous a. derived from fluor.—fluorescent lighting, form of artificial diffused lighting.

flurry (flur'-i) n. sudden, brief gust of wind; bustle;—v.t. agitate; fluster;—pr.p. flurr'ying.—pa.p. flurr'ied.

flush (flush) v.i. become suffused with blood; turn red in the face; blush;—v.t. cause to blush or turn red; cleanse with rush of water;—n. flow of water; rush of blood to face; mill-stream; freshness;—a. and adv. well supplied with, as money.

flush (flush) v.t. cause to start, as a hunter, a bird;—v.i. fly up quickly and suddenly from concealment;—n. flock of birds flying up suddenly.

flush (flush) n. run of cards of same suit.

flush (flush) v.t. level up;—a. being in the same plane.

fluster (flus'-ter) v.t. make hot and agitated; flurry;—v.i. be confused and flurried;—n. confusion; muddle.—flus'tered a.

flute (flōōt) n. wood-wind instrument,

with lateral holes, blown directly (i.e. without reed); stop in pipe-organ; (*Archit.*) vertical groove in shaft of column; similar groove as in lady's ruffle;—*v.t.* play (tune) on flute; make flutes or grooves in.—**flut'ed** *a.* ornamented with grooves, channels, etc.—**flut'er** *n.*—**flut'ing** *n.* action of playing flute; the ornamental vertical grooving on pillar, on glass, or in lady's ruffle.—**flut'ist** *n.* one who plays a flute. Also **flaut'ist.**—**flut'y** *a.* flute-like in tone.

flutter (flut'-er) *v.t.* cause to flap; throw into confusion; move quickly;—*v.i.* flap the wings; move with quick vibrations; (of heart) palpitate;—*n.* quick and irregular motion; nervous hurry; confusion; (*Colloq.*) a mild gamble.

fluvial (floo'-vi-al) *a.* pert. to river.

flux (fluks) *n.* act of flowing; fluidity; (*Phys.*) rate of flow; (*Med.*) morbid discharge of body-fluid, esp. blood; dysentery; excrement; (*Chem.*) substance added to another to promote fusibility; continuous process of change;—*v.t.* fuse; purge;—*v.i.* flow.—**flux'ion** *n.* flowing; abnormal discharge of fluid catarrh; fusion.

fly (flī) *v.t.* cause to fly; direct the flight of; flee from;—*v.i.* move through the air; travel by aeroplane; move rapidly; flee;—*pr.p.* **fly'ing.**—*pat.* **flew** (floo).—*pa.p.* **flown.**—*n.* a winged insect; a house-fly; fish-hook in imitation of fly; flap on a garment covering row of buttons.—**flies** *n.pl.* space above theatre stage where scenery is moved;—*a.* (*Slang*) wide-awake; nimble-witted.—**fly'-blow** *n.* larva of a fly.—**fly'-blown** *a.* tainted with fly-blow; maggoty.—**fly'-by-night** *n.* gadabout; cheat; cad (*abbrev.* fly);—*a.* flighty; unreliable.—**fly'er, fli'er** *n.*—**fly'-fish'ing** *n.* catching fish by artificial flies on hook.—**fly'ing** *n.* moving through air: air navigation;—*a.* capable of flight; swift.—**fly'ing-boat** *n.* seaplane with boat-like hull.—**fly'ing-but'tress** (*Archit.*) arched prop attached only at one point to mass of masonry whose outward thrust it is designed to counteract.—**fly'ing-col'umn** *n.* body of soldiers equipped for rapid movement and independent of main base.—**fly'ing-fish** *n.* fish which can leap from water and fly through the air.—**fly'ing-fox** *n.* tropical fruit-eating bat with fox-like face.—**fly'ing-machine'** *n.* aircraft.—**flying squad**, special mobile unit of police force.—**flying squirrel**, squirrel-like rodent with expanding fold of skin between front and hind legs.—**flying visit**, hasty, unexpected visit.—**fly'-leaf** *n.* blank page at beginning or end of book.—**fly'-over** *n.* carriageway carried over the top of another

one at a cross-roads.—**fly'-rail** *n.* hinged flap attached to table for supporting adjustable leaf.—**fly'-wheel** *n.* heavy-rimmed wheel attached to shaft to stabilise speed or accumulate kinetic energy.—**to fly off at a tangent**, digress from topic under discussion.—**to fly a kite**, obtain money by accommodation bills; test probable public reaction.

foal (fōl) *n.* young of mare or she-ass; colt or filly;—*v.t.* and *v.i.* bear a foal.

foam (fōm) *n.* froth; spume; bubbles of air on surface of effervescent liquid;—*v.i.* froth; bubble; gather foam.—**foam'ing** *a.*—**foam'ingly** *adv.*—**foam'-rub'ber** *n.* sponge-like aerated latex.—**foam'y** *a.* frothy.

fob (fob) *n.* small pocket in waistband for holding watch.—**a fob chain**, chain with seals, etc. dangling from fob.

fob (fob) *v.t.* cheat; impose on;—*n.* swindler.—*pr.p.* **fob'bing.**—*pat.* and *pa.p.* **fobbed.**—**to fob off**, impose on someone by deliberate trickery.

fo'c'sle See **forecastle.**

focus (fō'-kus) *n.* point at which rays meet after reflection or refraction; point of concentration;—*pl.* **fo'cuses**, **foci** (fō'-sī);—*v.t.* bring to focus; adjust; concentrate;—*v.i.* converge.—*pr.p.* **fo'cus(s)ing.**—*pa.p.* **fo'cus(s)ed.**—**fo'cal** *a.*—**in focus**, clearly outlined; well defined.—**out of focus**, distorted.

fodder (fod'-er) *n.* food for cattle;—*v.t.* supply with fodder.

foe (fō) *n.* enemy; adversary; hostile army.—**foe'man** *n.* enemy in war;—*pl.* **foe'men.**

foetus See **fetus.**

fog (fog) *n.* thick mist; watery vapour in lower atmosphere; cloud of dust or smoke obscuring visibility; cloudiness; (*Fig.*) mental confusion;—*v.t.* shroud in fog; perplex the mind;—*v.i.* become cloudy or obscured.—**fog'-bank** *n.* mass of fog over the sea.—**fog'-bound** *a.* hindered by fog from reaching destination.—**fog'gily** *adv.*—**fog'giness** *n.*—**fog'gy** *a.*—**fog'-horn** *n.* loud siren used during fog.—**fog'-sig'nal** *n.* detonator placed on railway track during fog.

fogy, fogey (fō'-gi) *n.* dull, old fellow.

foible (foi'-bl) *n.* weakness of character; failing.

foil (foil) *v.t.* frustrate; baffle; put off the scent; defeat;—*n.* track of hunted animal; frustration; defeat; blunt sword, with button on point, for fencing practice.

foil (foil) *n.* thin leaf of metal; thin leaf of metal placed under gems to increase their brilliancy or colour; thin coating of quicksilver amalgam on back of a mirror; (*Archit.*) a leaf-like ornament in windows, niches, etc. (*trefoil, quatrefoil,* etc.); (*Fig.*)

anything serving to set off something else.

foist (foist) v.t. palm off; insert surreptitiously or unwarrantably.—**foist'er** n.

fold (fōld) n. doubling over of flexible material; plait; coil (of rope); crease made by folding;—v.t. double over; enclose within folds; embrace; —v.i. be plaited or doubled.— **fold'er** n. one who or that which folds; file for holding papers, etc.

fold (fōld) n. enclosure for sheep; pen; flock of sheep; (Fig.) Church; congregation;—v.t. confine in fold or pen.

foliage (fō'-li-āj) n. leaves of plant in general; leafage.—**fo'liaged** a. having leaves.—**fo'liate** v.t. hammer (metal) into laminae or foil; (Archit.) ornament with leaf-design; number leaves (not pages) of a book.— **fo'liated** a.—**folia'tion** n.

folio (fō'-li-ō) n. sheet of paper once folded; book of such folded sheets; two opposite pages of ledger used for one account and numbered the same; (Print) page number in book; —a. pert. to sheets folded so as to make two leaves;—v.t. number the pages of a book on one side only.

folk (fōk) n. people in general, or as a class; race.—**folks** n.pl. (Colloq.) one's own family and near relations; (U.S.) people.—**folk'-dance** n. traditional country-dance.—**folk'-lore** n. popular superstitions or legends; study of traditional beliefs.—**folk'-lo'rist** n.—**folk'-song** n. traditional melody or ballad handed down from one generation to another.—**folk'-sto'ry**, or -tale, n. popular myth.

follicle (fol'-ik-l) n. (Bot.) one-celled seed vessel; (Zool.) small sac; (Anat.) gland, as in hair-follicle.—**follic'ular** a. pert. to follicle.

follow (fol'-ō) v.t. go after; move behind; adhere to (belief); practise (as trade or profession); comprehend; watch carefully; keep in touch with;—v.i. come after; pursue; occur as consequence;—n. act of following.—**foll'ower** n. one who comes after; disciple; supporter.— **foll'owing** n. supporters, adherents, vocation;—a. coming next after; (of a wind) favourable.—**to follow on**, come after interval has elapsed; (Cricket) have second innings when opponents are leading by certain number of runs.—**to follow up**, continue an action to get the maximum result; pursue an advantage.

folly (fol'-i) n. want of sense; foolish action.

foment (fo-ment') v.t. bathe with warm water; (Fig.) instigate.— **fomenta'tion** n. action of applying warm lotions; warm lotion applied. —**foment'er** n.

fond (fond) a. orig. foolish; doting; very affectionate.—**fond of**, much attached to; addicted to.—**fond'le** v.t. caress; stroke tenderly.—**fond'ly** adv.—**fond'ness** n.

fondant (fon'-dant) n. soft sugary sweetmeat.

font (font) n. stone basin for holding baptismal water.

food (fōōd) n. matter which one feeds on; solid nourishment; that which, absorbed by any organism, promotes growth; (Fig.) mental or spiritual nourishment.—**food'-stuff** n. nutritious edible commodity.

fool (fōōl) n. orig. imbecile; one who behaves stupidly; one devoid of common sense; simpleton; clown; dupe;—v.t. make a fool of; impose on; hoax;—v.i. behave like a fool.— **fool'ery** n.—**fool'-hard'ily** adv.—**fool'-hard'iness** n.—**fool'-hard'y** a. recklessly daring.—**fool'ish** a. ill-considered; stupid.—**fool'ishly** adv.—**fool'ishness** n.—**fool'ing** n. foolery.—**fool'proof** a. so devised that mishandling cannot cause damage.—**fools'cap** n. folio writing paper about 16¼ by 13¼ ins. —**a fool's errand**, fruitless errand.— **fool's paradise**, state of illusory happiness.

fool (fōōl) n. dessert consisting of purée of fruit mixed with cream or custard.

foot (foot) n. extremity of limb on which an animal stands or walks; base or support; bottom end; infantry; measure of length = 12 inches; unit in prosody, combination of syllables; margin at lower edge of printed page;—pl. **feet**.—v.t. traverse by walking; pay (a bill); put a new foot on;—v.i. dance; walk.—pr.p. **foot'ing**.—pa.p. **foot'ed**.—**foot'age** n. measurement in feet.—**foot'ball** n. ball used in games such as Rugby, Soccer; play with this ball.— **foot'baller** n.—**foot'breadth** n. width of foot.—**foot'-bridge** n. narrow bridge for foot-passengers.—**foot'ed** a. having feet or a foot (usually in compounds as two-footed, sure-footed).— **foot'-fall** n. step; sound of step.— **foot'gear** n. boots and shoes; stockings, socks.—**foot'hill** n. minor hill at base of higher range (usually pl.).— **foot'hold** n. support for foot; space to stand on.—**foot'ing** n. ground to stand on; status (in society).— **foot'lights** n.pl. row of screened lights along front of stage;—**foot'-loose** a. free to do as one likes.—**foot'man** n. liveried man-servant.—**foot'mark** n. footprint.—**foot'note** n. note of reference or explanation at foot of page.—**foot'pad** n. robber who frequents highways and byways on foot.—**foot'-pas'senger** n. pedestrian. —**foot'path** n. narrow path for pedestrians only.—**foot'plate** n. platform used by driver and fireman of locomotive.—**foot'-pound** *n.* unit of work being the energy required to lift 1 lb. vertically to height of 1 ft. against gravity.—**foot'print** *n.* impression made by foot.—**foot'rot** *n.* inflammatory disease affecting feet of sheep and cattle.—**foot'-rule** *n.* ruler or measure one foot long.—**foot'-scra'per** *n.* iron-barred device for cleaning muddy boots before entering a house.—**foot'slog** *v.i.* (*Slang*) tramp. —**foot'slogger** *n.* walker; foot-soldier. —**foot'-sol'dier** *n.* infantryman.— **foot'sore** *a.* having aching feet through over-walking.—**foot'step** *n.* tread; sound of this; print of foot.— **foot'stool** *n.* low stool for resting feet on.—**foot'wear** *n.* boots, shoes, etc. collectively.—**foot and mouth disease**, highly contagious disease of sheep, swine, and horned cattle.—**to put one's foot down**, refuse firmly.—**to put one's foot in it**, say something embarrassing.—**to fall on one's feet**, to be very lucky.

footle (fŏŏ'-tl) *v.i.* (*Colloq.*) bungle; be incompetent.

fop (fop) *n.* conceited, effeminate man; dandy.—**fop'pery** *n.* affectation in dress.—**fop'pish** *a.* vain.—**fop'pishly** *adv.*—**fop'pishness** *n.*

for (for) *prep.* in place of; instead of; because of; during; as being; considering; in return for; on behalf of; in spite of; in respect of;—*conj.* because.—**as for**, regarding.

forage (for'-ij) *n.* food for horses and cattle; search for this;—*v.t.* supply with provender; plunder;—*v.i.* rove in search of food; (*Fig.*) rummage. —**forage cap**, soldier's undress cap.

foramen (fo-rā'-men) *n.* small aperture, esp. in a bone.—*pl.* **foram'ina**. —**foram'inate(d)**, **foram'inous** *a.* perforated; porous.

forasmuch as (for-az-much') *conj.* seeing that; because; since.

foray (for'-ā) *n.* incursion into hostile territory to get plunder;—*v.t.* pillage.

forbade (for-bad') *pa.t.* of forbid.

forbear (for-bār') *v.t.* abstain from; avoid; bear with;—*v.i.* refrain from; control one's feelings.—*pa.t.* forbore'. —*pa.p.* forborne'.—**forbear'ance** *n.* restraint; leniency; patience.—**forbear'ing** *a.* long-suffering.

forbear (for'-bār) *n.* ancestor.

forbid (for-bid') *v.t.* prohibit; order to desist; exclude.—*pa.t.* **forbade** (for-bad') or **forbad'**.—*pa.p.* **forbid'den**.—**forbid'den** *a.* prohibited; illegal. —**forbid'ding** *a.* menacing.

force (fōrs) *n.* strength; energy; coercion; operation; body of soldiers, police, etc.; (*Mech.*) that which produces change in a body's state of rest or motion; (*Law*) unlawful violence.—**For'ces** *n.pl.* Army, Navy and Air Force;—*v.t.* compel; strain;

ravish; wring; (*Hort.*) cause plants to mature before normal time.— **force'able** *a.*—**forced** *a.* achieved by great effort, or under compulsion; lacking spontaneity.—**force'ful** *a.* full of energy; vigorous.—**force'fully** *adv.* —**fore'ible** *a.* having force; compelling; effective.—**forc'ibly** *adv.*— **forc'ibleness** *n.*—**forc'ing** *n.*—**to come into force**, become valid.—**to force the pace**, hasten more than necessary.— **forced landing** (*Aero.*) landing necessitated by mishap.

force (fōrs) *v.t.* stuff (as a fowl, etc.). —**force'meat** *n.* minced, well-seasoned meat, used as stuffing, etc.

forceps (for'-seps) *n.* surgical instrument like tongs used by surgeons, dentists, etc.

ford (ford) *n.* shallow part of stream, etc. where crossing can be made on foot;—*v.t.*—**ford'able** *a.*

fore (fōr) *a.* in front; forward; prior; —*adv.* in front, as opp. to *aft*;— *interj.* (*Golf*) a warning cry to person in the way.

forearm (fōr'-ärm) *n.* part of arm between elbow and wrist.

forearm (fōr-arm') *v.t.* take defensive precautions.

forebear (fōr'-bār) *n.* (*Scot.*) var. of for'bear.

forebode (fōr-bōd') *v.t.* predict (esp. something unpleasant); presage.— **forebod'ing** *n.* sense of impending evil or danger.

forecast (fōr'-kast) *n.* prediction;— *v.t.* and *i.* conjecture probable outcome: predict.—**fore'caster** *n.*

forecastle, fo'c's'le (fōk'-sl) *n.* (*Naut.*) upper - deck forward of foremast; forepart under deck, forming crew's quarters.

foreclose (fōr-klōz') *v.t.* deprive of right to redeem.—**foreclos'ure** *n.*

forecourt (fōr'-kōrt) *n.* outer or front court of building or group of buildings.

foredate (fōr-dāt') *v.t.* date beforehand; antedate.

foredoom (fōr-dōōm') *v.t.* judge in advance; predestine to failure, etc.

forefather (fōr'-fä-ther) *n.* ancestor.

forefinger (fōr'-fing-ger) *n.* finger next to thumb; index finger.

forefoot (fōr'-foot) *n.* one of front feet of quadruped.

forefront (fōr'-frunt) *n.* foremost place; centre of interest.

forego (fōr-gō') *v.t.* precede.—**fore'going** *a.* preceding; just mentioned. —**fore'gone** *a.* predetermined, as in a *foregone conclusion*.

forego Same as forgo.

foreground (fōr'-ground) *n.* part of ground nearest spectator; part of picture which seems nearest.

forehand (fōr'-hand) *n.* part of horse in front of rider:—*a.* done beforehand; (*Tennis*) used of stroke played with palm of hand facing net.

forehead (for'-ed, fōr'-hed) n. upper part of face above eyes; brow.

foreign (for'-in) a. situated outside place or country; alien; irrelevant; introduced from outside.—**for'eigner** n. native of another country; alien.

foreknow (fōr-nō') v.t. know or sense beforehand.—**foreknowl'edge** n.

foreland (fōr'-land) n. promontory; cape.

foreleg (fōr'-leg) n. front leg of animal.

forelock (fōr'-lok) n. lock of hair on forehead.—**to take time by the forelock,** seize chance.

foreman (fōr'-man) n. principal member and spokesman of jury; overseer of group of workmen.

foremast (fōr'-mást) n. mast in forepart of vessel, nearest bow.

forementioned (fōr-men'-shund) a. previously mentioned in speech or writing.

foremost (fōr'-mōst) a. first in place or time; first in dignity or rank.—**head foremost,** head first; headlong.

forename (fōr'-nām) n. first or Christian name.

forenamed (fōr'-nāmd) a. already mentioned.

forenoon (fōr'-nóón) n. part of day before noon; morning.

forensic (fo-ren'-sik) a. pert. to law-courts.—**forensic medicine,** medical jurisprudence.

forepart (fōr'-párt) n. part before the rest; beginning; bow of ship.

forerun (fōr-run') v.t. run before; herald.—**forerun'ner** n. messenger sent on in advance; harbinger; precursor.

foresaid (fōr'-sed) a. mentioned before.

foresail (fōr'-sāl or fō'-sl) n. lowest square sail on foremast.

foresee (fōr-sē') v.t. see beforehand; infer.—**fore'sight** n. wise fore-thought; prudence; (*Mil.*) front sight on gun.

foreshadow (fōr-shad'-ō) v.t. shadow or typify beforehand; suggest in advance.

foreshore (fōr'-shōr) n. part of shore between level of high tide and low tide.

foreshorten (fōr-short'-n) v.t. represent (in art) according to perspective.

foreshow (fōr-shō') v.t. prognosticate; foretell. Also **foreshew'**.

foresight (fōr'-sit) n. See foresee.

foreskin (fōr'-skin) n. skin covering the glans penis; prepuce.

forest (for'-est) n. tract of wooded, uncultivated land; area preserved for game-hunting, as *deer-forest*;—a. sylvan;—v.t. cover with trees.—**for'ester** n. one who has forest land, game, etc. under supervision.—**for'estry** n. science of growing timber.

forestall (fōr-stawl') v.t. orig. to buy up stock of goods before they reach market, so as to resell at maximum price; get in ahead of someone else.

forestay (fōr'-stā) n. (*Naut.*) rope reaching from foremast head to bowsprit end, to support mast.

foretaste (fōr'-tāst) n. taste beforehand; anticipation;—v.t. taste before possession.

foretell (fōr-tel') v.t. predict; prophesy.—pr.p. **foretell'ing.**—pa.p. **foretold'.**

forethought (fōr'-thawt) n. anticipation; provident care; foresight.

foretoken (fōr'-tō-ken) n. token or sign received beforehand; prophetic sign;—v.t. indicate beforehand.

forever (for-ev'-er) adv. always; eternally;—n. eternity.—**forev'ermore** adv. everlastingly.

forewarn (fōr-wawrn') v.t. warn or caution in advance.

forewoman (fōr'-wóóm-an) n. woman in charge of others in factory, shop, etc.

foreword (fōr'-wurd) n. preface; introductory note to a book.

forfeit (for'-fit) v.t. be deprived of, as punishment;—n. that which is forfeited; fine or penalty.—**for'feitable** a.—**for'feiture** n. act of forfeiting; state of being deprived of something as punishment; the thing confiscated.

forgather, foregather (for-gaTH'-er) v.i. (*Scot.*) to meet with friends socially.

forgave (for-gāv) pa.t. of verb forgive.

forge (forj) n. furnace with blast for heating iron red hot so that it can be hammered into shape; smithy; (*Fig.*) place where anything is fashioned or planned;—v.t. fashion into shape by heating and hammering; fabricate; counterfeit;—v.i. work with metals; commit forgery.—**forg'er** n.—**forg'ery** n. fraudulent imitation; that which is forged.

forge (forj) v.i. move forward steadily.—usually **to forge ahead.**

forget (for-get') v.t. lose remembrance of; neglect inadvertently; disregard;—pr.p. **forgett'ing.**—pa.t. **forgot'.**—pa.p. **forgot'** or **forgott'en.**—**forgett'-able** a.—**forget'ful** a. apt to forget; heedless; oblivious.—**forget'fulness** n.—**forget'-me-not** n. plant with small blue flowers, symbolic of friendship.

forgive (for-giv') v.t. pardon; cease to bear resentment against;—v.i. exercise mercy; grant pardon;—pa.t. **forgave'.**—pa.p. **forgiv'en.**—**forgiv'able** a.—**forgive'ness** n.—**forgiv'ing** a.

forgo (for-gō') v.t. renounce; abstain from possession or enjoyment.

fork (fork) n. implement or table utensil with two or more prongs at end; anything shaped like a fork; bifurcation of a road, etc.;—v.i. diverge into two;—v.t. pitch with fork, as hay; to lift with fork (as food).—**forked,** a. shaped like a fork; cleft.

forlorn (for-lorn') a. utterly lost; deserted; forsaken; wretched.—**forlorn'ly** adv.—**forlorn'ness** n.

form (form) n. shape or appearance; human body; state of health; model; style; method of arrangement of details; etiquette; long bench; class of school-children; official document with details to be filled in;—v.t. give shape to; construct;—v.i. develop.—**form'al** a. according to form; regular; methodical; conventional; ceremonious.—**formalisa'tion** n.—**form'alise** v.t. and i. give form to; make formal.—**form'alism** n. quality of being formal; insistence on conventional forms, esp. in religion or arts.—**form'alist** n.—**formal'ity** n.—**form'ally** adv.—**forma'tion** n. act of forming; structure; arrangement of troops, aircraft, etc.—**form'ative** a. giving form; conducing to growth.—**form'less** a. shapeless.—**good form,** correct etiquette.

formalin (for'ma-lin) n. aqueous solution of the organic gas formaldehyde, used as antiseptic and preservative and in making plastics.

format (for'ma, -mat) n. general get-up of a book, its size, shape, style of binding.

former (for'-mer) a. preceding in time; long past; first mentioned.—**for'merly** adv.

formic (for'-mik) a. pertaining to ants.—**formic acid,** fatty acid orig. obtained from ants.

formidable (for'-mi-da-bl) a. exciting fear or apprehension; overwhelming; terrible.—**for'midabil'ity, for'midableness** n.—**for'midably** adv.

formula (form'-u-la) n. prescribed form; conventional phrase; confession of faith; (*Math.*) general rule or principle expressed in algebraic symbols; (*Chem.*) series of symbols denoting the component parts of substance; (*Med.*) prescription;—*pl.* **form'ulas, formulae** (form'-u-lē).—**formula'tion** n.—**form'ulary** n. book of formulas, or prescribed ritual;—a. prescribed.—**form'ulate, form'ulise** v.t. reduce to a formula; express in definite form.

fornicate (for'-ni-kāt) v.t. have unlawful sexual intercourse.—**fornica'tion** n.—**for'nicator** n. (*fem.* **for'nicatress**)

forsake (for-sāk') v.t. abandon; leave or give up entirely;—*pa.t.* **forsook'.**—*pa.p.* **forsak'en.**—**forsak'en** a. deserted.

forsooth (for-sōōth') adv. in truth; indeed.

forswear (for-swār') v.t. renounce on oath; abjure;—v.i. swear falsely; commit perjury.—*pa.t.* **forswore'.**—*pa.p.* **forsworn'.**

forsythia (for-sīth'-i-a) n. genus of shrubs with yellow blossoms.

fort (fôrt) n. stronghold; small fortress; isolated trading station, or outpost.

forte (fôr'tā) n. strong point; that in which one excels.

forte (for'-tā) a. and adv. (*Mus.*) loud; loudly;—**fortis'simo** adv. very loudly.

forth (fôrth) adv. forwards, in place or time; out from concealment; into view; away—**forth'coming** a. ready to come forth or appear; available.—**forth'right** a. straightforward; frank;—n. straight path.—**forth'with** adv. immediately.

fortify (for'-ti-fī) v.t. strengthen; invigorate; corroborate.—**fortifica'tion** n. act of strengthening; defence work.

fortitude (for'-ti-tūd) n. power to endure pain or confront danger; resolute endurance.

fortnight (fort'-nīt) n. space of fourteen days; two weeks.—**fort'nightly** a. and adv. at intervals of a fortnight.

fortress (for'-tres) n. fortified place; stronghold.

fortuitous (for-tū'-i-tus) a. happening by chance; accidental.—**fortuitously** adv.—**fortu'itousness, fortu'ity** n.

fortune (for'-tūn) n. chance; that which befalls one; good or ill luck; possessions, esp. money or property.—**for'tunate** a. lucky; prosperous; successful.—**for'tunately** adv.—**for'tunateness** n.—**for'tune-tell'er** n. one who professes to reveal the future.

forty (for'-ti) a. and n. four times ten; symbol, as 40, XL.—**for'tieth** a. constituting one of forty equal parts;—n. fortieth part.—**forty winks,** nap.

forum (fō'-rum) n. market-place of ancient Rome where legal as well as commercial business was conducted; law-courts, as distinct from Parliament; tribunal.

forward (for'-ward) adv. towards a place in front; onwards in time; in progressive or conspicuous way;—a. near or at the forepart, as in a ship; early in season; progressive; (*Colloq.*) cheeky;—n. (football, hockey, etc.) player in front line;—v.t. promote; redirect (letter, parcel) to new address; dispatch.—**for'wardness** n.—**for'wards** adv. forward.

fosse (fos) n. ditch; moat, or trench.

fossil (fos'-il) n. portion of animal or vegetable organism, which has undergone process of petrifaction and lies in rock strata; (*Fig.*) antiquated person or thing;—a. pert. to or resembling fossil.—**fossilif'erous** a. bearing or containing fossils.—**fossil'ify, foss'ilise** v.t. turn into fossil; petrify;—v.i. become converted into fossil.

foster (fos'-ter) v.t. nourish; rear; (Fig.) promote; cherish.—**fos'ter-broth'er** n. male child fostered with another child of different parents.—**fos'ter-child** n. child reared by one who is not the parent.—**fos'ter daugh'ter, fos'ter-son, fos'ter-fath'er, fos'ter-moth'er, fos'ter-pa'rent** n.

fought (fot) pa.t. and pa.p. of verb **fight**.

foul (foul) a. filthy; containing offensive matter; obscene; stormy (of weather); contrary (of wind); full of weeds; entangled (of ropes); unfair;—n. breaking of rule (in sports);—v.t. make foul; obstruct deliberately; clog or jam;—v.i. become foul, clogged, or jammed; come into collision.—**foul'-mouthed** a. using obscene or profane language.—**foul'-play,** cheating; (Law) criminal violence; murder.

found (found) pa.t. and pa.p. of verb **find**.—**found'ling** n. small child found abandoned.

found (found) v.t. lay the foundation of; establish; endow;—v.i. rely; depend.—**founda'tion** n. act of founding; the base of a building; groundwork; underlying principle; endowment; endowed institution.—**founda'tioner** n. one who benefits by funds of endowed college or school; bursar.—**founda'tion-stone** n. one of the stones used in foundations of a building, esp. one laid with public ceremony.—**found'er** n. (fem. **found'ress**) one who establishes or endows.

found (found) v.t. melt (metal, etc.) and pour into a mould; cast.—**found'er** n.—**found'ing** n. metalcas'ing.—**found'ry, found'ery** n. works for casting metals; process of metalcasting.

founder (foun'-der) v.i. collapse; fill with water and sink; stick in boggy ground; become lame;—v.t. cause to founder.

fountain (foun'-tän) n. natural spring; artificial jet of water.—**fount** n. spring of water; source.—**fount'ain-head** n. source of stream; (Fig.) the origin.

four (för) a. one more than three; twice two;—n. sum of four units; symbol 4, IV.—**four'fold** a. quadruple; folded or multiplied four times.—**four'-in-hand** n. team of four horses drawing carriage; the carriage —**four'-post'er** n. bed with canopy supported on four posts.—**four'some** n. (Golf) game for four persons.—**four'-square** a. having four equal sides and angles.—**four'-stroke** a. of internal combustion engine firing once to every four strokes of piston.—**four'teen** n. sum of four and ten; the symbol 14, XIV.—**four'teenth** a. making one of fourteen equal parts; last in succession of fourteen.—

fourth a. next after third;—n. one of four equal parts; musical interval of four degrees.—**fourth'ly** adv.—**to go on all fours,** to go on one's hands and knees (or feet).

fowl (foul) n. bird; barn-door cock or hen; flesh of fowl;—pl. fowls, fowl.—v.i. catch or kill wild fowl.—**fowl'er** n. one who hunts wild fowl.—**fowl'ing-piece** n. light shot-gun for shooting wild fowl.

fox (foks) n. (fem. **vix'en**) animal of canine family, reddish-brown in colour, with large, bushy tail and erect ears; (Fig.) wily person;—v.t. mislead; spy on.—**fox'-earth** n. fox's burrow.—**fox'glove** n. tall plant with white or purple-pink bell-shaped flowers and leaves which yield digitalin.—**fox'-hole** n. (Mil.) small trench.—**fox'iness** n. quality of being foxy; decay (in timber); discoloration (in paper); state of being sour (of beer).—**fox'-ter'rier** n. popular breed of dog trained for unearthing foxes, or 'ratting.'—**fox'-trot** n. dance with syncopated rhythm.—**fox'y** a.

foyer (fwä'-yä) n. large room in theatre opening on to vestibule or staircase.

fracas (fra-ká') n. noisy quarrel; brawl.

fraction (frak'-shun) n. small portion; fragment; (Arith.) division of a unit.—**decimal fraction,** fraction expressed decimally.—**vulgar fraction,** fraction expressed with numerator above, and denominator below line.—**frac'tional** a.—**frac'tious** a. quarrelsome; peevish.—**frac'tiously** adv.—**frac'tiousness** n.—**frac'ture** n. act of breaking; breach or rupture; breaking of a bone;—v.t. break; crack;—v.i. become broken.—**compound fracture,** fracture of a bone, the jagged edge of which protrudes through the skin.—**simple fracture,** a fracture where surrounding tissues and skin are undamaged.

fragile (fraj'-il or -Il) a. easily broken; frail; brittle.—**fragil'ity** n.

fragment (frag'-ment) n. portion broken off; imperfect part; unfinished portion. — **fragment'al** a. (Geol.) composed of fragments of different rocks. — **frag'mentary** a. broken.

fragrant (frä'-grant) a. sweet smelling.—**fra'grance, fra'grancy** n. quality of being sweet-scented; perfume; pleasant odour.

frail (frål) a. fragile; easily destroyed; infirm; morally weak.—**frail'ly** adv.—**frail'ness, frail'ty** n. quality of being weak.

frame (främ) v.t. construct; contrive; provide with frame; put together, as a sentence; bring false charge against;—v.i. take shape;—n. anything made of parts fitted together;

skeleton of anything; structure; border round picture; mood of mind; glazed structure in which plants are protected from frost; structure upon which anything is stretched.—**frame'-up** n. faked charge; conspiracy.—**frame'work** n. fabric which supports anything; outline.—**fram'ing** n.

franc (frangk) n. coin (100 centimes), monetary unit of France, Belgium and Switzerland.

franchise (fran'-chīz) n. the right to vote in Parliamentary elections;—v.t. make free; enfranchise.

Franciscan (fran-sis'-kan) n. one of the order of friars founded by Francis of Assisi; one of the Grey Friars;—a. pert. to this order.

Franco (frangk'-ō) prefix, French, in combinations, as *Franco-Prussian*.

frank (frangk) a. open; candid; unreserved;—v.t. exempt from charge, esp. postage.—**frank'ly** adv. candidly.—**frank'ness** n. openness; honesty; candour.

frankincense (frangk'-in-sens) n. dry, perfumed resin, burned as incense.

franklin (frangk'-lin) n. formerly free-holder, holding his estate free from feudal obligations; country squire.

frantic (fran'-tik) a. mad; frenzied; raving.—**fran'tically** adv.

fraternal (fra-ter'-nal) a. pert. to brother or brethren; brotherly.—**frater'nally** adv.—**fraternisa'tion** n.—**frat'ernise** v.i. associate with others in friendly way.—**frat'erniser** n.—**frater'nity** n. brotherhood; group of men associated for common purpose; religious brotherhood; guild.

fratricide (frat'-ri-sīd) n. crime of killing a brother; one who commits this crime.—**fratricid'al** a.

fraud (frawd) n. deception deliberately practised; trickery; cheat; imposture.—**fraud'ulence**, **fraud'ulency** n.—**fraud'ulent** a.—**fraud'ulently** adv.

fraught (frawt) a. freighted; laden; filled.

fray (frā) n. affray; brawl; contest.

fray (frā) v.t. wear through by friction; ravel edge (of cloth); (Fig.) irritate, as nerves;—v.i. become frayed.

freak (frēk) n. sudden whim; prank; capricious conduct; something or someone abnormal.—**freak'ish** a.—**freak'ishness** n.

freckle (frek'-l) n. brownish spot on skin caused by sunburn; small spot;—v.t. colour with freckles;—v.i. become covered with freckles.—**freck'ly**, **freck'led** a.

free (frē) a. having political liberty; unrestricted; loose; independent; open; liberal; irregular; exempt from duties, or fees (as trade, education);—adv. without hindrance; gratis;—

v.t. set at liberty; emancipate; clear; disentangle.—**free'booter** n. one who wanders about for plunder; pillager.—**freed'man** n. one who has been freed from slavery.—**freed'om** n. liberty; franchise; immunity; indecorous familiarity.—**free'-fight** n. (Colloq.) a mêlée.—**free-hand**, drawn in easy, sweeping lines.—**free'-hand'ed** a. generous; liberal.—**free'hold** n. tenure of property in fee-simple, or fee-tail, or for life;—a. held by freehold.—**free'holder** n.—**free kick** (Football) kick allowed as compensation for opponents' breach of rules.—**free'lance** n. orig. mercenary soldier who sold services to any country, esp. used of journalist, not attached to particular newspaper.—**free'-love** n. doctrine that sexual relations should be unhampered by marriage, etc.—**free'man** n. man who is not a slave; one who enjoys full privileges of corporate body.—**freemas'son** n. orig. member of organisation of skilled masons; now, member of secret association for mutual assistance and social enjoyment.—**freemason'ic** a.—**freemas'onry** n. system practised by freemasons.—**free'-mind'ed** a. openminded; unworried.—**free'ness** n.—**free'-spoken** a. accustomed to speak without reserve.—**free'stone** n. building-stone composed of sand and grit, easily quarried, cut, and carved.—**free-think'er** n. one who professes to be independent of orthodox religious authority; rationalist.—**free'-think'ing**, **free'-thought** n.—**free trade**, policy of unrestricted international trade.—**free'-trad'er** n.—**free'-verse** n. form of verse unrestricted in length of line, metre, stanza-form, and generally without rhyme.—**free'-will** n. power of human will to choose without restraint;—a. voluntary.

freesia (frē'-zi-a) n. plant genus of the iris family.

freeze (frēz) v.t. harden into ice; congeal; preserve by refrigeration; paralyse with cold or terror;—v.i. become hardened into ice; become stiff with cold.—pa.t. **froze**.—pa.p. **froz'en**.—n. frost.—**freez'able** a.—**freez'ing-point** n. temperature at which liquid turns solid, esp. that at which water freezes, marked 32° F. or 0° C.

freight (frāt) n. cargo; load; charge for conveyance of goods;—v.t. load a ship, etc.—**freight'age** n. charge for transport of goods; freight.—**freight'er** n. one who freights a ship, etc.; freight-carrying boat or aircraft.

French (frensh) a. pert. to France or its inhabitants;—n. inhabitants or language of France.—**french bean**, kidney bean.—**french chalk**, hydrated magnesium silicate used as dry lubricant; variety of talc.—**french'-horn** n. musical wind-instrument with note like a hunting-horn.—**French'man** (fem. **French'woman**) n. native of France.—**french'pol'ish** n. polish for wood made of shellac dissolved in methylated spirit;—v.t. apply this polish.—**french window**, one functioning as door and window.—**to take french leave**, go away without permission.

frenzy (fren'-zi) n. violent agitation of mind; madness;—v.t. render frantic.—**fren'zied**, **fren'zical** a.—**fren'et'ic** (also **phrenet'ic**) a. mad; frenzied.

frequent (frē'-kwent) a. happening at short intervals; constantly recurring; repeated.—**frequent** (frē-kwent') v.t. visit often.—**fre'quency** n. state of occurring repeatedly; (Phys.) number of vibrations per second of recurring phenomenon. — **frequency modulation**, form of radio transmission in which carrier wave is modulated by varying its frequency.—**fre'quently** adv.

fresco (fres'-kō) n. method of mural decoration on walls of fresh, still damp, plaster;—v.t. paint in fresco.

fresh (fresh) a. vigorous; newly cut; not stale; brisk; original; unsalted; (Slang) impudent.—**fresh'en** v.t. make fresh;—v.i. grow fresh; become vigorous.—**fresh'ener** n.—**fresh'et** n. inundation caused by rains or melting snows; fresh-water stream.—**fresh'man** n. first-year University student. Also **fresh'er**.—**fresh'ness** n.—**fresh-wat'er** a. pert. to or living in water which is not salt.

fret (fret) v.t. wear away by friction; eat away; irritate;—v.i. wear away; be corroded; be vexed or peevish.—prp. **fret'ting**.—pa.p. **fret'ted**.—n. vexation; irritation; ruffled surface of water.—**fret'ful** a. querulous.—**fret'fully** adv.—**fret'fulness** n.

fret (fret) n. net-like pattern of interlacing strips.—**fret'-saw** n. small saw used in fretwork.—**fret'ted**, **fret'ty** a. ornamented with frets.—**fret'work** n. decorative, perforated work on wood or metal done by a fretsaw.

fret (fret) n. narrow bar of metal, gut, etc., marking note-positions on fingerboard of stringed instrument.

friable (frī'-a-bl) a. easily crumbled or reduced to powder.—**fri'ableness**, **friabil'ity** n.

friar (frī'-ęr) n. member of one of the four orders of mendicant monks.—**friar's balsam**, tincture of benzoin used to heal wounds.—**fri'ary** n. a monastery.

fricassée (frik-a-sē) n. dish of minced fowl, rabbit, etc. stewed with rich gravy sauce;—v.t. make a fricassée.

friction (frik'-shun) n. act of rubbing one thing against another; (Phys.) resistance which a body encounters

in moving across surface of another with which it is in contact; (Med.) massage; unpleasantness.—**fric'ative** a. produced by friction, as consonants sounded by friction of breath forced through narrow passage.—**fric'tional** a. caused by friction.

Friday (frī'-dā) n. sixth day of the week.

fridge (frij) n. (Colloq.) short for refrigerator.

fried (frīd) pa.t. and pa.p. of verb fry.

friend (frend) n. one attached to another by esteem and affection; intimate associate; supporter. — **Friend** n. member of the Quakers.—**friend'less** a. without friends.—**friend'lily** adv.—**friend'liness** n. friendly feeling.—**friend'ly** a. having the disposition of a friend; kind; propitious.—**friend'ship** n. attachment to a friend.—**Friendly Society**, voluntary organisation for mutual benefit of members in sickness, old age, unemployment, etc. — **Society of Friends**, the Quaker sect.

frieze (frēz) n. heavy woollen cloth.

frieze (frēz) n. (Archit.) the part of an entablature between the architrave and cornice; in house decoration upper part of wall, below cornice.

frigate (frig'-āt) n. fast 2-decked sailing ship of war of 18th and 19th centuries; now a large sloop designed for escort duties.—**frigate bird**, tropical sea-bird of prey.

fright (frīt) n. sudden fear; extreme terror; alarm; (Colloq.) an ugly person.—**fright'en** v.t. terrify; scare.—**fright'ened** a. timid.—**fright'ful** a. terrible; shocking.—**fright'fully** adv. terribly; (Colloq.) very.—**fright'fulness** n.—**fright'some** a. frightful.

frigid (frij'-id) a. very cold; unfeeling; passionless.—**frigid'ity** n. coldness.—**frig'idness** n.

frill (fril) n. a plaited or gathered edging of linen, etc.; similar edging of paper round pie-dish, etc.; ruffle; (Fig.) excessive ornament (as in style);—v.t. ornament with a frill; —v.i. become crinkled.

fringe (frinj) n. loose threads as ornamental edging of cloth; border; hair cut across forehead; outside edge of anything;—v.t. adorn with fringe; border.—**fringe benefit**, regular perquisite given in addition to pay.

frisk (frisk) v.i. leap; gambol; skip; (Colloq.) search a person;—n. frolic.—**frisk'ily** adv. playfully.—**frisk'iness** n.—**frisk'y** a. lively; frolicsome.

fritter (frit'-ęr) n. slice of fruit or meat dipped in batter and fried.

fritter (frit'-ęr) v.t. waste (time, energy, etc.) in futile way.—**fritt'erer** n.

frivolous (friv'-ol-us) a. trifling; silly; superficial.—**friv'olously** adv.—**friv'olousness**, **frivol'ity** n.

frizz, friz (friz) *v.t.* curl; crisp;—*n.* row of small curls.—**frizz'le** *v.t.* curl; in cooking, crisp by frying;—*n.* curled hair.

fro (frō) *adv.* from; back, as in *to and fro.*

frock (frok) *n.* woman's dress; monk's long, sleeved garment; child's outer garment.—**frock'-coat** *n.* man's double-breasted, black coat with long skirts.

frog (frog) *n.* amphibious, tailless animal (developed from tadpole); V-shaped horny pad on sole of horse's foot; V-shaped section of train or tram lines, where two sets of rails cross.—**frog'march** *n.* method of carrying troublesome prisoner, face downwards, with every limb held.—**frog'men** *n.* underwater swimmers.—**Frogs** or **Frog'gies** *n.pl.* nick-name given to Frenchmen.

frolic (frol'-ik) *n.* wild prank; merry-making; gaiety;—*a.* merry;—*v.i.* play wild pranks; gambol.—*pr.p.* **frol'icking.**—*pa.p.* **frol'icked.**—**frol'icsome** *a.* sportive.

from (from) *prep.* away; forth; out of; on account of; at a distance.

frond (frond) *n.* (*Bot.*) leaf, esp. of fern or palm.

front (frunt) *n.* forehead; human countenance; forepart; (*Mil.*) battle-zone; promenade at sea-side resort; (*Meteor.*) boundary of air masses of different temperature and density; —*a.* pert. to the front of, anything; —*adv.* to the front;—*v.t.* and *i.* have face or front towards any point.—**front'age** *n.* front part of a building. —**front'al** *a.* pert. to forehead or foremost part; (*Mil.*) direct, as an attack, without flanking movement;—*n.* ornamental cloth for altar front.— **front'let** *n.* band worn across forehead. —**to put a bold front on,** face bravely.

frontier (frun'-tēr) *n.* border of country;—*a.* bordering; pioneering. —**fron'tiersman** *n.* one who settles on a frontier.

frontispiece (frun'-tis-pēs) *n.* illustration facing title-page of book.

frost (frost) *n.* condition when water turns to ice, i.e. when temperature falls below 32° F.; severe cold; frozen dew; (*Fig.*) disappointment;—*v.t.* cover with hoar-frost; nip (as plants); sharpen, as a horse's shoe, to prevent slipping.—**frost'bite** *n.* freezing of the skin and tissues due to exposure to extreme cold.—**frost'-bit'ten** *a.*—**frost'ed** *a.* covered with frost or anything resembling it.— **frost'ily** *adv.*—**frost'iness** *n.*—**frost'y** *a.* accompanied with frost; chilly.

froth (froth) *n.* spume; foam;—*v.t.* cause to froth;—*v.i.* bubble.— **froth'iness** *n.*—**froth'y** *a.* light; foamy.

frown (froun) *v.i.* wrinkle the brow; scowl;—*v.t.* rebuke by stern look;— *n.* wrinkling of the brow to express disapproval or puzzlement.

frowsy (frou'-zi) *a.* musty; unkempt; slovenly.

frozen (frōz'-n) *pa.p.* of the verb freeze.

fructify (fruk'-ti-fī) *v.t.* make fruitful; fertilise;—*v.i.* bear fruit; (*Fig.*) materialise.—**fructif'erous** *a.* fruit-bearing.—**fructifica'tion** *n.* act or process of bearing fruit.

frugal (frōō'-gal) *a.* sparing; thrifty; economical; careful.—**frugal'ity** *n.* economy; thrift.

fruit (frōōt) *n.* edible produce or seed of a plant; offspring; consequence or outcome;—*v.i.* produce fruit.—**fruitar'ian** *n.* one who lives almost wholly on fruit.—**fruit'erer** *n.* (*fem.* **fruit'eress**) one who sells fruit.—**fruit'ful** *a.* producing fruit; abundant.—**fruit'fulness** *n.* productivity.—**fruit'ing** *n.* —**fruit'less** *a.* having no fruit; (*Fig.*) profitless; vain; empty.—**fruitlessness** *n.*—**fruit'y** *a.* resembling fruit; mellow; (*Colloq.*) salacious.

fruition (frōō-ish'-un) *n.* fulfilment of hopes; enjoyment from possession.

frumenty (frōō'-men-ti) *n.* wheat boiled in milk, sweetened and spiced. Also **fro'menty.**

frump (frump) *n.* dowdy, old-fashioned woman.

frustrate (frus'-trāt) *v.t.* bring to nothing; thwart.—**frustra'tion** *n.* disappointment; defeat.

fry (frī) *v.t.* dress and roast with fat in pan over fire;—*v.i.* be cooked in a frying-pan.—*pa.p.* **fried.**—*n.* dish of anything fried.

fry (frī) *n.* young fish just spawned; young children.

fuchsia (fū'-shi-a) *n.* genus of flowering plants, with drooping flowers of red and purple, or pink and white.

fuddle (fud'-l) *v.t.* make confused by drink;—*v.i.* tipple.

fudge (fuj) *n.* sweetmeat of consistency of soft tablet; space reserved in newspaper for last minute news; nonsense;—*v.t.* patch up; fake.

fuel (fū'-el) *n.* anything combustible to feed fire;—*v.t.* provide with fuel.

fug (fug) *n.* (*Colloq.*) stuffy atmosphere.

fugacious (fū-gā'-shus) *a.* fleeting; ephemeral.

fugitive (fū'-ji-tiv) *a.* escaping; fleeing; fleeting;—*n.* refugee; one who flees from justice.

fugue (fūg) *n.* (*Mus.*) musical composition for voices or instruments based on chief and subsidiary themes; (*Psych.*) form of amnesia.

fulcrum (ful'-krum) *n.* (*Mech.*) the pivot of a lever; (*Fig.*) means used to achieve purpose.—*pl.* **ful'crums, ful'cra.**

fulfil (fool-fil') *v.t.* carry into effect; execute; discharge; satisfy (as hopes).—*pr.p.* fulfil'ling.—*pa.p.* fulfilled'.—fulfil'ler *n.*—fulfil'ment *n.* accomplishment; execution.

fulgent (ful'-jent) *a.* shining; dazzling.—ful'gency *n.*—ful'gently *adv.*

full (fool) *a.* filled to capacity; crowded; complete; final; abundant; showing whole surface (as moon); ample (of dress-material); (*Colloq.*) drunk; clear and resonant (of sounds);—*n.* utmost extent; highest degree.—*adv.* quite; completely; very.—full'-blood'ed *a.* of pure race; vigorous.—full'-blown *a.* fully developed.—full'-dress *n.* dress worn on ceremonial occasions;—*a.* formal.—full moon, the moon with its whole disc visible.—full'ness, ful'ness *n.* copiousness; completeness; deep emotion.—full'-stop *n.* a period (in punctuation).—full'y *adv.* wholly.

full (fool) *v.t.* cleanse, shrink and thicken cloth in a mill;—*v.i.* become thick or felted.—full'er *n.* one who fulls cloth.—fuller's earth, clay used by fullers to absorb grease from newly woven cloth.

fulmar (fool'-mar) *n.* sea-bird, species of petrel.

fulminate (ful'-min-āt) *v.t.* cause to explode; detonate; (*Fig.*) remonstrate loudly;—*v.i.* flash; explode.—ful'minant *a.*;—*n.* explosive.—fulmina'tion *n.*—ful'minatory *a.*

fulsome (fool'-sum) *a.* excessive; nauseating; insincere.

fumarole (fum'-a-rōl) *n.* small fissure in volcano, from which gas and steam escape.

fumble (fum'-bl) *v.i.* grope blindly or awkwardly;—*v.t.* handle clumsily.

fume (fūm) *n.* pungent vapour from combustion or exhalation; (*Fig.*) excitement; rage;—*v.i.* smoke; be in a rage;—*v.t.* subject to fumes to darken colours, as oak.—fum'atory *n.* a smoke-chamber.

fumigate (fūm'-i-gāt) *v.t.* expose to poisonous gas or smoke, esp. for purpose of destroying germs.—fum'igator *n.* apparatus or substance used.

fun (fun) *n.* merriment; sport.—fun'nily *adv.*—fun'ny *a.* full of fun; comical; droll; odd.

function (fungk'-shun) *n.* performance; special purpose; office; ceremony; (*Math.*) quantity the value of which varies with that of another quantity; social entertainment;—*v.i.* operate; fulfil set task.—func'tional *a.* having special purpose; pert. to duty or office.—func'tionary *n.* official;—*a.* functional.

fund (fund) *n.* permanent stock or capital; invested sum, income of which is used for set purpose; store; ample supply;—*v.t.* establish fund for payment of interest.—fund'ed *a.* invested in public funds.

fundament (fun'-da-ment) *n.* lower part or seat of the body.—fundament'al *a.* pert. to foundations; basic; essential;—*n.* primary principle; origin; (*Mus.*) root of chord.—fundament'alism *n.* belief in literal truth of Bible.—fundament'alist *n.*

funeral (fū'-nē-ral) *n.* ceremony of burying or cremating the dead;—*a.* pert. to.—fu'nerary, funer'eal *a.*

fungus (fung'-gus) *n.* the lowest division of cellular cryptogamic plants, mushrooms, toadstools, moulds, etc.;—*pl.* fungi (fun'-jī), funguses (fung'-gus-ez).—fun'gicide *n.* preparation which destroys fungoid growths.—fung'oid, fung'ous *a.*

funicular (fū-nik'ū-lar) cable railway.

funk (fungk) *n.* (*Colloq.*) terror; panic; one who shrinks in terror;—*v.t.* and *i.* be terrified of or by.—funk'y *a.*—funk'-hole *n.* dug-out; job through which military service is avoided.

funnel (fun'-el) *n.* inverted metal cone with tube, used for filling vessels with narrow inlet; smoke-stack of steam-ship or railway engine.

fur (fur) *n.* short, soft hair of certain animals; animal pelts used for coats, necklets, etc.; game (rabbits, hares, etc.) as opposed to feathered game; coating on the tongue; deposit on inside of kettles, etc.—*v.t.* line with fur.—*pr.p.* fur'ring.—*pa.p.* furred.—fur'rier *n.* dealer in furs.—fur'riery *n.*—fur'ry *a.*

furbish (fur'-bish) *v.t.* polish; burnish.

furious (fū'-ri-us) *a.* raging; incensed; violent; savage.—fu'riously *adv.*—fu'riousness *n.*

furl (furl) *v.t.* roll, as a sail.

furlong (fur'-long) *n.* eighth of mile; 220 yards.

furlough (fur'-lō) *n.* leave of absence.

furmenty, furmity See frumenty.

furnace (fur'-nās) *n.* enclosed structure for generating of heat for smelting ores, warming houses, etc.

furnish (fur'-nish) *v.t.* supply; equip;—*v.i.* supply a room or house with furniture.—fur'nisher *n.*—fur'nishings *n.pl.* fittings, of a house, esp. furniture.

furniture (fur'-ni-tūr) *n.* that which is put into a house for use or ornament.

furore (foo-rōr'-ā) *n.* enthusiastic outburst; acclaim; craze.

furrow (fur'-ō) *n.* trench made by a plough; groove; deep wrinkle;—*v.t.* plough; mark with wrinkles.

further (fur'-THẹr) *a.* more remote; additional;—*adv.* to a greater distance; moreover.—fur'thermore *adv.* moreover; besides.—fur'thermost *a.* most remote.—fur'thest *adv.* and *a.*

most remote (far'ther, far'thest are preferred as comp. and superl. of *far*). further education, organised instruction other than at university after leaving school.

further (fur'-THẹr) *v.t.* help forward; promote.—**fur'therance** *n.* act of furthering.

furtive (fur'-tiv) *a.* done stealthily; sly.

fury (fū'-ri) *n.* rage; passion; frenzy; (*Myth.*) goddess of revenge; virago.

furze (furz) *n.* spiny, yellow-flowered evergreen plant, also called *gorse*, and (*Scot.*) *whin*.

fuse (fūz) *v.t.* melt (as metal) by heat; amalgamate;—*v.i.* become liquid;—*n.* tube filled with combustible matter, used in blasting or discharge of bombs, etc.; soft wire used as safety device in electric circuits. —**fusibil'ity** *n.*—**fu'sible** *a.* capable of being melted or liquefied.—**fu'sion** *n.* act of melting; state of being melted or blended.

fusee (fū'-zē') *n.* spindle-shaped wheel in clock or watch, round which the chain is wound; match used by smokers to light pipe in a wind.

fuselage (fū'-ze-lij or fū-ze-lázh') *n.* body of aircraft.

fusil (fū'-zil) *n.* light flint-lock musket.—**fusilier'** *n.* orig. soldier armed with a fusil; infantryman.—**fu'sillade** *n.* simultaneous discharge of firearms.

fuss (fus) *n.* bustle; unnecessary ado; —*v.i.* become agitated;—*v.t.* worry another with attentions.—**fuss'ily** *adv.*—**fuss'iness** *n.*—**fuss'y** *a.*

fust (fust) *n.* shaft of column; strong, musty smell;—*v.i.* have rank smell.—**fusty** *a.*

fustian (fust'-yạn) *n.* coarse cotton twilled fabric, including corduroy; (*Fig.*) bombast;—*a.* bombastic.

futile (fū'-tīl, fū'-til) *a.* ineffectual, unavailing, useless.—**futil'ity** *n.* uselessness.

future (fūt'-ûr) *a.* about to happen; that is to come hereafter;—*n.* time to come.—**fut'urism** *n.* time to come.—**fut'urism** *n.* modern aesthetic movement marked by complete departure from tradition.—**fut'urist** *n.*—**futurist'ic** *a.*

fuze Same as fuse.

fuzz (fuz) *n.* fine, light particles; fluff;—*v.i.* fly off in minute particles. —**fuzz'-ball** *n.* puff-ball.—**fuzz'iness** *n.* —**fuzz'y** *a.*

G

G-man (jē'-man) *n.* (*U.S. Colloq.*) armed officer of the Federal Bureau of Investigation.

gab (gab) *n.* (*Colloq.*) trifling talk;

chatter;—*v.i.* chatter; talk idly.—**the gift of the gab**, talent for talking.

gabardine (gab'-ạr-dēn) *n.* See gaberdine.

gabble (gab'-l) *v.i.* talk noisily or without meaning;—*n.* loud or rapid meaningless talk.—**gabb'ler** *n.*

gaberdine (gab'-ẹr-dēn) *n.* cloth of cotton or silk, with wool lining; material for raincoats; a loose upper garment worn by Jews.

gable (gā'-bl) *n.* end of house, esp. vertical triangular ends of building.

gad (gad) *v.i.* go about idly; rove; straggle; ramble.—**gad'about** *v.i.* wander idly;—*n.* pleasure-seeker, esp. woman who neglects her work.

gadfly (gad'-flī) *n.* cattle-biting fly; (*Fig.*) tormentor.

gadget (gaj'-et) *n.* (*Colloq.*) general term for any small mechanical contrivance.

Gael (gāl) *n.* Scottish Highlander of Celtic origin.—**Gael'ic** *a.*—*n.* language of Gaels.

gaff (gaf) *n.* barbed fishing spear; stick with iron hook for landing fish; (*Naut.*) spar for top of fore-and-aft sail;—*v.t.* seize with a gaff;—*v.i.* use the gaff.

gaff (gaf) *n.* (*Slang*) nonsense; silly talk.—**to blow the gaff** (*Slang*) be an informer.

gaffe (gaf) *n.* indiscretion; injudicious act.

gaffer (gaf'-ẹr) *n.* old man, esp. in country; foreman in factory, etc.

gag (gag) *n.* something thrust into or over mouth to prevent speech; words inserted by actor which are not in his part; (*Slang*) joke;—*v.t.* silence by force.

gage (gāj) *n.* pledge or pawn; glove, gauntlet, cast down as challenge; challenge;—*v.t.* give as security; pledge.

gage (gāj) *n.* kind of plum; greengage.

gage (gāj) *v.t.* See gauge.

gaggle (gag'-l) *v.i.* cackle like goose; —*n.* flock of geese.

gaiety (gā'-e-ti) *n.* mirth; merriment; glee; jollity.—**gai'ly** *adv.*

gain (gān) *v.t.* attain to, or reach; get by effort; get profit; earn; win; —*v.i.* have advantage or profit; increase; make an advance;—*n.* profit; advantage; increase; (*Radio*) degree of amplification.—**gain'ings** *n.pl.* winnings.—**gain'ful** *a.* profitable; lucrative.

gainsay (gān'-sā, gān-sā') *v.t.* contradict; deny;—*pa.p.* and *pa.t.* gainsaid'.

gait (gāt) *n.* manner of walking or running.

gaiter (gā'-tẹr) *n.* covering for ankle, fitting upon upper of shoe.

gala (ga'-lạ, gā'-lạ) *n.* show or festivity.—**ga'la-day**, *n.* holiday with rejoicing.

galactic (ga-lak'-tik) a. of, or pert. to, milk; lactic; pert. to a galaxy or Milky Way.

galantine (gal'-ạn-tin) n. dish made of meat or game boiled till tender, then set in a jelly and served cold.

galaxy (gal'-ạk-si) n. band of stars encircling the heavens; Milky Way.—gal'axy n. brilliant assembly of persons.

gale (gāl) n. wind between stiff breeze and hurricane.

galena (ga-lē'-na) n. sulphide of lead, principal ore from which lead is extracted.

gall (gawl) n. bile secreted in the liver; anything bitter; (Fig.) bitterness; spite.—gall'-bladd'er n. small sac on under side of liver, in which bile is stored.—gall'-stone n. concretion formed in gall-bladder.

gall (gawl) n. excrescence, produced by an insect, in a plant, e.g. the oak-apple.—gall'-ap'ple, gall'-nut n. oak-apple.

gall (gawl) v.t. fret and wear away by rubbing; vex, irritate;—n. skin-wound caused by rubbing.—gall'ing a. irritating.

gallant (gal'-ant) a. splendid; noble in bearing or spirit; brave; chivalrous; courteous to women; amorous (ga-lant');—n. brave, high-spirited man; courtly or fashionable man; a lover or paramour.—gall'antly adv.—gall'antry n. splendour of appearance; chivalry; polite attentions to ladies.

galleon (gal'-e-on) n. large, clumsy sailing-ship built up high at bow and stern.

gallery (gal'-ẹr-i) n. long corridor, hall, or room; room or rooms in which works of art are exhibited; uppermost tier of seats, esp. in theatre; audience or spectators; passage in mine; tunnel.

galley (gal'-i) n. low, one-decked vessel, navigated both with oars and sails; captain's boat on warship; kitchen of ship; (Print.) oblong tray on which type is placed when set up.—gall'ey-proof n. (Print.) proof taken from the galley on long strip of paper, before it is made up in pages.—gall'ey-slave n. one condemned to row in galleys.

galliard (gal'-yard) n. ancient dance in triple time.

Gallic (gal'-ik) a. pert. to ancient Gaul, or France; French.—gall'icise v.t. make French in opinions, manners, idiom, etc.

gallipot (gal'-i-pot) n. small, glazed earthenware pot.

gallivant (gal-i-vant') v.i. gad about, pleasure-seeking, esp. with those of the opposite sex.

gallon (gal'-on) n. measure of capacity containing four quarts.

gallop (gal'-op) n. fastest gait of horse, when it lifts forefeet together, and hind feet together; a ride at a gallop;—v.i. ride at a gallop; go at full speed;—v.t. cause to gallop.—gall'oping a. speedy; swift.

gallows (gal'-ōz) n. frame from which criminals are hanged.—gall'owes n.pl. (Scot.) pair of braces.—gall'ows-tree n. gallows.

galop (gal'-op, ga-lop') n. lively dance.

galore (ga-lōr') adv. abundantly; in plenty.

galosh, golosh (ga-losh', go-losh') n. rubber overshoe.

galumph (ga-lumf') v.i. prance triumphantly and awkwardly.

galvanism (gal'-va-nizm) n. obsolete term for science of electric currents.—galvan'ic a.—gal'vanise v.t. coat with zinc by electrodeposition; spur to activity.—gal'vanising n.—galvanom'eter n. instrument for measuring electric currents.—galvanised iron, iron coated with zinc as preventative against rust.

gamba (gam'-ba) n. (Mus.) short for viola da gamba, a cello-size viol; organ stop with gamba-like tone.

gambit (gam'-bit) n. in chess, opening move involving sacrifice of pawn.

gamble (gam'-bl) v.i. play for money; risk esp. by speculation;—v.t. lose in speculative ventures;—n. risky undertaking; speculation.

gamboge (gam-bōj', -bóōj') n. gum-resin of reddish-yellow colour used as a pigment.

gambol (gam'-bol) v.i. leap about playfully; skip and dance about;—n. dancing or skipping about; frolic.

game (gām) n. sport; pastime; sporting contest; play for stakes; victory in a game; jest; frolic; mockery, hence, object of ridicule; animals and birds protected by law and hunted by sportsmen;—a. pert. to animals hunted as game; brave; plucky;—v.i. gamble.—games n.pl. athletic contests, e.g. Olympic Games.—game'smanship n. art of winning by devious means without actually cheating.—game'ster n. gambler.—gam'ing a. playing cards, dice, etc. for money; gambling.—gam'y a. having flavour of dead game which has been kept uncooked for long time.—game'-cock n. breed of cock trained for cock-fighting.—game'-keeper n. man employed to breed game, prevent poaching, etc.—big game, all large animals hunted for sport, e.g. elephants, tigers, etc.—fair game (Fig.) person considered easy subject for jest.—to play the game, act in a sportsmanlike way.

game (gām) a. (Colloq.) of an arm or leg, crippled; crooked.

gamin (gam'-in) n. street-urchin,

child neglected and left to run wild.

gamma (gam'-a) n. third letter of Greek alphabet; γ.—**gamma rays**, electro-magnetic radiations, of great penetrative powers, given off by certain radioactive substances.

gammer (gam'-er) n. old woman.

gammon (gam'-on) n. thigh of pig, pickled and smoked.

gammon (gam'-on) n. hoax; humbug;—v.t. humbug.

gammy (gam'-i) a. (Colloq.) crippled; disabled.

gamp (gamp) n. (Colloq.) large, dilapidated umbrella; any umbrella.

gamut (gam'-ut) n. whole series of musical notes; scale; compass of a voice; entire range.

gander (gan'-der) n. male goose; simpleton.

gang (gang) n. people banded together for some purpose, usually bad; body of labourers working together;—v.t. (Radio, etc.) couple switches or controls.—**ganger** (gang'-er) n. foreman of a squad of workmen.—**gang'ster** n. hooligan; hardened criminal.

gangling (gang'-gling) a. lanky and loosely knit in build.

ganglion (gang'-gli-on) n. mass of nerve tissue, which receives and sends out nerve fibres; globular, hard tumour, situated on a tendon. —pl. **gang'lions, gang'lia.**

gangrene (gang'-grēn) n. first stage of mortification or death of tissue in the body;—v.t. and i. affect with, or be affected with, gangrene.— **gang'renous** a. mortified; putrefying.

gangway (gang'-wā) n. movable plank bridge thrown across gap between ship and shore; passage between rows of seats;—interj. make way, please!

gannet (gan'-et) n. solan goose, seafowl of the pelican tribe.

gantlet (gánt'-let) n. military or naval punishment of former times, in which the offender was made to run between files of men who struck him as he passed.—**to run the gantlet** (erroneously, **gauntlet**), undergo this ordeal; face any unpleasant ordeal.

gantry, gauntry (gan'-tri, gawn'-tri) n. structure to support a crane, railway-signals, etc.

gaol (jāl) n. confinement; prison; jail.—**gaol'er** n. [form of jail].

gap (gap) n. opening; breach.

gape (gāp) v.i. open wide, esp. the mouth; stare with open mouth;—n. act of gaping.—**the gapes,** disease of poultry and other birds, characterised by gaping.

gar (gár) n. fish of the pike family.

garage (gar'-ij, gar'-azh) n. covered enclosure for motor vehicles; fuel and repair station for motor vehicles;— v.t. place in a garage.

garb (gárb) n. clothing; mode or style of dress;—v.t. dress.

garbage (gár'-bij) n. offal; kitchen refuse; anything worthless.

garble (gár'-bl) v.t. distort by reproducing in part; pervert, as a story, a quotation, an account.

garden (gár'-dn) n. ground for cultivation of flowers, vegetables, etc.; pleasure grounds;—v.i. cultivate, or work in, a garden.—**gar'dener** n.—**gar'dening** n.—**market gardener**, one who raises fruit, vegetables, etc. for sale.—**common or garden** (Colloq.) quite ordinary.

Gardenia (gár-dē'-ni-a) n. genus of tropical shrubs with sweet-scented flowers.

gargantuan (gár-gan'-tū-an) a. immense, enormous, esp. of appetite.

gargle (gar'-gl) v.i. rinse (mouth or throat), use a gargle;—n. throat wash [O.Fr. gargouille, throat].

gargoyle, gargoil (gár'-goil) n. projecting spout, often in form of grotesque carving, found on old buildings and intended to carry off water from gutters.

garish (gár'-ish) a. gaudy; showy; glaring; dazzling.—**gar'ishness** n.

garland (gár'-land) n. wreath of flowers, branches, etc.; anthology or book of literary extracts;—v.t. ornament with garland.

garlic (gár'-lik) n. plant having bulbous root, strong onion-like smell, and pungent taste.

garment (gár'-ment) n. any article of clothing.

garner (gár'-ner) n. granary;—v.t. store in a granary; gather up.

garnet (gár'-net) n. red semi-precious stone, resembling ruby.

garnish (gár'-nish) v.t. adorn; embellish; ornament; (Cookery) make food attractive or appetising by decoration;—n. ornament; decoration.—**gar'nishment** n.

garret (gar'-et) n. upper floor of house immediately under roof; attic.

garrison (gar'-i-sn) n. body of troops stationed in fort, town, etc.; fort or town itself;—v.t. occupy with garrison.

garrotte (ga-rot') n. Spanish mode of execution by strangling, with iron collar affixed to post and tightened by screw; apparatus for this;—v.t. execute by strangulation; seize by throat, in order to throttle and rob.

garrulous (gar'-ū-lus) a. talkative; loquacious.

garter (gár'-ter) n. string or band worn near knee to keep stocking up; badge of highest order of knighthood in Great Britain;—v.t. bind with garter.

gas (gas) n. elastic fluid such as air, esp. one not liquid or solid at ordinary temperatures; such fluid, esp. coal-gas, used for heating or lighting; anaesthetic used by dentists; (*Slang*) empty talk; (*U.S. Colloq.*) petrol. — *pl.* gas'es. — *v.t.* poison with gas. — *v.i.* (*Slang*) talk emptily; talk unceasingly. — gaseous (gā'shus) *a.* like, or in the form of, gas. — ga'seousness *n.* — gasifica'tion *n.* — gas'ify *v.t.* convert into gas, as by action of heat, or by chemical processes. — gas'sy *a.* full of gas. — gas'-bag *n.* large bag for holding gas; (*Slang*) very talkative person. — gas'-burn'er *n.* piece of metal, with small nozzle or jet, fitted to end of gaspipe to spread the flame. — gas'-hold'er *n.* huge container for storing gas (popularly, but erroneously, called gasom'eter). — gas'-jar *n.* (*Chem.*) large glass-jar for collecting gas during experiment. — gas'-jet *n.* spread of flame from gas-burner; burner itself. — gas'-mains *n.* network of pipes leading from gas-holder. — gas'-mant'le *n.* dome-shaped gauze fitting on gas-burner which glows brightly when heated. — gas'-me'ter *n.* appliance to measure amount of gas consumed. — gas'-retort' *n.* large chamber or oven in which coal is heated to produce gas. — gas'-stove *n.* heating or cooking appliance in which gas is burned. — gas'-tar *n.* coal-tar. — gas'-trap *n.* bend in drain-pipe, filled with water, to prevent the escape of foul gases.

gas (gas) *n.* (*War*) any chemical substance—solid, liquid, or gas—used to cause poisonous or irritant effects on the human body. — gassed *a.* incapacitated by gas. — gas'-mask *n.* respirator designed to protect the eyes, nose, mouth and lungs against gas.

Gascon (gas'kon) *n.* native of *Gascony*, in S.W. France; boaster. — gasconade (gas-ko-nād') *n.* boasting talk; bravado.

gash (gash) *v.t.* make a long, deep cut in; — *n.* deep cut.

gasket (gas'ket) *n.* washer between parts such as a cylinder head and cylinder block.

gasolene, gasoline (gas'-ō-lēn) *n.* American name for petrol.

gasometer (gas-om'e-ter) *n.* chemical instrument for holding, testing, or mixing gases.

gasp (gasp) *v.i.* struggle for breath with open mouth; pant; — *v.t.* utter with gasps; — *n.* painful catching of the breath. — gas'per *n.* (*Colloq.*) cheap cigarette.

gasteropod (gas'-te-rō-pod) *n.* class of molluscs, e.g. snails and whelks.

gastric (gas'trik) *a.* pert. to stomach. — gastritis (gas-trī'tis) *n.* inflammation of stomach. — gas'tro-enteri'tis *n.* inflammation of stomach and intestines.

gastronomy (gas-tron'-o-mi) *n.* art of good eating; epicurism. — gas'tronome, gastron'omer *n.* one fond of good living. — Also gastron'omist. — gastronom'ic, gastronom'ical *a.*

gat (gat) *n.* (*Slang*) pistol or revolver.

gate (gāt) *n.* opening into enclosure, through fence, wall, etc.; entrance; device for stopping passage of water through dam or lock; number of people paying to watch a game; the money taken; — *v.t.* punish students by confinement. — gate'-crash *v.t.* attend a social function uninvited. — gate'way *n.* passage through fence or wall; entrance.

gateau (gā'-tō) *n.* cake.

gather (gaTH'-er) *v.t.* bring together; collect; pick; in sewing, draw into puckers; infer; — *v.i.* come together; congregate; increase; swell up and become full of pus (of a sore or boil); — *n.* pucker, plait, or fold in cloth. — gath'ering *n.* assemblage; crowd; abscess.

gauche (gōsh) *a.* shy and uncouth in manner. — gaucherie (gō'-she-rē) *n.* clumsiness.

gaucho (gou'-chō) *n.* native of S. American pampas, of Spanish descent.

gaudy (gawd'-i) *a.* tawdry; vulgarly gay; pretentious.

gauge (gāj) *v.t.* ascertain capacity of; measure ability of; estimate. — *n.* instrument for determining dimensions or capacity; standard of measure; test; distance between rails of railway. — gaug'er *n.* one who gauges, esp. exciseman who measures contents of casks.

Gaul (gawl) *n.* an old name for France; inhabitant of Gaul.

gaunt (gawnt) *a.* lean and haggard; pinched and grim; desolate; barren. — gaunt'ly *adv.*

gauntlet (gawnt'-let) *n.* glove with metal plates on back, worn formerly as armour; glove with long cuff. — to run the gauntlet, see gantlet. — to throw down, to take up, the gauntlet, give, accept, challenge.

gauss (gous) *n.* (*Elect.*) unit of magnetic flux density.

gauze (gawz) *n.* thin, transparent fabric of silk, linen, wire, etc. — gauz'iness *n.* — gauz'y *a.*

gave (gāv) *pa.t.* of give.

gavel (gav'-el) *n.* mallet; small wooden hammer used by chairman or auctioneer.

gavotte (ga-vot') *n.* old dance after the style of the minuet.

gawk (gawk) *n.* awkward person; simpleton; booby. — gawk'y *a.* foolish and awkward; clumsy.

gay (gā) *a.* lively; merry; light-hearted; showy; dissipated. — gay'ly, gai'ly *adv.* — gai'ety *n.* joyousness.

gaze (gāz) *v.i.* look fixedly; fix the eyes in steady or earnest look; stare;—*n.* fixed, earnest look; long, intent look.

gazelle (gą-zel') *n.* small antelope.

gazette (gą-zet') *n.* newspaper; official newspaper (*London Gazette*) for announcements of government appointments, military promotions, etc.;—*v.t.* publish in the official gazette.—**gazetteer** (gaz-e-tēr') *n.* formerly writer for gazette; now, geographical dictionary.

gear (gēr) *n.* apparatus; equipment; tackle; set of tools; harness; rigging; clothing; goods; utensils; set of toothed wheels working together to transmit power or change timing;—*v.t.* provide with gear; put in gear;—*v.i.* be in gear.—**gear'ing** *n.* series of toothed wheels for transmitting power, changing speed, etc.

gecko (gek'-ō) *n.* small, wall-lizard.

gee (jē) *interj.* command to draught animal to turn to off-side;—*n.* horse; also (*Colloq.*) **gee'-gee.**—**gee'-up** *interj.* command, esp. to horse, to go faster.

geese (gēs) *n.* plural of **goose.**

Geiger counter (gī'-ger) *n.* device for detecting radio-activity, etc.

geisha (gā'-shą) *n.* Japanese professional hostess and entertainer.

gel (jel) *n.* (*Chem.*) colloidal solution which has set into a jelly;—*v.i.* form a gel.—**gel'able** *a.* able to be congealed.—**gela'tion** *n.* solidifying by means of cold.

gelatine, gelatin (jel'-ą-tēn, -tin) *n.* glutinous substance obtained from animal connective tissue, used in foodstuffs, photographic film, glues, etc.—**gelatinous** (je-lat'-i-nus) *a.*—**gelat'inate, gelat'inise** *v.t.*

geld (geld) *v.t.* castrate.—**geld'ing** *n.* castrated animal, esp. horse.

gelder-rose See **guelder-rose.**

gelid (jel'-id) *a.* cold as ice.

gelignite (jel'-ig-nīt) *n.* gelatinised explosive used for blasting in mines.

gem (jem) *n.* precious stone of any kind; jewel; anything of great value;—*v.t.* adorn with gems.

geminate (jem'-i-nāt) *a.* doubled; existing in pairs.—**gemina'tion** *n.*

Gemini (jem'-i-nī) *n.pl.* third sign of the Zodiac which sun enters about 21st May; (*Astron.*) constellation containing two bright stars Castor and Pollux.

gen (jen) *n.* (*Army Slang*) information.

gendarme (zhong-dárm') *n.* an armed policeman in France.

gender (jen'-der) *n.* sex, male or female.

gene (jēn) *n.* hereditary factor transmitted by each parent to offspring which determines hereditary characteristics.

genealogy (jen-e-al'-o-ji) *n.* study of family history; family tree; pedigree.—**geneal'ogist** *n.*—**genealog'ical** *a.*

genera (jen'-ę-rą) *n. pl.* See **genus.**

general (jen'-e-rąl) *a.* relating to genus or kind; pert. to whole class or order; not precise, particular, or detailed; usual, ordinary, or prevalent;—*n.* that which embraces the whole or greater part; officer in British Army ranking immediately below field-marshal.—**gen'erally** *adv.* as a whole; for the most part; commonly.—**general'ity** *n.* indefiniteness; vagueness; vague statement.—**in general**, in most respects.—**general election**, one in which every constituency chooses a representative.

generalise (jen'-er-al-īz) *v.t.* reduce to general laws; make universal in application;—*v.i.* draw general conclusions from particular instances; speak vaguely.—**generalisa'tion** *n.* act of generalising; general conclusion from particular instances.

generate (jen'-ę-rāt) *v.t.* bring into being; produce.—**genera'tion** *n.* bringing into being; act of producing; that which is generated; step in family descent; all persons born about same time; average time in which children are ready to replace their parents (about 30 years).—**generative** (jen'-ę-rā-tiv) *a.* having power of generating or producing; prolific.—**gen'erator** *n.* one who, or that which, generates; apparatus for converting mechanical into electrical energy.

generic (je-ner'-ik) *a.* pert. to genus; of general nature.—**gener'ically** *adv.*

generous (jen'-ę-rus) *a.* noble-minded; free in giving; abundant; copious.—**gen'erously** *adv.*—**generos'ity** *n.* magnanimity; nobleness of heart and feeling; liberality in giving. Also **gen'erousness** *n.*

genesis (jen'-e-sis) *n.* origin; creation; production; birth.—*pl.* **geneses** (jen'-e-sēs).—**Gen'esis** *n.* (*Bib.*) first book of Old Testament.

genetic (je-net'-ik) *a.* pert. to origin, creation, or reproduction.—**genet'ics** *n.* scientific study of heredity.—**genet'icist** *n.*

Genevan (je-nē'-vąn) *a.* pert. to *Geneva*, in Switzerland.—**Geneva Conventions**, international agreements, signed at Geneva in 1864, 1868, 1906 and 1949, to provide for neutrality of hospitals, etc., in war.

genial (jēn'-yąl) *a.* kindly; sympathetic; sociable; of a climate, mild.—**geniality** (jē-ni-al'-i-ti) *n.* sociability; friendliness; cheerfulness.

genie (jē'-ni) *n.* sprite; goblin; jinnee.—*pl.* **genii** (jē'-ni-ī).

genital (jen'-i-tąl) *a.* pert. to generation, or to organs of generation.—**gen'itals** *n.pl.* external sexual organs.

genitive (jen'-i-tiv) *a.* pert. to, or indicating, source, origin, possession, etc.

genius (jē'-ni-us, jēn'-yus) *n.* one's mental endowment or individual talent; spirit of people, generation or locality; uncommon intellectual powers; person endowed with highest mental gifts.—*pl.* geniuses (jēn'-yus-ez).—**genius** (jē'-ni-us) *n.* tutelary deity supposed by ancients to preside over man's life and fortune.—*pl.* genii (jē'-ni-ī).

genocide (jen'-ō-sīd) *n.* deliberate killing-off of race or nation.—gen'ocidal *a.*

genre (zhong'-r) *n.* kind; sort; style.—genre painting, painting which portrays scenes in everyday life.

gent (jent) *n.* (*Colloq.*) a gentleman.

genteel (jen-tēl') *a.* possessing qualities belonging to high birth and breeding; well-bred; stylish; affectedly refined.—genteel'ly *adv.*—genteel'ness *n.*—gentility (jen-til'-i-ti) *n.*

gentian (jen'-shan) *n.* common name of Gentiana, plants whose root is used medicinally. — gentian violet, mixture of methyl dyes used as antiseptic and anti-bacterial agent.

Gentile (jen'-tīl) *n.* one who is not a Jew;—*a.* pert. to other nations as distinct from the Jews.

gentle (jen'-tl) *a.* kind and amiable; mild and refined in manner; quiet and sensitive of disposition; (*Arch.*) of good family;—*n.* (*Arch.*) one of good birth; larva of blue-bottle;—gen'tlefolk *n.pl.* persons of good breeding and family.—gen'tleness *n.*—gen'try (jen'-tri) *n.* class of people next below the nobility.

gentleman (jen'-tl-man) *n.* man of good breeding and refined manners; man of good family; polite term for a man.—*pl.* gen'tlemen.—gen'tlemanly *a.* well-behaved; courteous.—gen'tlewoman *n.* (*Arch.*) woman of good family or of good breeding.—gentleman's gentleman, a valet.—gentleman's agreement, one binding in honour but not legally.

genuflect (jen'-ū-flekt) *v.i.* bend the knee, esp. in worship.—genuflec'tion, genuflex'ion *n.*

genuine (jen'-ū-in) *a.* real; true; pure; authentic; unadulterated.—gen'uinely *adv.*—gen'uineness *n.*

genus (jē'-nus) *n.* race; class; order; kind; (*Nat. Hist.*) subdivision ranking next above species.—*pl.* gen'era.

geo-, ge- (jē'-o, jē) combining forms fr. Gk. *ge*, meaning earth, ground.

geodesy (jē-od'-e-si) *n.* mathematical survey and measurement of earth's surface, involving allowance for curvature.—geodet'ic, geodet'ical *a.*

geography (jē-og'-ra-fi) *n.* science of the earth's form, its physical divisions into seas, rivers, mountains, etc.; book on this.—geo'grapher *n.*—geograph'ic, geograph'ical *a.*

geology (jē-ol'-o-ji) *n.* science of earth's crust, rocks, strata, etc.—geolog'ical *a.*—geol'ogist *n.*

geometry (jē-om'-e-tri) *n.* mathematical study of the properties of lines, angles, surfaces, and solids; text-book on this.—geomet'ric(al) *a.* pert. to geometry.—geometri'cian, geom'eter *n.* one skilled in geometry.—geometrical progression (*Math.*) series of quantities in which each quantity is obtained by multiplying preceding term by a constant factor.

Georgian (jor'-ji-an) *a.* pert. to reigns of the six *Georges*, Kings of Great Britain; relating to *Georgia*, republic of Soviet Union, or *Georgia* in U.S.A.

georgette (jor-jet') *n.* fine semi-transparent silk fabric.

Georgic (jor'-jik) *n.* poem on husbandry.—geor'gic *a.* pert. to agriculture or rustic affairs.

geotropism (jē-ot'-ro-pizm) *n.* (*Bot.*) tendency of growing plant to direct its roots downwards.—geotrop'ic *a.*

geranium (je-rā'-ni-um) *n.* plant having showy flowers, and seed-vessels like a crane's bill; garden 'geranium' is of genus Pelargonium.

gerfalcon (jer'-fawl-kon, -faw-kn) *n.* large Arctic falcon.—Also gyr'falcon.

geriatrics (jer-i-at'-riks) *n.* medical study of old people; welfare of the old.

germ (jerm) *n.* rudimentary form of a living thing, animal or plant; microscopic organism; microbe; bud; that from which anything springs.—germ'icide *n.* substance for destroying disease-germs.—germici'dal *a.*

german (jer'-man) *a.* of the first degree (only used in *brother-german, sister-german, cousin-german*); closely allied.—germane (jer-mān') *a.* appropriate; relevant; allied; akin.

German (jer'-man) *a.* belonging to *Germany*;—*n.* native of Germany; German language.—German'ic *a.* pert. to Germany; Teutonic.—Ger'manise *v.t.* make German.—German measles, disease like measles, but less severe.

germanium (jer-mā'-ni-um) *n.* metallic element, noted for its semiconductor properties.—symbol Ge.

germinal (jer'-mi-nal) *a.* pert. to germ or seed-bud.

germinate (jerm'-in-āt) *v.i.* sprout; bud; shoot; begin to grow;—*v.t.* cause to grow.—germina'tion *n.*

gerontology (jer-on-tol'-o-ji) *n.* (*Med.*) branch of science that studies the decline of life, esp. of man.

gerrymander (jer-i-man'-der) *v.t.* arrange to private advantage electoral districts.

gerund (jer'-und) *n.* part of the

Latin verb used as a verbal noun.—
gerun'dial a. of the nature of a
gerund.—**gerun'dive** n. future participle passive of Latin verb expressing the action of having to be done.
gestation (jes-tā'-shun) n. carrying
young in womb; pregnancy.—
gestatory (jes'-ta-to-ri) a.
gesticulate (jes-tik'-ū-lāt) v.i. make
violent gestures or motions, esp.
with hands and arms, when speaking.—**gesticula'tion** n. act of gesticulating; gesture.—**gestic'ulatory** a.
gesture (jes'-tūr) n. motion of head,
hands, etc. as a mode of expression;
act indicating attitude of mind;
conciliatory approach.
get (get) v.t. procure; obtain; gain
possession of; come by; win, by
almost any means; receive; earn;
(Colloq.) understand;—v.i. become;
reach; bring one's self into a condition.—pa.t. **got**.—pa.p. **got**.—**getaway** (get'-a-wā) n. (Colloq.) escape.—
get'-up n. equipment; dress.
geyser (gī'-zer, gā'-zer) n. hot spring
which spouts water intermittently;
apparatus for heating water rapidly
by gas, electricity, etc.
ghastly (gást'-li) a. and adv. horrible;
shocking; ghostly.—**ghast'liness** n.
gherkin (ger'-kin) n. small species of
cucumber used for pickling.
ghetto (get'-ō) n. Jewish quarter in
city.
ghost (gōst) n. apparition of dead
person; spectre; disembodied spirit;
shadow; (Colloq.) a person who does
literary or artistic work for another,
who takes credit for it; duplicate
image on television.—**ghost'ly** a.—
Holy Ghost, Holy Spirit; third
element in the Trinity.
ghoul (gōōl) n. imaginary evil being
in East, supposed to rob graves and
feed on corpses.—**ghoul'ish** a.
giant (jī'-ant) n. (fem. **gi'antess**) man
of extraordinary bulk and stature;
person of unusual powers, bodily or
intellectual.—a. like a giant.
gib (jib) n. in machine or structure,
wedge-shaped piece of metal to hold
other parts in position; arm of a
crane.—Also **jib**.
gibber (jib'-er, gib'-er) v.i. speak
rapidly and inarticulately; chatter
like an ape.—**gibb'erish** n. meaningless speech; gabble; nonsense.
gibbet (jib'-et) n. gallows; post with
arm on which criminals were
executed by hanging;—v.t. to hang
on a gallows.
gibbon (gib'-on) n. tail-less, long-armed ape.
gibbous (gib'-us) a. protuberant;
humped; convex; of the moon, with
the bright part greater than a semicircle.
gibe, jibe (jīb) v.i. taunt; sneer at;
scoff at;—n. expression of censure

mingled with contempt; taunt; jeer.
giblets (jib'-lets) n. pl. internal
eatable parts of poultry.
giddy (gid-i') a. dizzy; feeling swimming sensation in the head; liable to
cause this sensation; whirling;
flighty; frivolous.—**gidd'ily** adv.-
gidd'iness n.
gift (gift) n. present; thing given;
donation; natural talent; faculty;
power;—v.t. present with; bestow.—
gift'ed a. talented.
gig (gig) n. light carriage with one
pair of wheels, drawn by one horse
ship's boat; rowing-boat.
gigantic (ji-gan'-tik) a. like a giant
of extraordinary size; huge.—**gigan'tically** adv.—**gigan'tism** n. (Med.)
abnormal overgrowth of the body or
limbs.
giggle (gig'-l) v.i. laugh in silly way
titter;—n. such a laugh.—**gigg'ler** n
—**gigg'ling** n.
gigolo (jig'-o-lō) n. professional male
dancing-partner.
gigot (jig'-ot) n. leg of mutton or of
lamb.
gild (gild) v.t. overlay with gold-leaf
or gold-dust; cover with anything
like gold; brighten; embellish.
gill (jil) n. measure of capacity containing fourth part of a pint.
gill (gil) n. organ of respiration in
fishes; flap below the beak of a bird;
flesh about the chin and jaws; radial
tissue on underside of mushrooms
and other fungi.
gill (gil) n. ravine or narrow valley,
with stream running through it.
Also **ghyll**.
gillie, gilly (gil'-i) n. in Scotland,
orig. male attendant on a chieftain;
now one who attends on sportsmen.
—Also (incorrectly) **ghill'ie**.
gillyflower (jil'-i-flou-er) n. clove-scented pink.
gilt (gilt) n. gold, or something
resembling gold, laid on the surface
of a thing;—a. yellow like gold;
gilded.—**gilt'-edged** a. having the
edges gilded; of the best quality.
gimbals (jim'-balz) n.pl. contrivance
of rings and pivots for keeping a
ship's compass, etc. always in a
horizontal position.
gimcrack (jim'-krak) n. fanciful
trifle; mechanical device;—a. showy
but worthless.
gimlet (gim'-let) n. small implement
with screw point and cross handle,
for boring holes in wood;—v.t. bore
with a gimlet.
gimmick (gim'-ik) n. originally in
the U.S., small device fitted to
gaming-machine to make it unfair;
trick-of-the-trade; any mannerism
or trick employed for purposes.
gimp (gimp) n. narrow fabric used as
edging for furniture or trimming for
dresses.

gin (jin) n. distilled spirit, flavoured with juniper berries.

gin (jin) n. snare or trap; machine for lifting or moving heavy weights; machine for separating seeds from cotton;—v.t. clear cotton of seeds by a gin; catch in a snare.

ginger (jin'-jer) n. plant with hot-tasting spicy root; ginger-beer; (Slang) spirit; a light reddish-yellow colour;—v.t. put life into; animate (with up).—gin'ger-ale n. aerated beverage.—gin'ger-beer n. effervescing beverage made by fermenting ginger, cream of tartar, and sugar, etc.—gin'ger-bread n. cake flavoured with ginger.—gin'ger-pop n. weak ginger-beer.—gin'ger-wine n. wine made by fermentation, from ginger with other ingredients. —gin'gery a. hot and spicy.

gingerly (jin'-jer-li) adv. cautiously.

gingham (ging'-am) n. cotton cloth.

gin rummy (jin-rum'-i) n. two-handed card game (or four-handed with partners).

gipsy, gypsy (jip'-si) n. one of nomadic tribe of Indian origin, that came by way of Egypt in 14th cent. —pl. gip'sies.

giraffe (ji-ráf') n. African animal, with spotted coat and very long neck and legs; (Arch.) camelopard.

gird (gerd) v.t. gibe; jeer.—gird'er n.

gird (gerd) v.t. encircle; put belt round; fasten clothes thus; equip with, or belt on, a sword.—pa.p. and pa.t. gird'ed or girt.—n. child's hoop. —gird'er n. principal piece of timber or iron in a floor to act as a supporting beam for joists; iron or steel beam as used in engineering.

girdle (ger'-dl) n. that which girds or encircles, esp. band which encircles the waist; belt; corset;— v.t. bind with belt or sash.

girl (gerl) n. female child; young unmarried woman. — girl'hood n. state of being a girl.—girl'ish a. like a girl.—Girl Guide, member of organisation for girls on the lines of Boy Scouts.

girt (gert) pa.t. and pa.p. of the v. gird;—v.t. gird; surround.

girth (gerth) n. band to hold saddle, blanket, etc. in place; measurement round a thing.

gist (jist) n. main point of question; substance or essential point of any matter.

give (giv) v.t. bestow; make a present of; grant; make over; cause to have; pledge, as one's word;—v.i. yield; give away; move.—pa.p. giv'en.— pa.t. gave.—given (giv'-n) a. granted; admitted; certain; inclined to.—to give away, hand over; divulge; betray. —to give over, cease from.

gizzard (giz'-ard) n. bird's strong muscular second stomach.

glacé (glá'-sā) a. of a cake, iced; of a kind of leather, polished or glossy.

glacier (glas'-i-er, glá'-sher) n. mass of ice, formed by accumulated snow which moves very slowly down a mountain; river of ice.—glacial (glá'-shal) pert. to ice or glaciers; icy; frozen; pert. to ice-age.—glacial period, Ice Age.

glad (glad) a. pleased; happy;—v.t. gladden; cheer; please.—glad'some a. joyful; cheerful.—glad eye (Colloq.) amorous glance.

glade (glād) n. grassy open space in a wood.

gladiator (glad'-i-ā-tor) n. literally, swordsman; in ancient Rome, professional combatant who fought in the arena.

gladiolus (glad-i-ō'-lus, glạ-dī'-o-lus) n. plant genus of iris family, with sword-shaped leaves;— pl. gladio'luses, or gladioli.

glair (glār) n. white of egg; size or gloss made from it; any viscous substance resembling white of egg; —v.t. smear with glair.

glamour (glam'-ur) n. deceptive or alluring charm.—glam'orous a.

glance (gláns) n. quick look; glimpse; flash; allusion or hint; oblique hit;— v.i. give a swift, cursory look; allude; fly off in an oblique direction.

gland (gland) n. cell or collection of cells secreting certain substances in plants and animals.—gland'ers n. disease of mucous membrane in nostrils of horses.—gland'ular, gland'ulous a. containing glands; consisting of glands.

glare (glār) n. strong, dazzling light; overwhelming glitter; showiness; fierce, hostile look;—v.i. shine with dazzling light; stare in fierce and hostile manner.—glar'ing a. brilliant; open and bold.

glass (glás) n. hard, brittle, generally transparent substance formed by fusing silica with fixed alkalis; articles made of glass, glass drinking-vessel; telescope; barometer; quantity contained in drinking glass.—a. made of glass;—v.t. to glaze.— glass'es n.pl. spectacles.—glass'y a. made of glass; vitreous; like glass; dull or lifeless.—glass'-blow'ing n. art of shaping and fashioning glass by inflating it through a tube, after heating. — glass'-blow'er n. — glass'-house n. greenhouse; (Slang) military prison.—glass'-pa'per n. paper coated with pulverised glass for polishing. —glass'ware n. articles made of glass. —cut glass, glass ornamented by cutting designs into it with a wheel. —ground glass, glass rendered untransparent by grinding.

glaucoma (glaw-kō'-mạ) n. (Med.) serious eye-disease with build-up of fluid in eyeball.

glaucous (glaw'-kus) a. sea-green; covered with grey-green bloom.

glaze (glāz) n. vitreous, transparent coating of pottery or porcelain; glossy coating;—v.t. furnish with glass; impart a glaze to.—**glaz'er** n. a workman who glazes pottery, cloth, or paper.—**glazier** (glā'-zi-er) n. dealer in glass; one who sets glass in windows, etc.

gleam (glēm) n. faint or transient ray of light; brightness; glow;—v.i. shoot or dart, as rays of light; flash; shine faintly.

glean (glēn) v.t. gather after reaper, as grain; collect with patient labour; pick up (information);—v.i. gather what is left by reapers.—**glean'er** n. —**glean'ings** n.pl. what is collected by gleaning.

glebe (glēb) n. land belonging to parish church.

glee (glē) n. mirth; joy; musical composition for three or more voices; a part song.

gleet (glēt) n. thin discharge from a mucous surface.

glen (glen) n. valley.

glengarry (glen-gar'-i) n. Scottish Highlander's cap, with two ribbons hanging down behind.

glib (glib) a. smooth; fluent; plausible; superficial; flippant.—**glib'ly** adv.—**glib'ness** n.

glide (glīd) v.i. move gently; go stealthily; move through the air without expending power;—n. sliding movement.—**glid'er** n. aeroplane capable of flight without motive power, by utilising air currents.

glimmer (glim'-er) v.i. shine faintly and unsteadily; flicker;—n. faint, unsteady light; flicker.

glimpse (glimps) n. momentary view; passing appearance; weak, faint light; faint notion;—v.t. catch a glimpse of; get passing view of; v.i. glimmer.

glissade (glē-sād') n. act of sliding down slope of ice or snow; dancing, gliding step sideways.

glisten (glis'-n) v.i. glitter; shine.

glitter (glit'-er) v.i. shine with bright, quivering light; sparkle; be showy and attractive;—n. bright, sparkling light.

gloaming (glō-ming) n. evening twilight.

gloat (glōt) v.i. feast the eyes, usually with wicked joy; exult maliciously.

globe (glōb) n. round body; sphere; heavenly sphere, esp. the earth; sphere with map of the earth or the stars; anything of this shape.—**glob'al** a. taking in the whole world. —**globose'**, **glob'ous** a. round, spherical (or nearly so).—**glob'ular** a. globe-shaped.—**globule** (glob'-ūl) n. small spherical particle of matter; tiny pill.—**glob'ulous** a.—**globe'-trot'ter** n.

hasty, sight-seeing traveller or tourist.

globulin (glob'-ū-lin) n. one of the soluble proteins of the blood.

glockenspiel (glok'-en-spēl) n. musical instrument consisting of a set of bells or metal bars struck with hammers, often from a keyboard.

glomerate (glom'-e-rāt) v.t. gather into a ball;—a. gathered into a cluster.—**glomera'tion** a.

gloom (glóóm) n. thick shade; partial or almost total darkness; melancholy.—v.i. become dark or threatening; be dejected; look sullen.—**gloom'y** a. dark and dreary. —**gloom'ily** adv.—**gloom'iness** n.

glory (glō'-ri) n. renown, praise; whatever brings honour; praise and adoration due to God; divine happiness; height of excellence or prosperity; splendour. — v.i. be proud; boast; exult triumphantly.— **gloriole** (glō'-ri-ōl) n. halo or circle of rays.—**glo'rious** a. illustrious; splendid; noble.—**glo'rify** v.t. exalt; praise; esp. extol in worship; make eternally blessed; shed radiance on.—**glo'rifier** n.—**glorifica'tion** n.—**glo'ry-hole** n. lumber-room.

gloss (glos) n. lustre from a smooth surface; polish;—v.t. make smooth and shining; render plausible (with over).—**gloss'y** a. smooth and shining.

gloss (glos) n. explanatory note upon some word or passage in a text, written in the margin or between the lines; glossary;—v.t. and i. to annotate.

glossary (glos'-a-ri) n. vocabulary of obscure or technical words; vocabulary to a book.

glottis (glot'-is) n. (Anat.) narrow opening at top of larynx or windpipe, between the vocal chords.— **glott'al** a.

glove (gluv) n. cover for hand and wrist with sheath for each finger.— **glov'er** n. one who makes or sells gloves.

glow (glō) v.i. shine with an intense or white heat; be bright or red; feel hot; burn;—n. white heat; incandescence; redness of colour; sensation of warmth.—**glow'ing** a. bright; warm; excited.

glower (glou'-er) v.i. stare sullenly; —n. sullen scowl.

glucose (glóó'-kōs) n. white crystalline sugar obtained from grapes, etc.; grape-sugar.

glue (glóó) n. unrefined gelatin, used as adhesive; adhesive made from animal tissue, casein, synthetic resins, etc.—v.t. join with glue.— **glu'ey** a.—**glu'eyness** n.

glum (glum) a. sullen; morose.

glut (glut) v.t. swallow greedily; feed till over-full; supply over-abundantly;—n. super-abundance; surfeit.

gluten (glōō'-ten) *n.* protein of wheat, etc.

glutton (glut'-n) *n.* one who eats too much; (*Fig.*) one eager for anything in excess; carnivore of weasel family, wolverine.—**glutt'onise** *v.t.* eat to excess; gormandise.—**glutt'onous** *a.* given to gluttony.—**glutt'ony** *n.*

glycerine (glis'-er-in, -ēn) *n.* sweet, colourless, odourless, syrupy liquid. —Also **glyc'erin.**

glycol (glī'-kol) *n.* compounds in the chain linking glycerine and alcohol.

glyph (glif) *n.* shallow vertical channel or carved fluting.

glyptic (glip'-tik) *a.* pert. to carving on stone.—**glyp'tics** *n.pl.* art of engraving on precious stones.— **glyp'tograph** *n.* engraving on gem or precious stone.

gnarl (márl) *n.* knot in wood or on trunk of tree.—**gnarled, gnar'ly** *a.* knotty; knobby.

gnash (nash) *v.t.* grind the teeth together, as in anger;—*n.* snap; sudden bite.

gnat (nat) *n.* kind of small mosquito.

gnaw (naw) *v.t.* wear away by scraping with the teeth; bite steadily; corrode;—*v.i.* use teeth in biting; cause steady pain.—*pa.p.* gnawed.

gneiss (nīs) *n.* crystalline rock, consisting of quartz, feldspar, and mica.

gnome (nōm) *n.* being, of diminutive size, guardian of precious metals hidden in earth; goblin.

gnomon (nō'-mon) *n.* pin, rod, or plate which casts shadow on sundial; indicator.

gnosis (nō'-sis) *n.* science; mystical knowledge.—**gnostic** (nost'-tik) *a.* pert. to knowledge; having special knowledge; pert. to Gnostics.— **Gnos'tics** *n.pl.* followers of religious sect in early Christian era who had esoteric spiritual knowledge.

gnu (nōō) *n.* kind of antelope, resembling an ox; the black wildebeest.

go (gō) *v.t.* pass from one place or condition to another; move along; be in motion; depart; elapse; put; be able to be put; result; contribute to result; tend to; pass away; become; fare.—*pa.p.* gone (gon).— *pa.t.* went.—*n.* going; vigour; (*Colloq.*) attempt; fashion.—**go'er** *n.* one who, or that which, goes.—**go'ing** *n.* state of ground, e.g. on race-course, etc.—**goings on** (*Colloq.*) usually in bad sense, strange behaviour.— **gone** *a.* lapsed; beyond recovery; weak and faint.—**go'-between'** *n.* intermediary.—**go'-by** *n.* intentional slight.—**go'-cart** *n.* framework on castors, for teaching infants to walk; baby-carriage.—**go'-kart** *n.* small four-wheeled chassis fitted with engine for racing.—**to go halves,** share equally with.—**to go in for,** sit an examination; choose as career.— **to go off,** depart; explode; disappear; become less efficient, popular, fashionable, fresh, etc.

goad (gōd) *n.* sharp, pointed stick for driving cattle; anything that urges to action;—*v.t.* drive with goad; urge on; irritate.

goal (gōl) *n.* in race winning-post; in football, hockey, etc., space marked by two upright posts and cross-bar; act of kicking or driving the ball between these posts; object of effort; end or aim.

goat (gōt) *n.* long-haired, ruminant quadruped with cloven hoofs, allied to the sheep, with backward-curving horns; 10th sign of Zodiac, Capricorn, which the sun enters on 22nd Dec.—**goatee** (gō-tē') *n.* small tuft of beard on chin.—**goat-herd** *n.* one who tends goats.—**goat'ish** *a.* rank-smelling, like a goat; wanton; lecherous.—**to get one's goat** (*Colloq.*) irritate.

gob (gob) *n.* lump or mouthful; clot of spittle; (*Colloq.*) mouth.—**gobb'et** *n.* mouthful; small lump, esp. of flesh.

gobble (gob'-l) *v.t.* eat hurriedly; swallow in lumps.—**gobb'ler** *n.* greedy eater.

gobble (gob'-l) *n.* throaty, gurgling cry of the turkey-cock;—*v.i.* make such a noise.—**gobbledegook'** *n.* official jargon.—**gobb'ler** *n.* turkey-cock.

goblet (gob'-let) *n.* drinking vessel without a handle.

goblin (gob'-lin) *n.* evil or mischievous sprite or elf; a gnome.

God (god) *n.* Supreme Being; Jehovah.—**god** *n.* person of more than human powers; divinity; idol; any person honoured unduly; any object esteemed as chief good;— *n.pl.* false deities; (*Colloq.*) gallery of theatre; audience therein.—**god'dess** *n.* female god or idol.—**god'head** *n.* divinity.—**god'ly** *a.* reverencing God; pious; devout.—**god'liness** *n.* holiness; righteousness. — **god'less** *a.* wicked; impious; acknowledging no God.—**god'send** *n.* unexpected piece of good fortune.—**god'speed** *n.* prosperous journey; wish for success given at parting.—**God'fear'ing,** *a.* devoutly religious. — **god'forsak'en,** dreary; dismal.

godchild (god'-chīld) *n.* one for whom person becomes sponsor at baptism.—**god'daughter** *n.*—**god'son** *n.* —**god'father** *n.* sponsor at baptism.— **god'mother** *n.*

godwit (god'-wit) *n.* wading-bird resembling curlew.

goggle (gog'-l) *v.i.* roll the eyes; stare;—*n.* rolling of the eyes;—*a.*

rolling; bulging; protruding (of the eyes).—**gogg'les** *n.pl.* spectacles.

goitre (goi'-ter) *n.* swelling on front of neck, the enlargement of thyroid gland.—**goi'trous** *a.* like goitre.

gold (gōld) *n.* precious metal of bright yellow colour; money; riches; bright yellow colour;—*a.* made of gold; of colour of gold; golden.—**gold'en** *a.* made of gold; having colour of gold; precious.—**gold'finch** *n.* a beautiful singing bird.—**gold'fish** *n.* small fish named from its colour.—**gold'smith** *n.* one who manufactures vessels and ornaments of gold.—**gold'-beat'er** *n.* one who beats gold into gold-leaf.—**gold'-dig'ger** *n.* one who digs or mines gold; (*Slang*) an unscrupulous flirt, expert at obtaining money from male friends.—**gold'-dust** *n.* gold in fine particles.—**gold'-leaf** *n.* gold beaten into an extremely thin leaf or foil, used for gilding.—**gold'-mine** *n.* mine from which gold is dug.—**gold'-rush** *n.* mad scramble to reach new gold-field.—**gold standard,** currency system under which bank-notes are exchangeable for gold at any time.—**golden age,** most flourishing period in history of a nation.—**golden eagle,** large, powerful eagle, so called from yellow-tipped feathers on its head.—**golden rod,** plant of the aster family.—**golden rule,** rule of doing as you would be done by.—**golden wedding,** fiftieth anniversary of one's wedding.

golf (golf) *n.* out-door game played with set of clubs and ball, in which ball is driven with fewest possible strokes, into succession of holes.—**golf'er** *n.*—**golf'-course** *n.*, **golf'-links** *n.pl.* ground on which game is played.

golliwog, gollywog (gol'-i-wog) *n.* black-faced, goggle-eyed fantastically dressed doll.

golly (gol'-i) *interj.* orig. minced oath; to express joy, sorrow, surprise, etc.

golosh (go-losh') *n.* rubber overshoe.

gonad (gon'-ad) *n.* (*Biol.*) primary sex gland; ovary or testis.

gondola (gon'-do-la) *n.* long, narrow, flat-bottomed boat, used in canals of Venice; passenger car of balloon or airship.—**gondolier** (gon-do-lēr') *n.* boatman who propels the gondola.

gone (gon) *pa.p.* of the verb go.—**gon'er** *n.* (*Slang*) one who is in a hopeless state.

gong (gong) *n.* circular metal plate which gives out deep note when struck with a soft mallet; anything used in the same way; (*Slang*) medal.

gonococcus (gon-o-kok'-us) *n.* (*Med.*) bacterium causing gonorrhea.—**gonorrhea** (gon-o-rē'-a) *n.* contagious discharge of mucus from membrane of urethra or vagina.

good (good) *a.* commendable; right; proper; suitable; excellent; virtuous; honest; just; kind; sound; valid; solvent; adequate; full, as weight, measure, etc.; skilful;—*n.* that which is good; welfare; well-being; profit; advantage;—*n.pl.* property; wares; merchandise;—*interj.* well! right!—*comp.* of adjective, bett'er. —*superl.* best.—**good'ish** *a.* (of quality) pretty good; (of quantity) fairly plentiful.—**good'ly** *a.* handsome; pleasant; agreeable; graceful. —**good'ness** *n.* quality of being good; —*interj.* used for emphasis.—**good'y** *a.* sentimentally good; obtrusively virtuous.—**good'-bye** *interj.* contraction of God be with you; farewell! —**good'-day** *interj.* greeting at meeting or parting.—**good'-eve'ning** *interj.* greeting at meeting or parting in evening.—**good'-fell'owship** *n.* jolly and sociable company.—**good'-for-nothing'** *a.* of no use or value; worthless; shiftless;—*n.* shiftless person; idler.—**Good Friday,** Friday before Easter.—**good'-hu'mour** *n.* happy or cheerful state of mind.—**good'-hu'moured** *a.*—**goodman'** *n.* master of the house.—**good'-morn'ing** *interj.* greeting at meeting or parting in morning. —**good'-na'ture** *n.* natural kindness of disposition; good temper.—**good'-na'tured** *a.*—**good'-night** *interj.* a salutation at parting for the night. —**good sense,** sound judgment.—**good'-tem'pered** *a.* not easily annoyed. —**good turn,** kindly action.—**good-wife'** *n.* mistress of household.—**good'-will** *n.* kindly disposition; (*Commerce*) right, on transfer or sale of a business, to the trade, and custom of that business.—**goods'-train** *n.* train of goods-waggons, as opposed to passenger-train.—**as good as,** same as.—**to be in someone's good graces,** be held worthy of favour.

googly (goo'-gli) *n.* in cricket, a ball which 'breaks' in a way opposite to that in which might be expected.

goose (goos) *n.* web-footed bird like a duck but larger; simpleton; tailor's smoothing-iron;—*pl.* **geese** (gēs).—**gosling** (goz'-ling) *n.* young goose.—**goose'-flesh** *n.* bristling state of the skin due to cold or fright.—**goose'-grass** *n.* popular name for Bedstraw, common weed found in hedges.—**goose'-quill** *n.* large wing-feather of a goose; pen made from it.—**goose'-step** *n.* (*Mil.*) ceremonial marching-step with legs kept stiff and lifted high at each step.

gooseberry (goos'-, gooz'-ber-i) *n.* thorny shrub cultivated for its fruit; fruit itself; (*Fig.*) chaperon to couple, unwanted third person.

gopher (gō'-fer) *n.* in America, ground-squirrel; kind of rat with pouched cheeks.

gore (gôr) *n.* thick or clotted blood; blood.—**gor'y** *a.* bloody.

gore (gôr) *v.t.* pierce with spear, horns, or tusks.

gore (gôr) *n.* triangular piece of land; tapering piece of material inserted in garment or sail, to widen it;—*v.t.* cut into a wedge-shape; supply with gore.

gorge (gorj) *n.* throat or gullet; narrow defile between mountains; full meal;—*v.t.* swallow with greediness;—*v.i.* feed greedily and to excess.

gorgeous (gor'-jus) *a.* splendid; showy.

Gorgon (gor'-gon) *n.* (*Myth.*) one of three sisters of terrifying aspect; any one, esp. a woman, who is terrifying or repellent-looking.—**gorgonesque'** *a.*

Gorgonzola (gor-gon-zō'-la) *n.* kind of ewe-milk cheese made in Italy.

gorilla (go-ril'-a) *n.* ape of great size and strength.

gormand (gor'-mand) *n.* earlier form of gourmand, greedy eater; glutton.—**gor'mandise** *v.t.* and *i.* eat greedily.

gorse (gors) *n.* prickly shrub, bearing yellow flowers; furze; whin.

goshawk (gos'-hawk) *n.* bird of hawk family, formerly used for hunting wild-geese.

gospel (gos'-pel) *n.* glad tidings; revelation of the Christian faith; story of Christ's life in first four books of New Testament; doctrine; anything accepted as infallibly true; —*a.* pert. to the gospel.—**gospeller** *n.* evangelist preacher.

gossamer (gos'-a-mer) *n.* filmy substance, like cobwebs, stretched on bushes or grass; any thin, gauzy material.

gossip (gos'-ip) *n.* idle talk about others; one who talks thus;—*v.i.* talk gossip; chat.—**goss'iper** *n.*

got (got) *pa.p.* and *pa.t.* of get.

Goth (goth) *n.* member of ancient Teutonic tribe, who invaded Roman Empire in 3rd cent.; barbarian; rude, ignorant person.—**Goth'ic** *a.* pert. to Goths or their language; barbarous; pert. to pointed-arch style of architecture;—*n.* language of Goths.

gouache (gooásh) *n.* water-colour painting with opaque colours mixed with water, gum, and honey; picture painted thus.

gouge (gouj) *n.* chisel with curved cutting edge, for cutting grooves or hollows;—*v.t.* cut or scoop out with a gouge; force out, as the eye of a person, with thumb or finger.

goulash (góó-lash') *n.* Hungarian stew seasoned with paprika.

gourd (góórd) *n.* one of a number of trailing or climbing plants, including pumpkin, cucumber, etc.; fleshy fruit of this plant; its dried rind used as water-bottle, drinking-vessel, etc.

gourmand (góór'-mong, -mand) *n.* greedy eater; a gormand;—*a.* gluttonous.—**gourmet** (góór'-mā, góór'-met) *n.* lover of good food.

gout (gout) *n.* acute inflammation and swelling of the smaller joints, esp. of the big toe; a disease of wheat; drop: splash.—**gout'iness** *n.*—**gout'y** *a.* diseased with, or subject to, gout.

gout (góó) *n.* taste; relish.

govern (guv'-ern) *v.t.* rule; direct; guide; control; regulate by authority;—*v.i.* exercise authority; administer laws.—**gov'ernable** *a.*—**gov'erness** *n.* woman with authority to control and direct; lady, usually resident in a family, in charge of children's education.—**gov'ernment** *n.* act of governing; exercise of authority; system of governing in state or community; ruling power in a state; executive power; ministry.—**governmen'tal** *a.*—**gov'ernor** *n.* one invested with supreme authority; ruler; guardian; tutor; director, as of a bank, etc.; regulator or mechanical device for maintaining uniform velocity, pressure, etc.; (*Slang*) father; 'sir', often guv'nor.

gowan (gou'-an) *n.* (*Scot.*) the wild daisy.

gown (goun) *n.* loose, flowing, upper garment; outer dress of a woman; official robe of professional men and scholars.

grab (grab) *v.t.* grasp suddenly; snatch; seize;—*n.* sudden clutch; greedy action.

grace (grās) *n.* charm; attractiveness; easy and refined motion, manners, etc.; accomplishment; favour; divine favour; short prayer of thanksgiving before or after meal; period of delay granted as favour; ceremonious title used when addressing duke, or achibishop;—*n.pl.* favour; esteem;—*v.t.* adorn; honour; add grace to.—**grace'ful** *a.* displaying grace or charm in form or action; elegant; easy.—**grace'fully** *adv.*—**grace'fulness** *n.*—**grace'less** *a.* wanting in grace or excellence, esp. divine grace; hence, depraved; degenerate; corrupt.—**grace'lessness** *n.*—**gracious** (grā'-shus) *a.* favourable; kind; friendly; acceptable; proceeding from divine grace.—**grace'-note** *n.* (*Mus.*) note that is an embellishment, not essential to the melody.—**good gracious!** exclamation of surprise.—**year of grace**, year of the Christian era.

gradation (gra-dā'-shun) *n.* successive stages in progress; degree; a step, or series of steps; the state of being graded or arranged in ranks; shading.

grade (grād) *n.* step or degree in rank, merit, quality, etc.; class or category; gradient;—*v.t.* arrange in order, degree, or class; classify.

gradient (grād'-yent) *a.* and *n.* the degree of slope (up or down) of a road or railway; an incline.

gradual (grad'-ū-el) *a.* proceeding by steps or degrees; progressive.

graduate (grad'-ū-āt) *v.t.* mark with degrees; divide into regular steps or intervals; grade;—*v.i.* take university degree;—*n.* one admitted to an academic degree.—**grad'uator** *n.* instrument for dividing line into regular intervals.—**gradua'tion** *n.*

graft, graff (gráft, gráf) *v.t.* insert bud or small branch of tree into another; transplant living tissue from one part of the body to another;—*n.* bud, etc. so inserted, or tissue transplanted.

graft (gráft) *v.i.* toil; exercise political privilege; use influence unfairly for self-advancement;—*n.* manual work; self-advancement by unfair means; bribery.

grail (grāl) *n.* cup; dish.—**The Holy Grail,** in medieval legends, cup or vessel used by Christ at the Last Supper.

grain (grān) *n.* kernel, esp. of corn, wheat, etc.; fruit of corn, wheat, rye, barley, oats, etc. (used collectively); small, hard particle; small portion; 20th part of scruple in apothecaries' weight; 24th part of pennyweight troy; arrangement of particles of any body which determines its comparative roughness; the direction of fibres of wood; texture; degree of coarseness of photographic image;—*v.t.* paint in imitation of grain of wood; form into grains, as sugar, etc.;—*v.i.* form grains, or assume a granular form. —**grained** (grānd) *a.* divided into small particles or grains; dyed in grain; rough.—**grain'ing** *n.* painting in imitation of the grain of the wood.— **against the grain,** i.e. against fibre of wood; hence (*Fig.*) against person's natural inclination, etc.

gram (gram) *n.* See gramme.

grammar (gram'-er) *n.* science of language; system of general principles for speaking and writing; text-book for teaching elements of a language.—**gramma'rian** (gra-mā'-ri-an) *n.* philologist; one who teaches grammar.—**grammat'ical** *a.* pert. to grammar; according to rules of grammar.

gramme (gram) *n.* unit of weight in metric system = 15.432 troy grains. —Also gram.

gramophone (gram'-o-fōn) *n.* instrument for reproducing sounds from vibrations engraved upon revolving disc; record player.

grampus (gram'-pus) *n.* blowing and spouting sea-creature of whale family.

granary (gran'-a-ri) *n.* store-house for threshed grain; barn.

grand (grand) *a.* great; high in power and dignity; illustrious; eminent; distinguished; superior; noble; sublime; final; indicating family relationship of the second degree;—*n.* (*Mus.*) grand piano; (*U.S. Slang*) a thousand dollars.— **grand'ad,** grand'-dad *n.* (*Colloq.*) grandfather; an old man.—**gran'dam** *n.* grandmother; an old lady.—**grand'child** *n.* son's or daughter's child.— **grand'daughter** *n.* son's or daughter's daughter. — **grandee** (gran-de') *n.* Spanish or Portuguese nobleman of highest rank.—**grandeur** (gran'-dūr) *n.* nobility of action; majesty; splendour.—**grand'father** *n.* a father's or mother's father.—**grand'father('s)-clock,** *n.* tall, old-fashioned clock, standing on the floor.—**Grand Guignol,** performance of plays of melodramatic or sensational type.—**grandiloquence** (gran-dil'-o-kwens) *n.* lofty words or phrases; bombast.—**grandil'oquent** *a.*—**grandiose** (gran'-di-ōs) *a.* imposing; bombastic. — **grand'ma,** grand'mamma, grand'mother *n.* a father's or mother's mother.—**grand'mother-clock** *n.* similar to grandfather-clock but smaller.—**grand'ness** *n.* greatness; magnificence.—**grand'pa,** grand'papa *n.* grandfather.—**grand'parent** *n.* grandfather or grandmother. —**grand piano,** large harp-shaped piano, with a horizontal frame.— **grand'sire** *n.* grandfather; ancestor.— **grand slam** (*Cards*) winning of all tricks at Bridge.—**grand'son** *n.* a son's or daughter's son.—**grand'stand** *n.* principal covered enclosure on racecourse, football ground, etc.

grange (grānj) *n.* farm-house with its barns, stables, etc.; barn.

granite (gran'-it) *n.* hard igneous rock, consisting of quartz, feldspar, and mica.—**granit'ic** *a.*—**granolith'ic** *a.* made of cement formed of pounded granite.

granny (gran'-i) *n.* a grandmother. —**grann'y-knot** *n.* (*Naut.*) knot, similar to reef-knot but less secure.

grant (gránt) *v.t.* allow; yield; concede; confer; admit as true;—*n.* bestowing; gift; allowance.

granule (gran'-ūl) *n.* a little grain; small particle.—**gran'ular** *a.* consisting of grains or granules.—**gran'ulate** *v.t.* form into grains; make rough on the surface;—*v.i.* to be formed into grains.—**gran'ulated** *a.*—**granula'tion** *n.* process of forming into grains; (*Med.*) development of new tissue in a wound, characterised by the formation of grain-like cells.

grape (grāp) *n.* fruit of the vine.—

graph   215   great

grape'-fruit n. sub-tropical citrus fruit similar to the orange or lemon but larger.—**grape'-hyacinth** n. (Bot.) small variety of hyacinth.—**grape'-shot** n. (Mil.) formerly, number of shot or bullets which scattered when fired from cannon.—**grape'-su'gar** n. kind of sugar, so called because found abundantly in grapes; dextrose.—**grape'-vine** n. grape-bearing vine plant; means of secret communication.—**sour grapes** (Fig.) things despised because unattainable.

graph (graf) n. diagram or curve representing variation in value of some phenomenon according to stated conditions;—v.t. show variation by means of a diagram.—**graph'ic(al)** a. pert. to writing or delineating; truly descriptive; vivid; picturesque.—**graph'ics** n. the art of drawing, esp. mechanical drawing. —**graph'ite** n. natural form of carbon used in making of 'lead' of pencils; plumbago; blacklead.—**graphol'ogy** n. the study of handwriting as an index of character.

grapnel (grap'-nel) n. iron instrument with hooks or claws for clutching; type of small anchor.

grapple (grap'-l) v.t. seize firmly; seize with grapnel;—v.i. come to grips;—n. grip; contest at close quarters.—**grapp'ling-i'ron** n. grapnel for clutching side of enemy ship.

grasp (grásp) v.t. seize firmly; clutch; take possession of; understand.—v.i. endeavour to seize;—n. firm grip of hand; power of seizing and holding; reach of arms; mental capacity.—**grasp'ing** a. seizing; greedy of gain.

grass (grás) n. pasture for cattle; reeds;—v.t. cover with grass; feed with grass; (Slang) lay information. —**grass'y** a.—**grass'hopper** n. jumping, chirping insect, allied to locust.— **grass'-land** n. permanent pastureland.—**grass'-snake** n. harmless variety of snake.—**grass'-wid'ow** n. wife left temporarily alone through absence of husband on business, etc.

grate (grāt) n. frame of bars for holding fuel in place while burning. —**grat'ing** n. partition of parallel or cross bars.

grate (grāt) v.t. rub into small bits with something hard; wear away by rubbing;—v.i. rub with harsh sound; irritate.—**grat'er** n. instrument with rough surface for grating.

grateful (grāt'-fóòl) a. thankful.

gratify (grat'-i-fī) v.t. give pleasure to; do favour to.—**grat'ifying** a.— **grat'ifier** n. one who gratifies.— **gratifica'tion** n. act of pleasing; satisfaction; delight.

gratin (gra'-tin) n. (Cookery) dish prepared with covering of breadcrumbs.

gratis (grā'-tis, gra'-tis) adv. for nothing; free; without charge.

gratitude (grat'-i-tūd) n. good will and kindness awakened by a favour received.

gratuity (grạ-tū'-i-ti) n. present; gift of money for services rendered; donation; tip.—**gratu'itous** a. free; voluntary.

grave (grāv) n. hole dug for dead body; place of burial; (Fig.) death. —**grave'-clothes** n.pl. shroud.—**grave'-stone** n. memorial stone set on or near grave; tomb-stone.—**grave'yard** n. burial-ground.

grave (grāv) a. serious; important.

grave (grāv) v.t. carve; engrave.— **graven image**, idol.

gravel (grav'-ẹl) n. small stones; coarse sand; small pebbles; (Med.) aggregation of minute crystals in the urine; disease of kidneys and bladder due to this;—v.t. cover with gravel;—pr.p. grav'elling.—pa.p. and pa.t. grav'elled.—**grav'elly** a.

gravid (grav'-id) a. heavy, esp. being with child; pregnant.

gravitate (grav'-i-tāt) v.i. obey law of gravitation; tend towards a centre of attraction; be naturally attracted to.—**gravita'tion** n. act of gravitating; force of gravity.

gravity (grav'-i-ti) n. weight; heaviness; seriousness; force of attraction of one body for another, esp. of objects to the earth.—**specific gravity**, relative weight of any substance as compared with weight of equal volume of water.

gravy (grā'-vi) n. juices from meat in cooking.—**grav'y-boat** n. dish for holding gravy.

gray, grey (grā) a. between black and white in colour; clouded; dismal; turning white; aged;—n. gray colour; gray horse.—**gray'ish** a. somewhat gray.—**gray'lag** n. common gray or wild goose.

grayling (grā'-ling) n. fish of salmon family.

graze (grāz) v.t. touch lightly in passing; abrade the skin thus;—n. light touch in passing; grazing.

graze (grāz) v.t. feed, as cattle, with grass; feed on grass;—v.i. eat grass or herbage.—**grazier** (grā'-zhẹr) n. one who pastures cattle for the market.

grease (grēs) n. soft melted fat of animals; thick oil as lubricant;— (grēs, grēz) v.t. apply grease to; (Slang) bribe.—**greas'y** a. like grease; oily; fat; (Fig.) unctuous.—**greas'ily** adv.—**grease'-gun** n. device for forcing lubricant into bearings under pressure.—**grease'-paint** n. kind of make-up, used by actors.

great (grāt) a. large in size or number; big; long in time or duration; admirable; eminent; uncommonly gifted; of high rank; mighty; pregnant; denoting relationship, either in the ascending or descending line; (*Slang*) splendid.—**great'coat** *n.* overcoat, esp. military.—**great'-grand'child** *n.* child of a grandchild. —**great'-grand'-pa'rent** *n.* father or mother of grand-parent.—**Great Bear** (or Ursa Major) group of stars in northern heavens, also known as The Plough, or Charles's Wain.

grebe (grēb) *n.* short-winged, tailless diving-bird.

Grecian (grē'-shạn) *a.* Greek; pert. to Greece;—*n.* native of Greece.—**Grecian nose**, one whose line is prolongation of line of forehead.—**Gre'co-Ro'man, Grae'co-Ro'man** *a.* pert. to both Greece and Rome.

greed (grēd) *n.* eager and selfish desire; covetousness; avarice.—**greed'y** *a.* having keen desire for food, drink, wealth, etc.; ravenous.

Greek (grēk) *a.* pert. to Greece; Grecian;—*n.* native of Greece; language of Greece.—**Greek Church**, 'Eastern,' or 'Orthodox' Church, which separated from Roman church in 1054.

green (grēn) *a.* of colour between blue and yellow; grass-coloured; emerald-coloured; containing its natural sap; unripe; inexperienced; easily deceived; sickly;—*n.* the colour; a communal piece of grass-covered land; grass-covered back-court of tenement building; mown turf on which game of bowls is played; (*Golf*) putting-green.—**greens** *n.pl.* fresh leaves or branches; green vegetables; one of the brassica family, with curled leaves.—**green'ery** *n.* vegetation.—**green'ish** *a.* somewhat green.—**green'ness** *n.* the quality of being green; freshness.—**green'-eyed** *a.* having green eyes; (*Fig.*) jealous. — **green-eyed monster**, jealousy. — **green'finch** *n.* common British singing-bird, yellowish-green in colour. —**green'fly** *n.* type of aphis.—**green'gage** *n.* small, yellowish, green-coloured plum.—**green'grocer** *n.* retailer of fresh vegetables, etc.—**green'heart** *n.* very hard S. American wood, much used in making of fishing rods.—**green'horn** *n.* raw youth; simpleton.—**green'house** *n.* building for rearing of plants; glass-house.—**green'room** *n.* retiring-room for actors in theatre.—**green'shank** *n.* wading bird of sandpiper and snipe family.—**green sickness** (*Med.*) chlorosis, kind of anaemia which attacks adolescent girls.—**green'sward** *n.* turf.

greet (grēt) *v.t.* salute; hail; meet.—**greet'ing** *n.* salutation at meeting someone; expression of good wishes.

greet (grēt) *v.i.* (*Scots*) weep.

gregarious (gre-gā-ri-us) *a.* living in flocks; fond of company.—**grega'riously** *adv.*

gremlin (grem'-lin) *n.* (*World War 2*) mischievous pixy haunting machinery and causing mishaps, esp. in aircraft.

grenade (gre-nād') *n.* explosive shell or bomb, thrown by hand or shot from rifle.—**grenadier** (gren-a-dēr') *n.* British Army, soldier in Grenadier Guards.

grew (grōō) *pa.t.* of **grow**.

grey (grā) *a.* Same as **gray**.—**Grey Friar**, a Franciscan, from the grey-coloured habit worn.—**grey matter**, grey substance forming the outer layer of brain and controlling active thought; (*Colloq.*) brains.

greyhound (grā'-hound) *n.* swift, slender dog, used in coursing and racing.

grid (grid) *n.* frame of bars; grating; grid-iron; luggage-carrier of motor-car; (*Elect.*) lead or zinc plate in storage battery; national system of main electric supply lines; series of squares superimposed on a map. (*Radio*) electrode in thermionic valve controlling the stream of electrons emitted by filament.

griddle (grid'-l) *n.* flat, iron plate for baking.

gridiron (grid'-ĩ-ẹrn) *n.* cooking utensil of parallel metal bars, for broiling meats, etc.

grief (grēf) *n.* deep sorrow; pain; cause of sorrow or distress.

grieve (grēv) *v.t.* cause grief; afflict; vex;—*v.i.* feel grief; be distressed.—**griev'ance** *n.* ground of complaint; cause of grief.—**griev'ous** *a.* painful; causing sadness.

griffin, griffon (grif'-in, -on) *n.* fabulous beast with eagle's head and wings, and lion's body; watchful overseer.

griffon (grif'-on) *n.* small flat-faced Belgian breed of dog.

grig (grig) *n.* cricket; lively creature.

grill (gril) *v.t.* broil on gridiron; (*Fig.*) to torment; subject to severe cross-examination;—*n.* cooking utensil or device for broiling meat, etc.; dish so cooked.

grille (gril) *n.* metal grating screening a window, etc.; entrance gate.

grilse (grils) *n.* young salmon on first return to fresh water from sea.

grim (grim) *a.* stern; severe; fierce; surly.

grimace (gri-mās') *n.* distortion of face to express contempt, dislike, mockery, etc.

grime (grīm) *n.* ingrained dirt; soot; —*v.t.* soil deeply; dirty; blacken.—**grim'y** *a.*

grin (grin) *v.i.* show the teeth as in laughter, derision, or pain;—*n.* the act of grinning.

grind (grīnd) *v.t.* crush to powder;

make sharp or smooth by rubbing; turn a crank-handle, esp. of a barrel-organ; grate;—v.i. work hard;—pa.p. and pa.t. ground.—n. action of grinding; laborious task.—grind'er n. one of the double teeth, used to masticate food.—grind'stone n. round revolving stone for grinding.

grip (grip) n. firm hold; grasp of the hand; clutch; mastery of a subject, etc.; handle; (U.S.) suitcase;—v.t. grasp or hold tightly; (Fig.) hold attention of.

gripe (grip) v.t. grip; oppress; afflict with pains of colic;—v.i. suffer griping pains; complain continually;—n. grasp; oppression; severe intestinal pain due to flatulence, etc.—gri'ping a.

grisly (griz'-li) a. grim; horrible.

grist (grist) n. supply of corn to be ground at one time; provision; (Fig.) profit; gain.

gristle (gris'-l) n. smooth, solid, elastic substance in animal bodies; cartilage.

grit (grit) n. coarse part of meal; particles of sand; coarse sandstone; (Fig.) courage; spirit;—pl. oats or wheat coarsely ground;—v.t. grind (the teeth); grate;—v.i. give forth a sound, as of sand under the feet.—pr.p. gritt'ing.—gritt'y a. consisting of grit; courageous.

grizzle (griz'-l) n. gray colour.—grizz'led a. gray; grayish.—grizz'ly a. gray;—n. grizzly bear.

groan (grōn) v.i. make low deep sound of grief or pain;—n. the sound.

groat (grōt) n. old English silver coin, worth fourpence.

groats (grōts) n.pl. hulled grain, esp. oats.

grocer (grō'-ser) n. dealer in domestic stores, etc.—gro'cery n. his trade.—gro'ceries n.pl. wares sold.

grog (grog) n. mixture of spirits, esp. rum and cold water.—grog'gy a. tipsy; unsteady on one's legs; shaky.

groin (groin) n. depression between belly and thigh; (Archit.) angular curve formed by intersection of two vaults; structure of timber, etc. to stop shifting of sand on sea-beach.

groom (grōom) n. servant in charge of horses; bridegroom;—v.t. tend or curry a horse.

groove (grōov) n. channel, esp. one cut by a tool, as a guide, or to receive a ridge; rut; (Fig.) routine.

grope (grōp) v.i. feel about; search blindly as if in the dark.

gross (grōs) a. coarse; indecent; rude or rough, as work; thick; solid; rank; overfed; total, not net;—n. twelve dozen; mass; bulk.—gross'ly adv.—gross'ness n.

grotesque (grō-tesk') a. wildly formed; irregular in design or form;

—n. whimsical figure; caricature.—grotesque'ness.

grotto (grot'-ō) n. natural, picturesque cave; artificial structure in gardens, etc. in imitation of such cave.—pl. grot'toes.

ground (ground) pa.p. and pa.t. of grind.

ground (ground) n. surface of the earth; dry land; territory; special area of land; soil; sea-bottom; reason; motive; basis; (Art) surface to work on;—v.t. establish; instruct in elementary principles; place on ground; (Aviat.) prevent from flying;—v.i. (Naut.) to run ashore.—grounds n.pl. dregs; sediment; enclosed lands round a building.—ground'less a. without reason.—ground'ed a. (Aviat.) unable to fly; (Radio) earthed.—ground'ing n. background of any design; thorough knowledge of essentials of a subject.—grounds'man, ground'man n. caretaker of football ground, cricket pitch, etc.—ground'work n. foundation; basis; essential part; first principles.—ground'-bait n. bait dropped to bottom in order to attract fish.—ground'-floor n. floor on a level, or nearly so, with ground.—ground'-nut n. pea-nut.—ground'-plan n. surface representation of building or sections of it.—ground'-rent n. rent paid to landlord for privilege of building on his ground.

groundsel (ground'-sel) n. yellow-flowered weed, often used as food for cage-birds.

group (grōop) n. number of persons or things near together; class; cluster, crowd, or throng; (Art) two or more figures forming artistic design;—v.t. arrange into groups;—v.i. fall into groups.—group'-cap'tain n. (Mil.) commissioned officer in the R.A.F. equivalent to captain in navy and colonel in army.

grouse (grous) n. a British game-bird.

grouse (grous) v.i. (Colloq.) grumble;—n. complaint.—grous'er n. one who grumbles.

grove (grōv) n. group of trees; small wood.

grovel (grov'-l, gruv'-l) v.i. lie face downward, from fear or humility; crawl thus; abase oneself.—grov'eller n.—grov'elling a. servile.

grow (grō) v.t. produce by cultivation; raise;—v.i. develop naturally; increase in size, height, etc.; become by degrees.—pa.p. grown (grōn).—pa.t. grew (grōo).—grow'er n.—growth (grōth) n. process of growing; gradual increase of animal and vegetable bodies; (Med.) tumour.—grown'-up n. adult.

growl (groul) v.i. make low guttural sound of anger; grumble.—growl'er n.

one who growls; (*Slang*) four-wheeled horse-drawn cab.

groyne (groin) *n.* breakwater made of wooden piles, etc. to prevent sand or shingle shifting.

grub (grub) *v.t.* dig superficially; root up;—*v.i.* dig; rummage; (*Fig.*) plod;—*n.* larva of a beetle; that which is dug up for food; hence (*Slang*) food.—**grub'ber** *n.*—**grub'biness** *n.* state of being grubby.—**grub'by** *a.* unclean; dirty, grimy.

grudge (gruj) *v.t.* be unwilling to give or allow; envy;—*n.* feeling of ill-will; resentment.—**grudg'ing** *a.* reluctant; regretful.

grue (gróó) *v.i.* shudder; feel horror. —**grue'some** *a.*

gruel (gróó'el) *n.* food made by boiling oatmeal in water; kind of porridge.—**gruel'ling** *n.* subjection to extreme physical effort;—*a.* exhausting.

gruff (gruf) *a.* rough in manner or voice.

grumble (grum'-bl) *v.i.* murmur with discontent; complain;—*n.* a complaint.

grumpy (grum'-pi) *a.* surly; irritable.

grunt (grunt) *v.i.* of a pig, make its characteristic sound; utter sound like this;—*n.* deep, guttural sound; a pig's sound.

gryphon (grif'-on) *n.* See **griffin**.

guano (gwa'-nō) *n.* agricultural fertiliser in form of solidified excrement of sea-birds.

guarantee (gar-an-tē') *n.* promise to be responsible for payment of debt, or performance of duty; assurance of truth, genuineness, permanence, etc. of something; person who gives such promise or assurance; guaranty; security;—*v.t.* warrant; answer for. —**guaranty** (gar'-an-ti) *n.* warrant or surety.—**guar'antor** *n.*

guard (gård) *v.t.* protect from danger; accompany for protection; defend; —*v.i.* watch by way of caution or defence; be in a state of defence or safety;—*n.* sentry; soldiers protecting anything; official in charge of coach or train; defence.—**Guards** *n.pl.* in the British Army, Royal Household Troops.—**guard'ed** *a.* cautious; wary.—**guard'ian** *n.* keeper; protector; (*Law*) one who has custody of a minor.—**guard'ianship** *n.*—**guards'-man** *n.* soldier in one of the regiments of Guards.—**to mount guard** (*Mil.*) go on sentry duty.

guava (gwa'-vạ) *n.* genus of tropical trees, bearing pear-shaped fruit.

gudgeon (guj'-un) *n.* small freshwater fish, allied to carp; gullible person.

gudgeon (guj'-un) *n.* pivot of axle of a wheel; pin which fixes piston to connecting-rod.

guelder rose (gel'-dẹr-rōz) *n.* species of *Viburnum*, the 'Snowball tree.'

Guernsey (gẹrn'-zi) *n.* (*Geog.*) one of the Channel Islands; breed of dairy cattle.—**guern'sey** *n.* knitted woollen shirt.

guerilla, guerrilla (gẹr-il'-a) *n.* member of band of irregular troops.

guess (ges) *v.t.* and *i.* estimate without calculation or measurement; judge at random; (*U.S.*) suppose;— *n.* rough estimate; random judgment.—**guess'work** *n.* result obtained by random estimate.

guest (gest) *n.* visitor received at another's house; one living in hotel, etc.—**guest'-house** *n.* boarding-house.

guffaw (guf-aw') *n.* burst of boisterous laughter.

guide (gid) *n.* one who shows the way; adviser; one who directs or regulates; an official accompanying tourists; conductor; book of instruction or information; Girl Guide;—*v.t.* lead; direct; act as guide to.—**guid'ance** *n.* direction; government.—**guide'-book** *n.* descriptive handbook for tourists, etc.— **guided missile**, powered projectile which can be directed to target by remote control.—**guid'er** *n.* officer in Girl Guides.

guild, gild (gild) *n.* corporation; society for mutual help, or with common object; society of merchants or tradesmen.—**guild'hall** *n.* hall where guild or corporation assembles, hence, town-hall.

guilder (gil'-dẹr) *n.* Dutch silver coin, worth about 2s. a Dutch florin. Also **gil'der**.

guile (gil) *n.* craft; cunning.— **guile'ful** *a.* characterised by cunning, deceit, or treachery.—**guile'less** *a.* artless; honest; innocent.

guillemot (gil'-e-mot) *n.* sea-bird, allied to penguins, auks, and divers.

guillotine (gil'-ō-tēn) *n.* machine for beheading by descending stroke of heavy knife; paper-cutting machine; in Parliament, drastic cut, imposed by government, of time allowed for debating a Bill.

guilt (gilt) *n.* fact or state of having offended; culpability; crime; offence. —**guilt'y** *a.* judged to have committed crime, offence, etc.; criminal; sinful; wicked.—**guilt'iness** *n.* criminality.—**guilt'less** *a.* innocent.

guinea (gin'-i) *n.* 21 shillings; formerly, gold coin of this value.— **guin'ea-fowl** *n.* fowl allied to pheasant.—**guin'ea-pig** *n.* small S. American rodent, resembling small pig; (*Fig.*) person used as subject for experimental tests.

guise (gīz) *n.* external appearance, esp. one assumed; behaviour; dress. —**guiser** (gī'-zẹr) **gui'sard** *n.* person in disguise; mummer.

guitar (gi-tár') *n.* stringed musical instrument resembling the lute, plucked with fingures.—**guitar'ist** *n.*

gulch (gulch) *n.* ravine; glutton.

gules (gūlz) *n.* and *a.* (*Her.*) red.

gulf (gulf) *n.* large bay; sea extending widely into the land; abyss; deep chasm; immeasurable depth.

gull (gul) *n.* long-winged sea-bird.

gull (gul) *n.* dupe; fool;—*v.t.* deceive; trick; defraud.—**gull'ible** *a.* easily imposed on; credulous.—**gullibil'ity** *n.* credulity.

gullet (gul'-et) *n.* food-passage from mouth to stomach; throat.

gully (gul'-i) *n.* channel worn by water; ravine; ditch; groove; (*Cricket*) a position in field.

gulp (gulp) *v.t.* swallow eagerly; swallow in large draughts;—*v.t.* gasp; choke;—*n.* large mouthful.

gum (gum) *n.* firm flesh in which teeth are set.—**gum'boil** *n.* abscess in gum.

gum (gum) *n.* a sticky substance issuing from certain trees; this substance prepared for adhesive purposes; kind of sweetmeat, jujube; abbrev. of chewing-gum;—*v.t.* stick with gum.—**gum'miness** *n.* state of being gummy.—**gum'my** *a.*—**gum'ar'able** *n.* gum obtained from various species of the acacia.—**gum'-boots** *n.pl.* boots made of rubberised fabric, reaching to knees.—**gum-tree** *n.* any species of eucalyptus tree.—**up a gum-tree** (*Slang*) in a difficult position; in a fix.—**chew'ing-gum** *n.* sticky sweetmeat for chewing, chief ingredient being chicle.

gumption (gum'-shun) *n.* common sense; resource.

gun (gun) *n.* weapon consisting mainly of a metal tube from which missiles are thrown by explosion; cannon, rifle, pistol, etc.; (*Sport*) one of a shooting party.—*v.t.* shoot with gun.—**gun'ner** *n.* one who works a gun; (*Mil.*) private in artillery regiment; (*Navy*) warrant officer having charge of ordnance.—**gun'nery** *n.* firing of guns; science of artillery.—**gun'ning** *n.*—**gun'-boat** *n.* small vessel of light draught fitted to carry one or more guns.—**gun'-cott'on** *n.* nitrocellulose with high nitrogen content used as explosive.—**gun'man** *n.* armed criminal or gangster.—**gun'-met'al** *n.* alloy of copper and tin or zinc.—**gun'pow'der** *n.* explosive mixture of saltpetre, sulphur, and charcoal.—**gun'-runn'er** *n.* one who smuggles fire-arms.—**gun'-smith** *n.* one who makes, repairs, deals in guns.—**gun'-stock** *n.* the wood in which barrel of gun is fixed.—**a son of a gun** (*Colloq.*) rascal.—**a big gun** (*Slang*) person of great importance.

gunny (gun'-i) *n.* strong, coarse sacking made from jute.

gunwale (gun'l) *n.* upper edge of side of boat or ship. Also **gun'nel.**

gurgle (gur'-gl) *n.* bubbling noise;—*v.i.* flow in a broken, noisy current.

Gurkha (goor'-kə) *n.* race of Nepal, India, who make excellent infantrymen. Also **Ghoor'ka, Goor'kha.**

gurnard, gurnet (gur'-nard, -net) *n.* spiny sea-fish with angular head.

gush (gush) *v.i.* flow out suddenly and copiously; (*Fig.*) display exaggerated and effusive affection;—*n.* sudden copious flow; affected display of sentiment.—**gush'er** *n.* gushing person; oil-well with big natural flow.

gusset (gus'-et) *n.* triangular piece of material inserted in garment to strengthen or enlarge it.

gust (gust) *n.* sudden blast of wind; burst of rain; outburst of passion.—**gust'y** *a.*

gust (gust) *n.* sense of pleasure in tasting food; relish; enjoyment.—**gust'o** *n.* enjoyment in doing a thing; taste.

gut (gut) *n.* intestine; material made from guts of animals, as for violin strings, etc.; catgut; narrow passage; strait;—*n.pl.* intestines; (*Colloq.*) courage; pluck;—*v.t.* remove the entrails from, esp. from fish; destroy interior of a building.

gutta percha (gut'-ə per'-chə) *n.* horny, flexible substance, hardened juice of a Malayan tree.

gutter (gut'-er) *n.* passage for water; tube or pipe for conveying rain from the eaves of a building; channel at side of road, etc. for carrying off the water;—*v.i.* of a candle, to melt away by the wax forming channels and running down in drops.—**gutt'er-press** *n.* sensational newspapers.—**gutt'er-snipe** *n.* neglected child.

guttural (gut'-ur-əl) *a.* pert. to the throat;—*n.* guttural sound.

guy (gī) *n.* (*Naut.*) rope or chain to steady other parts of ship's tackle; rope or chain to secure tent, airship, flagpole, etc.

guy (gī) *n.* effigy of *Guy* Fawkes to be burnt on 5th Nov.; ridiculously dressed person; (*U.S. Slang*) man;—*v.t.* ridicule; make fun of.

guzzle (guz'-l) *v.t.* and *i.* eat or drink greedily.—**guzz'ler** *n.*

gybe (jīb) *v.t.* (*Naut.*) of boom of fore-and-aft sail, to swing over to other side.

gymkhana (jim-kā'-nə) *n.* athletic display, esp. races.

gymnasium (jim-nā'-zi-um) *n.* building or part of one, equipped for physical training.—*pl.* **gymna'sis,** or **gymna'siums.**—**gymnast** (jim'-nast) *n.* one who teaches or practises gymnastic exercises.—**gymnas'tic** *a.*—**gymnas'tics** *n.pl.* muscular and bodily exercises.

gynaecology (jin- (or gin) -ē-kol'-o-ji) n. (*Med.*) science which deals with the disorders of women, particularly of reproductive organs—**gynaecol'o-gist** n.—Also **gynecol'ogy** etc.

gypsophila (jip-sof'-i-la) n. the 'Chalk Plant,' genus of hardy herbaceous perennial.

gypsum (jip'-sum) n. mineral, consisting mostly of sulphate of lime, which when burned in a kiln, and ground fine, is known as 'plaster of Paris'.

gypsy (jip'-si) n. See **gipsy**.

gyrate (jī'-rāt) v.i. revolve round central point; move in circle; move spirally.—**gy'ratory** a.—**gyra'tion** n. act of circling, or whirling round a fixed centre.

gyroscope (jī'-ro-skōp) n. disc or wheel so mounted that it can rotate about any axis.—**gyroscop'ic** a.

gyve (jīv) v.t. to shackle; to fetter;—n. (usually in pl.) fetters, esp. for leg.

H

ha (hā) *interj.* denoting surprise, joy, etc.

haar (hār) n. raw sea-mist, esp. on E. coast of Scotland.

habeas corpus (hā'-be-as kor'-pus) n. writ to governor of prison to produce prisoner, to determine legality of confinement.

haberdasher (hab'-er-dash-er) n. dealer in small articles of dress, ribbons, needles, etc.

habiliment (ha-bil'-i-ment) n. garment: usually in pl., dress.

habit (hab'-it n. custom; usage; tendency to repeat an action in same way; dress, esp. *riding-habit*;—v.t. dress; clothe.—**habit'ual** a. formed by habit.—**habit'uate** v.t. accustom to practice; familiarise.—**hab'itude** n. customary practice, thought, or feeling; confirmed practice.—**habitué** (ha-bit'-ū-ā) n. constant visitor; frequenter (of a place).

habitable (hab'-it-a-bl) a. fit to live in.—**hab'itant** n. inhabitant.—**hab'itat** n. natural home of animal or plant; place of residence.—**habita'tion** n. act of inhabiting; place of abode.

hachure (hash'-ūr) n. shading on map to show mountains;—v.t. mark with this.

hacienda (hà-thē-en'-da) n. ranch.

hack (hak) v.t. cut irregularly; notch; (*Football*) kick on the shin;—n. cut; notch; bruise; kick on the shin; blunt axe; pick-axe.—**hack'-saw** n. special saw for cutting metal.

hack (hak) n. horse let out for hire; horse worn out by over-work; drudge, esp. literary;—a. hackney-

ed; hired; mercenary; worn out by service;—v.t. let out for hire.

hackle (hak'-l) n. comb for flax; neck feathers of cock; flimsy substance unspun, e.g. raw silk; artificial fly for angling;—v.t. separate, as coarse part of flax or hemp from the fine; tear rudely asunder.

hackney (hak'-ni) n. horse for riding or driving; vehicle kept for hire;—v.t. make trite or commonplace.—**hack'ney, hackneyed** (hak'-nid) a. let out for hire; commonplace.

haddock (had'-uk) n. fish of cod family.

Hades (hā'-dēz) (*Myth.*) the underworld; hell.

hadj, hajj (hāj) n. Mohammedan pilgrimage to Mecca.—**had'ji, haj'ji** n. one who has made this pilgrimage.

haematite, hematite (he'-ma-tīt, hem'-a-tīt) n. form of iron-ore, so called because blood-coloured.

haemoglobin, hemoglobin (hē-mo-glō'-bin) n. colouring matter of red blood-corpuscles.

haemophilia (hē-mo-fil'-i-a) n. (*Med.*) tendency to excessive bleeding due to deficiency in clotting power of blood.—**haemophil'iac** n. sufferer from this.

haemorrhage, hemorrhage (hem'-or-āj) n. (*Med.*) flow of blood; discharge of blood from blood-vessels; bleeding.—**haemorrhag'ic** a.

haemorrhoids, hemorrhoids (hem'-or-oidz) n.pl. dilated veins around anus; piles.

haft (hāft) n. handle, esp. of knife; hilt;—v.t. set in a handle.

hag (hag) n. ugly old woman; witch; sorceress.—**hagg'ish** a. like a hag.—**hag'-rid'den** a. ridden by witches, as horse; troubled with nightmares.

haggard (hag'-ard) a. wild-looking; lean and ghastly;—n. untrained hawk.—**hagg'ardly** adv.

haggis (hag'-is) n. Scottish dish made from sheep's heart, lungs and liver, chopped up, with oatmeal, suet, onion, etc. and boiled in stomach-bag.

haggle (hag'-l) v.t. cut roughly; mangle;—v.i. dispute terms; bargain keenly;—n. chaffering.

hagiology (hā-ji-, hag-i-ol'-o-ji) n. history of lives of saints.—**hagiol'ogist** n.—**hagiog'raphy** n. branch of literature which treats of lives of saints.

ha-ha, haw-haw (ha-hā', haw-haw') n. fence or bank sunk in a slope.

hail (hāl) n. frozen rain falling in pellets;—v.t. rain hail.—**hail'stone** n. frozen rain-drops.

hail (hāl) v.t. greet; salute; call to;—n. greeting; call;—*interj.* exclamation of respectful salutation.—**hail-fellow well met** a. on friendly terms.—**to hail from**, to come from.

hair (hār) n. filament growing from skin of animal; such filaments collectively, esp. covering the head; bristles; anything small or fine.—**hair'iness** n.—**hair'y** a. covered with, made of, resembling hair.—**hair'breadth** (hār'-bredth), **hair's-breadth** n. very small distance;—a. very narrow.—**hair'-brush** n. brush for the hair.—**hair'-do** n. coiffure.—**hair'dresser** n. one who dresses or cuts hair; barber.—**hair'-oil** n. oil used for dressing and setting the hair.—**hair'-pin** n. two-legged pin for controlling hair.—**hair-pin bend**, bend of road in form of a U.—**hair'-rais'ing** a. (Fig.) terrifying.—**hair'-splitting** n. and a. minute distinctions in reasoning.—**hair'-spring** n. fine spring in a watch.—**hair'-trigg'er** n. trigger released by very slight pressure.

hajj See **hadj**.

hake (hāk) n. sea-fish of cod family.

halberd, halbert (hal-berd, -bert) n. ancient military weapon, combined spear and battle-axe.—**halberdier** (hal-ber-dēr') n. soldier armed with a halberd.

halcyon (hal'-si-un) n. kingfisher;—a. pert. to halcyon, said to nest on calm sea; hence, calm, esp. of days.

hale (hāl) a. robust; sound; healthy, esp. in old age.—**hale'ness** n.

half (háf) n.pl. **halves** (hávz) either of two equal parts of a thing;—a. forming a half;—adv. to extent of half;—v.t. divide into two equal parts.—**half'-and-half** n. mixture of two liquids, in equal proportions.—**half'-back** n. (Football) player behind the forwards.—**half'-baked** a. underdone; silly.—**half'-blood** n. relation between persons born of same father or same mother, but not of both.—**half'-bound** a. of a book, bound with leather on back and corners only.—**half'-breed** n. one whose parents are of different races.—**half'-bred** a. of mixed breed; mongrel; vulgar; ill-mannered.—**half'-broth'er** n. brother by one parent only.—**half'caste** n. half-breed, esp. one of mixed European and Asiatic parentage. — **half'-cock** n. middle position of cock of gun when retained by first notch.—**half'-crown** n. British coin worth 2s. 6d.—**half'-doz'en** n. six.—**half'-heart'ed** a. wanting in true affection; lukewarm.—**half'-meas'ure** n. inadequate means to achieve end.—**half'-nel'son** n. hold in wrestling.—**halfpenny** (hā'-pen-i) n. British coin worth ½d.; sometimes spelt **ha'penny**.—pl. **halfpence** (hā'-pens).—**half'-sov'ereign** n. British gold coin worth 10s.—**half'-tim'bered** a. built with framework of timber filled in with bricks, plastered rubble, etc.—**half'-ti'tle** n. name of book, or subdivision of book, occupying full page.—**half'-wit** n. imbecile; blockhead.—**half'-wit'ted** a.—**halve** (háv) v.t. divide into two equal portions; reduce to half the previous amount.

halibut (hal'-i-but) n. large, flat sea-fish, allied to the turbot and flounder.

halidom (hal'-i-dom) n. holy place or thing.

halitosis (hal-i-tō'sis) n. (Med.) foul or offensive breath.

hall (hawl) n. place of public assembly; passage-way at entrance of house; college in a university; a students' hostel.—**hall'-mark** n. mark used (at Goldsmiths' Hall, London) to indicate standard of tested gold and silver;—v.t. stamp with this mark.

Hallelujah, Halleluiah (hal-e-lōō'-yą) n. and interj. used in songs of praise to God.

halliard See **halyard**.

hallo, halloa (ha-lō') interj. exclamation to greet a person, etc.

halloo (ha-lōō') n. hunting cry; shout or call to draw attention;—v.t. encourage with shouts, esp. dogs in hunting.

hallow (hal'-ō) v.t. make holy; consecrate; to treat as sacred;—n. saint.—**Hallowe'en'** n. evening before All Hallows' or All Saints' day (31st Oct.).—**Hall'owmas** n. feast of All Hallows, All Saints, or All Souls (1st Nov.).

hallucinate (hal-ū'-sin-āt) v.t. produce illusion in the mind of.—**hallucina'tion** n. illusion; seeing something that is not present.—**hallu'cinative, hallu'cinatory** a.

halm, haulm (hawm) n. stalk of any kind of grain, beans, peas, etc.

halo (hā'-lō) n. circle of light round moon, sun, etc.; disc of light round head of sacred person.—pl. **ha'los, ha'loes**.

halogen (hal'-ō-jen) n. (Chem.) one of the elements chlorine, bromine, iodine and fluorine, all of similar characteristics.

halt (hawlt) n. stoppage on march or journey; stopping-place;—v.t. cause to stop;—v.i. make a stop.

halt (hawlt) a. lame; limping; crippled;—v.i. limp; falter;—n. limp; speech impediment.

halter (hawl'-ter) n. rope or strap with head-stall to fasten horses or cattle; noose for hanging a person;—v.t. fasten with a rope.

halve (háv) v.t. divide into two equal parts.

halyard, halliard (hal'-yard) n. (Naut.) rope for hoisting or lowering yards or sails.

ham (ham) n. region behind the knee; thigh of any animal, esp. hog's thigh cured by salting and smoking; (*Slang*) inexperienced person; amateur; bombastic actor.—**ham'-string** *n.* tendon at back of knee;—*v.t.* cripple by cutting this; (*Fig.*) frustrate; render helpless.

hamburger (ham'burg-er) *n.* minced steak and onions formed into round.

hamlet (ham'-let) *n.* small village.

hammer (ham'-er) *n.* tool, with heavy head at end of a handle, for beating metal, driving nails, etc.; contrivance for exploding charge of gun;—*v.t.* and *i.* beat with a hammer; (*Slang*) punish severely.—**hamm'erhead** *n.* rapacious kind of shark.—**hamm'er-toe** *n.* deformed toe which has grown bent upwards.—**to hammer out** (*Fig.*) find a solution by full investigation of all difficulties. —**to come under the hammer**, be sold by auction. — **hammer-and-tongs** (*Fig.*) vigorously.

hammock (ham'-ok) *n.* kind of hanging bed, consisting of a piece of canvas or net, and suspended by cords from hooks.

hamper (ham'-per) *n.* large covered basket for conveying goods.

hamper (ham'-per) *n.* fetter; (*Naut.*) cumbrous equipment;—*v.t.* put a fetter on; hence, to impede; to obstruct the movements of.

hamster (ham'-ster) *n.* rodent with large cheek-pouches.

hand (hand) *n.* extremity of arm beyond wrist; pointer on dial, e.g. on a watch; measure of hands' breadth, four inches; style of handwriting; cards dealt to player; manual worker; sailor; side; quarter; direction; agency; service; aid; help;—*v.t.* give with the hand; deliver; pass; hold out.—**hand'y** *a.* convenient; close at hand; clever with the hands.—**hand'y-man** *n.* one clever with his hands.—**hand'ily** *adv.*—**hand'less** *a.* clumsy; awkward. —**hand'-barr'ow** *n.* wheel-less barrow with handles at each end.—**hand'bill** *n.* printed sheet for circulation by hand; pruning-hook.—**hand'book** *n.* manual.—**hand'-cart** *n.* small cart drawn or pushed by hand.—**hand'-cuff** *n.* shackle around wrist connected by chain with one on other wrist; manacle;—*v.t.* manacle.—**hand'fast** *n.* firm hold; betrothal; pledge;—*v.t.* pledge one's word by handshake; betroth.—**hand'ful** *n.*—**hand'maid(en)** *n.* female servant.—**hand'-out** *n.* official information handed out to Press.—**hand'rail** *n.* rail of staircase, gallery, etc.—**hand'shake** *n.*—**hand-to-hand**, *a.* at close quarters.—**hand'-to-mouth** *a.* without thought of the future.—**hand'writing** *n.* way a person writes. —at first hand, direct from original source.—**in hand**, under control; under preparation.—**off'-hand** *adj.*

inconsiderate; careless;—*adv.* without preparation.—**on hand**, ready for distribution; available for disposal.—**with a heavy hand**, severely. —**high-handed** *a.* overbearing.—**old hand**, person with experience; veteran.—**second hand**, having already been used.—**to change hands**, become property of another.—**to gain the upper hand**, overcome.—**to set one's hand to**, make a start; undertake.—**to show one's hand**, reveal one's intentions.

handicap (hand'-i-kap) *n.* race or contest in which competitors' chances are equalised by starts given, weights carried, etc.; condition so imposed; (*Fig.*) disability; —*v.t.* impose such conditions.—**handicapped** *a.* and *n.* mentally or physically disabled (person).

handicraft (hand'-i-kraft) *n.* manual occupation or skill; work performed by hand.—**hand'iwork**, **hand'ywork** *n.* work done by the hands; a thing done by anyone in person.

handkerchief (hang'-ker-chif) *n.* small square of fabric for wiping nose.

handle (hand'-l) *v.t.* touch or feel with hand; manage; wield; deal with; deal in; treat well or ill;—*n.* part of thing made to hold it by; (*Fig.*) opportunity; pretext.—**hand'le-bar(s)** *n.* device to steer bicycle.—**hand'ler** *n.* one who handles or manages; one who leads animal in ring at cattle or dog show.

handsel, hansel (hand'-, han'-sel) *n.* gift on beginning something; New Year gift; earnest money; first use of anything;—*v.t.* be the first to use.

handsome (han'-sum) *a.* of fine appearance; generous.—**hand'somely** *adv.*—**hand'someness** *n.*

hang (hang) *v.t.* suspend; put to death by suspending from gallows; cover with, as wallpaper, pictures, etc.; fix on hinges; display;—*v.i.* be suspended; incline; be in suspense; cling to.—*pa.p.* and *pa.t.* hanged or hung.—*n.* slope; inclination; tendency.—**hang'-dog** *a.* having sneaking look.—**hang'er** *n.* that by which thing is suspended, e.g. *coat-hanger*; short broad sword.—**hang'er-on** *n.* follower or dependant (often disparagingly) —**hang'ing** *n.* death by suspension; that which is hung;—*a.* punishable by death; unfixed; floating.—**hang'-man** *n.* public executioner.—**hang'-over** *n.* depressing after-effects of drinking bout.—**to hang fire**, of fire-arms, be slow in going off; (*Fig.*) hesitate.—**to hang in the balance**, be in doubt or suspense.

hangar (hang'-er, hang'-ar) *n.* shed for aircraft.

hank (hangk) *n.* coil, esp. as measure of yarn (*Naut.*) ring at corner of sail.

hanker (hang'-kẹr) v.i. long for; crave.—**hank'ering** n. persistent longing for; craving.

hansom (han'-sum) n. light two-wheeled cab with the driver's seat at the back.

hap (hap) n. that which happens unexpectedly; chance;—v.i. befall.—**hap'less** a. unlucky.—**hap'ly** adv. by chance; perhaps.—**hap'haz'ard** a. random; without design;—adv. by chance.—**happ'en** v.i. come by chance; occur; take place.—**happ'ening** n. occurrence; event.

happy (hap'-i) a. lucky; fortunate; successful; prosperous; glad; content; apt; fitting.—**happ'ily** adv.—**happ'iness** n.

hara-kiri (há-ra-kē'-rē) n. method of suicide by disembowelment, practised by the Japanese.

harangue (hạ-rang') n. loud, noisy, public speech;—v.i. deliver a harangue.

harass (har'-ạs, ha-ras') v.t. fatigue; worry; attack repeatedly.—**har'assed** a.—**har'assing** a.—**har'assment** n.

harbinger (hár'-bin-jẹr) n. one who announces another's approach; forerunner.

harbour (hár-bur) n. shelter for ships; port; any shelter;—v.t. give shelter to; entertain as a guest; protect;—v.i. take shelter.—**har'bourage** n. shelter; entertainment.

hard (hárd) a. firm; solid; difficult; harsh; unfeeling; difficult to bear; strenuous; bitter, as winter; keen, as frost; of water, not making lather; (Slang) of alcoholic drinks, spirituous;—n. beach; firm ground.—**hard'en** v.t. make hard or more hard; strengthen; confirm in wickedness or obstinacy; make less sympathetic;—v.i. become hard.—**hard'ly** adv. with difficulty; scarcely; severely; roughly.—**hard'ship** n. severe toil or suffering; ill-luck; privation; suffering. — **hard-and-fast**, strict. — **hard'board** n. board made of compressed fibre.—**hard'-boiled** a. boiled till hard, e.g. of an egg; (Slang) tough; unfeeling.—**hard by**, near; close at hand.—**hard cash**, gold and silver coins, as opposed to paper-money.—**hard'currency** n. dollar, or any other currency convertible into dollars.—**hard'-hand'ed** a. having hard hands, as a labourer; (Fig.) severe.—**hard'-head'ed** a. shrewd; practical.—**hard'-heart'ed** a. merciless; unsympathetic.—**hard tack**, ship-biscuit, large coarse unsalted biscuit.—**hard up**, short of money; poor.—**hard'ware** n. articles made of iron, copper, or other metals, e.g. pots, pans, etc.—a **die-hard** (Fig.) one who clings desperately to long-held opinions.

hardy (hár'-di) a. robust; vigorous; bold; brave; daring; able to bear exposure.—**har'dily** adv.—**har'dihood** n. extreme boldness.—**har'diness** n.

hare (hár) n. rodent with long hind-legs, long ears, short tail, and divided upper lip;—v.i. (Colloq.) hasten.—**hare'bell** n. plant with blue bell-shaped flowers; bluebell of Scotland.—**hare'-brained** a. wild; heedless.—**hare'-lip** n. (Med.) congenital fissure in upper lip.—**hare and hounds**, paper-chase.

harem (hā'-rem, ha-rēm') n. apartment for females in Moslem house.

haricot (har'-i-kō, -kot) n. French bean; kidney-bean; stew of mutton and vegetables.

hark (hárk) v.i. listen;—interj. listen! hear!—**to hark back** (Fig.) return to some previous point in an argument.

harlot (hár'-lot) n. prostitute.—**har'lotry** n.

harm (hárm) n. injury; hurt; damage; misfortune;—v.t. hurt; injure.—**harm'ful** a. hurtful; injurious.—**harm'less** a.

harmony (hár'-mo-ni) n. agreement; concord; friendliness; peace; melodious sound; combination of musical notes to make chords; study of musical sounds in combination.—**harmon'ic** a. musical; concordant;—n. overtone.—**harmon'ica** n. mouth-organ.—**harmonious** (hár-mō'-ni-us) a. vocally or musically concordant; symmetrical; living in peace and friendship.—**har'monise** v.t. bring into harmony; cause to agree; reconcile; (Mus.) arrange into parts;—v.i. be in harmony; agree.—**har'moniser** n.—**har'monist** n. a harmoniser; musical composer.—**harmo'nium** n. small reed-organ the bellows of which are operated by foot-pressure.—**harmonic progression**, series of numbers whose reciprocals are in arithmetical progression.

harness (hár'-nes) n. equipment esp. of draught horse;—v.t. dress in armour; put harness on.

harp (hárp) n. stringed musical instrument played by hand;—v.i. play on the harp; (Fig.) dwell persistently upon a particular subject.—**harp'er** n. player on the harp; minstrel.—**harp'ist** n. player on the harp.—**harpsichord** (harp'-si-kord) n. keyboard instrument with mechanical plucking action.

harpoon (hár-pōōn') n. barbed spear with rope attached for catching whales, etc.

harpy (hár'-pi) n. (Myth.) ravenous monster, with head and breast of woman and wings and claws of vulture; a rapacious woman.

harridan (har'-i-dạn) n. haggard old woman; shrew; vixen.

harrier (har'-i-ẹr) n. kind of small hound for hunting hares; beagle; falcon; cross-country runner.

harrow (hăr'-ō) *n.* toothed agricultural implement to level, break clods, or cover seed when sown;—*v.t.* draw harrow over; (*Fig.*) distress greatly.—**harr'owing** *a.*

harry (har'-i) *v.t.* ravage; harass; plunder.

harsh (hársh) *a.* rough; unpleasing to the touch or taste; unfeeling.—**harsh'ness** *n.*

hart (hárt) *n.* male deer or stag, esp. over five years old.—**harts'horn** *n.* horn of the hart, formerly chief source of ammonia; solution of ammonia.—**hart's'-tongue** *n.* common British fern.

harum-scarum (hār'-um-skār'-um) *a.* reckless; wild;—*n.* rash person.

harvest (hár'-vest) *n.* (season for) gathering crops; crop itself;—*v.t.* gather in.—**har'vester** *n.* one who harvests; reaping machine.—**har'vest-bug, -mite** *n.* irritant mite, found in fruit-trees, grasses, etc. in late summer.—**har'vest-home** *n.* bringing home of harvest; social gathering to celebrate this.

hash (hash) *v.t.* chop into small pieces; mince;—*n.* dish of hashed meat and vegetables; (*Slang*) mess.

hashish, hasheesh (hash'-ēsh) *n.* leaves of the Indian hemp used as an intoxicant.

hasp (hasp) *n.* clasp passing over a staple for fastening a door, etc.

hassock (has'-ok) *n.* padded cushion for kneeling on in church; tuft of grass.

haste (hāst) *n.* speed; hurry;—*v.i.* hasten.—**hasten** (hā'-sn) *v.t.* urge forward; hurry on;—*v.i.* be in a hurry.—**hast'ener** *n.*—**hast'y** *a.* speedy; over-eager; rash; passionate.—**hast'ily** *adv.*—**hast'iness** *n.*

hat (hat) *n.* covering for head, usually with brim; red hat of cardinal.—**hat'ter** *n.* one who makes, or sells hats.—**hat'-trick** *n.* in cricket, taking of three wickets with successive balls; any three successive wins.—**top hat**, formal silk hat with high crown.—**pass round the hat**, take up a collection.

hatch (hach) *v.t.* bring forth young birds from the shell; incubate; plot; —*v.i.* come forth from the shell;—*n.* act of hatching; the brood hatched.—**hatch'ery** *n.* place for hatching eggs, esp. of fish.

hatch (hach) *n.* lower half of divided door; boards, etc. covering hatchway; hatchway.—**hatch'way** *n.* opening in a deck, floor or wall.

hatch (hach) *v.t.* shade with lines.

hatchet (hach'-et) *n.* small axe.—**hatch'et-faced** *a.* sharp featured.—**bury the hatchet**, make peace.

hate (hāt) *v.t.* dislike strongly; detest; *n.* strong dislike; hatred.—**hate'ful** *a.* full of hate; detestable;

ugly.—**hate'fulness** *n.*—**hat'red** *n.* aversion; ill-will; enmity; animosity.

haughty (haw'-ti) *a.* proud.—**haugh'tily** *adv.*—**haugh'tiness** *n.*

haul (hawl) *v.t.* pull with force; drag; steer ship closer to the wind; close-haul;—*v.i.* of wind, shift, veer;—*n.* hauling; catch; good profit or gain.—**haul'age** *n.* act of pulling; charge for hauling; carrying of goods, etc. by road.—**haul'er** *n.* one who hauls.—**haul'ier** *n.* carter; mine-worker who hauls coal to foot of the shaft.—**close'-hauled** *a.* (*Naut.*) of ship, with the sails trimmed to keep her close to the wind.

haulm (hawm) *n.* See **halm**.

haunch (hawnsh) *n.* body between ribs and thighs; hip; leg and loin of venison, etc.

haunt (hawnt) *v.t.* frequent; of ghosts, visit regularly;—*v.i.* loiter about a place;—*n.* place of frequent resort.—**haunt'ed** *a.*

hautboy (hō'-boi) *n.* older form of oboe.

have (hav) *v.t.* hold; be possessed or affected with; seize; bring forth; produce; be obliged (to do); (as an auxiliary verb, forms other tenses; —*pa.p.* and *pa.t.* **had**.

haven (hā'-vn) *n.* bay or inlet giving shelter for ships; harbour.

haver (hāv'-er) *v.i.* (*Scot.*) to talk nonsense.

haversack (hav'-er-sak) *n.* soldier's canvas ration-bag; similar bag for travellers.

havoc (hav'-ok) *n.* pillage; devastation; ruin.

haw (haw) *n.* red berry of hawthorn; hedge; enclosed garden.—**haw'finch** *n.* small bird of finch family.—**haw'thorn** *n.* thorny shrub.

hawk (hawk) *n.* bird of prey of falcon family;—*v.t.* and *i.* hunt birds with hawks, as in falconry.—**hawk'er** *n.* falconer.—**hawk'ing** *n.* sport of hunting birds with hawks; falconry.

hawk (hawk) *v.i.* clear the throat noisily.

hawk (hawk) *v.t.* carry about wares for sale; peddle.—**hawk'er** *n.* pedlar.

hawse (hawz) *n.* part of ship's bows with holes for cables.

hawser (haw'-zer) *n.* large rope.

hay (hā) *n.* grass mown and dried for fodder.—**hay'-cock** *n.* conical heap of hay.—**hay'-fev'er** *n.* irritation of nose and throat generally by pollen.—**hay'-rick** *n.*—**hay'-stack** *n.* a large pile of hay.—**hay'-seed** *n.*

hay (hā) *n.* old country-dance.

hazard (haz'-ard) *n.* chance; a chance; risk; danger; (*Golf*) inclusive term for all obstacles on golf-course;—*v.t.* expose to risk; run the risk of.—**haz'ardous** *a.* dangerous.

haze (hāz) *n.* misty appearance in the

air.—**haz'y** *a.* misty; unclear.—**haz'ily**
adv.—**haz'iness** *n.*

hazel (hā'-zl) *n.* nut-bearing small
tree; reddish-brown colour of the
nuts;—*a.* of this colour.—**ha'zel-nut**
n. nut of the tree.

he (hē) *pron.* 3rd pers. sing. masc.
nom.—**he'-man** *n.* (*Colloq.*) a very
virile man.

head (hed) *n.* upper part of man's or
animal's body; brain; upper part of
anything; top; chief part; chief;
leader; section of chapter; source of
stream; cape or headland; freedom
to go on;—*a.* chief; principal; of
wind, contrary;—*v.t.* lead; be at
head of; direct; hit (ball) with head;
—*v.i.* originate; form a head; make
for.—**head'y** *a.* impetuous; wilful;
apt to intoxicate.—**head'ily** *adv.*—
head'iness *n.* obstinacy.—**headache**
(hed'-āk) *n.* nerve-pain in head;
(*Colloq.*) worrying problem.—**head'-
dress** *n.* ornamental covering for head.
—**head'ing** *n.*—**head'lamp** *n.* head-
light.—**head'land** *n.* cape; promontory.—**head'light** *n.* strong light
carried on the front of locomotive,
motor-vehicle, etc.—**head'line** *n.*
summary of news in large print in
newspaper; caption.—**head'long** *adv.*
with head foremost; rashly;—*a.*
steep; reckless.—**head'man** *n.* chief,
esp. of tribe.—**head'most** *a.* most
advanced; foremost.—**head'-on** *a.*
meeting head to head.—**head'phone**
n. telephone-receiver to clip on head
(usually in pl.).—**head'quar'ters** *n.pl.*
(*Mil.*) residence of commander-in-
chief, general, or other important
officer; centre of operations.—**head'-
room** *n.* amount of space between
head and roof.—**head'stone** *n.* memorial stone at head of grave.—**head'-
strong** *a.* obstinate; stubborn.—
head'way *n.* progress made by ship
in motion; hence, progress of any
kind.—**head over heels**, upside down;
completely; deeply.—**to keep one's
head**, keep calm.

heal (hēl) *v.t.* make whole; restore to
health; make well;—*v.i.* become
sound.—**heal'er** *n.*

health (helth) *n.* soundness of body;
general condition of the body;
toast drunk in person's honour.—
health'y *a.* having, or tending to
give, health; sound; vigorous;—
health'iness *n.*—**health'ful** *a.* free
from disease; healthy.

heap (hēp) *n.* number of things lying
one on another; pile; mass; a great
quantity;—*v.t.* throw or lay in heap.

hear (hēr) *v.t.* perceive with the ear;
listen to; heed; (*Law*) try (a case);—
v.i. perceive sound; learn by report;
—*pa.p.* and *pa.t.* **heard** (herd).—
hear'ing *n.* act of perceiving sound;
sense by which sound is perceived;
audience; earshot.—**hear'say** *n.* rum-

our; report.—**hear! hear!** *interj.*
indicating approval of speaker's
words.

hearken (hár'-kn) *v.i.* listen.

hearse (hers) *n.* carriage for coffin.

heart (hárt) *n.* hollow, muscular
organ which makes blood circulate;
seat or source of life; seat of
emotions and affections; inner part
of anything; mind; soul; courage;
affection; playing-card marked with
figure of a heart.—**heart'y** *a.* cordial;
friendly; in good health; of a meal,
satisfying the appetite.—**heart'iness**
n.—**heart'less** *a.* without a heart;
unfeeling.—**heart'en** *v.t.* encourage;
incite; stimulate.—**heart'ache** *n.* sorrow; anguish.—**heart'-break** *n.* over-
powering sorrow.—**heart'-brok'en** *a.*
—**heart'burn** *n.* form of dyspepsia.—
heart'-burning *n.* discontent; secret
enmity.—**heart'-felt** *a.* deeply felt;
intense; sincere.—**heart's'-ease**, common pansy.—**heart'-sick** *a.* depressed;
disgusted.—**heart'-sink'ing** *n.* despondency.—**heart'-strings** *n.pl.* (*Fig.*)
affections; emotions.—**at heart**, at
bottom; inwardly.—**by heart**, by
memory.—**to wear one's heart on one's
sleeve**, show one's feelings openly.

hearth (hárth) *n.* fireside; home.

heat (hēt) *n.* hotness; sensation of
this; hot weather; warmth of
feeling; anger; excitement; sexual
excitement in animals, esp. female;
(*Sport*) eliminating race to decide
persons to compete further;—*v.t.*
make hot; excite;—*v.i.* become hot.
—**heat'ed** *a.* (*Fig.*) of argument, etc.
passionate; intense.—**heat'er** *n.*—
heat'-wave *n.* a spell of abnormally
hot weather.

heath (hēth) *n.* moor; shrub of genus
Erica.

heathen (hē'-THn) *n.* one not an
adherent of religious system; infidel;
pagan; (*Colloq.*) irreligious person;—
a. hea'thenish *a.*—**hea'thenism** *n.*
religious system of a heathen people.
—**hea'thendom** *n.* parts of world
where heathenism prevails.

heather (heTH'-er) *n.* small plant of
genus Erica; heath; ling;—*a.* of
colour of heather.—**heath'er-bell** *n.*
flower of the plant.

heave (hēv) *v.t.* lift with effort;
throw (something heavy); utter
(sigh); pull on rope, etc.; haul;—
v.i. rise and fall in alternate motions;
—*n.* heaving; effort to lift something;
rise and fall;—*pa.p.* and *pa.t.* **heaved**
or **hove**.—**to heave to**, bring a ship to
standstill.

heaven (hev'-n) *n.* sky; upper air;
abode of God; place of bliss;
supreme happiness.—**heav'enly** *a.*
pert. to heaven; pure; divine;
(*Colloq.*) excellent;—*adv.* in heavenly
manner.—**heav'enliness** *n.*—**in the
seventh heaven**, supremely happy.

heavy (hev'-i) *a.* weighty; striking or falling with force; large in amount, as debt; rough, as weather; clayey, as soil; sad; hard to bear; dull; serious, indigestible.—**heav'ily** *adv.*—**heav'iness** *n.*—**heav'y-hand'ed** *a.* awkward; oppressive.—**heav'y-head'ed** *a.* drowsy.—**heav'y-heart'ed** *a.* sad.—**heav'yweight** *n.* (*Boxing*) boxer exceeding 12 st. 7 lb. in weight.

hebdomadal (hem-dom'-a-dạl) *a.* weekly.—**hebdom'sdally** *adv.*

Hebrew (hē'-brōō) *n.* one of the ancient inhabitants of Palestine; Israelite; Jew; the language.—*fem.* He'brewess.—**Hebraic** (hē-brā'-ik) *a.* pert. to Hebrews, or to their language.—**He'braist** *n.* one versed in Hebrew.

heckle (hek'-l) *n.* comb for cleaning flax;—*v.t.* comb with hackle; ask awkward questions of speaker at public meeting.

hect-, hecto- (hekt, hek'-to) *prefix,* fr. Gk. *hekaton,* one hundred, combining to form derivatives used in metric system.

hectic (hek'-tik) *a.* flush; consumptive; feverish; (*Colloq.*) exciting.

Hector (hek'-tor) *n.* hero of Troy in war with Greeks.—**hec'tor** *n.* bully; blusterer;—*v.t.* and *i.* bully; bluster.

hedge (hej) *n.* fence of bushes; protecting barrier;—*v.t.* enclose with hedge; fence; obstruct; hem in;—*v.i.* bet on both sides to guard against loss; evade an issue.—**hedge'-bill** *n.* kind of hook for trimming hedges.—**hedge'hog** *n.* small quadruped, covered on upper part of its body with prickles.—**hedge'-hopp'ing** *n.* in aviation, flying very low.—**hedge'row** *n.* row of bushes forming hedge.—**hedge'-sparr'ow** *n.* small bird of sparrow family.

hedonism (hē'-do-nizm) *n.* belief in pleasure as chief good.—**he'donist** *n.*

heed (hēd) *v.t.* take notice of; care for; mind;—*n.* attention; notice; care; caution.—**heed'ful** *a.* watchful; cautious; attentive.—**heed'fulness** *n.*—**heed'less** *a.* careless; thoughtless.

heehaw (hē'-haw) *v.i.* bray, of an ass.

heel (hēl) *n.* hind part of foot, shoe, boot, or stocking; hind part of anything; spur; (*U.S.*) undesirable person;—*v.t.* add heel to, as in knitting.—**heel'-tap** *n.* small amount of liquor left in bottom of glass.—**heel of Achilles** (*Fig.*) vulnerable part.—down at heel, seedy; ill-shod.

heel (hēl) *v.i.* of ship, lean to one side.

hefty (hef'ti) *a.* vigorous; well-built.

hegemony (hē-gem'-on-i, hē'-jem-on-i) *n.* leadership; predominance.

heifer (hef'-ẹr) *n.* young cow that has not had a calf.

height (hīt) *n.* measurement from base to top; quality of being high; high position; small hill; eminence.—**height'en** *v.t.* make high or higher; intensify.

heinous (hā'-nus) *a.* extremely wicked; atrocious; odious.

heir (ār) *n.* (*fem.* heir'ess) person legally entitled to succeed to property or rank.—**heir'-appa'rent** *n.* person first in line of succession to estate, crown, etc.—**heir'loom** *n.* article which descends to heir along with inheritance; thing that has been in family for generations.

held (held) *pa.p.* and *pa.t.* of hold.

helical (hel'-i-kạl) *a.* pert. to helix; spiral.

helicopter (hel'i-kop-tẹr) *n.* aircraft which can rise or descend vertically.

heliocentric (hē-li-ō-sen'-trik) *a.* (*Astron.*) taking the sun as centre. Also **heliocen'trical.**

heliograph (hē'-li-ō-graf) *n.* signalling apparatus employing mirror to reflect the sun's rays; instrument for photographing the sun.—**heliograph'ic** *a.*—**heliog'raphy** *n.*

heliotrope (hē'-li-ō-trōp) *n.* plant with fragrant purple flowers; colour of the flowers, or scent; bloodstone.—**heliot'ropism** *n.* (*Bot.*) the tendency of plants to direct their growth towards light.

helium (hē'-li-um) *n.* (*Chem.*) inert, non-inflammable, very light gas.

helix (hē'-liks) *n.* spiral; (*Anat.*) outer rim of the ear.—*pl.* **helices** (hē'-li-sēz).—**hel'ical** *a.* spiral.

hell (hel) *n.* abode of the damned; lower regions; place of vice, misery, or torture.—**hell'ish** *a.* infernal.

hellebore (hel'-e-bōr) *n.* (*Bot.*) genus of plants, including Christmas rose.

Hellene (hel'-ēn) *n.* ancient Greek; subject of modern Greece.—*pl.* Hell'enes, Greeks.—**Hellen'ic** *a.* pert. to inhabitants of Greece.—**Hell'enism** *n.* adoption of the manners, culture, and language of Ancient Greeks; hence, Grecian culture.—**Hell'enist** *n.* Greek scholar.

helm (helm) *n.* (*Naut.*) tiller or wheel for turning rudder of ship; (*Fig.*) control; guidance;—*v.t.* steer; control.—**helms'man** *n.* steersman.

helm (helm) *n.* (*Arch.*) helmet.—**hel'met** *n.* defensive covering for the head.

helminth (hel'-minth) *n.* parasitic worm.—**helmin'thic** *a.*—**helmin'thoid** *a.* worm-shaped.—**helminthology** *n.* study of parasitic worms.

helot (hē'-lot, hel'-ot) *n.* serf in ancient Sparta; slave.—**he'lotism** *n.* slavery.—**he'lotry** *n.* serfdom.

help (help) *v.t.* aid; support; relieve; prevent;—*v.t.* lend aid;—*n.* aid; assistance; support; domestic servant.—**help'er** *n.*—**help'ful** *a.* helping; assisting; useful.—**help'fulness** *n.*—**help'ing** *n.* portion of food.—**help'less** *a.* not able to take care of oneself;

weak.—**help'mate** n. assistant; partner; wife or husband.

helter-skelter (hel-ter'-skel'-ter) adv. in disorder; in hurry and confusion. —n. fairground spiral chute.

helve (helv) n. handle of tool.

hem (hem) n. border, sewing;—v.t. fold over and sew down.

hemisphere (hem'-i-sfēr) n. half sphere; half of celestial sphere; half of the earth.—**hemispher'ical** a.

hemlock (hem'-lok) n. poisonous umbelliferous plant used as sedative.

hemp (hemp) n. plant whose fibre is used in manufacture of coarse cloth, ropes, etc.; hashish, narcotic made from Indian hemp.—**hemp'en** a.

hen (hen) n. female of any bird, esp. domestic fowl; female of certain crustaceans, e.g. lobster, crab, etc.—**hen'coop** n. large cage for poultry.—**hen'-part'y** n. (Slang) social gathering of women only.—**hen'-peck** v.t. domineer over husband.

hence (hens) adv. from this point; for this reason;—interj. go away! begone!—**hence'forth, hencefor'ward** adv. from now.

henchman (hensh'-man) n. servant; loyal supporter.

henna (hen'-a) n. Egyptian privet; red dye made from it.

hepatic (hep-at'-ik) a. pert. to the liver; liver-coloured.

hepta- (hep'-ta) prefix from Greek hepta, seven, combining to form derivatives.—**hep'tad** n. group of seven.—**hep'tagon** n. plane figure with seven sides.—**heptag'onal** a.

heptameter (hep-tam'-e-ter) n. line of verse of seven feet.

heptangular (hep-tang'-gū-lar) a. having seven angles.

her (her) pron. objective case of pronoun she;—also, possessive case used adjectivally.—**hers** pron. absolute possessive case.—**herself** pron. emphatic and reflexive form of she and her.

herald (her'-ald) n. officer who makes royal proclamations, arranges ceremonies, etc.; messenger; envoy; forerunner.—**heral'dic** a.—**her'aldry**, n. art or office of a herald; science of genealogies and armorial bearings.

herb (herb) n. plant with soft stem; plant of which parts are used for medicine, food, or scent.—**herbaceous** (her-bā'-shus) a. pert. to herbs.—**herb'age** n. herbs; green food for cattle.—**herb'al** a. pert. to herbs;—n. book on herbs.—**herb'alist** n. writer on, dealer in, herbs.—**herbarium** (her-bā'-ri-um) n. collection of specimens of dried herbs and plants.—pl. **herba'riums, herba'ria.**

Hercules (her'-kū-lēz) n. hero distinguished for his strength; hence any person of extraordinary strength and size.—**Hercule'an** a.

herd (herd) n. number of animals feeding or travelling together; drove of cattle; large number of people; herdsman;—v.i. go in a herd;—v.t. tend (a herd); drive together.—**herds'man** n. one who tends cattle.

here (hēr) adv. in this place; at or to this point.—**here'about, here'abouts** adv. about this place.—**hereaf'ter** adv. after this;—n. future existence.—**hereby'** adv. not far off; by means of this; by this.—**herein'** adv. in this.—**hereon'** adv. on this.—**hereto'** adv. to this.—**herewith'** adv. with this.

heredity (he-red'-i-ti) n. transmission of characteristic traits and qualities from parents to offspring.—**hered'itable** a. heritable.—**hered'itary** a. descending by inheritance

heresy (her'-e-si) n. opinion contrary to orthodox opinion or belief.—**her'etic** n. one whose opinions contradict orthodox faith.—**heret'ical** a.

heritable (her'-i-ta-bl) a. that can be inherited; attached to property or house, as opposed to movable.—**her'itage** n. that which may be inherited.—**her'itor** n. one who inherits; (Scot.) proprietor or landholder in a parish.

hermaphrodite (her-maf'-rō-dīt) n. and a. person or animal with characteristics of both sexes; having normally both sexual organs.

hermetic (her-met'-ik) a. pert. to doctrines or writings of occult character; pert. to alchemy or magic; magical.—**hermetic sealing,** air-tight closing of a vessel by fusion.

hermit (her'-mit) n. person living in seclusion, esp. from religious motives; recluse.—**her'mitage** n. his abode.

hernia (her'-ni-a) n. (Med.) external protrusion of internal part through the membrane (commonly called rupture).

hero (hē'-rō) n. (fem. **heroine** (her'-ō-in)) illustrious warrior; one greatly regarded for achievements or qualities; chief character in poem, play, or story;—pl. **he'roes.**—**he'roic** a. pert. to hero; courageous; illustrious; narrating exploits of heroes, as a poem; denoting verse in such poems.—**hero'ics** n.pl. high-flown language.—**heroism** (her'-ō-izm) n. courage; valour; bravery.

heroin (her'-ō-in) n. (Med.) sedative; narcotic drug derived from morphine.

heron, hern (her'-on, hern) n. long-legged, wading bird.—**her'onry** n. place where herons breed.—**her'onshaw, hern'shaw** n. young heron.

herpes (her'-pēz) n. skin disease.—**herpet'ic** a.

herpetology (her-pet-ol'-o-ji) n. natural history of reptiles.

herring (her'-ing) n. sea-fish, moving in shoals.—**herr'ing-bone** n. zig-zag pattern.—red herring, (*Fig.*) subject introduced into discussion to divert criticism from main issue.

hesitate (hez′-i-tāt) *v.i.* feel or show indecision; hold back.—hes′itant *a.* pausing; slow to decide.—hes′itance, hes′itancy *n.*—hes′itative *a.*—hesita′tion *n.* doubt; indecision.

heterodox (het′-er-o-doks) *a.* contrary to accepted opinion, esp. in theology; not orthodox; heretical.—het′erodoxy *n.*

heterodyne (het′-er-o-dīn) *n.* (*Radio*) audible beat produced when two waves of different frequency are superimposed.

heterogeneous (het-er-o-jē′-ne-us) *a.* composed of diverse elements; differing in kind; dissimilar.—heterogene′ity, heteroge′neousness *n.*

heterosexual (het-er-o-seks-ū-al) *a.* attracted to opposite sex.—heterosexuality *n.*

hew (hū) *v.t.* chop or cut with axe, etc.; cut in pieces; shape or form;—*pa.p.* hewed, or hewn.—*pa.t.* hewed.

hexa- (hek′-sa) *prefix* from Gk. *hex*, six, combining to form derivatives, e.g. hex′agon *n.* plane figure having six sides and six angles.—hexag′onal *a.*—hexahe′dron *n.* solid figure having six faces, e.g. a cube.

hexachord (hek′-sa-kord) *n.* (*Mus.*) diatonic series of six notes, with a semitone between third and fourth.

hexad (hek′-sad) *n.* group of six numbers.

hexameter (hek-sam′-e-ter) *n.* verse of six feet.

hexapod (hek′-sa-pod) *n.* six-footed animal.

hey (hā) *interj.* used to call attention. —hey′day *n.* time of fullest strength.

hiatus (hī-ā′-tus) *n.* gap in a series; opening; lacuna; pronunciation without elision of two adjacent vowels.

hibernate (hī′-ber-nāt) *v.i.* winter; pass the winter, esp. in torpid state. —hiberna′tion *n.*

hiccup (hik′-up) *n.* (erroneously hic′cough) audible spasm of breathing organs; sound itself;—*v.i.* to have this;—*pr.p.* hic′cupping.

hickory (hik′-or-i) *n.* N. American tree; its tough wood.

hidalgo (hi-dal′-gō) *n.* Spanish nobleman.

hide (hīd) *v.t.* put or keep out of sight; keep secret;—*v.i.* lie concealed; *n.* place of concealment.—*pa. p.* hid′den, hid.—*pa.t.* hid.—hid′den *a.* concealed; secret; mysterious.

hide (hīd) *n.* skin of animal; dressed skin of animal; human skin;—*v.t.* flog.—hide′-bound *a.* (*Fig.*) narrow-minded.—hiding *n.* flogging.

hideous (hid′-e-us) *a.* repulsive; revolting; frightful.—hid′eousness *n.*

hie (hī) *v.i.* and *refl.* go quickly; hurry on.

hiemal (hī′-e-mal) *a.* pert. to winter.

hierarch (hī′-er-ark) *n.* one who has authority in sacred things; chief priest.—hi′erarchal, hierarch′ical *a.*—hi′erarchy *n.* authority in sacred things; government by priests; organisation of priesthood according to grades; three orders of angels.

hieratic (hi-e-ra′-tik) *a.* of priests

hieroglyphic (hī-er-o-glif′-ik) *n.* emblem or symbol of sacred things;—*pl.* ancient Egyptian symbols used in place of letters; picture-writing.— Also hi′eroglyph *n.*—hieroglyph′ic, hiero-glyph′ical *a.*

higgledy-piggledy (hig′-l-di-pig′-l-di) *adv.* and *a.* in confusion.

high (hī) *a.* elevated; tall; far up; elevated in rank, etc.; chief; eminent; loud; angry, as words; strongly marked, as colour; dear; costly; extreme; sharp, as tone or voice; tainted, as meat; intoxicated; remote from equator, as latitude;— *adv.* far up; strongly; to a great extent.—high′ball *n.* (*U.S. Slang*) whisky and soda.—high′-born *a.* of noble birth.—high′-bred *a.* of noble breeding, thoroughbred.—high′brow *a.* and *n.* (*Colloq.*) intellectual, esp. in snobbish manner.—High Church, section of Anglican Church which attaches extreme importance to ecclesiastical rites and ceremonies. —high command (*Mil.*) commander-in-chief of armies and his staff.— High Court (*Law*) supreme court.— high-falu′tin′, high-falu′ting *a.* bombastic.—high-fidel′ity *a.* giving high-quality sound reproduction.—high′fre′quency *n.* (*Radio*, etc.) any frequency above audible range.— high′-flown *a.* elevated; extravagant. —high′-fly′er, high′-fli′er *n.* (*Fig.*) ambitious person.—high′lands *n.pl.* mountainous region, esp. in Scotland.—High′lander *n.* inhabitant of mountainous region, esp. highlands of Scotland.—high′-lights *n.pl.* (*Art.*) brightest parts of a painting; (*Fig.*) moments of crisis.—high′ness *n.* quality of being high; title of honour to princes and princesses.—high′-pitched *a.* of a shrill sound.—high′-road *n.* main road.—high seas, sea or ocean beyond the three-mile belt of coastal waters.—high′spir′ited *a.* ardent; daring.—high′-strung *a.* sensitive.—high tea, tea served with meat, fish, etc.—high treason, breach of allegiance from a subject to sovereign or government of country.— high′-wat′er *n.* high tide.—high′-way *n.* main road; public road; ordinary route.—high′wayman *n.* robber on public road.

hijack (hī′-jak) *v.t.* and *i.* commit highway robbery; hold up driver and steal vehicle and contents.

hike (hīk) *v.i.* walk; tramp;—*v.t.* to

carry on one's back;—*n.* journey on foot.—hik'er *n.*

hilarious (hi-lā'-ri-us) *a.* extremely funny.—hilar'ity *n.* mirth.

hill (hil) *n.* small mountain; mound.—hill'y *a.* full of hills.—hill'ock *n.* small hill.

hilt (hilt) *n.* handle of sword, dagger, etc.

him (him) *pron.* objective case of pronoun he.—himself' *pron.* emphatic and reflexive form of he and him.

hind (hīnd) *n.* female of stag.

hind, hinder (hīnd, hīnd'-ẹr) *a.* at the back; placed at the back; combining form in such words as hind'-leg.—hind'most, hind'ermost *a.* furthest behind; last.—hind'sight *n.* wisdom after the event.

hinder (hin'-dẹr) *v.t.* prevent from progressing; stop.—hin'derer *n.*—hin'drance *n.* obstruction; obstacle.

Hindustan (hin'-dōō-stan) *n.* (Geog.) country of upper valley of R. Ganges, India.—Hin'di, Hindee (hin'-dē) language spoken in India.—Hin'du, Hindoo (hin'-dōō) *n.* native of Hindustan; one who practices Hinduism.—Hindusta'ni, Hindoosta'nee *n.* chief language of Hindu India; also known as 'Urdu'.

hinge (hin'-j) *n.* movable joint, as that on which door, lid, etc. hangs; point on which thing depends;—*v.t.* attach with, or as with, a hinge;—*v.i.* turn on; depend on.

hinny (hin'-i) *n.* offspring of stallion and she-ass.

hint (hint) *n.* slight allusion; indirect suggestion;—*v.t.* and *i.* allude to indirectly.

hinterland (hint'-ẹr-land) *n.* district inland from coast or river.

hip (hip) *n.* upper part of thigh.

hip (hip) *n.* fruit of the wild-rose.

hippodrome (hip'-o-drōm) *n.* stadium for horse and chariot races; circus.

hippopotamus (hip-o-pot'-ạ-mus) *n.* African amphibious quadruped.—*pl.* hippopot'amuses, or hippopot'ami.

hire (hīr) *n.* payment for use of a thing; wages; hiring or being hired;—*v.t.* pay for use of thing; contract with for wages; take or give on hire.—hire'ling *n.* one who serves for wages.

hirsute (hir'-sūt) *a.* hairy; shaggy.

his (hiz) *pron.* and *a.* possessive case of the pronoun he, belonging to him.

hiss (hiss) *v.i.* make a prolonged sound like that of *ss* as in 'ass,' esp. to express disapproval.

history (his'-to-ri) *n.* study of past events; record of events in life of a nation, institution, etc.; description of animals, plants, etc. existing on the earth, called natural history.—historian (his-tō'-ri-ạn) *n.* writer or

student of history.—histor'ic *a.* pert. to history.—histor'ical *a.* of, or based on, history; belonging to the past.—historiog'rapher *n.* writer of history, esp. as official historian.

histrionic (his-tri-on'-ik) *a.* theatrical; affected.—histrion'ics *n.pl.* dramatic art.

hit (hit) *v.t.* strike; (Fig.) affect injuriously;—*v.i.* strike; light (upon).—*pr.p.* hit'ting.—*pa.p.* and *pa.t.* hit.—*n.* blow; stroke; success; lucky chance; best-selling popular song.

hitch (hich) *v.t.* raise with a jerk; fasten with loop, etc.; make a rope fast;—*v.i.* to be caught or fastened;—*n.* jerk; fastening, loop, or knot; (Fig.) difficulty. — hitch'er *n.* — to hitch-hike, travel by begging rides from motorists, etc.

hither (hiTH'-ẹr) *adv.* to or towards this place;—*a.* situated on this side.—hith'erto *adv.* up to now.

hive (hīv) *n.* place where bees live; (Fig.) industrious company;—*v.t.* gather or place bees in a hive;—*v.i.* enter a hive; take shelter together; live in company.

hives (hīvz) *n.* eruptive skin disease allied to chicken-pox.

hoar (hōr) *a.* gray with age; grayish-white.—hoar'y *a.* white or gray with age; venerable.—hoar'-frost *n.* white frost; frozen dew.

hoard (hōrd) *n.* stock or store, esp. if hidden away; treasure;—*v.t.* store secretly;—*v.i.* lay up a store.—hoard'er *n.*

hoarding (hōr'-ding) *n.* temporary wooden fence round house while builders are at work; screen on which advertisements are posted.

hoarse (hōrs) *a.* rough and harsh sounding; having hoarse voice.

hoax (hōks) *v.t.* deceive by amusing or mischievous story; play a trick upon for sport;—*n.* practical joke.—hoax'er *n.*

hob (hob) *n.* projecting nave of wheel; flat-topped casing of fireplace where things are placed to be kept warm.—hob'nail *n.* large-headed nail for boot-soles.

hob (hob) *n.* elf.—hobgob'lin *n.* mischievous elf; bogey.

hobble (hob'-l) *v.i.* walk lamely; limp;—*v.t.* tie legs together of a horse, etc.;—*n.* limping gait; fetter; rope for hobbling.

hobby (hob'-i) *n.* favourite pastime.—hobb'y-horse *n.* stick with horse's head used as child's toy-horse; at fairs, etc. horse in wooden merry-go-round.

hobnob (hob'-nob) *v.i.* drink together; be very friendly with.

hobo (hō'-bō) *n.* tramp (U.S. Slang).

hock (hok) *n.* joint of quadruped's hind leg between knee and fetlock.—Also hough.

hock (hok) *n.* German white wine.

hockey (hok'-i) *n.* team game played with a ball and curved sticks.

hocus (hō'-kus) *v.i.* hoax; stupefy with drugs.—**ho'cus-po'cus** *n.* juggler; juggler's trick; trickery.

hod (hod) *n.* small trough on a staff used by builders for carrying mortar, bricks, etc.

hodometer (ho-dom'-e-ter) *n.* instrument for measuring distance travelled.

hoe (hō) *n.* tool for breaking ground, scraping out weeds, etc.;—*v.t.* break up or weed with a hoe.—*pr.p.* **hoe'ing.**

hog (hog) *n.* swine; pig, esp. if reared for fattening; greedy or dirty fellow.—**hog'gish** *a.* like a hog. —**hog'-back, hog's'-back** *n.* crested hill-ridge; archwise ridge on road.

hog, hogg (hog) *n.* yearling sheep not yet shorn.—Also **hog'gerel, hog'get.**

Hogmanay (hog-ma-nā') *n.* (*Scot.*) last day of the year.

hogshead (hogz'-hed) *n.* large cask; liquid measure.

hoist (hoist) *v.t.* raise aloft, esp. of flags; raise with tackle, etc.;—*n.* elevator; lift.

hold (hōld) *v.t.* keep fast; grasp; support in or with the hands, etc.; own; detain; celebrate;—*v.i.* cling; not to give way; abide (by); keep (to); proceed; be in force;—*pa.p.* and *pa.t.* **held.**—*n.* grasp; grip; claim; binding power and influence. —**hold'ing** *n.* stocks held.—**hold'-all** *n.* kind of valise, or portable travelling-case, for holding clothes, etc.—**to hold up,** support; cause delay; obstruct; commit highway robbery.

hold (hōld) *n.* space below the deck of a ship, for cargo.

hole (hōl) *n.* a hollow; cavity; pit; den; lair; burrow; opening; (*Colloq.*) awkward situation;—*v.t.* make a hole in.—**hole-and-corner,** secret; underhand.

holiday (hol'-i-dā) *n.* a day or period of rest from work; religious festival.

hollow (hol'-ō) *n.* cavity; hole; depression; valley;—*a.* empty;—*v.i.* make a hollow in.—**holl'ow-eyed** *a.* with sunken eyes.

holly (hol'-i) *n.* evergreen shrub or tree with prickly leaves.

hollyhock (hol'-i-hok) *n.* tall flowering garden plant.

holocaust (hol'-o-kawst) *n.* burnt offering; wholesale sacrifice, destruction.

hol'ograph *n.* and *a.* any writing, as a letter, deed, will, etc. wholly in the hand-writing of the signer.

holster (hōl'-ster) *n.* leather case for a pistol.

holt (hōlt) *n.* otter's den.

holy (hō'-li) *a.* belonging to, or devoted to, God; sacred.—**ho'liness** *n.*—**ho'ly-day** *n.* (modern spelling, **hol'iday**) religious festival.—**Holy Ghost, Holy Spirit,** third Person of the Godhead or Trinity.—**Holy Land,** Palestine.—**ho'ly or'ders** *n.* office of clergyman; Christian ministry.

homage (hom'-āj) *n.* tribute; respect paid; reverence; deference.

home (hōm) *n.* one's fixed residence; dwelling-place; native place or country; institution for the infirm; —*a.* pert. to, or connected with, home; not foreign; domestic;—*adv.* to or at one's home; close.—**home'less** *a.*—**home'lessness** *n.*—**home'ly** *a.* plain; domestic.—**home'liness** *n.*—**home'-farm** *n.* farm attached to mansion or manor-house.—**home'land** *n.* one's native land.—**home'-made** *a.* made at home; plain.—**home'-sick** *a.* depressed in spirits through absence from home.—**home'-sickness** *n.*—**home'spun** *a.* spun or made at home; anything plain or homely.—**home'stead** *n.* farmhouse with out-buildings.—**Home Office,** department of British Government, under Home Secretary, which deals with internal administration of the country.

home (hōm) *v.i.* find the way home or to a target.—**hom'er** *n.* homing pigeon.

homeopathy (hō-me-op'-a-thi) *n.* treatment of disease by administration of very small doses of drugs. — Also **homoeop'athy.** — **ho'meopath, homeop'athist** *n.*—**homeopath'ic** *a.*

homicide (hom'-i-sīd) *n.* manslaughter.—**homici'dal** *a.*

homily (hom'-i-li) *n.* tedious discourse on religious or moral subject; sermon.

homoeopathy. See **homeopathy.**

homogeneous (ho-mo-jē'-ne-us) *a.* of the same kind or nature; similar. —**homogeneity** (ho-mo-je-nē'-i-ti) *n.* sameness; uniformity.

homograph (hom'-o-graf) *n.* word having same spelling as another, but different meaning and origin.

homologate (ho-mol'-o-gāt) *v.t.* approve; confirm.

homonym (hom'-o-nim) *n.* word having same pronunciation as another but different meaning, e.g. *air* and *heir.*

homosexuality (ho-mo-seks-ū-al'-i-ti) *n.* attraction between individuals of same sex.—**homosex'ual** *n.* person thus perverted.

hone (hōn) *n.* stone for sharpening knives.

honest (on'-est) *a.* upright; just; faithful.—**hon'esty** *n.* upright conduct; (*Bot.*) flowering plant with semi-transparent, silvery pods.

honey (hun'-i) *n.* sweet, thick fluid made by bees from nectar of flowers; sweetness;—*a.* sweet; luscious;—*pa.p.* and *a.* **honeyed** (hun'-id).—also

hon'ied a. sweet; (*Fig.*) flattering.—**hon'ey-bee** n. common hive-bee.—**hon'eycomb** n. structure of wax in hexagonal cells in which bees place honey, eggs, etc.; anything resembling this;—v.t. fill with cells or perforations.—**hon'ey-combed** a.—**honeydew** (hun'-i-dū) n. sweet sticky substance secreted by plants and certain aphides.—**hon'eymoon** n. holiday taken by newly-wed couple. Also, v.i.—**hon'eysuckle** n. climbing plant with yellow flowers; woodbine.

honk (hongk) n. cry of the wild goose.

honorary (on'-or-ar-i) a. conferred for sake of honour only; holding a position without pay.—**honorarium** (on-o-rā'ri-um) n. voluntary payment for services rendered.

honour (on'-or) n. high respect; renown; glory; source or cause of honour; high rank or position; title of respect given to a judge, etc.; chastity; court-card;—v.t. respect highly; confer mark of distinction on; accept or pay (bill, etc.) when due.—**hon'ours** n.pl. public marks of respect or distinction; distinction in examinations.—**hon'ourable** a. worthy of honour; upright; title of distinction or respect.—**hon'ourably** adv.—**hon'ourableness** n.—an affair of honour, duel.—**maid of honour**, lady attending queen or princess; kind of cheesecake.

hooch (hōóch) n. (*Slang*) alcoholic liquor.

hood (hood) n. covering for head and neck; appendage to graduate's gown designating his university and degree; folding roof of carriage or motor-car;—v.t. cover with a hood.—**hood'wink** v.t. blind by covering the eyes; impose on; deceive.—**hood'ed-crow,** n. greyish crow (also called **hood'ie-crow**).

hoodlum (hood'-lum) n. (*U.S.*) hooligan.

hoodoo (hōō'-dōō) n. cause of bad luck.

hoof (hōóf) n. horny casing of foot of horse, ox, sheep, etc.;—pl. hoofs, hooves.

hook (hook) n. bent piece of metal, etc. for catching hold, hanging up, etc.; curved tool for cutting grain, grass, etc.; bent piece of barbed steel for catching fish;—v.t. and i. fasten with a hook; catch a fish with a hook; (*Golf*) drive a ball in a curve to the left; (*Boxing*) to deliver a blow with bent elbow.—**hook'er** n. (*Rugby*) player in the scrummage, who tries to hook the ball back to his own side.—**hooks and eyes**, bent metallic clips and catches used for fastening clothing.

hooka, hookah (hoo'-ka) n. tobacco-pipe in which the smoke is drawn through water and a long tube.

hooligan (hōól'-i-gan) n. one of a gang of rough boys; a rowdy.—**hool'iganism** n.

hoop (hōóp) n. band for holding together staves of casks, etc.; circle of wood or metal as a toy;—v.t. bind with a hoop.—**hoop'la** n. game played by throwing rings at objects, won if encircled.

hoot (hōót) n. cry of an owl; cry of disapproval; laugh; sound of a motor-horn;—v.t. assail with hoots; —v.i. cry as an owl; cry out in disapproval.—**hoot'er** n. a factory siren.

hooves (hōóvz) pl. of hoof.

hop (hop) v.i. of persons, to spring on one foot; of animals or birds, leap or skip on all feet at once.—pr.p. hop'ping.—pa.p. and pa.t. hopped.—n. action of hopping; (*Aviat.*) one stage in a flight.—**hop'per** n. one who hops; device for feeding material into mill or machine; boat for carrying dredged mud, etc. out to sea.—**hop-o'-my-thumb** n. a dwarf.

hop (hop) n. climbing plant with bitter cones used to flavour beer, etc.—**hops** n.pl. cones of hop plant.—**hop'-bind (-bine)** n. stalk on which hops grow.

hope (hōp) n. desire; optimistic expectation; thing hoped for;—v.t. desire, with belief in possibility of obtaining;—v.i. feel hope.—**hope'ful** a.—**hope'fully** adv.—**hope'fulness** n.—**hope'less** a.—**hope'lessly** adv.—**hope'lessness** n.

hopscotch (hop'-skoch) n. child's game, played on squares drawn on ground.

horde (hōrd) n. troop of nomads or tent-dwellers; rabble or gang.

horizon (ho-rī'-zun) n. boundary of part of the earth seen from any given point; line where earth (or sea) and sky seem to meet.—**horizontal** (hor-i-zon'-tal) a. parallel to horizon; level.—**horizon'tally** adv.

hormone (hor'-mōn) n. secretion in plant or animal which stimulates physiological reaction in parts of the organism to which it passes.

horn (horn) n. hard organ growing from heads of cows, deer, etc.; tentacle of a snail; wind instrument of music; drinking cup; utensil for holding gunpowder; sounding contrivance on motors; either extremity of the crescent moon.—**horn'y** a. hard or callous.—**horn'beam** n. tree resembling a beech.—**horn'book** n. formerly primer for children, covered with horn to protect it.—**horn'-owl** n. owl with two tufts of feathers on its head.—**horn'pipe** n. old musical instrument; vigorous dance; lively tune for such dance.

hornet (hor'-net) n. large insect of the wasp family.

horography (ho-rog'-ra-fi) n. art of constructing watches, clocks, etc.—**horog'rapher** n.—**horol'oger**, **horol'ogist** n.—**horol'ogy** n. science of measuring time; art of making timepieces.—**horom'etry** n. art or method of measuring time by hours, etc.

horoscope (hor'-o-skōp) n. chart of the heavens which predicts the character of the individual.—**horoscop'ic** a.—**horos'copist** n. astrologer.—**horos'copy** n. art of prediction from a horoscope; disposition of the stars at a given moment.

horrible (hor'-i-bl) a. tending to excite horror, fear, dread.—**horr'ibly** adv.—**horr'ibleness** n.—**horr'id** a. frightful.—**horr'ify** v.t. strike with horror, dread, repulsion; shock.—**horrif'ic** a. causing horror.

horror (hor'-or) n. painful emotion of fear and repulsion; that which excites dread.

horse (hors) n. large hoofed quadruped used for riding, drawing vehicles, etc.; male of the horse species; mounted soldiers; in gymnastics, vaulting-block; frame for drying clothes on;—v.i. mount on a horse.—**hors'y** a. pert. to horses; fond of horses.—**hors'iness** n.—**horse'back** n. back of a horse.—**on horseback**, mounted.—**horse'-box** n. large kind of enclosed stall used for transport of horses.—**horse'-chest'nut** n. tree with conical clusters of flowers and large nuts; the nut.—**horse'-fly** n. stinging fly troublesome to horses.—**horse'-hair** n. hair from tail or mane of a horse; haircloth.—**horse'knack'er** n. one who buys old horses, slaughters them, and sells the hides, etc.—**horse'-laugh** n. loud boisterous laugh.—**horse'man** n.—**horse'manship** n.—**horse'-pis'tol** n. old kind of large pistol.—**horse'-play** n. rough boisterous play.—**horse'-pow'er** n. (abbrev. **h.p.**), power a horse is capable of exerting; estimated (in Mechanics) to be the power of lifting 33,000 lb. one foot high in one minute.—**horse'-ra'dish** n. plant used for sauce, salads, etc.—**horse'-sense** n. (Colloq.) common sense.—**horse'-shoe** n. horse's metal shoe, symbol of good luck.

horticulture (hor'-ti-kul-tūr) n. gardening.—**hortiticul'tural** a.—**horticul'turist** n.

hosanna (hō-zan'-a) n. cry of praise to God.

hose (hōz) n. stockings; socks; covering for legs and feet; flexible pipe for conveying water.—v.t. water with a hose.—**hose'-pipe** n. hose used by firemen for spraying water.—**hosier** (hōz'-yer) n. dealer in hosiery.—**hos'iery** n. knitted goods.

hospice (hos'-pis) n. traveller's house of rest at monastery.

hospitable (hos'-pit-a-bl) a. entertaining guests in a friendly and liberal fashion.—**hos'pitably** adv.—**hos'pitableness** n.—**hospital'ity** n. generous reception of guests.

hospital (hos'-pit-al) n. institution for the care of the sick.—**hospitalisa'tion** n. scheme for treatment in hospital.—**hos'pitalise** v.t.

host (hōst) n. one who lodges or entertains another; innkeeper; animal or plant with parasites living on it.—**host'ess**, woman who entertains guests.—**hostel** (hos'-tel) n. residence for students; communal lodging.—**hos'telry** n. inn.—**hos'teler**, **hos'teller** n. one living in a hostel.

host (hōst) n. large number; multitude; crowd; army.—**the heavenly host**, angels and archangels.

Host (hōst) n. the bread consecrated in the Eucharist.

hostage (hos'-tāj) n. one handed over to the enemy as security.

hostile (hos'-til) a. pert. to an enemy; unfriendly; opposed.—**hos'tilely** adv.—**hostil'ity** n. opposition;—pl. state or acts of warfare.

hostler, ostler (hos'-ler, os'-ler) n. man who attends to horses; groom at an inn.

hot (hot) a. of high temperature; very warm; of quick temper; passionate; (of dance music) with marked rhythm.—**hot'ly** adv.—**hot'ness** n.—**hot'-bed** n. in gardening, glass-covered bed for bringing on plants quickly; hence (Fig.) any place conducive to quick growth (e.g. of scandal, vice, etc.).—**hot'-blood'ed** a. high-spirited; passionate.—**hot'-dog** n. (Colloq.) sandwich roll with hot sausage inside.—**hotfoot'** adv. swiftly.—**hot'head** n. impetuous person.—**hot'-pot** n. dish of meat and vegetables cooked in a closed casserole.

hotchpotch, hotchpot (hoch'-poch, hoch'-pot) n. dish of many ingredients; a mixture.

hotel (hō-tel') n. house for accommodation of travellers—**hotel'keeper** n.

hound (hound) n. dog used in hunting, esp. by scent; despicable man;—v.t. chase as with hounds; incite; pursue.

hour (our) n. twenty-fourth part of a day, or 60 minutes; time of day; appointed time.—**hour'-glass** n. sandglass lasting an hour.—**hour'ly** adv.

house (hous) n. dwelling-place; legislative assembly; family; business firm; audience at theatre, etc.; dynasty;—pl. **houses** (houz'-ez)—**house** (houz) v.t. shelter; receive; store;—v.i. dwell.—**housing** (houz'-zing) n. providing of houses; covering for piece of mechanism.—**house'ful** n.—**house'less** a.—**house'hold** n. inmates of a house; family;—a. domestic.—**house'holder** n. tenant of a house,—

house'keeper n.—**housewife** (hous'-wīf) n. mistress of a family; (huz'-if) little case for materials used in sewing.— **housewifery** (hous'-wif-ri) n. business of a housewife.—**house'-boat** n. flat-bottomed barge, with house-like superstructure. — **house'-mar'tin** n. migrant bird allied to swallow.— **house'-physic'ian, -sur'geon** n. resident medical officer of a hospital, etc.— **house'-warm'ing** n. merrymaking to celebrate entry into new house.— **household gods,** (Fig.) articles in the house endeared by long association. — **household troops,** the Guards.

housel (houz'-el) n. the Eucharist.

housing (hou'-zing) n. saddle-cloth.—pl. trappings of a horse.

hove (hōv) pa.p. and pa.t. of heave.

hovel (hov'-el, huv'-el) n. small, mean house.

hover (hov'-er, huv'-er) v.i. hang fluttering in the air; loiter.—**hov'er-craft** n. amphibious craft which rides on cushion of air generated by jets.

how (hou) adv. in what manner; by what means; to what degree; in what condition.—**however** (hou-ev'-er) adv. in whatever degree; all the same.— **howsoev'er** adv. however.

howdah, houdah (hou'-da) n. canopied seat on an elephant's back.

howitzer (hou'-it-ser) n. form of gun, with a high trajectory.

howl (houl) v.i. utter a prolonged, wailing cry as that of a dog; cry; (Colloq.) laugh heartily;—v.i. utter with howling;—n. wail or cry.— **howl'er** n. one who howls; (Colloq.) ridiculous blunder.

hoyden (hoi'-dn) n. a bold girl; tomboy.—**hoy'denish** a.

hub (hub) n. central part of wheel.

hubble-bubble (hub'-l-bub'-l) n. hookah.

hubbub (hub'-ub) n. tumult, uproar.

huckaback (huk'-a-bak) n. coarse linen, much used for towels.

huckle (huk'-l) n. hip or haunch.— **huck'le-bone** n. hip-bone; ankle-bone.

huckleberry (huk'-l-ber'i) n. American shrub bearing black berries.

huckster (huk'-ster)n. retailer of small articles; mean, mercenary fellow.

huddle (hud'-l) v.t. crowd together; heap together confusedly;—v.i. press together in fear or confusion; cower;—n. crowd; tumult.—**to go into a huddle with** (Slang) meet in conference with.

hue (hū) n. colour; tint.—**hued** a.

hue (hū) n. outcry; now only used in **hue and cry,** loud outcry or clamour.

huff (huf) n. fit of petulance;—v.t. in game of draughts, remove opponent's 'man' which could have taken pieces but did not;—v.i. blow; take offence. —**huff'y** a. sulky.

hug (hug) v.t. embrace;—n. close embrace.

huge (hūj) a. very large; enormous.— **huge'ly** adv.—**huge'ness** n.

hulk (hulk) n. body of a ship, esp. dismantled ship; anything big and unwieldy;—pl. old government vessels formerly used as prisons.— **hul'king, hul'ky** a. unwieldy; clumsy.

hull (hul) n. husk of fruit, seed, or grain; frame or body of a vessel;— v.t. remove shell or husk.

hullabaloo (hul'-a-ba-lóó) n. uproar; outcry.

hum (hum) v.t. sing with lips closed; —v.i. make buzzing sound.—n. noise of bees; low confused droning. —**hum'ming-bird** n. tiny, brightly-coloured, tropical bird.

human (hū'-man) a. belonging to, or having qualities of, man or mankind.—**hu'manly** adv.—**hu'manness** n.—**humane** (hū-mān') a. having moral qualities of a man; kind.— **humane'ly** adv.—**humane'ness** n.— **hu'manism** n. system of philosophy which rejects the supernatural; literary culture.—**hu'manist** n. one who studies the humanities or classical literature; one who rejects the supernatural in religon.—**human-is'tic** a.—**hu'manise** v.t. render human or humane.—**human'ity** n. quality of being human; human nature; human race; kindness. — **humani'ties** n.pl. branches of polite learning, esp. Latin and Greek.—**humanita'rian** n. philanthropist.—**hu'mankind** n. whole race of man.

humble (hum'-bl) a. thinking lowly of oneself; mean; not proud; modest;—v.t. bring low; make meek. —**hum'bly** adv.—**hum'bleness** n.

humble-bee (hum'-bl-bē) n. bumble-bee.

humbug (hum'-bug) n. hoax; nonsense; imposter; kind of toffee sweetmeat;—v.t. hoax; deceive.

humdrum (hum'-drum) a. commonplace.

humeral (hū'-mer-al) a. pert. to the shoulder.—**hu'merus** n. long bone of upper arm.

humid (hū'-mid) a. damp; moist.— **hu'midly** adv.—**humid'ity, hu'midness,** n. dampness.

humiliate (hū-mil'-i-āt) v.t. humble. —**humil'iating** a.—**humilia'tion** n. abasement.—**humil'ity** n. state of being humble and free from pride.

hummock (hum'-ok) n. hillock.

humour (hū'-, ū'-mur) n. fluids of animal bodies; state of mind; mood; caprice; fun; comedy;—v.t. indulge; comply with mood of.—**hu'moral** a. pert. to bodily humours.—**humor-esque** (hūmor-esk') n. musical composition of fanciful character.—**hu'morist** n.—**hu'morous** a.—**hu'morously** adv.—**hu'moursome, hu'morsome** a. moody; capricious.

hump (hump) n. the hunch formed

by a crooked back; hillock; (*Slang*) depression;—*v.t.* bend into a hump shape; to carry on the back.—**hump'back** *n.* person with crooked back.—**hump-backed** *a.*

humus (hū'-mus) *n.* decayed organic matter in soil; mould.

hunch (hunsh) *n.* hump; (*Slang*) intuition;—*v.t.* arch into a hump.—**hunch'back** *n.* humpback.

hundred (hun'-dred) *n.* ten times ten; formerly, division of a county in England.—*a.* ten times ten.—**hun'dredfold** *a.* hundred times as much.—**hun'dredth** *a.* last of a hundred;—*n.* one of a hundred equal parts.—**hun'dred-weight** *n.* 112 lb. or twentieth part of a ton. Usually written *cwt.*

hung (hung) *pa.p.* and *pa.t.* of **hang**.

hunger (hung'-ger) *n.* discomfort or exhaustion caused by lack of food; craving for food; strong desire;—*v.i.* feel hunger; long for;—*v.t.* starve.—**hung'ry** *a.*—**hung'rily** *adv.*—**hung'er-strike** *n.* refusal of all food by a prisoner, as protest.

hunt (hunt) *v.t.* pursue animals or game for food or sport; search diligently after; drive away;—*v.i.* go out in pursuit of game; search;—*n.* act of hunting; chase; search; association of huntsmen.—**hun'ter** *n.* (*fem.* **hun'tress**) one who hunts; horse used in hunting; watch that has the face protected by metal cover.—**hun'ting-crop** *n.* short whip.—**hunts'man** *n.* man in charge of pack of hounds.—**hunt down**, persecute.

hurdle (hur'-dl) *n.* frame of interlaced twigs or wooden bars, for fencing;—*v.t.* enclose with hurdles; jump over.—**hur'dle-race** *n.* race in which competitors jump hurdles.

hurdy-gurdy (hur'-di-gur'-di) *n.* old-fashioned musical instrument; street-organ.

hurl (hurl) *v.t.* send whirling; throw with violence;—*n.* violent throw.

hurly-burly (hur'-li-bur'-li) *n.* tumult; bustle.

hurrah, hurra (hu-ra') *interj.* used as a shout of joy. Also **hurray'**.

hurricane (hur'-i-kan) *n.* wind of 60 m.p.h. or over; violent storm.—**hur'ricane-deck** *n.* upper deck of a ship.—**hur'ricane-lamp** *n.* oil-lamp, for use out of doors.

hurry (hur'-i) *v.t.* hasten; urge on;—*v.i.* move or act with haste;—*n.* quick motion.—**hur'ried** *a.* done in haste.—**hur'riedly** *adv.*

hurt (hurt) *v.t.* cause pain; wound or bruise; damage; wound feelings.—*v.i.* give pain;—*n.* wound, injury, or bruise.—**hurt'ful** *a.*—**hurt'fully** *adv.*

hurtle (hur'-tl) *v.t.* brandish; whirl;—*v.i.* move rapidly; rush violently.

husband (huz'-band) *n.* married man;—*v.t.* manage with economy;

formerly, to till the soil.—**hus'bandman** *n.* farmer.—**hus'bandry** *n.* farming; thrift or frugality.

hush (hush) *interj.* or *imper.* be quiet! silence!—*n.* silence or stillness;—*v.t.* make quiet; (with *up*) keep secret;—*v.i.* be silent.

husk (husk) *n.* dry, external covering of certain seeds and fruits; chaff of grain;—*pl.* waste matter; refuse;—*v.t.* remove outer covering.—**hus'ky** *a.* full of husks; dry, esp. of the throat, hence, rough in tone; hoarse.—**hus'kily** *adv.*—**hus'kiness** *n.*

husky (hus'-ki) *n.* Canadian-Indian sledge-dog; Eskimo; Eskimo language; sturdy fellow;—*a.* powerful and muscular.

hussar (hoo-zár') *n.* one of the light cavalry of European armies.

hussy (huz'-, hus'-i) *n.* ill-behaved woman; insolent or pert girl.

hustings (hus'-tingz) *n.* principal court of the city of London; any platform from which political campaign speeches are made.

hustle (hus'-l) *v.t.* jostle;—*v.i.* hurry; bustle;—*n.* speed.—**hus'tler** *n.*

hut (hut) *n.* small house or cabin.—**hut'ment** *n.* camp of huts.

hutch (huch) *n.* box; grain-bin; pen for rabbits; waggon in which coal is brought up from the mine.

hyacinth (hī'-a-sinth) *n.* bulbous plant, bearing spikes of bell-shaped flowers; purplish-blue colour; variety of zircon.

hyaena, hyena (hī-ē'-na) *n.* carnivorous mammal, allied to the dog.—**laughing hyaena**, spotted hyaena.

hybrid (hī'-brid) *n.* offspring of two animals or plants of different species; word compounded from different languages;—*a.* cross-bred.

hydrangea (hī-drān'-je-a) *n.* genus of shrubs producing brightly-coloured flowers.

hydrant (hī'-drant) *n.* water-pipe to which a hose can be attached; water-plug.

hydrate (hī'-drāt) *n.* (*Chem.*) compound of water with another compound or an element;—*v.t.* combine with water.—**hy'drated** *a.* combined with water.—**hydra'tion** *n.*

hydraulic (hī-drawl'-ik) *a.* pert. to hydraulics; relating to the conveyance of water; worked by water-power.—**hydraul'ics** *n.pl.* science of water conveyance or water-power.

hydro *n.* See **hydropathic**.

hydro- (hī'-dro) *prefix* combining to form derivatives.—**hydrocar'bon** *n.* compound of hydrogen and carbon.—**hydroceph'alus** (hī-dro-sef'-a-lus) *n.* (*Med.*) excess of cerebro-spinal fluid in the brain; water on the brain.—**hydrocephal'ic, hydroceph'alous** *a.*—**hydrochlo'ric** *a.* containing hydrogen and chlorine.—**hydrochloric**

acid, strong acid commonly called 'spirits of salts.'

hydrodynamics (hī-dro-dī-nam'-iks) n.pl. branch of physics which deals with flow of fluids, whether liquids or gases.—**hydrodynam'ic**, **hydrodynam'ical** a. — **hydrokinet'ics** n.pl. branch of hydrodynamics which treats of fluids in motion.

hydroelectric (hī-dro-e-lek'-trik) a. pert. to generation of electricity by utilising water-power or steam.

hydrogen (hī'-dro-jen) n. an inflammable, colourless, and odourless gas, the lightest of all known substances. —**hydrogen bomb** nuclear fusion bomb of enormous power.

hydrography (hī-drog'-ra-fi) n. science of measuring and describing seas, lakes, etc.

hydrology (hī-drol'-o-ji) n. science of the properties, laws, etc. of water.—**hydrolysis** (hī-drol'-i-sis) n. chemical process by which oxygen or hydrogen in water combines with some element of a compound, to form a new compound.—**hydrolyt'ic** a.

hydrometer (hī-drom'-e-tẹr) n. graduated instrument for measuring specific gravity.

hydropathy (hī-drop'-a-thi) n. treatment of diseases with water, including use of cold or warm baths. —**hydropath'ic** a.—n. establishment where such treatment is given; (Colloq.) abbrev. **hy'dro**.

hydrophobia (hī-dro-fō'-bi-a) n. acute infectious disease in man caused by bite of mad dog; rabies; extreme fear of water.

hydroplane (hī'-dro-plān) n. kind of flat-bottomed boat designed to skim over the surface of the water.

hydrostatic, hydrostatical (hī-drostat'-ik, -i-kal) a. pert. to hydrostatics.—**hydrostat'ics** n.pl. study of fluids (liquids or gases) at rest.—**hy'drostat** n. device for detecting presence of water.

hydrous (hī'-drus) a. containing water; containing hydrogen.

hygiene (hī'-jēn) n. medical science which treats of preservation of health.—**hygienic** (hī-jen'-ik) a.—**hygien'ics** n. science of health.

hygroscope (hī'-gro-skōp) n. instrument which indicates variations of humidity in the atmosphere, without showing its exact amount; **hygroscop'ic** a. capable of absorbing moisture from the atmosphere.

hymeneal (hi-me-nē'-al) a. pert. to marriage.

hymn (him) n. ode or song of praise, esp. religious one.—**hym'nal**, **hym'nary** n. hymn-book.—**hymnol'ogy** n. study or composition of hymns; hymns collectively.—**hymnol'ogist** n.

hyperbola (hī-pẹr'-bo-la) n. (Geom.) curve formed by section of cone

when cutting plane makes greater angle with the base than side of cone makes.—**hyperbol'ic** a.

hyperbole (hī-pẹr'-bo-lē) n. (Gram.) figure of speech which expresses much more or much less than the truth, for sake of effect; exaggeration.—**hyperbol'ic**, **hyperbol'ical** a.— **hyperbol'ically** adv.—**hyper'bolise** v.t.

hypercritic (hī-pẹr-krit'-ik) n. one critical beyond measure;—**hypercrit'ical** a. excessively critical.—**hypercrit'ically** adv.

hypersensitive (hī-pẹr-sen'-si-tiv) a. abnormally sensitive. — **hypersen'sitiveness**, **hypersensitiv'ity** n.

hypertrophy (hī-pẹr'-tro-fi) n. (Med.) abnormal enlargement of organ or part of body.—**hypertroph'ic**, **hyper'trophied** a.

hyphen (hī'-fen) n. mark (-) used to connect syllables or compound words;—v.t. connect with hyphen.—**hy'phenate** v.t. join with hyphen.—**hy'phenated** a.

hypnosis (hip-nō'-sis) n. abnormal sleep mentally responsive to suggestion.—**hypnot'ic** a. tending to produce sleep; pert. to hypnotism;—n. drug that induces sleep.—**hyp'notise** v.t. produce mental state resembling sleep.—**hyp'notism** n. art of inducing hypnosis.—**hyp'notist** n.

hypochondria (hip-ō-kon'-dri-a) n. mental disorder, characterised by melancholy and gloomy views, esp. about one's own health.—Also **hypochondriasis** (hip-ō-kon-drī'-a-sis). —**hypochon'driac** a. affected by hypochondria;—n. person so affected.

hypocrisy (hi-pok'-ri-si) n. pretence of goodness; feigning to be what one is not; insincerity.—**hypocrite** (hip'-o-krit) n. pretender to virtue or piety; deceiver.—**hypocrit'ical** a.—**hypocrit'ically** adv.

hypodermic (hī-po-dẹr'-mik) a. pert. to parts underlying the skin;—n. injection of drug beneath the skin by means of needle and small syringe.—**hypoder'mically** adv.

hypotenuse (hī-pot'-e-nūs) n. (Geom.) side of right-angled triangle opposite the right angle.

hypothesis (hī-poth'-e-sis) n.pl.—**hypoth'eses**, supposition used as basis from which to draw conclusions; theory.—**hypothet'ic**, **hypothet'ical** a. —**hypothet'ically** adv.

hyssop (his'-op) n. aromatic herb.

hysteria, **hysterics** (his-tē'-ri-a, hister'-iks) n. affection of nervous system, characterised by excitability and emotional disturbance.—**hyster'ic**, **hyster'ical** a.—**hyster'ically** adv.

I

I (I) *pron.* pron. of the first pers. sing.

iambus (I-am'-bus) *n.* metrical foot of two syllables, the first short or unaccented, and the second long or accented.—*pl.* iam'buses, iam'bi.—iam'bic *a.*

Iberian (I-bē'-ri-ạn) *a.* pert. to Iberia, viz. Spain and Portugal.

ibex (I'-beks) *n.* wild mountain goat.

ibis (I'-bis) *n.* stork-like wading bird.

ice (Is) *n.* frozen water; concreted sugar; sweetened cream or water in frozen condition; ice-cream;—*v.t.* cover with ice; freeze;—*pr.p.* ic'ing. —ice age (*Geol.*) Pleistocene period, the series of glacial epochs.—ice'-axe *n.* implement for cutting footholds in ice in mountaineering.—ice'berg *n.* detached portion of glacier floating in the sea.—ice'-bound *a.* surrounded by or jammed in ice.—ice'-break'er *n.* vessel designed to maintain an open passage through ice-bound waters.—ice'-cap *n.* glacier formed by accumulation of snow and ice on a plateau and moving out from the centre in every direction.—ice'-cream *n.* cream or substitute sweetened and congealed by freezing.—ice'-drift *n.* masses of floating ice.—ice'-field *n.* vast expanse of sea either frozen or covered with floating masses of ice.—ice'-float, ice'-floe *n.* large mass of floating ice.—ice'-hock'ey *n.* game played by skaters on ice with hard rubber disc (the puck). —ice'-pack *n.* drifting field of ice, closely packed together.—ice'-rink *n.* place, open or under cover, where ice-sports are played.—ice'-sheet *n.* enormous glac-ier covering a huge area.—ic'ily *adv.* spoken coldly.—ic'iness *n.*—ic'ing *n.* covering of sugar on cakes, etc.; formation of ice on parts of aircraft.—ic'y *a.* pert. to ice; ice-like; cold; chilling; frigid.—dry ice, solid carbon dioxide.—to break the ice, overcome initial awkwardness in company.

Icelander (Is'-lan-dẹr) *n.* native of Iceland.—Iceland'ic *a.* relating to Iceland.

ichneumon (ik-nū'-mun) *n.* small carnivore of mongoose family.—ichneumon fly, insect which destroys the larvae of certain insects by laying eggs in their bodies.

ichthyic (ik'-thi-ik) *a.* (*Zool.*) pert. to fish.

ichthyoid, ichthyoidal (ik'-thi-oid, -al) *a.* resembling fish.

ichthyology (ik-thi-ol'-o-ji) *n.* classification of fishes.—ichthyolog'ical *a.* —ichthyol'ogist *n.*

ichthyosaurus (ik-thi-o-saw'-rus) *n.* extinct marine reptile intermediate between a saurian and a fish.

icicle (Is'-i-kl) *n.* pendent conical mass of ice, built up by freezing of drops of water.

icon (I'-kon) *n.* image of Christ, angel, or saint, found in Greek and Orthodox Eastern Churches.—icon'ic, icon'ical *a.* pert. to icons.—icon'oclasm *n.* act of breaking images; attack on cherished beliefs of others.—icon'oclast *n.* breaker of images; one who exposes or destroys shams of any kind.—iconol'ater *n.* image-worshipper. — iconol'atry *n.* image-worship.—icon'oscope *n.* type of television camera.

id (id) *n.* (*Psych.*) primary source in individuals of instinctive energy.

idea (I-dē'-ạ) *n.* mental image of external object; way of thinking; vague belief; plan; aim.—ide'al *a.* existing in fancy only; satisfying desires;—*n.* imaginary type of perfection to be aimed at.—idealisa'tion *n.*—ide'alise *v.t.* represent or look upon as ideal; make or render ideal; refine.—ide'aliser *n.* idealist.—ide'alism *n.* tendency to seek the highest spiritual perfection; doctrine that the world is to be regarded as consisting of mind; opposite of *materialism* in science and *realism* in art and literature.—ide'alist *n.*—idealist'ic *a.* pert. to idealism; perfect.—ideal'ity *n.* ideal state.—ide'ally *adv.*

identical (I-den'-ti-kạl) *a.* not different.—iden'tically *adv.*—iden'ticalness *n.* sameness.

identify (I-den'-ti-fI) *v.t.* establish identity of; prove to be the same; recognise; associate (oneself) in interest, use, etc.;—*pa.p.* iden'tified. —iden'tifiable *a.*—identifica'tion *n.*

identity (I-den'-ti-ti) *n.* state of having the same nature or character with; absolute sameness; personal character; (*Math.*) an algebraic equation in which the two expressions are equal for all values of the letters involved.

ideograph (id'-e-ō-graf) *n.* picture, symbol, diagram, etc., suggesting an idea or object without naming it; character in Chinese and kindred languages.—id'eogram *n.* ideograph.—ideograph'ic, -al *a.*—ideog'raphy *n.*

ideology (I-de-ol'-o-ji) *n.* mental philosophy; political cult; abstract speculation.—ideolog'ic, ideolog'ical *a.* unrealistic; fanciful.—ideol'ogist *n.* theorist.—ide'ologue *n.* ideologist.

idiom (id'-i-um) *n.* peculiar mode of expression; colloquial speech; dialect.—idiomat'ic, idiomat'ical *a.*—idiomat'ically *adv.*

idiosyncrasy (id-i-o-sin'-krạ-si) *n.* peculiarity in a person; fad.—idiosyncrat'ic, idiosyncrat'ical *a.*

idiot (id'-i-ut) *n.* one mentally

deficient; born fool.—**id'iocy** n. permanent mental deficiency. — **idiot'ic**, **idiot'ical** a. senseless or stupid.—**idiot'ically** adv.

idle (ī'-dl) a. doing nothing; lazy; unused; frivolous;—v.t. spend in idleness;—v.i. be unoccupied; of machinery, to run off-load.—**i'dleness** n.—**i'dler** n.

idol (ī'-dul) n. image of a deity as object of worship; false god; object of excessive devotion.—**idol'ater** n. (fem. **idol'atress**).—**idol'atrise** v.t. worship as an idol.—**idol'atrous** a.—**idol'atrously** adv.—**idol'atry** n. worship of false gods; excessive admiration. —**idolisa'tion** n.—**i'dolise** v.t. make an idol of; venerate to excess.

idyll (ī'-dil, id'-il) n. short pastoral poem; picture of simple perfection. —**idyll'ic** a. pert. to idylls; blissful.

if (if) conj. on the condition or supposition that; whether; in case that.

igloo (ig'-lòò) n. dome-shaped house built by Eskimos; snow-hut.

igneous (ig'-ne-us) a. resembling fire; resulting from action of fire; fiery; burning.—**ignif'erous** a. bearing or producing fire.

ignis-fatuus (ig'-nis-fat'-ū-us) a. flickering light caused by marsh gas; Will o' the Wisp.

ignite (ig-nīt') v.t. set on fire; kindle;—v.i. catch fire.—**ignit'ible**, **ignit'able** a.—**igni'tion** n. act of setting on fire; part of internal combustion engine which produces spark.

ignoble (ig-nō'-bl) a. of low birth; mean; base; vulgar; dishonourable. —**igno'bleness** n.—**igno'bly** adv.

ignominy (ig'-nō-min-i) n. public disgrace; infamous conduct; infamy. —**ignomin'ious** a. disgraceful; dishonourable.—**ignomin'iously** adv.— **ignomin'iousness** n.

ignoramus (ig-nō-rā'-mus) n. ignorant person; vain pretender to knowledge; dunce.

ignorant (ig'-nō-rant) a. uninformed; unlearned; inexperienced.—**ig'norance** n.— **ig'norantly** adv.

ignore (ig-nōr') v.t. disregard; leave out of account; not to recognise.

iguana (i-gwä'-na) n. family of lizards; monitor lizard in S. Africa.

ilex (ī'-leks) n. common holly; genus of trees, including the holm oak.

ilk (ilk) a. the same.—**of that ilk**, applied when surname of a person is the same as name of his ancestral estate.

ill (il) a. bad or evil in any respect; sick; wicked; ugly; unfavourable; harsh;—n. evil of any kind; misfortune; pain; wickedness;—adv. badly; unfavourably; not rightly (compar. **worse**; superl. **worst**).— **ill'ness** n.

ill- (il) prefix implying badness.— **ill'-advised'** a. badly advised.—**ill'-affect'ed** a. not well disposed.—**ill'-blood** n. enmity.—**ill'-disposed'** a. not friendly; hostile. — **ill'-fa'ted** a. destined to bring misfortune.—**ill'-fa'voured** a. ugly; deformed.—**ill'-got**, **ill'-gott'en** a. not honestly obtained. —**ill'-hum'our** n. bad temper.—**ill'-na'tured** a. surly; cross.—**ill'-o'mened** a. inauspicious.—**ill'-starred** a. unlucky.—**ill'-tem'pered** a. habitually morose or cross.—**ill'-timed** a. inopportune.—**ill'-treat** v.t. misuse.— **ill'-will** n. bad feeling; enmity.

illegal (i-lē'-gal) a. unlawful.— **ille'galise** v.t. render unlawful.— **illegal'ity** n. unlawful act or state. —**ille'gally** adv.

illegible (i-lej'-i-bl) a. unreadable; indistinct.—**illeg'ibleness**, **illegibil'ity** n.—**illeg'ibly** adv.

illegitimate (i-le-jit-i-māt) a. not regular; unlawful; illegal; born out of wedlock;—n. bastard.—**illegit'imacy** n. bastardy; illegality.— **illegit'imately** adv.

illiberal (i-lib'-er-al) a. not liberal; not generous; narrow-minded.— **illiberal'ity** n.

illicit (i-lis'-it) a. prohibited; unlawful; forbidden.—**illic'itly** adv.— **illic'itness** n.

illimitable (i-lim'-it-a-bl) a. immeasurable.

illiterate (i-lit'-er-āt) a. unable to read or write;—n. person unable to read or write.—**illit'erateness**, **illit'eracy** n. inability to read or write.

illogical (i-loj'-i-kal) a. unsound; fallacious.—**illog'ically** adv.—**illogical'ity**, **illog'icalness** n.

illuminate (i-lū'-mi-nāt) v.t. enlighten, literally and figuratively; light up; embellish, as a book or manuscript with gold and colours. —**illu'minable** a.—**illu'minant** a. and n. source of light.—**illumina'tion** n. act of giving light; instruction; enlightenment; splendour; display of lights; decoration on manuscripts and books.—**illu'minative** a.; instructive.—**illu'minator** n.—**illu'mine** v.t. add light; enlighten; enhance.

illusion (i-lū'-zhun) n. false perception; deceptive appearance, esp. as a conjuring trick.—**illu'sionist** n. professional entertainer who produces illusions.—**illu'sive**, **illu'sory** a. deceiving by false appearances.— **illu'sively** adv.—**illu'siveness** n.

illustrate (il'-us-trāt, il-us'-trāt) v.t. exemplify, esp. by figures, diagrams, etc.; adorn with pictures.— **illustra'tion** n. pictorial representation accompanying printed description. —**illus'trative**, **illus'tratory** a.—**illus'tratively** adv.—**ill'ustrator**, n.

illustrious (i-lus'-tri-us) a. bright; shining; conferring honour; having honour or dignity.—**illus'triousness** n.

image (im'-ij) n. mental picture of any object; object set up for worship; statue; idol; likeness; representation of object on photograph, TV screen, etc.;—v.t. reflect; imagine.—**im'agery** n. images collectively; figures of speech; imagination.

imagine (im-aj'-in) v.t. form in the mind idea or image; conceive; picture; believe; suppose;—v.t. form image of; picture in mind.—**imag'inable** a.—**ima'ginableness** n.—**imag'inably** adv.—**ima'ginary** a. fanciful; unreal.—**imag'inative** a. gifted with creative faculty; fanciful.—**imagina'tion** n. mental faculty which forms ideas of external objects.—**imag'inatively** adv.—**imag'inativeness** n.

imago (i-mā'-gō) n. final, fully developed adult stage of insect development.

imam, imaum (i-mȧm', i-mawm') n. officer who leads the devotion and prayers in Mohammedan mosques.

imbecile (im'-be-sēl) a. mentally feeble; idiotic;—**imbecil'ity** n.

imbibe (im'bīb') v.t. drink in; absorb;—v.t. drink.—**imbib'er** n.

imbroglio (im-brōl'-yō) n. intricate, complicated plot; confusion.

imbue (im-bū') v.t. dye; stain; inspire.

imburse (im-burs') v.t. supply with money.

imitate (im'-i-tāt) v.t. follow, as pattern, model, or example; copy.—**im'itable** a.—**imita'tion** n. reproduction of original; copy; mimicry.—**im'itative** a. not original.—**im'itatively** adv.—**im'itativeness** n.—**im'itator** n.

immaculate (i-mak'-ū-lāt) a. spotless; pure; undefiled.—**immac'ulately** adv.—**immac'ulateness** n.—**Immaculate Conception**, dogma that the Blessed Virgin Mary was conceived and born without taint of sin.

immanent (im'-ȧ-nent) a. inherent.—**imm'anence, imm'anency** n.

immaterial (im-a-tē'-ri-ȧl) a. not consisting of matter; of no consequence; incorporeal; unimportant.

immature (im-a-tūr') a. not mature or ripe; raw; undeveloped; untimely.—**immature'ness, immatur'ity** n.

immeasurable (i-mezh'-ūr-ȧ-bl) a. incapable of being measured; illimitable; boundless.—**immeas'urably** adv.

immediate (i-mē'-di-āt) a. occurring at once; without delay; direct; present.—**imme'diacy** n.—**imme'diately** adv.—**imme'diateness** n.

immemorial (i-me-mōr'-i-ȧl) a. of great antiquity.—**immem'orable** a.—**immemo'rially** adv.

immense (i-mens') a. unlimited; very great; vast; huge; enormous.—**immense'ly** adv.—**immense'ness, immens'ity** n. infinity; boundlessness.

immerse (i-mȧrs') v.t. plunge into,

esp. a fluid; dip.—**immers'able, immers'ible** a.—**immersed'** a. submerged; engrossed. — **immer'ser** n. electric water-heater.—**immer'sion** n.

immigrate (im'-i-grāt) v.t. to migrate into a country.—**imm'igrant** n.—**immigra'tion** n.

imminent (im'-i-nent) a. threatening immediately to fall or occur.—**imm'inence** n. the near future.—**imm'inently** adv.

immobile (i-mob'-il) a. incapable of being moved; fixed; immovable.—**immob'ilise** v.t.

immoderate (i-mod'-ėr-āt) a. exceeding just bounds; excessive.—**immod'eracy, immod'erateness** n. extravagance. — **immod'erately** adv.—**immodera'tion** n.

immodest (i-mod'-est) a. wanting in modesty; indecent; impudent.—**immod'esty** n.

immolate (im'-ō-lāt) v.t. sacrifice; offer as a sacrifice; kill as a religious rite.—**immola'tion** n.—**imm'olator** n.

immoral (i-mor'-ȧl) a. uninfluenced by moral principle; contrary to divine law; wicked.—**immoral'ity** n. vice; profligacy.—**immor'ally** adv.

immortal (i-mor'-tȧl) a. not mortal; having eternal existence; undying; deathless;—n. one exempt from death or oblivion; divine being.—**immor'talise** v.t. make famous for all time.—**immortal'ity** n.

immovable (i-mōóv'-ȧ-bl) a. incapable of being moved; firmly fixed; fast.—**immov'ableness, immov'ability** n.—**immov'ably** adv.

immune (i-mūn') a. exempt; protected against infection.—**imm'unise** v.t. render immune.—**immunisa'tion** n.—**immun'ity** n.

immure (i-mūr') v.t. enclose within walls.

immutable (i-mūt'-ȧ-bl) a. invariable; unalterable.—**immutabil'ity, immut'ableness** n.

imp (imp) n. little demon; brat; mischievous child; a shoot; scion; graft;—v.t. graft.—**imp'ish** a. mischievous.

impact (im-pakt') v.t. press or drive forcibly together.—**im'pact** n. impulse communicated by one moving object striking another; effect.

impair (im-pār') v.t. diminish in value, excellence, or strength; injure; weaken.

impale (im-pāl') v.t. inclose with stakes; put to death by fixing on upright, sharp stake.—**impale'ment** n. fenced-in place.

impalpable (im-pal'-pȧ-bl) a. not capable of being felt or perceived by the senses, esp. by touch; not readily understood or grasped.—**impalpabil'ity** n.—**impal'pably** adv.

impart (im-pȧrt') v.t. bestow a share or portion of; grant; divulge.

impartial (im-pär'-shąl) *a.* not partial; without prejudice; not taking sides; unbiased.—**impartial'ity, impar'tialness** *n.*

impassable (im-pas'-ą-bl) *a.* incapable of being passed; impervious; impenetrable; pathless.—**impassabil'ity, impass'ableness** *n.*

impasse (im-pás, im'-pás) *n.* deadlock; dilemma; fix.

impassion (im-pash'-un) *v.t.* affect strongly with passion.—**impass'ionable, impass'ionate, impass'ioned** *a.* stirred by fervid emotion; ardent.

impassive (im-pas'-iv) *a.* not susceptible of pain or suffering; showing no emotion; calm.—**impass'ively** *adv.*—**impass'iveness, impassiv'ity** *n.*

impasto (im-pas'-tō) *n.* painting with thick layers of pigment on canvas.

impatient (im-pā'-shent) *a.* uneasy under trial or suffering; restless.—**impa'tience** *n.* want of patience.—**impa'tiently** *adv.*

impeach (im-pēch') *v.t.* charge with a crime or misdemeanour; call to account; challenge.—**impeach'able** *a.*—**impeach'ment** *n.* trial of minister of state or high public servant for official misconduct.

impeccable (im-pek'-ą-bl) *a.* not liable to sin or error; perfect.—**impeccabil'ity,** *n.*

impecunious (im-pe-kū'-ni-us) *a.* poor; hard up.—**impecunios'ity** *n.* dire poverty.

impede (im-pēd') *v.t.* stop progress of; hinder; obstruct.—**impe'dance** *n.* hindrance.—(*Elect.*) apparent resistance.—**imped'iment** *n.* that which hinders; stammer.—**imped'imenta** *n. pl.* baggage, esp. military.

impel (im-pel') *v.t.* drive or urge forward; induce; incite.—*pr.p.* **impel'ling.**—*pa.t.* and *pa.p.* **impelled'.**—**impel'lent** *a.* impelling;—*n.* force which impels.—**impel'ler** *n.*

impend (im-pend') *v.i.* hang over; threaten; be imminent.—**impend'ence, impend'ency** *n.*—**impend'ent** *a.* threatening.

impenetrable (im-pen'-e-trą-bl) *a.* incapable of being penetrated; obscure.—**impenetrabil'ity** *n.*

impenitent (im-pen'-i-tent) *a.* not repenting of sin; not contrite; obdurate.

imperative (im-per'-ą-tiv) *a.* authoritative; obligatory; absolutely necessary; peremptory.—**imper'atively** *adv.*

imperceptible (im-per-sep'-ti-bl) *a.* not discernible by the senses; minute. — **impercep'tibleness, imperceptibil'ity** *n.*—**impercep'tibly** *adv.*—**impercep'tive,** *a.* not having power to perceive.

imperfect (im-per'-fekt) *a.* wanting some part or parts; defective.—**imper'fectly** *adv.*—**imperfect'ion** *n.*

imperforate, imperforated (im-per'-fo-rāt, -ed) *a.* not perforated or pierced through.

imperial (im-pē'-ri-ąl) *a.* pert. to empire or emperor; sovereign; majestic;—*n.* tuft of hair on the lower lip.—**impe'rialism** *n.* system of government in an empire; policy of national territorial expansion.—**impe'rialist** *n.*

imperil (im-per'-il) *v.t.* bring into peril; endanger; hazard; risk.

imperious (im-pē'-ri-us) *a.* commanding; domineering; dictatorial; tyrannical.—**impe'riously** *adv.*—**impe'riousness** *n.*

imperishable (im-per'-ish-ą-bl) *a.* not liable to decay or oblivion; indestructible.—**imper'ishableness** *n.*—**imperishabil'ity** *n.*

impermanence (im-per'-man-ens) *n.* want of permanence or stability.

impersonal (im-per'-sun-ąl) *a.* having no personal reference; objective; (*Gram.*) form of verb used only in 3rd person singular with nominative *it,* e.g. *it hails.*—**imper'sonally** *adv.*

impersonate (im-per'-son-āt) *v.t.* represent in character or form; act part on the stage; imitate.—**imperona'tion** *n.*—**imper'sonator** *n.*

impertinent (im-per'-ti-nent) *a.* having no bearing on the subject; irrelevant; impudent; saucy; pert.—**imper'tinence** *n.*

imperturbable (im-per-tur'-bą-bl) *a.* incapable of being agitated; unmoved; composed.—**imperturbabil'ity** *n.*—**impertur'bably** *adv.*

impervious (im-per'-vi-us) *a.* impenetrable; impassable. — **imper'viableness, imperviabil'ity, imper'viousness** *n.*—**imper'viously** *adv.*

impetuous (im-pet'-ū-us) *a.* rushing with force and violence; ardent; hasty.—**impet'uously** *adv.*—**impet'uousness, impetuos'ity** *n.* precipitancy.

impetus (im'-pe-tus) *n.* force with which a body moves; momentum; boost.

impinge (im-pinj') *v.i.* (*with* on. upon, against) fall or dash against; touch on.

impious (im'-pi-us) *a.* not pious; wanting in reverence.—**im'piously** *adv.*—**im'piousness, impi'ety** *n.*

implacable (im-plak'-, im-plāk'-ą-bl) *a.* inexorable; not to be appeased; unrelenting. — **implac'ableness, implacabil'ity** *n.*

implant (im-plant') *v.t.* set in; insert; sow (seed); plant (shoots); settle in mind or heart.

implement (im'-ple-ment) *n.* weapon, tool, or instrument; utensil;—*v.t.* fulfil an obligation; give effect to; carry out.—**implemen'tal** *a.*

implicate (im'-pli-kāt) *v.t.* involve; include; entangle.—**implica'tion** *n.* implied meaning; entanglement.—

im′plicative *a.*—im′plicatively *adv.*—implic′it *a.* implied, though not actually expressed; without questioning.—implic′itly *adv.*

implore (im-plōr′) *v.t.* entreat earnestly; beseech.—implora′tion *n.*—implor′er *n.*—implor′ingly *adv.*

imply (im-plī′) *v.t.* to contain by implication; to involve the truth of; insinuate; denote.—*pr.p.* imply′ing.—*pa.p.* implied′.

impolite (im-po-līt′) *a.* uncivil; rude; discourteous.—impolite′ly *adv.*—impolite′ness *n.*

impolitic (im-pol′-i-tik) *a.* ill-advised; inexpedient.—impol′itely *adv.*

imponderable (im-pon′-der-a-bl) *a.* without perceptible weight; not able to be weighed;—*n.* unknown factor.—impon′derableness, imponderabil′ity *n.*

import (im-pōrt′) *v.t.* bring in from abroad; convey meaning; be of consequence to.—im′port *n.* that which is brought in from abroad; purport; meaning; consequence.—impor′tance *n.* consequence; value; significance.—impor′tant *a.* carrying or possessing weight or consequence; assuming air of gravity.—impor′tantly *adv.*—importa′tion *n.*

importune (im-por-tūn′) *v.t.* request with urgency; pester with requests; solicit.—impor′tunacy, impor′tunateness *n.*—impor′tunate *a.* earnestly solicitous; troublesome by begging.—impor′tunately *adv.*

impose (im-pōz′) *v.t.* levy; to lay, as charge or tax; enjoin or command;—*v.i.* (with *upon*) deceive; take advantage of person′s good-nature; overawe; impress.—impos′able *a.*—impos′ing *a.* commanding; grand.—imposi′tion *n.* that which is imposed; tax; burden; deception; exercise for school pupils as punishment.

impossible (im-pos′-i-bl) *a.* incapable of existing in conception or in fact; unattainable;—*interj.* absurd!—impossibil′ity *n.*

impostor (im-pos′-tur) *n.* one who assumes false character; deceiver; cheat.—impos′ture *n.* deception.

impotent (im′-po-tent) *a.* powerless; without sexual power (of a male).—im′potence, im′potency *n.*

impound (im-pound′) *v.t.* confine cattle in pound or pen; seize and retain.

impoverish (im-pov′-er-ish) *v.t.* reduce to poverty; exhaust fertility of land.—impov′erishment *n.*

impracticable (im-prak′-tik-a-bl) *a.* not able to be accomplished.—imprac′ticability, imprac′ticableness *n.*—imprac′tical *a.* not practical.

imprecate (im′-pre-kāt) *v.t.* invoke evil upon; curse.—impreca′tion *n.*—im′precatory *a.*

impregnable (im-preg′-na-bl) *a.* not to be taken by assault; not to be moved, impressed, or shaken.—impregnabil′ity *n.*—impreg′nably *adv.*

impregnate (im-preg′-nāt) *v.t.* make pregnant; render fertile; saturate.—impregna′tion *n.*

impresario (im-pre-sá′-ri-ō) *n.* organiser of public entertainment.

impress (im-pres′) *v.t.* take forcibly, persons or goods, for public service; commandeer.

impress (im-pres′) *v.t.* press in or upon; make mark or figure upon; fix deeply in mind; stamp.—im′press *n.* mark made by pressure; stamp; impression on mind.—impressibil′ity *n.* susceptibility.—impress′ible *a.* capable of being impressed.—impress′ibly *adv.*—impress′ion *n.* act of impressing; mark or stamp made by pressure; influence on mind; opinion; idea.—impress′ionable *a.* susceptible to influences; emotional.—impress′ive *a.* making deep impression on mind.—impress′ively *adv.*—impress′iveness *n.*

imprint (im-print′) *v.t.* mark by pressure; fix indelibly, as on mind; print.—im′print *n.* name of printer or publisher on title-page or at end of book.

imprison (im-prizn′) *v.t.* to put in prison.—impris′onment *n.*

improbable (im-prob′-a-bl) *a.* unlikely.—improbabil′ity *n.*—improb′ably *adv.*

improbity (im-prob′-i-ti) *n.* dishonesty.

impromptu (im-promp′-tū) *adv.* or *a.* offhand; without previous study.

improper (im-prop′-er) *a.* unsuitable; unfit; indecent.—improp′erly *adv.*—impropri′ety *n.*

improve (im-prōóv′) *v.t.* make better; make progress;—*v.i.* grow better.—improvabil′ity, improv′ableness *n.*—improv′able *a.*—improv′ably *adv.*—improve′ment *n.*—improv′ingly *adv.*

improvident (im-prov′-i-dent) *a.* not prudent or foreseeing; neglectful of future needs.—improv′idence *n.*

improvise (im-pro-vīz′) *v.t.* extemporise; make best of materials at hand; compose, speak or perform without preparation.—improvisa′tion *n.*—improvis′er *n.*

imprudent (im-prōó′-dent) *a.* lacking in prudence or discretion; injudicious; heedless.—impru′dence *n.*—impru′dently *adv.*

impudent (im′-pū-dent) *a.* shameless; wanting modesty; brazen; bold-faced; rude.—im′pudence *n.*—im′pudently *adv.*

impugn (im-pūn′) *v.t.* call in question; contradict; challenge accuracy of a statement.—impugn′able *a.*—impugn′er *n.*—impugn′ment *n.*

impulse (im′-puls) *n.* push; thrust; momentum; sudden thought; motive.—impul′sion *n.* impelling force;

incitement.—**impuls'ive** a. acting momentarily without due thought. —impuls'ively adv.—impuls'iveness n.

impunity (im-pūn'-i-ti) n. exemption from punishment, injury, or loss.

impure (im-pūr') a. not pure; mixed; adulterated; unchaste.—impure'ly adv.—impu'rity, impure'ness n.

impute (im-pūt') v.t. ascribe to (in bad sense); attribute to.—imput'able a.—imput'ableness, imputabil'ity n.—imputa'tion n.—impu'tative a. imputed.—imput'atively adv.

in (in) prep. within; inside of;—adv. inside; closely; immediately.—in as far as, to the extent that.—in as much as, inasmuch as, considering that.

inability (in-a-bil'-i-ti) n. want of strength, means, or power; impotence; incapacity.

inaccessible (in-ak-ses'-i-bl) a. not accessible; unapproachable; unattainable.—inaccessibil'ity n.—inaccess'ibly adv.

inaccurate (in-ak'-ūr-āt) a. not correct; erroneous.—inacc'uracy n.—inacc'urately adv.

inactive (in-ak'-tiv) a. idle; inert; lazy; (Chem.) not combining with other elements. — inac'tion n. — inact'ively adv.—inactiv'ity n.

inadequate (in-ad'-e-kwāt) a. insufficient; too cramped; incapable. —inad'equacy n.—inad'equately adv.—inad'equateness n.

inadmissible (in-ad-mis'-i-bl) a. that can not be allowed; improper.—inadmiss'ibly adv.

inadvertent (in-ad-vert'-ent) a. inattentive; thoughtless; careless.—inadvert'ence, inadvert'ency n.—inadvert'ently adv.

inadvisable See unadvisable.

inalienable (in-āl'-yen-a-bl) a. incapable of being separated or transferred.

inane (in-ān') a. empty; void; foolish; silly.—inani'tion n. state of being empty; exhaustion; starvation.—inan'ity n. silly remark.

inanimate (in-an'-i-māt) a. not animate; destitute of life or spirit.—inanima'tion n.—inan'imateness n.

inapplicable (in-ap'-lik-a-bl) a. not applicable; unsuitable; irrelevant; inappropriate.

inapposite (in-a'-poz-it) a. not apposite; inappropriate; inapplicable; irrelevant; not pertinent; out of place.—inap'positely adv.

inappreciable (in-a-prē'-shi-a-bl) a. not worth reckoning; not able to be valued.

inappropriate (in-a-prō'-pri-āt) a. unsuitable; unbecoming; at the wrong time.—inappro'priately adv.—inappro'priateness n.

inapt (in-apt') a. inappropriate; unsuitable.—inap'titude n.—inapt'ly adv.

inarticulate (in-ar-tik'-ūl-āt) a. un-

able to put one's ideas in words; not uttered distinctly; not jointed.—inartic'ulately adv.—inartic'ulateness n.—inarticula'tion n.

inasmuch adv. See in.

inattentive (in-a-tent'-iv) a. heedless; regardless; negligent.—inatten'tion, inattent'iveness n.

inaudible (in-awd'-i-bl) a. not able to be heard; noiseless; silent.—inaudibil'ity, inaud'ibleness n.—inaud'ibly adv.

inaugurate (in-aw'-gūr-āt) v.t. induct formally into office; install; set in motion; begin.—inau'gural, inau'guratory a.—inaugura'tion n. opening ceremony.—inau'gurator n.

inauspicious (in-aw-spish'-us) a. not auspicious; ill-fated; unlucky.—inauspic'iously adv.—inauspic'iousness n.

inborn (in'-born) a. born in or with; innate; natural; inherent; congenital.

inbred (in'-bred) a. innate; inherent. —in'breed v.t. mate animals of same blood-stock; marry within the family.—in'breeding n.

incalculable (in-kal'-kū-la-bl) a. countless; numberless; enormous.—incal'culableness n.

incandescent (in-kan-des'-ent) a. glowing with white heat and providing light.—incandes'cence n. white heat.

incantation (in-kan-tā'-shun) n. magical formula recited to produce a spell.—incan'tatory a.

incapable (in-kāp'-a-bl) a. not admitting of; not susceptible of; not capable; drunk.—incapabil'ity n.

incapacitate (in-kap-as'-i-tāt) v.t. render incapable.—incapacita'tion n. act of disqualifying. — incapac'ity n. want of capacity; inability; incapability.

incarcerate (in-kár'-ser-āt) v.t. imprison.

incarnate (in-kár'-nāt) v.t. embody in flesh, esp. in human form;—a. embodied in flesh.—incarna'tion n. embodiment; that which embodies and typifies an abstraction.

incautious (in-kaw'-shus) a. not cautious; careless; indiscreet; unwary; rash.—incau'tion, incau'tiousness n.—incau'tiously adv.

incendiary (in-sen'-di-ar-i) n. one who maliciously sets fire to property; agitator who inflames passions; fire bomb;—a. pert. to malicious burning of property; tending to inflame dissension.—incen'diarism n. arson.

incense (in-sens') v.t. enrage.

incense (in'-sens) n. aromatic substance, producing sweet-smelling smoke when burnt.

incentive (in-sent'-iv) a. inciting; provoking;—n. motive; spur; stimulus; encouragement.

inception (in-sep'-shun) n. beginning; start; origin.—**incep'tive** a.

incertitude (in-ser'-ti-tūd) · n. uncertainty.

incessant (in-ses'-ant) a. continuing or following without interruption; ceaseless; constant; perpetual.—**incess'ancy** n.—**incess'antly** adv.

incest (in'-sest) n. sexual intercourse within the forbidden degrees of relationship.—**incest'uous** a.

inch (insh) n. twelfth part of linear foot; small degree or quantity;—v.i. push forward by slow degrees; edge forward.

incident (in'-si-dent) a. falling upon, as ray of light upon reflecting surface; naturally attaching to; striking; liable to happen;—n. event; occurrence; episode; subordinate action.—**in'cidence** n. occurrence; range of influence.—**incident'al** a. happening.—**incident'ally** adv. by the way.—**incident'alness** n.

incinerate (in-sin'-er-āt) v.t. consume by fire; burn to ashes.—**incinera'tion** n.—**incin'erator** n. furnace for consuming refuse.

incipient (in-sip'-i-ent) a. beginning; originating; inceptive.—**incip'ience**, **incip'iency** n.

incise (in-sīz') v.t. cut into; carve; engrave.—**incision** (in-sizh'-un) n. act of cutting with sharp instrument; cut; gash.—**inci'sive** a. sharp; acute; biting; trenchant;—**inci'sively** adv.—**inci'siveness** n.

incite (in-sīt') v.t. move mind to action; spur on.—**incitation** (in-sit-ā'-shun) n. act of inciting; that which incites.—**incite'ment** n.motive; incentive.—**incit'er** n.

incivil (in-siv'-il) a. rude; uncivil.—**incivil'ity** n. want of courtesy; rudeness; impoliteness.

inclement (in-klem'-ent) a. not clement; unmerciful; severe; harsh; rainy; stormy.—**inclem'ency** n.—**inclem'ently** adv.

incline (in-klīn') v.t. cause to deviate from line; give tendency to; bend; turn from vertical;—v.i. deviate from vertical; be disposed.—**in'cline** n. ascent or descent; slope.—**inclina'tion** n. act of inclining; leaning; tendency towards; favour for one thing more than another; desire.—**inclined'** a. bent; disposed.

inclose, inclosure See **enclose**.

include (in-klōōd') v.t. confine within; comprise.—**inclu'sion** n. state of being included or confined.—**inclu'sive** a. taking in the stated limit, number, etc.; enclosing; embracing.—**inclu'sively** adv.

incognito (in-kog'-ni-tō) a. and adv. having identity concealed.

incoherent (in-kō-hēr'-ent) a. not connected or clear (of speech); confused.—**incoher'ence** n.—**incoher'ently** adv.

incombustible (in-kom-bust'-i-bl) a. not capable of being burned.—**incombustibil'ity, incombust'ibleness** n.—**incombust'ibly** adv.

income (in'-kum) n. gain from one's work or investments; profit; interest.—**in'comer** n. newcomer to a locality.—**in'coming** n. taking possession of house, farm, etc.; revenue;—a. accruing; ensuing.—**income tax**, tax levied on income.

incommensurable (in-kom-en'-sū-ra-bl) a. having no common measure of comparison.—**incommensurabil'ity, incommen'surableness** n.—**incommen'surably** adv.—**incommen'surate** a. not admitting of common measure; unequal; out of proportion.—**incommen'surately** adv.

incommode (in-ko-mōd') v.t. inconvenience; give trouble to.—**incommo'dious** a.—**incommo'diously** adv.

incommunicable (in-ko-mūn'-i-ka-bl) a. incapable of being communicated; not transferable.—**incommunicabil'ity** n.—**incommun'icableness** n.—**incommun'icably** adv.—**incommun'icative** a. reserved; not ready to impart information.

incomparable (in-kom'-par-a-bl) a. not admitting any degree of comparison with another; unrivalled.—**incomparabil'ity** n.—**incom'parableness** n.—**incom'parably** adv.

incompatible (in-kom-pat'-i-bl) a. incapable of existing side by side; unable to live together in harmony.—**incompatibil'ity, incompat'ibleness** n.—**incompat'ibly** adv.

incompetent (in-kom'-pe-tent) a. not efficient; inadequate; incapable.—**incom'petence** n.—**incom'petency** n.—**incom'petently** adv.

incomplete (in-kom-plēt') a. defective; imperfect; unfinished.—**incomplete'ly** adv.

incomprehensible (in-kom-pre-hen'-si-bl) a. incapable of being understood.—**incomprehensibil'ity, incompre-hen'sibleness** n.—**incomprehen'sibly** adv.—**incomprehen'sive** a. limited; not extensive.

incompressible (in-kom-pres'-i-bl) a. cannot be compressed or reduced in bulk.

inconceivable (in-kon-sēv'-a-bl) a. cannot be conceived in the mind; unthinkable.—**inconceivabil'ity, inconceiv'ableness** n.—**inconceiv'ably** adv.

inconclusive (in-kon-klōōs'-iv) a. not decisive; not settling a point.

incongruous (in-kong'-grōō-us) a. having nothing in common.—**incon'-gruent** a.—**incongru'ity** n.

inconsequent (in-kon'-se-kwent) a. illogical; irrelevant; rambling.—**incon'sequence** n.—**inconsequen'tial** a. not to the point; illogical; trivial.—**inconsequen'tially** adv.

inconsiderable (in-kon-sid'-er-a-bl)

a. unworthy of consideration; unimportant.

inconsiderate (in-kon-sid'-er-āt) *a.* thoughtless; careless of others' feelings; heedless; inattentive.—**inconsid'erately** *adv.*

inconsistent (in-kon-sist'-ent) *a.* liable to sudden and unexpected change; changeable; not agreeing.—**inconsist'ence, inconsist'ency** *n.*

inconsolable (in-kon-sōl'-a-bl) *a.* not to be comforted or consoled.

inconspicuous (in-kon-spik'-ū-us) *a.* scarcely noticeable or discernible.

inconstant (in-con'-stant) *a.* not constant or consistent; subject to change.—**incon'stancy** *n.* fickleness.—**incon'stantly** *adv.*

incontestable (in-kon-test'-a-bl) *a.* not to be contested; indisputable; undeniable; unquestionable.—**incontest'ably** *adv.*

incontinent (in-kon'-ti-nent) *a.* incapable of restraint;—*adv.* immediately; at once; straightway.—**incon'tinence, incon'tinency** *n.*—**incon'tinently** *adv.*

incontrovertible (in-kon-tro-ver'-ti-bl) *a.* unquestionable; indisputable.—**incontrovert'ibly** *adv.*

inconvenient (in-kon-vēn'-yent) *a.* awkward; unsuitable. — **inconven'ience** *v.t.* put to trouble or annoyance.—**inconven'ience, inconven'iency** *n.*—**inconven'iently** *adv.*

inconvertible (in-kon-vert'-i-bl) *a.* cannot be changed or exchanged.—**inconvertibil'ity** *n.*

incorporate (in-kor'-pō-rāt) *v.t.* and *v.i.* blend, as different ingredients; give material form to; constitute into corporation; become incorporated; embody;—*a.* united; formed into incorporation.—**incorpora'tion** *n.*—**incor'porative** *a.*

incorrect (in-ko-rekt') *a.* inaccurate; erroneous; false.—**incorrect'ly** *adv.*—**incorrect'ness** *n.*

incorrigible (in-kor'-i-ji-bl) *a.* beyond hope of reform or improvement in conduct.

incorrupt (in-kor-upt') *a.* pure; undefiled; not open to bribery.—**incorrup'tible** *a.* incapable of being corrupted; not subject to decay.

increase (in-krēs') *v.t.* make greater; extend; lengthen; — *v.i.* become greater.—**in'crease** *n.* growth; produce; profit; interest; offspring; enlargement; addition.—**increas'able** *a.*—**increas'ingly** *adv.*

incredible (in-kred'-i-bl) *a.* impossible to be believed; surpassing belief; amazing.—**incredibil'ity, -'ibleness** *n.*—**incred'ibly** *adv.*

incredulous (in-kred'-ū-lus) *a.* sceptical; hard of belief.—**incredu'lity, incred'ulousness** *n.*—**incred'ulously** *adv.*

increment (in'-kre-ment) *n.* increase; matter added; growth; annual addition to salary.—**increment'al** *a.*

incriminate (in-krim'-i-nāt) *v.t.* charge with crime; involve one in criminal action.—**incrim'inatory** *a.*

incrust, encrust (in-, en-krust') *v.t.* cover with crust;—*v.i.* form hard covering or crust on surface.—**incrusta'tion** *n.*

incubate (in'-kū-bāt) *v.i.* sit, as on eggs, for hatching; brood; of disease germs, pass through the stage between infection and appearance of symptoms;—*v.t.* hatch; ponder over.—**incuba'tion** *n.*—**in'cubator** *n.* cabinet, in which heat is automatically regulated, used to hatch eggs.

inculcate (in'-kul-kāt) *v.t.* (foll. by *in* or *on*) instil; implant.—**inculca'tion** *n.*—**in'culcator** *n.*

incumbent (in-kum'-bent) *a.* lying or resting upon; obligatory, as duty;—*n.* holder of ecclesiastical benefice.—**incum'bency** *n.* office or tenure of incumbent.

incur (in-kur') *v.t.* become liable to; bring upon oneself.—*pr.p.* incurr'ing.—*pa.t.* and *pa.p.* incurred'.

incurable (in-kūr'-a-bl) *a.* not able to be cured;—*n.* one beyond cure.—**incur'ableness, incurabil'ity** *n.*

incurious (in-kū'-ri-us) *a.* not inquisitive or curious; indifferent.—**incu'riously** *adv.*—**incu'riousness, incurios'ity** *n.*

incursion (in-kur'-shun) *n.* raid with hostile intention; attack.—**incur'sive** *a.*

incurve (in-kurv') *v.t.* curve inward;—*v.i.* bend inward.—**incur'vate** *v.t.* bend inward or upward;—*a.* curved inward or upward.

indebted (in-det'-ed) *a.* in debt; under an obligation; owing; grateful.—**indebt'edness** *n.*

indecent (in-dē'-sent) *a.* unbecoming; immodest; obscene.—**inde'cency** *n.* lack of decency.—**inde'cently** *adv.*

indecipherable (in-de-sī'-fer-a-bl) *a.* incapable of being deciphered; illegible.

indecision (in-de-sizh'-un) *n.* want of decision; irresoluteness; hesitancy.—**indeci'sive** *a.*—**indeci'sively** *adv.*—**indeci'siveness** *n.*

indecorous (in-de-kōr'-us, in-dek'-o-rus) *a.* unbecoming; contrary to good manners.—**indeco'rously** *adv.*—**indeco'rousness, indeco'rum** *n.*

indeed (in-dēd') *adv.* in reality; in truth; in fact; certainly.

indefatigable (in-de-fat'-i-ga-bl) *a.* incapable of being fatigued; untiring. — **indefat'igableness, indefatigabil'ity** *n.*—**indefat'igably** *adv.*

indefeasible (in-de-fēz'-i-bl) *a.* irrevocable; inalienable.—**indefeasibil'ity** *n.*—**indefeas'ibly** *adv.*

indefensible (in-de-fens'-i-bl) *a.* incapable of being justified; untenable; inexcusable.

indefinable (in-de-fīn'-a-bl) *a.* not

able to be defined.—**inde fin'ably** *adv.*

indefinite (in-def'-i-nit) *a.* having no known limits; (*Gram.*) not pointing out the person, thing, or time to which a part of speech refers.—**indef'initely** *adv.*—**indef'initeness** *n.* want of precision.—**indefinite article,** a, an.

indelible (in-del'-i-bl) *a.* not to be blotted out or erased; ineffaceable; ingrained.—**indelibil'ity, indel'ibleness** *n.*—**indel'ibly** *adv.*

indelicate (in-del'-i-kāt) *a.* offensive to purity of mind; indecorous.—**indel'icacy** *n.*—**indel'icately** *adv.*

indemnify (in-dem'-ni-fī) *v.t.* reimburse; give security against; free one from liability;—*pa.t.* and *pa.p.* **indem'nified.**—**indemnifica'tion** *n.*—**indem'nitor** *n.*—**indem'nity** *n.* agreement to render person immune from liability; compensation.

indemonstrable (in-de-mon'-stra-bl) *a.* cannot be demonstrated or proved.

indent (in-dent') *v.t.* cut into points; make notches or holes in; make an order (*upon* some one *for*); make duplicate copies of document; indenture; (*Print.*) begin first line of paragraph farther away from margin than remaining lines;—*v.i.* bargain. —**in'dent** *n.* cut or notch; dent; mark, as of tooth; official order for goods to be supplied.—**indenta'tion** *n.* hollow; depression.—**inden'ture** *n.* contract of apprenticeship; written agreement between two or more persons;—*v.t.* bind by indentures.

independent (in-de-pend'-ent) *a.* not subject to the control of others; unrelated; free; irrespective of.—**independ'ence, independ'ency** *n.*—**independ'ently** *adv.*

indescribable (in-de-skrīb'-a-bl) *a.* incapable of being described.

indestructible (in-de-struk'-ti-bl) *a.* not destroyable; imperishable.—**indestructibil'ity** *n.*—**indestruc'tibly** *adv.*

indeterminable (in-de-ter'-min-a-bl) *a.* cannot be determined, classified, or fixed.—**indeter'minableness** *n.*—**indeter'minably** *adv.*—**indeter'minate** *a.* not fixed in detail; indefinite.—**indeter'minately** *adv.*—**indeter'minateness, indetermina'tion** *n.*

index (in'-deks) *n.* directing sign; that which points out, esp. pointer or hand, which directs to anything; reference table in book; forefinger or pointing finger; ratio between measurement of given substance and that of fixed standard.—*pl.* **in'dexes.** —(*Math.*) figure or letter showing the power of a quantity; exponent of a power.—*pl.* **in'dices.**—*v.t.* provide with table of references; place in alphabetical order in index.—**in'dexer** *n.*

Indian (in'-di-an) *a.* pert. to India in

Asia, to East Indies, or to aborigines of America;—*n.* native of India, or one of the aboriginal inhabitants of America or West Indies.—**Indian summer,** period in autumn characterised by calms and no rain.—**Red Indian,** one of aboriginal races of New World.

indicate (in'-di-kāt) *v.t.* point out; be sign of; denote; show.—**indica'tion** *n.* mark; token; sign.—**indic'ative** *a.* pointing out; denoting.—**indic'atively** *adv.*—**in'dicator** *n.*—**in'dicatory** *a.*

indices (in'-di-ses) *n.pl.* (*Math.*) See index.

indict (in-dīt') *v.t.* charge with crime; accuse; summon for trial.—**indict'able** *a.*—**indict'ment** *n.* formal charge of crime.

indifferent (in-dif'-er-ent) *a.* without influence or weight; of no account; uninterested; careless; neither good nor bad.—**indiff'erence** *n.* freedom from prejudice or bias; unconcern. —**indiff'erently** *adv.*

indigenous (in-dij'-e-nus) *a.* born in a country; native.—**indig'enously** *adv.*

indigent (in'-di-jent) *a.* destitute of means of subsistence; needy; poor. —**in'digence** *n.*

indigested (in-di-jest'-ed) *a.* not digested; lacking order or system.—**indigestibil'ity** *n.*—**indigest'ible** *a.*—**indigest'ibly** *adv.*—**indigest'ion** *n.* inability to digest food or pain in doing so; dyspepsia.—**indigest'ive** *a.*

indignant (in-dig'-nant) *a.* moved by feeling of wrath, mingled with scorn or contempt.—**indig'nantly** *adv.*—**indigna'tion** *n.* righteous wrath.—**indig'nity** *n.* affront.

indigo (in'-di-gō) *n.* blue dye obtained from many plants, but also synthesised from naphthalene; —*a.* of deep-blue colour.

indirect (in-di-rekt') *a.* not direct; oblique; unfair; dishonest.—**indirec'tion** *n.* attempt to mislead; trickery. —**indirect'ly** *adv.*—**indirect'ness** *n.*

indiscernible (in-dis-ern'-i-bl) *a.* invisible; imperceptible.

indiscreet (in-dis-krēt') *a.* imprudent. — **indiscreet'ly** *adv.* — **indiscretion** (in-dis-kresh'-un) *n.* indiscreet act; rashness; mistake.

indiscriminate (in-dis-krim'-i-nāt) *a.* wanting discrimination.—**indiscrim'inately** *adv.*—**indiscrim'inating, indiscrim'inative** *a.*—**indiscrimina'tion** *n.*

indispensable (in-dis-pen'-sa-bl) *a.* absolutely necessary; not to be set aside. — **indispensabil'ity, indispens'ableness** *n.*—**indispens'ably** *adv.*

indispose (in-dis-pōz') *v.t.* render unfit; make slightly ill; render disinclined (toward).—**indisposed'** *a.* averse; not well; ill.—**indisposi'tion** *n.*

indisputable (in-dis'-pū-ta-bl) *a.* too obvious to be disputed; incontestable.

indissoluble (in-dis-ol'-ū-bl) *a.* not capable of being dissolved; perpetually binding or obligatory; inviolable.—**indiss'olubleness, indissolubil'ity** *n.*—**indiss'olubly** *adv.*

indistinct (in-dis-tingkt') *a.* not clearly defined or uttered; obscure; dim.—**indistinct'ive** *a.* not capable of making distinctions; not distinctive. —**indistinct'ly** *adv.*

indistinguishable (in-dis-ting'-gwish-ạ-bl) *a.* may not be distinguished. — **indistin'guishableness** *n.*—**indistin'guishably** *adv.*

indite (in-dīt') *v.t.* dictate what is to be uttered or written; compose; write.—**indite'ment** *n.*

individual (in-di-vid'-ū-ạl) *a.* not divided; single; peculiar to single person or thing; distinctive;—*n.* single being, animal, or thing.—**individualisa'tion** *n.*—**individ'ualise, individ'uate** *v.t.* particularise.—**individ'ualism** *n.*—**individ'ualist** *n.*—**individualist'ic** *a.*—**individual'ity** *n.* separate or distinct existence; personality.—**individ'ually** *adv.*

indivisible (in-di-viz'-i-bl) *a.* not divisible; not separable into parts; —*n.* infinitely small quantity.—**indivisibil'ity, indivis'ibleness** *n.*—**indivis'ibly** *adv.*

indoctrinate (in-dok'-trin-āt) *v.t.* teach; imbue with political or religious principles and dogmas.—**indoctrina'tion** *n.*

indolent (in'-do-lent) *a.* habitually lazy; indisposed to exertion.—**in'dolence, in'dolency** *n.* laziness.—**in'dolently** *adv.*

indomitable (in-dom'-it-ạ-bl) *a.* that cannot be overcome; unconquerable. —**indom'itably** *adv.*

Indonesia (in-do-nē'-zi-ạ) *n.* republic of S.E. Asia.—**Indone'sian** *a.* and *n.*

indoor (in'-dōr) *a.* being within doors; under cover; pert. to house affairs.—**in'doors** *adv.*

indubitable (in-dū'-bit-ạ-bl) *a.* undoubted; certain.—**indu'bitably** *adv.*

induce (in-dūs') *v.t.* bring in; persuade; produce or cause (as electricity).—**induce'ment** *n.* that which induces or persuades to action.—**induc'er** *n.*—**induc'ible** *a.*

induct (in-dukt') *v.t.* bring in or introduce; install or put formally into office.—**induc'tion** *n.* installation of person in benefice, charge or office; reasoning from the particular to the general; (*Elect.*) transfer of magnetic or electric state from electrified to non-electrified body, by proximity.—**induc'tional**.—**induc'tive** *a.* leading or drawing on.—**induc'tively** *adv.*—**induc'tor** *n.*

indulge (in-dulj') *v.t.* give freedom to; allow one his own way;—*v.i.* (usu. followed by *in*) give oneself to habit or practice of.—**indul'gence** *n.*

act of indulging; favour granted; remission of temporal penalty due for sin.—**indul'gent** *a.* compliant; very forbearing; liberal; tender.—**indul'gently** *adv.*

industry (in'-dus-tri) *n.* habitual diligence; steady application to work; assiduity; particular branch of trade or manufacture.—**indus'trial** *a.* pert. to industry or manufacture.—**indus'trialism** *n.* system of large-scale industry or manufacture.—**indus'trially** *adv.*—**indus'trious** *a.* diligent; assiduous, busy.—**indus'triously** *adv.*—**indus'triousness** *n.*

inebriate (in-ē'-bri-āt) *v.t.* make drunk; intoxicate; exhilarate;—*n.* habitual drunkard.—**inebria'tion, inebri'ety** *n.* drunkenness.—**ine'brious** *a.* stupidly drunk.

inedible (in-ed'-i-bl) *a.* not eatable; unfit for food.—**inedibil'ity** *n.*

ineffable (in-ef'-ạ-bl) *a.* incapable of being expressed in words; indescribable; unutterable.—**ineff'ableness, ineffabil'ity** *n.*—**ineff'ably** *adv.*

ineffaceable (in-e-fās'-ạ-bl) *a.* incapable of being rubbed out.—**ineffac'eably** *adv.*

ineffective (in-e-fek'-tiv) *a.* incapable of producing effect intended; useless; inefficient.— **ineffec'tively** *adv.* — **ineffec'tual** *a.* vain; fruitless; futile.—**ineffectual'ity, ineffec'tualness** *n.*—**ineffec'tually** *adv.*

inefficacy (in-ef'-i-kạ-si) *n.* want of power to produce proper effect.—**inefficca'cious** *a.*

inefficient (in-e-fish'-ent) *a.* not fitted to perform work; not capable; incompetent. — **ineffic'iency** *n.* — **ineffic'iently** *adv.*

inelastic (in-e-las'-tik) *a.* not elastic; rigid; unyielding.—**inelastic'ity** *n.*

inelegant (in-el'-e-gant) *a.* lacking in form or beauty; wanting grace or ornament.—**inel'egance, inel'egancy** *n.*—**inel'egantly** *adv.*

ineligible (in-el'-i-jibl) *a.* incapable of being chosen for or elected to office; unsuitable.—**ineligibil'ity** *n.*—**inel'igibly** *adv.*

ineluctable (in-e-luk'-tạ-bl) *a.* not able to be avoided; inevitable.—**ineluctabil'ity** *n.*

inept (in-ept') *a.* not apt; unsuitable; foolish.—**inept'itude** *n.*—**inept'ly** *adv.*

inequable (in-ē', or -e-kwạ-bl) *a.* not equable; not uniform; unfairly distributed.

inequality (in-ē-kwol'-i-ti) *n.* want of equality; disparity; dissimilarity; unevenness.

inequitable (in-ek'-wi-tạ-bl) *a.* not fair or just.

ineradicable (in-e-rad'-i-k -bl) *a.* incapable of being rooted out; deep-seated.

inert (in-ẹrt') *a.* without power of action or resistance; torpid; slow;

dull; lifeless; without active chemical properties.—**inertia** (in-ẽr'-shi-ạ) n. that property of matter by which it tends when at rest to remain so, and when in a motion to continue moving in a straight line.—**inert'ly** adv.—**inert'ness** n.

inescapable (in-es-kā'-pạ-bl) a. inevitable.

inessential (in-es-en'-shạl) a. not necessary; immaterial; not vital; of little consequence.

inestimable (in-es'-tim-ạbl) a. priceless; of untold value; invaluable.—**ines'timably** adv.

inevitable (in-ev'-it-ạ-bl) a. unavoidable; inescapable.—**inev'itability** n.—**inev'itably** adv.

inexact (in-eg-zakt') a. not exact; not strictly true.—**inexact'itude**, **inexact'ness** n.

inexcusable (in-eks-kū'-zạ-bl) a. not admitting excuse; unpardonable.—**inexcus'ably** adv.

inexhaustible (in-eg-zaws'-ti-bl) a. incapable of being exhausted; unfailing. — **inexhaustibil'ity** n. — **inexhaust'ibly** adv.—**inexhaus'tive** a. unfailing; cursory.

inexorable (in-egz'-or-ạ-bl) a. not to be persuaded or moved by entreaty; unyielding.—**inex'orableness**, **inexorabil'ity** n.—**inex'orably** adv.

inexpedient (in-eks-pē'-di-ent) a. not advisable; impolitic; undesirable at the moment.—**inexpe'dience**, **inexpe'diency** n.

inexpensive (in-eks-pens'-iv) a. cheap.

inexperience (in-eks-pē'-ri-ens) n. absence or want of experience.—**inexpe'rienced** a.

inexpert (in-eks-pẽrt') a. unskilled; clumsy; awkward.—**inexpert'ness** n.

inexplicable (in-eks'-pli-kạ-bl) a. incapable of being explained; unintelligible.—**inexplicabil'ity**, **inex'plicableness** n.—**inex'plicably** adv.

inexplicit (in-eks-plis'-it) a. not explicit; not clearly stated; ambiguous; equivocal.

inexpressible (in-eks-pres'-i-bl) a. cannot be expressed; indescribable.—**inexpress'ibly** adv.

inextinguishable (in-eks-ting'-gwish-ạ-bl) a. cannot be extinguished; unquenchable.

inextricable (in-eks'-tri-kạ-bl) a. not to be disentangled; incapable of being cleared up or explained.—**inex'tricably** adv.

infallible (in-fal'-i-bl) a. incapable of error; unerring; sure.—**infall'ibilism**, **infallibil'ity** n.—**infall'ibly** adv.

infamy (in'-fạ-mi) n. total loss of reputation; public disgrace; ill-fame.—**in'famous** a. of evil fame or reputation.—**in'famously** adv.

infant (in'-fạnt) n. young baby; (Law) person under 21;—a. pert. to infants or infancy.—**in'fancy** n.—**infant'icide** n. killing of newly-born child.—**in'fantile** a. pert. to infants; extremely childish.—**infantile paralysis**, infectious disease, poliomyelitis.

infanta (in-fan'-ta) n. princess of former Spanish or Portuguese royal families. — **infante** (in-fan'-tā) n. Spanish prince, other than heir.

infantry (in'-fạn-tri) n. foot-soldiers.

infatuate (in-fat'-ū-āt) v.t. inspire with foolish passion.—**infat'uated** a. greatly enamoured.—**infatua'tion** n. excessive and foolish love.

infect (in-fekt') v.t. affect (with disease); taint; influence emotions.—**infec'tion** n.—**infec'tious**, **infec'tive** a. causing infection; catching.—**infec'tiously** adv.

infelicity (in-fe-lis'-i-ti) n. unhappiness; anything not appropriate.—**infelic'itous** a.

infer (in-fẽr') v.t. draw as conclusion; deduce; conclude.—pr.p. **infer'ring**.—pa.t. and pa.p. **inferred**.—**infer'able** a.—**in'ference** n. deduction.—**inferen'tial** a. deduced or deducible by inference.—**inferen'tially** adv.

inferior (in-fē'-ri-or) a. lower in rank, order, etc.; of less value; poorer in quality;—n. person of lower rank.—**inferior'ity** n.—**infe'riorly** adv.—**inferiority complex**, in psycho-analysis, sub-conscious sense of inferiority which results in exaggerated self-assertion.

infernal (in-fẽr'-nal) a. pert. to lower regions; hellish.—**infernal'ity** n.—**infer'nally** adv.—**infer'no** n. hell; place resembling hell; furnace.—**infernal machine**, time bomb.

infertile (in-fẽr'-tīl) a. not fertile or productive; barren.—**infertil'ity** n.

infest (in-fest') v.t. haunt; swarm in numbers.—**infest'ed** a. covered with body parasites as lice, etc.; plagued.

infidel (in'-fi-del) a. unbelieving; sceptical;—n. one without religious faith; unbeliever; non-Christian; Mohammedan.—**infidel'ity** n. disbelief of Christianity; unfaithfulness to marriage contract; treachery.

infilter (in-fil'-tẽr) v.t. and i. filter in.—**infil'trate** v.i. enter gradually; pass through enemy's lines, one by one.

infinite (in'-fi-nit) a. unlimited in time or space; without end; (Math.) greater than any assignable quantity; immeasurable;—n. boundless-ness of universe; the Almighty.—**in'finitely** adv. exceedingly.—**in'finiteness** n.—**infinites'imal** a. infinitely small.—**infinites'imally** adv.—**infin'ity** n. unlimited and endless extent.

infinitive (in-fin'-it-iv) a. unlimited; designating mood of verb expressing action without limitation of persons or numbers.

infirm (in-fẽrm') a. not strong;

weak; disabled.—in firm'ary *n.* hospital.—in firm'ity, disease; failing.—infirm'ly *adv.*

inflame (in-flām') *v.t.* set on fire; arouse, as desire; provoke; be affected with inflammation.—in flam'mable *a.* catching fire easily.—inflammabil'ity *n.* quality of being inflammable.—in flam'mably *adv.*—inflamma'tion *n.* inflaming; in any part of the body heat, redness and pain.—in flam'matory *a.* ready to burst into flame; hot-tempered; rabble-rousing.

inflate (in-flāt') *v.t.* swell with air or gas; raise (price) artificially; increase (currency) abnormally.—inflat'ed *a.* swollen; bombastic.—in flat'ingly *adv.*—in fla'tion *n.* swelling; increase in amount of paper money issued.—in fla'tor, in fla'ter *n.*

inflect (in-flekt') *v.t.* bend inwards; modulate voice.—in flec'tion, in flex'ion *n.* bending inwards; variation in tone of voice; variation in terminations of words to express grammatical relations.—in flec'tional, in flex'ional *a.*—in flective *a.*—inflexibil'ity, in flex'ibleness *n.*—in flex'ible *a.* incapable of being bent; unyielding to influence or entreaty. in flex'ibly *adv.*

inflict (in-flikt') *v.t.* lay on; impose (a penalty, etc.); afflict with something painful.—in flic'tion *n.* burden.—in flic'tive *a.*

influence (in'-flŏŏ-ens) *n.* power over men or things; effect on mind;—*v.t.* act on mind; sway; induce.—influen'tial *a.* exerting influence; possessing great authority.—in fluen'tially *adv.*

influenza (in-flŏŏ-en'-za) *n.* (*Med.*) acute, viral, infectious, epidemic, catarrhal fever.

influx (in'-fluks) *n.* act of flowing in; arrival of many strangers in place; infusion.

infold, enfold (in-, en-fold') *v.t.* wrap up; enclose; encircle.

inform (in-form') *v.t.* make known to; tell;—*v.i.* give information.—inform'al *a.* without formality, unceremonious.—informal'ity *n.*—inform'ant *n.* one who imparts news.—informa'tion *n.* knowledge; news.—infor'mative *a.*—infor'matory *a.* full of information.—informed' *a.* educated.—inform'er *n.* one who gives information.

infraction (in-frak'-shun) *n.* breach; violation.

infrangible (in-fran'-ji-bl) *a.* not capable of being broken or violated.—infrangibil'ity *n.*

infra-red (in'-fra-red) *a.* pert. to invisible rays below red end of the spectrum.

infrequent (in-frē'-kwent) *a.* rare.—infre'quence, infre'quency *n.*—infrequently *adv.*

infringe (in-frinj') *v.t.* transgress.—

infringe'ment *n.* breach; breaking (of law).

infuriate (in-fū'-ri-āt) *v.t.* render furious; enrage; madden.

infuse (in-fūz') *v.t.* pour into; instil; inspire; steep in order to extract soluble properties.—infus'ible *a.* capable of being infused; not capable of fusion.—infusibil'ity *n.*—infu'sion *n.*

ingathering (in'-gaTH-er-ing) *n.* harvesting.

ingenious (in-jēn'-yus) *a.* skilled in invention; clever in design; skilfully contrived.—inge'niously *adv.*—inge'niousness, ingenu'ity *n.*

ingenuous (in-jen'-ū-us) *a.* frank, candid, artless, innocent.—ingen'uously *adv.*—ingen'uousness *n.*

ingle (ing'-gl) *n.* fire or fireplace.

inglorious (in-glō'-ri-us) *a.* without glory or honour; ignominious; disgraceful; shameful.—inglo'riously *adv.*—inglo'riousness *n.*

ingot (in'-got) *n.* metal casting, esp. of unwrought silver or gold.

ingrain, engrain (in-, en-grān') *v.t.* dye deeply; fix firmly in mind.—ingrain' *a.* dyed, before manufacture, into articles.—ingrained' *a.* deeply rooted.

ingrate (in'-grāt) *a.* ungrateful;—*n.* ungrateful person.—ingrat'itude *n.* want of gratitude; unthankfulness.

ingratiate (in-grā'-shi-āt) *v.t.* work oneself into favour with another.

ingredient (in-grēd'-yent) *n.* component part of any mixture.

ingress (in'-gres) *n.* entrance.

ingrowing (in'-grō-ing) *a.* growing inwards, esp. of toe-nail.—in'growth *n.*—in'grown *a.*

ingurgitate (in-gur'-ji-tāt) *v.t.* swallow hastily.—ingurgita'tion *n.*

inhabit (in-hab'-it) *v.t.* live or dwell in; occupy.—inhab'itable *a.* possible to be dwelt in.—inhab'itant *n.* one who inhabits; resident;—*a.* resident.—inhab'iter *n.*

inhale (in-hāl') *v.t.* breathe in, as air, draw into the lungs.—inhal'ant *n.* volatile medicine to be inhaled.—inhal'ant, inha'lent *a.*—inhala'tion *n.*

inhere (in-hēr') *v.i.* (usu. followed by *in*) exist in; belong naturally to; be a quality of; be vested in, as legal rights.—inher'ence, inher'ency *n.*—inher'ent *a.* existing in as an essential element.—inher'ently *adv.*

inherit (in-her'-it) *v.t.* receive by descent, or by will; fall heir to; derive (traits, etc.) from parents;—*v.i.* succeed as heir.—inher'itable *a.* heritable.—inher'itance *n.* what is inherited.—inher'itor *n.* (*fem.* inher'itress, inher'itrix).

inhibit (in-hib'-it) *v.t.* hold back; forbid; restrain.—inhibi'tion *n.* subconscious repressed emotion which controls person's behaviour.—inhib'itory *a.* prohibiting; restraining.

inhospitable (in-hos'-pi-ta-bl) *a.* averse to showing kindness to strangers or guests; discourteous.— **inhos'pitableness, inhospital'ity** *n.*— **inhos'pitably** *adv.*

inhuman (in-hū'-man) *a.* not human or humane; without feeling or pity. —**inhumane'** *a.* cruel.—**inhuman'ity** *n.*

inimical (in-im'-i-kal) *a.* like enemy; unfriendly.—**inim'ically** *adv.*

inimitable (in-im'-i-ta-bl) *a.* defying imitation; unique; incomparable.— **inim'itably** *adv.*

iniquity (in-ik'-wi-ti) *n.* gross injustice; wickedness.—**iniq'uitous** *a.*— **iniq'uitously** *adv.*

initial (i-nish'-al) *a.* occurring at beginning; commencing; early;— *v.t.* put one's initials to.—*pr.p.* **init'ialling.**—*pa.t.* and *pa.p.* **init'ialled.** —*n.* first letter of word, esp. name. —**init'iate,** *v.t.* begin; start (a movement, etc.); instruct in the rudiments of;—*n.* one who is initiated.— **initia'tion** *n.* act of introducing to or instructing in rudiments of.—**init'iative** *a.* serving to initiate;—*n.* first step; quality of showing enterprise. —**init'iator** *n.*—**init'iatory** *a.*

inject (in-jekt') *v.t.* throw in; force in; introduce (a fluid) under the skin by means of syringe.—**injec'tion** *n.* act of injecting; medicament so injected.—**injec'tor** *n.*

injudicious (in-jóó-dish'-us) *a.* illadvised; imprudent; lacking in judgment.—**injudic'iously** *adv.*— **injudic'iousness** *n.*

injunction (in-jungk'-shun) *n.* order or command; exhortation; precept.

injure (in'-jer) *v.t.* do wrong, injury, damage, or injustice to.—**inju'rious** *a.* causing injury or damage.— **inju'riously** *adv.*—**in'jury** *n.* wrong; damage; harm.

injustice (in-jus'-tis) *n.* unjust act; want of justice; unkindness; wrong.

ink (ingk) *n.* fluid, black or coloured, used for writing, printing and sketching;—*v.t.* cover or smear with ink.—**ink'iness** *n.*—**ink'y** *a.* resembling ink.

inkling (ink'-ling) *n.* hint or whisper; slight knowledge.

inland (in'-land) *a.* remote from sea; interior; carried on within a country; —*n.* interior part of country.— **inland revenue,** national income derived from taxes and duties.

in-laws (in-lawz') *n.pl.* (*Colloq.*) one's relations by marriage.

inlay (in-lā') *v.t.* ornament, by cutting out part of surface and inserting pieces of pearl, ivory, wood, etc., to form pattern.—*pa.p.* **inlaid'.**—*n.* inlaid pattern.

inlet (in'-let) *n.* entrance; small bay or creek; insertion.

inly (in'-li) *adv.* internally; inwardly; secretly.

inmate (in'-māt) *n.* dweller in house or institution; fellow-lodger.

inn (in) *n.* house which provides lodging accommodation for travellers; hotel.—**inn'-keeper** *n.* one who keeps an inn.—**Inns of Court,** four societies which possess exclusive right to call candidates to Bar.

innate (i-nāt') *a.* inborn; native; natural; inherent.—**innate'ly** *adv.*— **innateness** *n.*

inner (in'-er) *a.* farther in; interior; internal;—*n.* part of target next to bull's-eye or centre.—**in'most, inn'er-most,** *a.* farthest in.

innings (in'-ingz) *n.pl.* in games, a side's turn of batting.

innocent (in'-o-sent) *a.* free from guilt; blameless; sinless; simple;— *n.* guileless, unsuspecting person.— **inn'ocence, inn'ocency** *n.* freedom from guilt.—**inn'ocently** *adv.*

innocuous (in-ok'-ū-us) *a.* producing no ill effects.—**innoc'uously** *adv.*— **innoc'uousness** *n.*

innovate (in'-o-vāt) *v.t.* make changes by introducing something new.— **innova'tion** *n.*

innuendo (in-ū-en'-dō) *n.* allusive remark or hint (usually deprecatory); insinuation.

innumerable (i-nū'-mer-a-bl) *a.* not able to be numbered; countless.— **innumerabil'ity** *n.*—**innu'merableness** *n.*

inobservant (in-ob-zer'-vant) *a.* not observant.

inoculate (in-ok'-ū-lāt) *v.t.* insert, as bud of plant, in another plant for propagation; (*Med.*) introduce into the body pathogenic bacteria or living virus by means of hypodermic syringe; imbue strongly with opinions.—**inocula'tion** *n.*

inoffensive (in-o-fen'-siv) *a.* giving no offence.—**inoffen'sively** *adv.*—**inoffen'siveness** *n.*

inoperable (in-op'-er-abl) *a.* (*Surgery*) not able to be operated upon.— **inop'erative** *a.* not operating or in working order.

inopportune (in-op'(or-tūn) *a.* not convenient; untimely.—**inopportune'ly** *adv.*—**inopportun'ity** *n.*

inordinate (in-or'-di-nāt) *a.* excessive.—**inor'dinately** *adv.*

inorganic, inorganical (in-or-gan'-ik, -i-al) *a.* devoid of organised structure; not derived from animal or vegetable life.—**inorgan'ically** *adv.*

input (in'-póót) *n.* (*Elect.*) power supplied to battery, condenser, etc.; contribution.

inquest (in'-kwest) *n.* investigation; judicial inquiry presided over by coroner, with or without jury, into cause of person's death.

inquietude (in-kwī'-e-tūd) *n.* uneasiness either of body or of mind; restlessness.

inquire, enquire (in-, en-kwīr') *v.t.*

ask questions; make investigation; seek information;—*v.t.* ask about.— **inquir'er, enquir'er** *n.*—**inquir'ing** *a.* prying.—**inquir'ingly** *adv.*—**inquir'y, enquir'y** *n.* investigation; question.

inquisition (in-kwi-zish'-un) *n.* strict investigation; official inquiry; ecclesiastical tribunal.—**inquisi'tional** *a.*— **inquis'itive** *a.* apt to ask questions; curious to know.—**inquis'itively** *adv.* —**inquis'itiveness** *n.*—**inquis'itor** *n.* one whose official duty it is to make inquiries.—**inquisito'rial** *a.*—**inquisito'rially** *adv.*

inroad (in'-rōd) *n.* sudden incursion into enemy territory; sudden invasion; raid.

insalubrious (in-sa-lū'-bri-us) *a.* unhealthy; unwholesome.

insane (in-sān') *a.* unsound in mind. —**insane'ly** *adv.*—**insane'ness, insan'ity** *n.* lunacy; madness.

insanitary (in-san'-i-tar-i) *a.* unhealthy; unhygenic.

insatiable (in-sā'-sha-bl) *a.* not able to be satisfied; voracious.—**insa'tiableness, insatiabil'ity** *n.*—**insa'tiably** *adv.*

insatiate (in-sā'-shi-āt) *a.* not to be satisfied.—**insa'tiately** *adv.*—**insati'ety** (in-sa-tī'-et-i) *n.*

inscribe (in-skrīb') *v.t.* write upon; engrave; dedicate.—**inscrib'able** *a.*— **inscrib'er** *n.*—**inscrip'tion** *n.* writing upon; words inscribed on monument, coin, etc.; dedication of a book, etc.; title.

inscrutable (in-skróó'-ta-bl) *a.* not able to be searched into and understood; mysterious. — **inscrutabil'ity, inscrut'ableness** *n.*—**inscru'tably** *adv.*

insect (in'-sekt) *n.* invertebrate having body divided into three parts, head, thorax and abdomen, and with three pairs of jointed legs; —*a.* pert. to insects; small; insignificant.—**insec'ticide** *n.* killing insect pests by spraying, dusting, etc.; chemical preparation for killing insects.—**insectiv'orous** *a.* living on insects.

insecure (in-se-kūr') *a.* not securely fixed; unsafe.—**insecur'ity** *n.*

inseminate (in-sem'-i-nāt) *v.t.* sow; impregnate.—**insemina'tion** *n.* approach of spermatozoon to ovum; conception.

insensate (in-sen'-sāt) *a.* void of sense; stupid.—**insen'sately** *adv.*— **insen'sateness** *n.*

insensible (in-sen'-si-bl) *a.* not perceived by senses; unconscious.— **insensibil'ity, insen'sibleness** *n.*—**insen'sibly** *adv.*

insensitive (in-sen'-si-tiv) *a.* not sensitive; callous.—**insensitiv'ity, insen'sitiveness** *n.*

inseparable (in-sep'-a-ra-bl) *a.* not separable; always together;—*n.pl.* persons or things seldom seen apart.—**insep'arably** *adv.*

insert (in-sert') *v.t.* put in; place among.—in'sert *n.* anything inserted. —**inser'tion** *n.*

inset (in'-set) *n.* something set in; insertion.—**inset'** *v.t.* set in; insert.

inshore (in'-shōr) *a.* near to shore;— *adv.* in towards shore.

inside (in'-sīd) *prep.* or *adv.* within sides of; in the interior;—*a.* internal; interior;—*n.* part within; stomach; —*pl.* inward parts; guts.

insidious (in-sid'-i-us) *a.* advancing imperceptibly.—**insid'iously** *adv.*—**insid'iousness** *n.*

insight (in'-sīt) *n.* mental penetration; clear understanding; power of discernment.

insignia (in-sig'-ni-a) *n.pl.* symbols of authority, dignity, or office.

insignificant (in-sig-nif'-i-kant) *a.* having little importance, use, or value; trifling.—**insignif'icance, insignif'icancy** *n.*—**insignif'icantly** *adv.*

insincere (in-sin-sēr') *a.* not sincere. —**insincere'ly** *adv.*—**insincer'ity** *n.*

insinuate (in-sin'-ū-āt) *v.t.* introduce gently and adroitly; suggest by remote allusion;—*v.i.* ingratiate (oneself).—**insin'uating** *a.*—**insin'uatingly** *adv.*—**insinua'tion** *n.* gaining favour by artful means; hint; suggestion (*usu.* deprecatory).—**insin'uative** *a.*—**insin'uator** *n.*—**insin'uatory** *a.*

insipid (in-sip'id) *a.* tasteless; deficient in spirit, life, or animation.— **insip'idly** *adv.*—**insip'idness, insipid'ity** *n.* want of taste.

insist (in-sist') *v.i.* be urgent or pressing; (foll. by *on* or *upon*) to hold firmly to.—**insist'ence** *n.* refusal to give way.—**insist'ency** *n.* pertinacity. —**insist'ent** *a.*

insobriety (in-sō-brī'-et-i) *n.* drunkenness.

insole (in'-sōl) *n.* inner sole of boot or shoe.

insolent (in'-so-lent) *a.* proud and haughty; overbearing.—**in'solence** *n.* contemptuous rudeness or arrogance.—**in'solently** *adv.*

insoluble (in-sol'-ū-bl) *a.* incapable of being dissolved; inexplicable; not to be explained.—**insolubil'ity, insol'ubleness** *n.*—**insol'vable** *a.*

insolvent (in-solv'-ent) *a.* not able to pay one's debts; bankrupt;—*n.* bankrupt.—**insolv'ency** *n.*

insomnia (in-som'-ni-a) *n.* sleeplessness.—**insom'niac** *n.*

insomuch (in-sō-much') *adv.* so that; to such degree; in so far.

inspect (in-spekt') *v.t.* view narrowly and critically; examine officially as troops.—**inspec'tion** *n.* careful survey; official examination.—**inspec'tor** *n.* official examiner; police officer above sergeant; person appointed to inspect schools.—**inspec'torate** *n.* district under inspector; body of inspectors.—**inspecto'rial** *a.*

inspire (in-spīr') *v.t.* breathe into; infuse thought into; affect with influence; arouse;—*v.i.* draw air into lungs; inhale.—**inspir'able** *a.*—**inspira'tion** *n.* drawing in the breath; communication of ideas from supernatural source; bright idea.—**inspira'tional** *a.*—**inspir'atory** *a.* encouraging.—**inspired'** *a.* actuated by Divine influence.

instability (in-stą-bil'-i-ti) *n.* want of stability.

install, instal (in-stawl') *v.t.* place in position; induct, with ceremony, person to office of dignity.—**installa'tion** *n.* complete equipment of building for heating, lighting, etc.; generally, placing in position for use.—**instal'ment** *n.* periodical payment of part-cost of something; portion.

instance (in'-stans) *n.* urgency; case in point; example; illustration; occasion;—*v.t.* mention as example.—**in'stant** *a.* urgent; pressing; belonging to current month (usu. abbreviated to inst.);—*n.* moment.—**instantane'ity** *n.*—**instantan'eous** *a.* done in an instant; happening in a moment.—**instantan'eously** *adv.*—**instantan'eousness** *n.*—**in'stantly** *adv.* at once.

instead (in-sted') *adv.* in place of.

instep (in'-step) *n.* arched upper part of foot, near ankle.

instigate (in'-sti-gāt) *v.t.* urge forward; incite; bring about.—**instiga'tion** *n.* prompting; impulse, esp. to evil.—**in'stigator** *n.*

instil, instill (in-stil') *v.t.* put in by drops; infuse slowly; introduce by degrees (into the mind).—*pr.p.* **instil'ling.**—*pa.t.* and *pa.p.* **instilled'.**—**instilla'tion** or **instila'tion, instil'ment** or **instill'ment** *n.* act of instilling.

instinct (in-stingkt) *n.* intuition; natural inclination; (in *neurology*) compound reflex action; (in *psychology*) innate train of reflexes; inborn impulse or propensity; unconscious skill; intuition.—**in'stinct** *a.* urged from within; animated.—**instinc'tive** *a.* prompted by instinct; natural; spontaneous; involuntary. **instinc'tively, instinct'ly** *adv.*

institute (in'-sti-tūt) *v.t.* establish; found; appoint; set going; originate; —*n.* society or organisation established for promoting some public object; rule, law or principle.—**in'stitutes** *n.pl.* book of precepts, principles or rules; legal principles.—**institu'tion** *n.* act of establishing; established law or custom; institute—**institu'tional** *a.* pert. to institutions.—**institu'tionalise** *v.t.*—**institu'tionally** *adv.*—**institu'tive** *a.* set up by authority, instituted; **institutively** *adv.*—**institu'tor, institu'ter** *n.* founder.

instruct (in-strukt') *v.t.* teach; inform; order or command; give directions to.—**instruc'tion** *n.* tuition; education; order; mandate.—**instruc'tional** *a.* pert. to instruction.—**instruc'tive** *a.* conveying knowledge or information.—**instruc'tively** *adv.*—**instruc'tiveness** *n.*—**instruc'tor** *n.* (*fem.* **instruc'tress**).

instrument (in'-stroo-ment) *n.* tool or implement esp. for scientific purposes; person or thing made use of; means of producing musical sounds; (*Law*) formal document.—**instrument'al** *a.* serving as instrument or means; helpful; pert. to musical, surgical, or other instruments.—**instrument'alist** *n.* a player of musical instrument.—**instrumental'ity** *n.* quality of serving some purpose; good offices.—**instrument'ally** *adv.* indirectly; with musical instruments.—**instrumenta'tion** *n.* art of arranging musical compositions for instruments; orchestration; installation of scientific instruments in aircraft etc.

insubordinate (in-sub-or'-di-nāt) *a.* disobedient; rebellious. — **insubordina'tion** *n.*

insufferable (in-suf'-ęr-ą-bl) *a.* not able to be endured; intolerable.—**insuff'erably** *adv.*

insufficient (in-su-fish'-ent) *a.* not enough; deficient.—**insuffic'iency** *n.*

insular (in'-sū-ląr) *a.* pert. to island; surrounded by water; narrow-minded or prejudiced.—**insular'ity** *n.*

insulate (in'-sū-lāt) *v.t.* make into island; keep apart from contact with other people; bar passage of electricity, heat, sound, light, damp, or vibration by use of non-conducting materials.—**insula'tion** *n.* separation; isolation; (*Elect.*) prevention of leakage of current of electricity; material which insulates.—**in'sulator** *n.* contrivance used to insulate conductor from earth; non-conductor.

insulin (in'-sū-lin) *n.* hormone secreted in pancreas; organic drug for treatment of diabetes.

insult (in-sult') *v.t.* treat with insolence or contempt; abuse; affront.—**in'sult** *n.* gross abuse.

insuperable (in-sū'-per-ą-bl) *a.* not able to be got over or surmounted; invincible.—**insuperabil'ity** *n.* **insu'perably** *adv.*

insupportable (in-su-pōr'-tą-bl) *a.* not to be borne or endured.—**insupport'ableness** *n.*—**insupport'ably** *adv.*

insure (in-shōōr') *v.t.* make sure or certain; make safe (against); ensure; secure payment of sum in event of loss, death, etc., by contract and payment of sums called premiums.—**insur'able** *a.*—**insur'ance** *n.* contract between two parties whereby insurer agrees to indemnify insured upon the occurrence of a stipulated contingency.

insurgent (in-sur'-jent) *a.* against lawful authority; rebellious;—*n.* a rebel.—**insur'gency** *n.* incipient stage of revolt.

insurmountable (in-sur-moun'-ta-bl) *a.* not able to be surmounted or overcome.—**insurmountabil'ity** *n.*—**surmount'ably** *adv.*

insurrection (in-su-rek'-shun) *n.* rising against civil or political authority.—**insurrec'tional, insurrec'-tionary** *a.*—**insurrec'tionist** *n.*

insusceptible (in-su-sep'-ti-bl) *a.* not susceptible; not to be moved, affected, or impressed; proof against (disease, etc.).

intact (in-takt') *a.* untouched; uninjured.

intake (in'-tāk) *n.* that which is taken in; inlet of a tube.

intangible (in-tan'-ji-bl) *a.* not perceptible to touch; impalpable; difficult to envisage.—**intan'gibleness, intangibil'ity** *n.*—**intan'gibly** *adv.*

integer (in'-te-jer) *n.* whole of anything; whole number (as opposed to fraction or mixed number).—**in'tegral** *a.* denoting whole number or quantity; constituting essential part of whole;—*n.* whole number; (*Math.*) sum of differentials.—**in'tegrally** *adv.*—**in'tegrate** *v.t.* make entire; give sum or total.—**integra'tion** *n.* act of making a whole out of parts; making equal of white and coloured people.—**in'tegrator** *n.*—**integ'rity** *n.* state of being entire; wholeness; honesty; uprightness.

intellect (in'-te-lekt) *n.* faculty of reasoning and thinking; mental power; mind; understanding.—**intellect'ual** *a.* of high mental capacity; —*n.* one well endowed with intellect. —**intellect'ualism** *n.* doctrine that knowledge is derived from pure reason; over-emphasis on value of rational faculties.—**intellectual'ity** *n.* intelligence.—**intellect'ually** *adv.*

intelligent (in-tel'-i-jent) *a.* having good intellect; quick at understanding.—**intell'igence** *n.* inborn quickness of understanding; information. —**intell'igently** *adv.*—**intelligent'sia** *n.* intellectual or cultured classes.— **intell'igible** *a.* that can be understood; —**intell'igibleness, intelligibil'ity** *n.*— **intell'igibly** *adv.*—**intelligence quotient** (abbrev. I.Q.) numerical rating of general intelligence by use of psychological tests.

intemperate (in-tem'-per-ăt) *a.* immoderate; indulging to excess any appetite or passion; addicted to excessive use of intoxicating drink. —**intem'perance** *n.* excess of any kind; over-indulgence in intoxicating drink.—**intem'perately** *adv.*—**intem'-perateness** *n.*

intend (in-tend') *v.t.* and *v.i.* design; purpose; mean; have in mind.—

intend'ed *a.* and *n.* (*Colloq.*) betrothed.

intense (in-tens') *a.* to an extreme degree; very strong or acute; emotional.—**inten'sely** *adv.*—**intense'-ness, inten'sity** *n.* severity; ardour; earnestness.—**intensifica'tion** *n.*—**inten'sify** *v.t.* render more intense; increase;—*v.i.* become more intense. —*pa.t.* and *pa.p.* **inten'sified.**— **inten'sive** *a.* unrelaxed; increasing in force.—**inten'sively** *adv.*

intent (in-tent') *a.* having mind bent on object; eager; firmly resolved; absorbed;—*n.* intention; aim; view. —**inten'tion** *n.* aim; purpose. **inten'tional, inten'tioned** *a.* done purposely.—**inten'tionally** *adv.*—**intent'ly** *adv.* closely; attentively.— **intent'ness** *n.*

inter (in-ter') *v.t.* bury;—*pr.p.* **inter'-ring.**—*pa.t.* and *pa.p.* **interred'.**— **inter'ment** *n.* burial.

interact (in'-ter-akt) *n.* interlude; —*v.i.* act mutually on each other. —**interac'tion** *n.*

interbreed (in-ter-brēd') *v.t.* to crossbreed.—**interbreed'ing** *n.*

intercede (in-ter-sēd') *v.i.* act as peace-maker; plead in favour of; mediate.—**interced'er** *n.*—**intercess'ion** *n.* mediation.—**intercess'or** *n.* mediator.—**intercesso'rial, intercess'ory** *a.*

intercept (in-ter-sept') *v.t.* stop or obstruct passage of another;—*n.* —**intercep'ter, intercep'tor** *n.*—**intercep'tion** *n.*—**intercep'tive** *a.*

interchange (in-ter-chānj) *v.t.* exchange;—*v.i.* succeed alternately; —*n.* mutual exchange.— **interchange'-able** *a.* identical.—**interchangeabil'ity, interchange'ableness** *n.*

intercom (in'-ter-kom) *n.* internal telephonic system, generally of aircraft. — **intercommun'icate** *v.t.* exchange conversation or messages.

interconnect (in-ter-ko-nekt') *v.t.* and *v.i.* connect mutually and intimately.

intercourse (in'-ter-kōrs) *n.* communication; conversation; sexual connection.

interdepend (in-ter-de-pend') *v.i.* depend upon each other.—**interdepen'dence** *n.*—**interdepen'dent** *a.*— **interdepen'dently** *adv.*

interdict (in-ter-dikt') *v.t.* forbid; prohibit; restrain; lay under interdict.—**in'terdict** *n.* prohibition.— **interdic'tion** *n.*—**interdic'tive, interdic'tory** *a.* prohibitory.

interest (in'-ter-est) *v.t.* engage and keep attention of; arouse curiosity of; concern;—*n.* special attention; personal advantage; curiosity; profit per cent derived from money lent.— **in'terested** *a.* having share in; feeling interest in; partial.—**in'terestedly** *adv.* —**in'terestedness** *n.*—**in'teresting** *a.* appealing to or exciting interest or curiosity.—**in'terestingly** *adv.*—**com-**

pound interest, interest on principal and also on added interest.—**simple interest**, interest only on principal during time of loan.

interfere (in-ter-fēr') v.i. meddle; to intervene.—**interfer'ence** n. meddling with other people's business; uncalled-for intervention; (*Radio*, *TV*) anything which prevents proper reception.—**interfer'er** n.—**interfer'ingly** adv.

interim (in'-ter-im) n. time between; meantime;—a. for the time being; temporary.

interior (in-tē'-ri-or) a. inner; internal; inland, away from coast or frontiers;—n. inside part; inland part of country.—**inter'iorly** adv.

interject (in-ter-jekt') v.t. throw between; exclaim abruptly.—**interjec'tion** n. word of strong emotion or passion when suddenly uttered.—**interjec'tional, interjec'tionary, interject'ural** a.—**interjec'tionally** adv.

interlace (in-ter-lās') v.t. lace together; entwine; unite; interweave.

interlard (in-ter-lard') v.t. mix together, as fat with lean; diversify by mixture.

interlock (in-ter-lok') v.t. unite by locking together; fasten together so that one part cannot move without the other;—v.i. be locked or jammed together.

interlocution (in-ter-lo-kū'-shun) n. dialogue; conference.—**interloc'utor** n. (*Scots law*) (*Colloq.*) written document containing judgment or determination of court.—**interloc'utory** a.

interlope (in-ter-lōp') v.i. intrude into other people's affairs; gatecrash.—**interlo'per** n.

interlude (in'-ter-lūd) n. performance given between parts of an independent play; interval; incident during pause in proceedings.

intermarry (in-ter-mar'-i) v.i. connect families by marriage.—**intermarr'iage** n.

intermeddle (in-ter-med'-l) v.i. interfere in others' concerns.

intermediate (in-ter-mē'-di-āt) a. lying between two extremes; in middle position;—n. anything in between; examination preceding final one.—**interme'diacy** n. mediation.—**interme'dial** a. intermediate.—**interme'diary** a. acting between; intermediate;—n. go-between or mediator.—**interme'diately** adv.

interment (in-ter'-ment) n. burial.

intermezzo (in-ter-med'-zō) n. light dramatic entertainment between acts of tragedy, grand opera, etc.; interlude; (*Mus.*) short movement connecting more important ones in symphony, sonata, opera, etc.

interminable (in-ter'-min-a-bl) a. endless; unlimited.—**inter'minableness** n.—**inter'minably** adv.

intermingle (in-ter-ming'-gl) v.t. mingle or mix together.

intermit (in-ter-mit') v.t. give up for a time; interrupt;—v.i. cease for a time.—**intermis'sion** n. suspension; interval.—**intermiss'ive** a. coming after temporary cessations.—**intermit'tence, intermit'tency** n.—**intermit'tent** a. occurring at intervals; ceasing at intervals; coming and going.—**intermit'tently** adv.

intermix (in-ter-miks') v.t. and v.i. mix together.—**intermix'ture** n.

intern (in-tern') v.t. confine, esp. aliens or suspects in time of war;—**in'-tern** n. resident pupil; resident doctor in hospital; boarder.—**internee'** n. one confined to certain place.—**intern'ment** n.

internal (in-ter'-nal) a. interior; inner; inward; domestic, as opposed to foreign.—**inter'nally** adv.—**internal combustion**, process occurring by exploding in piston-fitted cylinders mixture of air and fuel, as petrol gas.

international (in-ter-nash'-un-al) a. pert. to relations between nations; —n. match between teams representing their respective countries; player in such a contest; organisation of socialists, founded in 1864 to further interests of working-classes in all countries.—**Internationale** n. party-song of communists.—**interna'tionalism** n. political theory for breaking down artificial barriers which separate nations.—**interna'tionalist** n.—**interna'tionally** adv.

internecine (in-ter-nē'-sīn) a. mutually destructive; pert. to civil war.

interplanetary (in-ter-plan'-e-tar-i) a. between planets.

interplay (in'-ter-plā) n. reciprocal action of two things; give and take.

Interpol (in'-ter-pol) n. word, from parts of *Inter*national Criminal *Pol*ice Commission, for organisation that co-operates with all countries to counter criminal activities.

interpolate (in-ter'-po-lāt) v.t. insert new (esp. misleading matter) into text of book or manuscript; foist in; interpose; (*Math.*) infer missing terms in known series of numbers. —**interpola'tion** n.—**inter'polator** n.

interpose (in-ter-pōz') v.t. and v.i. place or come between; thrust in the way; interfere.—**interpos'er** n.—**interposi'tion** n.

interpret (in-ter'-pret) v.t. explain meaning of; translate orally.—**inter'pretable** a. able to be explained. —**interpreta'tion** n. translation; meaning; artiste's version of a dramatic part or musical composition.—**inter'pretative** a.—**inter'preter** n.

interregnum (in-ter-reg'-num) a. time when throne is vacant between death or abdication of king and accession of successor.

interrelation (in-ter-re-lā'-shun) *n.* reciprocal or mutual relation.—**interrela'tionship** *n.*

interrogate (in-ter'-o-gāt) *v.t.* question; examine by questioning.—**interroga'tion** *n.* close questioning; question.—**interrogation mark**, mark (?) placed after question.—**interrog'ative** *a.* expressed in form of a question;—*n.* word used in asking questions.—**interrog'atively** *adv.*—**interr'ogator** *n.*—**interrog'atory** *a.*

interrupt (in-ter-rupt') *v.t.* break in upon; stop course of; break continuity of.—**interrup'tedly** *adv.*—**interrupter** *n.*—**interrup'tion** *n.* intervention; hindrance; obstruction; impediment. —**interrup'tive** *a.*

intersect (in-ter-sekt') *v.t.* cut into or between; divide into parts; cross one another.—**intersec'tion** *n.* point where lines, roads, etc., cut or cross one another.—**intersec'tional** *a.*

intersperse (in-ter-spers')*v.t.* scatter; mingle.—**intersper'sion** *n.*

interstellar (in-ter-stel'-ar) *a.* passing between, or situated among, the stars. Also **interstell'ary**.

interstice (in-ter'-stis) *n.* small gap or chink in an object or between two things; crevice.—**intersti'tial** *a.*

intertwine (in-ter-twīn) *v.t.* twine together.

interval (in'-ter-val) *n.* time or distance between; pause; break; (*Mus.*) difference in pitch between any two tones.

intervene (in-ter-vēn') *v.i.* come or be between; happen in the meantime; interfere; to interrupt.—**interven'er** *n.*—**interven'ient** *a.*—**interven'tion** *n.* act of coming between.—**interven'tionist** *n.* or *a.*

interview (in'-ter-vū) *n.* meeting for conference; meeting of reporter and person whose views he wishes to publish; *v.t.* have an interview with.—**interview'er** *n.*

interweave (in-ter-wēv') *v.t.* to weave together; to interlace; to connect closely;—*pa.t.* **interwove'**.—*pa.p.* **interwo'ven**.

intestate (in-tes'-tāt) *a.* not having made a valid will; not disposed of by will;—*n.* one who dies intestate.—**intest'acy** *n.* disposal of property of person who has died without leaving a valid will.

intestine (in-tes'-tin) *a.* internal; domestic; within a country; civil (of war, etc.);—*n.pl.* the canal forming lower part of digestive tract; bowels; entrails.—**intes'tinal** *a.*

intimate (in'-ti-met) *a.* familiar; closely-related; close;—*n.* intimate friend;—(-māt) *v.t.* make known; give notice of;—**in'timacy** *n.* state of being intimate; sexual relations.—**in'timately** *adv.*—**intima'tion** *n.* announcement.

intimidate (in-tim'-i-dāt) *v.t.* deter by threats; inspire with fear; frighten into action; cow.—**intimida'tion** *n.*—**intim'idator** *n.*

into (in'-tōō) *prep.* express motion to a point within, or a change from one state to another.

intolerable (in-tol'-e-ra-bl) *a.* insufferable; unbearable.—**intol'erableness** *n.*—**intol'erably** *adv.*—**intol'erance** *n.* want of forbearance; bigotry.—**intol'erant** *a.*—**intol'erantly** *adv.*

intone (in-tōn') *v.t.* utter or recite with long drawn out musical note or tone; chant;—*v.i.* modulate the voice.—**in'tonate** *v.t.* intone.—**intona'tion** *n.* expressive modulation of voice; accent; accuracy of pitch.

intoxicate (in-tok'-si-kāt) *v.t.* make drunk; excite beyond self-control.—**intox'icating** *a.* producing intoxication; heady.—**intox'icant** *n.* intoxicating liquor.—**intoxica'tion** *n.*

intra- (in'-tra) *prefix fr.* L. *intra*, within, inside of.

intractable (in-trak'-ta-bl) *a.* not to be managed or governed; unmanageable; stubborn; refractory.—**intractabil'ity, intract'ableness** *n.*—**intract'ably** *adv.*

intramural (in-tra-mū'-ral) *a.* within the walls.

intransigent (in-tran'-si-jent) *a.* refusing to compromise (esp. in political matters); irreconcilable;—*n.* one who adopts this attitude.—**intran'sigence** *n.* uncompromising attitude.

intransitive (in-tran'-si-tiv) *a.* not passing over; (*Gram.*) denoting such verbs as express an action which does not pass over to an object.

intrepid (in-trep'-id) *a.* free from fear or trepidation.—**intrepid'ity** *n.* undaunted courage.—**intrep'idly** *adv.*

intricate (in'-tri-kāt) *a.* involved; entangled; complicated; perplexed; obscure; difficult.—**in'tricacy, in'tricateness** *n.*—**in'tricately** *adv.*

intrigue (in-trēg') *n.* plot to effect some purpose by secret artifices; illicit love;—*v.i.* scheme; plot; carry on illicit love;—*v.t.* fascinate; arouse interest in; puzzle.—*pr.p.* **intrig'uing**.—**in'trigant, in'triguant, in-trig'uer** *n.* one who intrigues.—**intrig'uing** *a.* given to intrigues; arousing interest.—**intrig'uingly** *adv.*

intrinsic, intrinsical (in-trin'-sik, -si-kal) *a.* having internal value; inherent; real; natural; genuine.—**intrinsical'ity** *n.*—**intrin'sically** *adv.*

introduce (in-trō-dūs') *v.t.* lead or bring in; bring forward; make known formally (one person to another); begin.—**introduc'tion** *n.* act of introducing or bringing into notice; act of making persons formally acquainted with one another; preliminary section of a speech or discourse;

prologue; preface.—**introduc'tory, introduc'tive** a. serving to introduce; preliminary; initiating. — **introduc'- tively, introduc'torily** adv.

intromit (in-trō-mit') v.t. send in; let in; admit; to put in;—v.i. meddle with affairs of another.—**intromiss'ion** n. act of sending in or allowing in.

introspect (in-trō-spekt') v.t. inspect;—v.i. pre-occupy oneself with one's own thoughts and feelings.— **introspec'tion** n.—**introspec'tive** a.— **introspec'tively** adv.

introvert (in-trō-vert') v.t. turn inward;—n. in psycho-analysis, self-centred, introspective individual. Cf. *extrovert*.—**introver'sion** n.—**introver'sive, introver'tive** a.

intrude (in-trōōd') v.i. thrust oneself in; enter unwelcome into company; trespass;—v.t. force in.—**intrud'er** n. —**intru'sion** n. act of entering, without invitation, to annoyance of others.—**intru'sive** a.—**intru'sively** adv. —**intru'siveness** n.

intuition (in-tū-ish'-un) n. instinctive perception of a truth; direct understanding without reasoning.— **intuit'ional** a.—**intu'itive** a. having instinctively immediate perception of something.—**intu'itively** adv.

inundate (in'-un-dāt, in-un'-dāt) v.t. overflow; flood; overwhelm by force of numbers; fill more than is necessary.—**inunda'tion** n.

inure (in-ūr') v.t. accustom (to); habituate; harden (the body) by toil, etc.—**inure'ment** n.

invade (in-vād') v.t. enter with hostile intentions; attack; violate; encroach upon.—**invad'er** n.—**inva'sion** n.—**inva'sive** a.

invalid (in-val'-id) a. not valid; void; null; no longer in current use; of no legal force; weak.—**inval'idate** v.t. render invalid.—**invalida'tion** n. —**invalid'ity, inval'idness** n.

invalid (in'-va̧-lid, or -lēd) n. person enfeebled by sickness or injury;— a. ill; sickly; weak;—v.t. and v.i. send away as invalid.

invaluable (in-val'-ū-a̧-bl) a. incapable of being valued; priceless; of very great value.

invariable (in-vā'-ri-a̧-bl) a. not displaying change; always uniform; (*Math.*) constant.—**inva'riableness, invariabil'ity** n.—**inva'riably** adv.

invective (in-vek'-tiv) n. outburst of censure; abuse; vituperation; satire; —a. abusive; satirical.

inveigh (in-vā') v.i. rail against; denounce; to declaim against.— **inveigh'er** n.

inveigle (in-vē'-gl) v.t. entice by deception or flattery; allure; mislead into something evil; seduce.— **invei'glement** n.—**invei'gler** n.

invent (in-vent') v.t. devise something new; contrive; originate; think up

something untrue.—**inven'tion** n. act of producing something new; original mechanical contrivance; deceit, fiction, or forgery.—**inven'tive** a. able to invent; of ingenious turn of mind; resourceful.—**inven'tively** adv. —**inven'tor** n.

inventory (in'-ven-tor-i) n. detailed list of articles comprising effects of house, etc.; catalogue of movables;— v.t. make list of.

Inverness (in-ver-nes') n. kind of sleeveless cloak with cape hanging loosely over the shoulder.

inverse (in-vers') a. inverted; opposite in order or relation.—**inverse'ly** adv.—**inver'sion** n. act of inverting; state of being inverted; change of order or time.—**inver'sive** a.

invert (in-vert') v.t. turn over; put upside down; place in contrary order.—**inver'tedly** adv.—**inverted commas**, quotation marks ' ' or " ".

invertebrate (in-ver'-te-brāt) a. not having a vertebral column or backbone; spineless;—n. animal with no spinal column.

invest (in-vest') v.t. clothe, as with office or authority; dress; lay siege to; lay out capital with view to profit;—v.i. make purchase or investment.—**inves'titure** n. ceremony of installing any one in office.— **invest'ment** n. act of investing; capital invested to produce profit; blockade.—**inves'tor** n.

investigate (in-ves'-ti-gāt) v.t. inquire into; examine thoroughly.— **invest'igable** a. — **investiga'tion** n. thorough enquiry.—**inves'tigative** a. —**inves'tigator** n.—**inves'tigatory** a.

inveterate (in-vet'-er-āt) a. firmly established; obstinate; deep-rooted. —**invet'erately** adv.—**invet'eracy** n.

invidious (in-vid'-i-us) a. likely to provoke envy, ill-will, or hatred; offensive.—**invid'iously** adv.—**invid'-iousness** n.

invigilate (in-vij'-i-lāt) v.i. supervise candidates at examination.—**invig-ila'tion** n.—**invig'ilator** n.

invigorate (in-vig'-or-āt) v.t. give vigour; strengthen.—**invigora'tion** n.

invincible (in-vin'-si-bl) a. unconquerable; impregnable; insuperable. —**invincibil'ity** n.—**invin'cibly** adv.

inviolable (in-vī'-ol-a̧-bl) a. not to be profaned; sacred; holy.—**inviolabil'-ity, invi'olableness** n.—**invi'olably** adv. —**invi'olate** a. unprofaned; uninjured. —**invi'olately** adv.

invisible (in-viz'-i-bl) a. incapable of being seen; unseen. — **invisibil'ity, invis'ibleness** n.—**invis'-ibly** adv.

invite (in-vīt') v.t. ask by invitation; attract.—**invita'tion** n. act of inviting; spoken or written form with which invitation is extended.— **invit'er** n.—**invit'ing** a. alluring, attractive.—**invit'ingly** adv.

invocation (in-vō-kā'-shun) n. petition for divine help and guidance.—**invoc'atory** a.

invoice (in'-vois) n. detailed list of goods, with prices, sold or consigned to purchaser;—v.t. make such a list.

invoke (in-vōk') v.t. address solemnly in prayer; beg for assistance; implore; conjure up.

involuntary (in-vol'-un-ta-ri) a. outside control of will; unintentional; instinctive.—**invol'untarily** adv.—**invol'untariness** n.

involve (in-volv') v.t. envelop; wrap up; include; comprise; implicate (person); complicate (thing); entail; include; twine; interlace; overwhelm.—**involve'ment** n.

invulnerable (in-vul'-ne-ra-bl) a. incapable of being wounded or injured.—**invulnerabil'ity**, **invul'nerableness** n.—**invul'nerably** adv.

inward (in'-ward) a. placed within; towards the inside; interior; internal; spiritual;—n. that which is within.—esp. in pl., viscera;—adv. toward the inside; into the mind. Also **in'wards**;—**in'wardly** adv. in parts within; secretly; in mind or soul.

inwrought (in-rawt') a. ornamented with figures; inherent; interwoven.

iodine (ī'-o-dīn) n. a non-metallic chemical element.—**i'odise**, treat substances with compounds of iodine.—**iod'oform** n. powdered crystalline compound of iodine.

ion (ī'-on) n. electrically charged atom, molecule, or radical whose migration facilitates the passage of electricity through an electrolyte or gas.—**ion'ic** a. pert. to ions.—**ionisa'tion** n. splitting up of liquid during electrolysis or of gas during glow discharge, into ions.—**i'onise** v.t.—**ion'osphere** n. part of the Kennelly-Heaviside layer of ionised molecules in upper atmosphere which reflects radio-waves back to earth.

Ionic (i-on'-ik) a. pert. to Ionia, district of Asia Minor, esp. denoting second of Grecian orders of architecture, characterised by flutings and scrolled capitals.

iota (ī-ō'-ta) n. very small quantity; jot [name of smallest letter of Greek alphabet = I, ι].

ipecacuanha (ip-e-kak-ū-á'-na) n. Brazilian plant; drug prepared from the root of this plant, used as expectorant and emetic.

Iran (i-ran') n. native name of Persia.—**Irani** (i-rán'-i), a.—**Iran'ian** a. pert. to Persian;—n. Persian.

Iraq (i-rak') n. republic of Asia.—**Iraq'i** n. native of Iraq.

irascible (i-ras'-i-bl) a. easily provoked; hot-tempered.—**irascibil'ity** n.—**iras'cibly** adv.

irate (ī-rāt') a. angry; incensed; enraged.

ire (īr) n. anger; wrath.—**ire'ful** a. incensed; resentful.—**ire'fully** adv.—**ire'fulness** n.

iridescence (i-ri-des'-ens) n. rainbow-like display of colours, due to interference of light, seen on floating oil, some gem etc.—**irides'cent** a.

iridium (ī-rid'-i-um) n. silvery metallic chemical element of the platinum group.

iris (ī'-ris) n. rainbow; appearance resembling rainbow; thin coloured membrane surrounding pupil of the eye; apeture diaphragm of camera lens; genus of flowering plants;—pl. i'rises.

Irish (Ī-rish) a. pert. to Ireland;—n. early language spoken in Ireland, now known as Erse.—**I'rishism** n. mode of speaking, phrase, or idiom of Ireland.—**I'rishman**, **I'rish-woman** n.—**Irish Free State** self-governing state set up in 1922 in S. Ireland, later (Dec. 1937) known as Eire.—**Irish moss**, carrageen, form of edible seaweed.

irk (erk) v.t. weary; give pain to; trouble; distress (used impersonally as, it irks me).—**irk'some** a. wearisome; tiresome; tedious; annoying.—**irk'somely** adv.

iron (ī'-ern) n. most common of metallic element; instrument or utensil made of iron; instrument used, when heated, to press and smooth cloth; in golf, iron-headed club.—**i'rons** n.pl. fetters; manacles; leg-supports;—a. made of iron; robust; unyielding;—v.t. smooth with heated flat iron; fetter.—**i'ron-clad** a. covered with sheets of iron;—n. a naval vessel having parts above water plated with iron.—**i'ron-found'er** n. one who makes or founds iron-castings.—**i'ron-foun'dry** n.—**i'ron-lung** n. apparatus which maintains artificial respiration.—**i'ronmaster** n. proprietor of iron-works.—**i'ronmonger** n. dealer in hardware.—**i'ronmongery** n. hardware.—**i'ron-ore** n. rock containing iron-rich compounds.—**i'ron-ra'tion** n. ration of highly concentrated food for use in emergency.—**I'ronside** n. Cromwellian cavalryman.—**i'ronstone** n. ore of iron mixed with clay, etc.;—**i'ronwork** n. parts of structure made of iron; anything of iron;—pl. forge; rolling-mill or foundry.—**cast'-i'ron** n. or pig iron, iron obtained by smelting iron ore with charcoal, coke, or raw coal in blast furnace.—**Iron age**, period following Bronze age, when iron was substituted for bronze in the making of tools, weapons, and ornaments.—**Iron Curtain** (Fig.) political barrier between communist and non-communist states.—**to have too many irons in the fire,** attempt to ⟨o⟩ too many things at same time.—w..ile **the iron is hot,** at the opportune moment.

irony (I'-ro-ni) *n.* mode of speech in which meaning is opposite of that actually expressed; sarcasm; satire.—**iron'ic, iron'ical** *a.*—**iron'ically** *adv.*

irradiate (i-rā'-di-āt) *v.t.* throw light upon; illuminate; expose to X-rays;—*v.i.* emit rays; give forth light;—*a.* illumined with beams of light.—**irra'diance, irra'diancy** *n.* effulgence; splendour.—**irra'diant** *a.*—**irradia'tion** *n.*—**irra'diative** *a.*—**irra'diator** *n.*

irrational (i-rash'-un-al) *a.* incompatible with or contrary to reason.—**irrational'ity** *n.*—**irra'tionally** *adv.*

irreclaimable (i-re-klā'-ma-bl) *a.* beyond reformation; incorrigible.—**irreclaim'ably** *adv.*

irreconcilable (i-rek-on-sīl'-a-bl) *a.* incapable of being reconciled.—**irreconcil'ableness, irreconcilabil'ity** *n.*—**irreconcil'ably** *adv.*

irrecoverable (i-re-kuv'-er-a-bl) *a.* cannot be recovered; irreparable; irretrievable.—**irrecov'erableness** *n.*—**irrecov'erably** *adv.*

irredeemable (i-re-dēm'-a-bl) *a.* not redeemable; incorrigible; hopelessly lost.—**irredeem'ableness, irredeemabil'ity** *n.*—**irredeem'ably** *adv.*

irreducible (i-re-dūs'-i-bl) *a.* that which cannot be reduced or lessened.—**irreduc'ibleness, irreducibil'ity** *n.*—**irredu'cibly** *adv.*

irreflection (i-re-flek'-shun) *n.* want or absence of reflection or thought.

irrefragable (i-ref'-ra-ga-bl) *a.* unanswerable; undeniable.—**irrefraga-bil'ity**—**irref'ragably** *adv.*

irrefutable (i-re-fū'-ta-bl) *a.* that cannot be refuted.—**irrefutabil'ity** *n.*—**irrefu'tably** *adv.*

irregular (i-reg'-ū-lar) *a.* not regular; not according to rule; (*Gram.*) not inflected according to normal rules;—*n.* member of armed force outwith government control.—**irregular'ity** *n.*—**irreg'ularly** *adv.*

irrelative (i-rel'-a-tiv) *a.* not relative; unconnected.—**irrel'atively** *adv.*

irrelevant (i-rel'-e-vant) *a.* not to the point; not pertinent.—**irrel'evancy** *n.*—**irrel'evantly** *adv.*

irreligion (i-re-lij'-un) *n.* indifference or opposition to religious beliefs.—**irrelig'ious** *a.*—**irrelig'iously** *adv.*

irremediable (i-re-mēd'-i-a-bl) *a.* not to be remedied or redressed.—**irremed'iableness** *n.*—**irremed'iably** *adv.*

irremovable (i-re-mōō'-va-bl) *a.* fixed; steadfast.—**irremovabil'ity, irremov'ableness** *n.*—**irremov'ably** *adv.*

irreparable (i-rep'-ar-a-bl) *a.* that cannot be repaired or rectified.—**irreparabil'ity, irrep'arableness** *n.*—**irrep'arably** *adv.*

irreplaceable (i-re-plā'-sa-bl) *a.* that

cannot be replaced; indispensable; unique.

irreproachable (i-re-prō'-cha-bl) *a.* free from blame; upright; faultless.—**irreproach'ableness** *n.*—**irreproach'-ably** *adv.*

irresistible (i-re-zis'-ti-bl) *a.* incapable of being resisted; too strong, fascinating, charming, etc., to be resisted.—**irresistibil'ity** *n.*—**irresist'ibly** *adv.*

irresolute (i-rez'-ol-ūt) *a.* inconstant in purpose; unsettled; wavering.—**irres'olutely** *adv.*—**irres'oluteness, irreso-lu'tion** *n.*

irrespective (i-re-spek'-tiv) *a.* and *adv.* without taking account (of); without regard to; apart from.—**irrespec'tively** *adv.*

irresponsible (i-re-spon'-si-bl) *a.* not liable to answer (for consequences); carefree; without due sense of responsibility.—**irresponsibil'ity** *n.*—**irrespons'ibly** *adv.*

irresponsive (i-re-spon'-siv) *a.* not responsive (to); unenthusiastic.—**irrespons'iveness** *n.*

irretrievable (i-re-trē'-va-bl) *a.* incapable of recovery or repair.—**irretrievabil'ity, irretriev'ableness** *n.*—**irretriev'ably** *adv.*

irreverent (i-rev'-e-rent) *a.* not reverent; disrespectful.—**irrev'erence** *n.*—**irrev'erently** *adv.*

irreversible (i-re-ver'-si-bl) *a.* that cannot be reversed, turned back, or annulled.—**irrevers'ibly** *adv.*

irrevocable (i-rev'-ō-ka-bl) *a.* incapable of being recalled or revoked.—**irrevocabil'ity, irrev'ocableness** *n.*—**irrev'ocably** *adv.*

irrigate (ir'-i-gāt) *v.t.* water (by artificial channels).—**irr'igable, irr'igative** *a.* capable of being irrigated.—**irriga'tion** *n.* watering land by artificial channels.—**irriga'tor** *n.*

irritate (ir'-i-tāt) *v.t.* excite to anger; annoy; excite heat and redness in the skin by friction.—**irritabil'ity** *n.*—**irr'itable** *a.* easily annoyed; fretful.—**irr'itableness** *n.*—**irr'itably** *adv.*—**irr'itant** *a.* irritating;—*n.* that which irritates or causes irritation.—**irrita'tion** *n.* exasperation; anger; itching.—**irr'itative** *a.* tending to irritate.

irruption (i-rup'-shun) *n.* sudden invasion; breaking or bursting in; inroad.—**irrup'tive** *a.* rushing in or upon with violence.—**irrup'tively** *adv.*

isinglass (I-zing-glas) *n.* glutinous substance, prepared from swimming-bladder of various species of fish.

Islam, Islamism (iz'-lam, -izm) *n.* the religion of Mahomet; Mohammedanism.—**Islam'ic, Islamit'ic** *a.*

island (I'-land) *n.* piece of land surrounded by water; anything resembling this, e.g. street-refuge.—**is'lander** *n.* inhabitant of island.

isle (Il) *n.* island.—**isles'man** *n.* islander, esp. from the Hebrides.—**islet** (I'-let) *n.* tiny island.

ism (izm) *n.* any distinctive doctrine, theory, or practice.

iso- (I'-so) *prefix* fr. Gk. *isos*, equal, used in the construction of compound terms.

isobar (I'-sō-bar) *n.* line on map joining points of equal barometric pressure.—**isobar'ic** *a.*

isochromatic (I-sō-krō-mat'-ik) *a.* having the same colour.

isodynamic (I-sō-dī-nam'-ik) *a.* having equal force or power.

isohel (I-sō-hel) *n.* line on map joining places having same recorded amount of sunshine.

isohyet (I-sō-hī'-et) *n.* line on map joining places with equal rainfall.—**isohy'etal** *a.*

isolate (I'-so-lāt) *v.t.* place apart or alone; insulate; separate; disconnect.—**isola'tion** *n.* state of being isolated.—**isolation hospital**, hospital for infectious diseases.—**isola'tionist** *n.* one who advocates non-participation in world-politics.

isometric (I-sō-met'-rik) *a.* of equal measurement.

isomorphism (I-sō-morf'-izm) *n.* similarity of structure, esp. between crystals of different chemical substances.—**isomor'phic** *a.* — **isomor'phous** *a.*

isosceles (I-sos'-e-lēz) *a.* having two sides which are equal (of a triangle).

isotherm (I'-sō-therm) *n.* line on map joining places of equal temperature.—**isother'mal** *a.*

isotope (I-sō-tōp) *n.* (*Physics*) atom with slightly different nuclear mass but identical chemical properties to others.

Israel (iz'-ra-el) *n.* since 1948, name of Jewish State in Palestine; (*Bib.*) Jewish people.—**Israeli** (iz-rāl'-I) *n.* inhabitant of Israel.—**Is'raelite** *n.* (*Bib.*) descendant of Israel; Jew.—**Israelit'ic**, **Israelit'ish**, *a.* Jewish, Hebrew.

issue (ish'-ū) *n.* passing or flowing out; sending out; whole number sent out at one time; topic of controversy; morbid discharge from the body; outlet; edition; consequence; end; result; off-spring;—*v.t.* send out (a book, etc.); put into circulation, as notes; proclaim with authority; supply with equipment, etc.;—*v.i.* pass or flow out; come out; proceed; be born from.—**iss'ueless** *a.* childless.—**iss'uer** *n.* at issue, (point) to be debated.—**to join issue**, take opposite views on a point.

isthmus (isth'-mus, is'-mus) *n.* narrow neck of land connecting two larger parts.

it (it) *pron.* neuter pronoun of third person;—*n.* (*Colloq.*) sex appeal.

Italian (i-tal'-yạn) *a.* pert. to Italy, inhabitants or language;—*n.* native of Italy; the language; satinised cotton cloth.—**ital'ianise** *v.i.* make Italian.—**Ital'icism** *n.* word or phrase peculiar to Italians.

italics (i-tal'-iks) *n.pl.* printing type of Italian origin, having type sloping from right downwards, *as the letters in which these words are printed.*—**ital'icise** *v.t.* print thus.

itch (ich) *n.* irritation in skin; scabies; irrepressible desire;—*v.i.* feel irritation in the skin; be anxious to.—**itch'iness** *n.*—**itch'y** *a.*—**an itching palm**, grasping disposition.

item (I'-tem) *adv.* also; likewise (used in enumerating);—*n.* any of a list of things; entry in account or list; detail.—**i'temize** *v.t.* (*U.S.*) to give particulars.

iterate (it'-ẹ-rāt) *v.t.* repeat; do again.—**itera'tion**, it'erance *n.* repetition.—**it'erative**, it'erant *a.* repeating.

itinerant (I-tin-ẹ-rạnt) *a.* travelling from place to place; of no settled abode; wandering;—*n.* one who goes from place to place; wanderer.—**itin'eracy**, itin'erancy *n.* habit of wandering about the country.—**itin'erantly** *adv.*—**itin'erary** *n.* record of travel; route, line of travel; guide-book for travellers.

its (its) possessive case of *pron.* it.—**itself'** *pron.* neuter reciprocal pronoun applied to things; reflexive form of it.

ivory (I'-vor-i) *n.* hard, white bony substance constituting tusks of elephant, walrus, etc.—*n.pl.* teeth; piano keys.—*a.* made of or like ivory.—**black ivory**, Negro slaves.

ivy (I'-vi) *n.* climbing evergreen plant;—*pl.* i'vies.—**i'vied** *a.* covered with ivy.

J

jab (jab) *v.t.* poke sharply; stab;—*n.* sharp poke, stab, or thrust.

jabber (jab'-ẹr) *v.i.* chatter; speak quickly and indistinctly;—*v.t.* utter indistinctly;—*n.* rapid, incoherent talk.—**jabb'erer** *n.*—**jabb'eringly** *adv.*

jabot (zhá'-bō) *n.* frill of lace on woman's dress; orig. ruffle on man's shirt-front.

jacaranda (jak-a-ran'-dạ) *n.* tropical tree yielding rosewood.

jacinth (ja'-sinth) *n.* (*Geol.*) reddish-orange variety of zircon, used as gem; hyacinth.

Jack (jak) *n.* popular nickname and diminutive of *John*; fellow; labourer, as *steeple-jack*; sailor; knave in pack of cards; device to facilitate removal of boots, as *boot-jack*; device for turning roasting-spit; portable machine for raising heavy weights, esp. for raising motor vehicle to change tyre; (*Bowls*) white ball used as mark to be aimed at; flag or ensign; male of certain animals, as a *Jack-hare.*—**jack** *v.t.* raise with jack. Also **jack'-up**—**jack'-boot** *n.* long boot reaching above the knee.—**jack'-in-the-box'** *n.* child's toy comprising small figure which springs out of a box when lid is lifted.—**jack'-knife** *n.* strong clasp knife.—**jack o' lantern,** will o' the wisp.—**jack'-of-all'-trades** *n.* one who can turn his hand to anything.—**jack'-pot** *n.* cumulative pool, in poker, and other games; hidden treasure or windfall.—**jack-tar,** sailor.—**Union Jack,** the national flag of Gt. Britain.—**yel'low-jack** *n.* yellow fever.

jack (jak) *n.* a coat of mail; a jerkin worn over armour.—**black jack,** a leather bottle.

jackal (jak'-awl) *n.* a bushy-tailed carnivorous animal of Persia and India, allied to the dog.

jackanapes (jak'-a-naps) *n.* orig. a monkey; impertinent fellow; cheeky child.

jackaroo (jak'-a-róó) *n.* (*Austral. slang*) an English newcomer gaining experience in the Australian outback; a novice.

jackass (jak'-as) *n.* male ass; stupid fellow; blockhead.—**laughing jackass,** the giant kingfisher of Australia.

jackdaw (jak'-daw) *n.* bird of the crow family.

jacket (jak'-et) *n.* short, sleeved coat; outer covering or skin (as of potatoes); outer casing for boiler to keep in heat; loose dust-cover for book; —*v.t.* cover with a jacket.

Jacobean (jak-ō-bē'-an) *a.* pert. to reign of James I.

Jacobin (jak'-ō-bin) *n.* French Dominican friar, so called from monastery of *St. Jacques*, Paris; member of society of French Revolutionists in 1789; demagogue; variety of hooded pigeon;—*a.* (*Hist.*) extreme; turbulent; revolutionary.

Jacobite (jak'-ō-bit) *n.* adherent of James II or of his descendants, Old and Young Pretender;—*a.* pert. to followers of James II and Stuart supporters.—**Jac'obitism** *n.*

jaculation (jak-ū-lā'-shun) *n.* act of throwing, as a dart.—**jac'ulate** *v.t.* throw.

jade (jād) *n.* over-worked, worn-out horse; mean woman; hussy;—*v.t.* tire; harass.—**jad'ed** *a.* tired; weary; off-colour.

jade (jād) *n.* hard silicate of lime and magnesia, carved for ornaments.—**jade'ite** *n.* green silicate of sodium and aluminium, found in Burma.

jag (jag) *n.* notch; ragged protuberance; (*Slang*) inoculation; — *v.t.*

notch; stab.—**jag'ged, jag'gy** *a.* notched; rough-edged.—**jag'gedness** *n.*

jaguar (jag'-wàr) *n.* large spotted yellowish beast of prey, resembling leopard.

jail (jāl) *n.* prison. Also gaol.—**jail'bird,** *n.* prisoner; criminal.—**jail'er, jail'or,** *n.* one who has charge of prisoners.—**jail'-fe'ver,** *n.* typhus.

jalopy (ja-lop'-i) *n.* (*U.S. Slang*) old motor-car.

jam (jam) *n.* preserve made from fruit, boiled with sugar; (*Slang*) something easily obtained.

jam (jam) *v.t.* squeeze tight; wedge in; block up;—*v.i.* cease to function because of obstruction;—*pr.p.* jam'ming—*pa.p* jammed—*n.* crush; hold up (as of traffic); (Colloq.) tight corner—**jamming** *n.* (*Radio*) effect of interference as when signals of similar wave length collide.

jamb (jam) *n.* side-piece of door, fire-place, etc.

jambok (jam'-bok) *n.* long piece of hide used as a whip. Also **sjambok.**

jamboree (jam-bō-rē') *n.* international rally of Boy Scouts; friendly gathering; (*Euchre*) hand containing five highest cards making total of 16.

jangle (jang'-gl) *v.t.* ring with discordant sound;—*v.i.* sound out of tune; wrangle;—*n.* discordant sound; dispute.—**jang'ling** *n.*

janitor (jan'-i-tor) *n.* (*fem.* jan'itrix, jan'itress) door-keeper; porter.

January (jan'-ū-ar-i) *n.* first month, dedicated by Romans to *Janus,* the god with two faces.—**jan'us-faced** *a.* untrustworthy.

Japan (ja-pan') *n.* a N.E. Asiatic insular empire.—**Jap** *n.* abbrev. of Japanese; native of Japan;—*a.* pert. to Japan.—**Japanese'** *n.* native of Japan;—*a.* pert. to Japan, the people, or language.—**japan'** *v.t.* make black and glosey; lacquer with black varnish;—*pr.p.* japan'ning.—*pa.p.* japanned';—*n.* the black lacquer used in japanning.

jape (jāp) *v.t.* deride;—*n.* jest.

japonica (jap-on'-ik-a) *n.* garden shrub, the Japanese quince; the camellia.

jar (jàr) *n.* vessel narrower at top than at base, with or without handles.

jar (jàr) *n.* give forth discordant sound; vibrate discordantly; be inconsistent with; annoy;—*v.t.* cause to vibrate by sudden impact; shake physically or mentally;—*pr.p.* jar'ring,—*pa.p.* jarred.—*n.* harsh, grating sound.—**jar'ringly** *adv.*

jargon (jar'-gon) *n.* confused speech; gibberish; slang; the technical phraseology of experts.

jasmine (jas'-min) *n.* climbing plant with white or yellow flowers.—Also **jess'amine.**

jasper (jas'-per) n. precious stone; impure opaque form of silica.

jaundice (jån'-dis, jawn'-dis) n. disease, characterised by yellowness of skin and eyes.—jaun'diced a. affected with jaundice; (Fig.) jealous; prejudiced.

jaunt (jånt, jawnt) v.i. make an excursion;—n. outing; ramble.—jaunt'ing a. rambling.—jaunting car, vehicle used in Ireland, two wheeled, and with side seats back to back.

jaunty (jånt'-i, jawnt'-i) a. sprightly; airy; carefree.—jaunt'ily adv.—jaunt'iness n.

javelin (jav'-lin) n. light hand-thrown spear.

jaw (jaw) n. one of two bones forming framework of mouth and containing the teeth; mouth; part of any device which grips or crushes object held by it, as a vice; (Slang) loquacity;—pl. narrow entrance to a gorge;—v.t. scold.—jaw'-bone n. bone of mouth in which teeth are set.—jawed a. having jaws.

jay (jå) n. chattering, perching bird with gay plumage; (Fig.) foolish person.—jay'-walk'er n. pedestrian who disregards all traffic regulations.

jazz (jaz) n. syncopated music, derived from Negro spirituals;—a. discordant; raucous; garish;—v.t. and v.i. dance to jazz music.—jaz'zy a.

jealous (jel'-us) a. solicitous; zealously careful; envious; suspicious.—jeal'ously adv.—jeal'ousness, jeal'ousy n. envy; apprehension of rivalry.

jean (jēn, jån) n. strong, twilled, cotton cloth;—pl. (U.S.) overalls; (Colloq.) trousers.

jeep (jēp) n. light motor utility truck.

jeer (jēr) v.i. mock; deride;—v.t. treat scoffingly;—n. gibe.—jeer'ingly adv.

Jehovah (je-hō'-va) n. (Bib.) Hebrew name for God.

jejune (je-jōōn') a. empty; barren; uninteresting; dry.—jejune'ly ad.—jejune'ness n.

jelly (jel'-i) n. any gelatinous substance; the juice of fruit boiled with sugar.—jell v.i. stiffen.—jell'ied a. thick and stiff, like jelly.—jell'ify v.t. make into jelly;—v.i. become set like jelly.—jell'y-fish n. popular name given to certain marine animals with bell-shaped bodies.

jemmy (jem'-i) n. small crowbar, as used by burglars.

jennet (jen'-et) n. small Spanish horse.—Also ge(n)n'et.

jenny (jen'-i) n. travelling crane; spinning machine; (Cinema) portable electric dynamo; female ass; female bird, the wren (usually jenny-wren).

jeopardy (jep'-ard-i) n. danger; risk.—jeop'ard, jeop'ardise v.t. endanger; imperil.—jeop'ardous a. perilous.—jeop'ardously adv.

jerk (jerk) v.t. throw with quick motion; twitch; give sudden pull, twist, or push;—n. short, sudden thrust, or push; spasmodic twitching.—jerk'er n.—jerk'ily adv.—jerk'iness n.—jerk'y a. fitful; spasmodic; lacking rhythm.—physical jerks (Colloq.) gymnastics.

jerkin (jer'-kin) n. close-fitting jacket or waistcoat.

jerry-builder (jer'-i-bil'-der) n. one who builds flimsy houses of second-rate material.

Jersey (jer'-zi) n. largest of Channel Islands; cow of Jersey breed;—a. pert. to Jersey.—jer'sey n. a close-fitting, knitted, woollen jacket, vest, or pullover.

jessamine See jasmine.

jest (jest) n. joke; quip; object of ridicule;—v.i. joke.—jest'er n. one who jests; professional fool, originally attached to court or lord's manor.—jest'ful a. given to jesting.—jest'ingly adv.

Jesuit (jez'-u-it) n. one of religious order founded by Ignatius Loyola in 1543 under the title of The Society of Jesus.—Jesuit'ic, -al, a. pert. to, or resembling, a Jesuit; crafty.—Jes'uitism, Jesuitoc'racy n. government by Jesuits.

jet (jet) n. a variety of very hard, black lignite, capable of brilliant polish and much used for ornaments; —a. made of, or having the glossy blackness of jet.—jet'-black a. black like jet.—jet'tiness n.—jet'ty a. black as jet.

jet (jet) n. sudden rush, as of water or flame, from a pipe; spout or nozzle emitting water, gas, etc.;—v.t. spout forth.—jet propulsion, propulsion of machine by the backward discharge of high speed jets of gas.

jetsam (jet'-sam) n. goods thrown overboard to lighten ship in distress; goods washed ashore from wrecked ship.—jet'tison n. jetsam;—v.t. throw overboard, as cargo; (Fig.) to abandon, as a scheme.

jetty (jet'-i) n. breakwater built to protect harbour; landing-pier.

Jew (jōō) n. (fem. Jew'ess) Hebrew or Israelite; (Fig.) sometimes applied to one who drives a hard bargain.—Jew'ish a.—Jew'ishness n.—Jew'ry n. Judea; Jewish people; ghetto.—Jew's harp, small, lyre-shaped musical instrument held between the lips, sounded by means of a steel tongue struck with the finger.

jewel (jōō'-el) n. precious stone; ornament set with gem(s); highly valued person or thing;—v.t. adorn with jewels; fit (as a watch) with jewel for pivot-bearings;—pr.p. jew'elling;—pa.p. jew'elled.—jew'eller n. one who deals in jewels.—jew'ellery, jew'elry n. jewels collectively.

jib (jib) n. (*Naut.*) triangular stay-sail extended from outer end of jib-boom to fore topmast-head; projecting beam of crane or derrick;—v.t. swing (the sail) from one side to the other; — v.t. swing round (of sail) as course of ship is changed.—jib'-boom n. spar run out from the extremity of the bowsprit.

jib (jib) v.i. (of horse) to stand still and refuse to go on; move restively; (*Fig.*) refuse obstinately to go on with task.—to jib at, be reluctant to do something.

jibe (jib) n. sneering comment.—v.i. sneer.—pr.p. jib'ing.—pa.p. jibed.— Also gibe.

jiffy (jif'-i) n. (*Colloq.*) moment; instant.

jig (jig) n. lively dance; music for this; trick; tool used to guide cutting tools in the making of duplicate parts;—v.t. jerk up and down;—v.i. dance; bob up and down;—pr.p. jig'ging.—pa.p. jigged. —jig'-jog n. jerky motion.—jig'-saw n. machine fret-saw.—jig-saw puzzle, picture cut into irregular pieces for putting together again.

jigger (jig'-er) n. one who or that which jigs; mechanical device which operates with jerky movement esp. apparatus for washing and separating ores by shaking in sieves under water; iron-headed golf club for approach-shots; rest for billiard cue.

jiggery-pokery (jig'-er-i-pōk'-er-i) n. (*Colloq.*) underhand scheming.

jilt (jilt) n. one, esp. woman, who capriciously disappoints lover;— v.t. disappoint in love; break engagement to marry.

jingle (jing'-gl) v.t. cause to give sharp, tinkling sound;—v.i. tinkle; use repetitive sounds in poetry;—n. tinkling sound, as of bells; correspondence of sounds, rhymes, etc., in verse to catch the ear; light, covered two-wheeled cart.

jingo (jing'-gō) n. mild oath, as in *By Jingo*; one who expresses vehement patriotism.—jing'o, jing'o-istic a.—jing'oism n. political, chauvinistic principles of jingoes.

jinn (jin) n.pl. (*sing.* jin'nee) spirits of Mohammedan mythology, appearing as men and animals. Also Djinn, Ginn.

jinriksha (jin-rik'-sha) n. two-wheeled hooded carriage pulled by one or more men in Japan (*abbrev.* rick'shaw).

jitters (jit'-erz) n.pl. (*Slang*) state of nervous agitation. — jit'terbug n. (*U.S.*) a jazz-dancer; a person who panics easily.—jit'tery a.

jiu-jitsu See ju-jutsu.

jive (jīv) n. and v.i. lively modern dance; its music.

job (job) n. piece of work; (*Colloq.*) habitual employment or profession; —pl. lengths of defective cotton fabrics sold usually by weight;—a. lumped together (of miscellaneous articles).—v.i. do odd jobs; act as broker; use influence unscrupulously;—v.t. hire out for specified time (as horse); deal unscrupulously in business. — pr.p. job'bing.— pa.p. jobbed.—job'ber n. middleman, particularly in Stock Exchange; one who transacts public business to his own advantage; one who does odd jobs; one who hires out horses by day or hour.—job'bery n. underhand means to gain profit; fraudulent dealings. —job'bing a. not regularly employed; —n. odd jobs.

Job (jōb) n. (*Bib.*) Hebrew patriarch of the Old Testament; person accepting continued disaster with infinite patience. — a Job's comforter, one who aggravates distress of another while pretending to console him.

jockey (jock'-i) n. professional rider in horse-races; dealer in horses; one who cheats in business;—v.t. jostle against, in riding; manoeuvre for one's own advantage; trick;—v.i. cheat.—jock'eyism, jock'eyship n.

jocose (jō-kōs') a. given to jesting; waggish.—jocose'ly adv.—jocose'ness, jocos'ity n. the quality or state of being jocose.

jocular (jok'-ū-lar) a. given to jesting; merry.—jocular'ity n.—joc'ularly adv.

jocund (jok'-und) a. merry; gay; genial.—jocund'ity, jocund'ness n.— joc'undly adv.

jodhpurs (jod'-pôôrz) n.pl. long riding breeches, close-fitting from knee to ankle.

jog (jog) v.t. push with the elbow or hand; nudge; stimulate (as memory); —v.i. move on at slow pace; to plod on;—pr.p. jog'ging;—pa.p. jogged.— n. nudge; push to awaken attention; reminder.—jog'-trot, slow trot.

joggle (jog'-l) v.t. shake slightly; join by notches to prevent sliding apart;—v.i. shake; totter;—pr.p. jog'gling.—n. jolt; joint of two bodies by means of notches, that sliding apart is prevented; metal pin joining two pieces of stone.

join (join) v.t. bring together; fasten; unite; act in concert with; become member of; return to (as one's ship); —v.i. meet; unite in marriage, partnership, etc.; be in contact;—n. junction; fastening. — joind'er n. (*Law*) union.—join'er n. workman who does wood-work of buildings. —join'ery n. trade of joiner.—to join battle, begin fighting.—to join issue, to take different sides on point in debate.

joint (joint) n. place where two

things are joined; articulation of two or more bones in body; cut of meat with bone prepared for the table; (*Slang*) bar, restaurant, etc.;—*v.t.* unite; provide with joints; cut up, as meat;—*v.i.* fit like joints;—*a.* jointed; held in common.—**joint'ed** *a.* having joints.—**joint'ing** *n.* process of filling in brick-work, wood-work, etc., e.g. with mortar.—**joint'ly** *adv.* together; co-operatively.—**joint-stock company**, mercantile, banking, or co-operative association with capital made up of transferable shares.—**joint'ure** *n.* property settled on woman at marriage to be hers on decease of her husband.—**out of joint**, dislocated; (*Fig.*) disordered.

joist (joist) *n.* beam to which boards of floor or laths of ceiling are nailed.

joke (jōk) *n.* something said or done to provoke laughter; witticism; prank;—*v.t.* make merry with; banter;—*v.i.* make sport; be merry. —**jok'er** *n.* one who makes jokes or plays pranks; (*Slang*) fellow; (*Cards*) extra card in the pack, used in some games, such as poker.—**jok'ingly** *adv.*

jolly (jol'-i) *a.* jovial; handsome;—*v.t.* (*U.S.*) cajole;—*n.* (*Slang*) marine;—*adv.* very; exceptionally.—**jollifica'tion** *n.* celebration; noisy party.—**joll'iness, joll'ity** *n.* mirth.

jolt (jōlt) *v.t.* shake with sudden jerk;—*v.i.* shake, as a vehicle on rough ground;—*n.* sudden jerk.

Jonah (jō'-na) *n.* (*Bib.*) Hebrew prophet; (*Colloq.*) a person who brings bad luck, especially on board a ship.

jonquil (jon'-kwil) *n.* variety of narcissus, with small yellow flowers.

joss (jos) *n.* Chinese idol.—**joss'-stick** *n.* small stick of incense burned in a Chinese temple.

jostle (jos'-l) *v.t.* push against, esp. with elbow;—*v.i.* push;—*n.* push against.

jot (jot) *n.* iota; something negligible; —*v.t.* scribble down; make note of; —*pr.p.* **jot'ting**.—**jot'ter** *n.* one who jots down; notebook.—**not to care one jot or tittle**, not to care at all.

jougs (jōōgz) *n.* iron ring, in which criminal was held fast by neck; form of pillory in Scotland.

joule (jōōl, joul) *n.* (*Elect.*) unit of work; energy expended in 1 sec. by 1 ampere flowing through a resistance of 1 ohm.

journal (jur'-nal) *n.* diary; book recording daily transactions of business firm; daily newspaper; periodical.—**journalese'** *n.* term of contempt for second-rate literary style of journalists.—**jour'nalise** *v.i.* write for journal.—**jour'nalism** *n.*—**jour'nalist** *n.* one who writes professionally for newspaper or periodical. —**journalist'ic** *a.*

journey (jur'-ni) *n.* travel from one place to another; distance covered in specified time;—*v.i.* travel.—**jour'neyman** *n.* orig. one hired to work by the day; skilled artisan who has completed his apprenticeship.

joust (jōōst) *n.* mock encounter on horseback; tournament;—*v.i.* tilt.

Jove (jōv) *n.* Jupiter.—**jo'vial** *a.* orig. born under influence of planet Jupiter; convivial.—**jovial'ity, jo'vialness** *n.*—**jo'vially** *adv.*

jowl (joul) *n.* jawbone; cheek; the dewlap, of cattle.

joy (joi) *n.* gladness; exhilaration of spirits; —*v.i.* rejoice; exult; —*v.t.* gladden.—**joy'ance** *n.* gaiety.—**joy'ful** *a.*—**joy'fully** *adv.*—**joy'fulness** *n.*—**joy'less** *a.* dismal.—**joy'lessly** *adv.*—**joy'lessness** *n.*—**joy'ous** *a.* full of joy. —**joy'ously** *adv.*—**joy'ousness** *n.*—**joy'-ride** *n.* (*Slang*) pleasure ride, or stolen ride.—**joy'-stick** *n.* (*Colloq.*) control column of aircraft.

jubilant (jōō'-bi-lant) *a.* exulting; uttering songs of triumph.—**ju'bilantly** *adv.*—**ju'bilate** *v.i.* rejoice; exult. —**jubila'tion** *n.* rejoicing; exultation.

jubilee (jōō'-bi-lē) *n.* Jewish festival of emancipation celebrated every fiftieth year; (*R.C.Ch.*) year of indulgence granted orig. at fixed intervals, now at any time; fiftieth anniversary of any event; time of rejoicing.—**silver jubilee**, twenty-fifth anniversary.—**diamond jubilee**, sixtieth anniversary.

Judaism (jōō'-dā-izm) *n.* religious doctrines and rites of the Jewish people.—**Juda'ic, -al** *a.* pert. to Jews.—**Juda'ically** *adv.*

judge (juj) *n.* one who judges; officer authorised by the Crown to administer justice; arbitrator;—*v.t.* decide; hear and try case in court of law; give final opinion or decision; criticise;—*v.i.* act as judge; form opinion; come to conclusion.—**judge'ship** *n.* office of judge.—**judg(e)'ment** *n.* act of judging; legal decision arrived at by judge in court of law; discernment; special infliction of suffering or death; opinion. —**Judg(e)ment Day**, day on which God will pronounce the final judgment on mankind.

judicature (jōōd'-i-kā-tūr) *n.* power of dispensing justice; judges collectively; court of justice; judge's period of office.—**ju'dicable** *a.* capable of being tried or judged.—**ju'dicative** *a.* having power to judge.—**ju'dicatory** *a.* dispensing justice.—**judic'ial** *a.* pert. to court of justice or to judge; impartial.—**judic'ially** *adv.*—**judic'iary** *n.* judges of the Crown collectively; —*a.* pert. to courts of law; passing judgment or sentence.—**judic'ious** *a.* wise; prudent.—**judic'iously** *adv.*—**judic'iousness** *n.*

judo (jōō'-dō) n. form of ju-jitsu.

jug (jug) n. vessel of earthenware, glass, etc., with handle and spout;—v.t. to stew (rabbit or hare) in jug or covered vessel.

Juggernaut (jug'-er-nawt) n. chief idol among the Hindus: any fanatical idea for which people are prepared to sacrifice their lives; tyrannical force which crushes all obstacles.

juggle (jug'-l) v.i. deceive by artifice; perform conjuring tricks;—v.t. defraud;—n. trick by sleight of hand; imposture; verbal trickery.—jugg'ler n. conjurer; cheat.—jugg'lery n.

jugular (jug'-u-lar) a. pert. to neck or throat;—n. one of large veins of the neck.

juice (jōōs) n. sap; liquid constituent of fruits or vegetables; (Slang) petrol or electricity used in motor-car, aeroplane, etc.—juic'iness n.—juic'y a. full of juice.

ju-ju (jōō'-jōō) n. W. African fetish, as an idol, to which sacrifices are made; taboo.

jujube (jōō'-jōōb) n. shrub, native of Syria, with small, edible fruit; lozenge made of gelatine, fruit-juice, sugar, etc.

ju-jutsu (jōō-jut'-sōō) n. form of wrestling, originating in Japan.— Also ju-jit'su.

juke-box (jōōk'-boks) n. (Colloq.) gramophone which plays a tune when a coin is inserted.

julep (jōō'-lep) n. sweet drink, esp. one in which medicine is taken. Also ju'lap.

Julian (jōōl'-yan) a. pert. to Julius Caesar.—Julian Calendar, calendar as adjusted by Julius Caesar in 46 B.C. in which the year was made to consist of 365 days, 6 hours.

July (jōō-lī') n. seventh month of the year.

jumble (jum'-bl) v.t. mix in confused mass;—v.i. be in a muddle;—n. miscellaneous collection; chaotic muddle.—jum'ble-sale n. sale of second-hand goods for charity-fund.

jumbo (jum'-bō) n. huge person, animal, or thing.

jump (jump) v.i. spring over; skip (as page of book); risk; steal;—v.t. lift feet from ground and alight again; spring; twitch; coincide;—n. leap; bound; sudden, nervous start. —jump'iness n. nervous twitching. —jump'y a. nervous—jump'ing-jack n. toy figure, the limbs of which twitch when a string is pulled.—count'er-jump'er n. shop-assistant, esp. in drapery store.

jumper (jump'-er) n. loose tunic worn by sailors; knitted jersey.

junction (jungk'-shun) n. act of joining; place of joining; connection. —junc'ture n. joint; exigency.

June (jōōn) n. sixth month of the year.

jungle (jung'-gl) n. land covered with forest trees, tangled undergrowth, esp. dense forests of equatorial latitudes.—jung'le-fev'er n. severe form of malaria.

junior (jōōn'-yur) a. younger, esp. of son with same name as his father; of lower status;—n. young person; younger of two; minor; one in subordinate position.

juniper (jōō'-ni-per) n. evergreen shrub, with dark blue berries used in flavouring gin.

junk (jungk) n. flat-bottomed Chinese sailing vessel.

junk (jungk) n. pieces of old cordage used for oakum; useless, discarded articles; (Naut.) hard, dry salted meat; (Colloq.) narcotic drugs.

junket (jung'-ket) n. orig. cream cheese served on a rush-mat; dish of curds usually fruit-flavoured, and served with cream; merry-making; —v.i. feast; picnic;—v.t. entertain; —pr.p. jun'keting.—pa.p.—jun'keted. —jun'keting n. merrymaking; picnicking.

junta (jun'-ta) n. council of state in Spain and South America.

Jupiter (jōō'-pi-ter) n. in Roman mythology, the supreme god, equivalent to Greek Zeus. Also Jove; largest and brightest of the outer planets.

Jurassic (jōō-ras'-ik) a. (Geol.) of the middle system of Mesozoic rocks as found in the Jura mountains; oolitic.

juridical (jōō-rid'-ik-al) a. pert. to judge, or administration of justice. —jurid'ically adv.

jurisdiction (jōō-ris-dik'-shun) n. administration of justice; legal authority; limit within which this authority may be exercised.— jurisdic'tional, jurisdic'tive a.

jurisprudence (jōō-ris-prōō'-dens) n. science of law; study of fundamental principles underlying any legal system.—medical jurisprudence, forensic medicine, study of medicine as it concerns criminal law.

jurist (jōō'-rist) n. one versed in the law, esp. in Roman or civil law.

jury (jōō'-ri) n. body of citizens (12 in England, 15 in Scotland (except in civil cases)) selected and sworn to give a verdict from the evidence produced in court; committee chosen to decide the winners in a competition.—ju'ror n. one who serves on a jury. Also ju'ryman, ju'rywoman.

jurymast (jōō'-ri-mast) n. temporary mast erected in a ship to replace one broken or carried away in a storm.

just (just) a. straight; exact; complete; true; founded on fact; proper; well-deserved;—adv. exactly; nicely, closely; scarcely.—just'ly *adv.* in a just manner; deservedly; uprightly.—**jus′ness** *n.* fairness.

justice (jus′-tis) *n.* quality of being just; equity; merited reward or punishment; administration of law; judge; magistrate.—**jus′ticeship** *n.* office of a judge.—**justic′iary** *n.* judge; Lord Chief-Justice;—*a.* pert. to administration of law.—**Justice of the Peace (J.P.),** county or borough magistrate, commissioned to keep the peace in local areas.

justify (jus′-ti-fī) *v.t.* prove the justice of; excuse; adjust;—*pa.p.* just′ified.—**justifi′able** *a.* defensible; excusable.—**justifi′ableness** *n.* justifi′ably *adv.* justifica′tion *n.*—vindication; (*Theol.*) absolution. — **jus′tificative, jus′tificatory** *a.* having power to justify.—**jus′tifier** *n.*

jut (jut) *v.i.* project;—*pr.p.* jut′ting.—*pa.p.* jut′ted [a form of *jet*].

jute (jōōt) *n.* fibre of Indian plant used in manufacture of carpets, cordage, etc.

Jutes (jōōts) *n.pl.* Teutonic tribe which invaded Britain in 5th and 6th cents.

juvenile (jōō′-ven-īl) *a.* young; youthful; puerile;—*n.* young person; book written for children.—**juvenil′ity** *n.*—**juvenil′ia** *n.pl* works of author produced in childhood and early youth.

juxtapose (juks-ta-pōs′) *v.t.* place side by side.—**juxtaposi′tion** *n.* contiguity.

K

Kaffir, Kafir (kaf′-ėr) *n.* branch of Bantu group of natives, living in eastern part of S. Africa.—**kaffir corn,** variety of sorghum.—**Kaff′irs** *n.pl.* Stock Exchange term for S. African mine shares.

kail, kale (kāl) *n.* colewort; cabbage with curled leaves.—**kail′-yard** *n.* kitchen garden.

Kaiser (kī′-zėr, kā′-zėr) *n.* name from Latin *Caesar*, given to emperors of Old Holy Roman Empire, and to rulers of German Empire.

kale See kail.

kaleidoscope (ka-lī′-do-skōp) *n.* optical instrument, varying patterns being displayed on rotation.— **kaleidoscop′ic** *a.*

kalends See calends.

kalif See caliph.

kangaroo (kang-ga-rōō′) *n.* a marsupial found in Australia, having highly developed hindquarters and progressing by flying bounds.—**kangaroo′-grass** *n.* valuable fodder grass of Australia and S. Africa.

Kanuck, Canuck (ka-nuk′) *n.* Canadian: French Canadian.

kaolin (kā′-o-lin) *n.* China clay; fine porcelain clay chiefly produced from feldspar in China, U.S.A. and Cornwall by weathering.—**kaolin poultice,** antiseptic substitute for linseed poultice.

kapok (ka-pok′) *n.* silky white fibre developed in the fruit pods of the silk cotton-tree, used for stuffing pillows, etc.; vegetable down.

karob, carob (kar′-ob) *n.* the locust, evergreen Mediterranean tree; its pods provide succulent edible pulp; seed of the tree.

karroo, karoo (ka-rōō′) *n.* in S. Africa, one of the series of semi-barren terraces separating successive ridges of hills.

katathermometer (kat - a - ther-mom′-e-tėr) *n.* a combination of the wet and dry bulb thermometer, designed to give indication of total effect of temperature, humidity, evaporation, wind, etc., on ventilation conditions.

katydid (kā′-ti-did) *n.* green insect of grasshopper family.

kauri, kauri-pine (kou′-ri-pīn) *n.* coniferous tree of New Zealand giving valuable timber.—**kau′ri-gum** *n.* resinous gum dug up on sites of ancient kauri forests.

kava (kā′-va) *n.* narcotic beverage made from a Polynesian shrub of the pepper family.

kayak (kī′-yak) *n.* Eskimo seal-skin canoe.

keck (kek) *v.i.* to retch, as if about to vomit.

kedge (kej) *n.* small anchor used to keep a ship steady or for warping; —*v.t.* warp, as a ship; move ship by means of small anchors and hawsers.

kedgeree, kedjeree (kej′-e-rē) *n.* Indian dish: in European cookery, a breakfast dish of cold fish, boiled rice and eggs.

keek (kēk) *v.i.* and *n.* (*Scot.*) peep.

keel (kēl) *n.* length-wise beam of ship on which the frames rest; a low flat-bottomed barge used for coaling ships;—*v.i.* navigate; turn up the keel.—**keel′age** *n.* dues for ships at rest in a port or harbour.—**keel′haul** *v.t.* haul under keel of a ship by ropes attached to yard-arms on each side; form of punishment in British navy during the 17th and 18th cents.; rebuke a subordinate severely.—**keel′son** *n.* large vertical girder formed of plates and angles bolted to the top of a ship's keel.—**to keel over,** capsize.

keen (kēn) *a.* having fine cutting edge; penetrating; piercing (of wind); eager; intense (of frost); acrimonious.—**keen′ly** *adv.*—**keen′ness** *n.*

keen (kēn) *n.* in Ireland, lamentation or dirge for the dead; coronach;—*v.i.* wail over the dead before burial.

keep (kēp) *v.t.* retain possession of; detain; observe; carry out; have the care of; cause to continue; manage; commemorate;—*v.i.* remain in good condition; continue;—*pa.p.* **kept**.—*n.* care; guardianship; maintenance; food or fodder; chief tower or dungeon (or donjon) of a castle; stronghold.—**keep'er** *n.* one who keeps or guards; attendant; game-keeper; finger-ring to prevent another from slipping off.—**keep'ing** *n.* care; custody; harmony.—**keep'sake** *n.* anything given to recall memory of the giver.—**to keep well away from.**—**to keep company with**, associate with.—**to keep in touch with**, correspond with.—**to keep in with**, remain on friendly terms out of self-interest.—**to keep one's hand in**, maintain one's skill by occasional practice.—**to keep open house**, be very hospitable.—**to keep the peace**, be law-abiding.—**to keep up**, maintain (appearances, spirits, etc.); support.—**for keeps** (*Slang*) permanently.

keg (keg) *n.* small cask or barrel.

kelp (kelp) *n.* calcined ash of sea-weed, used as source of iodine; general name for large sea-weeds.

kelpie, kelpy (kel'-pi) *n.* (*Scot.*) water-spirit, usually in the form of a fearsome horse.

Kelt, Keltic Same as **Celt, Celtic**.

kelt (kelt) *n.* salmon which has just spawned.

kemp (kemp) *n.* coarse rough hairs in wool.

ken (ken) *v.t.* know; recognise; descry;—*n.* view; range of sight or knowledge.

kennel (ken'-el) *n.* house for dogs; pack of dogs;—*v.t.* to confine in a kennel; — *pr.p.* **kenn'elling**. — *pa.p.* **kenn'elled**.—**kenn'el-maid, kenn'elman** *n.* attendant on dogs.

kenspeckle (ken'-spek-l) *a.* conspicuous; well-known in a certain locality.

kentledge (kent'-lej) *n.* loose balance weights of a crane; pigs of iron placed in a ship's hold for permanent ballast.

kepi (kā'-pē) *n.* light military cap, flat-topped with a straight peak.

kept (kept) *pa.t.* and *pa.p.* of **keep**.

kerb (kerb) *n.* edge of pavement; curb.—**kerb'stone** *n.*

kerchief (ker'-chif) *n.* square of fine linen used by women to cover the head; any cloth used in dress, esp. on the head or round the neck.

kermess, kermis (ker'-mes) *n.* church-festival or fair in the Low Countries.

kern (kern) *n.* light-armed Irish foot-soldier; Irish peasant.

kern (kern) *n.* in Scotland, last sheaf of the harvest; harvest-home. Also **kirn**;—*v.i.* to harden, as corn in ripening; granulate.

kernel (ker'-nel) *n.* edible part of nut; little grain or corn; central or essential part; nucleus.

kerosene (ker'-o-sēn) *n.* American term for paraffin oil.

kersey (ker'-zi) *n.* coarse woollen cloth.

kerseymere (ker'-zi-mēr) *n.* fine light woollen twill cloth.

kestrel (kes'-trel) *n.* genus of small falcons.

ketch (kech) *n.* small two-masted coasting vessel.

ketchup, catchup, catsup (kech'-up) *n.* sauce made of mushrooms, tomatoes, etc.

kettle (ket'-l) *n.* metal vessel, with spout and handle, used for heating and boiling water.—**kett'ledrum** *n.* a musical percussion instrument of copper covered with vellum.—**kett'ledrum'mer** *n.*—**a pretty kettle of fish**, an awkward affair.

key (kē) *n.* low-lying island near the coast of Florida.

key (kē) *n.* instrument which shuts or opens a lock; instrument by which anything is screwed and turned, as a *watch-key*, etc.; spanner; highest central stone of an arch; lever in musical instrument, depressed by the fingers in playing; lever on a type-writer; wedge to secure firmly rail in chair on railway lines; any rough surface or a space between laths or wire-meshing to secure adhesion of plaster; winged husk containing the seed of ash, maple, etc.; (*Mus.*) set of related notes; solution; translation of a foreign book, or solutions to questions set; —*a.* critical; of vital importance.—**key'board** *n.* range of keys on keyed instrument; manual.—**key'hole** *n.* hole in door or lock for receiving key. — **key-industry**, industry on which vital interests of the country depend.—**key'-man** *n.* indispensable employee.—**key'-mon'ey** *n.* money demanded from new tenant as condition of granting a lease.—**key'-note** *n.* first tone of the scale in which passage is written.—**key'-ring** *n.* ring for keeping keys together.—**key'-sig'nature** *n.* (*Mus.*) essential sharps and flats placed at beginning of piece after the clef to indicate the key.—**key'stone** *n.* wedge-shaped central stone at the crown of an arch.—**all keyed up**, tense with expectation.—**House of Keys**, lower house of the Tynwald, legislature of Isle of Man.

khaki (kä'-kē) *a.* dust-coloured or buff;—*n.* cloth of this colour, used for soldiers' uniforms.

khamsin (kam'-sin) *n.* hot, dry, south wind which blows over Egypt, esp. in March to May.

khan (kàn) n. title of respect in Mohammedan countries of C. Asia and N. India; among Mongol races, king, prince, or chief.—**khan'ate** n. dominion of a khan.

khedive (ke-dēv') n. title of ruler of Egypt, from 1867 to 1922.

kia ora (kē'-a ōr'-a) interj. Maori salutation, 'Your health.'

kibbutz (ki-bôôts) n. Israeli communal settlement.

kibosh (kī'-bosh, ki-bosh') n. (Colloq.) nonsense; rubbish.—**to put the kibosh on**, to defeat; to get rid of.

kick (kik) v.t. hit with the foot;—v.i. strike out with the foot; show opposition; resist; recoil violently (of rifle, etc.);—n. blow with the foot; recoil of a gun; (Slang) stimulation; thrill.—**kick'-off** n. commencement of game of football.—**kick'-up** n. disturbance; shindy.—**to kick over the traces**, throw off all restraint; rebel openly.—**to kick the bucket** (Slang) die.—**drop'-kick** n. in rugby, kick made as ball, just dropped from the hand, rebounds from the ground.—**free'-kick** n. in association football, privilege granted to a player to kick the ball once without interference from opposing side.—**place'-kick** n. in rugby, kick allowed to side which has scored a try.

kickshaw (kik'-shaw) n. toy or trifle; light dainty dish.

kid (kid) n. young goat; leather made from the skin of a goat; (Slang) child;—pl. gloves of smooth kid leather;—a. made of this.

kid (kid) v.t. and i. (Slang) hoax; pretend;—n. pretence.—**kid'der** n. practical joker.

kidnap (kid'-nap) v.t. carry off, abduct, or forcibly steal a person.—**kid'napper** n.—**kid'napping** n.

kidney (kid'-ni) n. one of two glandular organs in the lumbar region which excrete urine; nature kind; temperament.—**kidney bean**, the kidney-shaped seed of any bean plant; haricot or French bean.

kieselghur (kē'-zl-gûr) n. fine earth, nearly pure silica, used in the manufacture of dynamite.

kilderkin (kil'-der-kin) n. small barrel; liquid measure.

kilerg (kil'-erg) n. (Physics) thousand ergs.

kill (kil) v.t. deprive of life; put to death; destroy; neutralise; to weaken; render inactive; pass (time);—n. the act of killing; animal killed in a field-sport.—**kill'er** n. one who kills; butcher or slaughterman; club for killing fish.—**kill'er-whale** n. grampus, smaller variety of whale, with immense jaws and capable of swallowing seals, porpoises, etc.—**kill'ing** a. depriving of life; very exhausting; (Colloq.) exceedingly

funny.—**kill'ingly** adv.—**kill'-joy** n. depressing fellow; gloomy person.

killock (kil'-ok) n. small anchor.—Also **kill'ick**.

Kilmarnock (kil-mar'-nok) n. flat, round tam-o'-shanter.

kiln (kil, kiln) n. large oven, generating great heat, in which materials are dried, calcined, or hardened (lime, malt, hops, etc.).—**kiln-dry** v.t. dry in a kiln.

kilo- (kil'-o) prefix fr. Gk. chilioi, one thousand, in the metric system denoting a thousand.—**kil'ocycle** n. unit of frequency, 1000 cycles or oscillations per second.—**kil'ogramme**, **kil'ogram** n. 1000 grammes, equal to 2.2046 lbs. avoirdupois.—**kil'olitre**, **kil'oliter** n. 1000 litres, equivalent of 35.31472 cubic feet and to 220.0967 imperial gallons.—**kil'ometre**, **kil'ometer** n. 1000 metres, 3280.899 English feet or nearly ⅝ of a mile.—**kilo'ton** n. unit of nuclear explosive force equivalent to 1000 tons of TNT.—**kil'owatt** n. 1000 watts, equivalent to 1.34 horsepower.—**kil'owatt-hour** n. one kilowatt expended for one hour, commonly called 'Board of Trade unit.'

kilt (kilt) n. short pleated skirt usually of tartan cloth, reaching from waist to knees;—v.t. tuck up or pleat vertically.—**kilt'ie** n. (Colloq.) soldier in Highland regiment.

kimono (ki-mō'-nō) n. over-garment with wide sleeves, worn in Japan by both men and women; dressing-gown in imitation of this.

kin (kin) n. family relations; relationship; consanguinity; affinity;—a. of the same nature or kind; kindred;—akin.—next of kin, person or persons closest in relationship to deceased person.

kinaesthesis (kin-ēs-thē'-sis) n. perception of muscular effort.—**kinaesthet'ic** a.

kind (kīnd) n. genus; sort; variety; class;—a. sympathetic; considerate; good; benevolent; obliging.—**kind'-heart'ed** a.—**kind'-heart'edness** n.—**kind'liness** n. benevolence.—**kind'ly** a. and adv.—**kind'ness** n. kind action.—**kind of** (Colloq.) somewhat; to a certain extent.—**in kind**, payment in goods, instead of money.

kindergarten (kin'-der-går'-tn) n. infant school.

kindle (kin'-dl) v.t. set on fire; light; excite (passions); inflame; enrage;—v.i. catch fire; grow warm or animated.—**kin'dling** n. act of starting fire; material for starting fire.

kindred (kin'-dred) n. relation by birth; affinity; relatives by blood or marriage;—a. related; cognate; allied; congenial.

kine (kīn) n.pl. plural form of cows.

kinematic, **kinematical** (kin-e-mat'-ik, -i-kal) *a.* pert. to pure motion.—**kinemat'ics** *n.pl.* branch of mechanics dealing with problems of motion.

kinetic, kinetical (ki-net'-ik, -i-kal) *a.* pert. to motion; imparting or growing out of motion.—**kinetic energy,** mechanical energy of a body by virtue of its motion; —*n. pl.* science which treats of changes in movements of matter produced by forces.

king (king) *n.* (*fem.* queen) ruler of country; sovereign; monarch; one distinguished above all others; playing-card with picture of a king; chief piece in game of chess; in draughts, man which is crowned.— **King'-at-Arms, King'-of-Arms** *n.* one of the three principal officers, under the Earl Marshal, of the College of Arms, with jurisdiction over heraldry and armoury.—**king'-cob'ra** *n.* larger snake than the common cobra; hamadryad.—**king'-cup** *n.* marshmarigold, species of buttercup.— **king'dom** *n.* quality and attributes of a king; country subject to a king; realm; sphere; domain; one of the three divisions (animal, vegetable, mineral) of Natural History.—**king'-fisher** *n.* bird with brilliant plumage. —**king'-hood** *n.* kingship; kingliness. —**king'let** *n.* puppet king; goldencrested wren.—**king-like, king'ly** *a.* royal.—**king'-pin** *n.* metal rod upon which steering stub axle of a motor-car is pivoted; the swivel-pin; (*Fig.*) important person. — King's (or Queen's) Bench, one of the three divisions of the English High Court of Justice.—King's (or Queen's) Counsel, honorary distinction conferred on eminent barristers giving them the right to wear a silk gown (hence, *to take silk*).—King's (or Queen's) evidence, evidence in a court-of-law given by an accomplice, on behalf of the prosecution, against a prisoner.—**king'ship** *n.* state or office of a king.—King's Proctor, Treasury solicitor who may intervene to stop decrees *nisi* in divorce being made absolute.—King's Regulations, the official regulations of the British Army or Navy.

kink (kingk) *n.* short twist, accidentally formed, in a rope, wire, etc.; mental twist; — *v.i.* and *t.* to twist spontaneously; to form a kink (in).

kinsfolk (kinz'-fōk) *n.* blood relations; kin; members of same family. —**kin'ship** *n.* state of being related by birth.—**kins'man, kins'wo'man** *n.* person of same kin or race with another.

kiosk (ki-osk') *n.* open pavilion or summer-house, supported by pillars; stall for the sale of periodicals, sweets, tobacco, etc.; band-stand.

kip (kip) *n.* (*Slang*) lodging; sleep.

kipper (kip'-er) *n.* herring, split, then smoked; male salmon when spent after spawning season;—*v.t.* cure fish by salting, smoking, or drying.

kirk (kerk) *n.* (*Scot.*) church.— **kirk'-sess'ion** *n.* lowest ecclesiastical court in Scotland, composed of the minister and elders of a church.

kirtle (ker'-tl) *n.* kind of short gown or jacket; outer petticoat.

kismet (kis'-met) *n.* fate or destiny.

kiss (kis) *v.t.* and *v.i.* touch with the lips, in affection or reverence; touch gently;—*n.* salute by touching with lips.—**kiss'able** *a.*—**kiss'-curl** *n.* small lock of hair at temples.— **kiss'er** *n.* one who kisses; (*Slang*) mouth.—**kiss of life,** mouth to mouth form of artificial respiration. **to kiss hands,** kiss the hand of sovereign on accepting office.

kit (kit) *n.* soldier's outfit, excluding his uniform; set of tools or implements; personal effects.—**kit'-bag** *n.* —**kit'-box** *n.* box for holding small tools.

kit (kit) *n.* contr. of *kitten.*—**kit'ty** *n.* pool in card games; (*Bowls*) jack.

kitchen (kich'-en) *n.* room in which food is prepared and cooked. — **kitchenette'** *n.* small room combining kitchen, pantry and scullery.— **kit'chen-gar'den** *n.* vegetable garden. —**kitch'en-maid** *n.*— **kitchen midden,** shell-heap or refuse-heap of prehistoric origin.

kite (kīt) *n.* bird of Falcon family; sheet of paper, etc., stretched over a light frame and flown by means of a cord attached and held from ground; (*Slang*) aircraft. — **kite-'fly'ing** *n.* effort to discover how the public will react to some proposal.

kith (kith) *n.* in phrase **kith and kin,** friends and acquaintances, as well as blood-relations.

kitten (kit'-n) *n.* young cat;—*v.i.* bring forth young cats.—**kitt'enish** *a.* like a kitten; playful.—**kitt'y** *n.* pet name for cat.

kittiwake (kit'-i-wāk) *n.* species of gull.

kittle (kit'-l) *v.t.* tickle;—*a.* difficult to manage; ticklish; intractable.— **kitt'ly** *a.* easily tickled.—**kittle cattle,** persons difficult to handle.

kiwi (kē'-wē) *n.* N.Z. flightless bird; apteryx; (*Slang*) New Zealander.

klaxon (klak'-son) *n.* electric (form. mechanical) horn on motor-cars [Protected Trade Name].

kleptomania (klep-tō-mā'-ni-a) *n.* uncontrollable impulse to steal.— **kleptoma'niac** *n.*

kloof (klōōf) *n.* ravine; gulley.

knack (nak) *n.* inborn dexterity; adroitness; mannerism; habit.— **knack'iness** *n.* skill.—**knack'y** *a.* handy; clever.

knacker (nak'-er) n. one who deals in and disposes of old, worn-out horses.—**knack'ery** n. slaughter-house for such horses.

knag (nag) n. knot in wood; peg; branch of deer's horn.—**knagg'y** a. knotty; rugged.

knap (nap) v.t. snap; split flints for walling;—pr.p. **knap'ping**.—**knap'per** n. one who breaks stones.—**knap'-ping-hamm'er** n.

knapsack (nap'-sak) n. leather bag for food and clothing, borne on the back; rucksack.

knapweed (nap'-wēd) n. name applied to many plants of genus *Centaurea*.

knar (när) n. knot in tree or in timber.—**knarred** a. knotty; gnarled.

knave (nāv) n. dishonest person; rascal; boy; servant; playing-card, the jack.—**knav'ery** n. roguery; trickery; sharp practice.—**knav'ish** a. villainous; mischievous; roguish.—**knav'ishly** adv.

knead (nēd) v.t. work up flour into dough; work or shape anything by pressure; blend together; massage.—**knead'er** n.

knee (nē) n. joint formed by the articulation of femur and tibia, the two principal bones of the leg; anything of wood or metal bent like a knee;—v.t. touch with the knees.—**knee'breech'es** n.pl. breeches reaching and fastened below knee-joints, as in court-dress.—**knee'-cap** n. patella, flattened bone in front of knee-joint; covering to protect knees, esp. of horses.—**knee'-reflex'** n. involuntary jerk given by the leg in response to tap on knee-cap.

kneel (nēl) v.i. fall on the knees; rest on the knees in prayer.—pa.t. and pa.p. **kneeled** or **knelt**.—**kneel'ing** n.

knell (nel) n. toll of a bell rung at a funeral or death; portent of doom;—v.i. toll;—v.t. summon by tolling bell.

knew (nū) pa.t. of **know**.

knickerbockers (nik'-er-bok'ers) n. pl. loose breeches gathered in at the knees.—**knick'ers** n.pl. woman's undergarments; drawers.

knick-knack (nik'-nak) n. trifle, toy, or trinket.

knife (nīf) n. cutting instrument;—pl. **knives** (nīvz)—v.t. stab with knife.—**knife'-board** n. board covered with leather for cleaning knives.—**to get one's knife into** (Colloq.) have a spite against.

knight (nīt) n. orig. in feudal times, young man admitted to privilege of bearing arms; person of rank below baronet, giving right to prefix *Sir* to his name; champion; minor piece in chess bearing a horse's head;—v.t. dub or create a knight.—**knight'-err'ant** n. knight who wandered about in search of adventures.—**knight'-err'antry** n.—**knight'hood** n. dignity or order of knights.—**knight'liness** n.—**knight'ly** a. and adv.—**knight bachelor**, one who has been knighted but not admitted to any particular Order.

knit (nit) v.t. form into a knot; tie; weave yarn or thread in a series of connected knots by means of needles or pins; cause to grow together, as a fractured bone; contract (the brows); unite closely;—v.i. be united closely.—pr.p. **knit'ting** **knit'ter** n. **knit'ting** n. work of a knitter; the net-work formed by knitting.—**knit'ting-need'le** n. long eyeless needle for knitting yarn into stockings, etc.—**knit'-wear** n. knitted garments.

knob (nob) n. rounded lump; hard protuberance or swelling; boss or stud; small round handle of door, etc.—**knobbed** a. set with knobs.—**knob'biness** n.—**knob'by** a. full of knobs; lumpy.—**knob'kerrie** n. in S. Africa, stick with large knob on the end, used as weapon.

knock (nok) v.t. and v.i. strike or beat with something hard or heavy; strike against; rap; (Colloq.) criticise;—n. stroke with something heavy; rap on a door; blow.—**knock'abouts** n.pl. acrobats who combine skill and fun on the stage.—**knock'er** n. ornamental metal attachment on a door.—**knock'-kneed** a. having the knees bent inward.—**knock'-out** n. blow in boxing-match which knocks out opponent; competition in which losers are eliminated at each stage.

knoll (nōl) n. small rounded hill; top of a hill; hillock; mound.

knot (not) n. complication of threads, cords, or ropes, formed by tying or entangling; ribbon folded in different ways worn as an ornament; cockade; bond of union; small group (of people); difficulty; hard lump, esp. of wood where branch has sprung from the stem; (Naut.) speed equal to one nautical mile (6,080 ft.) per hour;—v.t. form a knot in; entangle; tie.—pr.p. **knot'ting** —**knot'tiness** n.—**knot'ty** a. full of knots; rugged; difficult; puzzling; intricate.

know (nō) v.t. be aware of; have information about; be acquainted with; recognise; have experience; understand; have sexual intercourse with;—v.i. to have information or understanding.—pa.t. **knew** (nū).—pa.p. **known**.—**know'-all** n. conceited person who thinks he knows everything.—**know-how** n. specialised skill.—**know'ing** a. sly; cute; cunning; clever.—**know'ingly** adv.—**to know the ropes**, know from experience what to do.

knowledge (nol'-ej) *n.* understanding; acquaintance with; skill; information; learning; sexual intercourse.—**knowl'edgeable** *a.*

knuckle (nuk'-l) *n.* joint of a finger; knee-joint of ox, sheep, etc.;—*v.t.* strike with the knuckles;—*v.i.* bend the fingers.—**knuck'le-bones** *n.* a game, dibs.—**knuck'le-dust'er** *n.* iron or brass shield of rings fitting across the knuckles, used to deliver murderous blows.—**to knuckle down** or **under**, yield or submit.—**near the knuckle**, bordering on the indecent.

knur, knurr (nur) *n.* knot. See **knar**; wooden ball, used in game of **knur and spell**, the ball being projected into the air and hit with a bat.

koala (kō-ä'-la) *n.* small marsupial of arboreal habit, known in Australia as the Native Bear.

Koh-i-noor (kō'-i-nōr) *n.* famous diamond of 102 carats, one of the British Crown Jewels.

kohl (kōl) *n.* powdered antimony used in the East as cosmetic.

kohlrabi (kōl'-rā-bi) *n.* variety of cabbage with edible turnip-shaped stem.

kola (kō'-la) *n.* African tree whose seeds or nuts contain caffeine; an aerated water.

kolinsky (ko-lin'-ski) *n.* Siberian mink; its fur.

kolkhos (kōlk'-hos) *n.* collective farm in Soviet Russia.

kookaburra (kook'-a-bur'-a) *n.* laughing jackass of Australia; great kingfisher.

kop, kopje (kop', kop'-i) *n.* small flattened hill in S. Africa.

Koran (kō-rän', kō'-ran) *n.* sacred book of Islam.

kosher (kō'-sher) *a.* (of food) pure, clean, esp. meat, made ceremonially clean according to Jewish law.

kotow, kowtow (kō-, kou-tou') *v.i.* perform Chinese ceremony of prostration by touching the ground with forehead; abase oneself; fawn on someone;—*n.* an obsequious act.

kraal (krāl) *n.* Hottentot or Kaffir village consisting of group of huts encircled by a stockade.

Kraken (krá'-ken) *n.* huge fabulous sea-monster.

Kremlin (krem'-lin) *n.* citadel of a Russian town or city, esp. the citadel of Moscow, seat of Soviet government.

kris (kris) *n.* Malay dagger with a wavy blade.

Krishna (krish'-nå) *n.* in Hinduism the last incarnation of Vishnu.

krone (krōn'-e) *n.* silver coin of Denmark and Norway;—*pl.* kro'ner. —Also old coin of Austria and Germany;—*pl.* kro'nen.

Kroo (krôô) *a.* W. African Negro race living on the coast of Liberia.

krypton (krip'-ton) *n.* non-metallic chemical element belonging to the group of rare gases present in the atmosphere.

kudos (kū'-dos) *n.* (*Colloq.*) fame; glory; credit.

kuh-horn (kôô'-horn) *n.* curved horn used by Swiss herdsmen when tending herds.

Ku Klux Klan (kū'-kluks-klan) *n.* American secret society, founded c. 1865, to oppose granting of privileges to the freed Negroes.

kukri (kook'-ri) *n.* short curved knife with broad blade, used by Gurkhas.

kulak (kôô'-lāk) *n.* prosperous smallholder in Russia who resisted the efforts of the Soviet to nationalise agriculture.

kümmel (kim'-el) *n.* liqueur flavoured with cumin and caraway seeds.

Kurd (kôôrd) *n.* member of a war-like nomadic race inhabiting Kurdistan.

kyle (kīl) *n.* (*Scot.*) narrow channel.

kyloe (kī'-lō) *n.* breed of small long-horned cattle in Scottish Highlands.

Kyrie (kir'-i-ē) *n.* words and music of the **Kyrie Eleison** (kī'-ri-ē el-ē'-i-son, kir'-i-ē el-ī'-son) 'Lord, have mercy on us' part of service in the R.C. Church; response in the Anglican communion service after each of the Ten Commandments.

L

la (lä) *n.* (*Mus.*) syllable for sixth tone of scale in tonic sol-fa notation.

laager (lä'-ger) *n.* (*S. Afr.*) defensive encampment within a circle of waggons; (*Mil.*) parking place for army transport vehicles.

label (lā'-bel) *n.* paper, card, etc., affixed to anything, denoting its contents, ownership, destination, etc.; (*Fig.*) classifying phrase or word applied to persons, etc.; (*Archit.*) dripstone;—*v.t.* affix a label to; identify by a label.—*pr.p.* la'belling.—*pa.p.* la'belled.

labial (lā'-bi-al) *a.* pert. to lips; formed by the lips, as certain sounds such as *p, b, w, o*.—*n.* sound formed by the lips.—la'biate, *pl.p.*

labiodental (lā'-bi-ō-den'-tal) *a.* pert. to lips and teeth;—*n.* sound made with the lips and teeth.—la'bium *n.* lip or lip-like structure.—*pl.* la'bia.

laboratory (lab'-or-a-tor-i) *n.* place for experiments or research in science, pharmacy, etc.

labour (lā'-bor) *n.* exertion of body or mind; toil; work demanding patience and endurance; manual workers collectively or politically; (*Med.*) pains of childbirth;—*pl.* heroic achievements;—*v.i.* work strenuously; take pains; move with difficulty; (*Med.*) suffer pains of childbirth; (*Naut.*) pitch and roll.— **labo'rious** *a.* toilsome: industrious.— **labo'riously** *adv.*—**labo'riousness** *n.*— **la'boured** *a.* clumsy and forced, as of literary style.—**la'bourer** *n.* worker, esp. one who does manual work.— **Labour Exchange,** bureau set up in local areas by the Government, to direct available labour into appropriate channels.—**Labour Party,** political party which champions interests of the working classes.—**labour of love,** work undertaken without thought of reward.

labret (lā'-bret) *n.* ornament inserted into the lip, worn by some primitive tribes.—**lab'ral** *a.*—**la'brose** *a.* having thick lips.—**la'brum** *n.* liplike structure.—*pl.* **la'bra.**

laburnum (la-bur'-num) *n.* small tree, with hanging racemes of yellow flowers.—**labur'nin** *n.* alkaloid found in its unripe seeds.

labyrinth (lab'-i-rinth) *n.* system of intricate winding passages; maze; (*Med.*) passages of the internal ear.—**labyrinth'al, labyrinth'ine** *a.*

lac, lakh (lak) *n.* in India one hundred thousand, as a *lac of rupees.*

lac (lak) *n.* deep-red resinous substance, the excretion of an insect, and used as a dye.—**seed'-lac** *n.* resinous substance cleared from twigs, etc.

lace (lās) *n.* string or cord used for fastening dress, shoes, etc.; net-like fabric of linen, cotton, silk, with ornamental design interwoven by hand or machine;—*v.t.* fasten with a lace; ornament with lace; mix, as coffee, with a dash of brandy;— **lac'ing** *n.* fastening formed by a lace threaded through eye-holes.

lacerate (las'-er-āt) *v.t.* tear; rend; injure.—**lac'erable** *a.*—**lac'erate(d)** *a.* torn; mangled.—**lacera'tion** *n.*—**lac'erative** *a.* having power to tear or injure.

lachrymal (lak'-ri-mal) *a.* pert. to or producing tears, as *lachrymal* duct, the tear-duct.—*n.* small vessel, in ancient graves, supposed to contain tears of the bereaved.—**lach'rymary, lach'rymatory** *a.* containing tears; causing tears to flow;—*n.* lachrymal vase.—**lach'rymose, lac'rymose** *a.* tearful; morose.—**lach'rymosely** *adv.*

lack (lak) *v.t.* and *v.i.* be destitute of; want;—*n.* deficiency; shortage; need; want.—**lack'-lus'tre** *a.* dim.

lack-a-day (lak'-a-dā) *interj.* exclamation of sorrow, regret, or dismay.—**lackadai'sical** *a.* affectedly pensive; listless—**lackadai'sically** *adv.*

lackey (lak'-i) *n.* liveried manservant; footman;—*v.t.* or *v.i.* attend or serve as a lackey.

laconic (la-kon'-ik) *a.* pert. to the *Lacones,* or Spartans; (of style) brief; concise; expressing maximum meaning in the minimum of words. Also **lacon'ical.**—**lacon'ically** *adv.*—**lac'onism, lacon'icism** *n.* brief, pithy style of speech; terse, sententious saying.

lacquer (lak'-er) *n.* varnish consisting of solution of shellac in alcohol;— *v.t.* varnish.

lacrosse (la-kros') *n.* outdoor ballgame played with a *crosse* or stick which has a net at the end.

lacteal (lak-te-al) *a.* pert. to milk; milky; resembling chyle;—*n.* lymphatic vessel conveying chyle from intestines to thoracic duct.—**lac'tate** *n.* (*Chem.*) salt of lactic acid, and a base.—**lacta'tion** *n.* act of giving or secreting milk; period during which mother suckles child.—**lac'teous** *a.* resembling milk.—**lactes'cence** *n.* process of turning milky.—**lactes'cent** *a.* producing milk or white juice.— **lac'tic** *a.* pert. to milk; procured from milk or whey.—**lactif'erous** *a.* bearing or conveying milk; producing a thick, milky juice, as a plant.—**lac'tose** *n.* milk-sugar.

lacuna (la-ū'-na) *n.* hollow; hiatus; omission.—*pl.* **lacu'nae.**

lacustral (la-kus'-tral) *a.* pert. to lakes or swamps. Also **lacus'trine.**

lad (lad) *n.* (*fem.* lass) young man; boy; (*Colloq.*) reckless man.—**lad'die** *n.* young boy.

ladder (lad'-er) *n.* frame of wood, steel, ropes, etc., consisting of two sides connected by rungs for climbing up; anything resembling a ladder, as *stocking-ladder,* vertical break in the woven fabric;—*v.t.* cause ladder in a stocking;—*v.i.* develop ladder in a stocking.

lade (lād) *v.t.* load, esp. ship or waggon; draw (fluid) by means of ladle.—*pa.t.* **lad'ed.**—*pa.p.* **lad'en.**— *n.* (*Scot.*) watercourse; mill-race.— **lad'ing** *n.* act of loading; freight.

ladle (lā'-dl) *n.* long-handled spoon for drawing off liquid;—*v.t.* draw off with ladle.

lady (lā'-dl) *n.* woman of social distinction, position, or independent means; well-bred woman; wife.—*pl.* **la'dies.**—**La'dy** *n.* title given to wife of nobleman below duke; title of daughter of duke, marquis, or earl; courtesy title of wife of knight or baronet.—**la'dybird** *n.* small beetle usually yellow or red, feeding on plant lice. Also **la'dybug, la'dy-cow.**— **La'dy-day** *n.* 25th March, Feast of the Annunciation of the Virgin Mary.— **la'dy-in-wait'ing** *n.* lady in Court circles appointed to attend on Queen or Princess.—**la'dy-kil'ler** *n.* man who imagines he has a fascination for women.—**la'dy-like** *a.* gracious; fastidious; (of a man) effeminate.—**la'dy-love** *n.* sweetheart.—**la'dyship** *n.* title of lady.—**la'dy's-maid** *n.*

personal servant of lady.—**lady's man**, man who seems to prefer lady's company to that of men.

laevo-rotation (lē'-vō-rō-tā'-shun) n. counterclockwise or left-hand rotation.—**lae'vo-rota'tory** a.

lag (lag) v.t. bind round, as pipes, cistern etc., with non-conducting material to prevent loss of heat.

lag (lag) a. slow; tardy;—n. time-lapse; retardation;—v.i. move slowly; fall behind.—pr.p. **lag'ging**.—pa.p. **lagged**.—**lag'gard** n. slowcoach; listless person.—**lag'ging** a. loitering.—**lag'gingly** adv.

lag (lag) n. (Colloq.) convict.

lager-beer (lä'-ger-bēr) n. light beer.

lagoon (la-gōon') n. marsh, shallow pond, or lake, esp. one into which the sea flows.

laic (lā'-ik) a. lay; secular;—n. layman.—**la'ically** adv.—**la'icise** v.t. secularise.

laid (lād) pa.t. and pa.p. of the verb lay;—a. put down; (of paper) having slightly ribbed surface showing the marks of the parallel wires on which pulp was laid.—**laid up**, indisposed; (Naut.) dismantled; temporarily out of service, for repairs.

lain (lān) pa.p. of verb lie.

lair (lār) n. den or bed of wild animal; (Scot.) ground for a grave in cemetery.

laird (lārd) n. (Scot.) landed proprietor.

laissez-faire (les'-ā-fer') n. policy of non-interference. Also **lais'ser-faire'**.

laity (lā'-i-ti) n. the people, as distinct from the clergy.

lake (lāk) n. large sheet of water within land.—**lake'-dwell'ing** n. prehistoric dwelling built on piles some distance from lake-shore.—**lake'let** n. small lake.—**la'ky** a. pert. to lakes.—**Lake District**, the region in N.W. England noted for its many lakes and hills.

lake (lāk) n. deep-red colouring matter consisting of aluminous earth and cochineal.

lakh Same as lac.

Lallans (lal'-anz) n. literary form of broad Scots incorporating words from various dialects.

lam (lam) v.t. (Slang) beat; flog.

lama (lä'-ma) n. Buddhist priest in Tibet.—**La'maism** n. form of Buddhist religion practised in Tibet, Mongolia, etc.—**la'masery** n. Tibetan monastery.—**Da'lai La'ma** n. or **Grand Lama**, chief of the lamas.

lamb (lam) n. young sheep; flesh of lamb as food; young and innocent person;—v.i. bring forth lambs.—**lamb'kin, lamb'ling** n. little lamb.—**lamb'like** a. gentle.

lambent (lam'-bent) a. playing on the surface; gleaming; flickering.—**lam'bency** n.

lame (lām) a. crippled in a limb; hobbling; (Fig.) unsatisfactory, as an excuse; imperfect;—v.t. cripple.—**lame'-duck** n. defaulter; bankrupt.—**lame'ly** adv.—**lame'ness** n.—**lam'ish** a. rather lame.

lamé (la'-mā) n. textile containing metal threads.

lamella (la-mel'-a) n. thin plate-like scale.—pl. **lamell'ae**.—**lam'ellar, lam'ellate** a. composed of thin plates or scales.

lament (la-ment') v.i. utter cries of sorrow; bemoan; mourn for;—v.t. deplore;—n. heartfelt expression of sorrow; elegy or dirge.—**lam'entable** a. grievous; sad; mean.—**lam'entably** adv.—**lamenta'tion** n. audible expression of grief.—**lament'ed** a. mourned.—**lament'ing** a. grieving.—**lament'ingly** adv.

lamina (lam'-i-na) n. thin plate or scale lying over another;—pl. **lam'inae**.—**lam'inable, lam'inar, lam'inary** a. consisting of, or resembling, thin plates.—**lam'inate** v.t. cause to split into thin plates;—v.i. split into layers.—**lam'inate, -d** a. formed of thin plates; stratified.—**lamina'tion** n. arrangement in thin layers.—**laminif'erous** a. consisting of laminae.

Lammas (lam'-as) n. feast of first-fruits, on Aug 1st.

lamp (lamp) n. vessel containing oil to be burned by a wick, or gas from a jet; any light-giving contrivance.—**lamp'-black** n. fine soot formed by smoke of a burning lamp; soot formed by condensation of smoke from burning resinous substances; pigment from this soot.

lampoon (lam-pōon') n. bitter personal satire, usually in verse; abusive or scurrilous publication;—v.t. abuse in written satire.—**lampoon'er** n.—**lampoon'ery** n.

lamprey (lam'-pri) n. eel-like fish with sucking mouth by which it attaches itself to rocks, etc.

lance (läns) n. war-weapon consisting of spear-head on a long wooden shaft; sharp-pointed surgical instrument;—v.t. pierce with lance; open with lancet.—**lance'-cor'poral** n. private soldier with acting rank of corporal.—**lan'ceolate** a. (Bot.) having the shape of lance-head; tapering at both ends. Also **lan'ceolar**.—**lan'cer** n. cavalry soldier armed with lance;—pl. square dance, like quadrilles.—**lan'cet** n. small two-edged surgical knife.—**lan'cet-arch** n. narrow, pointed arch.—**lan'cet-win'dow** n. tall and pointed type of window.—**lan'ciform** a. shaped like lance.—**a free lance**, professional person who works on his own, not attached to a firm.

land (land) n. earth; solid matter of surface of globe; any area of the earth; ground; soil; inhabitants of a country; real estate;—*v.t.* set on shore;—*v.i.* go on shore; disembark; (*Aviat.*) bring aircraft to rest on land or water;—**land agent**, a person employed by estate-owner to manage farms, etc.—**land′-ar′my** *n.* one of the Women's Services recruited in both World Wars to work on the land.—**land′-breeze** *n.* off-shore current of air.—**land′-crab** *n.* crab, which lives on land but breeds in the sea.—**land′ed** *a.* pert. to, or possessing, real estate; (*Slang*) left in the lurch or in awkward situation.—**land′-fall** *n.* sighting of land by ship at sea.—**land′-girl** *n.* member of Women's Land Army.—**land-hold′er** *n.* proprietor of land.—**land′ing** *n.* disembarkation; level part of staircase between two flights of steps.—**land′ing-gear** *n.* wheeled undercarriage of aeroplane.—**land′ing-net** *n.* net used by anglers for landing fish already caught by rod.—**land′ing-place** *n.* point of disembarkation on quayside.—**land′ing speed** *n.* minimum airspeed at which an aircraft normally alights.—**land′ing-stage** *n.* small quayside or (sometimes) floating pier at which passengers and cargo are landed from sea-going vessels.—**land′lady** *n.* the owner of estate or property; one who lets rooms in a house; proprietrix of an inn.—**land′-lock** *v.t.* enclose by land.—**land′lord** *n.* lord of a manor; owner of houses rented to tenants; proprietor of an inn, etc.—**land′-lub′ber** *n.* landsman (term used by sailors); one who knows little or nothing about boats.—**land′mark** *n* mark to indicate boundary; outstanding or elevated object indicating general direction.—**land′-owner** *n.*—**land′rail** *n.* corn-crake.—**land′scape** *n.* portion of land which the eye can comprehend in a single view; pictorial representation of an inland scene.—**landscape gardener**, one employed professionally to lay out gardens according to plan.—**land′scapist** *n.* painter of landscape.—**land′slide** *n.* fall of rock from a hillside or cliff; (*Fig.*) sudden overwhelming change of public opinion.—**land′slip** *n.* landslide.—**lands′man** *n.* non-seafaring person.—**land′-tax** *n.* tax on land or property built on the land.—**land′ward** *a.* situated near the land; lying toward the land away from sea.

landau (lan′-daw) *n.* carriage, the top of which may be opened and thrown back.—**landaulet′, landaulette′** *n.* small type of landau; motor-car with folding hood.

landgrave (land′-grāv) *n.* German nobleman, corresponding in rank to earl in England.

lane (lān) *n.* track between hedges or across fields; narrow street or road; division of road or motorway.

language (land′-gwāj) *n.* speech; tongue; expression of ideas by words or written symbols; mode of speech peculiar to a nation.—**lang′uaged** *a.*—**dead language**, language not spoken now, as opposed to *living language.*

languid (lang′-gwid) *a.* listless; flagging from exhaustion.—**lang′uidly** *adv.*—**lang′uidness** *n.*—**lang′uish** *v.i.* droop with weariness; become wistful.—**lang′uishing** *a.* drooping; sentimental.—**lang′uishingly** *adv.*—**lang′uishment** *n.* tenderness of look.—**lang′uor** *n.* lassitude; sentimental softness.—**lang′uorous** *a.* languid.

langur (lang′-gŏŏr) *n.* Indian monkey.

laniferous (lan-if-ẹr-us) *a.* bearing wool; fleecy.

lank (langk) *a.* drooping; weak and thin; long and straight, as hair.—**lank′y** *a.* slender.—**lank′ly** *adv.*—**lank′ness, lank′iness** *n.*

lanolin, lanoline (lan′-ō-lin) *n.* oily substance obtained from wool.

lantern (lant′-ẹrn) *n.* a portable fixture, enclosing a light and protecting it from wind, rain, etc.; square turret placed over the junction of the cross in a cathedral; light chamber of a lighthouse.—**lant′ern-jaws** *n.* hollow cheeks.—**Chinese-lantern** coloured, collapsible paper-lantern.—**dark lantern**, lantern with sliding shutter to obscure light.—**magic lantern**, instrument by means of which are magnified images of pictures are thrown on a screen in a dark room.

lanthanum (lan′-than-um) *n.* white metallic element, one of the rare earths, allied to cerium, (symbol La).

lanyard, laniard (lan′-yǎrd) *n.* short rope or line for fastening; cord, with knife attached, worn round the neck.

lap (lap) part of clothing between waist and knees of a person who is sitting; part of the body thus covered; overlying part of any substance or fixture; circuit, as in motor-racing, etc.;—*v.t.* lay over or on; lead by full circuit;—*v.i.* be spread or laid on or over; be turned over or on; be made even.—**lap′dog** *n.* small pet dog.—**lapel′** *n.* part of coat or dress which laps over the facing.—**lapelled′** *a.*—**lap′ful** *n.* that which fills a lap.—**lap′pet** *n.* part of garment which hangs loose; fold of flesh.—**lap′peted** *a.*

lap (lap) *v.t.* wrap or twist round; enfold.

lap (lap) *v.i.* take up food or drink by licking; make sound like animal lapping its food;—*v.t.* lick up; wash or flow against;—*pr.p.* **lap′ping.**—*pa.p.* **lapped.**

lapidary (lap'-i-dar-i) *a.* pert. to stones or to art of cutting stones; pert. to inscriptions and monuments; —*n.* one skilled in cutting, polishing and engraving of precious stones; dealer in precious stones. Also **lapida'rian, lap'idarist, lap'idist.**—**lap'idifica'tion** *n.*—**lapid'ify** *v.t.* turn into stone;—*v.i.* become petrified.—*pr.p.* **lapid'ifying**—*pa.p.* **lapid'ified.**—**lap'islazu'li** *n.* opaque mineral, sapphire-blue in colour, used in jewellery.

Lapp (lap) *n.* and *a.* native of Lapland. Also *n.* **Lap'lander.**

lapse (laps) *v.i.* slip or fall; fail to maintain a standard of conduct; pass from one proprietor to another because of negligence;—*n.* slip or fall; gliding; passing of time; error of omission; failure to do one's duty. —**lapsed** *a.* no longer valid.

lapwing (lap'-wing) *n.* crested bird of plover family, commonly called peewit.

larboard (lar'-bōrd) *n.* obsolete nautical term for the left-hand side of a ship looking towards the bow. Now called *port.*

larceny (lár'-sen-i) *n.* theft.—**lar'cenist** *n.* thief.—**lar'cenous** *a.* pilfering.

larch (lárch) *n.* cone-bearing tree.

lard (lárd) *n.* clarified fat of pig;—*v.t.* smear with fat; stuff, as meat or fowl, with bacon or pork; (*Fig.*) embellish.—**lard'y** *a.*

larder (lárd'-er) *n.* pantry where meat and food stuffs are kept; supply of provisions.

large (lárj) *a.* of great size; extensive; liberal; numerous;—*adv.* in a large way.—**large'-heart'ed** *a.* generous; liberal.—**large'ly** *adv.*—**large'ness** *n.* bigness; magnanimity.—**larg'ish** *a.* fairly big.—**at large**, free; escaped from prison.

largess (lár'-jes) *n.* gift; donation. Also **lar'gesse.**

larghetto (lár-get'-ō) *a.* (*Mus.*) rather slow; less slow than *largo.*—**lar'go** *a.* and *adv.* slow.

lariat (lar'-i-at) *n.* lasso; rope or thong of leather, with noose for catching wild horses.

lark (lárk) *n.* frolic; prank;—*v.i.* play practical jokes.

lark (lárk) *n.* small, singing-bird;—**lark'spur** *n.* delphinium.

larva (lár-va) *n.* insect in the caterpillar, grub, or maggot stage.—*pl.* **lar'vae.**—**lar'val** *a.*

larynx (lar'-ingks) *n.* upper part of windpipe containing the vocal cords.—*pl.* **lar'ynges** (-injēs), **lar'ynxes.**—**laryn'geal, laryn'gean** *a.* pert. to the larynx.—**laryngi'tis** *n.* inflammation of the larynx.—**laryng'oscope** *n.* special mirror for examining larynx.

lascar (las'-kar) *n.* native East-Indian sailor.

lascivious (la-siv'-i-us) *a.* lustful.—**lasciv'iously** *adv.*—**lasciv'iousness** *n.*

laser (lā'-zer) *n.* device for the amplification of light rays into an intense beam.

lash (lash) *n.* thong of a whip; cord; stroke with a whip; satirical or sarcastic reproof; eyelash;—*v.t.* strike with lash; dash against, as waves; bind with rope; scourge with criticism;—*v.i.* ply the whip.—**lash'ing** *n.* act of whipping; ropes fastening anything securely;—*pl.* abundance.

lass (las) *n.* young woman; girl; sweetheart.—**lass'ie** *n.* little girl.

lassitude (las'-i-tūd) *n.* exhaustion of body or mind; languor.

lasso (las-óó') *n.* long rope with noose, used for catching wild horses; lariat.—*pl.* **lasso(e)s'.**

last (lást) *a.* following all the rest; most unlikely; final; supreme;—*adv.* finally; immediately before in time; in conclusion;—*n.* final appearance.—**at last**, finally.

last (lást) *n.* mould of human foot in wood or metal on which shoes are made or repaired;—*v.t.* fit with last.—**to stick to one's last**, attend diligently to one's business.

last (lást) *v.i.* continue in time; endure; suffice.—**last'ing** *a.* durable; permanent.

latch (lach) *n.* small piece of iron or wood used to fasten a door; catch;—*v.t.* fasten with latch. **latch'-key** *n.* key used for raising latch of door.

late (lāt) *a.* behindhand; coming after; delayed; earlier than the present time; no longer in office; deceased;—*adv.* after the usual time; not long ago; lately; far into the night, day, week, etc.—**late'ly** *adv.*—**late'ness** *n.* tardiness.—**lat'er** *a.* (comp. of *late*) subsequent.—**lat'est** *a.* (superl. of *late*) longest after the usual time; most recent or up-to-date.—**latter** (lat'-er) *a.* (var. of *later*) later or more recent; second of two just mentioned; modern.—**latt'erly** *adv.*—**lat'ish** *a.* somewhat late.—**of late**, recently.

lateen (la-tēn') *a.* applied to triangular type of sail.

latent (lā'-tent) *a.* not visible; dormant; hid; concealed.—**la'tence, la'tency** *n.*—**la'tently** *adv.*

lateral (lat'-e-ral) *a.* relating to the side.

latex (lā'-teks) *n.* the milky sap of trees, plants; the milky juice of the rubber tree.

lath (láth) *n.* thin, narrow slip of wood to support plaster, slates, etc.—*pl.* **laths** (láthz).

lathe (lāTH) *n.* machine-tool for turning articles of wood, metal, etc.

lather (láTH'-er) *n.* foam or froth made with soap and water; froth from sweat;—*v.t.* spread over with lather;—*v.i.* form lather.

Latin (lat´-in) *à.* pert. to *Latium*, part of ancient Italy with Rome as its centre, or to its inhabitants; written or spoken in the language of the Latins;—*n.* inhabitant or language of ancient Latium; member of one of the modern Latin races descended linguistically from the ancient Latins.—**Lat´inise** *v.t.* give Latin form to; translate into Latin; —*v.i.* use Latin words.—**Lat´inism** *n.* Latin idiom.—**Lat´inist** *n.* Latin scholar or expert.—**Latin Church**, Roman Catholic Church using Latin as its official language.—**Latin languages**, languages derived mainly from Latin as French, Italian, Spanish, Rumanian.—**Latin Quarter**, part of Paris where University and Art students live and work.

latitude (lat´-i-tūd) *n.* distance, measured in degrees, north or south of the Equator; angular distance of a heavenly body from the ecliptic; (*Fig.*) breadth of signification; deviation from a standard, esp. religious or ethical; scope; range.— **latitud´inal** *a.* pert. to latitude.— **latitudina´rian** *a.* broad; liberal, esp. in religious principles;—*n.* one indifferent to strictly orthodox religious principles. **latitudina´rianism** *n.*—**latitu´dinous** *a.* having latitude.

latrine (la-trēn´) *n.* water-closet, esp. in barracks, hospitals, etc.

latten (lat´-en) *n.* alloy of copper and zinc, with appearance of brass, used for church ornaments; sheet tin; iron-plate covered with tin.—**gold latten**, very thin sheet gold.

latter See **late**.

lattice (lat´-is) *n.* net-like framework of wood, metal, etc., formed by strips, laths, or bars crossing each other diagonally; window thus formed; arrangement of atoms in a crystal.—**latt´ice-work** *n.* a trellis.

laud (lawd) *v.t.* praise in words or singing; extol;—*n.* eulogy; praise;— *pl.* in R.C. services, the prayers immediately after matins.—**laudabil´ity** *n.* praiseworthiness.—**laud´able** *a.* commendable. — **laud´ableness** *n.* — **laud´ably** *adv.*—**lauda´tion** *n.* eulogy; act of praising highly.—**laud´atory** *a.* expressing praise.

laudanum (law´-dạ-num) *n.* preparation of opium in spirit of wine; tincture of opium.

laugh (laf) *v.i.* express mirth spontaneously; make an involuntary sound of amusement; be merry or gay;—*n.* mirth; laughter.—**laugh´-able** *a.* droll; ludicrous; comical.— **laugh´ableness** *n.*—**laugh´ably** *adv.*— **laugh´er** *n.*—**laugh´ing** *a.* happy; merry.—**laugh´ing-gas** *n.* nitrous oxide gas used as anaesthetic in

dentistry.—**laugh´ing-hyae´na** *n.* spotted hyaena.—**laugh´ing-jack´ass** *n.* great kingfisher of Australia.— **laugh´ingly** *adv.*—**laugh´ing-stock** *n.* object of ridicule.—**laugh´ter** *n.* merriment; audible expression of amusement.—**to laugh in (or up) one's sleeve**, laugh inwardly.

launch (lawnsh) *v.t.* throw through the air; cause to slide into the water as ship; initiate, as an attack; start a new activity;—*v.i.* go into the water; push out to sea; go forth; embark upon;—*n.* sliding of ship into water.

launch (lawnsh, lånsh) *n.* largest boat carried on warship or other vessel; a boat driven by steam, petrol, or electricity; a pinnace.

laundry (lawn´-dri, lån´-dri) *n.* place where clothes are washed, dried and ironed; process of washing clothes, etc.; clothes thus washed, etc.— **laun´der** *v.t.* wash linen;—*n.*—**laun´-derer** *n.*—**launderette** *n.* premises where washing and drying machines may be used for a fee.—**laun´dress** *n.* woman who washes and irons clothes.

laurel (lor´-el) *n.* evergreen shrub, used formerly to make wreaths symbolical of honour;—*pl.* (*Fig.*) honours;—*a.* consisting of laurel.— **lau´reate** *a.* crowned with laurel;—*n.* esp. in *Poet-Laureate*, poet attached to the Royal Household;—*v.t.* crown with laurel wreath.—**Lau´reate-ship** *n.* —**lau´relled** *a.*

lava (lå´-va) *n.* molten rock, ejected by volcano, hardening as it cools.

lave (låv) *v.t.* wash; bathe;—*v.i.* bathe; wash oneself.—**lav´atory** *n.* place for washing; privy.

lavender (lav´-en-dẹr) *n.* aromatic plant yielding an essential oil; pale-lilac colour of lavender-flowers.— **lav´ender-wat´er** *n.* perfume made of spirits of wine and lavender-oil.

lavish (lav´-ish) *a.* prodigal; over-generous; extravagant; ample;— *v.t.* expend or bestow extravagantly; squander. — **lav´ishly** *adv.* — **lav´ish-ment** *n.*—**lav´ishness** *n.*

law (law) *n.* rule established by authority; legal science; established usage; rule, principle, or maxim of science, art, etc.; legal profession; legal procedure; (*Theol.*) Jewish or Mosaic code, as distinct from Gospel.—**law´-abid´ing** *a.* well-behaved; conforming to the law.—**law´-ful** *a.* allowed by law; legitimate.— **law´fully** *adv.*—**law´fulness** *n.*—**law´-giver** *n.* legislator.—**law´less** *a.* not conforming to the law; violent.— **law´lessly** *adv.*—**law´lessness** *n.*—**Law´-Lord** *n.* a peer in the House of Lords who is a member of the highest Court of Appeal in England; (*Scot.*) judge of the Court of Session. —**law´-off´icer** *n.* legal adviser of

Government.—**law'-suit** n. process in law for recovery of a supposed right.—**law'yer** n. practitioner of law; solicitor.—**common law**, body of laws established more by custom than by definite legislation.—**written law**, statute law, codified and written down, as distinct from *Common law*.

lawn (lawn) n. stretch of closely-cut, carefully-tended grass.—**lawn'-mow'er** n. machine for cutting grass.—**lawn'-tenn'is** n. outdoor game played on a court of grass, gravel, etc., by two or four persons with racquets and balls.

lawn (lawn) n. fine linen or cambric.

lax (laks) a. slack; flabby; loose, esp. in moral sense; not constipated.—**la'xative** a. having purgative effect;—n. aperient.—**lax'ity, lax'ness** n. slackness; looseness of moral standards.—**lax'ly** adv.

lay (lā) v.t. place or put down; apply; exorcise; spread on a surface; wager; produce; prepare; sight or aim gun; set out dishes, etc. (on a table); charge, as with a responsibility;—v.i. produce eggs.—pa.p. **laid**.—n. situation.—**lay'er** n. one who, or that which lays, as bricklayer, hen, etc.; thickness or coating laid down; stratum of rock or vegetation; shoot of a plant partly covered with earth, thus laid to encourage propagation.—**lay'ering** n. artificial propagation of plants by layers.—**lay-by** n. parking area on verge of highway.—**lay'-off** n. slack time in industry.—**lay'-out** n. design or plan, as of a garden.—**to lay about one**, hit out vigorously in all directions.—**to lay down the law**, assert dogmatically.—**to lay in**, gather together, as a store of provisions.—**to lay oneself out to**, take great trouble over.—**to lay oneself open to**, expose oneself to (as attack, criticism).—**to be laid up**, be confined to bed by illness; (of a ship, motor, etc.) be temporarily out of service.—**to lay waste**, devastate; pillage.

lay (lā) n. song; a lyrical poem.

lay (lā) a. pert. to laity, as distinct from clergy; unprofessional.—**la'icise** v.t. deprive of clerical character.—**la'ity** n.—**lay'-broth'er** n. servant in monastery.—**lay'-fig'ure** n. jointed figure used by artists in imitation of the human form; nonentity.—**layman** n. one of the laity, or people; one who is not expert in a branch of knowledge.—**lay'-read'er** n. one not a clergyman, but authorised to read the lessons during a Church service.—**lay'-sis'ter** n. woman who serves the nuns in a convent.

layette (lā'yet') n. outfit for newborn baby.

laze (lāz) v.i. (Colloq.) be lazy; lounge;—n. lazy time.

lazy (lā'-zi) a. unwilling to work; slothful; indolent.—**la'zily** adv.—**la'ziness** n.—**la'zy-bed**, n. seed-bed for potatoes.—**la'zy-bones**, n. lazy fellow; idler.

lea (lē) n. meadow; pasturage.

leach (lēch) v.t. wash by causing water to pass through; (Bot.) remove salts from soil by percolation;—v.i. pass through by percolation;—n. vessel used for leaching. Also **letch**.—**leach'y** a.

lead (led) n. malleable bluish-grey metal, used for roofing, pipes, etc.; plummet for sounding ocean depths; thin strip of type metal to separate lines of print; graphite for pencils;—pl. sheets of lead for roof coverings;—a. made of, or containing lead.—**lead'ed** a. fitted with lead; set in lead.—**lead'en** a. made of lead; heavy; dull.—**lead'-pen'cil** n. pencil containing black lead.—**lead'-poi'soning** n. poisoning caused by lead being absorbed into the blood.—**swinging the lead** (Slang) trying to evade a job.

lead (lēd) v.t. show the way; guide; direct; persuade; precede; (Cards) to play first card of a round;—v.i. go in front and show the way; outstrip; conduct; tend to;—n. precedence; guidance; direction; principal part in a play; electric wire; first card played in a card-game; dog's leash.—**lead'er** n. guide; conductor; commander; leading editorial in a newspaper; (Mus.) performer who leads an orchestra or choir.—**lead'ership** n.—**lead'ing** n. direction; the act of guiding.—**lead'ing-art'icle** n. leader or editorial in a newspaper.—**lead'ing-lad'y, -man** n. actress or actor playing principal role.—**lead'ing-ques'tion** n. (Law) question so phrased as to suggest the answer expected.—**lead astray**, tempt from virtue.

leaf (lēf) n. thin shoot from the stem or branch of a plant; part of book containing two pages; side of double door or shutter; hinged flap; very thinly beaten plate, as of gold.—pl. **leaves**.—v.i shoot out leaves.—**leaf'age** n. foliage.—**leaf'iness** n.—**leaf'less** a.—**leaf'let** n. tiny leaf; printed sheet; brochure; tract.—**leaf'-mould** n. leaves decayed and reduced to mould, used as manure.—**leaf'y** a. full of leaves.—**to turn over a new leaf**, to reform.

league (lēg) n. old measure equal to three miles.

league (lēg) n. compact between nations or individuals for promoting common interests; association, as of football clubs;—v.i. combine in an association.

leak (lēk) n. crack, crevice, fissure, or hole in a vessel; oozing of liquid from such; (*Fig.*) escape of information; (*Elect.*) escape of electrical current;—*v.i.* let fluid into, or out of, defective vessel.—**leak'age** *n.* oozing quantity of liquid which passes through a defect in a vessel; (*Fig.*) giving away of secrets, news, etc.—**leak'iness** *n.*—**leak'y** *a.* having leaks.—**spring a leak**, develop crack or flaw.

leal (lēl) *a.* faithful; loyal; true.—**Land o' the Leal** (*Scot.*) heaven.

lean (lēn) *v.i.* incline; cause to rest against;—*v.i.* incline.—*pa.t.* and *pa.p.* **leaned** or **leant** (lent).—*n.* slope; a rest against.—**lean'ing** *n.* inclination (of body or mind).—**lean'-to** *n.* shed built against wall or house.

lean (lēn) *a.* thin; wanting in flesh or fat; (*Fig.*) empty; impoverished;—*n.* flesh of meat without fat.—**lean'ly** *adv.*—**lean'ness** *n.*

leap (lēp) *v.i.* spring; jump up or forward; vault;—*v.t.* pass over by leaping;—*pa.t.* **leaped** or **leapt** (lept).—*pa.p.* **leaped**, **leapt.**—*n.* jumping up or forward; (*Fig.*) sudden rise (as of book-sales).—**leap'-frog** *n.* game, in which one stoops down, and another vaults over his head.—**leap'-year** *n.* year of 366 days.

learn (lern) *v.t.* acquire knowledge; get to know; gain skill by practice;—*v.i.* gain knowledge; take example from.—*pa.t.* and *pa.p.* **learned** (lernd) or **learnt**.—**learned** (lern'-ed) *a.* having knowledge; erudite.—**learn'edly** *adv.*—**learn'edness** *n.*—**learn'er** *n.*—**learn'ing** *n.* that which is learned; literature; erudition.

lease (lēs) *n.* contract renting houses, etc. for a specified time; time covered by lease; any tenure;—*v.t.* grant possession of lands, etc., to another for rent; let for specified time.—*pr.p.* **leas'ing**.—*pa.p.* **leased**.—**leas'able** *a.*—**lease'hold** *a.* held on lease.—**lease'holder** *n.*

leash (lēsh) *n.* line by which hawk or dog is held; set of three hounds, or hares held in leash;—*v.t.* hold by a leash; bind.

least (lēst) *a.* (superl. of **little**) smallest; most minute;—*adv.* in the smallest degree;—*n.* smallest amount.—**at least**, at any rate; however.

leather (leTH'-er) *n.* skin of an animal dressed and prepared for use; anything made of leather;—*v.t.* apply leather to; (*Colloq.*) thrash with a strap.—**leath'ering** *n.* thrashing.—**leath'er-jack'et** *n.* crane-fly grub.—**leath'ern** *a.* made of leather.—**leath'ery** *a.* like leather; tough.—**patent leather**, leather with shiny surface.

leave (lēv) *n.* liberty granted; formal good-bye; furlough; permission to be absent from duty.—

to take one's leave of, bid farewell to.—**French leave**, absence without permission.

leave (lēv) *v.t.* quit; forsake; omit to remove; bequeath; permit; entrust;—*v.i.* cease; desist; depart from; withdraw.—*pr.p.* **leav'ing**.—*pa.p.* **left**.—**leav'ings** *n.pl.* things left; refuse.

leaven (lev'-n) *n.* substance which causes bread dough to rise; (*Fig.*) anything which causes general change in the mass;—*v.t.* raise with leaven.

lecher (lech'-er) *n.* man given to lewdness;—*v.i.* practise lewdness.—**lech'erous** *a.*—**lech'erously** *adv.*—**lech'erousness, lech'ery** *n.*

lectern (lek'-tern) *n.* reading-desk in a church.

lection (lek'-shun) *n.* portion of Scripture read during Church service.—**lec'tionary** *n.* book containing portions of Scripture to be read on particular days.—**lec'tor** *n.* reader.

lecture (lek'-tūr) *n.* discourse on any subject; formal reproof;—*v.t.* instruct by discourses; reprove;—*v.i.* deliver formal discourse.—**lec'turer** *n.* one who lectures; assistant to a University professor.—**lec'tureship** *n.*

led (led) *pa.t.* and *pa.p.* of verb **lead**.

ledge (lej) *n.* layer; projection, as from wall or cliff; a shelf; ridge of rock.

ledger (lej'-er) *n.* book in which business firm enters all debit and credit items;—*a.* stationary (only in compound words).—**led'ger-line** *n.* line with hook and sinker; (*Mus.*) additional line above or below stave. Also **leg'er**.

lee (lē) *n.* place protected from wind; shelter;—*a.* pert. to the part or side farthest from the wind.—**lee'-shore** *n.* shore on the lee-side of vessel.—**lee'-side** *n.* side of a vessel opposite to direction from which the wind is blowing.—**leeward** (lē'-ward, lōō'-ward) *a.* pert. to, or in, the direction towards which the wind is blowing.—**lee'-way** *n.* side movement of a vessel to the leeward of her course; loss of progress; (*Colloq.*) room to manoeuvre.

leech (lēch) *n.* blood-sucking worm used for blood-letting; (*Arch.*) physician.

leek (lēk) *n.* bulbous plant allied to onion; national emblem of Wales.

leer (lēr) *n.* furtive look expressive of malignity, lasciviousness, or triumph;—*v.i.* look thus.—**leer'ingly** *adv.*

lees (lēz) *n.pl.* sediment at bottom of wine-cask; dregs.

leet (lēt) *n.* (*Scot.*) selected list of candidates for a post.

left (left) *a.* on side of the body

westward when one is facing north. Also **left'-hand**.—*n.* side opposite to right; in legislative assemblies, left side of Speaker's chair where Opposition members sit, hence extreme or radical party;—*adv.* to or on the left.—**left'-hand** *n.* left side;—*a.* situated on left side; executed with the left hand.—**left'-hand'ed** *a.* using left hand more easily than the right; awkward.—**left'-hand'edness** *n.*—**left'ish** *a.* having political views which tend towards the left.—**left'-wing** *n.* political group with relatively radical views.

left (left) *pa.t.* and *pa.p.* of the verb leave.

leg (leg) *n.* limb of animal used in supporting the body and in walking; any support, as leg of table; one of the two divisions of forked object, as compasses; part of garment covering the leg; (*Cricket*) field to left of, and behind, batsman; (*Naut.*) ship's course covered on one tack. — *pr.p.* **leg'ging**. — *pa.t.* and *pa.p.* **legged**.—**legged** *a.*—**leg'ging** *n.* gaiter to cover legs.—**leg'gy** *a.* having disproportionately long legs.—**leg'less** *a.*—**leg'-pull** *n.* (*Slang*) practical joke.—**on one's last legs**, almost worn out.—**sea legs** become used to ship's motion.

legacy (leg'-ą-si) *n.* bequest; gift of personal property by will.—**leg'atary** *n.* legatee.—**legatee'** *n.* one who receives a legacy.

legal (lē'-gąl) *a.* pert. to, or according to, law; statutory; constitutional.—**legalisa'tion** *n.*—**le'galise** *v.t.* make lawful; sanction.—**legal'ity** *n.* conformity to law.—**le'gally** *adv.*—**legal tender**, money, which may be lawfully used in paying a debt.

legate (leg'-āt) *n.* Pope's highest diplomatic envoy; ambassador.—**leg'ateship** *n.*—**leg'atine** *a.* pert. to a legate.—**lega'tion** *n.* embassy; official residence of diplomatic minister at foreign court.

legato (le-gà'-tō) *adv.* (*Mus.*) in a smooth, gliding manner.

legend (lej'-end) *n.* orig. chronicle of lives of saints; marvellous story of ancient times; inscription on coin, medal, etc.—**leg'endary** *n.* book of, relater of, legends;—*a.* comprising legends; fabulous; strange.

legible (lej'-i-bl) *a.* capable of being read.—**leg'ibly** *adv.*—**leg'ibleness, legibil'ity** *n.*

legion (lē'-jun) *n.* in ancient Rome, body of infantry of from three to six thousand; military force; great number.—**le'gionary** *a.* pert. to legion or legions; containing a great number;—*n.* soldier of a legion.

legislate (lej'-is-lāt) *v.i.* make or enact laws.—**legisla'tion** *n.* act of legislating; laws made.—**leg'islative**

a. having power to make laws; constitutional.—**leg'islatively** *adv.*—**leg'islator** *n.* (*fem.* **leg'islatress**) one who enacts laws.—**leg'islature** *n.* body empowered to make laws.

legitimate (le-jit'-i-māt) *a.* lawful; born in lawful wedlock; justifiable; genuine;—*v.t.* render legitimate; legalise.—**legit'imacy** *n.* state of being legitimate.—**legit'imately** *adv.*—**legit'imateness** *n.*—**legitima'tion** *n.* act of investing with the rights and privileges of lawful birth.—**legit'imise** *v.t.* legitimate.—**legit'imism** *n.*—**legit'imist** *n.* one who upholds hereditary monarchical government.

leisure (lezh'-ôôr, lē'-zhur) *n.* freedom from occupation; spare time;—*a.* unoccupied.—**lei'surable** *a.*—**lei'sured** *a.* free from business duties.—**lei'surely** *a.* slow;—*adv.* slowly.

leitmotiv (līt'-mō-tēf) *n.* (*Mus.*) theme associated with a person or idea, constantly recurring in a composition; (*Fig.*) recurrent idea.

lemming, leming (lem'-ing) *n.* short-tailed migratory rodent of the vole family found in N. Europe.

lemon (lem'-on) *n.* oval-shaped fruit, pale yellow and very acid; tree of this fruit;—*a.* of the colour of lemon rind.—**lemonade'** *n.* drink made of lemon juice, sugar, and water.—**lem'on-squash** *n.* drink made of lemon juice and soda water.

lemon sole (lem'-on sōl) *n.* flat fish, allied to the sole proper.

lemur (lē'-mur) *n.* monkey-like mammal found in Madagascar.

lend (lend) *v.t.* grant temporary use of, let out money at interest; permit use of; afford; to serve for;—*v.i.* to make a loan.—*pa.p.* **lent**.—**lend'er** *n.*

length (length) *n.* measurement from end to end; extension; duration of time; extent; distance, as in a race; quantity of syllable or vowel in prosody.—**length'en** *v.t.* extend in length;—*v.i.* grow longer.—**length'ily** *adv.*—**length'iness** *n.*—**length'wise** *a.* in the direction of the length.—**length'y** *a.*

lenient (lē'-ni-ent) *a.* softening; acting without severity;—*n.* (*Med.*) emollient. — **le'nience, le'niency** *n.* clemency.—**le'niently** *adv.*—**len'itive** *n.* medicine which eases pain;—*a.* soothing; emollient.—**len'ity** *n.*

lens (lenz) *n.* (*Optics*) a piece of glass ground with one or both sides curved so as to refract rays of light, to modify vision; the crystalline biconvex tissue between cornea and retina of the eye; magnifying glass;—*pl.* **lens'es**.

Lent (lent) *n.* fast of 40 days from Ash Wednesday until Easter Day, commemorating the fast of Christ in the wilderness.—**lent'en** *a.* pert. to Lent; meagre.

lenticular (len-tik'-ū-lar) *a.* shaped like a lens or lentil; resembling a double-convex lens. Also **len'tiform.**—**len'toid** *a.* lens-shaped.

lentil (len'-til) *n.* plant allied to the bean, cultivated for its seeds.

lento (len'-tō) *adv.* (*Mus.*) slowly.

leonine (lē'-ō-nīn) *a.* of or like a lion.

leopard (lep'-ard) *n.* a large carnivorous member of the cat family.

leotard (lē'-ō-tard) *n.* skin-tight, one-piece garment worn by ballet dancers, etc.

leper (lep'-er) *n.* person afflicted with leprosy. (*Fig.*) outcast.—**lep'rosy** *n.* contagious disease affecting skin, tissues and nerves.—**lep'rous** *a.*

Lepidoptera (lep-i-dop'-te-ra) *n.pl.* order of insects having four wings, as moths, butterflies, etc.—**lepidop'teral, lepidop'terous** *a.*

leprechaun (lep'-re-Hawn) *n.* sprite; brownie referred to in Irish folk-lore.

Lesbian (lez'-bi-an) *a.* pert. to island of *Lesbos* (Mytilene) in the Aegean Sea, or to ancient school of lyric poets there; amatory;—*n.* woman sexually attracted to another woman.

lese-majesty (lēz'-maj'-es-ti) *n.* (*Law*) crime committed against the sovereign, or state; high treason.

lesion (lē'-zhun) *n.* (*Med.*) any change in structure or functioning of living tissues of the body; injury; (*Law*) loss or injury.

less (les) *a.* smaller in size; not equal to in number; lower; inferior;—*adv.* in a smaller or lower degree;—*n.* smaller portion; the inferior.—**less'en** *v.t.* make less; diminish;—*v.i.* contract; decrease.—**less'er** *a.* smaller; inferior.

lessee (les-ē') *n.* one to whom a lease is granted.

lesson (les'-n) *n.* reading; something to be learned by pupils; Scripture passage read aloud as part of Church service; reproof.

lest (lest) *conj.* for fear that.

let (let) *v.t.* allow; give permission; cause to do (foll. by *infin.* without *to*); grant use of, for hire;—*pr.p.* let'ting;—*pa.t.* and *pa.p.* let.—**to let alone**, refrain from interfering.—**to let blood**, relieve blood pressure by cutting a vein.—**to let down**, lower; (*Colloq.*) fail in a promise to a person.—**to let go**, release; allow to pass without comment.—**let'-off** *n.* exculpation **let'-up** *n.* (*Colloq.*) respite.

let (let) *v.t.* hinder;—*n.* hindrance.

lethal (lē'-thal) *a.* deadly; mortal.

lethargy (leth'-ar-ji) *n.* heavy drowsiness; lassitude; inertia.—**lethar'gic, lethar'gical** *a.* drowsy; apathetic.—**lethar'gically** *adv.*

letter (let'-er) *n.* symbol used to represent an articulate, elementary sound; written or printed communication; epistle;—*pl.* learning; erudition;—*v.t.* impress or form letters on; print in special lettering.—**lett'er-book** *n.* book in which copies of business letters are kept.—**lett'er-box** *n.* box for receiving letters; pillar-box.—**lett'er-card** *n.* paper, gummed at edges which may be folded and sealed, without use of envelope.—**lett'ered** *a.* literate; educated; inscribed with lettering.—**lett'erer** *n.*—**lett'er-file** *n.* device for holding letters for reference.—**lett'er-head** *n.* printed heading on business stationery.—**lett'ering** *n.* act of impressing letters; letters impressed.—**lett'er-press** *n.* machine for making copies of letters.—**letter of credit**, letter authorising money to be paid by a bank to the bearer.—**letters patent**, document conferring the exclusive right to use an invention or design.

lettuce (let'-us) *n.* common garden plant, with tender, green leaves used in salads.

leucocyte (lū'-ko-sīt) *n.* one of the white corpuscles of the blood, destroying bacteria.

levee (lev'-ā, lev'-ē) *n.* formal Royal reception.

levee (lev'-e, le-vē') *n.* (*U.S.*) river embankment, as in Mississippi Valley; quay.

level (lev'-el) *n.* line or plane parallel to the horizon; state of equality; grade; instrument for finding true horizontal line;—*a.* even; horizontal; equal in rank or degree; impartial;—*v.t.* make horizontal; reduce to the same height with something else; raze; make equal in rank, etc.; point a gun to the mark.—*pr.p.* lev'elling.—*pa.t.* and *pa.p.* lev'elled.—**lev'el-cross'ing** *n.* point at which road crosses railway at same level.—**lev'el-head'ed** *a.* prudent.—**lev'eller** *n.* one who believes in making all men equal.—**lev'elling** *n.* act of making a surface even with another; process of ascertaining the difference of elevation between two points.—**to be on the level**, be honest in one's dealings with another.

lever (lē'-ver) *n.* bar used to exert pressure or sustain a weight at one point of its length; crowbar for prizing open;—*v.t.* raise up; prize open.—**le'verage** *n.* action of a lever; mechanical advantage gained by its use.

leveret (lev'-er-et) *n.* a hare in its first year.

leviathan (le-vī'-a-than) *n.* whale; sea-monster; anything of colossal size.

levitation (lev-i-tā'-shun) *n.* act of making buoyant or light; phenomenon of heavy bodies being made to float in air by spiritual agencies.—**lev'itate** *v.t.*

levity (lev'-i-ti) n. lightness; buoyancy; want of seriousness.

levy (lev'-i) v.t. raise by assessment, as taxes; enlist or collect, as troops; impose, as a fine;—v.i. raise funds by a levy.—pa.p. lev'ied.—n. collection of assessment by authority or compulsion, for public services; money or troops thus collected.

lewd (lūd or lood) a. indecent; given to unlawful indulgence.—lewd'ly adv.—lewd'ness n.

lexicon (lek'-si-kon) n. dictionary, esp. of Greek, or Hebrew; word-building game played with pack of cards.—lex'ical a. pert. to a lexicon.—lexicog'rapher n. one who compiles a dictionary.—lexicograph'ic, -al a.—lexicog'raphist, lexicol'ogist n. expert in lexiconology.—lexicog'raphy n. process of compiling a dictionary.—lexicol'ogy n. science which deals with exact significance and use of vocabulary.

liable (lī'-a-bl) a. obliged in law; subject; answerable; responsible.—liabil'ity n. state of being liable; responsibility; obligation; tendency;—pl. debts.

liaison (lē-ā'-zŏng) n. union; connection; illicit intimacy between man and woman; (Mil.) contact maintained between one unit and another; sounding, as in French, of final consonant of a word before initial vowel or mute h of next word.—liase v.i.

liana (li-an'-a) n. climbing tropical plant.

liar (lī'-ar) n. one who tells lies.

libation (lī-bā'-shun) n. ceremonial pouring of wine in honour of a deity; liquid.

libel (lī'-bel) n. defamatory writing or public statement;—v.t. defame by a writing, picture, etc.; proceed against, by filing a libel.—pr.p. li'belling.—pa.t. and pa.p. li'belled.—li'beller n.—li'bellous a. defamatory.—li'bellously adv.

liberal (lib'-e-ral) a. open-minded; generous; unbiased; (in politics) favouring democratic ideals, and freedom of religion;—n. one who favours greater political and religious freedom; supporter of Whig or Liberal party.—liberalisa'tion n. process of gaining greater freedom.—lib'eralise v.t. cause to be freer or more enlightened.—lib'eralism n. principles upheld by Liberal party.—lib'eralist n.—liberal'ity n. generosity.—lib'erally adv.—lib'erate v.t. set free.—lib'eration n. act of setting free; state of being free from bondage.—lib'erator n. one who sets others free, esp. from tyranny.—Liberal Party, one of the political parties of Gt. Britain evolved in 1830 from the Whigs.

liberty (lib'-er-ti) n. freedom from bondage or restraint; power to act according to one's natural rights as an individual; privilege; freedom of act or speech unduly taken in social intercourse;—pl. rights, privileges, etc.—liber'tinage n. debauchery of libertine.—lib'ertine n. one who leads a dissolute life;—a. dissolute; debauched.—liberty man, sailor on leave.

libido (li-bē'-dō) n. the emotional craving behind all human impulse; esp. used by Freud to denote the sex-urge.—libid'inous a. lewd; obscene; lustful.—libid'inously adv.

Libra (lī'-bra) n. the balance, 7th sign of the Zodiac.

library (lī'-bra-ri) n. collection of books; room or building which contains it.—libra'rian n. keeper of a library.—libra'rianship n.

libretto (li-bret'-ō) n. words of an opera or oratorio.—librett'ist n. writer of librettos.

lice (līs) pl. of louse.

licence (lī'-sens) n. authority granted to do any act; legal permit authorising a person's right to marry, preach, practise medicine, sell tobacco, liquor, etc., keep a dog, possess car, radio, television, etc.; excess of liberty.—li'cense, li'cence v.t. permit by grant of authority; authorise.—li'censable a.—li'censed a.—licensee' n. one given a licence.—li'censer n.—licen'tiate n. one who has a licence to practise a profession.—licen'tious a. using excessive licence; dissolute.—licen'tiously adv.—licen'tiousness n.

lichen (lī-ken, lich'-en) n. one of an order of flowerless plants growing on rocks, tree-trunks, etc.; (Med.) skin eruption accompanied by itch and inflammation.

lichgate (lich'-gāt) n. roofed gateway or arch at entrance to churchyard where coffin may be left to await clergyman's arrival. Also lych'gate.—lich'-house n. mortuary.

licit (lis'-it) a. lawful; allowable.—lic'itly adv.

lick (lik) v.t. pass or draw the tongue over; to lap; take in by the tongue; touch lightly (as flames); (Colloq.) thrash; be superior over;—n. act of licking; (Scot.) small portion;—pl. a beating.—lick'er n.—lick'ing n.—lick'-spittle n. abject flatterer.

licorice, liquorice (lik'-o-ris) n. plant, root of which contains a sweet juice; brittle, black substance extracted from the roots of this plant, and used medicinally, esp. as laxative, and in confectionery.

lid (lid) n. cover of vessel or box; the covering of the eye.

lido (lē'-dō) n. pleasure resort; public swimming pool.

lie (lī) v.i. utter untruth; misrepresent; deceive; make false statement.—*pr.p.* ly'ing.—*pa.t.* and *pa.p.* lied.—*n.* deliberate falsehood.—li'ar *n.* one who utters a falsehood.—ly'ing *a.* addicted to telling lies.—a white lie, untruth uttered with good intention.

lie (lī) *v.i.* be in a horizontal position or nearly so; be situated; lean; be at rest; press upon.—*pr.p.* ly'ing.—*pa.t.* lay.—*pa.p.* lain.—*n.* manner of lying; relative position; direction.—lie'-abed' *n.* one not an early riser.—to lie doggo, remain in hiding.—to lie in, be in childbed.—to lie low, keep in background.—to lie off (*Naut.*) anchor some distance off shore.

lief (lēf) *adv.* gladly; willingly; freely.

liege (lēj) *a.* bound by feudal tenure; (of a lord) entitled to receive homage; sovereign;—*n.* vassal; feudal lord to whom allegiance is owed.—*pl.* citizens generally.

lien (lī'-en, lēn) *n.* (*Law*) legal charge upon real or personal property.

lieu (lū) *n.* place; room; stead.

lieutenant (lef-ten'-ant) *n.* deputy; officer who takes place of a superior in his absence; rank below a captain (*Army*) or below a commander (*Navy*).—lieuten'ant-col'onel *n.* rank below colonel.—lieuten'ant-command'er *n.* in British Navy, rank intermediate between that of lieutenant and commander.—lieuten'ant-gen'eral *n.* military rank intermediate between that of major-general and general. — lieuten'ant-gov'ernor *n.* State official ruling a province in a British dominion (e.g. Canada) under governor-general. — Lord'-Lieuten'ant *n.* King's deputy in Ireland (till 1922); governor of a county.

life (līf) *n.* existence; vitality; condition of plants, animals, etc., in which they exercise functional powers; span between birth and death; mode of living; narrative of a person's history.—*pl.* lives, men; persons.—life'-and-death' *a.* desperate.—life'-belt *n.* belt inflated, or made buoyant with cork, for keeping person afloat in water.—life'-boat *n.* special type of boat, designed for stability in stormy seas, for saving lives.—life'guard *n.* military bodyguard.—Life Guards, regiment of household cavalry.—life'-his'tory *n.* cycle of life of person, organism, etc.—life'-jack'et *n.* life-belt.—life'less *a.* inanimate; dead.—life'lessly *adv.*—life'lessness *n.*—life'-like *a.* like a living creature; resembling closely.—life'-long *a.* lasting a lifetime.—life'-preser'ver *n.* apparatus (as life-belt, -buoy, -line) for preserving or rescuing life; loaded cane for self-defence.—lif'er *n.* (*Colloq.*) criminal who has received a life-sentence.—life'-rent *n.* rent which one is legally entitled to receive during one's lifetime.

lift (lift) *v.t.* raise; take up and remove; elevate socially; exalt spiritually; steal; take passengers on a bus, etc.;—*v.i.* rise; be dispersed;—*n.* assistance; helping of a person by offering conveyance in one's car; elevator; rise in the ground; (*Aviat.*) air force acting at right angles on aircraft's wing, thereby lifting it.

ligament (lig'-a-ment) *n.* anything which binds one thing to another; (*Anat.*) strong bands connecting bones of the body.—ligament'al, ligament'ary, ligament'ous *a.*—li'gate *v.t.* bind; bandage.—liga'tion *n.* act of binding; state of being bound with a ligature.—lig'ature *n.* anything which binds; a bandage; (*Mus.*) line connecting two notes; (*Print.*) type consisting of two or more letters joined.

light (līt) *v.i.* come to by chance; alight; settle.—*pa.p.* light'ed, or lit.

light (līt) *a.* not heavy; easy; active; nimble; loose, as soil; moderate, as wind; spongy, as cake; not heavily armed, as a cruiser; unsettled; trifling; worthless; easily disturbed, as sleep.—light'en *v.t.* make less heavy; enliven;—*v.i.* become less heavy or gloomy.—light, light'ly *adv.*—light'er *n.* barge used in loading and unloading ships.—light'erage *n.* price paid for loading and unloading ships.—light'erman *n.*—light'-fing'ered, *a.* dexterous; thieving.—light'-foot'ed *a.* agile. —light'-hand'ed *a.* delicate of touch.—light'-head'ed *a.* delirious; giddy.—light'-heart'ed *a.* carefree; gay.—lights *n.pl.* lungs of slaughtered animal.—light'-weight *a.* (of a boxer) weighing less than 9 st. 9 lbs.—light'ness *n.*

light (līt) *n.* that form of radiant energy which stimulates visual perception; brightness; day; illuminated part of a scene or picture; point of view; aspect; spiritual enlightenment; key-word of an acrostic; opening admitting light into a building;—*a.* bright; not dark; whitish; pale (of colour);—*v.t.* give light or fire to;—*v.i.* begin to burn; (*Fig.*) express joy.—*pa.t.* and *pa.p.* light'ed or lit.—light'en *v.t.* illuminate.—light'er *n.* device for producing a flame. — light'house *n.* tower-like structure on sea-coast with powerful light to serve as warning to ships.—light'ing *n.* illumination; arrangement of lights.—light'ish *a.* rather light or pale in colour.—light'ness *n.*—light'ship *n.* floating lighthouse.—light'-year *n.* (*Astron.*) the distance in a year (calculated at 6 million

million miles) light travels.—**to see the light,** be born; to comprehend.—**foot'lights,** *n.pl.* row of electric lamps along edge of stage in a theatre.—**lit up** (*U.S. slang*) drunk.

lightning (lĭt'-nĭng) *n.* flash produced by an electrical discharge.—**light'ning conductor** *n.* metal conductor between highest point of building and earth, as a safety device to channel lightning. Also **lightning rod.**

ligneous (lĭg'-ne-us) *a.* woody.—**lig'nify** *v.t.* convert into wood.—**lig'nite** *n.* coal of recent origin; brown coal.—**lig'num-vit'ae** *n.* tree of America and Australia with wood of extreme hardness.

like (līk) *a.* equal; similar;—*n.* equal; person or thing resembling another; exact resemblance;—*adv.* (*Archaic*) in the same manner; to an equal degree;—*conj.* (*Vulgar*) as; as if.—**like'lihood** *n.* probability.—**like'ly** *a.* probable; credible; of excellent qualities;—*adv.* probably.—**lik'en** represent as similar; compare.—**like'ness** *n.* resemblance; image, picture, or statue.—**like'wise** *adv.* in like manner; also; moreover.

like (līk) *v.t.* be pleased with; enjoy; approve;—*v.i.* be pleased;—*n.* a liking.—**lik(e)'able** *a.* pleasant; congenial; attractive.—**lik(e)'ableness** *n.*—**lik'ing** *n.* fondness; taste.

lilac (lī'-lǎk) *n.* shrub, with flowerclusters, purple, pale mauve, or white in colour; pale mauve colour;—*a.* of lilac colour.

lilt (lĭlt) *n.* lively tune;—*v.t.* and *v.i.* sing.

lily (lĭl'-ĭ) *n.* bulbous plant, with fragrant flowers;—*a.* resembling a lily.—**lila'ceous** *a.* lily-like.—**lil'ied** *a.* adorned with lilies.—**lil'y-liv'ered** *a.* cowardly.—**lil'y-white** *a.* pure white; unsullied.—**lil'y-of-the-vall'ey** *n.* plant of the genus *Convallaria*.

limb (lĭm) *n.* extremity of human body, as arm or leg; branch of tree.

limber (lĭm'-bẽr) *n.* detachable front part of gun-carriage;—*v.t.* attach to gun-carriage.

limber (lĭm'-bẽr) *a.* easily bent; supple.—**to limber up,** perform gymnastic exercises.

limbo (lĭm-bō) *n.* region intermediate between heaven and hell in which souls of unbaptised children, etc. are confined after death; region of forgotten things; neglect; oblivion.

lime (līm) *n.* linden-tree;—*a.* pert. to linden-tree.

lime (līm) *n.* tree which produces sour kind of lemon; fruit of this tree.—**lime'-juice** *n.* juice of lime.

lime (līm) *n.* viscous substance; bird-lime; oxide of calcium;—*v.t.* smear with lime; ensnare; cement; manure with lime.—**lime'-kiln** *n.* furnace in which limestone is

heated to produce lime.—**lime'light** *n.* powerful light, as on a stage, produced by projecting oxy-hydrogen flame on ball of lime.—**lime'stone** *n.* rock consisting chiefly of carbonate of lime.—**lim'ous** *a.* slimy.—**lim'y** *a.* covered with or impregnated with lime; sticky; resembling lime.

limen (lī'-men) *n.* threshold of consciousness.—**li'minal** *a.*

limerick (lĭm'-er-ĭk) *n.* nonsense verse.

limit (lĭm'-ĭt) *n.* boundary; edge; utmost extent;—*v.t.* confine within certain bounds; curb; restrict the signification of.—**lim'itable** *a.* that may be bounded or restricted.—**lim'itary** *a.* placed at boundary, as a guard; restricted.—**limita'tion** *n.* act of restricting; state of being limited or confined; qualification.—**limita'tive,** lim'ited *a.* circumscribed; narrow.—**lim'itedly** *adv.*—**lim'itedness** *n.*—**lim'itless** *a.* boundless; infinite.—**limited liability,** said of joint stock company in which liability of shareholder is in proportion to amount of his stock.

limn (lĭm) *v.t.* draw or paint; illuminate manuscript.—**lim'ner** *n.* painter; one who decorates books with pictures.

limousine (lĭm'-ŏŏ-zēn) *n.* closed car.

limp (lĭmp) *v.i.* walk lamely; halt;—*n.* lameness.

limp (lĭmp) *a.* wanting in stiffness; flexible; (*Fig.*) lethargic; exhausted.

limpet (lĭm'-pet) *n.* small, conical shaped shell-fish which clings firmly to rocks.

limpid (lĭm'-pĭd) *a.* clear; translucent; crystal.—**limpid'ity, limp'idness** *n.*—**limp'idly** *adv.*

lin, linn (lĭn) *n.* waterfall; pool.

linchpin (lĭnsh'-pĭn) *n.* pin used to prevent a carriage-wheel from sliding off the axle-tree.

linctus (lĭngk'-tus) *n.* soothing cough mixture.—Also **linc'ture.**

linden (lĭn'-den) *n.* lime-tree.

line (lĭn) *n.* linen thread or string; slender cord; thread-like mark; (*Math.*) that which has length, but no breadth or thickness; boundary; row or continued series; progeny; verse; (*Colloq.*) short letter; course of conduct, thought, or policy; trend; trade, business or profession; system of buses, trains, or aircraft under one management; railway track; formation of naval vessels; regular infantry of an army; unit of measurement, $\frac{1}{12}$ of an inch; harmony; graceful cut (as of a costume, dress); path of scanning spot on TV screen;—*pl.* certificate of Church membership, marriage, etc.; punishment exercise; parts of play memorised by actor or actress;—

v.t. mark out with lines; form in line; border.—**line'eage** *n.* descendants from common progenitor; pedigree.—**lin'eal** *a.* composed of lines; pert. to, or in direction of, a line; directly descended from a common ancestor.—**lineal'ity** *n.*—**lin'eally** *adv.*—**lin'eament** *n.* feature; form; characteristic; outline of body or figure.—**lin'ear** *a.* pert. to, or consisting of, a line; drawn in lines.—**lin'early** *adv.*—**lin'eate(d)** *a.* marked by lines.—**linea'tion** *n.*—**lined** *a.* marked with lines; ruled.—**line'engraving** *n.* engraving lines on copper-plate.—**li'ner** *n.* steamship or passenger aircraft of regular transport line.—**liner** *train n.* express freight train linking large cities and running to scheduled timetable.—**lines'man** *n.* one employee who examines and repairs railway lines or telephone wires; official (at football or tennis match) who determines whether ball has crossed the outside line or not.—**line'-up** *n.* marshalling of forces, or resources.—**the line,** Equator.—**to shoot a line,** boast, usually of one's personal exploits.

line (līn) *v.t.* cover on the inside, as garment, pan, etc.—**lin'ing** *n.* material used to line garment, etc.

linen (lin'-en) *n.* thread or cloth made from flax; napery;—*a.* made of flax or linen.

ling (ling) *n.* fish of cod family.

ling (ling) *n.* common heather.—**ling'y** *a.*

linger (ling'-ger) *v.i.* delay; dally; loiter.—**ling'erer** *n.*—**ling'ering** *a.* protracted.

lingerie (lang'-zhe-rē) *n.* orig. linen goods; women's underclothing.

lingo (ling'-gō) *n.* language; (*Colloq.*) jargon.

lingual (ling'-gwal) *a.* pert. to the tongue;—*n.* sound or letter made by tongue, as *d.*—**ling'ually** *adv.*—**ling'uiform** *a.* shaped like tongue.—**ling'uist** *n.* fluent speaker of several languages.—**linguist'ic** *a.*—**linguist'ically** *adv.*—**linguist'ics** *n.* comparative philology.

liniment (lin'-i-ment) *n.* lotion or soft ointment.

link (lingk) *n.* single ring of chain; anything doubled and closed like a link; connection; ¹⁄₁₀₀ part of a chain (7.92 inches).—*v.t.* connect by link; (*Fig.*) combine for a common purpose;—*v.i.* be coupled.—**link'age** *n.* system of connections.

link (lingk) *n.* torch of tar and tow.—**link'-boy** or **-man** *n.* one who carried link and guided people.

link (lingk) *n.* bend of river.—**links** *n.pl.* flat ground near the sea, often a golf-course.

linnet (lin'-et) *n.* small British songbird of the finch family.

linoleum (lin-ō'-le-um) *n.* floorcloth of hessian impregnated with cement of linseed oil, cork, etc.

Linotype (līn'-o-tīp) *n.* type-setting machine in which the matter is cast in solid lines.

linseed (lin'-sēd) *n.* flax-seed.—**linseed cake,** compressed mass of husks of linseed, after oil has been pressed out, used for cattle feeding.—**linseed oil,** oil of linseed.

lint (lint) *n.* linen material with one side teased or scraped to a soft, woolly surface.

lintel (lin'-tel) *n.* horizontal beam or stone over doorway.

lion (lī'-un) *n.* (*fem.* **li'oness**) largest of the cat family, the male having a shaggy mane; (*Fig.*) person of fierce courage; celebrity; (*Astron.*) sign of the Zodiac (Leo).—**li'on-heart** *n.* courageous. Also **li'on-heart'ed** *a.*—**li'onise** *v.t.* to treat as a celebrity.—**the lion's share,** the biggest portion.

lip (lip) *n.* one of the two fleshy, outer edges of the mouth; edge of anything; brim; (*Slang*) impertinent talk;—*pl.* organs of speech as represented by the lips;—*v.t.* touch with the lips; speak.—**lipped** *a.* having a brim.—**lip'-read'ing** *n.* art of 'hearing' by reading motions of speaker's lips; this system as taught to the deaf.—**lip'-ser'vice** *n.* superficial devotion to person or cause.—**lip'stick,** cosmetic used by women to colour the lips.

liquefy (lik'-we-fī) *v.t.* transform to liquid; melt;—*v.i.* become liquid.—*pa.t.* and *pa.p.* liq'uefied.—**liquefa'cient** *a.*—**liquefac'tion** *n.* act of liquefying; state of being liquefied.—**liquefi'able** *a.*—**liq'uefier** *n.*—**liques'cency** *n.*—**liques'cent** *a.* melting.

liqueur (li- or lē-kēr') *n.* a preparation of aromatic distilled spirits.

liquid (lik'-wid) *a.* fluid; in state intermediate between solid and gas; flowing smoothly; (of sounds) pleasing to the ear;—*n.* substance intermediate between solid and gas which assumes shape of vessel which contains it; name applied to consonant which has smooth flowing sound (*l, m, n, r*).—**liq'uidate** *v.t.* make clear; settle debt; wind up affairs of bankrupt company; adjust; destroy;—*v.i.* (of business) to be wound up.—**liquida'tion** *n.*—**liquida'tor** *n.*

liquor (lik'-ur) *n.* any liquid or fluid, esp. alcoholic or spirituous fluid; decoction.

liquorice (lik'-o-ris) See **licorice**.

lira (lē'-ra) *n.* Italian coin; monetary unit.

lisle (līl) *n.* fine hard twisted cotton thread.

lisp (lisp) *v.i.* speak imperfectly, esp. substitute the sound *th* for *s*;—*v.t.*

pronounce with lisp;—*n.* habit of lisping.—lisp'ing *n.*

lissom (lis'-um) *a.* supple; flexible; lithe.—liss'omness *n.*

list (list) *n.* outer edge or selvedge of woven cloth; row or stripe; roll; catalogue; inventory; register; boundary line enclosing field of combat, esp. in *pl.* lists; field thus enclosed;— *v.t.* enter in catalogue or inventory; —*v.i.* enlist; engage in public service by enrolling.—short list, selection from which final choice will be made.

list (list) *v.i.* lean or incline; please; desire; (*Naut.*) heel over;—*v.t.* cause to heel over;—*n.* inclination to one side.

listen (lis'-n) *v.i.* attend closely; yield to advice.—list *v.t.* and *v.i.* listen (poetical).—list'ener *n.* one who listens; (*Radio*) one who hears broadcasts.—to listen in, hear broadcasts.

listless (list'-les) *a.* indifferent; languid; apathetic.—list'lessly *adv.*— list'lessness *n.*

lit (lit) *pa.t.* and *pa.p.* of verb light.

litany (lit'-an-i) *n.* earnest prayer of supplication used in public worship.

literal (lit'-e-ral) *a.* according to the letter; real; not figurative; word for word.—lit'eralness *n.*—lit'erally *adv.*

literary (lit'-er-ar-i) *a.* pert. to letters or literature; versed in literature.—lit'eracy *n.* state of being literate.—lit'erate *a.* educated; —*n.* one able to read and write.— litera'ti *n.pl.* men of letters.—litera'tim *adv.* letter by letter.—litera'ture *n.* art of writing prose or poetry; written works generally.

lithe (lïth) *a.* supple; pliant.—lithe'ly *adv.*—lithe'ness *n.*—lithe'some *a.*

lithograph (lith'-ō-graf) *v.t.* trace on stone, zinc, or aluminium, and transfer to paper by special process; —*n.* print from stone, etc.—lithog'rapher *n.*—lithograph'ic, -al *a.*— lithograph'ically *adv.*—lithog'raphy *n.* art of tracing designs on stone or metal, and taking impressions.

lithotomy (lith'-ot-o-mi) *n.* (*Surg.*) operation by which stones are removed from the bladder.

litigate (lit'-i-gāt) *v.t.* contest in law; —*v.i.* carry on lawsuit.—lit'igable *a.* —lit'igant *n.* person engaged in a lawsuit;—*a.* engaged in lawsuit.— litiga'tion *n.* judicial proceedings.— lit'igator *n.*—litigios'ity *n.*—litig'ious *a.* disputatious.

litmus (lit'-mus) *n.* bluish purple dye which turns *red* with an acid, and *blue* with an alkali.—litmus paper, paper impregnated with litmus, used to test solutions.

litotes (lī'-tō-tēz) *n.* figure of speech expressing strong affirmative by using negative of its contrary.

litre (lē'-tr) *n.* unit of volume in metric system, equal to 61.027 cubic inches, or 1.76 English pints.

litter (lit'-er) *n.* heap of straw as bedding for animals; vehicle containing bed carried on men's shoulders; stretcher; odds and ends left lying about; state of disorder; family of young pigs, puppies, etc., brought forth at the one birth;— *v.t.* bring forth young; scatter indiscriminately about; make untidy with odds and ends.

little (lit'-l) *a.* small in size, extent, or quantity; brief; slight; mean;—*n.* small quantity or space;—*adv.* in small quantity or degree (*comp.* less; *superl.* least).

littoral (lit'-or-al) *a.* pert. to the seashore.

liturgy (lit'-ur-ji) *n.* ritual for public worship in church, esp. Mass. —litur'gic, -al *a.*—litur'gically *adv.*

live (liv) *v.i.* have life; subsist; be conscious; dwell; enjoy life; keep oneself (as on one's income);—*v.t.* spend; pass;—*pr.p.* liv'ing;—*pa.p.* lived.—liv'able *a.* habitable.—liv'er *n.*—to live in, reside at one's place of business, esp. college or hospital.

live (līv) *a.* having life; quick; active; vital; burning, as coal; charged (with electricity, explosive, etc.).— lived (līvd) *a.* used in compounds as *long-lived, short-lived*.—live'-fence *n.* hedge. —lïv'en *v.t.* enliven.—live'-stock *n.* general term for horses, cattle, pigs, etc., on a farm.

livelihood (līv'-li-hòòd) *n.* means of earning one's living.

livelong (liv'-long) *a.* lasting throughout the whole day.

lively (līv'-li) *a.* animated; active; gay; light;—*adv.* briskly;—live'lily *adv.*—live'liness *n.*

liver (liv'-er) *n.* (*Anat.*) organ in body secreting bile; flesh of this organ in animals used as food.—liv'er-fluke *n.* trematode parasitic on sheep, etc.— liv'erish *a.* off-colour because of disordered liver.

livery (liv'-er-i) *n.* orig. special dress or food *delivered* by a lord to his household retinue; dress peculiar to certain group, as members of medieval guild; any characteristic uniform of employee, as of chauffeur; supply of food given out at stated intervals to horses, etc.; body of liverymen in London; garb.—liv'eried *a.* clothed in a livery.—liv'erycom'pany *n.* one of London's city companies, orig. trade guild.— liv'eryman *n.* one who wears a livery; a freeman of the city of London.—liv'ery-sta'ble *n.* a stable where horses and vehicles are kept for hire.

livid (liv'-id) *a.* black and blue; discoloured, as flesh, by bruising;

(*Colloq.*) enraged.—**livid'ity, liv'idness** *n.*

living (liv'-ing) *a.* having life; active; flowing (of water); resembling closely; contemporary;—*n.* livelihood; maintenance; mode of life; ecclesiastical benefice. — **living language**, language still in use.—**liv'ing-room** *n.* sitting-room.

lizard (liz'-ard) *n.* four-footed, scale-clad reptiles; dressed skin of this used in manufacturing handbags etc.

llama (lá'-ma) *n.* S. American two-toed ruminant, allied to the camel.

lo (lō) *interj.* look! behold!

loach (lōch) *n.* small river-fish.

load (lōd) *n.* burden; any heavy weight; cargo; (*Elect.*) amount of electrical energy drawn from a source; (*Fig.*) burden of anxiety;—*pl.* (*Colloq.*) plenty; heaps;—*v.t.* burden; put on, for conveyance; freight; overweight; charge (a gun); adulterate (as wine); weight with lead (as a cane); insert spool into (as a camera);—*v.i.* take on a load or cargo; charge a firearm; become loaded.—**load'ed** *a.* weighted.—**load'ing** *n.* act of loading; freight. **load'-line** *n.* line painted on side of a vessel to indicate maximum immersion when loaded (*Plimsoll mark*).—**load'stone** *n.* See **lode'stone.**

loaf (lōf) *n.* shaped portion of dough baked in oven; lump of sugar shaped like a cube, or a conical mass of sugar;—*pl.* loaves.

loaf (lōf) *v.i.* spend (time) idly; **loaf'er** *n.*

loam (lōm) *n.* rich, fertile soil.

loan (lōn) *n.* act of lending; that which is lent, esp. money for interest;—*v.t.* (chiefly *U.S.* usage) lend.—**loan'ee, loan'er** *n.*—**loan'-off'ice** *n.* pawnbroker's office.

loath, loth (lōth) *a.* unwilling; reluctant; disinclined.—**loath'ness** *n.*

loathe (lōTH) *v.t.* detest; abominate; —**loath'ing** *n.* disgust; repulsion.— **loath'ly** *adv.*—**loath'some** *a.* detestable; repugnant.—**loath'somely** *adv.* —**loath'someness** *n.*

lob (lob) *n.* dull, clumsy fellow; anything thick and heavy; (*Cricket*) slow underhand ball; (*Tennis*) ball rising high in air over opponent's head; — *v.t.* bowl underhand; hit (tennis ball, shuttle-cock) high into the air;—*v.i.* deliver a lob; walk clumsily; — *pr.p.* lob'bing. — *pa.p.* lobbed.—**lob'-worm** *n.* large earthworm used as bait.

lobby (lob'-i) *n.* narrow passage, or hall, forming the entrance to public building or private dwelling; waiting-room; hall of House of Commons where M.P.'s may meet their constituents.—**division lobby**, corridor in House of Commons to which members retire to vote.—**lobb'ying** *n.*

frequenting of the lobby to influence voting.

lobe (lōb) *n.* rounded division of an organ; lower, fleshy part of human ear; division of lung.—**lob'ar** *a.*

lobster (lob'-ster) *n.* edible, marine, long-tailed crustacean.—**lobster pot**, basket in which lobsters are trapped.

local (lō'-kal) *a.* pert. to particular place; confined to definite spot, district, or part of body; circumscribed;—*n.* some person or thing belonging to a district; suburban train.—**lo'cal, lo'cale** *n.* scene of an occurrence; scene of film-shot.— **localisa'tion** *n.* act of localising.— **lo'calise** *v.t.* assign to definite place; decentralise; cordon off.—**local'ity** *n.* position of a thing; neighbourhood.—**lo'cally** *adv.*—**locate'** *v.t.* set in a particular place; find exact position of.—**loca'tion** *n.* act of locating; situation; geographical position; out-of-doors site of a film production.—**loc'ative** *a.* pert. to a location.—**local anaesthetic**, anaesthetic injected to produce insensibility in one part of the body only. —**the local** (*Colloq.*) public-house.

loch (loH) *n.* lake, or arm of sea esp. in Scotland.—**loch'an** *n.* small loch.

lock (lok) *n.* strand or tress of hair; —*pl.* hair of the head.

lock (lok) *n.* device for fastening door, box, etc.; mechanism on gun released by trigger; enclosure in a canal with gate at each end for allowing vessels to pass from one level to another; hold in wrestling; —*v.t.* fasten with lock and key; hold tightly;—*v.i.* become fast; jam.— **lock'er** *n.* drawer or small cupboard. —**lock'et** *n.* small case, containing portrait, lock of hair, and worn on a chain.—**lock'fast** *a.* securely fastened.—**lock'-gate** *n.* canal sluice-gate. —**lock'-jaw** *n.* spasmodic contraction of jaw muscles; tetanus.—**lock'-nut** *n.* a second nut screwed on top of the first nut.—**lock'-out** *n.* refusal by employer to restart employees until trade dispute has been settled.—**lock'-smith** *n.* one who makes and repairs locks.—**lock'-up** *n.* prison.

locomotion (lō-kō-mō'-shun) *n.* act of moving from place to place.— **locomo'tive** *a.* capable of moving from one place to another;—*n.* railway engine.

locus (lō'-kus) *n.* exact position of anything; (*Math.*) path traced by a point in accordance with some mathematical law;—*pl.* **loci** (lō'-sī).

locust (lō'-kust) *n.* winged insect, allied to the grasshopper.—**lo'cust-tree,** *n.* false acacia; carob.

locution (lo-kū'-shun) *n.* speech; phrase.

lode (lōd) *n.* metallic vein; water-course.—**lode'star, load'star** *n.* star by which one steers, esp. Pole-star.—**lode'-stone, load'stone** *n.* magnetic iron ore.

lodge (loj) *n.* small country-house; cottage at entrance to an estate; porter's room in a college; branch of a society, as of Freemasons, or the building;—*v.i.* dwell in temporarily; reside; become embedded in;—*v.t.* deposit for preservation; lay flat; harbour; put (as money) in a bank; allege, as an accusation;—*pr.p.* **lodg'ing.**—**lodg'er** *n.* one who occupies rooms at weekly rent.—**lodg'ing(s)** *n.* room(s) let at weekly rent.

loft (loft) *n.* upper room; attic in space between top story and roof; gallery in church;—*v.t.* (*Golf*) strike a ball high.—**loft'ily** *adv.*—**loft'iness** *n.*—**loft'y** *a.* elevated; haughty.

log (log) *n.* roughly hewn piece o timber; apparatus to measure speed of a ship; record of ship's speed; log-book;—*a.* made of logs;—*v.t.* fell trees; keep a record of; fine.—*pr.p.* **logging.**—*pa.p.* **logged.**—**log'book** *n.* a daily record of a ship's voyage.—**log'-cab'in** *n.* hut made of lopped tree trunks.—**log'ger** *n.* lumberjack.—**log'ging** *n.* lumbering.—**log'line** *n.* line marked off in knots and fastened to a log for estimating ship's speed.—**log'-roll'ing** *n.* act of clearing logs, esp. from a neighbour's land, hence mutual help, esp. in politics.

loganberry (lō'-gan-ber-i) *n.* shrub, a cross between raspberry and blackberry.

logarithm (log'-a-rithm) *n.* index of the power to which a fixed number or base must be raised to produce the number; method of reducing arithmetical calculations to a minimum by substituting addition and subtraction for multiplication and division.—**logarith'metic(al), logarith'mic(al)** *a.*—**logarith'mically** *adv.*

loggerhead (log'-er-hed) *n.* blockhead; kind of turtle.—**at loggerheads,** at cross-purposes.

loggia (lōj'-a or loj'-ya) *n.* kind of open, elevated gallery with pillars.—*pl.* **loggias** (lōj'yas).

logic (loj'-ik) *n.* science of reasoning; (*Colloq.*) commonsense.—**log'ical** *a.* pert. to formal thought; skilled in logic; deducible.—**logical'ity, log'icalness** *n.*—**log'ically** *adv.*—**logic'ian** *n.*

logistic, -al (loj-is'-tik, -al) *a.* expert in calculating.—**logis'tics** *n.pl.* (used as *sing.*) art of calculating; (*Mil.*) branch of military science which deals with the moving of and providing for troops.

logogram (log'-ō-gram) *n.* symbol representing a whole word or phrase, as £ = pound.

loin (loin) *n.* part of animal or man above hips and on either side of

spinal column; ribs of a sheep;—*pl.* lower part of back.—**loin'-cloth** *n.* strip of cloth worn round the loins.

loiter (loi'-ter) *v.i.* linger; be slow in moving.—**loi'terer** *n.*—**loi'teringly** *adv.*

loll (lol) *v.i.* lounge about lazily; hang out, as tongue;—*v.t.* thrust out, as tongue.

Lollard (lol'-ard) *n.* a follower of John Wycliffe in England in 14th and 15th cents.

lolly (lol'-i) *n.* lump.—**lolly'pop, loll'ipop** *n.* fruit-flavoured toffee or frozen fruit juice on a stick; (*Slang*) money.

Londoner (lun'-dun-er) *n.* native or citizen of London.—**Lon'don-clay** *n.* blue clay found in London and Hampshire basin. — **London pride** (*Bot.*) kind of saxifrage.

lone (lōn) *a.* solitary; standing by itself.—**lone'liness, lone'ness** *n.*—**lone'ly** *a.* alone; unfrequented.—**lone'some** *a.* solitary.—**lone'somely** *adv.*—**lone'someness** *n.*

long (long) *a.* extended in distance or time; protracted; slow in coming; continued at great length;—*adv.* to a great extent; at a point of duration far distant;—*v.i.* desire.—**long'-bow** *n.* bow drawn by hand—so called to distinguish it from Cross-bow.—**long'-drawn** *a.* protracted.—**longeron** (lon'-jer-on) *n.* (*Aviat.*) a main longitudinal strength member of a fuselage or nacelle.—**longevity** (long-jev'-i-ti) *n.* uncommonly prolonged duration of life.—**long'hand** *n.* ordinary hand-writing (opp. *shorthand*).—**long'-head'ed** *a.* far-seeing; prudent.—**long'-hund'red** *n.* a hundred and twenty.—**long'ing** *n.* yearning; craving. — **long'ingly** *adv.* — **long'ish** *a.* rather long.—**longitude** (lon'-gi-tūd) *n.* angular distance east or west of given meridian, measured in degrees. —**longitud'inal** *a.* pert. to length or longitude; lengthwise.—**longitud'inally** *adv.*—**long'-range** *a.* having power to fire a great distance, as a gun; able to fly or sail great distances without refuelling, as aircraft, submarine, etc.—**long'shore** *a.* existing or employed on the shore.—**long'-shoreman** *n.* dock-labourer; one employed *along* the shore.—**long'-sight'edness** *n.* (*Med.*) hypermetropia. —**long'-stand'ing** *a.* having existed for some time.—**long'-suff'ering** *a.* patiently enduring.—**long'-wind'ed** *a.* able to run a great distance without becoming short of breath; tedious; loquacious.—**long'wise, long'ways** *a.* lengthwise.—**before long,** soon.

loo (lōō) *n.* card-game.

loofa, loofah (lōō-fa) *n.* fibrous interior of a plant of the gourd type, used as a brush.

look (look) *v.i.* turn one's eyes upon; seem to be; consider; face, as a dwelling;—*v.t.* express by a look;—*n.* act of directing one's gaze upon; facial expression generally; aspect; view;—**look'er** *n.*—**look'er-on** *n.* spectator.—**look'ing** *n.* search.—**look'ing-glass** *n.* mirror.—**look'-out** *n.* vigilance; place from which a watch is kept; person stationed to keep watch.—**to look after,** tend.—**look up to,** admire.

loom (loom) *n.* machine for weaving cloth from thread by interlacing threads called the *woof* through threads called the *warp*.

loom (loom) *v.i.* emerge indistinctly; appear over the horizon; menace; (*Fig.*) assume great importance.

loom (loom) *n.* kind of guillemot; puffin; ember-goose. Also **loon**.

loon (loon) *n.* rogue; rascal; (*Scot.*) lad.

loop (loop) *n.* doubling of string or rope, through which another string may run; ornamental fastening; (*Aviat.*) manoeuvre in which plane describes a circle;—*v.t.* fasten by a loop. — **looped** *a.* coiled; folded double; knotted.—**loop'-line** *n.* branch railway which leaves and later rejoins main-line.

loop (loop) *n.* narrow slit in walls of fortification; (*Fig.*) way out of difficult situation. Also **loop'hole**, **loop'holed** *a.*

loose (loos) *v.t.* free from constraint; untie; disconnect; discharge;—*v.i.* set sail;—*a.* free; unsewed; unbound; flowing; diffuse; careless; inaccurate; lax; inclined to diarrhoea.—**loose'-box** *n.* stable where horse is free to move about.—**loose'ly** *adv.*—**loos'en** *v.t.* make loose; unscrew;—*v.i.* become loose; become relaxed.—**loose'ness** *n.*—**loose'-tongued** *a.* indiscreet.—**to be at a loose end,** have nothing particular to do.—**to break loose,** escape.

loosestrife (loos'-strif) *n.* kinds of herbaceous plants with purple or yellow flowers.

loot (loot) *n.* plunder; act of plundering;—*v.t.* and *i.* plunder.

lop (lop) *v.t.* cut off, esp. top of anything; cut away superfluous parts.—*n.* act of lopping.—**lop'per** *n.*—**lop'ping** *n.*

lop (lop) *v.i.* hang down loosely.—**lop'-eared** *a.* having drooping ears.—**lop'-sid'ed** *a.* heavier on one side than the other, askew.

lope (lop) *v.i.* run with long, leisurely gait (as a mule);—*n.* easy gait, like a canter.

loquacious (lo-kwa'-shus) *a.* talkative; babbling; garrulous.—**loqua'ciously** *adv.*—**loqua'ciousness, loquas'ity** *n.* talkativeness.

loran (lo'-ran) *n.* (*Aviat.*) aircraft radar navigational device [*Long range aid to navigation*].

lord (lord) *n.* master; ruler; king; husband; proprietor of a manor; peer of the realm; courtesy title of son of duke or marquis, and eldest son of earl; holder of certain high government offices, as Chancellor, or Chief Justice, and of municipal offices, as Mayor, Provost, etc.; form of address accorded to bishops; Jehovah; God; Christ;—*v.i.* play the lord; domineer.—**lord'liness** *n.*—**lord'ling** *n.* petty lord.—**lord'ly** *a.* pert. to lord; imperious; proud; magnificent.—**lord'ship** *n.* state of being a lord; authority; (*with* his, your) formal mode of address in speaking to a *lord, bishop, provost,* etc.—**lords and ladies,** wild arum lily.—**Lord's Day,** Sunday.—**Lord's Supper,** sacrament of communion.—**Lord Chancellor,** president of House of Lords, and Keeper of the Great Seal.—**Lord-Lieutenant,** head of the magistrates of a county.—**House of Lords,** upper house in the British Parliament.

lore (lor) *n.* learning; erudition; knowledge.

lorgnette (lorn-yet') *n.* pair of eye-glasses with handle; opera-glass.

lorry (lor'-i) *n.* wagon for heavy loads.

lose (looz) *v.t.* be deprived of; mislay; forfeit; fail to win; miss; waste; destroy;—*v.i.* fail; suffer loss; become bewildered;—*pr.p.* los'ing.—*pa.t.* and *pa.p.* lost.—**los'able** *a.*—**los'er** *n.*—**los'ing** *a.* producing loss.—**loss** *n.* defeat; diminution; bereavement; harm; waste by escape or leakage; number of casualties in war.—**lost** *a.* mislaid; bewildered; bereft; squandered; damned.—**at a loss,** uncertain.

lot (lot) *n.* destiny; object used to determine something by chance; choice thus determined; separate part; large number; portion of ground;—*v.t.* allot.—**lot'tery** *n.* scheme by which prizes are given by drawing lots.—**a job-lot,** collection of articles, sold as one item.

loth (loth) *a.* See **loath**.

lotion (lo'-shun) *n.* fluid with healing, antiseptic properties esp. for skin infections.

lotus (lo'-tus) *n.* Egyptian water-lily; N. African shrub, the fruit of which was reputed to induce over-powering lethargy. Also **lo'tos**.

loud (loud) *a.* making a great sound; noisy; flashy; obtrusive; vulgar.—**loud, loud'ly** *adv.*—**loud'ness** *n.*—**loud'-speak'er** *n.* (*Radio*) transducer rendering received signals audible at a distance.

lough (loH) *n.* lake or arm of the sea.—**the Irish form of loch.**

louis (loo'-i) *n.* obsolete French gold coin worth 20 francs. Also **louis d'or**.

lounge (lounj) *v.i.* recline at ease;

loll; spend time idly;—*n.* act of lounging; sitting-room.—loung'er *n.* —lounge'-suit *n.* man's jacket-suit for day-time wear.

lour, lower (lour) *v.i.* frown; look threatening, as the sky;—*n.* scowl. —low'ering *a.*—low'eringly *adv.*

louse (lous) *n.* parasitic insect infesting hair and skin;—*pl.* lice.— lous'ily *adv.*—lous'iness *n.*—lous'y *a.* infested with lice; (*Slang*) mean; despicable.

lout (lout) *n.* clumsy fellow; bump-kin;—lout'ish *a.* awkward; clownish. —lout'ishly *adv.*

louvre (lóó'-vr) *n.* opening in roof of ancient buildings for ventilation; slot for ventilation in motor-car.— lou'vre-window *n.* window partially closed by outward sloping boards.

love (luv) *n.* affection; strong liking; charity; devoted attachment to one of the opposite sex; passion; object of affection; personification of love, *Cupid*; (*Tennis*) no score;— *v.t.* show affection for; be delighted with; admire passionately;—*v.i.* be in love; delight.—lov'able *a.* worthy of affection; engaging.—lov'ableness *n.*—love'-ap'ple *n.* tomato.—love'-bird *n.* small parrot with bright-coloured plumage.—love'-child *n.* illegitimate child.—love'-in-a-mist *n.* fennel. — love'-in-i'dleness *n.* the pansy.—love'-knot *n.* a bow of ribbon tied in a special way, as a token of love.—love'less *a.*—love'-lies-bleed'ing *n.* a garden-flower with reddish-purple spike-flowers.—love'-lily *adv.*—love'liness *n.*—love'-lock *n.* curl worn on forehead or over the temple.—love'lorn *a.* forsaken.— love'ly *a.* very beautiful.—love'-phil'tre, -pot'ion *n.* drink supposed to induce the emotion of love towards a chosen person.—lov'er *n.* one who loves, esp. one of the opposite sex; admirer, as of the arts.—lov'erlike *a.*—love'sick *a.* pining because of love.—love'some *a.* lovely. —love'-tok'en *n.* object, as a ring, given as a symbol of love.—lov'ing *a.* affectionate; loyal.—lov'ing-cup *n.* large drinking-vessel with two handles, passed round at a banquet. —lov'ingly *adv.*—lov'ingness *n.*

low (lō) *a.* not high; lying near the ground; shallow; not loud, as voice; moderate, as prices; lewd; weak; cold, as temperature; humble; (of dress) décolleté;—*adv.* not high; low, quiet (voice); cheaply.—low'-brow *n.* non-intellectual person.—Low Church, the evangelical sect of the English Church as opp. to *High Church.*—Low Countries, Netherlands. —low'-down *a.* mean; underhand.— low'er *v.t.* cause to descend; take down; humble; diminish resistance; make cheap; reduce pitch;—*a.*

(*compar.* of *low*) less exalted.—low'er-most *a.* lowest.—low'land *n.* country which is relatively flat in comparison with surrounding hilly district.— low'lander *n.* inhabitant of flat land, esp. in Scotland.—low'liness *n.*— low'ly *a.* humble; meek.—low'-spir'ited *a.* dejected.

low (lō) *v.i.* bellow as ox or cow;— *n.* noise made.

loyal (loi'-al) *a.* faithful to lawful government, sovereign, cause, or friend.—loy'alist *n.* faithful follower of a cause.—loy'ally *adv.*—loy'alty *n.* fidelity.

lozenge (loz'-enj) *n.* figure with two acute and two obtuse angles; small (medicated) sweetmeat.

lubber (lub'-er) *n.* heavy, clumsy fellow. Also, lubb'ard.—lubb'erly *a.*— lubb'erliness *n.*

lubricate (lóó'-bri-kāt) *v.t.* make smooth; smear with oil, grease, etc., to reduce friction.—lub'ric, -al *a.*— lub'ricant *n.* any oily substance used to reduce friction;—*a.* having the property of reducing friction.— lubrica'tion *n.*—lub'ricative *a.*—lub'ricator *n.*—lubric'ity *n.* slipperiness; lewdness.

luce (lóós) *n.* fresh-water fish, pike.

lucerne (lóó'-sern) *n.* alfalfa; a fodder plant.

lucid (lóó'-sid) *a.* shining; clear; easily understood, as of style; normally sane.—lucid'ity, lu'cidness *n.*—lu'cidly *adv.*

luck (luk) *n.* accidental fortune, good or bad; fate; chance.—luck'ily *adv.*—luck'iness *n.*—luck'less *n.* unfortunate.—luck'lessly *adv.*—luck'lessness *n.*—luck'y *a.* fortunate; fortuitous.—luck'y-bag *n.* receptacle containing assorted articles which one chooses from, by dipping into the bag. Also lucky dip.

lucre (lóó'-ker) *n.* material gain; profit, esp. ill-gotten; advantage.— lu'crative *a.* profitable.—lu'cratively *adv.*—filthy lucre (*Slang*) money.

lucubrate (lóó'-kū-brāt) *v.i.* study by lamp or at night.—lucubra'tion *n.* nocturnal study.

ludicrous (lóó'-di-krus) *a.* provoking laughter; ridiculous. — lu'dicrously *adv.*—lu'dicrousness *n.*

ludo (lóó'-dō) *n.* children's game played with counters and dice.

luff (luf) *v.i.* turn head of ship towards the wind; sail nearer the wind;—*n.* windward side of a ship.

lug (lug) *v.t.* pull with force; tug; haul;—*pr.p.* lug'ging.—*pa.t.* and *pa.p.* lugged.—lug'gage *n.* traveller's baggage, etc.—lug'ger *n.* small vessel with lugsails.—lug'sail *n.* square sail bent upon a yard which hangs obliquely to the mast.

lug (lug) *n.* (*Scot.*) ear.

lugubrious (lóó-gū'-bri-us) *a.* mournful; dismal.—lugu'briously *adv.*— lugu'briousness *n.*

lukewarm (lóók'-wawrm) *a.* moderately warm; tepid. Also **luke**.—luke'warmly *adv.*—luke'warmness *n.*

lull (lul) *v.t.* soothe to sleep; quieten; —*v.i.* become quiet gradually;—*n.* period of quiet in storm or noise.—lull'aby *n.* song sung to child to soothe it to sleep.

lum (lum) *n.* ventilating chimney in a mine; (*Scot.*) chimney.

lumbago (lum-bā'-gō) *n.* painful rheumatic affection of lumbar muscles.—lum'bar, lum'bal *a.* pert. to lower part of the back.

lumber (lum'-bẹr) *n.* anything useless and cumbersome; odds and ends hoarded; timber cut and split for market;—*v.t.* heap in disorder.—lum'berer *n.* feller of timber. Also **lum'berjack.**—lum'bering *n.*

lumber (lum'-bẹr) *v.i.* move heavily. —lum'berer *n.*—lum'bering *a.*

luminary (lóóm'-in-ạr-i) *n.* body which gives light, esp. one of the heavenly bodies; (*Fig.*) person of outstanding qualities.—lu'minant *a.* giving out light.—lumina'tion *n.*— lumines'cence *n.* quality of being luminescent; phosphorescence. — lumines'cent *a.*—luminif'erous *a.* yielding light.—lu'minous *a.* shining; glowing; (*Fig.*) lucid.—lu'minously *adv.*—lu'minousness, luminos'ity *n.*

lump (lump) *n.* small mass of matter of indefinite shape; swelling; (*Colloq.*) stupid, clumsy person;—*v.t.* throw into a mass; take in the gross.— lump'y *a.* full of lumps; uneven.—in the lump, taken as an aggregate.

lunar (lóó'-nạr) *a.* pert. to moon; measured by revolutions of moon. Also lu'nary.—lu'nacy *n.* madness.— lu'natic *a.* insane;—*n.* mad person. luna'tion *n.* period from one new moon to the next.—lunar month, period of moon's revolution, about 29½ days.—lunar year, period of twelve lunar months (354½ days).

lunch (lunsh) *n.* light meal taken between breakfast and dinner. Also lunch'eon.—*v.i.* lunch.—lunch'er *n.*

lune (lóón) *n.* anything in shape of half-moon.—*n.* watch-glass with flattened centre; detached bastion.

lung (lung) *n.* one of the two main organs of respiration in a breathing animal.—lunged *a.*

lunge (lunj) *n.* in fencing, sudden thrust;—*v.i.* thrust.

lupin, lupine (lóó'-pin) *n.* genus of leguminous plants, cultivated for their spikes of flowers.

lupine (lóó'-pin) *a.* like a wolf.

lurch (lurch) *n.* sudden roll of ship to one side; staggering movement; —*v.i.* stagger.—lurch'er *n.* kind of hunting-dog.

lurch (lurch) *n.* critical move in game of cribbage.—to leave in the lurch, desert in moment of need.

lure (lūr) *n.* decoy used by falconer to recall hawk; artificial bait;—*v.t.* entice; decoy.

lurid (lū'-rid) *a.* ghastly pale; extravagantly coloured; (*Fig.*) startling.—lu'ridly *adv.*

lurk (lurk) *v.i.* lie hid; lie in wait.— lurk'er *n.*

luscious (lush'-us) *a.* excessively sweet; cloying.—lusc'iously *adv.*— lusc'iousness *n.*

lush (lush) *a.* fresh; juicy.

lust (lust) *n.* longing desire; sexual appetite; craving; — *v.i.* desire passionately; have sexual appetites. —lust'ful *a.* sensual.—lust'fully *adv.* —lust'fulness *n.*—lust'iness *n.*—lust'ily *adv.*—lust'y *a.* robust.

lustre (lus'-tẹr) *n.* clearness; gloss; (*Fig.*) renown; chandelier with pendants of cut glass; cotton dress fabric with glossy, silky surface; pottery glaze.—lus'trous *a.* gleaming; bright.—lus'trously *adv.*

lute (lóót) *n.* stringed instrument like a guitar.—lut'enist, lut'er, lut'ist *n.* lute-player.

lutecium (lóó-tē'-si-um) *n.* metallic element (symbol Lu), one of the rare-earths group.

luxury (luk'-sū-ri) *n.* that which is not a necessity of life.—luxu'riance, luxu'riancy *n.*—luxu'riant *a.* in great abundance; dense or prolific as vegetation.—luxu'riantly *adv.*—luxu'riate *v.i.* grow or live luxuriously.—luxu'rious *a.* self-indulgent in appetite, etc.; sumptuous.—luxu'riously *adv.* —luxu'rious ness *n.*

lych-gate See lich-gate.

lyddite (lid'-īt) *n.* picric acid; powerful explosive.

lye (lī) *n.* alkaline solution of wood ashes and water; used in soap-making.

lying (lī'-ing) *a.* recumbent.—ly'ing-in *n.* confinement of a pregnant woman.

lying (lī'-ing) *a.* untruthful;—*n.* habit of untruthfulness.—ly'ingly *adv.*

lymph (limf) *n.* fluid, watery in appearance, contained in tissues and organs of the body; vaccine.— lymphat'ic *a.* pert. to lymph; sluggish.—lymphat'ics *n.pl.* vessels in the body containing lymph.—lymph'oid *a.* like lymph.

lynch (linsh) *v.t.* inflict, esp. capital punishment without recourse to forms of law.

lynx (lingks) *n.* animal of cat family with keen sight.—lynx'-eyed *a.* keen-sighted; vigilant.

lyre (līr) *n.* stringed, musical instrument in use among ancient Greeks. —ly'rate *a.* shaped like a lyre.— lyre'-bird *n.* Australian bird with tail feathers in shape of a lyre.—lyr'ic *n.*

orig. poem sung to music; short poem expressing emotions of poet. —lyr'ic, -al *a.* pert. to the lyre; suitable to be sung to musical accompaniment; used of poetry expressing emotion.—lyr'icism *n.* lyrical quality of poem; emotional expression.—lyr'ist, lyricist *n.*

M

ma'am (mȧm) *n.* contr. of madam.

macabre (ma-kȧ'-br) *a.* gruesome; ghastly; grim.

macadam (ma-kad'-am) *n.* road-surface material of crushed stones. —macad'amise *v.t.*

macaroni (mak-a-rō'-ni) *n.* paste of wheat flour made in long slender tubes; young fop of the 18th cent.— macaron'ic *n.* medley;—*a.* affected; kind of burlesque verse.

macaroon (mak'-ạ-róón) *n.* small cake made of white of egg, ground almonds and sugar.

macaw (mạ-kaw') *n.* S. American parrot.

mace (mās) *n.* a heavy metal club; staff carried as emblem of authority; billiard cue.—mace'-bear'er *n.* Also mac'er *n.*

mace (mās) *n.* part of nutmeg.

macerate (mas'-ẹr-āt) *v.t.* soften by soaking; (*Fig.*) mortify the flesh.— macera'tion *n.*

Mach Number (mȧH) *n.* ratio of air speed of an aircraft to the velocity of sound.

machete (ma-chā'-tā) *n.* heavy knife used to cut down sugar-canes.

Machiavellian (mak-i-ạ-vel'-yan) *a.* pert. to Machiavelli; unscrupulous; crafty;—*n.* one who practises the perfidious political doctrine of Machiavelli; unprincipled ruthless ruler.—Machiavell'ianism *n.*

machicoulis (mȧ-shē-kóó-lē') *n.* in fortification, loop-holed, projecting parapet, etc.—machic'olate *v.t.* form with machicolations.—machicola'tion *n.* opening for assailing besiegers from above.

machinate (mak'-in-āt) *v.t.* contrive with evil motive;—*v.i.* conspire.— machina'tion *n.* plotting, esp. with evil intent; intrigue.—machina'tor *n.*

machine (mạ-shēn') *n.* any contrivance for the conversion and direction of motion; engine; vehicle;—*v.t.* sew with machine or print with printing-machine.—machine'-gun *n.* automatic small-arms weapon. — machin'ery *n.* machines collectively; parts of machine; any combination of means to an end.—machine'-room *n.* room where printing by machine is done. —machine'-tool *n.* tool for cutting,

shaping and turning, operated by machinery.—machin'ist *n.* one who makes machinery; one who works at a machine.

mackerel (mak'-e-rel) *n.* edible sea-fish with blue and black stripes.

mackintosh (mak'-in-tosh) *n.* waterproof coat.

macrocosm (mak'-rō-kozm) *n.* the great universe.—macrocos'mic *a.*

macron (mak'-ron) *n.* short line put over vowel to show it is long in quantity or quality, *e.g.* ē.

macroscopic (mak-rō-skop'-ik) *a.* visible to naked eye; opp. of *microscopic.*

macula (mak'-ū-lạ) *n.* spot.—*pl.* mac'ulae.—mac'ulate *v.t.* spot.—macula'tion *n.* act of spotting; spot.

mad (mad) *a.* (*comp.* mad'der; *superl.* mad'dest) deranged in mind; insane; frenzied; angry; irrational, as a scheme.—mad'cap *n.* rash person; tomboy;—*a.* uncontrolled.—mad'den *v.t.* enrage; drive mad;—*v.i.* behave as a madman.—mad'ding *a.* distracted.—mad'dingly, mad'ly *adv.*— mad'house *n.* asylum; a mental home.—mad'man *n.* lunatic.—mad'ness *n.* insanity.

madam (mad'-ạm) *n.* formal mode of address to married or elderly woman; (*Colloq.*) arrogant woman; —*pl.* mad'ams.—madame (ma-dam') *n.* French form of Mrs. or Madam;— *pl.* mesdames (mā-dam').

madder (mad'-ẹr) *n.* plant yielding red dye.—mad'der-lake *n.* red pigment.

made (mād) *pa.t.* and *pa.p.* of make.

Madonna (ma-don'-a) *n.* Virgin Mary; statue of the Virgin.

madrepore (mad'-rẹ-pōr) *n.* white coral.

madrigal (mad'-ri-gạl) *n.* short love poem; unaccompanied part-song, popular in 16th and 17th cents.

maelstrom (māl'-strom) *n.* famous whirlpool off coast of Norway; any whirlpool; (*Fig.*) chaotic state of affairs.

maestoso (mȧ-es-tō'-sō) *a.* and *adv.* (*Mus.*) with dignity.

maestro (mȧ-es'-trō) *n.* master, esp. an eminent composer or conductor.

maffick (maf'-ik) *v.i.* exult riotously as on occasion of victory [fr. *Mafeking,* the relief of which was wildly celebrated in 1900].

magazine (mag-ạ-zēn') *n.* military storehouse; part of ship where ammunition is stored; compartment in rifle holding the cartridges; periodical containing miscellaneous articles.

magdalene (mag'-da-lēn) *n.* reformed prostitute. Also mag'dalen.

mage (māj) *n.* magician; wizard.

magenta (mạ-jen'-tạ) *n.* purplish dye from coal-tar.

maggot (mag'-ot) n. grub; larva of house-fly.—**magg'oty** a. full of maggots.

Magi (mā'-jī) n.pl. in the N.T. the Wise Men who came to visit infant Jesus.

magic (maj'-ik) n. feigned art of influencing nature or events by occult means; sorcery; charm.—**mag'ic(al)** a.—**mag'ically** adv.—**magician** n. sorcerer; conjurer.—**magic eye** n. visual tuning device on radio receiver.—**magic lantern**, early form of projector using slides.—**black magic**, magic by aid of evil spirits.

magisterial (maj-is-tē'-ri-al) a. pert. to or conducted by a magistrate; authoritative; judicial; overbearing.—**magiste'rially** adv.

magistrate (maj'-is-trāt) n. person vested with public judicial authority; justice of the peace.—**mag'istracy** n. official position of magistrate; body of magistrates.

magnanimity (mag-na-nim'-i-ti) n. greatness of mind; generosity of heart.—**magnan'imous** a.—**magnan'imously** adv.

magnate (mag'-nāt) n. eminent person, esp. wealthy business man.

magnesium (mag-nē'-zi-um) n. silvery-white metallic element (symbol Mg).—**magne'sia** n. magnesium oxide.—**magnesium sulphate**, Epsom salts.

magnet (mag'-net) n. lodestone; bar of iron which attracts or repels iron, etc., and, when suspended, points N. and S.; (Fig.) person or thing with powers of attraction.—**magnet'ic, -al** a. pert. to magnet; attractive.—**magnet'ically** adv.—**magnetic'ian, mag'netist** n. expert in magnetism.—**magnetis'able** a.—**magnetisa'tion** n.—**mag'netise** v.t. give magnetic properties to; attract;—v.i. become magnetic.—**mag'netism** n. natural cause of magnetic force; science of magnetic force; attraction.—**animal magnetism**, mesmerism.—**magne'to** n. small electric generator with permanent magnet.—**magnetic field**, sphere of influence of magnetic forces.—**magnetic needle**, small magnetised pivoted steel bar of mariner's compass which always points North.—**magnetic north**, north as indicated by pivoted bar of mariner's compass.—**magnetic poles**, two nearly opposite points on the earth's surface where dip of the needle is 90°.—**magnetic tape**, plastic tape for electro-magnetic sound recording and reproduction.

magnify (mag'-ni-fī) v.t. make greater; cause to appear greater; extol; exaggerate.—pa.p. **mag'nified**.—**magnif'ic, -al,** a. grand; splendid.—**magnif'ically** adv.—**magnifica'tion** n. act of magnifying.—**magnif'icative**, **magnif'icent** a. splendid; brilliant.—**magnif'icence** n.—**magnif'icently** adv.—**mag'nifier** n. one who or instrument which magnifies.

magnitude (mag'-ni-tūd) n. greatness; size.

magnum (mag'-num) n. wine-bottle holding two quarts.

magpie (mag'-pī) n. bird of the crow family, with chattering cry; idle chatterer; (a hit on) outermost ring but one, of a target.

Maharajah (ma-ha-rā'-ja) n. (fem. **Maharan'i** or **Maharan'ee**) the title of an Indian prince.

mah-jong (mà-jong') n. old Chinese gambling game.

mahogany (ma-hog'-an-i) n. tree, hard, reddish wood of which is used for furniture; its red-brown colour.

Mahomedan, Mahometan See Mohammedan.

mahout (ma-hout' or ma-hóót') n. elephant-driver or keeper.

maid (mād) n. unmarried woman; virgin; female servant.—**maid of all work**, general domestic servant.—**old maid**, elderly spinster; game of cards.—**maid'en** n. maid;—a. pert. to maid; unmarried; fresh; pure; unused; first.—**maid'enhair** n. kind of fern with delicate fronds.—**maid'enhood, maid'enhead** n. virginity; purity; hymen.—**maid'enliness** n.—**maid'enly** a. maiden-like.—**maiden name**, surname of woman before marriage.—**maiden over** (Cricket) one in which no runs are scored.—**maiden speech**, member's first speech, esp. in Parliament.—**maiden voyage**, first ocean voyage of new ship.

mail (māl) n. armour composed of steel rings or plates; armour in general;—v.t. clothe in armour.—**mailed fist**, physical force.

mail (māl) n. bag for carrying letters, etc., or its contents; post; person or means of conveyance for transit of letters, parcels, etc.;—v.t. post; send by mail.—**mail'-bag** n. sack in which letters are put for transit.—**mail'-boat, -plane, -train** n. means of conveyance of letters, etc.

maim (mām) v.t. deprive of use of a limb; disable; disfigure;—n. injury.—**maimed'ness** n.

main (mān) a. principal; first in size, importance, etc.; essential; sheer;—n. chief part; strength, as in might and main; wide expanse of land or ocean; principal pipe in water, gas, or electricity system.—**main'-brace** n. brace of the mainyard.—**to splice the main-brace**, hand out double ration of rum.—**main'chance** n. self-interest.—**main'-door** n. front door.—**main'land** n. continent as distinct from islands.—**main'ly** adv.—**main'-mast** n. principal mast of ship.—**main'sail** n. principal sail on mainmast.

maintain (măn-tān') v.t. and v.i. hold; sustain; preserve; defend, as an argument; affirm.—**maintain'able** a.—**maintain'er** n.—**main'tenance** n. means of support.

maison(n)ette (mā-zon-et') n. small compact house.

maize (māz) n. Indian corn, cereal.

majesty (maj'-es-ti) n. grandeur; exalted dignity; royal state; title of sovereign.—**majest'ic**, -al a. possessing majesty; splendid.

majolica (ma-jol'-i-ka) n. decorative, enamelled pottery.

major (mā'-jer) a. greater in number, quality, quantity, or extent; (Mus.) greater by a semi-tone;—n. person who has reached the age of 21; officer in the army ranking below lieutenant-colonel.—**ma'jor-dom'o** n. steward.—**ma'jor-gen'eral** n. army officer in rank below lieutenant-general.—**major'ity** n. greater number; difference between greater and lesser number; full legal age (21).

make (māk) v.t. cause to be or do; create; constitute; compel; appoint; secure; reckon; perform;—v.i. tend; contribute.—pa.t. and pa.p. **made**.—n. structure; texture; form; style; brand.—**make'-believe'** n. pretence; —v.i. pretend.—**mak'er** n. one who makes; poet.—**Mak'er** n. God.—**make'shift** n. temporary expedient.—**make'-up** n. layout of printed page, magazine, etc.; facial cosmetics; general characteristics. — **make'-weight** n. something added to scale to make up weight.—**to make bold**, dare to.—**to make good**, justify one's efforts.—**to make headway**, progress.—**to make up to**, make friendly advances.—**on the make**, striving for monetary gain.

malachite (mal'-a-kīt) n. green carbonate of copper.

maladjustment (mal-ad-just'-ment) n. inability to adjust oneself to environment.

maladministration (mal-ad-min-is-trā'-shun) n. faulty administration, esp. of public affairs.

maladroit (mal-a-droit') a. clumsy; awkward. — **maladroit'ly** adv. — **maladroit'ness** n.

malady (mal'-a-di) n. disease.

Malagasy (mal-a-gas'-i) n. native of, or language of, Madagascar; new name of the republic of M.

malaise (mal'-āz) n. feeling of bodily discomfort; squeamishness.

malaprop(ism) (mal'-a-prop-(izm)) n. ludicrous misuse of word, so called from Mrs. Malaprop, character in Sheridan's play, The Rivals.—**malaprop'ian** a.

malaria (ma-lā'-ri-a) n. fever caused by bite of mosquito.—**mala'rial**, a.

malcontent (mal'-kon-tent) a. discontented; rebellious.—**malcontent'ed** a.—**malcontent'edly** adv.—**malcontent'edness** n.—**malcontent'ly** adv.

male (māl) a. pert. to sex which begets young; masculine;—n. male animal.

malediction (mal-e-dik'-shun) n. evil-speaking; curse.—**maledict'ory** a. reviling.

malefactor (mal'-e-fak-tor) n. evil-doer; criminal.

malevolent (mal-ev'-o-lent) a. evilly-disposed; vindictive. Also **malev'olous**. — **malev'olence** n. ill-will; malignity.—**malev'olently** adv.

malformation (mal-for-mā'-shun) n. irregular formation.—**malformed'** a. deformed.

malice (mal'-is) n. ill-will; spite.—**malic'ious** a. spiteful; showing malice.—**malic'iously** adv.—**malic'iousness** n.—**with malice aforethought** (Law) with deliberate criminal intention.

malign (ma-līn) a. spiteful; pernicious; sinister;—v.t. traduce; vilify.—**malig'nancy** n. (of disease) virulence. Also **malig'nance**.—**malig'nant** a. evilly disposed; (of disease) virulent; likely to prove fatal.—**malig'nantly** adv.—**maligner** (ma-līn'-er) n.—**malig'nity** n. extreme malevolence; spite.—**malign'ly** adv.

malinger (ma-ling'-ger) v.i. feign illness in order to avoid duty.—**maling'erer** n. shirker.

mallard (mal'-ard) n. male of the common wild duck.

malleable (mal'-e-a-bl) a. capable of being hammered by beating; (Fig.) amenable; tractable.—**mall'eableness**, **malleabil'ity** n.—**mall'eate** v.t. hammer.—**mallea'tion** n.

mallet (mal'-et) n. small wooden hammer; long-handled wooden hammer used in croquet, polo, etc.

mallow (mal'-ō) n. plant of genus Malva, having emollient properties.

malnutrition (mal'-nū-tri'-shun) n. state of being undernourished; semi-starvation.

malodorous (mal-ō'-dor-us) a. having offensive odour.—**malo'dour** n.

malpractice (mal-prak'-tis) n. evil practice; professional impropriety or negligence.

malt (mawlt) n. barley or other grain steeped in water till it germinates, then dried in kiln for use in brewing;—v.t. make into malt;—v.i. become malt.—**malt'ing** n.—**malt'ster**, **malt'man** n. worker in a malt-house.

Maltese (mawl'-tēz) n. native of Malta;—a. pert. to Malta or to its people.—**Maltese cross**, cross, with four arms equal in length and forked at the ends.

maltreat (mal-trēt') v.t. ill-treat; handle roughly.—**maltreat'ment** n.

mamba (màm'-ba) n. poisonous black snake.

mamma (mam'-ă) n. milk-secreting gland in females.—pl. **mam'mae**.—**mam'mary** a.

Mammalia (mam-ā'-li-ă) n.pl. (Zool.) class of mammals or animals which suckle their young.—**mam'mal** n. one of the Mammalia.—**mamma'lian** a.

mammon (mam'-on) n. god of riches; wealth personified and worshipped.

mammoth (mam'-uth) n. extinct species of elephant of huge size;—a. colossal.

man (man) n. human being; adult male; manly person; male servant; husband; human race; piece used in chess, draughts, etc.—pl. **men**.—v.t. furnish with men; to fortify.—pr.p. **man'ning**.—pa.t. and pa.p. **manned**.—**man'-at-arms** n. soldier; feudal knight.—**man'-eater**, cannibal; tiger.—**man'ful** a. vigorous: sturdy.—**man'fully** adv.—**man'fulness** n.—**man'handle** v.t. (Naut.) handle a boat without mechanical aid; treat roughly.—**man'-hole** n. opening to admit a man to a drain, sewer, etc.—**man'hood** n. state of being a man; courage.—**man'-hour** n. work performed by one man in one hour.—**man'kind** n. human beings; male sex.—**man'liness** n.—**man'ly** a. bold; resolute; dignified; not effeminate.—**man'nish** a. like a man; masculine.—**man'nishly** adv.—**man'nishness** n.—**man-of-war**, naval vessel; orig. a soldier.—**man-of-war** bird, frigate bird.—**man'-pow'er** n. unit of power equal to one-eighth of a horse-power; total number of people in industry, armed forces, etc.—**man'slaughter** n. culpable homicide without malice aforethought.—**man in the street**, average man.

manacle (man'-ă-kl) n. handcuff;—v.t. fetter with handcuffs.

manage (man'-āj) v.t. direct; control by hand; cope with;—v.i. direct affairs; succeed.—**manageabil'ity** n. quality of being manageable.—**man'ageable** a. capable of being managed.—**man'agableness** n.—**man'agement** n. administration; directors controlling business.—**man'ager** n. (fem. **man'ageress**) one who manages; one in charge of business, etc.—**manage'rial** a.—**man'aging** a. interfering; meddlesome.

manatee (man'-ă-tē) n. sea-cow.

mandarin (man'-dă-rin) n. Chinese provincial governor; (Fig.) any high government official; small orange. Also **man'darine**.

mandate (man'-dāt) n. official order; precept; commission to act as representative of a body of people, esp. one granted by United Nations to a State to administer another.—**man'datary**, **man'datory** n. one to whom mandate is given by a **man'dator**.—**man'dated** a. committed to a mandate—**man'datory** a. containing a mandate; directory.

mandible (man'-di-bl) n. jaw; in vertebrates, lower jaw; in birds, upper or lower beak.—**mandib'ular** a. pert. to jaw.

mandolin, mandoline (man-dō-lin) n. musical instrument like a small guitar.

mandrake (man'-drāk) n. narcotic plant used in magic.—**mandrag'ore** n. mandrake.

mandrel (man'-drel) n. spindle of lathe. Also **man'dril**.

mandrill (man'-dril) n. large W. African baboon.

mane (mān) n. long hair on neck of animal.

manganese (mang'-gă-nēz) n. brittle metal which oxidises rapidly in humid atmosphere; (symbol Mn).—**mangane'sian**, **mangan'ic**, a.

mange (mānj) n. disease affecting skin of animals, causing hair to fall out.—**man'giness** n.—**man'gy** a. infected with mange.

mangel-wurzel (mang'-gl-wur'-zl) n. large kind of beet grown for cattle-fodder.

manger (mānj'-er) n. trough for holding fodder for cattle.

mangle (mang'-gl) n. rolling press for smoothing linen;—v.t. smooth with mangle.

mangle (mang'-gl) v.t. hack; mutilate.—**man'gler** n.

mango (mang'-gō) n. E. Indian tree; its fruit;—pl. **mang'o(e)s**.

mangold See mangel-wurzel.

mangrove (man'-grōv) n. tropical tree with prominent roots, found in tidal swamps and estuaries.

mania (mā'-ni-ă) n. madness; extravagant enthusiasm; obsession.—**ma'niac** n. madman;—a. raving; frenzied.—**mani'acal** a.

manicure (man'-i-kūr) n. care of hands and nails;—v.t. file, and polish nails.—**man'icurist** n.

manifest (man'-i-fest) a. clearly visible; apparent to mind or senses;—v.t. make clear; reveal;—n. detailed list of a ship's cargo.—**manifest'able**, **manifest'ible** a. capable of being clearly revealed.—**manifesta'tion** n. act of revealing; state of being revealed; display; disclosure.—**man'ifestly** adv. obviously.—**man'ifestness** n.—**manifest'o** n. public declaration of policy of a leader or party;—pl. **manifest'oes**.

manifold (man'-i-fold) a. various in kind or quality; numerous;—v.t. take many copies of by machine, such as a duplicator;—n. sheet of thin paper used in duplicating; (Mech.) pipe fitted with several lateral outlets.—**man'ifoldly** adv.

man(n)ikin (man'-i-kin) *n.* little man; dwarf; model of the human body for use of anatomy students; tailor's dummy.

manilla (ma-nil'-a) *n.* cheroot made in *Manila*, capital of the Philippine Islands. Also manil'a.— manil(l)a hemp, fibre used for making ropes, twine, sails, etc.—manil(l)a paper, stout wrapping paper.

manipulate (ma-nip'-ū-lāt) *v.t.* operate with the hands; falsify;—*v.i.* use the hands.—manipula'tion *n.*—manip'ular, manip'ulative, manip'ulatory *a.* —manip'ulator *n.*

manna (man'-a) *n.* food supplied miraculously to Israelites in wilderness; sweetish juice of the ash; (*Fig.*) spiritual nourishment.

mannequin (man'-i-kin) *n.* one employed to parade new fashions in clothes; dummy for similar purpose. Also man'equin.

manner (man'-er) *n.* way of doing anything; custom; style; person's habitual bearing;—*pl.* social behaviour; customs. — mann'ered *a.* having manners, esp. in compounds *well-mannered, ill-mannered;* affected.—mann'erism *n.* personal peculiarity of bearing, speech, etc.; affectation.—mann'eriness *n.* politeness; decorum.—mann'erly *a.* having good manners; decorum.—mann'erly *a.* having good manners; courteous; civil; respectful; — *adv.* civilly; respectfully.—to the manner born, having natural talent.

manoeuvre (ma-nōō'-ver, or ma-nū'-ver) *n.* strategic movement of armed forces; (*Fig.*) skilful management;—*pl.* peace-time exercises of armed forces;—*v.t.* direct skilfully; —*v.i.* perform manoeuvres.—manoeuv'rer *n.*

manor (man'-or) *n.* land belonging to lord; land in feudal times over which owner had full power.— man'or-house *n.* mansion on such an estate.—mano'rial *a.* pert. to manor.

mansard-roof (man'-sard rōōf) *n.* roof in which lower slope is nearly vertical and upper much inclined.

manse (mans) *n.* Scottish Presbyterian minister's residence.

mansion (man'-shun) *n.* large house; manor-house. — man'sion-house *n.* large residence.—Mansion House, official residence of Lord Mayor of London.

mantel (man'-tl) *n.* shelf above fireplace.—man'telpiece *n.* framework round fireplace.

mantilla (man-til'-a) *n.* shawl worn by Spanish women; short cape.

Mantis (man'-tis) *n.* genus of insects including stick-insects and leaf-insects.

mantle (man'-tl) *n.* loose outer garment; cloak; (*Fig.*) covering; finely-meshed fixture on a gas-jet, producing incandescent light; structure of the earth immediately below the crust;—*v.t.* cover; hide;— *v.i.* rise and spread; suffuse; flush.

manual (man'-ū-al) *a.* pert. to or made by hand;—*n.* text-book; service-book of R.C. Church; key-board of organ.—man'ually *adv.*

manufacture (man-ū-fakt'-ūr) *n.* making goods by hand or machine (esp. mass-production of goods); anything produced from raw materials;—*v.t.* make from raw materials; fabricate;—*v.i.* be engaged in manufacture.—manufact'ory *n.* place where such goods are made; factory.— manufact'ural *a.*—manufact'urer *n.*

manumit (man-ū-mit') *v.t.* give freedom to a slave; emancipate.— manumiss'ion *n.*

manure (ma-nūr') *v.t.* enrich soil with fertiliser;—*n.* any fertilising substance applied to soil to enrich it. —manur'er *n.*

manuscript (man'-ū-skript) *a.* written by hand;—*n.* book, etc., written by hand; author's script for publisher (*abbrev.* Ms, *pl.* Mss).

Manx (mangks) *a.* pert. to Isle of Man or its inhabitants;—*n.* Gadhelic language of Isle of Man.—Manx cat, tailless breed of cat.

many (men'-i) *a.* comprising a great number (*comp.* more; *superl.* most);— *n.* number of people or things.— man'ysided *a.* (of persons) all-round; talented.

Maori (mow'-ri) *n.* aborigine of New Zealand; language of the aborigines.

map (map) *n.* representation, esp. on a plane surface, of features of the earth, or of part of it; chart of the heavens; plan;—*v.t.* draw map of; fill in details in a blank map;— *pr.p.* map'ping.—*pa.t.* and *pa.p.* mapped.—to map out, plan in detail, as itinerary.

maple (mā'-pl) *n.* tree of sycamore kind from which sugar is extracted.

maquis (mā'-kē) *n.* in Corsica, brushwood-covered heath; scrub; bush;—*n.pl.* French guerrillas in World War 2.

mar (mār) *v.t.* injure; impair; disfigure. — *pr.p.* mar'ring. — *pa.p.* marred.

maraschino (mar-as-kē'-nō) *n.* sweet liqueur distilled from cherries.

marathon (ma'-ra-thon) *n.* long-distance race (approx. 26 miles).

maraud (ma-rawd') *v.i.* rove in quest of plunder; foray; loot.

marble (mār'-bl) *n.* hard limestone which takes on a brilliant polish, used for ornaments, statuary, etc.; little ball of marble, glass, etc., used in games;—*a.* made of marble; cold; insensible;—*v.t.* colour like streaked marble.—mar'bled *a.* veined like

marble, as paper, pottery, etc.—
mar'bly a. like marble.

marcasite (már'-ka-sīt) n. white
iron pyrites used in jewellery.—
marcasit'ic a.

marcel (már-sel') n. artificial hair
wave.

March (márch) n. third month of
year.

march (márch) n. border; frontier of
a territory, esp. of Scotland and
Wales—used esp. in pl. **march'es.**—
v.i. border.

march (márch) v.i. move in order, as
soldiers; to proceed at steady pace;
go to war;—v.t. cause to move in
military array;—n. distance march-
ed; musical composition to accompany a march; (Fig.) steady advance.
—**march'er** n. one who marches.—
dead'-march n. funeral march.

marchioness (már'-shon-es) n. wife
of a marquis.

marchpane (márch'-pān) n. See
marzipan.

mare (már) n. female of horse.—
mare's nest, discovery of exaggerated
importance; hoax. — **mare's tail**,
marsh plant.

margarine (már'-gar-ēn, már'-jer-
ēn) n. butter substitute made principally from vegetable oils.—(Colloq.
abbrev.) **marge** (marj).

marge (márj) n. margin; shore.—
mar'gin n. border; blank space at
top, bottom and sides, of a page;
allowance for contingencies.—**mar'-
ginal** a. pert. to margin; entered in
margin; (Fig.) of doubtful significance. — **mar'ginally** adv. — **marginal
seat**, Parliamentary seat held by
small majority.

marguerite (már'-ge-rēt) n. ox-eye
daisy.

marigold (mar'-i-gōld) n. plant
bearing yellow or orange flowers.

marijuana (már-i-hwan'-a) n. hemp
dried and used as tobacco for its
narcotic effect.

marine (ma-rēn') a. pert. to sea;
found in, or near, sea; pert. to
shipping;—n. soldier serving on
board a warship; naval force of a
country.—**mar'iner** n. sailor.

Mariolatry (mā-ri-ol'-a-tri) n. term
implying immoderate worship of the
Virgin Mary.—**Mariol'ater** n.

marionette (mar-i-o-net') n. puppet
worked by strings.

marital (mar'-i-tal) a. pert. to
husband or marriage.

maritime (mar'-i-tīm) a. pert. to
sea; bordering on sea; living near
sea; having overseas trade or naval
power.

marjoram (már'-jō-ram) n. aromatic
plant of mint family used in cookery.

mark (márk) n. visible sign; cross;
character made by one who cannot
write; stamp; proof; target; point;

attainable standard; assessment of
proficiency; flaw or disfigurement;
peculiarity or distinguishing feature;
(Running) starting post; indication
of position, depth, etc.;—v.t. make
a sign upon; stamp or engrave;
notice; assess, as examination paper;
—v.i. observe particularly.—**marked**
a. specific; notorious.—**mark'edly** adv.
noticeably. — **mark'er** n. one who
marks score at billiards, bridge, etc.;
bridge scoring-card; counter; ornamental strip, used to mark place in
book; buoy, beacon, used as indicator.—**mark'ing-ink** n. indelible ink for
marking initials on linen, etc.—
marks'man n. one expert at hitting
target.—**marks'manship** n. shooting
skill.—**to mark time**, move feet up and
down without moving forward; (Fig.)
remain at a standstill, as in one's
work.—**trade mark**, special symbol
marked on commodities to indicate
the maker.

mark (márk) n. medieval English
coin worth 13s. 4d.; German monetary unit.—**merk** (merk) old Scots
silver coin worth 13s. 4d.

market (már'-ket) n. trading-centre;
demand; price or value at a stated
time;—v.i. buy or sell;—v.t. produce
for sale in market.—**mar'ketable** a.
suitable for selling.—**mar'ketably** adv.
—**mark'et-gar'den** n. garden for growing fruit and vegetables sold in the
market.—**mark'et-place** n. open space
in which markets are held.—**mark'et-
price** n. the current price of a
commodity.

marl (márl) n. fine-grain clay, often
used as manure; soil containing
carbonate of lime, used in brickmaking;—v.t. manure with marl.—
marl'y a.

marline (már'-lin) n. small rope used
to secure a splicing.—**mar'line-spike**
n. pointed tool used to separate
strands of rope.

marmalade (már'-ma-lād) n. preserve made of pulp and peel of
oranges, lemons, grapefruit, etc.

marmoset (már'-mo-zet) n. small
monkey.

marmot (már'-mot) n. rabbit-like
rodent inhabiting slopes of Alps.

marocain (már'-rō-kān) n. dress
material with surface like morocco
leather.

maroon (ma-róón') n. orig. fugitive
Negro slave of the W. Indies;
—v.t. put ashore on desolate island;
isolate, cut off, by any means, in any
place.

maroon (ma-róón') a. brownish-
crimson;—n. kind of firework with
loud report.

marquee (már-kē') n. large field-tent;
awning outside public building.

marquetry (már'-ket-ri) n. decorative, inlaid wood; process of inlaying

wood with designs of coloured wood, etc. Also mar'queterie.

marquess, marquis (már'-kwês) n. in Britain, noble ranking next below duke. (fem. mar'chioness).—mar'quessate n. rank or dignity of marquis.—marquise (márkèz') n. in France, wife of marquis; type of gemmed ring.

marrow (mar'-ō) n. soft substance in cavities of bones; (Fig.) the essence of anything.—marr'owfat n. rich variety of green pea.—marr'owy a.—vegetable marrow, kind of edible gourd.

marry (mar'-i) v.t. unite, take, or give in wedlock;—v.i. enter into matrimony.—pa.t. and pa.p. marr'ied.—marriage (mar'-ij) n. legal union of husband and wife; ceremony by which two people of opposite sex become husband and wife.—marr'iageable a. of an age to be married.—marr'iageableness n.—marriage lines, official certificate of marriage.

Mars (márz) n. Roman god of war; planet nearest to the earth.—Mar'tian n. and a. pert. to planet Mars.

Marseillaise (már-sā-yez' or már-se-làz') n. French national anthem.

marsh (mársh) n. tract of low, swampy land; bog; fen;—a. pert. to swampy areas.—marsh'-fe'ver n. malaria.—marsh'-gas n. methane.—marsh'mall'ow n. red flowered plant growing in marshes; sweetmeat made from its root, or from gelatine.—marsh'y a. boggy; swampy.

marshal (már'-shal) n. orig. master of the horse; master of ceremonies; herald; highest military rank in French army, in British army (Field-Marshal), in R.A.F. (Air-Marshal);—v.t. dispose in order, as troops; (Fig.) arrange, as ideas.—pr.p. mar'shalling.—pa.t. and pa.p. mar'shalled.—marshalling yard, railway depot for goods-trains.

marsupial (már-sū'-pi-al) a. having external pouch, to carry young;—n. animal such as kangaroo.

mart (márt) n. market.

marten (már'-ten) n. kind of weasel, valued for its fur.

martial (már'-shal) a. pert. to war or to the Services; warlike; military.—Mar'tial a. pert. to Mars the god.—mar'tialism n.—mar'tially adv.—martial law, law enforced by military authorities in times of danger and superseding Civil law.

martin (már'-tin) n. kind of swallow.

martinet (mar'-ti-net) n. strict disciplinarian.

martingale (már'-tin-gāl) n. strap fastened to horse's girth to keep its head down; (Naut.) stay for a jib-boom. Also mar'tingal.

Martinmas (már'-tin-mas) n. feast of St. Martin, 11th Nov.

martyr (már'-ter) n. one who suffers punishment or sacrifice of his life for adherence to principles or beliefs;—v.t. put to death for refusal to abandon principles; (Fig.) constant sufferer.—mar'tyrdom n. suffering and sacrifice of martyr.—martyrol'ogy n. history of martyrs.

marvel (már'-vel) n. anything wonderful;—v.i. wonder exceedingly.—pr.p. mar'velling.—pa.t. and pa.p. mar'velled.—mar'vellous a. wonderful; astonishing. — mar'vellously adv. — mar'vellousness n.

Marxism (marks'-izm) n. socialist doctrines of Karl Marx (1818-83).—Marx'ian, Marx'ist a.—Marx'ist n.

marzipan (már'-zi-pan) n. paste made of ground almonds, sugar, egg, etc., used for cakes and sweetmeats. Also marchpane.

mascara (mas-ka'-ra) n. cosmetic preparation for darkening eyebrows and lashes.

mascot (mas'-kot) n. person or thing reputed to bring good luck.

masculine (mas'-kū-lin) a. male; strong; virile; (of a woman) mannish; (Gram.) of male gender.—mas'culineness, masculin'ity n.

mash (mash) v.t. beat to pulp or soft mass; mix malt with hot water;—n. thick mixture of malt and hot water for brewing; mixture of bran meal, boiled turnips, etc. given to horses and cattle.

mashie (mash'-i) n. golf-club with short iron head used for lofting ball. Also mash'y.

mask (mask) n. covering for face; plastic impression of human face, as death-mask; respirator; false face; disguise; fox's head; masquerade; (Fig.) pretext;—v.t. hide, as with mask;—v.i. assume disguise.

masochism (mas'-o-kizm) n. form of sex gratification by endurance of pain.—mas'ochist n.

mason (mā'-sn) n. builder in stone; freemason.—mason'ic a. pert. to freemasonry.—ma'sonry n. stonework; freemasonry.

masquerade (mask-er-ād') n. assembly of masked persons; disguise;—v.i. take part in masquerade; disguise oneself.

mass (mas) n. quantity of matter in body; shapeless lump; magnitude; crowd; chief portion;—v.t. collect in a mass;—v.i. assemble in numbers.—mass'ive a. forming mass; bulky; weighty.—mass'ively adv.—mass'iveness n.—mass media n. pl. means of communication with the majority of the people, e.g. TV, radio etc.—mass'-meet'ing n. large public meeting.—mass'-produc'tion n. cheap production in great quantities of commodity.—mass'y a. massive.—the masses, common people.

mass (mas) *n.* communion service in R.C. Church; the music to accompany high mass.—**high mass**, mass celebrated with music, incense, and ritual.—**low mass**, simple mass.

massacre (mas'-ạ-kẹr) *n.* ruthless slaughter; carnage;—*v.t.* slaughter indiscriminately.

massage (ma'sázh') *n.* curative treatment of physical disorders by rubbing, etc., carried out by specialist;—*v.t.* treat by massage.—**mass'agist, masseur'** *n.* (*fem.* **masseuse'**) specialist in massage.

massif (ma-sēf') *n.* group of mountains.

mast (mást) *n.* upright pole supporting rigging, sails, etc., or ship; upright post supporting wireless aerial, etc.;—*v.t.* furnish with mast or masts.—**mast'ed** *a.*—**mast'-head** *n.* top portion of ship's mast.—**to sail or serve before the mast**, sail as ordinary seaman.

mast (mást) *n.* fruit of oak, beech, esp. as food for swine.

master (más'-tẹr) *n.* one who directs and controls; employer of labour; proprietor; ship-captain; teacher; graduate in Arts, Science, etc., of a University; courtesy title given sons of family, esp. by servants; expert; famous artist, esp. an *old master*; one who leads a fox-hunt;—*a.* chief, dominant, pre-eminent;—*v.t.* become the master of; become expert at; overcome.—**mas'ter-at-arms** *n.* police officer on board warship.—**mas'terful** *a.* compelling; domineering.—**mas'terfully** *adv.*—**mas'terfulness** *n.*—**mas'terhand** *n.* expert.—**mas'ter-key** *n.* key which opens several locks.—**mas'terly** *a.* highly competent;—*adv.* with skill of an expert.—**mas'ter-mar'iner** *n.* captain of merchant or fishing vessel.—**mas'ter-mind** *n.* first-class mind; controlling power behind scheme.—**mas'terpiece** *n.* brilliantly executed work of art.—**mas'ter-stroke** *n.* masterly action.—**mas'ter-switch** *n.* electric switch which must be turned on before other switches will function.—**mas'tery** *n.* supremacy; superiority; victory.—**to be one's own master**, be independent.

mastic, mastich (mas'-tik) *n.* tree, yielding pale-yellow resin used in manufacture of varnish.

masticate (mas'-ti-kāt) *v.t.* chew.—**mas'ticable** *a.*—**mastica'tion** *n.* process of chewing.—**mastica'tor** *n.* mincing machine.—**mas'ticatory** *a.*

mastiff (mas'-tif) *n.* powerful breed of dog.

mastitis (mas-tī'-tis) *n.* (*Med.*) inflammation of the breast.

mastodon (mas'-to-don) *n.* extinct mammal resembling elephant.—**mastodon'tic** *a.*

mastoid (mas'-toid) *a.* pert. to or like female breast; nipple-shaped;—*n.* prominence on the temporal bone behind the human ear.

masturbate (mas'-tur-bāt) *v.i.* practise sexual self-gratification.—**masturba'tion** *n.*—**mas'turbator** *n.*

mat (mat) *n.* a coarse fabric of twine, rope, rushes, etc. for wiping the feet on; rug; heat-resisting covering for protecting surface of table; tangled mass of hair;—*v.t.* lay or cover with mats;—*v.i.* become a tangled mass.—*pr.p.* **mat'ting.**—*pa.t.* and *pa.p.* **mat'ted.**

mat, matt (mat) *a.* having a dull finish.

matador, matadore (mat'-ạ-dor) *n.* man who kills the bull in Spanish bullfight.

match (mach) *n.* splint of wood tipped with substance capable of ignition by friction; piece of rope for firing gun; fuse.—**match'-wood** *n.* small wood splinters used for making matches.

match (mach) *n.* person or thing equal to or resembling another; sporting contest; marriage; mate;—*v.i.* correspond in quality, quantity, etc.;—*v.t.* compete with; unite in marriage; be the same as, in colour, size, etc.—**match'less** *a.* peerless; unique.—**match'-ma'ker** *n.* one who schemes to bring about a marriage.

mate (māt) *n.* companion; fellow-worker; spouse; one of a pair (of animals, etc.); second-in-command on merchant ship; assistant;—*v.t.* match; marry;—*v.i.* pair.—**ma'ty** *a.* (*Slang*) friendly.

mate (māt) *v.t.* checkmate (chess).

mate, maté (má'-tā) *n.* tree of Brazil and Paraguay, the leaves of which are dried and used as tea.

mater (mā'-tẹr) *n.* mother; one of two membranes covering brain and spinal cord.

material (ma-tē'-ri-ạl) *a.* consisting of matter; corporeal; (of persons) not spiritually minded; essential; appreciable;—*n.* that from which something may be made; fabric.—**materialisa'tion** *n.*—**mate'rialise***v.t.* render material; give bodily form to;—*v.i.* become fact.—**mate'rialism** *n.* attitude to life which ignores all spiritual values.—**materialist'ic, -al** *a.* pert. to materialism.—**materialist'ically** *adv.*—**mate'rially** *adv.* appreciably.

materia medica (mat-tē'-ri-ạ med'-i-kạ) *n.* (*Med.*) substances used in the making of medicines, drugs, etc.; science relating to medicines and their curative properties.

maternal (ma-tẹr'-nạl) *a.* pert. to a mother; motherly.—**mater'nally** *adv.*—**mater'nity** *n.* and *a.* pert. to motherhood and childbirth.

mathematics (math-e-mat'-iks) *n.*

science of quantity and space, including arithmetic, algebra, trigonometry, geometry.—**mathemat'ic, -al** *a.* pert. to mathematics; accurate.—**mathemat'ically** *adv.*—**mathemati'cian** *n.*

matin (mat'-in) *n.* morning song;—*pl.* morning service in Anglican church; one of the canonical hours sung at midnight or daybreak. Also **mat'tins.**—**mat'inal** *a.*—**matinée** (mat'-ē-nā) *n.* afternoon performance in theatre or cinema.

matriarch (mā'-tri-ark) *n.* woman in position analogous to that of patriarch.—**matriar'chal** *a.*—**matriar'chalism** *n.*—**ma'triarchy** *n.* government exercised by a mother; society in which the female is predominant.

matrices (mat'-ri-sēz) *n.pl.* of matrix.

matricide (mat'-ri-sīd) *n.* murder of a mother; one who kills his mother.

matriculate (ma-trik'-ū-lāt) *v.t.* admit to membership, esp. of college;—*v.i.* enter by matriculation.—**matricula'tion** *n.*

matrimony (mat'-ri-mo-ni) *n.* marriage; wedlock.—**matrimo'nial** *a.*—**matrimo'nially** *adv.*

matrix (mā'-triks or mat'-riks) *n.* womb; cavity where anything is formed; mould, esp. for casting type; rock where minerals are embedded.—*pl.* **mat'rices, mat'rixes.**

matron (mā'-tron) *n.* married woman; woman in charge of nursing staff of hospital, etc.—**ma'tronly** *adv.* like a matron; mature; staid.

matter (mat'-er) *n.* that which occupies space and is the object of the senses; substance; cause of difficulty; subject of book, speech, etc.; occasion; moment; indefinite amount; (*Med.*) pus;—*v.i.* be of importance; to signify; (*Med.*) discharge pus.—*pr.p.* **matt'ering.**—*pa.p.* **matt'ered.**—**matt'er-of-fact** *a.* prosaic; unimaginative.

matting (mat'-ing) *n.* mat-work; straw, rushes, etc., as floor-covering.

mattock (mat'-ok) *n.* kind of pick-axe with only one end pointed, used for loosening soil.

mattress (mat'-res) *n.* case of canvas, ticking, etc., quilted and stuffed with hair, wool, kapok, or feathers, for a bed.

mature (ma-tūr') *a.* ripe; fully developed; (*Med.*) come to suppuration; due for payment, as a bill;—*v.t.* ripen; perfect;—*v.i.* become ripe; become due, as a bill.—**matur'able** *a.*—**mature'ly** *adv.*—**mature'ness** *n.* ripeness.—**matur'ity** *n.* ripeness, complete development.

matutinal (mat-ū-tī'-nal) *a.* morning; early.

maudlin (mawd'-lin) *a.* over-sentimental; tearful; fuddled.

maul (mawl) *n.* heavy wooden hammer;—*v.t.* beat; maltreat; mishandle.

maundy (mawn'-di) *n.* religious ceremony of washing feet of poor and distributing alms, in commemoration of Christ's washing of disciples' feet.

mausoleum (maw-sō-lē'-um) *n.* magnificent tomb.—**mausole'an** *a.*

mauve (mawv or mōv) *n.* reddish-purple dye;—*a.* having purple colour.

mavis (mā'-vis) *n.* song-thrush; throstle.

maw (maw) *n.* stomach of lower animals; in birds, the craw.

mawkish (mawk'-ish) *a.* sickly sweet; maudlin.—**mawk** *n.* maggot.—**mawk'ishly** *adv.*

maxillar, maxillary (mak-sil'-ar, -i) *a.* pert. to upper jaw-bone or jaw;—*n.* jaw-bone.—**maxill'a** *n.* upper jaw;—*pl.* **maxill'ae.**

maxim (mak'-sim) *n.* accepted principle; axiom; proverb; precept.

maximum (mak'-si-mum) *a.* greatest;—*n.* greatest number, quantity, or degree; highest point; peak.—*pl.* **max'ima.**—opp. *minimum.*—**max'imal** *a.* of greatest value.

may (mā) *v.i.* expressing possibility, permission, uncertainty, hope.—*pa.t.* might (mīt).—**may'be** *adv.* perhaps; possibly.

May (mā) *n.* fifth month of year; (*Fig.*) youthful prime; hawthorn (which blossoms in May);—**May'beet'le** *n.* cockchafer.—**May'-bloom** *n.* hawthorn blossom.—**May'day** *n.* international radio distress call.—**May'-fly** *n.* ephemeral insect; artificial fly for fishing.—**may'pole** *n.* pole with streamers, around which people danced on May-day.

mayhem (mā'-hem) *n.* (*Law*) offence of maiming by violence.

mayonnaise (mā'-on-āz') *n.* sauce or dressing of egg-yolk, vinegar, oil, etc. for salads.

mayor (mā'-or) *n.* (*fem.* **may'oress**) chief magistrate of city or borough.—**may'oral** *a.*—**may'orality** *n.*

maze (māz) *n.* network of intricate paths; labyrinth; (*Fig.*) confused condition; mental perplexity;—*v.t.* bewilder.—**ma'zy** *a.*—**ma'zily** *adv.*—**ma'ziness** *n.*

me (mē) *pron.* objective case of first pers. pronoun, '*I.*'

me (mē) *n.* third note in tonic sol-fa.

mead (mēd) *n.* fermented drink made of honey, yeast and water.

mead (mēd) *n.* meadow.

meadow (med'-ō) *n.* low, level tract of pasture ground.—**meadow-sweet** *n.* fragrant plant with creamy, feathery flowers.—**mead'owy** *a.*

meagre (mē'-ger) *a.* having little flesh; gaunt; scanty.—**mea'grely** *adv.*—**mea'greness** *n.*

meal (mēl) n. food eaten at one time.

meal (mēl) n. grain ground less finely than flour.—**meal'iness** n.—**meal'worn** n. insect found in meal stores.—**meal'y** a. like meal; powdery.—**meal'y-mouthed** a. apt to mince words.

mean (mēn) a. humble in rank or birth; lacking dignity; stingy; (Colloq.) disobliging.—**mean'ly** adv.—**mean'ness** n. small-mindedness; sordidness; want of dignity.

mean (mēn) a. in middle position; average; intervening;—n. middle-point of quantity, rate, position, or degree;—pl. resources; wealth; agency.—**mean'time, mean'while** adv. in the intervening time.—**means test**, inquiry into means to determine claim to pension or benefit.

mean (mēn) v.t. intend; signify;—v.i. form in the mind; be disposed; have meaning.—pa.t. and pa.p. **meant** (ment).—**mean'ing** n. sense; signification;—a. expressive.

meander (mē-an'-dẽr) v.i. flow with winding course; saunter aimlessly;—n. circuitous path; winding course of river (usually used in pl.).—**mean'dering** a. winding.

measles (mē'-zlz) n. (Med.) highly contagious disease, characterised by rash of bright red spots.—**meas'led, meas'ly** a. having measles; (Fig.) wretched; shoddy.—**German measles**, disease resembling measles but less severe.

measure (mezh'-ẽr) n. dimension reckoned by some standard; instrument for measuring; vessel of predetermined capacity; stately dance; metre; bar in music; course of action; act of Parliament; means to an end;—v.t. ascertain quantity or dimensions of; assess; distribute;—v.i. have ascertained value or extent; compare favourably with.—**meas'urable** a. capable of being measured; moderate. — **meas'urableness, measurability** n.—**meas'urably** adv.—**meas'ured** a. uniform; (of words) calculated. — **meas'ureless** a. boundless; infinite.—**meas'urement** n. dimension, quantity, etc., ascertained by measuring with fixed unit.—**meas'urer** n.

meat (mēt) n. flesh used as food; food of any kind.—**meat'iness** n.—**meat'y** a. full of meat; (Fig.) pithy; compact with ideas.

Mecca (mek'-a) n. reputed birthplace of Mahomet.—**mecca** n. (Fig.) focal point for people drawn together by common interest.

mechanic, -al (me-kan'-ik, -al) a. pert. to machines, mechanism, or mechanics; produced by machinery; automatic; acting without thought; base.—**mechan'ic** n. one who works with machines or instruments; skilled workman.—**mechan'ically** adv.—**mechanic'ian** n. machine-maker or repairer.—**mechan'ics** n. branch of applied mathematics which deals with force and motion;—**mechanisa'tion** n. change from animal to mechanical power in transport.—**mech'anise** v.t. make mechanical.—**mech'anised** a.—**mech'anism** n. construction of machine; machinery, esp. its parts collectively; (Fig.) technique.—**mechanist'ic** a.

medal (med'-al) n. piece of metal, like a coin, as memento or reward;—v.t. decorate with medal.—**medall'ic** a. pert. to medals.—**medall'ion** n. large medal; metal disc, with portrait in bas-relief; ornament containing miniature or hair.—**med'allist, med'alist** n. maker or student of medals; one awarded a medal.

meddle (med'-l) v.i. interfere officiously; tamper with.—**medd'ler** n.—**medd'lesome** a. interfering.—**medd'lesomeness** n.

medial (mē'-di-al) a. in, or passing through, the middle; pert. to a mean or average.—**me'dian** a. situated in the middle;—n. (Geom.) line drawn from vertex of triangle to middle point of opposite side.

mediate (mē'-di-āt) a. being between two extremes; intervening; not direct;—v.i. interpose between contending parties to effect reconciliation;—v.t. effect by mediation.—**me'diacy** n.—**me'diately** adv.—**me'diateness** n.—**media'tion** n. act of mediating; steps to effect reconciliation.—**me'diator** n. (fem. **me'diatress, me'diatrix**) n.—**mediato'rial; me'diatory** a.

medical (med'-i-kal) a. pert. to medicine or art of healing; medicinal.—**med'icable** a. capable of being cured.—**med'ically** adv.—**med'icament** n. any healing remedy.—**med'icate** v.t. treat with medicine; impregnate with anything medicinal.—**med'icated** a.—**medica'tion** n.—**med'icative** a. tending to heal.

medicine (med'-i-sin or med'-sin) n. substance used in treatment of disease; science of healing and prevention of disease.—**medic'inal** a. pert. to medicine; remedial.—**medic'inally** adv.—**medicine man**, magician with supposed powers of healing; witch-doctor.

medieval, mediaeval (med-i-ē'-val) a. pert. to or characteristic of the Middle Ages.—**medi(a)e'valist** n. one who makes special study of Middle Ages.

mediocre (mē'-di-ō-kẽr) a. middling; neither good nor bad; second-rate.—**medioc'rity** n. middle state.

meditate (med'-i-tāt) v.t. consider thoughtfully; intend;—v.i. ponder, esp. on religious matters.—**med'itated**

a. planned.—**medita'tion** *n.* deep thought.—**med'itative** *a.* given to reflection.—**med'itatively** *adv.*—**med'itativeness** *n.*

mediterranean (med-i-ter-rā'-ne-an) *a.* (of land) far from the sea; (of water) encircled by land.—**Mediterra'nean** *a.* pert. to the almost landlocked water between S. Europe and N. Africa.

medium (mē'-di-um) *n.* that which is in the middle; mean; agency; in spiritualism, intermediary professing to give messages from the spirit world (*pl.* me'diums); in bacteriology, substance used for cultivation of bacteria;—*pl.* me'dia, me'diums.—*a.* middle; average; middling.

medlar (med'-lar) *n.* tree with fruit like small apple.

medley (med'-li) *n.* miscellaneous collection of things; miscellany.

medulla (me-dul'-a) *n.* marrow in bone; inner tissue of gland; pith of hair or plants.—**medull'ar, -y** *a.*—**med'ullose** *a.* like pith.

meek (mēk) *a.* submissive; humble; gentle.—**meek'ly** *adv.*—**meek'ness** *n.* humility.

meerschaum (mēr'-shawm) *n.* fine, white clay used for the bowl of tobacco-pipes; pipe of this.

meet (mēt) *a.* fit; suitable.—**meet'ly** *adv.*—**meet'ness** *n.*

meet (mēt) *v.t.* encounter; join; find; satisfy; pay, as debt; await arrival, as of train;—*v.i.* converge at specified point; combine; assemble in company;—*pa.t.* and *pa.p.* met.— *n.* assembly of people, esp. as beginning of a hunt.—**meet'ing** *n.* coming together, as of roads, rivers; encounter; people gathered together for worship, entertainment, discussion, sport, etc.—**Meeting House,** Quakers' place of worship.

megacycle (meg'-a-sī-kl) *n.* (*Elect.*) one million cycles.

megalith (meg'-a-lith) *n.* huge stone. —**megalith'ic** *a.* pert. to huge ancient stone monuments or stone-circles.

megalomania (meg-a-lō-mā'-ni-a) *n.* form of insanity in which the patient has grandiose ideas of his own importance; lust for power.— **megaloma'niac** *n.*

megaphone (meg'-a-fōn) *n.* large speaking-trumpet used as amplifier to make human voice audible at a great distance.

megohm (meg'-ōm) *n.* (*Elect.*) one million ohms.

megrim (mē'-grim) *n.* See **migraine.** —*pl.* depression.

melancholy (mel'-an-kol-i) *n.* depression of spirits;—*a.* gloomy; depressed.—**melanchol'ia** *n.* morbid state of depression; abnormal introspectiveness.—**melanchol'ic,** *a.* depressed; caused by melancholy.

mêlée (mel'-ā) *n.* confused, hand-to-hand fight.

meliorate (mē'-lyo-rāt) *v.t.* improve; —*v.i.* become better.—**meliora'tion** *n.*—**meliora'tor** *n.*

melliferous (mel-if'-er-us) *a.* producing honey.—**mellif'ic** *a.* honeymaking. —**mellif'luence** *n.* —**mellif'luent, mellif'luous** *a.* flowing sweetly or smoothly.—**mellif'luently, mellif'luously** *adv.*

mellow (mel'-ō) *a.* soft and ripe; well-matured; genial; resonant, as voice; (*Slang*) somewhat intoxicated.—*v.t.* soften; ripen;—*v.i.* become soft or ripe; become maturely wise.— **mell'owly** *adv.*—**mell'owness** *n.*

melodeon (mel'-ō'-di-un) *n.* kind of accordion.

melodrama (mel-o-dram'-a) *n.* dramatic entertainment, sensational and crudely emotional; play of romantic sentiment and situation.— **melodramat'ic** *a.*

melody (mel'-ō-di) *n.* rhythmical succession of sounds forming agreeable musical air; tune.—**melod'ic** *a.* tuneful. — **melo'dious** *a.* tuneful; pleasing to ear.—**melo'diously** *adv.*— **melo'diousness** *n.*—**mel'odist** *n.* musical composer or singer.

melon (mel'-on) *n.* kind of gourd with sweet, juicy pulp, and centre full of seeds.

melt (melt) *v.t.* reduce to liquid state; dissolve; soften; (*Fig.*) make tender;—*v.i.* become liquid or molten; blend; vanish; (*Fig.*) become tender.—*pa.p.* melt'ed or molt'en.— **melt'ing** *n.* act of making liquid or molten;—*a.* softening; tender.— **melt'ingly** *adv.*

member (mem'-ber) *n.* limb, esp. of animal body; constituent part of complex whole; one of society, group, parliament, etc.—**mem'bered** *a.* having limbs.—**mem'bership** *n.* state of being member, or one of a society; members collectively.

membrane (mem'-brān) *n.* (*Anat.*) thin tissue forming or lining an organ of the body; sheet of parchment.—**membran'eous, mem'branous, membrana'ceous** *a.* pert. to, or resembling, membrane.

memento (mem-en'-tō) *n.* reminder of person or event; souvenir;—*pl.* memen'tos or memen'toes.

memoir (mem'-wár or mem'-oir) *n.* short, biographical sketch; scientific record of investigations on set subject;—*pl.* reminiscences.

memory (mem'-o-ri) *n.* faculty of retaining and recalling knowledge; recollection; remembrance; part of computer in which data is stored.— **memorabil'ia** *n. pl.* things worthy of note.—**mem'orable** *a.* noteworthy; remarkable.—**mem'orably** *adv.*—**mem'orandum** *n.* note or reminder;—*pl.*

memoran'dums, or **memoran'da.—memo'rial** a. serving as reminder; contained in memory;—n. anything intended to commemorate person or event; written petition presented to official governing body; record of historical events.—**mem'orise** v.t. commit to memory.

menace (men'-as) n. threat; potential danger;—v.t. threaten.—**men'acing** a. impending; threatening.—**men'acingly** adv.

ménage (mā-nàzh') n. household; house-wifery.

menagerie (men-aj'-ér-i) n. collection of caged wild animals for exhibition.

mend (mend) v.t. repair; set right; improve;—v.i. improve; convalesce; —n. mended place.—**mend'er** n.—**mend'ing** n.

mendacious (men'dā'-shus) a. given to telling lies; untruthful.—**menda'ciously** adv.—**mendac'ity** n. prevarication; tendency to lying; untruthfulness.

mendicant (men'-di-kant) a. begging; living as a beggar;—n. beggar.—**mend'icancy, mendic'ity** n. begging; poverty; living by alms.

menial (mē'-ni-al) a. pert. to domestic servant or service; servile; mean;—n. servant; person of mean character.—**men'ially** adv.

meninx (mē'-ningks) n. one of three membranes enveloping brain;—pl. **meninges** (men-in'-jēz).—**meningi'tis** n. (Med.) inflammation of the membranes of the brain.

meniscus (mē-nis'-kus) n. lens convex on one side and concave on the other; curved surface of liquid in a vessel; (Math.) crescent.—**menis'cal, menis'cate** a.—**menis'ciform** a. crescent-shaped.

menopause (men'-ō-pawz) n. change of life in a woman.

mensal (men'-sal) a. monthly.

menses (men'-sēz) n.pl. monthly discharge from uterus of female.—**men'strua** n.pl. the menses.—**men'strual** a. pert. to the menses.—**men'struate** v.i. discharge the menses.—**menstrua'tion** n.—**men'struous** a.

mensurable (mens'-ū-ra-bl) a. capable of being measured.—**mensurabil'ity** n.—**mens'ural** a.—**mensura'tion** n.—**mensura'tive**.

mental (men'-tal) a. pert. to the mind; (Colloq.) mentally-defective.—**mental'ity** n. intellectual power; mental attitude.—**men'tally** adv.—**mental deficiency**, subnormal intelligence.

menthol (men'-thol) n. a camphor obtained from oil of peppermint.—**menthola'ted** a.

mention (men'-shun) n. brief notice; casual comment;—v.t. notice; name.—**men'tionable** a. fit to be remarked on.

mentor (men'-tor) n. experienced and prudent adviser.—**mentor'ial** a.

menu (men'-ū) n. bill of fare; food served.

mercantile (mer'-kan-tīl) a. pert. to commerce.—**mercantile marine**, ships and men engaged in commerce.

mercenary (mer'-se-nar-i) a. working merely for money; hired; sordid; —n. hired soldier.—**mer'cenarily** adv.—**mer'cenariness** n.

mercer (mer'-ser) n. dealer in textiles or small wares.—**mer'cery** n.

merchandiser (mer'-chan-dī'-zer) n. coin-operated machine which automatically dispenses goods.

merchant (mer'-chant) n. one who engages in trade; wholesaler;—a. pert. to trade or merchandise.—**mer'chandise** n. commodities bought and sold in home or foreign markets.—**mer'chantman** n. ship carrying goods.—**merchant navy**, ships and men of the mercantile marine.

Mercury (mer'-kū-ri) n. Roman equivalent of Greek god, *Hermes*, messenger of the gods; planet nearest to the sun.—**mer'cury** n. metallic chemical element, symbol Hg, silvery white in colour, with very low melting point (also called *quicksilver*) and used in barometers, thermometers, etc.; messenger.—**mercu'rial** a. pert. to, or consisting of, mercury; sprightly; agile; erratic.—**mercu'rially** adv.—**mercu'ric** a. (Chem). pert. to compounds of bivalent mercury.—**mer'curous** a. (Chem.) pert. to compounds of univalent mercury.

mercy (mer'-si) n. forbearance; clemency; leniency shown to one guilty of crime or misdemeanour; compassion.—**mer'ciful** a. full of mercy; compassionate.—**mer'cifully** adv.—**mer'cifulness** n.—**mer'ciless** a. void of pity; callous; cruel.—**mer'cilessly** adv.—**mer'cilessness** n.

mere (mēr) n. pool or lake. Also **meer**.

mere (mēr) a. nothing but; simple.—**mere'ly** adv. purely; simply; solely.

meretricious (mer-e-trish'-us) a. pert. to harlot; (Fig.) tawdry; specious; cheap.—**meretric'iously** adv.—**meretric'iousness** n.

merge (merj) v.t. cause to be swallowed up; plunge or sink;—v.i. lose identity by being absorbed in something else; be swallowed up or lost.—**mer'ger** n. combine of commercial or industrial firms.

meridian (me-rid'-i-an) n. imaginary circle passing through the poles at right angles to equator; (Astron.) circle passing through the poles of the heavens and the zenith of observer; highest attitude of sun or star; midday;—a. pert. to midday; supreme.—**merid'ional** a. pert. to meridian; southerly.—**meridional'ity** n.—**merid'ionally** adv.

meringue (me-rang') n. sugar and white of egg, whipped till stiff, and baked in oven; cake of this, filled with whipped cream.

merino (me-rē'-nō) n. breed of sheep with very fine, thick fleece, orig. from Spain; dress fabric of this wool;—a. pert. to merino sheep or its wool.

merit (mer'-it) n. quality of deserving reward; excellence; worth;—pl. rights and wrongs, as of law case:—v.t. earn; deserve.—**meritoc'racy** n. rule by persons promoted for superior ability.—**mer'ito'rious** a. deserving reward.—**merito'riously** adv.—**merito'riousness** n.—**Order of Merit** (abbrev. O.M.) award for outstanding achievement.

merle (merl) n. blackbird.

merlin (mer'-lin) n. species of falcon.

mermaid (mer'-mād) n. imaginary sea-creature with upper body and head of woman, and tail of fish.—**mer'man** n. male equivalent of mermaid.

merry (mer'-i) a. gay; lively; (Colloq.) slightly intoxicated.—**merr'ily** adv.—**merr'iment, merr'iness** n. gaiety with noise and laughter; hilarity.—**merr'y-go-round** n. revolving machine with horses, cars, etc.—**merr'y-ma'king** n. festivity.—**merr'y-thought** n. forked bone of fowl's breast, wishbone.

mesh (mesh) n. space between threads of net;—pl. network; (Fig.) toils;—v.t. net; ensnare;—v.i. become interlocked.

mesmerism (mez'-mer-izm) n. exercising influence over will and actions of another; animal magnetism; hypnotism.—**mesmer'ic, -al** a. of or pert. to mesmerism.—**mesmerisa'tion** n.—**mes'merise** v.t. hypnotise.—**mes'meriser, mes'merist** n.

mesolithic (mes-ō-lith'-ic) a. of period between Palaeolithic and Neolithic ages.

meson (mēz'-on, mes'-on) n. unstable sub-atomic particle of positive, negative, or zero charge, and mass between that of electron and proton.

Mesozoic (mes-ō-zō'-ik) a. pert. to second geological period, including Triassic, Jurassic, and Cretaceous systems.

mess (mes) n. unpleasant mixture; disorder; muddle; — v.t. dirty; muddle.—**mess'y** a. dirty; untidy; chaotic.

mess (mes) n. dish of food served at one time; soft, pulpy food; number of people who eat together or the place, esp. in army, etc., as officers' mess;—v.t. supply with a mess;—v.i. eat in company.—**mess'-tin** n. soldier's cooking-vessel.

message (mes'-āj) n. communication sent by one person to another; errand; inspired utterance;—**mess'enger** n. one who delivers a communication; one employed to deliver goods from shop.

Messiah (me-sī'-a) n. promised Saviour of the Jews; Jesus Christ. Also **Messi'as.**—**Messi'ah'ship** n.—**Mes-sian'ic** a.

met (met) pa.t. and pa.p. of the verb meet.

metabolism (me-tab'-ol-izm) n. chemical change continually going on in cells of living matter.—**metabol'ic** a.—**metab'olise** v.t.

metal (met'-al) n. mineral substance, fusible and malleable, usually capable of conducting heat and electricity; stones used in macadamising roads; (Fig.) courage; mettle;—pl. railroad track;—v.t. cover with metal; lay or repair roads with metal.—**met'alled** a. covered with metal, as a road.—**metal'lic** a. pert. to, like, or consisting of, metal.—**metal'lically** adv.—**met'alline** v.t.—**met'allist** n. metal-worker.—**met'alloid** n. element which has both metallic and non-metallic properties, as arsenic;—a. pert. to or having property of metal. Also **metalloid'al.**—**base metals,** copper, lead, zinc, tin as distinct from precious metals, gold and silver.

metallurgy (met'-al-ur-ji) n. art of working metals or of obtaining metals from ores.—**metallur'gic** a.—**met'allurgist** n.

metamorphosis (met-a-mor'-fe-sis) n. change of form or structure; evolution; — pl. **metamor'phoses.** — **metamor'phic** a. subject to change of form.—**metamor'phism** n.—**metamor'phose** v.t. transform in form or nature.

metaphor (met'-a-for) n. figure of speech which makes an implied comparison between things which are not literally alike.—**metaphor'ic, -al** a.—**metaphor'ically** adv.—**mixed metaphor,** combination of metaphors drawn from different sources.

metaphrase (met'-a-frāz) n. literal, word for word translation from foreign language (opp. of paraphrase); repartee;—v.t. translate literally.

metaphysics (met-a-fiz'-iks) n. sing. science which investigates first causes of all existence and knowledge.—**metaphys'ical** a.—**metaphys'ically** adv.—**metaphysic'ian** n.

metatarsus (met-a-tár'-sus) n. front part of the foot.—**metatar'sal** a.

mete (mēt) v.t. measure.—**mete out,** distribute; allot, as punishment.

metempsychosis (me-tem-si-kō'-sis) n. transmigration of soul, after death, into another body.—pl. **metempsycho'ses.**

meteor (mē'-te-or) *n.* any rapidly passing, luminous body seen in the atmosphere; shooting star; (*Fig.*) dazzling but transiently famous person.—**meteor'ic** *a.* pert. to meteor; influenced by atmospheric conditions; (*Fig.*) dazzling; flashing.—**me'teorite** *n.* meteoric stone.—**me'teoroid** *n.* body in space which becomes a meteor on passing through the atmosphere of the earth.—**me'teorlite** *n.* meteorite.—**meteorolog'ical** *a.*—**meteorol'ogist** *n.*—**meteorol'ogy** *n.* science which treats of atmospheric phenomena, esp. in relation to weather forecasts.

meter (mē'-tẹr) *n.* instrument for measuring, esp. quantity.

methane (meth'-ān) *n.* inflammable, hydro-carbon gas; marsh gas.

method (meth'-od) *n.* manner of proceeding; orderliness; classification system. — **method'ic**, **-al** *a.* arranged systematically; orderly.—**method'ically** *adv.*

Methodism (meth'-od-izm) *n.* doctrines and teaching of the Methodists.—**Meth'odist** *n.* member of nonconformist sect founded in 18th cent. by Charles and John Wesley.

methyl (meth'-il) *n.* radical of wood-alcohol.—**meth'ylate** *v.t.* mix or treat with methyl alcohol.—**methylated spirits**, alcohol mixed with 10 per cent wood spirit and coloured with violet dye, etc.

meticulous (me-tik'-ū-lus) *a.* scrupulous as to detail; over-exact.—**metic'ulously** *adv.*—**metic'ulousness** *n.*

métier (māt'-yā) *n.* occupation for which one has special aptitude.

metonymy (me-ton'-i-mi) *n.* figure of speech in which the name of one thing is put for another associated with it, as 'the turf' for 'racing.'

metre (mē'-tẹr) *n.* unit of length in metric system, 39.37 Eng. inches.—**met'ric** *a.*—**metric system**, decimal system.

metre, meter (mē'-tẹr) *n.* in poetry, rhythmical group arrangement of syllables (long and short, accented and unaccented).—**met'rical** *a.* pert. to metre or measurement.—**met'rically** *adv.*—**metrol'ogy** *n.* science of weights and measures.—**met'ronome** *n.* (*Mus.*) instrument like inverted pendulum for beating time.

metropolis (me-trop'-o-lis) *n.* capital town of a country; principal ecclesiastical city.—*pl.* **metrop'olises**.—**metropol'itan** *a.* pert. to metropolis; pert. to the see of a metropolitan bishop;—*n.* bishop with jurisdiction over other bishops of the see.

mettle (met'-l) *n.* spirit; courage.—**mett'lesome** *a.* high-spirited; ardent.—**to be on one's mettle**, be roused to do one's best.

mew (mū) *n.* sea-gull.

mew (mū) *v.t.* shed or cast; confine, as in a cage; —*v.i.* moult;—*n.* cage for hawks, esp. at moulting season;—*pl.* stables, orig. place where king's falcons were kept.

mew (mū) *n.* cry of cat, sea-gull, etc.;—*v.i.* cry as a cat.

mezzanine (mez'-a-nīn) *n.* (*Archit.*) low storey between two higher ones; window in such; in theatre, floor below the stage.

mezzo (met'-zō) *a.* middle.—**mez'zo-sopran'o** *n.* type of voice between soprano and contralto.—**mez'zotint** *n.* method of copper-plate engraving. Also **mezzotint'o**.

miasma (mi-az'-mạ) *n.* harmful exhalations from decomposing matter. Also **mi'asm**.—*pl.* **miss'mata**, **mi'asms**.

mica (mī'-ka) *n.* group of mineral silicates capable of cleavage into very thin, flexible, and often transparent laminae.—**mica'ceous** *a.*

mice (mīs) *pl.* of mouse.

Michaelmas (mik'-l-mas) *n.* feast of St. Michael the archangel, 29th Sept.—**Michaelmas daisy**, flower of aster family.

microbe (mī'-krōb) *n.* minute organism; disease-germ.—**micro'bial**, **micro'bian, micro'bic** *a.*—**micro'bicide** *n.* substance which kills microbes.—**microbiol'ogy** *n.* science of microbes. —**microbiolog'ical** *a.*

microcephalous (mī-krō-sef'-ạ-lus) *a.* (*Anat.*) having very small head.

microcosm (mī'-krō-kozm) *n.* man, regarded as the epitome of the universe; community symbolical of humanity as a whole; miniature representation.—**microcos'mic**, **-al** *a.*

microfilm (mī'-krō-film) *n.* film used in micro-copying of books, etc.

micrometer (mī-krom'-e-tẹr) *n.* instrument for measuring very small distances or angles.

micron (mī'-kron) *n.* millionth part of metre.

micro-organism (mī'-krō-or'-ganizm) *n.* microscopic organism; microbe; germ.

microphone (mī'-krō-fōn) *n.* instrument for turning sound waves into electrical waves; (*Colloq.* abbrev. **mike**); instrument for making faint sounds louder.

microphotography (mī'-krō-fō-tog'-rạ-fi) *n.* process of photographic enlargement of minute objects for purposes of study; art of producing minute photographs which can be examined only by means of microscope.—**microphotog'raph** *n.*

microscope (mī'-krō-skōp) *n.* optical instrument for magnifying minute objects.—**microscop'ic, -al** *a.* pert. to microscope; visible only by aid of microscope; very minute.—**microscop'ically** *adv.*—**micros'copy** *n.*

micturition (mik-tū-rish'-un) n. (Med.) the passing of urine; morbid desire to pass urine frequently.—**mic'turate** v.i.

mid (mid) a. situated between extremes; middle.—**mid'day** n. and a. noon; pert. to noon.—**mid'land** a. in middle of land area;—n. central part of a country.—**Mid'lands** n.pl. central counties of England.—**mid'most** a. middle.—**mid'night** n. twelve o'clock at night.—**mid'-off, mid'-on** n. (Cricket) fielder standing on off (or on) side of batsman, not far from bowler.—**mid'-ship** a. in middle part of ship.—**mid'shipman** n. junior naval officer below a sub-lieutenant.—**mid'ships** adv. amidships.—**mid'summer** n. middle of summer; period of summer solstice, 21st June.—**mid'way** adv. halfway. — **mid'winter** n. middle of winter; period of winter solstice, 22nd Dec.

mid (mid) prep. amidst (Poet.).

midden (mid'-n) n. heap of ashes, dung, etc.

middle (mid'-l) a. equidistant from the extremes; intermediate; — n. middle point.—**midd'le-aged** a. pert. to period of life between 40 and 60. —**midd'leman** n. agent acting between producer and consumer (or retailer). —**midd'lemost** a. nearest the middle. —**midd'le-watch** n. (Naut.) period between midnight and 4 a.m.—**midd'le-weight** n. (Boxing) boxer of a weight between 10 st. 7 lbs. and 11 st. 6 lbs.—**midd'ling** a. of medium size, quality;—adv. moderately.— **Middle Ages,** period of European history from Fall of the Roman Empire (about A.D. 476) to Fall of Constantinople (1453).—**middle class,** section of community between aristocracy and working classes; bourgeoisie.—**Middle English,** English language as written and spoken between 1150–1500 (approx.).

midge (mij) n. gnat; very small person.—**midg'et** n. dwarf.

midinette (mē-dē-net') n. Parisian shop-girl.

midriff (mid'-rif) n. diaphragm.

midst (midst) n. middle;—prep. amidst.

midwife (mid'-wīf) n. woman who assists another at childbirth.—pl. **mid'wives.** — **midwifery** (mid-wif'-eri) n. practice of obstetrics.

mien (mēn) n. demeanour; bearing; look.

might (mīt) pa.t. of verb **may**.

might (mīt) n. power; strength; energy.—**might'iness** n. greatness.— **might'y** a. having great strength or power; exalted.

mignonette (min'-yo-net) n. sweet-scented, greenish-gray flowered plant.

migraine (mē-grān') n. severe head-ache and depression. Also **megrim.**

migrate (mī'-grāt) v.i. move one's residence from one place to another; (of birds) fly to another place or country in search of warmer climate or better feeding grounds.— **mi'grant** n. migratory bird:—a. accustomed to migrate.—**migra'tion** n. act of migrating; mass removal. —**mi'gratory** a.

milch (milch) a. giving milk.

mild (mīld) a. gentle; kind; calm, temperate, as weather.—**mild'ly** adv. —**mild'ness.**

mildew (mil'-dū) n. whitish coating of minute fungi on plants, leather etc.;—v.t. and i. taint or be tainted with mildew.—**mil'dewy** a.

mile (mīl) n. measure of length, 1760 yds.—**geographical or nautical mile,** one minute of a great circle of the earth, equal to 6080 ft.—**mile'age** n. distance in miles; rate of travel calculated in miles.—**mil'er** n. man or horse trained to run a mile-race. —**mile'stone** n. stone on roadside marking distance in miles; (Fig.) stage or crisis in one's life.

militant (mil'-i-tant) a. fighting; serving as soldier.—**mil'itancy** n. state of being warlike; fighting spirit.—**mil'itantly** adv.—**mil'itarism** n. emphasis on military power of a country;—opp. of pacifism.—**mil'itarist** n. supporter of militarism; student of military science and strategy. — **mil'itary** a. pert. to soldiers, arms, or war; warlike;—n. army; body of soldiers.—**mil'itate** v.i. stand opposed to; have adverse effect on (foll. by against).

militia (mi-lish'-a) n. citizen army, liable to be called out in emergency; branch of British military forces known as Territorial Force after 1907;—**milit'iaman** n.

milk (milk) n. white fluid secreted by female mammals for nourishment of their young; juice of certain plants; —v.t. draw milk from; (Colloq.) exploit a person;—v.i. give milk.— **milk and water** a. insipid.—**milk'en** a. like milk.—**milk'er** n. one who milks a cow; milking-machine; cow which yields milk.—**milk'ily** adv.—**milk'iness** n.—**milk'ing** n. quality of milk yielded at one time; drawing of milk from cow.—**milk'like** a.—**milk'maid** n. dairymaid or woman who milks cows.—**milk'man** n. man who milks cows; man who distributes milk, esp. from house to house.— **milk shake,** drink made of fruit juices and milk mixed in special shaker.—**milk'sop** n. weak, effeminate man.—**milk'-tooth** n. one of first, temporary teeth, lost in childhood. —**milk'y** a. like, full of, or yielding milk.—**Milky Way,** Galaxy, irregular, luminous belt of faint stars in the heavens.—**condensed milk**, milk with sugar added and evaporated to consistency of syrup.—**evaporated milk**, unsweetened condensed milk.

mill (mil) *n.* building equipped with machinery to grind corn, etc.; apparatus worked by hand, electricity, etc., for grinding; factory or the machinery used in manufacture;—*v.t.* grind; cut fine grooves on edges of, as of coins; full (cloth); dress or purify (ore);—*v.i.* go round in circles, as cattle, or crowds of people.—**mill′board** *n.* stout pasteboard used in book-binding.—**milled** *a.* having edges raised and grooved, as coins; fulled, as cloth; rolled into sheets, as metal.—**mill′ing** *n.* grinding in a mill; fulling cloth, or grooving raised edges of coin;—*a.* confused; without direction.—**mill′pond** *n.* pond supplying water for mill-wheel. — **mill′-race** *n.* swiftly moving current of water which turns mill-wheel.—**mill′stone** *n.* one of pair of round, flat stones used in grinding grain.—**mill′-wheel** *n.* water wheel for driving mill.

millennium (mil-en′-i-um) *n.* thousand years; esp. period of thousand years when Christ will reign on earth (*Rev.* 20); future time of perfect peace on earth.—**millenna′rian** *a.* lasting thousand years; pert. to millennium;—*n.* one who believes in millennium.—**mill′ennary** *a.* comprising a thousand;—*n.* a period of thousand years.—**millenn′ial** *a.* pert. to millennium.

milliped, millipede (mill′-e-ped, -i-pēd) *n.* insect with many legs.

miller (mil′-er) *n.* one who grinds corn.

millet (mil′-et) *n.* cereal grass bearing seeds of great nutritive value.

milli- (mil′-i) *prefix* one thousandth of.—**mill′igram, mill′igramme** *n.* one thousandth of a gram, ·0154 of a grain.—**mill′ilitre** *n.* one thousandth of a litre, ·061 cub. in.—**mill′imeter, mill′imetre** *n.* one thousandth of a metre, ·0394 in.

milliard (mil′-yard) *n.* thousand millions; (*U.S.*) billion.

milliner (mil′-in-er) *n.* one who makes or sells ladies' hats.—**mill′inery** *n.*

million (mil′-yun) *n.* thousand thousands (1,000,000); very large number.—**millionaire′** *n.* (*fem.* **millionair′ess**) one whose wealth amounts to a million (or more) pounds, francs, dollars.—**mill′ionary** *a.*—**mill′ionfold** *a.*—**mill′ionth** *n.* one of a million parts;—*a.* being one of a million parts.—**the millions**, the masses.

mime (mīm) *n.* farce in which scenes of real life are expressed by gesture only; actor in this;—*v.i.* act in mime; express by gesture only.—

mimet′ic(al) *a.* imitative.—**mim′ic** *v.t.* imitate; burlesque; ridicule.—*pr.p.* **mim′icking**;—*pa.p.* **mim′icked**.—*n.* one who mimics or caricatures;—*a.* feigned.—**mim′icry** *n.*

mimosa (mi-mō′-zạ) *n.* genus of leguminous plants, with small, fluffy, yellow flowers.

mina, myna, mynah (mī′-na) *n.* Indian bird allied to starling.

minar (mi′-nȧr) *n.* lighthouse; tower.—**min′aret** *n.* turret on Mohammedan mosque.

minatory (min′-ạ-tor-i) *a.* threatening.

mince (mins) *v.t.* chop into very small pieces; (*Fig.*) tone down; extenuate;—*v.i.* clip one's words; speak or walk with affected elegance. — *pr.p.* **minc′ing**; — *pa.p.* **minced** (minst).—*n.* meat chopped small or put through a mincer.—**minc′er** *n.* machine, with revolving blades, for chopping meat, etc.—**mince′meat** *n.* currants, raisins, spices, apple, suet and sugar, chopped and mixed together, as filling for Christmas pies.—**mince′-pie** *n.* small round pie filled with this.—**minc′ing** *a.* speaking or walking with affected elegance.—**minc′ingly** *adv.*

mind (mīnd) *n.* intellectual faculty; understanding; memory; opinion; inclination; purpose;—*v.t.* attend to; heed; object to; take care of;—*v.i.* be careful; intend.—**mind′ed** *a.* disposed.—**mind′er** *n.* one who looks after anything.—**mind′ful** *a.* attentive.—**mind′fully** *adv.*—**mind′fulness** *n.*—**mind′less** *a.* regardless.—**mind′-read′er** *n.* one who can sense another's thoughts.—**absence of mind**, forgetfulness.

mine (mīn) *poss. pron.* belonging to me.

mine (mīn) *n.* underground pit from which minerals are excavated; secret excavation under military position; explosive device concealed in ground or water; (*Fig.*) profitable source;—*pl.* mining industry;—*v.i.* and *t.* lay a mine or mines under; dig a mine or in a mine; burrow; (*Fig.*) undermine; sap.—**mine′field** *n.* area of land or stretch of the sea where mines have been laid down.—**mine′-lay′er** *n.* vessel which lays down submarine or floating mines.—**mi′ner** *n.* one who works in mine.—**mine′-sweep′er** *n.* vessel equipped for clearing minefield.

mineral (min′-er-ạl) *n.* substance taken from earth by mining;—*pl.* mineral waters;—*a.* pert. to minerals; containing minerals; (*Chem.*) inorganic.—**mineralisa′tion** *n.*—**min′eralise** *v.t.* convert into minerals; impregnate with minerals.—**min′eralist** *n.* expert in minerals.—**mineralog′ical** *a.*—**mineralog′ically** *adv.*

—**mineral'ogy** n. science of minerals and their classification.—**mineralogist** n.—**mineral waters**, waters, naturally impregnated with mineral substance, and used medicinally; effervescent imitation of this, such as soda-water, etc.

mingle (ming'-gl) v.t. mix; blend; join in;—v.i. become mixed;—n. jumble.—**ming'ler** n.—**ming'ling** n. blend.—**ming'lingly** adv.

mingy (min'-ji) a. (Slang) parsimonious; stingy.

mini (mi'-ni) prefix used in compound terms, meaning small.—**min'ibus** n. small bus.—**minicab** n. small taxi.

miniature (min'-i-a-tūr) n. small-sized painting done on ivory, etc.; anything on small scale;—a. minute;—v.t. depict on small scale.

minim (min'-im) n. anything very minute; (Med.) ₁/₆₀ of fluid drachm; drop; (Mus.) note equal to two crotchets.—**min'imal** a.—**min'imise** v.t. reduce to smallest proportions; undervalue.—**minimisa'tion** n.—**min'imum** n. least to which anything may be reduced.—pl. **min'ima**.

minion (min'-yun) n. favourite; servile flatterer.

minister (min'-is-ter) n. servant; agent or instrument; clergyman; one entrusted with a State department; ambassador;—v.i. act as servant; supply things needful.—**minister'ial** a.—**minister'ially** adv.—**min'istering** a. serving.—**ministra'tion** n.—**ministra'tive** a.—**min'istry** n. act of ministering; office or functions of minister; clergy; government department, as the Cabinet.

mink (mingk) n. animal of the weasel tribe; its brown fur.

minnow (min'-ō) n. small freshwater fish.

minor (mi'-nor) a. lesser; inferior in bulk, degree, importance, etc.; subordinate; (Mus.) lower by a semi-tone;—n. person under 21.—**minor'ity** n. state of being under age; the lesser number, oppos. of majority.—**minor key** (Mus.) key characterised by minor third, sixth, or seventh.

minster (min'-ster) n. church of monastery; cathedral.

minstrel (min'-strel) n. medieval bard who sang songs of his own composing; seaside entertainer.—**min'strelsy** n. profession of a minstrel; group of minstrels; collection of ballads.

mint (mint) n. place where money is coined; (Fig.) source of invention or supply;—v.t. make by stamping, as coins; to invent.

mint (mint) n. aromatic plant used for medicinal and culinary purposes.

minuet (min-ū-et') n. slow, stately dance; music for it. Also **minuette'**.

minus (mi'-nus) a. less; deducted from; deficient;—n. sign (—) of subtraction; amount less than nothing.—**minus'cule** a. small;—n. (Print.) lower-case letter.

minute (min-ūt') a. very small; slight; particular; exact.—**minute'ly** adv.—**minute'ness** n.—**minutiae** (min-ū'-shi-ē) n.pl. minute details.

minute (min'-it) n. 60th part of hour or degree; short draft.—pl. official record of affairs at a meeting; —v.t. make a note of.—**min'ute-glass** n. sand glass which, in running out, indicates minute of time.—**min'ute-gun** n. gun discharged every minute as signal of distress or mourning.

minx (mingks) n. pert, saucy girl.

Miocene (mi'-ō-sēn) a. (Geol.) belonging to Middle Tertiary period.

miracle (mir'-a-kl) n. wonder; supernatural happening; prodigy.—**Miracle Play**, medieval form of drama based on lives of Saints, or Biblical history.—**mirac'ulous** a. supernatural; extraordinary.—**mirac'ulously** adv.—**mirac'ulousness** n.

mirage (mi-räzh') n. optical illusion caused by image of object below horizon being reflected back from upper layer of the atmosphere; (Fig.) delusion.

mire (mir) n. slimy soil; mud; (Fig.) defilement;—v.t. plunge into or cover with mud;—v.i. sink in mud. —**mi'riness** n.—**mi'ry** a.

mirror (mir'-or) n. looking-glass; brilliantly polished reflecting surface; (Fig.) pattern; reflection.—v.t. reflect.

mirth (merth) n. gaiety; merriment; joyousness.—**mirth'ful** a. full of mirth; jovial; festive.—**mirth'fully** adv.—**mirth'fulness** n.—**mirth'less** a. without mirth.—**mirth'lessly** adv.

misadventure (mis-ad-ven'-tūr) n. unlucky adventure; mishap.

misalliance (mis-a-li'ans) n. unfortunate alliance, esp. in marriage.

misanthrope (mis'-an-thrōp) n. hater of mankind.—**misanthrop'ically** adv.—**misan'thropy** n. hatred of mankind.

misapply (mis-a-pli') v.t. apply wrongly or dishonestly.—**misapplica'tion** n.

misapprehend (mis-a-pre-hend') v.t. apprehend wrongly.—**misapprehen'sion** n.—**misapprehen'sive** a.

misappropriate (mis-a-prō'-pri-āt) v.t. use wrongly, esp. embezzle money.—**misappropria'tion** n.

misbegotten (mis-be-got'-n) a. unlawfully conceived; illegitimate.

misbehave (mis-be-hāv') v.t. behave badly, improperly or dishonestly.—**misbehav'iour** n.

misbelieve (mis-be-lēv') v.t. believe wrongly.—**misbelief'** n. belief in false ideas.

miscalculate (mis-kal'-kū-lāt) *v.t.* calculate wrongly.—**miscalcula'tion** *n.*

miscall (mis-kawl') *v.t.* call by wrong name; abuse.

miscarriage (mis-kar'-ij) *n.* failure; premature birth.—**miscarr'y** *v.i.* fail to fulfil intended effect; give birth prematurely.

miscast (mis-kàst') *v.t.* and *v.i.* allot unsuitably, as parts in a play;—*a.* wrongly allotted.

miscegenation (mis-i-jen-ā'-shun) *n.* mixture of races, esp. whites and Negroes.

miscellaneous (mis-el-ān'-i-us) *a.* mixed; heterogeneous.—**miscellan'eously** *adv.*—**miscellan'eousness** *n.*—**miscell'anist** *n.* writer of miscellanies.—**miscell'any** *n.* medley, esp. collection of writings on various subjects.—**miscellan'ea** *n.pl.* odds and ends.

mischance (mis-chàns') *n.* mishap; ill-luck; disaster;—*v.i.* happen disastrously.

mischief (mis'-chif) *n.* ill; damage; trouble.—**mis'chief-mak'er** *n.* one who makes trouble.—**mis'chievous** *a.* tending to stir up trouble; hurtful.—**mis'chievously** *adv.*—**mis'chievous ness** *n.*

misconceive (mis-kon-sēv') *v.t.* mistake.—**misconcep'tion** *n.*

misconduct (mis-kon'-dukt) *n.* bad management; dishonest conduct; adultery.—**misconduct'** *v.t.*

misconstrue (mis-kon-strōò')*v.t.* interpret wrongly.—**misconstruc'tion** *n.*

miscount (mis-kount') *v.t.* count wrongly; miscalculate;—*n.* wrong counting.

miscreant (mis'-kre-ant) *n.* infidel; vile, unprincipled wretch.

miscue (mis-kū) *n.* (*Billiards*) stroke spoiled by cue slipping.

misdeed (mis-dēd') *n.* evil deed, crime.

misdemeanour (mis-de-mēn'-ur) *n.* dishonest conduct; (*Law*) crime less than felony.

misdirect (mis-di-rekt') *v.t.* direct or advise wrongly.—**misdirec'tion** *n.*

miser (mī'-zer) *n.* one who hoards money.—**mi'serly** *a.* avaricious; niggardly.—**mi'serliness** *n.*

miserable (miz'-er-a-bl) *a.* unhappy; causing misery.—**mis'erableness** *n.*—**mis'erably** *adv.*

misericord (miz-er-i-kord') *n.* mercy; small dagger; seat-bracket on a choir-stall.

misery (miz'-e-ri) *n.* great unhappiness; extreme pain of body or mind;calamity.

misfire (mis-fīr') *n.* (of internal combustion engine, etc.) *v.i.* fail to start or fire.

misfit (mis-fit') *n.* bad fit;—*v.t.* make of the wrong size;—*v.i.* fit badly.

misfortune (mis-for'-tūn) *n.* ill-luck; calamity.

misgive (mis-giv') *v.t.* fill with doubt.—**misgiv'ing** *n.* distrust; suspicion.

misgovern (mis-guv'-ern) *v.t.* govern badly.—**misgov'ernment** *n.*

misguide (mis-gīd') *v.t.* lead astray; advise wrongly.—**misguid'ance** *n.*

mishandle (mis-han'-dl) *v.t.* maltreat; bungle.

mishap (mis-hap') *n.* ill-chance; accident.

mishit (mis-hit') *n.* faulty stroke.

misinform (mis-in-form') *v.t.* give wrong information to.—**misinform'ant, misinform'er** *n.*—**misinforma'tion** *n.* wrong information.

misinterpret (mis-in-ter'-pret) *v.t.* interpret or explain wrongly.—**misinterpreta'tion** *n.* misconception.—**misinter'preter** *n.*

misjudge (mis-juj') *v.t.* judge wrongly; miscalculate.—**misjudg(e)'ment** *n.*

mislay (mis-lā') *v.t.* lay down something in a place which cannot later be recollected.

mislead (mis-lēd') *v.t.* lead astray; delude; deceive—*pa.p.* misled'.—**mislead'ing** *a.*

mismanage (mis-man'-āj) *v.t* manage badly—**misman'agement** *n.*

misnomer (mis-nōm'-er) *n.* wrong name; incorrect designation.

misogyny (mis-oj'-i-ni, or mis-og'-i-ni) *n.* hatred of women.—**misog'ynist** *n.* woman-hater.

misplace (mis-plàs') *v.t.* place wrongly; mislay; bestow, as one's trust, on an unworthy person or object.

misprint (mis-print') *v.t.* make an error in printing;—*n.* error in printing.

mispronounce (mis-pro-nouns') *v.t.* pronounce wrongly.—**mispronuncia'tion** *n.*

misquote (mis-kwōt') *v.t.* quote wrongly.—**misquota'tion** *n.* inaccurate quotation.

misrepresent (mis-rep-re-zent') *v.t.* represent or relate falsely.—**misrepresenta'tion** *n.*

misrule (mis-rōōl') *n.* misgovernment.

Miss (mis) *n.* title of unmarried women; girl.—*pl.* Miss'es.

miss (mis) *v.t.* fail to hit, reach, find, catch, notice; be without; feel the want of; omit;—*v.i.* fail to hit; fall short of one's objective;—*n.* failure to hit, reach, find, etc.; escape.—**miss'ing** *a.* lost; absent;—**to miss the boat** (*Slang*) fail to seize opportunity.

missal (mis'-l) *n.* book containing R.C. service of the mass for a year.

missel (mis'-l) *n.* largest of European thrushes. Also **miss'el-thrush.**

misshape (mis-shāp') *v.t.* shape badly; deform;—*n.* deformity.—**misshap'en** *a.*

missile (mis'-il or -īl) *n.* that which is projected or shot with intent to damage;—*a.* capable of being thrown or shot.

mission (mish'-un) *n.* act of sending; duty on which one is sent; group of people sent abroad on a political errand or for spreading the Gospel; objective vocation.—**miss'ionary** *a.* pert. to missions or missionaries;—*n.* one sent to preach religion,—**miss'ioner** *n.* one who conducts a district evangelical campaign.

missive (mis'-iv) *n.* that which is sent, as a letter;—*a.* intended to be sent, or thrown.

misspell (mis-spel') *v.t.* spell wrongly. —**misspell'ing** *n.* error in spelling.

misspend (mis-spend') *v.t.* spend foolishly; squander.—*pa.t.* and *pa.p.* **misspent'**.

mist (mist) *n.* visible vapour in lower atmosphere;—*v.t.* or *v.i.* dim or be dimmed, as by a mist.—**mist'y** *a.* dim; obscured by a mist.— **mist'ily** *adv.*—**mist'iness** *n.*

mistake (mis-tāk') *v.t.* misunderstand;—*v.i.* err;—*n.* error in opinion, judgment, conduct, etc.—*pa.t.* **mistook'**.—*pa.p.* **mistak'en**—**mistak'able** *a.*—**mistak'en** *a.* guilty of error; erroneous.—**mistak'enly** *adv.*

mister (mis-ter) *n.* sir; title of courtesy to a man (*abbrev.* Mr.).

mistime (mis-tīm') *v.t.* time wrongly. —**mistimed'** *a.* inopportune.

mistletoe (mis'-l-tō, or miz'-l-tō) *n.* parasitic, evergreen plant with white berries.

mistress (mis'-tres) *n.* (*fem.* of **master**) woman in authority, as employer, teacher; kept woman; courtesy title given to married women (*abbrev.* Mrs. (mis'ez)).

mistrial (mis-trī'-al) *n.* trial made invalid by error in legal proceedings.

mistrust (mis-trust') *n.* want of confidence;—*v.t.* suspect; lack faith in.—**mistrust'ful** *a.* suspicious.—**mistrust'fulness** *n.*

misunderstand (mis-un-der-stand') *v.t.* interpret wrongly.—**misunderstand'ing** *n.* misconception; slight quarrel.

misuse (mis-ūz') *v.t.* use improperly; maltreat.—**misuse** (mis-ūs') *n.* improper use.—**misu'sage** *n.* abuse.

mite (mīt) *n.* very small coin, as *widow's mite*; half-farthing; any very small thing or person; small kind of arachnid, as *cheese-mite*.

mitigate (mit'-i-gāt) *v.t.* assuage; relieve; alleviate; temper.—**mit'igable** *a.* capable of being lessened.— **mitiga'tion** *n.* alleviation; abatement. —**mit'igative, mit'igatory** *a.*

mitre (mī'-ter) *n.* bishop's head-dress; right-angled joint made from two 45° cuts;—*v.t.* confer mitre on; join at an angle of 45°.—**mi'tred** *a.*

mitten (mit'-n) *n.* kind of glove with thumb, but palm and fingers all in one; knitted covering for wrist and hand, but leaving fingers and thumb exposed. Also **mitt.**

mix (miks) *v.t.* unite into a mass; blend;—*v.t.* become mingled; associate;—*n.* mess; confusion.—**mix'able, mix'ible**—**mixed** *a.* mingled; blended; chaotic; of both sexes.—**mix'edly** *adv.*—**mix'er** *n.* one who or that which mixes; (*Colloq.*) one who is sociable.—**mix'ture** *n.* act of mixing; that which is mixed, esp. liquid compound of drugs; (*Chem.*) combination of substances which retain their individual properties.—**mix'-up** *n.* (*Colloq.*) confusion.—**mixed marriage**, marriage between two people of different religions.— **mixed up** *a.* (*Colloq.*) maladjusted.

mizzen, mizen (miz'-n) *n.* aftermost of the fore-and-aft sails of a vessel. —**mizz'en-mast** *n.* the mast bearing the mizzen.

mnemonic, -al (ne-mon'-ik, -al) *a.* assisting the memory.—**mnemon'ics** *n.pl.* art of assisting memory; artificial aids to memory.

moan (mōn) *n.* low cry of grief or pain;—*v.i.* utter low, wailing cry;— *v.t.* lament.

moat (mōt) *n.* deep trench round castle, etc., usually filled with water.

mob (mob) *n.* disorderly crowd of people; rabble; populace; — *v.t.* attack in disorderly crowd; jostle; —*pr.p.* **mob'bing.**—*pa.p.* **mobbed.**— **mob'-law** *n.* lynch law.

mob (mob) *n.* frilled cap, tied under the chin, worn by women in 18th cent.

mobile (mō'-bīl) *a.* easily moved; changing; vacillating; (of troops) mechanised; *n.* three dimensional decoration with free-swinging parts. —**mo'bilise** *v.t.* prepare for active service; gather together available resources.—**mobilisa'tion** *n.*—**mobil'ity** *n.* state of being mobile.

moccasin (mok'-a-sin) *n.* shoe of soft leather worn by N. American Indians, etc.; bedroom slipper of similar shape. Also **moc'cassin.**

mock (mok) *v.t.* laugh at; ridicule; make a fool of; defy; feign;—*n.* ridicule; derision; jibe;—*a.* counterfeit; substitute.—**mock'er** *n.*—**mock'ery, mock'ing** *n.*—**mock'ing** *n.* mockery;—*a.* scornful; derisive.—**mocking bird**, N. American bird which imitates songs of other birds.—**mock orange**, syringa.—**mock turtle**, soup made of calf's head, to imitate turtle soup.— **mock'-up** dummy model.

mod (mod) *n.* musical festival to encourage study and practice of national songs, poetry, etc., esp. Gaelic songs, etc.

mode (mōd) *n.* manner, form, or method; custom; prevailing fashion; ancient form of musical scale; (*Gram.*) the *mood* of the verb.—

mo'dal a. relating to mode or form. —**modal'ity** n.—**mo'dish** a. fashionable.—**mo'dishly** adv.—**mo'dishness** n. —**modiste** (mōd-ēst') n. dress-maker.

model (mod'-el) n. exact, three-dimensional representation of an object, in miniature; pattern or standard to copy; one who poses for an artist; mannequin;—a. serving as a model;—v.t. make in model; copy from pattern or standard of conduct; shape;—v.i. practise modelling.—pr.p. mod'elling.—pa.p. mod'elled.—mod'eller n. one who makes models.—mod'elling n. art of working in plastic materials or of making models; shaping.

moderate (mod'-ęr-it) a. restrained; temperate; average; not extreme;—v.t. restrain; control;—v.i. become less violent or intense; act as moderator;—n. person of moderate opinions in politics, etc.—mod'erately adv.—mod'erateness n.—modera'tion n.—mod'erator n. (fem. mod'eratrix) one who acts as arbitrator; president of an assembly; material used to slow down neutrons in nuclear reactor.

modern (mod'-ęrn) a. pert. to present or recent time; up-to-date;—n. person living in modern times; one who is up-to-date in outlook and ideas.—modernisa'tion n.—mod'ernise v.t. bring up-to-date.—modernis'er n.—mod'ernist n. one who upholds modern ideas.— mod'ernly adv.— mod'ernness, moder'nity n.

modest (mod'-est) a. unassuming; restrained; decent; retiring in manner; not excessive.—mod'estly adv.—mod'esty n. absence of arrogance.

modicum (mod'-i-kum) n. small quantity.

modify (mod'-i-fī) v.t. moderate; alter the form or intensity of;—modifi'able a.—modifica'tion n. act of modifying; state of being modified; change of form, manner, or intensity. mod'ificative, mod'ificatory a. qualifying.—mod'ifier n.

modulate (mod'-ū-lāt) v.t. regulate, esp. pitch of the voice; adapt; (Mus.) change the key of;—v.i. (Mus.) pass from one key to another.—mod'ular a. pert. to mode, modulation, or module.—modula'tion n. act of modulating; changing of pitch of voice; (Mus.) transposition into new key; (Radio) variation of the amplitude, phase or frequency of continuous waves.—mod'ulator n. —mod'ule n. unit of measurement, standardised unit used in construction work, etc.

mohair (mō'-hār) n. silky hair of the Angora goat; fabric made from this.

Mohammedan (mo-ham'-ed-ạn) a. pert. to Mohammed or to Mohammedanism;—n. follower of Mohammed; Moslem. Also **Mahom'etan**,

Mahom'edan. — **Moham'medanism** n. religion of Mohammed; Islam.

moiety (moi'-e-ti) n. half; small share.

moire (mwàr) n. watered silk.

moist (moist) a. damp; humid; rather wet.—**moist'en** v.t. make moist; damp slightly.—**moist'ness**, **moist'ure** n. that which causes dampness; condensed vapour.—**moist'ureless** a. dry.

molar (mō'-lạr) a. grinding or able to grind;—n. back double-tooth for grinding.

molasses (mo-las'-ez) n. sing. dark-coloured syrup obtained from sugar; treacle.

mole (mōl) n. slightly raised, dark brown spot on the skin.

mole (mōl) n. small burrowing animal, with velvety fur, small eyes, and paws like miniature hands;—v.t. burrow.—**mole'hill** n. little mound of earth thrown up by mole when burrowing.—**mole'skin** n. fur of mole; kind of fustian, with soft surface like this.

mole (mōl) n. breakwater; pier built to form harbour.

molecule (mol'-e-kūl) n. smallest portion of substance which can retain independently characteristics of that substance.—**molec'ular** a.—molecular weight, weight of molecule of a substance in relation to weight of hydrogen atom.

molest (mō-lest') v.t. trouble; accost with sinister intent.—molesta'tion n.

mollify (mol'-i-fī) v.t. appease; placate; soften.—pr.p. moll'ifying.—pa.p. moll'ified.—moll'ifiable a.—mollifica'tion n. act of mollifying.

mollusc, mollusk (mol'-usk) n. invertebrate with soft, pulpy body and (usually) hard outer shell, as the oyster, snail, etc.—pl. moll'uses or mollus'ca.—mollus'can a. pert. to molluscs;—mollus'coid, -cous a.

mollycoddle (mol'-i-kod-l) n. milk-sop;—v.t. coddle.

molten (mōlt'-n) a. melted; of metals, liquified by intense heat.—molt'enly adv.

molybdenum (mol-ib'-de-num) n. rare metal, used for alloying special steels.

moment (mō'-ment) n. minute space of time; interval; importance; measure of a force by its effect in causing rotation. — mo'mentarily adv.— mo'mentariness n.—mo'mentary a. very brief.—mo'mently adv.—moment'ous a. of great importance.—moment'ously adv.—moment'ousness n.—moment'um n. impetus in a body; product of mass of a body multiplied by its velocity; (Fig.) increasing force; impetus.—pl. momen'ta.

monarch (mon'-ark) n. supreme ruler of a state; (Fig.) superior;—a. supreme.—**monarch'al** a. pert. to monarch; sovereign. — **monarch'ial**,

monarch'ic, -al *a.* pert. to monarch or monarchy. — **monarch'ically** *adv.* — **mon'archise** *v.t.* govern, as a king; to convert to monarchical government. —**mon'archism** *n.* principles of monarchy; devotion to royalist cause.— **mon'archist** *n.* advocate of monarchy; royalist.—**mon'archy** *n.* government of a state by single ruler such as king, etc.; kingdom or empire.

monastery (mon'-as-ter-i) *n.* settlement of monks.—**monaste'rial, monas'tic, -al** *a.* pert. to monasteries, monks, or nuns.—**monas'tic** *n.* monk. — **monasticism** (mon-as'-ti-sizm) *n.* monastic way of life.

monaural (mon-aw'-ral) *a.* pert. to, or having, one ear; not stereophonic.

Monday (mun'-dā) *n.* second day of week.

monetary (mun'-e-ta-ri) *a.* concerning money or the coinage; consisting of money.

money (mun'-i) *n.* any token, as coin, banknote, used as medium of exchange, and stamped by state authority; paper currency; wealth. —*pl.* (*Law*) **mon'eys.**—**mon'eyed** *a.* wealthy.—**mon'ey-grub'ber** *n.* miser. —**mon'ey-lend'er** *n.* one who lends out money and charges interest on sum lent.—**mon'ey-mak'ing** *a.* profitable. —**mon'ey-spin'ner** or **-spid'er** *n.* small red spider supposed to bring good luck.

monger (mung'-ger) *n.* trader; dealer, usually in compound words, as *fishmonger,* etc.

mongoose (mon'-gōōs) *n.* animal like a weasel, notable as snake-killer. —*pl.* **mong'ooses.** Also **mung'oose.**

mongrel (mung'-grel) *n.* animal of mixed breed;—*a.* impure; hybrid.

monition (mon-ish'-un) *n.* cautionary advice; admonition; notice.—**mon'itive** *a.* expressing caution or warning.—**monitor** *n.* (*fem.* **mon'itress, monitrix**) one who cautions; instructer; school prefect; (*Naut.*) shallow-draught, heavily armed warship for coastal service.—**mon'itor** *v.t.* listen to broadcast or view TV transmission for purpose of supervision or checking; track and record flight of aircraft, space craft, etc.— **monito'rial** *a.*—**monito'rially** *adv.*— **mon'itory** *a.* warning.

monk (mungk) *n.* orig. hermit; member of religious community living in monastery.—**monk'hood** *n.* state of being monk.—**monk'ish** *a.* pert. to monk; monastic.—**monks'hood** *n.* poisonous plant, aconite.

monkey (mung'-ki) *n.* long-tailed mammal of the order of Primates, exclusive of man and lemurs, but resembling man in organisation; mischievous child; weighted head of pile driver; hammer for driving home bolts; (*Slang*) £500.—*v.t.*

meddle with.—**monk'ey-jack'et** *n.* short, tight jacket worn by sailors. —**monk'ey-nut** *n.* pea-nut.—**monk'ey-puzz'le** *n.* Chile pine.—**monk'ey-trick** *n.* prank.—**monk'ey-wrench** *n.* wrench with movable jaw.

mono- (mon'-o) *prefix.* meaning sole, single.

monochrome (mon'-ō-krōm) *n.* painting in different tones of same colour.—**monochromat'ic, monochro'ic** *a.* of one colour only.—**monochro'matism** *n.* colour-blindness.

monocle (mon'-o-kl) *n.* single eyeglass.

monocracy (mon-ok'-ra-si) *n.* government by single person.

monogamy (mon-og'-a-mi) *n.* state or practice of being married to one person at a time.—**monog'amist** *n.*— **monog'amous** *a.*

monogram (mon'-ō-gram) *n.* two or more letters, as initials of a name, interwoven.—**monogrammat'ic** *a.*

monograph (mon'-ō-graf) *n.* treatise on single subject or branch of subject.—**monog'rapher, monog'raphist** *n.*—**monograph'ic, -al,** *a.*

monogynous (mon-oj'-in-us) *a.* (*Bot.*) having single pistil; (*Zool.*) mating with single female. Also **monogyn'ian.**—**monog'yny** *n.* custom of having only one wife.

monolith (mon'-o-lith) *n.* monument or column fashioned from single block of stone.—**monolith'al, monolith'ic** *a.* (*Fig.*) massive; uncompromising.

monologue (mon'-ō-log) *n.* dramatic scene in which actor soliloquises; dramatic poem for solo performer.

monomania (mon-ō-mā'-ni-a) *n.* mental derangement in which sufferer is obsessed by one idea.—**monoma'niac** *n.*—**monoma'niacal** *a.*

monoplane (mon'-ō-plān) *n.* aircraft with only one set of planes

monopoly (mon-op'-o-li) *n.* sole right to trade in certain commodities; exclusive possession or control; Protected Trade Name for game played with dice and counters. —**monop'olise** *v.t.* have a monopoly; take the lead, to exclusion of others. —**monop'oliser, monop'olist** *n.* one who has monopoly.—**monopolis'tic** *a.*

monosyllable (mon-ō-sil'-a-bl) *n.* word of one syllable.—**monosyllab'ic** *a.* having one syllable; speaking in words of one syllable.—**monosyl'labism** *n.*

monotheism (mon'-ō-thē-izm) *n.* doctrine of one God only.—**mon'otheist** *n.*—**monotheis'tic** *a.*

monotone (mon'-ō-tōn) *n.* single, unvaried tone or sound; series of sounds of uniform pitch; sameness of any kind;—*v.t.* and *v.i.* intone; chant.—**monot'onous** *a.* uttered in one tone; dull; unvaried.—**monot'-onously** adv.—**monot'ony** n. tedious uniformity of tone: sameness.

monotype (mon'-ō-tīp) n. (Print.) two-part machine for setting and casting type in individual letters, as distinct from linotype.—**monotyp'ic** a.

monovalent (mon'-ō-val-ent) a. (Chem.) having valency of one; univalent.—**mon'ovalency** n.

monoxide (mo-nok'-sīd) n. oxide containing one oxygen atom in a molecule.

Monseigneur (mŏng-sen'-yer) n. my lord; title (abbrev. Mgr.) given in France to princes, bishops, etc.—pl. **Messeigneurs** (mā-sen-yer') — **Monsignor** (mon-sin-yŏr') (abbrev. Mgr. or **Monsig.**) Italian title given to prelates.—pl. **monsignor'i.**

monsoon (mon-sóón') n. seasonal wind of S. Asia; very heavy rainfall season, esp. in India.—**monsoon'al** a.

monster (mon'-ster) n. creature of unnatural shape; prodigy; freak; person of abnormal cruelty or wickedness;—a. huge.—**monstros'ity** n. unnatural production; abnormal creature; freak.—**mon'strous** a. abnormal; horrible.—**monstrously** adv.

montage (mon'-tāj, -tázh) n. edited whole; (Cinema) final assembling of various shots of film into collection of unrelated pictures mounted to form one unit.

montbretia (mont-brē'-shi-a) n. bulb plant with brilliant orange flowers.

month (munth) n. one of twelve divisions of the year; period of 28 days, or four complete weeks.—**month'ly** a. lasting, performed in, a month;—n. publication, produced once each month;—adv. once a month.

monument (mon'-ū-ment) n. structure, as a tombstone, erected to memory of person, or event; ancient record; achievement of lasting value.—**monument'al** a. like, or worthy of monument; massive; colossal.—**monument'ally** adv.

moo (móó) v.i. make the noise of a cow; low;—n. lowing of cow.

mood (móód) n. mode; (Gram.) inflection of a verb expressing its function, as indicative, etc.

mood (móód) n. disposition; frame of mind; temper.—**mood'ily** adv.—**mood'iness** n. state of being moody; temporary depression of spirits.—**mood'y** a. peevish; sulky.

moon (móón) n. satellite which revolves round earth in period of a lunar month; any secondary planet; month; anything crescent-shaped or shining like moon;—v.i. gaze or wander about aimlessly.—**moon'beam** n. ray of moonlight.—**moon'-calf** n. monster; dolt.—**moon'-faced** a. having round, expressionless face.—

moon'light n., a.—**moonlit** a.—**moon'shine** n. light of moon; empty show; smuggled liquor.—**moon'stone** n. form of felspar.—**moon'struck** a. lunatic.

moor (móór) n. stretch of heath with peaty soil.—**moor'-cock**, **moor'-fowl** n. red grouse.—**moor'-hen** n. female moor-cock; water-hen. — **moor'ish**, **moor'y** a.—**moor'land** n. heath.

moor (móór) v.t. secure by cables and anchors, as a ship.—**moor'age** n. place where vessel or airship is moored; charge for mooring.—**moor'ing** n. act of securing ship, etc., by cables and anchors; the place where ship is moored.

moose (móós) n. N. American elk.

moot (móót) v.t. suggest for debate; discuss;—a. debatable;—n. in olden times, council.—**moot'able** a. capable of being debated.—**moot'-case**, **moot'-point** n. debatable case, or point.

mop (mop) n. bunch of yarn or rags attached to handle for washing or polishing; bushy head of hair;—v.t. wipe or polish with mop; wipe perspiration from.—pr.p. **mop'ping.**—pa.p. mopped.

mope (mōp) v.i. be dull or depressed; sulk.—**mop'ing** a. listless.—**mop'ishly** adv. dispiritedly.—**mop'ish** a. dull.—**mop'ishly** adv.—**mop'ishness** n.

moped (mō'-ped) n. pedal cycle fitted with auxiliary motor.

moquette (mō-ket') n. carpet and furnishing material.

moraine (mō-rān') n. rock debris which accumulates along the sides of glacier.

moral (mor'-al) a. pert. to conduct or duties of man; ethical; virtuous; chaste;—n. meaning implied in fable, allegory, etc.—pl. ethics; conduct, esp. concerning sex-relations; habits.—**moralisa'tion** n.—**mor'alise** v.t. explain in a moral sense; draw moral from;—v.i. reflect on ethical values of.—**mor'aliser** n. **mor'alist** n. one who moralises; one who studies or teaches ethics.—**moralist'ic** a.—**moral'ity** n. practice of moral duties; virtue; ethics; right or wrong of a thing; early form of pre-Shakespearian drama, in which the characters were virtues and vices of men personified.—**mor'ally** adv. in moral manner; practically.—**moral philosophy**, science of right living and just conduct of affairs; ethics.—**moral victory**, defeat, which in a deeper sense, is victory.

morale (mo-rál') n. mental state which causes people to face an emergency with spirit and fortitude.

morass (mo-ras') n. bog; marshy ground.

moratorium (mor-a-tō'-ri-um) n. act authorising the suspension of payments or reparations by bank or debtor state, for given period of time; the period of suspension of payments.

morbid (mor'-bid) *a.* diseased; unhealthy; (of the mind) excessively introspective.—**morbid'ity** *n.* state of being morbid.—**mor'bidly** *adv.*—**mor'bidness** *n.*

mordant (mor'-dant) *n.* substance which fixes dyes;—acid used in copper-plate engraving;—*a.* biting; corrosive; (*Fig.*) scathing; sarcastic.

more (mōr) *a.* greater in amount, degree, quality, etc.; in greater number; additional;—*adv.* in greater quantity, extent, etc.; besides;—*n.* something additional;—*superl.* most.

moreover (mōr-ō-ver) *adv.* besides; also; further.

morganatic (mor-gan-at'-ik) *a.* applied to marriage between man of high, esp. royal rank, and woman of lower station, the issue having no claim to his rank or property.—**morganat'ically** *adv.*

morgue (morg) *n.* mortuary where bodies of people killed in street accidents, etc., are taken to await identification.

moribund (mor'-i-bund) *a.* at point of death.

Mormon (mor'-mon) *n.* member of 'The Church of Jesus Christ of Latter-day Saints' professing theocracy and, formerly, polygamy; (*Fig.*) polygamist;—*a.* pert. to this sect.—**Mor'monism** *n.*

morn (morn) *n.* early part of the day.

morning (mor'-ning) *n.* first part of day between dawn and midday; (*Fig.*) first part of anything;—*a.* pert. to or happening in early part of day.—**mor'ning-coat** *n.* tail-coat with cutaway front.—**morn'ing-room** *n.* room used esp. in the morning, for breakfast, etc. — **morning watch** (*Naut.*) 4-8 a.m.

morocco (mo-rok'-ō) *n.* fine goatskin leather; any skin grained in imitation of goat-skin.

moron (mōr'-on) *n.* adult with mental development of 7 yr. old child.

morose (mō-rōs') *a.* sullen; gloomy; soured in nature.—**morose'ly** *adv.*—**morose'ness** *n.*

morphia (mor'-fi-a) *n.* alkaloid of opium; drug used to induce sleep and to deaden pain. Also **mor'phine.**

morphic (mor'-fik) *a.* pert. to shape or form.—**morphog'raphy** *n.* description of structure of organism.—**morpholog'ic, -al** *a.*—**morphol'ogist** *n.*—**morphol'ogy** *n.* science of structure and shape of organisms.

morris, morrice (mor'-is) *n.* dance popular in medieval England

morris (mor'-is) *n.* popular medieval outdoor game of draughts.—**nine men's morris**, this game played with nine stones.

morrow (mor'-ō) *n.* next day; (*Poet.*) morning.

Morse (mors) *n.* system of telegraphic signalling in which the alphabet is represented by various combinations of dots and dashes.

morsel (mor'-sel) *n.* mouthful; small piece.

mortal (mor'-tal) *a.* subject to death; fatal; meriting damnation, as sin; implacable, as foe:—*n.* human being.—**mortal'ity** *n.* death; deathrate; human race.—**mor'tally** *adv.* fatally; sorely.

mortar (mor'-tar) *n.* thick bowl of porcelain, etc., in which substances are pounded with a pestle; mill for pulverising ores; (*Mil.*) widemouthed piece of ordnance for short-distance firing of fin-stabilised bombs; cement made of lime, sand and water, used in building;—*v.t.* pound in a mortar; cement.—**mor'tar-board** *n.* square board used when mixing mortar; academic cap.

mortgage (mor'-gij) *n.* (*Law*) conveyance of property in security of a loan; deed effecting this;—*v.t.* pledge as security.—**mortgagee'** *n.* one to whom mortgage is given.—**mort'gager, mort'gagor** *n.* one who gives mortgage to mortgagee.

mortician (mor-tish'-an) *n.* (*U.S.*) undertaker.

mortify (mor'-ti-fi) *v.t.* discipline the flesh; humiliate; vex;—*v.i.* (*Med.*) become gangrenous.—*pa.t.* and *pa.p.* **mor'tified.**—**mortifica'tion** *n.* act of mortifying or state of being mortified; death of one part of living body; humiliation; (*Scots law*) charitable bequest; (*Med.*) gangrene.

mortise (mor'-tis) *n.* hole in piece of wood to receive the projection or tenon of another piece, made to fit it. Also **mor'tice.**—*v.t.* cut or make a mortise in; join with mortice.—*pr.p.* **mor'tising.**—*pa.p.* **mor'tised.**

mortuary (mor'-tū-ar-i) *n.* place for temporary reception of dead bodies;—*a.* pert. to burial.

mosaic (mō-zā'-ik) *a.* pert. to or made of mosaic;—*n.* inlaid work of coloured glass or marble; flooring or pattern made of this; (*Fig.*) patchwork.—**mosa'ically** *adv.*

Mosaic (mō-zā'-ik) *a.* (*Bib.*) pert. to *Moses.*

Moslem (moz'-lem) *n.* Mohammedan;—*a.* pert. to the Mohammedans or their religion. Also **Mus'lim.**—**Mos'lemism** *n.*

mosque (mosk) *n.* Mohammedan temple.

mosquito (mos-kē'-tō) *n.* gnat-like insect.—*pl.* **mosqui'to(e)s.**—**mosquito curtain, net,** net-covering to ward off mosquitoes.

moss (mos) *n.* small, thickly growing, cryptogamous plant which thrives on moist surfaces; lichen; bog; peat moor.—**moss'-grown** a. closely covered with moss.—**moss'iness** n.—**moss'-land** n. peat bog.—**moss'-rose** n. species of rose with moss-like growth on calyx.

most (mōst) a. (superl. of more) greatest number or quantity; greatest;—adv. in greatest degree.—**most'ly** adv. for most part.

mot (mō) n. pithy, witty saying.

mote (mōt) n. small particle; speck of dust.

motel (mō-tel') n. hotel composed of accommodation units for cars and their owners.

motet (mō-tet') n. musical composition for (unaccompanied) voices.

moth (moth) n. nocturnal winged insect; larva of this insect which feeds on cloth, esp. woollens.—**moth'-balls** n.pl. camphor balls to ward off moths from clothes.—**moth'-eat'en** a. eaten into holes by moth larva; (Fig.) decrepit.

mother (muTH'-ęr) n. female parent; mode of address to elderly woman; head of convent; origin of anything;—a. natural; native; original;—v.t. adopt as son or daughter; cherish.—**mother-coun'try** n. native land.—**moth'erhood** n. state of being mother.—**moth'ering** n. motherly care; old custom of visiting one's parents on fourth Sunday in Lent (Mothering Sunday).—**moth'er-in-law** n. mother of one's wife or husband.—**moth'erliness** n.—**moth'erly** a. pert. to mother; kindly.—**moth'er-of-pearl** n. iridescent lining of certain shells.—**Mother Superior**, head of convent.—**moth'er-tongue** n. one's native language.

motif (mō-tēf') n. dominant theme in literary or musical composition.

motion (mō'-shun) n. act of moving; movement; impulse; proposal made in assembly; (Med.) evacuation of bowels;—v.t. guide by gesture;—v.i. make significant movement.—**mo'tionless** a. still; immobile.—**mo'tion pic'ture** n. cinema film.

motive (mō'-tiv) n. that which incites to action; inner impulse; dominant theme; motif;—a. causing movement or motion;—v.t. impel.—**mo'tivate** v.t. incite.—**motiva'tion** n.—**mo'tiveless** a. without purpose or direction.—**motiv'ity** n. capacity to produce motion.

motley (mot'-li) a. parti-coloured; diversified;—n. jester's dress.

motor (mō'-tor) n. that which imparts motion; machine which imparts motive power; motor-car;—a. causing motion; (Anat.) producing muscular activity;—v.t. and v.i. travel by, or convey in, motor-driven vehicle.—**mo'torise** v.t. mechanise the army.—**mo'torist** n.—**motor-**

cade (mō'-tor-kād) n. (U.S.)motor cars in procession; 'cavalcade' of cars.—**motor spirit**, petrol, etc., used to drive motor-engine.—**mot'orway** n. highway designed for fast motor traffic.

mottle (mot'-l) v.t. mark with spots; dapple.—**mott'led** a.

motto (mot'-ō) n. short appropriate phrase added to armorial bearings; maxim or aphorism;—pl. mott'oes.

mould (mōld) n. hollow shape in which anything is cast or set; templet; (Fig.) character;—v.t. shape in mould; fashion; (Fig.) influence.—**mould'er** n.—**mould'ing** n. anything moulded, esp. relief ornamentation; art or process of making moulds.

mould (mōld) n. fine, soft soil; grave;—v.t. cover with mould.—**mould'er** v.i. decay; crumble away; turn to dust.

mould (mōld) n. minute fungus which grows on leather, cheese, etc., esp. if exposed to damp; mildew.—**mould'iness** n.—**mould'y** a.

moult (mōlt) v.t. and v.i. to cast or shed feathers, as of birds;—n. act of casting feathers.

mound (mound) n. heap of earth; knoll; earthwork for defensive purposes;—v.t. fortify with mound.

mount (mount) n. mountain or hill (abbrev. Mt.); that on which anything is mounted for exhibition; horse for riding;—v.t. raise up; ascend; get on horse; frame (picture); set (gem-stones); put on slide for microscope examination; stage a play;—v.i. rise up; get up; increase.—**mount'ed** a. raised; (of picture) having cardboard edging or backing.—**to mount guard**, be on sentry-duty; keep watch over.

mountain (mount'-ān or -in) n. high hill;—a. pert. to mountain; growing or living on mountain.—**mount'ain-ash** n. rowan-tree.—**mount'ain-dew** n. Scotch whisky.—**mountaineer'** n. one who lives on mountain; one who climbs high mountains.—**mountaineer'ing** n. sport of climbing mountains.—**mount'ainous** a. very steep; full of mountains; colossal.

mountebank (moun'-te-bangk) n. quack doctor; a charlatan.

mourn (mōrn) v.t. grieve over; lament;—v.i. express grief; wear mourning.—**mourn'er** n. one who mourns; one who attends funeral.—**mourn'ful** a. sad.—**mourn'fully** adv.—**mourn'fulness** n.—**mourn'ing** n. act of grieving; wearing of black as sign of grief; period during which such clothes are worn.—**mourn'ingly** adv.

mouse (mous) n. small rodent found in fields, or in houses; lead weight on cords of sash-windows.—pl. mice.—**mouse** (mouz) v.t. and v.i. catch mice; search for patiently or slyly; prowl.

—**mous'er** *n.* cat which catches mice.—**mous'y** *a.* resembling mouse, esp. in colour; smelling of mice; (*Fig.*) timid.

mousse (mōōs) *n.* dessert of frozen whipped cream, eggs, sugar and flavouring.

moustache (mus-tash') *n.* hair on upper lip.

mouth (mouth) *n.* opening between lips of men and animals through which food is taken; cavity behind lips containing teeth, tongue, palate, and vocal organs; opening as of bottle, cave, etc.; estuary of river; wry face.—*pl.* mouths (mouTHz).—**mouth'ful** *n.* as much as mouth conveniently holds; small amount.—*pl.* mouth'fuls.—**mouth'-or'gan** *n.* harmonica; Jew's harp; pan-pipes.—**mouth'piece** *n.* part of musical instrument, tobacco-pipe, cigarette-holder, etc., held in mouth; (*Fig.*) spokesman.

mouth (mouTH) *v.t.* utter with overloud voice; speak with exaggerated movement of mouth; rant.—**mouthed** *a.* having a mouth.

move (mōōv) *v.t.* set in motion; stir emotions of; prevail on; incite; propose for consideration; — *v.i.* change one's position, posture, residence, etc.; march; make proposal or recommendation;—*n.* act of moving; change of residence; movement, as in game of draughts.—**mov'able**, **move'able** *n.* article of furniture;—*pl.* (*Law*) furnishings of house which are not permanent fixtures;—*a.* able to be moved, or changed in time; shifting.—**movable feast**, church festival, date of which varies annually.—**mov'ableness** *n.*—**mov'ably** *adv.*—**move'ment** *n.* act of moving; deportment; part of machine which moves; organised activity of society; division of musical composition.—**mov'er** *n.* one who moves; one who tables motion; originator.—**mov'ies** *n.pl.* (*Colloq.*) cinema films or cinema theatre.—**mov'ing** *a.* causing to change place; in motion; affecting emotions; pathetic.—**moving picture** (*abbrev.* **movie**) cinematograph.—**moving staircase**, escalator.

mow (mō) *v.t.* cut with scythe; cut down in great numbers.—*pr.p.* mow'ing.—*pa.t.* mowed.—*pa.p.* mown—**mow'er** *n.* one who mows; machine for cutting crops.

mow (mō) *n.* heap of hay or corn.

much (much) *a.* (*comp.* more; *superl.* most) great in quantity or amount; abundant;—*n.* great quantity;—*adv.* to great degree or extent; almost.—**much'ness** *n.* state of being much.—**much'ly** *adv.* (*Colloq.*) much.—**much of a muchness**, more or less the same.

mucilage (mū'-si-lāj) *n.* gummy substance extracted from plants and animals; solution of gum in water.—**mucilag'inous** *a.* pert. to mucilage; slimy; viscous.

muck (muk) *n.* moist dung; anything vile or filthy;—*v.t.* manure; make filthy.—**muck'iness** *n.*—**muck'y** *a.* filthy.

mucus (mū'-kus) *n.* viscid fluid secreted by mucous glands.—**mu'coid**, **mu'cous** *a.* like mucus.

mud (mud) *n.* soft, moist earth; (*Fig.*) aspersions;—*v.t.* bury in mud; foul; stir up dregs in liquid;—*v.i.* be submerged in mud.—**mud'dily** *adv.*—**mud'diness** *n.*—**mud'dy** *a.* consisting of mire or mud; miry; cloudy; (*Fig.*) stupid;—*v.t.* soil with mud.—*pr.p.* mud'dying.—*pa.t.* and *pa.p.* mud'died.—**mud'-flat** *n.* stretch of mud below high-water mark.—**mud'-guard** *n.* screen to protect from mud-splashes.—**mud'-lark** *n.* one who fishes up odds and ends from mud of tidal rivers.—**mud'-pack** *n.* treatment with impregnated mud which has beneficial effect on the skin.

muddle (mud'-l) *v.t.* make muddy; confuse; bewilder; deal incompetently with.—*v.i.* be confused;—*n.* confusion; jumble;—**mudd'lehead** *n.* one who is confused in mind.—**mudd'leheaded** *a.*

muezzin (mōō-ez'-in) *n.* official in Mohammedan mosque who summons worshippers to prayer.

muff (muf) *n.* warm covering for both hands.

muffin (muf'-in) *n.* round, flat scone or cake.

muffle (muf'-l) *v.t.* wrap up for warmth or to hide something; deaden (sound of);—*n.* something used to deaden sound.—**muff'led** *a.* smothered (of sound); wrapped up.—**muff'ler** *n.* scarf.

mufti (muf'-ti) *n.* Mohammedan priest; civilian dress worn by soldiers when off duty.

mug (mug) *n.* earthenware or metal cup with or without handle; tankard; (*Slang*) face.

mug (mug) *n.* (*Slang*) dupe; sucker.

muggy (mug'-i) *a.* warm and humid, as weather; close, enervating.

mulatto (mū-lat'-ō) *n.* (*fem.* mulatt'ress) offspring of white person and Negro.

mulberry (mul'-ber-i) *n.* tree on the leaves of which silkworm feeds; fruit of this tree; purplish-brown colour.

mulch (mulsh) *n.* protective covering of straw, manure, etc., for roots of young plants;—*v.t.* treat with mulch.

mulct (mulkt) *n.* fine;—*v.t.* impose fine on; deprive of.

mule (mūl) *n.* hybrid offspring of male ass and mare; any hybrid animal; machine used in cotton-spinning; heelless bedroom-slipper; (*Fig.*) obstinate person.—**muleteer'** *n.* mule-driver.—**mul'ish** *a.* obstinate. —**mul'ishly** *adv.*—**mul'ishness** *n.*

mull (mul) *v.t.* heat, sweeten and spice (wine, ale, etc.).—**mulled** *a.*—**mull'er** *n.*

mull (mul) *n.* muddle;—*v.t.* bungle.

mull (mul) *n.* (*Scot.*) headland or promontory.

mullet (mul'-et) *n.* edible sea-fish.

mulligatawny (mul-i-ga-taw'-ni) *n.* rich soup flavoured with curry, thickened with rice.

mullion (mul'-yun) *n.* dividing up-right between lights of windows, panels, etc.—**mull'ion**, **munn'ion** *v.t.* divide by mullions.—**mull'ioned** *a.*

multicolour (mul'-ti-kul-ur) *a.* hav-ing many colours. Also **mul'ti-coloured.**

multifarious (mul-ti-fā'-ri-us) *a.* manifold; made up of many parts.—**multifa'riously** *adv.*—**multifa'riousness** *n.* diversity.

multilateral (mul-ti-lat'-er-al) *a.* having many sides or participants.

multi-millionaire (mul'-ti-mil'-yun-ār) *n.* person who is worth several million pounds.

multipartite (mul-ti-par'-tīt) *a.* hav-ing many parts.

multiple (mul'-ti-pl) *a.* manifold; of many parts; repeated many times; —*n.* (*Math.*) quantity containing another an exact number of times.—**mul'tiple-fiss'ion** *n.* repeated division. —**multiple shop**, or **store**, retail business with branches in different parts of town or country.

multiply (mul'-ti-plī) *v.t.* increase in number; add number to itself a given number of times;—*v.i.* in-crease; grow in number.—*pr.p.* **multiply'ing**.—*pa.t.* and *pa.p.* **mul'-tiplied**.—**mul'tiplex** *a.* multiple; (of telegraph) capable of transmitting numerous messages over same wire. —**mul'tipliable**, **mul'tiplicable** *a.* cap-able of being multiplied.—**multiplic-and'** *n.* number to be multiplied.—**multiplica'tion** *n.* act of multiplying; operation by which any given number may be added to itself any specified number of times (symbol used = ×).—**mul'tiplicative** *a.*—**mul'-iplicator** *n.* multiplier.—**multiplic'ity** *n.* state of being multiplied; great number.—**mul'tiplier** *n.* number by which another, the *multiplicand*, is multiplied.

multi-ply (mul'-ti-plī) *n.* plywood of more than three layers.

multiracial (mul-ti-rā-shall) *a.* pert. to, or consisting of many races.—**multira'cialism** *n.*

multisyllable (mul-ti-sil'-a-bl) *n.* word of many syllables.

multitude (mul'-ti-tūd) *n.* great number; numerousness; crowd.—**multitud'inous** *a.* made up of very great number.

multivalent (mul-tiv'-a-lent) *a.* (*Chem.*) with more than one valency. —**multiv'alence**, **multival'ency** *n.*

mum (mum) *a.* silent;—*n.* silence; (*Colloq.*) mother;—*interj.* be quiet. —**mum's the word**, keep it secret.

mumble (mum'-bl) *v.t.* utter indis-tinctly;—*v.i.* speak indistinctly;—*n.* indistinct utterance.—**mum'bler** *n.*

mumbo-jumbo (mum-bō jum'-bō) *n.* (*Hist.*) religious idol; hence, super-stitious practices, jargon, etc.

mumm, mum (mum) *v.t.* perform in dumb show; act in mask.—**mumm'er** *n.* one who acts in dumb show, esp. at Christmas; buffoon.—**mumm'ery** *n.* performance in dumb show.—**mumm'ing** *n.*

mummy (mum'-i) *n.* dead body preserved by embalming.—*pa.p.* **mumm'ified**. — **mummifica'tion** *n.*—**mumm'ify** *v.t.* embalm and dry as mummy;—*v.i.* become dried up.

mumps (mumps) *n.* highly infectious disease causing painful swelling of face and neck-glands.

munch (munsh) *v.t.* and *i.* chew noisily.—**munch'er** *n.*

mundane (mun-dān) *a.* pert. to this world.—**mun'danely** *adv.*

municipal (mū-nis'-i-pal) *a.* pert. to corporation or city.—**municipal'ity** *n.* town or district with its own administration.—**munic'ipally** *adv.*

munificence (mū-nif'-i-sens) *n.* liber-ality; generosity. — **munif'icent** *a.* very generous.—**munif'icently** *adv.*

muniment (mū'-ni-ment) *n.* strong-hold;—*pl.* title deeds; charter.—**mu'niment-room** *n.* fire-proof room for storing of valuable charters, legal documents, etc.

munition (mū-nish'-un) *v.t.* equip with weapons of war;—*n.* (usually *pl.*) military stores; weapons of war, as guns, etc.

murder (mur'-der) *n.* homicide with premeditated and malicious intent; —*v.t.* commit murder; kill; mar by incompetence.—**mur'derer** *n.* (*fem.* **mur'deress**) one guilty of murder.—**mur'derous** *a.* pert. to murder; bloody; homicidal.—**mur'derously** *adv.*

murk (murk) *a.* dark;—*n.* misty darkness; gloom.—**murk'y** *a.* dark; misty.—**murk'ily** *adv.* **murk'iness** *n.*

murmur (mur'-mur) *n.* low, un-broken sound, as of wind, water, etc.; complaint expressed in sub-dued tones; softly uttered speech; —*v.i.* make low sound; speak in subdued tones; complain; grumble. —*pr.p.* **mur'muring**.—*pa.p.* **mur'-mured**.—**mur'murer** *n.*

murrain (mur'-in) *n.* disease affect-ing cattle, esp. foot-and-mouth disease.

muscadel (mus'-ka-del) n. musk-flavoured grape; wine made from this grape; raisin. Also mus'cat, mus'catel, mus'cadine.

muscle (mus'-l) n. band of contractile fibrous tissue which produces movement in animal body; strength. —mus'cled a. having muscle. —mus'cular a. pert. to muscle; strong. —muscular'ity n.—mus'cularly ad

Muscovy duck (mus'-ko-vi duk) n. musk-duck of C. and S. America.

muse (mūz) v.i. think over dreamily; ponder; consider meditatively;—n. reverie; contemplation; inspiration. —mus'er n.—mus'ingly adv.

museum (mū-zē'-um) n. permanent collection of works of art, antiques, objects of natural history, the sciences, etc.; building housing such a collection.

mush (mush) n. pulp; (Amer.) porridge of maize meal.—mush'y a. [form of mash].

mushroom (mush'-room) n. edible fungus of very quick growth;—a. of rapid growth; shaped like a mushroom.

music (mū'-zik) n. art of combining sounds or sequences of notes into harmonious patterns; melody; musical composition or score.— mu'sical a. pert. to music; set to music; appreciative of music; trained or skilled in art of music.— mu'sically adv.—mu'sicalness n.— mu'sical-box n. clockwork box which when wound up plays tune.— mu'sic-case, -fol'io, -hold'er n. case, etc., for carrying sheet music.— mu'sic-hall n. theatre where light variety programmes are performed. —musi'cian n. skilled performer of musical compositions.—musicol'ogy n. scientific study of music.

musk (musk) n. fragrant substance obtained from gland of musk-deer; perfume of this; plant with musky perfume. — musk'-cat n. civet.— musk'-deer n. small, hornless deer of C. Asia with gland secreting commercial musk.— musk'ily adv.— musk'iness n.—musk'-mallow n. variety of mallow plant with faint musky smell.—musk'-ox n. sheep-like ox inhabiting Canadian Arctic.— musk'-rat n. large N. American water-rat with musk-gland, valued for its fur; musquash.—musk'-rose n. climbing rose with white blossoms faintly perfumed with musk.— musk'y a. having smell of musk.

musket (mus'-ket) n. (formerly) hand gun or matchlock.—mus'keteer n. soldier armed with musket.— mus'ketry n. muskets collectively; troops armed with muskets; musket-practice.

Muslim (mus'-lim) n. Same as Moslem.

muslin (muz'-lin) n. thin cotton cloth of open weave, white or coloured;—a. made of muslin.

musquash (mus'-kwosh) n. musk-rat, or its fur.

mussel (mus'-l) n. bi-valve shell-fish.

Mussulman (mus'-ul-man) m. Mohammedan; Moslem.—pl. Muss'ulmans.

must (must) v.i. be obliged; n. (Collog.) a necessity.

must (must) n. wine newly pressed from grapes but not fermented.

must (must) n. mouldiness.

mustang (mus'-tang) n. wild horse of the American prairies; bronco.

mustard (mus'-terd) n. plant with yellow flowers and pungent seeds; yellow powder, made from the seeds, used as condiment.—mus'tard-plas'ter n. poultice made with mustard.—wild mustard, charlock.— to be as keen as mustard, be full of zest.

muster (mus'-ter) v.t. assemble; gather together, as one's resources; —v.i. be assembled together;—n. assembling of troops, etc.—to pass muster, be just up to standard.

musty (mus'-ti) a. mouldy; stale; sour.—must'ily adv.—must'iness n. mouldiness.

mutable (mū'-ta-bl) a. subject to change; inconstant. — mutabil'ity, mu'tableness n. state or quality of being mutable.—mu'tably adv.—muta'tion n. (Biol.) complete divergence from racial type due to genetic change.—mu'tative, mu'tatory a.

mute (mūt) a. dumb; silent; not sounded, as 'l' of calm;—n. person who is dumb; professional mourner at funeral; 'stopped' consonant, such as b, d, p, t;—v.t. muffle sound of.—mute'ly adv.—mute'ness n.

mutilate (mū'-til-āt) v.t. maim; cut off; impair by removing essential part.—mutila'tion n.—mu'tilator n.

mutiny (mū'-ti-ni) n. insurrection against lawful authority, esp. military or naval;—v.i. rise in mutiny.— pa.p. mu'tinied—mu'tineer n.—mu'tinous a. rebellious; seditious.

mutter (mut'-er) v.t. speak indistinctly or in low voice.—mutt'erer n.—mutt'ering n.

mutton (mut'-n) n. flesh of sheep.— mutt'on-chop n. rib of mutton for boiling or grilling. — mutton-chop whiskers, side-whiskers shaped like mutton-chop.

mutual (mū'-tū-al) a. reciprocally acting or related; interchanged; done by each to the other. — mutual'ity n. the quality of being reciprocal.—mu'tually adv.

muzzle (muz'-l) n. the snout; mouth and nose of animal; cage-like fastening for mouth to prevent biting; open end of a gun;—v.t. put a muzzle on; gag; enforce silence.—

muzz'le-load'er n. gun loaded at muzzle, opp. of *breech-loader.*

muzzy (muzz'-i) a. dazed; bewildered; tipsy.

my (mī) *poss.* of belonging to me.

mycetes (mī-sē'-tēz) n.pl. fungi.— **mycetol'ogy** n. Same as mycol'ogy.— **mycol'ogist** n.—mycology (mī-kol'-o-ji) n. science of fungi.

myelin (mī'-e-lin) n. (*Zool.*) fatty substance forming the sheath of nerve fibres.—**myeli'tis** n. inflammation of spinal cord.—myelo-meningi'tis n. spinal meningitis.

myna(h) (mī'-na) n. Indian starling.

myoid (mī'-oid) a. pert. to muscles. —**myocardi'tis** n. inflammation of heart muscle.

myopia (mī-ō'-pi-a) n. short-sightedness.—**my'ope** n. short-sighted person.—**myop'ic** a.

myriad (mir'-ad) n. immense number;—a. countless.

myriapod (mir'-i-a-pod) n. (*Zool.*) animal with great number of legs, as millipedes.

myrmidon (mer'-mi-don) n. brutal fighter; one who carries out orders with ruthlessness.

myrrh (mer) n. aromatic gum resin. —myr'rhic, myr'rhy a.

myrtle (mer'-tl) n. evergreen plant with fragrant white flowers and glossy leaves.

myself (mī-self') pron. I or me, used emphatically, or reflexively.

mystery (mis'-ter-i) n. anything strange and inexplicable; puzzle; secrecy; (*Arch.*) craft or trade; medieval drama based on Scripture;—pl. rites known to and practised by initiated only.—**myster'ious** a. strange; occult; incomprehensible.—**myste'riously** adv.—**myste'riousness** n.

mystic (mis'-tik) a. pert. to mystery or to secret religious rites; symbolical of spiritual truth; strange;—n. one who believes in mysticism; one who seeks to have direct contact with the Divine by way of spiritual ecstasy.— **mys'tical** a. — **mys'tically** adv.—**mys'ticism** n. doctrine of the mystics; study of spiritual experience.—**mystifica'tion** n.—**mys'tify** v.t. perplex; puzzle.—pr.p. **mys'tifying.**—pa.p. **mys'tified.**

myth (mith) n. fable; legend embodying primitive faith in supernatural; invented story; imaginary person or thing.—**myth'ic, -al** a. pert. to myths; fabulous; non-existent— **myth'ically** adv.—**mythologic-al** pert. to mythology; legendary.—**mytholog'ically** adv.—**mythol'ogist** n. one who has studied myths of various countries; writer of fables.—**mythol'ogy** n. collection of myths; science of myths; treatise on myths.

myxomatosis (mik-sō-ma-tō-sis) n. deadly disease affecting rabbits.

N

Naafi (naf'-i) n. organisation providing canteens and shopping facilities for men and women in the services [*Navy, Army,* and *Air Force Institutes*].

nab (nab) v.t. (*Slang*) catch hold of.

nabob (nā'-bob) n. Mohammedan chief in India; Anglo-Indian who had acquired great wealth in India.

nacelle (na-sel') n. small streamlined housing on aircraft for engines, etc.

nadir (nā'-dir) n. point of heavens directly opposite zenith; lowest stage.

naevus (nē'-vus) n. birth-mark formed by cluster of dilated blood-vessels. Also neave (nēv).

nag (nag) n. small horse; any horse.

nag (nag) v.t. and v.i. worry by constant fault-finding; scold pertinaciously.—pr.p. **nag'ging.**—pa.t. and pa.p. **nagged.**—**nag'ger** n.

naiad (nā'-ad, or nī'-ad) n. (*Myth.*) nymph of fresh-water fountain and streams.—pl. **nai'ades.**

naif See **naive.**

nail (nāl) n. horny shield covering ends of fingers or toes; claw; strip of pointed metal with head, for fastening wood, etc.; British cloth measure, 2 inches;—v.t. fasten with nail; fix or secure; confirm or pin down; catch out or expose; seize hold of.—**nail'-brush** n. brush for cleaning finger-nails.—**nail'er** n. one who makes nails.—**nail'rod** n. coarse dark tobacco.—**on the nail,** immediately.

naïve (na-ēv', nāv) a. having unaffected simplicity; artless. Also **naif.**—**naive'ly** adv.—**naivete** (nä-ēv-tā') n. childlike ingenuousness. Also **naïv'ety.**

naked (nā'-ked) a. having no clothes; exposed; bare; nude; evident; simple; sheer.—**na'kedly** adv.—**na'kedness** n.— **naked eye,** human eye unassisted by glasses.

namby-pamby (nam'-bi-pam'-bi) a. lacking strength of character; weakly sentimental.

name (nām) n. term by which person or thing is known; designation; title; reputation; repute;—v.t. give name to; call or mention by name; nominate; specify; christen. —**name'less** a. without name; dishonoured; obscure.—**name'lessly** adv. —**name'ly** adv. that is to say.— **name'sake** n. person who bears same name as another.

nancy (nan'-si) n. effeminate youth; homosexual.—**nan'cy-pret'ty** n. (*Bot.*) saxifrage, also known as *London pride* or *none-so-pretty.*

nankeen (nen-kēn') n. calico fabric dyed buff by tanning solution.

nanny (nan'-i) n. child's nurse.—nan'ny-goat n. she-goat.

nap (nap) n. short sleep; doze;—v.i. indulge in short sleep; be unprepared.

nap (nap) n. fine hairy surface of cloth; pile of velvet.

nap (nap) n. card game.

nap (nap) v.t. of racing tipsters, to advise client to bet on certain horse as sure winner.

napalm (nā'-pám) n. jellied petrol, used in air-raids and having devastating burning effect.

nape (nāp) n. back part of the neck.

napery (nā'-per-i) n. household linen.

naphtha (naf'-tha, nap'-tha) n. inflammable liquid distilled from petroleum, wood, etc.—naph'thalene n. solid crystalline hydrocarbon distilled from coal-tar and familiar in form of moth-balls.

napkin (nap'-kin) n. cloth used for wiping hands or lips at table; serviette.

napoleon (na-pō'-lē-on) n. French gold coin of First and Second French empires, then worth 20 francs (15/10½); the game of nap.—Napoleon'ic a. pert. to Napoleon I or III.

nappy (nap'-i) n. baby's napkin.

narcissism (nar'-sis-izm) n. in psycho-analysis, abnormal love and admiration for oneself.—narciss'ist n.

Narcissus (nar-sis'-us) n. genus of bulbous plants including daffodil, jonquil and narcissus.

narcotic (nar-kot'-ik) a. producing stupor or inducing sleep;—n. substance which induces sleep, and in large doses, insensibility.—narco'sis n. state of unconsciousness or stupor produced by use of narcotics.

nark (nark) n. (Slang) police spy; informer; v.t. nag; complain persistently.

narrate (na-rāt', nar'-āt) v.t. relate; tell (story) in detail; give an account of; describe.—narra'tion n. account.—narr'ative n. tale; detailed account of events;—a. pert. to, containing, narration.—narr'atively adv.—narra'tor n. one who narrates.

narrow (nar'-ō) a. of little breadth; not wide or broad; limited; niggardly; bigoted;—v.t. make narrow;—v.i. become narrow;—n.pl. straits.—narrow gauge, of railway lines less than 4 ft. 8½ in. apart.—narr'owly adv.—narr'ow-min'ded a. bigoted; prejudiced.

narwhal (nàr'-whal) n. sea-unicorn; Arctic whale, with one large protruding tusk.

nasal (nā'-zal) a. pert. to the nose; modified by nose, as the sound of m;—n. nasal sound or letter. such as

m or n.—na'salise v.i. render (a sound) nasally. — na'sally adv. through the nose.—nasal organ, nose.

nascent (nas'-ent) a. at moment of being born; just beginning to exist.

nasturtium (nas-tur'-shi-um) n. (Bot.) common garden plant of the genus Tropaeolum.

nasty (nás'-ti) a. very dirty; impure; disgusting; unpropitious (of weather, etc.); ill-natured; indecent.—nas'tily adv.—nas'tiness n.

natal (nā'-tal) a. pert. to one's birth, place of birth or date of birth; native.—natal day, birthday.

natant (nā'-tant) a. (Bot.) floating on surface.—nata'tion n. swimming.—natato'res n.pl. birds with webbed feet adapted for swimming.—natato'rial a. natatory.—na'tatory a. used or adapted for swimming.

nation (nā'-shun) n. people inhabiting a country under same government; race of people.

national (nash'-un-al) a. pert. to nation; public; general;—n. member of nation.—nationalisa'tion n.—nat'ionalise v.t. make national. acquire and manage by the State; make nation of.—nat'ionalism n.—nat'ionalist n. one who advocates national independence.—national'ity n. quality of being nation or belonging to nation; one's nation; patriotism.—nat'ionally adv. — national anthem, hymn or song expressive of patriotism.—national debt, debt due from nation to individual creditors.—national health insurance, compulsory insurance against illness.—National Trust, society for preserving places of historic interest, or natural beauty.

native (nā'-tiv) a. pert. to one's birth; belonging by birth; indigenous; natural;—n. person born in a place;—pl. oysters reared in artificial bed.—na'tively adv.—nativ'ity n. time or circumstances of birth.—The Nativity, birth of Christ.

natterjack (nat'-er-jak) n. British species of toad.

natty (nat'-i) a. neat; trim.—natt'ily adv.

natural (nat'-ū-ral) a. in accordance with, belonging to, or derived from, nature; inborn; unconstrained; normal; unaffected; unassuming; true to life; illegitimate; (Mus.) not modified by a flat or sharp;—n. idiot; (Mus.) character (♮).—naturalisa'tion n.—nat'uralise v.t. give to alien the rights of native subject; accustom, as to climate.—nat'uralism n. natural condition or quality; realism.—nat'uralist n. one versed in natural history.—naturalis'tic a. in accordance with nature.—naturalis'tic a. in accordance with nature.—naturalis'tically adv.—nat'urally adv.—

nat'uralness n.—natural gas n. gas generated in petroleum bearing strata.—natural history, science which deals with the earth's crust and its productions.—natural philosophy of nature and of the physical properties of bodies; physics.—natural selection, evolution by survival of the fittest.

nature (nā'-tūr) n. world, universe, known and unknown; power underlying all phenomena in material world; essential qualities of a thing; natural disposition; innate character; sort; kind; vital functions of organs of the body; state of nakedness.—na'tured a. in compounds, good-, bad-na'tured, showing one's innate disposition.

naught (nawt) n. nothing; figure 0; zero;—adv. in no degree;—a. worthless.—naught'y a. not behaving well; mischievous; bad.—naught'ily adv.—naught'iness n.

nausea (naw'-si-a, naw'-s(h)e-ą) n. feeling of sickness or disgust; seasickness.—nau'seate v.i. feel nausea; become squeamish;—v.t. loathe; fill with loathing or disgust.—nau'seous a. loathsome; disgusting; producing nausea.—nau'seously adv.

nautch (nawch) n. Indian dance.

nautical (naw'-ti-kąl) a. pert. to ships, seamen, or to navigation.—nau'tically adv.—nautical mile, 6,046 to 6,108 ft.

nautilus (naw'-ti-lus) n. genus of molluscs with many-chambered spiral shells.—pl. nau'tiluses or nau'tili.—nau'tiloid a.

naval (nā'-vąl) a. pert. to ships, esp. warships; belonging to or serving with navy; nautical; marine; maritime.

nave (nāv) n. central piece from which spokes of a wheel radiate.

nave (nāv) n. middle or body of a church, extending from choir or chancel to main entrance.

navel (nā'-vl) n. umbilicus, place of attachment of umbilical cord to the body of the embryo, marked by rounded depression in centre of lower part of abdomen.

navicular (ną-vik'-ū-ląr) a. shaped like boat or canoe; relating to small ships or boats.

navigate (nav'-i-gāt) v.t. steer or manage ship when sailing; sail upon or through;—v.i. sail.—nav'igable a. may be sailed over or upon; seaworthy; steerable (of balloons).—navigabil'ity, nav'igableness n.—nav'-igably adv.—naviga'tion n. science of directing course of seagoing vessel or airborne craft and of ascertaining its position at any time; shipping; voyage.—nav'igator n.

navvy (nav'-i) n. labourer on construction of roads, railways, canals, etc.

navy (nā'-vi) n. fleet; warships of country with their crews and organisation.—na'vy-blue n. and a. dark-blue, colour of naval uniform.

nay (nā) (Arch.) adv. no; not only this, but;—n. denial.

Nazarene (naz'-ą-rēn) n. native of Nazareth; term used by Jews and Mohammedans for a Christian; name given to Jesus Christ.

naze (nāz) n. promontory; headland.

Nazi (nät'-zi) n. and a. member of National Socialist Party of Germany (1922-1945).—Naz'ism, Naz'iism n.

Neanderthal (nē-ánd'-der-täl) a. denoting man of earliest long-headed race in Europe.—nean'derthaloid a.

neap (nēp) a. low;—n. neap-tide.—neaped a. aground until first spring tide.—neap'tide n. tide whose rise and fall is least marked, 7¼ days after time of new moon and full moon.

near (nēr) adv. at or to a short distance;—prep. close to;—a. close; closely related; stingy;—v.t. and v.i. approach.—near'-by a. adjacent.—Near East, part of Asia nearest Europe.—near'-hand a. close at hand;—adv. nearly.—near'ly adv. closely; almost.—near'ness n.—near'side n. of horses, vehicles, etc., left side; side nearest pavement.—near'-sight'ed a. short-sighted.—near'sight'edness n.

neat (nēt) n. any bovine animal; cattle.—neat'-herd n.

neat (nēt) a. clean; unsoiled; pure; trim; undiluted; handy; precise; exact; net.—neat'ly adv.—neat'ness n.

neb (neb) n. bill or beak of bird; nose.

nebula (neb'-ū-lą) n. little cloud; a greyish speck on cornea of eye; celestial phenomenon consisting of vastly diffused gas throughout which fine dust in an incandescent state is distributed;—pl. neb'ulae.—neb'ular a.—nebulos'ity n. cloudiness; vagueness.—neb'ulous a. cloudy, hazy, indistinct; pert. to nebula.—neb'ulousness n.

necessary (nes'-e-sąr-i) a. needful; indispensable;—n. essential need.—nec'essarily adv.—nec'essariness n.

necessity (ne-ses'-i-ti) n. pressing need; compulsion; needfulness; poverty; requisite; essential.—necess'-itate v.t. make necessary or indispensable; force.—necess'itous a. poor; needy.

neck (nek) n. part of body joining head to trunk; narrower part of bottle, etc.; narrow piece of anything between wider parts;—v.t. (Slang) cuddle.—neck'erchief n. band of cloth or kerchief worn round neck and folded, tie-form, in front.—neck'lace n. string of beads or precious stones worn round neck.—neck'let n. neck ornament; small collar, usually of fur.

necro- (nek'-ro) *prefix,* fr. Gk. *nekros,* dead body, used in the construction of terms, signifying death in some form.—**necrol'ogy** *n.* register of deaths; collection of obituary notices.—**nec'romancy** *n.* art of predicting future events by conjuring up spirits of the dead; black magic.—**nec'romancer** *n.* sorcerer; wizard.—**necroman'tic** *a.* pert. to magic.—**necrop'olis** *n.* cemetery. —**nec'ropsy, necros'copy** *n.* postmortem.—**necro'sis** *n.* gangrene, mortification.—**necrot'ic** *a.*

nectar (nek'-tar) *n.* drink of the gods, with power of conferring immortality; any delicious beverage; honey-like secretion of gland of flowers.—**necta'real, necta'rean, necta'reous, nec'tarous** *a.* sweet as nectar; resembling nectar; delicious.—**nec'tared** *a.* flavoured with nectar; very sweet.—**nec'tarine** *a.* sweet as nectar; —*n.* smooth-skinned peach.—**nec'tary** *n.* honey-gland of flower.

need (nēd) *n.* want; necessity; requirement; poverty; destitution; urgency;—*v.t.* be in want of; require;—*v.t.* be under necessity.— **need'ful** *a.* needy; necessary.—**the needful,** amount of ready-cash required.—**need'fully** *adv.*—**need'fulness** *n.*—**need'ily** *adv.*—**need'iness** *n.* temporary lack of money.—**need'less** *a.* not needed.—**need'lessly** *adv.*—**need'lessness** *n.*—**need'y** *a.* in need.

needle (nēd'-l) *n.* short pointed instrument with eye, for passing thread through cloth, etc.; knitting-pin; anything like a needle, as hypodermic syringe, leaf of pine, etc.; reproducing point of record-player; pointer of speedometer, etc.; —*a.* denote evenly-matched game, boxing-match, etc.—**need'le-woman** *n.* sempstress.—**need'lework** *n.* sewing; embroidery.

ne'er (nār) *adv.* poetical form of *never.*—**ne'er-do-well** *a.* and *n.* good-for-nothing; worthless.

nefarious (ne-fā'-ri-us) *a.* wicked in extreme; iniquitous; monstrous.— **nefa'riously** *adv.*—**nefa'riousness** *n.*

negate (ne-gāt') *v.t.* deny; prove the contrary.—**nega'tion** *n.* act of denying; disavowal; contradiction.

negative (neg'-a-tiv) *a.* expressing denial, prohibition, or refusal; not positive; (*Elect.*) at lower potential; (*Algebra*) minus;—*n.* negative word; photographic or TV image in which lights and shades are reversed;—*v.t.* refuse to sanction; reject.—**neg'atively** *adv.*—**neg'ativeness** *n.*—**negative quantity** (*Math.*) quantity preceded by the minus sign.

negatron (neg'-a-tron) *n.* negative electron.

neglect (ne-glekt') *v.t.* disregard; take no care of; fail to do; omit through carelessness;—*n.* omission; disregard.—**neglect'edness** *n.*—**neglect'ful** *a.* careless; inclined to be heedless. —**neglect'fully** *adv.*

negligence (neg'-li-jens) *n.* want of due care; carelessness; habitual neglect.—**neg'ligent** *a.* careless; inattentive; untidy.—**neg'ligently** *adv.*—**neg'ligible** *a.* hardly worth noticing.

negotiate (ne-gō'-shi-āt) *v.t.* settle by bargaining; arrange; transfer (bill, etc.); surmount;—*v.i.* discuss finding terms of agreement; bargain.— **nego'tiable** *a.* capable of being negotiated; transferable; able to be surmounted.—**negotiabil'ity** *n.*—**nego-tia'tion** *n.*—**nego'tiant, nego'tiator** *n.* (*fem.* **nego'tiatrix**) one who negotiates. —**negotia'tory** *a.*

Negro (nē'-grō) *n.* member of African race with dark skin, fuzzy hair, broad nose and protruding lips;—*a.* pert. to black African race.— **Ne'gress** *n.* Negro woman.—**Ne'groid** *a.* resembling Negroes.

negus (nē'-gus) *n.* drink compounded of (port) wine, hot-water, spice and sugar.

neigh (nā) *v.i.* whinny;—*n.* cry of horse.

neighbour (nā'-bur) *n.* person who lives near another;—*a.* neighbouring;—*v.t.* adjoin; be near.—**neigh'bourhood** *n.* adjoining district and its people; proximity; vicinity.—**neigh'bouring** *a.* close by.—**neigh'bourly** *a.* friendly; sociable; helpful.—**neigh'bourliness** *n.*

neither (nē'-THer, nī'-THer) *a.* and *pron.* not the one or the other;— *adv.* not on the one hand; not either;—*conj.* nor yet.

nemesis (nem-ē'-si-a) *n.* hardy garden plant.

nenuphar (nen'-ū-far) *n.* the white water-lily.

neolite (nē'-ō-līt) *n.* dark-green silicate of aluminium and magnesium.

neolithic (nē-ō-lith'-ik) *a.* (*Geol.*) pert. to New Stone Age.

neology (nē-ol'-o-ji) *n.* introduction of new words into language; new doctrines in theology.—**neolo'gian, neol'ogist** *n.* one who coins new words or holds novel doctrines in religion.—**neolog'ic, neolog'ical** *a.*— **neol'ogise** *v.i.* coin new words.— **neol'ogism** *n.* newly-coined word or phrase.

neon (nē'-on) *n.* non-metallic gaseous element.—**neon-lamp, -sign, or -tube,** one containing neon gas and glowing with reddish-orange light.

neophyte (nē'-ō-fīt) *n.* one newly admitted to religious order or initiated into practice of secret rites; novice or tyro; proselyte or convert to R.C. Church.

neozoic (nē-ō-zō'-ik) *a.* (*Geol.*) denoting rock-formations of recent period.

nephew (nev'-ŭ, nef'-ŭ) n. brother's or sister's son; originally, grandson.

nephr-, nephro- (nef'-rō) prefix from Greek nephros, kidney.—**nephral'gia, nephral'gy** n. pain in kidney.—**neph'ric** a. pert. to kidneys.—**nephrit'ic(al)** a. pert. to (diseases of) kidneys.—**nephri'tis** n. Bright's disease, inflammation of kidney.

nepotism (nep'-o-tizm) n. favouritism in awarding appointments to one's relations.

neptunium (nep-tūn'-i-um) n. radioactive element produced when uranium is bombarded with neutrons

nereid (nē'-rē-id) n. (Myth.) nymph of the sea; (Zool.) sea-centipede; sea-worm.

nerve (nęrv) n. one of bundles of fibres which convey impulses from brain to muscles, etc., or to brain from skin, eyes, nose, etc., producing sensation; vein of leaf; sinew; tendon; courage; cool assurance; impudence;—pl. irritability; sensitiveness to fear, etc.;—v.t. give courage or strength to.—**nerved** a.—**nerve'less** a. lacking in strength or will; incapable of effort.—**nerve'lessness** n.—**nerv'y** a. nervous; timid; fidgety.

nervous (nęrv'-us) a. vigorous; easily stimulated; timid.—**nerv'ously** adv.—**nerv'ousness** n.

nescience (nesh'-yens, nesh'-ens) n. condition of complete ignorance; want of knowledge; agnosticism.—**nesc'ient** a. ignorant; agnostic.

nest (nest) n. egg-laying animal's breeding-place; any snug retreat; set of boxes, tables, etc., which fit into one another;—v.t. form nest for;—v.i. occupy or build nest.—**nest'ling** n. bird too young to leave nest.—**nest'-egg** n. egg left in nest to induce bird to lay; small sum of money put aside.

nestle (nes'-l) v.t. settle comfortably and close to one another; lie snugly.

net (net) n. open-work fabric of meshes of cord, etc.; sections of this used to catch fish, etc.; lace formed by netting; snare;—a. made of netting; reticulate; caught in net;—v.t. cover with, or catch in, net;—v.i. make net or network;—pr.p. net'ting—pa.t. and pa.p. net'ted.—net'ted a.—net'ting n. act or process of forming network; net-like fabric; snaring by means of net.—net'-ball n. game, the object of which is to propel football with hand into netted ring.—net'-fish n. any fish caught in net.—net'work n. anything made like, or resembling, net.

net, nett (net) a. left after all deductions; free from deduction;—v.t. gain or produce as clear profit;—

pr.p. net'ting.—pa.p. net'ted.—net price, cash price without discount.

nether (neTH'-er) a. lower; low-lying; lying below; belonging to lower regions.—**neth'ermost** a. lowest.

nettle (net'-l) n. common weed with fine stinging hairs which contain acrid fluid;—v.t. irritate; provoke; make angry.—**net'tle-rash** n. irritating eruption in skin.

neural (nū'-ral) a. pert. to nerves.

neuralgia (nū-ral'-ji-a) n. spasmodic or continuous pain in one or more nerves.—**neural'gic** a.

neurasthenia (nū-ras-thē'-ni-a) n. nervous debility characterised by lack of energy.—**neurasthen'ic** a.

neuritis (nū-rī'-tis) n. inflammatory condition of nerve.

neurology (nū-rol'-o-ji) n. study of the structure, function and diseases of nervous system.—**neurolog'ical** a.—**neurol'ogist** n.

neuron (nū'-ron) n. nerve cell.

neuropath (nū'-rō-path) n. person suffering from nervous disorder; neuropathist. — **neuropath'ic, neuropath'ical** a. pert. to nervous diseases.—**neuropath'ically** adv.—**neurop'athist** n. nerve specialist.—**neuropathol'ogy** n. pathology of nervous system.—**neurop'athy** n. diseased condition of nervous system.

neurosis (nū-rō'-sis) n. functional disorder of nervous system, not attributable to organic disease.—**neurot'ic** a. pert. to nerves;—n. highly-strung person of morbid mentality.

neuter (nū'-ter) a. neither masculine nor feminine; (Bot.) possessing neither stamens nor carpels;—n. imperfectly developed female, as the worker-bee; one who is neutral.

neutral (nū'-tral) a. taking neither side in war, etc.; indifferent; without bias; grey; intermediate (shade of colour); neither acid nor alkaline; asexual;—n. nation, person, not taking sides in dispute; position in gear-mechanism when no power is transmitted.—**neu'tralise** v.t. render neutral; make ineffective; counterbalance.—**neu'traliser** n.—**neutral'ity** n. state of being neutral.—**neu'trally** adv.

neutron (nū'-tron) n. minute particle in the nucleus of atom, having approx. same mass as proton (q.v.) but being electrically neutral.

never (nev'-er) adv. at no time; not ever; in no degree; (Colloq.) surely not.—**nev'ermore** adv. at no future time.—**nevertheless'** conj. none the less; for all that; notwithstanding.—never-never n. (Colloq.) hire purchase.

new (nū) a. not existing before; lately discovered or invented; not old.—**new'ish** a. somewhat new.—**new'ness** n.—**new'born** a. recently born; born anew.—**new'com'er** n. one who has just settled down in new place or post.—**new'-fang'led** a. lately devised; novel.—**new'-fash'ioned** a. latest in style.—**New Englander**, native or resident of any of the six N.E. states of U.S.A.—**New Red Sandstone** (*Geol.*) lower division of Triassic series of rocks.—**New Testament**, later of two main divisions of Bible.—**New World**, (*Hist.*) N. and S. America.

newel (nū'-el) n. post supporting balustrade to flight of stairs; central, upright post to which inner ends of steps of circular or spiral staircase are attached.

news (nūz) n.sing. report of recent happings; fresh information; tidings; —**news'agent** n. shop-keeper who sells newspapers.—**news'-bull'etin** n. latest news, esp. as disseminated by broadcasters.—**newscaster** n. reader of broadcast news bulletins.—**news'monger** n. busy-body; gossip.—**news'paper** n. journal, daily or weekly, giving latest news.—**news'print** n. cheap paper for newspapers.—**news'reel** n. cinematograph film depicting items of news and topical features.—**news'-ven'dor** n. one who sells newspapers, esp. on streets.

newt (nūt) n. long-tailed amphibian animal; water-lizard; eft.

next (nekst) a. nearest; immediately following in place or time;—*adv.* nearest or immediately after; on first future occasion;—*prep.* nearest to.—**next'ly** adv. in the next place.—**next'-of-kin** n. nearest blood-relative.

nexus (nek'-sus) n. tie, connection, or bond.

nib (nib) n. something small and pointed; beak of bird; point of pen.—**nibbed** a. having nib.

nibble (nib'-l) v.t. bite a little at a time; gnaw;—v.i. catch at (as fish); dally with;—n. tiny bite.

niblick (nib'-lik) n. golf-club with iron-head, designed for lofting.

nice (nīs) a. exact; difficult to decide; discriminating; delicate; dainty; (*Colloq.*) agreeable; attractive; handsome; kind.—**nice'ly** adv.—**nice'ness** n.—**nie'ety** n. precision; delicacy; exactness.

niche (nich) n. recess in wall for statue, bust, etc.

nick (nik) v.t. make notch in; indent; catch in time;—n. notch; slit; score; opportune moment.

nickel (nik'-el) n. silver white metallic element, used in alloys and plating; in U.S.A. five cent piece of nickel;—v.t. plate with nickel.—pr.p. **nick'elling**.—pa.p. **nick'elled**.—**nick'el-plat'ing** n. plating of metals with nickel to keep down rust.—**nick'el-sil'ver** n alloy of copper, nickel and zinc; German silver.

nickname (nik'-nām) n. name given in contempt, derision, or familiarity to some person, nation, or object.

nicotine (nik'-o-tēn) n. alkaloid present in tobacco plant; used in manufacture of insecticides.

nictate (nik'-tāt) v.i. wink. Also **nic'titate**.—**nictita'tion** n. rapid and involuntary blinking.

nidification (nid-i-fi-kā'-shun) n. act of building nest.—**nid'ify** v.i. build nest.

niece (nēs) n. daughter of brother or sister.

niggard (nig'-ard) n. very miserly person;—a. stingy. Also **nigg'ardly**.—**ni'ggardliness** n.

nigger (nig'-er) n. Negro, in derision or contempt; person of black colour.—**nigg'er-brown** a. dark-brown.

niggle (nig'-l) v.i. trifle away one's time; complain about trivial matters.—**nigg'ler** n.—**nigg'ling, nigg'ly** a.

nigh (nī) a. near;—adv. almost; near;—prep. near to.

night (nīt) n. time of darkness from sunset to sunrise; end of daylight; ignorance; death.—**night'ly** a. happening or done every night; of night;—adv. every night; by night.—**night'-bird** n. nocturnal bird such as owl; bad character who prowls about by night; one who habitually keeps late hours.—**night'cap** n. cap worn in bed; glass of spirits taken at bed-time.—**night'-club** n. establishment for dancing and entertainment remaining open until early morning.—**night'-dress**, **night'-gown** n. loose gown worn in bed.—**night'fall** n. close of day.—**night'-hawk** n. British nightjar.—**night'jar** n. goatsucker, nocturnal migrant bird.—**night'-light** n. small stubby candle or electric bulb of low wattage kept burning all night.—**night'long** a. persisting all night.—**night'mare** n. terrifying feeling of oppression arising during sleep; incubus.—**night'-school** n. school for continuation of studies after working hours.—**night'shade** n. plants of potato family, some with poisonous berries.—**night'-shift** n. employees who work regularly during night;—**night'-time** n. period of night; first hours of darkness.

nightingale (nīt'-ing-gāl) n. bird of thrush family, the male being renowned for its beautiful song.

nihil, nil (nī'-hil, nil) n. nothing; zero.—**ni'hilism** n. rejection of all religious and moral principles; in 19th cent. opposition in Russia to constituted authority or government.—**ni'hilist** n.—**nihilist'ic** a.

nimble (nim'-bl) a. light and quick in motion.—**nim'ble-fing'ered** a. dexterous; given to pilfering.—**nim'bleness** n.—**nim'bly** adv.

nimbus (nim'-bus) *n.* rain-cloud; in representation of saints, etc., circle of light surrounding head; halo;—*pl.* nim'bi.

nincompoop (nin'-kom-poóp) *n.* feeble character; simpleton; ninny.

nine (nin) *a.* and *n.* one more than eight.—**nine'fold** *a.* nine times repeated.—**nine'teen** *a.* and *n.* nine and ten.—**nine'teenth** *a.* and *n.*—**nine'tieth** *a.* tenth after eightieth.—**nine'ty** *a.* and *n.*—**ninth** *a.* first after eighth;—*n.*—**ninth'ly** *adv.*—**nine'-pins** *n.* game in which nine erect wooden pegs are to be knocked down by ball; skittles.—**the Nine**, the Muses.

ninny (nin'-i) *n.* fool; dolt; simpleton.

nip (nip) *v.t.* pinch sharply; detach by pinching; check growth (as by frost); smart.—*pr.p.* nip'ping.—*pa.t.* and *pa.p.* nipped.—*n.* pinch: sharp touch of frost; sip; small measure of spirits.—**nip'per** *n.* young boy; thief; great claw (as of a crab);—*pl.* small pincers.—**nip'piness** *n.* agility; touch of frost.—**nip'pingly** *adv.*—**nip'py** *a.* agile; nimble; sharp in taste; parsimonious; curt; smarting.

nipple (nip'-l) *n.* protuberance in centre of woman's breast by which milk is obtained during breast-feeding; outlet of mammary glands; teat; small metal projection in grease-gun.

Nippon (nip'-on) *n.* Empire of Japan.

Nirvana (nir-vá'-na) *n.* in Buddhism, state of blissful repose reached by one in whom all craving for existence is extinguished.

nisi (ni'-si) *conj.* unless.—**decree nisi** (*Law*) decree to take effect after period of time has elapsed unless some valid objection arises.

nit (nit) *n.* egg of insect-parasite.

nitre (ni'-ter) *n.* potassium nitrate; saltpetre, white crystalline solid used in manufacture of gun-powder, etc.—**ni'trate** *n.* salt of nitric acid.—**ni'trated** *a.* combined with nitric acid.—**ni'tric** *a.* pert. to nitre.—**nitric acid**, powerful, corrosive acid; aqua fortis.—**ni'tride** *n.* compound of metal with nitrogen.—**ni'trify** *v.t.* treat with nitric acid.—**ni'trite** *n.* salt of nitrous acid.—**nitrous oxide**, laughing gas, used as anaesthetic in dentistry.

nitro- (ni'-trò) *prefix* signifying formed by, or containing, *nitre.*—**ni'tro-glyc'-erine** *n.* powerful oily liquid explosive.

nitrogen (ni'-trò-jen) *n.* gaseous chemical element, colourless, odourless and tasteless, nearly four-fifths of atmosphere.—**nitrog'enous** *a.*

nitwit (nit'-wit) *n.* (*Colloq.*) blockhead; fool.—**nitwit'ted** *a.* stupid; irresponsible.

nix (niks) *n.* (*Slang*) nothing.

no (nò) *a.* not any;—*adv.* expresses negative reply to question or request; not at all;—*n.* refusal; denial; negative vote.—**noes** *n.pl.* term used in parliamentary proceedings.—**no'-ball** *n.* in cricket, ball not properly bowled.—**no man's land**, waste land; terrain between trenches of opposing forces.

nob (nob) *n.* (*Slang*) head.

nobble (nob'-l) *v.t.* grab; steal; lame deliberately horse entered for race.

nobelium (no-bèl'-i-um) *n.* element No. 102, synthesised in 1957 by bombarding curium with carbon ions.

nobility (nò-bil'-i-ti) *n.* class holding special rank, usually hereditary, in state; quality of being noble; grandeur; loftiness and sincerity of mind or character.

noble (nò'-bl) *a.* distinguished by deeds, character, rank, or birth; of lofty character; titled;—*n.* nobleman; peer; old English gold coin.—**no'bleman** *n.*—**no'bleness** *n.*—**no'bly** *adv.*—**the noble art**, boxing.

nobody (nò'-bod-i) *n.* no one; person of no importance.—*pl.* no'bodies.

nocturn (nok'-turn) *n.* service held during the night.—**noc'turne** *n.* painting of a night-scene; musical composition of gentle and simple character.—**noctur'nal** *a.* pert. to night; happening or active by night.—**noctur'nally** *adv.*

nod (nod) *v.t.* and *v.i.* incline head forward by quick motion, signifying assent or from drowsiness; be sleepy; sway; bow by way of recognition.—*pr.p.* nod'ding.—*pa.t.* and *pa.p.* nod'ded.—*n.* act of nodding.—**nod'der** *n.*

noddle (nod'-l) *n.* jocular expression for the head.—*v.i.* nod repeatedly.

node (nòd) *n.* knot; knob; (*Geom.*) point at which a curve crosses itself to form a loop; (*Elect.*) point in circuit carrying alternating currents at which voltage is a minimum; (*Astron.*) one of two points at which the orbit of planet intersects the plane of the ecliptic; (*Phys.*) point of permanent rest in vibrating body; (*Med.*) small protuberance; constriction; (*Bot.*) part of stem to which leaf is attached.—**nod'al** *a.* pert. to nodes.—**nodat'ed** *a.* knotted.—**noda'tion** *n.* act of making knots.—**nodif'erous** *a.* (*Bot.*) having nodes.—**nod'ose** *a.* full of knots.—**nod'ular** *a.* like a nodule.—**nod'ulated** *a.* having nodules.—**nod'ule** *n.* small node or swelling.

Noël (nò'-el) *n.* Christmas; carol.

nog (nog) *n.* small pot or mug; kind of strong ale.—**nog'gin** *n.* nog; small mug.

nohow (nò'-hou) *adv.* in no way; not at all.

noise (noiz) *n.* sudden or harsh

sound; glamour, din; outcry; gossip —*v.t.* spread by rumour;—*v.i.* sound loud.—**noise´less** *a.* making no noise; silent. — **noise´lessly** *adv.* — **noise´lessness** *n.*—**nois´y** *a.* making much noise; clamorous.—**nois´ily** *adv.*—**nois´iness** *n.*

noisome (noi´-sum) *a.* injurious to health; noxious; evil-smelling. — **noi´somely** *adv.*—**noi´someness** *n.*

noll (nol) *n.* crown of head.

nomad (nŏ´-mad) *a.* roaming from pasture to pasture;—*n.* wanderer; member of wandering tribe.— **nomad´ic** *a.* pert. to nomads; pastoral; having no fixed dwelling place. —**nomad´ically** *adv.*—**nom´adism** *n.*

nomenclator (nŏ´-men-klā-tor) *n.* one who gives names to things.— **no´menclatory, no´menclatural** *a.*—**no´menclature** *n.* system of naming; vocabulary of a science, etc.

nominal (nom´-in-al) *a.* pert. to a name; existing only in name; ostensible.—**nom´inally** *adv.* in name only; not really.

nominate (nom´-i-nāt) *v.t.* name; put forward the name of, as a candidate; propose; designate.—**nomina´tion** *n.* act of naming or nominating; power or privilege of nominating.—**nom´inative** *a.* (*Gram.*) denoting the subject;—*n.* noun or pronoun which is subject of verb.—**nom´inator** *n.* one who nominates.—**nominee´** *n.* one named or proposed for office.

non- (non) *prefix* from L. *non* = not, used in terms signifying absence or omission.—**non´-com´batant** *n.* member of armed forces whose duties do not entail active part in military operations; unarmed civilian.—**non´-commis´sioned** *a.* of ranks between private and second-lieutenant;— (*abbrev.*) **non´-com**. — **non´-commit´tal** *a.* avoiding direct statement as to one's opinions.—**non´-commu´nicant** *n.* one not a member of church or lax in attendance at holy communion. — **non´-conduc´tor** *n.* substance which will not conduct electricity, heat, or sound; insulator. **non´-ferr´ous** *a.* of metal containing no, or only merest trace of, iron.— **non´-stop** *a.* not stopping at intermediate stations, etc.; continuous.— **non-U** *a.* not used by the upper classes; vulgar or common.

nonage (non´-āj) *n.* legal infancy; minority (under 21 years of age).

nonagenarian (non-a-je-nā´-ri-an) *n.* one ninety years old or more;—*a.* relating to ninety.

nonagon (non´-a-gon) *n.* nine-sided plane figure.

nonchalance (non´-sha-lans) *n.* unconcern; coolness; indifference; carelessness.—**non´chalant** *a.*—**non´chalantly** *adv.*

nonconformist (non-kon-for´-mist) *n.* dissenter; protestant who refuses to comply with usages and rites of Church of England.—**nonconfor´ming** *a.*—**nonconfor´mity** *n.*

nondescript (non´-de-skript) *a.* not hitherto described; not easily described; vague; insignificant.

none (nun) *a.* and *pron.* no one; not anything.—**none´such, non´such** *n.* person or thing without rival or equal.—**none´-so-prett´y** *n.* common garden-plant, also known as *London pride* or *nancy pretty.*—**none** the less, nevertheless; all the same.

none (nōn) *n.* one of the canonical hours of R.C. Breviary.

nonentity (non-en´-ti-ti) *n.* negation of being; thing not existing; nonexistence; person of no importance; a mere nobody.

nonpareil (non-pa-rel´) *n.* person or thing without an equal; nonesuch; pattern of book edge marbling; printing type counting 6 points;—*a.* unrivalled; peerless; matchless.

nonplus (non´-plus) *n.* perplexity; puzzle; embarrassment; quandary; —*v.t.* bewilder completely; bring to standstill.

nonsense (non´-sens) *n.* lack of sense; absurdity; trifling.—**nonsen´sical** *a.*—**nonsen´sically** *adv.*

noodle (nŏŏ´-dl) *n.* simpleton; blockhead.

noodle (nŏŏ´-dl) *n.* strip of dough, made of wheat flour and eggs, often served in soups.

nook (nook) *n.* corner; secluded retreat.

noon (nŏŏn) *n.* midday; twelve o'clock by day.—**noon´day, noon´tide** *n.* and *a.* midday.

noose (nŏŏs) *n.* running loop with slip knot; snare; tight knot;—*v.t.* tie, catch in noose.

nor (nor) and not.

Nordic (nor´-dik) *a.* of or pert. to peoples of Germanic stock; longheaded, tall, blue-eyed and blond.

norm (norm) *n.* rule or standard; unit for comparison; standard type or pattern; model.—**nor´mal** *a.* conforming to type or natural law;—*n.* perpendicular to line, surface, or tangent at point of contact.—**normalisa´tion, normal´ity** *n.*—**nor´mally** *adv.* —**nor´mative** *a.* setting up norm; regulative.

Norse (nors) *a.* pert. to Scandinavia, its language or people;—*n.* old Scandinavian language.

north (north) *n.* region or cardinal point opposite to midday sun; part of world, country, etc., towards this point;—*adv.* towards or in north;— *a.* to, from, or in north.—**nor´therly** *a.* towards north; of winds, coming from north.—**nor´thern** *a.* pert. to north; in or of north.—**nor´therner** *n.* inhabitant of northern parts of country.—**nor´thernly** *adv.* in northern direction.—**nor'thernmost** a. situated at most northerly point.—**north'ward, north'wardly** a. situated towards north;—adv. in northerly direction.—**north'wards** adv.—**north'east (-west)** n. point between north and east (west);—a. pert. to, or from, north-east (-west).—**north'east'er (-west'er)** n. wind from north-east (-west).—**north'-east'erly (-west'erly)** a. towards or coming from north-east (-west). — **north'-east'ern (-west'ern)** a. belonging to north-east (-west).—**north'-east'ward (-west'ward)** a. towards north-east (-west).—**northern lights**, aurora borealis.—**nor'thing** n. motion or distance northward; difference of latitude as ship sails in northerly direction.—**North Pole**, northern extremity earth's axis.—**north'-star** n. pole star.

nose (nōz) n. organ for breathing and smelling; power of smelling; any projection resembling nose;—v.t. detect by smell; speak through nose; —v.i. smell; pry officiously.—**nose'-bag** n. bag containing food fastened to horse's head. — **nose'-dive** n. (Aviat.) sudden steep plunge directly towards objective;—v.i. perform this.—**nose'gay** n. bunch of sweet-smelling flowers; bouquet.—**nos'ing** n. moulded projecting edge of tread of step; beading round edge of board.

nosology (nos-ol'-o-ji) n. branch of medicine treating generally of diseases; systematic classification of phases of disease.—**nosolog'ical** a.—**nosol'ogist** n.

nostalgia (nos-tal'-ji-a) n. longing for what is past.—**nostal'gic** a.

nostril (nos'-tril) n. external opening of nose.

nostrum (nos'-trum) n. quack, secret remedy; patent medicine of doubtful efficacy.

not (not) adv. word expressing denial, negation, or refusal.

notable (nō'-ta-bl) a. worthy of notice;—n. person of distinction.—**notabil'ia** n.pl. things worth noting. —**notabil'ity** n. eminent person.—**not'ableness** n.—**not'ably** adv.

notary (nō'-ta-ri) n. notary-public, person, usually solicitor, authorised to record statements, take affidavits, etc., on oath.

notation (nō-tā'-shun) n. art of representing pitch and time of musical sounds by signs; any system of figures, signs and symbols which conveys information.

notch (noch) n. V-shaped cut or indentation; nick; run scored at cricket; v.t. make notches in; indent; score (a run).

note (nōt) n. mark; brief comment; memorandum; short letter; diplomatic paper; written or printed promise of payment; character to indicate musical tone; notice; distinction; fame; regard;—v.t. observe; set down in writing; attend to; heed.—**note'-book** n. book for jotting down notes, etc.—**not'ed** a. well-known; eminent; celebrated; distinguished; notorious. — **not'edly** adv.—**not'edness** n.—**note'-pa'per** n. small size of writing paper.—**note'-worthy** a. worthy of notice; remarkable.—**note of hand**, written promise to pay sum by certain time.

nothing (nuth'-ing) n. not anything; non-existence; nonentity; nought; zero; trifle; bagatelle;—adv. in no degree; not at all.—**noth'ingness** n.

notice (nō'-tis) n. act of noting; remarking, or observing; observation; cognisance; regard; note: heed; news; review; formal intimation;—v.t. observe; remark upon; treat with regard.—**no'ticeable** a. worthy of observation; conspicuous; attracting attention; appreciable.—**no'ticeably** adv.—**to give notice**, warn beforehand.—**to receive one's notice**, be informed that one is about to be dismissed.

notify (nō'-ti-fī) v.t. make known; report; give notice of or to; announce; inform;—pa.p. **no'tified.**—**no'tifiable** a. must be reported to appropriate authorities.—**notifica'tion** n. official notice.

notion (nō'-shun) n. mental apprehension; idea; conception; opinion; belief; fancy; inclination.

notoriety (nō-tō-rī'-et-i) n. state of being known, esp. in disreputable way; public exposure; discreditable publicity.—**noto'rious** a. known by all and sundry; infamous.—**noto'riously** adv.—**noto'riousness** n. notoriety.

notwithstanding (not-with-stand'-ing) adv. nevertheless; however; yet; prep. in spite of; despite;—conj. although.

nougat (nōō'-ga) n. sweetmeat of almonds, sugar and honey paste.

nought (nawt) n. nothing; zero;—adv. in no degree; not at all. Also **naught.**

noun (noun) n. (Gram.) word used as name of person, quality, or thing; substantive.

nourish (nur'-ish) v.t. supply with food; nurture; cherish; tend; encourage.—**nour'ishable** a.—**nour'ishing** a. nutritious.—**nour'ishment** n. food; nutriment.

nous (nous, or nōōs) n. mind; reason; commonsense; intelligence.

nova (nō'-va) n. new star, which appears suddenly.

novel (nov'-el) a. recent origin or introduction; new; recent; unusual; —n. fictitious prose tale dealing with adventures or feelings of imaginary persons.—**novelette'** n. shorter form of novel, with strong love-interest.

—nov'elist n. writer of novels.—nov'elty n. newness; something new or unusual.

November (nō-vem'-bẹr) n. eleventh month of the year.

novice (nov'-is) n. candidate for admission to religious order; one new to anything; inexperienced person; beginner or tyro.—novi'ciate, novi'tiate n. state or time of being novice; novice.

now (nou) adv. at the present time;—conj. this being the case;—n. present time.—now'adays adv. in these days.—now! now! form of admonition.—now and then, occasionally.

Nowel See Noël.

nowhere (nō'-hwär) adv. not in any place; (Colloq.) far behind.—no'wise adv. not in any manner or degree.

noxious (nok'-shus) a. hurtful; pernicious; unwholesome.—nox'iously adv.—nox'iousness n.

nozzle (noz'-l) n. projecting spout or vent; outlet end of pipe, hose, etc.

nuance (nōō-ans') n. shade or subtle variation in colour, tone of voice, etc.; (Mus.) delicate gradation of tone and expression in performance on instrument.

nubile (nū'-bil) a. of marriageable age.—nubil'ity n.

nucleus (nū'-klē-us) n. central mass which increases by successive accretions; starting point of project or idea; (Astron.) centre of sun-spot; denser core or head of comet; (Biol.) inner essential part of living cell; (Physics) core of atom, where nearly all the mass is concentrated, composed of protons and neutrons.—pl. nu'clei.—nuclear a.—nuclear energy, energy freed or absorbed during reactions taking place in atomic nuclei.—nuclear fission, disintegration of atomic nuclei.—nuclear reactor n. device for producing controlled chain reactions of neutrons.—nu'cleate v.t. gather into or round nucleus.—nu'cleated a. possessing nucleus.—nucleon'ics n. study of atomic nuclei

nude (nūd) a. bare; naked; uncovered;—n. picture or piece of sculpture in the nude.—nude'ly adv.—nu'dity, nude'ness n. nakedness.—nu'dism n. cult emphasising practice of nudity for health.—nu'dist n.

nudge (nuj) v.t. touch slightly with elbow in order to attract attention;—n. gentle push.

nugget (nug'-et) n. rough lump or mass, esp. of native gold.

nuisance (nū'-sạns) n. something harmful, offensive, or annoying; troublesome person; inconvenience.

null (nul) a. of no legal validity; void; invalid; of no importance;—n. something of no force, or value;

—v.t. annul; render void.—null'ify v.t. render useless; invalidate;—pa.p. null'ified.—nullifica'tion n. act of nullifying;—null'ifier n.—null'ity n. state of being null and void; suit to contest validity of marriage.

numb (num) a. lacking sensation or motion; insensible; chilled; benumbed;—v.t. benumb; to deaden.—numb'ness n.

number (num'-bẹr) n. sum or aggregate of quantities; collection of things; assembly; single issue of publication; song; piece of music;—pl. metrical feet or verses; poetry; rhythm;—v.t. count; reckon; estimate; tell;—v.i. amount to.—num'berer n.—num'berless a. innumerable.—numerabil'ity, nu'merableness n.—nu'merable a. may be numbered.

numeral (nū'-mẹr-ạl) a. designating a number;—n. sign or word denoting a number.—nu'merable a. able to be counted.—nu'merably adv.—nu'merally adv. according to number.—nu'merary a. belonging to, or integral part of, certain number.—nu'merate v.t. count; reckon.—numera'tion n.—nu'merator n. top part of fraction.—numer'ic(al) a. of, or in respect of, numbers.—numer'ically adv.—nu'merous a. many.—nu'merously adv.—nu'merousness n.

numismatic (nū-mis-mat'-ik) a. pert. to coins or medals;—n.pl. scientific study of coins and medals.—numis'matist n.—numismatol'ogy n. science of coins and medals in relation to archaeology and history.—numismatol'ogist n.

numskull (num'-skul) n. dolt; dunce; stupid person; blockhead.

nun (nun) n. female member of religious order, vowed to celibacy; white-hooded, fancy pigeon.—nun'nery n. convent of nuns.

nuncio (nun'-shi-ō) n. messenger; ambassador representing Pope at foreign court.

nuncupate (nung'-kū-pāt) v.t. and v.i. declare orally, as a will.—nuncupa'tion n.—nun'cupative a. declared orally.—nun'cupator n.—nun'cupatory a. oral; verbal.

nuptial (nup'-shạl) a. pert. to marriage;—pl. wedding ceremony; marriage.

nurl, knurl (nurl) v.t. roughen edge of circular object; mill; indent.—nur'ling n. milling on edge of coin.

nurse (nurs) n. person trained for care of sick or injured; woman tending another's child;—v.t. tend, as nurse; suckle; foster; husband; harbour (grievance); keep in touch with (parliamentary constituency); manage skilfully.—nurse'maid, nurs'ery-maid n. girl in charge of young children. — nurs'er n. — nurs'ery n. room for children; place for rearing plants.—nurs'eryman n. one who raises plants for sale.— nursery rhymes, jingling rhymes to amuse young children.—nursery school, kindergarten, for children of 2-5 years of age.—nurs'ling n. infant.—wet-nurse n. woman who suckles infant of another.

nurture (nur'-tūr) n. nurturing; rearing; breeding; nourishment;— v.t. nourish; cherish; tend; train; rear; bring up.—nurt'urer n.

nut (nut) n. fruit consisting of hard shell enclosing kernel; hollow metal collar, internal surface of which carries groove or thread into which thread of bolt fits;—n.pl. kitchen-coal, in small lumps free from coal-dust;—v.i. gather nuts;—pr.p. nut'-ting.—pa.t. and pa.p. nut'ted.— nut'-brown a. of colour of nut.— nut butter, butter substitute made from nut-oil.—nut'cracker n. instrument for cracking nuts; bird of crow family.—nut'hatch, nut'jobber, nut'pecker n. climbing bird, allied to titmice.—nut'shell n. hard shell enclosing kernel of nut.—nut'ter n.— nut'tiness n. taste of nuts.—nut'ting n.—nut'ty a. abounding in nuts; having nut-flavour.—a hard nut to crack, difficult problem to solve; person difficult to deal with.

nutmeg (nut'-meg) n. aromatic spice from fruit of Malay tree.

nutrient (nū'tri-ent) a. nourishing; —n. something nutritious.—nu'triment n. that which nourishes; food. —nutri'tion n. the act of nourishing. —nutri'tional, nutri'tious, nu'tritive, nu'tritory a. nourishing.

nux vomica (nuks vom'-ik-ạ) n. dried ripe seed of an E. Indian plant, from which strychnine and brucine are obtained.

nuzzle (nuz'-l) v.t. and v.i. rub with nose; nestle; cherish.

nylon (nī'-lon) n. synthetic polymeric amide which can be drawn into fibre resembling silk.

nymph (nimf) n. goddess inhabiting mountain, grove, fountain, river, etc.; girl distinguished by grace and charm.—nymph'al, nymph'-like a.— nymphet n. very young sexually attractive girl.—nymphoma'nia n. excessive sexual desire in women.— nymphoma'niac n.

nymph, nympha (nimf, -ạ) n. immature form of mites and certain insects.

O

O, oh (ō) interj. exclamation of address, surprise, sorrow, wonder.

oaf (ōf) n. changeling; dolt; lout;

awkward fellow.—pl. oafs or oaves.— oaf'ish a. loutish.

oak (ōk) n. forest-tree yielding hard, durable timber.—oak'en a. made of oak.—oak'ling n. young oak.— oak'-app'le n. swelling on oak-leaves caused by gall-fly.

oakum (ōk'-um) n. loose fibre used for caulking seams of ships.

oar (ōr) n. wooden lever with broad blade worked by the hands to propel boat; oarsman;—v.t. and v.i. row.—oared a. having oars.—oars'man n. rower.—oars'manship n. art of rowing.—to put in one's oar (Colloq.) meddle.

oasis (ō-ā'-sis) n. fertile spot in desert.—pl. oases (ō-ā'-sēz).

oast (ōst) n. kiln for drying hops or malt.—oast'-house n.

oat (ōt) n. but usually in pl. oats, grain of cereal plant, used as food; the plant.—oat'en a. made of oat-straw or oatmeal.—oat'cake n. thin cake of oatmeal.—oat'meal n. meal made from oats.—to sow one's wild oats, indulge in youthful follies before settling down.

oath (ōth) n. confirmation of the truth by naming something sacred, esp. God; blasphemous use of name of God; any imprecation.—pl. oaths (ōTHz).

obbligato (ob-li-gȧ'-tō) n. (Mus.) instrumental accompaniment in musical composition indispensable to proper rendering of piece;—also a. Also obliga'to.

obdurate (ob'-dū-rāt) a. hard-hearted; stubborn; unyielding.—ob'durately adv.—ob'duracy n. hard-heartedness; stubbornness.

obedient (ō-bē'-di-ent) a. subject to authority; willing to obey.—obe'diently adv.—obe'dience n. doing what one is told.

obeisance (ō-bā'-sạns) n. a bow or curtsy.

obelisk (ob'-ē-lisk) n. tall, four-sided pillar, ending in small pyramid; in printing, reference mark (†) also called 'dagger'; sign (÷ or —).

obese (ō-bēs') a. fat; fleshy.—obese'-ness, obes'ity n. excessive fatness.

obey (ō-bā') v.i. do as ordered; be obedient; submit to authority;— v.t. comply with orders.

obfuscate (ob-fus'-kāt) v.t. darken; confuse or bewilder.—obfusca'tion n. obscurity.

obituary (o-bit'-ū-ar-i) a. pert. to death of person;—n. biographical sketch of deceased person.

object (ob'-jekt) n. anything presented to the mind or senses; material thing; end or aim.—ob'jectless a. having no aim or purpose.—ob'ject-glass n. lens in telescope, etc., nearest to object viewed.

object (ob-jekt') v.t. offer in opposition; put forward as reason against; —*v.i.* protest against; feel dislike.— **objection** (ob-jek'-shun) *n.* adverse reason; difficulty or drawback; argument against.—**objec'tionable** *a.* disagreeable.—**objec'tionably** *adv.*—**objec'tor** *n.*

objective (ob-jek'-tiv) *a.* pert. to object; pert. to that which is external to mind; unbiassed;—*n.* point aimed at in military attack.— **objec'tively** *adv.*—**objectiv'ity** *n.*

oblate (ob-lāt') *a.* (*Geom.*) flattened at the poles; orange-shaped.— **oblate'ness** *n.*

oblation (ob-lā'-shun) *n.* something offered to God, or a god; gift to church for pious uses.—**oblate** *n.* person dedicated to service of God.

obligate (ob'-li-gāt) *v.t.* bind, esp. by legal contract; put under obligation. —**obliga'tion** *n.* binding power of promise or contract; favour; duty; legal bond.—**oblig'atory** *a.* compulsory.—**oblig'atorily** *adv.*

oblige (ō-blīj') *v.t.* lay under an obligation; do a favour to; compel; —*v.i.* contribute to entertainment. —**obliged'** *a.* grateful; indebted.— **oblige'ment** *n.* favour.—**oblig'ing** *a.* helpful; courteous.—**oblig'ingly** *adv.* —**oblig'ingness** *n.*

oblique (ob-lēk') *a.* slanting; inclined; indirect; obscure; underhand.—**oblique'ly** *adv.*—**oblique'ness**, **obliquity** (ob-lik'-wi-ti) *n.* slant or inclination; dishonesty.

obliterate (ob-lit'-e-rāt) *v.t.* blot out; efface.—**oblitera'tion** *n.* destruction; extinction.—**oblit'erative** *a.*

oblivion (ob-liv'-i-un) *n.* forgetting, or being forgotten; forgetfulness.— **obliv'ious** *a.* forgetful; heedless.— **obliv'iously** *adv.*—**obliv'iousness** *n.*

oblong (ob'-long) *a.* longer than broad;—*n.* (*Geom.*) rectangular figure with adjacent sides unequal.

obloquy (ob'-lo-kwi) *n.* abusive speech.

obnoxious (ob-nok'-shus) *a.* offensive; objectionable.—**obnox'iously** *adv.*—**obnox'iousness** *n.*

oboe (ō'-boi, ō'-bō) *n.* (*Mus.*) double-reed wood-wind instrument with conical bore; organ reed-stop.— **o'boist** *n.*

obscene (ob-sēn') *a.* indecent; filthy; disgusting.—**obscene'ly** *adv.* — **obscene'ness** *n.*—**obscenity** (ob-sen'-i-ti) *n.*

obscure (ob-skūr') *a.* dark; hidden; humble; abstruse;—*v.t.* dim; conceal; make doubtful.—**obscure'ly** *adv.* —**obscure'ness** *n.* quality of being obscure.—**obscu'rity** *n.* absence of light; state of retirement, or of being unknown; indistinctness; lack of clear expression; dubiety of meaning; humility.

obsequies (ob'-se-kwiz) *n.pl.* funeral rites; funeral.—**obse'quial** *a.*

obsequious (ob-sē'-kwi-us) *a.* servile; fawning.—**obse'quiously** *adv.*—**obse'-quiousness** *n.*

observe (ob-zerv') *v.t.* watch; note systematically; keep religiously; remark;—*v.i.* take notice; comment. —**observ'able** *a.*—**observ'ably** *adv.*— **observ'ableness** *n.*—**observ'ance** *n.* act of observing or paying attention; religious rite; rule or practice.— **observ'ant** *a.* quick to notice; alert; carefully attentive.—**observ'antly** *adv.* —**observa'tion** *n.* action or habit of observing; attentive watchfulness; comment; remark.—**observa'tional** *a.* —**observa'tionally** *adv.*—**observ'atory** *n.* building for observation and study of astronomical, etc., phenomena.— **observ'er** *n.* one who observes; attentive spectator; member of crew of aircraft who makes aerial observations.

obsess (ob-ses') *v.t.* haunt; fill the mind completely; preoccupy.—**obsession** (ob-sesh'-un) *n.* domination of mind by one idea.

obsolete (ob'-sol-ēt) *a.* out of date.— **ob'soletely** *adv.*—**ob'soleteness** *n.*— **obsoles'cent** *a.* becoming obsolete; going out of use.—**obsoles'cence** *n.*

obstacle (ob'-sta-kl) *n.* obstruction; hindrance.

obstetrics (ob-stet'-riks) *n.* (*Med.*) science dealing with care of pregnant women; midwifery.—**obstet'ric**, **obstet'rical** *a.*—**obstetric'ian** *n.* specialist in midwifery.

obstinate (ob'-sti-nāt) *a.* stubborn; unyielding.—**ob'stinately** *adv.*— **ob'stinateness** *n.*—**ob'stinacy** *n.* unreasonable firmness; stubbornness.

obstreperous (ob-strep'-e-rus) *a.* noisy; vociferous; turbulent. — **obstrep'erously** *adv.*—**obstrep'erousness** *n.*

obstruct (ob-strukt') *v.t.* block up; impede; hinder passage of; block out.—**obstruc'ter**, **obstruc'tor** *n.*—**obstruc'tion** *n.* act of obstructing; that which obstructs or hinders.—**obstruc'tive** *a.*—**obstruc'tively** *adv.*

obtain (ob-tān') *v.t.* gain; secure;— *v.i.* be customary; hold good.— **obtain'able** *a.* procurable.—**obtain'ment** *n.* acquirement.

obtrude (ob-trōōd') *v.t.* thrust forward unsolicited;—*v.i.* intrude.— **obtru'der** *n.*—**obtru'sion** *n.* act of obtruding.—**obtru'sive** *a.* tending to thrust itself upon the attention unduly.—**obtru'sively** *adv.*

obtuse (ob-tūs') *a.* blunt; stupid; (*Geom.*) greater than right angle, but less than 180°.—**obtuse'ly** *adv.*— **obtuse'ness** *n.*

obverse (ob'-vers) *a.* being a counterpart; facing the observer; of coin, bearing the head;—*n.* face of coin, medal, etc. (opp. of 'reverse'); counterpart.—**obverse'ly** *adv.*

obviate (ob'-vi-āt) *v.t.* intercept (as

difficulties); make unnecessary; avoid.

obvious (ob'-vi-us) *a.* easily seen or understood; evident; apparent.—ob'viously *adv.*—ob'viousness *n.*

occasion (o-kā'-zhun) *n.* opportunity; reason or justification; time of important occurrence;—*pl.* affairs or business;—*v.t.* cause; bring about.—oeca'sional *a.* occurring now and then; incidental; meant for special occasion.—oeca'sionally *adv.* from time to time.

occident (ok'-si-dent) *n.* part of horizon where sun sets; west.—oeciden'tal *a.* western;—*n.* native of western country.

occlude (o-klōōd') *v.t.* shut in or out; (*Chem.*) absorb gas.—oeclu'sion *n.*—occlu'sive *a.* serving to shut in or out.

occult (ok-ult') *a.* hidden from view; secret; mysterious; magical;—*v.t.* conceal; hide from view.—occult'ly *adv.*—oeculta'tion *n.* eclipse of heavenly body by another.—occult'ism *n.* doctrine or study of supernatural, etc.—occult'ness *n.* mystery; magic.

occupy (ok'-ū-pī) *v.t.* take possession of; inhabit; fill;—*pa.p.* and *pa.t.* oee'upied.—oee'upancy *n.* act of having or holding possession; tenure.—oee'upant *n.*—oecupa'tion *n.* occupancy; possession; temporary possession of enemy country by victor; employment; trade; business; profession.—oecupa'tional *a.*—oee'upier *n.* occupant; tenant.

occur (o-kur') *v.i.* come to the mind; happen.—*pr.p.* oeeur'ring.—*pa.p.* and *pa.t.* oecurred'.—oeeur'renee *n.* happening; event.

ocean (ō'-shan) *n.* open sea; one of the large divisions of this (Arctic, Antarctic, Atlantic, Indian, Pacific); sea.—oeeanio (ō-shi-an-ik, ō-si-an'-ik) *a.* pert. to ocean.—oeeanog'raphy *n.* scientific description of ocean phenomena.—oeeanog'rapher *n.*,—oeeanograph'ie, oeeanograph'ical *a.*—oeeanol'ogy *n.* branch of science which relates to the ocean.

ocelot (ō'-se-lot) *n.* S. Amer. quadruped of leopard family.

ochre (ō'-ker) *n.* natural earths used as yellow, brown, etc. pigments.—o'ohr(e)ous, o'ohry *a.*

oct-, octa-, octo- (okt, ok'-ta, ok'-to) *prefix* fr. Gk. *okto*, eight, combining to form derivatives.—oe'tagon *n.* plane figure with 8 sides and 8 angles.—oetag'onal *a.*—oetahe'dron *n.* solid figure with 8 plane faces.—oetahe'dral *a.*—oe'tane *n.* (*Chem.*) hydrocarbon of the paraffin series, found in petroleum.—oetang'ular *a.* having 8 angles.—oe'tant *n.* eighth part of circle; instrument for measuring angles, with arc of 45°.

octave (ok'-tāv) *n.* week following celebration of principal Church festival; day falling week after festival; stanza of 8 lines; (*Mus.*) interval of 8 diatonic notes comprising complete scale; note 8 tones above or below another; group of 8.

octavo (ok-tā'-vō) *n.* size of sheet of paper folded three times, thus making 8 leaves (average size = 6" × 9½''); hence, book having 8 leaves to the sheet—(*abbrev.*) 8vo.

octet (ok-tet') *n.* (*Mus.*) group of 8 musicians or singers; composition for such group; first 8 lines of sonnet.

October (ok-tō'-ber) *n.* tenth month.

octogenarian (ok-tō-je-nā'-ri-an) *a.* and *n.* (one) between 80 and 90 years of age.

octopus (ok'-to-pus) *n.* mollusc with 8 arms or tentacles covered with suckers.

ocular (ok'-ū-lar) *a.* pert. to eye, or to sight; visual;—*n.* eye-piece of optical instrument.—oe'ulist *n.* eye-surgeon.

odd (od) *a.* not even; not divisible by two; left over after round number has been taken; extra; surplus; casual; occasional; out-of-the-way; queer or eccentric; strange.—odd'ly *n.* peculiarity; queer person or thing.—odd'ly *adv.*—odd'ment *n.* something left over; part of broken set; remnant.—odd'ness *n.* state of being odd.—odds *n.pl.* difference in favour of one as against another; inequality; advantage or superiority; ratio by which one person's bet exceeds another's; likelihood or probability.—**Oddfellow**, member of a friendly society.

ode (ōd) *n.* orig. poem intended to be sung; now, lyric poem of exalted tone.

odium (ō'-di-um) *n.* hatred; general abhorrence; stigma.—o'dious *a.* hateful; offensive.—o'diously *adv.*—o'diousness *n.*

odour (ō'-dur) *n.* smell; fragrance; perfume; repute or estimation.—odorif'erous *a.* sweet-scented; (*Colloq.*) having strong or unpleasant smell.—odorif'erously *adv.*—odorif'erousness *n.*—o'dourless *a.*—o'dorous *a.* scented.—o'dorously *adv.*—o'dorousness *n.*

oecumenic, oecumenical (ek-ū-men'-ik, -i-kal) *a.* relating to whole Christian world or church; universal; world-wide.

oedema (ē-dēm'-a) *n.* dropsical swelling.—oedematous *a.*

oesophagus (ē-sof'-a-gus) *n.* (*Anat.*) gullet.—osophag'eal *a.*

of (ov, uv) *prep.* belonging to; from; proceeding from; relating to; concerning.

off (of) *adv.* away; in general, denotes removal or separation, also completion, as in *to finish off*:—*prep.* not on; away from;—*a.* distant; on farther side; discontinued; free;—

interj. begone! depart!—**off'ing** *n.* more distant part of sea visible to an observer.—**off'-chance** *n.* slight chance.—**off colour**, out of condition; indisposed.—**off-hand'** *a.* without preparation; free and easy;—*adv.* impromptu.—**off'-licence** *n.* permission to sell alcoholic liquors for consumption off the premises only.—**off-peak** *a.* pert. to slack as opposed to busy period.—**off'set** *n.* side-branch; sum set off against another as an equivalent; compensation; (*Print.*) smudging of clean sheet; process in lithography;—*v.t.* counterbalance or compensate.—**off'shoot** *n.* that which shoots off from main branch or channel; descendant.—**off-side'** *a.* (*Football, etc.*) of player, being in such a position that he may not, under penalty, touch ball himself nor interfere with an opponent or with play.—**off'spring** *n.* children; issue.—**off and on**, intermittently.

offal (of'-ąl) *n.* waste meat; entrails of animals; anything thrown away as worthless; refuse.

offence (o-fens') *n.* sin; crime; insult; wrong; resentment.—**offens'ive** *a.* causing or giving offence; used in attack; insulting;—*n.* attack; onset.—**offens'ively** *adv.*—**offens'iveness** *n.*

offend (o-fend') *v.t.* displease; wound feelings of;—*v.i.* do wrong; sin.—**offend'er** *n.*

offer (of'-ęr) *v.t.* present for acceptance or refusal; tender; bid, as a price; propose; attempt; express readiness to do;—*v.i.* present itself or to occur;—*n.* price bid; tender; proposal, esp. of marriage.—**off'ering** *n.* that which is offered.—**off'erer** *n.*

offertory (of'-ęr-tor-i) *n.* part of mass during which elements are offered up; collection during service.

office (of'-is) *n.* duty; service; function; official position; form of worship; religious service; place for doing business.—**off'ices** *n.pl.* parts of house in which domestic work is done, e.g. kitchens, stables, etc.; outhouses; act of kindness; help.—**off'icer** *n.* person who holds official position; one who holds commissioned rank in navy, army, airforce, etc.—**off'ice-bear'er** *n.* one who holds office, esp. in society or club.

official (of-ish'-ąl) *a.* pert. to office; authorised;—*n.* one holding office, esp. in public body.—**offic'ially** *adv.*—**offic'ialdom** *n.* officials collectively; their work, usually derogatively meant.

officiate (o-fish'-i-āt) *v.i.* perform duties of office; perform divine service.

officious (o-fish'-us) *a.* given to exaggerate the duties of office; meddlesome. — **offic'iously** *adv.* — **offic'iousness** *n.*

often (of'-n) *adv.* frequently.—(*Arch.*) **oft**, **oft'entimes**, *adv.*

ogle (ō'-gl) *v.i.* make eyes;—*v.t.* cast amorous glances at;—*n.* amorous glance.—**o'gler** *n.*

ogre (ō-gęr) *n.* (*fem.* o'gress) fabulous man-eating giant.—o'greish, o'grish *a.*

ohm (ōm) *n.* standard unit of electrical resistance.—**ohm'meter** *n.* instrument for measuring electrical current and resistance.

oil (oil) *n.* one of several kinds of light viscous liquids, obtained from plants, animal substances, and minerals, used as lubricants, illuminants, fuel, medicines, etc.;—*v.t.* apply oil to;—*v.i.* take oil aboard as fuel.—**oil'er** *n.*—**oil'y** *a.* consisting of, or resembling, oil; greasy; fawning;—**oil'ily** *adv.*—**oil'iness** *n.*—**oils** *n.pl.* (*Paint.*) short for 'oil-colours.'—**oil'cake** *n.* cake of compressed linseed, used as cattle-food.—**oil'can** *n.* can, fitted with tube, for oiling machinery.—**oil'cloth** *n.* kind of linoleum. — **oil'-col'ours** *n.pl.* (*Paint.*) colours made by grinding pigments in oil.—**oil'-field** *n.* region rich in mineral oil.—**oil'-paint'ing** *n.* one done in oil-colours.—**oil'skin** *n.* cloth made waterproof with oil;—*pl.* overcoat of this material.—**oil'-well** *n.* boring made in district yielding petroleum.

ointment (oint'-ment) *n.* unguent; soft, fatty substance for healing or beautifying the skin.

okapi (o-kä'-pē) *n.* African animal of giraffe family.

okay (ō-kā') *a.* and *adv.* abbrev. to O.K., expression signifying approval.

old (ōld) *a.* advanced in age; having lived or existed long; belonging to earlier period; not new or fresh; stale; out of date.—**old'en** *a.* old; ancient; pert. to past.—**old'ish** *a.* somewhat old.—**old'ness** *n.*—**old'fash'ioned** *a.* out of date; not modern.—**Old Harry**, devil; Satan.—**old maid**, elderly spinster; (*Cards*) round game.—**old man's beard**, wild clematis.—**old master**, old painting by famous artist, esp. of 15th and 16th cents.—**Old Nick**, devil.—**old style**, Julian calendar method (before 1752) of reckoning time.—**Old Testament**, first division of Bible.—**Old World**, Eastern hemisphere.

oleander (ō-lē-an'-dęr) *n.* evergreen rose-bay.

olfaction (ol-fak'-shun) *n.* smelling; sense of smell.—**olfac'tory** *a.* pert. to smelling.

oligarchy (ol'-i-gär-ki) *n.* government in which supreme power rests with a few.—**ol'igarch** *n.* member of oligarchy.—**oligarchal** (ol-i-gär'-kąl) *a.* Also **oligar'chie(al)**.

olive (ol'-iv) *n.* evergreen tree in Mediterranean countries; its oval, oil-yielding fruit; colour, of greyish, ashy green;—*a.* of the colour of unripe olive, or of the foliage.—**olivaceous** (o-liv-ā'-shus) *a.* olive-green.—**ol'ive-branch** *n.* emblem or offer of peace.

Olympia (ō-lim'-pi-ạ) (*Class. Hist.*) plain in ancient Greece, scene of Olympic Games.—**Olymp'iad** *n.* name given to period of four years between each celebration of Olympic Games.—**Olym'pic** *a.*—**Olym'pics** *n.pl.*

ombre (om'-bẹr) *n.* old card game.

ombudsman (om'-buds-mạn) *n.* official appointed to investigate complaints against official bodies.

omega (ō'-me-gạ) *n.* last letter of Greek alphabet; hence, the end.—**the alpha and omega,** beginning and end.

omelette, omelet (om'-ẹ-let) *n.* dish of eggs beaten up with water or milk and seasonings and cooked in frying-pan.

omen (ō'-men) *n.* sign of future event; foreboding;—*v.t.* fore-shadow by means of signs; augur; predict.

ominous (om'-i-nus) *a.* threatening; inauspicious.—**om'inously** *adv.*—**om'inousness** *n.*

omit (ō-mit') *v.t.* leave out; neglect;—*pr.p.* omit'ting;—*pa.p.* and *pa.t.* omit'ted;—*n.*—**omission** (ō-mish'-un) *n.* neglect; failure to do; that which is omitted or left undone.—**omiss'ible** *a.*—**omiss'ive** *a.* to send.

omnibus (om'-ni-bus) *n.* large, four-wheeled, horse-drawn, public vehicle; later, motor-bus.—(*abbrev.*) bus;—*a.* used in sense of 'several in one,' e.g. **omnibus** volume, book containing several works originally published separately; anthology.

omnipotent (om-nip'-o-tent) *a.* all-powerful, esp. of God; almighty.—**omnip'otently** *adv.*—**omnip'otence** *n.* unlimited power.

omnipresent (om-ni-prez'-ent) *a.* present in all places at same time.—**omnipres'ence** *n.*

omniscience (om-nish'-i-ens) *n.* infinite knowledge.—**omnis'ient** *a.*

omnivorous (om-niv'-ō-rus) *a.* all-devouring; eating every kind of food.—**omniv'orously** *adv.*

on (on) *prep.* above and touching; in addition to; following from; referring to; at; near; towards, etc.;—*adv.* so as to be on; forwards.

once (wuns) *adv.* at one time; formerly; ever;—*n.* one time.—**at once,** immediately.

oncoming (on'-kum-ing) *a.* approaching;—*n.* approach.

oncost (on'-kost) *n.* charges borne by a firm, exclusive of salaries and wages.

one (wun) *a.* lowest cardinal number; single; undivided; only; without others; identical;—*n.* figure 1;

unity; single specimen;—*pron.* particular but not stated person; any person.—**one'ness** *n.* unity; uniformity; singleness.—**one'self** *pron.* one's own self or person.—**one'-horse** *a.* drawn by one horse; (*Colloq.*) of no importance; insignificant.—**one-sid'ed** *a.* esp. of game, etc., limited to one side; considering one side only; partial; unfair.—**one'-way** *a.* denoting system of traffic circulation in one direction.

onerous (on'-ẹr-us) *a.* burdensome; oppressive.—**on'erously** *adv.*—**on'erousness** *n.*

ongoing (on'-gō-ing) *n.* going on; advance; procedure.

onion (un'-yun) *n.* edible, bulbous plant with pungent odour used as vegetable and flavouring.—**on'iony** *a.*

onlooker (on'-lóókẹr) *n.* spectator.

only (ōn'-li) *a.* single; sole;—*adv.* solely; singly; merely; exclusively;—*conj.* but then; except that; with this reservation.

onomatopoeia (on-ō-mat-ō-pē'-yạ) *n.* formation of word by using sounds that resemble or suggest object or action to be named.—**onomatopoe'ic** *a.*

onset (on'-set) *n.* violent attack; assault.

onslaught (on'-slawt) *n.* attack; onset.

onto (on'-tóó) *prep.* upon; on the top; on to.

onus (ō'-nus) *n.* burden; responsibility.

onward (on'-wạrd) *a.* and *adv.* advancing; forward.—**on'wards** *adv.* direction; ahead.

onyx (on'-iks) *n.* variety of quartz, in coloured layers, used for making cameos.

ooze (óóz) *n.* soft mud or slime; gentle flow; kind of deposit on bottom of sea;—*v.i.* flow gently; leak or percolate;—*v.t.* exude or give out slowly.—**ooz'y** *a.* slimy; muddy; miry.

opal (ō'-pạl) *n.* a mineral much used as gem.—**opales'cent** *a.* of changing iridescent colour, like opal.—**opalese'ence** *n.*—**o'paline** *a.* like opal;—*n.* semi-transparent white glass.

opaque (ō-pāk') *a.* not transparent; impenetrable to sight; dull-witted.—**opaqu'ely** *adv.*—**opaqu'eness** *n.*—**opa'city** *n.* opaqueness; obscurity.

open (ō'-pn) *a.* not shut or blocked up; allowing passage in or out; not fenced; without restrictions; available; exposed; frank and sincere;—*n.* unobstructed space;—*v.t.* set open; uncover; give access to; begin; cut or break into;—*v.i.* become open; begin; (*Theat.*) have first performance.—**o'pener** *n.*—**o'pening** *a.* first in order; initial;—*n.* hole or gap; open or cleared space;

opportunity; beginning. — **o'penly** *adv.* frankly.—**o'penness** *n.*—**o'pen-cast** *a.* (*Mining*) excavated from surface.—**o'pen-hand'ed** *a.* generous, liberal.—**o'pen-heart'ed** *a.* frank.—**o'pen-mind'ed** *a.* free from prejudices.

opera (op'-e-rạ) *n.* musical drama; theatre where opera is performed.—**operat'ic** *a.* pert. to opera.—**operet'ta** *n.* short light opera.—**grand opera,** opera in which no spoken dialogue is permitted.—**opera bouffe** (bóóf) farcical play set to music.—**op'era-glass** (or **glass'es**) *n.* small binocular used in theatres.—**op'era-hat** *n.* man's collapsible tall hat.

operate (op'-e-rāt) *v.t.* cause to function; effect;—*v.i.* work; produce effect; exert power; perform act of surgery; deal in stocks and shares.—**opera'tion** *n.* act of operating; method or mode of action; treatment involving surgical skill; movement of army or fleet.—**opera'tional** *a.* pert. to operations; in working order.—**op'erative** *a.* having the power of acting; exerting force; efficacious; —*n.* artisan or workman; factory-hand.—**op'erator** *n.*

ophthalmia (of-thal'-mi-ạ) *n.* (*Med.*) inflammation of eye.—**ophthal'mic** *a.* pert. to eye.—**ophthal'mist, ophthalmol'ogist** *n.* one skilled in the study of the eye.

opiate (ō'-pi-ăt) *n.* preparation of opium; narcotic;—*a.* containing opium; inducing sleep.

opine (ō-pīn') *v.t.* and *i.* to think.

opinion (ō-pin'-yun) *n.* judgment or belief; estimation; statement by expert.—**opin'ionated** *a.* dogmatic.—**opin'ionative** *a.* stubborn.—**opin'ionatively** *adv.*—**opin'ionativeness** *n.*

opium (ō'-pi-um) *n.* narcotic juice of kind of poppy.

opossum (ō-pos'-um) *n.* small American marsupial animal. Also **pos'sum.**

opponent (o-pō'-nent) *a.* opposite; opposing; antagonistic;—*n.* one who opposes.

opportune (op-or'tūn') *a.* well-timed;—**opportun'ely** *adv.*—**opportune'ness** *n.*—**opportun'ism** *n.* policy of doing what is expedient at the time.—**opportun'ist** *n.*—**opportun'ity** *n.* convenient time; good chance.

oppose (o-pōz') *v.t.* set against; resist; compete with.—**oppos'able** *a.*—**oppos'er** *n.*

opposite (op'-o-zit) *a.* contrary facing; situated in front; adverse; contrary; diametrically different;—*n.* contrary;—*prep.* and *adv.* in front of; on the other side.—**opp'ositely** *adv.* facing each other.—**opp'ositeness** *n.*—**opposition** (op-o-zish'-un) *n.* state of being opposite; resistance; contradiction; obstacle; party opposed to that in power

oppress (o-pres') *v.t.* govern with tyranny; treat severely.—**oppression** (o-presh'-un) *n.* harshness; severity; tyranny.—**oppres'sive** *a.* hard to bear.—**oppres'sively** *adv.*—**oppres'iveness** *n.*—**oppres'or** *n.*

opprobrium (o-prō'-bri-um) *n.* reproach; disgrace; infamy.—**oppro'brious** *a.* shameful.—**opprobriously** *adv.*—**oppro'briousness** *n.*

opt (opt) *v.i.* make a choice; choose.—**optative** (op-tā'-tiv, op'-tạ-tiv) *a.* expressing wish.—**op'tatively** *adv.*

optic (op'-tic) *a.* pert. to eye or sight; pert. to optics.—**op'tics** *n.* science which deals with light and its relation to sight.—**op'tical** *a.* pert. to vision; visual.—**op'tically** *adv.*—**optician** (op-tish'-ạn) *n.* one skilled in optics; maker of, or dealer in, optical instruments, esp. spectacles.

optimism (op'-ti-mizm) *n.* disposition to look on bright side.—**op'timist** *n.* believer in optimism; one who takes hopeful view.—**optimis'tical** *a.*—**optimis'tically** *adv.*

option (op'-shun) *n.* choice.—**op'tional** *a.* left to one's free choice.—**op'tionally** *adv.*

opulent (op'-ū-lent) *a.* wealthy;—**op'ulently** *adv.*—**op'ulence** *n.* wealth.

opus (ō'-pus) *n.* work; musical composition;—*pl.* **opera** (op'-e-rạ).

or (or) *conj.* introducing alternative; if not.

oracle (or'-ạ-kl) *n.* medium by which divine utterances were transmitted, often priest or priestess; shrine where ancient Greeks consulted deity; response given, often obscure; person of outstanding wisdom.—**orac'ular** *a.* authoritative; ambiguous; forecasting the future.—**orac'ularly** *adv.*

oral (ō'-rạl) *a.* spoken; not written; using speech; pert. to mouth.—**o'rally** *adv.*

orange (or'-ạnj) *n.* juicy, gold-coloured fruit; tree bearing it; reddish yellow colour;—*a.* reddish yellow in colour. — **or'angery** *n.* plantation of orange-trees.

orang-outang, orang-utan (ō-rang'-óó-tang', ō'-rang-óó'-tan) *n.* large man-like ape.

orate (ō-rāt') *v.i.* talk loftily; harangue.—**oration** (ō-rā'-shun) *n.* dignified public discourse.—**or'ator** *n.* one who delivers oration; one distinguished for gift of public speaking.—**orator'ical** *a.*—**orator'ically** *adv.*—**oratorio** (or-ạ-tō'-ri-ō) *n.* sort of sacred musical drama.—**or'atory** *n.* art of speaking in public; rhetorical skill; eloquence; chapel or small room for private devotions.

orb (orb) *n.* circle; sphere or globe; heavenly body; globe surmounted by cross, which forms part of regalia; (*Poet.*) eye. — **or'bit** *n.* (*Astron.*) path traced by one heavenly body in its revolution round another, by spacecraft circling the earth, or by aircraft circling a point; (*Fig.*) range of influence or action; eye-socket.—**or'bital** *a.*

orchard (or'-chẹrd) *n.* garden or enclosure containing fruit-trees.

orchestra (or'-kes-trẹ) *n.* space in theatre occupied by musicians; band of performers on musical instruments. — **orches'tral** *a.* — **or'chestrate** *v.t.* arrange music for performance by orchestra.—**orchestra'tion** *n.*

orchid, orchis (or'-kid, or'-kis) *n.* genus of plants with fantastically-shaped flowers.

ordain (or-dān') *v.t.* decree; enact; destine; appoint; admit to Christian ministry; confer holy orders upon. —**ordina'tion** *n.* act of ordaining or decreeing; admission to Christian ministry.

ordeal (or'-dē-ạl, or'-dēl) *n.* ancient method of trial by dangerous physical test; trying experience; test of endurance.

order (or'-dẹr) *n.* rank; class; group; regular arrangement; sequence; succession; method; regulation; command; mode of procedure; monastic society; one of the five styles of architecture; sub-division of class of plants or animals, made up of genera; honour conferred for distinguished services; instructions, by customer, of goods to be supplied; —*v.t.* arrange; command; require; regulate; systematise; give order for.—**or'derly** *a.* methodical; tidy; peaceable; (*Mil.*) of a junior officer, on duty to supervise daily routine; —*n.* soldier following officer to carry orders; in military hospital, soldier-attendant;—*adv.* in right order.—**or'derliness** *n.*—holy orders, generally, ordination to Christian ministry.—**to take orders**, accept instructions; (*Church*) be ordained. —**in order to**, for the purpose of.

ordinance (or'-din-ạns) *n.* established rule, religious rite, or ceremony; decree.

ordinary (or'-di-nạ-ri) *a.* usual; regular; habitual; normal; plain;— *n.* church-service book; time and place.—**or'dinarily** *adv.*

ordnance (ord'-nạns) *n.* collective term for heavy mounted guns; military stores.—**ordnance survey**, Government department which prepares official maps.

ore (ōr) *n.* native mineral from which metal is extracted.

organ (or'-gạn) *n.* musical instrument of pipes worked by bellows and played by keys; keyboard instrument simulating pipe organ by means of electronic oscillations; member of animal or plant exercising a special function.—**organ'ic** *a.* pert. to or

affecting bodily organs; having either animal or vegetable life; derived from living organisms; systematic; organised.—**organ'ically** *adv.*—**or'ganism** *n.* organised body; living body.—**or'ganist** *n.* player on organ.—**or'gan-grinder** *n.* player on barrel-organ.—**or'gan-loft** *n.* gallery for organ.—**or'gan-stop** *n.* series of pipes of uniform tone; one of series of knobs for controlling them.— **organic chemistry**, branch of chemistry dealing with compounds of carbon.

organdie (or'-gạn-di) *n.* transparent muslin.

organise (or'-gạ-nīz) *v.t.* furnish with organs; give definite structure; prepare for transaction of business; put into working order; unite in a society.—**organis'able** *a.*—**organisa'tion** *n.* act of organising; individuals systematically united for some work; society.—**or'ganiser** *n.*

orgasm (or'-gazm) *n.* extreme excitement, esp. sexual.—**orgas'tic** *a.*

orgy (or'-ji) *n.* drunken or licentious revel; debauch.—*pl.* orgies (or'-jiz).

oriel (ō'-ri-ẹl) *n.* projecting window; recess in room formed by such a window.

orient (ō'-ri-ẹnt) *a.* eastern; lustrous (applied to pearls);—*n.* east; Eastern countries;—*v.t.* place so as to face east; determine position of, with respect to east; take one's bearings. —**orien'tal** *a.* eastern; pert. to east; —*n.* Asiatic.—**o'rientate** *v.t.* and *i.* orient; bring into clearly understood relations.—**orienta'tion** *n.* act of determining east; sense of direction. —**orienteering** *n.* sport which involves running or ambling across country with a map and compass.

orifice (or'-i-fis) *n.* mouth or small opening.

origin (or'-i-jin) *n.* beginning; source; birth; nationality.—**original** (or-ij'-in-ạl) *a.* earliest; first; new, not copied or derived; thinking or acting for oneself;—*n.* model; pattern.—**orig'inally** *adv.*—**original'ity** *n.* initiative.—**orig'inate** *v.t.* bring into being;—*v.i.* begin; arise.—**origina'tive** *a.*—**origina'tion** *n.*—**orig'inator** *n.*

oriole (ō'-ri-ōl) *n.* brightly-coloured bird of thrush family.

ormolu (or'-mo-lōō) *n.* alloy of copper, zinc and tin, resembling gold; gilded bronze; preparation of gold-leaf used for gilding furniture.

ornament (or'-nạ-ment) *n.* decoration; any object to adorn or decorate;—*v.t.* adorn; beautify; embellish. —**ornament'al** *a.*—**ornament'ally** *adv.* —**ornamenta'tion** *n.* decoration.— **ornate'** *a.* richly decorated.—**ornate'ly** *adv.*—**ornate'ness** *n.*

ornitho- (or'-ni-tho) *prefix fr.* Gk. *ornis, ornithos,* bird, used in derivatives.—**ornithol'ogy** n. scientific study of birds.—**ornitholog'ical** a.—**ornithol'ogist** n.

orography, orology (or-og'-rạ-fi, or-ol'-o-ji) n. branch of physical geography dealing with mountains. —**orograph'ical, orolo'gical** a.

orphan (or'-fạn) n. and a. child bereft of one or both parents;—v.t. make an orphan.—**or'phanage** n. institution for orphans.—**or'phanhood** n.

orris (or'-is) n. kind of iris.—**orr'is-root** n. dried root, used in perfumery and medicine.

orthodox (or'-tho-doks) a. sound in opinions or doctrine; conventional. — **or'thodoxly** adv. — **or'thodoxy** n. soundness of faith, esp. in religion.

orthography (or-thog'-rạ-fi) n. correct spelling. — **orthog'rapher** n. — **orthograph'ic, orthograph'ical** a. — **orthograph'ically** adv.

orthopaedia (or-thō-pē'-di-ạ) n. treatment and cure of bone defects esp. in children. Also **orthop(a)e'dy.**—**orthopae'dic** a.—**orthopae'dics** n. surgery dealing with correction and cure of bone defects.—**orthopae'dist** n.

orthoptics (or-thop'-tiks) n. (Med.) theory and practice of remedial treatment for eye-muscle defects.

oscillate (os'-i-lāt) v.i. swing to and fro; vibrate; (Radio) set up wave motion in a circuit.—**oscilla'tion** n. pendulum-like motion; variation between extremes.—**os'cillator** n.— **os'cillatory** a.—**oscill'ograph** n. cathode ray tube for displaying waveforms.

osculate (os'-kū-lāt) v.t. and i. kiss. —**oscula'tion** n. kissing.—**os'culatory** a. pert. to kissing.

osier (ō-zi-ẹr) n. species of willow, used in basket-making; willow-branch.

osmosis (os-mō'-sis) n. (Chem.) tendency of fluid substances, if separated by porous membrane, to filter through it and become equally diffused. Also **os'mose.**—**osmot'ic** a.

osprey (os'-prā) n. fish-eating hawk.

oss- (os) prefix fr. L. os, ossis, bone, used in many derivatives.—**osseous** (os'-ē-us) a. pert. to bone; bony.—**oss'icle** n. small bone.—**ossif'erous** a. containing, or yielding, bones.—**ossifica'tion** n. hardening into bone. —**oss'ify** v.t. harden into bone;—v.i. become bone, of cartilage, etc.

ossifrage (os'-i-frāj) n. sea-eagle.

ostensible (os-ten'-si-bl) a. plausible; pretended; apparent.—**osten'sibly** adv. —**ostensibil'ity** n.

ostentation (os-ten-tā'-shun) n. vainglorious display; showing off.—**ostenta'tious** a. fond of display.—**ostenta'tiously** adv.—**ostenta'tiousness** n.

osteo- (os'-te-o) prefix fr. Gk. osteon, bone, used in derivatives, mainly medical.—**os'teo-arthri'tis** n. chronic inflammation of a joint.—**os'teoid** a. resembling bone. — **osteol'ogy** n. branch of anatomy dealing with bones.—**osteol'ogist** n.

osteopathy (os-te-o'-pạth-i) n. manipulative surgery.—**os'teopath** n. practitioner of this.—**osteopath'ic** a.

ostler (os'-lẹr) n. stableman at inn; groom. Same as **host'ler.**

ostracise (os'-trạ-sīz) v.t. exclude from society; boycott.—**ostracism** n. exclusion from society; social boycotting.

ostrich (os'-trich) n. large flightless bird.

other (uTH'-ẹr) a. and pron. not this; not the same; different; opposite; additional;—adv. otherwise.—**oth'erwise** adv. differently; in another way; —conj. else; if not.—**oth'erwhere** adv. elsewhere.—**every other,** every second (one); each alternate.

otitis (ō-tī'-tis) n. inflammation of ear.

otter (ot'-ẹr) n. fish-eating animal of weasel family.

Ottoman (ot'-o-man) a. pert. to Turks;—n. Turk; kind of divan without back or arms.

oubliette (óó-blē-et') n. underground dungeon.

ought (awt) auxil. v. be bound by moral obligation or duty.

ought (awt) n. form of 'nought'; nothing.

ounce (ouns) n. unit of weight, abbrev. oz.; in avoirdupois weight = $\frac{1}{16}$ of pound; in troy weight = $\frac{1}{12}$ of pound.

ounce (ouns) n. snow leopard.

our (our) a. belonging to us.—**ours** poss. pron. used in place of our with noun.—**ourselves** pron. pl. we.

oust (oust) v.t. put out; expel.

out (out) adv. on, at, or to, the outside; from within; from among; away; not in usual or right place; not at home; in bloom; disclosed; at a loss; on strike; unemployed;— a. outlying; remote;—prep. outside; out of;—interj. away! begone!—v.t. put out; knock out;—**out'er** a. being on the outside; away from the inside;—n. on target, ring farthest from the centre; shot recorded there.—**out'ermost, out'most** a. on extreme outside—**outer space** n. the universe outside the solar system.

outbalance (out-bal'-ạns) v.t. exceed in weight; be heavier than.

outbid (out-bid') v.t. bid more than; offer higher price.—pr.p. **outbid'ding.** —pa.p. **outbid'** or **outbid'den.**—pa.t. **outbid'.**

outboard (out'-bōrd) a. projecting beyond and outside hull of ship, e.g. of ladder; also, of detachable motor-engine fixed to stern of small-boat.

outbreak (out'-brāk) n. sudden

breaking out; burst, esp. of anger; beginning, esp. of epidemic or war.

outbuilding (out'-bild-ing) n. outhouse.

outburst (out'-burst) n. bursting out, esp. of anger, laughter, cheering, etc.

outcast (out'-cast) a. cast out as useless;—n. one rejected by society.

outclass (out-klas') v.t. surpass.

outcome (out'-kum) n. issue; result.

outcrop (out'-krop) n. coming out of stratum of rock, coal, etc., to surface of the ground.—**outcrop coal**, surface-coal.

outcry (out'-kri) n. loud cry; cry of distress, etc.

outdistance (out-dis'-tans) v.t. surpass in speed; get ahead of.

outdo (out-dōō') v.t. excel; surpass.

outdoor (out'-dōr) a. out of doors; in open air.—**out'doors** adv. outside.

outfit (out'-fit) n. supply of things required for any purpose; equipment; kit;—v.t. supply with equipment, etc.—**out'fitter** n. one who supplies clothes.

outflank (out-flangk') v.t. (Mil.) succeed in getting beyond flank of the enemy; (Fig.) outwit.

outgo (out-gō') v.t. go beyond;—n. (out'-gō) expenditure; outlay.—**out'-going** n. going out; expenditure;—a. departing.

outgrow (out-grō') v.t. surpass in growth; become too large or old for; grow out of.—**out'growth** n. offshoot.

outhouse (out'-hous) n. small building not attached to main house.

outing (out'-ing) n. excursion; trip.

outlandish (out'-land'-ish) a. remote; foreign; barbarous; queer; fantastic.

outlaw (out'-law) n. one beyond protection of the law; bandit;—v.t. declare to be outlaw.—**out'lawry** n.

outlay (out'-lā) n. expenditure; expenses.

outlet (out'-let) n. passage or way out; (Fig.) source of recreation.

outline (out'-lin) n. lines that bound a figure; boundary; sketch without details; rough draft; general plan;—v.t. draw in outline; sketch; summarise.

outlive (out-liv') v.t. live longer than.

outlook (out'-look) n. prospect; person's point of view.

outlying (out'-li-ing) a. remote; isolated.

outmoded (out-mō'-ded) a. out of fashion.

outnumber (out-num'-ber) v.t. exceed in number.

out-patient (out'-pā'-shent) n. patient who comes to hospital, infirmary, etc., for treatment but is non-resident.

outpost (out'-pōst) n. (Mil.) detachment on guard some distance from main body.

outpour (out-pōr') v.t. pour out;

flow over.—**out'pour, out'pouring** n. overflow.

output (out'-pōōt) n. production; amount of goods produced in given time.

outrage (out'-rāj) n. excessive violence; violation of others' rights; gross insult;—v.t. do grievous wrong or violence to; insult grossly; shock.—**outrageous** (out-rā'-jus) a. violent; atrocious.—**outra'geously** adv.

outride (out'rid') v.t. ride faster than; ride farther than; (Naut.) of ship, live through storm.—pa.p. outrid'den.—pa.t. outrode'.—out'rider n. servant on horseback who rides beside carriage.

outrun (out-run') v.t. exceed in speed; run farther than; run faster than.

outset (out'-set) n. beginning; start.

outside (out-sīd') n. outer surface; exterior; farthest limit;—a. pert. to outer part; exterior; external; outdoor;—adv. not inside; out of doors; in open air;—prep. on outer part of; beyond.—**outsi'der** n. one not belonging to particular party, set, etc.; horse considered to have no chance of winning particular race.

outsize (out'-siz) a. and n. larger than normal size, esp. of garments.

outskirt (out'-skert) n. generally in pl. out'skirts, outer skirt; border; suburbs of town.

outspoken (out-spō'-kn) a. not afraid to speak aloud one's opinions; bold of speech.

outstanding (out-stand'-ing) a. standing out; prominent; conspicuous; of debts, unpaid.

outstrip (out-strip') v.t. surpass in speed.

outward (out'-ward) a. pert. to outside; external;—adv. towards outside.—**out'wards** adv. outward.—**out'wardly** adv. externally.

outwit (out-wit') v.t. defeat by cunning.

ouzel (ōō'-zl) n. bird of thrush family.

ova (ō'-va) n.pl. eggs; female germ-cells.—**o'vary** n. one of two reproductive organs in female animal in which ova are formed and developed.—pl. o'varies.—**ovarial, ova'rian** (ō-vā'-ri-al, -an) a.

oval (ō'-val) a. egg-shaped; elliptical;—n. oval figure or thing.

ovation (ō-vā'-shun) n. enthusiastic burst of applause; triumphant reception.

oven (uv'-n) n. iron box or enclosed chamber in stove, range, etc., for baking or heating.

over (ō'-ver) prep. above; on; upon; more than; in excess of; across; from side to side of; throughout; etc.;—adv. above; above and beyond; too much; past; finished; across;—a. upper; outer; covering;

—*n.* (*Cricket*) number of balls delivered from each end alternately. —o'verall *a.* inclusive.

overall (ō'-ver-awl) *n.* garment worn for protection. Also *n. pl.*

overawe (ō-ver-aw') *v.t.* restrain by fear; daunt.

overbear (ō-ver-bār') *v.t.* bear down; repress.—**overbear'ing** *a.* domineering; bullying.

overboard (ō'-ver-bōrd) *adv.* over side of ship; out of ship into water.

overcast (ō-ver-kast') *v.t.* cloud; darken.—o'vercast *a.* cloudy.

overcharge (ō-ver-chárj') *v.t.* and *i.* load too heavily; charge at too high a price.

overcoat (ō'-ver-kōt) *n.* outdoor garment for men; greatcoat; topcoat.

overcome (ō-ver-kum') *v.t.* and *i.* conquer.

overdo (ō-ver-dōō') *v.t.* do too much; fatigue; exaggerate.—**overdone'** *a.* exaggerated;—*pa.t.* overdid'.

overdose (ō-ver-dōs') *v.t.* give excessive dose;—*n.* too great a dose.

overdraw (ō-ver-draw') *v.t.* and *i.* exaggerate; draw money in excess of one's credit.—o'verdraft *n.*

overdue (ō-ver-dū') *a.* unpaid at right time; not having arrived at right time.

overestimate (ō-ver-es'-ti-māt) *v.t.* estimate too highly.

overflow (ō-ver-flō') *v.t.* flow over; flood;—*v.i.* flow over edge, bank, etc.—o'verflow *n.* what flows over; flood; excess; pipe for surplus water.

overgrow (ō-ver-grō') *v.t.* grow beyond; cover with growth;—*v.i.* grow beyond normal size.—overgrown (ō-ver-grōn') *a.* covered with grass, weeds, etc.—o'vergrowth *n.*

overhaul (ō-ver-hawl') *v.t.* examine thoroughly and set in order; overtake in pursuit.—o'verhaul *n.* thorough examination, esp. for repairs; repair.

overhead (ō'-ver-hed) *a.* and *adv.* over the head; above; aloft; in sky. —**overhead charges, costs, overheads,** permanent expenses of running a business, over and above cost of manufacturing and of raw materials.

overhear (ō-ver-hēr') *v.t.* hear by accident.—*pa.p.* and *pa.t.* overheard'.

overlap (ō-ver-lap') *v.t.* and *i.* lap over; rest upon and extend beyond.

overlay (ō-ver-lā') *v.t.* spread over.

overleaf (ō'-ver-lēf) *adv.* on next page.

overlie (ō-ver-lī') *v.t.* lie on top of; smother baby by lying on it in bed.

overlook (ō-ver-look') *v.t.* look over; inspect; fail to notice; pardon.

overlord (ō'-ver-lord) *n.* one who is lord over another; feudal superior.

overnight (ō-ver-nīt) *adv.* through and during night.

overpower (ō-ver-pou'-er) *v.t.* conquer by superior strength; subdue; crush.

overrate (ō-ver-rāt') *v.t.* put too high a value on; assess too highly.

overreach (ō-ver-rēch') *v.t.* reach beyond.

override (ō-ver-rīd') *v.t.* ride over; ride too much; set aside; cancel.— *pa.p.* overrid'den.—*pa.t.* overrode'.

overrule (ō-ver-rōōl')*v.t.* rule against or over; set aside by superior authority.

overrun (ō-ver-run') *v.t.* run over; grow over, e.g. as weeds; take possession.

oversea, overseas (ō'-ver-sē, -sēz) *a.* and *adv.* from or to a country over sea; abroad.

oversee (ō-ver-sē') *v.t.* inspect; superintend; supervise.—overse'er (sē'-er) *n.* superintendent; supervisor.

overshadow (ō-ver-shad'-ō) *v.t.* cast shadow over; (*Fig.*) outshine (a person).

overshoot (ō-ver-shōōt') *v.t.* send too far; exceed.—*pa.p.* and *pa.t.* overshot'.

oversight (ō'-ver-sīt) *n.* failure to notice; unintentional neglect.

overspill (ō'-ver-spil) *n.* that which spills over; surplus population which leaves a town or district.

overstate (ō-ver-stāt') *v.t.* exaggerate.—overstate'ment *n.* exaggeration.

overstrain (ō-ver-strān') *v.t.* and *i.* strain too much; (*Fig.*) work too hard;—*n.* overwork.—overstrained' *a.*

overstrung (ō-ver-strung') *a.* in state of nervous tension; of piano, having some of the longer strings crossing others obliquely, in order to save space.

overt (ō'-vert) *a.* open to view; public.

overtake (ō-ver-tāk') *v.t.* come up with; pass; catch; take by surprise.

overthrow (ō-ver-thrō') *v.t.* throw over or down; upset; defeat.— o'verthrow *n.* defeat; ruin; fall.

overtime (ō'-ver-tīm) *n.* time beyond regular hours; extra wages paid for such.

overtone (ō-ver-tōn) *n.* (*Mus.*) harmonic; implied meaning over and above literal meaning.

overture (ō'-ver-tūr) *n.* opening of negotiations; proposal; (*Mus.*) orchestral introduction to opera, etc.

overturn (ō-ver-tern') *v.t.* and *i.* upset; turn over; capsize; subvert.

overweening (ō-ver-wē'-ning) *a.* thinking too much of oneself; vain; arrogant.

overweight (ō'-ver-wāt) *n.* excess weight; *a.* too heavy.

overwhelm (ō-ver-hwelm')*v.t.* crush; submerge; overpower.—**overwhelm'ing** *a.* decisive; irresistible.—overwhelm'ingly *adv.*

overwork (ō-ver-wurk') v.t. and i. work too hard.—o'verwork n.— **overwrought** (ō-ver-rawt') a. tired out; highly excited.

ovoid (ō'-void) a. egg-shaped; oval.

ovum (ō'-vum) n. female egg-cell; also, the embryo after fertilisation by the male sperm; egg.—pl. o'va.

owe (ō) v.t. be bound to repay; be indebted for.—owing a. requiring to be paid.

owl (oul) n. night bird of prey; (Fig.) dull, stupid-looking person.— owl'et n. small owl.—owl'ish a.

own (ōn) a. used to emphasise possession, e.g. my own money;— v.t. possess; acknowledge; admit;— v.i. confess.—own'er n. rightful possessor.—own'ership n. right of possession.

ox (oks) n. male cow.—pl. ox'en.

oxalic acid n. poisonous organic acid found in many plants.—ox'alate n. salt of oxalic acid.

oxide (ok'-sīd) n. compound of oxygen and another element or radical.—ox'idise v.t. and i. combine with oxygen to form oxide; of metals, rust.—oxida'tion, oxidisa'tion n.

oxygen (oks'-i-jen) n. colourless, odourless, and tasteless gas, forming about ¼ by volume of the atmosphere.—ox'ygenate, ox'ygenise v.t. combine or treat with oxygen.— oxygena'tion n.—oxygenous (ok-sij'-e-nus) a. pert. to, or obtained from, oxygen.

oyster (ois'-ter) n. an edible, bivalve shellfish.—oys'ter-catch'er n. wading-bird of plover family.

ozone (ō'-zōn) n. condensed and very active form of oxygen with peculiar, pungent odour; popularly, invigorating sea-side air.

P

pace (pās) n. step; length of a step in walking (about 30 inches); gait; rate of movement;—v.t. measure by steps; set the speed for;—v.i. walk in slow, measured fashion.—paced a. having a certain gait.—pac'er n. one who sets pace for another.

pachy- (pak'-i) prefix from Gk. pachus, thick.—pach'yderm n. thick-skinned quadruped, e.g. the elephant.—pachyder'matous a. thick-skinned; insensitive.

pacify (pas'-i-fī) v.t. appease; tranquillise.—pacif'icism, pac'ifism n. doctrine which advocates abolition of war; anti-militarism.—pacif'icist, pac'ifist n.—pacif'ic a. peaceful.— pacifica'tion n.—pacif'icatory a. conciliatory.—pac'ifier n.

pack (pak) n. bundle for carrying, esp. on back; lot or set; band (of animals); set of playing-cards; (Rugby) the forwards; mass of floating ice; army rucksack.—v.t. arrange closely in bundle, box or bag; stow away within; fill, press together; carry; load; (with off) to dismiss summarily;—v.i. collect in packs, bales, or bundles.—pack'age n. container or parcel; v.t.—package deal, offer that includes terms and conditions required to be accepted en bloc.—pack'er n.—pack'et n. small package; (Slang) large sum of money. —pack'-horse n. horse for carrying burdens, in panniers or in packs.— pack'ing n. any material used to pack, fill up, or make close.—pack'ing-case n. box in which to pack goods.— pack'-man n. pedlar.

pact (pakt) n. agreement; compact.

pad (pad) n. anything stuffed with soft material; cushion; shin-guard (in games); sheets of paper fastened together in block; foot or sole of certain animals; rocket launching base; —v.t. furnish with pad; stuff; expand; fill out or protect.—pr.p. padd'ing.— pa.p. and pa.t. padd'ed.—padd'ing n. material used in stuffing; unnecessary matter inserted in book or speech, etc.

pad (pad) n. easy-paced horse; path or road; footpad;—v.i. travel on foot.

paddle (pad'-l) n. short oar with broad blade at one or each end; blade of paddle-wheel; flipper;— v.t. and i. propel by paddles.

paddle (pad'-l) v.i. walk with bare feet in shallow water; dabble.

paddock (pad'-ok) n. small grass field or enclosure; on race-course, the enclosure where horses are saddled before race.

paddy (pad'-i) n. rice in the husk.

padlock (pad'-lok) n. detachable lock with hinged hoop to go through staple;—v.t. fasten with padlock.

padre (pá'-drā) n. title given to priest; chaplain with H.M. Forces.

paean (pē'-an) n. any shout, song, or hymn of triumph.

paediatrics, pediatrics (pē-di-at'-riks) n. (Med.) branch dealing with diseases of children.—paediatri'cian n.

pagan (pā'-gan) n. heathen; idolater; —a. heathenish; idolatrous.—pa'ganish a.—pa'ganise v.t.—pa'ganism n.

page (pāj) n. one side of leaf of book or manuscript;—v.t. number the pages of.—paginal (pa'-jin-al) a.— paginate (pa'-jin-āt) v.t. number the pages consecutively.—pagina'tion n.

page (pāj) n. formerly, boy in service of person of rank; boy-attendant, esp. in hotel;—v.t. summon by sending page.

pageant (paj'-ent, pā'-jent) n. show of persons in costume in procession, dramatic scenes, etc. usually illustrating history; spectacle.—page'-

antry *n.* a brilliant display; pomp.

pagoda (pạ-gō'-dạ) *n.* temple or sacred tower.

paid (pād) *pa.p.* and *pa.t.* of the verb **pay**.

pail (pāl) *n.* round, open vessel of wood, tin, etc., for carrying liquids; bucket.

paillasse See **pal'liasse**.

pain (pān) *n.* bodily or mental suffering; ache; penalty; — *pl.* trouble; exertion;—*v.t.* inflict bodily or mental suffering upon.—**pain'ful** *a.* full of pain; causing pain; distressing. — **pain'fully** *adv.* — **pain'fulness** *n.*—**pain'less** *a.*—**pain'lessly** *adv.* — **pain'lessness** *n.* — **pains'taking** *a.* carefully laborious.

paint (pānt) *n.* colouring matter for putting on surface with brush, etc.; —*v.t.* cover with paint; make picture of.—**pain'ter** *n.*—**pain'ting** *n.* making pictures; picture in paint.—**Painted Lady**, orange-red butterfly with black and white spots.

painter (pān'-tẹr) *n.* rope at bow of boat, used to fasten it to any other object.

pair (pār) *n.* two things of a kind; single article composed of two similar pieces, e.g. pair of scissors; courting, engaged, or married couple;—*v.t.* unite in couples;—*v.i.* be joined in couples; mate.

pal (pal) *n.* (*Colloq.*) mate or partner; friend.

palace (pal'-is) *n.* house of an emperor, king, bishop, or other great personage; magnificent house.—**palatial** (pạ-lā'-shạl) *a.*

palae-, pale- palaeo-, paleo- (pal'-ē-(-o)) *prefix* from Gk. *palaios*, ancient.—**palaeography** (pal-ē-og'-rạ-fi) *n.* ancient writings; art of deciphering ancient writings.—**palaeograph'ic** *a.*—**palaeog'rapher** *n.*—**palaeolith** (pal'-ē-ō-lith) *n.* unpolished stone implement of earlier stone age.—**palaeolith'ic** *a.*—**palaeology** (pal-ē-ol'-o-ji) *n.* archaeology.—**palaeol'ogist** *n.*—**palaeontology** (pal-ē-on-tol'-o-ji) *n.* study of fossils.—**palaeontol'ogist** *n.*—**paleontolog'ical** *a.*

palate (pal'-ạt) *n.* roof of the mouth; sense of taste; relish.—**pal'atable** *a.* agreeable to taste.—**pal'atably** *adv.*—**pal'atal** *a.* pert. to palate.

palaver (pạ-lā'-vẹr) *n.* idle talk.

pale (pāl) *a.* faint in colour; whitish; dim; wan;—*v.t.* make pale;—*v.i.* become pale.—**pale'ness** *n.* lack of colour; wanness.—**pal'ish** *a.* somewhat pale.—**pale'-face** *n.* name given to white person by Red Indians.

pale (pāl) *n.* pointed wooden stake; narrow board used for making fence; boundary;—*v.t.* enclose with stakes.—**pal'ing** *n.* fence formed of wooden stakes; fencing.

palette (pal'-et) *n.* board on which

painter mixes his colours.—**pal'ette-knife** *n.* thin-bladed knife for mixing colours.

palfrey (pawl'-, pal'fri) *n.* small saddle-horse.

palindrome (pal'-in-drōm) *n.* word or sentence the same when read backward or forward.

palisade (pal-is-ād') *n.* fence of pales or stakes driven into ground.

pall (pawl) *n.* large, usually black cloth laid over coffin at funeral; ecclesiastical mantle; (*Fig.*) covering.

pall (pawl) *v.t.* make tedious or insipid;—*v.i.* become tedious or insipid.

pallet (pal'-et) *n.* small, rude bed.

pallet (pal'-et) *n.* tool with flat wooden blade used by potters and other workers; low platform on which goods are stored to facilitate lifting.

palliasse (pal'-i-as, pal-yas') *n.* hard straw mattress. Also **paillasse**.

palliate (pal'-i-āt) *v.t.* lessen without curing; extenuate.—**pallia'tion** *n.*—**palliative** (pal'-i-ā-tiv) *a.* serving to mitigate.—*n.* that which excuses, mitigates, alleviates.

pallid (pal'-id) *a.* lacking colour; pale; wan.—**pall'idly** *adv.*—**pall'idness** *n.*—**pall'or** *n.* paleness.

palm (pàm) *n.* inner surface of hand, between wrist and fingers; lineal measure, reckoned as 3 or 4 inches; part of ski on which it runs;—*v.t.* conceal in palm; impose by fraud (with 'off').—**palmar** (pal'-mẹr) *a.* pert. to palm.—**pal'mate** *a.* having shape of hand; (*Zool.*) web-footed.—**palmist** (pá'-, or pal'-mist) *n.* one who tells fortunes by palm of hand.—**palmistry** (pá'- or pal'-mis-tri) *n.* telling fortunes by lines on hand.

palm (pàm) *n.* branchless, tropical tree having at its summit tuft of leaves shaped like palm of hand; branch or leaf of this tree as symbol of victory; prize of honour.—**palmer** (pá'-mẹr) *n.* in Middle Ages, one who visited the Holy Land; itinerant monk.—**palm'y** *a.* bearing palms; (*Fig.*) prosperous.—**Palm Sunday**, Sunday before Easter.

palpable (pal'-pạ-bl) *a.* that may be touched or felt; certain; obvious.—**pal'pably** *adv.*—**pal'pableness** *n.*—**pal'pate** *v.t.* examine with hand.—**palpa'tion** *n.* examination by touch.

palpitate (pal'-pi-tāt) *v.i.* beat rapidly, as heart; throb; pulsate.—**palpita'tion** *n.*

palsy (pawl'-zi) *n.* paralysis; loss of power of movement or feeling.—**pal'sied** *a.*

palter (pawl'-tẹr) *v.i.* trifle with; deal evasively; use trickery; dodge.—**pal'terer** *n.*—**pal'try** *a.* mean; worthless.—**pal'triness** *n.*

pampas (pam'-pạz) *n.pl.* vast grassy, treeless plains in S. America.

pamper (pam'-per) v.t. gratify unduly; over-indulge.—**pam'perer** n.

pamphlet (pam'-flet) n. thin, paper-covered, unbound book; short treatise on current topic.—**pamphleteer** (pam-fle-tēr') n. writer of pamphlets.

pan (pan) n. broad, shallow metal vessel for household use; anything resembling this; abbrev. of brain-pan, upper part of skull;—v.t. and i. wash gold-bearing soil in pan in order to separate earth and gold; move cinema or TV camera horizontally, while it is taking picture.

panacea (pan-a-sē'-a) n. cure for all diseases.

panache (pan-ash') n. plume of feathers used as head-dress; swaggering manner.

panama (pan-a-má') n. hat made of fine, strawlike material.

pancake (pan'-kāk) n. thin cake of batter fried in pan;—v.i. land aeroplane almost vertically and in level position.

panchromatic (pan-krō-mat'-ik) a. (Phot.) pert. to plates or films which, although reproduction is in monochrome, give to all colours their proper values.

pancreas (pan'-krē-as) n. (Anat.) digestive gland behind stomach; in animals when used as food, the sweetbread.—**pancreat'ic** a.

panda (pan-da) n. raccoon-like animal found in S. and E. borders of Tibet; bear-cat.

pandemic (pan-dem'-ik) a. of disease, universal; widely distributed; affecting a nation.

pandemonium (pan-de-mō'-ni-um) n. disorderly, noisy place or gathering; riotous uproar.

pander (pan'-der) n. (fem. **pan'deress**) one who ministers to evil desires and passions of others;—v.i. help to satisfy any unworthy desires.

pane (pān) n. sheet of glass in window; near end of hammer head.

panegyric (pan-e-jir'-ik) n. speech of praise.—**panegyr'ical** a.—**pan'egyrist** n. one who writes or pronounces a eulogy.—**pane'gyrise** v.t. praise highly

panel (pan'-el) n. rectangular piece of cloth, parchment, or wood; list of jurors; a jury; list of doctors registered to serve patients insured under National Health Service Act; group of people participating in TV or radio programme.—v.t. divide into, or decorate with, panels.—**pan'elling** n. panelled work.

pang (pang) n. sudden pain, physical or mental; throe.

panic (pan'-ik) n. sudden terror; infectious fear;—a. extreme and illogical (of fear);—v.i. be seized with sudden, uncontrollable fright. —pa.t. **pan'icked**.—**pan'icky** a.—

pan'ic-mong'er n. one who tries to create panic.—**pan'ic-strick'en** a. seized with paralysing fear.

pannier (pan'-yer) n. one of pair of baskets carried on each side of pack-animal.

panoply (pan'-o-pli) n. complete suit of armour.—**pan'oplied** a. fully armed.

panorama (pan-o-rá'-ma) n. complete view in every direction.—**panoram'ic** a.

pansy (pan'-zi) n. cultivated violet. Also called Heart's-ease or Love-in-Idleness; (Slang) effeminate man.

pant (pant) v.i. breathe quickly; gasp for breath; yearn (with for or after);—v.t. utter gaspingly;—n. gasp.

pantaloon (pan-ta-lóón') n. character in Italian comedy of former times;—pl. tight trousers.

pantechnicon (pan-tek'-ni-kon) n. storage place or van for furniture.

pantheism (pen'-thē-izm) n. doctrine that identifies God with the universe.—**pan'theist** n.—**pantheis'tic** (-al) a.—**pantheol'ogy** n. system which embraces all religions and all gods.

panther (pan'-ther) n. (fem. **pan'theress**) variety of leopard.

pantile (pan'-tīl) n. roofing tile curved like the letter S.

panto- (pan'-tō) prefix fr. Gk. pas, pantos, all, used in derivatives.—**pan'tograph** n. instrument for copying drawings, maps, etc., on enlarged, reduced, or same scale.

pantomime (pan'-tō-mīm) n. dramatic entertainment in dumb show; Christmas-time dramatic and spectacular entertainment;—v.t. and i. act or express by gestures only.—**pantomim'ic** a.—**pan'tomimist** n.

pantry (pan'-tri) n. small room for storing food or kitchen utensils.

pants (pants) n.pl. (Colloq.) trousers; short trousers of light fabric; men's drawers.

pap (pap) n. soft food for infants, etc.

pap (pap) n. nipple; teat; woman's breast; small round hill resembling nipple.

papacy (pā-pa-si) n. office and dignity of Pope; Popes collectively.—**papal** (pā'-pal) a.

papaw (pa-paw') n. palm-like S. American tree.

paper (pā'-per) n. material made by pressing pulp of rags, straw, wood, etc., into thin flat sheets; sheet of paper written or printed on; newspaper; article or essay; document; hangings for covering walls; set of examination questions;—n.pl. document(s) establishing one's identity; ship's official documents;—a. consisting of paper;—v.t. cover with paper.—**pa'pery** a.—**pa'per-chase** n. cross-country race in which runners going ahead lay trail of torn-up pieces of paper.—**pa'per-hang'er** n. tradesman who papers walls.—**pa'per-knife** n. knife with blunt blade for opening envelopes, etc.—**pa'per-mon'ey** n. official pieces of paper issued instead of gold, silver, etc. coins; bank-notes.

papier-mâché (pap'-yă-mà-shā) n. paper pulp, mixed with glue, etc., shaped or moulded into articles, e.g. trays, fancy boxes, etc.

papist (pā'-pist) n. supporter of the papal system; Roman Catholic.—**papist'ic(al)** a.—**pa'pistry** n. Popery.

papoose (pạ-pōós') n. American Indian baby.

papyrus (pạ-pī'-rus) n. species of reed, pith of which was used by ancients for making paper; manuscript on papyrus.

par (pár) n. equality of value; face value (of stocks and shares); (*Golf*) the number of strokes for hole or course in perfect play.

parable (par'-ạ-bl) n. fable or allegory with moral.—**parabol'ical** a.—**parabol'ically** adv.

parabola (pạ-ra'-bo-la) n. conic section made by plane parallel to side of cone.—**parabol'ic(al)** a.—**para'boloid** n. solid formed when parabola is revolved round its axis.

parachute (par'-ạ-shōōt) n. collapsible umbrella-like device used to retard descent of falling body.—**par'achutist** n.—**par'achute-troops** n.pl. See paratroops.

parade (pạ-rād') n. display; show; public walk or procession; muster of troops for drill or inspection; ground on which such muster takes place;—v.t. make display or spectacle of; marshal in military order;—v.i. march in military array; march in procession with display.

paradigm (par'-ạ-dim) n. example; model.—**paradigmat'ic** a.—**paradigmat'ically** adv.

paradise (par'-ạ-dīs) n. garden of Eden; Heaven; state of bliss.—**paradisaic** (par-a-di-sā'-ik), **paradisa'ical**, **paradisal** a. pert. to paradise or happiness.

paradox (par'-a-doks) n. statement seemingly absurd or self-contradictory, but really true.—**paradox'ical** a.—**paradox'ically** adv.

paraffin (par'-ạ-fin) n. white wax-like substance obtained from shale, coal-tar, etc.; oil from same source used as illuminant.

paragon (par'-ạ-gon) n. pattern of excellence; person or thing of highest excellence.

paragraph (par'-ạ-graf) n. distinct part of a writing; section of passage, indicated by the sign ¶ or begun on new line;—v.t. arrange in paragraphs.—**paragraph'ic** a.

parakeet (par'-ạ-kēt) n. small long-tailed parrot. Also **par'rakeet**, **par'-oquet**.

parallel (par'-ạ-lel) a. continuously at equal distance; precisely corresponding; similar;—n. line equidistant from another at all points; thing exactly like another; comparison; line of latitude;—v.t. represent as similar; compare.—pr.p. **par'alleling** or **par'allelling**.—pa.p. and pa.t. **par'alleled** or **par'allelled**.—**par'allelism** n. state of being parallel; comparison.

parallelogram (par-ạ-lel'-ō-gram) n. four-sided plane figure with both pairs of opposite sides parallel.

paralysis (pạ-ral'-i-sis) n. (*Med.*) loss of power of movement or sensation.—**paralyse** (par'-ạ-līz) v.t. affect with paralysis; cripple.—**paralyt'ic** a. pert. to paralysis;—n. one affected with paralysis.—infantile paralysis, poliomyelitis.

paramount (par'-ạ-mount) a. superior; chief. — **par'amountcy** n. — **par'amountcy** adv.

paramour (par'-ạ-mōór) n. partner in illicit love intrigue; mistress.

paranoia (par-ạ-noi'-ạ) n. (*Med.*) a form of chronic insanity, often characterised by delusions of grandeur, persecution, etc.—**paranoi'ac** a. and n.

parapet (par'-ạ-pet) n. low wall at the edge of bridge, quay, etc.; breastwork to protect soldiers, esp. mound along front of trench.

paraphernalia (par-ạ-fẹr-nā'-li-ạ) n. pl. personal belongings; furnishings or accessories; (*Law*) goods of wife beyond dowry.

paraphrase (par'-ạ-frāz) n. restatement of passage; free translation into same or another language; interpretation; versified passage of Scripture;—v.t. express in other words; interpret freely.

parasite (par'-ạ-sīt) n. formerly, one who habitually ate at table of another, repaying with flattery; hanger-on; toady; plant or animal that lives on another.—**parasit'ic** a.—**parasit'ically** adv.—**parasitol'ogy** n. study of parasites, esp. as causes of disease.—**parasitolog'ical** a.—**parasitol'ogist** n.

parasol (par'-ạ-sol) n. light umbrella used to protect against sun.

paratroops (par'-ạ-trōóps) n.pl. troops who descend by parachute from aircraft.—**par'atrooper** n.

parboil (pár'-boil) v.t. boil partially.

parcel (pár'-sẹl) n. bundle or package (wrapped in paper); number of things forming group or lot; piece of land;—v.t. divide into portions; distribute; wrap up.—pr.p. **par'celling**.—pa.p. and pa.t. **par'celled**.

parch (párch) v.t. scorch; shrivel with heat; dry to excess;—v.i. be scorched.

parchment (pàrch'-ment) n. skin of animal, prepared for writing on; document written on this.

pardon (pàr'-don) v.t. forgive; free from punishment; excuse;—n. forgiveness; remission of penalty.—**par'donable** a. excusable.—**par'donably** adv.—**par'donableness** n.—**par'doner** n. one who pardons; formerly, one who sold papal indulgences.

pare (pàr) v.t. cut or shave off; remove outer skin; peel.—**par'er** n.—**par'ing** n. action of paring; that which is pared off.

parent (pàr'-ent) n. father or mother; one who, or that which, brings forth or produces.—**par'entage** n. descent from parents; birth; extraction.—**parental** (pa-rent'-al) a. pert. to parents; affectionate.—**parent'ally** adv.

parenthesis (pa-ren'-the-sis) n. word or sentence inserted in passage independently of sequence and usually marked off by brackets, dashes, or commas;—**paren'theses** (-sēz) n.pl. round brackets ( ), used for this.—**parenthet'ic, parenthet'ical** a. interposed.—**parenthet'ically** adv.

pariah (par'-, pàr'-i-a) n. in S. India, one deprived of all religious or social rights; member of the lowest or no caste; outcast; yellow, ownerless dog in India.

parietal (pa-rī'-e-tal) a. pert. to a wall; pert. to wall of the body or its cavities.

parish (par'-ish) n. sub-division of county; orig. ecclesiastical district; district under priest or clergyman; —a. pert. to parish.—**parishioner** (pa-rish'-on-er) n. inhabitant of parish; member of parish church.

parity (par'-i-ti) n. equality; analogy.

park (pàrk) n. large enclosed piece of ground, usually with grass and trees, attached to country house; similar ground in towns, for public use; sports' ground; place for storing motor-cars, etc.;—v.t. enclose in park; leave unattended, as car.—**parking meter** n. coin operated meter, usually at kerbside of city streets, that charges for parking there.

parlance (pàr'-lans) n. way of speaking; form of speech.—**parley** (pàr'-li) n. meeting between leaders of opposing forces to discuss terms; —v.t. hold discussion about terms.

parliament (pàr'-la-ment) n. supreme legislature of United Kingdom, composed of House of Lords and House of Commons; any similar foreign assembly.—**parliament'ary** a. pert. to, enacted by, or according to, established rules of parliament; of language, admissible in parliamentary debate.—**parliamenta'rian** n. skilled debater in parliament.

parlour (pàr'-lur) n. family sitting-room; private room in an inn.

parlous (pàr'-lus) a. hard to escape from; perilous; critical.

parochial (pa-rō'-ki-al) a. pert. to parish; provincial; narrow-minded. —**paro'chially** adv.—**paro'chialism** n.

parody (par'-o-di) n. imitation of poem, song, etc., where style is the same but the theme ludicrously different; feeble imitation; — v.t. write parody of; burlesque in verse. —**par'odist** n.

parole (pa-rōl') n. word of honour, esp. promise given by prisoner of war.

paronomasia (par-ō-nō-mā'-zi-a) n. play on words; pun.—**par'onym** n. word similar in sound to another but different in spelling and meaning.

paroxysm (par'-ok-sizm) n. sudden, violent attack of pain, rage, laughter; at; convulsion.

parquet (pàr'-ket) n. flooring of wooden blocks.—**parquetry** (pàr-ke-tri)

parr (pàr) n. young salmon.

parricide (par'-i-sīd) n. one who murders his father, parent, near relative, or person who is venerated; crime itself.

parrot (par'-ot) n. tropical bird with bright plumage and short hooked beak; one who repeats words, actions, ideas, etc. of another.

parry (par'-i) v.t. ward off; turn aside; avoid; evade.

parse (pàrz) v.t. classify a word or analyse a sentence in terms of grammar.—**par'sing** n.

parsimony (pàr'-si-mon-i) n. stinginess; undue economy; excessive thrift.—**parsimo'nious** (pàr-si-mō'-ni-us) a. stingy; niggardly.—**parsimo'niously** adv.—**parsimo'niousness** n.

parsley (pàrs'-li) n. herb, used as garnish in cookery.—**cow parsley, wild chervil.**

parsnip (pàrs'-nip) n. root-vegetable, carrot-like in shape.

parson (pàr'-sn) n. clergyman; the incumbent of parish.—**par'sonage** n. residence of parson.—**parson's nose,** rump of fowl.

part (pàrt) n. portion of whole; share or lot; division; actor's role; duty; interest; melody in harmonic piece; —pl. accomplishments or talents; region;—v.t. divide; separate; share; —v.i. separate; take leave; part with or give up.—**part'ing** n. act of separating; leave-taking; division; dividing-line;—a. given on taking leave.—**part'ly** adv. in part; in some measure or degree.—**part'ible** a. divisible.—**partibil'ity** n. susceptibility of division.

partake (pàr-tāk') v.t. and i. have or take share in; take food or drink.— pa.p. **partak'en.**—pa.t. **partook'.**—**parta'ker** n.

parterre (pår-ter') n. ornamental arrangement of flower-beds; pit of theatre.

partial (pår'-shạl) a. affecting only part; not total; inclined to favour unreasonably.—**par'tially** adv.—**partial'ity** n. favouritism.

participate (pår-tis'-i-pāt) v.t. and i. share in; partake (with in).—**partic'ipant** n. partaker;—a. sharing.—**partic'ipator** n.—**participation** (pår-tis-i-pā'-shun) n.

participle (pår'-ti-si-pl) n. (Gram.) adjective formed from verb.—**particip'ial** a.

particle (pår'-ti-kl) n. minute portion of matter; least possible amount; atom.

parti-coloured (pår'-ti-kul-urd) a. partly of one colour, partly of another; variegated.

particular (pår-tik'-ū-lạr) a. relating to single person or thing, not general; considered apart from others; minute in details; fastidious in taste;—n. single point or circumstance; detail or item.—**partic'ularly** adv. especially; in high degree.—**particular'ity** n. quality or state of being particular; individual characteristic.—**partic'ularise** v.t. and i. mention one by one; give in detail; specify.—**particularisa'tion** n.

partisan (pår'-ti-zan) n. adherent, often prejudiced, of party or cause; member of irregular troops esp. in enemy-occupied country;—a. adhering to faction.—**par'tisanship** n.

partition (pår-tish'-un) n. division or separation; any of parts into which thing is divided; that which divides or separates, as wall, etc.;—v.t. divide into shares; divide by walls.—**par'titive** n. word expressing partition; distributive;—a. denoting part.

partner (pårt'-nẹr) n. partaker; sharer; associate, esp. in business; husband or wife; one who dances with another; in golf, tennis, etc., one who plays with another;—v.t. in games, play with another against opponents.—**part'nership** n. state of being partner; association of two or more persons for business.

partridge (pår'-trij) n. game-bird.

parturient (pår-tū'-ri-ẹnt) a. bringing forth or about to bring forth young; prolific.—**parturi'tion** n. act of bringing forth young.

party (pår'-ti) n. number of persons united in opinion; political group; social assembly; participator; accessory;—a. pert. to party or faction.—**par'ty-col'oured** a. parti-coloured.

parvenu (pår'-vẹ-nū) n. upstart; self-made person; one who has risen socially.

pasha (på'-shạ, pạ-sha') n. Turkish official of high rank.

pass (pås) v.t. go by, beyond, through etc.; spend; exceed; approve; disregard; circulate; send through; move;—v.i. go; elapse; undergo examination successfully; happen; die; circulate.—pa.p. **passed**, past.—pa.t. **passed**.—n. passage or way, esp. narrow and difficult one; passport; permit; condition; success in examination, etc.; in football, hockey, etc., passing of ball from one player to another.—**pass'able** a. fairly good; admissible; current.—**pass'ably** adv.—**pass'book** n. small book issued by bank in which are entered customer's deposits and withdrawals.—**pass'-key** n. latch-key; master-key.—**pass'port** n. official document, issued by State Department, granting permission to travel abroad.—**pass'word** n. (Mil.) selected word given to sentries, soldiers, etc. used to distinguish friend from enemy.—**to pass the buck** (Slang) shift responsibility to another.

passage (pas'-āj) n. act, time, or right of passing; movement from one place to another; voyage; fare for voyage; entrance or exit; corridor; part of book, etc.; the passing of law; encounter; incident.—**bird of passage**, migratory bird.

passé (på-sā') a. past one's best; out of date.

passenger (pas'-en-jẹr) n. traveller, esp. by some conveyance; (Colloq.) one of team who does not pull his full weight;—a. adapted for carrying passengers.

passe-partout (pås-pår-tōō') n. master-key; method of framing pictures with gummed tape.

passion (pash'-un) n. story of Christ's suffering and last agony; intense emotion, as of grief, rage, love; eager desire.—**pass'ionate** a. easily moved to anger; moved by strong emotions.—**pass'ionately** adv.—**pass'ionateness** n.—**pass'ionless** a.—**pass'ion-play** n. theatrical representation of Christ's passion.—**pass'ion-week** n. week preceding Easter.

passive (pas'-iv) a. suffering; submissive; acted upon, not acting.—**pass'ively** adv.—**pass'iveness** n.—**passiv'ity** n. state of being passive; inertia.

Passover (pås'-ō-vẹr) n. feast of Jews to commemorate the exodus from Egypt.

past (påst) a. pert. to former time; gone by; ended;—n. former state; bygone times; one's earlier life;—prep. beyond; after;—adv. by; beyond.—**past master**, former master of guild, freemasons, etc.; one adept or proficient.

paste (påst) n. soft composition, as of flour and water; dough prepared for pies, etc.; any soft mixture or adhesive; pounded meat or fish;

fine glass for making artificial gems;
—*v.t.* fasten with paste; (*Slang*)
thrash.—**pasty** (pās'-ti, pas'-ti) *n.* pie
enclosed in paste and baked without
dish;—*a.* (pās'-ti) like paste.—
pas'try (pās'-tri) *n.* crust of pies and
tarts; articles of food made of paste
or dough.—**pasteboard** (pāst'-bōrd) *n.*
stiff, thick paper;—*a.* made of
pasteboard; flimsy or unsubstantial.

pastel (pas'-tel) *n.* coloured crayon;
drawing made with such crayons.—
pastel shades, delicate and subdued
colours, esp. in fabrics.

pastern (pas'-tern) *n.* part of horse's
leg between fetlock and hoof.

pasteurisation (pas-ter-I-zā-shun) *n.*
sterilisation of milk, etc. by heating
to 140° F. or over and then cooling.
—**pas'teurise** *v.t.*

pastille (pas-tēl') *n.* small lozenge,
aromatic or medicated.

pastime (pás'-tīm) *n.* that which
amuses and makes time pass
agreeably; recreation.

pastor (pás'-tor) *n.* minister of
gospel.—**pas'toral** *a.* pert. to shepherds or rual life; pert. to office of
pastor;—*n.* poem describing rural
life; idyll.—**pas'torally** *adv.*—**pas'torate**
n. jurisdiction of spiritual pastor.—
pas'torship *n.*

pasture (pás'-tūr) *n.* grass for food of
cattle; ground on which cattle
graze;—*v.t.* feed on grass;—*v.i.*
graze.—**past'urable** *a.*—**past'urage** *n.*
pasture-land; business of grazing
cattle.

pat (pat) *n.* light, quick blow, esp.
with hand or fingers; small lump,
esp. of butter;—*v.t.* strike gently.—
pr.p. **pat'ting**.—*pa.p.* and *pa.t.* **pat'ted**.

pat (pat) *a.* apt; at right moment;—
adv. opportunely.—**pat'ness** *n.*

patch (pach) *n.* piece of material
used to mend hole, rent, etc.; spot
on surface of anything; small spot of
black silk formerly worn on cheek by
ladies;—*v.t.* mend with patch; repair
clumsily.—**patch'y** *a.* full of patches;
unequal.—**patch'work** *n.* work made
by sewing together pieces of cloth of
different material and colour.

pate (pāt) *n.* top of the head; head.

patella (pa-tel'-a) *n.* knee-cap.

patent (pā'-tent, pat'-ent) *a.* open;
evident; open to public perusal, as
letters patent; protected by patent;
—*n.* short for *letters patent*, official
document granting right, privilege,
title, or exclusive right to invention; invention itself.—**patent** (pā'-
tent) *v.t.* secure or protect by
patent.—**pa'tently** *adv.* openly; evid-
ently.—**patentee** (pā-ten-tē', pat-en-
tē') *n.* one who has secured patent.
—**patent leather**, leather with varnished surface.

paternal (pa-ter'-nal) *a.* pert. to
father; fatherly; hereditary.—**pater**-

nally *adv.*—**pater'nity** *n.* relation of
father to his offspring.

paternoster (pat-er-nos'-ter) *n.*
Lord's Prayer.

path (path) *n.* way, course, or track;
course of action, conduct, or procedure.—**path'finder** *n.* pioneer.—
path'way *n.* narrow footway.

pathetic (pa-thet'-ik) *a.* affecting or
moving the tender emotions; causing
pity; touching.—**pathet'ically** *adv.*

patho- (pa'-tho) *prefix* fr. Gk. *pathos*,
suffering, feeling, used in derivatives.
—**pathogen'esis**, **pathog'eny** *n.* origin
and development of disease.—
pathogenet'ic, **pathogen'ic** *a.* causing
disease.—**pathol'ogy** *n.* science and
study of diseases.—**patholog'ic**, **patholog'ical** *a.*—**patholog'ically** *adv.*—
pathol'ogist *n.*

pathos (pā'-thos) *n.* power of exciting
tender emotions; deep feeling.

patient (pā'-shent) *a.* bearing trials
without murmuring; not easily made
angry; calm;—*n.* person under
medical treatment.—**pa'tiently** *adv.*
—**pa'tience** *n.* quality of enduring
with calmness; card-game for one.

patina (pa-tē'-na, pat'-i-na) *n.* film
formed on antique bronze; gloss on
other antique surfaces.

patio (pát'-i-ō) *n.* inner court of
Spanish house.

patois (pat'-wá) *n.* dialect; jargon.

patriarch (pā'-tri-ārk) *n.* father and
ruler of family, esp. in Biblical
history; highest dignitary in Eastern
church; venerable old man.—**patri-
arch'al** *a.*—**pat'riarchate** *n.* jurisdiction
of patriarch.—**pat'riarchy** *n.* government by head or father of tribe.

patrician (pa-trish'-an) *a.* pert. to
senators of ancient Rome; of high
birth; noble or aristocratic;—*n.*
person of high birth.

patricide See **parricide**.

patrimony (pat'-ri-mō-ni) *n.* right or
estate inherited from one's father or
ancestors; heritage.—**patrimo'nial** *a.*
—**patrimo'nially** *adv.*

patriot (pā'-tri-ot, pat'-ri-ot) *n.* one
who loves his country.—**patriot'ic** *a.*
filled with patriotism.—**patriot'ically** *adv.*—**pa'triotism** *n.* love for, and
loyalty to, one's country.

patrol (pa-trōl') *v.t.* and *i.* go round
camp, garrison, etc. in order to
protect it; make a reconnaissance.
—*pr.p.* **patrol'ling**.—*pa.p.* and *pa.t.*
patrolled'.—*n.* going of rounds by
guard; man or men who go the
rounds; small body of troops for
reconnoitring, etc.

patron (pā'-trun) *n.* (*fem.* **pa'troness**)
man under whose protection another
has placed himself; guardian saint;
one who has right of appointment to
church living or benefice; regular
customer.—**pa'tronage** *n.* support or
encouragement given to person or

cause; condescending manner; in trade, regular custom.—**patronise** (pat'-ro-nīz) v.t. act as patron to; assume air of superior towards; frequent, as customer.—**pat'ronising** a.—**pat'ronisingly** adv.

patronymic (pat-ro-nim'-ik) n. name derived from parent or ancestor; surname.

patter (pat'-ẽr) v.i. make quick succession of small taps, like those of rain falling.

patter (pat'-ẽr) v.t. speak rapidly and indistinctly; mutter;—v.i. talk glibly or mechanically;— n. chatter; prattle; jargon of profession or class.

pattern (pat'-ẽrn) n. model, example, or guide to be copied, or worthy of imitation;—a. model; ideal;—v.t. design from pattern; imitate.— **pat'ternmaker** n. worker in foundry who makes patterns for moulds.

patty (pat'-i) n. little pie.

paucity (paw'-si-ti) n. fewness; scarcity.

paunch (pawnsh, pánsh) n. belly.

pauper (paw'-pẽr) n. (fem. **pau'peress**) poor person, esp. one supported by the public.

pause (pawz) n. short stop or rest; hesitation; break in speaking, reading, or writing;—v.i. make short stop; cease for a time.

pavan, pavane (pạ-van') n. old-time stately dance.

pave (pāv) v.t. form level surface with stone, brick, etc.; make smooth and even; (Fig.) prepare.—**pave'ment** n. paved road or footpath; side-walk for pedestrians; (U.S.) traffic way.

pavilion (pạ-vil'-yun) n. orig. tent; hence, anything like tent, e.g. garden summer-house; club-house on playing-field, etc.

paw (paw) n. foot of animal having claws; (Slang) hand;—v.t. and i. scrape with the forefoot; (Colloq.) attempt unwelcome caress.

pawky (pawk'-i) a. (Scot.) sly; artful; cunning.

pawn (pawn) n. something deposited as security for money borrowed; pledge;—v.t. deposit as security for loan; pledge.—**pawn'broker** n. one who lends money on something deposited with him.—**pawn'shop** n. place of business of pawnbroker.

pawn (pawn) n. piece of lowest rank in the game of chess; (Fig.) person who is a mere tool in the hands of another.

pay (pā) v.t. discharge one's obligations to; give money, etc., for goods received or services rendered;—v.i. recompense; be worth the trouble. —pa.p. and pa.t. paid (pād).—n. reward; compensation; wages; salary.—**pay'able** a. justly due; profitable.—**payee** (pā-ē') n. one to whom money is paid.—**pay'er** n. one

who pays.—**pay'ment** n. discharge of debt; recompense.—**paying guest**, boarder or lodger.

pea (pē) n. the fruit, growing in pods, of a leguminous plant; the plant.— pl. **peas**.—**pea'-nut** n. ground-nut.— **sweet pea**, garden annual, bearing sweet-scented flowers.

peace (pēs) n. calm; repose; freedom from disturbance, war, or hostilities. —**peace'able** a. in state of peace; disposed to peace; not quarrelsome. —**peace'ably** adv.—**peace'ableness** n. —**peace'ful** a.—**peace'fully** adv.— **peace'fulness** n.—**peace'maker** n.

peach (pēch) n. juicy stone-fruit with whitish flesh, and velvety skin; the tree; a soft pale orange-pink colour. —**peach'y** a. like a peach.

peacock (pē'-kok) n. (fem. **pea'hen**) bird remarkable for beauty of its plumage, and large tail; vain person.—**pea'fowl** n. peacock or hen.

peak (pēk) v.i. waste or pine away.— **peak'y** a. thin, sickly.

peak (pēk) n. sharp top of hill; pointed end of anything; projecting part of cap-brim; maximum point of curve or record.—**peaked** a. pointed; projecting.

peal (pēl) n. loud sound, or succession of loud sounds, as of thunder, bells, laughter, etc.; set of bells attuned to each other;—v.t. and i. sound loudly; celebrate.

pear (pãr) n. sweet, juicy fruit of oval shape; tree on which it grows.

pearl (pẽrl) n. hard, smooth, lustrous substance, found in several molluscs, particularly pearl oyster, and used as gem; something very precious; small size of printing type, between ruby and diamond; colour of pearl, creamy grey;—a. made of pearls; pert. to pearls;—v.t. take a round form like pearls.—**pearl'y** a. of colour of pearls; like pearls; abounding in pearls; clear; pure.—**pearl'iness** n.— **moth'er-of-pearl** n. inside surface of pearl-oyster.—**pearl'ies** n.pl. London coster-mongers; their ornate dress.

peasant (pez'-ạnt) n. rural labourer; rustic;— a. rural.— **peas'antry** n. peasants collectively.

pease (pēz) n.pl. peas collectively.

peat (pēt) n. brown, fibrous turf, formed of decayed vegetable matter, used as fuel.—**peat'y** a. like peat.— **peat'-bog, peat'-moss** n. marshland of which the foundation is peat.— **peat'-hag** n. pool in peaty ground.

pebble (peb'-l) n. small, roundish stone; transparent and colourless rock-crystal used for lenses.— **pebb'led, pebb'ly** a. full of pebbles.

peccable (pek'-ạ-bl) a. liable to sin. —**peccabil'ity** n.—**pecc'ant** a. sinful.

peccadillo (pek-ạ-dil'-ō) n. trifling offence; slight mistake; indiscreet action.—pl. **peccadil'loes**.

peck (pek) *n*. measure of capacity for dry goods.

peck (pek) *v.t.* and *i*. strike with beak; pick up with beak; eat little quantities at a time;—*n*. (*Colloq.*) kiss.—**peck′er** *n*. that which pecks; (*Slang*) spirits; courage.—**peck′ish** *a*. (*Colloq.*) somewhat hungry.

pectoral (pek′-tor-al) *a*. pert. to breast.

peculate (pek′-ū-lāt) *v.t.* embezzle; steal.—**pecula′tion** *n*.—**pec′ulator** *n*.

peculiar (pe-kūl′-yar) *a*. belonging solely to; appropriate; particular; singular; strange.—**pecul′iarly** *adv*.—**peculiar′ity** (pe-kū-li-ar′-i-ti) *n*. something that belongs to only one person, thing, class, people; distinguishing feature; strangeness.

pecuniary (pe-kū′-ni-a-ri) *a*. pert. to or consisting of, money.

pedagogue (ped′-a-gog) *n*. schoolmaster; pedantic teacher.—**pedagogic** (ped-a-goj′-ik), **pedagog′ical** *a*.—**pedagogy** (ped′-a-goj′-i), **pedagog′ics** *n*. science of teaching.

pedal (ped′-al) *a*. pert. to foot;—*n*. mechanical contrivance to transmit power by using foot as lever.—*v.t.* and *i*. use pedals of organ, piano, etc.; propel bicycle by pedalling.—*pr.p.* ped′al(l)ing.—*pa.p.* and *pa.t.* ped′al(l)ed.

pedant (ped′-ant) *n*. one who insists on petty details of book-learning, etc.; one who shows off his learning. —**pedant′ic(al** *a*.—**pedant′ically** *adv*.—**ped′antry** *n*.

peddle (ped′-l) *v.i.* travel from place to place selling small articles;—*v.t.* sell or hawk goods thus.—**ped′lar** *n*. one who peddles goods; door-to-door hawker. Also **ped′(d)ler**.

pedestal (ped′-es-tal) *n*. support or foundation; base of statue, etc.

pedestrian (pe-des′-tri-an) *a*. going on, performed on, foot; of walking; commonplace;—*n*. walker; one who journeys on foot.

pedigree (ped′-i-grē) *n*. line of ancestors; genealogy;—*a*. having documented line of ancestors.

pediment (ped′-i-ment) *n*. (*Archit.*) the triangular ornamental facing of portico, door, or window, etc.— **pedimen′tal** *a*.

pedlar (ped′-lar) *n*. See peddle.

pedology (ped-ol′-o-ji) *n*. study of soil.—**pedol′ogist** *n*.

pedometer (pe-dom′-e-ter) *n*. device measuring distance walked by recording number of steps.

peek (pēk) *v.i.* peep; peer; look slyly through half-closed eyes;—*n*. sly or furtive glance.

peel (pēl) *v.t.* strip off the skin, bark, or rind; free from covering;—*v.i.* come off, as skin or rind;—*n*. outside skin of fruit; rind or bark.

peel (pēl) *n*. square fortified tower.

peep (pēp) *v.i.* look through a crevice; look furtively or slyly; emerge slowly;—*n*. sly glance.— **peep′-show** *n*. small exhibit, viewed through an aperture containing magnifying glass.

peep (pēp) *v.i.* cry, as a chick.

peer (pēr) *n*. (*fem.* peer′ess) equal in any respect; nobleman; member of House of Lords; associate.—**peer′age** *n*. rank of peer; body of peers.— **peer′less** *a*. having no equal.—**peer′lessly** *adv*.—**peer′lessness** *n*.

peer (pēr) *v.i.* look intently.

peevish (pē′-vish) *a*. fretful; irritable; hard to please; childish.—**peev′ishly** *adv*.—**peev′ishness** *n*.—**peeve** *v.t.* annoy; irritate.

peewit (pē′-wit *n*. See **pewit**.

peg (peg) *n*. wooden nail or pin; excuse; drink, esp. whisky, with soda; step or degree;—*v.t.* fix or mark with peg;—*v.i.* to persevere.

Peking (pē-kin′(g) *n*. (*Geog.*) capital of China; kind of silk stuff.—**Pekingese′** *n*. native of Peking; breed of Chinese lap-dog. *abbrev.* **peke**.

pelagian (pe-lā′-ji-an) *a*. pert. to deep sea.—*n*. animal living in deep sea.—**pelagic** (pe-laj′-ik) *a*. pert. to open sea.

Pelargonium (pel-ar-gō′-ni-um) *n*. large genus of flowering plants including geranium.

pelican (pel′-i-kan) *n*. large waterfowl, with enormous pouch beneath its bill.

pellet (pel′-et) *n*. little ball; pill; small shot.

pell-mell (pel-mel′) *adv*. in utter confusion; helter-skelter.

pellucid (pe-lū′-sid) *a*. perfectly clear; translucent.—**pellu′cidly** *adv*. —**pellu′cidness** *n*.

pelmet (pel′-met) *n*. canopy at top of window, esp. to conceal curtain rods.

pelt (pelt) *n*. raw hide; undressed skin of fur-bearing animal.

pelt (pelt) *v.t.* strike with projectiles;— *v.i.* of rain, etc. fall heavily; throw projectiles.

pelvis (pel′-vis) *n*. (*Anat.*) bony cavity at base of human trunk.— **pel′vic** *a*.

pemmican (pem′-i-kan) *n*. beef or venison, dried, pounded, and compressed into cakes.

pen (pen) *n*. instrument for writing with ink; large wing-feather (a quill) used for writing;—*v.t.* write; compose and set down.—*pr.p.* pen′ning. —*pa.p.* and *pa.t.* penned.—**penknife** (pen′-nif) *n*. pocket-knife, formerly used for splitting and preparing quill for writing.—**pen′name** *n*. assumed name of author.

pen (pen) *n*. small enclosure, as for sheep; coop.—*v.t.* confine in pen; shut in.

penal (pē′-nal) *a*. pert. to punishment.—**pe'nalise** v.t. impose penalty upon; handicap.—**pe'nally** adv.—**penalty** (pen'-al-ti) n. punishment for crime or offence; in games, handicap imposed for infringement of rule.

penance (pen'-ans) n. act intended to express repentance, atonement.

penchant (pong'-shong) n. inclination.

pencil (pen'-sil) n. artist's fine brush; crayon or stick of black lead enclosed in wood or other case, used for writing or drawing;—v.t. draw, write with pencil. — **pen'cilled** a.— **pen'cilling** n. works of pencil or fine brush; fine markings.

pendant (pen'-dant) n. hanging ornament, esp. locket or earring; lamp or chandelier hanging from ceiling; addition.—**pen'dent** a. suspended; hanging; projecting.—**pen'dently** adv.—**pen'ding** a. in suspense; undecided;—prep. during; until.

pendulous (pen'-du-lus) a. hanging loosely; swinging.—**pen'dulously** adv. —**pen'dulousness** n.—**pen'dulum** n. body suspended from fixed point, and swinging freely; swinging rod with weighted end which regulates movements of clock, etc.

penetrate (pen'-e-trāt) v.t. enter into; to pierce; pervade or spread through; touch with feeling;—v.i. make way to, or through.—**pene'trating** a.— **pen'etrable** a.—**pen'etrably** adv.—**penetrabil'ity** n.—**penetra'tion** n. power of penetrating; insight; acuteness. — **pen'etrative** a. piercing; discerning.

penguin (pen'-gwin) n. flightless seabird inhabiting S. temperate and Antarctic regions.

penicillin (pen-i-sil'-in) n. extract from the mould penicillium, used to prevent growth of bacteria.

peninsula (pe-nin'-su-la) n. portion of land nearly surrounded by water, and connected with mainland by isthmus.

penis (pē'-nis) n. male organ of generation.

penitent (pen'-i-tent) a. contrite; repentant;—n. one who repents of sin.—**pen'itently** adv.—**pen'itence** n. —**penitential** (pen-i-ten'-shal) a.— **peniten'tially** adv.—**penitentiary** (pen-i-ten'-sha-ri) a. pert. to penance;— n. office, or officer, of papal court, who prescribes penance; house of correction; (U.S.) gaol.

pennant (pen'-ant) n. very long, narrow flag tapering to point. Also **penn'on**.

pennon (pen'-on) n. narrow piece of bunting, esp. on lance, etc.; streamer; wing of bird.—**penn'oned** a.

penny (pen'-i) n. bronze coin, twelfth part of shilling; small sum.—pl. **pennies** (pen'-iz) denoting number of coins, and **pence** (pens) amount of pennies in value.—**penn'iless** a. with-

out money; poor.—**pennyweight** (pen'-i-wāt) n. troy weight of 24 grains (abbrev. dwt.).—**penn'yworth** n. as much as is given for penny; small quantity.—**penny farthing** (Colloq.) early form of bicycle with one very large wheel and one small one.

pennyroyal (pen'-i-roi-al) n. perennial aromatic herb of mint family.

pension (pen'-shun) n. annual grant of money for past services; annuity paid to retired officers, soldiers, etc.; —v.t. grant pension to.—**pen'sionable** a. entitled, or entitling, to pension. —**pen'sioner** n.

pension (pong'-sē-ōng) n. boarding-house.

pensive (pen'-siv) a. thoughtful; deep in thought; musing; melancholy.—**pen'sively** adv.—**pen'siveness** n.

pent (pent) a. confined; shut up.

penta- (pen'-ta) prefix fr. Gk. pente, five, used in derivatives.—**pen'tagon** n. (Geom.) plane figure having five angles and five sides.—**pentag'onal** a. —**pen'tagram** n. five-pointed star, formerly magic symbol.—**pentam'eter** n. verse of five feet.

penthouse (pent'-hous) n. outhouse attached to main building, its roof sloping down from the wall; self-contained flat or room on roof-top.— **pent'roof** n. roof with slope on one side only.

penult (pē-nult', pe'-nult) n. last syllable but one of word.—**penultimate** (pe-nult'-im-āt) a. next before the last;—n. last syllable but one; last member but one of series.

penumbra (pen-um'-bra) n. in eclipse, partially shadowed region which surrounds perfect or full shadow; half-shadow.

penury (pen'-ū-ri) n. extreme poverty; want or indigence; scarcity.— **penurious** (pe-nū'-ri-us) a. miserly; poor; scanty.—**penu'riously** adv.— **penu'riousness** n.

peony (pē'-o-ni) n. plant of buttercup family having globular flowers.

people (pē'-pl) n. body of persons that compose community, tribe, nation, or race; populace as distinct from rulers;—pl. inhabitants;—v.t. populate.

pep (pep) n. (Slang) vigour; energy.

pepper (pep'-er) n. pungent, spicy condiment obtained from E. Indian plant; red or green fruit of capsicum used as vegetable;—v.t. sprinkle with pepper; pelt with missiles.—**pepp'ery** a. having qualities of pepper; pungent; (Fig.) irritable.—**pepp'eriness** n. —**pepp'ercorn** n. berry of pepper-plant something of insignificant value.— **pepp'ermint** n. pungent plant which yields volatile oil; essence got from this oil; lozenge flavoured with this.

pepsin, pepsine (pep'-sin) n. ferment formed in gastric juice of vert-

ebrates serving as aid to digestion.
—pep'tic a. pert. to pepsin and to
digestion;—n.pl. medicines that promote digestion.

perambulate (per-am'-bū-lāt) v.t.
walk through or over;—v.i. walk
about; stroll.—perambula'tion n.—
peram'bulator n. one who perambul-
ates; small carriage for child.—
perambulatory a.

perceive (per-sēv') v.t. obtain knowledge of through the senses; see,
hear, or feel; understand.—perceiv'-
able a.—perceiv'ably adv.—perceiv'er
n.—perceptible (per-sep'-ti-bl) a. capable of being perceived.—percep'tibly
adv. — percep'tibility n. — perception
(per-sep'-shun) n. faculty of perceiving; intuitive judgment.—percep'tive a. having perception.—
perceptiv'ity n. power of perception.

percentage (per-sen'-tij) n. rate per
hundred.—per centum (abbrev. per
cent) by, in, or for, each hundred.

perch (perch) n. edible fresh-water
fish.

perch (perch) n. roosting bar for
birds; high place; lineal measure.
measure of area.—v.t. place on perch;
—v.i. alight or settle on perch; roost.

perchance (per-chàns') adv. perhaps.

percipient (per-sip'-i-ent) a. perceiving;—n. one able to perceive.—
percip'ience, percip'iency n.

percolate (per'-kō-lāt) v.t. and i. pass
slowly through small openings, as
liquid; filter.—percola'tion n.—per'-
colator n. filtering machine; coffee-
pot fitted with filter.

percuss (per-kus') v.t. strike sharply.
—percus'sion n. impact; vibratory
shock; section of orchestra comprising instruments played by striking; (Med.) tapping body to determine condition of internal organ.—
percus'sive a.

perdition (per-dish'-un) n. utter
loss; ruin.

peregrinate (per'-e-gri-nāt) v.i.
travel from place to place; journey.
—peregrina'tion n. wandering about.
—peregrina'tor n.—per'egrine n. kind
of hawk or falcon.

peremptory (per'-emp-tō-ri) a. dictatorial; non-debatable; decisive.—
per'emptorily adv.—per'emptoriness n.

perennial (pe-ren'-i-al) a. lasting
through the year; lasting; everlasting; lasting more than two years;
—n. plant lasting for such a time.—
perenn'ially adv.

perfect (per'-fekt) a. complete;
finished; faultless; correct; excellent.
perfect' or per'fect v.t. finish or complete; make perfect; improve.—
per'fectly adv.—perfect'ible a. capable
of becoming perfect.—perfectibil'ity n.
—perfec'tion n. state of being perfect.

perfidy (per'-fi-di) n. treachery;
breach of faith; violation of trust.—

perfid'ious a. treacherous.—perfid'-
iously adv.—perfid'iousness n.

perforate (per'-fō-rāt) v.t. bore
through; pierce; make series of holes
in.—perfora'tion n. act of perforating;
hole, or series of holes.

perforce (per-fōrs') adv. of necessity.

perform (per-form') v.t. accomplish;
fulfil; represent on stage;—v.i. do;
play, as on musical instrument.—
perform'ing a. trained to act part or
do tricks.—perform'er n.—perform'-
ance n. execution or carrying out;
thing done; degree of efficiency.

perfume (per'-fūm) n. sweet scent or
fragrance; substance which emits
agreeable scent.—perfume' v.t. scent.
—perfum'er n. maker or seller of
perfumes.—perfum'ery n. perfumes in
general; art of making perfumes.

perfunctory (per-fungk'-tō-ri) a. indifferent; superficial.—perfunc'torily
adv.—perfunc'toriness n.

pergola (pēr'-gō-la) n. arbour or
covered walk formed of growing
plants trained over trellis-work;
elevated balcony.

perhaps (per-haps') adv. it may be;
possibly.

peril (per'-il) n. danger; hazard;—
v.t. expose to danger; risk.—per'ilous
a. full of peril.—per'ilously adv.—
per'ilousness n.

perimeter (pe-rim'-e-ter) n. (Geom.)
outer boundary of plane figure; sum
of all its sides; circumference;
boundary.—perimet'rical a.

period (pē'-ri-od) n. particular portion of time; time in which heavenly
body makes revolution; series of
years; cycle; conclusion; punctuation
mark (.), to end a sentence;—pl.
menstruation; — a. of furniture,
dress, play, etc., belonging to
particular period in history.—
period'ic a. recurring at regular
intervals.—period'ical a. periodic;
pert. to periodical;—n. publication,
esp. magazine issued at regular
intervals.—period'ically adv.—period-
icity (pē-ri-o-dis'-it-i) n. tendency to
recur at regular intervals.

peripatetic (per-i-pa-tet'-ik) a. walking about; pert. to philosophy of
Aristotle;—n. disciple of philosophy
of Aristotle; one whose business,
etc. obliges him to do lot of walking
about.—peripatet'icism n.

periphery (pē-rif'-e-ri) n. length
round circular surface; circumference.—periph'eral a.

periphrasis (pē-rif'-ra-sis) n. roundabout way of speaking or writing.—
pl. periph'rases.—periphras'tic a.—
periphras'tically adv.

periscope (per'-i-skōp) n. optical
instrument (used in trench warfare,
submarines, etc.) to enable observer
to view surrounding objects from a
lower level.

perish (per'-ish) *v.t.* and *i.* die; waste away; be destroyed.—**perishable** *a.* liable to perish, decay, etc., e.g. fish, fruit, etc.

peritoneum (per-i-to-ne'-um) *n.* membrane which lines abdominal cavity, and surrounds intestines.—**peritoni'tis** *n.* inflammation of it.

periwig (per'-i-wig) *n.* wig; peruke.

periwinkle (per'-i-wing-kl) *n.* edible shell-fish known as 'winkle'.

periwinkle (per'-i-wing-kl) *n.* trailing shrub with blue flowers.

perjure (per'-jur) *v.t.* violate one's oath (used reflex.);—**per'jured** *a.* guilty of perjury.—**per'jury** *n.* false testimony; crime of violating one's oath. — **per'jurer** *n.* — **perjur'ious** *a.* guilty of perjury.

perk (perk) *a.* pert; smart;—*v.t.* make spruce or trim;—*v.i.* become brisk and lively again (*with* up).—**perk'y** *a.* jaunty; pert; trim.

permanent (per'-ma-nent) *a.* remaining unaltered; lasting.—**per'manently** *adv.*—**per'manence**, **per'manency** *n.* quality of being permanent; continuance in same state.—**permanent way**, railway lines.

permanganate (per-mang'-gan-āt) *n.* salt of acid of manganese, esp. potash salt.

permeate (per'-mē-āt) *v.t.* penetrate and pass through the texture of; saturate.—**per'meable** *a.* admitting of passage of fluids; capable of being magnetised.—**per'meably** *adv.*—**per'meability** (per-mē-a-bil'-i-ti) *n.* rate of diffusion of gas or liquid in a substance. — **permea'tion** *n.* — **permeative** (per'-mē-a-tiv) *a.* capable of permeating.

permit (per-mit') *v.t.* allow; give leave or liberty to;—*v.i.* give leave. —**permit** (per'mit) *n.* written permission. — *pr.p.* **permit'ing.** — *pa.p.* and *pa.t.* **permit'ed.**—**permis'ion** *n.* authorisation; leave or licence granted.—**permis'ible** *a.* allowable. —**permiss'ibly** *adv.*—**permiss'ive** *a.* allowing.—**permiss'ively** *adv.*

permute (per-mūt') *v.t.* change the order of.—**permut'able** *a.* capable of being permuted or exchanged.—**permut'ably** *adv.*—**permut'ableness**, **permutabil'ity** *n.*—**permuta'tion** *n.* (*Math.*) arrangement of a number of quantities in every possible order.

pernicious (per-nish'-us) *a.* destructive or harmful; wicked.—**perni'ciously** *adv.*—**perni'ciousness** *n.*

pernickety (per-nik'-e-ti) *a.* (*Colloq.*) unduly fastidious about trifles.

peroration (per-o-rā'-shun) *n.* concluding part of oration.—**per'orate** *v.i.* make peroration; (*Colloq.*) deliver a speech.

peroxide (per-ok'-sīd) *n.* (*Chem.*) oxide whose molecules have two linked oxygen atoms;—*v.t.* (*Colloq.*)

bleach hair with peroxide of hydrogen.—**peroxide of hydrogen**, liquid used in solution as bleach and antiseptic.

perpendicular (per-pen-dik'-ū-lar) *a.* exactly upright or vertical; at right angles to plane of horizon; at right angles to given line or surface; —*n.* line at right angles to plane of horizon; line at right angles to any line or plane; latest of the styles of English Gothic architecture.—**perpendic'ularly** *adv.*

perpetrate (per'-pe-trāt) *v.t.* commit (esp. crime); be guilty of.—**perpetra'tion** *n.*—**per'petrator** *n.*

perpetual (per-pet'-ū-al) *a.* continuing indefinitely; everlasting.—**perpet'ually** *adv.*—**perpet'uate** *v.t.* not to allow to be forgotten.—**perpetua'tion** *n.*—**perpetuity** (per-pe-tū'-i-ti) *n.* state of being perpetual.

perplex (per-pleks') *v.t.* make intricate, or difficult; bewilder.—**perplex'ed** *a.* puzzled; bewildered.—**perplex'ing** *a.* puzzling.—**perplex'ity** *n.* bewilderment; embarrassment.

perquisite (per'-kwiz-it) *n.* casual payment in addition to salary, etc.; gratuity. — **perquisi'tion** *n.* careful search.

perry (per'-i) *n.* fermented drink made from the juice of pears.

persecute (per'-se-kūt) *v.t.* subject to persistent ill-treatment; harass; worry.—**persecu'tion** *n.*—**per'secutor** *n.*

persevere (per-se-vēr') *v.i.* persist; not give in.—**perse'vering** *a.*—**perseve'ringly** *adv.*—**perseve'rance** *n.*

persiflage (per'-si-fläzh) *n.* idle banter.

persist (per-sist') *v.i.* continue firmly in a state in spite of obstacles.—**persis'tent** *a.* steady; persevering; lasting. — **persis'tently** *adv.* — **persis'tence**, **persis'tency** *a.* perseverance; continuous effort; obstinacy.

person (per'-sun) *n.* human being; individual; body of human being; character in play.—**per'sonable** *a.* attractive in appearance.—**per'sonage** *n.* person, esp. of rank or social position.—**per'sonal** *a.* pert. to, peculiar to, or done by, person; pert. to bodily appearance; directed against person.—**per'sonally** *adv.* in person; individually.—**personal'ity** *n.* individuality; distinctive personal qualities; one who has achieved fame in entertainment, sport, etc.—**personal'ities** *n.pl.* offensive remarks made to, or about, person.—**per'sonate** *v.t.* assume character of; pretend to be. —**persona'tor** *n.*—**in person**, by one's self.

personnel (per-sun-el') *n.* persons employed in public service, business, etc.; staff.

personify (per-son'-i-fī) *v.t.* endow inanimate objects or abstract ideas with human attributes; be outstanding example of.—*pa.p.* and *pa.t.* person'ified.—personifica'tion *n.*

perspective (per-spek'-tiv) *n.* art of drawing objects on plane surface to give impression of looking at objects themselves; relative distance of objects to eye, indicated by convergence of their receding lines; (*Fig.*) right proportion.

perspicacious (per-spi-kā'-shus) *a.* quick-sighted; of acute discernment. — perspic'ciously *adv.* — perspicacity (per-spi-kas'-i-ti) *n.* quick mental insight.—perspicuous (per-spik'-ū-us) *a.* clear to the understanding; lucid. —perspic'uously *adv.*—perspic'uousness *n.*—perspicuity (per-spi-kū'-i-ti) *n.* clearness.

perspire (per-spīr') *v.t.* emit through pores of the skin;—*v.i.* sweat.— perspira'tion *n.* process of perspiring; moisture emitted.

persuade (per-swād')*v.t.* influence by argument, etc.; induce.—persuasive (per-swā'-siv) *a.* having power of persuading; winning.—persua'sively *adv.* — persua'siveness *n.* — persuasion (per-swā'-zhun) *n.* act or quality of persuading; settled opinion or conviction; belief; sect.—persua'sible *a.* open to persuasion.

pert (pert) *a.* lively; bold; forward; saucy.—pert'ly *adv.*—pert'ness *n.*

pertain (per-tān') *v.i.* belong; concern; relate to.

pertinacious (per-ti-nā'-shus) *a.* adhering to opinion, etc. with obstinacy; persevering; resolute.— pertina'ciously *adv.*—pertina'ciousness *n.*—pertinacity (per-ti-nas'-i-ti) *n.*

pertinent (per'-ti-nent) *a.* related to subject or matter in hand; to the point.—per'tinently *adv.*—per'tinence, per'tinency *n.*

perturb (per-turb') *v.t.* disturb; trouble greatly.—perturbation (per-tur-bā'-shun) *n.* mental uneasiness; disorder or confusion.

peruke (pe-rōok', per-ūk') *n.* wig.

peruse (pe-rōoz', per-ūz') *v.t.* read through; examine.—peru'sal *n.*

pervade (per-vād') *v.t.* spread through whole of.—pervasion *n.*— perva'sive *a.* having power to pervade.

perverse (per-vers') *a.* obstinately wrong; refusing to admit error; self-willed.—perverse'ness, perver'sity *n.*

perversion (per-ver'-shun) *n.* turning from true purpose, use, or meaning; corruption; unnatural manifestation of sexual desire.—perver'sive *a.* tending to pervert.

pervert (per-vert') *v.t.* turn from its proper purpose; lead astray; corrupt. —pervert (per'-vert) *n.* one who has deviated from normal, esp. from right to wrong.

pessimism (pes'-i-mizm) *n.* gloomy view of life or events (opp. of *optimism*); melancholy.—pess'imist *n.* —pessimis'tic *a.*—pessimis'tically *adv.*

pest (pest) *n.* harmful thing or person; (*Colloq.*) nuisance.—pestif'erous *a.* pestilential; carrying disease.

pester (pes'-ter) *v.t.* trouble or vex persistently; annoy.

pesticide (pes'-ti-sīd) *n.* pest killer.

pestilence (pes'-ti-lens) *n.* infectious or contagious, deadly disease.— pes'tilent *a.* producing disease; noxious.—pestilential (pes-ti-len'-shal) *a.* pert. to, or producing, pestilence; destructive.

pestle (pes'-to, pes-l) *n.* instrument for pounding substances in mortar.

pet (pet) *n.* animal or person regarded with affection; favourite; darling;— *a.* favourite;—*v.t.* make pet of; treat with indulgence.—*pr.p.* pet'ting.— *pa.p.* and *pa.t.* pet'ted.

pet (pet) *n.* sudden fit of ill-temper.

petal (pet'-al) *n.* coloured flower-leaf. —pet'aled, pet'alled *a.* having petals.

petard (pet-ärd') *n.* formerly, kind of small bomb; kind of firework; paper cracker.—hoist with his own petard, beaten by his own weapons.

peter out (pē'-ter-out) *v.i.* (*Mining*) of vein, seam, etc., become exhausted; give out.

petition (pe-tish'-un) *n.* earnest request or prayer, esp. one presented to sovereign or parliament;—*v.t.* and *v.i.* present petition to; entreat.— petit'ionary *a.*—petit'ioner *n.*

petrel (pet'-rel) *n.* small sea-bird.

petrify (pet'-ri-fī) *v.t.* turn into stone; make hard like stone; (*Fig.*) make motionless with fear;—*v.i.* become like stone.—*pa.p.* and *pa.t.* pet'rified.

petro- (pet'-ro) *prefix* fr. L. and Gk. *petra*, rock, stone, used in derivatives.—petrog'raphy *n.* science of describing and classifying rocks.— petrograph'ic(al) *a.* — petrol'ogy *n.* branch of geology dealing with structure, and classification of rocks, their origin and sequence of formation.—petrolog'ic(al) *a.*—petrous (pe'-trus) *a.* pert. to rock; rocky; hard.

petroleum (pe-trō'-le-um) *n.* rock-oil, mineral oil drawn from the earth by means of wells.—pet'rol *n.* motor-spirit; (*U.S.*) gasoline.

petticoat (pet'-i-kōt) *n.* woman's underskirt.

pettifogger (pet'-i-fog-er) *n.* one given to mean dealing in small matters.—pett'ifog *v.i.*—pett'ifoggery *n.* low trickery; wrangling over trifles.—pett'ifogging *a.* underhand; paltry.

petty (pet'-i) *a.* small; unimportant; trivial; small-minded; of lower rank. —pett'ily *adv.*—pett'iness *n.*—petty cash, small items of expenditure, esp. in an office.—petty officer, non-commissioned officer in Navy.

petulant (pet'-ū-lant) *a.* given to small fits of temper; inclined to complain; irritable.—pet'ulantly *adv.*

—pet'ulance, pet'ulancy n. peevishness; crossness; fretfulness.

petunia (pē-tū'-ni-ạ) n. flowering plants of the tobacco family; purplish red.

pew (pū) n. long, fixed bench in church.

pewit (pē'-wit) n. lapwing. Also **pee'wit**.

pewter (pū'-tẹr) n. alloy of tin and lead; ware made of this;—a. made of pewter.

phaeton (fā'-ton) n. light, four-wheeled, open carriage.

phalanger (fa-lan'-jẹr) n. flying squirrel.

phalanx (fal'-angks, fā'-langks) n. in ancient Greece, company of soldiers in close array; any compact body of people.—pl. phal'anxes.

phallus (fal'-us) n. penis.—pl. phall'i.—phall'ic a.

phantasm (fan'-tazm) n. imaginary vision; phantom; spectre; illusion.—phantas'mal, phantas'mic a.—phantasmagoria (fan-taz-mạ-gō'-ri-ạ) n. exhibition of optical illusions; hence, crowd of dim figures.—phantasmagor'ic a.—phan'tasy n. See **fantasy.**—phan'tom (fan'-tom) n. apparition; spectre; ghost;—a. spectral.

Pharisee (far'-i-sē) n. (Bib.) Jewish sect noted for their strict observance of forms of the Law.—**Pharisaic** (far-i-sā'-ik), **Pharisa'ical** a. pert. to or like the Pharisees; hypocritical. — Pharisa'ically adv. — Pharisa'ism, Pharisee'ism n.

pharmaceutical (fár-mạ-sū'-tik-ạl) a. pert. to pharmacy.—pharmaceu'tics n.pl. science of pharmacy.—pharmaceu'tist n.

pharmacy (fár'-mạ-si) n. science of compounding and dispensing drugs and medicines; chemist's shop; drug-store.—phar'macist n. one skilled in pharmacy.—pharmacol'ogy n. study of drugs.—pharmacol'ogist n.—pharmacopoeia (fár-mạ-kō-pē'-yạ) n. standard and authoritative book containing list of medicinal drugs with information on their preparation and dosage.

pharynx (far'-ingks) n. cavity at back of mouth, opening into gullet.—pl. phar'ynges (far-in'-jē-ạl, far-in-jē'-ạl) a. Also pharyn'gal. — pharyngitis (far-in-jī'-tis) n. (Med.) inflammation of pharynx.

phase (fāz) n. (Astron.) aspect of moon or planet; stage in development; aspect of subject or question.—pha'sic a.

pheasant (fez'-ạnt) n. game-bird.

phenacetin (fe-nas'-e-tin) n. drug used as antipyretic.

phenomenon (fe-nom'-e-non) n. anything appearing or observed, esp. if having scientific interest; remarkable person or thing;—pl. phenom'-

ena.—phenom'enal a. remarkable; extraordinary.—phenom'enally adv.

phew (fū) interj. expressing disgust.

phial (fī'-ạl) n. small glass bottle; vial.

philander (fi-lan'-dẹr) v.i. flirt; amuse oneself with love-making.—philan'derer n.

philanthropy (fi-lan'-thro-pi) n. love of mankind.—philanthrop'ic, philanthrop'ical a.—philanthrop'ically adv.—philan'thropist n. one who loves and seeks to do good to his fellow-men. Also phil'anthrope.

philately (fi-lat'-e-li) n. practice of stamp-collecting. — philat'elic a. — philat'elist n.

philharmonic (fil-har-mon'-ik) a. loving harmony or music; musical.

philistine (fil'-is-tīn, -tin) n. (Fig.) person with no love of music, painting, etc.; uncultured person.

philology (fi-lol'-o-ji) n. scientific study of origin, development, etc. of languages.—philolog'ical a.—philologian (fi-lol-ō'-ji-ạn) philol'ogist n. student of philology.

philosophy (fi-los'-o-fi) n. lit. 'love of wisdom'; originally, any branch of investigation of natural phenomena; now, study of beliefs regarding God, existence, conduct, etc. and of man's relation with the universe; calmness of mind; resignation.—philos'opher n. student of philosophy.—philosophic (fil-o-sof'-ik), philosoph'ical a. wise; calm.—philosoph'ically adv.—philos'ophise v.i. theorise; moralise.—moral philosophy, study of ethics.—natural philosophy, branch of scientific study, physics.—philosopher's stone, substance sought for by alchemists of old, supposed to transform base metals into gold.

philtre, philter (fil'-tẹr) n. love potion.

phlebitis (fle-bī'-tis) n. inflammation of vein.—phlebit'ic a.—phlebot'omy n. (Surg.) blood-letting.

phlegm (flem) n. mucous substance discharged from throat by expectoration; calmness; sluggishness. — phlegmatic (fleg-mat'-ik) a. cool and collected.—phlegmat'ically adv.

phlox (floks) n. genus of garden plants.

phobia (fō'-bi-ạ) n. morbid dread of anything; used esp. as suffix, e.g. claustrophobia, hydrophobia, etc.

Phoenix, Phenix (fē'-niks) n. (Myth.) fabulous Arabian bird, said to be reborn from its own ashes; symbol of immortality; paragon.

phone (fōn) n., v.t. and i. (Colloq.) abbrev. of tel'ephone.

phone (fōn) n. sound made in speaking.—phon'ic a. pert. to sound, esp. to speech sounds; phonetic.—phon'ics n.pl. used as sing. phonetics; acoustics.

phonetic (fō-net'-ik) *a.* pert. to voice; pert. to vocal sounds. Also **phonet'ical** *a.*—**phonet'ically** *adv.*—**phonet'ics** *n.* branch of study of language which deals with speech sounds, and their symbols.—**phonetic'ian** *n.* student of phonetics.—**phonet'icise** *v.t.*—phonetic spelling, simplified system of spelling in which same letter or symbol is always used for same sound.

phoney (fō'-ni) *a.* (*Slang*) sham.

phono- (fō'-nō) *prefix* fr. Gk. *phonē,* sound, used in many derivatives.—**pho'nograph** *n.* early type of gramophone.—**phonol'ogy** *n.* study of phonetic structure and development of a language.—**phonolog'ic(al)** *a.*—**phonol'ogist** *n.*

phosphate (fos'-fāt) *n.* salt of phosphoric acid.—**phosphate of lime,** commercially, bone-ash.—**phos'phide** *n.* compound of phosphorus with another element.—**phos'phite** *n.* salt of phosphorous acid.

phosphorus (fos'-for-us) *n.* yellowish wax-like substance giving out pale light in dark.—**phos'phorous** *a.*—**phosphorescence** (fos-for-es'-ens) *n.* giving out of light without heat, as phosphorus, decaying fish, etc.—**phosphoresc'ent** *a.*—**phosphor'ic** *a.*

photo (fō'-tō) *n.* (*Colloq.*) abbrev. of photograph.

photo- (fō'-tō) *prefix* fr. Gk. *phos, photos,* light, used in derivatives.—**photo'copy** *n.* photographic replica of document.—**photoelectricity** *n.* electricity produced by the action of light.—**photo-finish,** in racing, photo taken at finish to show correct placing of contestants.—**photogen'ic** *a.* producing light; photographic; of person, having features, etc. that photograph well.

photography (fō-tog'-ra-fi) *n.* art of producing pictures by chemical action of light on a sensitive plate or film.—**pho'tograph** *n.* picture so made;—*v.t.* take photograph of.—**photog'rapher** *n.*—**photograph'ic, photograph'ical** *a.*—**photograph'ically** *adv.*—**photogravure** (fō'-tō-gra-vūr) *n.* method of producing prints from photos etched on a metal plate;—*v.t.* reproduce thus;—*n.* print so made. — **photolithography** (fō-tō-li-thog'-ra-fi) *n.* process of printing in which the subject is reproduced photographically on a litho plate.

photometer (fō-tom'-e-ter) *n.* device for measuring intensity of light.

photon (fō'-ton) *n.* unit of measurement of light-intensity.

Photostat (fō'-tō-stat) *n.* photographic apparatus for direct copies of documents, etc.—*v.t.* copy thus.—**photostat'ic** *a.* [Protected Trade Name].

phrase (frāz) *n.* group of words forming part of sentence; short pithy expression; (*Mus.*) short part of longer passage;—*v.t.* express suitably in words.—**phraseogram** (fra'-ze-ō-gram) *n.* in shorthand, symbol used to represent phrase.—**phraseol'ogy** *n.* choice of words used in speaking or writing.

phrenology (fre-nol'-o-ji) *n.* character reading from shape of head.—**phrenolog'ic(al)** *a.* — **phrenolog'ically** *adv.*—**phrenol'ogist** *n.*

phut (fut) *n.* onomatopœic word.—**to go phut** (*Colloq.*) collapse; break down.

physic (fiz'-ik) *n.* (*Arch.*) art of healing; drug; medicine in general;—*v.t.* give dose of physic to.—**physician** (fi-zish'-an) *n.* medical doctor.

physical (fiz'-ik-al) *a.* pert. to physics; pert. to nature; bodily, as opposed to mental or moral; material.—**phys'ically** *adv.*

physics (fiz'-iks) *n.* sciences (excluding chemistry and biology) which deal with natural phenomena, e.g. motion, force, light, sound, electricity, etc. Also called '*Natural Philosophy.*'—**physicist** (fiz'-i-sist) *n.*

physiognomy (fiz-i-on'-o-mi) *n.* art of judging character from contours of face; face itself.—**physiognom'ic, physiognom'ical** *a.*—**physiog'nomist** *n.*

physiography (fiz-i-og'-ra-fi) *n.* study and description of natural phenomena; physical geography.—**physiog'rapher** *n.*

physiology (fiz-i-ol'-o-ji) *n.* science which deals with functions and life processes of plants, animals, and human beings.—**physiolog'ical** *a.*—**physiol'ogist** *n.*

physiotherapy (fiz-i-ō-ther'-a-pi) *n.* application of massage, light, heat, etc., for treatment of disabilities.

physique (fi-zēk') *n.* bodily structure and development.

pi (pī) *n.* Greek letter π, esp. as mathematical symbol for ratio of circumference of circle to its diameter, approx. $3\frac{1}{7}$, or 3.14159.

piano (pē-à'-nō) *adv.* (*Mus.*) softly.—**pianis'simo** *adv.* very softly.

piano (pē-á'-nō) *n. abbrev.* of **pianoforte** (pē-à-nō-for'-tā) *n.* musical instrument having wires of graduated tension, struck by hammers moved by notes on keyboard.—**pianist** (pē'-a-nist, pē-an'-ist) *n.* one who plays piano.

piastre (pi-as'-ter) *n.* monetary unit of some Eastern countries, Turkey, Egypt, etc.

piazza (pē-at'-sa, pē-az'-a) *n.* open square, surrounded by buildings.

pibroch (pē'-broH) *n.* selection of music for Scottish bagpipes.

picador (pik-a-dor') *n.* mounted bullfighter.

picaroon (pik'-a-roón) *n.* rogue; pirate.—**picaresque** (pik-a-resk') *a.* of a novel, episodic, connected by central character; dealing with lives and adventures of rogues.

piccalilli (pik-a-lil'-i) *n.* pickle of vegetables.

piccaninny (pik'-a-nin-i) *n.* small child; Negro baby.

piccolo (pik'-o-lō) *n.* small flute, octave higher than ordinary flute.

pick (pik) *v.t.* peck at, like birds with their bills; pierce with pointed instrument; open with pointed instrument, as lock; pluck, as flowers, etc.; raise or lift (*with* up); choose or select; pluck strings of musical 'nstrument;—*v.i.* eat daintily or without appetite; find fault with (*with* on);—*n.* sharp-pointed tool, used for breaking up earth, etc.; choice; right of selection; the best of anything.—**pick'axe** *n.* instrument for breaking up ground.—**pick'ing** *n.* act of one who picks; stealing;—*pl.* gleanings; perquisites.—**pick'pocket** *n.* one who steals from pockets.—**pick'-me-up** *n.* drink that acts as stimulant.—**pick-up** *n.* device holding stylus in record player.

pick-a-back (pik'-a-bak) *adv.* on the shoulders.

picket (pik'-et) *n.* sharpened stake (used in fortifications, etc.); peg; guard posted in front of army; party sent out by trade unions to prevent men from working during strike;—*v.t.* fence with pickets; post, as guard; beset with pickets.

pickle (pik'-l) *n.* brine or vinegar in which fish, meat, or vegetables are preserved; food preserved in brine or vinegar; difficult situation;—*v.t.* preserve with salt or vinegar.—**pick'led** *a.* (*Slang*) drunk.—**pick'les** *n.pl.* vegetables in spiced vinegar.

picnic (pik'-nik) *n.* pleasure excursion with meal out of doors; agreeable situation;—*v.i.* go on a picnic.—*pr.p.* **pic'nicking**—*pa.p.* and *pa.t.* **pic'nicked.**

Pict (pikt) *n.* one of ancient race, formerly inhabiting E. Scotland.—**Pic'tish** *a.*

pictorial (pik-tō'-ri-al) *a.* pert. to pictures; illustrated.—**picto'rially** *adv.*

picture (pik'-tūr) *n.* representation of objects or scenes on paper, canvas, etc., by drawing, painting, photography, etc.; mental image; likeness or copy; illustration; picturesque object; vivid description in words;—*v.t.* draw or paint image or representation of; describe graphically; recall vividly.—**picturesque** (pik-tū-resk') *a.* making pleasing picture.—**picturesque'ly** *adv.*—**picturesque'ness** *n.*—**pic'ture-house,** *n.* cinema.

pidgin (pij'-in) *n.* corruption of English word *business.*—**pidgin** or **pigeon English,** jargon used in China between foreigners and natives.

pie (pi) *n.* (*Cookery*) dish of meat or fruit covered with paste and baked; (*Print.*) confused mass of type.

pie (pi) *n.* magpie.—**piebald** (pī'-bawld) *a.* streaked with any two colours.—**pied** *a.* piebald; variegated.

piece (pēs) *n.* part; bit; portion; single object; separate example; coin; counter in chess, draughts, etc.; literary work; musical composition; gun;—*v.t.* mend; put together.—**piece'meal** *adv.* gradually.—**piece'work** *n.* work paid for by amount done.—**piece of eight,** old Spanish dollar.

pier (pēr) *n.* piece of solid, upright masonry, as support or pillar for arch or bridge; structure built out over water as landing-stage.—**pier'glass** *n.* tall mirror, esp. wall-mirror between two windows.

pierce (pērs) *v.t.* thrust into, esp. with pointed instrument; make hole in;—*v.i.* enter; penetrate.—**pierc'ing** *a.* sharp; keen.—**pierc'ingly** *adv.*

pierrot (pē'-er-ō) *n.* member of troupe of seaside entertainers.

piety (pī'-e-ti) *n.* quality of being pious; devotion to religion; affectionate respect for one's parents.—**pi'etist** *n.* sanctimonious person.—**pietist'ic** *a.*—**pi'etism** *n.*

pig (pig) *n.* hoofed domestic animal, reared for its flesh; oblong mass of smelted metal, as pig-iron;—*v.i.* bring forth pigs.—**pigg'ish** *a.* pert. to, or like, pigs; dirty; greedy.—**pigg'ery** *n.* place where swine are kept.—**pig'tail** *n.* tail of pig; queue or plait of hair hanging from back of head; roll of twisted tobacco.—**pig'-head'ed** *a.* obstinate.—**pig'-nut** *n.* earth-nut.—**pig'sty** *n.* covered enclosure for pigs; dirty house or room.

pigeon (pij'-un) *n.* bird of dove family; simpleton or dupe.—**pig'eon-Eng'lish** See **pidgin-English.**—**pig'eon-heart'ed** *a.* timid.—**pig'eon-hole** *n.* little division in desk for holding papers, etc.;—*v.t.* place in pigeonhole of desk, etc.; shelve for future reference; classify. — **pig'eon-toed** *a.* having turned-in toes.

pigment (pig'-ment) *n.* paint; colouring matter; colouring matter in animal tissues and cells.—**pigmenta'tion** *n.* colouration esp. of stain.

pike (pik) *n.* sharp point; old weapon with long, wooden shaft with flat-pointed steel head; voracious fresh-water fish.

pilaster (pi-las'-ter) *n.* rectangular column, esp. as part of wall.

pilchard (pil'-chard) *n.* sea-fish resembling herring, but smaller.

pile (pil) *n.* mass of things; heap; large building or mass of buildings;

electric battery, with alternate plates; nuclear reactor; (*Colloq.*) large fortune;—*v.t.* throw into pile or heap; accumulate (up).

pile (pīl) *n.* beam driven vertically into ground to support building, bridge, etc.;—*v.t.* drive piles into; support with piles.—**pile'-driv'er** *n.* engine for driving in piles.

pile (pīl) *n.* fur; hair; nap of fabric.

piles (pīlz) *n.pl.* haemorrhoids.

pilfer (pil'-fer) *v.t.* and *i.* steal in small quantities.

pilgrim (pil'-grim) *n.* traveller, esp. one who journeys to visit holy place. —**pil'grimage** *n.* the journey.

pill (pil) *n.* small ball of medicine, to be swallowed whole; anything disagreeable that has to be endured; (*Slang*) any ball.—**pill'-box** *n.* (*Mil.*) small concrete fort.

pillage (pil'-āj) *n.* act of plundering; plunder, esp. in war;—*v.t.* plunder.

pillar (pil'-ar) *n.* slender upright structure of stone, iron, etc.; column; support.—**pill'ared** *a.*—**pill'-ar-box** *n.* hollow iron pillar in which letters can be posted.

pillion (pil'-yun) *n.* pad put behind saddle on horse or motor-cycle to seat second person.

pillory (pil'-o-ri) *n.* frame with holes for head and hands in which offenders were formerly exposed to pelting and ridicule;—*v.t.* punish thus; expose to ridicule and abuse.—*pr.p.* pill'orying.—*pa.p.* and *pa.t.* pill'oried.

pillow (pil'-ō) *n.* cushion for head, esp. for person in bed;—*v.t.* place on pillow.—**pill'ow-case**, **pill'ow-slip** *n.* removable covering for pillow.

pilot (pī'-lot) *n.* person qualified to take charge of ship, where knowledge of local waters is needed; one qualified to operate aircraft; steersman; guide;—*v.t.* direct course of; guide through dangers or difficulties. —**pi'lot-cloth** *n.* heavy, blue, woollen cloth for overcoats.—**pi'lot-fish** *n.* tropical fish, said to guide sharks to their prey.—**pilot light**, a small jet of gas kept burning in order to light cooker, geyser, etc.—**pilot officer** (*R.A.F.*) officer of equivalent rank to second lieutenant in Army or act. sub-lieut. R.N.—**pilot scheme**, small-scale experimental scheme.

pimpernel (pim'-per-nel) *n.* annual plant of primrose family.

pimple (pim'-pl) *n.* small, red, pustular spot on the skin.—**pim'pled**, **pim'ply** *a.*

pin (pin) *n.* short, thin piece of stiff wire with point and head for fastening soft materials together; wooden or metal peg or rivet; (*Golf*) thin metal or wooden stick (with flag) to mark the position of hole; trifle;—*pl.* (*Slang*) legs;—*v.t.* fasten with pins; seize and hold fast.

—*pr.p.* pin'ning.—*pa.p.* and *pa.t.* pinned.—**pin'cushion** *n.* small pad in which pins are stuck.—**pin'-mon'ey** *n.* orig. sum of money settled on wife for private expenses; hence, wife's dress allowance.—**pin'point** *v.t.* (*R.A.F.*) locate (target) with great accuracy.—**pin'-prick** *n.* prick with pin; (*Fig.*) petty annoyance or irritation.—**pin table** *n.* type of bagatelle used for gambling.—**pin-up** (*Colloq.*) girl's photograph pinned up on the wall; subject of such a photograph.

pinafore (pin'-a-fōr) *n.* type of apron.

pincers (pin'-serz) *n.pl.* tool for gripping, composed of two limbs crossed and pivoted; nippers; pliers; claw of lobster, crab, etc.—**pincer-movement** (*Mil.*) two-fold attack converging on enemy's position.

pinch (pinsh) *v.t.* nip or squeeze, e.g. between thumb and finger; stint; make thin, e.g. by hunger; (*Slang*) steal; (*Slang*) arrest;—*v.i.* press hard; be miserly;—*n.* as much as can be taken up between thumb and finger; nip; emergency.—**pinched** *a.* (*Fig.*) thin and hungry-looking.

pinchbeck (pinsh'-bek) *n.* zinc and copper alloy; cheap jewellery;—*a.* flashy; tawdry.

pine (pīn) *n.* coniferous tree with evergreen, needle-like leaves; its wood.—**pi'ney**, **pi'ny** *a.* abounding with pines. — **pineapp'le** *n.* tropical plant and its fruit; anana.—**pine'-cone** *n.* fruit of pine.—**pine'-need'le** *n.* leaf of pine-tree.

pine (pīn) *v.i.* waste away from grief, anxiety, etc.; languish; wither; desire eagerly.

ping (ping) *n.* sound of bullet going through air.—**ping'-pong** *n.* table-tennis.

pinion (pin'-yun) *n.* outermost joint of bird's wing; feather; small wheel with teeth working into teeth of larger wheel;—*v.t.* restrain by binding arms to body; shackle.

pink (pingk) *n.* clove-scented garden-flower; light crimson colour; scarlet colour of fox-hunter's coat;—*a.* of pale crimson colour.

pink (pingk) *v.t.* pierce; ornament edge with scallops, etc.

pink (pingk) *v.i.* of motor-engine, make metallic, knocking sound.

pinnace (pin'-as) *n.* warship's boat; light sailing-vessel.

pinnacle (pin'-a-kl) *n.* slender turret elevated above main building; rocky mountain peak; summit; (*Fig.*) climax.

pint (pīnt) *n.* liquid measure.

pioneer (pī-o-nēr') *n.* (*Mil.*) one of advance body clearing or repairing road for troops; explorer; one who prepares way for others;—*v.i.* open way or originate.

pious (pī'-us) *a.* having love for God; marked by pretended or mistaken devotion.

pip (pip) *n.* seed of apple, orange, etc.

pip (pip) *n.* disease in mouth of fowls.—**to have the pip**, be depressed, or irritable.

pip (pip) *n.* star on officer's shoulder; each spot on domino, playing-card, dice, etc.; shrill staccato note.

pip (pip) *v.t.* (*Colloq.*) wound; fail.

pipe (pīp) *n.* tubular instrument of music; long tube; tube of clay, wood, etc. with bowl for smoking; bird's note; wine-measure, usually 126 gallons; pipeful of tobacco; funnel;—*pl.* bagpipes;—*v.t.* perform on a pipe; utter in shrill tone; convey by means of pipes; ornament with fancy edging;—*v.i.* play on pipe, esp. the bagpipes; whistle.—**piped** (pīpt) *a.* furnished with pipe; tubular; conveyed by pipes.—**pi'ping** *a.* giving forth shrill sound; steaming hot;—*n.* act of playing on pipe; system of pipes (for gas, water, etc.); kind of cord trimming for ladies' dresses; ornamentation made on cakes by forcing icing through small nozzle.—**pi'per** *n.*—**pipe'-clay** *n.* fine, whitish clay used in manufacture of tobacco-pipes;—*v.t.* whiten with pipe-clay.—**pipe'-line** *n.* long line of piping for conveying water or oil.—**pipe'-ma'jor** *n.* (*Mil.*) commander of pipe-band.

pipette (pi-pet') *n.* thin glass tube used for withdrawing small quantities of liquid.

pipit (pip'-it) *n.* small bird, like lark.

pippin (pin'-in) *n.* one of several kinds of apple.

piquant (pē'-kant) *a.* agreeably pungent to taste; (*Fig.*) arousing curiosity.—**pi'quantly** *adv.*—**piquancy** (pē'-kan-si) *n.* pungency.

pique (pēk) *v.t.* irritate; hurt pride of; displease; stimulate;—*pr.p.* piq'uing.—*n.* annoyance from slight.

piqué (pē'-kā) *n.* stiff, ribbed cotton fabric.

pirate (pī'-rāt) *n.* sea-robber; vessel manned by sea-robbers; publisher, etc. who infringes copyright;—*v.t.* and *i.* act as pirate; plunder; infringe copyright.—**pirat'ical** *a.*—**pirat'ically** *adv.*—**pi'racy** *n.*

pirouette (pir-oō-et') *n.* spinning round on one toe;—*v.i.* do this.

piscatology (pis-ka-tol'-o-ji) *n.* study of fishes.—**piscator** (pis-kā'-tor) *n.* angler; fisherman.—**piscato'rial**, **pis'catory** *a.* pert. to fishes or fishing.—**pis'ciform** *a.* fish-shaped.

pistachio (pis-ta'(tā')-shi-ō) *n.* nut of Asiatic tree, used for flavouring.

pistil (pis'-til) *n.* seed-bearing organ of flower, consisting of stigma, style, and ovary.

pistol (pis'-tl) *n.* small hand-gun.

piston (pis'-tun) *n.* closely fitting metal disc moving to and fro hollow cylinder, e.g. as in steam-engine, motor-car, etc.

pit (pit) *n.* deep hole in ground, esp. one from which coal, etc. is dug; abyss of hell; area for cock-fighting, etc.; in theatre, cheaper priced seats behind orchestra stalls; in motor-racing, base where cars are re-filled, etc.; small indentation in the skin left by pustule of e.g. smallpox;—*v.t.* mark with little hollows, as by pustules; place in pit; put forward as antagonist in contest.—**pitt'ed** *a.* marked with small hollows.—**pit'fall** *n.* pit lightly covered, intended to entrap animals; (*Fig.*) hidden danger.

pitch (pich) *n.* thick, black, sticky substance obtained by boiling down tar;—*v.t.* cover over, smear with pitch. — **pitch'iness** *n.* — **pitch'-black**, **pitch'-dark** *a.* very dark.—**pitch'blende** *n.* natural ore consisting mainly of uranium oxide, source of radium.—**pitch'-pine** *n.* pine abounding in resinous matter.

pitch (pich) *v.t.* throw, toss, fling; set up (tent, camp, wickets, etc.); set keynote of;—*v.i.* alight; plunge or fall forward; slope down; of ship, plunge.—*n.* act of tossing or casting or, in golf, lofting ball; throw or cast; degree of elevation or depth; highest point; plunging motion of vessel lengthwise; degree of acuteness of musical note; (*Cricket*) ground between wickets; station for street vendor; distance between consecutive threads of screw, or between successive teeth of gear.—**pitched** (picht) *a.* sloping; fully arranged for and deliberately entered upon, as *pitched battle.*—**pitch'er** *n.*—**pitch'fork** *n.* fork for tossing hay, etc.; tuning-fork;—*v.t.* lift with a pitch-fork; (*Fig.*) thrust suddenly into.—**pitch and toss**, gambling game, played by tossing coins.

pitcher (pich'-er) *n.* jug.

pith (pith) *n.* spongy substance in plant stems; thin whitish layer beneath citrus peel; essential substance; force or vigour.—**pith'y** *a.* consisting of pith; forceful; energetic. —**pith'ily** *adv.*—**pith'iness** *n.*—**pith'less** *a.*

pittance (pit'-ans) *n.* very small or insufficient portion or allowance.

pituitary (pi-tū'-i-tari) *a.* secreting mucus. — **pituitary gland**, ductless gland at base of brain.

pity (pit'-i) *n.* sympathy for others' suffering; cause of grief;—*v.t.* feel grief for.—*pa.t.* and *pa.p.* pit'ied.—**pit'ying** *a.*—**pit'yingly** *adv.*—**pit'iable** *a.* deserving pity.—**pit'iably** *adv.*—**pit'iful** *a.* full of pity; tender; exciting pity.—**pit'ifully** *adv.*—**pit'iless** *n.*—**pit'iless** *a.* hard-hearted.

—pit'ilessly *adv.*—pit'ilessness *n.*—pit'-
eous *a.* fitted to excite pity: wretched.
—pit'eously *adv.*—pit'eousness *n.*

pivot (piv'-ut) *n.* pin on which wheel
or other body turns; that on which
important results depend;—*v.i.* turn
as on pivot.

pixy, pixie (pĭk'-si) *n.* fairy or elf.

pizzicato (pit-si-kä'-tō) *a.* (*Mus.*)
direction for stringed instruments
denoting that strings be plucked
with fingers.

placable (plak'-ạ-bl, plā'-kạ-bl) *a.*
readily appeased; willing to forgive.
—placabil'ity, plac'ableness *n.*—placate
(plạ-kāt') *v.t.* appease.—placa'tory *a.*
conciliatory.

place (plās) *n.* orig. open space in
town; particular part of space: spot;
locality; building; rank; position;
priority of position; stead; duty;
office or employment; (*Sport*) position among the first three competitors to finish;—*v.t.* put in particular
spot; find position for: appoint; fix;
put; identify.—placed *pa.p.* of the
verb;—*a.* in race, etc., to be first,
second, or third at the finish.—
place'-kick *n.* (*Rugby*) one made by
kicking ball after it has been placed
on ground for the purpose.—to give
place, to make room for.

placenta (plạ-sen'-ta) *n.* (*Med.*) the
soft, spongy substance through
which the mother's blood nourishes
foetus; after-birth.—placen'tal *a.*

placid (plas'-id) *a.* calm; peaceful.—
plac'idly *adv.*—placid'ity *n.* mildness;
serenity.

plagiarise (plā'-ji-ạr-īz) *v.t.* steal
words, ideas, etc. of another and use
them as one's own.—pla'giarism *n.*
act of plagiarising; literary theft.—
pla'giarist *n.*—pla'giary *n.* plagiarism;
plagiarist.

plague (plāg) *n.* deadly, epidemic,
infectious disease; pestilence; (*Colloq.*) nuisance;—*v.t.* vex;—annoy.—
pr.p. plag'uing;—*pa.p.* and *pa.t.*
plagued;—plaguey (plāg'-gi) *a.)*

plaice (plās) *n.* flat-fish allied to
flounder.

plaid (plăd. plad) *n.* long, woollen
garment, usually with tartan pattern, worn as wrap by Scottish
Highlanders.

plain (plān) *a.* level; flat; even;
evident; clear; simple; ordinary;
without decoration; not beautiful;
—*adv.* clearly;—*n.* tract of level
country.—plain'ly *adv.*—plain'ness *n.*
—plain'-sail'ing *n.* unobstructed
course of action.—plain'-song *n.*
traditional chants of R.C. church,
sung in unison.

plaint (plānt) *n.* a lamentation.—
plain'tiff *n.* one who sues in court of
law; prosecutor.—plain'tive *a.* sad;
mournful.—plain'tively *adv.*

plait (plat plāt) *n.* fold; braid of

hair, straw, etc.;—*v.t.* interweave
strands of hair, straw, etc. Also
pleat.

plan (plan) *n.* drawing representing
a thing's horizontal section; diagram; map; project; design; scheme;
—*v.t.* make plan of: arrange beforehand.—*pr.p.* plan'ning.—*pa.p.* and
pa.t. planned.

plane (plān) *n.* carpenter's tool for
smoothing wood;—*v.t.* make smooth
with plane.—pla'ner *n.*

plane (plān) *n* any tree of genus
Platanus; (*Scot.*) sycamore.

plane (plān) *n.* flat, level surface;
(*Geom.*) surface such that, if any
two points on it be joined by
straight line, that line will lie
wholly on surface;—*a.* perfectly
level; pert. to plane.—plane geometry,
branch of geometry which deals with
plane, not solid, figures.

plane (plān) *n.* abbrev. of 'aeroplane';
wing of aeroplane or glider;—*v.i.*
glide.

planet (plan'-et) *n.* celestial body
revolving round sun as distinct from
fixed stars.—planetarium (plan-e-tā'-
ri-um) *n.* working model of planetary
system.—plan'etary *a.* pert. to planets; revolving in fixed orbit; (*Astrol.*)
under influence of planet.

plank (plangk) *n.* thick, heavy board;
policy in political programme;—
v.t. lay with planks.—plank'ing *n.*
structural planks esp. of ships.

plankton (plangk'-tun) *n.* minute
animal and vegetable organisms
floating in ocean.

plant (plänt) *n.* living organism
belonging to vegetable kingdom,
generally excluding trees and shrubs;
slip or cutting; machinery, tools,
etc., used in industrial undertaking;
—*v.t.* set in ground for growth;—
v.i. sow seeds, or set shoots, in
ground.—plantation (plạn-tā'-shun)
n. area planted with trees: large
estate, esp. in a colony.—plan'ter *n.*
one who plants; the owner of
plantation.

plantain (plan'-tān) *n.* roadside
weed with broad leaves.

plantain (plan'-tān) *n.* tropical tree
of banana family; its fruit.

plaque (plak) *n.* thin, flat, ornamental tablet hung on wall or inserted
into wall.

plasm (plazm) *n.* (*Biol.*) living
matter of cell; protoplasm.—plas'ma
n. (*Med.*) protoplasm; fluid part of
blood; hot ionised gas neutrally charged.—plasmat'ic, plas'mic *a.*

plaster (plås'-ter) *n.* composition of
lime, water, and sand, for coating
walls; gypsum, for making ornaments, mouldings, etc.; (*Med.*)
adhesive, curative application;
(*Surg.*) composition used to hold
limb, etc. rigid;—*v.t.* cover with

plaster, as wound; smooth over or conceal.—plas′terer *n.*

plastic (plas′-tik) *a.* capable of moulding or of being moulded; pliable;—*n.* substance capable of being moulded.—plas′tics *n.pl.* synthetic resins and natural substances (other than rubber) which can be moulded under heat or pressure.—plasticity (plas-tis′-i-ti) *n.* quality of being plastic.—plastic art, art of representing figures in sculpture or by modelling in clay.—plastic surgery, art of restoring damaged parts of body by grafting on sound tissue.

plate (plāt) *n.* shallow, round dish from which food is eaten; plateful; flat, thin sheet of metal, glass, etc.; utensils of gold or silver; thin sheet of vulcanite, or metal, to hold artificial teeth; (*Photog.*) short for 'photographic plate';—*v.t.* cover with thin coating of gold, silver, or other metal; protect with steel plates, e.g. as ship.—pla′ter *n.* shipyard worker who fixes steel plates on ship.—plate′-arm′our *n.* very heavy, protective armour for warships.—plate′-glass *n.* thick glass, rolled in sheets and used for windows, mirrors, etc.—plate′-lay′er *n.* railroad worker who lays down or repairs rails.—photographic plate or film, thin sheet of glass or celluloid coated with sensitive emulsion.

plateau (pla-tō′) *n.* tract of level, high ground; flat portion of line in graph. — *pl.* plateaus, plateaux (pla-tōz′, pla-to′).

platform (plat′-form) *n.* wooden structure raised above level of floor, as stand for speakers; landing-stage at railway-station; (*Fig.*) policy of political party.

platinum (plat′-in-um) *n.* hard, silvery-white, malleable metal.—platin′ic, plat′inous *a.*—plat′inoid *n.* metal found associated with platinum, e.g. iridium.

platitude (plat′-i-tūd) *n.* commonplace remark; dullness of writing or speaking.—platitu′dinous *a.*

Plato (plā′-tō) *n.* Greek philosopher (427-347 B.C.).—Platonic (pla-ton′-ik), Platon′ical *a.* pert. to Plato or to his philosophy.—Platonic love, spiritual affection between man and woman without sexual desire.

platoon (pla-tōōn′) *n.* (*Mil.*) small body of soldiers employed as unit.

platter (plat′-ẹr) *n.* large, shallow plate.

platypus (plat′-i-pus) *n.* the duck-bill, a small, aquatic, furred animal of Australia, has bill like duck, burrows, lays eggs, but suckles its young.

plaudit (plaw′-dit) *n.* enthusiastic applause.

plausible (plaw′-zi-bl) *a.* having appearance of being true; apparently right; fair-spoken.—plaus′ibly *adv.*—plausibil′ity.

play (plā) *v.t.* and *i.* frolic; flutter; amuse oneself; take part in game; gamble; act part on stage; perform on musical instrument; operate; delude;—*n.* free movement; scope; activity; action; amusement; fun; frolic; sport; gambling; dramatic piece or performance.—play′er *n.* one who plays; actor; performer on musical instrument; gambler.—play′able *a.*—play′ful *a.* fond of play or fun; lively.—play′fully *adv.*—play′bill *n.* bill to advertise play.—play′boy *n.* habitual pleasure-seeker.—play′house *n.* theatre.—play′mate *n.* playfellow.—play′-pen *n.* portable wooden enclosure for small children to play in.—play′thing *n.* toy.—playwright (plā′-rīt) *n.* writer of plays; dramatist.—play′ing-card *n.* one of set of cards, usually 52 in number, used in card-games.

plea (plē) *n.* (*Law*) defendant's answer to plaintiff's declaration; excuse; entreaty.

plead (plēd) *v.t.* allege in proof or vindication; offer in excuse; (*Law*) argue at bar;—*v.i.* carry on lawsuit; present answer to declaration of plaintiff; urge reasons in support of or against; beg or implore.—plead′er *n.*—plead′ing *a.* entreating;—*n.* art of conducting cause as advocate; entreaty; supplication;—*n.pl.* written statements of plaintiff and defendant in support of their claims.—plead′ingly *adv.*

please (plēz) *v.t.* excite agreeable sensations in; gratify; delight; satisfy;—*v.i.* like or think fit; choose; give pleasure. — pleasant (plez′-ant) *a.* fitted to please; cheerful; lively; merry; agreeable.—pleas′antly *adv.*—pleas′antness *n.*—pleasantry (plez′-ant-ri) *n.* playfulness in conversation; joke; humorous act;—*pl.* pleas′antries.—pleasing (plē′-zing) *a.* agreeable.—plea′singly *adv.*—pleasure (plezh′-ẹr) *n.* agreeable sensation; gratification; amusement; diversion; choice.— pleas′urable *a.*—pleas′urably *adv.*

pleat (plēt) *n.* flattened fold; crease.

plebeian (ple-bē′-an) *a.* pert. or belonging to the common people; vulgar; popular.

plebiscite (pleb′-i-sīt, pleb′-i-sit) *n.* vote of whole community or nation.

plectrum (plek′-trum) *n.* small instrument used for plucking strings of lyre, guitar, etc.

pledge (plej) *n.* something deposited as security; sign or token of anything; drinking to health of; solemn promise;—*v.t.* deposit in pawn; leave as security; drink the health of.

Pleistocene (plīs′-tō-sēn) *n.* (*Geol.*)

deposits of last glacial period, following Tertiary.

plenary (plē'-na-ri) *a.* full, entire, complete; unqualified; (of an assembly) fully attended.—**ple'narily** *adv.*—**ple'nariness** *n.*—**plenipotentiary** (plen-i-pō-ten'-sha-ri) *n.* ambassador with full powers;—*a.* possessing full powers.—**plenish** (plen'-ish) *v.t.* furnish; provide with necessary stock.—**plenitude** (plen'-i-tūd) *n.* fullness; repletion; abundance.

plenty (plen'-ti) *n.* full supply; abundance; sufficiency. — **plenteous** (plen'-tē-us) *a.* copious; ample; rich.—**plen'teously** *adv.*—**plen'teousness** *n.*—**plen'tiful** *a.* abundant; ample.—**plen'tifully** *adv.*—**plen'tifulness** *n.*

plethora (pleth'-o-ra) *n.* excess of red corpuscles in blood; (*Fig.*) superabundance.

pleura (plŏŏ'-ra) *n.* (*Med.*) membrane lining chest and covering lungs.—*pl.* **pleu'rae.**—**pleu'ral** *a.*—**pleu'risy** *n.* (*Med.*) inflammation of pleura.

pliable (plī'-a-bl) *a.* easily bent; easily influenced. Also **pliant** (plī'-ant).—**pli'ably, pli'antly** *adv.*—**pliabil'ity, pli'ancy** *n.*

pliers (plī'-erz) *n.pl.* pincers with flat grip.

plight (plīt) *n.* condition of distressing kind; predicament.

plight (plīt) *n.* solemn promise; pledge;—*v.t.* pledge, as one's word of honour; betroth.

plimsolls (plim'-sols) *n.pl.* rubber-soled shoes with canvas uppers.

plinth (plinth) *n.* square slab, forming base of column; projecting band running along foot of wall.

Pliocene (plī'-o-sēn) *n.* (*Geol.*) deposits belonging to latest Tertiary period.

plod (plod) *v.t.* tread heavily;—*v.i.* walk or work laboriously; toil or drudge.—**plod'der** *n.*—**plod'ding** *a.*

plot (plot) *n.* small patch of ground; plan of field, farm, etc. drawn to scale;—*v.t.* to draw a graph of.—*pr.p.* **plott'ing.**—*pa.p.* and *pa.t.* **plott'ed.**

plot (plot) *n.* plan of play, novel, etc.; complicated scheme; conspiracy;—*v.t.* plan;—*v.i.* conspire.

plough (plou) *n.* implement with heavy cutting blade for turning up soil;—*v.t.* turn up with plough; furrow; advance laboriously; reject candidate in examination;—*v.i.* till soil with plough.—**plough'share** *n.* heavy iron blade of plough which cuts into ground.—**the Plough** (*Astron.*) seven stars constituting the Great Bear.

plover (pluv'-er) *n.* lapwing.

ploy (ploi) *n.* (*Colloq.*) manoeuvre.

pluck (pluk) *v.t.* pull off; pick, as flowers; strip off feathers; pull with sudden force:—*n.* pull or twitch; act of plucking; courage or spirit.—**pluck'y** *a.* brave; spirited.—**pluck'ily** *adv.*—**pluck'iness** *n.*

plug (plug) *n.* anything used to stop hole; bung; cake of compressed tobacco; (*Elect.*) device for easy connecting and disconnecting of circuit; *abbrev.* for sparking-plug;—*v.t.* stop with plug; insert plug in; shoot; (*Slang*) advertise by repetition;—*pr.p.* **plugg'ing.**—*pa.p.* and *pa.t.* **plugged.**

plum (plum) *n.* round or oval stone-fruit; tree that bears it; good appointment or position; dark purplish colour.—**plum'-cake, plum'-pudd'ing** *n.* cake or pudding containing raisins, currants, etc.—**plum'-duff** *n.* (*Colloq.*) suet pudding made of flour and raisins.

plumage (plŏŏ'-māj) *n.* bird's feathers.

plumb (plum) *n.* plummet; weight of lead attached to line, to determine perpendicularity; perpendicular position;—*a.* perpendicular;—*adv.* perpendicularly; (*U.S., Colloq.*) utterly, absolutely;—*v.t.* adjust by plumb-line; take depth of water with plummet.—**plumber** (plum'-er) *n.* artisan who attends to water and sewage system of building.—**plumbing** (plum'-ing) *n.* trade of plumber; system of water and sewage pipes in building.—**plumb'-line** *n.* weighted string for testing the perpendicular.—**plumb'-bob** *n.* weight at the end of this line.

plume (plŏŏm) *n.* feather or tuft of feathers; crest on helmet;—*v.t.* furnish with plumes; strip of feathers; (*Fig.*) boast of.

plummet (plum'-et) *n.* plumb-line.

plump (plump) *a.* of rounded form; moderately fat.—**plump'ness** *n.*

plump (plump) *v.i.* fall or sit down heavily and suddenly; vote for one candidate;—*v.t.* drop or throw abruptly;—*a.* direct; abrupt; down-right;—*adv.* heavily; abruptly.

plunder (plun'-der) *v.t.* take by force;—*n.* robbery by force; property so obtained.—**plun'derer** *n.*

plunge (plunj) *v.t.* thrust forcibly into; to immerse suddenly in liquid;—*v.i.* throw oneself headlong into; (*Colloq.*) gamble recklessly;—*n.* act of plunging; dive; sudden rush.—**plun'ger** *n.* cylindrical rod used as piston in pumps.

plural (plŏŏ'-ral) *a.* more than one; (*Gram.*) denoting more than one person or thing;—*n.* (*Gram.*) word in its plural form.—**plu'rally** *adv.*—**plu'ralism** *n.* holding of more than one appointment, benefice, etc. simultaneously.—**plu'ralist** *n.*—**pluralis'tic** *a.*—**plural'ity** *n.* large number; holding of two or more offices, etc.

simultaneously; majority of votes.

plus (plus) *n.* symbol of addition (+); positive quantity; extra quantity;—*a.* to be added; (*Math.*, *Elect.*, *etc.*) positive;—*prep.* with addition of.—**plus-fours'** *n.pl.* wide knickerbockers worn by golfers.

plush (plush) *n.* fabric with velvety nap.

Pluto (plōō'-tō) *n.* (*Myth.*) god of Lower World.—**Pluto'ian** *a.* pert. to Pluto or infernal regions; subterranean; dark.—**Pluto'nic** *a.* Plutonian.—**pluto'nium** *n.* radioactive element resulting from disintegration of neptunium.

plutocracy (plōō-tok'-ra-si) *n.* government by rich; wealthy class.—**plu'tocrat** *n.* wealthy person.—**plutocrat'ic** *a.*

ply (plī) *v.t.* wield; work at steadily; practise with diligence; urge;—*v.i.* work steadily; of boat, motor vehicle, etc. to run regularly for hire.—*pa.p.* and *pa.t.* **plied.**

ply (plī) *n.* fold; plait; bend; twist; strand of yarn; thickness.—*pl.* **plies.** —**ply'wood** *n.* board made of two or more thin layers of wood cemented together.

pneumatic (nū-mat'-ik) *a.* pert. to air or gas; inflated with wind or air operated by compressed air.

pneumonia (nū-mō'-ni-a) *n.* acute inflammation of lung.—**pneumon'ic** *a.* pert. to lungs.

poach (pōch) *v.t.* cook food in hot salted water; cook eggs by breaking them into pan of boiling water.

poach (pōch) *v.t.* and *i.* take game or fish without permission or by illegal methods.—**poach'er** *n.*—**poach'ing** *n.*

pock (pok) *n.* pustule on skin, as in smallpox.—**pock'mark** *n.* pit left in skin by pock.

pocket (pok'-et) *n.* small pouch or bag inserted into garment; socket, cavity, or hollow; (*Mil.*) isolated area held by enemy;—*v.t.* put in pocket; take surreptitiously, esp. money; accept without resentment, as insult.—**pock'et-book** *n.* small book or case for holding money or papers. —**pock'et-mon'ey** *n.* money for small, personal expenses.—**in pocket,** having funds.

pod (pod) *n.* seed-vessel of plant, as peas, beans, etc.;—*v.t.* produce pods; remove pods from peas or beans.

podge (poj) *n.* short, fat person.—**podg'y** *a.* short and fat; thick.

poem (pō'-em) *n.* composition in verse; opp. to 'prose.'—**po'esy** *n.* art of composing poems.—**po'et** *n.* (*fem.* **po'etess**) author of poem.—**poet'ic(al)** *a.* pert. to poetry; possessing imaginative beauties of poetry.—**poet'ically** *adv.*—**poet'ics** *n.* principles

of art of poetry; criticism of poetry. —**poetry** (pō'-et-ri) *n.* language of imagination expressed in verse;—**poetaster** (pō'-et-as-ter) *n.* would-be poet.—**poetic justice,** ideal justice, in which crime is punished and virtue rewarded.—**poetic licence,** latitude in grammar or facts, allowed to poets. —**poet laureate,** official court poet.

poignant (poi'-nant) *a.* acutely painful; sharp; pungent.—**poig'nantly** *adv.*—**poig'nancy** *n.*

point (point) *n.* sharp or tapering end of anything; dot or mark; dot in decimal system; punctuation mark; full stop; (*Geom.*) that which has position but no magnitude; item or detail; gist of argument; effective part of speech, story, etc.; moment of time; purpose; physical quality in animals, esp. for judging purposes; (*Geog.*) headland; movable rail changing train to other rails; plug-position for electrical apparatus; one of 32 direction marks of compass; unit of scoring in certain games; (*Print.*) unit of measurement of size of type (72 points = 1 inch); (*Cricket*) position of fieldsman to immediate right of batsman;—*v.t.* sharpen; give value, force, etc. to words, etc.; aim or direct; fill up joints with mortar;—*v.i.* show direction or position; of dog, indicate position of game by standing facing it.—**point'ed** *a.* having sharp point; sharp; direct; telling; of remark, etc., aimed at particular person; (*Archit.*) pert. to style having pointed arches, i.e. Gothic.—**point'edly** *adv.*—**point'edness** *n.*—**point'less** *a.* having no point; blunt; irrelevant; insipid.—**point'er** *n.* one who, or that which, points; index; rod, stick for pointing on blackboard; indicator; breed of dog trained to stop and point at game.—**point'ing** *n.* filling crevices of walls with mortar.—**point'-blank** *a.* aimed horizontally;—*adv.* at short range; hence (*Fig.*) directly; plainly.—**point'-to-point'** *n.* (*Racing*) steeple-chase horse-race.

poise (poiz) *v.t.* place or hold in balanced or steady position;—*v.i.* hover; balance;—*n.* equilibrium; carriage of head, body, etc.; (*Fig.*) self-possession.

poison (poi'-zn) *n.* substance which kills or injures when introduced into living organism; that which has evil influence on health or moral purity; —*v.t.* give poison to; infect; corrupt. —**poi'soner** *n.*—**poi'sonous** *a.*—**poi'sonously** *adv.*—**poi'son-pen** *n.* writer of malicious, anonymous letters.

poke (pōk) *v.t.* push or thrust against with pointed object, e.g. with finger, stick, etc.; stir; thrust in;—*v.i.* make thrusts; pry;—*n.* thrust or push.—**po'ker** *n.* metal rod for stirring fire.—**po'ky** a. small; confined.

poke (pōk) n. sack; (*Scot.*) small bag.

poker (pō'-kẹr) n. card-game in which players bet on value of their hands.—**po'ker-faced** a. having an inscrutable expression.

polar (pō'-lẹr) a. pert. to North or South Poles; pert. to magnetic poles (points on earth's surface where magnetic needle dips vertically); pert. to either pole of magnet; magnetic; directly opposed; having polarity.—**polar'ity** n. state of being polar; condition of having opposite poles; power of being attracted to one pole, and repelled from other.

polarise (pō'-lạ-rīz) v.t. give polarity to; (*Chem.*) separate the positive and negative charges on molecule; (*Light*) to confine vibrations of light waves to certain directions, e.g. to plane. —**polarisa'tion** n.

pole (pōl) n. long, rounded piece of wood or metal; measure of length = 5¼ yards; measure of area = 30¼ yards;—v.t. propel with pole.

pole (pōl) n. either of ends of axis of sphere, esp. of earth (in latter case called North Pole and South Pole); either of opposite ends or terminals of magnet, electric battery, etc.— **pole'-star** n. North Star; (*Fig.*) guide.

polecat (pōl'-kat) n. small, carnivorous animal, resembling weasel.

polemic (po-lem'-ik) a. controversial; —n. controversy.—**polem'ics** n.pl. art of controversy; controversial writings or discussions, esp. religious. Also **polem'ical** a.—**polem'ically** adv.

police (po-lēs') n. civil force which maintains public order; internal government of country or city;— v.t. control with police; keep in order.—**police'-con'stable, police'man** (*fem.* police'-wo'man), police'-off'icer n. member of police force.—**police'-court** n. court for trial of minor offences. — **police'-off'ice, police'-sta'tion** n. headquarters of police, and temporary prison.

policy (pol'-i-si) n. course of action adopted.

policy (pol'-i-si) n. document containing contract of insurance.

poliomyelitis (pol-i-ō-mī-e-lī'-tis) n. (*Med.*) inflammation of grey matter of spinal cord.—*abbrev.* **polio**.

polish (pol'-ish) v.t. make smooth and glossy; make polite and cultured;— v.i. become polished;—n. smooth, glassy surface; substance used in polishing; (*Fig.*) refinement: elegance of manners.—**pol'isher** n.

polite (po-līt') a. courteous; well-bred. —**polite'ly** adv.—**polite'ness** n.

politic (pol'-i-tik) a. prudent; wise; shrewd; advisable.—**pol'itics** n.pl. art of government; political affairs. —**pol'iticly** adv.—**polit'ical** a. pert. to

state or its affairs; pert. to politics. —**polit'ically** adv.—**politician** (pol-i-tish'-ạn) n. one versed in science of government; member of political party.

polka (pōl'-kạ) n. a lively dance in duple time.

poll (pōl) n. (top of) head; register of persons; list of persons entitled to vote; place of voting; number of votes recorded; statistical test of public opinion;—v.t. cut off top of, e.g. tree; cut off horns of cattle; canvass; receive (votes); cast vote;— v.i. vote.—**poll'-tax** n. tax on each person.—**poll'ing-booth** n. voting-place at election.

pollen (pol'-ẹn) n. fertilising dust of flower.—**poll'inate** v.t. fertilise flower by conveying pollen to pistil.

pollute (po-lūt') v.t. make foul; defile; profane.—**pollu'tion** n.

polo (pō'-lō) n. game like hockey played on ponies; short for **wa'terpo'lo**, ball game played by swimmers.

poltroon (pol-trōōn') n. coward.— **poltroon'ery** n. cowardice.

poly- (pol'-i) *prefix* fr. Gk. *polus*, many, much, used in derivatives.— **polyan'dry** n. custom by which wife is shared between several husbands.—**polyan'thus** n. (*Bot.*) kind of primula.—**pol'ychrome** n. picture, statue, etc. in several colours; a. many-coloured, also **polychromat'ic**, **polychro'mic**, **pol'ychromous**.

polygamy (po-lig'-ạ-mi) n. practice of having more than one wife at once.—**polyg'amous** a.—**polyg'amist** n.

polyglot (pol'-i-glot) a. pert. to, or speaking, several languages;—n. person who speaks several languages; book, esp. Bible in different languages.

polygon (pol'-i-gon) n. plane figure with more than four sides or angles. —**polyg'onal** a.

polyhedron (pol-i-hē'-dron) n. (*Geom.*) solid figure with many faces, usually more than six.

polymorphous (pol-i-mor'-fus) a. assuming many forms. Also **polymor'phic**.—**polymor'phism** n.

polyp, polype (pol'-ip) n. small, marine animal with tube-like tentacles, e.g. sea-anemone; polypus.— **pol'ypus, pol'yp** n. (*Med.*) small tumour in the mucous membrane of the nose, etc.—**pol'ypous** a.

polysyllable (pol-i-sil'-ạ-bl) n. word of three or more syllables.—**polysyllab'ic** a.

polytechnic (pol-i-tek'-nik) a. pert. to many arts and sciences;—n. school or college of applied arts and sciences.

polytheism (pol'-i-thẹ-izm) n. belief in existence of many gods, or in more than one.—**pol'ytheist** n.— **polytheist'ic** a.

pomade (po-mad') *n.* scented ointment for hair. Also **poma'tum.**

pomegranate (pom'-gra-nāt) *n.* large fruit with many seeds in red pulp.

pomeranian (pom-er-ā'-ni-an) *n.* small breed of dog with bushy tail, sharp pointed muzzle, prick ears and long silky hair.—*Abbrev.* **pom.**

pommel (pum'-el) *n.* knob of sword hilt; front part of saddle;—*v.t.* strike repeatedly; beat with fists.—*pr.p.* **pomm'elling.**—*pa.p.* and *pa.t.* **pomm'elled.**

pomp (pomp) *n.* splendid display or ceremony; magnificence.—**pomp'ous** *n.* showy with grandeur; of person, self-important; of language, inflated.—**pomp'ously** *adv.*—**pomp'ousness** *n.*—**pompos'ity** *n.* vain-glory.

pompon (pom'-pon) *n.* ball of coloured wool worn in front of shako, etc.; small, compact chrysanthemum or dahlia.

pond (pond) *n.* pool of standing water.

ponder (pon'-der) *v.t.* weigh in mind; consider attentively;—*v.i.* meditate; muse; deliberate (on).—**pon'derer** *n.*

ponderous (pon'-der-us) *a.* very heavy; weighty; massive; unwieldy; dull or lacking in spirit.—**pon'derously** *adv.*—**pon'derousness** *n.*—**ponderos'ity** *n.*—**pon'derable** *a.* having appreciable weight.—**pon'derableness** *n.*

poniard (pon'-yard) *n.* thin dagger.

pontiff (pon'-tif) *n.* Pope; bishop; high priest.—**pontif'ical** *a.* belonging to high priest; popish; pompous and dogmatic.—**pontif'ically** *adv.*—**pontif'icate** *n.* state, dignity, or term of office of priest, bishop, or pope.—**pon'tificate** *v.i.* act the pontiff; speak in bombastic manner.

pontoon (pon-tóón') *n.* low, flat-bottomed boat used as support in building temporary bridge; bridge of boats.

pontoon (pon-tóón') *n.* card-game, vingt et un.

pony (pō'-ni) *n.* small horse; (*Slang*) £25.

poodle (póó'-dl) *n.* a breed of dog with thick, curly hair.

pooh (póó) *interj.* exclamation of scorn.—**pooh-pooh** *v.t.* (*Colloq.*) express contempt for.

pool (póól) *n.* small body of still water; small pond; deep place in river.

pool (póól) *n.* collective stakes in various games; place where stakes are put; variety of snooker; combination to fix prices and divide business; common fund of money or goods; group providing for common needs;—*v.t.* put into common fund;—*v.i.* form pool.

poop (póóp) *n.* raised deck at stern of ship;—*v.t.* break over poop of.

poor (póór) *a.* having little or no money; without means; needy; miserable; wretched; unfortunate; feeble; unproductive; of inferior quality.—**poor'ly** *adv.* in want; inadequately; with little or no success; without spirit;—*a.* somewhat ill; out of sorts.—**poor'ness** *n.*—**poor-spir'ited** *a.* cowardly.

pop (pop) *n.* abrupt, small explosive sound; shot; effervescing drink, e.g. ginger-beer, etc.;—*v.i.* make sharp, quick sound; go or come unexpectedly or suddenly; dart;—*v.t.* put or place suddenly; (*Slang*) pawn.—*adv.* suddenly.—*pr.p.* **pop'ping.**—*pa.p.* and *pa.t.* **popped.**—**pop-shop** *n.* (*Colloq.*) pawnshop.

Pope (pōp) *n.* Bishop of Rome and head of R.C. Church.—**popish** (pō'-pish) *a.*—**pope'dom** *n.*—**popery** (pō'-pe-ri) *n.* R.C. religion (a Protestant term, often used offensively).

popinjay (pop'-in-jā) *n.* parrot; formerly in archery, mark like parrot, to be shot at; vain, conceited fellow.

poplar (pop'-lar) *n.* tree noted for slender tallness.

poplin (pop'-lin) *n.* corded fabric of silk and worsted.

poppy (pop'-i) *n.* bright flowered plant one species of which yields opium.

populace (pop'-ū-las) *n.* common people; masses.—**pop'ulate** *v.t.* people.—**popula'tion** *n.* total number of people in country, town, etc.—**pop'ulous** *a.* thickly inhabited.

popular (pop'-ū-lar) *a.* pert. to common people; finding general favour; easily understood.—**pop'ularly** *adv.*—**pop'ularise** *v.t.* make popular; make familiar, plain, easy, etc. to all.—**popularisa'tion** *n.*—**popular'ity** *n.* public favour.

porcelain (pors'-lan, por'-se-lān) *n.* finest kind of earthen ware; china-ware.—**porcelain clay,** kaolin.

porch (pōrch) *n.* covered entrance to doorway.

porcupine (por'-kū-pīn) *n.* large quadruped of rodent family, covered with spines.

pore (pōr) *n.* minute opening in skin for passage of perspiration.—**por'ous** *a.* full of pores.—**por'ousness** *n.*—**porosity** (pō-ros'-i-ti) *n.*

pore (pōr) *v.i.* look at with steady attention, esp. in reading or studying; ponder.

pork (pōrk) *n.* flesh of swine used for food.—**por'ky** *a.* like pork; fat; greasy.—**por'ker** *n.* hog fattened for eating.

pornography (por-nog'-ra-fi) *n.* obscene literature or pictures.—**pornog'rapher** *n.*—**pornograph'ic** *a.*

porphyry (por'-fi-ri) *n.* rock with a dark, reddish-purple ground mass.

porpoise (por'-pus) *n.* blunt-nosed

mammal 5 to 8 feet long, frequenting Northern Seas; dolphin.

porridge (por'-ij) n. breakfast dish made by stirring oatmeal into boiling, salted water.

porringer (por'-in-jer) n. small bowl-shaped dish meant for holding porridge.

port (pört) n. harbour; town with harbour; haven; refuge.

port (pört) n. city gate; gateway.—**port'-hole** n. window in side of ship.

port (pört) n. demeanour;—v.t. (Mil.) carry (a rifle) slanting upwards across body. — **port'ly** a. dignified in appearance; corpulent.

port (pört) n. strong, sweet wine.

port (pört) n. left side of ship, looking towards bow (formerly larboard);—v.t. and i. turn (helm) to left side.

portable (pört-abl) a. easily carried.

portage (pör'-täj) n. act of carrying or transporting goods; charge for transport; in N. America, carrying of goods, boats, etc. between two navigable bodies of water.

portal (pört'-al) n. gate or entrance; smaller of two gateways side by side.

portcullis (pört-kul'-is) n. strong grating hung over gateway of castle, etc. to be lowered as aid to defence.

portend (pör-tend') v.t. foretell; give warning in advance; be an omen of.—**por'tent** n. omen, esp. of evil.—**portent'ous** a. serving to portend; ominous.

porter (pör'-ter) n. door- or gate-keeper; U.S. sleeping-car attendant; one employed to carry baggage, esp. at stations or hotels; dark-brown, bitter beer.—**por'terage** n. fee for hire of porter.

portfolio (pört-fō'-li-ō) n. flat case for holding documents, drawings, etc.; papers themselves; office of minister of state; list of investments.

portico (pör'-ti-kō) n. (Archit.) row of columns in front of entrance to building; colonnade; covered walk.

portion (pör'-shun) n. piece; part; share; helping of food; destiny;—v.t. divide into shares; give dowry to.—**por'tionless** a.

portmanteau (pört-man'-tō) n. leather travelling-bag; suitcase—**portmanteau word**, one made up from two others combining their meaning.

portray (pör-trä') v.t. represent by drawing, painting, acting, or imitating; describe vividly in words.—**portray'al** n.—**portray'er** n.—**portrait** (pör'-trit) n. picture of person, esp. of face; graphic description of person in words.—**por'traiture** n.

pose (pōz) n. attitude or posture of person, natural or assumed; mental attitude or attitudinising.—v.t. place in position for the sake of effect; lay

down or assert;—v.i. assume attitude; affect or pretend to be of certain character.—**poseur** (pō-zer') n. (fem.) **poseuse** (pō-zez') affected, attitudinising person.

pose (pōz) v.t. puzzle; embarrass by questioning.—**po'ser** n.

posh (posh) a. (Slang) smart; stylish.

position (pō-zish'-un) n. place or station; manner of arrangement; social standing; employment; state of affairs.—**posi'tional** a.

positive (poz'-i-tiv) a. formally laid down; clearly stated; absolute; confident; (Elect.) not negative; plus; (Math.) pert. to quantity greater than zero; (Colloq.) utter; downright; — n. in photography, print in which lights and shadows are not reversed.—**pos'itively** adv.—**pos'itiveness** n.—**pos'itivism** n. philosophical system which recognises only matters of experience.—**pos'itivist** n.—**positive pole**, of magnet, north-seeking-pole.—**positive sign**, sign (+ read plus) of addition.

posse (pos'-e) n. company or force, usually with legal authority; in America, men, under orders of sheriff, maintaining law.

possess (po-zes') v.t. own or hold as property; have as attribute; seize or obtain; enter into and influence.—**possessed'** a. influenced, as by evil spirit; demented.—**possession** n. ownership; occupancy; state of being possessed; thing possessed.—**possess'ive** a. denoting possession.—**possess'ively** adv.—**possess'or** n.

possible (pos'-i-bl) a. capable of being or of coming into, being; liable to happen; worthy of consideration;—n. highest attainable mark or score.—**poss'ibly** adv.—**possibil'ity** n. that which is possible.

post (pōst) n. piece of timber or metal, set upright as support; prop or pillar;—v.t. attach to post or wall, as notice or advertisement.—**post'er** n. placard for posting up in public place.

post (pōst) n. fixed place; military station or soldiers occupying it; office of trust, service, or emolument; trading settlement; formerly, stage on road for riders carrying mail; postman; established conveyance of letters; mail;—v.t. station or place; send by post; travel with speed.—**post'age** n. cost of conveyance by post.—**post'al** a. pert. to mail-service. — **post'al-or'der** n. (abbrev. P.O.) money order issued by one post-office authorising payment at another.—**post'man** n. one who collects and delivers letters.—**post'mark** n. mark which cancels postage-stamp.—**post'master** n. manager of post-office. — **post'master-gen'eral** n. chief of post-office department of government.—post'-card *n.* stamped card on which message may be sent through post.—post'-chaise, post'-coach *n.* four-wheeled carriage hired by those who travelled with post-horses.—post'haste *n.* haste or speed in travelling;—*a.* expeditious;—*adv.* with speed.—post'-horse *n.* one of number kept for hiring out to travellers by post-chaise.—post'-off'ice *n.* office where letters and parcels are received for distribution; government postal department.—post'age-stamp *n.* adhesive stamp, affixed to postal packets to indicate payment.

post- (pōst) *adv.* and *prefix* fr. L. *post*, after, behind, used in many compound words.—post-date' *v.t.* put on document, letter, etc., date later than actual one.—post'grad'uate *a.* of academic study, etc., undertaken after university degree.— *n.* one so doing.—post'-mor'tem *a.* after death; —*n.* dissection of body after death; autopsy.—post'-na'tal *a.* after birth.

posterior (pos-tē'-ri-or) *a.* coming after; situated behind; later; hinder; —*n.* rump.—poste'riorly *adv.*—poster'ity (pos-ter'-it-i) *n.* future generations; descendants.

postern (pōs'-tern) *n.* back door or gate;—*a.* rear; private.

posthumous (pos'-tū-mus) *a.* born after death of father; published after death of author; occurring after death.—post'humously *adv.*

postilion, postillion (pos-til'-yun) *n.* rider on near horse of team drawing carriage.

postpone (pōst-pōn') *v.t.* put off till later; to delay.—postpone'ment *n.*

postprandial (pōst-pran'-di-al) *a.* after dinner.

postscript (pōst'-skript) *n.* something added to letter after signature; *abbrev.* PS.

postulate (pos'-tū-lāt) *v.t.* assume without proof; lay down as self-evident; stipulate;—*n.* proposition assumed without proof.—postula'tion *n.*—postulatory (pos'-tū-lā-tor-i) *a.*

posture (pos'-tūr) *n.* the position of body, figure, etc. or of its several members; attitude;—*v.i.* assume an artificial or affected attitude.—pos'tural *a.*

posy (pō'-zi) *n.* small bouquet.

pot (pot) *n.* rounded vessel of metal, earthenware, etc., used for cooking, holding fluids, etc.; contents of pot; —*v.t.* plant in pots; preserve (as jam, etc.); abridge; shoot at; in billiards, pocket.—*pr.p.* pot'ting.—*pa.p.* and *pa.t.* pot'ted.—potsherd (pot'-sherd) *n.* piece of broken pot.—pot'-bell'ied *a.* corpulent.—pot'-boil'er *n.* literary or artistic work produced solely for sake of money.—pot'-hang'er, pot'-hook *n.* hook on which pots were

hung over open fires; letter shaped like pot-hook, used in learning to write.—pot'-hole *n.* cavity formed in rock by action of stones in eddy of stream; hole in roadway.—pot'-luck *n.* whatever may happen to have been provided for meal.—pot'-shot *n.* shot at random.

potable (pō'-ta-bl) *a.* drinkable.—potation (pō-tā'-shun) *n.* drink.

potash (pot'-ash) *n.* powerful alkali obtained from wood-ashes. Also pot'ass.—potass'ium *n.* metallic base of potash.—pot'ash-water, aerated water.

potato (pō-tā'-tō) *n.* edible tuber widely grown for food.—*pl.* pota'toes

potent (pō'-tent) *a.* having great authority or influence; powerful; mighty; procreative.—po'tently *adv.* —po'tency *n.* moral or physical power; influence; energy; efficacy.—po'tentate *n.* one who possesses power; prince.—potential (pō-ten'-shal) *a.* latent; existing in possibility but not in actuality;—*n.* inherent capability; (*Elect.*) level of electric pressure.—poten'tially *adv.*—potentiality (pō-ten-shi-al'-i-ti) *n.* possibility, as distinct from actuality; power of capacity.—potential difference (*Elect.*) difference of pressure between two points; voltage.

potion (pō'-shun) *n.* dose, esp. of liquid, medicine, or poison; draught.

pottage (pot'-aj) *n.* soup or stew; (*Bib.*) dish of lentils.

potter (pot'-er) *n.* maker of earthenware vessels.—pott'ery *n.* vessels made of earthenware; place where it is made; art of making it.

potter (pot'-er) *v.i.* work or act in feeble, unsystematic way; to loiter; to dawdle.

pouch (pouch) *n.* small bag or sack; pocket; bag-like receptacle in which certain animals, e.g. kangaroo, carry their young;—*v.t.* pocket.

pouf, pouffe (pōōf) *n.* large drum-shaped cushion, used as seat.

poult (pōlt) *n.* young fowl.—poultry (pōl'-tri) *n.* fowls.—poult'erer *n.* dealer in poultry.

poultice (pōl'-tis) *n.* hot, moist mixture of bread, mustard, linseed, etc. applied to sore, etc.;—*v.t.* apply poultice to.

pounce (pouns) *v.i.* spring upon suddenly; swoop;—*n.* swoop or sudden descent.

pound (pound) *n.* measure of weight (*abbrev.* lb.), 16 ounces avoirdupois, or 12 ounces troy; unit of British money (*abbrev.* £), 20 shillings.—pound sterling, British standard pound of 20 shillings as gold coin or paper note.—pound'age *n.* commission, allowance, or charge of so much per pound.—pound'al *n.* unit of force.

pound (pound) v.t. and i. beat or strike; crush to pieces; walk, run, etc., heavily.

pound (pound) n. enclosure for animals;—v.t. shut up in one.

pour (pōr) v.i. come out in stream, crowd, etc.; flow freely; rain heavily;—v.t. cause to flow, as liquid from vessel; shed.

pout (pout) v.i. thrust out the lips, as in displeasure, etc.; look sullen or sulky;—n. protrusion of the lips.—**pout'er** n. one who pouts; pigeon with power of inflating its crop.

poverty (pov'-er-ti) n. state of being poor; poorness; lack of means.

powder (pou'-der) n. dust; solid matter in fine dry particles; medicine in this form; short for gunpowder, face-powder, etc.;—v.t. reduce to powder; pulverise; sprinkle with powder;—v.i. fall into powder; crumble.—**pow'dery** a. like powder.—**pow'der-mag'azine** n. place where powder is stored.—**pow'der-puff** n. pad of soft material used for applying face-powder to skin.

power (pou'-er) n. capacity for action; energy; might; agency or motive force; authority; one in authority; influence or ascendancy; nation; mechanical energy; (Math.) product arising from continued multiplication of number by itself.—**pow'erful** a. having great power; intense; capable of producing great effect.—**pow'erfully** adv.—**pow'erfulness** n.—**pow'erless** a.—**pow'erlessly** adv.—**pow'erlessness** n.—**pow'er-house**, **pow'er-sta'tion** n. building where electric power is generated.

pox (poks) n. disease attended with pustules on skin, as small-pox; (Arch.) syphilis.

practice (prak'-tis) n. performance or execution, as opposed to theory; custom; systematic exercise for instruction; training; exercise of profession.—**prac'tise** v.t. put into action; do habitually; exercise profession; exercise oneself in; train;—v.i. perform certain acts customarily; exercise profession.—**prac'ticable** a. capable of being accomplished or put into practice; capable of being used, e.g. weapon, road, etc.—**prac'ticably** adv.—**prac'ticableness** n.—**practicabil'ity** n.—**prac'tical** a. pert. to practice or action; adapted to actual circumstances; useful; virtual.—**prac'tically** adv.—**prac'ticalness** n.—**practical'ity** n.—**practitioner** (prak-tish'-un-er) n. one engaged in profession, esp. law or medicine.—**general practitioner** (abbrev. G.P.) one who practises in all branches of medicine and surgery.

pragmatic, pragmatical (pragmat'-ik, -i-kal) a. pert. to state affairs; pert. to business; concerned with practical consequences; matter-of-fact; officious or meddlesome.—**pragmat'ically** adv.—**pragmat'icalness** n.—**prag'matise** v.t. represent imaginary thing as real.—**prag'matist** n.

prairie (prā'-ri) n. large tract of grass-land, destitute of trees.—**prai'rie-schoon'er** n. large, covered waggon, formerly used by emigrants going from east to west America.—**prai'rie-wolf** n. coyote.

praise (prāz) v.t. express approval or admiration; glorify;—n. approval of merit; commendation.—**praise'worthy** a.—**praise'worthiness** n.

pram (pram) n. baby-carriage.

prance (prans) v.i. spring or bound like high-spirited horse; swagger; caper, esp. of children;—n. prancing movement.—**pranc'er** n.—**pranc'ing** n.

prank (prangk) n. mischievous trick.

prate (prāt) v.t. and i. talk idly; utter;—n. chatter.

prattle (prat'-l) v.i. utter childishly; babble;—n. childish talk.

prawn (prawn) n. edible crustacean of shrimp family.

pray (prā) v.t. ask earnestly; entreat;—v.i. make request or confession, esp. to God; pay one's devotions to God.—**pray'er** n. one who prays; earnest entreaty; words used; thing asked for; petition, esp. to public body.—n.pl. family worship; divine service.

preach (prēch) v.i. and t. deliver sermon; speak publicly on religious subject; advocate.—**preach'er** n.—**preach'ify** v.i. moralise.

preamble (prē-am'-bl) n. introductory part of discourse, story, etc.; preface.

prebend (preb'-end) n. stipend of canon of cathedral chapter.—**preb'endal** a.—**preb'endary** n. clergyman in receipt of prebend.

precarious (prē-kā'-ri-us) a. depending on will or pleasure of another; depending on circumstances; uncertain; dangerous; perilous.—**preca'riously** adv.—**preca'riousness** n.

precaution (prē-kaw'-shun) n. care taken beforehand.—v.t. forewarn.—**precau'tionary** a.

precede (prē-sēd') v.t. go before in place, time, rank, or importance.—**preced'ent** a. preceding; going before in time;—**pre'cedent** n. something done, or said, that may serve as example.—**preced'ently** adv.—**precedence** (prē-sē'-dens) n. act of preceding; priority in position, rank, or time.—**preced'ing** a. going before in time, place, or order; previous.

precentor (prē-sen'-tur) n. one who leads choir in cathedral.

precept (prē'-sept) n. instruction intended as rule of conduct; maxim; exhortation.—**precep'tive** a.—**precep'-**

tor *n.* (*fem.* **precep'tress**) teacher; instructor.

precinct (prē'-singt) *n.* enclosure within walls of sacred or official buildings; boundary or limit.—*pl.* ground attached to ecclesiastical building.

precious (presh'-us) *a.* of great value or price; costly; highly esteemed; over-refined; — *adv.* extremely. — **prec'iously** *adv.*—**prec'iousness** *n.*—**preciosity** (pres(h)-i-os'-i-ti) *n.* affected refinement.

precipice (pres'-i-pis) *n.* very steep place, as cliff-face.—**precip'itous** *a.* very steep.—**precip'itously** *adv.*—**precip'itousness** *n.*

precipitate (pre-sip'-i-tāt) *v.t.* throw headlong; urge on eagerly; hasten occurrence of; (*Chem.*) cause to separate and fall to bottom, as substance in solution; of vapour, condense;—*v.i.* (*Chem.*) fall to bottom of vessel, as sediment;—*n.* (*Chem.*) sediment;—*a.* headlong; rash or over-hasty.—**precip'itately** *adv.*—**precip'itable** *a.* (*Chem.*) that may be precipitated.—**precipitabil'ity** *n.*—**precip'itance, precip'itancy** *n.* rash haste.—**precip'itant** *a.* falling headlong; too hasty.—**precip'itantly** *adv.*—**precipita'tion** *n.* rash haste; falling headlong; condensation of vapour; sum total of rain-, hail- and snowfall —**precip'itative** *a.* tending to precipitate.—**precip'itator** *n.*

précis (prā-sē') *n.* concise statement.

precise (pre-sīs') *a.* exact; definite; formal; prim.—**precise'ly** *adv.*—**precise'ness** *n.*—**precision** (pre-sizh'-un) *n.* accuracy; definiteness;—*a.* done with, or capable of, great accuracy.

preclude (pre-klōōd') *v.t.* shut out; hinder.—**preclu'sion** *n.*—**preclu'sive** *a.* shutting out; hindering beforehand.

precocious (pre-kō'-shus) *a.* ripe or developed too soon; having mental powers or bodily growth developed at early age; premature.—**preco'ciously** *adv.*—**preco'ciousness, preco'city** *n.*

precognition (prē-kog-nish'-un) *n.* previous knowledge; (*Scots Law*) examination of witnesses before trial.

preconceive (prē-kon-sēv') *v.t.* form opinion or idea of beforehand.—**preconcep'tion** *n.*

precursor (prē-kur'-sor) *n.* forerunner.—**precur'sive, precur'sory** *a.*

predatory (pred'-a-tō-ri) *a.* living by preying on others; plundering; pillaging.

predecessor (prē-dē-ses'-ur) *n.* one who has preceded another in office, position, etc.

predestine (prē-des'-tin) *v.t.* destine beforehand; foreordain.—**predes'tinate** *v.t.* determine beforehand; foreordain.—**predestina'tion** *n.* (*Theol.*) doctrine that salvation or damnation of individuals has been foreordained by God; determination beforehand of future events; destiny; fate.—**predestina'rian** *n.* believer in this doctrine.

predicable (pred'-i-ka-bl) *a.* able to be predicated;—*n.* anything that can be affirmed of something.—**predicabil'ity** *n.*

predicament (pre-dik'-a-ment) *n.* awkward plight; trying situation.

predicate (pred'-i-kāt) *v.t.* affirm; assert; declare;—*n.* that which is predicated.—**predica'tion** *n.* assertion; affirmation.—**pred'icative** *a.* affirming.—**pred'icatively** *adv.*

predict (prē-dikt') *v.t.* tell beforehand; foretell; prophesy.—**predic'table** *a.*—**predic'tion** *n.* prophecy.—**predic'tive** *a.* foretelling; prophetic.—**predic'tor** *n.*

predigest (prē-di-jest') *v.t.* subject food to artificial digestion before eating.

predilection (prē-di-lek'-shun) *n.* partiality.

predispose (prē-dis-pōz') *v.t.* incline beforehand; give tendency or bias to; influence.—**predisposi'tion** *n.*

predominate (prē-dom'-i-nāt) *v.i.* surpass in strength, influence, or authority; rule; prevail.—**predom'inance, predom'inancy** *n.* ascendancy; superiority.—**predom'inant** *a.* having ascendancy; controlling.—**predom'inantly** *adv.*

pre-eminent (prē-em'-i-nent) *a.* distinguished; outstanding.—**pre-em'inently** *adv.*—**pre-em'inence** *n.*

preen (prēn) *v.t.* trim with the beak; smarten oneself.

prefab (prē-fab') *n.* (*Colloq.*) prefabricated house.

prefabricate (prē-fab'-ri-kāt) *v.t.* build houses and ships in standardised units in factories for rapid assembly on sites or ship-yards.—**prefabrica'tion** *n.*

preface (pref'-as) *n.* introductory remarks at beginning of book, or spoken before discourse; foreword;—*v.t.* furnish with preface.—**pref'atory** *a.* introductory.

prefect (prē'-fekt) *n.* ancient Roman magistrate; governor of French civil department; senior boy in school, appointed to maintain discipline.—**pre'fectship** *n.* office or jurisdiction of prefect.

prefer (prē-fer') *v.t.* like better; choose rather; promote to office or dignity.—**pref'erable** *a.* worthy of preference; more desirable.—**pref'erably** *adv.*—**pref'erableness** *n.*—**pref'erence** *n.* act of preferring one thing before another; what is preferred; choice.—**preferential** (pref-e-ren'-shal) *a.* giving or receiving preference.—**preferen'tially** *adv.*—**prefer'ment** *n.* advancement or promotion.

prefix (prē'-fiks) *n.* letter, syllable, or word put at beginning of another word to modify its meaning.—**prefix** (prē-fiks') *v.t.* place at beginning.

pregnable (preg'-na-bl) *a.* able to be taken by assault or force.

pregnant (preg'-nant) *a.* being with child; fruitful; full of meaning.—**preg'nantly** *adv.*—**preg'nancy** *n.*

prehensile (prē-hen'-sil) *a.* (*Zool.*) capable of grasping.

prehistory (prē-hist'-or-i) *n.* period before written records were kept.—**prehistor'ic** *a.*

prejudice (prej'-ū'dis) *n.* opinion, favourable or unfavourable, formed without fair examination of facts; harm; bias;—*v.t.* bias; influence;—**prejudicial** (prej-ū-di'-shal) *a.* injurious.—**prejudi'cially** *adv.*

prelate (prel'-at) *n.* bishop, or other Church dignitary of equal or higher rank.—**prel'acy** *n.*

preliminary (pre-lim'-i-na-ri) *a.* introductory; preparatory;—*n.* introduction; preparatory measure; (often used in *pl.*).

prelude (prel'-ūd) *n.* introductory performance or event; musical introduction; preliminary;—*v.t.* to serve as forerunner to.—**prelu'sive**, **prelu'sory** *a.* introductory.

premature (pre'-, prē'-ma-tūr) *a.* ripe before natural time; untimely; over-hasty.—**premature'ly** *adv.*—**premature'ness**, **prematur'ity** *n.* early flowering or maturity.

premeditate (prē-med'-i-tāt) *v.t.* think, consider, or revolve in the mind beforehand.

premier (prē'-mi-er, prem'-yer) *a.* first; chief or principal; most ancient; —*n.* prime minister.—**prem'iership** *n.*

première (pre-myer') *n.* first public performance of play or film.

premise (pre-mīz') *v.t.* set forth as introductory to main subject; lay down propositions on which reasonings rest.—**premise** (prem'-is) *n.* Also **pre'miss**, proposition previously supposed or proved; proposition from which inference or conclusion is drawn.—**prem'isses** *n.pl.* building with its adjuncts.

premium (prē'-mi-um) *n.* recompense; prize; fee paid to learn trade or profession; money paid for insurance; amount exceeding par value of shares or stock.—**at a premium**, above par; in great demand.

premonition (prē-mo-nish'-un) *n.* previous warning; presentiment.—**premon'itor** *n.* forewarner.—**premon'itory** *a.* giving previous warning or notice.—**premon'itorily** *adv.*

pre-natal (prē-nā'-tal) *a.* previous to birth.

preoccupy (prē-ok'-ū-pī) *v.t.* take possession of before another; engage attention of.—**preoc'cupied** *a.* occupied previously; engrossed in thought.—**preoc'cupancy** *n.* act of taking possession of before others.—**preoccupa'tion** *n.*

prepaid (prē-pād') *a.* paid in advance.

prepare (pre-pār') *v.t.* make ready for use; fit for particular purpose; provide; fit out;—*v.i.* make things ready; make oneself ready.—**preparation** (prep-a-rā'-shun) *n.* act of making ready for use; readiness; substance, esp. medicine or food, specially made up for use.—**prepar'ative** *a.* tending to prepare for; —*n.* anything which serves to prepare.—**prepar'atively** *adv.*—**prepar'atory** *a.* preliminary; introductory. —**preparedness** (pre-pār'-ed-nes) *n.*

preponderate (pre-pon'-der-āt) *v.i.* exceed in power, numbers, etc.; to outweigh.—**prepon'derance** *n.* superiority of power, numbers, etc.—**prepon'derant** *a.*—**prepon'derantly** *adv.*

prepossess (prē-po-zes') *v.t.* possess beforehand; influence person etc. beforehand; prejudice favourably.—**prepossess'ing** *a.* attractive.—**prepossess'singly** *adv.*—**prepossess'sion** *n.*

preposterous (pre-pos'-ter-us) *a.* contrary to nature or common sense; utterly absurd.—**prepos'terously** *adv.*—**prepos'terousness** *n.*

prerogative (prē-rog'-a-tiv) *n.* exclusive right or privilege by reason of rank, position, etc.—*a.* privileged.

presage (pres'-āj) *n.* omen.—**presage** (prē-sāj') *v.t.* foretell; forebode; have presentiment of.

presbyter (prez'-bi-ter) *n.* in Episcopal churches, one ordained to second order in ministry; member of presbytery. — **Presbyterian** (prez-bi-tē'-ri-an) *n.* one belonging to Presbyterian Church;—*a.* pert. to Presbyterian Church.—**Presbyte'rianism** *n.*—**pres'bytery** *n.* body of elders in Christian Church; court of all pastors within certain district, and one ruling elder from each church; space in cathedral between altar and choir.

prescience (prē'-shi-ens) *n.* foreknowledge.—**pre'scient** *a.*

prescribe (pre-skrīb') *v.t.* lay down authoritatively; set out rules for; (*Med.*) order or advise use of.—**prescrib'er** *n.*—**pre'script** *n.* direction; ordinance.—**prescription** (pre-skrip'-shun) *n.* act of prescribing or directing; doctor's direction for use of medicine.—**prescrip'tive** *a.* acquired by immemorial use.

present (prez'-ent) *a.* being in certain place; here or at hand; now existing; —*n.* present time.—**pres'ence** *n.* state of being present; nearness or proximity; personality; mien or appearance; apparition.—**pres'ently** *adv.* at once; soon; by and by.

present (pre-zent') *v.t.* introduce into presence of; exhibit or offer to notice; offer as gift; bestow; aim, as weapon;—**pres'ent** *n.* gift.—**present'able** *a.* fit to be presented.—**presenta'tion** *n.* act of presenting; state of being presented; that which is presented.—**present'ment** *n.* act or state of presenting; representation; laying of formal statement before court or authority.

presentiment (prē-sen'-ti-ment) *n.* foreboding.

preserve (prē-zėrv') *v.t.* keep from injury or destruction; keep in sound state;—*n.* that which is preserved, as fruit, etc.; medium used in preserving; place for the preservation of game, fish, etc.—**preser'ver** *n.*—**preser'vable** *a.*—**preserva'tion** *n.* act of preserving or keeping safe; state of being preserved; safety.—**preser'vative** *n.* that which preserves;—*a.* having power of preserving.—**preser'vatory** *a.* tending to preserve;—*n.* that which preserves.

preside (prē-zīd') *v.i.* be chairman of meeting; direct; control; superintend.—**president** (prez'-i-dent) *n.* head of society, company, association, etc.; elected head of republic.—**pres'idency** *n.* presidentship.—**presiden'tial** *a.* pert. to president, his office, dignity, etc.—**pres'identship** *n.*

press (pres) *v.t.* push or squeeze; crush; hug; drive with violence; hurry; urge steadily; force; solicit with importunity; constrain; smooth by pressure;—*v.i.* exert pressure; strive eagerly; crowd; hasten;—*n.* instrument or machine for squeezing, compressing, etc.; printing-machine; printing and publishing; newspapers collectively; crowd; stress; cupboard.—**press'ing** *a.* urgent; persistent.—**press-a'gent** *n.* one employed to advertise and secure publicity.—**press'-cutt'ing** *n.* item cut out of newspaper.—**to go to press**, of newspaper, to start printing.

press (pres) *v.t.* force to serve in navy or army; take for royal or public use; to requisition.—**press'-gang** *n.* (*Hist.*) men employed to obtain recruits for navy (or army), by force.

pressure (presh'-ůr) *n.* the act of pressing; state of being pressed; influence; authority.—**pressure group** *n.* group seeking to influence the government on a particular issue.

pressurisation (presh-ů-rī-zā'-shun) *n.* maintenance of same pressure inside aircraft at high altitudes.—**pressurise** *v.t.*

prestidigitation (pres-ti-dij-i-tā'-shun) *n.* conjuring; sleight of hand.—**prestidig'itator** *n.* conjurer (conjuror); juggler; magician.

prestige (pres-tēzh', pres'-tij) *n.* standing; reputation; power to impress.

presto (pres'-tō) *adv.* (*Mus.*) quickly.

presume (prē-zūm') *v.t.* take for granted; accept without proof; assume;—*v.i.* act in forward manner; take liberties.—**presum'able** *a.* probable.—**presum'ably** *adv.*—**presumption** (prē-zum'-shun) *n.* strong probability; that which is taken for granted; arrogance of opinion or conduct; boldness.—**presumptive** (prē-zum'-tiv) *a.* presuming; probable; likely.—**presump'tively** *adv.*—**presump'tuous** *a.* forward; taking liberties.—**presump'tuously** *adv.*—**presump'tuousness** *n.*

presuppose (prē-su-pōz') *v.t.* assume beforehand.—**presupposi'tion** *n.*

pretend (pre-tend') *v.t.* assert falsely; counterfeit; make believe;—*v.i.* lay claim (to); make pretence; sham.—**preten'der** *n.* one who simulates or feigns; claimant, esp. to the throne.—**pretence'** *n.* simulation; act of laying claim; assumption; pretext.—**preten'sion** *n.* act of advancing claim, esp. false claim; right alleged or assumed.—**pretentious** (pre-ten'-shus) *a.* presumptuous and arrogant.—**preten'tiously** *adv.*—**preten'tiousness** *n.*

preter- (prē'-tėr) *prefix* meaning beyond, above.—**preternat'ural** *a.* beyond what is natural; abnormal.

pretext (prē'-tekst) *n.* ostensible reason or motive which cloaks real reason; pretence.

pretty (prit'-i) *a.* of beauty that is charming and attractive, but not striking or imposing; neat and tasteful; elegant; pleasing;—*adv.* moderately; fairly; rather.—**prett'ily** *adv.*—**prett'iness** *n.*

prevail (pre-vāl') *v.i.* gain upper hand or mastery; succeed; be current; be in force; induce.—**prevail'ing** *a.*—**prev'alent** *a.* most generally received; extensively existing; rife.—**prev'alently** *adv.*—**prev'alence** *n.*

prevaricate (pre-var'-i-kāt) *v.i.* evade the truth; quibble.—**prevarica'tion** *n.* deviation from truth.—**prevar'icator** *n.*

prevent (pre-vent') *v.t.* keep from happening; stop.—**prevent'able** *a.*—**preven'tion** *n.* obstruction; hindrance; preventive.—**preven'tive** *a.* tending to ward off;—*n.* that which prevents; antidote to keep off disease.

preview (prē'-vū) *n.* showing of exhibition, etc., before official opening.

previous (prē'-vi-us) *a.* preceding; happening before.—**pre'viously** *adv.*—**pre'viousness** *n.*

prey (prā) *n.* animal hunted and killed for food by another animal; victim; spoil; plunder;—*v.i.* seize and devour; pillage; weigh heavily.

price (prīs) *n.* amount at which thing is valued, bought, or sold; value;

cost; reward;—*v.t.* fix price of; ask cost of.—**price'less** *a.* beyond any price.—**price'lessness** *n.*

prick (prik) *n.* sharp-pointed instrument; dot, mark, or puncture made by sharp point; sharp, stinging pain; hence, (*Fig.*) remorse; spur;—*v.t.* pierce slightly with sharp point; incite; affect with sharp pain; sting; erect (the ears).—**prick'er** *n.* sharp-pointed instrument.—**prick'-eared** *a.* having pointed ears.

prickle (prik'-l) *n.* small sharp point; thorn; spike; bristle;—*v.t.* prick slightly; cover with small points;—*v.i.* feel tingling sensation.—**prick'ly** *a.* full of prickles; tingling.—**prick'liness** *n.*—**prick'ly-pear** *n.* kind of cactus.

pride (prīd) *n.* state or quality of being proud; too high opinion of oneself; self-esteem.—**pride'ful** *a.* arrogant.—**pride'fully** *adv.*—**to pride oneself on (upon)**, take credit for.

priest (prēst) *n.* (*fem.* **priest'ess**) clergyman; in R.C. and Episcopal churches, one of order between deacon and bishop; in pagan times, one who officiated at altar, or performed rites of sacrifice.—**priest'like, priest'ly** *a.*—**priest'liness** *n.*—**priest'hood** *n.* office or duty of priest; priests collectively.

prig (prig) *n.* conceited person who professes superior culture, etc.—**prig'gish** *a.*

prim (prim) formal and precise; affectedly nice; prudish;—*v.t.* shape or arrange with precision.—**prim'ly** *adv.*—**prim'ness** *n.*

prima (prē'-ma) *a.* first.—**prima donna**, principal female singer in opera.—**prima facie case**, case based on sufficient evidence to go to jury.

primal (prī'-mal) *a.* first; original; chief.—**pri'mary** *a.* first in order of time, development, importance; preparatory; elementary;—*n.* that which stands highest in rank or importance.—**pri'marily** *adv.* in first place.—**pri'mariness** *n.*—**primary colours**, basic colours from which others can be formed—for pigments, red, yellow and blue, for colour photography, red, green and blue.

primate (prī'-māt) *n.* chief dignitary in church; archbishop. — **primacy** (prī'-ma-si) *n.* office or dignity of archbishop.

Primates (prī-mā'-tēz) *n.pl.* highest order of mammals.

prime (prīm) *a.* first in time; original; first in degree or importance; foremost; of highest quality; (*Math.*) that cannot be separated into factors;—*n.* earliest stage; spring; youth; full health; best portion;—*v.t.* prepare firearm by charging with powder; instruct beforehand; introduce charge of liquid or fuel into pump or engine before starting it.—

pri'mer *n.* one who, or that which, primes, esp. percussion cap, etc. used to ignite powder of cartridges, etc. small, elementary book used in teaching.—**prime'ly** *adv.*—**prime'ness** *n.*—**pri'ming** *n.* powder, etc. used to fire charge in firearms; preparatory coat of paint on bare surface.—**prime minister**, first minister of state.—**prime number**, number divisible without remainder only by itself or unity.

primeval (prī-mē'-val) *a.* original; prehistoric.—**prime'vally** *adv.*

primitive (prim'-i-tiv) *a.* pert. to beginning or origin; earliest of its kind; old-fashioned; plain and rude.—**prim'itively** *adv.*—**prim'itiveness** *n.*

primogeniture (prī-mō-jen'-i-tūr) *n.* state of being first-born child; right of eldest son to inherit parents' property.—**primogen'ital, primogen'itary** *a.*—**primogen'itor** *n.* earliest ancestor.

primordial (prī-mor'-di-al) *a.* existing from beginning; first in order; primeval.

primrose (prim'-rōz) *n.* plant bearing pale-yellow flowers in spring; this colour.

primula (prim'-ū-la) *n.* genus of plants including primrose.

prince (prins) *n.* (*fem.* **princess'**) ruler or chief; son of king or emperor.—**prince'dom** *n.* jurisdiction, rank, or estate of prince.—**prince'let, prince'-ling** *n.* young prince; petty prince.—**prince'ly** *a.* pert. to, or worthy of, prince; stately; dignified.—**prince'-liness** *n.*—**Prince Consort**, husband of reigning queen.

principal (prin'-si-pal) *a.* chief in importance; first in rank, etc.;—*n.* chief person in authority; most important thing; leader; head of certain institutes, esp. a university, college, or school; chief actor in crime; person for whom another is agent; sum of money lent and yielding interest.—**prin'cipally** *adv.*—**prin'cipalship** *n.* office or dignity of principal.—**principal'ity** *n.* territory or dignity of prince; sovereignty.

principle (prin'-si-pl) *n.* fundamental truth or law; moral rule; uprightness; honesty; element.—**prin'cipled** *a.* guided by certain rules of conduct.

print (print) *v.t.* impress; reproduce words, pictures, etc. by pressing inked types on paper, etc.; produce in this way; write in imitation of this; publish;—*n.* impression or mark left on surface; printed cotton fabric; printed lettering; engraving; photograph.—**print'er** *n.* one engaged in printing of books, newspapers, etc.—**printed circuit** (*Elect.*) one formed of copper foil etched on dielectric surface.—**print'ing-press** *n.* printing-machine.

prior (prī'-or) *a.* previous; former;

earlier;—*n.* (*fem.* **pri'oress**) superior of a priory; one next to abbot.—**prior'ity** *n.* precedence; preference in regard to privilege.—**pri'ory** *n.* religious household, headed by prior or prioress.

prise (prīz) *n.* lever;—*v.t.* force open.

prism (prizm) *n.* (*Geom.*) solid whose bases are any similar, equal, and parallel plane figures, and whose sides are parallelograms; (*Optics*) transparent figure of this nature, usually with triangular ends.—**prismat'ic(al)** *a.*—**prismat'ically** *adv.*

prison (priz'-n) *n.* building, for confinement of criminals; jail; any place of confinement;—*v.t.* imprison.—**prisoner** (priz'-ner) *n.* one confined in prison; one captured in war.

pristine (pris'-tīn) *a.* belonging to earliest time; original; former.

private (prī'-vąt) *a.* not public; belonging to or concerning individual; peculiar to oneself; personal; secluded; secret; of soldier, not holding rank;—*n.* common soldier.—**pri'vately** *adv.*—**pri'vateness** *n.*—**privacy** (priv'-ą-si, prī-vą-si) *n.* state of being in retirement from company; solitude; seclusion; secrecy.

privateer (prī-vą-tēr') *n.* armed private vessel commissioned by government to attack enemy ships.

privation (prī-vā'-shun) *n.* state of being deprived; destitution; want.

privet (priv'-et) *n.* evergreen shrub.

privilege (priv'-i-lej) *n.* special right or advantage;—*v.t.* grant some special favour to.—**priv'ileged** *a.* enjoying special right or immunity.

privy (priv'-i) *a.* private; confidential; secret; admitted to knowledge of secret;—*n.* latrine.—**priv'ily** *adv.*—**priv'ity** *n.* connivance.—**privy** to, secretly informed of.—**Privy Council**, council which advises sovereign on matters of government.

prize (prīz) *n.* reward for success in competition; reward for merit; thing striven for; thing won by chance, e.g. in lottery.—*v.t.* value highly.—**prize'-fight** *n.* professional boxing-match. — **prize'-fighter** *n.*

prize (prīz) *n.* enemy ship or property captured in naval warfare.

probable (prob'-ą-bl) *a.* likely; having more evidence for than against.—**prob'ably** *adv.*—**probabil'ity** *n.* likelihood; appearance of truth; possibility of occurrence.

probate (prō'-bāt) *n.* process by which last will and testament is legally authenticated after testator's death; official copy of will.

probation (prō-bā'-shun) *n.* proving; proof; trial or test of person's character, conduct, ability, etc.; testing of candidate before admission to full membership; system of

releasing offenders, esp. juveniles, and placing them under supervision of **Probation Officer**.—**proba'tional** *a.*—**proba'tionary** *a.* serving to test.—**proba'tioner** *n.* person undergoing probation.

probe (prōb) *n.* (*Med.*) instrument for examining wound, ulcer, cavity, etc.; investigation; exploratory space vehicle;—*v.t.* explore wound, etc. with probe; (*Fig.*) examine thoroughly.

probity (prob'-i-ti) *n.* integrity; rectitude.

problem (prob'-lem) *n.* matter proposed for solution; question difficult of solution; puzzle.—**problemat'ic(al)** *a.* questionable; uncertain; doubtful.—**problemat'ically** *adv.*

proceed (prō-sēd') *v.i.* move onward; advance; renew progress; come forth; take legal proceedings.—**proceed'ing** *n.* going forward; movement;—*pl.* (*Law*) steps of prosecuting charge, claim, etc.;—**proceeds** (prō'-sēdz) *n.pl.* produce; sum realised by sale.—**procedure** (prō-sēd'-ūr) *n.* method of proceeding.

process (prō'-ses) *n.* continued forward movement; lapse (of time); method of operation; (*Anat.*) projecting part or growth; (*Law*) procedure;—*v.t.* subject to some process, as food or material.—**procession** (prō-sesh'-un) *n.* marching forward; regular progress.—**proces'sional** *a.* pert. to procession;—*n.* hymn sung during church procession.—**pro'cess-ser'ver** *n.* sheriff's officer; bailiff.

proclaim (prō-klām') *v.t.* make known by public announcement; publish.—**proclaim'ant**, **proclaim'er** *n.* one who proclaims.—**proclamation** (prok-la-mā'-shun) *n.* official public announcement.

proclivity (prō-kliv'-i-ti) *n.* inclination; proneness; aptitude.

procrastinate (prō-kras'-ti-nāt) *v.i.* put off till some future time.—**procrastina'tion** *n.* dilatoriness.—**procras'tinator** *n.*

procreate (prō'-krē-āt) *v.t.* bring into being; beget; generate.—**procrea'tion** *n.* reproduction of species; generation.—**pro'creative** *a.* having power to beget; productive.—**pro'creativeness** *n.*—**pro'creator** *n.*

proctor (prok'-tor) *n.* one who manages affairs of another; procurator; university official in charge of discipline.—**procto'rial** *a.*—**proc'torship** *n.*—**King's Proctor**, Crown solicitor in divorce suits, who may intervene when collusion is alleged to have occurred.

procuration (prok-ū-rā'-shun) *n.* management of another's affairs; instrument empowering person to transact affairs of another.—**proc'-**

urator n. one who acts for another in legal affairs.—**proc'urator-fis'cal** n. in Scotland, public prosecutor.

procure (prō-kūr') v.t. acquire; obtain; get.—**procur'able** a. obtainable.—**procure'ment** n. act of procuring or obtaining; management.—**procur'er** n. (fem. **proc'uress**) one who procures; one who supplies woman for immoral purposes.

prod (prod) v.t. poke with something pointed; goad;—n. pointed instrument for prodding.—pr.p. **prod'ding**.—pa.p. and pa.t. **prod'ded**.

prodigal (prod'-i-gạl) a. wasteful; spending recklessly;—n. spendthrift.—**prod'igally** adv.—**prodigal'ity** n. reckless extravagance.

prodigy (prod'-i-ji) n. portent; anything unusual and unnatural; person or thing causing wonder; marvel; very gifted child; monster.—**prodigious** (prō-dij'-us) a.—**prodig'iously** adv.—**prodig'iousness** n.

produce (prō-dūs') v.t. bring forth; give birth to; yield; make; cause; of play, present it on stage; (Geom.) of line, extend in length.—**produce** (prod'-ūs) n. that which is produced; crops.—**produc'er** n.—**produc'ible** a.

product (prod'-ukt) n. that which is produced.—**produc'tion** n. act of producing; things produced.—**produc'tive** a. having the power to produce; creative; fertile; efficient.—**produc'tively** adv.—**produc'tiveness, productiv'ity** n.

profane (pro-fān') a. not sacred; irreverent; blasphemous; given to swearing;—v.t. treat with irreverence; put to wrong or unworthy use; desecrate; pollute or defile.—**profane'ly** adv.—**profane'ness** n.—**profan'er** n.—**profanation** (prof-ạ-nā'-shun) n. act of violating sacred things.—**profanity** (pro-fan'-i-ti) n. profaneness; irreverence; use of oaths and bad language.

profess (pro-fes') v.t. make open declaration of; confess publicly; affirm belief in; pretend to knowledge or skill in.—**professed'** a. openly acknowledged.—**professedly** (pro-fes'-ed-li) adv.—**profession** (pro-fesh'-un) n. act of professing; that which one professes; occupation or calling, esp. one requiring learning.—**profes'sional** a. pert. to profession or calling; engaged in game or sport for money, as opposed to amateur;—n. one who makes livelihood in sport or games (abbrev. pro).—**profes'sionally** adv.

professor (pro-fes'-ẹr) n. one who makes profession; senior teacher in university.—**professorial** (pro-fe-sō'-ri-ạl) a.—**professo'rially** adv.—**profes'sorship** n.

proffer (prof'-ẹr) v.t. offer—n. offer made.—**proff'erer** n.

proficient (pro-fish'-ẹnt) a. thorough-

ly versed or qualified in any art or occupation; skilled; adept.—n. expert.—**profi'ciently** adv.—**profi'cience, profi'ciency** n. expertness.

profile (prō'-fīl, prō'-fēl) n. outline or contour; portrait in side view; sideface; short biographical sketch;—v.t. draw outline of.

profit (prof'-it) n. advantage or benefit; excess of returns over expenditure; pecuniary gain in any transaction or occupation;—v.t. be of service to;—v.i. gain advantage; grow richer.—**prof'itable** a. yielding profit or gain; advantageous; helpful.—**prof'itably** adv.—**prof'itableness** n.—**profiteer** (prof-i-tēr') n. one who makes excessive profits;—v.i. make such profits.

profligate (prof'-li-gāt) a. abandoned to vice; dissolute;—n. depraved person.—**prof'ligately** adv.—**prof'ligateness** n.—**prof'ligacy** (prof'-li-gạ-si) n. vicious and dissolute manner of living.

profound (prō-found') a. deep; learned; deeply felt.—**profound'ly** adv.—**profound'ness** n.—**profun'dity** n. depth of place, skill, feeling.

profuse (prō'fūs') a. giving or given generously; lavish; extravagant.—**profuse'ly** adv.—**profuse'ness, profusion** (prō-fū'-zhun) n. lavishness; great abundance.

progeny (proj'-e-ni) n. descendants; children; race.—**progen'itive** a. pert. to production of offspring.—**progen'itor** n. (fem. **progen'itress, progen'itrix**) ancestor.

prognosis (prog-nō'-sis) n. forecast; (Med.) foretelling course of disease.—pl. **progno'ses**.—**prognostic** (prognos'-tik) a. predicting;—n. prediction.—**prognos'ticate** v.t. foretell.—**prognostica'tion** n.—**prognos'ticator** n.

programme, program (prō'-gram) n. plan of intended proceedings at public entertainment, etc.; outline of policy; set of actions to be performed by a computer;—v.t. prepare a computer for a given operation.—**programmer** n.

progress (prog'-res, prō'-gres) n. moving forward; advancement; development.—**progress** (prō-gres') v.i. move forward; advance; develop; improve.—**progression** (prō-gresh'-un) n. onward movement; progress.—**progres'sional** a.—**progres'sive** a. moving forward gradually; improving; favouring progress or reform.—**progres'sively** adv.—**progres'siveness** n.

prohibit (prō-hib'-it) v.t. forbid; prevent; hinder; interdict by authority.—**prohib'iter, prohib'itor** n.—**prohibition** (prō-hi-bish'-un) n. act of forbidding; interdict; forbidding by law of manufacture, importation, sale, or purchase of alcoholic liquors.—**prohibi'tionist** n. one in favour of prohibition.—**prohib'itive, prohib'itory** *a.* exclusive.—**prohib'itively** *adv.*

project (prō-jekt') *v.t.* throw or cast forward; plan; contrive; scheme; throw photographic image on screen; —*v.i.* jut out; protrude.—**project** (proj'-ekt) *n.* plan; scheme.—**projectile** (prō-jek'-til) *n.* heavy missile, object thrown.—**projec'tion** *n.* act of projecting; something that juts out; plan; delineation; representation on plane of curved surface or sphere.—**projec'tive** *a.*—**projec'tor** *n.* apparatus for throwing photographic images, esp. films, on screen.

proletarian (prō-le-tā'-ri-an) *a.* pert. to proletariat; belonging to commonalty;—*n.* one of the proletariat.—**proletariat** (prō-le-tā'-ri-at) *n.* propertyless wage-earners who live by sale of their labour.

proliferous (prō-lif'-e-rus) *a.* (*Biol.*) reproducing freely by cell division; developing anthers. — **prolif'erously** *adv.*—**prolif'erate** *v.t.* bear;—*v.i.* reproduce by repeated cell division; increase.—**prolifera'tion** *n.* increase.

prolific (prō-lif-ik) *a.* fruitful; abundantly productive.—**prolif'ically** *adv.*

prolix (prō'-liks) *a.* long drawn out; diffuse; verbose; wordy.—**prolix'ly** *adv.*—**prolix'ness** *n.*—**prolix'ity** *n.*

prologue (prō'-log) *n.* preface to discourse, poem, book, or performance, esp. address spoken before dramatic performance;—*v.t.* preface.

prolong (prō-long') *v.t.* lengthen out; extend duration of.—**prolonga'tion** *n.* act of lengthening out; extension.

prom (prom) *n.* (*Colloq.* abbrev.) promenade concert; promenade at seaside resort.

promenade (prom-e-nâd', -nâd') *n.* leisurely walk, esp. in public place; place adapted for such walk;—*v.i.* walk for pleasure.—**promena'der** *n.*

prominent (prom'-i-nent) *a.* sticking out; projecting; conspicuous; distinguished. — **prom'inently** *adv.*—**prom'inence, prom'inency** *n.* state of being prominent; projection.

promiscuous (prō-mis'-kū-us) *a.* mixed without order; confused; not limited to particular individual or class.—**promis'cuously** *adv.*—**promiscuousness, promiscuity** (prom-is-kū'-i-ti) *n.* indiscriminate sexual relations.

promise (prom'-is) *n.* undertaking to do or not to do something; cause for hope;—*v.t.* give one's word to do or not to do something; give cause for expectation; undertake; agree to give;—*v.i.* assure by promise; give grounds for hope.—**prom'ising** *a.* likely to turn out well or to succeed.

promissory (prom'-i-sor-i) *a.* containing promise.—**promissory note,** written agreement to pay sum to named person at specified date.

promontory (prom'-on-tor-i) *n.* point of high land jutting out into sea.

promote (prō-mōt') *v.t.* move forward; move up to higher rank or position; encourage growth of; float new business venture or company. —**promo'ter** *n.* supporter; initiator, esp. of new business venture, etc.—**promo'tion** *n.* advancement; preferment; higher rank, or position, encouragement.—**promo'tive** *a.*

prompt (promt) *a.* ready and quick to act; done at once; punctual;—*v.t.* suggest; aid memory of (actor or speaker).—**prompt'ly** *adv.*—**prompt'er** *n.*—**prompt'itude, prompt'ness** *n.* readiness; quickness of decision and action.—**prompt'-side** *n.* (*abbrev.* P.S.) right side of stage (facing audience).

promulgate (prom'-ul-gāt) *v.t.* proclaim; publish.—**promulga'tion** *n.*

prone (prōn) *a.* lying face downwards; steep; inclined; naturally disposed.—**prone'ly** *adv.*—**prone'ness** *n.* tendency.

prong (prong) *n.* one of pointed ends of fork; spike.

pronoun (prō'-noun) *n.* (*Gram.*) word used instead of noun.—**pronom'inal** *a.*

pronounce (prō-nouns') *v.t.* speak distinctly; utter formally or officially; declare or affirm.—**pronounced'** *a.* strongly marked; very definite.—**pronounce'able** *a.*—**pronounce'ment** *n.* formal declaration.—**pronoun'cer** *n.*—**pronoun'cing** *a.* teaching or indicating pronunciation.—**pronunciation** (prō-nun-si-ā'-shun) *n.* mode of uttering words.

proof (prōof) *n.* something which proves; test or trial; demonstration; evidence that convinces mind and produces belief; argument; standard strength of alcohol; (*Print.*) trial impression from type;—*a.* firm in resisting; impenetrable;—*v.t.* render proof against.—**proof'ing** *n.* act of rendering materials impenetrable to water; substance used in this.—**proof'-read'er** *n.* one who corrects printer's proofs.—**proof'-spir'it** *n.* mixture of alcohol and water, containing not less than standard quantity of alcohol.

prop (prop) *v.t.* support; sustain.—*n.* that which supports; stay.

propaganda (prop-a-gan'-da) *n.* scheme for propagating doctrine or set of principles; beliefs thus spread.—**propagan'dise** *v.t.* and *i.* spread propaganda.—**propagan'dist** *n.*

propagate (prop'-a-gāt) *v.t.* cause to multiply by generation; breed; spread knowledge of; transmit or carry forward;—*v.i.* breed.—**prop'agator** *n.*—**propaga'tion** *n.*

propel (prō-pel') *v.t.* drive forward; press onward by force; push.—*pr.p.* **propell'ing.** — *pa.p.* **propelled.** — **propell'ant** *n.* fuel for rocket motor.—**pro-**

pell'er n. revolving shaft with blades for driving ship or aeroplane.

propensity (prŏ-pen'-si-ti) n. bent of mind; leaning or inclination; disposition; natural tendency.

proper (prop'-ẽr) a. particular; individual; belonging to oneself; befitting one's nature; correct or according to usage; thorough or complete;—adv. (Colloq.) very.—**prop'erly** adv.

property (prop'-ẽr-ti) n. essential quality; ownership; thing owned; possessions; estate;—pl. theatrical requisites, as scenery, dresses, etc.

prophecy (prof'-e-si) n. foretelling future events; prediction.—**prophesy** (prof'-e-si) v.t. foretell; predict;—v.i. utter predictions.—pr.p. **proph'esying.**—pa.p. and pa.t. **proph'esied.**—proph'et n. (fem. **proph'etess**) one who foretells future events; in Bible, inspired teacher or revealer of Divine Will—**prophet'ic(al)** a.

prophylactic (prof-i-lak'-tik) a. (Med.) preventive;—n. medicine or treatment tending to prevent disease. — **prophylax'is** n. preventive treatment of disease,.

propinquity (prŏ-ping'-kwi-ti) n. nearness in time or place; nearness in blood relationship.

propitiate (prŏ-pish'-i-āt) v.t. conciliate; gain favour of.—**propitia'tion** n. appeasement; conciliation.—**propi'tiator** n.—**propi'tiatory** a.—**propitious** (prŏ-pish'-us) a. favourable; kind; auspicious.—**propi'tiously** adv.—**propi'tiousness** n.

proportion (pro-pōr-'shun) n. relative size, number, or degree; comparison; relation; equal or just share; relation between connected things or parts; equality of ratios;—n.pl. dimensions;—v.t. divide into equal or just shares.—**propor'tionable** a. capable of being proportioned or made proportional.—**propor'tionably** adv.—**propor'tional** a. pert. to proportion. — **propor'tionally** adv. — **propor'tionate** a. adjusted so as to correspond in size, amount, or degree; proportional.—**propor'tioned** a. having suitable dimensions or measurements.—**propor'tionment** n.

propose (pro-pōz') v.t. offer for consideration; nominate;—v.i. form plan; intend; offer oneself in marriage.—**propo'sal** n. act of proposing; what is offered for consideration; offer, esp. of marriage.—**propo'ser** n.—**proposi'tion** n. proposal; statement; assertion.—**proposi'tional** a.

proprietor (prŏ-prī'-e'tor) n. (fem. **propri'etress, propri'etrix**) owner of property; owner. — **propri'etary** a. pert. to owner; made and sold by individual or firm having exclusive rights of manufacture and sale.—**propri'etorship** n.

propriety (prŏ-prī'-e-ti) n. properness; correct conduct.—**the propri'eties** n.pl. manners and conventions observed in polite society.

propulsion (prŏ-pul'-shun) n. act of driving forward.—**propul'sive, propul'sory** a. tending, or having power, to propel.

prorogue (prŏ-rōg') v.t. adjourn for indefinite time (esp. parliament);—**proroga'tion** n.

prosaic (prŏ-zā'-ik) a. dull; commonplace.—**prosa'ically** adv.

proscenium (prŏ-sē'-ni-um) n. part of stage in front of curtain.

proscribe (prŏ-skrīb') v.t. outlaw; prohibit.—**proscrib'er** n.—**proscrip'tion** n. prohibition; denunciation.—**proscrip'tive** a.

prose (prōz) n. ordinary language in speech and writing; language not in verse;—a. pert. to prose; not poetical;—v.i. speak or write in dull, tedious manner.—**pro'sy** a. dull and tedious.—**pro'sily** adv.—**pro'siness** n.

prosecute (pros'-e-kūt) v.t. follow or pursue with a view to an end; (Law) proceed against judicially;—v.i. carry on a legal suit.—**prosecu'tion** n. (Law) institution and carrying on of suit in court of law; party by which legal proceedings are instituted.—**pros'ecutor** n. (fem. **pros'ecutrix**) one who prosecutes; public prosecuting counsel.

proselyte (pros'-e-līt) n. convert to some party or religion;—v.t. convert.—**pros'elytise** v.t. make converts.—**pros'elytism** n.

prosody (pros'-o-di) n. art of versification.—**prosodiacal** (pros-ŏ-dī'-a-kal), **prosodial** (pro-sō'-di-al), **prosodic** (pro-sod'-ik) a.—**pros'odist** n. one skilled in prosody.

prospect (pros'-pekt) n. that which eye sees at one time; wide view; anticipation; reasonable hope; promise of future good.—**prospect'** v.t. and i. search or explore (region), esp. for oil, etc.—**prospec'tive** a. looking forward; pert. to future.—**prospec'tively** adv.—**prospec'tor** n.—**prospec'tus** n. circular or pamphlet outlining main features of proposed commercial undertaking, new publication, school, hotel, etc.

prosper (pros'-pẽr) v.t. cause to succeed;—v.i. succeed; do well.—**prosper'ity** n. success.—**pros'perous** a. thriving; successful; doing well.—**pros'perously** adv.

prostate (pros'-tāt) n. small gland at neck of bladder in males.

prostitute (pros'-ti-tūt) n. woman who hires herself for sexual intercourse; harlot;—v.t. make prostitute of; sell basely; put to base use.—**prostitu'tion** n.

prostrate (pros'-trāt) a. lying on ground face downwards; mentally or physically exhausted;—**prostrate'** v.t. lay flat on ground; bow down in adoration.—**prostra'tion** n.

protagonist (prō-tag'-on-ist) n. principal actor in Greek drama; leading character; participant.

protect (prō-tekt') v.t. defend; guard; put a tariff on imports.—**protec'tion** n. defending from injury or harm; state of being defended; that which defends.—**protec'tionism** n. doctrine of protecting industries by taxing competing imports.—**protec'tive** a. sheltering. — **protec'tively** adv. — **protec'tor** n.

protégé (pro-tā-zhā') n. (fem. protégée) one under care or patronage of another.

protein (prō'-tē-in, prō'-tēn) n. one of group of complex nitrogenous substances forming constituent of living cells.

protest (prō-test') v.i. assert formally; make declaration against;— v.t. affirm solemnly; object to.— **protest** (prō'-test) n. declaration of objection.—**protestant** (prot'-es-tant) n. one who holds opposite opinion. —**Prot'estant** a. pert. or belonging to any branch of Western Church outside Roman communion;—n. member of such church.—**Prot'estantism** n.—**protesta'tion** n. solemn declaration, esp. of dissent.

proto- (prō'-tō) prefix original; primitive.—**pro'toplasm** n. semi-fluid substance forming basis of primitive tissue of animal and vegetable life; living matter.—**protoplasmat'ic, protoplas'mic** a.—**prototype** (prō'-tō-tīp) n. original from which anything is copied; pattern.—**pro'totypal, prototyp'ie(al)** a.—**Protozoa** (prō-tō-z;'-ạ) n.pl. first or lowest division of animal kingdom.—**protozoon** (prō-tō-zō'-on) n. member of this division. —**protozo'al, protozo'an** a.

protocol (prō'-to-kol) n. original copy; rough draft of terms signed by negotiating parties as basis of formal treaty or agreement; diplomatic usage.

proton (prō'-ton) n. (Phys.) positively charged particle; a constituent of atomic nuclei.

protract (prō-trakt') v.t. lengthen; draw out; prolong; delay; defer.— **protrac'ted** a. prolonged; long drawn out; tedious.—**protrac'tion** n.—**protrac'tive** a. prolonging; delaying.— **protrac'tor** n. mathematical instrument for measuring angles.

protrude (prō-trōōd') v.t. and i. stick out; project; thrust forward.— **protru'sion** n. act of thrusting forward; state of being protruded or thrust forward; that which protrudes.—**protru'sive** a. thrusting forward.

protuberant (prō-tū'-be-rạnt) a. bulging; swelling out; prominent.— **protu'berantly** adv.—**protu'berance** n. swelling; prominence.

proud (proud) a. having excessive conceit of oneself; haughty; arrogant; self-respecting.—**proud'ly** adv.— **proud flesh**, excessive granulation in tissue of healing wound.

prove (prōōv) v.t. try by experiment; ascertain by evidence; demonstrate; show; endure; suffer; establish validity of (will, etc.).—v.i. turn out (to be, etc.); be found by trial; make trial.—pr.p. **prov'ing.**—pa.p. and pa.t. **proved.**—pa.p. (Scots Law) **prov'en.**—**prov'able** a.—**prov'ably** adv.

provender (prov'-en-der) n. dry food for beasts, e.g. corn, hay, oats; fodder, hence, provisions; food.

proverb (prov'-erb) n. short pithy expression of truth or moral; adage. —**prover'bial** a. pert. to proverb; well-known.—**prover'bially** adv.

provide (prō-vīd') v.t. get or make ready for future use; prepare; supply; furnish;—v.i. make preparation; set forth as previous condition. —**provid'ed** (that), **provid'ing** (that) conj. on condition that.—**providence** (prov'-i-dens) n. foresight; wise economy; God's care; event regarded as act of God.—**Prov'idence** n. God.— **prov'ident** a. prudent; thrifty.— **prov'idently** adv.—**providential** (prov-i-den'-shạl) a. effected by divine foresight; fortunate; lucky.—**providen'tially** adv.—**provi'der** n.

province (prov'-ins) n. division of country or empire; administrative district; district under jurisdiction of archbishop; sphere of action; department of knowledge; one's special duty.—**the provinces** n.pl. any part of country outside capital.— **provincial** (prō-vin'-shạl) a. pert. to province or provinces; countrified; unpolished;—n. inhabitant of province or provinces.—**provin'cially** adv.

provision (prō-vizh'-un) n. act of providing; measures taken beforehand; store esp. of food (generally in pl.); condition or proviso;—v.t. supply with provisions.—**provis'ional** a. temporary.—**provis'ionally** adv.

provoke (prō-vōk') v.t. excite or stimulate to action, esp. arouse to anger or passion; bring about or call forth. — **provok'ing** a. — **provocation** (prov-o-kā'-shun) n. that which provokes.—**provocative** (prō-vok'-ạtiv) a. serving to provoke.—**provoc'atively** adv.—**provoc'ativeness** n.

provost (prov'-ost) n. person appointed to preside, as head of certain colleges or religious communities; chief magistrate of Scottish towns.—**provost-marshal** (prov-ō'-mȧr-shạl) n. officer in charge of military police.

prow (prou) n. forepart of ship.

prowess (prou'-es) *n.* bravery; valour.

prowl (proul) *v.i.* roam about, esp. in search of prey;—*n.* act of prowling.

proximate (prok'-si-măt) *a.* next or nearest; closest; immediately following or preceding.—**prox'imately** *adv.*—**proxim'ity** *n.* being next in time, place, etc.; immediate nearness.—**prox'imo** *adv.* in or of coming month.

proxy (prok'-si) *n.* agent or substitute; one deputed to act for another; writing empowering one person to vote for another.

prude (próód) *n.* person affecting excessive propriety in sexual matters.—**prud'ish** *a.* like prude.—**prud'ery** *n.* affected coyness.

prudent (próó'-dent) *a.* cautious; careful; not extravagant.—**pru'dently** *adv.*—**pru'dence** *n.* caution.—**pruden'tial** *a.*—**pruden'tially** *adv.*

prune (próón) *n.* dried plum.

prune (próón) *v.t.* cut off dead parts, etc.; remove anything superfluous.—**pru'ning-hook** *n.* knife with curved blade.

Prussia (prush'-a) *n.* (*Geog.*) formerly leading State of Germany.—**Pruss'ian** *n.* and *a.*—**prussic acid**, hydrocyanic acid, violent and rapid poison.

pry (prī) *v.i.* look curiously; peer.—*pa.p.* and *pa.t.* **pried** (prīd).—**pri'er, pry'er** *n.*

psalm (sám) *n.* sacred hymn.—**the Psalms** (*Bib.*) book of Old Testament.—**psalmist** (sám'-ist, sal'-mist) *n.* writer of psalms.—**psalmody** (sá'-mo-di) *n.* art or practice of singing sacred music; psalms collectively.—**psal'modist** *n.* singer of psalms.—**Psalter** (sawl'-ter) *n.* Book of Psalms.—**psal'tery** *n.* obsolete stringed instrument like zither.

psephology (sef-ol-oj-i) *n.* statistical study of elections.

pseud(o)- (sū'-dō) *prefix* used to signify false; pretended.—**pseudonym** (sū'-dō-nim) *n.* fictitious name assumed, esp. by author; nom de plume.—**pseudon'ymous** *a.*

pshaw (shaw) *interj.* expressing contempt.

psittacosis (sit-a-kō'-sis) *n.* (*Med.*) fatal disease found in parrots.

psychiatry (sik-I'-atri, sī-kī'-a-tri) *n.* study of mental disorders.—**psychi'atrist** *n.* specialist in mental disorders.—**psychiat'ric(al)** *a.*

psychic, psychical (sī'-kik, -ki-kal) *a.* pert. to soul, spirit, or mind; spiritualistic. — **psy'chically** *adv.* — **psy'chic** *n.* one sensitive to spiritualistic forces; medium.—**psy'chicist** *n.*

psycho-analysis (sī'-kō-an-al'-i-sis) *n.* process of studying unconscious mind; method of treating mental disturbances, in which causes are traced to forgotten memories and repressions affecting mind unconsciously removed.—**psy'cho-an'alyse** *v.t.* treat thus.—**psy'cho-an'alyst** *n.*—**psy'cho-analy'tic(al)** *a.*

psychology (sī-kol'-o-ji) *n.* scientific study of mind and its activities.—**psycholog'ical** *a.*—**psycholog'ically** *adv.*—**psychol'ogist** *n.*

psychopath (sī'-kō-path) *n.* sufferer from mental disease.—**psycopath'ic** *a.*

psychosis (sī-kō'-sis) *n.* general term for any disorder of mind.—*pl.* **psycho'ses.**

psychotherapy (sī-kō-ther'-a-pi) *n.* treatment of disease through mind.

ptarmigan (tár'-mi-gan) *n.* bird of grouse family whose plumage turns white in winter.

pterodactyl (ter-o-dak'-til) *n.* extinct flying reptile with bat-like wings.

ptomaine (tō'-mān, to-mān') *n.* poisonous amino compounds found in putrefying organic matter.

pub (pub) *n.* (*Colloq.*) public-house.

puberty (pū'-ber-ti) *n.* earliest age at which individual is capable of reproduction.—**pubescence** (pū-bes'-ens) *n.* period of sexual development; puberty.—**pubes'cent** *a.*

public (pub'-lik) *a.* of, or pert. to, people; not private or secret; open to general use; accessible to all; serving the people;—*n.* community or its members; section of community.—**pub'licly** *adv.*—**pub'lican** *n.* keeper of public-house.—**publica'tion** *n.* making known to public; proclamation; book, periodical, magazine, etc.—**pub'licise** *v.t.* make widely known; advertise.—**pub'licist** *n.* one versed in international law.—**publicity** (pub-lis'-i-ti) *n.* state of being generally known; notoriety; advertisement.—**pub'lic-house** *n.* inn, or tavern for sale of alcoholic liquors.—**public prosecutor**, legal officer appointed to prosecute criminals in serious cases.—**public school**, large school, usually endowed, and managed by board of governors; elementary or primary school, esp. in Scotland; council-school.

publish (pub'-lish) *v.t.* make generally known; proclaim; print and issue for sale; put into circulation.—**pub'lisher** *n.*

puce (pūs) *a.* brownish-purple.

puck (puk) *n.* rubber disc used instead of ball in ice-hockey.

pucker (puk-er) *v.t.* and *i.* gather into small folds or wrinkles; wrinkle;—*n.* wrinkle.

pudding (póó'-ding) *n.* name of various forms of cooked foods, usually in soft mass, served as dessert; meat cooked in covering of flour; (*Naut.*) rope-fender.—**black pudding**, kind of sausage stuffed with blood, meal, suet, and other ingredients.

puddle (pud'-l) *n.* small pool of dirty

water;—*v.t.* make muddy; stir about molten pig-iron to remove carbon and make it malleable;—*v.i.* make muddy.—**pudd'ling** *n.*—**pudd'ler** *n.*

puerile (pū'-ẽr-īl) *a.* boyish; childish; silly.—**pu'erilely** *adv.*—**pueril'ity** *n.* childishness.

puerperal (pū-ẽr'-pẽr-al) *a.* pert. to, or caused by, child-birth.—**puerperal fever** (*Med.*) fever developing after child-birth.

puff (puf) *n.* short blast of breath or wind; small quantity of smoke, etc.; whiff; light pastry; soft pad for applying powder; exaggerated praise;—*v.i.* send out smoke, etc. in puffs; breathe hard; pant; swell up; —*v.t.* send out in puff; blow out; smoke hard; cause to swell; praise unduly.—**puff'er** *n.*—**puff'ing** *n.* act of praising unduly.—**puff'ingly** *adv.*—**puff'y** *a.* inflated; swollen; breathing hard.—**puff'iness** *n.*—**puff'add'er** *n.* venomous African viper.—**puff'-ball** *n.* ball-shaped fungus.

puffin (puf'-in) *n.* sea-bird of auk family with parrot-like beak.

pug (pug) *n.* small, snub-nosed dog; monkey; fox; shunting-locomotive. —**pug'-faced** *a.* monkey-faced.—**pug'-nose** *n.* snub nose.

pug (pug) *v.t.* make clay plastic by grinding with water; fill in spaces with mortar;—*n.* clay prepared for brickmaking.

pugilism (pū'-ji-lizm) *n.* art of fighting with fists; boxing.—**pu'gilist** *n.* boxer.—**pugilist'ic** *a.*

pugnacious (pug-nā'-shus) *a.* given to fighting; quarrelsome.—**pugna'ciously** *adv.*—**pugnacity** (pug-nas'-i-ti) *n.* inclination to fight.

puke (pūk) *v.i.* and *t.* vomit.

pukka (puk'-a) *a.* (*Anglo-Ind.*) real.

pulchritude (pul'-kri-tūd) *n.* beauty.

pule (pūl) *v.i.* whimper; whine.

pull (pool) *v.t.* draw towards one; drag; haul; tug at; gather; row boat;—*v.i.* draw; tug;—*n.* tug; strain; effort; (*Colloq.*) unfair advantage; (*Print.*) rough proof; (*Golf*) curving shot to left.—**pull'er** *n.* —**pull'over** *n.* jersey put on by pulling over head.

pullet (pool'-et) *n.* young hen.

pulley (pool'-i) *n.* small wheel with grooved rim on which runs rope.

pulmo- (pul'-mō) *prefix.*—**pulmonary** (pul'-mo-na-ri) *a.* pert. to lungs.—**pulmon'ic** *a.* pert. to lungs.

pulp (pulp) *n.* soft, moist mass of animal or vegetable matter; soft, succulent part of fruit; material of which paper is made;—*v.t.* reduce to pulp; remove pulp from.—**pul'py** *a.* like pulp.—**pul'piness** *n.*

pulpit (pŏŏl'-pit) *n.* elevated place in church for preacher; desk.

pulsate (pul'-sāt, pul-sāt') *v.t.* throb, as heart; vibrate; quiver.—**pulsa'tion** *n.* throbbing.—**pul'sative, pul'satory** *a.* capable of pulsating; throbbing.

pulse (puls) *n.* throbbing of heart or blood-vessels, esp. of arteries; place, esp. on wrist, where this beat is felt; any measured beat.—*v.i.* throb.

pulse (puls) *n.* leguminous plants or their seeds, as beans, peas, etc.

pulverise (pul'-vẽr-īz) *v.t.* reduce to fine powder; smash;—*v.i.* fall as dust. —**pulverisa'tion** *n.*—**pul'veriser** *n.*

puma (pū'-ma) *n.* carnivorous animal of the cat family; the cougar; the American panther.

pumice (pū'-mis, pum'-is) *n.*—**pum'ice-stone**, light, porous variety of lava, used for cleaning, polishing, etc.

pummel (pum'-el) *n.* pommel;—*v.t.* pommel; beat with fists.

pump (pump) *n.* appliance used for raising water, putting in or taking out air or liquid, etc.;—*v.t.* raise with pump; free from water by means of pump; (*Fig.*) extract information;—*v.i.* work pump; raise water with pump.—**pump'-room** *n.* room at spa for patrons who drink waters.

pump (pump) *n.* thin-soled dancing-shoe.

pumpkin (pump'-kin) *n.* plant of gourd family; its fruit, used as food.

pun (pun) *n.* play on words similar in sound but different in sense;—*v.i.* use puns.

punch (punsh) *n.* drink made of spirits or wine, flavoured with lemon-juice, sugar, etc.

punch (punsh) *n.* tool used for making holes or dents; machine for perforating tickets;—*v.t.* perforate, dent, or stamp with punch.

punch (punsh) *v.t.* strike with fist; beat; of cattle, drive;—*n.* blow with the fist; (*Slang*) energy.

punctilio (pungk-til'-i-ō) *n.* fine point of etiquette.—**punctil'ious** *a.* strict in observance of rules of conduct, etc.—**punctil'iously** *adv.*—**punctil'iousness** *n.*

punctual (pungk'-tū-al) *a.* arriving at fixed time; prompt; not late.—**punc'tually** *adv.*—**punctual'ity** *n.*

punctuate (pungk'-tū-āt) *v.t.* separate into sentences, clauses, etc. by periods, commas, etc.; emphasise; interrupt at intervals.—**punctua'tion** *n.* system of separating by use of punctuation marks.

puncture (pungk'-tūr) *n.* act of pricking; small hole made by sharp point;—*v.t.* to make hole with sharp point.

pungent (pun'-jent) *a.* sharply affecting taste or smell; stinging; sarcastic; caustic.—**pun'gently** *adv.*—**pun'gency** *n.*

punish (pun'-ish) *v.t.* cause offender to suffer for offence; inflict penalty or pain; chastise.—**pun'ishable** *a.*—**pun'ishment** *n.* penalty inflicted for crime; chastisement; correction.—**punitive** (pū'-ni-tiv) *a.* pert. to or inflicting punishment.

punnet (pun'-et) *n.* small, shallow chip basket for fruit.

punt (punt) *n.* flat-bottomed boat;—*v.t.* and *i.* propel boat by means of pole.

punt (punt) *v.t.* and *i.* kick football, when dropped from hands, before it touches the ground;—*n.* such kick.

punt (punt) *v.i.* (*Colloq.*) back horses. —**punt'er** *n.*

puny (pū'-ni) *a.* small and feeble;

pup (pup) *n.* puppy or young dog; conceited, foppish fellow;—*v.i.* bring forth puppies or whelps.

pupa (pū'-pa) *n.* inactive stage preceding adult stage in metamorphosis of some insects.—*pl.* **pupae** (pū'-pē).

pupil (pū'-pil) *n.* youth or scholar of either sex; boy or girl under age of puberty and so under care of guardian or tutor; ward; small circular opening in centre of iris of eye.—**pu'pilage, pu'pillage** *n.* state of being pupil; period of time during which one is pupil or minor.—**pu'pilary, pu'pillary** *a.* pert. to pupil or ward; pert. to pupil of eye.

puppet (pup'-et) *n.* small figure with jointed limbs manipulated by wires; marionette; person whose actions are controlled by another.—**pupp'etry** *n.* puppet-show.

purchase (pur'-chas) *v.t.* buy;—*n.* thing bought; any advantageous hold that may be secured in order to exert force.—**pur'chasable** *a.*—**pur'chaser** *n.*

pure (pūr) *a.* free from all extraneous matter; blameless; chaste; innocent; theoretical, not applied.—**pure'ly** *adv.* entirely; solely.—**pure'ness** *n.*—**pu'rity** *n.* freedom from all extraneous matter; innocence; chastity.

purge (purj) *v.t.* purify; cleanse; clear out; clear from guilt, etc.; remove undesirable or suspect members; cleanse bowels by taking cathartic medicine;—**purgative** (pur'-ga-tiv) *a.* having power of purging; —*n.* medicine which will cause evacuation of bowels.—**pur'gatory** *a.* tending to cleanse; purifying; expiatory;—*n.* in R.C. faith, place where souls of dead are purified by suffering; (*Fig.*) place or state of torment.—**purgato'rial** *a.*

purify (pū'-ri-fī) *v.t.* make pure, clear, or clean; free from impurities; free from guilt;—*v.i.* become pure. —*pa.p.* and *pat.t.* **pu'rified.**—**purifica'tion** *n.* act of removing impurities; act of cleansing, esp. from guilt or sin.—**pu'rificative** *a.*—**pu'rificator** *n.*—**pu'rificatory** *a.* tending to cleanse.—**pu'rifier** *n.*

purist (pū'-rist) *n.* stickler for correctness, esp. of style.

Puritan (pū'-ri-tan) *n.* a member of the extreme Protestant party, who desired further *purification* of the Church after the Elizabethan reformation.—**pu'ritan** *n.* person of extreme strictness in morals or religion; bigot; kill-joy;—*a.* pert. to Puritans or to puritan.—**puritan'ic(al)** *a.*—**puritan'ically** *adv.*—**pu'ritanism** *n.* doctrine and practice of Puritans; narrow-mindedness; bigotry.

purl (purl) *n.* embroidered border; knitting-stitch that is reverse of plain stitch;—*v.t.* ornament with purls;—*v.i.* knit in purl. Also **pearl**.

purl (purl) *v.i.* flow with gentle murmur.

purloin (pur-loin') *v.t.* steal; pilfer.

purple (pur'-pl) *n.* colour between crimson and violet from mixture of red and blue; robe of this colour;—*a.* purple-coloured; dark-red;—*v.t.* make or dye purple colour;—*v.i.* become purple.—**born to the purple**, of princely rank.

purport (pur'-pōrt) *n.* meaning; apparent meaning; import; aim.—**purport** (pur-pōrt') *v.t.* mean; be intended to seem.

purpose (pur'-pos) *n.* object in view; aim; end; plan; intention; effect; purport;—*v.t.* intend; mean to.—**pur'posely** *adv.* intentionally; deliberately.—**pur'poseful** *a.* determined; resolute.—**pur'posefully** *adv.* —**pur'poseless** *a.* aimless.—**pur'poselessly** *adv.*—**pur'posive** *a.* done with purpose.—**pur'posiveness** *n.*

purr (pur) *n.* low, murmuring sound made by cat when pleased; sound made by smooth-running machinery; —*v.i.* make this sound.

purse (purs) *n.* small bag to carry money in; money offered as prize; money;—*v.t.* wrinkle up; pucker.—**purs'er** *n.* (*Naut.*) officer in charge of accounts.—**purse'-strings** *n.pl.* power to control expenditure.

pursue (pur-sū') *v.t.* run after; chase; aim at; seek; continue;—*v.i.* go on; proceed; prosecute at law.—**pursu'er** *n.* one who pursues; (*Scots Law*) plaintiff.—**pursu'ance** *n.* act of pursuing.—**pursu'ant** *a.* done in consequence, or performance, of anything.—**pursuit'** (pur-sūt') *n.* act of pursuing; chase; attempt to catch; profession; occupation.—**pursuivant** (pur'-swi-vant) *n.* state messenger; officer of College of Arms ranking below herald.

purulent (pū'-rū-lent, pur'-ū-lent) *a.* pert. to pus; septic; suppurating.—**pu'rulence, pu'rulency** *n.*

purvey (pur-vā') *v.t.* furnish or provide; supply, esp. provisions;—*v.i.* cater.—**purvey'ance** *n.* act of purveying; supplies.—**purvey'or** *n.*

purview (pur'-vū) n. stipulation or condition; scope; range; limits.

pus (pus) n. yellowish-white matter produced by suppuration.

push (pŏŏsh) v.t. move or try to move away by pressure; drive or impel; press hard; press or urge forward; shove; thrust;—v.i. make a thrust; press hard in order to move;—n. thrust; pressure applied; emergency; enterprise; (Mil.) attack on large scale; (Colloq.) dismissal from post, etc.—push'er n.—push'ful, push'ing a. given to pushing oneself or one's claims; self-assertive.—push'ingly adv.

pusillanimous (pū-si-lan'-i-mus) a. cowardly; faint-hearted.—pusillan'imously adv.

puss (pŏŏs) n. familiar name for cat; hare; young girl.—puss'y n. dim. of puss; cat.

pustule (pus'-tūl) n. small swelling or pimple containing pus.—pus'tular, pus'tulous a.

put (pŏŏt) v.t. place; set; lay; apply; state; propose; urge; throw; cast;—v.i. place.—pr.p. putting (pŏŏt'-ing).—pa.p. and pa.t. put.—n. throw, esp. of heavy weight.—to put about, (Naut.) alter ship's course.

putrefy (pū'-tre-fī) v.t. and i. corrupt; decompose; rot.—pa.p. and pa.t. pu'trefied.—putrefac'tion n. process of putrefying; rotting of animal or vegetable matter; rottenness; decomposition.— putrefac'tive a.—putres'cence n. tendency to decay; decay; rottenness.—putres'cent a.—putrid (pū'-trid) a. in a state of decay.—putrid'ity, pu'tridness n.

putt (put) v.t. and i. (Golf) hit ball on putting-green in direction of hole; (Scot.) throw (weight or iron ball) from shoulder;—n. stroke so made in golf; throw of weight.—putt'er n. one who putts; short golf-club.

puttee (put'-ē) n. strip of cloth wrapped from ankle to knee, to act as legging.

putty (put'-i) n. kind of paste or cement, of whiting and linseed-oil; polishing powder used by jewellers; mixture of fine lime (without sand) and water, used by plasterers;—v.t. fix, fill up, etc. with putty.

puzzle (puz'-l) n. perplexing question; problem; conundrum;—v.t. perplex; bewilder; (with out) to solve after hard thinking;—v.i. be bewildered.—puzz'ling a. bewildering; perplexing.

Pygmy, Pigmy (pig'-mi) n. one of race of dwarf Negroes of C. Africa.—pl. Pyg'mies, Pig'mies.—pyg'my, pig'my n. very small person or thing; dwarf;—a. diminutive.

pyjamas (pi-, pī-ja'-maz) n.pl. loose trousers, worn by Mohammedans; sleeping-suit. Also paja'mas.

pylon (pī'-lon) n. gateway of ancient Egyptian temple; large metal tower, to support power-transmission cables.

pyorrhoea (pī-o-rē'-a) n. (Med.) discharge of pus; dental disease characterised by discharge of pus from gums.

pyramid (pir'-a-mid) n. solid figure on triangular, square, or polygonal base, and with sloping sides meeting at apex; structure of this shape, esp. ancient Egyptian (usually with square base);—n.pl. (Billiards) game similar to snooker.—pyramidal a. pert. to, or having form of, pyramid.—pyram'idally adv.

pyre (pīr) n. pile of wood for burning dead body; funeral pile.

pyrethrum (pir-eth'-rum) n. (Bot.) genus of herbaceous perennial plants.

pyrite (pī'-rīt) n. yellow mineral formed of sulphur and iron; iron pyrites.—pyrites (pir-ī'-tēz, pī'-rīts) n.pl. name for many compounds of metals with sulphur or arsenic, esp. iron pyrites, or copper pyrites.—pyrit'ic, pyritif'erous, pyr'itous a.

pyrography (pī-rog'-ra-fi) n. producing design on wood with heated metal point; pokerwork.

pyrolatry (pī-rol'-a-tri) n. fire-worship.

pyromania (pī-rō-mā'-ni-a) n. mania for setting things on fire.—pyroma'niac n. sufferer from this.

pyrotechnics (pī-rō-tek'-niks) n.pl. art of making fireworks; art of displaying them. Also pyrotech'ny.—pyrotech'nic a.

python (pī'-thon) n. large, non-poisonous snake that kills prey by crushing it; spirit; soothsayer.—Py'thoness n. (Myth.) priestess of Apollo at Delphi; witch.

pyx (piks) n. vessel in which consecrated bread or Host is kept; box at Royal Mint, London, in which specimen coins are kept for trial and assay;—v.t. test by assay.

Q

quack (kwak) v.i. cry like duck; act as quack;—n. cry of duck or like sound; one who pretends to skill in an art esp. in medicine; charlatan;—a. pert. to quackery.—quack'ery n.—quack'salver n. quack doctor.

Quadragesima (kwod-ra-jes'-i-ma) n. (Eccl.) season of Lent, lasting for 40 days.—Quadrages'imal a.

quadrangle (kwod'-rang-gl) n. in geometry, plane figure having four equal sides and angles; square or court surrounded by buildings (abbrev. quad.).—quadrang'ular a.

quadrant (kwod'-rant) n. fourth part

of area of circle; arc of 90°; instrument for taking altitude of heavenly bodies; in gunnery.

quadrate (kwod'-rāt) a. having four equal sides and four right angles; square; divisible by four (used chiefly in anatomical names);—n. square;—**quadrate'** v.i. square; agree; suit.—**quadrat'ic** a. pert. to, or resembling, square; square; (Alg.) involving second but no higher power of unknown quantity, esp. in **quadratic equation.**—**quadrature** (kwod'-ra̱-tūr) n. act of squaring or reducing to square; position of a heavenly body when its relation to earth and sun forms angle of 90°.

quadrennial (kwod-ren'-i-a̱l) a. occurring once in four years; comprising four years.—**quadren'nially** adv.—**quadrenn'ium** n. four years.

quadricentennial (kwod-ri-sen-ten'-i-a̱l) a. pert. to period of four hundred years;—n. four hundredth anniversary.

quadrilateral (kwod-ri-lat'-e̱r-a̱l) a. having four sides;—n. (Geom.) plane figure having four sides.

quadrille (ka̱-dril', kwo-dril') n. 18th cent. card game; square dance, also, its music.

quadrillion (kwo-dril'-yun) n. million raised to fourth power, represented by unit with 24 ciphers annexed; in French and U.S. notation, with 15 ciphers annexed.

quadripartite (kwod-ri-pär'-tīt) a. divided into four parts.

quadroon (kwod-rŏŏn') n. offspring of mulatto and white; one who is one-fourth Negro.

quadruped (kwod'-rŏŏ-ped) n. animal having four feet:—a. having four feet.

quadruple (kwod'-rŏŏ-pl) a. fourfold;—n. fourfold amount; sum four times as great as another;—v.t. multiply by four;—v.i. be multiplied by four.—**quad'ruplet** n. one of four children born at a birth.—**quadru'plicate** v.t. multiply by four;—n. one of four things corresponding exactly;—a. fourfold.—**quadruplica'tion** n.

quaff (kwaf) v.t. swallow in large draughts.

quag (kwag) n. marshy spot; bog.—**quagg'y** a. boggy.—**quagmire** (kwag'-mīr) n. soft, wet land, yielding under feet.

quaich, quaigh (kwāH) n. shallow, bowl-shaped drinking vessel.

quail (kwāl) v.i. lose spirit; cower.

quail (kwāl) n. game-bird allied to partridge.

quaint (kwānt) a. curious and fanciful.—**quaint'ly** adv.—**quaint'ness** n.

quake (kwāk) v.i. tremble or shake with fear, cold, or emotion; quiver;—n. shaking or trembling.

Quaker (kwā-ke̱r) (fem. **Qua'keress**) member of Society of Friends, sect founded in 17th cent. by George Fox.—**Qua'kerism** n.

qualify (kwol'-i-fī) v.t. ascribe quality to; describe (as); prepare by training for special duty; furnish with legal title to; limit; diminish;—v.i. make oneself competent; render oneself fit for.—**qual'ifier** n.—**qual'ifiable** a.—**qualifica'tion** n. act of qualifying; endowment or acquirement that fits person for office or employment; modification; restriction.

quality (kwol'-i-ti) n. property inherent in body; essential attribute, or distinguishing feature, or characteristic of anything; character or nature; degree of excellence; excellence of character; rank or high birth.

qualm (kwäm) n. sudden attack of faintness or nausea; scruple of conscience.

quandary (kwon'-da̱-ri, kwon-dā'-ri) n. state of perplexity; predicament; dilemma.

quantify (kwon'-ti-fī) v.t. fix or express quantity of; modify with respect to.—**quantifica'tion** n.

quantity (kwon'-ti-ti) n. property of things ascertained by measuring; amount; bulk; certain part; considerable amount; number; (Pros.) the length or shortness of vowels, sounds, or syllables;—pl. abundance; profusion.—**quantitative** (kwon'-ti-tā-tiv) a. relating to quantity.—**quantity surveyor**, specialist estimator of costs of erecting buildings, etc.

quantum (kwon'-tum) n. large quantity or amount; specified, desired, or required amount; sufficient amount.—**quantum theory**, in physics, theory that energy transferences take place not continuously, but in multiples of minimum quantity or quantum.

quarantine (kwor-a̱n-tēn) n. period of compulsory isolation during incubation period of any infectious disease, or for statutory period in certain cases, e.g. ships;—v.t. put under quarantine.

quarrel (kwor'-e̱l) n. rupture of friendly relations; angry altercation; dispute;—v.i. dispute; wrangle; disagree.—**pr.p. quarr'elling.**—**pa.p.** and **pa.t. quarr'elled.**—**quarr'eller** n.—**quarr'elsome** a. apt to quarrel; irascible; contentious.

quarrel (kwor'-e̱l) n. heavy square-headed arrow for crossbow; diamond-shaped pane of glass;- glazier's diamond.

quarry (kwor'-i) n. excavation whence stone is dug for building; source from which material or (Fig.) information may be extracted;—v.t. dig from quarry.—**pa.p.** and **pa.t. quarr'ied.**

quarry (kwor'-i) *n.* orig. game hunted with hawks; object of pursuit; prey.

quart (kwort) *n.* fourth part of gallon; two pints.

quarter (kwor'-ter) *n.* fourth part; in avoirdupois weight, fourth of 1 cwt., or 28 lb.; in dry measure, 8 bushels; one of four cardinal points of compass; (*Her.*) one of four parts into which shield is divided by quartering; term in school, etc.; part of ship's side aft of mainmast; region; territory; part of town, or county; merciful treatment granted to enemy;—*pl.* lodgings, esp. for soldiers; shelter;—*v.t.* divide into four equal parts; divide up traitor's body; furnish with shelter;—*v.i.* have temporary residence.—**quar'tering** *n.* assignment of quarters for soldiers; (*Her.*) partition of shield into compartments.—**quar'terly** *a.* consisting of fourth part; occurring every quarter of year;—*n.* magazine published quarterly;—*adv.* by quarters; once in quarter of year.—**quar'ter-day** *n.* one of four days in year, when rents fall due.—**quar'terdeck** *n.* part of deck of ship which extends from stern to mainmast; (*Fig.*) officers of naval vessel.—**quar'termaster** *n.* (*Mil.*) officer in charge of quarters, clothing, stores, etc.; (*Naut.*) petty officer who attends to steering, signals, etc.—**quar'termaster-ser'geant** *n.* N.C.O. assistant to quartermaster.—**quar'ter-ses'sions** *n.* court held quarterly by justices of peace.—**quar'ter-staff** *n.* long, stout staff, formerly weapon.

quartern (kwor'-tern) *n.* orig. quarter of peck, stone, or pint; now generally used only in **quartern-loaf**, weighing four pounds.

quartet, quartette (kwor-tet') *n.* (*Mus.*) composition of four parts, each performed by single voice or instrument; set of four who perform this; group of four.

quarto (kwor'-tō) *a.* denoting size of book in which paper is folded to give four leaves to sheet (*abbrev.* 4to);—*n.* book, size of fourth of sheet.

quartz (kworts) *n.* kinds of mineral found in massive and in hexagonal crystals.

quash (kwosh) *v.t.* crush; quell; (*Law*) annul, or make void.

quasi (kwā'-si, kwä'-sē) *as if; as it were; in a certain sense or degree; seeming; apparently; it is used as adj. or adv. and as prefix to noun, adj. or adv.

quatercentenary (kwo-ter-sen-tē'-na-ri, kwa'-ter-sen'-ti-na-ri) *n.* 400th anniversary.

quaternary (kwo-ter'-na-ri) *a.* consisting of four; by fours.—*n.* number four.

quatrain (kwot'-rān) *n.* stanza of four lines, generally rhyming alternately.

quaver (kwā'-ver) *v.i.* shake, tremble, or vibrate; sing or play with tremulo; —*v.t.* utter or sing with quavers or trills;—*n.* trembling, esp. of voice; (*Mus.*) note equal to half crochet.

quay (kē) *n.* landing-place used for loading and unloading of ships; wharf.

queen (kwēn) *n.* consort of king; woman who is sovereign of kingdom; sexually active female of a group of social insects; woman who is pre-eminent; piece in chess.—*v.i.* act part of queen (as in *to queen it*).—**queen'ly** *a.* majestic.—**queen'liness** *n.*—**queen'-hood** *n.*—**queen'-bee** *n.*—**queen'-con'sort** *n.* wife of king.—**queen'-dow'ager** *n.* widow of king.—**queen'-moth'er** *n.* queen-dowager who is also mother of reigning monarch.—**queen'-re'gent** *n.* queen who reigns as regent.—**queen-reg'nant** *n.* queen reigning in her own right.—**Queen's Bench,** one of three divisions of English High Court of Justice.—**Queen's Counsel,** honorary distinction conferred on eminent barristers giving them right to wear silk gown (hence, *to take silk*).—**Queen's Messenger,** courier appointed by Foreign Office to carry despatches.—**Queen's Proctor,** Treasury solicitor who may intervene to stop decrees *nisi* in divorce being made absolute.—**Queen's Regulations,** official regulations for organisation of British Army or Navy.

queer (kwēr) *a.* odd; singular; quaint; open to suspicion; indisposed;—*v.t.* (*Slang*) spoil.—*n.* (*Slang*) homosexual.—**queer'ly** *adv.*—**queer'ish** *a.* somewhat queer.—**queer'ness** *n.*—in **Queer Street** (*Slang*) in trouble or difficulty, esp. financially.

quell (kwel) *v.t.* subdue; put down; suppress forcibly.

quench (kwensh) *v.t.* extinguish; put out, as fire or light; cool or allay; repress; stifle; slake (thirst);—*v.i.* become cool. — **quench'able** *a.* — **quench'less** *a.* — **quench'er** *n.*

quern (kwern) *n.* primitive stone handmill for grinding grain.

querulous (kwer'-ū-lus) *a.* peevish; fretful; whining; discontented.—**quer'ulously** *adv.*—**quer'ulousness** *n.*

query (kwē'-ri) *n.* question; inquiry; mark of interrogation;—*v.t.* inquire into; call in question; mark as of doubtful accuracy;—*v.i.* express doubt.

quest (kwest) *n.* search; act of seeking; thing sought;—*v.i.* search; seek.

question (kwest'-yun) *n.* interrogation; inquiry; that which is asked; subject of inquiry or debate; (subject of) dispute; matter of doubt or difficulty; problem;—*v.t.* inquire of by asking questions; be uncertain of; challenge; take objection to; interrogate;—**quest'ionable** *a.* doubtful; suspicious. — **quest'ionably** *adv.* — **quest'ionableness** *n.*—**quest'ioner** *n.*—**quest'ion-mark** *n.* mark of interrogation.—**out of the question,** not to be thought of.—**to beg the question,** assume as fact something which is to be proved.

questionnaire (kes-ti-on-ār') *n.* list of questions drawn up for formal answer, with view to establishing statistics. Also **ques'tionary.**

queue (kū) *n.* tie of wig; pig-tail; file of people awaiting their turn;—*v.i.* form, join queue.

quibble (kwib'-l) *n.* evasion of point in question by stressing unimportant aspect of it; equivocation or pretence;—*v.i.* use quibbles; trifle in argument.—**quibb'ler** *n.*

quick (kwik) *a.* alive; living; smart; animated; sprightly; ready or prompt; sensitive; rapid; hasty; impatient;—*n.* sensitive flesh under nails; part of tissue keenly susceptible to pain; (*Fig.*) one's tenderest susceptibilities;—*adv.* also **quick'ly,** rapidly; speedily; promptly; with haste.—**quick'ness** *n.*—**quick'en** *v.t.* make alive; make active; hasten; stimulate;—*v.i.* become alive; move with greater rapidity.—**quick'ener** *n.* —**quick'ening** *n.* making or becoming quick; first movement of foetus in womb.—**quick'lime** *n.* unslaked lime. —**quick'sand** *n.* sand, readily yielding to pressure, esp. if loose and mixed with water.—**quick'set** *n.* living plant, esp. hawthorn, planted as hedge;—*a.* formed, as hedge, of living plants.—**quick'silver** *n.* mercury.—**quick'-step** *n.* march at rate of 120 paces minute; lively dance.

quid (kwid) *n.* portion suitable for chewing, esp. of tobacco; cud.

quid (kwid) *n.* (*Slang*) pound sterling.

quiesce (kwi-es') become still or silent.—**quiescent** (kwi-es'-ent) *a.* still; inert.—**quies'cently** *adv.*—**quies'-cence, quies'cency** *n.*

quiet (kwi'-et) *a.* still; peaceful; placid; not showy;—*n.* calm; peace; tranquillity;—*v.t.* reduce to state of rest; calm; allay; soothe;—*v.i.* become quiet.—**qui'eten** *v.t.* and *i.* quiet.—**qui'etly** *adv.*—**qui'etness** *n.*— **qui'etude** *n.* freedom from noise or alarm; repose.—**quietus** (kwi-ē'-tus) *n.* final acquittance, of debt, etc.; (*Fig.*) extinction.

quiff (kwif) *n.* curl over forehead.

quill (kwil) *n.* large, strong, hollow feather of goose, swan, etc.; this used as pen; pen; prickle, as of porcupine; weavers' bobbin; plectrum.

quilt (kwilt) *n.* bed-coverlet made of two pieces of material sewn together, filled with padding and stitched across in patterns; eiderdown;— *v.t.* stitch together, like quilt, with soft filling; pad.

quinary (kwi'-na-ri) *a.* consisting of, or arranged in, fives.

quince (kwins) *n.* hard, yellow, acid fruit.

quincentenary (kwin-sen-tē'-na-ri, kwin-sen'-te-na-ri) *n.* five-hundredth anniversary.

quinine (kwi-nēn', kwi-nīn') *n.* bitter alkaloid obtained from cinchona bark; used as tonic and febrifuge.

quinquagesima (kwin-kwa-jes'-i-ma) *n.* period of fifty days.— Quinquagesima Sunday, Sunday before Ash Wednesday, so called because fifty days before Easter.

quinquennial (kwin-kwen'-i-al) *a.* occurring once in five years, or lasting five years.—**quinquenn'ially** *adv.*—**quinquenn'iad, quinquenn'ium** *n.* period of five years.

quinsy (kwin'-zi) *n.* inflammation and suppuration of tonsils.

quintessence (kwin-tes'-ens) *n.* among Pythagoreans, fifth essence in natural bodies, in addition to four elements, earth, air, fire, water; pure essence of anything; essential part of thing.—**quintessen'tial** *a.*

quintet, quintette (kwin-tet') *n.* (*Mus.*) composition for five performers; company of five singers or players; set of five.

quintillion (kwin-til'-yun) *n.* number produced by involving million to fifth power; unit with 30 ciphers following; in French and American notation, unit with 18 ciphers.

quintuple (kwin'-tū-pl) *a.* multiplied by five; fivefold.—**quin'tuplets** *n.pl.* five children at a birth (*Colloq.* quins).

quip (kwip) *n.* smart, sarcastic turn of phrase; gibe; witty saying.

quire (kwir) *n.* 24 sheets of writing-paper, twentieth part of ream; twenty-four sheets of same size, each having single fold.

quirk (kwerk) *n.* sudden turn or twist; artful evasion; quibble; witty saying; knack.—**quirk'y** *a.*

quisling (kwiz'-ling) *n.* treacherous betrayer of one's country to enemy.

quit (kwit) *v.t.* depart from; leave; cease from; give up; let go; satisfy claim;—*v.i.* depart; stop doing thing;—*a.* released from obligation; free;—*pr.p.* quitt'ing.—*pa.p.* and *pa.t.* quitt'ed.—**quitt'ance** *n.* discharge from debt; receipt; requital.— **quitt'er** *n.* (*Colloq.*) person easily discouraged.—**to be quits,** be equal with another person by repayment (of money, or good, or evil).

quitch-grass (kwich'-gras) *n.* couch-grass.

quite (kwīt) *adv.* completely; wholly; entirely; totally; to considerable extent; positively.

quiver (kwiv'-er) *n.* case or sheath for holding arrows.—**quiv'erful** *n.* (*Fig.*) numerous family.

quiver (kwiv'-er) *v.i.* shake with tremulous motion; tremble; shiver; —*n.* act of quivering; tremor; shiver.

Quixote (kwiks'-ot) *n.* hero of romance of Miguel Cervantes (1547-1616).—**quixot'ic** *a.* like Don Quixote; ideally and extravagantly romantic. — **quixot'ically** *adv.* — **quix'otism.** — **quix'otry** *n.*

quiz (kwiz) *n.* puzzle or riddle; game in which two sides answer questions on general knowledge.— *pl.* **quiz'zes.**—*v.t.* puzzle; tease; eye rudely or contemptuously; interrogate.—**quiz'zer** *n.*—**quiz'zical** *a.*

quoin (koin) *n.* (*Archit.*) external angle, esp. of building; corner-stone; (*Print.*) small wooden or metal wedge used to lock types in galley, etc.

quoit (koit) *n.* flat, iron etc. ring to be pitched at fixed object in play;— *pl.* game of throwing these on to peg; —*v.i.* play at quoits.

quondam (kwon'-dam) *a.* former; that was once.

quorum (kwō'-rum) *n.* number of members that must be present at meeting to make its transactions valid.

quota (kwō'-ta) *n.* proportional part or share.

quote (kwōt) *v.t.* copy or repeat passage from; cite; state price for; —*n.* (*Slang*) quotation;—*pl.* quotation marks.—**quota'tion** *n.*—**quota'-tion-marks** *n.pl.* marks used to indicate beginning and end of quotation.

quotidian (kwō-tid'-i-an) *a.* daily;— *n.* thing returning daily, esp. fever.

quotient (kwō'-shent) *n.* number resulting from division of one number by another.

R

rabbi (rab'-I), **rabbin** (rab'-in) *n.* Jewish teacher of Law.—**rabbin'ic(al).**

rabbit (rab'-it) *n.* small, burrowing rodent mammal, like hare, but smaller; (*Slang*) duffer; poor performer at sport.—**rabb'it-hutch** *n.* box for rearing tame rabbits.— **rabb'itry, rabb'it-warr'en** *n.* breeding-place of wild rabbits.

rabble (rab'-l) *n.* noisy, disorderly crowd; common herd;—*v.t.* mob; hustle.

rabies (rā'-bēz) *n.* canine madness; hydrophobia.—**rab'id** *a.* suffering from rabies; furious; fanatical.—**rab'-idly** *adv.*—**rab'idness, rabid'ity** *n.*

raccoon, racoon (ra-kōōn') *n.* mammal of N. America, of bear family.

race (rās) *n.* descendants of common ancestor; distinct variety of human species; peculiar breed, as of horses, etc.; lineage; descent.—**ra'cial** *a.* pert. to race or lineage.—**rac'ially** *adv.*—**ra'cialism, ra'cism** *n.* animosity shown to peoples of different race.

race (rās) *n.* running; swift progress; rapid motion; contest involving speed; strong current of water, esp. leading to water-wheel which it drives;—*v.t.* cause to run rapidly;— *v.i.* run swiftly, of engine, etc., move rapidly and erratically.—**ra'cer** *n.* one who races; racehorse, car, etc., used for racing.—**race'course, race'-ground** *n.* ground for horse-races.— **race'horse** *n.* horse bred to run for stake or prize.—**race'-track** *n.* track used for racing.—**rac'ing** *n.*

rack (rak) *n.* instrument for stretching; instrument of torture by which limbs were stretched to point of dislocation; hence, torture; open framework for displaying books, bottles, hats, baggage, etc.; framework in which hay is placed;—*v.t.* stretch almost to breaking point; overstrain; torture; extort excessive rent; place in rack.—**racked** *a.*— **rack'ing** *a.* agonising (pain). — **rack railway**, mountain railway worked by rack and pinion.—**rack'rent** *n.* excessive rent.

rack (rak) *n.* thin, driving clouds; ruin; destruction;—*v.i.* drift, as vapour.

racket, racquet (rak'-et) *n.* bat used in tennis, etc.;—*pl.* ball game played in paved court with walls; snow-shoe.

racket (rak'-et) *n.* confused, clattering noise; din; occupation by which much money is made illegally;—*v.i.* make noise or clatter.—**racketeer'** *n.* extortioner; gangster.

racy (rā'-si) *a.* spicy; pungent; spirited (of story).—**ra'cily** *adv.*—**ra'ciness** *n.*

radar (rā'-där) *n.* radiolocation (fr. init. letters of *ra*dio, *d*etection, and *r*anging).

radial (rā'-di-al) *a.* pert. to ray, radius, or radium; branching out like spokes of wheel.

radian (rā'-di-an) *n.* unit of circular measure, angle subtended at centre of circle by arc equal in length to radius (= 57°·3).

radiant (rā'-di-ant) *a.* emitting rays; beaming; radiating;—*n.* (*Opt.*) luminous point from which rays of light emanate.—**ra'diance, ra'diancy** *n.* radiant intensity; brilliancy; splendour. —**ra'diantly** *adv.*

radiate (rā'-di-āt) *v.i.* branch out

like spokes of wheel; emit rays; shine;—*v.t.* emit rays, as heat, etc. —*a.* formed of rays diverging from centre; radially symmetrical.—**radia'tion** *n.* emission and diffusion of rays from central point;—**ra'diator** *n.* device which emits rays; energy in form of electro-magnetic waves; apparatus for radiating heat; in motorcars apparatus to cool circulating water in watercooling system.

radical (rad'-i-kạl) *a.* pert. to root; original; basic; complete; thorough; of advanced liberal views;—*n.* root; primitive word; politician who advocates thorough reforms; (*Math.*) quantity expressed as root of another.—**Rad'icalism** *n.* root and branch political reform.—**rad'ically** *adv.*—**rad'icalness** *n.*

radicle (rad'-i-kl) *n.* (*Anat.*) initial fibril of nerve.

radio- (rā'-di-ō) *prefix* used in formation of compound terms referring to *radius* of forearm.—**ra'diocar'pal** *a.* pert. to radius and wrist.— **ra'dio-mus'cular** *a.* pert. to radius and muscles.—**ra'dio-ul'nar** *a.* pert. to radius and ulna.

radio- (rā'-di-ō) *prefix* used in formation of compound terms with meaning 'of rays,' 'of radiation,' 'of radium,' as in —**ra'dioac'tive** *a.* emitting invisible rays which penetrate matter.—**ra'dioactiv'ity** *n.*— **radiog'rapher** *n.* one who takes X-ray photographs—**radiog'raphy** *n.*—**radiol'ogy** *n.* science of radio-activity in medicine.—**radiol'ogist** *n.*—**radiother'apy**, **ra'diotherapeu'tics** *n.* treatment of disease by radium or X-rays.

radio (rā'-di-ō) *n.* wireless telephony or telegraphy; wireless; broadcasting; apparatus for reception of broadcast; radio telegram.—**ra'diogram** *n.* telegram transmitted by radio; combination of radio receiver and gramophone.—**radio telescope** *n.* apparatus for receiving radio signals or echoes from outer space.

radish (rad'-ish) *n.* herb with edible root.

radium (rā'-di-um) *n.* metallic, radioactive element which undergoes spontaneous disintegration, giving off corpuscular and wave radiations.

radius (rā'-di-us) *n.* straight line from centre of circle to circumference; spoke of wheel; ray; distance from any one place; bone on thumb side of forearm; movable arm of sextant.—*pl.* rad'ii.

radon (rā'-don) *n.* gaseous, radioactive element, formed by disintegration of radium; radium emanation.

raff (raf) *n.* promiscuous heap; mob; worthless fellow.—**raf'fish** *a.*—see also riff-raff.

raffia (raf'-i-ạ) *n.* fibre from cultivated palm used for mats, baskets, etc.

raffle (raf'-l) *n.* lottery in which several persons subscribe towards or beyond value of article, ultimate possessor being decided by lot;— *v.t.* sell by raffle.

raft (raft) *n.* improvised float of planks fastened together; logs chained together for transportation down river.

rafter (raft'-ẹr) *n.* sloping beam, from ridge to eaves, to which roofcovering is attached;—*v.t.* provide with rafters.

rag (rag) *n.* fragment of cloth; remnant; patch; (*Slang*) newspaper; —*pl.* mean attire;—*a.* made of rags. —**rag'a-muffin** *n.* a dirty and disreputable person.—**rag'-tag** *n.* rabble; riff-raff.—**rag'-time** *n.* popular dance music, marked by strong syncopation;—**rag'-wort** *n.* roadside plant with bright, yellow flowers.

rag (rag) *v.t.* tease; torment; play practical jokes on; nag;—*v.i.* be noisy and riotous.—*pr.p.* rag'ging.— *pa.t.* and *pa.p.* ragged.—*n.* disorderly row (esp. by university students).

rage (rāj) *n.* violent excitement; extreme anger; craze; fashion;—*v.i.* be furious; rave; proceed violently (as storm, battle, etc.).—**ra'ging** *a.* —**ra'gingly** *adv.*

ragged (rag'-ed) *a.* worn to tatters; dressed in rags; jagged; slip-shod; not rhythmical.—**ragg'edly** *adv.*— **ragg'edness** *n.*—ragged robin, cuckoogilly-flower, crimson-flowered wild plant.

ragout (rạ-gōō') *n.* cubes of meat, stewed and highly seasoned; hash.

raid (rād) *n.* hostile incursion depending on surprise; surprise visit by police; attack on town by hostile aircraft;—*v.t.* make sudden attack upon.—**raid'er** *n.*

rail (rāl) *n.* piece of timber or metal extending from one post to another; bars of steel on which the wheels of vehicles run; track for locomotives; railway; horizontal bar for support; top of ship's bulwarks;—*v.t.* enclose with rails; send by railway.—**rail'head** *n.* farthest point to which rails have been laid.—**rail'ing** *n.*—*pl.* form of fence of upright iron-bars joined by horizontal bars.—**rail'road** *n.* railway.—**rail'way** *n.* road on which steel rails are laid for wheels to run on; system of such rails.

rail (rāl) *v.i.* use insolent language; utter abuse; reproach.—**rail'er** *n.*— **rail'lery** *n.* good-humoured banter.

raiment (rā'-mẹnt) *n.* clothing; dress; apparel.

rain (rān) *n.* condensed moisture, falling in drops from clouds; shower;—*v.t.* and *v.i.* fall as rain; pour down like rain.—**rain'bow** *n.*

arch showing seven prismatic colours and formed by refraction and reflection of sun's rays in falling rain in part of sky opposite sun.—**rain'-cloud** *n.* nimbus.—**rain'coat** *n.* light, rain-proof overcoat.—**rain'fall** *n.* fall of rain; amount of rain, in inches, or centimetres, which falls in particular place in given time.—**rain'-gauge** *n.* instrument for measuring rainfall.—**rain'iness** *n.*—**rain'less** *a.*—**rain'-proof** *a.* impervious to rain. —*n.* over-garment made from shower-proof cloth.—**rain'-storm** *n.*—**rain'-tight** *a.* impervious to rain.—**rain'y** *a.*

raise (rāz) *v.t.* cause to rise; elevate; promote; build up; collect; produce by cultivation; rear; levy; give up (siege); heighten (voice);—*n.* ascent; (*Colloq.*) increase in wages.—**rais'able** *a.*—**raised** *a.* elevated.—**rais'ing** *n*:—**to raise Cain, a dust, the devil, hell, etc., make a scene.**—**to raise the wind,** obtain ready-money.

raisin (rā'-zn) *n.* a dried grape.

raj (räj) *n.* sovereignty;—**ra'jah, ra'ja** *n.* king, prince, or noble of Hindu race.

rake (rāk) *n.* long-handled implement with cross-bar toothed for smoothing earth, etc.; agricultural machine used in hay-making;—*v.t.* and *v.i.* scrape with toothed implement; draw together, as mown hay; sweep or search over; ransack; scour; fire shot lengthwise into ship, etc.

rake (rāk) *n.* (*Hist.*) dissolute man of fashion; libertine.—**ra'kish** *a.*—**ra'kishly** *adv.*

rake (rāk) *n.* angle of inclination; inclination of masts from perpendicular; projection of upper parts of stem and stern beyond keel of ship; —*v.i.* incline from perpendicular.—**ra'kish** *a.* having backward inclination of masts; stylish or speedy-looking.—**ra'kishly** *adv.*

rally (ral'-i) *v.t.* and *v.i.* reassemble; collect and restore order; recover (strength, health); return ball (in tennis.)—*pr.p.* rall'ying.—*pa.t.* and *pa.p.* rall'ied.—*n.* act of rallying; assembly; outdoor demonstration; exchange of strokes in tennis; type of motoring contest over timed and observed routes to a given assembly point.

rally (ral'-i) *v.t.* attack with raillery; tease;—*n.* banter.

ram (ram) *n.* male sheep; tup; swinging beam with metal head for battering; hydraulic engine; beak projecting from bow of warship;—*v.t.* consolidate loose material with rammer; drive against with violence; butt; cram; press down.—*pr.p.* ram'ming.—*pa.t.* and *pa.p.* rammed. —**rammer** *n.* one who, or that which, rams.

ramble (ram'-bl) *v.i.* walk without

definite route; talk or write incoherently;—*n.* short stroll or walk.—**ram'bler** *n.* one who rambles; climbing-rose.—**ram'bling** *a.*

ramify (ram'-i-fi) *v.t.* and *v.i.* branch out in various directions.—*pa.p.* **ram'ified.**—**ramifica'tion** *n.* branch; sub-division from main structure.

ramp (ramp) *v.i.* climb, as plant; creep up; leap; rear up on hind legs; frolic; rage;—*n.* leap; bound; romp; inclined surface.

ramp (ramp) *n.* bare-faced swindle.

rampage (ram-pāj') *n.* state of excitement or passion, as on the rampage;—*v.i.* rush about, in rage; act violently.

rampant (ramp'-ant) *a.* leaping; rearing; climbing; violent; prevalent; rank; (*Her.*) erect on one of hind-legs.—**ramp'ancy** *n.*

rampart (ram'-part) *n.* mound of earth around fortified place; that which provides security; — *v.t.* strengthen with ramparts.

ramrod (ram'-rod) *n.* rod to ram down charge of gun; rod for cleaning barrel of rifle.

ramshackle (ram'-shak-l) *a.* tumble-down; beyond repair; crazy. Also **ram'shackled, ram'shackly.**

ran (ran) *pa.t.* of run.

ranch (ranch) *n.* prairie stock-farm; —*v.i.* keep a ranch.—**ranch'er** *n.* man employed on ranch.

rancid (ran'-sid) *a.* having rank smell; smelling or tasting like stale fat; tainted.—**ran'cidly** *adv.*—**ran'cidness, ranced'ity** *n.*

rancour (rang'-kur) *n.* bitter ill-feeling.—**ran'corous** *a.* evincing intense and bitter hatred; malignant. —**ran'corously** *adv.*

rand (rand) *n.* border, margin; thin inner sole; strip of flesh or leather; high land above river valley, as The Rand in Transvaal.

random (ran'-dum) *a.* done haphazardly; aimless;—*n.* in phrase, **at random,** haphazard.

rang (rang) *pa.t.* of ring.

range (rānj) *v.t.* set in row; rank; rove over;—*v.i.* extend; roam; be in line with; pass from one point to another; fluctuate between, as prices, etc.;—*n.* rank; row; block of buildings; long and wide kitchen stove; line of mountains; compass of voice; distance to target; place for practice shooting; pasture land; ranch.—**rang'er** *n.* keeper of park or forest; Girl Guide aged 16 and upwards.—**rang'ers** *n.pl.* body of mounted troops.—**ran'gy** *a.* roaming.

rank (rangk) *n.* row; soldiers standing side by side; grade in armed services; status; class; social position; title; eminence;—*pl.* common soldiers;—*v.t.* arrange in class, order, or division; place in line or abreast;

take rank over;—*v.i.* be placed in rank or class; possess social or official distinction.—**rank'er** *n.* commissioned officer risen from ranks.

rank (rangk) *a.* growing too thickly; offensively strong of smell; rancid; gross; vile; excessive.—**rank'le** *v.i.* be inflamed; become more violent; remain a sore point with.—**rank'ly** *adv.*—**rank'ness** *n.*

ransack (ran'-sak) *v.t.* search thoroughly.

ransom (ran'-sum) *n.* price paid for release of prisoner;—*v.t.* redeem from captivity.

rant (rant) *v.i.* rave; talk noisily;—*n.* noisy and meaningless declamation; wild gaiety.—**rant'er** *n.*

rap (rap) *n.* smart, light blow; knock on door, etc.; tap;—*v.t.* and *v.i.* deliver smart blow; knock;—*pr.p.* **rap'ping**.

rap (rap) *n.* Irish coin, counterfeited and current during reign of George I, hence expression, not worth a rap.

rapacious (ra-pā'-shus) *a.* subsisting on prey; greedy; grasping.—**rapa'ciously** *adv.*—**rapa'city** *n.*

rape (rāp) *n.* carnal knowledge of female against her will; act of snatching or carrying off by force;—*v.t.* ravish or violate.

rape (rāp) *n.* annual of cabbage family, seeds of which yield vegetable oils.

rapid (rap'-id) *a.* very quick; fast; speedy; hurried; descending steeply.—**rap'ids** *n.pl.* part of river where current rushes over rocks or through narrow gorge.—**rapid'ity** *n.*—**rap'idly** *adv.*—**rap'idness** *n.*

rapier (rā'-pi-er) *n.* light, slender, pointed sword, for thrusting only.

rapine (rap'-in) *n.* act of plundering; pillage; plunder; depredation.

rapport (ra-por') *n.* harmony; agreement.

rapprochement (ra-prosh'-mong) *n.* reconciliation; restoration of friendly relations.

rapt (rapt) *a.* snatched away; intent; in state of rapture.—**rap'ture** *n.* extreme joy; ecstasy; bliss; exultation.—**rap'turous** *a.* ecstatic; exulting.—**rap'turously.**

rare (rār) *a.* underdone (of meat).

rare (rār) *a.* uncommon, few and far between; thin, not dense, as air; extremely valuable; of highest excellence; singular.—**rarefac'tion** *n.* act of rarefying; decrease of quantity of gas in fixed volume.—**rarefy** (rar'-e-fi or rā'-re-fi) *v.t.* make rare or less dense;—*v.i.* become less dense;—*pa.p.* **rar'efied.**—**rare'ly** *adv.*—**rare'ness** *n.*—**rar'ity** *n.* thinness; something rare or seldom seen.

rascal (ras'-kal) *n.* rogue; scoundrel; trickster; scamp;—*a.* mean; low.—**rascal'ity** *n.* knavery; base villainy.

—**rapscall'ion** *n.* low, mean wretch.—**ras'cally** *a.*

rash (rash) *a.* quick; rapid; without reflection; precipitate.—**rash'ly** *adv.*—**rash'ness** *n.*

rash (rash) *n.* skin eruption.

rasher (rash'-er) *n.* slice of bacon.

rasp (rasp) *v.t.* rub or file; scrape (skin) roughly; speak in grating manner; irritate;—*n.* form of file with one side flat and other rounded; rough, grating sound.—**rasp'ing** *a.* emitting harsh, grating sound; irritating.—**rasp'ingly** *adv.*

rasp (rasp) *n.* contr. of *rasp*-berry.—**rasp'berry** *n.* plant, cultivated for its fruit; fruit of plant; (*Slang*) derisory noise.

raster (ras'-ter) *n.* in television, rectangular illumination formed on screen of cathode ray tube by scanning rays.

rat (rat) *n.* rodent; one who deserts his party; one who works at less than established wage;—*v.i.* hunt rats; abandon party or associates.—*pr.p.* **rat'ting.**—*pa.t.* and *pa.p.* **rat'ted.**—**rat'ter** *n.* rat-catcher; terrier.—**rat'ting** *n.*—**rat-race** (*Colloq.*) unscrupulous rivalry.

ratable See rate.

ratch (rach) *n.* ratchet; ratchet-wheel.—**ratch'et** *n.* pivoted catch engaging with teeth of ratchet-wheel to prevent backward motion.—**ratch'et-wheel** *n.* circular wheel having angular teeth to engage ratchet.

rate (rāt) *n.* established measure; degree; standard; proportion; ratio; value; price; movement;—*pl.* local taxation;—*v.t.* estimate value; settle relative scale, rank, or position of; levy rates from;—*v.i.* have rank.—**rat'able, rate'able** *a.* liable to payment of local rates.—**ratabil'ity** *n.*—**rat'al** *a.* pert. to rates.—**rat'ing** *n.* assessment; (*Naut.*) enlisted seaman.—**rate'payer** *n.* one assessed for local rates.

rate (rāt) *v.t.* take to task; chide.

rather (ràTH'-er) *adv.* preferably; on other hand; somewhat.

ratify (rat'-i-fi) *v.t.* confirm or sanction officially.—**ratifica'tion** *n.*

ratio (rā'-shi-ō) *n.* relation one quantity has to another; proportion; rate.

ratiocinate (rash-i-os'-i-nāt) *v.i.* reason; argue.—**ratiocina'tion** *n.* deductive reasoning from premises.—**ratioc'inative, ratioc'inatory** *a.*

ration (rā'-shun, ra'-shun) *n.* allotted portion; allowance of food, etc., to armed forces;—*pl.* provisions;—*v.t.* limit to fixed amount.

rational (rash'-on-al) *a.* sane; sensible; reasonable; fair; just; (*Math.*) quantity expressed in finite terms or whose root is whole number.—**rationalisa'tion** *n.* unification of control for buying, producing and distributing goods, to secure greater efficiency and profits.—**rat'ionalise** v.t.—**rat'ionalism** n. philosophy which makes reason sole guide.—**rat'ionalist** a.—**rationalist'ic(al)** a.—**rationalist'ic-ally** adv.—**rational'ity** n. power or faculty of reasoning.—**rat'ionally** adv.—**rat'ionalness** n.

ratline, ratlin, rattling (rat'-lin) n. (Naut.) one of the horizontal lines of rope-ladder for climbing rigging.

ratsbane (ratz'-bān) n. rat poison.

rattle (rat'-l) v.i. clatter; speak (on), eagerly and noisily; move along;—v.t. shake briskly; disconcert, or ruffle;—n. rapid succession of clattering sounds; loud, rapid talk or talker; toy for making a noise.—**ratt'le-snake** n. American poisonous snake.—**ratt'ling** n. clattering;—a. smart; brisk; lively; first-rate;—adv. extremely; very.

raucous (raw'-kus) a. hoarse; harsh; rough.—**rau'cously** adv.

ravage (rav'-āj) v.t. lay waste; despoil; plunder; sack;—n. ruin; destruction.

rave (rāv) v.i. talk in delirium or with great enthusiasm.—**ra'ver** n.—**ra'ving** n. delirious; wild talk;—a. delirious.

ravel (rav'-el) v.t. entangle; make intricate; fray out;—v.i. become twisted; fall into confusion.—pr.p. **rav'elling.** — n. complication; entanglement.

raven (rāv'-en) n. crow with glossy black plumage predatory in habit;—a. glossy black.

raven, ravin (rav'-en) v.t. and v.i. devour; be ravenous;—n. rapine; plunder; spoil.—**rav'ener** n. a plunderer.—**rav'enous, rav'ined** a. famished; voracious; eager for prey.—**rav'enously** adv.

ravine (ra-vēn') n. deep gorge; gully.

ravish (rav'-ish) v.t. seize and carry away by violence; violate; enrapture; charm eye or ear.—**rav'isher** n.—**rav'ishing** a. entrancing.—**rav'ishingly** adv.—**rav'ishment** n.

raw (raw) a. not cooked; not covered with skin; bleak; chilly and damp unpractised;—n. sore.—**raw'boned** a. having little flesh.—**raw'-hide** n. compressed untanned leather.—**raw'ly** adv.—**raw'ness** n.—**raw deal,** undeserved treatment.

ray (rā) n. narrow beam of light; path along which light and electromagnetic waves travel in space; heat radiation; one of number of lines diverging from common point or centre; gleam (of hope, truth, etc.);—v.t. and v.i. radiate; send forth rays.—**rayed** a. having rays.

ray (rā) n. flat-fish allied to skate.

rayon (rā'-on) n. artificial silk made from various forms of cellulose.

raze, rase (rāz) v.t. level to ground; destroy completely; demolish.

razor (rā'-zur) n. cutting appliance for shaving.—**ra'zor'-back** n. kind of hog.—**ra'zor-bill** n. sea-bird, of Auk family.—**ra'zor-shell** n. mollusc with razor-shaped shell.

re (rē) abbrev. for with reference to.

reach (rēch) v.t. extend; stretch; touch by extending hand; arrive at; come to; obtain; gain;—v.i. stretch out hand; strain after; be extended; arrive;—n. easy distance; mental range; scope; grasp; straight stretch of water.

react (rē-akt') v.i. respond to stimulus; resist the action of another body by an opposite effect; (Chem.) cause or undergo chemical or physical change when brought in contact with another substance.—**reac'tion** n. action in opposite direction to another; response to stimulus; revulsion of feeling.—**reac'tionary** a. tendency to reaction.—n. one opposed to progressive ideas.—**reac'tionist** n. reactionary.—**reactiva'tion** n. restoration of atom or molecule to activated state.—**reac'tive** a. having power to react.—**reac'tor** n. apparatus for generating heat by nuclear fission.

read (rēd) v.t. peruse and understand written or printed matter; read and utter; any indicating instrument (as gas-meter); study, esp. at university;—v.i. perform act of reading; find mentioned in writing or print; surmise.—pa.t. and pa.p. **read** (red).—**read** (rēd) n. reading; perusal.—**read** (red) a. versed in books; learned.—**read'able** (rēd-) a. well written; informative; interesting; legible.—**read'ably** (rēd) adv.—**read'er** (rēd-) n. one who reads; one whose office is to read prayers; senior university lecturer; one who determines suitability for publication of manuscripts offered to publisher; corrector of printer's proofs; reading-book.—**read'ing** (rēd-) a. pert. to reading;—n. act of reading; public recital of passages from books; interpretation of book; formal recital of bill or enactment.—**reading room,** room for silent reading and study.

readdress (rē-a-dres') v.t. address again.

readjust (rē-a-just') v.t. put in order again.—**readjust'ment** n.

ready (red'-i) a. prepared; fitted for use; handy; prompt; quick; willing; easy; apt;—adv. in state of preparation; beforehand.—**read'ily** adv.—**read'iness** n.—**read'y-made** a. not made to measure.—**ready money,** cash in hand.—**read'y-reck'oner** n. book of tabulated calculations.

reagent (rē-ā'-jent) n. substance employed to bring about characteristic reaction in chemical analysis.—**rea'gency** n.

real (rē´-ǫl) *a.* actual; not sham; not assumed; (*Law*) heritable.—**real'ty** *n.* actuality; fact; truth; (*Law*) realty.—**re'ally** *adv.* actually; indeed; —*interj.* is that so?—**re'altor** *n.* dealer in real estate.—**re'alty** *n.* fixed permanent nature of real property. —**real estate, real property,** freehold lands and property.

real (rē´-ǫl, rā-äl´) *n.* obsolete Spanish coin.

realise (rē´-ǫl-īz) *v.t.* make real; yield (profit); convert into money; apprehend.—**realisa'tion** *n.*—**re'alism** *n.* practical outlook on life; representation in art or letters of real life.— **re'alist** *n.*—**realis'tic** *a.* pert. to realism; actual; practical; true to life.—**realis'tically** *adv.*

realm (relm) *n.* kingdom; province; region.

ream (rēm) *n.* paper measure of 472 to 516 sheets, usually 480 sheets.

ream, reem (rēm) *v.t.* enlarge hole with reamer.—**ream'er** *n.* machine-tool for this.

reap (rēp) *v.t.* cut down ripe grain for harvesting; harvest; receive as fruits of one's labour.—**reap'er** *n.* harvester; reaping-machine.

reappear (rē-a-pēr´) *v.i.* appear second time.—**reappear'ance** *n.* second appearance.

rear (rēr) *n.* back of hindmost part; part of army or fleet behind others. —**rear'most** *a.* last of all; at very back. —**rear'-ad'miral** *n.* lowest rank of admiral.—**rear'guard** *n.* troops detailed to protect main body from rear attacks.—**rear'ward** *n.* rear-guard; hind or latter part;—*a.* in, or to, rear.

rear (rēr) *v.t.* raise; bring to maturity, as young; breed, as cattle; build;— *v.i.* rise up on hind legs, as horse.

rearm (rē-arm´) *v.t.* equip fighting services with new types of weapons of offence and defence.—**rearm'ament** *n.*

rearrange (rē-a-rānj´) *v.t.* arrange anew; set in different order.— **rearrange'ment** *n.*

reason (rē´-zn) *n.* faculty of thinking; power of understanding; intelligence; cause; motive; purpose; excuse;— *v.i.* exercise rational faculty; deduce from facts; argue with;—*v.t.* discuss by arguments.—**rea'sonable** *a.* rational; just; fair.—**rea'sonableness** *n.*— **rea'sonably** *adv.*—**rea'soner** *n.*—**rea'-soning** *n.*—**in reason,** in moderation.

reassemble (rē-a-sem´-bl) *v.t.* and *v.i.* assemble or bring together again.

reassure (rē-a-shōōr´) *v.t.* free from fear; allay anxiety; restore confidence. — **re'-assure'** *v.t.* re-insure against loss.—**re-assur'ance, re'assur'-ance** *n.* confirmation repeated; further insurance.—**reassur'ing** *a.* comforting.

rebate (re-bāt´) *v.t.* blunt; allow as discount;—*n.* deduction; discount.

rebec, rebeck (rē´-bek) *n.* musical instrument, forerunner of viol.

rebel (reb´-ǫl) *n.* one who resists lawful government; insurgent; revolter; revolutionist; one who is defiant;—*a.* rebellious.—**rebel** (re-bel´) *v.i.* take up arms against state or government; revolt.—*pr.p.* **rebel'-ling.**—*pa.t.* and *pa.p.* **rebelled'.**— **rebell'ion** *n.* organised resistance to authority; mutiny.—**rebell'ious** *a.*— **rebell'iously** *adv.*—**rebell'iousness** *n.*

rebind (rē-bīnd´) *v.t.* bind anew, esp. volume.—**rebound'** *n.* and *a.*

rebirth (rē-berth´) *n.* state of being born again spiritually; reincarnation; renaissance.

rebore (rē-bōr´) *v.t.* smooth and enlarge bores of cylinders of internal combustion engine.—**rebor'ing** *n.*

rebound (rē-bound´) *v.i.* leap back; recoil; bound repeatedly;—*v.t.* cause to fly back;—*n.* rebounding; recoil.

rebuff (re-buf´) *n.* blunt refusal; snub;—*v.t.* beat back; check; snub.

rebuke (re-būk´) *v.t.* censure; reprove; reprimand; find fault with;— *n.* reprimand; severe talking to.

rebut (re-but´) *v.t.* butt or drive back; refute; repel; disprove;— *pr.p.* **rebut'ting.**—*pa.t.* and *pa.p.* **rebut'ted.**—**rebut'table** *a.*—**rebut'tal** *n.* refutation of argument.

recalcitrate (re-kal´-si-trāt) *v.i.* kick back; be refractory.—**recal'citrant** *n.* one who defies authority;—*a.* refractory; wilfully disobedient.— **recal'citrance, recalcitra'tion** *n.*

recall (rē-kawl´) *v.t.* call back; annul or revoke; call to mind; remember; —*n.* act of recalling; summons.

recant (re-kant´) *v.t.* take back opinions; retract;—*v.i.* unsay.—**re-canta'tion** *n.*

recapitulate (rē-ka-pit´-ū-lāt) *v.t.* relate in brief substance of previous discourse;—*v.i.* sum up what has been previously said.—**recapitula'tion** *n.* summary.—**recapit'ulatory** *a.*

recapture (rē-kap´-tūr) *v.t.* capture back; regain;—*n.* act of retaking.

recast (rē-kast´) *v.t.* cast or mould again; remodel; throw back; add up figures in column, second time.

recede (re-sēd´) *v.i.* move back; retreat; withdraw; ebb.—**reced'ing** *a.*

receipt (rē-sēt´) *n.* act of receiving; written acknowledgment of money received; place where moneys are officially received;—*pl.* cash-drawings;—*v.t.* give receipt for.

receive (re-sēv´) *v.t.* take; accept; acquire; welcome or entertain; hold; take or buy stolen goods.— **receiv'able** *a.*—**receiv'er** *n.* one who receives; receptacle, place of storage, etc.; radio-receiving set; ear-piece of telephone; vessel for containing gases.—**receiv'ing** *n.*

recent (rē'-sent) *a.* that has lately happened; new.—**re'cently** *adv.*—**re'centness** *n.*

receptacle (re-sep'-tak-l) *n.* vessel; container.

reception (rē-sep'-shun) *n.* receiving; welcome; ceremonial occasion when guests are announced; quality of signals received in broadcasting.—**recep'tible** *a.* receivable.—**recep'tionist** *n.* official in hotel, etc., who receives guests or clients.—**recep'tive** *a.* able to grasp ideas quickly.—**recep'tiveness, receptiv'ity** *n.*

recess (rē-ses') *n.* a withdrawing; suspension of business; vacation, as of legislative body; retired place; niche in wall.—**recessed'** *a.* fitted with recess.—**reces'sion** *n.* act of withdrawing; period of reduced trade or business.—**reces'sional** *a.* pert. to recession;—*n.* hymn sung as clergyman leaves chancel.—**reces'sive** *a.* receding.—**recess'iveness** *n.*

recharge (rē-charj') *v.t.* charge again; reload gun, etc.

recidivist (re-sid'-i-vist) *n.* one who relapses into crime;—**recidivism** *n.*

recipe (res'-i-pe) *n.* prescription; (*Cooking*) ingredients and method for given dish.

recipient (re-sip'-i-ent) *a.* receptive; —*n.* one who receives.

reciprocal (re-sip'-ro-kal) *a.* moving backwards and forwards; alternating; mutual; complementary;—*n.* quantity arising from dividing unity by any quantity.—**recip'rocally** *adv.* —**recip'rocalness** *n.*—**recip'rocate** *v.t.* make return for; interchange;— *v.i.* move backwards and forwards; alternate.—**recip'rocating** *a.* applied to mechanism of which the parts move backwards and forwards alternately. Also **recip'rocatory.**—**reciproca'tion** *n.* mutual giving and receiving.—**recip'rocative** *a.*—**reciprocity** (res-i-pros'-i-ti) *n.* action and reaction; discharge of mutual duties or obligations.

recite (rē-sīt') *v.t.* and *v.i.* repeat aloud.—**reci'tal** *n.* act of reciting; what is recited; detailed narration; musical or dramatic performance by a single person.—**recita'tion** *n.* reciting; repetition of poem from memory.—**recitative'** *n.* declamation to musical accompaniment, as in opera;—*a.* in style of recitative.—**reci'ter** *n.*

reck (rek) *v.t.* and *v.i.* take account (of); heed; care (for).—**reck'less** *a.* rashly negligent.—**reck'lessly** *adv.*—**reck'lessness** *n.*

reckon (rek'-n) *v.t.* and *v.i.* count; estimate; think.—**reck'oner** *n.* one who reckons; table of calculations (usu. ready reckoner).—**reck'oning** *n.* computing; calculation; way of thinking.

reclaim (rē-klām') *v.t.* call back; demand return of; bring into state of productiveness, as salt marshes, etc.; win back from error or sin.—**reclaim'able** *a.*—**reclaim'ably** *adv.*—**reclama'tion** *n.*

recline (re-klīn') *v.t.* lean back;— *v.i.* repose; rest.—**reclin'er** *n.*

recluse (re-klóós') *a.* secluded from the world; solitary;—*n.* anchorite; hermit.

recognise (rek'-og-nīz) *v.t.* know again; identify; acknowledge; notice; —**recognis'able** *a.* capable of being recognised. — **recognis'ably** *adv.* — **recog'nisance** *n.* acknowledgment of person or thing; avowal; obligation; sum pledged as surety.—**recogni'tion** *n.* recognising; acknowledgment.—**recog'nitory** *a.*

recoil (re-koil') *v.i.* start, roll, bound, fall back; draw back; rebound;—*n.* return motion; starting or falling back.

recollect (rek'-o-lekt) *v.t.* recall; remember.—**recollec'tion** *n.* power of recalling ideas; remembrance; memory.—**recollec'tive** *a.*

recommend (rek-o-mend') *v.t.* speak well of; commend to one's care; entrust; approve; praise.—**recommend'able** *a.*—**recommenda'tion** *n.* recommending.—**recommend'atory** *a.*

recompense (rek'-om-pens) *v.t.* repay; reward; make up for; punish; —*n.* repayment; requital.

reconcile (rek-on-sīl') *v.t.* conciliate anew; restore to friendship; make agree; become resigned (to).—**rec'oncilable** *a.*—**reconcilement, reconcilia'tion** *n.* renewal of friendship; harmonising of apparently opposed ideas, etc.; (*Bib.*) expiation; atonement.—**reconcil'iatory** *a.*

recondite (rek'-on-dīt) *a.* obscure; little known.—**recondite'ness** *n.*

recondition (rē-kon-dish'-un) *v.t.* restore to sound condition; renovate; to repair.

reconnaissance (re-kon'-ā-sans) *n.* examination or survey, by land or air, for engineering or military operations.

reconnoitre (rek-on-noi'-ter) *v.t.* make reconnaissance of;—*v.i.* make reconnaissance; scout;—*n.* preliminary survey.

reconsider (rē-kon-sid'-er) *v.t.* consider again; take up for renewed discussion.

reconstitute (rē-kon'-sti-tūt) *v.t.* constitute anew; reconstruct; restore substance to original form.—**reconstit'uent** *a.*—**reconstitu'tion** *n.*

reconstruct (rē-kon-strukt') *v.t.* rebuild; enact (crime) on actual spot. —**reconstruc'tion** *n.*

record (re-kord') *v.t.* commit to writing; make note of; register (vote); inscribe; make sound record;

—*v.i.* speak, sing, etc. for reproduction on gramophone record.—**record** (rek'-ord) *n.* register; authentic copy of any writing; personal history; list; catalogue; finest performance or highest amount ever known; disc, cylinder, roll, etc. for mechanical reproduction of sound;—*pl.* public documents.—**recor'der** *n.* one who registers writings or transactions; (*Law*) chief judicial officer of city or borough; instrument for reproducing sounds as wavelengths on discs or magnetic tape; ancient, flute-like musical instrument.—**recor'ding** *n.* making, or reproduction of, sound by mechanical means.—**off the record**, unofficial.

recount (rē-kount') *v.t.* count again; relate; recite; enumerate;—*n.* second enumeration, esp. of votes at election.

recoup (rē-kōōp') *v.t.* recover equivalent for what has been lost; compensate.—**recoup'ment** *n.*

recourse (re-kōrs') *n.* application made to another in difficulty; resorting to.

recover (re-kuv'-er) *v.t.* get back; win back; revive; cure; rescue; (*Law*) obtain (damages) as compensation;—*v.i.* regain health.—**recov'erable** *a.*—**recov'ery** *n.* regaining possession; restoration to health; amends for bad start.

re-cover (rē-kuv'-er) *v.t.* put fresh cover on.

recreant (rek'-re-ant) *a.* cowardly; false;—*n.* coward.—**rec'reancy** *n.*

recreate (rek'-rē-āt) *v.t.* give fresh life to; restore; reanimate; cheer.—**recrea'tion** *n.* pleasurable interest; pastime; amusement.—**recrea'tional, recrea'tive** *a.*

recriminate (re-krim'-i-nāt) *v.t.* and *v.i.* charge accuser with similar crime.—**recrimina'tion** *n.* countercharge; mutual abuse and blame.—**recrim'inative, recrim'inatory** *a.*

recrudesce (rē-krōō-des') *v.i.* revive.—**recrudes'cence** *n.*—**recrudes'cent** *a.*

recruit (re-krōōt') *v.t.* repair by fresh supplies; renew in strength; enlist persons for army, navy, etc.;—*v.i.* gain health, spirits, etc.; obtain new adherents;—*n.* newly-enlisted soldier; fresh adherent.—**recruit'al, recruit'ing, recruit'ment** *n.*

rectangle (rek'-tang-gl) *n.* four-sided figure with four right angles.—**rectang'ular** *a.*

rectify (rek'-ti-fī) *v.t.* set right; correct; purify; convert alternating current into direct current;—*pa.t.* and *pa.p.* **rec'tified.**—**rectifi'able** *a.*—**rectifica'tion** *n.*—**rec'tifier** *n.* one who corrects; device for converting alternating current into direct; transformer; one who refines spirits by repeated distillations.

rectilineal, rectilinear (rek-ti-lin'-e-al, -ar) *a.* consisting of, or bounded by, right lines.—**rectilin'eally** *adv.*—**rectilinear'ity** *n.*

rectitude (rek'-ti-tūd) *n.* moral uprightness.

rector (rek'-tor) *n.* clergyman of Church of England who has charge of parish; incumbent of Episcopal church in Scotland or U.S.A.; headmaster of certain senior secondary schools in Scotland; nominal head of Scottish university.—**rec'toral** *a.* pert. to rector or rectory.—**recto'rial** *a.* rectoral;—*n.* in Scottish universities, rectorial election.—**rec'torate, rec'torship** *n.* office of rector.—**rec'tory** *n.* house of rector.

rectum (rek'-tum) *n.* lower end of large intestine.—*pl.* **rec'ta.**—**rec'tal** *a.*

recumbent (re-kum'-bent) *a.* reclining.—**recum'bence, recum'bency** *n.*—**recum'bently** *adv.*

recuperate (re-kū'-per-āt) *v.i.* win back health and strength; convalesce; recover.—**recupera'tion** *n.* convalescence; slow return to health.—**recu'perative, recu'peratory** *a.*

recur (re-kur') *v.i.* happen again;—*pr.p.* **recur'ring.**—*pa.t.* and *pa.p.* **recurred.**—**recur'rence, recur'rency** *n.*—**recur'rent** *a.*

recusant (rek'-ū-zant) *a.* obstinate in refusal;—*n.* dissenter or nonconformist.—**rec'usance, rec'usancy** *n.*

red (red) *a.* (*comp.* **red'der**; *superl.* **red'dest**) of colour of arterial blood, rubies, etc.; connected with bloodshed, revolution, left-wing politics, etc.;—*n.* colour of blood; socialist; communist; Russian soldier; danger signal.—**red'den** *v.t.* make red;—*v.i.* become red; blush; flush.—**red'ly** *adv.*—**red'ness** *n.* state of being red; blushing.—**red admiral**, British butterfly, black with red band, and white spots.—**red'breast** *n.* robin.—**redbrick**, facetiously descriptive of newer English universities.—**red'cap** *n.* military policeman.—**red'coat** *n.* British soldier, because of bright scarlet tunic.—**Red Cross**, international emblem of organisations for relief of sick and wounded in wartime.—**red'-currant** *n.* shrubby bush bearing small red berries.—**red'-deer** *n.* common stag or hind.—**red ensign**, flag of mercantile marine.—**red flag**, danger signal, as on railway; national flag of Soviet Russia; international communist anthem.—**red'-hand'ed** *a.* (*Fig.*) in very act, orig. of murderer.—**red herring**, common herring, cured by drying, smoking and salting; (*Colloq.*) any topic introduced to divert attention.—**red'-hot** *a.* heated to redness; eager; enthusiastic.—**Red'-Ind'ian** *n.* copper-coloured aboriginal native of N. America.—**red'-lead** *n.* oxide of lead, used as pigment.—**red'-let'ter** *a.* applied to principal holy saints' days of Church calendar—hence, any memorable (day).—**red pepper**, chillies; cayenne pepper.—**red'poll, red'pole** *n.* smallest British finch.—**red polls**, hornless cattle, bred in E. Anglia.—**red'shank** *n.* shore bird of Plover family.—**red'-shirt** *n.* follower of Garibaldi (1807-82); revolutionary.—**red'skin** *n.* N. American Indian.—**red'start** *n.* British song-bird of thrush family.—**red tape**, slavish adherence to official regulations.—**red'wing** *n.* song-bird, resembling song-thrush.—**to paint the town red**, indulge in drunken celebration.—**to see red**, become infuriated.

redeem (re-dēm') *v.t.* purchase back; regain, as mortgaged property; take out of pawn; ransom; deliver from sin; make good.—**redeemable** *a.*—**redeem'ableness** *n.*—**redeem'er** *n.*

redemption (rē-demp'-shun) *n.* buying back; deliverance from sin; Atonement.—**redemp'tioner** *n.*—**redemp'tive** *a.* redeeming.—**redemp'tory** *a.* paid as ransom.

red-hot poker (red-hot pō'-ker) *n.* ornamental plant of the lily family.

redirect (rē-di-rekt') *v.t.* direct again; readdress communication.—**redirec'tion** *n.*

redistribute (rē-dis-trib'-ūt) *v.t.* deal out again.—**redistribu'tion** *n.*

redolent (red'-ō-lent) *a.* diffusing strong or fragrant odour; scented; (*Fig.*) reminiscent (of).—**red'olence** *n.*

redoubt, redout (re-dout') *n.* military detached fieldwork; central part within field fortifications for final stand.

redoubtable (re-dou'-ta-bl) *a.* dreaded; formidable; valiant.—**redoubt'ed** *a.* redoubtable.

redound (re-dound') *v.i.* contribute or turn to; conduce (to); recoil; react (upon).

redraft (rē-draft') *v.t.* draw up second time;—*n.* second copy.

redress (rē-dres') *v.t.* make amends for; set right; compensate; adjust; dress second time;—*n.* reparation; amendment; relief; remedy.—**redress'er** *n.*—**redress'ible** *a.*

reduce (re-dūs') *v.t.* diminish in number, length, etc.; lower; degrade; slim; impoverish; subdue; capture (as fort).—**reduced'** *a.* impoverished.—**reduc'ible** *a.* capable of being reduced.—**reduc'tion** *n.* subjugation; diminution; curtailment.—**reduc'tive** *a.* having power of reducing.—**reduc'tively** *adv.*—**reducing agent** (*Chem.*) reagent for abstracting oxygen or adding hydrogen.

redundant (re-dun'-dant) *a.* superfluous; no longer serving useful purpose.—**redun'dance, redun'dancy** *n.*—**redun'dantly** *adv.*

re-echo (rē-ek'-ō) *v.t.* echo back; reverberate;—*v.i.* resound;—*n.* echo of echo.

reed (rēd) *n.* tall hollow-stemmed grass growing in water or marshes; in certain wind-instruments, thin strip of cane or metal which vibrates and produces musical sound; musical instrument made of hollow joint of some plant; pastoral pipe; arrow; pastoral poetry;—*v.t.* thatch with reeds; fit with reed.—**reed'ed** *a.* covered with reeds.—**reed'en** *a.* consisting or made of reeds.—**reed'iness** *n.*—**reed'-war'bler, reed'-wren** *n.* bird which frequents marshes in S. England.—**reed'y** *a.* abounding with reeds, possessing harsh and thin tone of reed, as certain voices.

reef (rēf) *n.* portion of square sail which can be rolled up and made fast to yard or boom;—*v.t.* reduce area of sail by taking in reef.—**reef'er** *n.* one who reefs; midshipman; sailor's close-fitting jacket; cigarette, doped with marijuana.—**reef'knot** *n.* (*Naut.*) square knot; one in which ends lie parallel with cord and will not slip.

reef (rēf) *n.* ridge of rock near surface of sea; outcrop of lode or vein.

reek (rēk) *n.* smoke; vapour; fume;—*v.i.* emit smoke or smell; steam.—**reek'ing** *a.* smelling strongly.—**reek'y** *a.* smoky.

reel (rēl) *n.* bobbin or spool for winding thread, film, etc.; portion of thread, film, etc. so wound.—*v.t.* wind upon reel; draw (in) by means of reel.—**to reel off**, enumerate or recite rapidly.

reel (rēl) *v.i.* stagger; sway from side to side; whirl; be dizzy.

reel (rēl) *n.* sprightly dance-tune; Scottish dance for two or more couples.

reeve (rēv) *v.t.* to pass line through hole in block, ring-bolt, etc., for purpose of pulling larger rope after it.

reeve (rēv) *n.* in early times, bailiff; steward.

refection (re-fek'-shun) *n.* refreshment; simple repast; lunch.—**refec'tory** *n.* dining-hall in monastery, convent, or college.

refer (re-fer') *v.t.* send back; transfer to another court; appeal to; direct to; assign to;—*v.i.* have reference to; offer, as testimony in evidence of character, etc.; allude (to).—*pr.p.* refer'ring.—*pa.t.* and *pa.p.* referred'.—**ref'erable, refer'rible** *a.* may be referred or assigned to.—**referee'** *n.* arbitrator; one named by candidate for post as willing to give testimony of character, etc.; umpire; neutral judge in various sports.—**ref'erence** *n.* appeal to the judgment of another; relation; one of whom inquiries can be made; passage in book to which reader is referred; quotation; testimonial.—**referen'dum** n. popular vote for ascertaining national will on single issue.—**referen'tial** a. containing reference.

refine (re-fin') v.t. purify; reduce crude metals to finer state; clarify; improve; free from coarseness, vulgarity, etc.;—v.i. become pure; improve in accuracy, excellence, or good taste.—**refined'** a. purified or clarified; polished; well-bred.—**refin'edly** adv.—**refine'ment** n.—**refin'ery** n. place for refining sugar, oil, etc.

reflect (re-flekt') v.t. throw back, esp. rays of light, heat, radio or sound waves, from surfaces; mirror;—v.i. throw back light, heat, etc.; meditate.—**to reflect on**, disparage.—**reflec'ted** a. cast or thrown back (as light); folded back on itself; reflexed.—**reflect'ible** a.—**reflect'ing** a. thoughtful; throwing back rays of light, etc.—**reflect'ingly** adv.—**reflec'tion** n. reflecting; return of rays from surface; image given back from mirror, etc.; meditation; contemplation.—**reflect'ive** a. meditative.—**reflect'ively** adv.—**reflect'iveness** n.—**reflect'or** n. reflecting surface.

reflex (rē'-fleks) a. turned backwards; introspective; reflective; reflected; (Mech.) produced by reaction; (Physiol.) denoting involuntary action of motor nerves under stimulus; involuntary; automatic;—n. reflection; reflected image; reflex-action;—v.t. bend back; reflect.—**reflex'ible, reflect'ible** a.—**reflexibil'ity** n.—**reflex'ive** a. bending or turned backwards; reflective.—**reflex'ively** adv.—**reflex'ly** adv.

reflux (rē'-fluks) n. flowing back; ebb;—a. re'fluent.—**ref'luence** n.

reform (rē-form') v.t. form again; reconstruct; restore; reclaim; to amend; improve;—v.i. amend one's ways; improve;—n. amendment; improvement; correction. — **refor'mable** a.—**reforma'tion** n. act of forming or shaping again; change for better; religious movement of 16th cent. in which large section of church broke away from Rome.—**refor'mative** a. forming again; aiming at reform.—**refor'matory** a. tending to reform;—n. former name for approved school.—**reformed'** a. formed again or in new fashion; amended; reclaimed.—**refor'mer** n.

refract (re-frakt') v.t. bend sharply back; cause to deviate, as rays of light.—**refrac'table** a.—**refrac'ted** a.—**refrac'ting** a. serving to refract; refractive.—**refraction** n.—**refrac'tive** a. having power to turn from direct course; pert. to refraction.

refractory (re-frak'-to-ri) a. sullen; stubborn.—**refrac'torily** adv.—**refrac'toriness** n.

refrain (re-frān') v.t. hold back; restrain;—v.i. abstain.—**refrain'ment** n.

refrain (re-frān') n. chorus recurring at end of each verse of song; constant theme.

refresh (re-fresh') v.t. make fresh again; revive; renew; enliven; provide with refreshment; freshen up.—**refresh'er** n. one who, or that which, refreshes; extra fee paid to legal counsel, in addition to retaining fee.—**refresh'ing** a. invigorating; reviving.—**refresh'ment** n. restoration of strength; that which adds fresh vigour—hence, pl. food and drink.

refrigerate (re-frij'-ẽr-āt) v.t. make cold or frozen; preserve food, etc., by cooling;—v.i. become cold.—**refrigera'tion** n.—**refrig'erative, refrig'eratory** a. cooling.—**refrig'erator** n. apparatus and plant for manufacture of ice; chamber for preserving food by mechanical production of low temperatures.

refuge (ref'-ūj) n. shelter; asylum; retreat; a street-island;—v.t. shelter; find shelter for;—v.i. take shelter.—**refugee'** n. one who flees from danger or persecution.

refulgent (re-ful'-jent) a. shining; splendid.—**reful'gence** n. splendour. Also **reful'gency.**

refund (rē-fund') v.t. return; repay.—**re'fund** n. repayment.

refuse (re-fūz') v.t. deny or reject; decline; — v.i. decline something offered; not comply.—**refu'sal** n. act of refusing; option.

refuse (ref'-ūs) a. rejected; worthless;—n. waste matter; garbage; trash.

refute (re-fūt') v.t. prove to be false.—**refu'table** a.—**refuta'tion** n.

regain (rē-gān') v.t. recover; retrieve; get back; reach again.

regal (rē'-gal) a. pert. to king; kingly; royal.—**regalia** (re-gā'-li-a) n.pl. insignia of royalty, as crown, sceptres, etc.—**regal'ity** n. royalty; sovereignty.—**re'gally** adv.

regale (re-gāl') v.t. entertain in sumptuous manner; refresh;—v.i. feast;—n. banquet; feast.—**regale'ment** n. refreshment.

regard (re-gård') v.t. observe; gaze; consider; pay respect to;—n. aspect; esteem; account; gaze; heed; concern; — pl. compliments; good wishes.—**regard'able** a.—**regard'ful** a. heedful.—**regard'fully** adv.—**regard'ing** prep. concerning.—**regard'less** a. without regard; careless; neglectful.—**regard'lessly** adv.

regatta (re-gat'-a) n. series of races in which yachts, rowing boats, etc. participate.

regenerate (rē-jen'-ẽr-āt) v.t. and v.i. give fresh life or vigour to; recreate the moral nature;—a. born anew; changed from natural to spiritual state; regenerated.—**regen'-**

eracy, regenera'tion n.—regen'erative a.
—regen'eratively adv.

regent (rē'-jẹnt) a. holding office of regent;—n. one who governs kingdom during minority, absence, or disability of sovereign.—re'gency n. office and jurisdiction of regent.

regicide (rej'-i-sīd) n. one who assassinates king.—regici'dal a.

régime (rā-zhēm') n. style of rule; administration; ordered mode of dieting.

regimen (rej'-i-men) n. orderly government; systematic method of dieting.

regiment (rej'-i-mẹnt) n. body of soldiers commanded by senior officer;—v.t. form into regiment; systematise.—regiment'al a. pert. to regiment;—n.pl. uniform worn by troops of regiment.—regimenta'tion n. control of lives of people without consulting them;—regimented a.

region (rē'-jun) n. territory of indefinite extent; district; part of body.—re'gional a.—re'gionally adv.

register (rej'-is-tẹr) n. written account; official record; list; book in which record is kept; alphabetical index; archive; catalogue; roll; registrar; mechanical contrivance which registers; (Mus.) row of organ pipes or harpsichord strings with same tone colour; organ stop; compass of voice or instrument;—v.t. record; enrol.—reg'istrable a.—reg'istered a. enrolled.—reg'istrant n. one who registers.—reg'istrar n. official who keeps register or record of transactions.—registra'tion n.—reg'istry n. act of registering; office for registering births, deaths and marriages; agency for supplying domestic servants, etc.—registered post, method of postal delivery by which mail is insured.

regius (rē'-ji-us) a. appointed by crown.

regnal (reg'-nạl) a. pert. to reign of monarch.—reg'nancy n. rule; reign; predominance.—reg'nant a. reigning; ruling by hereditary right.

regress (rē-gres') n. passage back; power of passing back; re-entry;—v.i. go or fall back; return to former state.—regres'sion n. returning; retrogression.—regress'ive a.

regret (re-gret') v.t. grieve over; lament; deplore;—pr.p. regret'ting.—pa.t. and pa.p. regret'ted.—n. grief; sorrow; remorse.—regret'ful a.—regret'fully adv.—regret'table a. lamentable.—regret'tably adv.

regular (reg'-ū-lạr) a. conforming to rule; periodical; symmetrical; orderly; habitual; straight; level; natural; standing (army); (Colloq.) out and out; (Mus.) strict;—n. soldier belonging to permanent, standing army.—reg'ularise v.t. make regular.

—regularisa'tion n.—regular'ity n. conformity to rule; uniformity.—reg'ularly adv.

regulate (reg'-ū-āt) v.t. adjust by rule, method, etc.; dispose; arrange; rule; control.—regula'tion n. state of being reduced to order; bye-law; order.—reg'ulative a. tending to regulate.—reg'ulator n. one who, or that which, regulates; mechanical contrivance for regulating motion.

regurgitate (re-gur'-ji-tāt) v.t. throw, flow, or pour back;—v.i. be thrown or poured back.—regurgita'tion n.

rehabilitate (rē-ha-bil'-i-tāt) v.t. restore to former position; increase capabilities of disabled person.—rehabilita'tion n.

rehash (rē-hash') v.t. mix and use second time;—n. old materials used over again.

rehearse (re-hẹrs') v.t. and v.i. repeat aloud; practise (play, etc.); recite; recapitulate.—rehear'sal n. trial performance of a play, opera, etc.

reign (rān) n. royal authority; period during which sovereign occupies throne; influence;—v.i. possess sovereign power.

reimburse (rē-im-burs') v.t. refund; pay back; give equivalent of.—reimburse'ment n.—reimbur'ser n.

rein (rān) n. strap of bridle to govern horse, etc.; means of controlling; restraint;—pl. means of exercising power;—v.t. govern with rein or bridle; restrain.

reincarnate (rē-in-kär'-nāt) v.t. embody again in flesh.—reincarna'tion n. belief in re-birth of human soul in another body.

reindeer (rān'-dēr) n. deer of colder regions.—rein'deer-moss n. winter food of reindeer.

reinforce (rē-in-fōrs') v.t. strengthen with new force, esp. of troops or ships; corroborate.—reinforce'ment n. additional troops or ships to strengthen fighting forces; steel bar incorporated in reinforced concrete.—reinforced concrete n. concrete strengthened by inclusion of steel nets, rods, etc.

reinstate (rē-in-stāt') v.t. restore to former position.—reinstate'ment n.

reissue (rē-ish'-ū) v.t. issue again; republish;—n. new issue; reprint.

reiterate (rē-it'-ẹr-āt) v.t. repeat again and again.—reit'erant a. reiterating.—reitera'tion n.

reive, reave (rēv) v.t. steal; rob;—pa.p. reft.—reiv'er, reav'er n. (Arch.) robber; freebooter.

reject (re-jekt') v.t. cast from one; throw away; refuse; put aside;—n. person or thing rejected as not up to standard.—rejec'table a.—rejec'tion n.

rejoice (re-jois') v.t. give joy to; cheer; gladden;—v.i. exult.—rejoic'ing n. act of expressing joy;—pl.

public expression of joy; festivities.
—rejoic'ingly adv.

rejoin (rē-join') v.t. unite again; meet again; enter again, as society, etc.;—v.i. reply.—rejoin'der n. curt, abrupt reply.

rejuvenate (rē-jōō'-ven-āt) v.t. make young again.—rejuvena'tion n.—rejuvenesce' v.i. grow young again.—rejuvenes'cence n.—rejuvenes'cent a.—reju'venise v.t. rejuvenate.

relapse (re-laps') v.i. slide back, esp. into state of ill-health, error;—n. falling back; return of symptoms after convalescence.

relate (re-lāt') v.t. narrate; recount; tell;—v.i. have relation (to); refer (to).—relat'ed a. connected by blood or marriage; akin.—rela'tion n. telling; account; feeling between persons or nations; connection between things; kindred; connection by consanguinity or affinity; relative.—rela'tional a. indicating some relation.—rela'tionship n.

relative (rel'-a-tiv) a. not absolute; connected; related;—n. person connected by blood or affinity.—rel'atively adv. comparatively.—rel'ativeness n.—relativ'ity n. being relative; doctrine in philosophy that knowledge is not absolute but conditioned; (Phys.) theory of space-time continium.

relax (re-laks') v.t. make less severe or stern; loosen;—v.i. become loosened or feeble; unbend; become less severe.—relaxa'tion n. recreation; mitigation; alleviation.—relax'ing a. enervating.

relay (rē-lā') n. supplies stored at successive stages of route; gang of men, fresh set of horses, etc., ready to relieve others;—v.t. pass on, as message, broadcast, etc.—relay race, race between teams of which each runner does part of distance.

release (re-lēs') v.t. set free; allow to quit; exempt from obligation;—n. liberation; exemption; discharge; catch for controlling mechanical parts of machine.

relegate (rel'-e-gāt) v.t. send away; banish; demote.—relega'tion n.

relent (re-lent') v.i. give up harsh intention; yield.—relent'less a. showing no pity or sympathy.—relent'lessly adv.—relent'lessness n.

relevant (rel'-e-vant) a. pertinent to case in hand; appropriate.—rel'evance, rel'evancy n.—rel'evantly adv.

reliable (re-lī'-a-bl) a. trustworthy; honest; creditable.—reliabil'ity, reli'ableness n. quality or state of being reliable.—reli'ably adv.—reli'ance n. trust; confidence; dependence.—reli'ant a. confident; trusting.

relic (rel'-ik) n. something surviving from past; part of body of saint or martyr, preserved with religious

veneration;—pl. corpse; remains of what is past.

relict (rel'-ikt) n. widow.

relief (re-lēf') n. removal or alleviation of pain, distress, etc.; help, comfort; remedy; one who relieves another at post; prominence; sculptured figure standing out from plane surface.

relieve (re-lēv') v.t. alleviate; free from trial, evil, or distress; release from post by substitution of another; remedy; indemnify; lighten (gloom, etc.).—reliev'ing a. serving to relieve.

religion (re-lij'-un) n. belief in supernatural power which governs universe; recognition of God as object of worship; system of faith and worship; reverence; holiness.—relig'ionist, relig'ionary, relig'ioner n. one who makes inordinate professions of religion.—religio'sity n. tendency towards religiousness.—relig'ious a. pious; teaching religion; conscientious.—relig'iously adv.

relinquish (re-ling'-kwish) v.t. give up; cede; resign.—relin'quishment n.

relish (rel'-ish) v.t. taste with pleasure; like immensely;—v.i. have pleasing taste; savour;—n. savour; flavour; what is used to make food more palatable, as sauce; appetite; zest.

reload (rē-lōd') v.t. recharge or refill.

reluctant (re-luk'-tant) a. unwilling; disinclined.—reluct'ance n.—reluc'tancy n.—reluc'tantly adv.

rely (re-lī') v.i. trust; depend; confide;—pa.t. and pa.p. relied'.—reli'er n.

remain (re-mān') v.i. stay; continue; abide; last;—n.pl. corpse.—remain'der n. what remains; remnant.

remand (re-mánd') v.t. send back to prison accused person pending further inquiries;—n. such recommittal.—remand home, place of detention for young delinquents.

remark (re-márk') v.t. take notice of; express in words or writing; regard; speak; say; comment;—n. comment; notice; heed;—v.i. make remark (on).—remark'able a. extraordinary.—remark'ableness n.—remark'ably adv.

remedy (rem'-e-di) n. means of curing or relieving disease, trouble, etc.; cure; antidote;—v.t. restore to health; heal; cure; put right.—pa.p. rem'edied.—reme'diable a. curable.—reme'dial a. affording remedy.

remember (re-mem'-ber) v.t. retain in memory; recollect; reward; remind;—v.i. have in mind.—remem'berable a.—remem'brance n. act of remembering; state of being remembered; recollection; memory; token; keepsake.—remem'brancer n. one who or that which reminds; officer of Exchequer.

remind (rē-mīnd') v.t. recall to memory.—**remind'er** n. that which reminds.

reminisce (rem-i-nis') v.i. call to mind;—**reminiscence'** n. state of calling to mind; recollection; remembrance; something recalling past events;—pl. autobiographical notes; memoirs.—**reminis'cent** a.

remiss (re-mis') a. not energetic or exact in duty; careless in fulfilling engagements.—**remis'sion** n. abatement; diminution; pardon; forgiveness of sin.—**remiss'ive** a. slackening; moderating.—**remiss'ly** adv.—**remiss'ness** n. slackness; neglect.

remit (re-mit') v.t. send back; refer; transfer; send accused for trial to higher court; transmit to distance, as money; return; restore; decrease; forgive; refrain from exacting;—v.i. abate in force; slacken off;—pr.p. **remit'ting**;—pa.t. and pa.p. **remit'ted**.—n. remission.—**remit'ment**, **remit'tal** n. remit.—**remit'tance** n. transmitting money to distant place; money sent. —**remit'tent** a. increasing and decreasing at periodic intervals.

remnant (rem'-nant) n. fragment of cloth; scrap; residue; remainder.

remonstrate (re-mon'-strāt) v.t. strongly protest;—v.i. present strong reasons against; speak strongly against course of conduct.—**remon'strance** n. formal protest.—**remon'strant** n. one who remonstrates;—a. expostulatory.—**remonstra'tion** n. **remon'strative**, **remon'stratory** a.

remorse (re-mors') n. self-reproach; repentance.—**remorse'ful** a. penitent; repentant.—**remorse'fully** adv. — **remorse'less** a. relentless; pitiless.

remote (re-mōt') a. far back in time or space; not near; slight; unlikely.—**remote'ly** adv.—**remote'ness** n.

remove (re-móóv') v.t. take or put away; dislodge; transfer; withdraw; extract; dismiss from post; eject;—v.i. change place or residence;—n. removal; change of place; move.—**removabil'ity** n.—**remo'vable** a. not permanently fixed.—**remo'vably** adv. —**remo'val** n. removing; transferring to another house; dismissal from post; departure.—**removed'** a. denoting nearness of relationship, as **cousin once removed**, parent's cousin or child of cousin.—**remo'ver** n.

remunerate (re-mū'-ne-rāt) v.t. reward for services; recompense.—**remu'nerable** a. that may, or should be, remunerated.—**remunera'tion** n. reward; salary.—**remu'nerative** a. lucrative; well-paid.

renaissance (re-nā'-sans) n. rebirth; Renaissence period of revival of learning in fourteenth to sixteenth cents.

renascent (re-nas'-ent) a. springing into being again; regaining lost

vigour.—**renas'cence** n. See **renaissance**.

rend (rend) v.t. tear asunder; pull to pieces; split;—pa.t. and pa.p. **rent**.

render (ren'-der) v.t. give in return; deliver up; supply; present; translate; reproduce music; portray; extract animal fats by heating; clarify.—**ren'derable** a.—**ren'derer** n. —**ren'dering** n. act of rendering; translation; version.—**rendi'tion** n. surrender; translation; version; interpretation.

rendezvous (ren'- or rong'-de-vóó) n. place of resort; appointed place for meeting;—v.i. assemble at prearranged place.

renegade (ren'-e-gād) n. faithless to principle or party; deserter;—a. false; traitorous.—**renege'** v.t. and v.i. deny; desert; turn renegade; revoke at cards.—**rene'ger** n.

renew (re-nū') v.t. and v.i. restore; renovate; revive; begin again.—**renew'able** a.—**renew'al** n. revival; restoration.

rennet (ren'-et) n. preparation from animal intestines, used for curdling milk and in preparation of cheese.

renounce (re-nouns') v.t. disavow; give up; resign; reject;—v.i. fail to follow suit at cards.—**renounce'ment**, **renuncia'tion** n.

renovate (ren'-o-vāt) v.t. render as good as new; renew.—**renova'tion** n. renewal;—pl. repairs and improvements.—**ren'ovator**, **ren'ovater** n.

renown (re-noun') n. reputation; fame.—**renowned'** a. famous; noted; eminent.

rent (rent) pa.t. and pa.p. of rend;—n. opening; tear; split; breach.

rent (rent) n. periodical payment for use of something, esp. land, houses; rental; hiring charge;—v.t. lease; hold by lease; hire;—v.i. be leased or let for rent.—**rent'able** a.—**rent'al** n. rent-roll; annual amount of rent. —**rent'er** n.

renunciation (re-nun-si-ā'-shun) n. surrender of claim; disavowal; rejection.—**renunciat'ory** a.

reorganise (re-or'-ga-nīz) v.t. organise anew.

repair (re-pār') v.t. restore to good state after injury; mend; retrieve; redress;—n. restoration; reparation; patching; mending.—**repair'able** a.—**repair'er** n.

reparable (rep'-a-ra-bl) a. that can be made good.—**rep'arably** adv.—**repara'tion** n. making amends; compensation; atonement.

repartee (rep-ar-tē') n. apt, witty reply.

repast (re-past') n. meal; victuals.

repatriate (rē-pā'-tri-āt, re-pat'-ri-āt) v.t. restore to one's own country; bring back prisoners of war and refugees from abroad.—**repatria'tion** (rē-pat'-ri-ā-shun) n.

repay (rē-pā') *v.t.* pay back; make requital for; compensate;—*pa.t.* and *pa.p.* repaid'.—repay'able *a.* meant to to be repaid.—repay'ment *n.*

repeal (rē-pēl') *v.t.* revoke, annul, as deed, will, law, or statute; cancel; abolish;—*n.* revocation; annulment.—repeal'able *a.*

repeat (re-pēt') *v.t.* say or do again; reiterate; echo; recite piece learnt by heart; rehearse; recur; regurgitate (of food);—*n.* repetition; encore.—repeat'able *a.*—repeat'ed *a.* frequent; recurring.—repeat'edly *adv.*—repeat'er *n.* one who, or that which, repeats; fire-arm which may be discharged many times in quick succession; watch which strikes last hour and appropriate quarter; (*Arith.*) a decimal in which same figure(s) repeat ad infinitum.—repeat'ing *n.*

repel (re-pel') *v.t.* drive back; repulse; oppose; excite revulsion in;—*v.i.* have negative electrical power; cause repugnance;—*pr.p.* repel'ling.—*pa.t.* and *pa.p.* repelled'.—repel'lence, repel'lency *n.* state of being repellent.—repel'lent *a.* driving back; distasteful;—*n.* that which repels.—repel'ler *n.*

repent (re-pent') *v.t.* and *v.i.* feel regret for a deed or omission.—repent'ance *n.* sorrow or regret; contrition; penitence.—repent'ant *a.*

repercuss (rē-per-kus') *v.t.* and *v.i.* beat or drive back, as sound or air.—repercus'sion *n.* act of driving back; rebound; echo; indirect consequence.—repercus'sive *a.* driving back.

repertoire (rep-er-twàr') *n.* list of plays, operas, musical works, dramatic rôles at hand for theatrical company or individual.—rep'ertory *n.* repertoire; treasury; magazine;—*a.* pert. to stock plays of resident company.

repetition (rep-e-tish'-un) *n.* act of repeating; thing repeated.—repet'itive *a.* involving much repetition.

repine (rē-pīn') *v.i.* fret or vex oneself; be discontented; complain; murmur.—repin'er *n.*—repin'ing *n.*

replace (rē-plās') *v.t.* put back into place; substitute for.—replace'able *a.*—replace'ment *n.* restoration; person or thing substituted for another.

replenish (rē-plen'-ish) *v.t.* fill up again; restock; refill; furnish; supply.—replen'ishment *n.*

replete (re-plēt') *a.* full; sated.—replete'ness, reple'tion *n.* satiety; fullness.

replica (rep'-li-ka) *n.* exact copy of work of art, esp. by artist of original; facsimile.

reply (re-plī') *v.t.* and *v.i.* return an answer; respond; rejoin.—*pa.t.* and *pa.p.* replied';—*n.* answer; rejoinder; response.

report (re-pōrt') *v.t.* relate; take down in writing; give an account of; communicate; narrate;—*v.i.* make official statement; furnish in writing account of speech, etc.; betake oneself as to superior officer;—*n.* official statement of facts; rumour; noise; reverberation, as of gun; account of proceedings, debates, etc.; reputation.—report'er *n.* one who reports, esp. for newspapers.—report'ing *n.*

repose (re-pōz') *v.t.* rely on; lean (on); confide (in); calm; deposit;—*v.i.* rest; sleep; recline;—*n.* sleep; relaxation.—reposed' *a.* calm; tranquil.—repos'it *v.t.* lodge in place of safety.—repos'itory *n.* place where valuables are deposited for safety; shop; magazine; depot; store-house.

reprehend (rep-re-hend') *v.t.* find fault with; blame; rebuke.—reprehen'sible *a.* unworthy.—reprehen'sibly *adv.*—reprehen'sive *a.* containing reproof.—reprehen'sively *adv.* — reprehen'sory *a.* given in reproof.

represent (rep-re-zent') *v.t.* exhibit counterpart or image of; recall by description or portrait; pretend to be; allege; act or play the part of; personate; imitate; deputise for; be member (of parliament, etc.) for.—represent'able *a.*—representa'tion *n.* describing, or showing; description; account; dramatic performance; protest; act of representing (in parliament, etc.).—representa'tional *a.*—represent'ative *a.* typical; representing all shades of opinions; portraying;—*n.* agent, delegate, or substitute; local member of parliament.

repress (re-pres') *v.t.* keep down or under; put down; reduce to subjection; quell; check.—repress'er, repress'or *n.*—repress'ible.—repress'ibly *adv.*—repres'sion *n.* check; restraint.—repress'ive *a.* designed to repress.

reprieve (re-prēv') *v.t.* remit or commute sentence; grant temporary relief; give respite to;—*n.* temporary suspension of execution of sentence; rest or relief.

reprimand (rep'-ri-mand) *v.t.* reprove severely; chide.—*n.* sharp rebuke.

reprint (rē-print') *v.t.* print again.—re'print *n.* new impression.

reprisal (re-prī'-zal) *n.* act of retaliation.

reproach (re-prōch') *v.t.* censure; upbraid; rebuke; reprove; charge (with);—*n.* reproof; rebuke; discredit.—reproach'ful *a.* expressing censure.—reproach'fully *adv.*

reprobate (rep'-rō-bāt) *v.t.* disapprove with extreme dislike; exclude from hopes of salvation;—*a.* disallowed; rejected; abandoned to error; cast off by God;—*n.* profligate; hardened sinner; scoundrel.—reproba'tion *n.* condition of those preordained to hell; censure.

reproduce (rē-prō-dūs') v.t. produce again; produce likeness or copy of; imitate;—v.i. propagate; generate.—**reprodu'cible** a.—**reproduc'tion** n. repeat; facsimile; process of multiplication of living individuals.—**reproduc'tive** a. pert. to reproduction; yielding return or profits; fertile.—**reproduc'tiveness, reproductiv'ity** n.

reproof (re-prōōf') n. reprimand; rebuke; censure.—**reprove'** v.t. charge with fault; rebuke.—**reprov'able** a. calling for censure.—**reproval** n. reproof.

reptile (rep'-til) n. creeping vertebrate animal moving on its belly; grovelling person;—a. creeping; grovelling; low; mean.—**reptil'ian** a. belonging to reptiles.

republic (re-pub'-lik) n. state, without hereditary head, in which supremacy of people or its elected representatives is formally acknowledged; commonwealth.—**repub'lican** a. pert. to republic;—n. one who favours republican system of government; one of two great traditional political parties of U.S.A. —**repub'licanism** n.

repudiate (re-pū'-di-āt) v.t. cast off; reject; discard; disclaim; disown.—**repudia'tion** n. rejection; disavowal. **repu'diator** n.

repugn (re-pūn') v.t. and v.i. oppose; resist; make stand against.—**repug'nance** n. state or condition of being repugnant.—**repug'nancy** n. settled or habitual feeling of aversion.—**repug'nant** a. contrary; distasteful; offensive; adverse; refractory.

repulse (re-puls') v.t. beat or drive back; repel decisively; reject; rebuff; —n. defeat; check; rebuff; rejection. —**repul'sion** n. act of driving back; state of being repelled; feeling of aversion; repugnance.—**repul'sive** a. loathsome; disgusting.—**repul'sively** adv.—**repul'siveness** n. repulsion.— **repul'sory** a. repulsive.

repute (re-pūt') v.t. account or consider; hold; reckon;—n. good character; reputation; credit; esteem.— **reputa'tion** n. estimation in which person is held; repute; good name; fame; renown.—**rep'utable** a. held in esteem; respectable; creditable.— **rep'utably** adv.—**reput'edly** adv. generally believed.

request (re-kwest') v.t. ask for earnestly; petition; beg;—n. expression of desire for; suit; demand. —**request'er** n.

requiem (rek'-wi-em) n. mass for souls of dead; dirge; music for such mass.

require (re-kwīr') v.t. insist upon having; claim as by right; make necessary; demand; need; lack.— **require'ment** n. act of requiring; want; need; essential condition.

requisite (rek'-wi-zit) a. necessary; needful; essential;—n. something indispensable.—**requisi'tion** n. levy of necessaries made by military force; written order for materials or supplies; formal demand;—v.t. demand supplies or materials, esp. for troops; request formally; seize.

requite (re-kwīt') return equivalent in good or evil; repay; reward; retaliate on.—**requi'tal** n. compensation; retaliation.

reredos (rēr'-dos) n. elaborately carved screen or wall panelling, behind church altar.

rescind (re-sind') v.t. annul; cancel; revoke; repeal; reverse.—**rescind'able** a.—**recis'sion** n. act of abrogating or annulling.—**rescis'sory** a. having power of rescinding.

rescue (res'-kū) v.t. free from danger or evil; set at liberty;—pr.p. res'cuing —n. deliverance.—res'cuer n.

research (re-serch') n. diligent search or inquiry; scientific study to discover facts; scrutiny;—a. pert. to research;—v.i. examine with care.— **research'er** n.

resemble (re-zem'-bl) v.t. be like or similar to; compare; liken.—**resem'blance** n. likeness; similarity.— **resem'bling** a.

resent (re-zent') v.t. consider as injury or affront; be angry at.— **resent'er** n.—**resent'ful** a. full of, or readily given to, resentment.— **resent'fully** adv.—**resent'ment** n. deep sense of affront; indignation.

reserve (re-zerv') v.t. hold back; set apart; keep for future use; retain;— a. acting as reserve;—n. what is reserved; supply of stores for future use; troops, etc., held back to assist when necessary; men discharged from armed forces but liable to be recalled in emergency; funds set aside for contingencies; minimum price acceptable at auction; reticence; concealment of feelings; area of land for particular purpose.— **reserva'tion** n. what is kept back; booking of hotel-room, etc.; proviso or condition; tract of land reserved for public use.—**reserved'** a. kept back; retained or booked for another; uncommunicative.—**reser'vedly** adv.—**reser'vedness** n.—**reser'vist**, member of armed force belonging to reserves.

reservoir (rez'-er-vwàr) n. enclosed area for storage and filtering of water; basin; cistern.

reset (rē-set') v.t. set over again, as page of printed matter; re-plant.

reset (re-set') v.t. and v.i. (Scots Law) receive, knowingly, stolen goods; hide and harbour deserter or criminal;—pr.p. reset'ting.—pa.t. and pa.p. reset'ted.—reset'ter n.

reshuffle (rē-shuf'-l) v.t. to rearrange

(cards, etc.);—*n.* rearrangement.

reside (re-zīd') *v.i.* dwell permanently; abide; live; be inherent in.—**res'idence** *n.* act of dwelling in place; house; abode.—**res'idency** *n.* residence, esp. official residence of British government agent at foreign court.—**res'ident** *a.* dwelling; residing;—*n.* one who resides in place.—**residen'tial** *a.* pert. to resident or residence; pert. to part of town consisting mainly of dwelling-houses.

residue (rez'-i-dū) *n.* balance or remainder.—**resid'ual** *a.* remaining after part is taken away.—**resid'uary** *a.* pert. to residue or part remaining. —**resid'uum** *n.* what is left after process of purification; balance or remainder.

resign (re-zīn') *v.t.* and *v.i.* relinquish formally (office, etc.); yield to; give up; submit to.—**resigna'tion** *n.* giving up, as claim, possession, office; abdication; relinquishment; patience. —**resigned'** *a.* surrendered; submissive; patient.—**resigned'ly** *adv.*

resilience (rē-zil'-i-ens) *n.* springing back or rebounding; elasticity, esp. of mind.—**resil'ient** *a.* leaping or springing back; rebounding; possessing power of quick recovery.

resin (rez'-in) *n.* gum-like substance obtained from sap of some trees and plants or synthetically, e.g. by polymerisation of phenol; rosin;— *v.t.* dress or coat with resin.— **resina'ceous** *a.* resinous.—**res'inous** *a.* of, or like resin.

resist (re-zist') *v.t.* and *i.* stand against; oppose; withstand; strive against; hinder.—**resis'tance** *n.* opposition; hindrance; opposition offered to passage of electric current; power to resist disease; in physics, forces tending to arrest movement;— **resis'tant** *n.* one who, or that which, resists.—**resis'tant, resis'tent** *a.* offering or making resistance.—**resis'ter** *n.*—**resistibil'ity, resis'tibleness** *n.* quality or state of being resistible.— **resis'tible** *a.*—**resis'tibly, resis'tingly** *adv.*—**resist'less** *a.* irresistible; unable to resist.—**resist'lessly** *adv.*—**resist'lessness** *n.*—**resis'tor** *n.* coil or similar apparatus possessing electrical resistance.—**resistance box,** box with number of resistance-coils.—**resistance coil,** coil of insulated wire whose resistance has been adjusted to stated value.— **resistance movement,** organised, underground movement in occupied country against invader.

resolute (rez'-o-lūt) *a.* having decided purpose; determined;—*n.* determined person.—**res'olutely** *adv.*— **res'oluteness** *n.* determination.—**reso-lu'tion** *n.* intention; firmness; decision of court or vote of assembly; motion or declaration; courage; boldness.

resolve (re-zolv') *v.t.* separate component parts of; solve and reduce to different form; make clear; unravel; (*Math.*) solve;—*v.i.* determine; decide; purpose; dissolve; determine by vote;—*n.* act of resolving; that which is resolved on; firm determination.—**resol'vable** *a.*—**resolved'** *a.* determined.—**resol'vedly** *adv.*—**resolv'edness** *n.*

resonant (rez'-o-nant) *a.* resounding; echoing; sonorous; ringing.—**res'onance** *n.* phenomenon exhibited by vibrating systems, brought into oscillation by periodic disturbance, frequency of which is equal to that of system.—**res'onate** *v.i.* resound;— **res'onator** *n.* tube etc., exhibiting resonance.

resort (re-zort') *v.i.* betake oneself; go; have recourse; apply (to); frequent; — *n.* frequented place; haunt; recourse; aid.—**last resort, last resource.**

resound (re-zound') *v.t.* sound back; send back sound;—*v.i.* echo; reverberate;—*n.* echo.—**resound'ing** *a.*

resource (re-sōrs') *n.* that to which one resorts, or on which one depends, for supply or support; skill in improvising; shift; means;—*pl.* pecuniary means; wealth.—**resource'ful** *a.* clever in devising fresh expedients; ingenious. — **resource'fully** *adv.* — **resource'fulness** *n.*

respect (re-spekt') *v.t.* esteem; honour; treat carefully; pay heed to; concern; relate to;—*n.* consideration; deference;—*pl.* good wishes.— **respec'table** *a.* worthy of respect; reputable; moderate.—**respectabil'ity** *n.*—**respec'tably** *adv.*—**respect'ful** *a.* deferential; reverential; polite.— **respect'fully** *adv.*—**respect'fulness** *n.*— **respec'ting** *prep.* regarding; concerning.—**respec'tive** *a.* relative; not absolute; particular; own; several. —**respec'tively** *adv.* relatively.

respire (re-spīr') *v.t.* and *v.i.* breathe; take rest.—**respir'able** *a.* fit to be breathed.—**respira'tion** *n.* process of breathing.—**respira'tional, respirative** (res'- or rē-spir'-) *a.* respiratory.— **res'pirator** *n.* appliance for covering mouth and nostrils in order to purify air breathed in, or for inhalation of medicated vapours; gas-mask.—**respiratory** (res'- or res-pī'-) *a.* pert. to respiration.

respite (res'-pit, res'-pīt) *n.* temporary intermission; suspension of execution of capital sentence; suspension of labour; stop; reprieve;— *v.t.* grant respite to; reprieve; relieve by interval of rest; delay.

resplendent (re-splen'-dent) *a.* shining with brilliant lustre; very bright; dazzling.—**resplen'dence, resplen'dency** *n.*—**resplen'dently** *adv.*

respond (re-spond') *v.i.* answer:

reply; suit; react.—**respon'dent** *a* answering;—*n.* (*Law*) one who answers in certain proceedings, esp. in divorce suit; defendant.

response (re-spons') *n.* answer or reply; part of liturgy said or sung by choir and congregation in answer to versicles of priest; in R.C. church, anthem after morning lessons, etc. —**responsibil'ity** *n.* state of being responsible; that for which any one is responsible; duty; charge; obligation.—**respon'sible** *a.* accountable; trustworthy; rational.—**respon'sibly** *adv.*—**respon'sive** *a.* able, ready, or inclined, to respond; correspondent. —**respon'sively** *adv.*—**respon'siveness** *n.*

rest (rest) *n.* repose; cessation from motion or labour; that on which anything rests or leans; place where one may rest; pause;—*v.t.* lay at rest;—*v.i.* cease from action; repose; stand (on); sleep; be dead; remain (with), for decision, etc.; trust; be undisturbed.—**rest'ful** *a.* soothing; peaceful; quiet.—**rest'fully** *adv.*— **rest'fulness** *n.*—**rest'less** *a.* unsettled; uneasy.—**rest'lessly** *adv.*—**rest'lessness** *n.*—**to lay to rest,** bury.

rest (rest) *v.i.* remain; continue to be; depend;—*n.* remainder.

restaurant (res'-to-rong, res'-torant) *n.* place where customers are provided with meals on payment; tea-room; cafe.—**restaurateur** (res-to'rạ-ter) *n.* proprietor of restaurant.

restitute (res'-ti-tūt) *v.t.* restore.— **restitu'tion** *n.* act of restoring, esp. to rightful owner; reparation, compensation.—**res'titutive** *a.*—**res'titutor** *n.*

restive (res'-tiv) *a.* impatient; fidgety; uneasy; stubborn.—**res'tively** *adv.*— **res'tiveness** *n.*

restore (re-stōr') *v.t.* give back; recover from ruin or decay; repair; renew; heal; revive; cure.—**restor'able** *a.*—**restora'tion** *n.* recovery; reconstruction; re-establishment of monarchy by return of Charles II in 1660.—**restor'ative** *a.* having power to renew strength, vigour, etc.;—*n.* remedy for restoring health and vigour.—**restor'atively** *adv.*

restrain (re-strān') *v.t.* hold back; hinder; check.—**restrain'able** *a.*—**restrain'ment** *n.*—**restraint'** *n.* repression; hindrance; imprisonment.

restrict (re-strikt') *v.t.* restrain within bounds; limit.—**restric'ted** *a.* limited.—**restric'tedly** *adv.*—**restric'tion** *n.* act of restricting; state of being restricted; limitation; restraint.— **restric'tive** *a.* having the power to restrict.—**restric'tively** *adv.*—**restrictive practice**, usage in industry which impedes efficiency or fair trading.

result (re-zult') *v.i.* follow, as consequence; happen; terminate;—*n.* issue; effect; outcome; answer to calculation.—**resul'tant** *a.*

resume (re-zūm') *v.t.* renew; recommence; summarise.—**résumé** (rā-zū-mā') *n.* summing up; summary; abstract.—**resum'able** *a.*—**resump'tion** *n.* fresh start.—**resump'tive** *a.*

resurge (re-surj') *v.i.* rise again.— **resur'gence** *n.*—**resur'gent** *a.* rising again (from the dead).—**resurrect'** *v.t.* restore to life; use once more; take from grave.—**resurrec'tion** *n.* resuscitation of body after death and its reunion with soul; Christ's rising from grave after Crucifixion; revival. —**resurrec'tional, resurrec'tionary** *a.*— **resurrec'tionist, resurrec'tion-man** *n.* one who exhumed bodies from grave for anatomical purposes.

resuscitate (re-sus'-i-tāt) *v.t.* restore to life one apparently dead;—*v.i.* come to life again.—**resus'citable** *a.*— **resus'citant** *n.* — **resuscita'tion** *n.* — **resus'citative** *a.*—**resus'citator** *n.*

retail (rē-tāl') *v.t.* sell in small quantities; tell frequently.—**re'tail** *a.* denoting sale in small quantities;— *n.* sale in small quantities.—**retail'er** *n.*—**retail'ment** *n.*

retain (re-tān') *v.t.* continue to keep; hold; reserve.—**retain'able** *a.*—**retain'er** *n.* one who retains; adherent or follower; dependant; fee paid to secure services of, esp. barrister.— **retain'ment** *n.*

retaliate (re-tal'-i-āt) *v.t.* and *v.i.* repay in kind; return like for like; revenge.—**retalia'tion** *n.*—**retal'iative, retal'iatory** *a.*—**retal'iator** *n.*

retard (re-tárd') *v.t.* hinder progress; make slow or late; impede.— **retarda'tion** *n.* delaying; diminishing velocity; rate of loss of velocity; delayed mental development in children.—**retard'ment** *n.*

retch (rech) *v.i.* strain at vomiting.

retention (re-ten'-shun) *n.* act or power of retaining; stoppage; (*Med.*) inability to urinate. — **reten'tive** *a.*—**reten'tively** *adv.*—**reten'tiveness** *n.*

reticent (ret'-i-sẹnt) *a.* reserved; taciturn; uncommunicative. — **ret'icence, ret'icency** *n.*—**ret'icently** *adv.*

reticule (ret'-i-kūl) *n.* little net-work bag; lady's work-bag.—**retic'ular, retic'ulary** *a.* having form of net; formed with interstices.—**retic'ulate** *v.t.* cover with net-like lines; make like net:—*a.* Also **retic'ulated,** netted; having lines crossing like net-work, as leaf.—**reticula'tion** *n.*

retina (ret'-i-nạ) *n.* sensory layer of eye from which sense impressions are passed to brain.—**ret'inal** *a.*

retinue (ret'-i-nū) *n.* body of hired servants or followers; train of attendants; suite.

retire (re-tīr') *v.t.* compel one to retire from office:—*v.i.* go back; withdraw; retreat; give up formally one's work or office; go to bed.— **reti'ral** *n.* act of retiring.—**retired'** *a.*

secluded; private; withdrawn from one's daily work.—**retired'ly** *adv.*—**retired'ness, retire'ment** *n.* act of retiring; state of being retired.—**retir'ing** *a.* reserved; modest; pert. to withdrawal from work or office.

retouch (rē-tuch) *v.t.* improve photographic negative or print.

retort (re-tort') *v.t.* repay in kind; hurl back (charge, etc.);—*v.i.* make smart reply;—*n.* vigorous reply; vessel in which substances are distilled.

retrace (rē-trās') *v.t.* trace over again; go back the same way; draw over former tracing.—**retrace'able** *a.*

retract (re-trakt') *v.t.* and *i.* draw back or in; take back, as statement; go back on one's word.—**retrac'table, retrac'tible** *a.* able to be retracted.—**retracta'tion** *n.* recantation.—**retrac'tile** *a.* (*Zool.*) capable of being drawn back or inwards, as claws, etc.—**retrac'tion** *n.*—**retrac'tive** *a.* ready to retract.—**retrac'tively** *adv.*

retread (rē-tred') *v.t.* tread again; renew worn tread on outer cover of rubber tyre;—*n.* tyre with renewed tread.

retreat (re-trēt') *n.* retiring or withdrawing; military signal for retiring; military call, at sunset, on bugle; place of seclusion; period of retirement for prayer and meditation;—*v.i.* move back; retire before enemy.—**retreat'ing** *a.* sloping backward, as forehead or chin.

retrench (re-trensh') *v.t.* cut down (expense, etc.); curtail; diminish; lessen; —*v.i.* economise. — **retrench'ment** *n.* diminution of expenditure; economy.

retribution (ret-ri-bū'-shun) *n.* suitable return, esp. for evil deeds; requital; vengeance.—**retribute** (re-tri'-būt, ret'-ri-būt) *v.t.* pay back.—**retrib'utive, retrib'utory** *a.*

retrieve (re-trēv') *v.t.* gain back; recover; re-establish (former position, fortune, etc.); repair; (of dog) find and bring back shot game.—**retriev'able** *a.*—**retriev'ably** *adv.*—**retriev'al, retrieve'ment** *n.*—**retriev'er** *n.* dog trained to find and bring back game.

retrocede (rē-trō-sēd') *v.t.* go or move back.—**retroces'sion** *n.* act of going back.

retrograde (ret'-rō-, rē'-trō-grād) *v.i.* move backward; deteriorate; decline;—*a.* tending to backward direction; deteriorating; reactionary; retrogressive.—**retrograda'tion** *n.*—**ret'rogress** *v.i.* move backwards; deteriorate.—**retrogres'sion** *n.* act of going backward; decline into inferior state.—**retrogress'ive** *a.* reactionary; degenerating.—**retrogress'ively** *adv.*

retrospect (ret'-rō-, rē'-trō-spekt) *n.* looking back; survey of past events; review.—**retrospec'tion** *n.*—**restrospec'tive** *a.* tending to look back; applicable to past events; of laws, rules, etc., having force as if enacted at earlier date.—**retrospec'tively** *adv.*

retroussé (rg-troô'-sā) *a.* turned up, as end of nose; pug.

retry (rē-trī') *v.t.* try again; put on trial second time.

return (re-turn') *v.t.* bring, give, or send back; restore; report officially; elect; yield (profit);—*v.i.* go or come back; recur; reply;—*n.* coming back to same place; profit; official report, esp. as to numbers; repayment; restitution.—**return'able** *a.* capable of being returned; required to be delivered up.—**return'ing-off'icer** *n.* officer who makes returns of writs, juries, etc.; presiding officer at election.

reunion (rē-ūn'-yun) *n.* union formed anew after separation; social gathering.—**reunite'** *v.t.* unite again; join after separation;—*v.i.* join and cohere again.

reveal (re-vēl') *v.t.* disclose; discover by supernatural power; show.—**reveal'able** *a.*—**reveal'er** *n.*—**reveal'ment** *n.* disclosure; revelation.—**revealed law,** divine law.

reveille (re-val'-i, re-vāl'-ye) *n.* bugle-call or roll of drums sounded in military establishments at daybreak to rouse inmates.

revel (rev'-el) *v.i.* make merry; carouse; delight (in);—*pr.p.* **rev'elling.**—*pa.t.* and *pa.p.* **rev'elled.**—*n.* noisy celebration;—*pl.* entertainment, with music and dancing.—**rev'eller** *n.*—**rev'elry** *n.* noisy and spontaneous festivity.

revelation (rev-e-lā'-shun) *n.* act of revealing; knowledge of God, or of divine things, imparted to man by Him; (*Bib.*) last book of New Testament — Apocalypse. — **revela'tional, rev'elatory** *a.*

revenge (re-venj') *v.t.* return injury for injury; avenge;—*n.* revenging; infliction of injury for injury; passion for vengeance.—**revenge'ful** *a.* full of revenge; vindictive.—**revenge'fully** *adv.*—**revenge'fulness** *n.*

revenue (rev'-e-nū) *n.* income derived from any source, esp. annual income of state or institution; proceeds; receipts; profits.—**in'land-rev'enue** *n.* public money from income tax, excise, etc.

reverberate (re-ver'-ber-āt) *v.t.* and *v.i.* send back, as sound; reflect, as light or heat; re-echo.—**reverb'erant** *a.* resounding.—**reverbera'tion** *n.*—**rever'berative** *a.* tending to reverberate.—**rever'berator** *n.*—**rever'beratory** *a.* producing reverberation.

revere (re-vēr') *v.t.* reverence.—**rever'able** *a.* worthy of respect.—

rev'erance n. respect and esteem; veneration; bow, curtsey, or genuflection; title applied to clergyman; —v.t. revere: venerate.—**rev'erend** a. worthy of reverence; venerable; title of respect given to clergy (abbrev. Rev.).—**rev'erent** a. with reverence.— **reveren'tial** a. respectful.—reveren'tially, rev'erently adv.

reverie, revery (rev'-er-i) n. state of mind, akin to dreaming; rhapsody; musing.

reverse (re-vers') v.t. change completely; give contrary decision; annul; overturn; repeal; transpose; invert;—v.i. change direction; come back;—n. side which appears when object is turned round; opposite or contrary; crest-side of coin or medal; check; defeat; misfortune;—a. turned backward; opposite; upside-down.—**rever'sal** n. reversing, changing, overthrowing, annulling.—**reversed'** a. turned in opposite direction; inverted; annulled.—**rever'sedly** adv.—reversibil'ity n.—**rever'sible** a. capable of being used on both sides or in either direction.—**rever'sibly** adv.—**rever'sion** n. returning or reverting; deferred annuity; interest which reverts to landlord after expiry of lease.—**rever'sional, revers'ionary** a. involving reversion; returning to person after time or event.—**revers'ive** a. tending to cause reversion.—**rever'so** n. left-hand page of book.

revert (re-vert') v.i. return to former state or rank; come back to subject; turn backwards;—v.t. turn back or reverse.—**revert'ible** a.

review (re-vu') v.t. re-examine; revise; consider critically (book); inspect troops, etc.—n. revision; survey; inspection, esp. of military forces; critical notice of book, etc.; periodical devoted to critical articles, etc.—**review'er** n. one who writes critical reviews; examiner; inspector.

revile (re-vil') v.t. abuse; vilify; defame.—**revile'ment** n.—**revil'er** n.

revise (re-viz') v.t. look over and correct; review and amend;—n. review; further printer's proof.—**revi'sal** n. review; re-examination.—**revi'sion** n. revisal; revised copy of book or document.—**revi'ser, revi'sor** n. proof-reader.—**revi'sional, revi'sionary** a. pert. to revision.—**revi'sory** a. having power to revise.—**Revised Version**, new translation of Bible in 1881 (New Testament) and 1884 (Old Testament).

revive (re-viv') v.i. come back to life, vigour, etc.; awaken;—v.t. resuscitate; re-animate; renew; refresh (memory). — **revivabil'ity** n. — **revi'vable** a. capable of being revived.—**revi'vably** adv.—**revi'val** n. reviving or being revived; renewed activity;

wave of religious enthusiasm; awakening; reappearance of old play, etc.—**revi'valism** n. religious fervour during evangelical revival.—**revi'valist** n. one who promotes religious revivals.—**revi'ver** n. stimulant.—**revivifica'tion** n. renewal of life and energy.—**reviv'ify** v.t. reinvigorate.

revoke (re-vok') v.t. annul; repeal; reverse (decision);—v.i. at cards, fail to follow suit;—n. neglect to follow suit at cards.—**revoke'ment** n. revoking.—**revok'er** n.—**rev'ocable** a. able to be revoked.—**rev'ocableness, revocabil'ity** n.—**rev'ocably** adv.—**revoca'tion** n. repeal; reversal.—**rev'ocatory** a.

revolt (re-volt') v.i. renounce allegiance; rise in rebellion; feel disgust;—v.t. shock; repel;—n. rebellion; mutiny; disgust.—**revol'ter** n.—**revol'ting** a. disgusting.—**revol'tingly** adv.

revolution (rev-o-lu'-shun) n. motion of body round its orbit or focus; turning round on axis (but preferably, rotation); radical change, esp. in constitution of country after revolt.—**revolu'tionary** a. pert. to revolution; marked by great and violent changes;—n. one who participates in revolution. — **revolu'tionise** v.t. change completely.

revolve (re-volv') v.i. turn round on axis; rotate; meditate;—v.t. cause to turn; rotate; reflect upon.—**revol'vable** a.—**revol'ver** n. pistol with several revolving loading chambers.

revue (re-vu') n. theatrical entertainment with music and sketches.

revulsion (re-vul'-shun) n. violent change of feeling; repugnance; reaction; counter-irritant.—**revul'sive** a. tending to revulsion.

reward (re-wawrd') v.t. give in return for; recompense;—n. what is given in return; return for voluntary act; money offered for recovery of articles or assistance in any form.—**reward'er** n.

rhabdo- (rab'-do) prefix used in formation of scientific compound terms, signifying a rod or rod-like.—**rhab'doid** a. rod-shaped.—**rhab'domancy** n. divination by divining-rod, usually of hazel, to trace presence of minerals or metals under ground.

rhapsody (rap'-so-di) n. collection of verses; passages gathered together without natural connection; wild, rambling composition or discourse; (Mus.) imaginative composition in free style.—**rhapsod'ie(al)** a. in wild, irregular style; gushing.—**rhapsod'ically** adv.—**rhap'sodise** v.t. and v.i. sing or recite, as rhapsody; be ecstatic over.—**rhap'sodist** n. one who recites or composes rhapsody.

rhea (re'-a) n. S. American three-toed ostrich.

rheostat (re'-o-stat) n. (Elect.) instrument for controlling and varying resistance.—rheostat'ic a.

rhesus (rē'-sus) n. small Indian monkey.—rhe'sian a.—rhesus factor, (Med.) inherited characteristic of red blood-cells classed as rhesus positive or negative.

rhetoric (ret'-o-rik) n. art of persuasive speech; declamation; artificial eloquence; exaggerated oratory.—rhetor'ical a. oratorical; declamatory; bombastic. — rhetorical question, question put for effect, not requiring an answer.—rhetor'ically adv.—rhetori'cian n. teacher of principles of rhetoric.

rheum (room) n. fluid secreted by mucous glands and discharged from nostrils or eyes during catarrh; tears; spleen.—rheumat'ic, rheumat'ical a. pert. to or suffering from rheumatism.—rheum'atism n. group of diseases with sharp pains and swelling in muscles and joints.—rheum'atoid a. resembling rheumatism.—rheum'y a. full of watery humour (esp. eyes); damp.—rheumatoid arthritis, severe chronic inflammation of joints.

rhinal (rī'-nal) a. pert. to nose.

rhinoceros (rī-nos'-e-ros) n. thick-skinned mammal with strong horn (sometimes two) on nose.

rhod-, rhodo- (rōd, rō'-dō) prefix signifying rose-coloured.—rho'dium n. metallic chemical element related to ruthenium and palladium whose salts are rosy-red; rose-wood.—rhododen'dron n. evergreen flowering shrub with attractive blossoms.

rhombus (rom'-bus) n. (Geom.) parallelogram whose sides are all equal, but whose angles are not right angles.—rhomb n. lozenge or diamond-shaped figure; rhombus.—rhom'bic, rhom'biform, rhom'boid, rhomboi'dal a. having shape of rhomboid.—rhom'boid n. parallelogram like rhombus, but having only opposite sides and angles equal.

rhone (rōn) n. eaves-gutter which collects rain from roof. Also rone.—rhone'-pipe n. pipe which drains rain-water from rhone.

rhubarb (roo'-barb) n. two plants, familiar rhubarb of kitchen-garden, and eastern variety whose roots are used as purgative.

rhyme, rime (rīm) n. identity of sound in word endings of verses; verses, usually two, in rhyme with each other; couplet; word answering in sound to another word;—v.t. put into rhyme;—v.i. make verses.—rhy'mer, rhym'ster n. one who makes rhymes; minor poet.

rhythm (rithm) n. measured flow of sound, as in music and poetry, or of action, as in dancing; periodic movement, as in heart pulsations;

regular recurrence; symmetry.—rhyth'mic(al) a.—rhyth'mically adv.—rhyth'mics n. science of rhythm.

rib (rib) n. one of arched bones springing from vertebral column; anything resembling rib; wire support of umbrella, etc.—v.t. furnish with ribs.—pr.p. rib'bing.—pa.t. and pa.p. ribbed.—rib'bing n. arrangement of ribs.

ribald (rib'-ald) a. vulgar; indecent; —n. ribald person.—rib'aldry n. indecent language or conduct; obscenity.—rib'aldish, rib'aldrous a.

ribbon, riband, ribband (rib'-un, rib'-and) n. fillet, commonly of silk or satin, as trimming or fastening for dress; coloured piece of silk as war-medal; part of insignia of order of knighthood.

rice (rīs) n. annual grass plant, cultivated in Asia, principal food of one-third of world.—rice'-pa'per n. paper made from pith of small tree.

rich (rich) a. wealthy; abounding in possessions; well supplied; fertile; of food, highly seasoned; harmonious (voice); in engines, of petrol-air mixture, containing excess of petrol;—n. wealthy classes.—rich'es n.pl. wealth; opulence; plenty. — rich'ly adv.—rich'ness n. opulence; wealth.

rick (rik) n. stack of grain or hay; sprain; wrench;—v.t. pile up in ricks.

rickets (rik'-ets) n. rachitis, infantile disease marked by defective development of bones.—rick'etiness n. being rickety; tottering state; shakiness.—rick'ety a. affected with rickets; shaky; unstable; insecure.

rickshaw (rik'-shaw) n. Japanese jinriksha, a light two-wheeled, hooded vehicle on springs, drawn by one man.

ricochet (rik'-ō-shā, -shet) n. glancing rebound of object after striking flat surface at oblique angle;—v.t. and v.i. rebound.—pr.p. ricochet'ting.—pa.t. and pa.p. ricochet'ted.

rid (rid) v.t. free; deliver; relieve of; disencumber.—pr.p. rid'ding.—pa.t. and pa.p. rid.—rid'dance n. deliverance.—a good riddance, welcome relief.

ridden (rid'-n) pa.p. of ride.

riddle (rid'-l) n. large sieve;—v.t. separate, as grain from chaff, with riddle; pierce with holes as in sieve.—ridd'lings n.pl. coarse material left in sieve.

riddle (rid'-l) n. enigma; puzzling fact, thing, person;—v.i. speak in, make, riddles.

ride (rīd) v.t. be mounted on horse, bicycle, etc.; cover distance;—v.i. be carried on back of animal; be borne along in vehicle; lie securely at anchor; float lightly;—pr.p. rid'ing.—pa.t. rode;—pa.p. rid'den.—

n. act of riding; journey, on horse-back, in vehicle, etc.; riding-track;—**rid′er** n. one who rides; addition to document; supplement to original motion or verdict.—**rid′ing** a. used for riding on; used by rider;—n. track prepared for riding exercise.—**rid′ing-light** n. white light on forestay of vessel at anchor.—**riding-whip**, light whip with short lash.—**to ride over**, tyrannise.—**to ride rough-shod**, show no consideration for others.—**riding the marches**, ceremonial riding round boundaries of town or burgh.

ridge (rij) n. line of meeting of two sloping surfaces; long narrow hill; strip of upturned soil between furrows; highest part of roof;—v.t. form into ridges;—v.i. rise in ridges; wrinkle.—**ridged** a. having ridges on its surface.—**ridge′way** n. road built along the crest of hill.—**ridg′y** a. rising in ridges.

ridicule (rid′-i-kūl) n. mockery; sarcasm; irony; derision;—v.t. satirise; mock; make fun of.—**rid′iculer** n.—**ridic′ulous** a. ludicrous; droll; laughable.—**ridic′ulously** adv.

Riding (rī′-ding) n. one of the three divisions of Yorkshire.

rife (rīf) a. prevailing; prevalent; abundant; plentiful.—**rife′ly** adv.—**rife′ness** n.

riff-raff (rif′-raf) n. refuse; rabble.

rifle (rī′-fl) v.t. search and rob; plunder.—**ri′fler** n.—**ri′fling** n. pillaging.

rifle (rī′-fl) v.t. groove; channel;—n. musket whose barrel is grooved.—**ri′fling** n. arrangement of grooves in gun-barrel.—**Ri′fleman** n. private in Rifle Brigade; man armed with rifle.

rift (rift) n. cleft; fissure; ford;—v.t. and v.i. cleave; split.

rig (rig) v.t. provide (ship) with spars, ropes, etc.; equip; clothe;—pr.p. **rig′ging**.—pa.t. and pa.p. **rigged**.—n. manner in which masts and sails of vessel are rigged; equipment used in installing machinery, etc.; costume; style of dress.—**rig′ger** n.—**rig′ging** n. system of ropes and tackle, esp. for supporting mast or controlling sails; adjustment of different components of aircraft.—**rig′-out** n. outfit;—v.t. supply with complete outfit.

rig (rig) n. trick; dodge; swindle;—v.i. romp;—v.t. raise prices by prior arrangement, hence, **to rig the market**; obtain favourable results by trickery.

right (rīt) a. straight; proper; upright; true; not left; on same side as right hand; conservative or so inclined; perpendicular;—adv. in right manner; equitably; very; correctly; properly; exactly; to the right hand;—n. that which is correct; uprightness; just claim; legal title; that which is on right side, or opposite to left; political party inclined towards preservation of status quo;—v.t. set upright; do justice to; righten;—v.i. recover proper or natural position; become upright.—**right′en** v.t. set right.—**right′ful** a. legitimate; lawful; true; fair.—**right′fully** adv.—**right′fulness** n. justice.—**right′ly** adv. correctly.—**right′ness** n. correctness; justice.—**right′-about** adv. in or to opposite direction.—**right′-ang′led** a. having ninety degrees.—**right′-hand** a. belonging to right hand; pert. to most reliable assistant or man.—**right′-of-way** n. right of individual to pass over another's lands.—**right off** immediately.

righteous (rī′-chus) a. doing what is right; free from sin; just; upright; godly.—**right′eously** adv. in righteous manner.—**right′eousness** n. holiness; godliness; uprightness; honesty.

rigid (rij′-id) a. stiff; not easily bent; strict.—**rigid′ity** n. resistance to change of form; stiffness; severity.—**rig′idly** adv.—**rig′idness** n.

rigmarole (rig′-ma-rōl) n. meaningless, rambling statements.

rigor (rig′-or) n. (Med.) attack of cold and shivering, accompanied by rise of temperature and perspiration.—**rig′orism** n. strictness.—**rig′orist** n. person of strict principles.—**rigor mortis**, stiffening of body after death.

rigour (rig′-ur) n. being rigid; harshness; strictness.—**rig′orous** a. severe; stiff; austere; strict.—**rig′orously** adv.—**rig′orousness** n.

rile (rīl) v.t. anger; exasperate; irritate.

rill (ril) n. small brook; streamlet.—**rill′-marks** n.pl. narrow furrows left on sands by receding tide.

rim (rim) n. margin; brim; border; metal ring forming outer edge of road-wheel;—v.t. furnish with rim;—pr.p. **rim′ming**.—pa.t. and pa.p. **rimmed**.—**rim′less** a.

rime (rīm) n. white or hoar frost; frozen dew or vapour.—**ri′my** a.

rind (rīnd) n. external covering or coating of trees, fruits, cheese, bacon, etc.; skin; peel; husk; bark;—v.t. strip off rind; peel.

rinderpest (rin′-der-pest) n. cattle plague.

ring (ring) n. small circle of gold, etc. esp. on finger; band, coil, rim; circle formed for dance or sports; round enclosure, as in circus, auction mart, etc.; area within roped square for boxing, etc.; combination of persons to control prices;—v.t. encircle; put ring through animal's nose;—**ring′-dove** n. pigeon, whose neck has ring-shaped, white mark.—**ring′ing** n.—**ring′leader** n. leader of people associated together.—**ring′less** a.—**ring′let** n. small ring; long curl of hair.—**ring′-mas′ter** n. one who directs performance in circus-ring.—ring'-worm n. contagious fungal disease of skin.

ring (ring) v.t. cause to sound, esp. by striking; produce, by ringing;—v.i. give out resonant sound, as bell; chime; resound; continue sounding, as ears; tingle;—pa.t. rang, rarely rung.—pa.p. rung.—n. resonant note; chime (of church bells).—to ring down, cause theatre curtain to be lowered.—to ring false, sound insincere.—to ring changes upon, vary.

rink (ringk) n. broad strip, 18 to 21 feet wide, of bowling-green; covered-in place for skating or curling; members of side at bowls or curling.

rinse (rins) v.t. wash out, by filling with water, etc., and emptying.

riot (ri'-ot) n. tumultuous disturb-ance of peace; tumult; uproar; broil; profusion; luxury;—v.i. make, or engage in, riot; revel; disturb peace.—ri'oter n.—ri'oting n.—ri'ot-ous a. unruly; rebellious.—ri'otously adv.—ri'otousness n.—to read the riot act (Colloq.) scold and threaten punish-ment.—to run riot, behave wildly, without restraint.

rip (rip) v.t. rend; slash; tear off or out; slit; saw wood along direction of grain;—v.i. tear; move quickly and freely;—pr.p. rip'ping.—pa.t. and pa.p. ripped.—n. rent; tear dissipated person.—rip'per n.—rip'-ping a. (Colloq.) splendid.—rip'pingly adv.—rip'cord n. cord to withdraw parachute from pack.—rip'-saw n. saw with large teeth for cutting timber in direction of grain.

riparian (ri-pā'-ri-an) a. pert. to, or situated on, banks of river.

ripe (rip) a. mature; fully developed; sound (judgment, etc.); ready (for). —v.i. ripen.—ripe'ly adv.—rip'en v.t. hasten process of riping; mature;—v.i. grow ripe; come to perfection.—ripe'ness n.

riposte (ri-post') n. quick return thrust in fencing; smart reply; repartee.—v.t. reply smartly.

ripple (rip'-l) n. dimpling of surface of water; little wave; subdued sound;—v.t. cause ripple in;—v.i. flow into little waves.

rise (riz) v.i. ascend; get up; get out of bed; appear above horizon; originate; swell; increase; adjourn; revolt; reach higher rank;—pr.p. ri'sing.—pa.t. rose.—pa.p. ris'en.—n. act of rising; that which rises or seems to rise; increase, as of price, etc.; source; elevation, as of voice. —ri'ser n. one who, or that which, rises; vertical part of step.—ri'sing n. getting up; revolt; insurrection; —a. nearing; approaching.

risible (riz'-i-bl) a. very prone to laugh; capable of exciting laughter; mirth-provoking.

risk (risk) n. danger; peril; hazard; amount covered by insurance; person or object insured;—v.t. ex-pose to danger or possible loss.—risk'er n.—risk'y a.

risotto (ri-zot'-tō) n. Italian dish based on rice, cooked in fat.

rissole (ris'-ōl) n. fried meat-ball or fish-cake.

rite (rit) n. practice or custom, esp. religious; form; solemnity; cere-monial.—rit'ual a. pert. to rites; ceremonial;—n. manner of perform-ing divine service; prescribed book of rites.—rit'ualism n. insistence on decorous ceremonial in public wor-ship and administration of Sacra-ments.—rit'ualist n.—ritualist'ic a.—rit'ually adv.

rival (ri'-val) n. competitor; op-ponent;—a. competing;—v.t. vie with; strive to equal or excel; emulate;—pr.p. ri'valling.—pa.t. and pa.p. ri'valled.—ri'valry n. keen competition.

rive (riv) v.t. rend asunder; split; cleave;—v.i. be split or rent asunder. —pa.t. rived.—pa.p. rived, riv'en.

river (riv'-er) n. natural stream of water flowing in channel; abund-ance.—riv'erain, riv'erine a. situated near or on river.—riv'er-bas'in n. area drained by river and tributaries.—riv'er-bed n. channel of river.

rivet (riv'-et) n. iron or steel pin with strong flat head at one end, used for uniting two overlapping plates, etc. by hammering down stub end;—v.t. fasten with rivets; clinch; fasten firmly.—riv'eter n.

rivulet (riv'-ū-let) n. little river.

roach (rōch) n. carp-like fresh-water fish.

road (rōd) n. way prepared for passengers, vehicles, etc.; direction; way; route; place where vessels may ride at anchor.—road'-block n. ob-struction placed across road.—road'-hog n. motorist who drives to the danger of others.—road'house n. restaurant, hotel, etc., on main-roads.—road'stead n. anchorage pro-viding part shelter for vessel while off shore.—road-test' n. try-out of vehicle on road; report of such test. —road'way n. carriage-way of road. —to take to the road, adopt life of tramp.

roam (rōm) v.t. and v.i. wander; ramble; rove;—n. ramble; walk.—roam'er n.

roan (rōn) a. having coat in which main colour is thickly interspersed with another, esp. bay or chestnut mixed with white or grey;—n. roan horse; smooth-grained sheep-skin, dyed and finished.

roar (rōr) v.t. and v.i. shout; bawl; squall; make loud, confused sound; laugh loudly;—n. sound of roaring;

loud cry.—roar'ing n. act or sound of roaring—roar'ingly adv.—Roaring Forties, area of Southern Ocean between 40° and 50° S. latitude where strong W. and N.W. winds are prevalent.—roaring trade, brisk, profitable business.

roast (rōst) v.t. cook by exposure to open fire or in oven; expose to heat (as coffee, etc.); (Slang) reprimand; —v.i. become over-heated;—n. what is roasted, as joint of meat;—a. roasted.—roas'ting n.

rob (rob) v.t. plunder; steal;—pr.p. rob'bing.—pa.t. and pa.p. robbed.— rob'ber n.—rob'bery n.

robe (rōb) n. long outer garment; ceremonial dress denoting state, rank, or office; gown;—v.t. invest with robe; dress.—rob'ing n.

robin (rob'-in) n. small red-breasted bird of thrush family; robin-redbreast.

robot (rō'-bot) n. automaton; mechanical man; machine which performs operations as if by human brain; (Fig.) person of machine-like efficiency.

robust (rō-bust') a. strong; muscular; sound; vigorous.—robust'ious a. boisterous; violent.—robust'ly adv.—robust'ness n.

rock (rok) n. large mass of stone; (Geol.) natural deposit of sand, earth, or clay when in natural beds; firm foundation; defence, fortress, strength; sweetmeat in long cylindrical form.—rock'ery n. small mound of stones planted with Alpine plants. —rock'iness n.—rock'y a. rugged; resembling rocks; unfeeling.—rock'-bott'om a. lowest possible;—n. fundamental principles.—rock'-cake n. currant cake with hard crust.—rock'crys'tal n. transparent quartz.— rock'-salt n. unrefined sodium chloride found in natural deposits.—the Rock, Gibraltar.—on the rocks (Colloq.) having no money.

rock (rok) v.t. sway to and fro; put to sleep by rocking; lull; shake;— v.i. be moved, backward and forward; reel; totter.—rock'er n. curving piece of wood on which cradle or chair rocks; rocking-horse or -chair. —rock'y a. disposed to rock; shaky. —rock'ing n. act or state of moving to and fro.—rock'ing-chair n. chair mounted on rockers.—rock'ing-horse n. wooden horse mounted on rockers; hobby-horse.—off one's rocker (Slang) eccentric.

rocket (rok'-et) n. firework or projectile propelled into the air by combustion of inflammable material within it; (Slang) reprimand;—v.i. soar up; increase rapidly in price, etc.—rock'etry n. science of rocket propulsion.

rococo (rō-kō'-kō) n. style of architecture, overlaid with fantastic ornamentation.

rod (rod) n. slender, straight, round bar, stick, or switch; birch rod for punishment; cane; emblem of authority; fishing-rod; English linear measure, pole or perch; (U.S. Slang) gun.

rode (rōd) pa.t. of ride.

rodent (rō'-dent) a. gnawing;—n. gnawing animal, as rabbit, rat.

rodeo (rō-dā'-ō) n. round-up of cattle to be branded or marked; exhibition and contest in steer-wrestling and buck-jumping.

roe (rō) n. small deer of forests of N. Scotland; female hart.—roe'buck n. male of roe.

roe (rō) n. eggs or spawn of fish.

roentgen (runt'-gen) n. (Nuclear Physics) measuring unit of radiation dose. See also Röntgen.

rogue (rōg) n. vagrant; vagabond; rascal; plant which is substandard or varies from rest of crop;—v.t. and i. remove rogues from crop.—rog'uery n. tricks; cheating; fraud.—rog'uish a. dishonest; rascally.—rog'uishly adv. —rog'uishness n.—rogue'-el'ephant n. elephant of dangerous temper living apart from herd.—rogues' gallery, collection of photographs of convicted criminals kept by police.

roist, roister (roist, rois'-ter) v.i. bluster; bully; swagger.—rois'ter, rois'terer n.

rôle (rōl) n. part played by actor in drama, hence, conspicuous part or task.

roll (rōl) v.t. turn over and over; move by turning on axis; form into spherical body; bind by winding; level with roller; beat with rapid strokes; utter (vowels, letter r) with full, long-drawn sound;—v.i. move forward by turning; revolve upon axis; keep falling over and over; sway; reel; rock from side to side;— n. rolling; piece of paper, etc. rolled up; object thus shaped; bread baked into small oval or rounded shapes; official document; list; register; catalogue; continuous sound; full cork-screw revolution of aeroplane about its longitudinal fore and aft axis during flight.—roll'able a.—roll'-call n. calling over list of names.—rolled gold, plate of alloy with thin sheets of gold welded firmly to surface.—roll'er n. revolving cylinder of wood, stone, metal, etc.; vehicle or implement embodying heavy cylinder(s) for levelling ground; cylinder which distributes ink over type in printing; long, swelling wave; long, broad bandage.— roller'-skate n. skate with wheels or rollers instead of steel runner.—roll-film n. photographic film rolled on to spool.—roll'ing a.—roll'ing-mill n. ap-

paratus for rolling pieces of metal into rods, bars, sheets, plates, etc. --
roll'ing-pin n. cylindrical piece wood or glass for rolling out paste or dough. —**roll'ing-plant, roll'ing-stock** n. locomotives, carriages, wagons, etc. of railway.—**rolling stone** (*Fig.*) person incapable of settling down in one place.
rollicking (rol'-iking) a. jovial; carefree; high-spirited.
roly-poly (rō'-li-pō'-li) n. in baking, sheet of paste covered with filling and rolled.
Roman (rō'-man) a. pert. to Rome or Roman people; pert. to R.C. religion; in printing, upright letters as distinguished from *Italic* characters; expressed in letters, not in figures, as I, IV, i, iv, etc. (as distinguished from Arabic numerals, 1, 4, etc.);— n. native, citizen, resident of Rome. —**Roman'ic** a. pert. to Rome or its people; pert. to languages which sprang out of Latin;— **Romance languages,** languages of certain countries in southern Europe, developed from Latin and including Italian, Spanish, French, Provençal, Roumanian, Romansch, etc.;—a. pert. to these languages.—**ro'manise** v.t. convert to Roman Catholicism;—v.i. use Latin expressions; conform to R.C. opinions or practices.—**Ro'manism** n. tenets of Church of Rome.— **Ro'manist** n.—**Rom'ish** a. relating to Rome or to R.C. church.—**Rom'ist** n. Roman Catholic.—**Roman candle,** firework which throws out differently coloured stars.—**Roman Catholic,** member or adherent of section of Christian Church which acknowledges supremacy of Pope;—a. pert. to Church of Rome.—**Roman Catholicism,** doctrines and tenets of R.C. church.—**Roman holiday,** unpleasant event providing entertainment for some.
romance (rō-mans') n. narrative of knight-errantry in Middle Ages; ballad of adventures in love and war; historical novel; story depending mainly on love-interest; highly-coloured falsehood; (*Mus.*) composition sentimental and expressive in character;—v.i. write or tell romances; lie unblushingly.—**roman'cer, roman'eist** n.—**romanesque'** a. (*Paint.*) representing subjects and scenes appropriate to romance; resembling Roman architecture;—n. portrayal of fabulous or fanciful subjects; any form of architecture derived from Roman, as Byzantine, Lombard, etc. —**roman'tic** a. pert. to romance or romanticism; fanciful; sentimental; imaginative. — **roman'tically** adv. — **roman'ticism** n. reactionary movement in literature and art against formalism and classicism; state of being romantic.

Romany, (rom'-a-ni) n. gipsy; language of gipsies.
romp (romp) v.i. leap and frisk about in play; frolic;—n. tom-boy; boisterous form of play.—**romp'ers** n.pl. child's overall, with leg openings.
Röntgen rays (runt'-gen räz) n.pl. X-rays.—**rönt'gen** n. unit of dosage or quantity of radiation. —**rönt'genise** v.t. submit to action of X-rays.
rood (rōód) n. fourth part of acre; cross or crucifix, esp. one placed in church over entrance to choir.—**rood'-arch** n. arch between nave and chancel of church.—**rood'-loft** n. small gallery over rood-screen of church.—**rood'-work** n. open-work screen, separating choir form nave in Gothic churches.
roof (rōóf) n. outside structure covering building; framework supporting this covering; upper part of hollow structure or object, as of cave, mouth, etc.; ceiling;—v.t. cover with roof; shelter.—**mansard roof,** roof having break in slope, lower part being steeper than upper.
rook (rook) n. in chess, one of four pieces placed on corner squares of board; also known as castle.
rook (rook) n. bird of crow family; swindler; card-sharper;—v.t. cheat; swindle.—**rook'ery** n. colony of rooks and their nests; overcrowded, slum tenement.
room (rōóm) n. (enough) space; apartment or chamber; scope; opportunity; occasion;—pl. lodgings; — v.i. lodge. — **room'ful** a. — **room'ily** adv.—**room'iness** n. spaciousness.—**room'y** a. spacious; wide.
roost (rōóst) n. pole on which birds rest at night; perch;—v.i. to perch. —**roost'er** n. cock.
root (rōót) n. part of plant which grows down into soil; plant whose root is edible, as beetroot; part of anything which grows like root, as of tooth, etc.; source; origin; vital part; basis; bottom; word from which other words are derived; (*Math.*) factor of quantity;—v.t. plant and fix in earth; impress in mind; establish firmly;—v.i. enter earth, as roots; be firmly fixed or established. — **root'-crop** n. plant grown for value of roots, e.g. turnip.—**root'ed** a. firmly established. —**root and branch,** entirely; completely.
root (rōót) v.t. and i. turn up with snout, as swine; rummage.
rope (rōp) v.t. stout cord of several twisted strands of fibre or metal wire; row of objects strung together, as pearls, etc.;—v.t. fasten with rope; lasso.—**rope'-cord** n. ornamental cord used by upholsterers.— **rope'-dane'er** n. one who performs on rope raised above ground.—**rope'-ladd'er, rope'-bridge,** etc. n.—**ro'pery**

n. place where ropes are made.—**ro'piness** *n.* stringiness; stickiness.—**ro'ping** *a.*

rorqual (ror'-kwǎl) *n.* genus of whale.

rosary (rō'-zą-ri) *n.* string of beads on which prayers are counted.

rose (rōz) *n.* genus (*Rosa*) of plant family Rosaceae; flower of such plants; delicate shade of pink; rosette; perforated nozzle of tube, as on watering-can.—**ro'seal** *a.* resembling rose in colour or fragrance.—**ro'seate** *a.* rosy; of rose colour; blooming.—**rose'-bay** *n.* willow-herb with showy spikes of large pink or purple flowers.—**rose'bud** *n.* bud of rose.—**rose'coloured** *a.* having colour of rose; unwarrantably optimistic. Also **rose'hued**.—**ro'sery** *n.* nursery for rearing rose-bushes.—**rose'-wa'ter** *n.* water tinctured with roses by distillation.—**rose'-win'dow** *n.* circular window with series of mullions diverging from centre.—**rose'wood** *n.* dark-red hardwood from S. America.—**ros'ily** *adv.*—**ros'iness** *n.*—**ros'y** *a.* like rose; blooming; red; blushing; bright; favourable.

rosemary (rōz'-mą-ri, rōz'-mā-ri) *n.* small, fragrant evergreen shrub.

rosette (rō-zet') *n.* like rose, as bunch of ribbon; rose-shaped architectural ornament.—**roset'ted** *a.*

rosin (roz'-in) *n.* residue from distillation of turpentine;—*v.t.* rub or cover with rosin.—**ros'iny** *a.*

roster (ros'-tęr) *n.* list or plan showing turns of duty; register of names.

rostrum (ros'-trum) *n.*—*n.pl.* **ros'trums**, **ros'tra**, beak of bird; beak of ship; raised platform; pulpit.—**ros'tral** *a.* pert. to rostrum, beak, or snout.—**ros'trate**, **ros'trated** *a.* beaked.

rot (rot) *v.t.* and *v.i.* decompose naturally; corrupt; putrefy;—*pr.p* **rot'ting.**—*pa.t.* and *pa.p.* **rot'ted**.—*n.* rotting; decay; disease of sheep, as foot-rot; form of decay which attacks timber, usually **dry'-rot**; (*Slang*) nonsense.

rota (rō'-tą) *n.* wheel; course; roster, list, or roll; (*Mus.*) round; ecclesiastical tribunal in R.C. church.—**ro'tal** *a.*

rotary (rō'-tąr-i) *a.* turning, as wheel; rotatory;—*n.* type-cylinder printing-machine; international association of business men's clubs.—**Rota'rian** *n.* member of Rotary Club.

rotate (rō-tāt') *v.t.* cause to revolve;—*v.i.* move round pivot; go in rotation; revolve; spin.—**rota'tion** *n.* turning, as wheel or solid body on its axis; serial change, as *rotation of crops*.—**rota'tional** *a.*—**rota'tor** *n.*—**ro'tatory** *a.* turning on axis, as wheel; going in circle; following in succession.

rote (rōt) *n.* mechanical repetition of words.

rotor (rō'-tor) *n.* revolving portion of dynamo, motor, or turbine; revolving aerofoils of helicopter.

rotten (rot'-n) *a.* putrefied; decayed; corrupt; (*Slang*) bad; worthless.—**rott'enly** *adv.*—**rott'enness** *n.*—**rott'er** *n.* (*Slang*) worthless, unprincipled person.

rotund (rō-tund') *a.* round; circular; spherical; plump.—**rotun'da** *n.* circular building or apartment, covered by dome.—**rotun'dity**, **rotund'ness** *n.* globular form.

rouble, **ruble** (róó'-bl) *n.* Russian monetary unit; divided into 100 kopeks.

roué (róó'-ā) *n.* libertine; profligate.

rouge (róózh) *n.* red powder used by jewellers as polish-material; cosmetic for tinting lips or cheeks;—*v.t.* and *i.* tint with rouge.

rough (ruf) *a.* not smooth; rugged; uneven; unhewn; shapeless; uncut; unpolished; rude; harsh; stormy; approximate;—*adv.* in rough manner;—*n.* coarse fellow; crude, unfashioned state; parts of golf-course adjoining fairway;—*v.t.* make rough; roughen; rough-hew; shape out in rough and ready way.—**rou'ghage** *n.* fibrous portions of food which promote intestinal movement.—**rough'cast** *n.* method of finishing outside plaster-work by covering with mixture of lime and pebbles or gravel.—**rough diamond**, uncut diamond; person of ability, but uncouth.—**rough'en** *v.t.* make rough;—*v.i.* become rough.—**rough'-hew** *v.t.* hew coarsely; give first form to thing.—**rough'-house** *n.* rag; horse-play.—**rough'ly** *adv.*—**rough'-neck** *n.* in U.S. (*Colloq.*), ill-mannered fellow.—**rough'ness** *n.*—to rough it, to put up with hardship and discomfort.

roulette (róó-let') *n.* game of chance, played with revolving disc and ball.

round (round) *a.* circular; spherical; globular; whole; total; not fractional as a sum; large; plump; smooth; plain; fair; candid; decided, as assertion; (of vowel) pronounced with rounded lips;—*n.* circle; globe; circuit; cycle; series; carousal; toasts; certain amount (of applause); walk by guard to visit posts, sentries, etc.; beat of policeman, milkman, etc.; game (of golf); stage in knock-out competition, as cup-tie football; short bout between two boxers; step of ladder; ammunition unit; circular dance; short canonic vocal piece;—*adv.* on all sides; circularly; back to starting point; on every side of; about;—*v.t.* make circular or cylindrical; go round; smooth; polish;—*v.i.* grow or become full in form.—**round'about** *a.* indirect;

circuitous;—n. merry-go-round; obstacle at cross-roads to compel traffic to slow down.—**roun'del** n. kind of dance; small circular shield. —**roun'delay** n. round or country dance; air or tune with refrain.—**round'ers** n. outdoor game with ball and stick.—**Round'head** n. Puritan (so called from practice of cropping hair close).—**round'-houses** n. in merchant navy, cabin built on after part of quarter-deck; sentry-box or guard-room.—**round'ly** adv. vigorously; bluntly; openly. — **round'ness** n. —**round'-rob'in** n. petition, etc. having signatures arranged in circular form so as to give no clue to order of signing.—**round'-shot** n. cannon-ball.—**rounds'man** n. person who delivers goods on prescribed beat.—**round'-up**, n. collecting cattle into herds; throwing cordon round area by police or military;—v.t. collect and bring into confined space. —**to round off**, bring to grand con-clusion.—**to come round**, recover consciousness.

round (round) v.t. and v.i. whisper.—to round on, inform against; scold.

roup (roup) n. (Scot.) sale of goods by auction.

rouse (rouz) v.t. wake from sleep; excite to action; agitate; startle.—v.i. awake from sleep or repose.—**rous'er** n.—**rous'ing** a.—**rous'ingly** adv.

rout (rout) n. tumultuous crowd; rabble; defeat of army or confusion of troops in flight;—v.t. defeat and throw into confusion.

rout (rout) v.t. turn up with snout.

route (root) n. course or way which is travelled or to be followed;—v.t. direct along particular way. —**en route**, on way.

routine (roo-tēn') n. procedure adhered to by order or habit;—a. according to rule.

rove (rōv) v.t. wander or ramble over;—v.i. wander about; ramble.—**ro'ver** n. wanderer; robber or pirate; senior Boy Scout.—**rov'ing** n. and a.

row (rō) n. persons or things in straight line; rank; file; line.

row (rō) v.t. impel (boat) with oars; transport, by rowing;—n. spell of rowing; trip in rowing-boat.—**row'-boat, row'ing-boat** n. boat impelled solely by oars.—**row'er** n.—**row'lock** n. space cut just above gunwale to take weight and thrust of oars; two thole-pins for same purpose.

row (rou) n. noisy disturbance; dispute; brawl.—**row'dy** a. noisy and rough; — n. hooligan. — **row'dyism, row'diness** n.

rowan (rou-an) n. mountain-ash.

rowel (rou'-el) n. spiked wheel of spur.

royal (roi'-al) a. pert. to crown; worthy of king or queen; kingly;—n. standard size of paper; small sail

above top-gallant-sail; third shoot of stag's antlers.—**roy'alism** n. principles of government by king.—**roy'alist** n. adherent to sovereign, or one attached to kingly government.—**roy'ally** adv.—**roy'alty** n. kingship; kingly office; person of king or sovereign; members of royal family; royal prerogative; royal domain; payment to owner of land for right to work minerals, or to inventor for use of invention, or to author on sales of book.—**royal burgh**, (Scot.) town holding charter granted by sovereign.—**royal commission**, committee of experts appointed by the Crown to investigate matter of public interest or administration.

rub (rub) v.t. subject to friction; abrade; chafe; remove by friction; wipe; scour; touch slightly;—v.i. become frayed or worn with friction. —pr.p. rub'bing.—pa.t. and pa.p. rubbed.—n. rubbing; difficulty, drawback.—**rub'ber** n. one who or that which rubs; masseur or masseuse.—**rubb'ing** n. applying friction to surface; impression taken of coin, inscriptions on brass, etc. by covering with paper, etc. and rubbing lightly.—**to rub in**, emphasise by constant reiteration.

rubber (rub'-er) n. caoutchouc; gum elastic; india-rubber for erasing pencil marks; — pl. overshoes; galoshes;—a. made of rubber.—**rubb'erised** a. impregnated with rubber, as rubberised fabrics.—**rubb'er-neck** n. tourist eager to see every important sight.

rubber (rub'-er) n. series of three games at various card games; series of odd number of games or contests at various games.

rubbish (rub'-ish) n. waste matter; anything worthless; refuse; nonsense.—**rubb'ish-heap** n.—**rubb'ishy** a.

rubble (rub'-l) rough stones used to fill up spaces between walls, etc.

Rubicon (rōō-bi-kon) n. stream in Italy, between Roman Italy and Cisalpine Gaul.—**to cross the Rubicon**, take decisive, irrevocable step in adventurous undertaking, as Caesar did when, by crossing, he virtually declared war against the republic.

rubicund (rōō'-bi-kund) a. ruddy; florid; rosy; reddish.—**rubicun'dity** n.

rubric (rōō'-brik) n. medieval manuscript in which initial letter was illumined in red; heading or portion of such work, printed in red, hence, title of chapter, statute, etc. originally in red; matter definitely settled by authority;—v.t. illumine with or print in red; enact.—**ru'bricate** v.t. mark in red; formulate as rubric.—**rubrician** (rōō-brish-an) n. one versed in rubrics.—**ru'bricist** n. strict adherent to rubrics; formalist.

ruby (rōō'-bi) *n.* precious stone, transparent variety of corundum; purple-tinged red colour; carbuncle; —*a.* having dark-red colour of ruby.

ruche (rōōsh) *n.* pleated trimming for dresses.

ruck, ruckle (ruk, ruk'-l) *v.t.* wrinkle; crease;—*v.i.* be drawn into folds;—*n.* fold.

ruck (ruk) *n.* rank and file; common herd.

rucksack (rook'-sak) *n.* pack carried on back by climbers, etc.

ruction (ruk'-shun) *n.* disturbance; row.

rudd (rud) *n.* British fresh-water fish.

rudder (rud'-er) *n.* flat frame fastened vertically to stern of ship or aircraft, which controls direction; anything which guides, as bird's tail-feathers.

ruddy (rud'-i) *a.* of red colour; rosy. —**rudd'ier** *a.* redder. — **rudd'iest** *a.* reddest.—**rudd'ily** *adv.*—**rudd'iness** *n.*

rude (rōōd) *a.* roughly made; uncivil; rustic.—**rude'ly** *adv.*—**rude'ness** *n.*

rudiment (rōō'-di-ment) *n.* beginning; germ; vestige; (*Biol.*) imperfectly developed or formed organ; —*pl.* elements (of knowledge, etc.); elementary text-book.—**rudimen'tal, rudimen'tary** *a.*—**rudimen'tarily** *adv.*

rue (rōō) *v.t.* and *v.i.* lament; regret; repent of.—*n.* sorrow; remorse.—**rue'ful** *a.* woeful; mournful; sorrowful.—**rue'fully** *adv.*

rue (rōō) *n.* aromatic, bushy, ever-green shrub.

ruff (ruf) *n.* broad, circular collar, plaited or fluted; something puckered; bird, male ringed with ruff or frill of long, black, red-barred feathers; (*fem.*) reeve; breed of domestic pigeons.—**ruffed** *a.*

ruff (ruf) *n.* trumping at cards when one cannot follow suit;—*v.t.* trump.

ruffian (ruf'-i-an) *n.* rough, lawless fellow;—*a.* brutal.—**ruff'ianism** *n.*—**ruff'ianly** *adv.*

ruffle (ruf'-l) *v.t.* make into ruff; draw into wrinkles, plaits, or folds; furnish with ruffles; roughen surface of; crumple; disorder; annoy;—*v.i.* flutter; jar; grow rough;—*n* strip of plaited cloth, attached to garment; frill; agitation; commotion.

rug (rug) *n.* thick, woollen wrap; mat for floor.

rugby (rug'-bi) *n.* code of football, played with teams of 15 players in which ball is handled.

rugged (rug'-ed) *a.* rough; uneven; jagged; coarse; harsh; homely.—**rugg'edly** *adv.*—**rugg'edness** *n.*

rugose, rugous (rōō'-gōs, -gus) *a.* wrinkled; corrugated.—**ru'gosely** *adv.*—**rugos'ity** *n.*

ruin (rōō'-in) *n.* downfall; misery; remains of demolished or decayed city, fortress, castle, etc.; state of being decayed;—*v.t.* bring to ruin; injure; spoil; mar.—**ru'ins** *n.pl.* ruined buildings, etc.—**ruins'tion** *n.* overthrow; destruction; decay.—**ru'iner** *n.*—**ru'inous** *a.* fallen to ruin; decayed; injurious; destructive.—**ru'inously** *adv.*

rule (rōōl) *n.* act, power of directing; government; sway, control; authority; prescribed law; established principle; regulation; habitual practice; standard; test; instrument to draw straight lines; ruler; (*Print.*) thin strip of metal, used for printing lines;—*v.t.* govern; control; determine; mark with straight lines;—*v.i.* have command; order by rule; prevail.—**ru'ler** *n.* one who rules; governor; sovereign; instrument for drawing lines.—**ru'ling** *a.* governing; controlling; managing;—*n.* authoritative decision; point of law settled by court.

rum (rum) *n.* spirit distilled from fermented molasses.—**rum'-runn'er** *n.* bootlegger.

rum (rum) *a.* queer; odd; droll; strange.—**rumm'y** *a.* rum; queer.

rumble (rum'-bl) *v.i.* make low, vibrant, continuous sound; reverberate;—*v.t.* rattle; (*Slang*) detect; —*n.* dull, vibrant, confused noise, as of thunder; rumour.

ruminant (rōō'-mi-nant) *n.* animal which chews cud, as sheep, cow;—*a.* chewing cud.—**ru'minate** *v.t.* chew over again; ponder over;—*v.i.* chew cud; meditate.—**rumina'tingly** *adv.*—**rumina'tion** *n.*—**ru'minative** *a.*—**ru'minator** *n.*

rummage (rum'-āj) *v.t.* search into or through; ransack;—*v.i.* make search;—*n.* careful search; lumber.—**rumm'ager** *n.*

rummy (rum'-i) *n.* simple card game.

rumour (rōō'-mur) *n.* current report; common talk;—*v.t.* put round as rumour.

rump (rump) *n.* end of backbone of animal; buttocks; hinder part.

rumple (rum'-pl) *v.t.* make uneven; crease; crumple;—*n.* irregular fold or plait.

rumpus (rum'-pus) *n.* uproar.

run (run) *v.i.* move rapidly on legs; hurry; contend in race; stand as candidate for; travel or sail regularly; extend; retreat; flee; flow; melt; turn;—*v.t.* drive, push, or thrust; maintain regularly, as bus-service; operate; evade (blockade); smuggle; incur (risk).—*pr.p.* run'ning.—*pa.t.* ran.—*pa.p.* run.—*n.* flow; channel; regular, scheduled journey; pleasure trip by car, etc.; working session of machine; ground for feeding poultry, etc.; vogue; point gained in cricket etc.; great demand; period play holds the stage; (*Mus.*) rapid scale passage.

—run'about n. light motor-car, esp. for short distance work; gadabout. —run'away n. fugitive.—run'ner n. one taking part in race; messenger; bookmaker's assistant; long stem which runs along ground; one of curved pieces on which sleigh slides; formerly, detective officer; device for facilitating movement of sliding doors, etc.; narrow strip of carpet; smuggler.—run'ner-up n. one who gains second place.—run'ning a. flowing; entered for race, as horse; continuous (as order, account); discharging (pus); cursive; easy in style;—n. moving quickly; chance of winning.—run'ning-board n. narrow platform along locomotive, motor-car, etc. to provide step for entering or leaving.—running commentary, broadcast description of event by eye-witness.—running in, operating new machine with a light load.—running knot, knot made to tighten when rope is pulled.—run'way n. prepared track on airfields for landing and taking-off.—also ran, unsuccessful competitor.—in the long run, in the end; ultimately.—run of the mill, ordinary.—to run amok, go mad.—to run off, repeat from memory; cause to flow out; print further copies.—to run on, continue talking; dwell on.—to run out, come to an end; dismiss batsman out of his crease at cricket.—to run riot, give way to excess.—to run to earth, capture after long pursuit.

rune (rōōn) n. letter or character of old Teutonic and Scandinavian alphabets; magic symbol; mystery. —run'ic a.

rung (rung) pa.p. of ring.

rung (rung) n. stave of ladder; cross-bar.

runnel (run'-el) n. small brook or rivulet.

runt (runt) n. small, weak specimen of any animal; mean, contemptible person; stem of cabbage.

rupee (rōō-pē') n. Indian monetary unit.

rupture (rup'-tūr) n. breaking or bursting; state of being violently parted; breach between individuals or nations; hernia; breaking of bodily organ or structure;—v.t. part by violence; burst (as blood-vessel).

rural (rōō'-ral) a. pert. to country or farming; rustic.—ru'ralise v.t. make rural;—v.i. live in country; become rural.—ru'ralism n.—ru'rally adv.

ruse (rōōz) n. artifice; trick; stratagem; wile.

rush (rush) v.t. carry along violently and rapidly; take by sudden assault; hasten forward;—v.i. speed:—n. impetuous, forward movement; heavy current of water, air, etc.; eager demand; stampede of cattle.

—rush'er n. one who acts precipitately; slave-driver.

rush (rush) n. name of plants, found in marshy places; stem as material for baskets, etc.; straw.—rush'-bott'omed a. of chair with seat made of rushes.—rush'-can'dle, rush'-light n. primitive form of light made from peeled rush, dried and dipped in boiling fat or grease.—rush'en a. made of rushes.—rush'y a.

rusk (rusk) n. biscuit or light, hard bread.

Russian (ru'-zhan) a. pert. to Russia;—n. general name for Slav races in Russia; inhabitants of Russia; Russian language.—Russian wolf-hound, borzoi.

russet (rus'-et) a. of reddish-brown colour; homespun cloth dyed this colour; type of dessert apple.

rust (rust) n. film on metals caused by oxygenation; fungus disease of plants;—v.t. corrode with rust; impair by inactivity;—v.i. become rusty; dissipate one's powers by inaction.—rust'ily adv.—rust'iness n.—rust'y a. covered with rust; rust-coloured; impaired by neglect or disuse; out of practice.

rustic (rus'-tik) a. pert. to country; rural; awkward;—n.peasant.—rustically adv.—rus'ticate v.t. banish from college for time;—v.i. live in country.—rustica'tion n.—rustic'ity n. state of being rustic; rustic manners; simplicity.

rustle (rus'-l) v.i. make sounds, like rubbing of silk cloth or dry leaves;—v.t. steal, esp. cattle;—n. soft, whispering sound.—rus'tler n. hustler cattle-thief.—rus'tling n.

rut (rut) n. furrow made by wheel; settled way of living; groove;—v.t. form ruts (in)—pr.p. rut'ting.—pa.t. and pa.p. rut'ted.

rut (rut) n. time of sexual excitement among animals, esp. of deer;—v.i. be in heat.

ruth (rōōth) n. pity; compassion.—ruth'ful a.—ruth'fully adv.—ruth'less a. pitiless; cruel.—ruth'lessly adv.—ruth'lessness n.

rye (rī) n. kind of grass allied to wheat; in U.S., whisky made from rye.—rye'-grass n. grass-like plant as fodder for cattle.

S

Sabbath (sab'-ath) n. seventh day of week, day of rest; Sunday; Lord's Day.—Sabbata'rian n. member of certain sects who observe Saturday as Sabbath; strict observer of Sabbath.—Sabbata'rianism n.—Sabbat'ic, -al a. pert. to Sabbath; rest-bringing.—Sabbatical year, in Jewish ritual, every seventh, in which lands were left untilled, etc.; year interrupting one's normal course of work, wholly devoted to further study or one's special subject.

sable (sā'-bl) *n.* small carnivorous mammal of weasel tribe; sable fur; (*Her.*) tincture or colour black;—*pl.* mourning garments; — *a.* black; made of sable.

sabot (sab'-ō) *n.* wooden shoe worn by peasantry of France and Belgium.

sabotage (să'-bo-tàzh) *n.* wilful damage or destruction of property perpetrated for political or economic reasons.—sab'oteur *n.*

sabre (sā'-ber) *n.* sword with broad blade, curved toward point; cavalry sword;—*v.t.* wound with sabre.— sabreur' *n.* cavalry man.

sac (sak) *n.* pouch-like structure or receptacle in animal or plant; cyst-like cavity.

saccharin, saccharine (sak'-a-rin) *n.* white crystalline solid substance, with intensely sweet taste.—sac'charine *a.* pert. to sugar; over-sweet; sickly sentimental.—saccharin'ity *n.* —sac'charise *v.t.* to convert into sugar.—sac'charose *n.* cane-sugar.— sac'charous *a.* sugary.

sacerdotal (sas-er-dō'-tạl) *a.* pert. to priests, or to order of priests.— sacerdo'talism *n.* system of priesthood; priestcraft; exaltation of sacred character of priests.—sacerdo'talist *n.*—sacerdo'tally *adv.*

sachet (să'-shā) *n.* small container.

sack (sak) *n.* large bag; contents of sack; measure or weight; (*Colloq.*) dismissal from employment;—*v.t.* put into sacks; (*Colloq.*) dismiss.— sack'cloth *n.* coarse fabric used for making sacks; in Scripture, garment worn in mourning.—sack'ful *n.*— sack'ing *n.* coarse cloth or canvas.— sack'-race *n.* race in which legs of contestants are encased in sacks.

sack (sak) *n.* old name for various kinds of dry wines, esp. Spanish sherry.

sack (sak) *v.t.* plunder or pillage; lay waste;—*n.* pillage of town; devastation.—sack'age, sack'ing *n.*

sackbut (sak'-but) *n.* early form of trombone.

Sacrament (sak'-rạ-ment) *n.* ceremonial observance in Christian Church enjoined by Christ esp. the Eucharist; Lord's Supper; solemn oath; sacred obligation; materials used in sacrament.—sacramen'tal *n.* observance, ceremony, or act of nature of sacrament instituted by R.C. Church;—*a.* belonging to, or of nature of, sacrament.—sacramen'tally *adv.*—sacramenta'rian *n.* one who believes in sacraments to confer grace and salvation.—sacramenta'rianism *n.*—sacramen'tary *a.* pert. to

sacraments of Lord's Supper or to sacramentarians.

sacred (sā'-kred) *a.* holy; pert. to worship of God; religious; dedicated. — sa'credly *adv.*—sa'credness *n.*

sacrifice (sak'-ri-fis, or -fīz) *v.t.* consecrate ceremonially to deity; surrender for sake of obtaining some other advantage; to offer up;—*v.i.* make offerings to God on altar;—*n.* anything consecrated and offered to divinity; anything given up for sake of others.—sac'rificer *n.*—sacrifi'cial *a.* pert. to sacrifice.—sacrifi'cially *adv.*

sacrilege (sak'-ri-lej) *n.* profanation of sacred place or thing; church robbery.—sacrile'gious *a.* violating sacred things; desecrating.—sacrile'giously *adv.*—sacrile'giousness *n.*— sacrile'gist *n.*

sacrist (sā'-krist) *n.* sacristan; church official in charge of books and music scrolls.—sac'ristan *n.* officer in church having care of sacristy or vestry; sexton; minor canon.—sac'risty *n.* vestry.

sacrosanct (sak'-rō-sangkt) *a.* inviolable and sacred in highest degree.—sacrosanc'tity *n.*

sad (sad) *a.* sorrowful; affected with grief; sombre-coloured;—*v.t.* sadden. —sad'den *v.t.* make sad or sorrowful; —*v.i.* become downcast.—sad'ly *adv.* —sad'ness *n.*

saddle (sad'-l) *n.* rider's seat on horse, cycle, etc.; joint of mutton or venison; ridge of hill;—*v.t.* put saddle upon; burden with.—sadd'le-backed *a.* having low back, with elevated head and neck (of horse).— sadd'le-bag *n.* one of two bags united by strap and hanging on either side of horse.—sadd'le-bow *n.* arch in front of saddle.—sadd'le-cloth *n.* cloth placed upon saddle.—sadd'le-girth *n.* band passing under belly of horse to hold saddle in place.— sadd'ler *n.* one who makes saddles and harness for horses.—sadd'lery *n.* materials for making saddles and harness; occupation of saddler.— sadd'le-shaped *a.*

sadism (sā'-dizm, să'-dizm) *n.* infliction of pain for pleasure, esp. sexual. —sa'dist *n.* one who practises this; inhumane person.—sadis'tic *a.*

safari (sa-fá'-rē) *n.* hunting-expedition for big game.

safe (sāf) *a.* free from harm; unhurt; sound; protected; sure;—*n.* fireproof chest for money and valuables; case with wire-gauze panels to keep meat, etc. fresh.—safe'-con'duct *n.* passport to pass through dangerous zone.—safe'-depos'it *n.* strong-room where valuables are stored.—safe'-guard *n.* protection; precaution; escort;—*v.t.* make safe; protect.— safe'ly *adv.*—safe'ness *n.*—safe'ty *n.*— safe'-ty-catch *n.* contrivance to pre-

vent accidental discharge of gun.—
safety curtain, fire-resisting curtain
between stage and auditorium.—
safe'ty-lamp n. lamp with cylinder of
wire-gauze to minimise danger of
igniting *fire-damp* in mines.—
safe'ty-ra'zor n. one in which blade
fits into holder with guard.—
safe'ty-valve n. automatical valve to
relieve too high pressure in boiler;
outlet for pent-up emotion.

saffron (saf'-run) n. plant whose
stigmas yield yellow saffron used as
flavouring and colouring in cookery;
—a. deep yellow.

sag (sag) v.i. sink in middle; give
way; tire.—pr.p. **sagg'ing**.—pa.p.
sagged.—n. droop.

saga (sä'-gạ, sä'-gạ) n. collection of
ancient Scandinavian myths and
legends of Viking heroes; series of
novels describing life of family.

sagacious (sạ-gā'-shus) a. acute;
shrewd. — **saga'ciously** adv. — **saga'-
ciousness**, **sagac'ity** n. shrewdness;
wisdom.

sage (sāj) n. dwarf shrub of mint
family.—**sage'-green** a. grey mixed
with green.

sage (sāj) a. wise; discerning;—n. wise
man.—**sage'ly** adv.—**sage'ness** n.

sago (sā-,gō) n. dry, granulated
starch, prepared from pith of several
palms.

sahib (sá'-ib) n. courtesy title in
India for European or high-born
Indian.

said (sed) pa.t. and pa.p. of say;
before mentioned; already specified;
aforesaid.

sail (sāl) n. sheet of canvas to catch
wind for propelling ship; sailing
vessel; journey upon water; arm of
windmill;—v.t. navigate; pass in
ship; fly through;—v.i. travel by
water; begin voyage.—**sail'able** a.
navigable.—**sail'less** a.—**sail'or** n.
mariner; seaman.—**sail'plane** n. glider.—**sail'-yard** n. spar on which sails
are extended.—**full sail**, with all sails
set.—**under sail**, have sails spread.—
to sail close to the wind, sail with sails
of ship barely full; run great risks.—
to sail under false colours, act under
false pretences.

sainfoin (sān'-foin) n. perennial,
tough-rooted forage plant.

saint (sānt) n. outstandingly virtuous
person; one of blessed in heaven; one
canonised by R.C. Church; angel;—
v.t. canonise.—**saint'ed** a. pious;
hallowed; sacred.—**saint'hood** n.—
saint'like, **saint'ly** a. devout, godly;
pious.—**sa'int'liness** n.—**saint's day**,
day of celebration of particular
saint.—**All-Saints' Day**, 1st November.—**St. Andrew's Day**, 30th November.—**St. Anthony's fire**, erysipelas.
—**St. Bernard**, dog famous for
rescuing travellers lost in snow.—

St. David's Day, 1st March.—**St.
Elmo's fire**, electrical appearances
sometimes seen about masts of
ships, steeples, etc.—**St. George's
Day**, 23rd April.—**St. John's wort**,
bright-yellow blossoming plant.—
St. Leger, horse-race for three-year-
olds.—**St. Martin's summer**, warm,
damp weather at end of autumn.—
St. Patrick's Day, 17th March.—**St.
Swithin's Day**, 15th July.—**St. Valentine's Day**, 14th February.—**St. Vitus's
dance**, chorea. — **Latter-day Saints**,
Mormons.—**patron saint**, saint held to
be protector.

sake (sāk) n. behalf; purpose;
account; regard.—**for the sake of**, on
behalf of.

sake (sá'-kē) n. national beverage of
Japan, fermented from rice.

sal (sal) n. salt (much used in compound words pert. to chemistry and
pharmacy).—**sal'-ammo'niac** n. ammonium chloride.—**sal'-vola'tile** n.
ammonium carbonate.

salaam, **salam** (sạ-läm') n. salutation of respect in East;—v.t. greet.

salacious (sạ-lā'-shus) a. lustful;
lewd; lecherous.—**sala'ciously** adv.—
sala'ciousness, **salac'ity** n.

salad (sal'-ạd) n. green uncooked
vegetables or fruit dressed with salt,
vinegar, oil or spices.—**sal'ad-cream**
n. prepared dressing for salads.—
salad days, early years of youthful
inexperience.—**sal'ad-oil** n. olive-oil.

salamander (sal-a-man'-dẹr) n.
small amphibian, allied to newt
(medieval salamander was fabulous
creature believed to live and delight
in fire).—**salaman'driform**, **salaman'-
drine** a. pert. to or shaped like
salamander; fire-resisting.

salami (sa-lä'-mē) n. Italian salted
sausage.

salary (sal'-ạ-ri) n. fixed remuneration for services rendered, or non-
mechanical work.—**sal'aried** a.

sale (sāl) n. exchange of anything for
money; public exposition of goods;
auction; special disposal of stock at
reduced prices.—**sale'able**, **sal'able** a.
capable of being sold.—**sale'ableness**
n.—**sale'ably** adv.—**sale'-room** n. auc-
tion-room.—**sales'man** n. shop-assistant.—**sales'manship** n. art of selling
goods.—**sales'woman** n.—**sale of work**,
sale of articles contributed by
members of organisation to raise
funds.

salient (sā'-li-ẹnt) a. moving by
leaps; projecting outwards; springing; prominent, striking, noteworthy;—n. external angle formed
by intersection of adjacent surfaces;
projecting angle in line of fortifications, system of trenches.—**sa'liently**
adv. pertinently.

saline (sāl'-īn, sạ-līn') a. of or containing salt; salty;—n. fruit salt

used as aperient.—**salinif'erous** a. producing salt.—**salin'ity** n. salty quality; degree of saltness.

saliva (sa-lī'va) n. digestive fluid secreted in mouth by salivary glands.—**sali'val** a. pert. to saliva.—**sal'ivary** a. pert. to, producing, saliva.—**sal'ivate** v.t. produce secretion of saliva.—**saliva'tion** n.

sallow (sal'-ō) n. small tree, allied to willow.

sallow (sal'-ō) a. of pale-yellow colour; of pale complexion.—**sall'owish** a. somewhat sallow.—**sall'owness** n.

sally (sal'-i) n. sudden eruption; issuing of troops to attack besiegers; sortie; witticism;—v.i. issue suddenly;—pa.t. and pa.p. sall'ied.

salmon (sam'-un) n. silver-scaled fish with orange-pink flesh.—**salm'on-col'our** n. orange-pink.—**salm'on-fly** n. artificial fly for catching salmon with rod and line.—**salm'on-fry** n. salmon under two years old.—**salm'on-trout** n. sea- or white-trout, fish resembling salmon in colour but smaller.

salon (sa-lŏng') drawing-room; exhibition of pictures; intellectual or social gathering.

saloon (sa-lōōn') n. public reception-room; public dining-room; principal cabin in steamer.—**saloon'-bar** n. well-appointed section of public-house.

salsify, salsafy (sal'-si-fi, sal'-sa-fi) n. herb of chicory family, used in cookery.

salt (sawlt) n. sodium chloride or common salt, used for seasoning food and preservation of meat, etc.; compound resulting from reaction between acid and base; savour; piquancy; wit; old sailor;—pl. (Med.) saline cathartics, as Epsom, Rochelle, etc.;—a. containing or tasting of salt; pungent; (Colloq.) expensive;—v.t. season or sprinkle with salt.—**salt'ing** n. salt marsh.—**salt'less** a. without salt; tasteless; wersh.—**salt'-lick** n. salt for animals to lick.—**salt'-marsh** n. pasture land liable to be overflowed by sea.—**salt'ness** n. salt taste; state of being salt.—**salt'y** a. saltish.—salt of the earth, persons of highest reputation or worth.—to take with a grain of salt, be sceptical of.

saltant (sal'-tant) a. leaping; jumping.—**sal'tate** v.i.—**salta'tion** n.

saltire, saltier (sal-tīr) n. cross in the shape of an X, or St. Andrew's cross.

saltpetre (sawlt'-pē-ter) n. common name for nitre or potassium nitrate.

salubrious (sa-lū'-bri-us) a. wholesome; healthy.—**salu'briously** adv.—**salu'briousness** n.

saluki (sa-lōō'-ki) n. gazelle-hound, native to Persia and Arabia.

salutary (sal'-u-ta-ri) a. wholesome; resulting in good; healthful; promotive of public safety; beneficial.—**sal'utarily** adv.—**sal'utariness** n.

salute (sa-lūt') v.t. address with kind wishes; recognise superior by sign; honour by discharge of cannon, by striking colours, etc.; greet; kiss;—n. greeting showing respect.—**saluta'tion** n. words uttered in welcome.—**salu'tatory** a. welcoming.

salvation (sal-vā'-shun) n. preservation from destruction; redemption; safety.—Salvation Army, organisation for revival of religion among the masses.—**salva'tionist** n. member of Salvation Army.

salve (salv) v.t. save ship or property from danger or destruction.—**salvabil'ity** n.—**sal'vable** a. capable of being reconstructed in spite of damage.—**sal'vage** n. compensation to persons who assist in saving ship or cargo, or property from destruction; property so saved.

salve (salv, sáv) n. healing ointment applied to wounds or sores;—v.t. anoint with such; heal; soothe (conscience).

salver (sal'-ver) n. tray, generally of silver, for presenting refreshments, letters, etc.

salvo (sal'-vō) n. guns fired simultaneously, or in succession as salute; sustained applause or welcome from large crowd;—pl. sal'vo(e)s.

Samaritan (sa-mar'-i-tan) n. native or inhabitant of Samaria; kind-hearted, charitable person.

samba (sam'-ba) n. dance of Brazilian origin; music for such dance.

same (sām) a. identical; not different; unchanged; uniform.—**same'ly** adv.—**same'ness** n. near resemblance; uniformity.

samite (sam'-it) n. rich silk material.

samovar (sam'-o-vár) n. Russian tea-urn.

Samoyed (sam'-ō-yed) n. Ugrian race.—Sam'oyede n. breed of dog.

sampan (sam'-pan) n. Chinese light river-vessel. Also san'pan.

samphire (sam'-fīr) n. herb found on rocks and cliffs, St. Peter's wort; sea-fennel.

sample (sam'-pl) n. specimen; example;—v.t. try; test; taste.—**samp'ler** n. one who makes up samples; beginner's exercise in embroidery.

sanable (san'-a-bl) a. curable.—**sanabil'ity, san'ableness** n.—**san'ative** a. having power to cure or heal.—**san'ativeness** n.—**sanato'rium** n. (pl. **sanato'ria**) institution for treatment of tuberculosis; institution for convalescent patients.—**san'atory** a.

sanctify (sangk'-ti-fi) v.t. set apart as sacred or holy; hallow; consecrate;

—*pa.t.* and *pa.p.* sanc'tified.—sanct-anim'ity *n.* religious devotion.—sanctifica'tion *n.* sanctifying or making holy.—sanc'tified *a.* hallowed.—sanc'tifiedly *adv.*—sanctimo'nious *a.* hypocritically pious.—sanctimo'niously *adv.*—sanctimo'niousness, sanc'timony *n.* holiness; devoutness; (*Ironically*) affected piety.—sanc'tity *n.* quality of being sacred; state of being pure and devout; inviolability.

sanction (sangk'-shun) *n.* authorisation; approval; legal use of force to secure obedience to law;—*v.t.* and *v.i.* confirm; authorise.—sanc'tions *n.pl.* measures to enforce fulfilment of international treaty obligations.—sanc'tionary *a.* ratifying.

sanctuary (sangk'-tū-a-ri) *n.* holy place; shrine; eastern part of choir of church; refuge for fugitives.—sanc'tum *n.* sacred place; private room or study.—sanctum sanctorum, holy of holies in Jewish temple; private place.

sand (sand) *n.* fine grains of quartz or other mineral matter formed by disintegration of rocks;—*n.pl.* sandy beach; desert region;—*v.t.* sprinkle or cover with sand.—sand'-bag *n.* bag filled with sand or earth.—sand'-bank *n.* shoal of sand thrown up by sea or river estuary.—sand'-blast *n.* jet of sand driven by blast of air or steam, for finishing metal surfaces, etc.—sand'-dune *n.* ridge of loose sand.—sand'ed *a.* sprinkled with sand.—sand'-glass *n.* hour-glass.—sand'iness *n.* state of being sandy; sandy colour.—sand'-mar'tin *n.* small swallow.—sand'-paper *n.* paper or cloth coated with glue and then sprinkled over with sand, as abrading agent for smoothing wood, etc.—*v.t.* smooth with sandpaper.—sand'-piper *n.* wading bird of plover family.—sand'-pit *n.* place from which sand is dug out.—sand'-shoe *n.* shoe with canvas uppers and rubber soles.—sand'stone *n.* type of sedimentary rock.—sand'y *a.* like or covered with sand; not firm or stable; yellowish-brown.

sandal (san'-dal) *n.* shoe with flat sole, bound to foot by straps.—san'dalled *a.*

sandal-wood (san'-dal-wŏŏd) *n.* fragrant heartwood of santalum, used in East for trinket-boxes, incense and perfumery.

sanderling (san'-der-ling) *n.* wading-bird of plover family; ruddy plover.

sandwich (sand'-wich) *n.* two thin pieces of bread and butter, with thin slice of meat, etc., between them;—*v.t.* make into sandwich; form of alternating layers; insert or squeeze in between.—sand'wich-man *n.* man carrying two advertising boards, one slung before and one behind him.

sane (sān) *a.* of sound mind; reasonable.—sane'ly *adv.*—sane'ness *n.*

sang-froid (song-frwä') *n.* composure of mind.

sanguine (sang'-gwin) *a.* florid; warm; hopeful; bloodthirsty.—san'guinarily *adv.*—san'guinariness *n.*—san'guinary *a.* bloodthirsty; murderous.—san'guinely *adv.*—san'guineness *n.* fulness of blood; ardour; confidence. — sanguin'eous *a.* bloody; blood-red; containing blood.—sanguin'ity *n.* sanguineness; relationship by blood.—sanguiv'orous *a.* blood-feeding, as fleas, vampires, etc.

sanitary (san'-i-ta-ri) *a.* pert. to health; hygienic.—sanitar'ian *n.* one interested in hygienic reforms.—san'itarily *adv.*—sanita'tion *n.* measures taken to promote health; hygiene.—sanito'rium *n.* hospital for treatment of special or chronic diseases; health retreat.—sanitary towel, pad used during menstruation.

sanity (san'-i-ti) *n.* state of being sane.

sans (sanz) *prep.* (*Arch.*) without.

sanserif (san-ser'-if) *n.* type face without serifs at termination of lines, e.g. SANSERIF.

Santa Claus (san'-ta klawz) *n.* traditional *Father Christmas* of children.

sap (sap) *n.* watery juice of plants.—sap'less *a.*—sap'ling *n.* young tree; youth.—sap'piness *n.* juiciness.—sap'py *a.* juicy.—sap'-rot *n.* dry rot in timber.—sap'-wood *n.* alburnum, exterior part of wood of tree next to bark.

sap (sap) *n.* tunnel driven under enemy positions;—*v.t.* and *v.i.* undermine; impair insidiously; exhaust gradually;—*pr.p.* sap'ping.—*pa.t.* and *pa.p.* sapped.—sap'per *n.* member of Royal Engineers.

sapid (sap'-id) *a.* savoury; tasty.—sapid'ity *n.*—sap'idless *a.* tasteless.—sap'idness *n.*

sapient (sā'-pi-ent) *a.* wise; sage; shrewd.—sa'pience *n.*—sa'piently *adv.*

saponaceous (sap-o-nā'-shus) *a.* resembling soap; slippery.—sapon'ify *v.t.* to convert into soap.

sapor (sā'-por) *n.* taste; flavour.—saporif'ic *a.* producing taste.—sapor'os'ity *n.*

sapphire (saf'-ir) *n.* precious stone of various shades of blue;—*a.* deep, pure blue.

saraband, sarabande (sar'-a-band) *n.* slow, stately dance.

sarcasm (sar'-kazm) *n.* taunt; veiled sneer; irony.—sarcas'tic, -al *a.* bitterly satirical; taunting.—sarcas'tically *adv.*

sarcology (sar-kol'-o-ji) *n.* branch of anatomy which treats of soft parts of body.

sarcophagus (sar-kof'-a-gus) *n.* stone coffin; monumental chest or

vase of stone, erected over graves.—
pl. sarcoph'agi.

sard (sård) *n.* rare variety of cornelian.

sardine (sár-dēn') *n.* small fish of herring family, esp. pilchard.

sardonic (sár-don'-ik) *a.* bitter, scornful, derisive.—sardon'ically *adv.*

sardonyx (sár'-don-iks) *n.* semi-precious stone.

sari (sár'-ē) *n.* light cotton cloth with fancy-coloured border used as robe by Hindu women; long scarf of embroidered gauze or silk.

sark (sárk) *n.* shirt; chemise.—sar'king *n.* linen for shirt-making; thin boards to hold slates or tiles on roofs.

sarong (sa-rong') *n.* garment draped round waist by Malays.

sarsaparilla (sár-sa-pa-ril'-a) *n.* plant with roots yielding medicinal sarsaparilla, a mild diuretic.

sartorial (sár-tō'-ri-al) *a.* pert. to tailor.

sash (sash) *n.* silken band; belt or band, usually decorative, worn round body.

sash (sash) *n.* frame of window which carries panes of glass.

Sassenach (sas'-e-naH) *n.* lowlander; name given in Scotland to Englishman.

Satan (sā'-tan) *n.* devil.—satan'ic, -al *a.* devilish; infernal; diabolical.—satan'ically *adv.*

satchel (sach'-el) *n.* small bag for books.

sate (sāt) *v.t.* satisfy appetite of; glut.

sateen (sa-tēn') *n.* glossy cloth for linings, etc. Also satteen'.

satellite (sat'-el-līt) *n.* obsequious follower; (*Astron.*) secondary body which revolves round planets of solar system; moon.—earth satellite, object launched into space by man to orbit earth for scientific purposes.—satellite town, town built to absorb overspill from large city. satelli'tic *a.*

satiate (sā'-shi-āt) *v.t.* satisfy appetite of; surfeit; sate;—*a.* filled to satiety; glutted; surfeited.—satiabil'ity *n.*—sa'tiable *a.* capable of being satisfied.—satia'tion *n.*—satiety (sa-tī'-e-ti) *n.* state of being satiated; feeling of having had too much.

satin (sat'-in) *n.* silk fabric with smooth, lustrous surface;—*a.* made of satin;—*v.t.* give satin finish to.—sat'inet *n.* thin kind of satin; glossy cloth to imitate satin.—sat'in-wood *n.* hard yellow wood, valued in cabinet work for veneers.—sat'iny *a.*

satire (sat'-īr) *n.* literary composition holding up to ridicule vice or folly of times; use of irony, sarcasm, or wit.—satir'ic, -al *a.*—satir'ically *adv.*—satir'icalness *n.*—sat'irise *v.t.* make object of satire.—sat'irist *n.*

satisfy (sat'-is-fī) *v.t.* gratify fully; pay, fulfil, supply adequately; convince; content;—*v.i.* give content; supply to full; make payment;—*pa.t.* and *pa.p.* sat'isfied.—satisfac'tion *n.* complete enjoyment; contentment; recompense; payment.—satisfac'torily *adv.*—satisfac'toriness *n.*—satisfac'tory *a.* yielding content; agreeable.—sat'isfying *a.* affording satisfaction.—sat'isfyingly *adv.*

saturate (sat'-ū-rāt) *v.t.* soak thoroughly; steep; drench;—*a.* saturated.—satura'tion *n.* complete penetration; condition of being saturated; solution of body in solvent, until solvent can absorb no more.—satura'tor *n.* contrivance for saturating air of factory, etc. with water-vapour.

Saturday (sat'-ur-dā) *n.* seventh day of week.

Saturn (sat'-urn) *n.* father of Jupiter; sixth of major planets.—Saturna'lia *n.pl.* festival in ancient Rome in honour of Saturn; time of unrestrained license; orgy.—saturna'lian *a.*—Satur'nian *a.* pert. to epoch of Saturn; primitive; golden.—sa'turnine *a.* gloomy, sluggish.

satyr (sat'-er) *n.* (*Myth.*) lascivious forest god, half man and half goat; lecherous person.—satyri'asis *n.* excessive desire for sexual intercourse in men. Also satyroma'nia.—satyroma'niac *n.* a man with unrestrainable sexual desires.— satyr'ical *a.*

sauce (saws) *n.* liquid seasoning for food; condiment; relish; (*Colloq.*) impudence;—*v.i.* season with sauce; give interest to; be pert in speech or manner.—sauce'-boat, sauce'-tureen' *n.* dish with lip for serving sauce.—sauce'pan *n.* metal pot with lid and long handle.—sau'cy *a.* bold; pert.—sau'cily *adv.*—sau'ciness *n.*

saucer (saw'-ser) *n.* orig. curved plate put under cup to catch spilt liquid.

sauerkraut (sour'-krout) *n.* German dish of shredded white cabbage laid in layers, pressed in casks and allowed to ferment.

sault (sō) *n.* rapid in river, esp. in Canada.

saunter (sawn'-ter, sán'-ter) *v.i.* stroll; loiter; linger;—*n.* leisurely walk or stroll.—saun'terer *n.*—saun'tering *n.*—saun'teringly *adv.*

saurian (saw'-ri-an) *n.* lizard-like reptile;—*a.* resembling lizard. Also saur'oid *a.*

sausage (saw'-sāj) *n.* meat minced and seasoned and enclosed in thin membranous casing.—sau'sage-roll *n.* meat minced and seasoned in roll of flour paste and cooked.

savage (sav-āj') *a.* wild; uncivilised; primitive; cruel;—*n.* man in native state of primitiveness; barbarian;—

v.t. tear at and worry;—*v.i.* play savage.—**sav'agely** *adv.*—**sav'ageness, sav'agery** *n.* ferocity.

savanna, savannah (sa̤-van'-a̤) *n.* in tropical America grass-covered treeless plain.

savant (sav'-ong, sa'-vant) *n.* man of learning.

save (sāv) *v.t.* rescue from danger, evil, etc.; redeem; protect; secure; maintain (face, etc.); lay by; hoard; spare; except;—*v.i.* lay by money; economise; — *prep.* except; — *conj.* but.—**sav'able, save'able** *a.* retrievable.—**sa'ver** *n.*—**sa'ving** *a.* frugal; thrifty; delivering from sin; implying reservation;—*prep.* excepting; with apology to;—*n.* economy;—*pl.* earnings or gains put by for future.—**sa'vingly** *adv.*—**sa'vings-bank** *n.* bank for deposit of small savings.

saveloy (sav'-e-loi) *n.* highly-seasoned dried sausage, made of salted pork.

saviour (sāv'-yur) *n.* one who saves from destruction or danger; deliverer or redeemer; Jesus Christ.

savory (sā'-vor-i) *n.* aromatic potherb.

savour, savor (sā'-vur) *n.* taste; flavour; relish; quality or character;—*v.t.* like; taste or smell with pleasure; relish;—*v.i.* have particular smell or taste; resemble.—**sa'vourily** *adv.*—**sa'vouriness** *n.*—**sa'vourless** *a.*—**sa'voury** *a.* tasty;—*n.* tasty dish at beginning or end of dinner.

savoy (sa̤-voi') *n.* hardy winter variety of cabbage with wrinkled leaves.

savvy, savvey (sav'-i) *v.t.* (*Slang*) understand;—*n.* intelligence.

saw (saw) *n.* old saying; maxim; proverb.

saw (saw) *n.* hand or mechanical tool with serrated edge, used for cutting;—*v.t.* and *v.i.* cut with saw;—*pa.t.* sawed.—*pa.p.* sawed or sawn.—**saw'bones** *n.* (*Slang*) surgeon.—**saw'dust** *n.* small particles of wood, etc.—**saw'er** *n.* one who saws; sawyer.—**saw'fish** *n.* tropical ray-like fish with long flat serrated beak.—**saw'mill** *n.* place where logs are sawn by mechanical power.—**saw'yer** *n.* one who saws timber; beetle with sawlike mandibles.

Saxe (saks) *a.* pert. to Saxony; of light blue shade:—*n.* light-blue shade. Also **Saxony blue.**

saxhorn (saks'-horn) *n.* brass windinstrument.

saxifrage (sak'-si-frāj) *n.* popular name of various plants, mostly true rock plants.

Saxony (sak'-sun-i) *n.* very fine quality of wool.

saxophone (sak'-sō-fōn) *n.* brass wind-instrument, with single reed and conical bore.

say (sā) *v.t.* utter with speaking voice; state; express; repeat; recite; —*pa.t.* and *pa.p.* said (sed).—*n.* something said; what one has to say; share in decision.—**say'er** *n.* speaker.—**say'ing** *n.* verbal utterance; spoken or written expression of thought; proverbial expression; maxim.

say (sā) *n.* trial; assay; proof by trial.

say (sā) *n.* thin silk; kind of serge used for linings, aprons, etc.—**sayette'** *n.* light stuff, made of pure wool, adapted for linings, etc.

scab (skab) *n.* crust forming over wound or sore; skin disease, resembling mange, which attacks horses, cattle and sheep; potato-disease; disease of apple and pear; blackleg; despicable person;—*v.i.* heal over; form scab;—*pa.t.* and *pa.p.* scabbed.—*pr.p.* scab'bing.—**scab'bed** *a.* covered with scabs; paltry; vile.—**scab'bedness, scab'biness** *n.*—**scab'bily** *adv.* vilely.—**scab'by** *a.* scabbed.

scabbard (skab'-ard) *n.* sheath for sword, dagger, or bayonet.

scabies (skā'-bi-ēz) *n.* skin disease caused by burrowing mite; itch.

scabiosa (skā-bi-ō'-sa) *n.* Also **sca'bious,** annual and perennial plants of teasel family.

scabrid (skab'-rid) *a.* (*Bot.*) having rough, file-like surface.—**scab'rous** *a.* rough; (*Bot.*) having wart-like excrescences; harsh.

scad (skad) *n.* horse-mackerel.

scaffold (skaf'-old) *n.* temporary erection, of timber or metal, used in building, framework; platform, esp. for execution of criminal;—*v.t.* furnish with scaffold; prop up; sustain.—**scaff'olding** *n.*

scald (skawld) *v.t.* burn with moist heat or hot liquid; cleanse by rinsing with boiling water; heat milk to approaching boiling-point; —*n.* injury by scalding.

scale (skāl) *n.* pan of balance; balance itself; machine for weighing, chiefly in *pl.*; Libra, one of signs of zodiac;—*v.t.* weigh; measure.

scale (skāl) *n.* bony plate-like outgrowth from skin of certain mammals, reptiles, and fishes; thin layer or flake on surface;—*v.t.* deprive of scales;—*v.i.* come off or peel in thin layers.—**scaled** *a.* having scales.—**scale'less** *a.*—**scal'iness** *n.*—**scal'ing** *n.* removing of scales.—**scal'y** *a.* covered with scales; resembling scales.

scale (skāl) *n.* ladder; series of steps; ratio between dimensions as shown on map, etc. to actual distance, or length; scope; graduated dial on instrument; (*Mus.*) succession of notes arranged in order of pitch; gamut;—*v.t.* climb by ladder; clamber up; mount.

scalene (skạ-lĕn') a. uneven; (*Geom.*) having all three sides unequal;—n. scalene triangle.

scall (scawl) n. scabbiness; scurf; leprosy;—a. mean; paltry; low.—**scalled, scald** a. scabby.

scallion (skal'-yun) n. variety of shallot.

scallop, scollop (skal'-op, skol'-op) n. mollusc with ribbed, fan-shaped shell; fringed, ornamental curved edge;—v.t. cut edge of material into scallops.

scallywag (skal'-i-wag) n. scamp; worthless fellow; scapegrace. Also seal'awag, scall'awag.

scalp (skalp) n. hairy skin of head; skin and hair torn off dead by Indian warriors as token of victory;—v.t.deprive of scalp.

scalpel (skalp'-el) n. small, straight surgical knife with convex edge.

scamp (skamp) n. scoundrel; rascal; rogue;—v.t. execute work carelessly; skimp.

scamper (skam'-per) v.i. run about; run away in haste;—n. hasty flight.

scampi (skam'-pi) n.pl. crayfish, prawns.

scan (skan) v.t. examine closely; measure (verse) by its metrical feet; (*Radar*) traverse area with electronic beams;—v.i. be metrically correct;—pr.p. scan'ning.—pa.t. and pa.p. scanned.—**scan'ning** n. (*Television*) process of dissecting picture to be transmitted.—**scan'sion** n. act of scanning poetry.

scandal (skan'-dal) n. malicious gossip; disgrace; injury to person's character; — v.t. defame. — **scan'dal-bear'er, scan'dal-mong'er** n. one who delights in retailing malicious scandal and gossip.—**scan'dalise** v.t. shock popular morals; defame; disgrace.—**scan'dalous** a. giving offence; libellous; disgraceful.—**scan'dalously** adv.—**scan'dalousness** n.

scant (skant) a. inadequate;—v.t. put on short allowance;—adv. scarcely; not quite;—n. scarcity.—**scant'ily** adv. — scant'iness n. — **scant'ly** adv. sparingly.—**scant'ness** n. scantiness; insufficiency.—**scant'y** a.

scantle (skan'-tl) v.t. divide into small pieces.—**scant'let** n. fragment. —**scant'ling** n. little piece; measured portion; size of cross-section; narrow length of timber.

scape (skāp) n. escape; escapade; freak;—v.t. and i. escape from; avoid; shun.—**scape'goat** n. one who has to shoulder blame due to another. —**scape'grace** n. graceless, good-for-nothing fellow.

scaphoid (skaf'-oid) a. boat-shaped.

scapula (skap'-ū-lạ) n. shoulder-blade.—**scap'ular** a. pert. to scapula; —n. bandage for shoulder blade.

scar (skár) n. permanent mark left on skin after healing of wound, burn; blemish;—v.t. mark with scar;—v.t. heal with scar.

scar (skár) n. precipitous bank or cliff.

scarab (skar'-ạb) n. black-winged beetle; gem cut in shape of this beetle, as amulet.

scaramouch (skar'-ạ-mouch) n. buffoon in motley dress; personage in old Italian comedy.

scarce (skārs) a. not plentiful; wanting; rare; uncommon; scanty; —adv. hardly.—**scarce'ly** adv. with difficulty; hardly; only just.—**scarce'-ness, scarce'ity** n. lack; deficiency.

scare (skār) v.t. terrify suddenly; alarm; drive away by frightening;—n. sudden alarm; panic.—**scare'crow** n. figure set up to frighten away birds; miserable-looking person.—scare'-mong'er n. alarmist.

scarf (skárf) n. long, narrow, light article of dress worn loosely about neck; necktie; muffler.—pl. scarfs, scarves.

scarf (skárf) v.t. unite lengthways two pieces of timber.—n. joint for connecting timbers lengthways.

scarify (skar'-i-fi) v.t. scratch the skin; stir surface soil of; lacerate; criticise unmercifully.—pa.t. and pa.p. scar'ified.—scarifica'tion n.— scar'ifier n.

scarlatina (skárlạ-tē'-nạ) n. disease inducing rash and inflamed tonsils.

scarlet (skár'-let) n. bright red colour; cloth of scarlet colour;—a. of this colour;—v.t. redden;—v.i. blush. scar'let-fe'ver n. scarlatina.—**scar'let-hat** n. cardinal's hat.—**scarlet pimpernel**, small annual herb.—**scar'let-run'ner** n. bean plant with twining stem and scarlet flowers.

scarp (skárp) n. steep slope of ditch in fortifications;—v.t. make steep.— **scarped** a. steeply sloping.

scathe, scath (skāth) n. injury; damage;—v.t. injure; damage.— **scath(e)'less** a. unhurt; unharmed; undamaged.—**sca'thing** a. cutting; biting.—**sca'thingly** adv.

scatology (skat-ol'-o-ji) n. study of fossilised excrement of animals; obscene literature.—**scatolog'ical** a.

scatter (skat'-er) v.t. strew about; sprinkle around; put to rout; disperse;—v.i. take to flight; disperse. —**scatt'er-brain** n. giddy, thoughtless person.—**scatt'er-brained** a.—**scatt'ered** a. widely separated; distracted; wandering.—**scatt'erer** n.—**scatt'ering** n. effect of irregularly reflected light; (*Radio*) general re-radiation of wave-energy when ray meets obstacle in its path;—a. dispersing; sporadic.—**scatt'eringly** adv.

scavenger (skav'-en-jer) n. one employed in cleaning streets, etc.; animal which feeds on carrion;—v.t.

scavenge. — **scav'enge** v.t. cleanse streets, etc.

scenario (sen-à'-ri-ō') n. motion-picture script.—**scenar'ist** n.

scene (sēn) n. stage of theatre; place, time of action of novel, play, etc.; sub-division of play; spectacle, show, or view; episode; unseemly display of temper.—**scen'ery** n. stage-scenes; natural features of landscape.—**scene'-shift'er** n. one who manages scenery in theatrical representation.—**scen'ic** a. pert. to scenery, esp. of theatre; theatrical; picturesque.—**scenograph'ic**, -al a. drawn in perspective.—**scenograph'ically** adv.—**sceno'graphy** n.

scent (sent) v.t. track by sense of smell; perfume to; detect; become suspicious of;—v.i. smell;—n. odour; fragrance; aroma; paper trail in game of hare and hounds.—**scent'ed** a. perfumed.—**to put off the scent**, mislead wilfully.

sceptic, skeptic (skep'-tik) n. one who doubts esp. existence of God, or doctrines of Christianity; rationalist; agnostic; unbeliever;—a. sceptical.—**scep'sis, skep'sis** n. scepticism.—**scep'tical** a. doubting; disbelieving; incredulous.—**scep'tically** adv.—**scep'ticalness** n.—**scep'ticise** v.i. doubt everything.—**scep'ticism** n. doubt in absence of conclusive evidence; doubt of existence of supernatural or of god; agnosticism.

sceptre (sep'-ter) n. ornamental staff baton, as symbol of royal power; mace; royal dignity.—**scep'tred** a. invested with sceptre.

schedule (shed'-ūl, in U.S. sked'-) n. written or printed scroll of paper; smaller document forming part of principal document, deed, etc.; official list; inventory; time-table; v.t. note and enter in list.

schema (skē'-ma) n. plan; synopsis; scheme;—pl. **sche'mata**.—**schemat'ic** a.—**schemat'ically** adv.

scheme (skēm) n. plan; design; system; plot; draft; outline; tabulated statement;—v.t. plan; contrive; —v.i. intrigue; plot.—**sche'mer** n. intriguer.—**sche'ming** n. and a. planning; intriguing; plotting.—**sche'mist** n. schemer.

scherzo (sker'-tsō) n. (Mus.) composition of lively, playful character.

schipperke (ship'-, skip'-per-ki) n. smallish, alert, tailless dog.

schism (sizm) n. split of community into factions; division of church or religious denomination.—**schismat'ic** a.—n. one who separates from church; dissenter.—**schismat'ical** a. schismatic.—**schismat'ically** adv.

schist (shist) n. metamorphic rock which splits into thin irregular plates.—**schista'ceous** a. slate-coloured.—**schist'ic, schist'ous, schist'ose** a.

schizo- (skiz', skīz'-o) prefix fr. Greek, schizein, cleave, used in compound terms.—**schiz'oid** a. exhibiting slight symptoms of schizophrenia.—**schizophren'ia** n. hallucinatory mental disorder known as split personality—**schizophren'ic** a.

scholar (skol'-ar) n. schoolboy or schoolgirl; student; learner; disciple; learned person; holder of scholarship.—**schol'arly** a. learned.—**schol'arship** n. learning; grant; exhibition; bursary.—**scholas'tic** a. pert. to schools, scholars, or education; pedantic; very subtle and abstruse; formal;—n. Jesuit student who has not taken Holy Orders.—**scholas'tically** adv.

scholiast (skō'-li-ast) n. ancient commentator or annotator of classical texts.—**scholias'tic** a.—**scho'lium** n.—pl. **scho'lia**, marginal note.

school (skōōl) n. shoal (of fish, whales, etc.).

school (skōōl) n. institution giving instruction in any subject; academy; seminary; institute; group of writers, artists, thinkers, etc. with methods in common; branch of study; system; habit or practice;—v.t. educate; discipline; instruct; tutor.—**school'-boy** n. boy attending school.—**school'fellow, school'mate** n. contemporary at school.—**school'ing** n. instruction in school; education.—**school'mast'er** n. master in charge of school; male teacher in school.—**school'room** n. place for teaching in.—**school'teach'er** n. one certificated to teach.—**boarding school**, residential school.—**grammar school**, secondary school where emphasis is on teaching of academic subjects.—**preparatory school**, private school which prepares young boys for public schools in England.—**public school**, in England, endowed school whose headmaster is member of the Headmasters' Conference; in Scotland, state-aided school, elementary or primary.

schooner (skōō'-ner) n. sailing-vessel, having two masts, fore-and-aft rigged; extra large glass for holding beer; in N. America, long drink.

schottische (sho-tēsh') n. round dance resembling polka; music for this dance.—**Highland schottische**, lively dance to strathspey tunes.

sciatica (sī-at'-i-ka) n. neuralgia of sciatic nerve.—**sciat'ic, -al** a. pert. to, hip region.—**sciat'ically** adv.

science (sī'-ens) n. systematic knowledge of natural or physical phenomena; truth ascertained by observation, experiment, and induction; ordered arrangement of facts; theoretical knowledge as distinguished from practical; knowledge of principles and rules of invention, construction, mechanism, etc. as distinguished from art.—**scientif'ic**, **-al** *a.*—**scientif'ically** *adv.*—**sci'entism** *n.* outlook and practice of scientist.—**sci'entist** *n.* person versed in science, esp. natural science.—**Christian Science** religious doctrine of faith-healing.

scimitar (sim'-i-tər) *n.* short sabre with curved, sharp-edged blade.

scintilla (sin-til'-ə) *n.* spark; gleams; least particle; atom.—**scin'tillant** *a.* emitting sparks; sparkling.—**scin'tillate** *v.i.* emit sparks; sparkle; glisten.—**scintillating** *a.* (*Colloq.*) witty.—**scintilla'tion** *n.* glittering; escent flash from high-energy particle.

sciolism (sī'-ō-lizm) *n.* superficial knowledge used to impress others.

scion (sī'-on) *n.* slip for grafting; offshoot; young member of family; descendant; heir.

scissors (siz'-ərz) *n.pl.* instrument of two sharp-edged blades pivoted together for cutting; small shears.

scler-, **sclero-** (sklēr, sklē'-ro) *prefix* hard, used in compound terms, implying hardness or dryness.—**scle'ra** *n.* fibrous membrane forming outer coat of eyeball.—white of eye.—**scler'al** *a.* hard, bony.—**scleri'tis** *n.* inflammation of sclera of eye.—**scleroder'ma**, **scleroder'mia** *n.* chronic skin disease characterised by hardness.—**scleroder'matous** *a.* (*Zool.*) possessing hard, bony, external structure.—**scleroder'mic**, **scleroder'mous**, **sclerodermit'ic** *a.* pert. to scleroderma; having hard outer skin.—**scle'roid** *a.* of hard texture.—**sclero'ma** *n.* hardening of tissues.—**sclero'sal** *a.* pert. to sclerosis.—**sclero'sis** *n.* hardening of organ as result of excessive growth of connective tissue.—**sclerot'ic** *a.* hardened; pert. to sclera.—*n.* external hard coat of eye; sclera.—**scle'rous** *a.* hard; bony.

scoff (skof) *v.t.* mock at;—*v.i.* jeer;—*n.* expression of scorn; object of derision.—**scoff'er** *n.*—**scoff'ingly** *adv.*

scoff (skof) *v.t.* (*Slang*) eat greedily.

scold (skōld) *v.t.* and *v.i.* find fault (with); chide; rebuke;—*n.* nagging, brawling woman.—**scold'er** *n.*—**scold'ing** *n.* harsh rebuke.

sconce (skons) *n.* wall bracket for carrying light; lantern for candle; projecting screen, to provide cover; protection for head, hence head itself, wits; breastwork, bulwark;—*v.t.* defend with sconce.

scone (skon, skōn) *n.* (*Scot.*) thin, flat cake baked on griddle or in oven.

scoop (skōōp) *n.* article for ladling; kind of shovel; hollow piece of wood for baling boats; publication of exclusive news in newspaper;—*v.t.* ladle out, shovel, lift, dig or hollow out with scoop; publish exclusive news; gain, as in scoop the pool.

scope (skōp) *n.* range of activity; space for action; room; outlet; aim; length of cable when ship is at anchor.

scorbutic (skor-bū'-tik) *a.* affected with, or relating to, scurvy.

scorch (skorch) *v.t.* burn surface of; shrivel; char; singe; wither;—*v.i.* be burnt on surface; dry up; parch; drive at excessive speed.—**scorched-earth policy**, destroying everything of value in path of hostile army.—**scorch'er** *n.* anything which scorches; furious driver.—**scorch'ing** *a.* burning superficially; oppressively hot.—**scorch'ingly** *adv.*

score (skōr) *n.* cut notch, line, stroke; tally-mark, reckoning, bill, account; number twenty; number of points, runs, goals, etc. made in game; musical composition written out with the parts one above the other;—*v.t.* mark with lines, scratches; cut; orchestrate; record; make (points, etc.) in game; cross out;—*v.i.* add point, run, goal, etc. in game; achieve success.—**scor'er** *n.* one who keeps official record of points, runs, etc. made in game; one who makes point, run, etc. in game.—**scor'ing** *n.*—**score'-book**, **-card**, **-sheet**, **scor'ing-card** *n.* for recording points, etc.—**to score off**, gain advantage over.

scoria (skō'-ri-ə) *n.* dross or slag from smelting of metal ores mass of volcanic clinker.

scorn (skorn) *n.* disdain or contempt; object of derision;—*v.t.* despise; spurn.—**scorn'ful** *a.*—**scorn'fully** *adv.*

Scorpio (skor'-pi-ō) *n.* Scorpion, 8th sign of zodiac.—**scor'pion** *n.* arthropod having slender tail which ends in poisonous sting; whip armed with points like scorpion's tail.

scot (skot) *n.* formerly, tax, fine.—**scot'-free** *a.* unhurt; exempt from payment.

Scot (skot) *n.* native of Scotland.

Scotch (skoch) *a.* pert. to Scotland or its inhabitants; Scots (a form usually preferred in Scotland); Scottish;—*n.* Scots; Scots dialect; Scotch whisky.—**Scotch** (**Scottish**) **bluebell**, harebell.—**Scotch fir**, indigenous pine in Britain—also known as **Scotch pine**.—**Scotch kail**, broth.—**Scotch'man** *n.* Scotsman.—**Scotch mist**, very fine rain.—**Scotch terrier**, small short-legged, rough-coated dog.—**Scotch thistle**, national emblem of Scotland.

scotch (skoch) *v.t.* support, as wheel, by placing some object to prevent its rolling; kill project in initial stages;—*n.* prop. wedge, strut.

scotch (skoch) *v.* wound slightly; maim; hack; abrade;—*n.* scratch; notch; mark.

Scots (skotz) *n.* dialect of English spoken in Lowland Scotland;—*a.*

pert. to Scotland; Scottish.—**Scots'-man**, **Scots'woman** n. native of Scotland.—**Scots Greys**, oldest dragoon regiment in British army.—**Scots Guards**, one of five regiments forming Foot Guards of Household Troops.

Scot(t)ice (skot'-i-sē) adv. in Scots language, dialect, or manner.—**Scott'icism** n. idiom, expression, or word peculiar to Scots language or people.—**Scott'icise** v.t. make conform to Scots ways or speech.

Scottish (skot'-ish) a. pert. to Scotland or its people; Scots; Scotch.

scoundrel (skoun'-drel) n. rascal; villain; vagabond.—**scoun'drelism** n. rascality; baseness.—**scoun'drelly** a. villainous; rascally.

scour (skour) v.t. clean by hard rubbing; purge violently; flush out;—v.i. clean by rubbing; be purged to excess;—n. clearing action of swift, deep current or rush of water.—**scour'er** n.

scour (skour) v.t. search thoroughly; range over; rake;—v.i. rove over; scurry along.

scourge (skurj) n. whip made of leather thongs; lash; punishment; affliction; pest; one who inflicts pain;—v.t. flog; lash; chastise; devastate.

scout (skout) n. one sent out to reconnoitre; look-out; Boy Scout; reconnaissance aeroplane; college man-servant at Oxford;—v.t. reconnoitre; spy out.—**scout'master** n. adult instructor in Boy Scouts.

scout (skout) v.t. reject with contempt.

scow (skou) n. large flat-bottomed barge, with square ends; lighter for carrying deck-loads.

scowl (skoul) v.i. wrinkle brows in displeasure; frown sullenly; look sullen or annoyed;—n. angry frown.

scrabble (skrab'-l) v.t. scribble; scrawl;—v.i. scratch with hands.

scrag (skrag) n. anything thin, lean, gaunt; raw-boned person; long, thin neck; lean end of neck of mutton;—v.t. wring neck of.—**scrag'ged** a. rough and uneven; rugged.—**scrag'gedness**, **scrag'giness** n.—**scrag'gily** adv.—**scrag'gly** a. rough and unkempt-looking.—**scrag'gy** a. lean; jagged.

scram (skram) interj. (Slang) clear out!

scramble (skram'-bl) v.i. move by crawling, climbing, etc. on all fours; clamber; struggle with others for;—v.t. cook eggs by stirring when broken, in frying-pan;—n. scrambling; disorderly proceeding; cross-country motor-cycle race.—**scram'bling** a. climbing; struggling.

scrap (skrap) n. small piece or fragment; material left over;—pl. odds and ends;—v.t. throw out; discard;

—pa.t. and pa.p. **scrapped**.—pr.p. **scrap'ping**.—**scrap'-heap** n. rubbish heap.—**scrap'-met'al** n. fragments of metal collected for remelting.—**scrap'pily** adv.—**scrap'piness** n.—**scrap'py** a. consisting of odds and ends; fragmentary.

scrap (skrap) n. (Slang) fight.

scrape (skrāp) v.t. abrade; grate; scratch; remove by rubbing; clean or smooth thus;—v.i. produce grating noise by rubbing; live parsimoniously; scratch in earth, as fowls;—n. act or sound of scraping; scratch; predicament.—**scrap'er** n. miser; fiddler; metal bar for scraping mud off soles of shoes; tool with thin blade for scraping.

scratch (skrach) v.t. mark narrow surface wound with claws, nails, etc.; abrade skin; erase; scrape; withdraw name of entrant for race or competition;—v.i. use claws or nails in tearing, abrading; strike out name from list of competitors;—n. slight wound, mark, or sound made by sharp instrument; one who concedes start in distance, time, etc. to other competitors;—a. brought together in hurry, as scratch team; denoting competitor without handicap.—**scratch'er** n.—**scratch'y** a.

scrawl (skrawl) v.t. write or draw untidily; scribble;—v.i. write unskilfully and inelegantly;—n. careless writing; scribble.—**scrawl'er** n.

scrawny (skraw'-ni) a. lean; scraggy; rawboned; gaunt.—**scraw'niness** n.

scream (skrēm) v.t. and v.i. utter piercing cry; shriek; laugh immoderately;—n. shrill cry; uncontrollable fit of laughter; laughter-provoking incident.—**scream'ing** a.

scree (skrē) n. pile of débris at base of hill.

screech (skrēch) v.i. utter harsh, shrill cry; scream;—n. shrill and sudden, harsh cry.—**screech'-owl** n. owl with persistent harsh call.

screed (skrēd) n. long letter or passage; long boring speech; list of grievances, etc.

screen (skrēn) n. anything provided to shelter from heat, light, draught, or observation; partition cutting off part of ecclesiastical building from rest; coarse riddle for grading coal, etc.; surface on which image is projected; troops thrown out towards enemy to protect main body;—v.t. provide with shelter; protect from blame; conceal; riddle; film; project image on screen; subject person to political scrutiny.—**screen'ing** n. (Nuclear Physics) reduction in intensity of radiations on passing through matter.—**smoke'-screen** n. dense smoke to conceal movements.

screw (skrōō) n. in mechanics, machine consisting of inclined plane wound round cylinder; cylinder with spiral ridge running round it; turn of screw; twist to one side; skinflint; moral pressure; (*Slang*) wages;—*v.t.* fasten with screw; press or stretch with screw; twist round; treat harshly; obtain by pressure; extort;—*v.i.* assume spiral motion.—**screw'-driv'er** *n.* tool for turning screws.—**screw'-nail** *n.* small nail with flat, slotted head and fine thread.—**screw'-propell'er** *n.* revolving shaft carrying two or more fan-like blades or flanges to create forward thrust of ship.—**screw'y** *a.* tortuous, like thread or motion of screw; (*Slang*) crazy.

scribble (skrib'-l) *v.t.* and *i.* write carelessly; write worthless stuff; scrawl;—*n.* something scribbled.—**scribb'ler** *n.* bad or careless writer; writer of trifles; author.—**scribb'ling** *a.* used for scribbling;—*n.* careless writing.

scribble (skrib'-l) *v.t.* to card or tease wool.

scribe (skrib) *n.* writer; official writer; clerk; copyist; secretary; author; official copyist and expounder of Jewish law;—*v.t.* write off edge of board so as to fit another edge or surface;—*v.i.* write.—**seri'bal** *a.* pert. to scribe.—**seri'ber** *n.* sharp-pointed instrument to mark off metal work.

scrimmage (skrim'-āj) *n.* confused struggle; tussle for ball in football; scrum. Also **scrumm'age**.

scrimp (skrimp) *v.t.* make too small; stint;—*a.* scanty.—**scrimped** *a.* stinted.—**scrimp'ly** *adv.*—**scrimp'ness** *n.*—**scrimp'y** *a.*

scrimshanker (skrim'-shangk-er) (*Slang*) *n.* one who is work-shy.

scrip (skrip) *n.* small bag or wallet; satchel.

scrip (skrip) *n.* writing; interim certificate of holding bonds, stock, or shares.—**scrip issue** *n.* bonus share issue.

script (skript) *n.* type, used in printing and typewriting, to imitate handwriting; handwriting; producer's version of words of play, or of scenes and words of film; text of spoken part in broadcast.

scripture (skrip'-tūr) *n.* anything written; sacred writing; passage from Bible.—**the Scriptures**, Old and New Testaments.—**scrip'tural, scrip'ture** *a.* biblical.

scrivener (skriv'-ęn-ęr) *n.* one who draws up contracts or other documents; one who places money at interest on behalf of clients; public writer; notary.

scrofula (skrof'-ū-lạ) *n.* tuberculosis of lymphatic glands.—**scrof'ulous** *a.*

scroll (skrōl) *n.* roll of paper or parchment; writing formed into roll; list; flourish at end of signature; curved head of violin.—**scrolled** *a.* formed like, or contained in, scroll.

scrotum (skrō'-tum) *n.* external muscular sac which lodges testicles of male.—**scrot'al** *a.*

scrounge (skrounj) *v.t.* and *v.i.* (*Slang*) cadge. — **scroun'ger** *n.* — **scroun'ging** *n.*

scrub (skrub) *v.t.* clean with hard brush and water; scour; rub;—*v.i.* be penurious;—*pa.t.* and *pa.p.* **scrubbed** — *pr.p.* **scrub'bing**. — *n.* underwood; brushwood.—**scrub'ber** *n.* one who, or that which, scrubs.—**scrub'bing** *n.* and *a.*—**scrub'bing-board** *n.* corrugated board for scouring clothes.—**scrub'by** *a.* mean and small; stunted; covered with scrub; unshaved.—**scrub'-wood** *n.* small, stunted tree.

scruff (skruf) *n.* back of neck; nape.

scruffy (skruf'-i) *a.* scurfy; unkempt.

scrum (skrum) *n.* (*Abbrev.*) scrummage (in rugby football).—**scrum'-half** *n.* half-back in rugby.—**scrumm'age** *n.* scrimmage; in rugby, pushing mass of rival forwards waiting for ball to be inserted.

scrumptious (skrum'-shus) *a.*(*Slang*) delicious.

scruple (skrōō'-pl) *n.* small weight equal to 20 troy gr. apothecaries' weight or 1.296 grammes (symbol, ℈); very small quantity; feeling of doubt; conscientious objection;—*v.i.* hesitate from doubt; have compunction.—**scru'pulous** *a.* extremely conscientious; attentive to small points.—**scru'pulously** *adv.*—**scru'pulousness, scrupulos'ity** *n.*

scrutiny (skrōō'-ti-ni) *n.* close search; critical examination; searching look or gaze; official re-examination of votes cast at election.—**scruta'tor** *n.*—**scru'tinate, scru'tinise** *v.t.* examine into critically.—**scru'tiniser, scrutineer'** *n.* one who makes close examination.—**scru'tinisingly** *adv.*

scud (skud) *v.i.* move quickly; run before gale;—*v.t.* slap;—*pr.p.* **scud'ding**.—*pa.t.* and *pa.p.* **scud'ded**.—*n.* act of moving quickly; cloud drifting rapidly in strong wind.

scuff (skuff) *v.t.* graze against one in passing;—*v.i.* shuffle along without raising feet.

scuffle (skuf'-l) *v.i.* struggle at close quarters; fight confusedly;—*n.* confused fight, or struggle; rough and tumble.—**scuff'ler** *n.*

scull (skul) *n.* short light oar pulled with one hand; light racing boat;—*v.t.* propel boat by two sculls; propel boat by oar placed over stern and worked, in figure of eight.—**scull'er** *n.*

scullery (skul'-ęr-i) *n.* small room off kitchen where rough work is done.

scullion (skul'-yun) *n.* male underservant who did menial work; low, dirty fellow.

sculpture (skulp'-tūr) n. art of reproducing objects out of hard material by means of chisel; carved work; copper-engraving;—v.t. represent, by sculpture.—**sculp'tor** n. (fem. **sculp'tress**) one who carves or moulds figures.—**sculp'tural** a.

scum (skum) n. impurities which rise to surface of liquids; foam or froth, if of dirty appearance; vile person or thing; riff-raff;—v.t. take scum off; skim;—v.i. throw up scum.—pr.p. **scum'ming**—pa.t. and pa.p. **scummed**.—**scum'my** a. covered with scum.

scupper (skup'-ẹr) n. channel alongside bulwarks of ship to drain away water from deck through scupperholes;—v.t. throw into scupper; endanger; slaughter; sink.

scurf (skurf) n. dry scales on skin, esp. of head; dandruff.—**scurf'iness** n.—**scurf'y** a. covered with scurf.

scurrilous (skur'-i-lus) a. obscenely vulgar; foul-mouthed; indecent; abusive; vile.—**scurril'ity**, **scur'rilousness** n. vulgar language; vile abuse. —**scur'rilously** adv.

scurry (skur'-i) v.i. hurry along; run hastily.—pa.t. and pa.p. **scurr'ied**.— **scurr'y**, **scurr'ying** n.

scurvy (skur'-vi) n. (Med.) disease due to lack of vitamin C; scorbutus; —a. afflicted with disease; scurfy; mean; low.—**scur'vily** adv. meanly; vilely.—**scur'viness** n.

scut (skut) n. short tail, as of hare.

scutcheon (skuch'-un) n. shield for armorial bearings; name-plate; plate to which door-knob is fixed.

scutter (skut'-ẹr) v.i. run away hastily.

scuttle (skut'-l) n. wide-mouthed vessel for coal.

scuttle (skut'-l) n. hole with cover, for light and air, cut in ship's deck; hinged cover of glass to close porthole;—v.t. make hole in ship, esp. to sink it.—**scutt'ler** n. one who scuttles; one who wrecks project.

scuttle (skut'-l) v.i. rush away.

scythe (sīTH) n. mowing implement with long curved blade swung by bent handle held in both hands;— v.t. cut with scythe.

sea (sē) n. mass of salt water covering greater part of earth's surface; named broad tract of this; expanses of inland water, when salt; billow, or surge; swell of ocean; flood; large quantity.—**sea'-anem'one** n. beautifully coloured marine animal, found on rocks.—**sea'-board** n. coast-line and neighbourhood; seashore.—**sea'-borne** a. carried on sea or on sea-going vessel.—**sea'-coast** n. shore or border of land adjacent to sea.— **sea'-dog** n. seal; old, experienced

sailor.—**sea'farer** n. sailor.—**sea'faring** a.—**sea'-fenn'el** n. samphire.—**sea'-front** n. land adjoining sea; esplanade facing sea; part of building facing sea.—**sea'-girt** a. encircled by sea.— **sea'-go'ing** a. pert. to vessels which make long voyages by sea.—**sea'-gull** n. any gull.—**sea'-horse** n. small fish with horse-like head; hippopotamus; walrus.—**sea'-legs** n.pl. ability to walk on ship's deck in rough seas.— **sea'-level** n. level of sea at mean-tide. —**sea'-li'on** n. lion-headed type of seal.—**Sea Lord**, naval member of Board of Admiralty.—**sea'man** n. deck-hand on mercantile ship; rating in British Navy.—**sea'manlike**, **sea'manly** a.—**sea'manship** n. art of managing and navigating ship at sea.—**sea'-mew** n. seagull; any gull. —**sea'-mile** n. geometrical mile, distance varying with latitude, mean value being 6076.8 ft.—**sea'-pink** n. species of thrift which grows on sandy shores.—**sea'plane** n. aeroplane which can take off from and alight on sea.—**sea'port** n. town with harbour.—**sea'scape** n. picture representing maritime scene.—**Sea'-Scout** n. member of special branch of Boy Scouts who receive training in seamanship, etc.—**sea'-ser'pent** n. fabulous sea-monster.—**sea'shore** n. (Law) ground between ordinary high-water mark and low-water mark.— **sea'sickness** n. nausea and vomiting, produced by rolling and pitching of vessel at sea.—**sea'side** n. and a. land adjacent to sea.—**sea'-trout** n. salmon-trout.—**sea'-wall** n. embankment to prevent flooding.—**sea'ward** a. and adv. towards sea.—**sea'-wa'ter** n. salt-water.—**sea'-way** n. rate of progress of vessel under way; inland waterway for ocean-going ships.—**sea'weed** n. collective name for large group of marine plants (Algae).—**sea'worthy** a. fit for proceeding to sea.—**sea'worthiness** n.—**sea'wrack** n. sea-weed thrown up by sea.—**at sea**, away from land; bewildered.—**half-seas over**, half-drunk, tipsy.—**high seas**, open sea.

seal (sēl) n. aquatic animal with flippers as limbs.—**seal'er** n. ship, or person, engaged in seal-fishing.— **seal'ery** n. seal-fishing station.— **seal'skin** n. dressed skin of furred-seal; —a. made of seal-skin.

seal (sēl) n. piece of metal or stone engraved with device for impression on wax, lead, etc.; impression made by this (on letters, documents, etc.); that which closes or secures; symbol, token, or indication; arrangement for making drain-pipe joints air-tight;—v.t. affix seal to; confirm; ratify; settle, as doom; shut up; close up joints, cracks, etc. —**sealed** a. having seal affixed;

ratified.—**seal'ing-wax** n. wax composed of shellac and turpentine tinted with colouring matter.—**seal'-ring** n. signet ring.—**Great Seal**, official seal of United Kingdom, used to seal treaties, etc.—**Privy Seal**, official seal affixed to state documents of minor importance.

sealyham (sēl'-i-ęm) n. small rough-coated terrier with very short legs.

seam (sēm) n. line of junction of two edges, e.g. of two pieces of cloth, or of two planks; thin layer, esp. of coal;—v.t. join by sewing together; scar.—**seam'less** a. having no seams; woven in one piece.—**seam'ster** n. (fem. **seam'stress, semp'stress**) one who sews.—**seam'y** a. sordid.

seance (sā'-ǫns) n. session of public body; meeting of spiritualists.

sear (sēr) v.t. brand with hot iron; dry up; wither; cauterise; render callous;—a. dry; burned; hardened.

sear (sēr) n. catch in lock of firearm.

search (sęrch) v.t. examine in order to find; probe into;—v.i. look for; seek; explore;—n. quest; inquiry; investigation.—**search'er** n. one who searches; custom-house officer.—**search'ing** a. thorough; keen; trying; severe.—**search'ingly** adv.—**search'ingness** n.—**search'light** n. electric arclight which sends beam in any direction.—**search'-warr'ant** n. warrant to enable police to enter premises of suspected person.

season (sē'-zn) n. one of four divisions of year; busy holiday period; fashionable time of year for society; appropriate time; period; time; interval; (Colloq.) season-ticket;—v.t. habituate; give relish to; spice; mature;—v.i. grow fit for use; become adapted to climate; become accustomed to.—**sea'sonable** a. suitable for season; opportune; timely.—**sea'sonableness** n.—**sea'sonably** adv.—**sea'sonal** a. depending on, or varying with, seasons.—**sea'sonally** adv.—**sea'soning** n. flavouring.—**sea'-son-tick'et** n. one valid for season or period.—**close season**, time when something is not permitted.

seat (sēt) n. thing made or used for sitting on; manner of sitting (of riding, etc.); right to sit (e.g. in council, etc.); sitting part of body; part of trousers which covers buttocks; locality of disease, trouble, etc.; country-house; parliamentary constituency—v.t. place on seat; cause to sit down; assign seat to; fit up with seats; establish;—v.i. rest; lie down.—**seat'ed** a. fixed; settled.—**seat'ing** n. fitting up with seats.

sebaceous (s-bā'-ę-shus) a. made of, or pert. to, tallow or fat; secreting oily matter.

secant (sē'-kąnt, sek'-ąnt) a. cutting; incising; dividing into two parts;—n. straight line which cuts another line, curve, or figure; straight line drawn from centre of circle through one end of arc, and terminated by tangent drawn through other end.

secateurs (sek-a-tęrz') n.pl. small hand pruning shears.

secede (sę-sēd') v.i. withdraw formally from federation, etc.—**sece'der** n. one who secedes.—**seces'sion** n. seceding from fellowship, alliance, etc.; withdrawal; departure.

seclude (sę-klood') v.t. shut up apart; guard from or remove from sight.—**seclud'ed** a. living apart; retired; remote.—**seclud'edly** adv.—**seclu'sion** n.—**seclu'sive** a. retiring.

second (sek'-und) a. next to first; other; another; inferior; subordinate;—n. one who, or that which, follows first; one next and inferior; one assisting, esp. principal in duel or boxing-match; sixtieth part of minute; moment;—n.pl. coarse kind of flour; inferior quality, brand, etc. of commodity or article;—v.t. support, esp. motion before meeting or council; encourage. — **second'** v.t. 'lend' official of one department to another for special duties.—**second'ed** a. so transferred.—**second childhood**, dotage.—**sec'ond-class** a. of inferior order; mediocre.—**sec'ond-cous'in** n. child of first cousin.—**sec'onder** n. one who supports another.—**sec'ond-hand** a. not new; used or worn; indirect.—**sec'ond-lieuten'ant** n. lowest commissioned rank in British Army.—**sec'ondly** adv. in second place.—**second'ment** n. temporary transfer of official to another department.—**second nature**, acquired habit.—**sec'ond-rate** a. of inferior quality, value, etc.—**sec'ond-sight** n. prophetic vision.—**to play second fiddle**, play or act subordinate part.

secondary (sek'-un-dąr-i) a. succeeding next in order to first; of second place, origin, rank; second-rate; inferior; unimportant; pert. to education and schools intermediate between elementary schools and university.—**secondary colour**, colour obtained by combination of two primary colours—**sec'ondarily** adv. in subordinate manner; not primarily.—**sec'ondariness** n.

secret (sē'-kret) a. meant to be kept from general knowledge; concealed; unseen; private;—n. something concealed; mystery;—**se'crecy** n. keeping or being kept secret; retirement; privacy; concealment.—**se'cretly** adv.—**se'cretness** n. secrecy.—**se'cretive** a. uncommunicative; underhand.—**se'cretively** adv.—**se'cretiveness** n.

secretary (sek'-re-tą-ri) n. one employed to deal with papers and correspondence, keep records, etc.;

confidential clerk; minister in charge of particular department of government; escritoire.—**secreta'rial** a. pert. to duties of secretary.—**secreta'riat, secreta'riate** n. administrative office or officials controlled by secretary.—**Secretary of State**, cabinet minister in charge of certain important government departments; in U.S., equivalent of Foreign Secretary.—**sec'retaryship** n. office or post of secretary.

secrete (se-krēt') v.t. hide; conceal;—a. separate; distinct.—**secre'ta** n.pl. products of secretion.—**secre'tion** n. substance made by gland out of blood or body-fluids; process of so secreting.—**secre'tional** a.—**secre'tive** a. promoting or causing secretion.—**secre'tor** n. secreting organ or gland.—**secre'tory** a. secretion-forming.

sect (sekt) n. body of persons with some special doctrines; religious denomination; party; faction; scion.—**secta'rian** a. pert. to sect; narrow-minded; bigoted. Also **secta'rial**.—n. one of sect; bigot; partisan.—**secta'rianism** n. bigoted devotion to sect.—**sec'tary** n. one of sect.

section (sek'-shun) n. cutting or separating by cutting; part separated from rest; division; portion; piece; sub-division of subject matter of book, chapter, statute; signature; representation of portion of building or object to show its construction and interior; (*Geom.*) plane figure formed by cutting solid by another plane; line formed by intersection of two surfaces; smallest military unit, four sections forming platoon; (*Bot.* and *Zool.*) thin slice of matter mounted on slide for microscopic examination.—**sec'tional** a. pert. to, made up of sections; partial; local.

sector (sek'-tur) n. portion of circle enclosed by two radii; mathematical measuring instrument; (*Mil.*) definite length of trench or front line.—**sec'toral** a.

secular (sek'-ū-lạr) a. worldly; temporal, as opposed to spiritual; lay; civil; profane;—n. layman; clergyman, not bound by vow of poverty and not belonging to religious order.—**secularisa'tion** n.—**sec'ularise** v.t. convert from spiritual to secular use; make worldly.—**sec'ularism** n. doctrine which advocates moral code independent of religious considerations.—**sec'-ularist** n.—**secular'ity** n. worldliness; indifference towards religion.—**sec'ularly** adv.

secure (se-kūr') a. free from care, anxiety, fear; safe; fixed;—v.t. make safe, certain, fast; close, confine effectually; obtain; insure; assure.—**secur'able** a.—**secur'ance** n. assurance; confirmation.—**secure'ly** adv.—**secure'ness** n. free from anxiety.—**secur'er** n.—**secur'ity** n. being secure; what

secures; protection; assurance; anything given as bond or pledge; measures against espionage.—**secur'ities** n.pl. general term for shares, bonds, etc. bought and sold on Stock Exchange.—**security risk** n. person considered politically unsuitable for state employment.

sedan (se-dan') n. (*Hist.*) closed conveyance with chair inside for one, carried on two poles; sedan-chair.

sedate (se-dāt') a. staid; not excitable; calm.—**sedate'ly** adv.—**sedate'ness** n. calmness; composure; primness.—**seda'tion** n. use of sedatives for calming; state of being so calmed.—**sed'ative** a. tending to calm; soothing;—n. agent which soothes.

sedentary (sed'-en-tạ-ri) a. sitting much; inactive.—**sed'entariness** n.

sedge (sej) n. rush-like plant growing in swampy grounds; marsh-grass.—**sedge'-war'bler** n. reed-warbler.—**sedg'y** a.

sediment (sed'-i-mẹnt) n. matter which settles to bottom of liquid; dregs.—**sedimen'tary** a. composed of sediment, esp. of rock as deposits by water action.—**sedimenta'tion** n.

sedition (se-dish'-un) n. act aimed at disturbing peace of realm; insurrection.—**sedi'tionary** n. one who incites sedition.—**sedi'tious** a. pert. to, tending to excite sedition.—**sedi'tiously** adv.—**sedi'tiousness** n.

seduce (se'dūs') v.t. lead astray; induce person to surrender chastity.—**seduce'ment** n. seduction.—**sedu'cer** n.—**sedu'cible** a. corruptible.—**seduc'tion** n. act of seducing.—**seduc'tive** a.—**seduc'tively** adv.—**seduc'tiveness** n.

sedulous (sed'-ū-lus) a. diligent; steady; persevering.—**sedu'lity** n.—**sed'ulousness** n.—**sed'ulously** adv.

see (sē) n. diocese or jurisdiction of bishop; province of archbishop.—**the Holy See**, papal court.

see (sē) v.t. perceive by eye; behold; observe; note; mark; understand; visit; meet with;—v.i. have power of sight; consider; give heed; understand; apprehend.—p.a.t. saw.—pa.p. seen.—**se'er** n. one who sees; one who foresees events, has second-sight; prophet.—**see'ing** conj. considering; since;—n. act of perceiving; sight.

seed (sēd) n. embryo, fertilised ovule, which gives origin to new plant; one grain of this; such grains saved for sowing; that from which anything springs; origin; source; progeny; offspring; children; descendants; generation; first principle;—v.t. sow with seed; remove seeds from; arrange draw for sports tournament, so that best players, etc. should not be drawn against each other in earlier rounds;—v.i. produce seed.—**seed'ed** a. sown; matured.—**seed'ily**

adv. in seedy manner.—**seed'iness** *n.* being seedy or off colour; shabbiness. —**seed'less** *a.*—**seed'ling** *n.* young plant.—**seeds'man** *n.* one who deals in seeds.—**seed'y** *a.* abounding with seeds; run to seed; exhausted; worn out; miserable looking.—**to run to seed**, go to waste or ruin.

seek (sēk) *v.t.* make search for; look for; ask for; strive after;—*v.i.* make search.—*pa.t.* and *pa.p.* **sought**.— **seek'er** *n.*

seem (sēm) *v.i.* appear (to be or to do); look; pretend;—*v.t.* suit.— **seem'ing** *a.* appearing like; apparent; plausible;—*n.* appearance; judgment.—**seem'ingly** *adv.*—**seem'liness** *n.*—**seem'ly** *a.* fit; becoming;—*adv.* in decent or proper manner.

seep (sēp) *v.i.* ooze; trickle; drip; drain slowly.—**seep'age** *n.*

seer (sēr) *n.* one who foresees events; prophet.—**seer'ship** *n.*

seesaw (sē'-saw) *n.* game in which two children sit at opposite ends of plank supported in middle and swing up and down; to-and-fro motion;—*a.* moving up or down;— *v.i.* move upward and downward.

seethe (sēTH) *v.t.* boil, cook, or soak in hot water;—*v.i.* be violently agitated;—*pa.t.* **seethed** or **sod**.—*pa.p.* **seethed** or **sodd'en**.

segment (seg'-ment) *n.* part cut off from figure by line; part of circle contained between chord and arc of that circle; section; portion; part;— *v.t.* and *v.i.* separate into segments. —**segmen'tal** *a.* relating to segment. —**seg'mentary**, **seg'mentate** *a.* having form of segment.—**segmenta'tion** *n.*— **segment'ed** *a.*

segregate (seg'-re-gāt) *v.t.* and *v.i.* set or go apart from rest; isolate; separate;—*a.* set apart; separate from others.—**segrega'tion** *n.*—**segrega'tionist** *n.* one who believes in racial separation.

seigneur (sān'-yer) *n.* feudal lord of manor; title; respectful address.— **seign'iorage**, **seign'orage** *n.* anything claimed by sovereign or feudal superior as prerogative.—**seignioral'ty** *n.* authority of seigneur.—**seignio'rial**, **seigneu'rial**, **signo'rial** *a.* manorial.— **seign'iory**, **seign'ory** *n.* lordship or feudal domain; manorial rights.

seine (sān, sēn) *n.* seine-net, open bag-net for sea-fishing;—*v.t.* catch fish with this.

seism (sīsm) *n.* earthquake.—**seis'mal**, **seis'mic** *a.* pert. to or produced by earthquake.—**seis'mogram** *n.* record of earthquake made by seismograph.—**seis'mograph** *n.* instrument which records distance and intensity of earth tremors.—**seismolog'io**, **-al** *a.* —**seismol'ogist** *n.* one versed in seismology.—**seismol'ogy** *n.* study of earthquakes.

seize (sēz) *v.t.* grasp; take hold of; arrest; capture; comprehend;—*v.i.* of bearing parts or piston of machine, to stick tightly through excessively high temperature.—**seiz'able** *a.*—**seiz'ure** *n.* act of seizing; thing or property seized; apoplectic stroke.

select (sē-lekt') *v.t.* choose; elect; prefer;—*a.* of choice quality; chosen; exclusive;—*n.* best people.—**selec'ted** *a.*—**selec'tedly** *adv.*—**selec'tion** *n.* selecting; things selected; variety of articles for sale; book containing select pieces; (*Mus.*) medley of airs. —**selec'tive** *a.* discriminating.—**selec'tively** *adv.*—**selectiv'ity** *n.* (*Radio*) ability to discriminate between signals of differing frequencies.—**selec'tor** *n.* one who, or device which, selects.

self (self) *n.* one's individual person; one's personal interest; ego; selfishness.—*pl.* **selves** (selvz);—*a.* of colour, uniform, same throughout; same;— *prefix* used in compounds.—**self'abandon'ment** *n.* disregard of self.— **self'-abnega'tion** *n.* self-denial.—**self'assur'ance** *n.* self-confidence.—**self'cen'tred** *a.* egoistic.—**self'-con'fidence** *n.* reliance on one's own powers.— **self'-con'fident** *a.*—**self'-con'sciousness** *n.* embarrassed state of mind due to belief that one is object of critical judgment.—**self'-con'scious** *a.*—**self'contained'** *a.* of reserved nature; complete in itself; (of house) having separate entrance, detached.—**self'defence'** *n.* act of defending one's person or justifying one's actions.— **self'-deni'al** *n.* unselfishness, to point of deprivation.—**self'-determina'tion** *n.* free-will; right of people to work out its own destiny, free from interference from without.—**self'-gov'erning** *a.* autonomous.—**self'-gov'ernment** *n.*—**self'-indul'gence** *n.* undue gratification of one's desires.—**self'-in'terest** *n.* selfishness.—**sel'fish** *a.* lacking consideration for others; mercenary; greedy.—**self'ishly** *adv.*—**self'ishness** *n.* —**self'less** *a.* unselfish.—**self'-pit'y** *n.* morbid pleasure in nursing one's woes.—**self'-possessed'** *a.* calm and collected; composed; undisturbed.— **self'-preserva'tion** *n.* instinctive impulse to avoid injury or death.— **self'-reli'ant** *a.* not relying on others. —**self'-reli'ance** *n.*—**self'-respect'** *n.* proper regard for one's own reputation. — **self'-respect'ing** *a.* — **self'respect'ful** *a.*—**self'-right'eous** *a.* thinking oneself faultless; priggish; hypocritical; sanctimonious.—**self'-sac'rifice** *n.* foregoing personal advantage for sake of others.—**self'same** *a.* identical.—**self'-satisfac'tion** *n.* personal reassurance; (in bad sense) smug conceit.—**self'-sat'isfied** *a.*—**self'-seek'er** *n.* one who seeks only his own profit or pleasure.—**self'-seek'ing** *a.*—

self-service a. said of stores where customers help themselves to goods.—**self'-start'er** n. automatic contrivance used for starting internal-combustion engine.—**self'-styled** a. so-called; self-assumed; would-be. —**self'-suffi'cient** a. sufficient in itself; relying on one's ownpowers.—**self'-supporting** a. not dependent on others for living.

sell (sel) v.t. dispose of for equivalent, usually money; deal in; betray for money; delude; have for sale; promote sale of;—v.i. fetch price; be in demand;—pa.t. and pa.p. **sold**.—n. deception; hoax.—**sell'er** n. vendor.

selvage, selvedge (sel'-vāj) n. edge of cloth finished to prevent ravelling out.

semantic (se-man'-tik) a. pert. to meaning of words.—**seman'tics** n.pl. branch of linguistic research concerned with studying changes in meaning of words.

semaphore (sem'-ạ-fōr) n. post with movable arm or arms used for signalling; system of signalling by human or mechanical arms.

semblable (sem'-blạ-bl) a. similar; resembling;—n. likeness.—**sem'blance** n. real or seeming likeness; appearance; image; form; figure.

semen (sē'-men) n. secretion formed by male reproductive organs, containing fertilising spermatozoa.

semester (se-mes'-tẹr) n. half-year session in universities.

semi- (sem'-i) prefix, half, partly, imperfectly, etc., used in construction of compound terms.—**sem'i-an'nual** a. half-yearly.—**sem'i-an'nular** a. forming semicircle.—**sem'ibreve** n. (Mus.) half length of breve and equivalent to two minims or four crotchets (symbol ⌑).—**sem'icircle** n. half circle.—**sem'icircled, semicir'cular** a.—**sem'icolon** n. punctuation mark (;) used to separate clauses of sentence requiring more marked separation than indicated by comma.—**sem'i-detached'** a. (of house) joined by party-wall with another house.—**sem'i-fi'nal** n. match, round, etc. qualifying winner to contest final.—**semi'quaver** n. (Mus.) one half of a quaver.—**sem'itone** n. (Mus.) half a tone.

seminal (sem'-i-nạl) a. pert. to seed of plants or semen of animals; radical; reproductive.—**sem'inate** v.t. sow; propagate; disseminate.—**semina'tion** n. act of sowing; seeding.—**seminif'erous** a. seed-bearing.

seminar (sem'-in-ar) n. group of advanced students pursuing research in subject.

seminary (sem'-in-ạr-i) n. place of education; academy; school or college; training college for R.C. priesthood; breeding-ground or nursery;—a. trained in seminary.—**sem'inarist** n. R.C. priest educated in foreign seminary.

Semite (sem'-īt, sē'-mīt) n. one of group of races, speaking allied languages; includes Jews, Arabs and Syrians.—**Semit'ic** a. pert. to Semites.

semolina (sem-ō-lē'-nạ) n. hard grains of wheat after milling;—used in production of spaghetti, macaroni, etc. Also **sem'ola**.

sempiternal (sem-pi-tẹr'-nạl) a. everlasting.—**sempiter'nity** n. duration without end.

senate (sen'-at) n. supreme legislative assembly in ancient Rome; Upper House, in legislature, e.g. U.S and some British Dominions; governing body in many universities.—**sen'ator** n. member of senate.—**senato'rial** a.—**sen'atorship** n.—**sena'tus** n. governing body in certain universities.

send (send) v.t. cause to go; transmit; forward; despatch; depute; cast; confer;—v.i. despatch messenger; transmit message;—pa.t. and pa.p. **sent**.—**to send down**, expel from college or university; rusticate.

senescence (se-nes'-ẹns) n. state of growing old; old age.—**senes'cent** a. growing old.

senile (sē'-nīl) a. pert. to old age; aged; doting.—**senil'ity** n. degenerative physical conditions accompanying old age; old age.

senior (sē'-nyur, sē'-ni-ẹr) a. older; superior in rank or standing; prior; —n. person older, of higher rank, of longer service, than another; aged person.—**senior'ity** n. state of being older; priority; superiority.—**senior service**, navy.

senna (sen'-a) n. purgative drug from dried pods of shrubs and herbs of genus Cassia.

sennet (sen'-et) n. (Arch.) flourish of trumpets.

sennight (sen'-īt) n. (Arch.) week.

señor (se-nyōr') n. Spanish form of address; sir; gentleman; equivalent to Mr.;—**seno'ra** n. lady; madam; Mrs.—**senori'ta** n. Miss.

sensation (sen-sā'-shun) n. what we learn through senses; excited feeling or state of excitement; exciting event.—**sen'sate, sen'sated** a. perceived by senses.—**sensa'tional** a. pert. to perception by senses; producing great excitement.—**sensa'tionalist** n.—**sensa'tionally** adv.

sense (sens) n. any of bodily faculties of perception or feeling; sensitiveness of any of these faculties; mental alertness; consciousness; significance; meaning; coherence; good judgment; prudence;—pl. wits; faculties;—v.t. perceive; suspect; understand.—**sense'less** a. insensible; unfeeling; foolish; absurd.—**sense'lessly** adv.—**sense'lessness** n.

sensible (sen'-si-bl) *a.* capable of being perceived by senses; characterised by good sense; perceptible; aware; conscious; reasonable; wise; sensitive.—**sensibil'ity** *n.* power of experiencing sensation; capacity of feeling.—**sen'sibly** *adv.*

sensitise (sen'-si-tīz) *v.t.* render sensitive; in photography, render film, paper, etc. sensitive to action of light.

sensitive (sen'-si-tiv) *a.* acutely affected by impressions; receptive to stimuli; responsive to slight changes; reacting to light rays; easily upset by criticism;—*n.* one who is sensitive.—**sen'sitively** *adv.* —**sen'sitiveness** *n.*—**sensitiv'ity** *n.* sensitiveness; keen sensibility.

sensory (sen'sory) *a.* pert. to senses; conveying sensations, as nerve-fibres.

sensual (sen'-sū-ąl) *a.* self-indulgent; carnal; voluptuous; lewd.—**sensualisa'tion** *n.*—**sen'sualise** *v.t.* make or render sensual; debase by gratifying carnal appetites.—**sen'sualism** *n.* fleshly indulgence; luxurious living. —**sen'sualist** *n.* one given to loose mode of life; voluptuary.—**sensualist'ic** *a.*—**sensual'ity** *n.* lewdness; debauchery.—**sen'sually** *adv.*—**sen'suous** *a.* apprehended by senses.— **sen'suously** *adv.*—**se''suousness** *n.*

sentence (sen'-tęns) *n.* combination of words, expressing thought; opinion; maxim; judgment passed on criminal by judge; decision;—*v.t.* condemn.—**senten'tious** *a.* abounding with maxims; short and energetic; pithy; pompously moralising.— **senten'tiously** *adv.*—**senten'tiousness** *n.*

sentient (sen'-shi-ęnt) *a.* capable of feeling; perceiving by senses; sensitive.—**sen'tiency** *n.* consciousness at sensory level.—**sen'tiently** *adv.*

sentiment (sen'-ti-męnt) *n.* abstract emotion; tendency to be moved by feeling rather than by reason; saying; idea; opinion.—**sentimen'tal** *a.* romantic; emotional; foolishly tender.—**sentimen'talism, sentimental'ity** *n.* superficiality of feeling.— **sentimen'talist** *n.* one given to sentimental talk; one swayed by emotions. —**sentimen'tally** *adv.*

sentinel (sen'-ti-nęl) *n.* guard; sentry; —*a.* acting as sentinel; watching.

sentry (sen'-tri) *n.* soldier on guard; sentinel.—**sen'try-box** *n.* small shelter used by sentry.—**sen'try-go** *n.* sentry duty.

sepal (sep'-ąl, sē'-pąl) *n.* (*Bot.*) leaf-like member of outer covering, or calyx, of flower.

separate (sep'-ą-rāt) *v.t.* part in any manner; divide; disconnect; detach; sever; put apart;—*v.i.* part; withdraw; become disunited;—*a.* divided; apart; 'ndividual.—**separabil'ity**

n.—**sep'arable** *a.*—**sep'arableness** *n.*—**sep'arably** *adv.*—**sep'arately** *adv.*—**sep'arateness** *n.*—**separa'tion** *n.* act of separating; state of being separate. —**sep'aratism** *n.* act or policy of separating or withdrawing from any union; secession.—**sep'aratist** *n.* one who secedes from church or political union; seceder; home-ruler.

sepia (sē'-pi-a) *n.* brown pigment obtained from cuttlefish; the colour.

sepoy (sē'-poi) *n.* (*Hist.*) native of India employed as soldier in British service.

sepsis (sep'-sis) *n.* (*Med.*) tissue infected by bacteria; putrefaction. —**sep'tic** *a.* pert. to sepsis; caused by blood-poisoning or putrefaction; infected; putrefying. Also **sep'tical**. —**septicae'mia, septicē'mia, septae'-mia** *n.* invasion of blood and tissues by bacteria; blood-poisoning.—**sep'tically** *adv.*—**septicae'mic septicē'mic** *a.*

sept (sept) *n.* clan, race, or family from common progenitor.

September (sep-tem'-bęr) *n.* ninth month of year.

septenary (sep'-tę-na-ri) *a.* consisting of seven; lasting seven years; occurring once in seven years.— **septen'nial** *a.* continuing seven years; occurring once in every seven years. —**septen'nium** *n.* a period of seven years.

septet, septette (sep-tet') *n.* (*Mus.*) composition for seven voices or instruments.

septic *a.* See **sepsis**.

septuagenarian (sep-tū-aj-e-nā'-ri-ąn) *n.* person between seventy and eighty years of age.—**septuag'enary** *a.* consisting of seventy; seventy years old;—*n.* septuagenarian.

Septuagesima (sep-tū-ą-jes'-i-ma) *n.* third Sunday before Lent, seventy days before Easter.—**septuages'imal** *a.* pert. to seventy.

septuple (sep'-tū-pl) *a.* sevenfold.

sepulchre (sep'-ul-kęr) *n.* tomb; grave; burial vault.—**sepul'chral** *a.* pert. to burial, etc.; funereal; mournful.—**sep'ulture** *n.* act of burying dead.

sequel (sē'-kwęl) *n.* consequence; issue; end; continuation, complete in itself, of novel or narrative previously published.

sequence (sē'-kwęns) *n.* connected series; succession; run of three or more cards of same suit in numerical order; part of scenario of film.— **se'quent** *a.* following; succeeding;— *n.* sequence.—**sequen'tial** *a.* in succession.—**sequen'tially** *adv.*

sequester (se-kwes'-tęr) *v.t.* put aside; separate; seclude; withdraw from society; (*Law*) put into hands of trustee; sequestrate;—*v.i.*—**se-ques'tered** *a.* withdrawn from public; secluded.—**seques'trable** *a.* liable to

sequestration.—sequestra'tion n. retirement; act of entrusting to neutral party.

sequin (sē'-kwin) n. ornamental metal disc on dresses, etc.; formerly Venetian gold coin.

seraglio (se-ral'-yō) n. harem or women's quarters.

seraph (ser'-af) n. angel of highest order;—pl. **ser'aphs, ser'aphim**—**seraph'ic** a.—**seraph'ically** adv.

Serb, Serbian (sĕrb, sĕr'-bi-an) a. pert. to Serbia;—n. native of Serbia, chief state of Yugoslavia.

sere (sēr) a. dry; withered.

serenade (ser-e-nād') n. music of quiet, melodious character sung or played at night below person's window, esp. by lover;—v.t. entertain with serenade.—**serena'der** n.

serendipity (ser-en-dip'-i-ti) n. knack of stumbling upon interesting finds unexpectedly.

serene (se-rēn') a. clear and calm; unclouded; bright; quiet; composed; sedate;—n. clearness; calmness.—**serene'ly** adv.—**serene'ness, seren'ity** n.

serf (sĕrf) n. under feudalism, labourer attached to estate; bondman; vassal; drudge.—**serf'age, serf'dom, serf'hood** n.

serge (sĕrj) n. hard-wearing worsted fabric.

sergeant, serjeant (sár'-jent) n. non-commissioned officer in army, ranking above corporal; police officer ranking between inspector and constable; in law, name (often *Serjeant*) given, until 1875, to certain English barristers.—**Ser'geant-at-arms** n. officer attendant on Speaker of House of Commons, charged with preservation of order.—**ser'geant-ma'-jor** n. highest non-commissioned officer.

serial (sē'-ri-al) a. consisting of series; appearing in successive parts or instalments; (*Mus.*) based on note rows in place of scales;—n. periodical publication; tale or other writing published in successive numbers of periodical.—**se'rialise** v.t. publish as serial.—**se'rially** adv. in regular series or order.—**se'riatim** adv. point by point; one after another; in regular order.

series (sē'-rēz, sē'-ri-ēz) n.sing. and pl. succession of related objects or matters; sequence; order; books, bound and printed in same style; (*Elect.*) end-to-end arrangement of batteries or circuits traversed by same current.

serif (ser'-if) n. (*Printing*) fine line at end of stems and arms of unconnected Roman type letters, as M, K, l, y, etc. Also **ser'iph**.

serious (sē'-ri-us) a. grave in manner or disposition; earnest; important; attended with danger; in earnest.—

se'riously adv. solemnly; gravely; dangerously.—**se'riousness** n.

sermon (ser'-mun) n. discourse of religious instruction, spoken from pulpit; serious address;—v.t. tutor; lecture; harangue.—**ser'monise** v.i. preach earnestly; compose sermon; dogmatise.—**sermoni'ser** n.

serous (sē'-rus) a. pert. to serum; watery.—**seros'ity** n. state of being serous; serous fluid.

serpent (ser'-pent) n. snake; reptile without feet; treacherous person; kind of firework; (*Mus.*) ancient bass wind instrument;—v.i. curl or wind round; encircle;—a. deceitful.—**ser'pentine** a. relating to, or like, serpent; winding; crafty; treacherous;—n. green magnesian mineral, with spotted appearance;—v.i. wind in and out like serpent.—**ser'pentinely** adv.

serrate, serrated (ser'-āt, -ed) a. notched like saw.—**serra'tion** n. formation in shape of saw.—**ser'rature** n. series of notches.

serried (ser'-id) a. in close order.

serum (sē'-rum) n. watery secretion; whey; thin straw-coloured fluid, residue of plasma; such fluid, used for inoculation or vaccination.

servant (ser'-vant) n. personal or domestic attendant; one who serves or obeys orders; menial; helper.—**civil servant**, government employee.

serve (sĕrv) v.t. work for; be servant to; wait on; attend; help; distribute, as rations, etc.; promote; advance; forward; satisfy;—v.i. work under another; carry out duties; be useful, suitable, or enough; in tennis, resume play by striking ball diagonally across court;—n. in tennis, act of serving ball.—**serv'able** a.—**ser'ver** n. one who serves; salver or small tray.

service (ser'-vis) n. state of being servant; work done for another; act of kindness; department of State employ; employment of persons engaged in this; military, naval, or air-force duty; use; form of divine worship; regular supply, as water, bus, rail, etc.; (*Law*) serving of process or summons; turn for serving ball at tennis, fives, etc.; set of dishes, etc.;—v.t. perform service for, e.g. motor-cars, etc.; also **ser'ving**.—**ser'viceable** a. useful; helpful; in fair working order.—**serviceabil'ity, ser'viceableness** n. usefulness.—**ser'viceably** adv.—**service dress**, ordinary uniform.—**active service**, military service against enemy.—**din'ner-, ta'ble-, tea-ser'vice**, complete set of appropriate dishes.—**senior service**, Royal Navy.—**the Services**, Army, Navy, and Royal Air Force.

service (ser'-vis) n. small fruit-tree resembling mountain ash.

serviette (ser-vi-et') *n.* table-napkin.

servile (ser'-vil) *a.* pert. to servant; mean; fawning; menial.—**ser'vilely** *adv.*—**servil'ity** *n.* slavery; bondage; slavishness.

servitor (ser'-vi-tor) *n.* male attendant.—**ser'vitude** *n.* state of subjection to master; slavery; bondage.

sesame (ses'-a-me) *n.* annual plant cultivated in India and Asia Minor for seeds yielding oil.

sesqui- (ses'-kwi) *prefix* denoting proportion 3 : 2.—**sesqui'teral, sesquial'terate, sesquial'terous** *a.* one and half more.—**sesquicenten'nial** *a.* pert. to century and half;—*n.* 150th anniversary. — **sesquipeda'lian** *a.* measuring a foot and half long; applied humorously to any long technical word or to one given to using unnecessarily long words.

session (sesh'-un) *n.* sitting of court, council, etc. for transaction of business; term during which court, council meet for business; school term; period between meeting and prorogation of parliament; meeting. —**ses'sional** *a.* pert. to session(s).—**Court of Session,** Supreme Civil Court of Scotland.

set (set) *v.t.* cause to sit; seat; place; plant; make ready; put up; adjust; arrange (of hair) while wet; (of razor, etc.) give fine edge; reduce from dislocated or fractured state, as limb; adapt, as words to music; compose type-matter; let; place brooding fowl on eggs; crouch or point, as dog, to game;—*v.i.* go down; strike root; become fixed or rigid; congeal; begin;—*pr.p.* set'ting. —*pa.t.* and *pa.p.* set.—**to set at naught,** defy.—**to set back,** impede.— **to set on foot,** start (some project, plan, etc.).—**to set out,** start on journey; begin; mark out.—**to set sail,** begin voyage.—**to set to,** apply oneself vigorously.

set (set) *n.* number of things or persons associated as being similar or complementary or used together, etc.; manner in which thing is set, hangs, or fits, as dress; attitude or posture; young plant, or slip for planting out; tendency, drift; group or clique; setting of sun; organised equipment to form ensemble of scene for stage representation; apparatus for reception (or transmission) of radio or TV signals and broadcasts; (*Tennis*) series of games forming unit for match-scoring purposes; wooden or granite block or sett;—*a.* fixed; firm; regular; arranged; formal; determined.—**set'**: **back** *n.* check to progress.—**set'square** *n.* flat triangular drawing instrument for making or testing angles.

sett (set) *n.* stone paving block, rectangular in shape.

settee (se-tē') *n.* couch or sofa.

setter (set'-er) *n.* hunting-dog of spaniel family.

setting (set'-ing) *n.* fixing, adjusting, or putting in place; descending below horizon, as of sun; bezel which holds precious stone, etc. in position; mounting of scene in play or film; background.

settle (set'-l) *v.t.* put in place, order, arrangement, etc.; fix; establish; make secure or quiet; decide upon; bring (dispute) to end; calm; pay; colonise;—*v.i.* become stationary; come to rest; (cause to) sink to bottom; subside; take up permanent residence in; dwell; become calm; become clear (of liquid).—**set'tled** *a.* fixed; permanent; decided; quiet; adjusted by agreement.—**sett'lement** *n.* act of settling; state of being settled; colonisation; colony; (*Law*) transfer of real or personal property to trustees; sum secured to person. —**sett'ler** *n.* one who makes home in new country; colonist.—**sett'ling** *n.* act of making settlement; act of subsiding; adjusting of matters in dispute;—*pl.* sediment; dregs; lees.

settle (set'-l) *n.* high-backed bench.

seven (sev'-n) *a.* one more than six; —*n.* number greater by one than six.—**sev'en-fold** *a.* repeated seven times; increased to seven times size; —*adv.* seven times as much or as often.

seventeen (sev'-en-tēn) *a.* one more than sixteen;—*n.* sum of ten and seven.—**sev'enteenth** *a.* and *n.* seventh after tenth.

seventh (sev'-enth) *a.* constituting one of seven equal parts;—*n.* one of seven equal parts.—**seventh heaven,** supreme ecstasy.—**sev'enthly** *adv.*

seventy (sev'-n-ti) *a.* seven times ten;—*n.* sum of seven times ten.— **sev'entieth** *a.* constituting one of seventy equal parts—*n.* one of seventy equal parts.

sever (sev'-er) *v.t.* divide by violence; sunder; cut or break off;—*v.i.* divide.—**sev'erable** *a.*—**sev'erance** *n.* separation; partition.

several (sev'-er-al) *a.* more than two; some; separate; distinct; various; different;—*pron.* several persons or things.—**sev'erally** *adv.*

severe (se-vēr') *a.* serious; painful; very searching.—**severe'ly** *adv.*—**severe'ness, sever'ity** *n.* sternness; harshness; austerity.

sew (sō) *v.t.* fasten together with needle and thread; join with stitches;—*v.i.* practise sewing.— **sew'er** *n.* one who sews.—**sew'ing** *n.* and *a.*—**sew'ing-machine** *n.* automatic machine for sewing.

sewage (sū'-āj) *n.* drainage; excrement carried off by system of underground pipes.—**sew'age-farm** *n.*

establishment where sewage is treated to provide sludge or manure.

sewer(sū'-ẹr, sŏŏ'-ẹr) n. underground drain to remove waste water and refuse.—**sew'erage** n. underground system of pipes to carry off water and refuse.

sex (seks) n. state of being male or female; characteristics which distinguish male and female organisms; males or females collectively; sexual intercourse.—**sex appeal**, what makes person sexually desirable or attractive.—**sex'ual** a. pert. to sex or sexes; pert. to genital organs.—**sexual intercourse**, coition.—**sexual'ity** n. quality of being sexual.—**sex'ually** adv.—**sexy** a. sexually provocative.

sexagenary (sek-saj'-e-nạ-ri) a. pert. to number sixty; proceeding by sixties.—**sexagenar'ian** n. person of age of sixty.

Sexagesima (sek-sa-jes'-i-ma) n. second Sunday before Lent, sixty days before Easter.—**sexages'imal** a. pert. to number sixty.

sexcentenary (sek-sen-tē'-nạ-ri, or sek-sen'-te-nạ-ri) n. and a. (of) 600th anniversary; (of) space of 600 years.

sexennial (seks-en'-yạl) a. continuing for six years; happening once every six years. Also **sexten'nial**.—**sexenn'ially, sexten'ially** adv.

sextant (seks'-tạnt) n. sixth part of circle; instrument used in surveying and navigation for measuring altitudes of celestial bodies.

sextet (seks-tet') n. musical composition for six voices or instruments; company of six singers or instrumentalists.

sexton (seks'-tun) n. church lay-officer acting as caretaker and may also be grave-digger.

sextuple (seks-tū-pl) a. sixfold; six times as many;—v.t. multiply by six.

sforzando (sfor-tsán'-dō) a. (Mus.) forced and adv.; strongly accented.

shabby (shab'-i) a. torn or worn to rags; poorly dressed; faded; worn; mean; dishonourable.—**shabb'ily** adv.—**shabb'iness** n.

shack (shak) n. roughly built wooden hut.

shackle (shak'-l) n. metal loop or staple; U-shaped steel link with pin closing free ends;—pl. fetters; manacles; anything which hampers; restraints;—v.t. fetter; hamper.

shade (shād) n. partial darkness; place sheltered from light, heat, etc.; screen; darker part of anything; tint; hue; very minute difference; shadow; ghost; translucent screen for lamp;—pl. region of dead;—v.t screen from light or a source of heat; darken; represent shades in drawing.—**sha'ded** a.—**sha'dily** adv. in shady manner.—**sha'diness** n.—**sha'ding** n. interception of light; tinting picture

or drawing to show parts in relief.—**sha'dy** a. in shade; disreputable; not respectable; doubtful.

shadow (shad'-ō) n. patch of shade; dark figure projected by anything which intercepts rays of light; darker part of picture; gloom; inseparable companion; phantom; gloom; slight trace;—v.t. cast shadow over; follow and watch closely; outline.—**shad'ow-box'ing** n. boxing practice, without opponent.—**shad'ower** n. one who dogs footsteps of another.—**shad'owiness** n. state of being shadowy or indistinct.—**shad'owing** n. gradation of light and colour; shading.—**shad'owy** a. full of shadow; serving to shade; faintly representative; obscure; unreal.

shaft (shaft) n. straight rod, stem, or handle; shank; stem of arrow; arrow; anything long and slender; well of elevator; vertical passage down to mine; part of column between base and capital; revolving rod for transmitting power; stem of feather; pole of carriage.

shag (shag) n. coarse, matted wool or hair; shredded strong tobacco;—a. rough; shaggy.—**shag'giness** n.—**shag'gy** a. with rough hair or wool; rugged; unkempt.

shagreen (shạ-grēn') n. untanned leather made from belly skins of sharks, rays, etc.; imitation of this used in making luxury goods.

shake (shāk) v.t. cause to move with quick vibrations; weaken stability of; impair resolution of; trill, as note in music; agitate;—v.i. tremble; shiver; totter;—pa.t. shook.—pa.p. shak'en.—n. shaking; vibration; jolt; severe shock to system; friendly grasping of hands; (Mus.) trill; (Colloq.) moment.—**shake'down** n. temporary substitute for bed.—**shak'en** a. weakened; agitated.—**shak'ily** adv.—**shak'iness** n.—**shak'y** a. unsteady; tottering; unreliable.—**to shake off**, get rid of.

shako (shak'-ō) n. military peaked headdress.

shale (shāl) n. (Geol.) indurated clay or mud which splits into thin plates.

shall (shal) v.i. and aux. expressing futurity, obligation, command, or intention.

shallot (shạ-lot') n. bulbous plant like onion.

shallow (shal'-ō) a. having little depth of water; superficial; not sincere;—n. shoal, flat, or sand-bank.—**shall'owly** adv.—**shall'owness** n.

shalt (shalt) 2nd pers. sing. of shall.

sham (sham) n. trick, fraud, or device which, deludes; counterfeit; imitation;—a. counterfeit; false;—v.t. counterfeit; pretend;—v.i. make false pretences;—pr.p. sham'ming.—pa.t. and pa.p. shammed'.

shamble (sham'-bl) v.i. walk unsteadily with shuffling gait.

shambles (sham'-blz) n.pl. slaughterhouse; hence scene of carnage, disorder, muddle.

shame (shām) n. emotion caused by consciousness of wrong in one's conduct; cause of disgrace; dishonour; ignominy;—v.t. cause to feel shame; disgrace; degrade.—**shame'-faced** a. bashful; modest; shy;—**shame'facedly** adv.—**shame'facedness**, n. excessive shyness.—**shame'ful** a. disgraceful.—**shame'fully** adv.—**shame'fulness** n.—**shame'less** a. brazenfaced; immodest.—**shame'lessly** adv.—**shame'lessness** n.

shammy See chamois.

shampoo (sham-pōō') n. fluid for washing hair; v.t. wash with this;—n. act of shampooing.—**shampoo'er** n.

shamrock (sham'-rok) n. small trefoil plant; national emblem of Ireland.

shandy, shandygaff (shan'-di-gaf) n. mixture of beer and ginger-beer or lemonade.

shanghai (shang-hī') v.t. drug or render unconscious man so that he may be shipped as member of crew; crimp;—pa.t. and pa.p. shanghaied'.

shank (shangk) n. lower part of leg, from knee to ankle; shin-bone; stem of anchor, pipe, etc.; shaft of column; long connecting part of appliance.

shantung (shan-tung') n. silk cloth with rough, knotted surface.

shanty (shant'-i) n. mean dwelling; shack.

shanty (shant'-i) n. sailor's song, sung while working capstan or windlass. Also chant'y.

shape (shāp) v.t. to mould or make into form; figure; devise;—v.i. assume form;—n. form; figure; outline; pattern; jelly, etc. turned out of mould.—**shap'able, shape'able** a. shapely.—**shape'less** a. without regular shape or form; deformed; ugly.—**shape'lessness** n.—**shape'liness** n. beauty of shape.—**shape'ly** a. well-proportioned.

shard (shārd) n. broken fragment, esp. of earthenware; hard wing-case of beetle.

share (shār) n. pointed, wedge-shaped, cutting blade of plough.

share (shār) n. part allotted; portion; division; lot; unit of ownership in public company entitling one to share in profits; quota;—v.t. give or allot share; enjoy with others; divide; distribute; allot;—v.i. partake; participate.—**share'holder** n. one who possesses share(s) in company, etc.—**shar'er** n.

shark (shārk) n. general name applied to certain voracious marine fishes with sharp teeth in mouth placed on underside of head; swindler; sharper; cheat.—**shark'skin** n. stiff, smooth-finished rayon fabric.

sharp (shārp) a. having cutting edge or fine point; having ready perception; quick; shrewd; acid; acrid; witty; pungent; painful; artful; strongly marked, esp. in outline; shrill; (Mus.) raised semi-tone in pitch; (symbol ♯) —n. acute sound esp. note;—v.i. play sharper; cheat in bargaining, etc.;—adv. punctually.—**sharp'en** v.t. give keen edge or fine point to; make more eager; make more acid; (Mus.) raise semi-tone.—**sharp'ener** n. one who, or that which, sharpens; instrument for putting fine point on lead-pencil, etc.—**sharp'er** n. swindler; cheat; rogue.—**sharp'-eyed** a. very observant.—**sharp'ly** adv.—**sharp'ness** n.—**sharp'-shoot'er** n. skilled, long-range marksman. — **sharp'-shoot'ing** n. — **sharp'-sight'ed** a.—**sharp'-wit'ted** a. having acute mind.

shatter (shat'-er) v.t. break into many pieces; smash;—v.i. fly in pieces.

shave (shāv) v.t. pare away; cut close, esp. hair of face with razor; cut off thin slices; miss narrowly; graze;—v.i. shave oneself;—pa.p. shaved or sha'ven.—n. act of shaving; thin slice; narrow escape; close miss.—**sha'ver** n. (Slang) young lad.—**sha'ving** n. act of shaving; what is shaved off.—**close or near shave**, very narrow escape from danger.

shaw (shaw) n. small wood; thicket, grove; stem of plant with leaves, as potato, etc.

shawl (shawl) n. cloth used by women as loose covering for neck and shoulders.

she (shē) pron. feminine pronoun of third person; female (used humorously as noun); also, in compound-words, as she-bear.

sheaf (shēf) n. bundle of stalks of wheat, rye, oats, or other grain; any similar bundle; sheave;—pl. sheaves.

shear (shēr) v.t. clip or cut through with shears or scissors; clip wool (from sheep); fleece; reap; cut by exerting lateral pressure;—v.i. divide with scissor-like action; split across owing to its lateral flow.—pa.t. sheared, shore.—pa.p. shorn, sheared of metal.—n. deviation; curve;—pl. cutting instrument, consisting of two blades movable on pin; large pair of scissors.—**shear'er** n.—**shear'ing** n. operation of clipping or cutting with shears; wool, etc. cut off with shears.—**shear'ling** n. sheep only once sheared.

sheath (shēth) n. close-fitting cover, esp. for knife or sword; scabbard.—**sheathe** v.t. put into sheath; envelop.

—**sheath'ing** n. that which sheathes.
—**sheath'-knife** n. knife with fixed blade fitting into sheath.

sheave (shēv) n. grooved pulley-wheel.

sheave (shēv) v.t. bind into sheaves.

shed (shed) n. roofed shelter.

shed (shed) v.t. cause to proceed, or flow out; spill; let fall; cast off, as hair, feathers, spread; radiate; separate; divide.—pr.p. **shed'ding**.—pa.t. and pa.p. **shed**.—n. parting, as of hair; watershed.

sheen (shēn) n. gloss; glitter.

sheep (shēp) n. sing. and pl. ruminant mammal, valued for flesh and fleecy wool; simple, bashful person; —pl. church congregation.—**sheep'-cot**, **sheep'-cote** n. shelter for sheep.—**sheep'-dog** n. breed of dog trained to herd sheep.—**sheep'-farm** n. sheep-run.—**sheep'-fold** n. sheep-cote.—**sheep'-hook** n. shepherd's crook.—**sheep'ish** a. like sheep; bashful; shy and embarrassed.—**sheep'ishly** adv.—**sheep'ishness** n.—**sheep'-pen** n. sheep-cote.—**sheep's eyes**, fond, languishing glances.—**sheep'-shank** n. knot or hitch for temporarily shortening rope, etc.; something slender or weak.— **sheep'-shear'er** n. — **sheep'-shear'ing** n.—**sheep'skin** n. skin of sheep; leather, parchment, or rug made from this.—**black sheep**, disreputable member of family; rogue.

sheer (shēr) a. pure; unmixed; absolute; downright; perpendicular; of linen or silk, very fine;—adv. quite; completely.

sheer (shēr) v.i. deviate from right course; (with off) move away;—**sheerlegs** n. type of derrick with pair of inclined struts.

sheet (shēt) n. broad expanse; broad piece of cloth spread on bed; broad piece of paper; newspaper; broad expanse of water; broad, thinly expanded portion of metal or other substance;—v.t. cover, as with sheet.—**sheet'-copp'er**, **-i'ron**, **-lead**, **-met'al**, etc. n. appropriate metal in broad, thin sheets.—**sheet'ing** n. process of forming into sheets; calico or linen cloths used for bed coverings;—**sheet'-light'ning** n. sudden glow on horizon due to reflection of forked lightning.

sheet (shēt) n. rope attached to lower lee corner of sail; ship's sail;—pl. open space at bow or stern of undecked boat.—**sheet'-anch'or** n. large anchor carried for emergencies; chief support.

shekel (shek'-l) n. old Hebrew weight, and coin;—pl. (Colloq.) money; coins; cash.

sheldrake (shel'-drāk) n. (fem. **shel'duck**) genus of wild duck.

shelf (shelf) n. board fixed horizon-tally on frame, or to wall, for holding things; sandbank in sea, or ledge of rocks, rendering water shallow; reef; shoal;—pl. **shelves** (shelvz).

shell (shel) n. hard outer protective covering of many animals, particularly molluscs; outer covering of eggs of birds; protective covering of certain seeds; projectile fired from gun; outer part of structure left when interior is removed; inner coffin; system of orbital electrons around nucleus of atom.—**shell'back** n. old sailor; barnacle.—**shelled** a. having shell; stripped of shell; damaged by shellfire.—**shell'-egg** n. egg of domestic fowl.—**shell'fish** n. aquatic animal with external covering of shell; crustacean; mollusc.—**shell'-proof** a. capable of withstanding bombs or high-explosives.

shellac (she-lak') n. thermoplastic resin obtained by refining lac (q.v.).

shelter (shel'-ter) n. place or structure giving protection; that which covers or defends; place of refuge; asylum;—v.t. screen from wind or rain;—v.i. take shelter.—**shel'terer** n.

shelve (shelv) v.t. furnish with shelves; place on shelf; put aside as unfit for use; defer;—v.i. slope gradually; incline.—**shel'ving** n. act of fitting up shelves; material.—**shel'vy** a. sloping; shallow.

shepherd (shep'-erd) n. (fem. **shep'herdess**) one who tends sheep; pastor of church;—v.t. watch over and guide.—**shep'herd's-crook** n. long staff, with end curved.—**shep'herd's-pie**, n. minced meat, potatoes, and onions baked in oven.—**shepherd's tartan**, kind of small black and white check pattern.

sherbet (sher'-bet) n. cooling drink used in East, of fruit juice diluted with iced-water and sweetened; in Britain, usually synthetic effervescent powder.

sherd. See **shard**.

sheriff (sher'-if) n. in England, chief officer of Crown in every county; in Scotland, law-officer of Crown; in U.S., police official with many functions.—**sher'iffdom**, **sher'iffship** n. office or jurisdiction of sheriff.

Sherpa (sher'-pa) n. one belonging to N.E. Nepal tribe, often employed as porter or guide on Himalayan mountaineering expeditions.

sherry (sher'-i) n. Spanish wine of amber colour.

shibboleth (shib'-bo-leth) n. party cry or watchword.

shield (shēld) n. broad piece of armour carried on arm; buckler; anything which protects or defends; escutcheon on which are placed bearings in coats of arms; trophy in shape of shield;—v.t. protect; defend.

shieling (shē'-ling) n. Highland hut or cottage, used by shepherds. Also **sheal'ing.**

shift (shift) v.t. change position (of); remove; move; change, as clothes; —v.i. move; change place, course; manage or contrive;—n. change; expedient; squad or relay of workmen; time of their working; woman's undergarment.—**shift'er** n. one employed to shift scenery, articles, etc.; trickster.—**shift'iness** n. trickiness of character or behaviour.—**shift'ing** a. changing place or position; unreliable.—**shift'less** a. lacking in resource or character; not to be depended upon.—**shift'lessness** n.—**shift'y** a. not to be trusted; unreliable.—**to shift one's ground,** veer round in argument.—**to make shift,** manage or contrive somehow.

shillelagh, shillelah (shi-lāl'-a) n. oak or blackthorn sapling; cudgel. Also **shillal'ah.**

shilling (shil'-ing) n. British silver coin of the value of twelve pence.

shilly-shally (shil'-i-shal'-i) n. foolish trifling; indecision;—v.i. waver.

shimmer (shim'-er) v.i. shine with faint, tremulous light; gleam; glisten;—n. faint, quivering light or gleam.—**shimm'ering** n.

shimmy (shim'-i) v.i. wobble.

shin (shin) n. fore-part of leg, between ankle and knee; shank;—v.i. climb (up) with aid of arms and legs; swarm (up).—**shin'-bone** n. tibia, larger of two bones of leg.

shindy (shin'-di) n. excessive noise and tumult; uproar.

shine (shin) v.i. give out or reflect light; radiate; beam; gleam; glisten; perform in brilliant fashion;—pa.t. and pa.p. **shone.**—v.t. cause to shine; polish shoes, etc.—pa.t. and pa.p. **shined.**—n. brightness; gloss.—**shi'ner** n.—**shi'ning** a. glistening; splendid.—**shi'niness** n.—**shi'ny** a. bright; glossy; unclouded.

shingle (shing'-gl) n. rounded water-worn pebbles, occurring near high water mark of sea-beaches or on banks of rivers.—**shing'ly** a.

shingle (shing'-gl) n. thin wooden slat, used as roofing tile; style of hairdressing for women;—v.t. cover with shingles or tiles; crop women's hair close at nape of neck.

shingles (shing'-glz) n.pl. (Med.) Herpes Zoster, acute inflammation of nerve ganglia in spine, accompanied by severe pain, later eruption, usually round waist.

Shinto (shin'-tō) n. native religion of Japan.—**Shin'toism** n. principles of Shinto.

shinty (shin'-ti) n. ball-game played in parts of Scotland, intermediate between hockey and Irish hurley; stick used.

ship (ship) n. sailing-vessel with three masts, all square-rigged; any seagoing vessel;—v.t. put on board ship for transportation; engage for service on ship; place object in position, as oar; receive on deck force of wave;—v.i. embark;—pr.p. **ship'ping.**—pa.t. and pa.p. **shipped.**—**ship'-break'er** n. one who breaks up obsolete ships.—**ship'-brok'er** n. agent for shipping-company; one who transacts marine-insurance deals.—**ship'builder** n. one who constructs ships.—**ship'building** n.—**ship'-chand'ler** n. one who deals in equipment for ship.—**ship'-chand'lery** n.—**ship'-mas'ter** n. captain or commander of ship.—**ship'mate** n. fellow-sailor.—**ship'ment** n. process of shipping; that which is shipped; cargo.—**ship'mon'ey** n. formerly, tax leviable on port-towns to furnish navy.—**ship'own'er** n.—**ship'per** n. one who forwards goods by ship.—**ship'ping** n. collective body of ships.—**ship'ping-a'gent** n. one who arranges shipment of goods or passengers.—**ship'shape** a. in seamanlike manner; hence, trim, tidy;—adv. properly.—**ship'way** n. sloping berth on which ships are built.—**ship'wreck** n. loss of ship by mischance; ruin.—**ship'wright** n. carpenter actively engaged in building or repairing ships.—**ship'yard** n. place where ships are built or repaired.

shire (shir) n. territorial division, usually identical with county; county.

shirk (sherk) v.t. evade; try to avoid (duty, etc.);—n. one who seeks to avoid duty.—**shirk'er** n.

shirt (shert) n. garment worn on upper part of body by men and boys; jersey worn in field games; woman's blouse.—**shirt'-front** n. detachable front.—**boiled shirt,** shirt with starched front for evening-wear.—**to keep one's shirt on** (Slang) to keep cool and unruffled.

shiver (shiv'-er) v.i. quiver or shake from cold or fear; tremble; shudder; —n. shaking or shuddering caused by cold, fear; vibration.—**shiv'ery** a. inclined to shiver; timid to excess.

shiver (shiv'-er) n. small piece or splinter;—v.t. and i. break into many small pieces or splinters; shatter.

shoal (shōl) n. large number of fish swimming together; great quantity;—v.i. form into shoals; crowd together.

shoal (shōl) n. sandbank or bar; shallow water;—a. shallow;—v.i. become shallow.—**shoal'y** a. full of shoals or shallows.

shock (shok) n. violent concussion when bodies collide; clash; percussion; conflict; emotional disturbance;

paralytic stroke; effect of electric discharge through body;—*v.t.* strike against suddenly; strike with surprise, horror, or disgust.—**shock'-absorb'er** *n.* anything to lighten a blow or shock.—**shock'er** *n.* highly sensational tale of no literary merit.—**shock'ing** *a.* appalling; frightful; repulsive; offensive.—**shock'ingly** *adv.*—**shock'ingness** *n.*—**shock'proof** *a.* able to withstand shocks.

shock (shok) *n.* disordered mass of hair;—*a.* shaggy; bushy.—**shock'-head, -ed** *a.*

shock (shok) *n.* group of sheaves of grain.

shod (shod) *pa.t.* and *pa.p.* of verb shoe.

shoddy (shod'-i) *n.* inferior textile material;—*a.* made of shoddy; pert. to shoddy; inferior; of poor material; second rate.

shoe (shōō) *n.* covering for foot, but not enclosing ankle; metal rim nailed to horse's hoof; plate of iron or slip of wood, nailed to bottom of runner of sledge;—*v.t.* furnish with shoes; put shoes on;—*pr.p.* shoe'ing.—*pa.t.* and *pa.p.* shod.—**shoe'-black** *n.* one who polishes shoes.—**shoe'-brush** *n.*—**shoe'-horn** *n.* curved piece of horn, metal, etc. used to help foot into shoe.—**shoe'-lace** *n.* shoe-string for fastening shoe on foot.—**shoe'less** *a.*—**shoe'maker** *n.*—**shoe'-string** *n.* a shoe-lace.

shone (shon) *pa.t.* and *pa.p.* of shine.

shoo (shōō) *interj.* go away!—*v.t.* scare or drive away.

shook (shook) *pa.t.* of shake.

shoot (shōōt) *v.t.* discharge missile from gun, etc.; kill or wound with such missile; fire; hit; cast (net); propel quickly; thrust out; pass swiftly over (rapids); photograph episode of motion-picture; — *v.i.* move swiftly and suddenly; let off gun, etc.; go after game with gun; jut out; sprout; bud; dart through (as pain); advance; kick towards goal-mouth;—*pa.t.* and *pa.p.* shot.—*n.* shooting; expedition to shoot; young branch or stem; inclined plane down which coal, rubbish, etc. slide; chute; rapid or fall in stream.—**shoot'er** *n.* one who shoots; implement for shooting.—**shoot'ing** *n.* act of discharging fire-arms, etc.; act of killing game.—**shoot'ing-brake** *n.* dual purpose motor-car, to carry passengers and (or) heavy luggage.—**shoot'ing-gall'ery** *n.* long room for practice with miniature rifles.—**shoot'ing-star** *n.* incandescent meteor.— **shoot'ing-stick** *n.* walking-stick which can be converted into seat.—**to shoot a line** (*Slang*) exaggerate.

shop (shop) *n.* building where goods are made, or bought and sold; workshop;—*v.i.* visit shops to purchase articles;—*pr.p.* shop'ping.—*pa.t.* and *pa.p.* shopped.—**shop'-assis'tant** *n.* one employed in retail trade.—**shop'-count'er** *n.* table in shop on which transactions are completed.—**shop'keeper** *n.* one who keeps retail shop.—**shop'keeping** *n.*—**shop'-lift'er** *n.* one who makes petty thefts from shop counters.—**shop'ping** *n.* visiting shops with view to purchasing.—**shop'soiled, shop'worn** *a.* soiled by long exposure in shop.—**shop'-stew'ard** *n.* trade-union representative of workers in factory, etc.—**shop'-walk'er** *n.* one employed in large shop to superintend staff and to assist customers.—**to talk shop,** talk exclusively about one's daily business or particular interests.

shore (shōr) *pa.t.* of shear.

shore (shōr) *n.* land adjoining sea or lake.

shore (shōr) *n.* strong beam set against wall of building or ship to prevent movement during alterations;—*v.t.* support by post or buttress; prop.

shorn (shorn) *pa.p.* of shear;—*a.* cut off; having hair or wool cut off or sheared.

short (short) *a.* having little length; not long in space; not extended in time; limited in quantity; hasty of temper; crumbling in mouth; pronounced with less prolonged accent; brief; near; pithy; abrupt; destitute; crisp;—*adv.* suddenly; abruptly;—*n.* short film to support feature film; short-circuit;—*pl.* short trousers reaching down to above knees.—**short'age** *n.* insufficient supply.—**short'bread, short'cake** *n.* rich, brittle form of sweet cake.—**short'-cir'cuit** *n.* passage of electric current by shorter route;—*v.t.* cause short-circuit. — **short'-coming** *n.* failing; fault; defect.—**short'-cut** *n.* quicker way of reaching place or of accomplishing task, etc.—**short'en** *v.t.* make shorter; render friable, as short-bread, with butter or lard; diminish; reduce; — *v.i.* contract; lessen. — **short'ening** *n.* lard used when baking crisp pastry.—**short'fall** *n.* deficiency.—**short'hand** *n.* system of rapid reporting by signs or symbols; stenography.—**short'-hand'ed** *a.* not having full staff on duty.—**short'ly** *adv.* soon; in few words.—**short'ness** *n.*—**short shrift,** summary treatment.—**short'-sight'ed** *a.* not able to see distinctly objects some distance away; lacking in foresight.—**short'-sight'edly** *adv.*—**short'-sight'(edness)** *n.*—**short'-tem'pered** *a.* easily roused to anger.—**short time,** not working usual full hours.—**short waves** (*Radio*) term loosely applied to wavelengths below 200 metres.—**short'-wind'ed** *a.* asthmatic; easily made out of breath.

—in short,briefly.—little short of, almost.

shot (shot) *pa.t.* and *pa.p.* of shoot.

shot (shot) *n.* act of shooting; injection; skilled marksman; one of small pellets in cartridge; heavy, round missile, formerly fired from cannon; range of such; charge of blasting powder; stroke in billiards, tennis, etc.; cast of fishing-nets; photographic exposure; film-sequence.—**shot'-fir'ing** *n.* method of blasting in mines.—**shot'-gun** *n.* smooth-bore gun for shooting small game.—**big shot**, important person.

should (shood) *v.* and *aux.* used with pronouns I or we; auxiliary used after words of opinion, intention, desire, probability, obligation, etc.

shoulder (shōl'-dẽr) *n.* ball and socket joint formed by humerus (bone of upper arm) with scapula (shoulder-blade); upper joint of foreleg of animal; anything resembling human shoulder, as prominent part of hill, surface flanking motorway; —*v.t.* push forward with shoulders; bear (burden, etc.); accept (responsibility);—*v.i.* push forward through crowd.—**shoul'der-belt** *n.*—**shoul'der-blade, -bone** *n.* flat bone of shoulder; scapula.—**to give one the cold shoulder**, treat coldly.

shout (shout) *n.* loud, piercing cry; call for help;—*v.t.* and *v.i.* utter loud, sudden cry.

shove (shuv) *v.t.* push; press against; jostle;—*v.i.* push forward;—*n.* act of pushing; push.

shovel (shuv'-l) *n.* spade with broad blade slightly hollowed; scoop;—*v.t.* lift with shovel;—*v.i.* use shovel; —*pr.p.* shov'elling.—*pa.t.* and *pa.p.* shov'elled.—**shov'eller** *n.*

show (shō) *v.t.* present to view; point out; display; disclose; explain; demonstrate; prove; conduct; guide;—*v.i.* appear; be visible; come into sight;—*pa.p.* shown or showed.—*n.* act of showing; that which is shown; exhibition; sight; parade; display; likeness.—**show business**, the entertainment world collectively.—**show'case** *n.* glass case for display.—**show'down** *n.* laying down of cards, face upwards, at poker or other card games; open disclosure of truth, clarification.— shower (shō'-ẽr) *n.*—**show'ily** *adv.* ostentatiously.— **show'iness** *n.*— **show'man** *n.* proprietor of show at fair, etc.; one employed in such; self-advertising person.—**show'manship** *n.*—**show'-room** *n.* room where goods are laid out for inspection.— **show'y** *a.* gaudy; attracting attention; loud; ostentatious.—**to show off**, make ostentatious display.—**to show up**, stand out prominently; expose; hold up to ridicule.

shower (shou'-ẽr) *n.* brief fall of rain or hail; anything coming down like rain; great number;—*v.t.* wet with rain; give abundantly;—*v.i.* rain; pour down.—**show'er-proof** *a.* impervious to rain.—**show'ery** *a.* raining intermittently.

shrapnel (shrap'-nẹl) *n.* shell to explode over, and shower bullets on, enemy; shell-splinters.

shred (shred) *n.* narrow piece cut or torn off; strip; bit; rag; tatter; scrap;—*v.t.* cut or tear to shreds; tear into strips;—*pr.p.* shred'ding.— *pa.t.* and *pa.p.* shred'ded.

shrew (shrōō) *n.* small insectivorous mammal; quarrelsome woman; scold; termagant.—**shrew'ish** *a.* having manners of shrew.—**shrew'ishly** *adv.*— shrew'ishness *n.*

shrewd (shrōōd) *a.* discerning; knowing; artful; cunning.—**shrewd'ly** *adv.*—**shrewd'ness** *n.*

shriek (shrēk) *v.i.* and *i.* scream; screech;—*n.* loud, shrill cry.

shrift (shrift) *n.* confession made to priest; absolution.—**short shrift**, summary treatment.

shrike (shrīk) *n.* bird which preys on birds, etc. and impales victims on thorns; butcher-bird.

shrill (shril) *a.* piercing; high-pitched; —*v.i.* make such sound.—**shrill'y** *adv.*

shrimp (shrimp) *n.* small edible crustacean allied to prawns; small, puny person; object of contempt; dwarf;—*v.i.* catch shrimps with net. —**shrimp'er** *n.*

shrine (shrīn) *n.* case in which sacred relics are deposited; tomb of saint; place of worship, esp. by wayside; sacred place.

shrink (shringk) *v.i.* become wrinkled by contraction; shrivel; contract; dwindle; recoil;—*v.t.* cause to contract;—*pa.t.* shrank, shrunk.—*pa.p.* shrunk.—**shrink'age** *n.* act or amount of shrinking.—**shrunk'en** *a.* contracted; shrivelled.

shrive (shrīv) *v.t.* give absolution to; confess (used reflexively);—*v.i.* receive confessions.

shrivel (shriv'-l) *v.t.* and *v.i.* cause to contract; wither;—*pr.p.* shriv'elling. —*pa.t.* and *pa.p.* shriv'elled.

shroud (shroud) *n.* that which clothes or covers; winding-sheet;— *pl.* strongest of wire-rope stays which support mast athwartships; cords of parachute;—*v.t.* enclose in winding-sheet; cover with shroud; screen; conceal.

shrove (shrōv) *n.* shrift; shriving;— *pa.t.* of verb shrive.—**Shrove'tide** *n.* period immediately before Lent, ending on Shrove Tuesday.

shrub (shrub) *n.* plant of smaller growth than tree; bush; low, dwarf tree.—**shrub'bery** *a.* collection of shrubs.—**shrub'by** *a.*

shrug (shrug) v.i. raise and narrow shoulders in disdain, etc.—v.t. move (shoulders) thus;—pr.p. shrug'ging. —pa.t. and pa.p. shrugged.

shudder (shud'-er) v.i. tremble violently, esp. with horror or fear; shiver; quake;—n. trembling or shaking; shiver.—shudd'ering n. and a. trembling; shivering.

shuffle (shuf'-l) v.t. throw into disorder; mix (cards); scrape (feet) along ground;—v.i. change position of cards in pack; practise shifts; prevaricate; move in slovenly manner; scrape floor with foot in dancing;—n. artifice or pretext; rapid, scraping movement of foot in dancing.—shuff'ler n.

shun (shun) v.t. keep clear of; get out of way of; avoid;—pr.p. shun'ning.— pa.t. and pa.p. shunned.

shunt (shunt) v.t. move to one side; move (train) from one line to another;—v.i. go aside; turn off.—n. act of shunting.—shunt'er n. railway employee who shunts rolling-stock. —shunt'ing n.

shut (shut) v.t. close to hinder ingress or egress; fasten; secure; bar; forbid entrance to;—v.i. close itself; become closed;—pr.p. shut'ting.—pa.t. and pa.p. shut.—a. closed; made fast.—shut'down n. stoppage of work. —shut'ter n. one who, or that which, shuts; movable screen for window; automatic device in camera which allows light from lens to act on film or plate for predetermined period.— to shut down, stop working; close (business, etc.).—to shut up, close; fasten securely; (Colloq.) stop talking.

shuttle (shut'-l) n. instrument used in weaving for shooting thread of woof between threads of warp; similar appliance in sewing-machine; —v.t. and v.i. move backwards and forwards.—shutt'lecock n. cork with fan of feathers for battledore or badminton.—shuttle service, transport service on short route with only one vehicle operating between two points.

shy (shī) a. timid; modest; bashful; cautious;—v.i. start suddenly aside; —pa.t. and pa.p. shied.—shy'ly, shi'ly adv.—shy'ness n.—to fight shy of, avoid.

shy (shī) v.t. throw; fling;—pa.t. and pa.p. shied.—n. throw; cast; trial.

sib (sib) a. having kinship; related by blood;—n. blood relation.

sibilance (sib'-i-lans) n. hissing sound; quality of being sibilant. Also sib'liancy.—sib'ilant a.—n. letter uttered with hissing of voice.

Sibyl (sib'-il) n. name applied to certain votaresses of Apollo, endowed with prophetic power; prophetess; fortune-teller; witch.—sib'yllie, sib'ylline a. prophetic; occult.

siccate (sik'-āt) v.t. to dry.—sicca'tion n. act or process of drying.— sic'cative a. drying.

sick (sik) a. inclined to vomit; ill; ailing; disgusted; tired of; morbid; —v.t. make sick; sicken;—v.i. become sick; sicken.—sick'-bay n. place set aside on ship for treating sick.— sick'-ben'efit n. allowance made to insured person while ill and off duty. —sick'en v.t. make sick; disgust;— v.i. become sick; be filled with abhorrence.—sick'ening a.—sick'eningly adv. — sick'-head'ache n. migraine.—sick'-leave n. leave of absence on account of illness.— sick'liness n. state of being sickly.— sick'-list n.—sick'ly a. somewhat sick; ailing; infirm.—sick'ness n.

sickle (sik'-l) n. reaping-hook with semi-circular blade and short handle.

side (sīd) n. one of surfaces of object; one of edges of plane figure; margin; verge; border; any part viewed as opposite to another; part of body from hip to shoulder; slope, as of hill; one of two parties, teams, or sets of opponents; body of partisans; sect or faction; bias given to ball by striking it on side; side-spin; affectation;—a. being on side; lateral; indirect; incidental;—v.i. (with with) embrace opinions of another; give support to one of two or more contending parties.—side'-arms n.pl. weapons carried on side of body.—side'board n. piece of furniture designed to hold utensils, etc. in dining-room.—side'car n. small box- or canoe-shaped body attached to motor-cycle.—side effect n. subsidiary symptom or result.—side'-issue n. subsidiary to main argument. —side'line n. form of profitable work ancillary to one's main business.— side'ling a. and adv. sideways; aslant.—side'long a. lateral; oblique; not directly forward;—adv. obliquely; on side.—sid'er n. supporter.— side-saddle, saddle for woman on horseback, not astride, but with both feet on one side of horse.— side'-show n. minor entertainment; subordinate affair.—side'-slip n. involuntary skid sideways;—v.i. skid. —sides'man n. officer, who assists churchwarden; church usher.—side'-splitting a. laughter-provoking.— side'-step n. step to one side;—v.i. step to one side.—side'-track v.t. shunt into siding; postpone indefinitely; shelve;—n. railway siding.—side'-view n. oblique view.— side'-walk n. (U.S.) pavement.—side'ways adv. to-wards or from the side; edgewise;—a. lateral.—sid'ing n. short line of rails on which trains or wagons are shunted from main line. —si'dle v.i. move sideways; edge alongside;—v.t. cause to move sideways.—**side by side,** close together; alongside.

sidereal (sī-dē'-rē-ǝl) a. relating to constellations and fixed stars; measured by apparent motion of stars.—**sidereal year,** period during which earth makes revolution in its orbit with respect to fixed star.

siege (sēj) n. investiture of town or fortified place by hostile troops; continuous effort to gain (affection, influence, etc.); seat; position; rank;—v.t. besiege.—**state of siege,** suspension of civil law and assumption of power by military authorities.

sienna (sē-en'-a) n. natural yellow earth which provides pigment.—**burnt sienna,** pigment giving reddish-brown tint.—**raw sienna,** pigment giving a yellowish-brown tint.

sierra (sē-er'-a) n. chain of mountains with saw-like ridge.

siesta (sē-es'-ta) n. rest or sleep in afternoon.

sieve (siv) n. utensil with wire netting for separating fine part of substance from coarse;—v.t. sift.

sift (sift) v.t. separate coarser portion from finer; sieve; examine closely.

sigh (sī) v.i. make deep, single respiration, as expression of exhaustion or sorrow;—v.t. utter sighs over;—n. long, deep breath, expressive of sorrow, fatigue, regret, or relief.

sight (sīt) n. act of seeing; faculty of seeing; that which is seen; view; glimpse; anything remarkable; show; exhibition; inspection; (Colloq.) pitiful object; device on firearm to assist eye in correct aiming;—v.t. catch sight of; see; give proper elevation and direction to instrument;—v.i. take aim by means of sight.—**sightless** a. blind; invisible.—**sight'lessly** adv.—**sight'lessness** n. blindness.—**sight'liness** n. comeliness.—**sight'ly** a. pleasing to eye; graceful;—**sight'-read'er** n. one who reads at sight, as music, etc.—**sight'-read'ing** n.—**sight'-see'ing** n. viewing of places or objects of interest.—**sight'-se'er** n.—**sec'ond-sight** n. gift of prophetic vision.—**at sight,** immediately; without study.

sigma (sig'-ma) n. Greek letter (Σ, σ, s) corresponding to letter s.—**sig'mate, sig'moid** a. curved like letter S.

sign (sīn) n. movement, mark, or indication to convey meaning; token; symbol; omen; signboard; password; (Math.) character indicating operation to be performed, as +, ×, ÷, =, etc.; (Mus.) any character, flat, sharp, dot, etc.; (Astron.) twelfth part of ecliptic or zodiac;—v.t. represent by sign; affix signature to; ratify;—v.i. make signal, sign, or gesture; append one's signature.—**sign'board** n. board dis-

played outside or near building, etc. advertising business.—**sign'-man'ual** n. signature appended by one to legal instrument; specifically, royal signature.—**sign'-paint'er** n. one who paints signs for inns, shops, etc.—**sign'post** n. post supporting signboard, to show way, placed at cross-roads.

signal (sig'-nal) n. sign to give notice of some occurrence to persons at distance; sign; token; semaphore, esp. on railway: communication made by electro-magnetic waves;—v.t. communicate by signals;—v.i. make signals;—pr.p. sig'nalling;—pa.t. and pa.p. sig'nalled.—a. eminent; extraordinary; conspicuous.—**sig'nal-box, -cab'in** n. place from where railway signals are manipulated.—**sig'nalise** v.t. render noteworthy.—**sig'naller** n. one who signals; member of Signal Corps in British Army.—**sig'nally** adv. eminently.—**sig'nalman** n. one who works railway signals.

signatory (sig'-na-tor-i) a. and n. (one) bound by signature to terms of agreement.

signature (sig'-na-tūr) n. sign, stamp, or mark impressed; person's name written by himself.—**signature tune,** introductory tune associated with specific programme, etc.

signet (sig'-net) n. seal, esp. privy seal, one of three royal seals used for authenticating documents.—**sig'net-ring** n. finger-ring on which is engraved monogram or initials of owner.—**Writer to the Signet,** in Scotland, solicitor corresponding to English attorney.

signify (sig'-ni-fī) v.t. make known by sign; convey notion of; denote; imply; indicate; mean;—v.t. express meaning; be of consequence;—pa.t. and pa.p. sig'nified.—**signif'icance** n. importance; force; meaning.—**signif'icant** a. important.—**signif'icantly** adv.—**significa'tion** n. act of signifying; meaning; sense.—**signif'icative** a.—**signif'icatory** a. having meaning.

silage (sī'-lāj) n. compressed fodder, orig. packed green in silo for preservation.

silence (sī'-lens) n. stillness; quietness; calm; dumbness; secrecy;—v.t. cause to be still; forbid to speak; hush; calm; refute.—**si'lent** a. free from sound; indisposed to talk; unpronounced; as vowel or consonant.—**si'lently** adv.—**si'lentness** n.

silhouette (sil-ōō-et') n. picture cut from black paper upon light ground; outline of object seen against light;—v.t. represent in outline; cause to stand out in shadow against light background.

silica (sil'-i-ka) n. main component of most rocks, occurring as sand, flint, quartz, crystal, etc.—**sil'icate** n. salt of silicic acid.—**sil'icated** a. combined or coated with silica.—**silicate of soda**, water-glass;—p.a.p. **silic'ified**.—**sil'icon** n.—**sil'icones** n.pl. group of organo-silicon compounds including oils as lubricants, water-repellents, etc., also solid plastics.—**silico'sis** n. (Med.) chronic fibrosis of lung, caused by inhaling dust.—**silicot'ic** a. affected by silicosis.

silk (silk) n. fine, soft, lustrous thread from cocoons made by larvae of certain moths, esp. silk-worm; thread or fabric made from this; (Colloq.) King's Counsel;—a. made of silk.—**silk'en** a. made of, or resembling, silk; soft; smooth; silky. —**silk'iness** n. quality of being soft and smooth to touch.—**silk'-screen** display-printing process using silk stencil.—**silk'worm** n. caterpillar of moth which produces silk.—**silk'y** a. made of, or pert. to, silk; silk-like; smooth; glossy; soft.—**to take silk**, to become King's (Queen's) Counsel.

sill (sil) n. base or foundation; horizontal member of stone, brick, or wood at bottom of window frame, door, or opening.

sillabub, syllabub (sil'-ạ-bub) n. (cook) milk or cream beaten up with sugar into froth; dish of sponge-cakes, fruits, and wine, covered with whipped cream; anything light.

silly (sil'-i) a. weak in intellect; foolish; senseless; stupid; innocent; —n. silly person; booby;—adv. in silly fashion.—**sill'ily** adv.—**sill'iness** n. foolishness.—**silly point**, in cricket, stance of fielder on off-side, in front of, and close to, batsman.

silo (si'-lō) n. large grain store or elevator; pit in which green crops are preserved for future use as fodder; —v.t. preserve in silo.

silt (silt) n. fine, alluvial, soil particles, deposited from water; mud; slime; sediment;—v.t. choke or obstruct with silt (generally with up);—v.i. become filled up with silt; ooze; percolate.

silvan, sylvan (sil'-vạn) a. pert. to woods or groves; wooded; rural.

silver (sil'-ver) n. soft, white, metallic element; silverware; silver coins; anything resembling silver; — a. made of, or resembling, silver; white or grey, as hair; having pale lustre, as moon; soft and melodious, as voice or sound; bright; silvery;— v.t. coat or plate with silver; apply amalgam of tin-foil and quicksilver to back of mirror; tinge with white or grey;—v.i. become gradually white, as hair.—**silver birch**, forest tree with thin, silvery bark.—**sil'ver-fox** n. fox now bred in captivity for its glossy, silver-tipped, black fur.— **sil'ver-gilt** n. silver or silver-plate

with thin coating of gold;—a. pert. to silver so covered.—**sil'veriness** n. —**sil'verise** v.t. coat or cover thinly with film of silver.—**silver lining**, prospect of better times to come.— **sil'vern** a. made of, or resembling, silver.—**silver paper**, tin-foil, quality of tissue-paper used for wrapping.— **sil'ver-plate** n. metallic articles coated with silver.—**sil'ver-pla'ted** a.—**sil'ver-pla'ting** n. deposition of silver on another metal by electrolysis.— **sil'verside** n. upper part of round of beef suitable for salting.—**sil'versmith** n. worker in silver.—**sil'verware** n. articles made of silver.—**silver wedding**, 25th anniversary of marriage. —**sil'very** a. like silver; white; (of sound) soft and clear.

simia (sim'-i-a) n. anthropoid ape; monkey or ape generally.—**sim'ian** a. Also **sim'ial**.

similar (sim'-i-lạr) a. like; resembling; exactly corresponding.—**similar'ity** n. quality or state of being similar.—**sim'ilarly** adv.

simile (sim'-i-le) n. statement of point of resemblance between two things which differ in other respects; similitude.

similitude (si-mil'-i-tūd) n. state of being similar or like; resemblance; likeness.

simmer (sim'-er) v.t. cause to boil gently;—v.i. be just below boiling-point;—n. gentle, gradual heating.

simnel (sim'-nel) n. rich plum-cake offered as gift at Christmas, Easter, or Mid-Lent.

simony (sim'-on-i, sī'-mon-i) n. offence of offering or accepting money or other reward for nomination or appointment to ecclesiastical office.—**si'monist** n. one who practices simony.

simoom (si-móóm') n. hot, dry, sand-laden wind of N. Africa, Syria, Arabia. Also **simoon**.

simper (sim'-per) v.i. smile in silly, affected manner; smirk;—n. smile with air of silliness or affectation.— **sim'perer** n.

simple (sim'-pl) a. single; not complex; entire; mere; plain; honest; clear; intelligible; simple-minded;— n. something not compounded; ingredient; medicinal herb.—**sim'ple-heart'ed** a. artless; sincere.—**simple interest**, money paid on principal borrowed but not on accrued interest as in compound interest.— **sim'ple-mind'ed** a. ingenious; frank; unsuspecting.—**sim'pleness** n. quality or state of being simple; artlessness; innocence; weakness of intellect.— **sim'pleton** n. person of weak intellect. —**simplic'ity** n. artlessness of mind; clearness; simpleness.—**simplifica'tion** n. act of making clear; thing simplified.—**sim'plify** v.t. make simple, plain, or easy;—*pa.t.* and *pa.p.* **sim'plified.**—**sim'ply** *adv.* in simple manner; plainly; absolutely.

simulacrum (sim-ū-lā'-krum) *n.* image; phantom.—*pl.* **simula'cra.**

simulate (sim'-ū-lāt) *v.t.* assume appearance of; feign; mimic.—**simula'tion** *n.*—**sim'ulator** *n.*

simultaneous (sim-ul-tā'-nē-us) *a.* existing or occurring at same time.—**simultane'ity, simulta'neousness** *n.* quality or state of happening at same time.—**simulta'neously** *adv.*

sin (sin) *n.* transgression against divine or moral law; moral depravity; wickedness; evil; immorality; crime; trespass;—*v.i.* depart from path of duty prescribed by God; violate rule of duty; do wrong.—*pr.p.* **sin'ning.**—*pa.t.* and *pa.p.* **sinned.**—**sin'ful** *a.* wicked; unholy.—**sin'fully** *adv.*—**sin'fulness** *n.* depravity; moral corruption.—**sin'ner** *n.* one who sins.—**original sin,** inherent tendency to sin, legacy from original sin of Adam.—**venial sin,** pardonable lapse into wrongdoing.

since (sins) *adv.* from then till now; subsequently; ago;—*prep.* at some time subsequent to; after;—*conj.* from time to that; seeing that; because that; inasmuch as.

sincere (sin-sēr') *a.* not assumed; straightforward. — **sincere'ly** *adv.* — **sincere'ness, sincer'ity** *n.* state or quality of being sincere; honesty of mind; truthfulness; genuineness.

sine (sīn) *n.* (*abbrev.* sin) (*Math.*) perpendicular drawn from one extremity of arc to diameter drawn through other extremity; function of one of two acute angles in right-angle triangle, ratio of line subtending this angle to hypotenuse.

sinecure (sī'-nē-kūr, sin'-e-kūr) *n.* orig. ecclesiastical benefice without cure of souls; office, position, etc. with salary but without duties.—**si'necurist** *n.*

sinew (sin'-ū) *n.* ligament which joins muscle to bone; muscle; nerve;—*pl.* strength; source of strength.—**sin'ewed** *a.* having sinews; strong; firm.—**sin'ewiness** *n.*—**sin'ewy** *a.* well braced with sinews; muscular.

sing (sing) *v.t.* utter with musical modulations of voice; celebrate in song;—*v.i.* utter sounds with melodious modulations of voice; pipe, twitter, chirp, as birds; hum, as kettle on boil; reverberate.—*pa.t.* **sang** or **sung.**—*pa.p.* **sung.**—**sing'er** *n.* one who sings; vocalist.—**sing'ing** *n.* art of singing; vocal music; humming noise (in ear, etc.).

singe (sinj) *v.t.* burn slightly surface of; scorch; char.—*pr.p.* **singe'ing.**—*n.* superficial burn.

single (sing'-gl) *a.* sole; alone; separate; individual; not double;

unmarried; straightforward; upright;—*n.* unit; (*Cricket*) one run; (*Tennis*) game confined to two opponents; ticket valid for journey in one direction only;—*v.t.* (with *out*) select from among number; pick; choose.—**sing'le-breast'ed** *a.* of garment, buttoning on one side only.—**sing'le-deck'er** *n.* passenger vehicle having no roof seats.—**sing'le-entry** *n.* in book-keeping, entry of transaction on one side only of account.—**sing'le-hand'ed** *a.* and *adv.* unassisted.—**single'-mind'ed** *a.* honest; upright; sincere.—**sing'leness** *n.* state of being single; honesty of purpose; sincerity.—**sing'le-stick** *n.* fencing with basket-hilted ash-stick.—**sing'ly** *adv.* one by one; by oneself; individually; alone.

singlet (sing'-glet) *n.* undervest.

singleton (sing'-gl-ton) *n.* (*Cards*) hand containing only one card of some suit.

singsong (sing'-song) *n.* drawling, monotonous fashion of speaking; droning; impromptu gathering where all join in communal singing;—*a.* monotonous; droning.

singular (sing'-gū-lạr) *a.* existing by itself; denoting one person or thing; individual; unique;—*n.* single instance; word in singular number.—**sing'ularise** *v.t.* make singular or unique.—**singular'ity** *n.* state of being singular; anything unusual or remarkable; strangeness of manner; oddity.—**sing'ularly** *adv.* in singular manner; strangely.

sinister (sin'-is-tẹr) *a.* on left hand; evil-looking; unlucky; threatening; (*Her.*) side of escutcheon on left of person standing behind it.—**sin'isterly** *adv.* in sinister manner.—**sin'istral** *a.* to the left; reversed.

sink (singk) *v.t.* cause to sink; submerge; lower out of sight; dig;—*v.i.* fall; subside; descend; penetrate (into); decline in value, health, or social status; be dying; droop; decay; become submerged;—*pa.t.* **sank** or **sunk.**—*pa.p.* **sunk.**—*n.* receptacle for washing up; place notoriously associated with evil-doing; filthy dwelling-place; cesspool.—**sink'er** *n.* weight fixed to anything to make it sink, as on net, fishing-line, etc.—**sink'ing** *n.* operation of excavating; subsidence; settling; abatement.

Sino-Japanese (sī'-no-jap-ạ-nēz') *a.* pert. to China and Japan.

sinology (sī-nol'-o-ji) *n.* branch of knowledge which deals with Chinese language, culture, etc.—**sinol'ogist, sin'ologue** *n.* one versed in Chinese culture and language.

sinter (sin'-tẹr) *v.t.* and *i.* fuse into a mass under heat without actually melting.

sinuate (sin'-ū-āt) v.t. and i. bend in and out; wind; turn.—**sin'uous** a. bending in and out; of serpentine form; morally crooked; supple.—**sinuos'ity** n. quality of being sinuous.—**sin'uously** adv.

sinus (sī'-nus) n. opening; hollow; cavity; groove or passage in tissues leading to deep-seated abscess, usually in nose or ear.—**sinusi'tis** n. inflammation of sinus, esp. of bones of forehead or jaws.

Sioux (sōō) n. member of tribe of N. American Indians; their language. pl. Sioux (sōō, sōōz).

sip (sip) v.t. and v.i. drink in very small quantities; taste.—pr.p. sip'ping.—pat. and pa.p. sipped.—n. portion of liquid sipped with lips; mouthful.

siphon, syphon (sī'-fon) n. bent tube or pipe by which liquid can be transferred from one receptacle to another; bottle with internal tube and lever top, for holding and delivering aerated water;—v.t. draw off by means of siphon.—**si'phonage, sy'phonage** n. action of siphon.

sir (ser) n. title of respect to man; title of knight or baronet.

sire (sīr) n. father; one who stands in relation of father as king or emperor; male parent of animal (applied esp. to horses);—pl. ancestors;—v.t. beget (of animals).

siren (sī'-ren) n. (Myth.) one of several nymphs said to sing with such sweetness that sailors were lured to death; mermaid; sweet singer; seductive alluring woman; form of horn which emits series of loud, piercing notes as warning signal of approaching danger; steamwhistle or hooter;—a. pert. to, or resembling siren; alluring; seductive.

sirloin (ser'-loin) n. upper part of loin of beef.

sirocco (si-rok'-ō) n. hot southerly wind from Africa, blowing in Italy.

sirrah (sir'-a) n. (Archaic) term formerly applied to man to express contempt.

sisal (sis'-al, sī'-sal) n. fibre plant, native to Yucatan, used for making rope.

sissy (sis'-i) n. (Colloq.) effeminate man or boy.

sister (sis'-ter) n. female whose parents are same as those of another; woman of same faith; female of same society, convent, abbey; nun; nurse in position of authority;—a. standing in relation of sister; related; of similar nature to, as institute, college, etc.—**sis'ter-german** n. full sister.—**sis'terhood** n. state of being sister; society of women united in one faith or order.—**sis'ter-in-law** n. husband's or wife's sister; brother's wife.—pl. sis'ters-in-law.—**sis'ter-like**, **sis'terly** a. like sister; befitting sister; affectionate.

sit (sit) v.i. rest upon haunches, seat, etc.; remain; rest; perch, as birds; (of hen) to cover eggs for hatching; be officially engaged in transacting business, as court, council, etc.; be in session; be representative in Parliament for constituency; pose for portrait;—v.t. keep good seat upon, as on horseback; place upon seat; put carefully in position; compete in (examination).—pr.p. sit'ting.—pat. and pa.p. sat.—**sit'ter** n. one who sits; one who poses for artist; easy catch, shot, or target; bird sitting on eggs.—**sit'ting** n. state of resting on seat, etc.; act of placing oneself on seat; session; business meeting; occasion when food is served to group of people; clutch of eggs for incubation;—a. resting on haunches; perched.—**sit'ting-room** n. parlour; small drawing-room.—**sit-down strike**, form of strike in which strikers refuse to leave place of work.—**to sit for**, represent in parliament; pose for artist.

site (sīt) n. place, situation; plot of ground for or with, building; position; place where anything is fixed;—v.t. place in position.

situate (sit'-ū-āt) v.t. give site to; place; locate;—a. located; situated.—**situa'ted** a. resident; located; conditioned.—**situa'tion** n. condition; place or position; site; job; office.

six (siks) a. one more than five;—n. sum of three and three; symbol 6 or VI.—**six'er** n. hit scoring six at cricket.—**six'fold** a. six times as much or as many.—**six'footer** n. person six feet in height.—**six'pence** n. British silver coin of value of six pennies.—**six'penny** a. worth sixpence; bought or sold for sixpence; paltry· cheap.—**six'-shoot'er** n. six-chambered revolver.—**six'teen** n. and a. six and ten, symbol 16 or XVI.—**six'teenth** a. sixth after tenth;—n. one of sixteen equal parts; (Mus.) semiquaver.—**sixth** a. next in order after fifth; one of six equal parts;—n. (Mus.) interval comprising six degrees of staff, as A to F.—**sixth'ly** adv.—**six'ty** a. six times ten; three score;—n. symbol 60 or LX.—**six'tieth** a. next in order after fiftyninth; one of sixty equal parts;—n.—**at sixes and sevens**, in disorder and confusion.

size (sīz) n. bulk; bigness; dimensions; extent;—v.t. arrange according to size.—**si'zeable** a. of large size.—**size up**, estimate possibilities of; take measure of.

size (sīz) n. substance of gelatinous nature, like weak glue;—v.t. treat with size.

sizzle (siz'-l) v.i. make hissing noise;

shrivel up;—n. hissing, sputtering noise; extreme heat.—**sizz'ling** n.

sjambok (shàm'-bok) n. short, heavy horse-whip, made of strip of dried, rhinoceros hide.

skate (skāt) n. steel blade to attach to boot, for gliding over ice;—v.i. travel over ice on skates.—**ska'ter** n. —**ska'ting** n.—**ska'ting-rink** n. stretch of ice (usually under cover) for skating; ice-rink.—**roll'er-skate** n. skate with castors in place of steel blade.

skate (skāt) n. flat fish of ray family.

skean (skēn) n. Scottish Highland dagger or dirk; long knife. Also **skeen**, **skene**.—**skean'-dhu** (dòò) n. dirk worn in top of stocking.

skein (skān) n. small hank, of fixed length, of thread, silk, or yarn; knot of thread or yarn; flight of wild geese or swans.

skeleton (skel'-e-ton) n. bony framework providing support for human or animal body; framework, as of building, plant, etc.; general outline; —a. pert. to skeleton; containing mere outlines. Also **skel'etal**.— **skeleton crew**, **staff**, **etc.**, minimum number employed on essential duty. —**skel'eton-key** n. key to open or pick lock by avoiding wards.

skep (skep) n. beehive made of straw; light basket.

skerry (sker'-i) n. rocky isle; reef.

sketch (skech) n. first rough draft of design; outline; drawing in pen, pencil, or similar medium; essay or account, in light vein; short, humorous one-act play;—v.t. draw outline of; make rough draft of; plan by giving principal ideas of;— v.i. draw; make sketches.—**sketch'er** n.—**sketch'ily** adv.—**sketch'iness** n. lack of detail.—**sketch'y** a. inadequate; incomplete.

skew (skū) a. awry; askew; off straight;—adv. awry; obliquely;—n. anything set at angle to some other object;—v.t. put askew; turn aside; —v.i. walk sideways; shy; skid.— **skew'bald** a. of horse, bay and white in patches.—**skewed** a. distorted.— **skew'-eyed** a. squinting.

skewer (skū'-er) n. pointed rod for fastening meat to keep it in form while roasting;—v.t. fasten with skewers.

ski (skē; in Norway, shē) n. long wooden runner strapped to foot, for running, sliding and jumping over snow;—v.i. run, slide, or jump on skis.—**skier** (skē'-er, shē'-er) n.

skid (skid) n. piece of timber to protect side of ship from injury; drag placed under wheel to check speed on steep gradient; loss of grip between wheels of vehicle and road surface; inclined plane down which logs, etc. slide;—v.i. slide along without revolving; slip;—v.t. slide log down incline; place on skids.

skid'pan n. (Motoring) large, greased, flat area of ground for demonstration of, and tuition in, skid control.

skiff (skif) n. light, narrow scullingboat for one rower; light, small boat.

skill (skil) n. practical ability and dexterity; knowledge; expertness; aptitude.—**skil'ful** a. expert; skilled; adept.—**skil'fully** adv.—**skil'fulness** n. —**skilled** a.

skillet (skil'-et) n. small, long-handled metal vessel for heating water, stewing vegetables, etc.

skim (skim) v.t. remove from surface of liquid; glide over lightly and rapidly; read in superficial way; graze;—v.i. pass lightly over; glide along; hasten over superficially.— pr.p. **skim'ming**—pa.t. and pa.p. **skimmed**.—n. matter which forms on surface of liquid; scum.—**skim'mer** n.—**skim'-milk** n. milk from which cream has been removed.

skimp (skimp) v.t. stint; do imperfectly;—v.i. be mean; economise in petty fashion;—a. scanty; spare; meagre.—**skimp'y** a. scant; meagre.

skin (skin) n. external covering of animal bodies; hide; pelt; exterior coat of fruits and plants; husk or bark; thick scum; coating;—v.t. strip off skin or hide of; flay; graze; peel; swindle;—v.i. peel off; become covered with skin.—**skin'-deep** a. superficial. — **skin'diver** n. underwater-swimmer who does not wear a diving suit; frogman.—**skin'-flint** n. miser.—**skin'-graft'ing** n. transplanting healthy skin to wound to form new skin.—**skin'ner** n. dealer in hides; furrier.—**skin'niness** n. leanness.—**skin'ny** a. having thick skin; very lean or thin; mean.—**skin'-tight** a. fitting close to skin.—**skin'-tights** n.pl. theatrical costume fitting close to limbs.—**to have a thick skin**, be not at all sensitive.—**by the skin of one's teeth**, very narrowly.

skip (skip) v.t. leap over lightly; omit;—v.i. leap lightly, esp. in frolic; frisk; clear rope swung in play under one's feet; run away hastily; pay hurried visits.—pr.p. **skip'ping**.— pa.t. and pa.p. **skipped**.—n. light leap, spring, or bound.—**skip'per** n. one who skips; type of butterfly.

skip (skip) n. box with hinged door, working in mine-shaft, for hoisting ore, etc.; bucket for transporting minerals, etc.

skip (skip) n. captain of bowling or curling team;—v.t. and i. do this.

skipper (skip'-er) n. captain of ship or team.

skirl (skerl) v.i. scream shrilly;—n. shrill, high-pitched scream; music of bagpipe.

skirmish (sker'-mish) n. irregular,

minor engagement between two parties of soldiers; brush;—*v.i.* take part in skirmish.—**skir'misher** *n.*

skirt (skẻrt) *n.* lower part of coat, gown; outer garment of woman fitted to and hanging from waist; petticoat; edge of part of dress; flap; border; margin; edge; rim; diaphragm of animal; midriff of beef;—*v.t.* border; round edge of;—*v.i.* be on border.—**skirt'ing** *n.* material for women's skirts; border.—**skirt'ingboard** *n.* narrow board between plaster of internal wall and floor.

skit (skit) *n.* satirical gibe; lampoon; caricature; burlesque; — *v.t.* burlesque; write skit upon;—*v.i.* leap aside; shy.—**skitt'ish** *a.* frisky; fickle; volatile; timid.—**skitt'ishly** *adv.*—**skitt'ishness** *n.*

skittles (skit'-lz) *n.pl.* nine-pins, game to overturn nine skittles.

skive (skiv) *v.t.* in shoe-making, pare away edges of leather; grind (diamonds).

skivvy (skiv'-i) *n.* (*Colloq.*) domestic servant.

skoff (skof) *n.* in S. Africa, food;—*v.t.* (*Slang*) eat greedily; bolt food.

skua (skū'-a) *n.* family of Arctic or Antarctic birds, allied to gulls.

skulk (skulk) *v.i.* sneak out of way; lurk; act sullenly;—*n.* one who skulks.

skull (skul) *n.* bony framework which encloses brain; cranium.—**skull'cap** *n.* brimless cap fitting close to head.

skunk (skungk) *n.* N. American animal, allied to weasel, which defends itself by emitting evil-smelling fluid; base, mean person.

sky (skl) *n.* apparent vault of heaven; heavens; firmament.—*pl.* **skies.**—*pa.t.* and *pa.p.* **skied.**—**sky'-blue** *n.* and *a.* azure.—**sky'-high** *a.* and *adv.* at great elevation; carried away with excitement.—**sky'lark** *n.* bird which sings as it soars;—*v.i.* indulge in boisterous byplay.—**sky'-lark'ing** *n.* noisy frolicking and horse-play.—**sky'light** *n.* glazed opening in roof or ceiling.—**sky'line** *n.* horizon.—**sky'-pi'lot** *n.* clergyman.—**sky'scraper** *n.* lofty building with many storeys.

slab (slab) *n.* thickish, flat, rectangular piece of anything; concrete paving-block; thick slice of cake, etc.;—*v.t.* cut in form of slabs.

slack (slak) *a.* not taut; not closely drawn together; not holding fast; remiss; easy-going;—*n.* part of rope which hangs loose; quiet time.—**slack, slack'en** *v.t.* loosen; moderate; relax; diminish;—*v.i.* become slack; relax; dodge work; flag.—**slack'er** *n.* one who shirks work.—**slack'ly** *adv.*—**slack'ness** *n.*—**slacks** *n.pl.* trousers worn by men or women.

slack (slak) *n.* finer screenings of coal;

dross.—**slack'heap** *n.* dump for slack.

slag (slag) *n.* refuse after smelting of ores; scoriae of volcano.—**slag'gy** *a.*

slain (slān) *pa.p.* of verb **slay.**

slake (slāk) *v.t.* quench; extinguish; of quicklime, combine with water; slacken;—*v.i.* become mixed with water; become extinct; diminish.—**slaked lime,** hydrate of lime formed by mixing quicklime and water.

slam (slam) *v.t.* shut noisily; bang; hit; win all, or all but one, of tricks at cards.—*pr.p.* **slam'ming**;—*pa.t.* and *pa.p.* **slammed.**—*n.* act of slamming; bang.—**slam (grand or little)** thirteen or twelve tricks taken at Bridge.

slander (slan'-der) *n.* false or malicious statement about person; defamation of character by spoken word; calumny;—*v.t.* injure by maliciously uttering false report; defame.—**slan'derer** *n.*—**slan'derous** *a.*—**slan'derously** *adv.*—**slan'derousness** *n.*

slang (slang) *n.* word or expression in common colloquial use but not regarded as standard English; jargon peculiar to certain sections of public; argot;—*a.* pert. to slang;—*v.t.* revile; scold.—**slang'ily** *adv.*—**slang'iness** *n.*—**slang'y** *a.*

slant (slant) *v.t.* turn from direct line; give sloping direction to;—*v.i.* lie obliquely; slope; incline;—*n.* slope; gibe; oblique point of view (on);—*a.* inclining; sloping; oblique.—**slan'ted** *a.* biassed.—**slan'tingly** *adv.*—**slant'ly, slant'wise** *adv.* in slanting direction or manner; aslant.

slap (slap) *n.* blow with open hand or flat instrument;—*v.t.* strike with open hand or something flat.—*pr.p.* **slap'ping**;—*pa.t.* and *pa.p.* **slapped.**—**slap'-bang** *adv.* suddenly; violently.—**slap'-dash** *adv.* impetuously;—*a.* careless; slipshod.—**slap'-up** *a.* (*Colloq.*) grand.

slash (slash) *v.t.* cut by striking violently; make gashes in; slit;—*v.i.* strike violently with edged weapon;—*n.* long cut; gash; cutting stroke; large slit in garment.—**slash'er** *n.*

slat (slat) *n.* narrow strip of wood or stone; lath.—**slat'ted** *a.* covered with slats.

slate (slāt) *n.* form of shale which splits readily into thin leaves; prepared piece of such stone for roofing houses, etc.; table for writing upon; dark blue-grey colour;—*a.* made of slate; bluish-grey;—*v.t.* cover with slates; reprimand.—**slate'-clay** *n.* shale.—**sla'ter** *n.* one who shapes slates or covers roofs with slates; wood-louse.—**sla'ting** *n.* act of covering with slates; roof-covering thus put on; severe reprimand; harsh criticism.—**sla'ty** *a.*

slattern (slat'-ern) *n.* slut; sloven.—

slatt'ernliness n.—slatt'ernly a. like slattern;—adv. in slovenly manner.

slaughter (slaw'-tẽr) n. act of slaughtering; massacre; butchery; bloodshed; killing of animals to provide food;—v.t. kill; slay in battle; butcher.—slaugh'terer n.—slaugh'terhouse n. place where cattle are slaughtered.—slaugh'terous a. murderously-inclined; destructive. —laugh'terously adv.

slave (slāv) n. person held legally in bondage to another; bondman; vassal; serf; drudge; one who has lost power of resistance to bad habit or vice;—v.i. work like slave; toil unremittingly.—slave'-dri'ver n. overseer in charge of slaves at work; exacting task-master.—sla'ver n. person or ship engaged in slave traffic.—sla'very n. condition of slave compelled to perform compulsory work for another; bondage; servitude; drudgery.—slave'-tra'der n.—sla'vey n. (Slang) domestic servant, esp. general servant.—sla'vish a. pert. to slaves; menial; drudging; servile; fawning; base; mean.—sla'vishly adv. —sla'vishness n.—white slavery, traffic in white women and girls for immoral purposes.

slaver (slăv'-ẽr) n. saliva running from mouth; gross flattery; sentimental nonsense;—v.t. smear with saliva from mouth;—v.i. slobber; talk in weakly sentimental fashion. —slav'erer n.

slay (slā) v.t. kill; murder; assassinate; slaughter.—pa.t. slew.—pa.p. slain.—slay'er n.

sled, sledge (sled, slej) n. vehicle on runners, for conveying loads over snow or ice; sleigh;—v.t. convey on sled;—v.i. ride on sled.

sledge (slej) n. large, heavy hammer. —sledge'-hamm'er n. heavy hammer with long handle.

sleek (slēk) a. having smooth surface; glossy; plausible; ingratiating;—v.t. make smooth; calm; soothe;—v.i. glide; sweep smoothly.—adv. smoothly; neatly; skilfully.—sleek'ly adv.—sleek'ness n.

sleep (slēp) v.i. rest by suspension of exercise of powers of body and mind; become numb (of limb); slumber; doze; repose; rest; be dead.—pa.t. and pa.p. slept.—n. slumber; repose; rest; death.—sleep'er n. one who sleeps; berth in railway sleeping-car; strong, horizontal piece of timber on railway line.—sleep'ily adv. in drowsy manner.—sleep'iness n.—sleep'ing a.—sleep'ing-bag n. bag of thick material, waterproofed on outside, for sleeping in open.—sleep'ing-part'ner n. business associate who takes no active part in management.—sleep'ing-pill n. medicine used for inducing sleep;

opiate.—sleep'ing-sick'ness n. tropical disease, common among natives of C. and W. Africa; trypanosomiasis. —sleep'less a. wakeful; restless; alert. —sleep'lessly adv.—sleep'lessness n. —sleep'-walk'er n. one who walks in sleep or in trance; somnambulist. —sleep'-walk'ing n.—sleep'y a. drowsy.

sleet (slēt) n. mixture of melting snow and rain;—v.i. snow or hail with rain.—sleet'iness n.—sleet'y a.

sleeve (slēv) n. part of garment which covers arm; casing or protective cover;—v.t. furnish with sleeves.—to laugh up one's sleeve, be inwardly amused at someone.

sleigh (slā) n. sled or sledge;—v.i. drive in sleigh.

sleight (slīt) n. feat so dexterously performed that performance escapes observation.—sleight'-of-hand n. legerdemain; conjuring.

slender (slen'-dẽr) a. thin or narrow; weak.—slen'derly adv.—slen'derness n.

sleuth (slōōth) n. track of man or beast, as followed by scent; bloodhound; detective.—sleuth'-hound n. blood-hound.

slew (slōō) pa.t. of slay.

slew, slue (slōō) v.t. and i. turn about for positioning purposes round fixed point; swing round.

slice (slīs) v.t. and i. cut off thin flat pieces; strike ball so that line of flight diverges well to right;—n. thin, flat piece cut off; broad, flat, thin knife for serving fish; share or portion; stroke at golf, etc. in which ball curls away to right or left.—sli'cer n.

slick (slik) a. smooth; sleek; smooth-tongued; quick in reply; smart; deft; clever;—adv. deftly; cleverly; at once;—v.t. sleek.

slide (slīd) v.i. slip smoothly along; slip, glide, esp. over ice; pass imperceptibly; deteriorate morally;—v.t. move something into position by pushing along surface of another body; thrust along; pass imperceptibly.—pr.p. slid'ing.—pa.t. slid.—pa.p. slid or slidd'en.—n. sliding; track on ice made by sliding; sliding part of mechanism; anything which moves freely in or out; photographic plate-holder; transparency for projection; chute; narrow glass rectangle to carry small object to be examined under microscope; woman's hair clip; moving part of trombone or trumpet.—slid'er n. one who slides.—slide'-rule n. mathematical device for rapid calculations

slight (slīt) a. trifling; inconsiderable; slim; slender;—n. contempt by ignoring another; disdain; insult;—v.t. ignore; disdain; insult.—slight'ing n. scorn; disrespect;—a. disparaging. —slight'ingly adv.—slight'ly adv. not seriously.—slight'ness n.

slim (slim) *a.* of small diameter or thickness; slender; thin; slight; unsubstantial;—*v.i.* reduce weight by diet and exercise.—**slim'ly** *adv.*

slime (slīm) *n.* soft, sticky, moist earth or clay; greasy, viscous mud; mire; mucus; viscous secretion of snails, etc.; fawning words or actions.—**slim'ily** *adv.* in a slimy manner.—**slim'iness** *n.*—**sli'my** *a.* consisting of, or covered with slime.

sling (sling) *n.* pocket of leather, etc. with string attached at each end for hurling stone; catapult; swinging throw; strap attached to rifle; hanging bandage, for supporting arm or hand; rope, chain, etc. for hoisting weights;—*v.t.* throw by means of sling; hoist or lower by slings; suspend;—*pa.t.* and *pa.p.* **slung.**—**sling'er** *n.*

sling (sling) *n.* (*U.S.*) iced drink of sweetened gin (or rum) with nutmeg.

slink (slingk) *v.i.* move in stealthy, furtive manner.—*pa.t.* and *pa.p.* **slunk.**

slip (slip) *v.t.* move object secretly into another position; loosen; release (dog); omit; miss; overlook; escape;—*v.i.* lose one's foothold; move smoothly along surface of; withdraw quietly; slide, stumble; make mistake; lose one's chance; fall into fault.—*pr.p.* **slip'ping.**—*pa.t.* and *pa.p.* **slipped.**—*n.* act of slipping; unintentional error; stumble; false step; twig for grafting; leash for dog; long, narrow piece; woman's underskirt or petticoat; pinafore; covering for pillow; in cricket, position on off-side, behind wicket; fieldsman in this position; small oilstone; sideslip; potters' clay thinned with water;—*pl.* wings of theatre; slipway in shipbuilding yard.—**slip'-knot** *n.* running knot which slips along rope around which it is made, forming loop.—**slip'per** *n.* light shoe for indoor use; dancing-shoe.—**slip'perily** *adv.*—**slip'periness**, **slip'piness** *n.* condition of being slippery.—**slip'pery** *a.* not affording firm footing; unstable; untrustworthy; wily.—**slip'py** *a.* slippery; lively; quick.—**slip'-shod** *a.* having shoes down at heel; slovenly; inaccurate.—**slip'-stream** *n.* stream of air driven astern by fast-moving vehicle.—**slip'way** *n.* long inclined plane down which ships are launched.

slit (slit) *v.t.* cut lengthwise; cut open; sever; rend; split;—*v.i.* be slit.—*pr.p.* **slit'ting.**—*pa.t.* and *pa.p.* **slit.**—*n.* straight, narrow cut; narrow opening in box.—**slit trench** *n.* narrow trench for one.

slither (sliTH'-ẽr) *v.i.* slide (down slope, etc.);—*a.* slippery.—**slith'ery** *a.* slippery.

sliver (slit'-vẽr, sliv'-ẽr) *v.t.* divide into long, thin strips;—*v.i.* split; become split off;—*n.* piece cut lengthwise.

sloe (slō) *n.* blackthorn; fruit of blackthorn. — **sloe'-gin** *n.* liqueur from gin and sloes.

slog (slog) *v.t.* hit wildly and vigorously;—*v.i.* work or study with dogged determination; trudge along;—*pr.p.* **slog'ging.**—*pa.t.* and *pa.p.* **slogged.**—*n.* wild swipe at ball; hard and tiring spell of work.—**slog'ger** *n.*

slogan (slō'-gan) *n.* war-cry of Highland clan; distinctive phrase used by political party; catchword for focusing public interest.

sloop (slōōp) *n.* one-masted sailing vessel; (*Hist.*) small warship rated below frigate; (*Navy*) warship of about 1,000 tons displacement for escort and general duties.

slop (slop) *n.* water carelessly spilled; puddle;—*pl.* semi-liquid food; water in which anything has been washed;—*v.t.* spill; soil by spilling over;—*v.i.* overthrow or be spilled.—*pr.p.* **slop'ping.**—*pa.t.* and *pa.p.* **slopped.**—**slop'-ba'sin**, **slop'-bowl** *n.* basin or bowl for holding dregs from tea-cups.—**slop'pily** *adv.*—**slop'piness** *n.*—**slop'py** *a.* muddy; weak; untidy; mawkishly sentimental.

slope (slōp) *n.* upward or downward inclination; slant; side of hill; position of rifle resting on shoulder;—*v.t.* form with slope; place slanting;—*v.i.* be inclined; (*Slang*) make off.—**slo'ping** *a.* inclined from straight line or plane.—**slope arms!** military command to place rifle on shoulder.

slosh (slosh) *n.* soft mud; (*Slang*) sentimental gush; heavy blow;—*v.t.* (*Slang*) to hit wildly.

slot (slot) *n.* broad flat wooden slat, for holding together larger pieces of timber.

slot (slot) *n.* hollow or defile between two ridges or hills; wide ditch; slit cut out for reception of object or part of machine; slit where coins are inserted into automatic machine;—*v.t.* make slot in.—*pr.p.* **slot'ting.**—*pa.t.* and *pa.p.* **slot'ted.**—**slot'-machine'** *n.* automatic machine worked by insertion of coin.

slot (slot) *n.* track of deer; spoor.

sloth (slōth) *n.* lethargy; indolence.—**sloth'ful** *a.* inactive; sluggish; lazy.—**sloth'fully** *adv.*—**sloth'fulness** *n.*

sloth (slōth, sloth) *n.* mammal of S. America which clings mostly to branches of trees.

slouch (slouch) *n.* ungraceful, stooping manner of walking or standing; shambling gait;—*v.i.* shamble;—*v.t.* cause to hang down loosely.—**slouch'-hat** *n.* soft hat with broad, flexible brim.—**slouch'y** *a.*

slough (slou) *n.* bog; swamp.

slough (sluf) *n.* cast-off outer skin, esp. of snake; dead tissue which separates from healthy tissues in sores;—*v.t.* cast off, or shed;—*v.i.* separate as dead matter which forms over sore; drop off.

sloven (sluv'-n) *n.* one careless of dress, or negligent of cleanliness; slut.—slov'enliness *n.*—slov'enly *a.*—*adv.* in slipshod manner.

slow (slō) *a.* not quick; gradual; indicating time later than true time; mentally sluggish; dull; wearisome; —*adv.* slowly;—*v.t.* render slow; retard; reduce speed of;—*v.i.* slacken speed.—slow'ooach *n.* laggard.—slow'ly *adv.*—slow'ness *n.*—slow in the uptake (*Colloq.*) slow-witted.

slow-worm (slō'-wurm) *n.* blindworm, legless lizard.

sludge (sluj) *n.* mud at bottom of waterways; slimy matter from sewage in sedimentation tank.—slud'gy *a.* muddy; miry; oozy.

slug (slug) *n.* sluggard; hindrance; land-snail, common pest in gardens.—slug'gard *n.* person habitually lazy; drone;—*a.* lazy; sluggish; slothful.—slug'gish *a.* habitually indolent; slothful; slow-moving.—slug'gishly *adv.*—slug'gishness *n.*

slug (slug) *n.* small thick disc of metal; piece of metal fired from gun; solid line of type cast by Linotype process.

slug (slug) *v.i.* strike heavily; slog.

sluice (slōōs) *n.* valve or shutter for regulating flow of water from reservoir; flood-gate or water-gate; artificial channel along which stream flows; rough-and-ready wash; sluicing;—*v.t.* provide with sluices; wash out, or pour over with water; to wash by dipping one's head in stream.

slum (slum) *n.* squalid house, street, or quarter of town;—*v.i.* visit slums.—*pr.p.* slum'ming.

slumber (slum'-ber) *v.i.* sleep lightly; be in state of inactivity;—*n.* light sleep; doze.—slum'berer *n.*—slum'berous, slum'brous *a.* inducing slumber; drowsy.

slump (slump) *n.* sudden, sharp fall in prices or volume of business done; industrial or financial depression;—*v.i.* decline suddenly in value, volume, or esteem; sink when crossing snow, boggy ground, etc.

slump (slump) *v.t.* lump together in mass;—*a.* gross; total, without detailing items.

slung (slung) *pa.t.* and *pa.p.* of sling.

slunk (slungk) *pa.t.* and *pa.p.* of slink.

slur (slur) *v.t.* pass over lightly; bring into disrepute; insult; blur type, in printing; pronounce indistinctly; (*Mus.*) sing or play in smooth, gliding style; run one into other, as notes.—*pr.p.* slur'ring.—*pa.t.* and *pa.p.* slurred.—*n.* slight mark or stain; stigma; implied insult; (*Mus.*)

mark, thus (⌣ or ⌢) connecting notes sung to same syllable, or made in one continued breath; tie.

slush (slush) *n.* half-melted snow mixed with mud; trashy literature; —*v.t.* flush place with water.—slush'y *a.*

slut (slut) *n.* dirty, untidy woman; slattern.—slut'tish *a.* untidy and dirty.—slut'tishly *adv.*—slut'tishness *n.*

sly (slī) *a.* artfully cunning.—sly'ly, sli'ly *adv.*—sly'ness, sli'ness *n.*

smack (smak) *v.t.* make loud, quick noise (with lips) as in kissing or after tasting; slap loudly; strike;—*v.i.* make sharp, quick noise with lips;—*n.* this noise; loud kiss; slap.

smack (smak) *v.i.* have taste or flavour; give suggestion (of);—*n.* slight taste.

smack (smak) *n.* small fishing vessel.

small (smawl) *a.* little in size, number, degree, etc.; not large; unimportant; short; weak; slender; mean;—*n.* small or slender part, esp. of back.—small'ish *a.* rather small.—small'ness *n.*—smalls *n.pl.* (*Colloq.*) small articles of clothing.—small'-arms *n.pl.* hand firearms, e.g. rifles, pistols, etc.—small'-talk *n.* light conversation.

smallpox (smawl'-poks) *n.* infectious disease, characterised by fever and eruption developing into pustules; variola.

smarm (smarm) *v.t.* and *v.i.* anoint; smooth, esp. hair; (*Colloq.*) fawn; ingratiate.—smar'my *a.* unctuous; fawning.

smart (smart) *n.* sharp pain; (*Fig.*) pang of grief;—*v.i.* feel such pain;—*a.* causing sharp, stinging pain; clever; active; shrewd; trim; neat; well-dressed.—smart'ly *adv.*—smart'ness *n.*—smarten (smar'-tn) *v.t.* and *v.i.* make or become smart; make brighter.

smash (smash) *v.t.* break into pieces; shatter; hit hard; ruin;—*v.i.* break into pieces; dash violently against; of business firm, fail;—*n.* crash; heavy blow; accident, wrecking vehicles; bankruptcy.—smash'ing *a.* crushing; (*Slang*) excellent.

smatter (smat'-er) *v.i.* talk superficially;—smatt'ering *n.* slight, superficial knowledge.

smear (smēr) *v.t.* rub over with greasy, oily, or sticky substance; daub; impute disgrace to;—*n.* stain; disparaging imputation.—smear'iness *n.* smear'y *a.* marked with smears.

smell (smel) *n.* sense of perceiving odours by nose; act of smelling; odour; scent;—*v.t.* perceive by nose; (*Fig.*) suspect;—*v.t.* use nose; give out odour;—*pr.p.* smell'ing.—*pa.p.* and *pa.t.* smelled or smelt.—smell'ing *n.*—smell'y *a.* having unpleasant smell.—smell'ing-salts *n.pl.* scented ammonium carbonate used to relieve faintness, etc.

smelt (smelt) n. small fish of salmon family.

smelt (smelt) v.t. melt or fuse ore to extract metal.—**smel'tery** n. place for smelting ores.—**smel'ting** n.

smile (smīl) v.i. to express pleasure, approval, etc. by curving lips; look happy;—v.t. express by smile;—n. pleasant facial expression.—**smi'ling** a. cheerful; joyous.—**smi'lingly** adv.

smirch (smerch) v.t. smear over; dirty; soil; stain;—n. stain.

smirk (smerk) v.i. smile in affected or conceited manner;—n. affected or silly smile.

smite (smīt) v.t. hit hard; strike with hand, fist, weapon, etc.; defeat;—v.i. strike;—pa.p. smote (smōt);—pa.t. smote.—**smi'ter** n.

smith (smith) n. one who shapes metal, esp. with hammer and anvil; blacksmith. — **smith'y** n. smith's workshop; forge.

smitten (smit'-n) pa.p. of smite.

smock (smok) n. woman's garment; smock-frock.—**smock'-frock** n. coarse linen smock, worn over clothes, by farm-labourers—.**smock'ing** n. gathering of dress, blouse, etc. into honeycomb pattern.

smog n. mixture of smoke and fog in atmosphere (from smoke and fog);—**smog mask** n. worn for protection against smog.

smoke (smōk) n. cloudy mass of particles that rises from fire or anything burning; spell of tobacco-smoking; (Colloq.) cigar or cigarette;—v.t. consume (tobacco, opium, etc.) by smoking; expose to smoke (esp. in curing fish, etc.);—v.i. give off smoke.—**smo'ker** n. one who smokes tobacco; railway-carriage, in which smoking is permitted.—**smo'king** n.—**smo'kiness** n.—**smo'ky** a. emitting smoke; filled with smoke; like smoke.—**smo'kily** adv.

smooth (smōōTH) a. not rough; level; polished; gently flowing; calm; plausible;—v.t. make smooth; polish; calm; make easy;—adv. in smooth manner.—**smooth'ly** adv.—**smooth'ness** n.

smote (smōt) pa.p. and pa.t. of smite.

smother (smuTH'-er) v.t. destroy by depriving of air; suffocate; conceal;—v.i. be suffocated; be without air;—n. thick smoke or dust.

smoulder (smōl'-der) v.i. burn slowly without flame; (Fig.) of feelings, esp. anger, resentment, etc. suppressed.

smudge (smuj) n. smear; stain; dirty mark; blot;—v.t. smear; make dirty;—v.i. become dirty.—**smud'gy** a.

smug (smug) a. self-satisfied; complacent.—**smug'ly** adv.—**smug'ness** n.

smuggle (smug'-l) v.t. import or export goods secretly to evade

customs duties. — **smug'gler** n. — **smug'ling** n.

smut (smut) n. black particle of dirt; disease of cereals, etc.; lewd or obscene talk or writing;—v.t. blacken; smudge;—pr.p. smutt'ing.—pa.p. and pa.t. smut'ted.—**smut'ty** a. soiled with smut; obscene; lewd.—**smut'tily** adv.—**smut'tiness** n.

snack (snak) n. share; slight, hasty meal.—**snack'-bar, -coun'ter, -room** n. part of restaurant for service of light, hurried meals.

snaffle (snaf'-l) n. horse's bridle, with mouth-bit jointed in middle but without curb;—v.t. put one on horse.

snaffle (snaf'-l) v.t. (Slang) steal; purloin.

snag (snag) n. stump projecting from tree-trunk; stump sticking up in river, impeding passage of boats; obstacle, drawback, or catch.

snail (snāl) n. slow-moving mollusc with spiral shell.—**snail'ery** n. place where edible snails are reared.

snake (snāk) n. long, scaly, limbless reptile; serpent; treacherous person.—**snak'y** a. pert. to, or resembling, snake; full of snakes.—**a snake in the grass**, (Fig.) hidden enemy.

snap (snap) v.t. break abruptly; crack; seize suddenly; snatch; bite; shut with click; (Photog.) take snapshot of;—v.i. break short; try to bite; utter sharp, cross words; make quick, sharp sound;—pr.p. snap'ping.—pa.p. and pa.t. snapped.—n. act of seizing suddenly, esp. with teeth; bite; sudden breaking; quick, sharp sound; small spring catch; crisp gingerbread biscuit; short spell of frosty weather; (Photog.) short for snapshot; card-game;—a. sudden; unprepared.—**snap'per** n. one who snaps; fresh-water turtle.—**snap'pish** a. short-tempered.—**snap'pishness** n.—**snap'py** a. snappish; lively; brisk; (Colloq.) smartly dressed.—**snap'-dragon** n. (Bot.) Antirrhinum.—**snap'shot** n. hasty shot; **snap out of it,** desist.

snare (snār) n. running noose of cord or wire, to trap animals or birds; trap; anything by which one is deceived; — n.pl. catgut strings across lower head of side-drum;—v.t. catch with snare; entangle.

snarl (snärl) v.i. growl like angry dog; speak in surly manner;—n. growling sound; surly tone of voice.—**snar'ler** n.

snarl (snärl) n. tangle or knot of hair, wool, etc.; complication.

snatch (snach) v.t. seize hastily; grasp;—v.i. make quick grab or bite (at);—n. quick grab; small bit or fragment.

sneak (snēk) v.i. creep or steal away; slink;—v.t. (Slang) steal;—n. mean, cowardly fellow; tell-tale.—**sneak'er** *n.*—**sneak'ing** *a.* mean; cowardly; secret.—**sneak'ingly** *adv.*—**sneak'iness, sneak'ingness** *n.* quality of being sneaky; slyness.—**sneak'y** *a.* somewhat sneaking; mean; underhand.

sneer (snēr) *v.i.* show contempt by facial expression; smile, speak, or write scornfully;—*n.* look of contempt; scornful utterance.—**sneer'er** *n.*—**sneer'ing** *a.*—**sneer'ingly** *adv.*

sneeze (snēz) *v.i.* expel air through nose with sudden convulsive spasm and noise.

snick (snik) *n.* small cut; notch; nick;—*v.t.* cut; notch; clip; hit cricket-ball with edge of bat.

sniff (snif) *v.i.* draw in breath through nose with sharp hiss; express disapproval, etc. by sniffing; snuff;—*v.t.* take up through nose; smell;—*n.* act of sniffing; that which is sniffed.—**snif'fle** *v.i.* sniff noisily through nose; snuffle.—**snif'fler** *n.* one who sniffles.—**snift** *v.i.* sniff; snuff.—**snift'er** *v.i.* sniff; sniffle;—*n.* sniff; (*Slang*) small drink, esp. of whisky.

snigger (snig'-ẹr) *v.i.* laugh in half-suppressed manner; giggle;—*n.* sly laugh.

snip (snip) *v.t.* clip off with scissors; cut;—*n.* single, quick stroke, as with scissors; bit cut off; (*Slang*) in betting, certainty;—*pr.p.* **snip'ping.** —*pa.p.* and *pa.t.* **snipped.**—**snip'per** *n.* —**snip'pet** *n.* fragment.

snipe (snīp) *n.* gamebird, frequenting marshy places;—*v.i.* (*Mil.*) shoot from cover;—*v.t.* hit by so shooting. —*pr.p.* **snip'ing.**—*pa.p.* and *pa.t.* **sniped.**—**snip'er** *n.*

snivel (sniv'-l) *n.* running at nose; sham emotion; whining, as of child. —*v.i.* run at nose; show real or sham sorrow; cry, or whine, as children.— *pr.p.* **sniv'elling.**—*pa.p.* and *pa.t.* **sniv'elled.**—**sniv'eller** *n.*

snob (snob) *n.* one who ignores those he considers his social inferiors; cobbler.—**snob'bery** *n.*—**snob'bish** *a.*— **snob'bishly** *adv.*—**snob'bishness** *n.*

snood (snōōd) *n.* ribbon or net to hold back hair; fine, short line fixing fish-hook to line.

snook (snōōk) *n.* gesture of contempt, by placing thumb at point of nose and extending fingers.—**to cock a snook,** do this.

snooker (snōō'-kẹr) *n.* billiard table game;—*v.t.* thwart.

snoop (snōōp) *v.i.* (*Colloq.*) pry into; —*n.* one who acts thus. Also **snoop'er.**

snooze (snōōz) *n.* short sleep;—*v.i.*

snore (snōr) *v.i.* breathe noisily during sleep;—*n.* such breathing.— **snor'er** *n.*

snort (snort) *v.i.* force air with violence through nose, as horses;

express feeling by such sound;—*v.t.* express by snort;—*n.*

snout (snout) *n.* projecting nose of animal, esp. of pig; any projection like snout.

snow (snō) *n.* frozen vapour which falls in flakes; snowfall; mass of flakes on ground; (*Slang*) narcotic drug, in powdered form;—*v.t.* cover with snow.—**snow'y** *a.* covered with, full of snow; white.—**snow'ily** *adv.*— **snow'iness** *n.*—**snow'ball** *n.* round mass of snow rolled together; shrub bearing white flowers, guelder-rose; *v.t.* pelt with snowballs;—*v.i.* throw snowballs.—**snow'-blind'ness** *n.* temporary blindness by glare of sun from snow.—**snow'drift** *n.* mass of snow driven into heap by wind.— **snow'drop** *n.* bulbous plant bearing white flowers in early spring.— **snow'fall** *n.* falling of snow; amount of snow falling.—**snow'-flake** *n.* small, thin, feathery mass of snow.— **snow'-line** *n.* line on mountain above which snow never melts.—**snow'-shoe** *n.* light, wooden framework for travelling over deep snow.—**snow'-storm** *n.*—**snow'-white** *a.*

snub (snub) *v.t.* check or rebuke with rudeness or indifference; repress intentionally;—*n.* intentional slight; rebuff; check;—*a.* of nose, short, flat, and slightly turned-up.

snuff (snuf) *n.* charred part of wick of candle or lamp;—*v.t.* nip this off; extinguish.—**snuff'ers** *n.pl.* instrument resembling scissors, for nipping off snuff from wick.

snuff (snuf) *v.t.* draw up or through nostrils; sniff; smell; inhale;—*v.i.* draw air or snuff into nose; take snuff;—*n.* powdered tobacco for inhaling through nose; sniff.— **snuff'er** *n.*

snuffle (snuf'-l) *v.i.* breathe hard through nose; sniff continually;—*n.* act of snuffling; nasal twang.— **snuf'fler** *n.*

snug (snug) *a.* cosy; trim; comfortable; sheltered.—**snug'ly** *adv.*—**snug'ness** *n.* cosiness.—**snug'gery** *n.* cosy room.—**snug'gle** *v.i.* lie close to, for warmth or from affection.

so (sō) *adv.* in this manner or degree; in such manner; very; to such a degree, an extent (*with* as or that); case being such; accordingly;—*conj.* therefore; in case that;—*interj.* well!—**so long!** (*Colloq.*) good-bye.— **so'-so** *a.* (*Colloq.*) fair; middling; tolerable;—*adv.* fairly.

soak (sōk) *v.t.* steep; wet thoroughly; —*v.i.* lie steeped in water or other fluid; drink to excess;—*n.* soaking; act of soaking; heavy rain; hard drinker.—**soak'ing** *a.* wetting thoroughly; drenching;—*n.* drenching by rain.

soap (sōp) *n.* compound of oil or fat

with alkali, used in washing;—*v.t.* and *v.i.* apply soap to.—soap'y *a.* pert. to soap; covered with soap; (*Fig.*) flattering; oily.—soap'iness *n.*—soap'-bub'ble *n.* bubble from soapsuds.—soap'-suds *n.pl.* foamy mixture of soap and water.

soar (sōr) *v.i.* fly high; mount into air; (*Fig.*) rise far above normal.

sob (sob) *v.i.* catch breath, esp. in weeping;—*pr.p.* sob'bing.—*pa.p.* and *pa.p.* sob'bed.—*n.* convulsive catching of breath, esp. in weeping or sighing.

sober (sō-bēr) *a.* temperate; not intoxicated; exercising cool reason; subdued;—*v.t.* and *v.i.* make or become sober.—so'berly *adv.*—so'berness *n.*—sobriety (sō-brī'-e-ti) *n.* habit of being sober; habitual temperance; moderation; seriousness.

soccer (sok'-ēr) *n.* (*Colloq.*) association football.

sociable (sō'-sha-bl) *a.* inclined to be friendly; fond of company.—so'ciably *adv.*—so'ciableness *n.*—sociabil'ity *n.* friendliness; geniality.

social (sō'-shal) *a.* pert. to society; affecting public interest; pert. to upper classes, world of fashion, etc.; companionable; convivial;—*n.* social meeting.—so'ciably *adv.*

socialism (sō'-shal-izm) *n.* system, aiming at public ownership of means of production, etc.—so'cialise *v.t.* make social; transfer industry, etc. from private to public ownership.—socialisa'tion *n.*—so'cialist *a.* pert. to socialism.—socialist'ic *a.*

society (so-sī'-e-ti) *n.* people in general; community; people of culture and good breeding in any community; upper classes; world of fashion; fellowship; company; association; club.

sociology (sō-shi-ol'-o-ji) *n.* social science.—sociolog'ical *a.*—sociol'ogist *n.* a student of sociology.

sock (sok) *n.* half-stocking, esp. for men.

sock (sok) *v.t.* (*Slang*) hit hard.

socket (sok'-et) *n.* hollow into which anything is fitted; cavity of eye, tooth, etc.;—*v.t.* provide with, or place in, socket.

sod (sod) *n.* flat piece of earth with grass; turf.

soda (sō'-da) *n.* name applied to various compounds of sodium, e.g. *baking-soda, caustic soda, washing-soda.* See sodium; (*Colloq.*) soda-water.—so'da-wa'ter *n.* drink made by charging water with carbonic acid gas.

sodden (sod'-n) *a.* soaked; soft with moisture; drunken; stupid.

sodium (sō'-di-um) *n.* white metallic element, base of soda (symbol Na.) sodium bicarbonate, compound of sodium and carbon, used in cooking,

medicine, etc.; baking-soda.—sodium carbonate, washing-soda. — sodium chloride, common household salt.

sofa (sō'-fa) *n.* long couch, with raised back.

soft (soft) *a.* yielding easily to pressure; not hard; easily shaped or moulded; smooth; gentle; quiet; weak; weak in intellect; containing no alcohol; 'c' and 'g,' pronounced with sibilant sound;—*adv.* softly; quietly.—soft'ish *a.* somewhat soft.—soft'ly *adv.* quietly.—soft'ness *n.*—soft'-head'ed *a.* weak in intellect.—soft'-heart'ed *a.* gentle; merciful.

soften (sof'-n) *v.t.* make soft or softer; lighten; mitigate; tone down; make less loud;—*v.i.* become soft or softer.—soft'ening *n.* becoming soft or softer.

soggy (sog'-i) *a.* soaked with water; sodden.

soil (soil) *v.t.* make dirty; stain;—*v.i.* become dirty; show stains;—*n.* dirty mark.

soil (soil) *n.* top layer of earth's surface.

soirée (swá-rā') *n.* social evening, reception.

sojourn (sō'-jurn, so-jurn') *v.i.* stay for short time;—*n.* short stay.

solace (sol'-as) *n.* comfort in grief; consolation;—*v.t.* console.

solan (sō'-lan) *n.* large sea-bird like goose; gannet. Also so'lan-goose.

solar (sō'-lar) *a.* pert. to, caused by, measured by sun.—so'larise *v.t.* and *v.i.* expose to sun's rays.—solarium (sō-lar'-i-um) *n.* room or balcony, esp. in hospital, etc. for sun-bathing. —*pl.* solar'ia.—solar plexus (*Med.*) network of nerve tissue at back of stomach.—solar system, sun and nine planets revolving round it.

sold (sōld) *pa.p.* and *pa.t.* of sell.

solder (sol'-der, sōl'-der, sod'-er) *n.* easily melted alloy for joining metals;—*v.t.* join with this.

soldier (sōl'-jer) *n.* man in military service; private or N.C.O. as distinguished from commissioned officer.—sol'diery *n.* soldiers collectively; troops.

sole (sōl) *n.* flat of foot; under part of boot or shoe; lower part of anything, or that on which anything rests; small flat-fish, used for food;—*v.t.* supply with sole.

sole (sōl) *a.* alone; only.—sole'ly *adv.* alone; only.—sole'ness *n.*

solecism (sol'-e-sizm) *n.* gross breach of grammar; or etiquette.—sol'ecist *n.* one guilty of solecisms.—solecist'ic, solecist'ical *a.*—solecist'ically *adv.*

solenoid (sol'-e-noid) *n.* coil acting as magnet when electrified.

solemn (sol'-em) *a.* marked with religious ceremony; impressive; grave; inspiring awe or dread.—sol'emnly *adv.*—sol'emnness *n.*—sol'-

emnise v.t. perform with ritual ceremony or legal form; celebrate, esp. festival.—**solemnisa'tion** n.—**solem'nity** n. sacred rite or celebration; seriousness.

sol-fa (sol-fä') v.i. sing notes of scale with sol, fa, etc.;—n. use of these in singing;—a. pert. to system of musical notation.

solicit (so-lis'-it) v.t. ask with earnestness; petition; entreat;—v.i. accost, esp. of prostitute.—**solic'itant** n. petitioner.—**solicita'tion** n. earnest. request; invitation; petition.—**solic'itous** a. anxious; earnest.—**solic'itously** adv.—**solic'itousness**, **solic'itude** n. being solicitous; uneasiness; anxiety; concern.

solicitor (so-lis'-i-tor) n. person legally qualified to represent another in court of law.

solid (sol'-id) a. not in liquid or gaseous state; hard; firm; not hollow; sound; unanimous; (Geom.) having length, breadth, and thickness;—n. firm, compact body; (Geom.) that which has length, breadth and thickness; (Physics) substance which is not liquid nor gaseous.—**sol'idly** adv. firmly; unitedly; unanimously.—**soldar'ity** n. state of being solidly united in support of common interests, rights, etc.—**solid'ity** n. compactness; hardness; firmness.—**sol'idness** n.

solidify (so-lid'-i-fi) v.t. make solid or firm; harden;—v.i. become solid.

soliloquy (so-lil'-o-kwi) n. talking to oneself; monologue, esp. by actor alone on stage.—**solil'oquise** v.i. recite soliloquy.

solitaire (sol-i-tär') n. single gem, esp. diamond, set by itself; game for one, played on board with marbles; (Cards) game for one, patience.

solitary (sol'-i-tar-i) a. living alone; done or spent alone; lonely; secluded; single; sole;—n. hermit; recluse.—**sol'itarily** adv.—**sol'itariness** n.—**sol'itude** n. being alone; loneliness; lonely place or life.

solo (sō'-lō) n. musical composition played or sung by one person.—pl. **solos** (sō'-lōz) (Aviat.) flight by single person;—**so'lo-whist** n. card game;—a. done or performed by one person; unaccompanied; alone.—**soloist** (sō'-lō-ist) n. (Mus.) performer of solos.

Solomon's seal figure of six-pointed star, made by two triangles.

solstice (sol'-stis) n. either of two points in sun's path at which sun is farthest N. or S. from equator; they mark mid-summer and mid-winter.—**solstitial** (sol-sti'-shal) a.

soluble (sol'-ū-bl) a. capable of being dissolved in liquid; able to be solved or explained.—**solubil'ity** n.

solution (so-lū'-shun) n. process of finding answer to problem; answer itself; dissolving gas, liquid, or solid, esp. in liquid; mixture so obtained; commonly, mixture of solid in liquid; separation;—v.t. coat with solution, as puncture.

solve (solv) v.t. orig. loosen or separate parts of; work out; find answer to; explain; make clear.—**sol'vable** a. able to be worked out.—**sol'ver** n.—**sol'vent** a. having power to dissolve another substance; able to pay one's debts;—n. substance, able to dissolve another substance.—**sol'vency** n. being able to pay one's debts.

sombre (som'-ber) a. dark; gloomy; melancholy.—**som'brely** adv.—**som'breness** n. darkness; gloominess.

some (sum) a. denoting indefinite number, amount, or extent; amount of; one or other; certain; particular; (Colloq.) remarkable;—(pron.) quantity; portion; particular persons not named; — adv. approximately. —**some'body** n. person not definitely known; person of importance.—**some'how** adv. in one way or another; by any means.—**some'one** n. somebody; person not named.—**some'such** a. denoting person or thing of kind specified.—**some'thing** n. thing not clearly defined; indefinite quantity or degree;—adv. in some degree.—**some'time** adv. at time not definitely stated; at one time or other; at future time;—a. former.—**some'times** adv. at times; now and then; occasionally.—**some'what** n. more or less; something;—adv. to some extent; rather.—**some'where** adv. in unnamed or unknown place.

somersault (sum'-er-sawlt) n. leap in which one turns head over heels;—v.i. make such a leap.

somnambulate (som-nam'-bū-lāt) v.i. walk in one's sleep.—**somnambula'tion** n. act of walking in sleep.—**somnam'bulism** n. habit of walking in sleep; sleep-walking.—**somnam'bulist** n. a sleep-walker.

somnolent (som'-no-lent) a. sleepy; drowsy.—**som'nolently** adv. drowsily.—**som'nolence** n. sleepiness; drowsiness. Also **som'nolency.**—**somnoles'cent** a. half-asleep.

son (sun) n. male child; male descendant; native of place; disciple.—**son'-in-law** n. husband of one's daughter.

sonata (so-nä'-ta) n. musical composition in three or four movements.—**sonatina** (so-na-tē'-na) n. short sonata.

song (song) n. singing; poem, or piece of poetry, esp. if set to music; piece of music to be sung; musical sounds made by birds; (Colloq.) mere trifle.—**song'ster** n. (fem. **song'stress**) one who sings.

sonic (son'ik) *a.* pert. to sound waves.
—**sonic bang**, shock waves occuring when aircraft breaks the sound barrier.

sonnet (son'-et) *n.* poem of fourteen lines, with definite rhyme scheme.—**sonneteer** *n.* writer of sonnets.

sonorous (so-nō'-rus) *a.* giving out deep, loud sound when struck; resonant; high-sounding.—**sono'rously** *adv.*—**sonor'ity**, **sono'rousness** *n.*

soon (sōon) *adv.* in short time; shortly; without delay; early.

soot (soot) *n.* black powdery substance formed by burning of coal, etc.—**soot'y** *a.* pert. to soot; covered with soot; black.—**soot'iness** *n.*

sooth (sōoth) *n.* truth; reality;—*a.* true; faithful.—**sooth'sayer** *n.* one who claims ability to foretell future.—**sooth'saying** *n.*

soothe (sōoTH) *v.t.* please with soft words or kind actions; calm; comfort; allay, as pain.—**sooth'ing** *a.*—**sooth'ingly** *adv.*

sop (sop) *n.* piece of bread, etc., dipped in liquid; anything given to pacify; bribe;—*v.t.* steep in liquid;—*pr.p.* **sop'ping**—*pa.p.* and *pa.t.* **sopped.**—**sop'ping** *a.* soaked; wet through.—**sop'py** *a.* soaked.

sophism (sof'-izm) *n.* specious argument; clever but fallacious reasoning. — **soph'ist** *n.* — **soph'istry** *n.*—**sophis'tic**, **sophis'tical** *a.*—**sophis'tically** *adv.*—**sophis'ticate** *v.t.* deceive by using sophisms; make artificial; falsify.—**sophis'ticated** *a.* wise in ways of world; not genuine; artificial.—**sophistica'tion** *n.*

sopor (sō'-por) *n.* coma.—**soporif'ic** *a.* causing or inducing sleep;—*n.* drug which induces deep sleep.—**soporif'erous**, **so'porose**, **so'porous** *a.* causing sleep; sleepy.—**soporif'erously** *adv.*—**soporif'erousness** *n.*

soprano (sō-prá'-nō) *n.* highest type of female or boy's voice; soprano singer;—*pl.* **sopra'nos.**

sorcery (sor'-ser-i) *n.* witchcraft; magic; enchantment.—**sor'cerer** *n.* magician.—*fem.* **sor'ceress**, witch.

sordid (sor'-did) *a.* filthy; squalid; meanly avaricious.—**sor'didly** *adv.*—**sor'didness** *n.*

sore (sōr) *a.* painful when touched; causing pain; tender; severe; intense; distressed; grieved; angry;—*adv.* painfully; intensely;—*n.* place where pain is felt; ulcer; boil.—**sore'ly** *adv.*—**sore'ness** *n.*

sororal (so-rō'-ral) *a.* pert. to sisters; sisterly.—**soror'icide** *n.* murder, or murderer, of sister.

sorrel (sor'-el) *n.* meadow plant, herb with sour taste.

sorrel (sor'-el) *a.* reddish-brown;—*n.* (horse of) reddish-brown colour.

sorrow (sor'-ō) *n.* pain of mind; grief; sadness; distress; cause of

grief, etc.;—*v.i.* feel pain of mind; grieve.—**sorr'ower** *n.*—**sorr'owful** *a.* causing sorrow; sad; unhappy.—**sorr'owfully** *adv.*—**sorr'owfulness** *n.*

sorry (sor'-i) *a.* feeling regret; mean; shabby; worthless.—**sorr'ily** *adv.*—**sorr'iness** *n.*

sort (sort) *n.* kind or class; persons or things having same qualities; quality; character; order or rank;—*v.t.* classify; put in order.—**sort'er** *n.*—**out of sorts**, unwell.

sortie (sor'-tē) *n.* sally by besieged forces to attack besiegers; flight by warplane.

S. O. S. (es-ō-es) *n.* international code-signal call of distress, esp. by wireless in Morse; desperate appeal.

sot (sot) *n.* confirmed drunkard.—**sot'tish** *a.* pert. to sot; stupid through drink.

sou (sōo) *n.* small French coin.

sough (suf, sou, *Scot,* sooH) *n.* low murmuring, sighing, or whistling sound, as of wind through trees;—*v.i.* make this sound.

sought (sawt) *pa.p.* and *pa.t.* of **seek.**

soul (sōl) *n.* spiritual and immortal part of human being; seat of emotion, sentiment, and aspiration; centre of moral and intellectual powers; vigour; energy; spirit; essence; human being.—**soul'ful** *a.* full of soul, emotion, or sentiment.—**soul'fully** *adv.*—**soul'less** *a.* without soul; not inspired.

sound (sound) *a.* healthy; in good condition; solid; entire; reliable; solvent, as business firm;—*adv.* soundly; completely.—**sound'ly** *adv.* thoroughly.—**sound'ness** *n.*

sound (sound) *n.* long, narrow stretch of water.

sound (sound) *v.t.* find depth of water, by means of line and lead; (*Fig.*) try to discover opinions of;—*v.i.* find depth of water; dive suddenly, of whale.—**sound'ing** *n.* measuring depth of water, esp. with weighted line.

sound (sound) *n.* that which is heard; distance to which sound is heard; earshot; noise; report;—*v.t.* cause to make sound; utter; play on; signal; examine with stethoscope;—*v.i.* make noise; be conveyed by sound; appear; seem.—**sound'ing** *a.* making sound; resonant.—**sound-barrier**, shock-waves formed when moving object reaches speed in excess of that of sound.—**sound'track** *n.* strip on one side of cinema film on which sound is recorded.—**sound-waves** *n.pl.* vibrations of air producing sound.

soup (sōop) *n.* liquid food made by boiling meat or vegetables.

sour (sour) *a.* acid; having sharp taste; pungent; rancid; of milk, turned; of soil, cold and wet; (*Fig.*)

cross;—*v.t.* and *v.i.* make or become sour.—**soured** *a.* embittered.—**sour'ly** *adv.*—**sour'ness** *n.*

source (sōrs) *n.* spring; origin.

souse (sous) *v.t.* steep in brine; pickle; soak;—*n.* pickle made with salt; brine; anything steeped in it; drenching.

south (south) *n.* cardinal point of compass opposite north; region lying to that side;—*a.* pert. to, or coming from south;—*adv.* towards south;—*v.i.* move towards south.—**southerly** *a.* (suTH'-ẽr-li) *a.* pert. to south.—**south'ern** *a.* in, from, or towards, south.—**south'erner** *n.* native of south of country, etc.—**south'ernly** *adv.* towards south. — **south'ernmost** *a.* lying farthest towards south.—**south'ward** *a.* and *adv.* towards south;—*n.* southern direction.—**south'wardly** *a.* and *adv.*—**south'wards** *adv.*—**sou'west'er** *n.* strong wind from south-west; waterproof hat.

souvenir (sōō-ve-nēr', sōō-ven-ẽr') *n.* keepsake; memento.

sovereign (suv'-ran, sov'-ran, suv'-ẽr-in, sov'-ẽr-in) *n.* ruler; (*Hist.*) British gold coin;—*a.* supreme in power; chief; efficacious in highest degree.—**sov'ereignty** *n.* right to exercise supreme power.

soviet (sov'-yet, sō'-vi-et) *n.* council.—**Sov'iet** *n.* elected local or national governing body in Russia. Also *a.*—**Soviet Union**, short for 'Union of Socialist Soviet Republics,' i.e. Russia;—*abbrev.* U.S.S.R.

sow (sou) *n.* female pig; in smelting, bar of cast iron.

sow (sō) *v.t.* scatter or deposit (seed); spread abroad; disseminate;—*v.i.* scatter seed.—*pa.p.* **sown** (sōn) or **sowed** (sōd).—*pa.t.* **sowed.**—**sow'er** *n.*

soy (soi) *n.* sauce made from soy-bean (soya-bean).—**soy'-bean, soy'a-bean** *n.* seed of plant of Far East, yielding oil (for margarine), flour, cattle fodder, and fertiliser.

spa (spä) *n.* place with mineral spring.

space (spās) *n.* expanse of universe; area; room; period of time; extent; empty place;—*v.t.* place at intervals. —**spa'cious** (spā'-shus) *a.* roomy; capacious; extensive. — **spa'ciously** *adv.*—**spa'ciousness** *n.*

spade (spād) *n.* digging-tool, with flat blade and long handle.—**spade'-work** *n.* toilsome work preliminary to main task.

spade (spād) *n.* (*Cards*) one of two black suits, marked by figure like pointed spade.

spaghetti (spa-get'-ti) *n.* foodstuff, thin strings of flour paste.

span (span) *pa.t.* of spin.

span (span) *n.* distance between thumb and little finger, when fingers are fully extended; this distance as measure = 9 in.; short distance or

period of time; distance between supports of arch, roof, etc.; of aeroplane, distance from wing-tip to wing-tip; pair, of horses or oxen harnessed together;—*v.t.* reach from one side of to other; extend across. —*pr.p.* **span'ning.**—*pa.p.* and *pa.t.* **spanned.**—**span'ner** *n.* tool for tightening screw-nuts; wrench.

spangle (spang'-gl) *n.* small piece of glittering metal, used to ornament dresses;—*v.t.* adorn with spangles;—*v.i.* glitter.

spaniel (span'-yel) *n.* breed of dogs with long, drooping ears; fawning person.

spank (spangk) *v.t.* slap;—*n.* slap.

spar (spär) *v.i.* fight with fists, in fun or in earnest; dispute, esp. in fun;—*pr.p.* **spar'ring.**—*pa.p.* and *pa.t.* **sparred.**

spar (spär) *n.* pole or beam.

spare (spär) *v.t.* and *v.i.* use frugally; do without; save; leave unhurt;—*a.* frugal; scanty; scarce; thin; lean; in reserve; not in use;—*n.* that which is held in reserve.—*pl.* **spares** or **spare'-parts,** duplicate parts of machine.—**spare'ly** *adv.*—**spare'ness** *n.* thinness; leanness.—**spar'ing** *a.* frugal; saving; scanty; merciful.—**spar'ingly** *adv.*

spark (spärk) *n.* small glowing or burning particle; flash of light; trace of anything; electric flash;—*v.i.* send out sparks.—**spark off** *v.t.* (*Fig.*) initiate suddenly.—*pl.* **sparks** (*Naut. Slang*) wireless operator.—**spark'ing-plug** *n.* in internal-combustion engines, device for providing electric spark for ignition.

sparkle (spärk'-l) *n.* small spark; glitter; gleam;—*v.i.* emit small flashes of light; gleam; emit little bubbles; effervesce.—**spark'ler** *n.* one who, or that which, sparkles; (*Slang*) diamond.—**spark'ling** *a.* flashing; gleaming; of wines, effervescent.

sparrow (spar'-ō) *n.* small brown bird of finch family.—**sparr'ow-grass** *n.* asparagus.—**sparr'ow-hawk** *n.* one of falcon family.

sparse (spärs) *a.* thinly scattered; scanty; rare.—**sparse'ly** *adv.*—**sparse'-ness** *n.* scantiness.

spasm (spazm) *n.* sudden, involuntary contraction of muscle(s); sudden, convulsive movement, effort, emotion, etc.; fitful effort; paroxysm. **spasmod'ic** *n.* medicine for relieving spasms.—**spasmod'ic(al)** *a.* pert. to spasms; fitful.—**spasmod'ically** *adv.* by fits and starts.—**spas'tic** *a.* (*Med.*) pert. to spasms; in rigid condition, due to spasm; applied to children suffering from cerebral palsy;—*n.* such child.—**spas'tics** *n.pl.* (*Med.*) condition showing tendency to spasm or muscular contraction.

spat (spat) *pa.t.* of spit.

spat (spat) *n.* kind of cloth gaiter,

reaching above ankle. Usu. in *pl.* **spats.**
spate (spāt) *n.* flood in river, esp. after heavy rain; inundation.
spatial (spā'-shạl) *a.* pert. to space.—**spa'tially** *adv.*
spatter (spat'-ẹr) *v.t.* cast drops of water, mud, etc. over; splash;—*v.i.* fall in drops;—*n.* slight splash.
spatula (spat'-ū-lạ) *n.* broad-bladed knife for spreading paints, ointments; (*Med.*) small instrument for holding down tongue during examination of throat.
spawn (spawn) *n.* eggs of fish, frogs; offspring;—*v.t.* and *v.i.* of fish, frogs, cast eggs; produce offspring.
speak (spēk) *v.i.* utter words; tell; deliver discourse;—*v.t.* utter; pronounce; express in words; address;—*pr.p.* speak'ing.—*pa.p.* spo'ken.—*pa.t.* spoke or (*Arch.*) spake.—**speak'er** *n.* one who speaks; orator.—**the Speaker,** president of British House of Commons.—**speak'ing** *n.*—*a.* having power to utter words; eloquent; (*Fig.*) lifelike, e.g. of picture.
spear (spēr) *n.* long, pointed weapon, used in fighting, hunting, etc.;—*v.t.* pierce or kill with spear.—**spear'-head** *n.* iron point, barb, or prong of spear; leader of advance; (*Mil.*) deep penetration, on narrow front, into enemy position.
special (spesh'-ạl) *a.* pert. to species or sort; particular; beyond usual; distinct; intimate.—**spe'cially** *adv.*—**spe'cialise** *v.t.* make special or distinct; adapt for particular purpose;—*v.i.* devote oneself to particular branch of study.—**specialisa'tion** *n.* act of specialising.—**spe'cialist** *n.* one trained and skilled in special branch.—**specialist'ic** *a.*—**speciality** (spesh-i-al'-i-ti), **specialty** (spesh'-ạl-ti) *n.* special characteristic of person or thing; special product; that in which person is highly skilled.
species (spē'-shēz, -shiz) *n.* kind; variety; sort; class; subdivision of more general class.
specific (spe-sif'-ik) *a.* pert. to species; peculiar to; well defined; precise;—*n.* (*Med.*) infallible remedy.—**specif'ically** *adv.*—**specific gravity,** weight of substance proportionate to weight of equal volume of water.
specification (spes-i-fi-kā'-shun) *n.* act of specifying.—**spe'cify** *v.t.* state definitely; give details of; indicate precisely.—**specifi'able** *a.*
specimen (spes'-i-men) *n.* part of anything, or one of number of things, used to show nature and quality of whole; sample.
specious (spē'-shus) *a.* having fair appearance; superficially fair or just; apparently acceptable, esp. at first sight.—**spe'ciously** *adv.*—**spe'-ciousness** *n.*
speck (spek) *n.* small spot; particle; very small thing; stain;—*v.t.* mark with specks.—**speck'le** *n.* small speck or spot;—*v.t.* mark with small spots.—**speck'led** *a.* spotted; variegated.—
spectacle (spek'-tạ-kl) *n.* sight; show; thing exhibited; pageant.—**spec'tacles** *n.pl.* arrangement of lenses, to help defective or weak eyesight. — **spec'tacled** *a.* wearing spectacles.—**spectac'ular** *a.* showy; grand; making great display.—**spectac'ularly** *adv.*
spectator (spek-tā'-tor) *n.* one who looks on; onlooker.
spectre (spek'-tẹr) *n.* ghost; apparition.—**spec'tral** *a.* pert. to spectre; ghostly; pert. to spectrum.—**spec'trally** *adv.*—**spec'troscope** *n.* instrument for studying spectra.—**spec'trum** *n.* coloured band into which ray of light can be separated as in rainbow; *pl.* **spectra.**
speculate (spek'-ū-lāt) *v.i.* make theories or guesses; meditate; engage in risky commercial transactions.—**specula'tion** *n.* act of speculating; theorising; guess; practice of buying shares, etc. in hope of selling at high profit.—**spec'ulative** *a.* given to speculation.— **spec'ulatively** *adv.* — **spec'ulator** *n.*—**spec'ulatory** *a.* speculative.
sped (sped) *pa.p.* and *pa.t.* of speed.
speech (spēch) *n.* power of speaking; what is spoken; faculty of expressing thoughts in words; enunciation; remarks; conversation; language; formal address; oration.—**speech'less** *a.* without power of speech; dumb; silent.—**speech'lessly** *adv.*—**speech'lessness** *n.*—**speech'ify** *v.i.* make boring speech.—**speech'ifier** *n.*
speed (spēd) *n.* swiftness of motion; rate of progress; velocity;—*v.t.* cause to move faster; aid; bid farewell to;—*v.i.* move quickly or at speed beyond legal limit;—*pa.p.* and *pa.t.* sped.—**speed'y** *a.* quick; rapid.—**speed'ily** *adv.*—**speedom'eter** *n.* instrument indicating speed.—**speed'way** *n.* track for motor-cycle racing.—**speed'well** *n.* small plant of genus Veronica.
spell (spel) *n.* word or words supposed to have magical power; magic formula; fascination.—**spell'bind** *v.t.* hold as if by spell; fascinate.—**spell'-bound** *a.* fascinated; enchanted.
spell (spel) *n.* turn of work or duty, esp. to relieve another; brief period of time.
spell (spel) *v.t.* read letter by letter; mean;—*v.i.* form words with proper letters;—*pa.p.* and *pa.t.* spelled or spelt.
spend (spend) *v.t.* and *v.i.* pay out; pass, as time; employ; exhaust.—**spent** *a.* exhausted; worn out; inefficient; of fish, having deposited spawn.—**spen'der** *n.* one who spends.

—**spend'thrift** n. one who spends money foolishly;—a. extravagant.

sperm (sperm) n. fertilising fluid of male animals; semen.—**sperm'-oil** n. oil obtained from sperm-whale.—**sperm'-whale** n. large whale, valuable for oil and spermaceti.—**spermaceti** (sper-ma-sē'-ti, sper-ma-set'-i) n. wax-like substance obtained from head of sperm-whale, used for making candles, etc.—**spermat'ic, spermat'ical** a. pert. to sperm.

spew, spue (spū) v.t. and v.i. eject from stomach; vomit.

Sphagnum (sfag'-num) n. bog-moss.

sphere (sfēr) n. round, solid body; ball; globe; revolution; orbit; range of influence, etc.; field of action; position;—v.t. put in sphere; encircle.—**sphe'ral** (sfē'-ral) a.—**spheric** (sfer'-ik) a.—**spher'ical** a.—**spher'ically** adv.—**spheric'ity** n. roundness.—**spheroid** (sfē'-roid) n. body almost, but not quite, spherical, e.g. orange, earth, etc.—**spheroi'dal** a. having form of spheroid. Also **spheroi'dic, spheroi'dical.**—**spher'ular, spher'ulate** a.

sphinx (sfingks) n. (Myth.) monster, with winged body of lion and head of woman, which proposed riddles to passers-by, and strangled all unable to solve them; statue of this; (Fig.) enigmatic person.

spice (spīs) n. aromatic substance, used for seasoning; spices collectively; (Fig.) anything that adds flavour, etc.;—v.t. season with spice.—**spi'cey** a. seasoned with spices; aromatic; suggestive.—**spi'cily** adv.

spick (spik) n. spike; nail;—a. neat; tidy.—**spick and span,** fresh and new; neat, clean.

spider (spī'-der) n. small, eight-legged insect-like animal that spins web to catch flies, etc.—**spi'dery** a. like spider; full of spiders; very thin.—**spider-man** n. steel scaffold erector.

spigot (spig'-ut) n. peg for stopping hole in cask; part of water-tap which controls flow.

spike (spīk) n. sharp-pointed piece of metal or wood; large nail; ear of corn, etc.; (Bot.) flower-cluster growing from central stem;—v.t. supply, set, fasten, or pierce with spikes.—**spi'ky** a.

spill (spil) v.t. cause to flow out; pour out; shed (blood); upset;—v.i. flow over; be shed; be lost or wasted;—n. overflow; fall or tumble, as from vehicle, horse, etc;—pa.p. and pa.t. spilled or spilt.—**spill'er** n.

spill (spil) n. thin strip of wood or twist of paper, for lighting fire, pipe, etc.; peg.

spin (spin) v.t. twist into threads; cause to revolve rapidly; whirl; draw out tediously, as story; prolong;—v.i. make thread; revolve rapidly; move swiftly;—n. rapid whirling motion; short, quick run or drive;—pr.p. spin'ning.—pa.p. and pa.t. spun or (Arch.) span.—**spin'ner** n. one who spins.—**spin-dryer** n. clothes dryer employing centrifugal force.

spinach (spin'-āj) n. vegetable used for food.

spindle (spin'-dl) n. long, slender rod, used in spinning, for twisting and winding thread;—v.i. grow long and slender.—**spin'dly** a. long and slender.

spindrift (spin'-drift) n. spray blown from surface of sea.

spine (spīn) n. thorn; backbone; back of book.—**spi'nal** a. pert. to spine or backbone.—**spine'less** a. having no spine; weak of character.—**spi'ny** a. full of spines; like spine; thorny; prickly.—**spi'nous** a. full of spines; prickly.—**spinal column,** backbone.

spinet (spin'-et) n. small type of harpsichord.

spinnaker (spin'-a-ker) n. triangular sail.

spinney (spin'-i) n. small wood; grove.

spinster (spin'-ster) n. unmarried woman.—**spin'sterhood** n.

spire (spīr) n. winding line like threads of screw; curl; coil.—**spi'ral** a. winding; coiled;—n. spiral curve; coil; whorl.

spire (spīr) n. blade of grass; stalk; slender shoot; anything tall and tapering to point; (tapering part of) steeple; peak;—v.t. furnish with spire;—v.i. rise high, like spire.—**spi'ral** a. like spire.—**spi'ry** a.

spirit (spir'-it) n. vital force; immortal part of man; soul; spectre; ghost; disposition; temper; mental vigour; courage; essential character; liquid got by distillation, esp. alcoholic;—v.t. carry away mysteriously; put energy into.—**spir'its** n.pl. state of mind; mood; distilled alcoholic liquor.—**spir'ited** a. full of spirit and vigour; lively.—**spir'edly** adv.—**spir'itedness** n.—**spir'itless** a. without spirit or life; lacking energy; listless.—**spir'itless** adv.—**spir'ituous** a. containing alcohol; distilled.—**spir'it-lev'el** n. instrument for finding or testing horizontal line.

spiritual (spir'-i-tū-al) a. pert. to spirit or mind; not material; pert. to sacred things; holy;—n. Negro sacred song or hymn.—**spir'itually** adv.—**spir'itualise** v.t. make pure in heart.—**spir'itualism, spir'itism** n. religious belief that spirits of dead can communicate with living people.—**spir'itualist** n.—**spir'itualistic** a.

spit (spit) n. pointed rod put through meat for roasting; sandy point of land projecting into sea;—v.t. thrust spit through.

spit (spit) v.t. eject from mouth; expel;—v.i. eject saliva from mouth;

expectorate; hiss, esp. of cats;—*n.* saliva; act of spitting; light fall of fine rain; exact likeness;—*pr.p.* spit'ting. — *pa.p.* spat. — *pa.t.* spat (*Arch.* spit).—spit'ter *n.*—spit'tle *n.* saliva ejected from mouth; sputum. —spittoon' *n.* vessel for spittle; cuspidor.

spit (spit) *n.* in digging, depth of spade.

spite (spīt) *n.* malice; ill-will;—*v.t.* treat maliciously; try to injure; vex; annoy.—spite'ful *a.* full of ill-feeling; desirous of thwarting.— spite'fully *adv.*—spite'fulness *n.*—in spite of, in defiance of.

splash (splash) *v.t.* spatter water, mud, etc. over; soil thus; print in bold headlines;—*v.i.* dash or scatter, of liquids; dabble in water; fall in drops;—*n.* sound of object falling into liquid; water, mud, etc. dashed about; spot; daub; patch of colour.—splash'y *a.* wet and muddy.

splatter (splat'-ẽr) *v.t. and i.* splash continuously; spatter.

splay (splā) *v.t.* slope; slant; spread outwards;—*a.* turned outwards; flat and broad; *n.* sloped surface of opening, as window.—splay'-foot *n.* flat foot.

spleen (splēn) *n.* ductless organ lying to left of stomach; (*Fig.*) ill-humour; spite; irritability.

splendid (splen'-did) *a.* magnificent; gorgeous; (*Colloq.*) excellent.—splen'didly *adv.*—splendour (splen'-dẽr) *n.* brilliant lustre; pomp.

splenetic (sple-net'-ik) *a.* pert. to spleen; affected with spleen; morose; irritable.—splenetic (splen'-e-tik) *n.* one suffering from disease of spleen; remedy for this.—splen'ic *a.* pert. to spleen.

splice (splīs) *v.t.* join, as two ends of rope, by weaving strands together; join, as wood, etc.; (*Colloq.*) marry;— *n.* union of two ends of ropes, etc.

splint (splint) *n.* piece split off; rigid piece of material for holding broken limb in position; bony excrescence on inside of horse's leg;—*v.t.* bind with splints.—splint'er *n.* piece of wood, metal, etc. split off;—*v.t. and i.* break off into long, thin pieces; shiver.—splint'er group, defecting section of larger group.

split (split) *v.t.* cut lengthwise; cleave; tear apart; separate;—*v.i.* break asunder; cut lengthwise; dash to pieces; betray secret;—*n.* crack; fissure; breach in political party;— *pl.* sitting down with legs stretched apart until they are flat on floor.— *pr.p.* split'ting.—*pa.p.* and *pa.t.* split. —split'ting *n.* cleaving or rending;— *a.* severe; distressing.—to split hairs, make fine distinctions.

splutter (splut'-ẽr) *v.t.* utter incoherently with spitting sounds;—*v.i.*

emit such sounds; speak confusedly; —*n.* such sounds or speech; confused noise.—splutt'erer *n.*

spoil (spoil) *v.t.* damage; injure; plunder; cause to decay; harm character of by indulgence;—*v.i.* go bad; decay;—*n.* booty; prey; plunder;—*pa.p.* and *pa.t.* spoiled or spoilt.

spoke (spōk) *pa.t.* of the verb speak. —spoken (spōk'-n) *pa.p.*,—spokes'man *n.* one deputed to speak for others; representative.

spoke (spōk) *n.* one of small bars connecting hub of wheel with rim; rung of ladder; hand-spike.—to put a spoke in one's wheel, frustrate or thwart.—spoke'shave *n.* tool for planing wood.

spoliate (spō'-li-āt) *v.t.* spoil; plunder;—*v.i.* practise plundering.— spo'liative *a.* tending to diminish.— spolia'tion *n.* robbery; destruction.— spo'liator *n.*

sponge (spunj) *n.* marine animal of cellular structure, outer coating of whose body is perforated to allow entrance of water; skeleton of this animal, used to absorb water; act of cleaning with sponge; sponge-cake; (*Colloq.*) parasite; sponger; hanger-on;—*v.t.* wipe, cleanse, with sponge; —*v.i.* live at expense of others.— spong'er *n.*—spongy (spunj'-i) *a.* sponge-like; of open texture; full of small holes; absorbent; wet and soft, esp. of ground.—spong'iness *n.* —sponge'-cake *n.* light, sweet cake.— to throw up the sponge, acknowledge defeat.

sponsor (spon'-sur) *n.* one who promises for another; surety; godfather or godmother; guarantor;— *v.t.* support; act as guarantor or patron of.—sponso'red *a.* of radio or TV programmes, subsidised by advertiser.—sponso'rial *a.*—spon'sorship *n.*

spontaneous (spon-tā'-ne-us) *a.* of one's own free-will; voluntary; produced by some internal cause, said of physical effects, as combustion, growth, etc.—sponta'neously *adv.* — spontaneity (spon-ta-nē'-i-ti), sponta'neousness *n.*

spoof (spóof) *n.* swindle;—*v.t.* fool.

spook (spóok) *n.* ghost; apparition. —spook'ish, spook'y *a.* pert. to ghosts.

spool (spóol) *n.* small cylinder for winding thread, yarn, etc.; reel; bobbin; photographic roll-film.

spoon (spóon) *n.* implement, with bowl at end of handle, for carrying food to mouth, etc.; golf-club with wooden head;—*v.t. and v.i.* use, lift with spoon.—spoon'ful *n.* quantity spoon can hold; small quantity; (*Med.*) half ounce.—spoon'bill *n.* long-legged wading bird.—spoon'-feed *v.t.* feed with spoon; (*Fig.*) do overmuch for person.

F.D.

P

spoonerism (spóón'-ẹr-izm) *n.* transportation of letters of spoken words, causing humorous effect, e.g. *half-warmed fish* for 'half-formed wish.'

spoor (spóór) *n.* track or trail of wild animal.

sporadic (spo-rad'-ik) *a.* occurring singly here and there; occasional. Also **sporad'ical.**—**sporad'ically** *adv.*

spore (spōr) *n.* in flowerless plants, e.g. in ferns, minute cell with reproductive powers; germ; seed.

sporran (spor'-ạn) *n.* large pouch worn in front of kilt.

sport (spōrt) *n.* that which amuses; diversion; pastime; merriment; object of jest; mockery; outdoor game or recreation; freak of nature; (*Colloq.*) broad-minded person; good loser;—*v.t.* display in public; show off;—*v.i.* play; take part in out-door recreation.—**sports** *n.pl.* games; athletic meetings.—**sport'ing** *a.* pert. to sport or sportsmen; willing to take chance.—**sport'ive** *a.* pert. to sport; playful.—**sports'man, sports'woman** *n.* —**sports'manship** *n.* practice or skill of sportsman; fair-mindedness; generosity towards opponent.

spot (spot) *n.* speck; blemish; pimple; place; locality; (*Colloq.*) small quantity of anything; drink; —*v.t.* cover with spots; stain; (*Colloq.*) detect; recognise;—*v.i.* become marked.—*pr.p.* spot'ting.— *pa.p.* and *pa.t.* spot'ted.—**spot'less** *a.* without spot or stain; scrupulously clean; pure; innocent.—**spot'lessly** *adv.*—**spot'lessness** *n.*—**spot'ted, spot'ty** *a.* marked with spots or stains; irregular.—**spot'tedness, spot'tiness** *n.* —**spot'ter** *n.* one who spots.—**on the spot,** immediately—**spot check,** random or unannounced check or test.

spouse (spouz) *n.* married person, husband or wife.—**spous'al** *a.* pert. to spouse, marriage;—*n.* marriage.— **spous'als** *n.pl.* marriage; nuptials.

spout (spout) *v.t.* throw out, as liquid through pipe; utter in pompous manner; recite;—*v.i.* gush out in jet; speak volubly, esp. in public; of whale, force up column of water when breathing through spiracle; blow;—*n.* projecting tube, pipe, etc., for pouring liquid; pipe or tube for leading off rain from roof.—**spout'er** *n.*—**up the spout** (*Slang*) in pawn.

sprain (sprān) *v.t.* wrench or twist muscles or ligaments of joint; overstrain;—*n.*

sprat (sprat) *n.* small sea-fish, allied to herring.

sprawl (sprawl) *v.i.* sit or lie with legs outstretched or in ungainly position; spread out irregularly; write carelessly and irregularly;—*n.* act of sprawling.

spray (sprā) *n.* twigs; small, graceful branch with leaves and blossoms; sprig.—**spray'ey** *a.*

spray (sprā) *n.* fine droplets of water driven by wind from tops of waves, etc.; shower of fine droplets of any liquid, e.g. medicine, perfume, etc.; spraying-machine; atomiser; —*v.t.* sprinkle with shower of fine drops. —**spray'er** *n.* spraying-machine.

spread (spred) *v.t.* stretch out; extend; cover surface with; scatter; unfold, as wings; convey from one to another, as disease; set and lay food on table;—*v.i.* extend in all directions; become spread, scattered, circulated, etc.;—*n.* extension; expanse; range;—*pa.p.* and *pa.t.* spread.—**spread'ing** *n.*—**spread'-ea'gle** *n.* eagle with wings stretched out;— *a.* with arms and legs stretched out; bombastic; extravagant;—*v.t.* tie up person, with outstretched limbs.

spree (sprē) *n.* drinking-bout; bout of reckless amusement.

sprig (sprig) *n.* small shoot or twig; ornament in form of spray; scion; youth; small, headless nail.

spright (sprīt) *n.* (*Arch.*) sprite.— **spright'ly** *a.* lively; airy; vivacious.— **spright'liness** *n.*

spring (spring) *v.i.* leap; jump; shoot up, out, or forth; appear; recoil; result, as from cause; issue, as from parent or ancestor; appear above ground; thrive;—*v.t.* cause to spring up; game; cause to explode, as mine; develop leak; release, as catch of trap;—*n.* leap; bound; jump; recoil; contrivance of coiled or bent metal with much resilience; resilience; flow of water from earth; fountain; any source of supply; origin; season of year;—*pa.p.* sprung. —*pa.t.* sprang or sprung.—**spring'er** *n.* one who springs; breed of spaniel.— **spring'y** *a.* elastic; light in tread or gait.—**spring'iness** *n.*—**spring tide,** tide that happens near time of new moon and full moon, and rises higher than ordinary tides.

springbok (spring'-bok) *n.* S. African gazelle.

sprinkle (spring'-kl) *v.t.* scatter small drops of water, sand, etc.; scatter on; baptise with drops of water; cleanse;—*v.i.* scatter (liquid or fine substance);—*n.* small quantity scattered; occasional drops of rain.— **sprin'kler** *n.* one who sprinkles.— **sprin'kling** *n.* act of scattering; small quantity falling in drops.

sprint (sprint) *v.i.* and *n.* run at full speed.—**sprin'ter** *n.*

sprite (sprīt) *n.* spirit; apparition; elf; fairy.

sprocket (sprok'-et) *n.* toothlike projection on outer rim of wheel; wheel with such projections.

sprout (sprout) *v.i.* begin to grow; spring up;—*n.* shoot; bud.—**Brussels**

sprouts, miniature cabbages growing on stalk.

spruce (sproos) a. neat in dress; smart; dapper; trim;—v.t. and v.i. smarten up; dress smartly.—spruce'ly adv.—spruce'ness n.

spruce (sproos) n. common name of some coniferous trees, esp. spruce-fir; its wood.

spry (sprī) a. nimble; agile; gay.

spud (spud) n. small spade-like implement; (Colloq.) potato.

spue (spū) v.t. and v.i. See spew.

spume (spūm) n. froth; foam; scum;—v.i. froth; foam.—spu'mous a. consisting of froth or scum; foamy.—spu'my a. foamy.

spunk (spungk) n. wood that readily takes fire; match; (Fig.) spirit.—spunk'y a. plucky.

spur (spur) n. pricking instrument worn on horseman's heels, used as goad; (Fig.) incitement, instigation; projection on leg of cock; mountain projecting from range; projection;—v.t. apply spurs to; urge to action;—v.i. ride hard; press forward;—pr.p. spur'ring;—pa.p. and pa.t. also a. spurred.

spurge (spurj) n. plant of several species, having acrid, milky juice.

spurious (spū'-ri-us) a. not genuine or authentic; counterfeit; false.—spu'riously adv.—spu'riousness n.

spurn (spurn) v.t. reject with disdain; scorn to accept;—n. disdainful rejection.

spurt (spurt) v.t. force out suddenly in stream; squirt;—v.i. gush out with force; make short, sudden, and strong effort, esp. in race;—n. sudden, strong flow from opening; short, sudden effort.

sputter (sput'-ęr) v.t. throw out with haste and noise; utter excitedly and indistinctly;—v.i. scatter drops of saliva, as in excited speech; speak rapidly; fly off with crackling noise, as sparks from burning wood;—n. act of sputtering; sound made.—sputt'erer n.

sputum (spūtum) n. spittle; saliva.—pl. spu'ta.

spy (spī) n. one who enters enemy territory secretly, to gain information; secret agent; one who keeps watch on others;—pl. spies.—v.t. catch sight of; notice; discern;—v.i. act as spy;—pa.p. and pa.t. spied (spīd).—spy'-glass n. small telescope.

squabble (skwob'-l) v.i. contend in debate; wrangle; dispute noisily;—n. petty, noisy quarrel; brawl.

squad (skwod) n. (Mil.) small party of soldiers at drill, etc.; party of men at work.

squadron (skwod'-run) n. division of cavalry regiment comprising two 'troops'; warships grouped into unit; Royal Air Force formation of two or more 'flights.'—squad'ron-lead'er n. (R.A.F.) rank equivalent to Lieut.-Commander in Navy or Major in Army.

squalid (skwol'-id) a. mean and dirty, esp. through neglect; filthy; foul.—squal'idly adv.—squal'idness, squal'or n. filth.

squall (skwawl) v.t. and i. scream or cry out violently;—n. loud scream; sudden gust of wind.—squall'y a.

squander (skwon'-dęr) v.t. waste; dissipate.—squan'derer n. spendthrift.

square (skwār) n. plane figure with four equal sides and four right angles; anything shaped like this; in town, open space of this shape; carpenter's instrument for testing or drawing right angles; (Math.) product of number or quantity multiplied by itself;—a. square-shaped; rectangular; rightly fitted; fair; balanced, as accounts; settled, as account or bill; (Slang) old-fashioned;—adv. directly;—v.t. make like square; place at right angles; (Math.) multiply by itself; balance; settle; put right; (Colloq.) win over by bribery; (Golf) draw level with opponent;—v.i. agree exactly; fit; suit.—square'ly adv. in square form; honestly; fairly.—square'ness n.—squa'rish a. nearly square.—square dance, old-fashioned dance for four couples.—square'-leg n. (Cricket) fielder who stands to batsman's left.—square'-rigged a. (Naut.) having chief sails stretched along yards slung horizontally to mast by middle.—square root, number or quantity which, when multiplied by itself, produces number of which it is the square root.—to square up, settle debts.

squash (skwosh) v.t. beat or crush flat; squeeze to pulp; (Fig.) suppress;—v.i. fall into soft, flat mass;—n. anything soft and easily crushed; soft drink with flavour of crushed fruit; packed crowd; short for squash rackets, game payed in walled court with small hollow rubber ball.

squat (skwot) v.i. sit on heels; crouch, as animal; settle on land without having title to it;—a. short and thick; sitting close to ground;—pr.p. squat'ting.—pa.p. and pa.t. squat'ted.—squat'ter n. one who squats; one who settles on land without legal right.

squaw (skwaw) n. Red Indian woman.

squawk (skwawk) n. shrill, harsh cry;—v.i. to utter such a cry.

squeak (skwēk) n. short, sharp, shrill sound; sharp, unpleasant, grating sound;—v.i. utter such sound.—squeak'er n.—squeak'y a.

squeal (skwēl) *n.* long, shrill cry;—*v.i.* utter long, shrill cry; (*Slang*) turn informer.

squeamish (skwēm'-ish) *a.* easily made sick; easily shocked; over-scrupulous; fussy.

squeegee (skwē'-jē) *n.* brush or broom, with rubber edge on head, for clearing water from deck of ship, floor, pavement, etc.;—*a.* (*Colloq.*) not straight. Also squil'gee.

squeeze (skwēz) *v.t.* press or crush; compress; extract by pressure; cause to pass, esp. by force; hug; subject to extortion;—*v.i.* force one's way; press;—*n.* pressure; close hug; crowd.

squelch (skwelch) *n.* crushing blow; suppression; sound made when withdrawing feet from sodden ground;—*v.t.* crush down;—*v.i.* make sound of squelch.

squib (skwib) *n.* small firework; short satire.

squid (skwid) *n.* kind of cuttle-fish.

squint (skwint) *a.* looking obliquely; having eyes turned in different directions; looking with suspicion; —*v.t.* cause to squint;—*v.i.* have eyes turned in different directions; glance side-ways;—*n.* act, habit of squinting; (*Med.*) strabismus; hasty glance.

squire (skwīr) *n.* formerly, knight's attendant; esquire; country gentleman; landed proprietor; lady's escort;—*v.t.* escort (lady).

squirm (skwirm) *v.i.* move like snake, eel, worm, etc.; wriggle.

squirrel (skwir'-el) *n.* small graceful animal with bushy tail, living in trees and feeding on nuts; its fur.

squirt (skwert) *v.t.* and *v.i.* eject, or be ejected, in jet; spurt;—*n.* instrument for squirting; syringe; thin jet of liquid.

stab (stab) *v.t.* pierce or wound with pointed instrument; hurt feelings of; —*v.i.* strike with pointed weapon; —*n.* blow or wound so inflicted; sudden pain;—*pr.p.* stab'bing;—*pa.p.* and *pa.t.* stabbed.—stab'ber *n.*

stabilise (stab'-i-līz, stā'-bi-līz) *v.t.* make stable, steady, fixed, etc.— stabilisa'tion *n.*—stab'iliser *n.* that which stabilises.—stabil'ity *n.*

stable (stā'-bl) *a.* firmly fixed; established; steady; resolute;— sta'bly *adv.*—sta'bleness *n.* stability.

stable (stā'-bl) *n.* building for horses, usually divided into stalls; racehorse-trainer's establishment;— *v.t.* put into, or keep in, stable;— *v.i.* be in stable.

staccato (stak-kä'-tō) *a.* and *adv.* (*Mus.*) direction to play notes in abrupt, disconnected fashion; short; sharp, and distinct.

stack (stak) *n.* large heap or pile, esp. of hay, straw, or wood; number of chimneys standing together; tall chimney, esp. of factory; chimney of locomotive; funnel of steamer; precipitous shaft of rock;—*v.t.* heap or pile up; arrange pack of cards for cheating.

stadium (stā'-di-um) *n.* ancient Greek measure; arena for foot-races; sportsground;—*pl.* sta'dia.

staff (stáf) *n.*—*pl.* staffs or staves (stāvz) pole or stick used in walking, climbing, etc. or for support or defence; prop; comfort; stick, as emblem of office or authority; flagpole; (*Mus.*) five lines and four spaces on which music is written.— (with *pl.* staffs) body of persons working in office, school, etc.; (*Mil.*) body of officers, attached to army commander;—*v.t.* provide with staff.

stag (stag) *n.* male of red or other large deer.—stag'hound *n.* Scottish deer-hound.—stag party (*Slang*) party for men only.

stage (stāj) *n.* raised floor or platform esp. of theatre, etc.; theatrical profession; dramatic art or literature; scene of action; degree of progress; point of development; stopping-place;—*v.t.* put (play) on stage.—sta'ging *n.* scaffolding.—stagy (stā'-ji) *a.* theatrical; affectedly theatrical; artificial.—sta'giness *n.*— stage-coach *n.* public passenger coach between towns.—stage'-whis'per *n.* whisper but loud enough for audience to hear.—old stager, person of long experience, esp. actor.

stagger (stag'-er) *v.i.* walk or stand unsteadily; reel; totter; hesitate;— *v.t.* cause to reel; cause to hesitate; distribute over period; arrange in zigzag fashion;—*n.* unsteady movement.—stagg'ers *n.pl.* disease of horses, cattle, etc.—stagg'erer *n.*— stagg'ering *a.* amazing; astounding.

stagnate (stag'-nāt) *v.i.* cease to flow; be motionless; be dull.— stag'nant *a.* of water, not flowing; hence, foul; impure.—stag'nantly *adv.* —stagna'tion *n.* stagnating; dullness.

staid (stād) *a.* sober and quiet; steady; sedate; grave.—staid'ly *adv.* —staid'ness *n.*

stain (stān) *v.t.* and *v.i.* discolour; spot; blot; dye; colour, as wood, glass, etc.; (*Fig.*) mark with guilt;— *n.* discoloration; spot; dye; taint of guilt; disgrace.—stain'less *a.* without stain; not liable to stain or rust, esp. of kind of steel.—stained-glass, glass with colours fused into it.

stair (stār) *n.* steps one above the other for connecting different levels. —stairs *n.pl.* flight of steps.—stair'-case *n.* space in which flight of steps is placed. Also stair'way.

stake (stāk) *n.* sharpened stick or post; post to which one condemned to be burned, was tied; money laid down as wager; interest in result of enterprise:—*pl.* money to be contended for;—*v.t.* secure or mark out with stakes; wager; risk; pledge.—at stake, risked; in danger.

stalactite (stal'-ak-tīt, stạ-lak'-tīt) *n.* deposit of carbonate of lime, hanging like icicle from roof of cave.—**stalac'tic, stalactit'ic** *a.*

stalagmite (stal'-ag-mīt, stạ-lag'-mīt) *n.* deposit of carbonate of lime rising from floor of cave.

stale (stāl) *a.* not fresh; kept too long, as bread; tasteless; musty; having lost power to please; common;—*v.t.* make tasteless; spoil novelty of;—*v.i.* lose freshness.—**stale'ly** *adv.*—**stale'ness** *n.*

stalemate (stāl'-māt) *n.* (*Chess*) position, resulting in drawn game; deadlock; standstill.

stalk (stawk) *n.* stem of plant, leaf, etc.; tall chimney.

stalk (stawk) *v.i.* steal up to game cautiously; walk in stiff and stately manner;—*v.t.* steal up to (game, etc.); track down;—*n.* stealing up to game; stiff, stately gait.—**stalk'er** *n.*

stall (stawl) *n.* compartment for animal in stable; erection for display and sale of goods; seat in cathedral or collegiate church, reserved for ecclesiastical dignitary; front seat in theatre, etc.; sheath for injured finger;—*v.t.* and *v.i.* place or keep in stall; come to standstill; of engine of motor-car, stop running unintentionally; of aircraft, lose flying speed and controllability.

stall (stawl) *n.* ambush; decoy;—*v.i.* (*U.S.*) evade question in conversation or under interrogation.

stallion (stal'-yun) *n.* uncastrated male horse, esp. one kept for breeding.

stalwart (stawl'-wạrt) *a.* sturdy; strong; brave; steadfast;—*n.* strong, muscular person; staunch supporter.—**stal'wartly** *adv.*

stamen (stā'-men) *n.* (*Bot.*) male organ of flowering plant, pollen-bearing part.—**stamina** (stam'-i-nạ) *n.* power of endurance; vigour.—**stam'inal** *a.*

stammer (stam'-er) *v.i.* speak with repetition of syllables or hesitatingly; stutter;—*v.t.* halting enunciation; stutter.—**stamm'erer** *n.*—**stamm'ering** *n.* stammer; stutter.

stamp (stamp) *v.t.* put down foot with force;—*v.t.* set down (foot) heavily or with force; make mark on; affix postage stamp; distinguish by mark; brand; fix deeply;—*n.* act of stamping; instrument for making imprinted mark; mark imprinted; die; piece of gummed paper printed with device, as evidence of postage, etc.; character; form.—**stamp'er** *n.*

stampede (stam-pēd') *n.* sudden, frightened rush, esp. of herd of cattle, crowd, etc.;—*v.t.* put into state of panic;—*v.i.* take part in stampede; rush off in general panic.

stance (stans) *n.* position of feet in certain games, e.g. golf, cricket, etc.; site; stand or stall in market-place; station, esp. for buses.

stanch, staunch (stawnsh) *v.t.* check flow (of blood).

stanchion (stan'-shun) *n.* upright support; iron bar, used as prop.

stand (stand) *v.i.* remain at rest in upright position; be situated; become or remain stationary; stop; have position, order, or rank; consist; place oneself; offer oneself as candidate; adhere to; persist; insist; be of certain height; (*Naut.*) hold course or direction; (*Colloq.*) treat;—*v.t.* endure; sustain; maintain; resist; withstand; admit;—*pa.p.* and *pa.t.* **stood.**—*n.* place where one stands; structure for spectators; piece of furniture on which things may be placed; stall for display of goods; resistance.—**stand'-by** *n.* something in reserve.—**stand'-off, stand'-off'ish** *a.* haughty; reserved; aloof.—**stand'-off'ishness** *n.*—**stand'point** *n.* point of view.—**stand by** to be in state of readiness.—**stand down, withdraw.**—**stand out, project; be conspicuous.**

standard (stan'-dạrd) *n.* flag; banner; accepted basis of measurement; criterion; upright support;—*a.* serving as established rule, model, etc.; having fixed value; uniform; standing upright.—**stan'dardise** *v.t.* make of, or bring to, uniform level.—**standardisa'tion** *n.*

standing (stan'-ding) *a.* established by law, custom, etc.; settled; not flowing; erect;—*n.* duration; existence; reputation. — standing army, force maintained in peacetime. — standing orders, permanent rules.

stanza (stan'-zạ) *n.* group of lines or verses of poetry having definite pattern; loosely, division of poem.—**stanzaic** (stan-zā'-ik) *a.*

staple (stā'-pl) *n.* settled market; chief commodity, unmanufactured material; fibre of wool, cotton, flax, etc.;—*a.* established in commerce; settled; regularly produced for market; principal; chief;—*v.t.* of textiles, grade according to length and quality of fibre.—**sta'pler** *n.*

staple (stā'-pl) *n.* U-shaped piece of metal to drive into a surface for securing wire etc.—**sta'pler** *n.* mechanical device for fastening papers together with wire staples.

star (stár) *n.* shining celestial body; asterisk; leading actor or actress;—*v.t.* set or adorn with stars; cast (in play) as leading actor;—*v.i.* shine, as star; play principal part.—**star'let** *n.* small star.—**star'light** *n.*—**star'lit** *a.*—**star'ry** *a.*—**starr'iness** *n.*—**star'fish** *n.* marine animal allied to sea-urchin.—**starry-eyed** *a.* idealistic.

starboard (stär'-bōrd) *n.* right-hand side of ship, looking forward;—*a.* pert. to, or on, this side;—*v.t.* put (helm) to starboard.

starch (stärch) *n.* substance forming main food element in bread, potatoes, etc. and used, mixed with water, for stiffening linen, etc.; (*Fig.*) formality; primness;—*v.t.* stiffen with starch.—**starch'y** *a.* pert. to, containing, starch; stiff; formal; prim.—**starch'ily** *adv.*—**starch'iness** *n.*

stare (stär) *v.i.* look fixedly; gaze;—*v.t.* be obvious to; visible to;—*n.* fixed, steady look.—**sta'rer** *n.*—**sta'ring** *n.* and *a.*

stark (stärk) *a.* stiff; rigid; strong; downright; utter;—*adv.* completely.—**stark'ly** *adv.*—**stark'ness** *n.* stiffness.

starling (stär'-ling) *n.* iridescent brownish-black bird.

start (stärt) *v.i.* make sudden movement; spring; begin;—*v.t.* cause to move suddenly; set going; begin; alarm;—*n.* sudden involuntary movement; act of setting out; beginning; in sports, advantage of lead in race.—**start'er** *n.*—**by fits and starts,** spasmodical.

startle (stärt'-l) *v.t.* cause to start; excite by sudden alarm; give fright to;—*v.i.* move abruptly, esp. from fright.—**start'ling** *a.* alarming; astonishing.—**start'lingly** *adv.*

starve (stärv) *v.i.* suffer from cold or hunger; die of hunger;—*v.t.* cause to suffer or die from lack of food, warmth, etc.—**starva'tion** *n.*—**starve'-ling** *a.* hungry; lean;—*n.* one weak from lack of food.

state (stāt) *n.* condition of person or thing; place or situation; rank; high position; formal dignity; politically organised community; civil powers of such;—*a.* pert. to state; governmental; royal; public; ceremonial;—*v.t.* set forth; express in words.—**sta'ted** *a.* fixed; regular; settled.—**state'ly** *a.* dignified; imposing; majestic. — **state'liness** *n.* — **state'ment** *n.* formal account.—**state'craft** *n.* political sagacity.—**state'less** *a.* without nationality.—**state'-room** *n.* private cabin in ship.—**states'man** *n.* one skilled in art of government; able politician.—**states'manlike** *a.*—**states'manly** *a.*—**states'manship** *n.*

static (stat'-ik) *a.* pert. to bodies at rest, or in equilibrium; motionless;—*n.* (*Radio*) atmospherics.—**stat'ical** *a.* static.—**stat'ics** *n.pl.* mechanics of bodies at rest.

station (stā'-shun) *n.* place where thing or person stands; position; situation; condition of life; rank;

regular stopping-place for railway trains; local or district office for police force, fire-brigade, etc.;—*v.t.* put in position; place; set.—**sta'tionary** *a.* not moving; fixed; regular; stable.

stationer (sta'-shuner) *n.* one who deals in writing materials.—**sta'tionery** *n.* wares sold by stationer.—**Stationery Office,** Government department responsible for publication and sale of all official reports, etc.

statistics (sta-tis'-tiks) *n.pl.* numerical data collected systematically, summarised, and tabulated; science of collecting and interpreting such information.—**statis'tic(al)** *a.*—**statistically** *adv.*—**statistician** (sta-tis-tish'-an) *n.* one skilled in statistics.—**sta'tist** *n.* statistician.

statue (stat'-ū) *n.* image of person or animal, carved out of solid substance or cast in metal.—**stat'uary** *n.* art of making statues; collection of statues; one who makes statues; sculptor.—**statuesque** (stat-ū-esk') *a.* like statue; immobile.—**statuette** (stat-ū-et') *n.* small statue.

stature (stat'-ūr) *n.* height of person or animal.

status (stā'-tus) *n.* position; rank.—**status-symbol** *n.* possession conferring sense of social superiority.

statute (stat'-ūt) *n.* law passed by legislature; Act of Parliament; permanent rules governing operations of corporation, institution, etc.—**stat'utable** *a.*—**stat'utory** *a.*

staunch (stawnsh) *a.* firm; loyal; trustworthy. — **staunch'ly** *adv.* — **staunch'ness** *n.*

stave (stāv) *n.* one of curved strips of wood forming cask; rung of ladder; staff; five lines and spaces on which musical notes are written; verse or stanza;—*v.t.* fit with staves; break stave(s) of (cask); knock hole in side of; ward off; defer;—*pa.p.* and *pa.t.* staved or stove.

stay (stā) *v.t.* restrain; check; stop; support; satisfy; last;—*v.i.* remain; continue in place; dwell;—*n.* remaining in place; halt; support; postponement.—**stays** *n.pl.* laced corset.—**stay'er** *n.*

stay (stā) *n.* (*Naut.*) strong rope or wire to support mast or spar;—*v.t.* support or incline to one side with stays; put on other tack;—*v.i.* change tack; go about.

stead (sted) *n.* place; use; benefit; advantage; service; place of abode; frame of bed.—**in stead, in place.**—**in good stead, of service.**—**stead'ing** *n.* outhouses of farm.

steadfast (sted'-fast) *a.* firmly fixed; steady; constant.—**stead'fastly** *adv.*—**stead'fastness** *n.*

steady (sted'-i) *a.* firm; constant; uniform; temperate; industrious;

reliable;—*n.* (*Colloq.*) regular boy or girl friend—*v.t.* make steady; support;—*v.i.* become steady;—*pr.p.* **stead'ying.**—*pa.p.* and *pa.t.* **stead'ied.** —*n.* support.— **stead'ier** *a.* — **stead'iest** *a.*—**stead'ily** *adv.*—**stead'iness** *n.*

steak (stāk) *n.* slice of meat or fish.

steal (stēl) *v.t.* take by theft; get by cunning or surprise; win gradually by skill, affection, etc.;—*v.i.* take what is not one's own; move silently, or secretly;—*pa.p.* **sto'len** (stō'-len).—*pa.t.* **stole** (stōl).—**stealth** (stelth) *n.* secret means used to accomplish anything; concealed act.—**steal'thy** *a.* done by stealth.—**stealth'ily** *adv.*—**stealth'iness** *n.*

steam (stēm) *n.* vapour rising from boiling water; water in gaseous state; any exhalation of heated bodies;—*a.* worked by steam;—*v.t.* apply steam to; cook or treat with steam;—*v.i.* give off steam; rise in vapour; move under power of steam. —**steam'y** *a.*—**steam'iness** *n.*—**steam'er** *n.* steamship; vessel for cooking or washing by steam.

steed (stēd) *n.* horse.

steel (stēl) *n.* hard, malleable metal, made by mixing carbon in iron; tool or weapon of steel; instrument for sharpening knives;—*a.* made of steel; hard; unfeeling;—*v.t.* point, edge, with steel; harden; make obdurate.—**steel'y** *a.* made of, or like, steel; hard; obdurate; relentless.—**steel'iness** *n.*

steep (stēp) *a.* having abrupt slope; precipitous; difficult; (*Colloq.*) exorbitant, esp. of prices;—*n.* precipice.—**steep'ly** *adv.*—**steep'en** *v.t.* and *v.i.* make, or become, steep.

steep (stēp) *v.t.* soak in liquid; drench; saturate;—*v.i.* be soaked;—*n.* act of steeping; liquid used.

steeple (stē'-pl) *n.* church tower with spire.—**steep'lechase** *n.* horse-race in which ditches, hedges, etc. must be jumped; cross-country foot-race.—**stee'plejack** *n.* skilled workman who climbs steeples, tall chimneys, etc.

steer (stēr) *n.* young male ox; bullock.

steer (stēr) *v.t.* guide course of (ship, motor-car, etc.) by means of rudder, wheel, etc.;—*v.i.* guide ship, motor-car, etc.; direct one's course. —**steer'age** *n.* act of steering; part of ship allotted to passengers paying lowest fare.—**steer'er, steers'man** *n.* helmsman of ship.—**steer'age-way** *n.* sufficient movement of vessel through water to enable it to answer helm.—**steer'ing-gear** *n.* mechanism for steering.

stellar (stel'-ạr) *a.* pert. to, or about, stars; starry.—**stell'ate, stell'ated** *a.* arranged in form of star; star-shaped; radiating.—**stell'iform** *a.* star-shaped. —**stell'ular** *a.* like little stars.

stem (stem) *n.* principal stalk of tree or plant; slender stalk of plant; slender shaft resembling stalk; branch of family; curved or upright piece of timber or metal to which two sides of ship are joined;—*v.t.* remove stem of;—*pr.p.* **stem'ming.**—*pa.p.* and *pa.t.* **stemmed.**

stem (stem) *v.t.* check; stop; dam up; —*pr.p.* and *pa.t.* **stemmed.**

stench (stensh) *n.* strong, offensive odour.

stencil (sten'-sil) *n.* thin sheet of metal, paper, etc. pierced with pattern or letters, so that when brushed over with paint, ink, etc., design is reproduced; design so reproduced;—*v.t.* mark or paint thus;—*pr.p.* **sten'cilling.**—*pa.p.* and *pa.t.* **sten'cilled.**

stenography (sten-og'-rạ-fi) *n.* short-hand writing.—**stenog'raphist** *n.*—**stenograph'ic, stenograph'ical** *a.*

stentorian (stent-or'-i-ạn) *a.* of voice, extremely loud.

step (step) *v.i.* move and set down foot; walk slowly;—*v.t.* set or place, as foot; measure in paces; (*Naut.*) set up (mast);—*n.* act of stepping; complete movement of foot in walking, dancing, etc.; distance so covered; manner of walking; footprint; footfall; tread of stair; degree of progress; act; measure; grade; (*Naut.*) socket for mast;—*pl.* portable ladder;—*pr.p.* **step'ping.**—*pa.p.* and *pa.t.* **stepped.**—**step'per** *n.*—**step'ping-stone** *n.* stone for stepping on when crossing stream, etc.; (*Fig.*) aid to success.

step- (step) *prefix*, showing relationship acquired by remarriage.—**step'father** *n.* second, or later, husband of one's mother. Similarly **step'mother, step'brother, step'sister.**

steppe (step) *n.* vast, treeless plain, as in Siberia.

stereo- (ster'-e-ō) fr. Gk. *stereos*, solid, used in many derivatives.—**ster'eogram, ster'eograph** *n.* double photograph of same scene, for use in stereoscope.

stereophony (stē-rē-of'-o-ni) *n.* sound recording and reproduction giving three-dimensional effect. — **stereophon'ic** *a.*

stereoscope (ster'-e-, stē'-rē-ō-skōp) *n.* optical instrument in which two pictures taken at different viewpoints are combined into one image, with effect of depth and solidity.—**stereoscop'ic(al)** *a.* — **stereoscop'ically** *adv.* —**stereo'scopy** *n.*

stereotype (ster'-e-, stē'-rē-ō-tīp) *n.* metal printing plate produced from papier-maché mould of original type; —*a.* pert. to stereotypes;—*v.t.* make stereotype from; print from stereotypes; fix unalterably; (*Fig.*) make always same.—**ste'reo typed** *a.*—**ste'-**

reotyper, ste'reotypist n.—stereo-typog'-raphy n.

sterile (ster'-il, ster'-il) a. barren; (Med.) germ-free.—ster'ilise v.t.—sterilisa'tion n.—ster'iliser n.—steril'ity n. barrenness.

sterling (ster'-ling) a. pert. to standard value, weight, or purity; of solid worth; genuine; pure; denoting British money;—n. British money; **sterling area**, groups of countries using currency based on British sterling.

stern (stern) a. severe; strict; rigorous.—stern'ly adv.—stern'ness n.

stern (stern) n. after part of ship; rump or tail of animal.—stern'most a. farthest astern.

stertor (ster'-tor) n. heavy, sonorous breathing.—ster'torous a. snoring; characterised by snoring sound.—ster'torously adv.

stet (stet) v.i. word used by proof-readers as instruction to printer to cancel previous correction.

stethoscope (steth'-o-skōp) n. instrument for listening to action of lungs or heart.—stethoscop'ic a.

stevedore (stēv'-e-dōr) n. one who loads and unloads ships.

stew (stū) v.t. cook slowly in closed vessel; simmer;—v.i. be cooked slowly; feel uncomfortably warm;—n. stewed meat.

steward (stū'-ard) n. one who manages another's property; on ship, attendant on passengers; catering-manager of club; official who manages race-meeting, assembly, etc.—stew'ardess n. fem. female steward.—stew'ardship n. office of steward; management.

stick (stik) n. small branch cut off tree or shrub; staff; walking-stick; rod; (Print.) instrument in which types are arranged.

stick (stik) v.t. stab; pierce; jab; puncture; fasten; cause to adhere; fix; thrust; (Colloq.) endure;—v.i. pierce; adhere closely; remain fixed; stop; halt; be unable to proceed; be puzzled;—pa.p. and pa.t. stuck.—stick'er n. one who perseveres.—stick'y a. adhesive; viscous; tenacious; (Colloq.) embarrassing; painful.—stick'iness n.—stick'ing-plaster n. adhesive bandage for small wounds, cuts, etc.—stuck up, conceited.

stickler (stik'-ler) n. one who stubbornly insists on importance of some trivial point.—a **stickler for**, one who is punctilious about.

stickle (stik'-l) n. prickle; spine.—stick'leback n. small spiny-backed fresh-water fish.

stiff (stif) a. not easily bent; moved with difficulty; firm; hard; thick; stubborn; formal in manner; (Colloq.) high in price; (Slang) fool; corpse.—stiff'ly adv.—stiff'ness n.—

stiff'en v.t. and v.i. make or become stiff or stiffer.—stiff'ener n. one who, or that which, stiffens.—stiff'-necked a. stubborn.

stifle (stī'-fl) v.t. and v.i. choke; suppress sound of; repress.—sti'fling a. airless.

stigma (stig'-ma) n. brand; mark of disgrace; stain on character; blemish on skin.—stigmata (stig'-ma-ta) n.pl. marks resembling five wounds of Christ.—stigmat'ic(al) a. pert. to, or marked with, stigma; giving reproach.—stigmat'ically adv.—stig'matise v.t. hold up to disgrace.

stile (stīl) n. arrangement of steps for climbing fence or wall.

stiletto (sti-let'-ō) n. small dagger; pointed instrument used in needle-work;—a. descriptive of women's shoes with very high pointed heels.

still (stil) a. motionless; silent; quiet; of wine, not sparkling;—n. stillness; (Cinema) enlargement of one unit of film;—v.t. quiet; silence;—adv. to this time; yet;—conj. yet; however.—still'y a. still; quiet;—adv. silently; quietly.—still'ness n.—still'-birth n. state of being dead at time of birth.—still'-born a.—still life (Art) inanimate objects as subject of painting.

still (stil) n. apparatus for distilling alcoholic liquors.

stilt (stilt) n. pole with foot-rest, for walking raised from ground;—v.i. walk on stilts.—stilt'ed a. (Fig.) formal; stiff; pretentious.

stimulus (stim'-ū-lus) n. incentive; stimulant;—pl. stim'uli.—stim'ulate v.t. rouse to activity; excite; increase vital energy of.—stim'ulant a. serving to stimulate;—n. that which spurs on; (Med.) any agent or drug which increases temporarily action of any organ of body.—stimula'tion n.—stim'ulative a. and n.

sting (sting) n. pointed organ often poisonous, of certain animals, insects, or plants; thrust, wound, or pain of one; any acute pain;—v.t. thrust sting into; cause sharp pain to; hurt feelings; incite to action; (Slang) overcharge;—v.i. use sting;—pa.p. and pa.t. stung.—sting'er n.—sting'ing a. sharp.—sting'ingly adv.

stingy (stin'-ji) a. meanly avaricious; miserly.—stin'gily adv.—stin'giness n.

stink (stingk) v.i. give out strongly offensive smell;—pa.p. stunk (stungk).—pa.t. stank (stangk) or stunk.—stench.—stink'er n.—stink'ing a.—stink'ingly adv.

stint (stint) v.t. limit; keep on short allowance; skimp;—v.i. be frugal;—n. limitation of supply or effort; allotted task.—stint'ed a. limited.

stipend (stī'-pend) n. money paid for person's services.—stipend'iary a. receiving salary;—n. one who performs services for a fixed salary.

stipple (stip'-l) v.t. and i. engrave, draw, or paint by using dots;—n.—stipp'ler n.—stipp'ling n.

stipulate (stip'-ū-lāt) v.i. arrange; settle definitely; insist on in making agreement.—**stipula'tion** n. specified condition.—**stip'ulator** n.

stir (ster) v.t. set or keep in motion; move; rouse; incite;—v.i. begin to move; be in motion;—pr.p. stir'ring.—pa.p. and pa.t. stirred.—n. act of stirring; commotion.—stir'rer n.—stir'ring a. active; exciting; rousing;—n. act of stirring.

stirrup (stir'-up) n. metal loop hung from strap, for foot of rider on horse.—stir'rup-cup n. drink given to departing rider.

stitch (stich) n. in sewing, single pass of needle; loop or turn of thread thus made; in knitting, crocheting, etc., single turn of yarn or thread round needle or hook; (Fig.) bit of clothing; sharp, sudden pain in side;—v.t. and v.i. form stitches; sew.—stitch'er n.—stitch'ing n. work done by sewing.

stoat (stōt) n. ermine or weasel, esp. in its summer fur of reddish-brown colour.

stock (stok) n. stump or post; stem or trunk of tree or plant; upright block of wood; piece of wood to which barrel, lock, etc. of firearm are secured; ancestry; family; domestic animals on farm; fund; supply of goods trader has on hand; government securities; capital of company; quantity; supply; juices of meat, etc. to form liquid used as foundation of soup; type of cravat; garden plant bearing fragrant flowers; gillyflower;—pl. frame of timber supporting ship while building; old instrument of punishment in form of wooden frame with holes in it;—v.t. lay in supply for future use; store; keep for sale;—a. used, or available, for constant supply; commonplace; conventional.—stock'breed'er n. one who raises cattle, horses, etc.—stock'broker n. one who buys and sells stocks or shares for others.—stock'broking n.—stock exchange, building in which stockbrokers meet to buy and sell stocks and shares.—stock'ist n. one who keeps supply of certain goods.—stock'-still a. motionless.—stock'-ta'king n. act of preparing inventory of goods on hand.

stockade (sto-kād') n. enclosure or pen made with posts and stakes;—v.t. surround, enclose, or defend by erecting line of stakes.

stocking (stok'-ing) n. woven or knitted covering for foot and leg.

stocky (stok'-i) a. short and stout; thickset.—stock'ily adv.

stodge (stoj) v.i. stuff; cram.—stodg'y a. heavy; indigestible; (Fig.) dull and uninteresting.—stodg'iness n.

Stoic (stō'-ik) n. disciple of Greek philosopher Zeno (342-270 B.C.).—sto'ic n. one who suffers without complaint; one indifferent to pleasure or pain.—sto'ical a.—sto'ically adv.—sto'icism n.

stoke (stōk) v.t. and v.i. stir up, feed, or tend (fire).—stok'er n.—stoke'hole n. mouth of furnace.

stole (stōl) n. long, loose garment, reaching to feet; long scarf worn by bishops, priests, etc. during mass; woman's long scarf.

stolid (stol'-id) a. dull or stupid; not easily excited.—stol'idly adv.—stol'idness, stolid'ity n.

stomach (stum'-ak) n. chief digestive organ in animal; appetite; desire; spirit;—v.t. put up with; endure. — stomachic (stum-ak'-ik), stomach'ical a. pert. to stomach; aiding digestion.—n. (Med.) medicine for aiding digestion.

stone (stōn) n. hard matter of which rock is made; piece of rock; measure of weight equal to 14 lb.; hard centre of certain fruits; gem; concretion in kidneys or bladder; calculus; testicle;—a. made of stone, stoneware;—v.t. pelt with stones; remove stones from, as from fruits.—sto'ny a. like stone; full of stones; (Fig.) hard; pitiless.—sto'nily adv.—sto'niness n.—stone'-blind a. entirely blind.—stone'crop n. creeping plant found on old walls, etc.; wall-pepper.—stone'-dead a. quite dead; lifeless.—stone'-deaf a. completely deaf.—stone'-ma'son n. worker in stone.—stone'-wall v.t. and i. offer stubborn resistance.—stone'ware n. earthenware.—sto'ny-broke a. (Slang) quite penniless.

stood (stood) pa.p. and pa.t. of stand.

stooge (stooj) n. (Slang) one who bears blame for others; actor serving as butt of another's jokes;—v.i. act as stooge.

stook (stook) n. group of sheaves of corn, etc. set up in field;—v.t. set up in stooks.

stool (stool) n. chair with no back; low backless seat for resting feet on; seat for evacuating bowels; discharge from bowels.—stool-pi'geon n. pigeon used to trap other pigeons; person used as decoy.—to fall between two stools (Fig.) lose both of two opportunities.

stoop (stoop) v.i. bend body; lean forward; have shoulders bowed forward; bow one's head; submit; condescend; swoop down, as bird of prey;—v.t. cause to lean forward;—n. stooping carriage of head and shoulders.

stop (stop) v.t. fill up opening; keep

from going forward; bring to halt; obstruct; check; suspend; withhold; desist from; bring to end; punctuate; —*v.i.* cease to go forward; halt; leave off;—*pr.p.* stop'ping—*pa.p.* and *pa.t.* stopped;—*n.* act of stopping; state of being stopped; halt; halting-place; pause; delay; hindrance; device for checking movement; (*Mus.*) device for altering or regulating pitch; set of organ pipes; lever for putting it in action; aperture admitting light to a camera lens.—**stop'page** *n.* state of being stopped; act of stopping; obstruction; cessation; deduction from wages.—**stop'per** *n.* one who, or that which stops; plug for closing mouth of bottle, etc.;—*v.t.* close opening with stopper.—**stop'ping** *n.* material for filling up cracks, holes, etc.—**stop'-cock** *n.* short pipe with key or tap, for regulating flow of liquid from vessel.—**stop'-gap** *n.* that which closes gap or opening; makeshift; temporary substitute.—**stop'-press** *n.* news put into newspaper after printing has begun.—**stop'-watch** *n.* special watch used for exact timing. —**full stop**, in punctuation, period.

store (stōr) *n.* great quantity; abundance; reserve supply; stock; place for keeping goods; shop; warehouse; that part of a computer which registers data fed in;—*v.t.* collect; accumulate; hoard; place in warehouse.—**sto'rage** *n.* act of placing goods in warehouse; space occupied by them; price paid.—**store'-catt'le** *n.* cattle kept for fattening.

storey, story (stō'ri) *n.* horizontal division of building; set of rooms on one floor;—*pl.* sto'reys, sto'ries.— **storeyed, sto'ried** (stō'-rid) *a.* having storeys or floors.

stork (stork) *n.* large bird allied to heron.

storm (storm) *n.* violent wind; tempest; assault on fortified place; commotion; outburst of emotion;— *v.t.* assault;—*v.i.* raise tempest; rage; fume.—**storm'y** *a.* tempestuous; violent; passionate.—**storm'ily** *adv.* —**storm'iness** *n.*—**storm'-bound** *a.* delayed by storms.

story (stō'ri) *n.* narrative of facts or events; account; tale; anecdote; (*Colloq.*) falsehood;—*pl.* sto'ries.— **storied** (stō'-rid) *a.* told in story; having history.—**sto'ry-tell'er** *n.* one who tells stories; novelist; romancer.

stoup (stōŏp) *n.* flagon; holy-water basin.

stout (stout) *a.* strong; robust; bold; resolute; fat; bulky;—*n.* strong, dark-coloured beer; porter.—**stout'ly** *adv.*—**stout'ness** *n.*—**stout'-heart'ed** *a.* brave; courageous.

stove (stōv) *n.* apparatus with enclosed fire, for cooking, warming room, etc.;—*v.t.* heat; keep warm.

stove (stōv) *pa.p.* and *pa.t.* of stave.

stow (stō) *v.t.* fill by packing closely; arrange compactly; conceal.—**stow'-age** *n.* act of packing closely; space for stowing goods; charge made for stowing goods.—**stow'away** *n.* one who hides on ship to obtain free passage.

straddle (strad'-l) *v.i.* spread legs wide; stand or walk with legs apart;—*v.t.* bestride something (target);—*n.* act of straddling;—*adv.* astride.

strafe (strāf) *v.t.* bombard heavily.

straggle (strag'-l) *v.i.* wander from direct course; get dispersed; lag behind.—**stragg'ler** *n.*—**stragg'ling** *a.*

straight (strāt) *a.* passing from one point to another by nearest course; without bend; direct; honest; upright; frank; (*Slang*) of whisky, etc. undiluted;—*n.* straightness; straight part, e.g. of racing-track;—*adv.* directly; without ambiguity; at once.—**straight'ly** *adv.*—**straight'en** *v.t.* and *i.*—**straight'ener** *n.*—**straight'away** *adv.* straightforward; (*Colloq.*) at once.—**straightfor'ward** *a.* proceeding in straight course; honest; frank; simple. — **straightfor'wardly** *adv.* — **straightfor'wardness** *n.*—**straight'ness** *n.*

strain (strān) *n.* race; breed; stock.

strain (strān) *v.t.* stretch tight; stretch to full or to excess; exert to utmost; injure by over-exertion; wrench; force; stress; pass through sieve; filter;—*v.i.* make great effort; filter;—*n.* act of straining; violent effort; injury caused by over-exertion; sound; tune; style; manner; tone of speaking or writing.—**strain'-er** *n.* filter; sieve.

strait (strāt) *a.* narrow; strict; difficult;—*n.* narrow channel of water connecting two larger areas; difficulty; financial embarrassment. —**strait'ly** *adv.* strictly; narrowly.— **strait'en** *v.t.* make strait; narrow; restrict; put into position of difficulty.—**strait-jack'et, -waist'coat** *n.* garment for restraint of violent lunatics.—**strait'laced** *a.* puritanical.

strand (strand) *n.* edge of sea or lake; shore;—*v.t.* cause to run aground; drive ashore; (*Fig.*) leave helpless;—*v.i.* run aground; be driven ashore.—**strand'ed** *a.*

strand (strand) *n.* single string of wire, rope, hair, etc.;—*v.t.* make rope by twisting strands together.

strange (strānj) *a.* foreign; belonging to another person or place; unaccustomed; not familiar; uncommon; odd; wonderful, extraordinary; shy; inexperienced.—**strange'ly** *adv.* —**strange'ness** *n.*—**stran'ger** *n.* one from another country, town, place, etc.; unknown person.

strangle (strang'-gl) *v.t.* kill by

squeezing throat; choke; stifle; suppress.—**strang'ler** n.—**strang'ulate** v.t.—**strangula'tion** n.

strap (strap) n. long, narrow strip of leather, cloth, or metal; strop;—v.t. fasten, bind, chastise with strap; sharpen (razor);—pr.p. **strap'ping**.—pa.p. and pa.t. **strapped**.—**strap'ping** n.—a. tall and handsome.

stratagem (strat'-ə-jem) n. artifice in war; scheme for deceiving enemy; ruse.

strategy (strat'-e-ji) n. art of conducting military or naval operations; generalship.—**strategic** (stra-tej'-ik, stra-tē'-jik) a. pert. to, based on, strategy.—**strateg'ics** n.pl. strategy.—**strateg'ical** a.—**strateg'ically** adv.—**strat'egist** n. one skilled in strategy.

strathspey (strath-spā') n. lively Scottish dance; music played for it.

stratify (strat'-i-fī) v.t. form or deposit in strata or layers;—pa.p. and pa.t. **strat'ified**.—**stratifica'tion** n.

stratosphere (stra-tō-sfēr) n. layer of atmosphere, six miles or more above earth.

stratum (strā'-tum, strat'-um) n. bed of earth, rock, coal, etc. in series of layers; any bed or layer; class in society;—pl. **stra'ta**.—**stra'tus** n. low, horizontal bands of cloud.

straw (straw) n. stalk of corn, etc. after grain has been thrashed out; collection of such used for fodder, etc.; thing of very little value;—a. made of straw.

strawberry (straw'-be-ri) n. creeping plant of genus Fragaria; its fruit, red berry.

stray (strā) v.i. wander from path; get lost; digress; (Fig.) err;—a. wandering; strayed; lost;—n. stray animal; lost child.

streak (strēk) n. line, or long band, of different colour from background; stripe; flash of lightning; trait; strain;—v.t. mark with streaks.—**streaked**, **streak'y** a. striped.

stream (strēm) n. flowing body of water, or other liquid; river, etc.; current; course; steady flow of air or light, or people;—v.i. issue in stream; flow or move freely; stretch in long line; float or wave in air;—v.t. send out in stream; send forth rays of light.—**stream'er** n. long, narrow flag; pennant; beam of light shooting up from horizon.—**stream'let** n. little stream.—**stream'line** n. line of current of air; shape of body (e.g. motor-car, ship, etc.) calculated to offer least resistance to air or water when passing through it;—v.t. design body of this shape; (Fig.) eliminate everything that tends to reduce efficiency.

street (strēt) n. road in town or village.—**street'-walk'er** n. prostitute.

strength (strength) n. quality of being strong; capacity for exertion; ability to endure; power or vigour; force; potency of liquid; intensity; force of expression; vigour of style; support; security; force in numbers, e.g. of army.—**strength'en** v.t. and i.—**strength'ener** n.

strenuous (stren'-ū-us) a. urgent; energetic; full of, requiring effort; bold; earnest.—**stren'uously** adv.—**stren'uousness** n.

stress (stres) n. force; pressure; strain; emphasis; accent; (Mech.) force producing change in shape of body;—v.t. lay stress on.

stretch (strech) v.t. pull out; tighten; reach out; strain; exaggerate;—v.i. be drawn out; be extended; spread;—n. extension; strain; effort; expanse; scope; long line or surface; direction; course; unbroken period of time.—**stretch'er** n. one who, or that which, stretches; frame or litter for carrying sick or wounded; brick or stone laid lengthwise along line of wall.—**to stretch a point**, make concession.

strew (strōō) v.t. scatter; spread loosely;—pa.p. **strewed** or **strewn**.—pa.t. **strewed**.

stricken (strik'-n) a. struck; smitten; afflicted (with illness, age, etc.).

strict (strikt) a. stern; severe; exacting; rigid; unswerving; defined; without exception; accurate; restricted.—**strict'ly** adv.—**strict'ness** n.—**stric'ture** n. severe criticism.

stride (strīd) n. long step, or its length;—v.t. to pass over with one long step;—v.i. to walk, with long steps;—pa.p. **stridden** (strid'-n).—pa.t. **strode**.

strident (strī'-dent) a. harsh in tone; grating; jarring.—**stri'dently** adv.

strife (strīf) n. conflict; struggle for victory.

strike (strīk) v.t. hit; smite; punish; dash against; collide; sound; cause to sound; occur; impress; afflict; cause to light, as match; lower, as flag or sail; take down, as tent; ratify; conclude; cancel;—v.i. hit; deliver blow; dash; clash; run aground; stop work for increase of wages, etc.; take root, of plant;—n. stoppage of work to enforce demand; (Colloq.) find, esp. in prospecting for gold; stroke of luck;—pa.p. **struck**, or **strick'en** (obsolete).—pa.t. **struck**.—**stri'ker** n. one who, or that which, strikes.—**stri'king** a. impressive.—**stri'kingly** adv.

string (string) n. cord; twine; thick thread; chain; succession; series; stretched cord of gut or wire for musical instrument; (Colloq.) all race-horses from certain stable;—pl. stringed musical instruments collectively.—**without strings**, (of offer, agreement, etc.) without restrictive conditions; unconditionally; — v.t. furnish with strings; put on string; —v.i. stretch out into line; form strings; become fibrous;—pa.p. and pa.t. **strung.**—**stringed** (stringd) a. having strings.—**string'y** a. fibrous; of person, long and thin.—**string'iness** n.—**string-beans** n.pl. French beans.

stringent (strin'-jent) a. strict; rigid; severe.—**strin'gently** adv.—**strin'gency** n.

strip (strip) v.t. pull or tear off; peel; skin; lay bare; divest;—v.i. take off one's clothes;—n. long, narrow piece of anything;—pr.p. **strip'ping.** —pa.p. and pa.t. **stripped** (stript).—**strip'ling** n. youth;—**striptease** n. display of undressing.

stripe (strip) n. narrow line, band, or mark; strip of material of different colour from rest; chevron; weal;—v.t. mark with stripes; lash.—**striped** (stript) a.

strive (striv) v.i. try hard; make effort; struggle; contend;—pa.p. **striv'en.**—pa.t. **strove**—**stri'ver** n.

stroke (strōk) n. blow; paralytic fit; sound of bell or clock; mark made by pen, pencil, brush, etc.; completed movement, as in swimming, rowing, etc.; rower nearest stern who sets pace; entire movement of piston from one end to other of cylinder; single, sudden effort in business, diplomacy, etc.;—v.t. set time and pace for rowers.

stroke (strōk) v.t. pass hand gently over; caress; soothe;—n. act of stroking.

stroll (strōl) v.i. walk leisurely; saunter; ramble;—n. leisurely walk.—**stroll'er** n.

strong (strong) a. powerful; muscular; able to resist attack; healthy; firm; solid; steadfast; violent; intense; not easily broken.—**strong'ly** adv.—**strong'-box** n. box for storage of valuables; safe.—**strong'hold** n. fortified place. — **strong'-room** n. chamber or vault for storage of valuables.

strontium (stron'-shum) n. (Chem.) yellowish, reactive, metallic element (symbol Sr.).

strop (strop) n. strip of leather for sharpening razor;—v.t. sharpen on strop;—pr.p. **strop'ping.**—pa.p. and pa.t. **stropped** (stropt).

structure (struk'-tūr) n. building; manner of building; arrangement of parts or elements; organisation.—**struc'tural** a.—**struc'turally** adv.

struggle (strug'-l) v.i. contend; strive;—n. violent physical effort; strife.—**strugg'ler** n.

strum (strum) v.t. and v.i. play badly and noisily on (stringed instrument). —pr.p. **strum'ming.**—pa.p. and pa.t. **strummed.**

strut (strut) v.i. walk pompously; walk with affected dignity;—n. pompous gait.—pa.p. and pa.t. **strut'ting.**—pa.p. and pa.t. **strut'ted.**

strut (strut) n. rigid support; support for rafter; brace;—v.t. brace.

strychnine (strik'-nēn, or -nin, or -nin) n. highly poisonous alkaloid; (Med.) nerve and spinal stimulant.

stub (stub) n. stump of tree; short, remaining part of pencil, cigarette, etc.;—v.t. clear (ground) by rooting up stumps of trees; strike toe against fixed object;—pr.p. **stub'bing.**—pa.p. and pa.t. **stubbed.**—**stubbed** a.—**stub'by** a.—**stub'biness** n.

stubble (stub'-l) n. short ends of cornstalks left after reaping; short growth of beard.—**stubb'led** a. covered with stubble.—**stubb'ly** a.

stubborn (stub'-orn) a. fixed in opinion; obstinate; headstrong.—**stubb'ornly** adv.—**stubb'ornness** n.

stucco (stuk'-ō) n. plaster of lime, sand, etc. used on walls, and in decorative work.

stuck (stuk) pa.p. and pa.t. of stick.—**stuck'-up** a. (Colloq.) conceited.

stud (stud) n. movable, double-headed button; ornamental button or knob; large flat-headed nail; boss;—v.t. furnish with studs; set thickly in, or scatter over;—pr.p. **stud'ding.**—pa.p. and pa.t. **stud'ded.**

stud (stud) n. collection of horses or other animals kept for breeding; place where they are kept.—**stud'-book** n. official book for recording pedigrees of thoroughbred animals.

student (stū'-dent) n. one who studies; scholar at university or other post-school institution.—**stu'dentship** n. scholarship at university.

studio (stū-di-ō) n. workroom of artist, sculptor, etc.; room equipped for filming or televising;—pl. **stu'dios.**

studious (stū'-di-us) a. given to, or fond of, study; thoughtful; contemplative; painstaking; careful (of); deliberate.—**stu'diously** adv.

study (stud'-i) n. thoughtful attention; meditation; aim; room for study; preliminary sketch by artist; musical composition embodying teaching points;—v.t. set mind to; examine carefully; scrutinise; ponder over;—v.i. read books closely to gain knowledge.—**studied** (stud'-id) pa.p. and pa.t.;—also a. examined closely; carefully planned.

stuff (stuf) n. textile fabric, esp. woollen; goods; belongings; useless matter; trash;—v.t. fill by pressing closely; cram; (Cook.) fill with seasoning; fill skin, e.g. of animal, bird, etc. to preserve as specimen;—v.i. (Colloq.) eat greedily.—**stuff'ing** n.—**stuffed shirt**, (Slang) pompous person.

stuffy (stuf'-i) a. badly ventilated; airless.—**stuff'iness** n.

tultify (stul'-ti-fī) v.t. make to look ridiculous; make ineffectual; destroy the force of.—**stultifica'tion** n.

tumble (stum'-bl) v.i. trip in walking and nearly fall; fall into error;—v.t. cause to trip; mislead;—n. wrong step; error.—**stum'blingly** adv.—**stum'bling-block** n. obstacle.

stump (stump) n. part of tree left after trunk is cut down; part of limb, tooth, etc. after main part has been removed; remnant; in cricket, one of three upright rods forming wicket;—v.t. reduce to stump; cut off main part; in cricket, to dismiss batsman by 'breaking' wicket when he is out of his ground; (Colloq.) puzzle; tour (district) making political speeches;—v.i. walk noisily.—**stump'y** a. full of stumps; short and thick.

stun (stun) v.t. knock senseless; daze; stupefy; amaze;—pr.p. **stun'ning**.—pa.p. and pa.t. **stunned** (stund).—**stun'ner** n.—**stun'ning** a. stupefying; (Slang) excellent.

stunt (stunt) v.t. check growth of; dwarf.—**stunt'ed** a. underdeveloped; dwarfed.

stunt (stunt) n. any spectacular feat of skill or daring, if for display or publicity.

stupefy (stū'-pe-fī) v.t. make stupid; deprive of full consciousness; dull senses.—**stupefac'tion** n.

stupendous (stū-pen'-dus) a. astonishing, esp. because of size, power, etc.; amazing.—**stupen'dously** adv.—**stupen'dousness** n.

stupid (stū'-pid) a. slow-witted; unintelligent; foolish.—**stu'pidly** adv.—**stupid'ity, stu'pidness** n.

stupor (stū'-por) n. complete or partial loss of consciousness; dazed state.

sturdy (stur'-di) a. robust; strongly built.—**stur'dily** adv.—**stur'diness** n.

sturgeon (stur'-jun) n. fish, whose roe is made into caviare, and whose air-bladder is made into isinglass.

stutter (stut'-er) v.i. and v.t. speak with difficulty, esp. with repetition of initial consonants; stammer;—n. act of stuttering.—**stutt'erer** n.

sty (stī) n. place to keep pigs in; hence, any filthy place.

sty, stye (stī) n. small abscess on eyelid.

style (stīl) n. pointed instrument for writing on waxed tablets; engraving-tool; manner of expressing thought in writing, speaking, etc.; in games, manner of play and bodily action; mode of dress; fashion; fine appearance; mode of address; title; sort, kind, make, shape, etc. of anything;—v.t. give title, official or particular, in addressing or speaking of (person); term; name; call.—**sty'lise** v.t. in art, make conform to convention.—

sty'lish a. fashionable; correct.—**sty'lishly** adv.—**sty'lishness** n.—**sty'list** n. one who is master of style.—**sty'lus** n. style; pen.

stymie (stī'-mi) n. (Golf) position on putting-green resulting from one player's ball coming to rest between hole and opponent's ball; (Fig.) thwart.

styptic (stip'-tik) a. astringent;—n. (Med.) any substance used to arrest bleeding.

suave (swāv, swâv) a. pleasant; agreeable; bland.—**suave'ly** adv.—**suav'ity** n.

sub (sub) n. (Colloq.) shortened form of subaltern, sub-lieutenant, subscription.

subaltern (sub'-al-tern, su-bawl'-tern) n. (Mil.) commissioned officer under rank of captain; first or second lieutenant;—a. of lower rank.

subaqueous (sub-ā'-kwe-us) a. living, lying, or formed under water.—**subaquat'ic** a.

subconscious (sub-kon'-shus) a. pert. to unconscious activities of mind; partially conscious;—n. subconscious mind.—**subcon'sciously** adv.

subcutaneous (sub-kū-tā'-ne-us) a. under skin.

subdivide (sub-di-vīd') v.t. divide part, or parts of, into other parts; divide again;—v.i. be subdivided.—**subdivi'sion** n.

subdue (sub-dū') v.t. bring under one's power; conquer; bring under control; reduce force or strength of; soften.—**subdued'** a.—**subdu'er** n.—**subdu'able** a.

sub-edit (sub-ed'-it) v.t. be assistant editor.—**sub-ed'itor** n.

subhuman (sub-hū'-man) a. less than human.

subject (sub'-jekt) a. under power of another; owing allegiance; subordinate; dependent; liable to; prone; exposed;—n. one under power of another; one owing allegiance; person, animal, etc. used as object of experiment, etc.; matter under consideration; topic; theme.—**subject** (sub-jekt') v.t. bring under control of; subdue; cause to undergo; submit.—**subjec'tion** n. act of bringing under power or control; state of being under control.—**subjec'tive** a. pert. to subject; existing in or relating entirely to one's own mind.—**subjec'tively** adv.—**subjec'tiveness** n.—**subjectiv'ity** n. theological doctrine that bases religious beliefs on subjective experience.

subjugate (sub'-joo-gāt) v.t. force to submit; conquer.—**subjuga'tion** n.—**sub'jugator** n.

sublease (sub-lēs') n. lease granted to another tenant by one who is himself tenant;—v.t.

sublet (sub-let') v.t. let to another

tenant property, of which one is tenant.

sub-lieutenant (sub-lef-ten'-ant) *n.* naval officer ranking below lieutenant.—**sub-lieuten'ancy** *n.*

sublimate (sub'-lim-āt) *v.t.* (*Chem.*) convert solid direct into vapour; purify thus; in psycho-analysis, direct repressed impulses, esp. sexual, towards new aims and activities;—*n.* (*Chem.*) vapourised substance.—**sublima'tion** *n.*

sublime (sub-līm') *a.* exalted; elevated; high in place; eminent; majestic; grandiose;—*n.* that which is sublime; —*v.t.* purify; exalt.—**sublime'ly** *adv.* —**sublimity** (sub-lim'-i-ti) *n.*

subliminal (sub-lim'-in-al) *a.* in psychology, below level of consciousness; latent.

submarine (sub-ma-rēn') *a.* situated, living, or able to travel under surface of sea;—*n.* submersible boat, esp. one armed with torpedoes.

submerge (sub-merj') *v.t.* put under water; cover with water; (*Fig.*) overwhelm;—*v.i.* go under water.—**submer'gence** *n.*

submit (sub-mit') *v.t.* put forward for consideration; surrender;—*v.i.* yield oneself to another; surrender; —*pr.p.* submit'ting;—*pa.p.* and *pa.t.* submit'ted.—**submis'sion** *n.* act of submitting; surrender; humility; meekness.—**submis'sive** *a.* obedient; docile; humble.—**submis'sively** *adv.*—**submis'siveness** *n.* docility.

subnormal (sub-nor'-mal) *a.* below normal.

subordinate (sub-or'-di-nāt) *a.* lower in rank, importance, power, etc.;—*n.* one of lower rank, etc. than another; one under orders of another;—*v.t.* make or treat as subordinate; make subject.—**subor'dinately** *adv.*—**subor'dinacy, subor'dinateness** *n.* state of being subordinate.—**subordina'tion** *n.*

suborn (sub-orn') *v.t.* induce (person) to commit perjury; bribe to do evil. —**suborna'tion** *n.*—**suborn'er** *n.*

subpoena (sub-pē'-na) *n.* (*Law*) writ summoning person to appear in court (under penalty for non-appearance);—*v.t.* issue such.

subscribe (sub-skrīb') *v.t.* write underneath; sign name at end of paper or document; contribute;—*v.i.* promise in writing to give sum of money to cause; (*with* to) pay in advance for regular supply of newspaper, etc., use of telephone; agree with or support.—**subscrib'er** *n.*—**subscrip'tion** *n.* act of subscribing; name or signature of subscriber; money subscribed or signature of subscriber; money subscribed or gifted; fee for membership of society, club, etc.

subsequent (sub'-se-kwent) *a.* fol-

lowing or coming after in time; happening later.—**sub'sequently** *adv.* —**sub'sequence, sub'sequency** *n.*

subserve (sub-serv') *v.t.* serve in small way; help forward.—**subser'vient** *a.* serving to promote some purpose; servile.—**subser'viently** *adv.* —**subser'vience, subser'viency** *n.* state of being subservient.

subside (sub-sīd') *v.i.* sink or fall to bottom; settle; sink to lower level; collapse; abate.—**subsi'dence** *n.* act of subsiding.

subsidiary (sub-sid'-i-a-ri) *a.* pert. to subsidy; aiding; helping; supplementary; secondary; auxiliary;—*n.* one who, or that which, helps; auxiliary; accessory.

subsidy (sub'-si-di) *n.* financial aid; government grant, e.g. to encourage certain industries.—**sub'sidise** *v.t.* pay subsidy to.

subsist (sub-sist') *v.i.* continue to be; exist; live (on);—*v.t.* support with food; feed.—**subsist'ent** *a.* having real being; existing.—**subsist'ence** *n.* act of subsisting; livelihood.

subsoil (sub'-soil) *n.* layer of earth lying just below top layer.

substance (sub'-stans) *n.* essence; stuff, material, etc. of which anything is made; matter; essential matter of speech, discussion, etc.; real point; property.—**substantial** (sub-stan'-shal) *a.* pert. to or having substance; material; really existing, i.e. not imaginary.—**substan'tially** *adv.* — **substantiate** (sub-stan'-shi-āt) *v.t.* make substantial; give substance to; bring evidence for; establish truth of; confirm.—**substantia'tion** *n.*—**sub'stantive** *a.* real; solid; fixed; expressing existence.—**sub'stantively** *adv.*

substitute (sub'-sti-tūt) *v.t.* put in place of another; exchange.—*v.i.* take place of another;—*n.* one who, that which, is put in place of another.—**substitu'tion** *n.*—**substitu'tional, substitu'tionary** *a.*

subtenant (sub-ten'-ant) *n.* tenant who rents house, farm, etc. from one who is himself tenant.

subtend (sub-tend') *v.t.* (*Geom.*) of line, extend under or be opposite to, e.g. angle.

subterfuge (sub'-ter-fūj) *n.* that to which person resorts to escape from difficult situation, to conceal real motives, to avoid censure, etc.; underhand trick.

subterranean (sub-te-rā'-ne-an) *a.* being or lying under surface of earth. Also **subterra'neous.**

sub-title (sub'-tī-tl) *n.* additional title of book; half-title; film caption.

subtle (sut'-l) *a.* delicate; acute; discerning; ingenious; evasive.—**subt'ly** *adv.*—**subt'leness, subtlety** (sutl'-ti) *n.* quality of being subtle; artfulness; acuteness; a fine distinction.

subtract (sub-trakt') v.t. take away (part) from rest; deduct one number from another to find difference.—**subtrac'tion** n.—**subtrac'tive** a.

subtropical (sub-trop'-i-kạl) a. designating zone just outside region of tropics.

suburb (sub'-urb) n. residential district on outskirts of town;—pl. outskirts.—**suburb'an** a.—**suburb'ia** n. suburbs and their inhabitants.

subvention (sub-ven'-shun) n. government grant; subsidy.

subvert (sub-vert') v.t. turn upside down; overthrow, esp. government; destroy; ruin utterly; corrupt.—**subver'sion** n. act of subverting; entire overthrow.—**subver'sive** a.

subway (sub'-wā) n. underground passage; underground railway.

succeed (suk-sēd') v.i. come immediately after; follow in order; take place of;—v.i. come next in order; become heir (to); achieve one's aim; prosper.—**succeed'er** n. successor.—**success'** n. accomplishment; attainment; outcome; prosperity; one who has achieved success.—**success'ful** a.—**success'fully** adv. — **success'fulness** n. — **succession** (suk-sesh'-un) n. act of following in order; sequence; line of descendants; act or right of entering into possession of property, title, etc., of another, esp. of one near of kin.—**succes'sive** a. following in order; consecutive.—**succes'sively** adv.—**succes'sor** n. one who succeeds or takes place of another; heir to throne or title.

succinct (suk-singkt') a. closely compressed; expressed in few words; terse; concise.—**succinct'ly** adv.—**succinct'ness** n. terseness.

succour (suk'-ur) v.t. help, esp. in great distress; comfort;—n. aid; support.

succulent (suk'-ū-lẹnt) a. full of juice; juicy.—**succ'ulently** adv.—**succ'ulence** n. juiciness.

succumb (su-kum') v.i. yield; die.

such (such) a. of like kind; of that kind; of same kind; similar; of degree, quality, etc. mentioned; certain or particular;—pron. used to denote certain person or thing; these or those.—**such'like** a. similar; —pron. similar things (but not defined); this or that.

suck (suk) v.t. draw into mouth (by using lips and tongue); draw liquid from (by using mouth); roll (sweet) in mouth; drink in; absorb;—v.i. draw in with mouth; drink from mother's breast;—n. act of drawing with mouth; milk drawn from mother's breast.—**suck'er** n. one who, or that which, sucks; organ by which animal adheres by suction to

any object; shoot of plant from roots or lower part of stem; (U.S. Slang) person easily deceived.—**suck'ing** a. drawing nourishment from mother's breast; young; inexperienced.—**suck'le** v.t. give suck to; feed at mother's breast.—**suck'ling** n. young child or animal not yet weaned.

suction (suk'-shun) n. act of sucking or drawing in, etc.; 'force' that causes one object to adhere to another when air between them is exhausted.—**suc'torial** a.

sudden (sud'-n) a. happening without warning; done with haste.—**sud'denly** adv.—**sud'denness** n.—**all of a sudden,** suddenly; unexpectedly.

suds (sudz) n.pl. hot water in which soap has been dissolved; froth and bubbles on it.

sue (sū) v.t. (Law) seek justice by taking legal proceedings; prosecute; —v.i. begin legal proceedings; petition; entreat.

suède (swād) n. soft, lamb or sheep-skin leather dressed on under side.

suet (sū'-et, sŏŏ'-et) n. hard animal fat around kidneys and loins.—**su'ety** a.

suffer (suf'-ẹr) v.t. endure; undergo; bear; be affected by; allow; tolerate; —v.i. undergo pain, etc.; sustain loss.—**suff'erable** a. able to be suffered; bearable.—**suff'erance** n. toleration.—**on sufferance,** permitted but with reluctance.

suffice (su-fīs') v.t. satisfy;—v.i. be enough; meet needs of; be satisfied. —**sufficient** (su-fish'-ẹnt) a.—**suffi'ciently** adv.—**suffi'ciency** n.

suffix (suf'-iks) n. letter or syllable added to end of word; affix.—**suffix'** v.t. add to end.

suffocate (suf'-ō-kāt) v.t. kill by choking; smother; stifle;—v.i. be choked or smothered.—**suff'ocating** a. choking.—**suff'ocatingly** adv.—**suffoca'tion** n.

suffragan (suf'-rạ-gạn) a. assisting; —n. assistant bishop.

suffrage (suf'-rāj) n. vote; right to vote; approval. — **suffragette** n. woman who agitated for women's right to parliamentary vote.

suffuse (su-fūz') v.t. pour from underneath and spread over; flood. —**suffu'sion** n.

sugar (shŏŏg'-ạr) n. sweet, crystalline substance obtained from certain plants; any sweet substance like sugar; (Fig.) sweet words; flattery; —v.t. sweeten with sugar;—v.i. turn into sugar.—**sug'ary** a. made of, tasting of, or containing sugar; sweet; flattering.—**sug'ariness** n.—**sug'ar-cane,** tall grass whose sap yields sugar.—**sug'ar-loaf** n. cone-shaped mass of hard, refined sugar.

suggest (su-jest') v.t. bring forward;

propose; hint; insinuate.—**sugges'ter** n.—**sugges'tion** n. proposal; hint.—**sugges'tive** a. tending to call up idea to mind; hinting at; tending to bring to mind indecent thoughts; improper. — **sugges'tively** adv. — **sugges'tiveness** n.

suicide (sū'-i-sīd) n. one who kills himself intentionally; this act.—**suicidal** (sū-i-sī'-dạl) a. — **suici'dally** adv.

suit (sūt) n. act of suing; petition; request; action in court of law; courtship; series or set of things of same kind or material; set of clothes; any of four sets in pack of cards;—v.t. fit; go with; become; be adapted to; meet desires of;—v.i. agree; be convenient.—**suit'able** a. proper; appropriate; becoming.—**suit'ably** adv.—**suitabil'ity, suit'ableness** n.—**suit'ing** n. suit of clothes; material suitable for making this.—**suit'or** n. one who sues; wooer; lover.—**suit'-case** n. flat travelling-bag for holding clothes, etc.

suite (swēt) n. retinue; number of things used together; (Mus.) series of dances or other pieces.

sulk (sulk) v.i. be silent owing to ill-humour, etc.; be sullen;—n. sullen fit or mood.—**sulks** n.pl. sullen mood.—**sulk'y.**—**sulk'ily** adv.—**sulk'iness** n.

sullen (sul'-en) a. gloomily ill-humoured; morose.—**sull'enly** adv.—**sull'enness** n.

sully (sul'-i) v.t. soil; stain; (Fig.) disgrace;—v.i. be sullied.

sulphate (sul'-fāt) n. salt of sulphuric acid.—**sul'phide** n. compound of sulphur with metal or other element.—**sul'phite** n. salt of sulphurous acid.

sulphonamide (sul-fon'-a-mīd) n. antibacterial drug containing sulphur and ammonium.

sulphur (sul'-fur) n. yellow element, burning with blue flame and giving off suffocating odour; brimstone.—**sulphu'ric** a. pert. to, obtained from, sulphur.—**sul'phurous** a. pert. to, like, containing sulphur; sulphureous; (Fig.) hellish; profane.—**sul'phury** a. like sulphur.—**sulphuric acid,** colourless acid, having strong corrosive action.

sultan (sul'-tạn) n. Mohammedan prince or ruler.—**sulta'na** n. wife, mother, or daughter of sultan; kind of raisin.

sultry (sul'-tri) a. hot, close, and oppressive; sweltering.—**sul'trily** adv.—**sul'triness** n.

sum (sum) n. result obtained by adding together two or more things, quantities, etc.; full amount; total; aggregate; summary; quantity of money; arithmetical problem;—v.t. (generally with up) add up; find total amount; make summary of main parts.—**pr.p. summ'ing.**—**pa.p.**

and pa.t. **summed.**—**summa'tion** n. act of summing up; addition; total reckoning.

summary (sum'-ạ-ri) a. expressed in few words; concise; done quickly and without formality;—n. abridgement of chief points of longer document, speech, etc.; epitome.—**summ'arily** adv.—**summ'arise** v.t.—**summ'arist** n.

summer (sum'-er) n. warmest of four seasons of year, season between spring and autumn; commonly, months of June, July, and August;—pl. 'years,' in counting age;—a. pert. to period of summer;—v.i. pass summer.—**summ'ery** a. like summer.—**summ'er-house** n. permanent garden-shelter or outhouse.

summit (sum'-it) n. highest point; top.

summon (sum'-on) v.t. demand appearance of, esp. in court of law; cite; send for; gather up (energy, etc.).—**summ'oner** n.—**summ'ons** n. (Law) document ordering person to appear in court; any authoritative demand;—v.t.

sump (sump) n. lowest part of excavation, esp. of mine, in which water collects; well in crank-case of motor vehicle for oil.

sumptuary (sump'-tū-ạ-ri) a. pert. to, regulating, expenditure.—**sump'tuous** a. costly; lavish.—**sump'tuously** adv.—**sump'tuousness, sumptuosity** n. splendour, lavishness.

sun (sun) n. luminous body round which earth and other planets revolve; its rays; any body forming centre of system;—v.t. expose to sun's rays; warm (oneself) in sunshine;—pr.p. **sunn'ing.**—**pa.p.** and pa.t. **sunned.**—**sun'ny** a.—**sun'niness** n.—**sun'bathe** v.i. expose body to sun.—**sun'beam** n. ray of sunlight.—**sun'-blind** n. shade for protecting windows from sun.—**sun'burn** n. darkening of skin, due to exposure to sun;—v.t. and v.i. darken by exposure to sun.—**sun'burned, sun'burnt** a.—**sun'dew** n. insectivorous bog plant.—**sun'-di'al** n. device for showing time by shadow which raised pin casts on plate marked with hours.—**sun'down** n. sunset; broad-brimmed hat.—**sun'flower** n. tall plant with large, round, yellow-rayed flower-heads.—**sun'light** n. light of sun.—**sun'lit** a.—**sun'rise** n. dawn; east.—**sun'set** n. descent of sun below horizon; time of its disappearance; west. — **sun'shade** n. parasol.—**sun'shine** n. light of sun; (Fig.) cheerfulness.—**sun'shiny** a.—**sun'spot** n. dark, irregular patches seen periodically on surface of sun; freckle.—**sun'stroke** n. feverish and sudden prostration caused by undue exposure to very strong sunlight.

sundae (sun'-dā) n. ice-cream served with crushed fruit.

Sunday (sun'-dā) n. first day of week.

sunder (sun'-der) v.t. separate; divide;—v.i. come apart.—**sun'dry** a. separate; several; various.—**sun'dries** n.pl. sundry things; odd items.—**all and sundry,** all collectively and individually; everybody.

sup (sup) v.t. sip; eat with spoon, as soup;—v.i. have supper; sip;—n. small mouthful; sip;—pr.p. sup'ping. —pa.p. and pa.t. supped.

super (sū'-per) n. supernumerary (actor); (Colloq. abbrev.) superintendent; (Colloq.) superfine, super-excellent, etc.; first-rate.

superable (sū'-per-abl) a. able to be overcome.

superabound (sū-per-a-bound') v.i. be exceedingly abundant.—**superabund'ant** a. much more than enough; excessive. — **superabund'antly** adv. — superabund'nce n.

superannuate (sū-per-an'-ū-āt) v.t. pension off because of age, etc.— **superannua'tion** n. state of being superannuated; pension of superannuated person; contribution made by employee.

superb (sū-perb') a. grand; splendid; stately; elegant.—**superb'ly** adv.— superb'ness n.

supercharge (sū-per-chärj') v.t. charge or fill to excess.—**supercharg'er** n. in internal-combustion engine, device for forcing extra supply of petrol mixture into cylinders.

superciliary (sū-per-sil'-i-a-ri) a. pert. to eyebrow.—**supercil'ious** a. lofty with pride; haughty and indifferent.—**supercil'iously** adv.—supercil'iousness n.

supererogation (sū-per-er-ō-gā'-shun) n. doing more than duty or necessity requires.—**superog'ative,** superog'atory a.

superficial (sū-per-fish'-al) a. lying on surface; not deep; slight.— superfi'cially adv.—superficial'ity (fish-i-al'-i-ti). Also superfi'cialness.

superfine (sū-per-fīn) a. fine above others; of first class quality; very fine or subtle.

superfluous (sū-per'-flŏŏ-us) a. more than is required or desired; useless. —super'fluously adv.—superflu'ity n. state of being superfluous; quantity beyond what is required; superabundance.—super'fluousness n.

superhuman (sū-per-hū'-man) a. more than human; divine; excessively powerful.

superimpose (sū-per-im-pōz') v.t. lay upon another thing.—superimposi'tion n.

superintend (sū-per-in-tend') v.t. manage; supervise; direct; control; —v.i. supervise. — superinten'dence,

superinten'dency n.—superinten'dent a. superintending;—n. police officer above inspector.

superior (sū-pē'-ri-or) a. upper; higher in place, position, rank, quality, etc.; surpassing others; being above, or beyond, power or influence of; supercilious; snobbish; —n. one who is above another; head of monastery or other religious house.—superior'ity n.

superlative (sū-per-la-tiv) a. of or in the highest degree; surpassing all others; supreme.—super'latively adv.

supermarket (sū'-per-mar-ket) n. large self-service store.

supernal (sū-per'-nal) a. pert. to things above; celestial; exalted.

supernatural (sū-per-nat'-ū-ral) a. beyond powers or laws of nature; spiritual.—supernat'urally adv.

supernumerary (sū-per-nū'-mer-ar-i) a. exceeding number required; over and above what is necessary; —n. person or thing in excess; actor with no speaking part.

superscribe (sū-per-skrīb') v.t. write or engrave on outside or top of.— superscrip'tion n.

supersede (sū-per-sēd') v.t. set aside; replace by another person or thing; take place of.—superses'sion n.

supersonic (sū-per-son'-ik) a. pert. to sound-waves of too high frequency to be audible; denoting speed greater than that of sound.

superstition (sū-per-stish'-un) n. belief in, or fear of, what is unknown, mysterious, or supernatural. —supersti'tious a.—supersti'tiously adv. —supersti'tiousness n.

superstructure (sū-per-struk'-tūr) n. structure built on top of another; part above foundation.—superstruc'tive, superstruc'tural a.

supervene (sū-per-vēn') v.i. happen in addition, or unexpectedly; follow closely upon.—superve'nient a. happening in addition.—superven'tion n. act of supervening.

supervise (sū-per-vīz') v.t. oversee; superintend; inspect; direct and control.—supervision (vizh'-un) n. act of supervising; superintendence; inspection.—supervisor (vī'-zor) n.— supervi'sory a. pert. to supervision.

supine (sū'-pīn) a. lying on one's back; (Fig.) indolent; inactive.— supine'ly adv.—supine'ness n.

supper (sup'-er) n. last meal of day.

supplant (su-plant') v.t. displace (person) esp. by unfair means; take place of.—supplant'er n.

supple (sup'-l) a. easily bent; flexible; (Fig.) docile;—v.t. and v.i. make or become supple.—supp'ly adv.—supp'leness n.

supplement (sup'-le-ment) n. something added to supply deficiency; appendix; special number of newspaper; extra charge.—**supplement'** v.t. fill up or supply deficiency; add to; complete.—**supplement'al** a.—**supplement'ary** a. additional.

suppliant (sup'-li-ant) a. supplicating; asking humbly; beseeching;—n. one who supplicates.—**supp'liantly** adv.—**supp'licant** a. supplicating;—n. suppliant.—**supp'licate** v.t. and v.i. ask humbly; beg earnestly; petition.—**supplica'tion** n.—**supp'licatory** a.

supply (su-pli') v.t. provide what is needed; furnish; fill place of;—n. act of supplying; what is supplied; stock; store; temporary substitute for another.—**supplies'** n.pl. food or money; sums of money granted by parliament to meet public expenditure.—**suppli'er** n. one who supplies.

support (su-pōrt') v.t. keep from falling; bear weight of; sustain; tolerate; encourage; furnish with means of living; confirm; defend;—n. advocacy; maintenance or subsistence; one who, or that which, supports.—**suppor'ters** n. pl. (Her.) figures placed one on each side of escutcheon.

suppose (su-pōz') v.t. assume as true without proof; advance or accept as possible or probable fact, condition, etc.; imagine.—**supposed'** a. imagined; put forward as authentic.—**supposedly** adv.—**suppos'able** a.

supposition (sup-o-zish'-un) n. act of supposing; assumption; that which is supposed; belief without proof.—**supposi'tional** a.—**supposi'tionally** adv. — **supposititious** (su-poz-i-tish'-us) a. spurious.

suppository (su-poz'-i-tor-i) n. (Med.) substance introduced into rectum or other canal of body.

suppress (su-pres') v.t. subdue; overpower and crush; conceal.—**suppression** (su-presh'-un) n. act of crushing or subduing; state of being suppressed.—**suppress'ive** a. tending to suppress.—**suppress'or** n. device to eliminate electrical interference.

suppurate (sup'-ū-rāt) v.i. form pus.—**sup'purative** a.—**suppura'tion** n.

supreme (sū-prēm') a. holding highest authority; most excellent; greatest possible; uttermost.—**supreme'ly** adv.—**supreme'ness** n.—**supremacy** (sū-prem'-a-si) n.

surcharge (sur-chárj') v.t. make additional charge; overload.—**surcharge** (sur-chárj, sur-charj') n. excessive charge or burden; additional words or marks superimposed on postage stamp.

sure (shŏor) a. certain; positive; admitting of no doubt; secure.—**sure'ly** adv. certainly; undoubtedly; securely.—**sure'ness** n.—**surety** (shŏor'-ti) n. certainty; that which makes sure; security against loss or damage; one who makes himself

responsible for obligations of another.

surf (surf) n. foam or broken water of sea breaking on shore or reefs, etc.—**surf'y** a.—**surf'-ri'ding** n. sport, consisting in riding on long, narrow boards over surf.

surface (sur'-fās) n. external layer or outer face of anything; outside; exterior;—a. involving surface only;—v.t. cover with special surface; smooth;—v.i. come to surface.

surfeit (sur'-fit) v.t. overfeed; fill to satiety;—n. excess in eating and drinking.—**sur'feiter** n.—**sur'feiting** n.

surge (surj) n. rolling swell of water; large wave or billow;—v.i. swell; more forward.—**sur'gent, sur'gy** a.

surgeon (sur'-jun) n. medical man qualified to perform operations; one who practises surgery.—**sur'gery** n. branch of medicine dealing with cure of disease or injury by manual operation; doctor's consulting-rooms.—**sur'gical** a. pert. to surgeons or surgery.—**sur'gically** adv.

surly (sur'-li) a. unfriendly; uncivil; sullen.—**sur'lily** adv.—**sur'liness** n.

surmise (sur-mīz') v.t. imagine or infer without proper grounds; make guess; conjecture;—n. supposition; guess.

surmount (sur-mount') v.t. rise above; overcome.—**surmount'able** a.

surname (sur'-nām) n. name added to baptismal or Christian name; family name.

surpass (sur-pas') v.t. go beyond; excel; outstrip.—**surpass'ing** a. excellent; exceeding others.

surplice (sur'-plis) n. white vestment worn over cassock by clergy of Anglican Church.

surplus (sur'-plus) n. excess beyond what is wanted;—a. more than enough.

surprise (sur-prīz') v.t. fall or come upon unawares; capture by unexpected attack; strike with astonishment;—n. astonishment; unexpected event, piece of news, gift, etc.—**surpris'al** n. act of surprising or state of being surprised.—**surpris'ing** a. remarkable.—**surpris'ingly** adv.

surrealism (su-rē'-al-izm) n. 20th cent. phase in art and literature of expressing subconscious in images without coherence, as in dream.—**surre'alist** n.—**surrealis'tic** a.

surrender (su-ren'-der) v.t. hand over to power of another; resign; yield;—v.i. cease resistance; give oneself up into power of another; capitulate;—n. act of surrendering.—**surren'derer** n.

surreptitious (sur-ep-tish'-us) a. stealthy; furtive.—**surrepti'tiously** adv.

surround (su-round') v.t. be on all sides of; encircle; (Mil.) cut off from communication or retreat;—n. that which surrounds; border or framework. — **surroun'dings** n.pl. things which environ; neighbourhood.

surtax (sur'-taks) n. extra tax;—v.t.

surveillance (sur-vā'-lạns, sur-vā'-yạns) n. close watch; supervision.

survey (sur-vā') v.t. look over; view as from high place; take broad, general view; determine shape, extent, etc. of tract of land.— **survey** (sur'-vā) n. general view, as from high place; attentive scrutiny; measured plan; set of statistics.— **survey'or** n. one versed in art of surveying, i.e. measuring and mapping surfaces.—**survey'orship** n.

survive (sur-vīv') v.t. live longer than; outlive or outlast;—v.i. remain alive.—**survi'val** n. living longer than, or beyond, life of another person.—**survi'vor** n. one who lives longer than another; one who remains alive in spite of event which might have caused death.

susceptible (su-sep'-ti-bl) a. capable of; readily impressed; sensitive; touchy; amorous.—**suscep'tibly** adv.—**suscep'tibleness** n.—**susceptibil'ity** n. sensitiveness;—pl. sensitive spots in person's nature.—**suscep'tive** a. receptive of emotional impressions.

suspect (sus-pekt') v.t. imagine existence or presence of; imagine to be guilty; conjecture; mistrust.—**sus'pect** n. suspected person;—a. inspiring distrust.

suspend (sus-pend') v.t. cause to hang; bring to stop temporarily; debar from office or privilege; keep undecided.—**suspen'der** n. one who suspends; contrivance for supporting sock or stocking;—pl. (U.S.) braces.—**suspense'** n. state of being suspended; state of uncertainty; indecision.—**suspen'sion** n. delay or deferment; temporary withdrawal.—**suspen'sor** n. something which suspends.—**suspen'sory** a. pert. to suspension; hanging.—**suspension bridge**, one supported by flexible cables.

suspicion (sus-pish'-un) n. act of suspecting; doubt; mistrust; slight trace or hint.—**suspic'ious** a. feeling suspicion; mistrustful; arousing suspicion.—**suspic'iously** adv.

sustain (sus-tān') v.t. keep from falling or sinking; nourish or keep alive; endure or undergo.—**sustain'able** a.—**sustain'er** n.—**sustenance** (sus'-te-nạns) n. food, nourishment.

suture (sū'-tūr) n. act of sewing; sewing up of wound; material used for this; connection or seam, between bones of skull;—v.t. join by stitching.—**su'tural** a.—**su'tured** a.

suzerain (sū-ze'-rān) n. feudal lord; paramount ruler.—**su'zerainty** n. dominion.

svelte (svelt) a. supple; lithe; lissom.

swab (swob) n. mop for rubbing over floors, decks, etc.; (Surg.) absorbent pad;—v.t. clean with mop or swab.—pr.p. **swabb'ing**.—pa.t. and pa.p. **swabbed**.—**swabb'er** n.

swaddle (swod'-l) v.t. bind tightly with, or as with, bandages.—**swadd'ling-band, -cloth** n. long binder formerly wrapped round infants.

swag (swag) n. bundle; stolen goods or booty; in Australia, tramping bushman's pack.

swagger (swag'-er) v.i. strut; boast or brag;—n. defiant or conceited —**swagg'erer** n.—**swagg'ering** a.

swain (swān) n. country lad; rustic lover; (Colloq.) suitor.

swallow (swol'-ō) n. migratory, passerine, insectivorous bird. — **swall'ow-tail** n. forked tail.

swallow (swol'-ō) v.t. receive into stomach through mouth and throat; absorb; accept without criticism;—v.i.;—n. act of swallowing; amount taken at one gulp.—**swall'ower** n.

swamp (swomp) n. wet, spongy, low-lying ground; marsh;—v.t. cause to fill with water, as boat;—v.i. founder.—**swam'py** a.

swan (swon) n. large, web-footed bird of goose family.—**swan'nery** n. place where swans are bred.—**swan'-shot** n. shot of large size.—**swan'-song** n. song which, according to myth, swan sings before dying; last work of poet, composer, etc.

swank (swangk) v.i. (Slang) show off; swagger;—n. (Slang) showing off; swagger; bluff.—**swank'y** a.

swap See swop.

sward (swawrd) n. land covered with short green grass; turf;—v.t. cover with sward.

swarm (swawrm) n. large number of insects esp. in motion; cluster of honey-bees leaving hive to form colony elsewhere; great multitude or throng;—v.i. of bees, emigrate in swarm; collect in large numbers.

swarm (swawrm) v.i. climb with arms and legs.

swarthy (swawr'-ᴛʜi) a. dark in hue; of dark complexion; sunburnt.

swashbuckler (swash'-buckler) n. swaggering bully; braggart.—**swash'buckling** a. bragging.

swastika (swas'-ti-kà) n. symbol in form of Greek cross with ends of arms bent at right angles, all in same direction, thus ⍷. Used as badge of Nazi party. Also called *fylfot*.

swat (swot) v.t. hit smartly; kill insects.

swathe (swāᴛʜ) v.t. bind with bandage; envelop in wraps;—n. bandage.

sway (swā) v.t. cause to incline to one side or other; influence;—v.i. incline or be drawn to one side or other; swing unsteadily; totter;—n. swaying or swinging movement; control.

swear (swâr) *v.t.* utter, affirm or declare on oath;—*v.i.* utter solemn declaration; (*Law*) give evidence on oath; use name of God profanely; curse;—*pa.p.* sworn.—*pa.t.* swore.—swear'er *n.*—swear'ing *n.* use of profane language.—swear'word *n.* (*Colloq.*) profane word.

sweat (swet) *n.* moisture excreted from skin; perspiration; state of sweating; toil or drudgery;—*v.t.* cause to excrete moisture from skin; exude from skin; employ at low wages;—*v.i.* excrete moisture from skin; toil or drudge at.—sweat'er *n.* warm, woollen jersey or jacket.—sweat'y *a.*—sweat'ily *adv.*—sweat'iness *n.*

sweep (swēp) *v.t.* pass brush over to remove loose dirt; scan rapidly;—*v.i.* pass with swiftness or violence; move with dignity; extend in curve; effect cleaning with broom;—*n.* act of sweeping; reach of stroke; curving gesture or movement; powerful drive forward, covering large area; long, heavy oar; one who sweeps chimneys; sail of windmill; (*Colloq.*) sweepstake; — *pa.p.* and *pa.t.* swept.—sweep'er *n.*—sweep'ing *a.* moving swiftly; of great scope; comprehensive.—sweep'ingly *adv.*—sweep'-stake(s) *n.* gambling on horse-racing, in which participators' stakes are pooled.

sweet (swēt) *a.* tasting like sugar; having agreeable taste; fragrant; melodious; pleasing to eye; gentle; affectionate; dear or beloved; likeable;—*n.* sweetmeat; dish served as dessert; darling.—sweet'en *v.t.* make sweet, pleasing, or kind; make pure and salubrious.—sweet'ening *n.* act of making sweet; ingredient which sweetens.—sweet'ly *adv.* (*Colloq.*) smoothly. — sweet'ness *n.* — sweet'-bread *n.* pancreas of animal, as food.—sweet'heart *n.* lover or beloved person; darling.—sweet'meat *n.* small confection chiefly of sugar or chocolate.—sweet'-pea *n.* plant, bearing bright, sweet-scented flowers.—sweet'-will'iam *n.* garden-plant, bearing clusters of small pink or red flowers.

swell (swel) *v.t.* increase size; dilate; augment;—*v.i.* grow larger; expand; rise in waves; grow louder; be filled with emotion;—*n.* act of swelling; increase in bulk, intensity, importance, etc.; slow heaving and sinking of sea after storm; (*Mus.*) crescendo followed by diminuendo; (*Colloq.*) dandy;—*a.* (*Slang*) excellent;—*pr.p.* swell'ing.—*pa.p.* swoll'en or swelled.—*pa.t.* swell'ed.—swell'ing *n.* act of swelling; state of being swollen; protuberance.

swelter (swel'-tẹr) *v.i.* be oppressive, or oppressed, with heat; perspire profusely;—*n.* heated or sweaty state.—swel'try *a.*

swerve (swẹrv) *v.i.* depart from straight line; wander or turn aside from duty, custom, etc.;—*v.t.* cause to bend or turn aside;—*n.* act of swerving.

swift (swift) *a.* quick, rapid; prompt; moving quickly. — swift'ly *adv.* — swift'ness *n.* speed.

swift (swift) *n.* long-winged, quick-flying migratory bird, resembling swallow.

swill (swil) *v.t.* and *v.i.* drink greedily; rinse or flush;—*n.* act of swilling; pig-food; slops.—swill'er *n.*—swill'ings *n.pl.* hogwash.

swim (swim) *v.i.* propel oneself in water by means of hands, feet, or fins, etc.; float on surface; move with gliding motion;—*v.t.* cross or pass over by swimming; cause to swim;—*n.* act of swimming; spell of swimming;—*pr.p.* swimm'ing.—*pa.t.* swam.—*pa.p.* swum or swam.—swimm'er *n.*—swimm'ingly *adv.* easily, successfully.

swim (swim) *v.i.* be dizzy or giddy;—*n.* dizziness or unconsciousness.

swindle (swin'-dl) *v.t.* and *v.i.* cheat or defraud; obtain by fraud;—*n.* act of defrauding; false pretences.—swind'ler *n.*

swine (swīn) *n. sing.* and *pl.* pig; hog; person of bestial disposition or habits.—swine'herd *n.*—swin'ish *a.* like swine; gross.—swin'ishly *adv.*

swing (swing) *v.i.* move to and fro, esp. as suspended body; sway; vibrate; turn on pivot; progress with easy, swaying gait; wheel round;—*v.t.* fix up so as to hang freely; move to and fro; cause to wheel about point; brandish;—*n.* act of swinging or causing to swing; extent, sweep, or power of anything swung; seat suspended by ropes, on which one may swing.—*pa.p.* and *pa.t.* swung.—swing'er *n.*—swing'ing *a.*—swing'ingly *adv.*—to swing the lead (*Slang*) malinger.

swipe (swīp) *v.t.* strike with wide, sweeping blow, as with bat, racket, etc.;—(*Slang*) steal by snatching;—*n.* hard stroke.

swirl (swẹrl) *n.* eddy of wind or water; whirling motion;—*v.i.* form eddies;—*v.t.* carry along with whirling motion.

swish (swish) *n.* whistling or hissing sound;—*v.i.* move with hissing or rustling sound;—*v.t.* flourish; flog;—*a.* (*Slang*) smart.

switch (swich) *n.* flexible twig or rod; tufted end of animal's tail; tress of false hair; stiff-bristled brush or broom; on railway, movable rail for transferring carriages from one set of lines to another; (*Elect.*) device for making, breaking, or transferring electric current; act of switching;— *v.t.* strike with switch; whisk; sweep with stiff broom; shift or shunt (train) to another track; (*Elect.*) turn electric current off or on with switch; transfer one's thoughts to another subject; transfer.—**switch'-back** *n.* sharply undulating road or railway.—**switch'board** *n.* set of switches at telephone exchange.

swither (swiTH'-er) *v.i.* hesitate; vacillate.

swivel (swiv'-l) *n.* ring turning on pivot, forming connection between two pieces of mechanism;—*v.i.* swing on pivot;—*v.t.* cause to turn as on pivot.—*pr.p.* swiv'elling.—*pa.p.* and *pa.t.* swiv'elled.

swollen (swōln) *a.* swelled;—*pa.p.* of swell.

swoon (swóón) *v.i.* faint;—*n.*

swoop (swóóp) *v.t.* catch up with sweeping motion;—*v.i.* sweep down upon prey, as hawk; pounce;—*n.* sweeping downward flight of bird of prey; pounce.

swop, swap (swop) *v.t.* and *v.i.* exchange; barter;—*n.* exchange;— *pr.p.* swop'ping.—*pa.p.* and *pa.t.* swopped.

sword (sōrd, sord) *n.* weapon for cutting or thrusting, having long blade; emblem of judicial punishment; destruction by war; military power.—**sword'-arm, -hand** *n.* right arm or hand.—**sword'play** *n.* fencing. —**swords'man** *n.* one skilful with sword.—**swords'manship** *n.*—**sword-stick, -cane** *n.* cane or walking-stick containing slender sword.—**to cross swords**, oppose in fight, controversy, argument.

swore (swōr) *pa.t.* of **swear**;—**sworn** *pa.p.* of same verb.

swot (swot) *v.t.* and *v.i.* (*Slang*) study hard or long;—*n.* one who studies hard.

sybarite (sib'-a-rīt) *n.* person devoted to luxury and pleasure.—**sybarit'ic, sybarit'ical** *a.*

sycamore (sik'-a-mōr) *n.* tree with broad leaves, allied to plane-tree and maple; kind of fig-tree of Egypt and Asia Minor.

sycophant (sik'-ō-fant) *n.* tale-bearer or informer; flatterer, or one who fawns on rich or famous; parasite;— *a.* servile; obsequious.—**syc'ophancy** *n.*—**sycophan'tic, sycophan'tical** *a.*

syllable (sil'-a-bl) *n.* sound uttered at single effort of voice, and constituting word, or part of word;—*v.t.* divide into syllables; articulate.— **syllab'ic** *a.* pert. to, or consisting of, syllable(s).—**syllab'ically** *adv.*

syllabus (sil'-a-bus) *n.* compendium containing heads of discourse; outline of topics treated of, as in book, lectures, etc.

syllogism (sil'-ō-jizm) *n.* formal

statement of argument.—**syll'ogise** *v.t.* and *v.i.*—**syllogis'tic, syllogis'tical** *a.*—**syllogis'tically** *adv.*

sylph (silf) *n.* elemental spirit of air; fairy or sprite; graceful girl.— **syl'phid** *n.* little sylph.—**sylph'like** *a.* graceful and slender.

sylvan (sil'-van) *a.* forest-like; a- bounding in forests; rural, rustic.— **syl'viculture** *n.* forestry.

symbol (sim'-bol) *n.* something that represents something else; emblem; conventional sign.—**symbol'ic, symbol'ical** *a.*—**symbol'ically** *adv.*—**sym'-bolise** *v.t.* stand for, or represent; represent by symbol or symbols.— **sym'bolism** *n.* representation by symbols; system of symbols; investing of practice with symbolic meaning; in art and literature, to invest ordinary objects with imaginative meanings.—**sym'bolist** *n.*

symmetry (sim'-e-tri) *n.* due proportion between several parts of object; exact correspondence; beauty of form.—**symmet'ric, symmet'rical** *a.* —**symmet'rically** *adv.*—**symmet'ricalness** *n.*—**sym'metrise** *v.t.*

sympathy (sim'-pa-thi) *n.* fellow-feeling; sharing of emotion, interest, desire, etc.; compassion or pity.— **sympathet'ic(al)** *a.* exhibiting or expressing sympathy; compassionate; congenial.—**sympathet'ically** *adv.* —**sym'pathise** *v.i.* feel or express sympathy; agree.—**sym'pathiser** *n.*

symphony (sim'-fo-ni) *n.* harmony of sound; (*Mus.*) composition for full orchestra, consisting usually of four contrasted sections or movements.—**symphon'ic** *a.*—**sym'phonist** *n.* composer of symphonies.—**symphonic poem**, composition of symphonic scope.

symposium (sim-pō'-zi-um) *n.* drinking together; convivial gathering, esp. one at which interchange of ideas takes place; series of short articles by several writers dealing with common topic;—*pl.* sympo'sia.

symptom (sim'-tom) *n.* (*Med.*) perceptible change in body or its functions, which indicates disease; sign of existence of something else. —**symptomat'ic, symptomat'ical** *a.*

synagogue (sin'-a-gog) *n.* Jewish place of worship.—**synagogical** (sin-a-goj'-i-kal) *a.*

synchromesh (sin'-krō-mesh) *a.* of gearbox with mechanical device to ensure silent gear change in car.

synchronise (sin'-krō-nīz) *v.i.* agree in time; be simultaneous;—*v.t.* cause to occur at same time.— **synchronisa'tion** *n.*—**syn'chronism** *n.*— **syn'chronal** *a.*—**syn'chronous** *a.*

syncopate (sin'-kō-pāt) *v.t.* (*Gram.*) contract, as word, by taking one or more letters or syllables from middle; in music, alter rhythm by accenting usually unaccented note, or causing accent to fall on rest, or silent beat. —syncopa'tion n.

syndicate (sin'-di-kāt) n. body of persons associated to carry out enterprise; association of industrialists or financiers formed to carry out industrial project;—v.t. control by syndicate.

syndicalism (sin'-di-kal-izm) n. movement aiming at replacing State by federation of trade unions, and transferring control of production to unions of workers.—syn'dicalist n.—syndicalis'tic a.

syndrome (sin'-drōm) n. of symptoms.

synod (sin'-od) n. church court, superior to presbyteries, but subordinate to General Assembly; convention or council.—syn'odal, synod'ic, synod'ical a.—synod'ically adv.

synonym (sin'-o-nim) n. word which has same meaning as another.—synon'ymous a.—synon'ymously adv.

synopsis (si-nop'-sis) n. general outlook, view; summary.—pl. synop'ses (sēz).—synop'tic, synop'tical a.—synop'tically adv.

syntax (sin'-taks) n. part of grammar that treats of construction of sentences, and correct arrangement of words therein; rules governing sentence - construction. — syntac'tic, syntac'tical a.—syntac'tically adv.

synthesis (sin'-the-sis) n. combination or putting together; combining of parts into whole (opp. to analysis); (Chem.) uniting of elements to form compound;—pl. syntheses (sin'-the-sēz).—synthet'ic, synthet'ical a. pert. to, consisting in synthesis; not derived from nature; artificial; spurious—synthet'ically adv.—syn'thesise, syn'thetise v.t. combine by synthesis—syn'thesist, syn'thetist n.

syphilis (sif'-i-lis) n. contagious venereal disease.—syphilit'ic a.

syringa (sir-ing'-ga) n. lilac; applied to mock-orange, shrub with large white flowers.

syringe (sir-inj, sir'-inj) n. tube and piston serving to draw in and then expel fluid; squirt;—v.t. inject by means of syringe.

syrup (sir'-up) n. fluid separated from sugar in refining.—syr'upy a.

system (sis'-tem) n. assemblage of objects arranged after some distinct method; scheme of created things regarded as forming complete whole; universe; organisation; classification; set of doctrines or principles; body as functional unity.—systemat'ic, systemat'ical a.—systemat'ically adv.—sys'tematise, sys'temise v.t.—systematisa'tion, systemisa'tion n.

T

tab (tab) n. tag; label; check.

tabard (tä'-bard) n. sleeveless tunic worn over armour by knights; tunic emblazoned with Royal arms, worn by heralds.

tabby (tab'-i) n. stout kind of watered silk; striped cat, esp. female; (Colloq.) old maid;—a. striped;—v.t. give watered finish to, as silk.—tabb'y-cat n. striped or brindled female cat.

tabernacle (tab'-er-na-kl) n. movable shelter esp. for religious worship by Israelites; nonconformist meeting-place for worship.

table (tā'-bl) n. smooth flat surface of wood, etc. supported by legs, as article of furniture; flat surface, esp. slab bearing inscription; food served on table; memorandum-book; systematic arrangement of figures, facts, etc. as multiplication table; index, scheme, or schedule; synopsis; —a. pert. to or shaped like table;—v.t. form into table or catalogue; lay down, as money in payment of bill; set down in writing for subsequent consideration.—ta'ble-land n.—ta'ble-ten'nis n. game of indoor-tennis played on table; ping-pong.

tableau (tab'-lō) n. vivid representation of scene in history, art, etc. by group of persons appropriately dressed and posed;—pl. tableaux (tab'-lōz).

tablet (tab'-let) n. anything flat on which to write; pad; slab of stone with inscription; (Scot.) sweetmeat cut in small, flat squares.

tabloid (tab'-loid) n. (U.S.) newspaper, giving topical events in compressed form.

taboo, tabu (ta-bōō') n. system among natives of Pacific islands by which certain objects and persons are set aside as sacred or accursed; political, social, or religious prohibition;—a. prohibited; proscribed; —v.t. forbid use of; ostracise.

tabor, tabour (tā'-bur) n. small drum like tambourine.

tabular (tab'-ū-lar) a. pert. to, or resembling, table in shape; having broad, flat top; arranged systematically in tables or columns.—tab'ularise v.t.—tab'ularly adv.—tab'ulate v.t. reduce to tabular form.

tachometer (tak-om'-e-ter) n. instrument for indicating the speed at which a shaft is revolving.

tacit (tas'-it) a. implied, but not expressed; silent.—tac'itly adv.—tac'iturn a. silent; reserved of speech. —taciturn'ity n. habitual silence or restraint.—tac'iturnly adv.

tack (tak) *n.* small sharp-pointed nail; long stitch; ship's course in relation to position of sails; (*Fig.*) course of action; reliance; stickiness, as of gum, varnish, etc.; (*Slang*) food; —*v.t.* fasten with long, loose stitches; append; nail with;—*v.i.* change ship's course by moving position of sails.—tack′er *n.*—tack′iness *n.* stickiness.—tack′y *a.* sticky; viscous.

tackle (tak′-l) *n.* mechanism of ropes and pulleys for raising heavy weights; rigging, etc. of ship; equipment or gear; (*Rugby*) move by player to grasp and stop opponent; —*v.t.* harness; fix by ropes and pulleys; lay hold of; undertake;—*v.i.* perform operation of tackling.—tack′ling *n.* gear; rigging of ship.

tact (takt) *n.* right thing to do or say to avoid giving offence.—tact′ful *a.*—tact′fully *adv.*—tact′ile *a.* capable of being touched or felt; tangible.—tact′less *a.* wanting in tact.

tactics (tak′-tiks) *n. sing.* science of disposing of military forces to best advantage; adroit management of situation.—tac′tic, -al *a.*—tac′tically *adv.*—tactic′ian *n.*

tadpole (tad′-pōl) *n.* young of frog in its first state before gills and tail are absorbed.

taffeta (taf′-e-ta) *n.* light-weight glossy silk of plain weave.

taffrail, tafferel (taf′-rāl, taf′-e-rel) *n.* rail round stern of ship.

tag (tag) *n.* metal point at end of shoelace, etc.; tab on back of boot; tie-on label; appendage; catchword; hackneyed phrase; ragged end; refrain;—*v.t.* fit with tags; add on; follow behind;—*pr.p.* tag′ging.—*pa.t.* and *pa.p.* tagged.—tag′-end *n.* tail-end.

tail (tāl) *n.* prolongation of animal's spine; back, lower, or inferior part of anything; reverse side of coin; queue; train of attendants; upward or downward stroke of letter, minim, crotchet, etc.; rear horizontal unit of aircraft;—*pl.* tail-coat;—*v.t.* furnish with tail; extend in line; trail; cut off stalk.—tail′-coat *n.* man's evening-dress coat with tails.—tailed *a.*—tail′less *a.*—tail′-light *n.* rear-light of vehicle.—tail′-plane *n.* stabilising surface at rear of aircraft.

tailor (tāl′-or) *n.* (*fem.* tail′oress) one who makes clothes;—*v.t.* and *v.i.* make men's suits, women's costumes, etc.—tail′oring *n.* work of tailor.—tail′or-made *a.* made by tailor; perfectly fitting.

taint (tānt) *v.t.* impregnate with something poisonous; contaminate; —*v.i.* be infected with incipient putrefaction;—*n.* corruption; (*Fig.*) moral blemish.

take (tāk) *v.t.* grasp; capture; entrap; remove; win; choose; assume; suppose; photograph;—*v.i.* be effective; catch; please; go; direct course of; resort to;—*pr.p.* ta′king.—*pa.t.* took. —*pa.p.* ta′ken.—*n.* fish caught at one time; drawings at theatre performance.—take′-off *n.* mimicry; caricature; (*Aviat.*) moment when aircraft leaves ground.—ta′ker *n.*—ta′king *n.* act of taking or gaining possession; —*pl.* cash drawings of shop, theatre, etc.;—*a.* attractive; infectious.—ta′kingly *adv.*—ta′kingness *n.* quality of being attractive.—to take after, resemble in face or character.—to take in hand, undertake.—to take in vain, blaspheme.—take to, become addicted to; feel liking for (person). —take-over bid, attempt to gain control of company by acquiring majority of shares.

talc (talk) *n.* fine, slightly perfumed toilet-powder; soft mineral with soapy feel; commercial name for *mica*.—tal′cose *a.* pert. to or composed of talc.—tal′cum *n.* powdered talc, as toilet powder.

tale (tāl) *n.* narrative; story; false report; reckoning.—tale′-bear′er *n.* one who spitefully informs against another.—old wives' tale, far-fetched story.

talent (tal′-ent) *n.* ancient weight and denomination of money; faculty; special or outstanding ability.—tal′ented *a.* gifted.

talisman (tal′-is-man) *n.* object endowed with magical power of protecting wearer from harm; lucky charm.—talisman′ic, -al *a.*

talk (tawk) *v.t.* and *v.i.* converse; speak; discuss;—*n.* conversation short dissertation; rumour; gossip. —talk′ative *a.* loquacious; chatty.—talk′atively *adv.*—talk′ativeness *n.*—talk′er *n.* one who talks; gossip.—talk′ie *n.* (*Slang*) sound-film.—to talk big, boast.—to talk round, persuade. —to talk shop, talk exclusively of one's daily occupation.

tall (tawl) *a.* high in stature; lofty; (*Slang*) excessive; exaggerated.—tall′ness *n.*

tallboy (tawl′-boi) *n.* high chest of drawers.

tallow (tal′-ō) *n.* animal fat melted down and used in manufacture of candles, etc.—tall′ow-can′dle *n.*—tall′ow-chand′ler *n.* one who sells tallow-candles.

tally (tal′-i) *n.* stick notched to indicate purchases made, and afterwards split in two, one part being kept by seller, other by buyer; duplicate of business account; match; identity label;—*pl.* tall′ies.—*v.t.* score with corresponding notches; make to fit;—*v.i.* correspond; conform;—*pa.t.* and *pa.p.* tall′ied.—tall′ier *n.* one who keeps tally.

talon (tal′-on) *n.* hooked claw of bird

of prey.—**tal'oned** a. having talons.

tamarind (tam'-a-rind) n. tropical tree, bark and pods used for medicines, etc.; hard wood used for furniture.

tamarisk (tam'-ar-isk) n. Mediterranean evergreen shrub with pink and white flowers.

tambour (tam'-boor) n. small flat drum; circular embroidery-frame.

tambourine (tam-boo-reen') n. round, shallow, single-sided drum with jingling metal discs.

tame (tām) a. domesticated; subdued; insipid; dull;—v.t. domesticate; discipline; curb; reclaim.—**tame'able** a.—**tame'ly** adv.—**tame'ness** n.—**tam'er** n.

Tamil (tam'-l) n. Dravidian language spoken in S. India and Ceylon.

tam o' shanter (tam'-ō-shan'-ter) n. round woollen cap.—abbrev. **tam'my**.

tamp (tamp) v.t. ram down; plug shot-hole with clay during blasting.

tamper (tam'-per) v.i. meddle; interfere with; corrupt; alter (as document, cheque) with malicious intent.—**tam'perer** n.

tan (tan) n. bark of oak, etc. bruised to extract tannic acid for tanning leather; yellowish brown colour; sunburn;—v.t. convert skins into leather by soaking in tannic acid; make bronze-coloured; toughen; (Colloq.) thrash;—v.i. become sunburned;—pr.p. **tan'ning**.—pa.t. and pa.p. **tanned**.—**tan'ner** n. one who works in tannery.—**tan'nery** n. place where leather is made.—**tan'nic** a. pert. to tannin.—**tan'nin** n.

tandem (tan'-dem) adv. one behind other;—n. pair of horses so harnessed; bicycle for two people one behind other.

tang (tang) n. projection or prong (of tool) which fits into handle; pungent smell or taste; distinctive flavour;—v.t. furnish (tool) with tang.—**tanged, tang'y** a.

tangent (tan'-jent) n. (Geom.) line which touches curve but, when produced, does not cut it;—a. touching but not intersecting.—**tangen'tial** a. pert. to, or in direction of, tangent.—**tangen'tially** adv.

tangerine (tan'-je-rēn) n. small sweet orange.

tangible (tan'-ji-bl) a. palpable; concrete.—**tangibil'ity, tan'gibleness** n.—**tan'gibly** adv.

tangle (tang'-gl) n. knot of ravelled threads, hair, etc.; edible species of seaweed; confusion;—v.t. form into confused mass; ravel; muddle.

tango (tang'-gō) n. S. American dance of Spanish origin.

tank (tangk) n. large basin, cistern, or reservoir; immerser for photographic films; part of railway engine, motor-car, etc. where water, petrol, etc. is stored; tracked armoured fighting vehicle;—v.t. store or immerse in tank.—**tank'age** n. storage of water, oil, gas, etc. in tank; cost of this; liquid capacity of tank; fertilising agent from refuse of fats.—**tank'er** n. vessel designed to carry liquid cargo.

tankard (tang'-kard) n. large drinking-vessel with handle.

tansy (tan'-si) n. perennial plant common in hedgerows, bearing small yellow flowers.

tantalise (tan'-ta-līz) v.t. torment by keeping just out of reach something ardently desired; tease; provoke.—**tantalis'ing** a.—**tantalis'ingly** adv.—**tan'talus** n. locked case containing visible spirit decanters.

tantamount (tan'-ta-mount) a. equivalent in value or significance.

tantrum (tan'-trum) n. fit of bad temper.

tap (tap) v.t. strike lightly;—v.i. strike gentle blow;—pr.p. **tap'ping**.—pa.p. **tapped**.—n. rap.

tap (tap) n. hole, pipe, or screw-device with valve, through which liquid is drawn; plug or bung; liquor of particular brewing in cask; instrument of hardened steel for cutting internal screw-threads; (Elect.) connection made at intermediate point on circuit;—v.t. pierce to let fluid flow out; furnish (cask) with tap; —v.i. — pr.p. **tap'ping**.—pa.p. **tapped**.—**tap'per** n. one who taps.—**tap'-room** n. bar, of inn or hotel.—**tap'-root** n. root of plant which goes straight down into earth without dividing.—**on tap**, of liquor, drawn from cask; (Fig.) at hand.

tape (tāp) n. narrow piece of woven material used for tying, fastening clothes, etc.; strip marking winning post on race-track; strip of paper used in printing telegraph instrument; plastic strip coated with ferromagnetic substance for sound-recording; strip of paper or linen marked off in inches used for measuring;—v.t. tie with tape or finish with loops of tape; measure; record on tape.—**tape'-machine'** n. teleprinter.—**tape'-meas'ure** n. inch-tape.—**tape-recorder** n. machine for recording sound on magnetic tape.—**tape'worm** n. flat, segmented parasitic worm.—**punched tape**, perforated computer tape representing data.—**red tape**, officialdom.

taper (tā'-per) n. long wick coated thinly with wax; small light;—a. narrowing gradually towards end;—v.i. narrow gradually;—v.t. cause to narrow.—**ta'pering** a. narrowing gradually.—**ta'peringly** adv.

tapestry (tap'-es-tri) n. fabric covering for furniture, walls, etc.

tapioca (tap-i-ō-ka) n. farinaceous

substance in irregular grains, obtained from manioc.

tapir (tā'-pir) n. piglike mammal with short, flexible proboscis.

tappet (tap'-et) n. small lever connected with valves of steam-engine cylinder; small cam; in internal combustion engine, short steel rod conveying to valve-stem movement imparted by lift of cam.

tar (tár) n. (Arch.) sailor.

tar (tár) n. dark-brown or black viscid liquid, used for waterproofing, road-laying, and as preservative;—v.t. smear, cover, or treat with tar.—pr.p. tar'ring.—pa.t. and pa.p. tarred.—tar'-mac n. mixture of tar and small stones for road-surfacing.—tar'ry a.—to tar and feather, smear with tar and roll in feathers, as punishment.—to be tarred with the same brush or stick, have the same faults as another.

tarantella (tar'-an-tel'-a) n. Italian dance with rapid, whirling movements; music for it.

tarantula (ta-ran'-tū-la) n. hairy, venomous spider of S. Europe.

tardy (tár'-di) a. slow; dilatory; late; backward.—tar'dily adv.—tar'diness n.

tare (tār) n. vetch, used for cattle-fodder; weed, prob. darnel, growing among corn.

tare (tār) n. allowance made for weight of container, such as cask, crate, etc. in reckoning price of dutiable goods; weight of vehicle when empty.

targe (tárj) n. small, round shield.

target (tár'-get) n. mark to aim at in shooting practice, esp. flat circular board with bull's eye in centre of series of concentric circles; butt; object of attack.

tariff (ta'-rif) n. list of goods on which duty is payable; list of charges, as in hotel, etc.

tarn (tárn) n. small lake among mountains.

tarnish (tár'-nish) v.t. lessen lustre of; (Fig.) sully, as one's reputation; —v.i. become dull, dim, or sullied.

tarpaulin (tár-paw'-lin) n. canvas sheet treated with tar to make it waterproof; oilskin coat, hat, etc.

tarragon (tar'-a-gon) n. perennial herb cultivated for its aromatic leaves.

tarry (tar'-i) v.i. stay; linger; delay; stay behind;—pr.p. tar'rying.—pa.t. and pa.p. tar'ried.

tart (tárt) a. sour to taste; acid; (Fig.) caustic; severe.—tart'ish a. rather sour.—tart'ly adv.—tart'ness n.

tart (tárt) n. fruit baked in oven with covering of paste; small pastry cake containing fruit or jam; (Slang) girl; prostitute.—tart'let n.

tartan (tár'-tan) n. woollen cloth of coloured checks, each genuine Scot-tish clan possessing its own pattern; —a. made of tartan.

Tartar (tár-tar) n. native of Tartary. Also Ta'tar.—tar'tar n. irritable, quick-tempered person.

tartar (tár'-tar) n. crude potassium tartrate; crust deposited in wine cask during fermentation (purified, it is called cream of tartar; in crude form, argol); acid incrustation on teeth.—tarta'reous, tar'tarous a.—tartar'ic a. pert. to, or obtained from, tartar.—tartaric acid, organic hydroxy-acid found in many fruits.—cream of tartar, purified form of tartar used medicinally and as raising-agent in baking.

task (task) n. specific amount of work imposed by another; set lesson; drudgery; uncongenial labour;—v.t. impose task on; exact.—task'-force n. body of soldiers sent to do specific operation.—task'master n. (Arch.) overseer. — to take to task, rebuke call in question.

tassel (tas'-l) n. ornamental fringed knot of silk, wool, etc.; pendent flower of some plants.—tass'elled a. ornamented with tassel(s).

taste (tāst) v.t. perceive or test by tongue or palate; appraise flavour of by sipping; experience;—v.i. try food with mouth; eat or drink very small quantity; have specific flavour; —n. act of tasting; one of five senses; flavour; appreciation; judgement; small amount.—taste'ful a. having or showing good taste.—taste'fully adv.—taste'fulness n.—taste'-less a. insipid.—taste'lessly adv.—taste'lessness n.—tast'er n. one whose palate is trained to discern subtle differences in flavour, as tea-taster.—tast'ily adv.—tast'y a. having good taste; savoury.

tat (tat) v.i. make tatting.—tat'ting n. lace-like edging.

tatter (tat'-er) n. rag; shred of cloth or paper hanging loosely;—v.t. and v.i. tear or hang in tatters.—tatter-dema'lion n. ragged fellow.—tatt'ered a. ragged; torn in small pieces.

tattle (tat'-l) v.i. prattle; gossip;—n. chatter.—tatt'ler n. gossip.

tattoo (ta-tōō') n. beat of drum or bugle as signal; sudden rapping; military pageant, usually at night; —v.i. beat tattoo.

tattoo (ta-tōō') v.t. prick coloured designs, initials, etc. into skin with indelible coloured inks;—n. such design.—tattoo'er n.

tau (tou) n. Greek letter T.

taught (tawt) pa.t. and pa.p. of verb teach.

taunt (tawnt) v.t. reproach with severe or insulting words; gibe at; sneer at;—n. gibe; sarcastic remark. —taunt'er n.

taut (tawt) a. tight; fully stretched.

—taut′en *v.t.* make tight.—taut′ness *n.*

tautology (taw-tol′-o-ji) *n.* needless repetition of same idea in different words in sentence.—tautolog′ic,-al *a.* —tautolog′ically *adv.*—tautol′ogism *n.*

tavern (tav′-ern) *n.* licensed house for sale of liquor; inn; hostelry.— tav′erner *n.* inn-keeper.

taw (taw) *n.* large marble for children's game; line in which marble is thrown.

tawdry (taw′-dri) *a.* showy but cheap; gaudy; flashy.—taw′drily *adv.* —tawd′riness *n.*

tawny (taw′-ni) *a.* of yellow-brown colour.—taw′niness *n.*

tax (taks) *n.* levy imposed by State on income, property, etc.; burden; severe test;—*v.t.* impose tax on; subject to severe strain; accuse.— tax′able *a.* capable of being taxed; subject to taxation.—tax′ableness, taxabil′ity *n.*—tax′ably *adv.*—taxa′tion *n.*—tax′-free *a.* exempt from taxation.—tax′payer *n.*

taxi (taks′-i) *n.* motor-car for hire, fitted with taximeter; any car plying for hire;—*v.i.* travel by taxi; of aircraft, travel on ground (or surface of water) under its own power;—*pr.p.* tax′ying, tax′i-ing.—*pa.p.* tax′ied.— tax′i-cab *n.*—tax′i-driv′er, tax′i-man *n.* —tax′imeter *n.* instrument which registers mileage and fare of journey by taxi.

taxidermy (taks′-i-der-mi) *n.* art of preparing pelts of animals for exhibition.—tax′idermist *n.*

tea (tē) *n.* dried and prepared leaf of tea-plant, grown in India, Ceylon, etc.; infusion of dry tea in boiling water; any infusion of plant leaves, or of chopped meat; meal at which tea is drunk.—tea′-cadd′y, -can′ister *n.* air-tight box for holding tea.— tea′-cake *n.* flat, round, slightly sweet scone.—tea′-cloth *n.* ornamental cloth for tea-table or tray.— tea′-co′sy *n.* padded cover to keep tea-pot hot.—tea′-gar′den *n.* tea-plantation; public garden where afternoon tea is served.—tea′-kett′le *n.* smallish-sized kettle.—tea′-par′ty *n.* social entertainment at which tea is served.—tea′-room *n.* restaurant where tea, coffee, etc. are served.— tea′-ser′vice, tea′-set *n.* cups, saucers, plates, etc. for use at tea table.— tea′spoon *n.* small-sized spoon.—tea′-spoonful *n.*—tea′-tast′er *n.* one trained to test quality of tea by tasting.— tea′-tray *n.* small tray holding tea-cups, etc.—tea′-urn *n.* vessel with tap near bottom rim, for serving tea to large numbers.—storm in a teacup, quarrel over nothing.

teach (tēch) *v.t.* instruct; educate; discipline;—*v.i.* follow profession of teacher.—*pa.t.* and *pa.p.* taught (tawt).—teachabil′ity *n.*—teach′able *a.*

—teach′ableness *n.*—teach′er *n.* one who instructs; one trained to teach in school.—teach-in *n.* (*U.S.*) marathon university debate bringing together the best exponents of divergent views on a chosen subject.

teak (tēk) *n.* tree of E. Indies yielding very hard, durable timber.

teal (tēl) *n.* web-footed water-fowl like duck.

team (tēm) *n.* two or more oxen, horses, or other beasts of burden harnessed together; group of people working together for common purpose; side of players in game.— team′ster *n.* one who drives team.— team′wise *adv.*—team′work *n.* co-operation among members of group.

tear (tēr) *n.* small drop of fluid flowing from eyes, under emotional stimulus; transparent drop;—*pl.* grief; sorrow.—tear′-drop *n.* tear.— tear′ful *a.* weeping.—tear′fully *adv.*— tear′fulness *n.*—tear′-gas *n.* irritant poison gas causing abnormal watering of eyes.—tear′less *a.* dry-eyed.

tear (tār) *v.t.* pull apart forcibly; rend; lacerate;—*v.i.* move violently; rush; rage;—*pr.p.* tear′ing.—*pa.t.* tore.—*pa.p.* torn.—*n.* rent fissure.

tease (tēz) *v.t.* comb or card, as wool or flax; raise pile of cloth; harass; annoy in fun; chaff.—teas′er *n.* poser; difficult question to answer.— teas′ing *a.*

teat (tēt) *n.* nipple of female breast; dug of animal; rubber or plastic nipple of feeding-bottle.

technical (tek′-nik-al) *a.* pert. to any of the arts, esp. to useful or mechanical arts; connected with particular art or science; accurately defined; involving legal point.— technical′ity *n.* state of being technical; term peculiar to specific art; point of procedure.—tech′nically *adv.* —tech′nicalness *n.*—technic′ian *n.* expert in particular branch of knowledge.—tech′nics *n.pl.* arts in general; industrial arts.—technique (tek-nēk′) *n.* skill acquired by thorough mastery of subject; method of handling materials of art; executive ability. —technolog′ic, -al *a.* pert. to technology.—technol′ogist *n.*—technol′ogy *n.* science of mechanical and industrial arts, as contrasted with fine arts; technical terminology.

teddy-bear (ted′-i-bār) *n.* toy-bear for children.

tedious (tē′-di-us) *a.* wearisome; protracted; irksome; monotonous. —te′diousness *n.*—te′diously *adv.*— te′dium *n.* wearisomeness; monotony.

tee (tē) *n.* mark aimed at in games, such as quoits, bowls; tiny cone of sand, wooden peg, etc. on which golf-ball is placed for first drive of each hole; teeing-ground which marks beginning of each hole on golf-course.—*v.t.* to place on tee.

teem (tēm) *v.t.* produce; bring forth;—*v.i.* bring forth, as animal; be prolific; be stocked to overflowing.—**teem′ing** *a.* prolific; abundant.

teem (tēm) *v.t.* pour; empty;—*v.i.* rain in torrents.

teens (tēnz) *n.pl.* years of one's age, thir*teen* to nine*teen*.—**teen′-a′ger** *n.* young person, 13-19 years of age.

teepee (tē′-pē) *n.* (*U.S.*) wigwam, one of conical tents of N. American Indians. Also **te′pee′**.

teething (tēTH′-ing) *n.* process, in babyhood, of cutting first teeth.—**teethe** *v.i.* cut first teeth.

teetotal (tē-tō′-tal) *a.* pert. to teetotalism; abstemious.—**teeto′taler**, **teeto′taller** *n.* one who abstains from intoxicating liquors.—**teeto′talism** *n.*

tee-totum (tē-tō′-tum) *n.* toy-top with letters on four sides.

tegestologist (tej-es-tol′-ō-gist) *n.* collector of beer-mats.

tegument (teg′-ū-ment) *n.* covering, of animal body.—**tegumen′tal** *a.*

telecast (tel-ē-kast) *v.t.* broadcast by television.—**telecaster** *n.*

telecommunication (tel′-i-ko-mūn-i-kā′-shun) *n.* communication by telegraph, telephone, etc.

telegram (tel′-e-gram) *n.* message sent by telegraph.—**telegram′mic** *a.*

telegraph (tel′-e-graf) *n.* electrical apparatus for transmitting messages by code to distance; signalling device for transmitting messages;—*v.i.* send message by telegraph; signal.—**tele′grapher** (or te-leg′-), **tel′egraphist** (or te-leg′-) *n.* one who operates telegraph.—**telegraph′ic**, **-al** *a.*—**telegraph′ically** *adv.*—**tele′graphy** *n.* electrical transmission of messages to distance.

telemeter (te-lem′-e-ter) *n.* instrument for determining distances; (*Elect.*) instrument for reading valves at distance.—**telemetry** *n.*

telepathy (te-lep′-a-thi) *n.* occult communication of facts, feelings, etc. between mind and mind at distance; thought-transference. — **telepath′ic** *a.*—**telepath′ically** *adv.*

telephone (tel′-e-fōn) *n.* electrical instrument by which sound is transmitted and reproduced at distance;—*v.t.* and *v.i.* communicate by telephone.—**telephon′ic** *a.*—**teleph′onist** *n.* telephone-operator.—**tele′phony** *n.* art or process of operating telephone.

telephoto (tel-e-fōt-ō) *a.* pert. to narrow angle, long focal length lens for distance photography.

teleprinter (tel-e-prin′-ter) *n.* electrical apparatus like typewriter by which typed messages are sent and received by wire.

telescope (tel′-e-skōp) *n.* optical instrument for magnifying distant objects;—*v.t.* slide or drive together, as parts of telescope;—*v.i.* be impacted violently.—**telescop′ic**, **-al** *a.* pert. to or like telescope.—**telescop′ically** *adv.*

teletypewriter (tel-e-tīp′-rīt-er) *n.* invention by which material typed on one typewriter is by electrical control simultaneously typed on machines at distance.

television (tel-e-vizh′-un) *n.* transmission of visual images by electromagnetic wireless waves or direct line.—**tel′evise** *v.t.* transmit by television.

tell (tel) *v.t.* recount or narrate; divulge; reckon; discover;—*v.i.* produce marked effect; betray (as secret); report;—*pa.t.* and *pa.p.* told.—**tell′er** *n.* narrator; bank-clerk who pays out money; Member of House of Commons who counts votes; enumerator.—**tell′ing** *a.* effective; impressive; striking.—**tell′ingly** *adv.*—**tell′-tale** *n.* one who betrays confidence; informer;—*a.* tending to betray.—**to tell off**, detail for special duty; (*Slang*) scold.

temerity (te-mer′-i-ti) *n.* rashness.

temper (tem′-per) *v.t.* mingle in due proportion; bring (metal) to desired degree of hardness and elasticity by heating, cooling, and re-heating; regulate;—*n.* due proportion; condition achieved by tempering; (*Fig.*) balanced attitude of mind; composure; anger; irritation.—**tem′pered** *a.* having certain consistency, as clay, or degree of toughness, as steel; having certain disposition, as *good-tempered*, *bad-tempered*.—**tem′peredly** *adv.*—**tem′pering** *n.*

tempera (tem′-per-a) *n.* painting medium in which no oil is used.

temperament (tem′-per-a-ment) *n.* emotional mood; natural disposition; (*Mus.*) adjustment of natural scale to adapt it for all keys.—**temperamen′tal** *a.* liable to moods; passionate.

temperance (tem′-per-ans) *n.* moderation; self-discipline, esp. of natural appetites; total abstinence from, or moderation in, consumption of intoxicating liquors; sobriety.

temperate (tem′-per-et) *a.* moderate; abstemious; sober; (of climate) equable; not extreme.—**tem′perately** *adv.*—**tem′perateness** *n.*—**tem′perature** *n.* degree of heat or cold of atmosphere or of living body; (*Colloq.*) fevered condition.—**temperate zones**, areas of earth between Polar Circles and Tropics.—**to run a temperature**, become fevered.

tempest (tem′-pest) *n.* wind storm of great violence; (*Fig.*) violent commotion.—**tempes′tuous** *a.* pert. to tempest; violent.—**tempes′tuously** *adv.*—**tempes′tuousness** *n.*

Templar (tem'-plar) n. one of religious order of knights founded in 12th cent. for protection of Holy Sepulchre; lawyer with chambers in Temple, London.

template (tem'-plět) n. pattern of wood or metal cut to shape required for object.

temple (tem'-pl) n. place of worship; place dedicated to pagan deity; Christian church.

temple (tem'-pl) n. part of forehead between outer end of eye and hair.—**tem'poral** a.

tempo (tem'-pō) n. (Mus.) time; degree of speed or slowness.

temporal (tem'-por-al) a. pert. to time or to this life; transient; secular; political as opposed to ecclesiastical.—**temporal'ity** n. material welfare;—pl. material possessions, esp. ecclesiastical.—**tem'porally** adv.—**tem'porariness** n.—**tem'porality** n. laity.—**tem'porarily** adv.—only for a time.—**tem'porariness** n.—**tem'porary**, **tempora'neous** a. lasting only for a time; fleeting.—**tem'porise** v.i. act to gain time; compromise.—**tem'poriser** n.—**tem'porising** n.

tempt (temt) v.t. attempt; induce to do something wrong; entice.—**tempta'tion** n. inducement to do evil; attraction.—**tempt'er** n. (fem. tempt'-ress) one who tempts, esp. Satan.—**tempt'ing** a. attractive; seductive.—**tempt'ingly** adv.—**tempt'ingness** n.

ten (ten) a. twice five; one more than nine;—n. number nine and one; figure or symbol representing this, as 10, x.—**ten'fold** a. ten times repeated;—adv. ten times as much.—**tenth** a. next after ninth; being one of ten equal divisions of anything;—n. one of ten equal parts; tenth part of anything; tithe.—**tenth'ly** adv.

tenable (ten'-a-bl) a. capable of being held, or logically maintained.—**tenabil'ity**, **ten'ableness** n.

tenacious (te-nā'-shus) a. holding fast; adhesive; retentive; pertinacious.—**tena'ciously** adv.—**tena'ciousness** n.—**tena'city** n.

tenant (ten'-ant) n. (Law) one who has legal possession of real estate; one who occupies property for which he pays rent;—v.t. hold or occupy as tenant.—**ten'ancy** n. act of holding land or property as tenant; property held by tenant.—**ten'antable** a. fit for occupation by tenant.—**ten'antry** n. tenants or employees collectively on estate.

tench (tensh) n. fish of carp family.

tend (tend) v.i. have bias or inclination.—**ten'dency** n. inclination; bent.—**tenden'tious** a. (of writings) having biased outlook.

tend (tend) v.t. look after; minister to.—**ten'der** n. vessel supplying

larger one with stores, etc., or landing passengers; truck attached to locomotive, with water and fuel.

tender (ten'-der) v.t. offer in payment or for acceptance;—v.i. make offer or estimate;—n. offer, esp. contract to undertake specific work, or supply goods; estimate.—**legal tender**, currency recognised as legally acceptable in payment of debt.

tender (ten'-der) a. soft; easily impressed; delicate; expressive of gentler passions; immature; sore; not tough (of meat).—**ten'derfoot** n. one not yet hardened to prairie life; novice; Boy Scout before he has passed third-class test.—**ten'derly** adv.—**ten'derness** n.

tendon (ten'-don) n. tough fibrous cord attaching muscle to bone.—**ten'dinous** a.

tendril (ten'-dril) n. spiral shoot of climbing plant by which it clings to another body.

tenement (ten'-e-ment) n. building divided into separate flats and let to different tenants.

tenet (ten'-et) n. opinion, dogma, or principle held as true.

tenfold See **ten**.

tennis (ten'-is) n. game for two or four players, played in prepared court by striking ball with racquets across net; lawn-tennis.—**tenn'is-court** n. specially marked-out court where tennis is played.

tenon (ten'-on) n. end of piece of wood shaped for insertion into cavity (mortise) in another piece to form join;—v.t. join with tenons.—**ten'on-saw** n. thin saw used in cutting tenons.

tenor (ten'-or) n. general drift of thought; purport; (Mus.) highest male adult voice; one who sings tenor;—a. pert. to tenor voice.

tense (tens) n. (Gram.) form of verb which indicates time of action.

tense (tens) a. stretched; strained almost to breaking point; unrelaxed; alert.—**tense'ly** adv.—**tense'ness** n.—**tensibil'ity**, **tensil'ity** n. quality of being tensile.—**ten'sible**, **ten'sile** a. capable of being stretched or subjected to stress, as metals; capable of being made taut, as violin strings.—**ten'sion** n. act of stretching; strain; state of being nervously excited; (of metals) pulling stress as opposed to compressive stress.—**ten'sor** n. body-muscle which stretches.

tent (tent) n. portable canvas shelter;—v.i. live in tent; pitch tent.

tentacle (ten'-takl) n. long flexible appendage in many lower animals for touching, grasping, and sometimes moving; feeler.—**tentac'ular** a.

tentative (ten'-ta-tiv) a. experimental; trying;—n. something done as feeler towards general opinion.—ten'tatively adv.

enter (ten'-ter) n. machine for stretching cloth by means of hooks;—v.t. stretch on hooks.—ten'ter-hook n. one of sharp hooks by which cloth is stretched on tenter.—on tenterhooks, state of anxiety.

enuity (te-nū'-i-ti) n. smallness of diameter; thinness.—ten'uous a. slender; gossamer-like; over-subtle.—ten'uousness n.

enure (ten'-ūr) n. holding of office, property, etc.; conditions govering occupancy.

epee (tē'-pē) n. Indian tent. Also **tee'pee.**

epid (tep'-id) a. moderately warm; luke-warm.—tepid'ity, tep'idness n.

ercentenary (ter-sen-tē'-na-ri or ter-sen'-te-na-ri) n. 300th anniversary of event;—a. pert. to period of 300 years.

erebene (ter'-e-bēn) n. 'turpentine or petroleum derivative used as solvent or paint thinner.—tereb'ic a. pert. to turpentine.—ter'ebinth n. turpentine-tree.—terebinth'ine a.

eredo (te-rē'-dō) n. ship-worm.

ergiversate (ter'-ji-ver-sāt) v.i. use subterfuges; vacillate.—tergiversa'tion n.—ter'giversator n.

erm (term) n. boundary; limit, esp. of time; period during which law-courts are sitting; fixed day when rent is due; period during which schools, universities, etc. are open; word or expression with specific meaning; (Math.) member of compound quantity;—pl. mode of expression; stipulation; relationship; charge for accommodation, etc., or for instruction given;—v.t. call.—terminolog'ical a. pert. to specific language used.—terminolog'ically adv.—terminol'ogy n. technical words.—to come to terms, reach agreement.

ermagant (ter'-ma-gant) n. quarrelsome, shrewish woman;—a. scolding; quarrelsome.

erminate (ter'-min-āt) v.t. set limit to; end;—v.i. come to end; finish.—ter'minable a. capable of being terminated; liable to cease.—ter'minal n. extremity; place of assembly for airline passengers; terminus; (Elect.) metal attachment for connecting end of circuit;—a. pert. to end; belonging to terminus; occurring in, or at end of term.—ter'minally adv.—termina'tion n. finish; conclusion; ending of word.—termina'tional a.—ter'minative a. serving to terminate; definite.—ter'minatively adv.—ter'minus n. end; farthest limit; railway-station, airport, etc.—pl. ter'mini, ter'minuses.

ermite (ter'-mīt) n. insect found in tropical countries.

tern (tern) n. sea-bird allied to gull.

tern (tern) n. that which consists of three;—a. threefold.—ter'nal, ter'nary a. consisting of three; proceeding by threes; (Chem.) comprising three compounds.—ter'nate a. arranged in threes.—ter'nion n. group of three.

terra (ter'-a) n. earth, as in various Latin phrases.—terr'a-cot'ta n. reddish, brick-like earthenware.—terr'a-fir'ma n. dry land.—terr'a-incog'nita n. unexplored territory.—terra'nean a. belonging to surface of earth.—terra'neous a. growing on land.—terrene' a. pert. to earth; earthy.

terrace (ter'-as) n. raised shelf of earth; row of linked houses.

terrain (ter'-ān) n. tract of land.

terrestrial (ter-es'-tri-al) a. pert. to earth; existing on earth; earthly, as opp. to celestial;—n. inhabitant of earth.

terrible (ter'-i-bl) a. calculated to inspire fear or awe; frightful; dreadful; (Colloq.) excessive.—terr'ibleness n.—terr'ibly adv.

terrier (ter'-i-er) n. breed of small sized dog, originally trained for hunting foxes, badgers, etc.

terrify (ter'-i-fī) v.t. inspire with terror.—pa.t. and pa.p. terr'ified.—terrif'ic a. causing terror; (Colloq.) tremendous.—terrif'ically adv.

territory (ter'-i-to-ri) n. large tract of land; part of country which has not yet attained political independence.—territo'rial a. pert. to territory; limited to certain district;—Territorial n. member of voluntary home-defence force in Britain.

terror (ter'-or) n. extreme fear; violent dread; one who or that which causes terror.—terrorisa'tion n.—terr'orise v.t. fill with terror; rule by intimidation.—terr'oriser n.—terr'orism n. mass-organised ruthlessness.—terr'orist n.—terr'or-strick'en, -struck a. paralysed with fear.

terse (ters) a. (of speech, writing, etc.) concise; succinct; brief; laconic; (of persons) abrupt.—terse'ly adv.—terse'ness n.

tertian (ter'-shan) a. (Med.) occurring every third day;—n. fever, with paroxysms occurring at intervals of forty-eight hours.

tertiary (ter'-shar-i) a. of third formation or rank; (Geol.) pert. to era of rock formation following Mezozoic.

terza-rima (ter'-tsa-rē'-ma) n. form of stanza-arrangement of iambic pentameter lines in groups of three, rhyming aba, bcb, cdc.

tessellate (tes'-e-lāt) v.t. make mosaic paving with square-cut stones.

test (test) n. critical examination; standard; grounds for admission or exclusion; (Chem.) reagent; substance used to analyse compound into its several constituents; touchstone;—v.t. make critical examination of; put to proof; (Chem.) analyse nature and properties of compound.—**test'-case** n. (Law) case tried for purpose of establishing precedent.—**test'er** n.—**test'ing** n.—a. demanding endurance. — **test'-match** n. cricket-match between international sides. — **test'-pi'lot** n. experienced pilot engaged int esting flying qualities of new types of aircraft.—**test'-tube** n. glass tube rounded and closed at one end,

test (test) v.t. (Law) attest and date; —v.i. make will.—**test'able** a. capable of being bequeathed by will.—**test'acy** n. state of being testate.—**tes'tate** a. having left valid will.—**testa'tor** n. (fem. **testa'trix**) one who makes will.

testament (tes'-ta-ment) n. solemn declaration of one's will; one of two great divisions of Bible.—**testamen'tal, testamen'tary** a. pert. to testament or will; bestowed by will.

testicle (tes'-ti-kl) n. one of two male reproductive glands.—**testic'ular** a.—**testic'ulate, -d** a. having testicles; resembling testicle in shape.—**test'is** n. testicle.—pl. test'es.

testify (tes'-ti-fī) v.i. bear witness; affirm or declare solemnly; give evidence upon oath.—v.t. bear witness to.—**tes'tifier** n.

testimony (tes'-ti-mon-i) n. solemn declaration; witness; proof of some fact; in Scripture, two tables of law; divine revelation as whole.—**testimo'nial** a. containing testimony;—n. written declaration testifying to character and qualities of person; written tribute to person's worth.

testy (tes'-ti) a. fretful; irascible.—**test'ily** adv.—**test'iness** n.

tetanus (tet'-a-nus) n. disease in which bacillus causes spasms of violent muscular contraction; lockjaw.—**tetan'ic** a.

tether (teTH'-er) n. rope or chain fastened to grazing animal to keep it from straying;—v.t. restrict movements of.

tetra- (tet'-ra) prefix meaning four.

tetrahedron (tet-ra-hē'-dron) n. solid figure enclosed by four triangles.—**tetrahe'dral** a.

tetrameter (te-tram'-e-ter) n. verse of four measures.

tetrapod (tet'-ra-pod) a. having four feet;—n. four-footed animal.

tetrarch (tet'-rark) n. Roman governor of fourth part of province.—**tet'rarchate, tet'rarchy** n. office of tetrarch; province ruled by tetrarch.—**tet'rarchic, -al** a.

text (tekst) n. original words of author, orator, etc. as distinct from paraphrase or commentary; verse of Scripture chosen as theme of sermon.—**text'-book** n. manual of instruction.—**tex'tual** a. pert. to text or subject-matter; based on actual text or wording.—**tex'tually** adv.

textile (teks'-til) a. pert. to weaving; capable of being woven;—n. fabric made on loom.

texture (teks'-tur) n. that which is woven; manner of weaving threads in fabric; quality of surface of woven material; disposition of several parts of anything in relation to whole.

thallium (thal'-i-um) n. (Chem.) rare metal (symbol Tl) bluish white and soft.

than (THan) conj. introducing adverbial clause of comparison and occurring after comparative form of adjective or adverb.

thane (thān) n. in Anglo-Saxon community, member of class between freemen and nobility.

thank (thangk) v.t. express gratitude for favour;—n. expression of gratitude (usually in pl.).—**thank'ful** a. grateful; appreciative.—**thank'fully** adv.—**thank'fulness** n. gratitude.—**thank'less** a. ungrateful.—**thank'lessly** adv.—**thank'lessness** n. ingratitude.—**thank'-off'ering** n. gift made as token of gratitude.—**thanks'giving** n. act of rendering thanks; service held as expression of thanks for Divine goodness.—**Thanksgiving Day** (U.S.), usually last Thursday in November.

that (THat) demons. pron. or a. (pl. those) pointing out person or thing, or referring to something already mentioned; not this but other;—rel. pron. who or which;—conj. introducing noun cl., adjective cl., or adverbial cl. of purpose, result, degree.

thatch (thach) n. straw, rushes, heather, etc. used to roof cottage, or cover stacks of grain; (Colloq.) hair;—v.t. roof with thatch.—**thatch'er** n.—**thatch'ing** n. act or craft of roofing with thatch; materials used.

thaumaturgy (thaw'-ma-tur-ji) n. art of working miracles; conjuring.—**thau'maturge** n. miracle worker; magician; conjurer.

thaw (thaw) v.t. cause to melt by increasing temperature; liquefy;—v.i. melt, as ice, snow, etc.; become warmer; (Fig.) become genial;—n. melting of ice or snow.

the (THe, emphatic THē) a. or definite article, placed before nouns, and used to specify general conception, or to denote particular person or thing;—adv. by so much; by that amount, as the more, the merrier.

theatre (thē'-a-ter) n. playhouse; stage; lecture or demonstration room for anatomy studies; room in hospital where surgical operations are performed; field of military,

...aval, or air operations.—**theat′ric,-
l** a.—theat′rically adv.—theat′ricals
..pl. dramatic performances, esp. by
.mateurs.

...ee (THē) pron. objective case of
.hou.

...eft (theft) n. act of stealing; that
.which is stolen.

...eir (THãr) a. and pron. of them;
.ossessive case of they.—theirs poss.
.ron., form of their used absolutely.

...em (THem) pron. objective and
.lative case of they.

...eme (thēm) n. subject-matter of
.writing, discourse, etc.; brief essay;
(Mus.) groundwork melody recur-
.ing at intervals.—the′ma n. subject
.or discussion.—themat′ic a. pert. to.
.—themat′ically adv.—theme′-song n.
.ecurring melody.

...emselves (THem-selvz′) pron. pl.
.of himself, herself, and itself.

...en (THen) adv. at that time (past
.or future); immediately afterwards;
.hereupon; that being so; for this
.reason;—conj. moreover; therefore.
.—now and then, occasionally.

...ence (THens) adv. from that place;
.from that time; for that reason.—
.hence′forth adv. from that time on.
.—thencefor′ward adv. thenceforth.

...eodolite (thē-od′-ō-līt) n. instru-
.ment for measuring angles, used in
.surveying.

...eology (thē-ol′-o-ji) n. science
.which treats of religion, and rela-
.tions between God and man.—
.theolog′ian n. one learned in theology.
.—theolog′ic, -al a. pert. to theology.
.—theolog′ically adv.—theol′ogise v.t.
.theorise upon theological matters.—
.theologis′er n.—theol′ogist n. student
.of, authority on, theology.

...eorem (thē′-or-ẹm) n. (Math).
.proposition to be proved by logical
.reasoning; algebraical formula.—
.theoremat′ic, -al a.

...eory (thē′-o-ri) n. supposition put
.forward to explain something;
.speculation; exposition of general
.principles as distinct from practice
.and execution; (Colloq.) general
.idea; notion.—theoret′ic, -al a. pert.
.to or based on theory; speculative
.as opp. to practical.—the′orise v.t.
.form theory; speculate.—the′oriser,
.the′orist n.

...eosophy (thē-os′-ō-fi) n. form of
.religious philosophy claiming special
.insight into the nature of God.—
.theos′ophist n.—theosoph′ic, -al a.

...erapeutic (ther-ạ-pū′-tik) a. pert.
.to healing.—therapeu′tically adv.—
.therapeu′tics n. branch of medicine
.concerned with treatment and cure
.of diseases.—therapeu′tist n.

...erapy (ther′-ạ-pi) n. remedial
.treatment, as radio-therapy, for cure
.of disease by radium.

...here (THãr) adv. in that place;

farther off—opp. to here;—interj.
expressing surprise, alarm.—there′-
about, there′abouts adv. near that
place, number, or quantity.—there-
aft′er adv. after that time; accordingly.—thereat′ adv.—thereby′ adv. by
that means; in consequence.—
there′fore conj. and adv. for that or
this reason; consequently; accordingly.—therein′ adv. in that, or this
place, time, or thing; in that
particular.—thereinaft′er adv. afterwards in same document.—thereof′
adv. of that or this.—thereon′ adv. on
that or this.—thereto′ adv. to that or
this.—there′upon adv. upon that or
this; consequently; immediately.—
therewith′ adv. with that or this;
straightway.

therm (therm) n. term used in
Britain for thermal unit (abbrev.
B.Th.U.), amount of heat required
to raise 1 lb. of water through 1°F.;
(of household gas supply) measuring
100,000 British thermal units.—
ther′mae n.pl. hot springs; Roman
baths.—ther′mal a. pert. to heat; n.
rising column of warm air.—ther′mic
a. caused by heat.—ther′mically adv.
—thermatol′ogy n. medical treatment
of ailments by hot springs, etc.

thermionic (ther-mi-on′-ik) a. pert.
to emission of electrons from heated
cathode.—thermionic current (Radio)
flow of electrons from cathode to
plate of thermionic valve.—thermion′-
ics n. science dealing with emission
of electrons from substances under
action of heat.

thermochemistry (ther-mo-kem′-is-
tri) n. branch of science which deals
with changes of heat during chemical
processes.

thermodynamics (ther-mo-di-nam-
iks) n. branch of science which deals
with conversion of heat into
mechanical energy.

thermoelectricity (ther-mo-el-ek-
tris′-i-ti) n. electricity developed by
action of heat on two different
metals.—thermoelec′tric, -al a.

thermograph (ther′-mo-graf) n. instrument for continuously registering varying temperatures on graph.

thermometer (ther-mom′-e-ter) n.
instrument for measuring temperature.—thermomet′ric, -al a.—thermo-
met′rically adv.—thermom′etry n.—
clinical thermometer, small thermometer for measuring temperature of
human body.

thermoplastic (ther-mo-plas-tik) a.
capable of being melted by heat.

Thermos (ther′-mos) n. vacuum
flask [Protected Trade Name].

thermostat (ther′-mo-stat) n. instrument which controls temperature automatically, used in refriger-
ators, hot-water tanks, etc.—ther-
mostat′ic a.—thermostat′ically adv.—

thermostat'ics n. science dealing with equilibrium of heat.

thesaurus (the-saw'-rus) n. treasury of knowledge, etc.; lexicon; encyclopaedia.

these (THēz) *demons. a.* and *pron. pl.* of **this**.

thesis (thē'-sis) n. basis of argument; dissertation, esp. for higher University degree.—*pl.* **the'ses**.

thew (thū) n. muscle; sinew; brawn; (*Fig.*) mental vigour.—usu. *pl.*

they (THā) *pron. pers.* of he, she, it; indefinitely, for number of persons.

thick (thik) a. dense; foggy; muddy; not thin; abundant; packed; frequent; muffled; mentally dull;—n. thickest part;—*adv.* thickly; to considerable depth; fast.—**thick'en** *v.t.* make thick;—*v.i.* become thick. —**thick'ening** n. something added to liquid, as cornflour, to thicken it.— **thick'et** n. shrubbery.—**thick-head'ed** a. dull mentally.—**thick'ly** *adv.*— **thick'ness** n. quality of being thick; measurement of depth between opposite surfaces; layer.—**thick'-set** a. closely planted; sturdily built.

thief (thēf) n. (*pl.* thieves) one who steals goods and property of another.—**thieve** *v.t.* take by theft;— *v.i.* steal.—**thiev'ery** n.—**thiev'ish** a. addicted to stealing.—**thiev'ishly** *adv.* —**thiev'ishness** n.

thigh (thī) n. part of leg between knee and trunk.

thimble (thim'-bl) n. cap to protect tip of middle finger from needle, in sewing.—**thim'bleful** n. very small amount of liquid.

thin (thin) a. having little depth or thickness; dilute; lean; fine;—*adv.* sparsely; not closely packed;—*v.t.* make thin;—*v.i.* grow or become thin; slim.—**thin'ly** *adv.*—**thin'ness** n. —**thin'ning** n. practice of removing some plants to give remainder richer soil in which to mature.

thine (THīn) *pron.* (*poss.* form of thou) belonging to thee; thy.

thing (thing) n. material or inanimate object; entity; specimen; commodity; event; person (in pity or contempt);—*pl.* belongings; clothes; furniture.—**thing'amy**, **thing'umabob**, **thing'umajig**, **thing'ummy** n. word used for name one has forgotten.

think (thingk) *v.t.* conceive; to believe; consider;—*v.i.* reason; form judgment; deliberate; imagine; recollect.—*pa.t.* and *pa.p.* thought (thawt).—**think'able** a.—**think'er** n. sage or philosopher.—**think'ing** a. reflective; rational.

third (thėrd) a. next after second; forming one of three equal divisions; —n. one of three equal parts; (*Mus.*) interval of three diatonic degrees of scale.—**third estate**, commons. — **third'ly** *adv.* — **third man**

(*Cricket*) fielder standing on off-side between point and slip.—**third'-rate** a. inferior; shoddy.

thirst (thėrst) n. desire to drink; suffering endured by long abstinence from drinking; (of soil) drought. (*Fig.*) craving;—*v.i.* crave for something to drink; wish for earnestly.— **thirst'er** n.—**thirst'ily** *adv.*—**thirst'iness** n.—**thirst'y** a. having desire to drink; dry; eager for.

thirteen (thėr'-tēn) a. ten and three; —n. sum of ten and three; symbol representing thirteen units, as 13, XIII.—**thir'teenth** a. next in order after twelfth; being one of thirteen equal parts;—n. one of these parts.

thirty (thėr'-ti) a. three times ten;— n. sum of three times ten; symbol representing this, as 30, XXX.— **thir'tieth** a. next in order after twenty-ninth; being one of thirty equal parts;—n. thirtieth part.

this (THis) *demons. pron.* and a. denoting person or thing near at hand, just mentioned, or about to be mentioned.

thistle (this'-l) n. one of numerous prickly plants of genus Carduus, with yellow or purple flowers; national emblem of Scotland.— **this'tle-down** n. feathery down of thistle seeds.—**thist'ly** a. overgrown with thistles.

thither (THiTH'-er) *adv.* to that place; to that point, end, or result.— **thith'erward** *adv.* toward that place.

thole (thōl) *v.t.* pin in gunwale of boat to keep oar in rowlock.

thole (thōl) *v.t.* and *i.* (*Scot.*) endure.

thong (thong) n. narrow strap of leather.

thorax (thō'-raks) n. part of body between abdomen and neck; chest-cavity containing heart, lungs, etc. —**thorac'ic** a.

thorn (thorn) n. sharp, woody shoot on stem of tree or shrub; prickle; (*Fig.*) anything which causes trouble or annoyance.—**thorn'y** a. full of thorns; prickly; (*Fig.*) beset with difficulties.

thorough (thur'-ō) a. passing through or to end; complete; absolute.— *adv.* through.—**thor'oughbred** a. (of animals) pure bred from pedigree stock; (of people) aristocratic, hence high-spirited;—n. animal (esp. horse) of pure breed.—**thor'oughfare** n. passage through; unobstructed passage.— **thor'oughly** *adv.*—**thor'oughness** n.

those (THōz) a. and *pron. pl.* of that.

thou (THou) *pron. pres.*, *2nd sing.* denoting person addressed.

though (THō) *conj.* granting; admitting; even if; notwithstanding; however.

thought (thawt) *pa.t.* and *pa.p.* of think.

thought (thawt) n. act of thinking; that which one thinks; reflection; opinion.—**thought'ful** a. contemplative; considerate.—**thought'fully** adv.—**thought'fulness** n.—**thought'less** a.; heedless; impulsive; inconsiderate.—**thought'lessly** adv.—**thought'lessness** n.—**thought'-read'er** n. one who professes to read another's thoughts.—**thought'-read'ing** n.—**thought'-trans'ference** n. telepathy.

thousand (thou'-zand) a. consisting of ten hundred; used indefinitely to express large number;—n. number ten hundred; symbol representing any large number.—**thou'sandfold** a. multiplied by thousand.—**thou'sandth** a. constituting one of thousand equal parts; next in order after nine hundred and ninety-nine;—n. thousandth part.

thrall (thrawl) n. slave; bondsman; servitude;—**thral'dom** n. bondage.

thrash (thrash) v.t. separate grain from chaff by use of flail or threshing-machine; thresh; flog. Also thresh. — **thrash'er** n. — **thrash'ing, thresh'ing** n. act of thrashing grain, etc.; corporal punishment; flogging.—**thrash'ing- thresh'ing-machine'**, n. agricultural machine for thrashing grain.—**to thrash out**, argue about from every angle.

thrawn (thrawn) a. (Scot.) twisted; obstinate; perverse.

thread (thred) n. very thin twist of wool, cotton, linen, silk, etc.; filament as of gold, silver; prominent spiral part of screw; (Fig.) consecutive train of thought;—v.t. pass thread through eye of needle; string together, as beads; pick one's way with deliberation.—**thread'bare** a. shabby; (Fig.) hackneyed; trite.

threat (thret) n. menace.—**threat'en** v.t. menace; declare intention to do harm to; portend.—**threat'ener** n.—**threat'ening** a. menacing; portending something undesirable; (of clouds or sky) lowering.—**threat'eningly** adv.

three (thrē) a. two and one;—n. sum of two and one; symbol of this sum, 3 or iii.—**three'-cor'nered** a. having three corners; triangular; of election contest, having candidates of three political parties.—**three-dimensional** a. giving effect of depth as well as length and breadth.—**three'-fold** a. triple. –**three halfpence**, (thrē-hā'-pens) 1½d.—**three-legged race**, race run by pairs of competitors, right leg of one being tied to left leg of other.—**threepenny bit**, (thrip'-ni-bit) coin worth three pennies.—**three'-ply** a. having three layers or thicknesses; having three strands twisted together, as wool.—**three'-quar'ter** n. (Rugby) one of four backs behind half-backs. — **three'score** a. and n. sixty.—**three'some** n. game (as golf)

played by three players; dance performed by three people.

thresh See thrash.

threshold (thresh'-ōld) n. door-sill; piece of wood or stone immediately under door.

thrice (thrīs) adv. three times; repeatedly.

thrift (thrift) n. thriving condition; economical management; frugality; plant, sea-pink.—**thrift'ily** adv.—**thrift'iness** n. frugality.—**thrift'less** a. extravagant; wasteful.—**thrift'lessly** adv.—**thrift'y** a. (comp. **thrift'ier**; superl. **thrift'iest**) economical; frugal.

thrill (thril) n. emotional excitement; throb;—v.t. pierce; stir deeply; arouse emotional response;—v.i. feel glow of excitement, enthusiasm, etc.—**thrill'er** n. novel, play, or film, etc. with sensational plot.—**thrill'ing** a. causing a thrill; exciting.—**thrill'ingly** adv.

thrive (thrīv) v.i. prosper; grow abundantly; develop healthily.—pa.t. throve and thrived.—pa.p. thriven (thriv'-n) thrived.—**thri'ving** a. flourishing; prosperous.

throat (thrōt) n. forepart of neck; passage connecting back of mouth with lungs, stomach, etc.; narrow section.—**throat'iness** n. quality of having throaty or muffled voice.—**throat'y** a. guttural; muffled.

throb (throb) v.i. pulsate; beat rapidly, as heart;—pr.p. **throb'bing**.—pa.t. and pa.p. **throbbed**.—n. pulsation; palpitation; beat.

throe (thrō) n. suffering; pain;—pl. pains of childbirth.—**to be in the throes of**, struggle with task.

thrombosis (throm-bō'-sis) n. formation of blood clot in vein or artery during life.

throne (thrōn) n. chair of state; royal seat; bishop's seat in cathedral; sovereign power and dignity;—v.t. place on royal seat; exalt.—pr.p. **thron'ing**.—pa.p. **throned**.

throng (throng) n. multitude; crowd;—v.t. and i. mass together; crowd.

throttle (throt'-l) n. windpipe; valve controlling pressure or flow, lever or pedal operating this;—v.t. choke by external pressure on windpipe; shut off steam in steam-engine; (Fig.) suppress; silence;—v.i. open or close throttle of an engine.

through (thrōō) prep. from end to end of; going in at one side and out other; by passing between; across; along; by means of; as consequence of;—adv. from one end or side to other; from beginning to end.—a. (of railway train) passing from one main station to another without stops; unobstructed; (U.S.) finished.—**through and through**, completely.—**throughout'** adv. and prep. wholly; completely; during entire time of.—

to pull through, recover from serious illness.

throw (thrō) v.t. fling, cast, or hurl; send; venture, at dice; twist into thread, as silk; mould clay; unseat; shed, as snake's skin; produce off-spring, as animal; spread carelessly; —v.i. cast dice; hurl;—pr.p. throw'-ing.—pa.t. threw.—pa.p. thrown.—n. act of throwing; round in wrestling-match.—throw'-back n. one who reverts to ancestral type.—throw'er n.—thrown a. twisted.—to throw down the gauntlet, challenge.—to throw light on, elucidate.—to throw up, vomit.—to throw up the sponge, admit defeat.

thrum (thrum) n. fringe of threads left on loom after web is cut off.

thrum (thrum) v.t. strum on instrument.

thrush (thrush) n. song-bird, esp. mavis.

thrush (thrush) n. (Med.) disease affecting mouth, tongue and lips of children; disease affecting feet of horses, etc.

thrust (thrust) v.t. push or drive with force; pierce;—v.i. make a push; attack with pointed weapon; intrude; push way through;—pa.t. and pa.p. thrust.—n. stab; attack; assault; horizontal outward pressure; force developed by jet engine, etc.; stress acting horizontally, as in machinery.—thrust'er n.—thrust'ful a.—thrust'fully adv.—thrust'fulness n.

thud (thud) n. dull sound made by blow or heavy fall;—v.i. make sound of thud.

thug (thug) n. (Hist.) professional robber of N. India; cut-throat; ruffian; (U.S.) gangster.—thug'gery, thug'gism n. gangsterism.

thumb (thum) n. short, thick finger of human hand; part of glove which covers this;—v.t. manipulate awk-wardly; soil with thumb-marks; (Slang) hold up thumb, solicit lift from passing motorist.—thumbed a. having thumbs; soiled with thumb-marks.—thumb'-nail n.—thumb-nail sketch, miniature; succinct descrip-tion.—thumb'-stall n. sheath like glove thumb for injured thumb.—thumb'screw n. old instrument of torture by which thumb was com-pressed till joint broke.—by rule of thumb, by rough and ready method.

thump (thump) n. blow of fist; sudden fall of heavy body or weight thud;—v.t. beat with something heavy;—v.i. strike or fall with thud. —thump'er n. — tub'-thump'er n. (Slang) street-corner orator.

thunder (thun'-dẹr) n. rumbling sound after lightning-flash; very loud noise;—v.t. rage with loud voice;—v.i. rumble with thunder; roar.—thun'der-bolt n. imagined solid body accompanying lightning;

(Fig.) anything totally unexpected and unpleasant.—thun'der-clap n. peal of thunder.—thun'dering n. thunder; booming, as of guns.—a. making loud noise.—thun'derous a. thundery; booming like thunder.—thun'derously adv.—thun'der-storm n. storm of thunder and lightning with torrential rain.—thun'der-struck a. struck by lightning; (Fig.) speechless with amazement.—thun'dery a. pert. to thunder; sultry.—to steal some-one's thunder, win applause expec-ted by someone else.

Thursday (thurz'-dā) n. fifth day of week.

thus (THus) adv. in this or that manner; to this degree; so.

thwack (thwak) v.t. beat; flog.

thwart (thwawrt) a. lying across; transverse; athwart;—v.t. hinder; frustrate; baulk;—n. seat across or athwart rowing-boat;—adv. and prep. across.—thwar'ting a.—thwart'-ships adv. across ship.

thy (THI) poss. a. of or belonging to thee [contr. fr. thine].

thyme (tIm) n. small flowering-shrub cultivated for aromatic leaves.

thymus (thI'-mus) n. small ductless gland in upper part of chest.

thyroid (thI'-roid) a. signifying cartilage of larynx or gland of trachea. — thyroid gland, ductless gland situated in neck.

thyself (THI-self) pron. reflex. or emphatic, of person, thou or thee.

tiara (tI-ár'-a) n. triple, gem-studded crown worn by Pope on ceremonial occasions; gem-studded head-dress or coronet worn by ladies.

tibia (tib'-i-a) n. shin-bone; inner and usually larger of two bones of leg, between knee and ankle;—pl. tib'iae. —tib'ial a. pert. to tibia.

tic (tik) n. facial muscular twitching.

tick (tik) n. parasitic blood-sucking insect.

tick (tik) n. cover for bed-mattress, pillow, etc. stuffed with wool, etc.—tick'ing n. strong cotton or linen used for mattress covers, etc.

tick (tik) n. (Slang) credit; trust.

tick (tik) v.i. make small, recurring, clicking sound, as watch; beat steadily;—n. sound made by watch ticking; (Colloq.) very short time.—tick'er n. anything which ticks regularly; (Colloq.) watch or clock; tape-machine; heart.

tick (tik) v.t. mark lightly;—n. small mark placed after word, item, etc. in checking; very small piece.—ticked a. spotted.—to tick off, (Colloq.) rebuke.

ticket (tik'-et) n. piece of cardboard or paper entitling admission, travel by public transport, participation in function, lottery, etc.; (Colloq.) summons—v.t. mark with ticket.—

tick'et-of-leave n. permit for convict to be at liberty with certain restrictions, before expiry of sentence.

tickle (tik'-l) v.t. touch skin lightly so as to excite nerves and cause laughter; to amuse;—v.i. itch; be gratified.—**tick'ler** n.—**tick'lish** a. difficult to understand or solve; requiring skilful handling.—**tick'lishly** adv.—**tick'lishness** n.

tiddler (tid'-ler) n. (Colloq.) stickleback.

tiddley-winks (tid'-li-wingks) n.pl. game in which players flick counters into dice-cup.

tide (tīd) n. time; season, as in eventide, Eastertide; periodical rise and fall of ocean; (Fig.) trend.—to tide over, manage temporarily; surmount meantime.—**ti'dal** a. pert. to tide.—**tidal basin**, harbour which is affected by tides.—**tidal wave**, mountainous wave as caused by earthquake, etc.—**tide'less** a. having no tides.—**tide'-tab'le** n. table giving times, throughout year, of high-water.—**ebb**, or low, tide, falling level of sea.—**flood**, or high, tide, rising level of sea.—**neap tide**, minimum tide.—**spring tide**, maximum tide.

tidings (tī'-dingz) n.pl. news; information.

tidy (tī'-di) a. neat; orderly; (Colloq.) comfortable; of fair size;—n. chairback cover;—v.t. put in order;—pa.t. and pa.p. ti'died.—**ti'dily** adv.—**ti'diness** n.

tie (tī) v.t. fasten by rope, string, etc.; fashion into knot; bind together, as rafters, by connecting piece of wood or metal; (Fig.) hamper; (Mus.) connect two notes;—v.i. (Sport) make equal score, etc.—pr.p. ty'ing.—pa.t. and pa.p. tied.—n. knot; necktie; fastening; connecting-link; equality of score; draw; (Mus.) curved line connecting two notes.—**tie'-beam** n. horizontal timber connecting two rafters.—**ti'er** n.

tier (tēr) n. row or rank.

tiff (tif) n. slight quarrel.

tiffany (tif'-a-ni) n. kind of gauze or very thin silk.

tiger (tī'-ger) n. (fem. ti'gress) fierce carnivorous quadruped of cat tribe; (U.S.) jaguar; (S. Afr.) leopard.—**ti'ger-cat** n. wild cat; ocelot.—**ti'g(e)rish** a. like tiger; fierce.—**ti'ger-lil'y** n. tall Chinese lily with flaming orange flowers.—**ti'ger-moth** n. variety of of moth with streaked or spotted wings.

tight (tīt) a. firm; compressed; not leaky; fitting close or too close to body; neat; tense; restricted for want of money; dangerous; (Colloq.) mean; (Slang) drunk;—adv. firmly. —**tight'en** v.t. make tight or tighter; make taut;—v.i. become tight or

tighter.—**tight'ly** adv.—**tight'ness** n.— **tight'rope** n. strong, taut rope, or steel wire on which rope-dancers perform. —**tights** n.pl. close-fitting woven hose and trunks in one.

tike (tīk) n. dog; a cur; Yorkshireman.

tilde (til'-dā) n. mark (~) over letter n in Spanish, to indicate following y sound.

tile (tīl) n. thin piece of slate or baked clay, used for roofs, walls, floors, drains, etc.; (Slang) silk top-hat;— v.t. cover with tiles.—**ti'ler** n. one who makes or lays tiles; kiln for firing tiles. Also **ty'ler** n.—**ti'lery** n. place where tiles are made.

till (til) n. money-box or drawer in shop counter; cash-register.

till (til) prep. as late as; until;—conj. till time when.

till (til) v.t. cultivate; plough soil, sow seeds, etc.—**till'age** n. act of preparing soil for cultivation; cultivated land.—**till'er** n.—**tilth** n. cultivated land; state or depth of cultivation of soil.

tiller (til'-er) n. bar used as lever, esp. for turning rudder.

tilt (tilt) v.t. raise one end of; tip up; thrust, as lance; forge with tilt-hammer;—v.i. charge on horseback with lance, as in tournament; heel over;—n. thrust, as with lance; tilt-hammer; inclination forward.—**tilt'er** n.—**tilt'-ham'mer** n. heavy hammer used in iron works and tilted by wheel.—**to run full tilt**, run very rapidly.

tilt (tilt) n. tent; canvas covering of vehicle; small canvas awning over stern-sheets of boat;—v.t. cover with awning.

timber (tim'-ber) n. trees felled and prepared as building material; trees collectively; rib of ship;—v.t. furnish with timber.—**tim'bered** a. furnished with timber; built of timber.

timbre (tam'-br, tim'-ber) n. tone-quality in sound of human voice or instrument.

time (tīm) n. particular moment; period of duration; past, present, and future, as sequence; epoch; system of measuring duration, as Greenwich time; opportunity; occasion; (Mus.) rhythmical arrangement of beats;— pl. period characterised by certain tendencies, as Victorian times; term indicating multiplication, as four times four;—v.t. ascertain time taken, as by racing competitor; select precise moment for; (Mus.) measure;—v.i. keep or beat time.— **time'-bomb** n. delayed-action bomb. —**time'-gun** n. gun fitted with device which causes it to fire at given time. —**time'-hon'oured** a. venerable.— **time'-keep'er** n. one who keeps record of men's hours of work; clock or watch.—**time'-lag** n. period of time which elapses between cause and effect.—**time'less** *a.* eternal; unending.—**time'lessly** *adv.*—**time'liness** *n.*—**time'ly** *a.* in good time; opportune.—**timeous, timous** (tīm-us) *a.* (*Scots Law*) in good time.—**time'ously, tim'ously** *adv.*—**time'-piece** *n.* clock.—**time'-serv'er** *n.*—**time'-serv'ing** *n.* selfish opportunism.—**time'-ta'ble** *n.* tabulated list of duties; roster; booklet containing times of departure and arrival of trains, etc.—**time'-worn** *a.* aged; decayed.—**tim'ing** *n.*—**Greenwich time**, British standard time settled by passage of sun over meridian at Greenwich.—**to do time** (*Slang*) serve sentence of imprisonment.—**to mark time**, keep feet moving on one spot; (*Fig.*) delay.

timid (tim'-id) *a.* wanting courage; lacking in self-confidence; shy.—**timid'ity** *n.* shyness; diffidence.—**tim'idly** *adv.*—**tim'idness** *n.*—**tim'orous** *a.* frightened; very timid;—**tim'orously** *adv.*—**tim'orousness** *n.*

timpani, (tim'-pa-ni) *n. pl.* kettle drums of orchestra.

tin (tin) *n.* soft, whitish-grey metal, very malleable and ductile, used for tin-plating; tin-can;—*a.* made of tin or plated with tin;—*v.t.* plate with tin; preserve, as food, in airtight tin-plated container.—*pr.p.* **tin'ning**—*pa.p.* and *pa.t.* **tinned**.—**tin'foil** *n.* wafer-thin sheets of tin; so-called 'silver-paper.'—**tin'-op'ener** *n.* gadget for opening tins containing food, etc.—**tinned** *a.* preserved in tin; plated with tin.—**tin'ner, tin'man** *n.* tin-miner; one who makes tin-plate.—**tin'ning** *n.*—**tin'ny** *a.* like tin; making sound like tin when struck.—**tin'-plate** *n.* sheet-iron coated with tin, to protect from oxidation.—**tin'-pot** *a.* valueless; trivial.—**tin'smith** *n.* worker in tin or tin-plate industry.—**tin'ware** *n.* utensils, etc. made of tin.

tincture (tingk'-tūr) *n.* tinge or shade of colour; (*Fig.*) faint taste; veneer; (*Pharm.*) solution of substance in alcohol;—*v.t.* tinge; (*Fig.*) affect to small degree.

tinder (tin'-der) *n.* anything inflammable used for kindling fire from spark.

tine (tīn) *n.* prong of fork; spike of harrow; branch of deer's antler.—**tined** *a.*

ting (ting) *n.* sharp, metallic sound, as of bell; tinkle;—*v.t.* and *v.i.* tinkle.—**ting'-a-ling** *adv.* tinkling repeatedly.

tinge (tinj) *v.t.* colour slightly; imbue; temper;—*pr.p.* **ting(e)'ing**.—*n.* faint touch.

tingle (ting'-gl) *v.i.* feel faint thrill;—*v.t.* ring;—*n.* pricking sensation.

tinker (tingk'-er) *n.* mender of pots, kettles, etc.; rough and ready

worker; (*Colloq.*) untidy person;—*v.i.* do work of tinker; (*Colloq.*) meddle; dabble.

tinkle (tingk'-l) *v.t.* cause to make small, quick, metallic sounds; clink;—*v.i.* make series of quick, sharp sounds; jingle;—*n.* small, sharp, clinking sound.

tinsel (tin'-sel) *n.* very thin, glittering, metallic sheets, used in strips for decorations, etc.; (*Fig.*) anything showy or flashy;—*a.* gaudy; showy and cheap;—*v.t.* decorate with tinsel; make gaudy;—*pr.p.* **tin'selling** *pa.t.* and *pa.p.* **tin'selled**.—**tin'selly** *a.* showy; meretricious.

tint (tint) *n.* hue or dye; faint tinge; colour with admixture of white;—*v.t.* give faint colouring to; tinge.

tiny (tī'-ni) *a.* (*comp.* **ti'nier**; *superl.* **ti'niest**) very small; diminutive.

tip (tip) *n.* point of anything small; end;—*v.t.* form point on; cover tip of;—*pr.p.* **tip'ping**—*pa.p.* **tipped**.—**tip'toe** *adv.* on tips of toes;—*v.i.* walk on tips of toes; walk stealthily.—**on tiptoe**, quietly; all agog.—**tip'top** *a.* first-rate.

tip (tip) *v.t.* touch lightly; tap; tilt; cant, as liquid; weigh down, as scales; (*Slang*) give useful hint to; recompense with small gratuity;—*v.i.* fall to one side; give gratuity;—*n.* light stroke; private information; advice; gratuity; refuse-dump.—**tip'ping** *n.*—**tip'ster** *n.* one who sells tips regarding horse-racing, etc.—**tip'-tilt'ed** *a.* (of nose) slightly turned up.—**to tip off**, warn.

tippet (tip'-et) *n.* short cape of cloth or fur.

tipple (tip'-l) *v.i.* drink small quantities frequently; indulge habitually in intoxicating drinks;—*v.t.* drink excessively;—*n.* strong drink.—**tipp'ler** *n.*

tipsy (tip'-si) *a.* intoxicated; staggering.—**tip'sily** *adv.*—**tip'siness** *n.*—**tip'sy-cake** *n.* sponge-cake soaked in sherry.

tirade (tī-rād') *n.* long denunciatory speech.

tire (tīr) *v.t.* weary or fatigue;—*v.i.* become wearied, bored, or impatient.—**tired** *a.* wearied; bored.—**tired'ness** *n.*—**tire'less** *a.* unwearied; indefatigable.—**tire'lessly** *adv.*—**tire'some** *a.* exhausting; dull; provoking.

tire (tīr) *n.* attire; apparel; head-dress;—*v.t.* dress.

tire, tyre (tīr) *n.* hoop of iron placed round wheel; solid rubber hoop round carriage-wheels; outer rubber tube of cycle or motor-car wheel.

tissue (tish'-ū) *n.* fine cloth interwoven with gold, etc.; fabric of cells in living organisms; unbroken series; web;—*a.* made of tissue;—*v.t.* make into tissue.—**tis'sued** *a.* made of or resembling tissue.—**tis'sue-pa'per** *n.*

very soft, white or coloured semi-transparent paper.

tit (tit) *n.* small bird, e.g. titmouse.

tit (tit) *n.* small blow, as in phrase, tit for tat, blow for blow; retaliation.

tit (tit) *n.* teat.

Titan (tī'-tạn) *n.* (*fem.* Ti'taness) person of magnificent physique or of brilliant intellectual capacity;—*a.* colossal; mighty.—**Titan'ic** *a.* epic.—**titanium** *n.* metallic element of great strength and heat resistance (symbol Ti).

titbit (tit'-bit) *n.* choice morsel. Also **tid'bit**.

tithe (tīth) *n.* tenth part; orig. tenth part of produce of land and cattle allotted to upkeep of Church and clergy, later paid in form of tax; small portion;—*v.t.* levy tithe.

titian (tish'-ạn) *a.* rich auburn.

titillate (tit'-il-lāt) *v.t.* tickle, usually in sense of stimulating mind, palate, etc.—**titilla'tion** *n.* process of titillating; any pleasurable sensation.—**titilla'tive** *a.*

titivate (tit'-i-vāt) *v.i.* and *v.t.* (*Slang*) put finishing touches to one's general appearance.

title (tī'-tl) *n.* inscription put over, or under, or at beginning of, anything; designation; appellation denoting rank or pre-eminence; that which constitutes just claim or right; (*Law*) legal proof of right of possession; title-deed.—**ti'tled** *a.* having title, esp. aristocratic title.—**ti'tle-deed** *n.* document of proof of legal ownership of property.—**ti'tle-role** *n.* part in play from which it takes its name.

titmouse (tit'-mous) *n.* small bird which builds in holes of trees; tit; tomtit.—*pl.* **tit'mice**.

titrate (tī'-trāt) *v.t.* determine amount of ingredient in solution by adding quantities of standard solution until required chemical reaction is observed.—**titra'tion** *n.*

titter (tit'-er) *v.i.* give smothered laugh; giggle;—*n.* restrained laugh.

tittle (tit'-l) *n.* minute particle; jot.

titular (tit'-ū-lạr) *a.* pert. to or of title; nominal; ruling in name but not in deed.—**titular'ity** *n.*—**tit'ularly** *adv.*—**tit'ulary** *a.* titular;—*n.* nominal holder of title.

to (tōō) *prep.* expressing motion towards; as far as; regarding; unto; upon; besides; compared with; as to; indicating indirect object; preceding infinitive mood of verb;—*adv.* forward; into customary position; on.

toad (tōd) *n.* amphibian resembling frog, but brownish with dry warty skin, and short legs; (*Fig.*) mean, detestable person.—**toad'-in-the-hole** *n.* meat or sausages cooked in batter.—**toad'stool** *n.* fungus resembling mushroom.—**toad'y** *n.* obsequious flatterer;—*v.i.* flatter excessively; fawn on;—*pr.p.* **toad'ying**.—*pa.t.* and *pa.p.* **toad'ied**.—**toad'yism** *n.* sycophancy.

toast (tōst) *v.t.* dry or warm by exposure to fire; crisp and brown (as bread) before fire, under grill, etc.; drink to health of;—*v.i.* drink toast;—*n.* slice of bread crisped and browned on both sides by heat of fire, etc.; person in whose honour toast is drunk.—**toast'er** *n.* one who or that which toasts; electrical table device for toasting bread.—**toast'ing-fork**, or **-iron** *n.* long-handled fork for toasting bread, etc. at open fire.—**toast'-mast'er** *n.* one who formally announces toasts at public function.

tobacco (to-bak'-ō) *n.* plant, dried leaves of which are used for chewing, smoking, or as snuff.—*pl.* **tobacc'os**.—**tobacc'onist** *n.* one who sells tobacco, cigarettes, matches, etc.

toboggan (to-bog'-ạn) *n.* sledge used for coasting down snow-clad hill slopes;—*v.i.* slide down hills on sledge.—**tobog'ganing** *n.*

toby (tō'-bi) *n.* small jug in shape of old man wearing three-cornered hat.

toccata (tok-ká'-ta) *n.* (*Mus.*) composition for organ or piano which tests player's technique.

tocsin (tok'-sin) *n.* alarm-bell or its ringing sound.

today (tōō-dā') *n.* present day;—*adv.* on this day; at present time.

toddle (tod'-l) *v.i.* walk with short, hesitating steps, as child.—**todd'ler** *n.* child just learning to walk.

toddy (tod'-i) *n.* drink of whisky, sugar, and hot water.

to-do (tōō-dōō') *n.* commotion; fuss.

toe (to) *n.* one of five small digits of foot; forepart of hoof; part of boot, shoe, or stocking covering toes;—*v.t.* touch or reach with toe.—**toe'cap** *n.* additional cap on toe of boot or shoe.—**toed** *a.* having toes.

toff (tof) *n.* (*Slang*) dandy; swell.

toffee, toffy (tof'-i) *n.* hard sweet-meat made of sugar, butter, etc. boiled together.

tog (tog) *n.* (*Slang*) dress.—usu. in *pl.*

toga (tō'-ga) *n.* loose outer garment worn by Roman citizens.

together (tōō-geTH'-er) *adv.* in company; in or into union; simultaneously; in same place.

toggle (tog'-l) *n.* cigar-shaped bar of wood put through eye of rope, to prevent it slipping through loop of another rope;—*v.t.* fix with toggle.

toil (toil) *v.i.* labour; move with difficulty;—*n.* drudgery; exertion; task.—**toil'er** *n.* one who works hard.—**toil'ful, toil'some** *a.* laborious.—**toil'somely** *adv.*—**toil'someness** *n.*

toil (toil) *n.* net or snare; mesh.—usu. *pl.*

toilet (toil'-et) *n.* orig. dressing-table or its cover; process of dressing; mode of dressing; lavatory. Also **toilette** (twä-let').—**toil'et-pa'per** *n.* thin paper for lavatory use.

token (tō'-ḳen) *n.* sign; symbol; concrete expression of esteem; card of certain value exchangeable for goods, as *book-token;—adj.* symbolic.—**to'ken-pay'ment** *n.* deposit paid as token of later payment of full debt.

told (tōld) *pa.t.* and *pa.p.* of verb **tell**.

tolerate (tol'-ẹr-āt) *v.t.* suffer to be done; endure.—**tol'erable** *a.* endurable; passably good.—**tolerabil'ity, tol'erableness** *n.*—**tol'erably** *adv.*—**tol'erance** *n.* forbearing; long-suffering.—**tol'erant** *a.* forbearing; long-suffering.—**tol'erantly** *adv.*—**tolera'tion** *n.* practice of allowing people to worship as they please; granting to minorities of political liberty.—**tolera'tor** *n.*

toll (tōl) *n.* tax, esp. for right to use bridge, ferry, public road, etc.; cross-roads where toll was formerly exacted from travellers;—*v.i.* exact toll.—**to take toll of**, cause great loss.

toll (tōl) *v.t.* cause to ring slowly, as bell, esp. to signify death;—*v.i.* peal with slow, sonorous sounds;—*n.* sound of bell tolling.

tom (tom) *n.* male animal as *tom-cat.*—**tom'boy** *n.* hoyden; romping, mischievous girl.—**tom'fool** *n.* complete fool.—**tomfool'ery** *n.* nonsensical behaviour.—**Tom Thumb**, midget.

tomahawk (tom'-a-hawk) *n.* war-hatchet used by N. American Indians.

tomato (to-mä'-tō) *n.* plant with red or yellow fruit much used in salads;—*pl.* **toma'toes**.

tomb (tóóm) *n.* grave; underground vault.—**tomb'stone** *n.* stone erected over grave.

tome (tōm) *n.* book; large, heavy volume.

tommy (tom'-i) *n.* bread; rolls; provisions, esp. as formerly given to workmen instead of wages.—**tomm'yrot** *n.* (*Slang*) utter nonsense.

tommy-gun (tom'-i-gun) *n.* automatic short-barrelled, light machine-gun.

tomorrow, to-morrow (tóó-mor'-ō) *n.* day after today;—*adv.* on following day.

tomtit (tom'-tit) *n.* small bird, tit-mouse.

tom-tom (tom'-tom) *n.* small drum used by Indian and African natives; gong.

ton (tun) *n.* (var. of **tun**) weight consisting of 20 cwt. or 2240 lb.; measure of capacity varying according to article being measured; (*Slang*) 100 m.p.h.;—**ton'nage** *n.* cubical content (100 cub. ft.) or burden (40 cub. ft.) of ship in *tons*; duty on ships estimated per ton; shipping collec-

tively assessed in tons. Also **tun'nage**.

tone (tōn) *n.* quality or pitch of musical sound; modulation of speaking or singing voice; colour-values of picture; (*Mus.*) one of larger intervals of diatonic scale; (*Med.*) natural healthy functioning of bodily organs;—*v.t.* give tone or quality to; modify colour or general effect of, as in photograph; tune (instrument);—*v.i.* blend (with).—**to'nal** *a.* pert. to tone.—**tonal'ity** *n.* quality of tone or pitch; system of variation of keys in musical composition; colour-scheme of picture.—**to'nally** *adv.*—**tone'-deaf** *a.* unable to distinguish musical intervals.—**toned** *a.* having tone.—**tone'-poem** *n.* descriptive orchestral composition.—**to tone down**, modify, as loudness of sound, brilliance of colour, etc.—**to tone in**, cause to harmonise;—*v.i.* blend (with).

tongs (tongz) *n.pl.* implement consisting of pair of pivoted levers, for grasping.

tongue (tung) *n.* flexible muscular organ in mouth used in tasting, swallowing, and for speech; facility of utterance; language; anything shaped like tongue; clapper of bell; narrow spit of land.—**tongued** *a.* having tongue.—**tongue'-tied** *n.* having tongue defect causing speech-impediment; (*Fig.*) speechless through shyness.—**tongue'-twist'er** *n.* number of words, usually alliterative, difficult to repeat rapidly.—**to hold one's tongue**, be silent.

tonic (ton'-ik) *a.* pert. to tones or sounds; having invigorating effect;—*n.* medicine which tones up system; anything invigorating; (*Mus.*) key-note.—**ton'ically** *adv.*—**ton'icity** *n.*—**tonic sol-fa**, system of musical notation.

tonight, (tóó-nīt) *n.* this night; night following this present day;— *adv.* on this night.

tonsil (ton'-sil) *n.* one of two oval-shaped lymphoid organs on either side of pharynx.—**tonsil(l)i'tis** *n.* inflammation of tonsils.

tonsure (ton'-shúr) *n.* act of shaving part of head as token of religious dedication; shaved crown of priest's head.—**ton'sor** *n.* barber.—**tonso'rial** *a.* pert. to shaving.—**ton'sured** *a.* shaven; having tonsure.

too (tóó) *adv.* over; in addition; more than enough; moreover.

took (took) *pa.t.* of **take**.

tool (tóól) *n.* implement or utensil operated by hand, or by machinery; cutting or shaping part of machine; means to end;—*v.t.* cut, shape, or mark with tool, esp. to chisel stone.

toot (tóót) *v.t.* cause to sound, as motor-horn;—*n.* unmusical sound; hoot.—**toot'le** *v.i.* make short, sharp sounds, as on flute, horn, whistle etc.

tooth (tŏŏth) n. bone projection in gums of upper and lower jaws of vertebrates; prong as of comb, saw, rake; cog of wheel;—pl. **teeth**.—v.t. provide with teeth; indent; interlock.—**tooth'-comb** n. small comb with teeth very close together.—**toothed** a. having teeth.—**tooth'-pick** n. small pointed quill or stick for removing particles of food lodged between teeth.—**a sweet tooth**, fondness for sweet foods.

top (top) n. highest part of anything; upper side; highest rank; first in merit, as of examination-candidates; (Naut.) platform surrounding head of lower-mast. Also pl. **tops**.—a. highest; most eminent; excellent;—v.t. cover on the top; rise above; cut off top of; hit, as golf-ball, above centre; surpass;—v.i. be outstanding;—pr.p. **top'ping**.—pa.t. and pa.p. **topped**.—**top'-boot** n. riding-boot.—**top'-coat** n. overcoat.—**top'-ful** a. brimming over.—**top'-hat** n. tall silk-hat.—**top'-heav'y** a. having top too heavy for base.—**top'-hole** a. (Slang) excellent.—**top'most** a. supreme; highest.—**top'notch** a. describing persons of high ability or anything which is super-excellent.—**top'per** n. (Slang) top hat; something placed on top;—**top'ping** n. act of lopping off top of something;—**top'pingly** adv.—**top'-sail** n. square sail on top-mast.

top (top) n. child's toy made to spin by means of string or by whipping.

topaz (tŏ'paz) n. gem-stone, translucent and of varied colours.

tope (tŏp) v.i. drink hard or to excess.—**to'per** n.

topee (tŏ-pē') n. cork or pith helmet worn by Europeans in tropical climates.

topiary (tŏ'-pi-ar-i) a. pert. to landscape gardening; cut into ornamental shapes, as trees, hedges, etc. Also **topa'rian**.—**to'piarist** n.

topic (top'-ik) n. subject of essay, discourse, or conversation; branch of general subject.—**top'ical** a. pert. to place; up-to-date; concerning local matters.—**top'ically** adv.

topography (to-pog'-ra-fi) n. description of place; scientific description of physical features of region.—**topog'rapher** n.—**topograph'ic, -al** a.—**topograph'ically** adv.

topple (top'-l) v.t. throw down; overturn;—v.i. overbalance.

topsy-turvy (top'-si-tur'-vi) adv. upside down;—a. turned upside down;—n. disorder.

tor (tor) n. rocky hill.

torch (torch) n. piece of wood or rope soaked in inflammable liquid, and used as light.—**torch'-bear'er** n.—**electric torch**, small hand-light

containing electric battery and bulb.

toreador (tor-e-a-dor') n. bullfighter.

torment (tor'-ment) n. extreme pain of body; anguish of mind; misery; cause of anguish.—**torment'** v.t. inflict pain upon; torture; vex; tease.—**torment'ing** a.—**tormen'tingly** adv.—**tormen'tor, tormen'ter** n.

tornado (tor-nā'-dō) n. violent gust of wind; whirling progressive wind-storm causing wide-spread devastation;—pl. **torna'does**.

torpedo (tor-pē'-dō) n. cigar-shaped under-water projectile with high-explosive charge; electric ray.—pl. **torpe'does**.—v.t. attack, hit, or sink with torpedoes. — **torpe'do-boat** n. small, swift naval vessel armed chiefly with torpedoes.

torpid (tor'-pid) a. numb; lethargic; physically or mentally inert.—**torpid'ity** n. inactivity; lethargy.—**tor'pidly** adv.—**tor'pidness** n.—**tor'por** n. numbness; sluggishness; mental inertia.—**torporif'ic** a. causing torpor.

torque (tork) n. collar of gold wires twisted together. Also **torc**; (Mech.) rotating force in mechanism.

torrent (tor'-ent) n. swift-flowing stream; downpour, as of rain; (Fig.) rapid flow as of words;—a. rushing.—**torren'tial** a.—**torren'tially** adv.

torrid (tor'-id) a. dried with heat; arid. — **tor'ridness** n. — **torrid zone**, broad belt lying between Tropics of Cancer and Capricorn.

torsion (tor'-shun) n. act of turning or twisting; (Mech.) force with which twisted wire or similar body tends to return to original position.—**tor'sional** a.

torso (tor'-sō) n. trunk of human body; statue without head and limbs.

tort (tort) n. (Law) private injury to person or property for which damages may be claimed.—**tor'tious** a.—**tor'tiously** adv.

tortoise (tor'-tis or tor'-toiz) n. toothless land turtle, encased in dome-shaped scaly box-like shell;—**tor'toise-shell** n. mottled brown outer shell of hawksbill tortoise;—a. mottled.

tortuous (tor'-tū-us) a. full of twists; crooked; devious; circuitous; deceitful.—**tor'tuose** a. wreathed; twisted. — **tortuos'ity** n. — **tor'tuously** adv.—**tor'tuousness** n.

torture (tor'-tūr) n. act of deliberately inflicting extreme pain as punishment or reprisal; anguish; torment;—v.t. put to torture; inflict agony on.—**tor'turer** n.—**tor'turing** a. agonising; causing torment.

tosh (tosh) n. (Slang) nonsense.

toss (tos) v.t. throw upwards with jerk; cause to rise and fall; agitate violently;—v.i. be tossed; roll and tumble; be restless;—n. fling; sudden fall from horseback; distance anything is tossed.—**toss'er** *n.* one who tosses.—**toss'ing** *n.*—a toss-up, spinning of coin to decide issue; even chance.—**to toss off,** swallow in one gulp; do work easily and quickly.

tot (tot) *n.* anything small, esp. child; small drinking-cup; dram.

tot (tot) *v.t.* add; count up;—*n.* total.

total (tō'-tạl) *a.* full; complete; utter; absolute;—*n.* whole; sum; aggregate; —*v.t.* sum; add; —*v.i.* amount to.—**totalita'rian** *a.* relating to one-party dictatorial form of government.—**to'talisator**, **to'taliser**, (*Colloq.*) **the tote** *n.* automatic betting-machine at horse and dog races.—**total'ity** *n.* whole sum; entirety.—**to'tally** *adv.*—**to'talness** *n.*

totem (tō'-tẹm) *n.* natural object, such as animal or plant, taken by primitive tribe as emblem of their hereditary relationship with that object; image of this.—**to'tem-pole** *n.* ornamental staff with *totem.*

totter (tot'-ẹr) *v.i.* walk with faltering steps; sway; shake; reel.—**tott'erer** *n.* —**tott'ering** *a.* shaky; insecure.— **tott'eringly** *adv.*—**tott'ery** *a.* shaky; unsteady.

toucan (tŏŏ-kán', or tŏŏ'-kạn) *n.* bird of Brazil with long orange beak and black plumage.

touch (tuch) *v.t.* come in contact with; finger; reach; attain to; concern; meddle with; treat of, superficially; move deeply; equal in merit; (*Slang*) borrow from;—*v.i.* be in contact; take effect on;—*n.* contact; sense of feeling; quality of response in handling of instrument or colour; individual style of execution; unique quality; trace or tinge; test; mild attack; (*Football*) part of field beyond touch-lines.— **touch'able** *a.* capable of being touched.—**touch'ableness** *n.*—**touch and go,** precarious situation.— **touch-down** *n.* (*Rugby*) handling of ball on ground behind goal-line.—**touched** *a.* (*Slang*) crazy.—**touch'er** *n.*—**touch'ily** *adv.*— **touch'iness** *n.*—**touch'ing** *a.* pathetic; —*prep.* referring to.—**touch'ingly** *adv.*—**touch'ingness** *n.*—**touch'-judge** *n.* linesman at rugby match.—**touch'-line** *n.* side line of football-field.— **touch'stone** *n.* Lydian stone, variety of schist, used for testing purity of gold and silver by streak impressed by it on stone; (*Fig.*) criterion; standard of judgment.—**touch'y** *a.* easily offended.—**touch at** (of ships) call at.—**touch-down** (of aircraft) *v.i.* and *n.* make contact with ground on landing.—**touch on,** refer to briefly.

tough (tuf) *a.* flexible but not brittle; not easily broken; firm; difficult to chew; stout-hearted; vigorous; hardy; difficult to solve; (*U.S. Slang*) vicious;—*n.* bully; gangster.—**tough-en'** *v.t.* make tough, or hardy;—*v.i.*

become tough.—**tough'ish** *a.* rather tough.—**tough'ly** *adv.*—**tough'ness** *n.*

toupee (tŏŏ-pē') *n.* tuft or artificial lock of hair to cover bald patch. Also **toup'et.**

tour (tŏŏr) *n.* journey from place to place in country; excursion; spell of duty;—*v.t.* travel round; visit as part of tour.—**tour'ism** *n.*—**tour'ist** *n.* one who makes tour; sightseer.

tournament (tŏŏr'-nạ-mẹnt) *n.* mock-fight, common form of contest and entertainment in medieval times; any sports competition or championship.

tourniquet (tŏŏr'-ni-kā, or -ket) *n.* surgical instrument for arresting haemorrhage by compression; bandage or pad tightened and periodically released, used to arrest bleeding.

tousle (tou'-zl) *v.t.* make untidy by pulling, as hair; dishevel.—**tous'led** *a.* untidy.

tout (tout) *v.i.* solicit custom;—*n.* one who pesters people to be customers; hanger-on at racing-stables.

tow (tō) *v.t.* drag through water by rope; pull along with rope;—*n.* act of pulling; rope used for towing; coarse fibre of hemp used in rope-making.—**tow'age** *n.* act of or charge for towing.—**tow(ing)-path** *n.* path alongside canal used by horses towing canal barge.—**to take in tow** (*Fig.*) take charge of.

toward (tō'-ård) **towards** (tō'-årdz) *prep.* in direction of; near (of time); with respect to; regarding;—*adv.* nearly; at hand.

towel (tou'-ẹl) *n.* cloth for drying skin, or for domestic purposes.— **tow'elling** *n.* soft fabric for making towels.—**to throw in the towel,** acknowledge defeat.

tower (tou'-ẹr) *n.* lofty, round or square stone structure; fortress;—*v.i.* be lofty; soar; excel.—**tow'ered** *a.* having towers.—**tow'ering** *a.* lofty; (*Fig.*) violent.

town (toun) *n.* collection of houses, etc. larger than village; inhabitants of town;—*a.* pert. to town.—**town'-clerk** *n.* official in charge of administrative side of town's affairs.— **town'-coun'cil** *n.* group of representatives, elected by ratepayers to manage municipal affairs.—**town'-ship** *n.* parish.

toxicology (tok-si-kol'-o-ji) *n.* science of poisons, their effects, etc.— **toxe'mia,** *n.* blood-poisoning.—**toxe'-mic** *a.*—**tox'ic** *a.* poisonous.—**tox'-ically** *adv.*—**tox'icant** *a.* poisonous;— *n.* poison.—**toxicolog'ical** *a.*—**toxicol'-ogist** *n.*—**tox'in** *n.* poison usually of bacterial origin.

toxophilite (tok-sof'-i-līt) *n.* student of, or expert in, archery.

toy (toi) *n.* child's plaything; bauble; trifle;—*v.i.* dally; trifle.

race (trās) *n.* mark; footprint; vestige; minute quantity; remains; outline;—*v.t.* pass through; copy or draw exactly; follow track of; work out step by step; walk or tread;—*v.i.* move.—**trace′able** *a.* capable of being traced or detected; attributable.—**trace′ableness** *n.*—**trace′ably** *adv.* —**tra′cer** *n.* one who traces.—**tra′cery** *n.* ornamental openwork formed in head of Gothic window; any delicate and intricate pattern of lines.— **tra′cing** *n.* traced copy of drawing.— **tra′cing-pa′per** *n.* specially prepared, transparent paper for tracing design, etc.

race (trās) *n.* strap, rope, chain, by which horse pulls vehicle.—**trace′-horse** *n.* draught-horse hitched on in front of horse and lorry to draw heavy loads up steep hill.

trachea (trā′-ke-a, tra-kē′-a) *n.* windpipe between lungs and back of throat.—*pl.* **trache′ae.**—**tra′cheal** *a.*

track (trak) *n.* mark left by something; footprint; pathway trodden out by usage; laid-out course for racing; (of railway) permanent way; (of motor-vehicles) distance between road-wheels on one axle; (*Fig.*) evidence; trace;—*v.t.* follow trail or traces of; record course of.—**track′er** *n.* one who or that which tracks, or tows canal boat by rope.

tract (trakt) *n.* region of indefinite extent; continuous period of time; dissertation; short treatise on practical religion.—**tractabil′ity** *n.* quality or state of being tractable.—**trac′-table** *a.* docile; amenable to reason. —**trac′tableness** *n.*—**trac′tably** *adv.*— **trac′tile** *a.* capable of being drawn out; (of metals) ductile.—**tractil′ity** *n.*—**trac′tion** *n.* act of drawing solid body along plane; propelling force of vehicle. — **trac′tional** *a.* — **trac′tion-en′gine** *n.* locomotive, steam-driven for haulage.—**trac′tive** *a.* pulling.— **trac′tor** *n.* traction-engine; motor-vehicle for drawing agricultural machinery.

trade (trād) *n.* business of buying and selling; commerce; occupation, esp. in industry, shopkeeping, etc.; employees collectively in particular trade; vocation;—*v.t.* carry on trade; engage in commerce;—*v.t.* exchange.—**trade′-mark** *n.* registered name or device on maker's goods.— **trade′-name** *n.* registered name given by manufacturer to proprietary article.—**trad′er** *n.* merchant (wholesale or retail); trading-vessel.— **trades′man** *n.* shopkeeper; skilled workman.—**trade′-un′ion, trades′-un′-ion** *n.* legally recognised association of employees, etc.—**trade′-un′ionist** *n.* —**trade′-wind** *n.* one of two prevailing winds which blow steadily between tropics and Equator; in Northern Hemisphere it is N.E. wind, in Southern Hemisphere, S.E.—**trad′ing** *n.*—**to trade in,** give in part exchange. —**to trade on,** exploit.

tradition (tra-dish′-un) *n.* belief, custom, etc. transmitted by word of mouth from age to age.—**tradi′tional** *a.* handed down from age to age.— **traditionalist** *n.*—**traditionalism** *n.*

traduce (tra-dūs′) *v.t.* defame character of; misrepresent; calumniate.— **traduce′ment** *n.* calumny.—**tradu′cer** *n.* slanderer.

traffic (traf′-ik) *n.* commerce; barter; illegal buying and selling, as *drug-traffic*; movement of people, vehicles, etc. to and fro; people, vehicles, etc. collectively in any given area;—*v.i.* carry on trade; do business, esp. illegally;—*v.t.* barter;—*pr.p.* **traff′-icking.**—*pa.t.* and *pa.p.* **traff′icked.**— **traff′icker** *n.*—**traff′ic-lights** *n.pl.* indicator fitted with red, amber and green lights erected at street crossings to control traffic.

tragedy (traj′-e-di) *n.* serious and dignified dramatic composition in prose or verse with unhappy ending; sad or calamitous event.—**trage′dian** *n.* actor in or writer of tragedy.— **trage′dienne** *n. fem.*—**trag′ic, -al** *a.* pert. to tragedy; distressing; calamitous.—**trag′ically** *adv.*—**trag′i-com′edy** *n.* drama combining tragedy and comedy; romance.

trail (trāl) *v.t.* draw along ground or through water; drag; follow track of; carry rifle loosely in hand, parallel with ground; make track by treading ground;—*v.i.* dangle loosely, touching ground; drag one foot wearily after other;—*n.* track followed by hunter; visible trace left by anything; scent of hunted animal; part of gun-carriage which rests on ground during firing; mode of carrying rifle at trailing position; tail of meteor.—**trail′er** *n.* vehicle towed by another; (*Cinema*) advance excerpt shown as advertisement of coming film.—**trailing edge** (*Aviat.*) rear-edge of aerofoil.

train (trān) *v.t.* discipline; instruct or educate; submit person to arduous physical exercise, etc. for athletics; teach animal to be obedient; cause plant to grow in certain way; aim, as gun;—*v.i.* exercise body or mind to achieve high standard of efficiency;—*n.* retinue; procession of people; line of carriages drawn by locomotive; trailing back-folds of dress; string of pack-animals; sequence of events, ideas, etc.; trail of gunpowder to lead fire to explosive charge.—**trained** *a.* skilled; fully qualified.—**train′ee** *n.* one who is training.—**train′er** *n.* one who supervises training.—**train′ing** *n.*—**to put in train,** set things going.

trait (trā or trāt) n. distinguishing feature, esp. in character.

traitor (trā'-tor) n. (fem. **trait'ress**) one who betrays person, country, or cause.—**trait'orous** a. guilty of treachery; pert. to treason or traitors.—**trait'orously** adv.

traject (tra-jekt') v.t. throw across; cast through.—**trajec'tion** n. crossing; act of throwing across.—**trajec'tory** n. curve of projectile in flight through space.

tram (tram) n. tramcar; public vehicle running on rails on roadway; truck, tub, etc. running on rails;—v.t. convey by tram;—**tram'-way** n. system for transport of passengers by tramcars.

trammel (tram'-el) n. long net for catching birds or fishes; shackle for training horse to walk slowly; anything which impedes movement;—v.t. impede; hinder; confine;—pr.p. **tramm'elling.**—pa.p. **tramm'elled.**

tramp (tramp) v.t. tread heavily; walk over or through;—v.i. go/on walking tour; plod; wander as vagrant;—n. homeless vagrant; long walk; cargo-boat with no regular route.—**tramp'er** n.

trample (tram'-pl) v.t. tread heavily underfoot; (Fig.) oppress; treat with contempt;—v.i. tread rapidly;—n. act of trampling.—**tramp'ler** n.

trance (trans) n. state of complete insensibility, due to morbid nervous condition, or produced by hypnotism; ecstasy.

tranquil (trang'-kwil) a. calm; serene; undisturbed.—**tranquill'ity** n. serenity; composure (of mind).—**tran'quilliser** n. sedative or muscle-relaxant drug.—**tran'quilness** n.

transact (tranz-akt') v.t. carry through; negotiate;—v.i. do (business).—**transac'tion** n. act of transacting (business).—**transac'tion** n. act of transacting business;—pl. records.

transalpine (tranz-al'-pīn) a. north of Alps (as from Rome).

transatlantic (tranz-at-lan'-tik) a. across the Atlantic.

transcend (tran-send') v.t. go beyond; excel; surpass.—**transcen'dence, transcen'dency** n. quality of being transcendent.—**transcen'dent** a. supreme in excellence; surpassing all.—**transcenden'tal** a. abstruse; intuitive.—**transcenden'talism** n.—**transcenden'talist** n.—**transcenden'tally** adv.

transcontinental (tranz-kon-ti-nen'-tal) a. crossing continent.

transcribe (tran-skrīb') v.t. copy out; write over again; reproduce in longhand or typescript notes taken in shorthand; (Mus.) rearrange composition for another instrument or voice.—**transcrib'er** n.—**trans'cript** n. something transcribed; written copy.—**transcrip'tion** n. act of copying.

transducer (trans-dū'-ser) n. device which transforms input of one form of energy into output of another.

transept (tran'-sept) n. transverse portion of church at right angles to nave.

transfer (trans-fer') v.t. move from one place to another; transport; remove; convey, as property, legally to another;—pr.p. **transfer'ring.**—pa.t. and pa.p. **transferred'.**—**trans'fer** n. removal from one place to another.—**transferabil'ity, transferribil'ity** n.—**trans'ferable, transfer'rible** a.—**transfer'or, transfer'er** n.

transfigure (trans-fig'-ūr) v.t. change outward appearance of; make more beautiful or radiant.—**transfigura'tion** n. change of form.—**The Transfiguration**, miraculous outward transformation of Christ when on the Mount.

transfix (trans-fiks') v.t. pierce through; impale; (Fig.) astound.

transform (trans-form') v.t. change form, nature, character of; transmute;—v.i. be changed.—**transform'able** a.—**transforma'tion** n. change of outward appearance or inner nature.—**transfor'mer** n. one who or that which transforms; electrical device for changing voltage up or down.

transfuse (tranz-fūz') v.t. pour, as liquid, from one receptacle into another; (Med.) transfer blood from one person to vein of another in compatible blood-group; (Fig.) imbue.—**transfu'sion** n.

transgress (tranz-gres') v.t. overstep a limit; violate law or commandment;—v.i. offend by violating law; sin.—**transgres'sion** n. act of violating civil or moral law; offence; crime.—**transgres'sor** n.

tranship, transship (tran-ship') v.t. transfer from one ship to another.

transient (tran'-zi-ent) a. fleeting; ephemeral; not permanent.—**tran'sience** n. quality of being transient.—**tran'siently** adv.

transistor (tran-sis'-tor) n. small semi-conductor device which performs the functions of a thermionic valve without the necessity of a heating current.—**transis'torise** v.t. fit with transistors.

transit (tran'-zit) n. conveyance or passage over or across.—**transi'tion** n. passage from one place to another; change from one state or condition to another.—**transi'tional, transi'tionary** a.—**transi'tionally** adv.—**trans'itive** a. having power of passing across.—**trans'itively** adv.—**trans'itiveness** n.—**trans'itorily** adv.—**trans'itoriness** n. state of being transitory.—**trans'itory** a. continuing for brief while only; ephemeral; transient.

translate (tranz-lāt') v.t. remove from one place to another; change from one medium to another; turn from one language to another;—*v.i.* be capable of translation.—**transla′tion** *n.*—**transla′tor** *n.*

transliterate (tranz-lit′-ę-rāt) *v.t.* write words of language in alphabetic symbols of another.—**translitera′tion** *n.*—**translit′erator** *n.*

translucent (tranz-lōō′-sęnt) *a.* semi-transparent; diffusing light but not revealing definite contours of object as *frosted glass.*—**translu′cence**, translu′cency *n.*—**translu′cently** *adv.*—**translu′cid** *a.* translucent.

transmigrate (tranz′-mī-grāt) *v.i.* pass from one country to another as permanent residence; (of soul) pass at death into another body or state. —**transmigra′tion** *n.*—**trans′migrator** *n.*—**transmi′gratory** *a.*

transmit (tranz-mit′) *v.t.* send from one person or place to another; communicate; hand on, as by heredity;—*pr.p.* **transmit′ting.**—*pa.t.* and *pa.p.* **transmit′ted.**—**transmissibil′ity** *n.*—**transmis′sible**, **transmit′tible** *a.* —**transmis′sion** *n.*—**transmit′tal** *n.* transmission. — **transmit′tance** *n.*— **transmit′ter** *n.*

transmontane (tranz-mon-tān′) *a.* across, or beyond, mountains.

transmute (tranz-mūt′) *v.t.* change from one nature, species, form, or substance into another.—**transmu′table** *a.* capable of being changed in form.—**transmu′tableness** *n.*—**transmutabil′ity** *n.*—**transmu′tably** *adv.*—**transmuta′tion** *n.* act or process of transforming; in alchemy, supposed change of baser metals into gold; (*Geom.*) reduction of figure or area to another having same superficial extent or solidity.—**transmu′tative** *a.* —**transmu′ter** *n.*

transom (tran′-sum) *n.* horizontal cross-bar in window; lintel; beam across stern-post of ship; horizontal strut to give support.

transparent (tranz-pār′-ęnt) *a.* that may be distinctly seen through; pervious to light; clear; (*Fig.*) obvious.—**transpar′ency** *n.* (*Photog.*) picture on transparent film for projection or viewing against light.— **transpar′ently** *adv.*—**transpar′entness** *n.*

transpire (tran-spīr′) *v.t.* emit through pores of skin;—*v.i.* exhale; (*Fig.*) come out by degrees; (*Colloq.*) happen—**transpira′tion** *n.*

transplant (tranz-plant′) *v.t.* remove and plant elsewhere; (*Surg.*) graft live tissue from one part of body to another.

transport (tranz-pōrt′) *v.t.* convey from one place to another; banish, as criminal, to penal colony; (*Fig.*) overwhelm emotionally.—**trans′port** *n.* transportation; conveyance of people or commodities; vehicles collectively used in conveyance of passengers; troop-ship; (*Fig.*)

passion; ecstasy.—**transpor′table** *a.*— **transporta′tion** *n.* act of transporting from place to place; banishment, for felony.—**transpor′ted** *a.* (*Fig.*) carried away with emotion.

transpose (tranz-pōz′) *v.t.* alter order of words; (*Mus.*) change key of composition.—**transpo′sable** *a.*— **transpo′sal** *n.* change of order.— **transposi′tion** *n.* substitution; (*Mus.*) raising or lowering of original key.

transubstantiate (tran-sub-stan′-shi-āt) *v.t.* change into another substance.—**transubstantia′tion** *n.* doctrine that 'whole substance' of bread and wine in Eucharist is changed into flesh and blood of Christ,

transverse (tranz-vęrs′) *a.* lying in cross-wise direction;—*adv.* cross-wise.—**transverse′ly** *adv.*

trap (trap) *n.* device, mechanical or otherwise, for catching animals, vermin, etc.; snare; U-shaped bend in pipe; light two-wheeled carriage; (*Fig.*) stratagem; deliberate plot to catch person unawares;—*v.t.* catch in snare, or by stratagem;—*pr.p.* **trap′ping.**—*pa.p.* **trapped.**—**trap′-door** *n.* hinged door in floor, or leading to loft.—**trap′per** *n.* one who traps animals, esp. for their pelts.

trap (trap) *n.* horse-cloth; trapping;— *pl.* one's belongings, luggage, etc.;— *v.t.* adorn.—**trap′pings** *n.pl.* ornaments, gay coverings, esp. those on horse in olden times.

traipse (trāps) *v.i.* trail along.

trapezium (trą-pē′-zi-um) *n.* quadrilateral with only one pair of sides parallel; (*Anat.*) one of bones of wrist;—*pl.* **trape′zia**, **trape′ziums.**— **trapeze′** *n.* horizontal cross-bar swing. —**trap′ezoid** *n.* quadrilateral with no sides parallel.—**trapezoid′al** *a.*

trash (trash) *v.t.* lop off;—*n.* worthless refuse; loppings of trees, bruised sugar-canes, etc.—**trash′ery** *n.* trash. —**trash′ily** *adv.* **trash′iness** *n.*—**trash′y** *a.* worthless; shoddy.

trauma (trau′-ma) *n.* injury; deep seated emotional disturbance.

travail (tra′-vāl) *n.* painful, arduous labour; pains of childbirth;—*v.i.* labour with difficulty; suffer pangs of childbirth.

travel (trav′-el) *v.t.* journey over; pass;—*v.i.* move; journey on foot or in vehicle; tour, esp. abroad;—*pr.p.* **trav′elling.**—*pa.t.* and *pa.p.* **trav′elled.** —*n.* act of travelling; journey;—*pl.* prolonged journey, esp. abroad; book describing journeys.—**trav′elled** *a.* having sojourned extensively, esp. abroad.—**trav′eller** *n.* one who travels widely; travelling representative of business firm. Also **commercial travel-ler.**—**traveller's cheque**, cheque issued by bank and payable at any bank in area visited by traveller.—**trav′elling** *a.* mobile.

traverse (trav'-ẹrs) *a.* lying across; built crosswise; sailing in zig-zag fashion;—*n.* anything set across; partition; course cut across face of precipice;—*v.t.* cross; thwart; obstruct; survey scientifically; rake with gun fire from end to end; pivot laterally; discuss, as topic, from every angle;—*v.i.* turn, as on pivot; walk sideways;—*adv.* athwart; crosswise.—**trav'ersable** *a.*—**trav'erser** *n.*

travesty (trav'-es-ti) *n.* burlesque imitation of work; parody;—*v.t.* caricature.

trawl (trawl) *v.t.* catch fish with trawl;—*v.i.* drag with trawl;—*n.* trawl-net, shaped like large bag with one end open.—**trawl'er** *n.* one who fishes with trawl; fishing-vessel which uses trawl-net.—**trawl'ing** *n.*

tray (trā) *n.* flat, shallow vessel for carrying things; salver.

treachery (trech'-ẹr-i) *n.* violation of allegiance or faith; treason; perfidy.—**treach'erous** *a.* disloyal; perfidious.—**treach'erously** *adv.*

treacle (trē'-kl) *n.* thick dark-brown syrup from sugar during refining; molasses.—**trea'cly** *a.* sweet, thick and sticky.

tread (tred) *v.i.* walk; move with stately or measured step; (of fowls) copulate; crush or step on by mistake;—*v.t.* step or walk on; crush with foot; oppress; operate with foot, as treadle;—*pr.p.* **tread'ing.** —*pa.t.* **trod.**—*pa.p.* **trod** or **trod'den.**—*n.* act of stepping; pace; that which one steps on, as surface of horizontal step of flight of stairs; sole of boot or shoe; part of rubber tyre in contact with ground.—**tread'ing** *n.*—**tread'le, tred'dle** *n.* foot-lever; pedal;—*v.i.* work treadle.—**tread'ler** *n.*—**tread'mill** *n.* mill worked by treading upon steps on periphery of wheel; (*Fig.*) drudgery.—**to tread on a person's toes or corns,** to offend his sensibilities.

treason (trē'-zn) *n.* disloyalty; treachery.—**trea'sonable** *a.* pert. to or involving treason.—**trea'sonableness** *n.*—**trea'sonably** *adv.*—**high treason,** violation by subject of allegiance to Sovereign or State.

treasure (trezh'-ūr) *n.* accumulated wealth; hoard of valuables; that which has great worth;—*v.t.* hoard; collect; value; cherish, as friendship.—**treas'urer** *n.* person appointed to take charge of funds of society, church, club, etc.—**treas'ure-trove** *n.* any money, treasure, etc., of unknown ownership, found buried, which becomes property of Crown.—**treas'ury** *n.* place where treasure, hoarded wealth, or public funds are deposited; (*Fig.*) storehouse of facts and information; anthology.—**Treas'ury** *n.* government department which controls management of public revenues.—**treas'ury-note** *n.* British paper currency.

treat (trēt) *v.t.* handle; entertain with food or drink; pay for another's entertainment or refreshment; behave towards; apply remedy to; consider as topic for discussion; discourse on;—*v.i.* discourse; come to terms of agreement; give entertainment;—*n.* entertainment; something that gives special pleasure; (*Colloq.*) one's turn to pay for another's entertainment.—**treat'er** *n.*—**treat'ing** *n.* act of standing treat.—**treat'ise** *n.* dissertation on particular theme.—**treat'ment** *n.* act or mode of treating person or subject; method of counteracting disease or of applying remedy for injury.—**treat'y** *n.* agreement between states; pact.

treble (treb'-l) *a.* threefold; triple; (*Mus.*) playing or singing highest part;—*n.* highest of four principal parts in music; soprano part; soprano voice;—*v.t.* multiply by three;—*v.i.* become three times as much;—*pa.p.* **treb'led.**—**treb'ly** *adv.*

tree (trē) *n.* perennial plant, having trunk, bole, or woody stem with branches; anything resembling crosslike form of tree; cross of Christ.—**tree'less** *a.* devoid of trees; bare.—**shoe'-tree** *n.* foot-shaped mould for preserving shape of shoe.—**family tree,** genealogical table of ancestry.

trefoil (trē'-foil) *n.* plant with leaves comprising three leaflets; clover; (*Archit.*) ornament of three cusps in circle resembling three-leaved clover.

trek (trek) *v.i.* travel by ox-wagon; migrate, esp. large body of people;—*n.* journey by ox-wagon; mass-migration.—**trek'ker** *n.*

trellis (trel'-is) *n.* light-weight lattice structure of spars for screens, doors.—**trell'ised** *a.*—**trell'is-work** *n.*

tremble (trem'-bl) *v.i.* shake involuntarily from fear, cold, etc.; quiver; quake;—*n.* involuntary shaking; quiver.—**trem'bler** *n.*—**trem'bling** *n.*—**trem'blingly** *adv.*—**trem'bly** *a.* shaky;—*adv.* shakily.—**trem'ulant, trem'ulous** *a.* quivering; quaking.—**trem'ulously** *adv.*—**trem'ulousness** *n.*

tremendous (tre-men'-dus) *a.* awe-inspiring; formidable; momentous; (*Colloq.*) great.—**tremen'dously** *adv.*—**tremen'dousness** *n.*

tremolo (trem'-ō-lō) *n.* quivering of singing voice.—**trem'ulant** *n.* organ-device to procure tremolo effect.

tremor (trem'-or) *n.* involuntary quiver; momentary thrill; shaking, as caused by earthquake.—**trem'or-less** *a.* steady.

trench (trensh) *n.* cut or dig, as ditch; turn over soil by digging deeply; fortify with ditch;—*v.i.* encroach;—*n.* ditch; deep ditch formed by earth piled up to protect soldiers from enemy fire.—**trenchancy** n. quality of being trenchant.—**trenchant**, **trench'ing** a. sharp; (*Fig.*) caustic; biting.—**trench'-coat** n. knee-length belted waterproof coat.—**trench'er** n. one who digs trenches. — **trench'ing** n. — **trench'mortar** n. short range mortar.

trencher (tren'-sher) n. formerly wooden plate for holding food; bread-board.—**a good trencherman**, one who has hearty appetite.

trend (trend) v.i. run or stretch in certain direction;—n. inclination; tendency.

trepan (tre-pan') n. (*Surg.*) cylindrical saw for removing bone from skull;—v.t. operate with trepan.—**trepanning** n.

trepidation (trep'-idā-shun) n. involuntary trembling; alarm; fluster.

trespass (tres'-pas) v.i. cross unlawfully boundary line of another's property; intrude; encroach; violate moral law;—n. **tres'passer** n.

tress (tres) n. lock, curl, plait, or strand of hair; ringlet;—v.t. form into ringlets or plaits; braid.—**tressed** a. having tresses.

trestle (tres'-l) n. movable wooden frame consisting of two pairs of braced legs; similar metal or stone construction supporting bridge.

trews (trōōz) n.pl. tartan trousers, as worn by soldiers of some Highland regiments.

triad (trī'-ad) n. union of three; (*Chem.*) trivalent atom; (*Mus.*) chord of three notes; poem with triple grouping.

trial (trī'-al) n. act of trying, testing, or proving properties of anything; experimental examination; affliction; judicial examination in law-court of accused person; temptation.

triangle (trī'-ang-gl) n. (*Math.*) figure bounded by three lines and containing three angles; anything like triangle; (*Mus.*) small percussion instrument consisting of bar of steel bent in shape of triangle.—**tri'angled** a.—**triang'ular** a. having three angles; shaped like triangle.—**triangular'ity** n.—**triang'ularly** adv.—**the eternal triangle**, three persons, two of them husband and wife, the third lover of one of them.

tribe (trīb) n. family, race, or succession of generations descending from same progenitor; nation of barbarian clans each under one leader; (*Colloq.*) very large family.—**trib'al** a.—**trib'alism** n. tribal feeling; clannishness.—**trib'ally** adv.—**tribes'-man** n. one of tribe.

tribulation (trib-ū-lā'-shun) n. severe affliction; prolonged suffering, esp. of mind.

tribune (trib'-ūn) n. in ancient Rome, magistrate chosen by people to defend their rights; champion of masses; raised platform or pulpit.—**tribu'nal** n. bench on which judge or magistrates sit; court of justice.—**trib'unary** a.—**trib'unate**, **trib'uneship** n. office or functions of tribune.

tribute (trib'-ūt) n. payment made by one state to another as price of peace and protection; contribution; personal testimony to achievements or qualities of another.—**trib'utary** a. paying tribute; subordinate; contributory; (of river) flowing into main river;—n. state liable for tribute; stream flowing into larger river.

trice (trīs) n. moment; **in a trice**, at once.

tricentenary (trī-sen'-te-na-ri) n. space of three hundred years; three-hundredth anniversary. Also **tercen'tenary**.

trichology (tri-kol'-o-ji) n. study of hair and diseases affecting it.

trichotomy (trī-kot'-ō-mi) n. division into three parts.

trick (trik) n. artifice designed to deceive; conjurer's sleight of hand; prank for mischief; mannerism; dexterity; cards played out in one round, and taken by player with winning card; spell at helm of ship;—v.t. deceive; hoax; mystify.—**trick'er** n. cheat.—**trick'ery** n. act of playing tricks; fraud.—**trick'ily** adv.—**trick'iness** n. quality of being tricky; intricacy.—**trick'ish** a. prone to play tricks.—**trick'ishly** adv.—**trick'ishness** n.—**trick'ster** n. cheat; swindler.—**trick'y** a. full of tricks; requiring great dexterity of hand; intricate.

trickle (trik'-l) v.i. flow gently in slow, thin stream;—n. thin flow of liquid; rill.—**trick'let** n. little rill.

tricolour (trī-kul-or) n. national flag of three colours, esp. French National Flag.

tricorn (trī'-korn) a. having three horns, or points;—n. three-cornered hat.

tricycle (trī'-si-kl) n. three-wheeled cycle,—**tri'cyclist** n.

trident (trī'-dent) n. three-pronged spear, symbol of Neptune; any three-pronged instrument, such as fish-spear.—**tri'dent**, **trident'ate**, **tri'dented** a. having three prongs.

triennial (trī-en'-al) a. lasting for three years; happening once every three years.—**trienn'ially** adv.

trifle (trī'-fl) n. anything of little value or importance; paltry amount; dessert of sponge-cake, etc.;—v.i. speak or act lightly.—**tri'fler** n.—**tri'fling** a. trivial.—**tri'flingly** adv.

triform (trī'-form) a. having triple form.

trifurcate (trī'-fur-kāt) a. having three branches or forks. Also

trifurca'ted.—trifur'cate *v.t.* divide into three branches.

trigger (trig'-er) *n.* catch of firearm which, when pulled, releases hammer of lock; device fitted on wheel for retarding speed of vehicle going down steep incline.

triglyph (trī'-glif) *n.* triple-grooved ornament in frieze of Doric column.—**triglyph'ic, -al** *a.*

trigonometry (trig-o-nom'-et-ri) *n.* branch of mathematics which deals with relations between sides and angles of triangle.—**trig'onomet'ric, -al** *a.*—**trigonomet'rically** *adv.*

trilateral (trī-lat'-er-al) *a.* having three sides; arranged by three parties.—**trilat'erally** *adv.*

trilby (tril'-bi) *n.* (*Colloq.*) man's soft felt-hat.

trilinear (trī-lin'-ē-ar) *a.* consisting of three lines.

trilingual (trī-ling'-gwal) *a.* expressed in three languages; speaking three languages.

trilith (trī'-lith) *n.* ancient monument of two upright stones and third across top.—**trilith'ic** *a.*

trill (tril) *v.t.* and *v.i.* sing or play (instrument) with tremulous quality; pronounce, as letter 'r';—*n.* shake or vibration of voice, produced by singing, in rapid alternation, two notes; consonant, such as 'r' pronounced with trill.

trillion (tril'-yun) *n.* million million million (British) i.e. 1 with 18 ciphers; million million (U.S.) i.e. 1 with 12 ciphers.

trilogy (tril'-o-ji) *n.* group of three plays, novels, etc. with common theme, or common central character.

trim (trim) *a.* neat; firm; compact; in good order or health;—*adv.* neatly;—*v.t.* put in order; dress; decorate; balance; clip shorter; adjust wick, as lamp; (*Naut.*) arrange sails according to wind-direction;—*v.i.* balance; fluctuate between two parties, so as to appear to favour each;—*pr.p.* **trim'ming.**—*pa.t.* and *pa.p.* **trimmed.**—*n.* dress; decoration; disposition; state of bodily fitness or mental alertness; state of readiness.—**trim'ly** *adv.*—**trim'mer** *n.* one who trims; instrument for clipping; one who, for expediency, supports whichever party is in power; time-server.—**trim'ming** *n.* that which trims, edges, or decorates.—**trim'ness** *n.* neatness; compactness; readiness for use.

trinitrotoluene (trī-nī-trō-tol'-ū-ēn) *n.* (*abbrev.* **T.N.T.**) high explosive produced by adding toluene to nitric and sulphuric acids.

Trinity (trin'-i-ti) *n.* union in one Godhead of Father, Son, and Holy Ghost; any combination of three people or things as one.—**Trinita'rian**

a. pert. to doctrine of Trinity;—*n.* one who believes in this doctrine.—**Trinita'rianism** *n.*—**Trinity Sunday,** Sunday following Whitsunday.

trinket (tring'-ket) *n.* small ornament worn as ring, brooch, etc.; ornament of little value.—**trin'ketry** *n.* trinkets.

trinomial (trī-nō'-mi-al) *a.* (*Bot. Zool.*) having three names as of *order, species* and *sub-species;* (*Math.*) consisting of three terms connected by sign × or — ;—*n.* trinomial quantity.

trio (trē'-ō, or trī'-o) *n.* group of three persons performing together; (*Mus.*) work for three voices, or players.

trip (trip) *v.t.* cause to stumble; loose, as ship's anchor; start up, as machine;—*v.i.* walk or dance lightly; stumble over obstacle; make false step; (*with* up) detect in another's statement, error of fact.—*pr.p.* **tripp'ing.**—*pa.p.* **tripped.**—*n.* quick, light step; short journey for pleasure; false step; indiscretion in speech or conduct.—**trip'-ham'mer** *n.* tilt-hammer used in forges.—**trip'per** *n.* one who trips; holiday-maker, esp. day-excursionist.

tripartite (trī-pár'-tīt, or trip'-ár-tīt) *a.* divided into three parts; having three corresponding parts; arranged or agreed to, by three parties or nations, as *tripartite pact.*

tripe (trīp) *n.* large stomach of ruminating animal, esp. of sheep, or ox, prepared for food; (*Colloq.*) entrails; (*Slang*) rubbish.

triphthong (trif'-thong) *n.* a syllable containing three vowels together, as in *beauty.*

triple (trip'-l) *a.* consisting of three united; three times repeated; treble;—*v.t.* make three times as much or as many;—*v.i.* become trebled.—**trip'let** *n.* three of kind; three consecutive verses rhyming together; (*Mus.*) three notes played in time of two; (*Colloq.*) one of three children born at a birth.—**trip'lex** *a.* threefold.—**trip'licate** *a.* threefold; made three times as much;—*n.* third copy corresponding exactly to two others of same kind;—*v.t.* treble; make three copies of.—**triplica'tion** *n.* act or process of trebling.

tripod (trī'-pod) *n.* stool, vessel, etc. on three-legged support; three-legged, folding-stand for camera, theodolite, etc.;—*a.* having three legs.—**trip'od'al** *a.*

tripos (trī'-pos) *n.* honours degree exam at Cambridge University.

triptych (trip'-tik) *n.* writing-tablet in three parts; altar-piece or picture in three panels, side panels hinged to fold back on centre one.

trireme (trī'-rēm) *n.* Greek or Roman galley or war-vessel with three banks of oars.

trisect (trī-sekt') *v.t.* divide into three equal parts, as line or angle.—**trisec'tion** *n.*

trisyllable (trī- or tri-sil'-ạ-bl) *n.* word of three syllables.—**trisyllab'ic, -al** *a.*—**trisyllab'ically** *adv.*

trite (trīt) *a.* made stale by use; hackneyed; banal.—**trite'ly** *adv.*—**trite'ness** *n.*

triumph (trī'-umf) *n.* victory; conquest; rejoicing; great achievement; —*v.i.* celebrate victory with pomp and ceremony; achieve supremacy; prevail; exult.—**trium'phal** *a.* pert. to triumph; expressing joy for success. —**trium'phant** *a.* rejoicing for victory; successful.—**trium'phantly** *adv.*

triumvir (trī-um'-vir) *n.* one of three men sharing governing power in ancient Rome;—*pl.* **trium'virs**.—**trium'virate** *n.* coalition of three men in office or authority.

trivalent (trī'-vạ-lẹnt) *a.* (*Chem.*) having valency of three; capable of combining with three atoms of hydrogen.—**tri'valence** *n.*

trivet (triv'-et) *n.* three-legged stool, table or support; iron tripod for standing pot or kettle close to fire.

trivial (triv'-i-ạl) *a.* paltry; of little consequence.—**trivial'ity** *n.* state or quality of being trivial; trifle; anything insignificant.—**triv'ially** *adv.*—**triv'ialness** *n.*—**trivia** *n.pl.*

trochee (trō'-kē) *n.* in English prosody, metrical foot of two syllables, first one accented, as *ho'ly*.

trod, trodden *pa.t., pa.p.* of tread.

troglodyte (trog'-lō-dīt) *n.* cave-dweller; kind of ape; hermit.—**trog'lodytism** *n.*

troll (trōl) *n.* in Scandinavian mythology, mischievous hump-backed cave-dwellers.

troll (trōl) *v.t. and i.* roll; fish with baited line trailing behind boat;—*n.* round or catch.—**troll'er** *n.* one who or that which trolls.—**troll'ey, troll'y** *n.* form of truck, body of which can be tilted over; light two-wheeled hand-cart; pulley to connect electric tramcar with overhead wires; low truck running on rails.—**troll'ey-bus** *n.* omnibus with overhead trolley but not running on rails.—**troll'ey-car** *n.* (*U.S.*) electric tramcar.

trollop (trol'-op) *n.* slattern;—*v.i.* draggle; be slovenly.—**troll'opy** *a.*

trombone (trom'-bōn) *n.* deep-toned brass musical instrument. — **trom'bonist** *n.*

troop (trōop) *n.* large assembly of people; body of cavalry; light-horse, or dragoons; command of this; troupe;—*pl.* soldiers collectively; army;—*v.i.* flock; gather in crowd.—**troop'-carri'er** *n.* transport-plane for troops.—**troop'er** *n.* non-commissioned cavalryman; troop-horse; troop-

ship; (*U.S.*) mounted policeman, esp. of Royal Canadian Mounted Police.—**troop'-ship** *n.* vessel for transporting soldiers.—**trooping the colour**, ceremony held at public mounting of garrison-guards.

trope (trōp) *n.* word or phrase used metaphorically.

trophy (trō'-fi) *n.* orig. pile of arms taken from vanquished enemy; memorial of victory; memento; mural decoration, as stag's antlers; prize, esp. for sports, etc.

tropic (trop'-ik) *n.* one of two circles of celestial sphere, situated 23½° N. (*Tropic of Cancer*) and 23½° S. (*Tropic of Capricorn*) of Equator, and marking point reached by sun at greatest declination north and south; one of two corresponding parallels of latitude on terrestrial globe; — *pl.* region (torrid zone) between tropics of Cancer and Capricorn.—**trop'ic, -al** *a.* pert. to or within tropics; (of climate) very hot.

troposphere (trop'-ō-sfēr) *n.* lower layer of atmosphere below stratosphere.

troppo (trop'-pō) *adv.* (*Mus.*) too much.—**non troppo**, moderately.

trot (trot) *v.i.* (of horse) move at sharp pace; (of person) move along fast;—*v.t.* cause to trot;—*pr.p.* **trot'ting**.—*pa.p.* **trot'ted**.—*n.* normal pace of horse; quick walk.—**trot'ter** *n.* one who trots; horse which trots; foot of animal; (*Colloq.*) foot.

troth (troth) *n.* truth; fidelity;—*v.t.* plight.—**to plight one's troth**, become engaged to be married.

trouble (trub'-l) *v.t.* stir up; vex; perplex; (*Colloq.*) bother;—*v.i.* take pains; feel anxiety;—*n.* disturbance; agitation of mind; unrest; ailment; inconvenience.—**troub'ler** *n.*—**troub'lesome** *a.* difficult; vexatious; irksome.—**troub'lesomely** *adv.*—**troub'lesomeness** *n.*—**troub'lous** *a.* disturbed.

trough (trof) *n.* long, open vessel for water or fodder for animals; channel; depression, as between waves; part of cyclone where atmospheric pressure is lowest.

trounce (trouns) *v.t.* beat severely; defeat completely.

troupe (trōop) *n.* company or troop, esp. of actors, acrobats, etc.—**troup'er** *n.* actor or entertainer.

trousers (trou'-zẹrs) *n.pl.* man's two-legged outer garment extending from waist to ankles; slacks.—**trou'sered** *a.* wearing trousers.—**trou'ser-press**, or **-stret'cher** *n.* device for keeping trousers in shape.

trousseau (trōo'-sō) *n.* bride's outfit of clothes.

trout (trout) *n.* fish, resembling salmon but smaller, found in lake, river, and sea.

trowel (trou'-el) *n.* mason's tool for

spreading and dressing mortar; garden tool for scooping out earth, plants, etc.

troy-weight (troi'-wāt) *n.* system of weight for precious metals and gems.

truant (tróó'-ant) *n.* one who wastes time; pupil who absents himself from school;—*a.* wandering from duty; idle;—*v.i.* play truant.—tru'ancy, truant'ship *n.*

truce (tróós) *n.* temporary cessation of hostilities; armistice; lull.

truck (truk) *v.t.* exchange; barter;—*v.i.* deal with by exchange;—*n.* exchange of commodities; (*Colloq.*) rubbish.

truck (truk) *n.* small wooden wheel; open wagon for heavy transport by rail; porter's barrow for heavy luggage; lorry.—truck'age *n.* transport by trucks; cost of such transport.—truck'le *n.* small wheel or castor; truckle-bed; (*Fig.*) fawn on.—truck'le-bed *n.* low bed on castors.

truculent (truk'-ū-lent) *a.* fierce; aggressive;—truc'ulence, truc'ulency *n.*—truc'ulently *adv.*

trudge (truj) *v.t.* go on foot; plod along;—*n.* wearisome walk.

true (tróó) *a.* genuine; exact; loyal; trustworthy;—*v.t.* adjust accurately; straighten;—*adv.* truly; conforming to type (of plants, etc.).—true'-blue *n.* (*Fig.*) person of unquestionable loyalty.—true'ness *n.*—tru'ism *n.* self-evident truth.—tru'ly *adv.*

truffle (truf'-l) *n.* tuber-shaped edible underground fungus.

trug (trug) *n.* mason's hod; gardener's shallow wooden basket.

trull (trul) *n.* drab; trollop.

trump (trump) *n.* trumpet; its sound; Jew's harp.—trump'et *n.* wind instrument of brass, with bell-shaped mouth; powerful reed-stop of pipe-organ;—*v.t.* proclaim by trumpet; bellow; (*Fig.*) praise loudly;—*v.i.* play on trumpet; (of elephant) utter cry through trunk.—trum'pet-call *n.* summons on trumpet; call to action.—trum'peter *n.*—trum'peting *n.*—to blow one's own trumpet, praise oneself.

trump (trump) *n.* one of suit of cards which takes any card of another suit; (*Colloq.*) good-natured fellow;—*v.t.* play trump-card; take trick with trump.—trump'-card *n.* (*Fig.*) best means to desired end.

trump (trump) *n.* impose upon; deceive.—trum'pery *n.* anything showy but of little value; rubbish.—to trump up, concoct.

truncate (trung'-kāt) *v.t.* cut off; lop.—trunc'ate, -d *a.*

truncheon (trun'-shun) *n.* short staff; policeman's baton; baton of office, as of Earl Marshal.

trundle (trun'-dl) *n.* anything capable of being rolled; small wheel or

castor; low truck;—*v.t.* roll on little wheels; bowl, as child's hoop, barrel, etc.;—*v.i.* roll.

trunk (trungk) *n.* stem of tree; body minus head and limbs; torso; shaft of column; main part of anything; main lines of railway, bus, or telephone system; large box with hinged lid, for storage or as luggage;—*pl.* short, tight-fitting pants, esp. for swimming.—trunc'al *a.* pert. to trunk.—trunk'-call *n.* long-distance telephone call.—trunk'-line *n.* main line of railway, bus, telegraph, or telephone system.—trunk'-road *n.* road connecting important centres.

trunk (trungk) *n.* proboscis of elephant.

truss (trus) *n.* bundle, as hay or straw; tuft of flowers on top of long stem; framework of beams constructed to bear heavy loads; (*Med.*) appliance to keep hernia in place;—*v.t.* bind or pack close; support, as bridge-span, with truss; skewer, as fowl, before cooking.—to truss up, tie very firmly.

trust (trust) *n.* confidence; reliance; implicit faith; moral responsibility; property used for benefit of another; combine of business firms in which shareholders turn over stock to board of trustees;—*v.t.* rely upon; have faith in; credit; entrust; hope; believe;—*v.i.* confide in;—*a.* held in trust.—trust'-deed *n.* (*Law*) document conveying property to trustee.—trustee' *n.* person to whom trust is committed.—trustee'ship *n.*—trust'er *n.*—trust'ful *a.* having implicit faith.—trust'fully *adv.*—trust'fulness *n.*—trust'ily *adv.* confidently.—trust'iness *n.*—trust'ing *a.* confiding.—trust'ingly *adv.*—trust'worthiness *n.*—trust'worthy *a.* worthy of trust; reliable.—trust'y *a.* (*comp.* trust'ier *superl.* trust'iest).

truth (tróóth) *n.* honesty; conformity to fact or reality; veracity; true statement.—truth'ful *a.* honest; reliable.—truth'fully *adv.*—truth'fulness *n.*—truth'less *a.*

try (trī) *v.t.* test; attempt; examine judicially; refine, as metals;—*v.i.* endeavour;—*pa.t.* and *pa.p.* tried.—*n.* trial; effort; in Rugby football, points gained when player manages to place ball over back line of opponents; (*Colloq.*) attempt.—tried *a.* proved; afflicted.—tri'er *n.* one who tries.

tryst (trīst) *n.* appointment to meet; place appointed for meeting; fair;—*v.t.* make appointment.—*v.i.* agree on rendezvous.

Tsar (tsár) *n.* same as Czar.

tsetse (tset'-se) *n.* African fly; bite fatal to animals, causing in men *sleeping-sickness.*

tub (tub) *n.* open, wooden vessel used for washing clothes, etc.; small cask;

slow, cumbersome boat;—*v.i.* (*Colloq.*) have bath.—**tub'by** *a.* shaped like tub; (of persons) squat and portly.

uba (tū'-ba) *n.* (*Mus.*) largest brass instrument of orchestra with coiled tube and wide, bell-shaped mouth;—*pl.* tu'bae, tu'bas.

ube (tūb) *n.* long hollow cylinder for conveyance of liquids, gas, etc.; pipe; siphon; *abbrev.* for tube-railway; (*Anat.*) cylindrical-shaped organ; flexible container with screw cap for holding paint, solder, glue, etc.; stem of plant; inner rubber tyre of bicycle or motor-car wheel; (*U.S.*) thermionic valve.—**tu'bing** *n.* act or process of making tubes; length of tube, esp. rubber.—**tu'bular** *a.*, **tu'bulate**, **-d**, **tu'bulous**, **tu'bulose** *a.*—**tu'bule** *n.* small tube.

uber (tū'-ber) *n.* fleshy, rounded underground root, containing buds for new plant, as of *potato*, etc.; (*Med.*) swelling.—**tu'berous**, **tu'berose** *a.* having tubers; knobby.

ubercle (tū'-ber-kl) *n.* small swelling; nodule; (*Med.*) morbid growth, esp. on lung causing *tuberculosis*.—**tu'bercled** *a.*—**tuber'cular**, **tuber'culate**, **-d**, **tuber'culose**, **tuber'culous** *a.*—**tuber'culin** *n.* liquid extract from tubercle bacillus, used in testing for, or in treatment of, tuberculosis.—**tuberculo'sis** *n.* (*Colloq. abbrev.* T.B.) disease caused by infection with tubercle bacillus.—**tuber'culum** *n.* tubercle.

uberose (tū'-be-rōs, or tūb'-rōz) *n.* bulbous plant with creamy-white flower-spikes.

tuck (tuk) *v.t.* make fold(s) in cloth before stitching down; roll up, as sleeves; cram; enclose snugly in bed-clothes;—*n.* flat fold in garment to shorten it, or as ornament; (*Slang*) food, esp. sweets, cakes, etc.

Tuesday (tūz'-dā) *n.* third day of week.

tuft (tuft) *n.* cluster; bunch of something soft, as hair, feathers, etc.; imperial (beard);—*v.t.* adorn with, arrange in tufts.—**tuft'ed** *a.*

tug (tug) *v.t.* pull with effort; haul along; jerk forward;—*v.i.* pull with great effort; comb, as hair, with difficulty;—*pr.p.* tug'ging.—*pa.t.* and *pa.p.* tugged.—*n.* strong pull; tussle; small steamboat used to tow larger vessel.—**tug'-boat** *n.* small but powerful boat used for towing.—**tug'-of-war** *n.* contest in which two teams pull at either end of rope, until losing team is drawn over centre-line.

tuition (tū-ish'-un) *n.* private coaching for examination; teaching.

tulip (tū'-lip) *n.* bulbous plant of order Liliaceae.

tulle (tōōl) *n.* fine silk net used for dresses, etc.

tumble (tum'-bl) *v.i.* fall heavily; trip over; toss from side to side; turn head over heels; perform acrobatic tricks; slump, as prices;—*v.t.* overturn; shoot, as rabbit;—*n.* act of tumbling; toss; somersault.—**tum'ble-down** *a.* ramshackle; derelict.—**tum'bler** *n.* one who tumbles; acrobat; kind of pigeon which appears to perform somersaults when in flight; glass drinking-vessel; spring catch of lock.—**tum'bling** *n.* act of falling or turning somersault.

tumbrel (tum'-brel) **tumbril** (tum'bril) *n.* dung-cart; low open cart in which victims of French Revolutionists were conveyed to guillotine; ducking-stool for scolds.

tumefy (tū'-me-fī) *v.t.* cause to swell;—*v.i.* swell; develop into tumour;—*pa.t.* and *pa.p.* tu'mefied.—**tumefac'tion** *n.* swelling; tumour.

tumid (tū'-mid) *a.* swollen; turgid; pompous.—**tumes'cence** *n.* state of swelling; turgidity.

tumour (tū'-mor) *n.* (*Med.*) morbid, parasitic over-growth of tissue, sometimes accompanied by swelling; cancer.—**tu'morous** *a.*

tumult (tū'-mult) *n.* commotion; violent uproar; mass hysteria; storm.—**tumult'uous** *a.* confused; uproarious; disturbing.—**tumult'uously** *adv.*—**tumult'uousness** *n.*

tumulus (tū'-mū-lus) *n.* artificial burial mound; barrow;—*pl.* tu'muli.—**tu'mular**, **-y**, **tu'mulous** *a.*

tun (tun) *n.* large cask; measure of liquid; vat in brewery;—*v.t.* store in casks.—**tun'nage** *n.* tax formerly levied on imported wine.

tuna (tōō'-na) *n.* prickly pear; tunny-fish.

tundra (tun'-dra) *n.* cold desert; zone north of Arctic Circle.

tune (tūn) *n.* melody; rhythmical arrangement of notes and chords in particular key; quality of being in pitch; temper of mind;—*v.t.* adjust to proper pitch; harmonise; adapt or make efficient; (*Radio*) adjust circuit to give resonance at desired frequency.—**tu'nable** *a.*—**tu'nableness** *n.*—**tu'nably** *adv.*—**tune'ful** *a.* melodious; harmonious.—**tune'fully** *adv.*—**tune'fulness** *n.*—**tune'less** *a.* without melody; discordant; silent.—**tu'ner** *n.*—**tu'ning-fork**, *n.* steel two-pronged instrument giving specified note when struck.—(*Fig.*) out of tune, at variance.—to tune in (*Radio*) adjust receiver to desired wavelength.

tungsten (tung'-sten) *n.* hard grey metallic element used in alloys, special forms of steel, and for filaments in electric lamps.

tunic (tū'-nik) *n.* short-sleeved knee-length garment worn by women and boys in ancient Greece and Rome; girl's dress for gymnastics: jacket of uniform, as worn by soldiers, policemen, etc.

tunnel (tun'-el) n. arched subterranean passage usually as track for railway-line; — v.t. cut tunnel through; excavate;—pr.p. **tunn'elling**,—pa.t. and pa.p. **tunn'elled**.

tunny (tun'-i) n. edible fish of mackerel family found in Mediterranean, larger variety found off coasts of U.S.A.; tuna fish.

turban (tur'-ban) n. Oriental male head-dress comprising long strip of cloth swathed round head or cap; close-fitting cap or scarf head-dress worn by women.

turbid (tur'-bid) a. clouded; muddy; (Fig.) disturbed. — **tur'bidly** adv. — **tur'bidness, turbid'ity** n.

turbine (tur'-bīn or -bin) n. horizontal water-wheel with curved floats on periphery; rotary engine driven by steam, or water striking on curved vanes of wheel, or drum.;—**tur'binal** a. coiled like spiral.—**tur'bo-jet'** n. jet propelled gas turbine aero engine.— **turbo-prop** n. jet engine in which turbine is coupled to propeller.

turbot (tur'-bot) n. large sea-fish.

turbulent (tur'-bū-lent) a. disturbed; in violent commotion; swirling. —**tur'bulence, tur'bulency** n.

tureen (tu-rēn' or tū-rēn) n. large, deep dish with removable cover, for serving soup.

turf (turf) n. surface soil containing matted roots, grass, etc.; sward; sod; peat; race-course;—pl. **turfs, turves**.—v.t. cover with turf, as lawn. —The Turf, horse-racing and betting.

turgid (tur'-jid) a. swollen; (Fig.) bombastic.—**turgid'ity, tur'gidness** n.

Turk (turk) n. native of Turkey; Ottoman; fierce person; Mohammedan.—**Turkey carpet**, wool carpet with brilliant colours and thick pile.— **Turkey red**, brilliant red dye; cotton cloth dyed with this.—**Turkish** a. pert. to Turks or Turkey.—**Turkish bath**, steam or hot air bath after which person is rubbed down, massaged, etc.—**Turkish delight**, soft sweetmeat. — **Turkish towel**, orig. rough surfaced towel; towel of cotton fabric with loops uncut, giving it specially absorbent qualities.—**Turk'oman** n. one of the Turkish race living in C. Asia.

turkey (tur'-ki) n. large, gallinaceous bird, bred for food, esp. at Christmas.

turmeric (tur'-mer-ik) n. E. Indian plant; root of this powdered, and used in dyes, medicines, condiments, curry-powder, etc.

turmoil (tur'-moil) n. commotion; harassing; labour; upset.

turn (turn) v.t. move round; cause to revolve; deflect; form on lathe; apply; convert; upset or nauseate;

—v.i. rotate; hinge; depend; become giddy, nauseated, or upset; (of tide), change from ebb to flow or the reverse; become sour, as milk;—n. act of turning; change of direction, single revolution, as of wheel; bend, action, as good turn; action done in rotation with others; short walk; single performance, as on variety stage; crisis.—**turn'coat** n. renegade —**turn'er** n. one who or that which turns; one who turns things on lathe.—**turn'ing** n. act of turning; deflection; winding; junction of two roads or streets.—**turn'ing-point** n. decisive moment; crisis.—**turn'key** n. one in charge of prison keys; warder —**turn'-out** n. production, as of factory; strike; number of people at any gathering; carriage and horses, driver, etc.—**turn'over** n. total sales made by business in certain period; tart of paste folded over filling of jam, or fruit.—**turn'pike** n. gate across road at point where toll is due —**turn'-stile** n. revolving gate for controlling admission of people.— **turn'-ta'ble** n. revolving circular platform for turning locomotives; revolving plate on which gramophone records are played.—**turn'-up** n. disturbance; domestic upheaval.—**turn about**, alternately.—**to turn down**, decline, as offer; reject, as application. —**to turn in**, bend inwards; hand in; go to bed.—**to turn upon**, attack suddenly; retort. — **to turn one's head**, make one conceited.—**turn the tables on**, reverse conditions.—**turn turtle**, turn upside down.—**in turn**, in sequence.—**on the turn**, at moment of changing as tides.

turnip (tur'-nip) n. plant with large globular root much cultivated for food and cattle-fodder.

turpentine (tur'-pen-tīn) n. oily liquid extracted by distillation of resin exuded by coniferous trees.— (Colloq. abbrev.) **turps**.

turpitude (tur'-pi-tūd) n. revolting baseness.

turquoise (tur'-koiz or -kwoiz) n. bluish-green gem.—**tur'quoise-green** n. pale jade colour.

turret (tur'-et) n. small tower on building; revolving gun-tower on ship, tank, or aircraft; rotating holder for cutting tools on a lathe or for lenses on a camera.—**turr'eted** a.

turtle (tur'-tl) n. marine tortoise with hard shell;—**hawksbill turtle**, yields tortoiseshell,—**green turtle**, is used for soup.—**mock'-tur'tle** n. soup of calf's head with curry flavouring.—**to turn turtle** (Naut. slang) capsize.

turtle (tur'-tl) n. kind of pigeon. Also **tur'tledove**.

tusk (tusk) n. long, protruding side-tooth of certain animals such as elephant, wild boar, walrus.—

tusked *a.*—**tusk'er** *n.* elephant with fully developed tusks.—**tusk'y** *a.*

tusser (tus'-ėr) *n.* silkworm of India; rather coarse fawn-coloured silk fibre spun by tusser; hard-wearing, uneven-textured fawn silk fabric, from this fibre.

tussle (tus'-l) *n.* struggle; scuffle.

tussock (tus'-ok) *n.* tuft, or hillock of grass.

tut (tut) *interj.* irritated sound

tutelage (tū'-te-lăj) *n.* guardianship; state or period of being under this.—**tu'telar, tu'telary** *a.* having protection over person or place.

tutor (tū'-tor) *n.* (*fem.* **tu'toress**) (*Law*) one in charge of minor; private teacher; university lecturer who supervises studies of undergraduates;—*v.t.* teach; prepare another for special examination by private coaching; discipline; have guardianship of.—**tuto'rial** *a.* pert. to tutor;—*n.* extra tuition given by college tutor.—**tuto'rially** *adv.*—**tu'toring** *n.*—**tu'torship** *n.*

tuxedo (tuk-sē'-dō) *n.* (*U.S.*) dinner-jacket.

twaddle (twod'-l) *n.* inane conversation; nonsensical talk;—*v.i.* talk inanely.—**twadd'ler** *n.*

twain (twān) *n.* two; pair.—**in twain**, in two parts; asunder.

twang (twang) *n.* sharp, sound made by tense string sharply plucked; nasalised speech;—*v.t.*

tweak (twēk) *v.t.* twist and pull with sudden jerk; nip sharply;—*n.* sharp pinch.

tweed (twēd) *n.* woollen twilled fabric esp. for costumes, coats, suits;—*a.* of tweed.

tweezers (twēz'-ėrz) *n. sing.* small pair of pincers.

twelve (twelv) *a.* one more than eleven; two and ten; dozen;—*n.* sum of ten and two; symbol representing twelve units, as 12, xii.—**twelfth** *a.* next after eleventh; constituting one of twelve equal parts;—*n.* one of twelve equal parts.—**twelve'-month** *n.* year.—**twelve-tone** *a.* (*Mus.*) of twelve tone scale.

twenty (twen'-ti) *a.* twice ten; nineteen and one;—*n.* number next after nineteen; score; symbol representing twenty units, as 20, xx.—**twen'tieth** *a.* next after nineteenth;—*n.* one of twenty equal parts.

twice (twis) *adv.* two times; doubly.

twiddle (twid'-l) *v.t.* play with; twirl idly;—*v.i.* spin round; trifle with.—**to twiddle one's thumbs**, have nothing to do.

twig (twig) *n.* small shoot or branch of tree.—**twig'gy** *a.* covered with twigs.

twilight (twi'-lit) *n.* half-light preceding sunrise or immediately after sunset; faint, indeterminate light;—*a.* partially illuminated; obscure.

twill (twil) *n.* fabric woven with diagonal ribbing;—*v.t.* weave this.

twin (twin) *n.* one of two born at one birth; exact counterpart;—*a.* twofold; being one of two born at one birth; consisting of two identical parts; growing in pairs.—**twin-set** *n.* woman's matching jumper and cardigan.

twine (twin) *n.* cord composed of two or more strands twisted together; string; tangle;—*v.t.* twist together, as fibres; entwine; encircle;—*v.i.* wind; coil spirally.—**twi'ning** *a.* winding; coiling.

twinge (twinj) *n.* sudden, acute spasm of pain; pang;—*v.t.* effect momentarily with sudden pain.

twinkle (twing'-kl) *v.i.* blink; sparkle; (of eyes) light up; (of feet) move quickly and neatly;—*n.* gleam of amusement in eyes; flicker; quick movement of feet; sparkle.—**twink'ler** *n.*—**twink'ling** *n.* twinkle.

twirl (twirl) *v.t.* whirl round; flourish;—*v.i.* turn round rapidly;—*n.* rapid, rotary motion; flourish.

twist (twist) *v.t.* contort; coil spirally; wind; encircle; distort; form from several fibres wound together;—*v.i.* become tangled; wriggle; be united by winding round each other; coil; follow roundabout course; (*Fig.*) cheat;—*n.* cord; string; coil; single strand of rope; small roll of tobacco.—**twist'ed** *a.*—**twist'er** *n.* one who, or that which, twists; swindler.

twit (twit) *v.t.* taunt; tease.—*pr.p.* **twit'ting**;—*pa.t.* and *pa.p.* **twit'ted**.

twitch (twich) *v.t.* pull suddenly with slight jerk; snatch;—*v.i.* be suddenly jerked; contract with sudden spasm as muscle; quiver;—*n.* sudden spasmodic contraction of fibre or muscle.—**twitch'ing** *n.*

twitter (twit'-ėr) *n.* chirping sound; slight trembling of nerves; half-suppressed laugh;—*v.i.* chirp; talk rapidly and nervously; titter.—**twitt'ering** *n.* agitation.

two (tóó) *a.* one and one;—*n.* sum of one and one; symbol representing two units, as 2, ii; pair.—**two'-edged** *a.* having two sharp edges, as sword; (*Fig.*) ambiguous.—**two'-faced** *a.* having two faces; hypocritical.—**two'-fold** *a.* double; doubly.—**two'-hand'ed** *a.* requiring two hands or two players; ambidextrous.—**two'-ply** *a.* having two strands or two layers.—**two'-sid'ed** *a.* having two surfaces or aspects; (of cloth) reversible;(*Fig.*) double-dealing.—**two'-stroke** *a.* denoting an internal combustion engine making one explosion to every two piston-strokes.

tycoon (ti-kóón') *n.* head of great business combine; magnate.

tympanum (tim'-pạn-um) *n.* drum; (*Anat.*) cavity of middle-ear; eardrum; (*Archit.*) flat, triangular space between sides of pediment; similar space over door between lintel and arch.—*pl.* **tym'pana.**—**tym'panal** *a.* like drum; pert. to middle ear.—**tym'panist** *n.* one who plays drum or any percussion instrument.

type (tīp) *n.* mark or impression of something; model; pattern; person representative of group or of certain quality; (*Biol.*) individual specimen representative of species; (*Print.*) metal block on one end of which is raised letter, etc. required for letterpress printing; such blocks collectively; style or form of printing;—*v.t.* typify; represent in type; reproduce by means of typewriter;—*v.i.* use typewriter.—**type'found'er** *n.* one who casts type for printing.—**type'-script** *n.* typewritten document.—**type'-set'ting** *n.* process or occupation of preparing type for printing.—**type'write** *v.t.* produce by means of typewriter.—**type'writer** *n.* machine with keyboard operated by fingers, which produces printed characters on paper; operator of such machine.—**type'writing** *n.*—**type'-written** *a.*—typic, -al (tip'-ic, -ạl) *a.* pert. to type; symbolic; true to type.—**typical'ity** *n.*—**typ'ically** *adv.*—**typ'icalness, typifica'tion** *n.*—**ty'pifier** *n.*—**typ'ify** *v.t.* represent by image; symbolise; exemplify.—*pa.p.* **typ'ified.**—**typ'ing** *n.* act of typing; script typed.—**typ'ist** *n.* one who operates typewriter.—**typog'rapher** *n.* printer.—**typograph'ic, -al** *a.* pert. to printing.—**typog'raphy** *n.* art of printing; style or mode of printing.

typhoid (tī'-foid) *a.* resembling typhus; pert. to enteric fever;—*n.* infectious disease characterised by severe diarrhoea. Also called *enteric fever.*—**typhoid'al** *n.*

typhoon (tī-fóòn') *n.* cyclonic hurricane occurring in China seas.—**typhon'ic** *a.*

typhus (tī'-fus) *n.* highly contagious disease caused by virus conveyed by body lice.—**ty'phous** *a.*

tyrant (tī'-rạnt) *n.* harsh, despotic ruler; any person enforcing his will on others, cruelly and arbitrarily.—**tyran'nic, -al, tyrannous** (tir'-ạn-us) *a.*—**tyran'nically** *adv.*—**tyr'annously** *adv.*—**tyran'nicalness** *n.*—**tyr'annise** *v.i.* exert authority ruthlessly;—*v.t.* subject to tyrannical authority.—**tyranny** (tir'-ạ-ni) *n.* despotic government; cruelly harsh enforcement of authority.

tzigane (tsig-à'-ni) *n.* Hungarian gipsy.

U

U *a.* (*Slang*) as used by the upper classes or in the best circles; elegant; fashionable.

ubiquity (û-bik'-wi-ti) *n.* existing in all places at same time; omnipresence.—**ubiq'uitous** *a.* being everywhere.—**ubiq'uitously** *adv.*—**ubiq'uitousness** *n.* omnipresence.

udder (ud'-ẹr) *n.* milk-gland of certain animals, as cow.

ugh! (uh) *interj.* exclamation of disgust.

ugly (ug'-li) *a.* offensive to sight; of disagreeable aspect; dangerous, (of *situation*).—**ug'liness** *n.*

ukulele (û-kŏŏ-lā'-li) *n.* small four-stringed instrument like guitar.

ulcer (ul'-sẹr) *n.* superficial sore discharging pus; (*Fig.*) source of corruption.—**ul'cerate** *v.i.* suppurate.—**ul'cerated** *a.*—**ulcera'tion** *n.* state of discharging pus.—**ul'cered** *a.* having ulcers.—**ul'cerous** *a.* pert. to ulcer.

ullage (ul'-āj) *n.* amount which cask lacks of being full.—**ull'ing.**

ulna (ul'-nạ) *n.* inner and larger of two bones of forearm.—*pl.* **ul'nae.**—**ul'nar** *a.*

ulster (ul'-stẹr) *n.* long loose overcoat or mackintosh usually with hood.

ulterior (ul-tē'-ri-or) *a.* situated on farther side; beyond; (of *motives*) undisclosed; not frankly stated.

ultimate (ul'-ti-mẹt) *a.* farthest; final; primary; conclusive.—**ul'timately** *adv.*—**ultima'tum** *n.* final proposition; final terms offered as basis of treaty.—*pl.* **ultima'tums, or ultima'ta.**—**ul'timo** *a.* in month preceding current one (*abbrev.* **ult.**).

ultra (ul'-trạ) *a.* beyond; extreme; in combination words with or without hyphen.

ultramarine (ul-trạ-mạ-rēn') *a.* situated beyond sea;—*n.* bright-blue pigment.

ultramontane (ul-trạ-mon'-tān) *a.* being beyond mountains, esp. Alps; —*n.* advocate of extreme or ultrapapal views.—**ultramon'tanism** *n.*—**ultramon'tanist** *n.*

ultrasonics (ul-trạ-son'-iks) *n.* science of mechanical vibrations of frequencies greater than those normally audible to ear.

ultra-violet (ul-trạ'-vī-o-let) *a.* beyond limit of visibility at violet end of spectrum.

ululant (ûl'-û-lạnt) *a.* howling; hooting.—**ul'ulate** *v.i.* howl; hoot.—**ulula'tion** *n.*

umbel (um'-bẹl) *n.* (*Bot.*) flowercluster, stalks of which rise from common centre on main stem.

umber (um'-ber) *n.* natural earth pigment, yellowish-brown in colour when *raw*, reddish-brown when calcined or *burnt*.

umbilic. -al (um-bil'-ik, -al) *a.* pert. to umbilicus or navel.—**umbilic'ular** *a.* pert. to navel.—**umbilical cord** (*Anat.*) fibrous cord joining foetus to placenta.

umbra (um'-bra) *n.* shadow; (*Astron.*) complete shadow cast by earth or moon in eclipse.—**um'bral** *a.*

umbrage (um'-brāj) *n.* shadow; (*Fig.*) feeling of resentment.—**umbra'geous** *a.* shady.—**to take umbrage,** feel resentful.

umbrella (um-brel'-a) *n.* circular covering of silk or other material on framework of spokes, carried as protection against rain.—**umbrell'a-stand** *n.* stand for holding umbrellas.

umpire (um'-pīr) *n.* person chosen to arbitrate in dispute; person chosen to see that rules of game are properly enforced; referee.

umpteen (ump'-tēn) *a.* (*Slang*) innumerable.

un- *prefix* before nouns, adjectives, and adverbs, adding negative force; before verbs, expressing reversal of action.

unabashed (un-a-basht') *a.* unashamed.

unabated (un-a-bā'-ted) *a.* not diminished; fully maintained.

unabridged (un-a-brijd') *a.* not shortened; (of text) in full.

unaccented (un-ak-sent'-ed) *a.* not accented; unstressed.—**unaccent'uated** *a.* not accented.

unaccommodating (un-a-kom'-ō-dāt-ing) *a.* not compliant; disobliging.

unaccompanied (un-a-kum'-pa-nid) *a.* not accompanied; sung or played on instrument without piano, organ, or orchestral accompaniment.

unaccountable (un-a-kount'-able) *a.* inexplicable.

unadorned (un-a-dornd') *a.* not adorned; plain; void of ornament.

unadulterate, -d (un-a-dul'-te-rāt) *a.* not adulterated; pure.

unaffected (un-a-fekt'-ed) *a.* not affected; unmoved; straightforward; sincere.—**un'affect'edly** *adv.* simply; void of affectation.

unalloyed (un-a-loid') *a.* not alloyed; pure; (*Fig.*) complete; unqualified.

unalterable (un-awl'-ter-a-bl) *a.* not capable of alteration; fixed; permanent.—**unalterabil'ity, unal'terableness** *n.*—**unal'terably** *adv.*—**unal'tered** *a.* unchanged.

unanimous (ū-nan'-i-mus) *a.* all of one mind; agreed to by all parties.—**unanim'ity** *n.* state of being unanimous.—**unan'imously** *adv.*

unanswerable (un-an'-ser-a-bl) *a.* not answerable; irrefutable; conclusive.—**unanswerabil'ity, unan'swerableness** *n.*

unappreciated (un-a-prē'-shi-ā-ted) *a.* not appreciated; not valued.—**unappre'ciative** *a.* not appreciative; lacking in gratitude.

unapproachable (un-a-prōch'-a-bl) not approachable; inaccessible; (of person) having aloof manner.—**unapproach'ableness** *n.*

unarm (un-arm') *v.t.* disarm; render harmless;—*v.i.* lay down arms.—**unarmed'** *a.* defenceless.—**unar'moured** *a.* (of ships, etc.) not protected by armour-plating.

unashamed (un-a-shāmd') *a.* not ashamed; unabashed; brazen.

unassailable (un-a-sāl'-a-bl) *a.* not assailable; irrefutable; invincible.—**unassailed'** *a.*

unassimilated (un-a-sim'-i-lā-ted) *a.* not assimilated.—**unassim'ilable** *a.* not capable of mixing thoroughly.—**unassim'ilating** *a.*

unattached (un-a-tachd') *a.* not attached; dangling; not posted to particular regiment.

unattested (un-a-test'-ed) *a.* not attested; unsupported by evidence of witness.

unavailing (un-a-vāl'-ing) *a.* not availing; fruitless; having no result.—**unavailabil'ity** *n.*—**unavail'able** *a.* not procurable; not at one's disposal.—**unavail'ingly** *adv.* fruitlessly.

unavoidable (un-a-void'-a-bl) *a.* not avoidable; inevitable; inescapable; incapable of being made null and void.—**unavoid'ableness** *n.*—**unavoid'ably** *adv.*—**unavoid'ed** *a.*

unaware (un-a-wār') *a.* having no information.—*adv.* unawares.—**unawares'** *adv.* unexpectedly; without previous warning.

unbalance (un-bal'-ans) *v.t.* upset; unhinge.—**unbal'anced** *a.* not balanced; lacking equipoise, or mental stability; not adjusted or equal on credit and debit sides (of ledger).—**unbal'ance, imbalance** *n.*

unbearable (un-bār'-a-bl) *a.* not bearable; intolerable; (of pain) excruciating.—**unbear'ableness** *n.*—**unbear'ably** *adv.*

unbecoming (un-bē-kum'-ing) *a.* not becoming; not suited to wearer; (of behaviour) indecorous.—**unbecom'ingly** *adv.*—**unbecom'ingness** *n.*

unbeknown (un-bē-nōn') *a.* unknown.—**unbeknownst'** *adv.* without knowledge of.

unbelief (un-bē-lēf') *n.* scepticism.—**unbelievabil'ity** *n.*—**unbeliev'able** *a.*—**unbelieved'** *a.*—**unbeliev'er** *n.* sceptic.—**unbeliev'ing** *a.* not believing in divine revelation.—**unbeliev'ingly** *adv.*

unbend (un-bend') *v.t.* free from bent position; straighten; relax; loose, as anchor;—*v.i.* become relaxed; become more friendly.—**unbend'ing** *a.*

not pliable; rigid; (*Fig.*) coldly aloof; resolute.—**unbend'ingly** *adv.*—**unbent'** *a.* straight.

unbias (un-bī'-as) *v.t.* rid of prejudice. —**unbi'as(s)ed** *a.* unprejudiced; impartial.

unblemished (un-blem'-isht) *a.* not blemished; faultless; (of character) pure; perfect.

unbodied (un-bod'-id) *a.* freed from body; incorporeal.

unbolt (un-bōlt') *v.t.* withdraw bolt from; unfasten.—'-ed *a.* unfastened.

unbolted (un-bōlt'-ed) *a.* (of grain) unsifted; not having bran separated by bolter.

unborn (un-born') *a.* not yet born.

unbosom (un-bóóz'-um) *v.t.* disclose freely; reveal intimate feelings.

unbound (un-bound') *a.* not bound; free; without outer binding, as book. —**unbound'ed** *a.* abundant; irrepressible.—**edly** *adv.*—**edness** *n.*

unbowed (un-boud') *a.* not bowed; invincible.

unbridle (un-brī'-dl) *v.t.* remove bridle from, as horse.—**unbri'dled** *a.* unrestrained; violently passionate.

unbroken (un-brō'-kn) *a.* complete; whole; (of horse) untamed;inviolate; continuous.

unburden (un-bur'-dn) *v.t.* relieve of burden; (*Fig.*) relieve mind of anxiety.—**unbur'dened** *a.*

uncalled (un-kawld') *a.* not summoned.—**uncalled for,** superfluous; gratuitous.

uncanny (un-kan'-i) *a.* weird; unearthly; frightening—**uncann'ily** *adv.* —**uncann'iness** *n.*

unceasing (un-sēs'-ing) *a.* not ceasing; continual;—**unceas'ingly** *adv.*

unceremonious (un-ser-e-mōn'-i-us) *a.* not ceremonious; informal; abrupt.—**unceremon'iously** *adv.*—**unceremon'iousness** *n.*

uncertain (un-ser'-ten) *a.* not certain; not positively known; unreliable; insecure.—**uncer'tainly** *adv.* —**uncer'tainness** *n.*—**uncer'tainty** *n.* state of being or that which is uncertain; lack of reassurance.

uncharted (un-chär'-ted) *a.* not shown on map; unexplored.

unchristian (un-kris'-tyan) *a.* not Christian; contrary to principles of Christianity; pagan; not humanitarian.—**unchris'tianly** *adv.*

uncial (un'-shal) *a.* pert. to type of script, found in ancient MSS;—*n.* uncial letter or manuscript.—**un'cialise** *v.t.* form like uncials.

unciform (un'-si-form) *a.* shaped like hook.—**un'cinal**, **un'cinate** *a.* hooked.

uncircumcised (un-sir'-kum-sīzd) *a.* not circumcised; Gentile; (*Fig.*) unregenerate.

uncivil (un-siv'-il) *a.* not civil; rude. —**uncivilised'** *a.* barbarous.—**unciv'illy** *adv.* discourteously.

unclassified (un-clas'-if-īd) *a.* not classified; not secret or confidential of roads, minor.

uncle (ung'-kl) *n.* brother of one's father or mother; any elderly man; (*Slang*) pawnbroker.—**Uncle Sam** (*Fig.*) United States of America; typical American citizen.

unclean (un-klēn') *a.* not clean; filthy; ceremonially unsanctified; obscene.—**uncleanliness** *n.* (un-klen'-li-nes). — **uncleanly** (un-klēn'-li or -klen'-li) *adv.*—**unclean'ness** *n.*

uncock (un-kok') *v.t.* let down hammer of gun without exploding charge.

uncommitted (un-kom-it'-ed) *a.* not pledged to support any particular faction or theory; not under obligation.

uncommunicative (un-ko-mū'-ni-kā'-tiv) *a.* not communicative; discreet; taciturn.—**uncommu'nicable** *a.* not capable of being shared or communicated.—**uncommu'nicableness** *n.* —**uncommu'nicated** *a.*

uncompromising (un-kom-prō-mī'-zing) *a.* not compromising; making no concession; rigid.—**uncom'promisingly** *adv.*

unconcern (un-kon-sern') *n.* lack of concern; apathy.—**unconcerned'** *a.* not concerned; disinterested; apathetic; not involved.—**unconcer'nedly** *adv.*—**edness** *n.*

unconditioned (un-kon-dish'-und) *a.* not subject to conditions; absolute; instinctive.—**uncondi'tional** *a.* complete; absolute; without reservation. —**uncondi'tionally** *adv.*

unconscious (un-kon-shus) *a.* insensible;—*n.* (*Psych.*) that part of mind inaccessible to will.

uncongenial (un-kon-jē'-ni-al) *a.* not congenial; temperamentally disagreeable. — **uncongenial'ity** *n.* — **uncon'genially** *adv.*

unconnected (un-kon-ek'-ted) *a.* not connected; disjointed; incoherent; unrelated.

unconscionable (un-kon'-shun-a-bl) *a.* beyond reason; unscrupulous; excessive.—**uncon'scionableness** *n.*—**uncon'scionably** *adv.*

unconstitutional (un-kon-sti-tū'-shun-al) *a.* not constitutional; contrary to constitution, as of society or state.—**unconstitutional'ity** *n.*—**unconstitu'tionally** *adv.*

unconstrained (un-kon-strānd') *a.* not constrained; not embarrassed; voluntary.—**unconstrain'edly** *adv.*—**unconstraint'** *n.*

unconventional (un-kon-ven'-shun-al) *a.* not conventional; original; bohemian. — **unconventional'ity** *n.* — **unconven'tionally** *adv.*

unconverted (un-kon-ver'-ted) *a.* not converted; unchanged in heart; heathen; not changed in opinion;

(*Rugby*) of try, not converted into goal.—**unconver'tible** *a.*

uncouth (un-kóóth') *a.* awkward in manner; strange; unpolished;—**un couth'ly** *adv.*—**uncouth'ness** *n.*

uncover (un-kuv'-ẹr) *v.t.* remove cover of; expose to view; leave un protected;—*v.i.* take off one's hat.

unction (ungk'-shun) *n.* act of anointing with oil, as in ceremony of consecration or coronation; anoint ing dying, according to last rites administered by R.C. Church; (*Med.*) ointment; act of applying ointment; unguent; (*Fig.*) that which soothes; insincere emotion; gush.—**unctuos'ity** *n.* quality or state of being unctuous.—**unc'tuous** *a.* oily; (*Fig.*) excessively suave.— **unc'tuously** *adv.*—**unc'tuousness** *n.*— **extreme unction**, R.C. rite of anoint ing the dying.

uncultivable (un-kul'-tiv-ạ-bl) *a.* not capable of being cultivated; waste.—**uncul'tivated** *a.* not cul tivated; not tilled; (*Fig.*) un developed.—**uncul'tured** *a.* not cul tured; not educated.

uncurb (un-kurb') *v.t.* free from curb. —**uncurbed'** *a.* not curbed; un restrained.

undamped (un-dampt') *a.* not damp ed; dry; (*Fig.*) not downhearted or dispirited.

undaunted (un-dawn'-ted) *a.* not daunted; fearless; intrepid.—**un daun'tedly** *adv.*

undeceive (un-de-sēv') *v.t.* free from deception or illusion.—**undeceived'** *a.*

undecided (un-dē-sī'-ded) *a.* not settled; irresolute; vacillating.— **undeci'dable** *a.* not capable of being settled.—**undeci'dedly** *adv.*

undecipherable (un-dē-sī'-fẹr-ạ-bl) *a.* impossible to decipher; illegible.

undeclared (un-dē'-klârd') *a.* not declared; (of taxable goods at customs) not admitted as being in one's possession during customs' examination.

undefined (un-dẹ-fīnd') *a.* not de fined; vague; not made clear by definition.—**undefin'able** *a.* not cap able of being defined.

undeniable (un-de-nī'-ạ-bl) *a.* not capable of being refuted or denied; certain; obvious.—**undeni'ably** *adv.* palpably; certainly.

under (un'-dẹr) *prep.* below; be neath; subjected to; less than; liable to; included in; in care of; during period of; bound by;—*adv.* in a lower degree or position; less; —*a.* subordinate; lower in rank or degree.—**under age**, younger than 21 years.—**under arms**, mobilised for active service.—**under fire**, exposed to enemy assault.—**under one's breath**, in whisper.

underact (un-dẹr-akt') *v.t.* or *v.i.* act

in play in colourless, ineffective way.

underbid (un-dẹr-bid') *v.t.* bid price less than real value of article; sell goods more cheaply than another; make lower bid at bridge than cards justify.

underbred (un-dẹr-bred') *a.* of inferior manners; vulgar.

underbrush (un'-dẹr-brush) *n.* under growth of shrubs and bushes.

undercarriage (un'-dẹr-kar-ij) *n.* (*Aviat.*) landing-gear of aircraft.

undercharge (un-dẹr-chárj') *v.t.* charge less than true price.

underclothes (un'-dẹr-klōTHz) *n. pl.* garments worn below outer clothing, esp. next skin; underclothing; lingerie.—**un'derclothing** *n.*

undercurrent (un'-dẹr-kur-ẹnt) *n.* current under surface of main stream, sometimes flowing in con trary direction; (*Fig.*) hidden ten dency;—*a.* hidden.

undercut (un-dẹr-kut') *v.t.* cut away from below, as coal seam; strike from beneath; sell goods cheaply to capture market or monopoly;—*a.* produced by cutting away from below.—**un'dercut** *n.* meat on under side of sirloin; (*Boxing*) punch from underneath.

underdo (un-dẹr-dóó') *v.t.* cook insufficiently. — **underdone'** *a.* not sufficiently cooked; rave.

underdog (un'-dẹr-dog) *n.* (*Fig.*) person who fares badly in struggle.

underdose (un-dẹr-dōs') *v.t.* give insufficient dose (of medicine) to.— **un'derdose** *n.* insufficient dose.

underestimate (un-dẹr-es'-ti-māt) *v.t.* miscalculate value of; rate at too low figure;—*n.* inadequate valua tion. Also **underestimation**.

underfeed (un-dẹr-fēd') *v.t.* provide insufficient food; undernourish.—**un derfed'** *a.*

underfelt (un'-dẹr-felt) *n.* felt laid underneath carpet.

underfoot (un-dẹr-fóót') *adv.* be neath feet; (*Fig.*) in subjection.

undergarment (un'-dẹr-gár-mẹnt) *n.* garment worn underneath outer clothes.

undergo (un-dẹr-gō') *v.t.* bear; suffer; participate in.—*pr.p.* **undergo'ing**.— *pa.t.* **underwent'**.—*pa.p.* **undergone'**.

undergraduate (un-dẹr-grad'-ū-ẹt) *n.* student attending classes for first degree at university.

underground (un'-dẹr-ground) *a.* below ground; subterranean; (*Fig.*) secret;—*n.* underground railway system; subway; (*Fig.*) secret organ isation or resistance movement.— **underground'** *adv.* below surface of earth; (*Fig.*) secretly.

undergrowth (un'-dẹr-grōth) *n.* small trees, shrubs, or plants growing beside taller trees.

underhand (un'-dẹr-hand) *adv.* by

secret means; fraudulently; (*Tennis*) served or played with racquet kept below waist-level; secretly; clandestine; slyly.—**underhan'ded** *a.* secret.

underived (un-dē-rīvd') *a.* not derived; original; natural.

underlay (un-dẹr-lā') *v.t.* lay underneath; support by something put below;—*v.i.* incline from perpendicular;—*n.* floor covering laid underneath carpet.

underlie (un-dẹr-lī') *v.t.* lie beneath; (*Fig.*) be basis of.—**underly'ing** *a.*

underline (un-dẹr-līn') *v.t.* mark with line below, for emphasis; emphasise. (*Fig.*) inference.

underling (un'-dẹr-ling) *n.* one who holds inferior position; subordinate member of staff;.weakling.

underman (un-dẹr-man') *v.t.* supply, as ship, with too small a crew; employ too small a staff, for work on hand.—**undermanned'** *a.*

undermentioned (un'-dẹr-men-shund) *a.* referred to below or later in text.

undermine (un-dẹr-mīn') *v.t.* excavate for purpose of mining, blasting, etc.; erode; (*Fig.*) sap, as one's energy; weaken insidiously, as another's faith.

underneath (un-dẹr-nēth') *adv.* and *prep.* beneath; below; in lower place.

undernourished (un-dẹr-nur'-ishd) *a.* insufficiently nourished.

underpay (un-dẹr-pā') *v.t.* pay inadequately for work done; exploit. —**underpay'ment** *n.*

underpin (un-dẹr-pin') *v.t.* support or reconstruct lower part of structure without affecting upper part.

underproof (un'-dẹr-próóf) *a.* containing less alcohol than proof-spirit.

underrate (un-dẹr-rāt') *v.t.* rate too low; underestimate.—**un'derrate** *n.* price lower than real value.

under-secretary (un'-dẹr-sek'-re-tạ-ri) *n.* assistant-secretary, esp. of Government department. — Parliamentary Under-Secretary, M.P. acting as secretary to Minister with portfolio. — Permanent Under-Secretary, Civil Servant who is head of State department.

undersell (un-dẹr-sel')*v.t.* sell cheaper than another.—**undersell'er** *n.*

undershot (un'-dẹr-shot) *a.* (of mill-wheel) turned by water flowing under; (of lower jaw) projecting.

undersign (un-dẹr-sīn') *v.t.* write one's name at foot of or underneath; subscribe.—**undersigned'** *a.* and *n.*

underskirt (un'-dẹr-skẹrt) *n.* petticoat.

understand (un-dẹr-stand') *v.t.* comprehend; grasp significance of.

understate (un-dẹr-stāt') *v.t.* state less strongly than truth warrants; minimise.—**un'derstatement** *n.*

understudy (un'-dẹr-stud-i) *n.* actor

ready to deputise for principal actor (or actress) at moment's notice; —*v.t.* study theatrical part for this purpose.

undertake (un-dẹr-tāk') *v.t.* take upon oneself as special duty; embark on; agree (to do); warrant;—*v.i.* be under obligation to act for another; make arrangements for burial.—*pa.t.* undertook'.—*pa.p.* underta'ken.—**underta'ker** *n.* contractor; one who manages burial.—**un'dertaking** *n.* project; guarantee.

undertone (un'-dẹr-tōn) *n.* low, subdued tone of voice or colour; (*Fig.*) inference.

undertow (un'-dẹr-tō) *n.* undercurrent of wave after it has reached shore.

undervalue (un-dẹr-val'-ū) *v.t.* set too low a price on; esteem lightly;—*n.* underestimate.—**un'dervalua'tion** *n.*

underwear (un'-dẹr-wār) *n.* underclothes.

underwent (un-dẹr-went') *pa.t.* of undergo'.

underwork (un-dẹr-wurk') *v.t.* (*Fig.*) undermine; contrive secretly;—*v.i.* do less work than is due; slack.— *pa.t.* and *pa.p.* un'derworked, un'derwrought.—**un'derwork** *n.* inadequate labour; slacking; subordinate task.

underworld (un'-dẹr-wurld) *n.* nether regions; Hades; antipodes; section of community which lives by vice and crime.

underwrite (un-dẹr-rīt') *v.t.* write under something else; subscribe; append one's signature to insurance policy (esp. marine insurance) whereby one guarantees to compensate for loss or damage on payment of certain premium per cent; undertake to buy shares not bought by public, and thereby guarantee success of issue of business capital.—*pr.p.* underwri'ting.—*pa.t.* underwrote'.—*pa.p.* underwrit'ten.—**un'derwriter** *n.*

undeserved (un-de-zẹrvd') *a.* not merited; unwarranted.—**undeser'ving** *a.* not deserving; unworthy.—**undeser'vingly** *adv.*

undesirable (un-dē-zīr'-ạ-bl) *a.* not desirable; having no appreciable virtues;—*n.* person of ill-repute.— undesirabil'ity, undesir'ableness *n.*— undesir'ably *adv.*

undetermined (un-de-tẹr'-mind) *a.* not determined; undecided.—**undeter'minable** *a.*—**undeter'minate** *a.* indeterminate; vague.

undeterred (un-de-tẹrd') *a.* not deterred.

undeveloped (un-de-vel'-opt) *a.* immature; (of land) not yet exploited; potential not fully realised.

undeviating (un-dē'-vi-ā-ting) *a.* not deviating; resolute in pursuing a straight course.

undiscriminating (un-dis-krim'-inā-ting) a. not discriminating; not critical.

ndisposed (un-dis-pōzd') a. not disposed; disinclined; not sold off or distributed.

ndisputed (un-dis-pū'-ted) a. not disputed; unchallenged. — **undispu'table** a. indisputable.—**undispu'tableness** n.—**undispu'tedly** adv.

ndo (un-dóó') v.t. reverse what has been done; loose; unfasten.—pa.t. undid'.—pa.p. **undone'.—undo'er** n.—**undo'ing** n. act of reversing what has been done; ruin, esp. of reputation. —**undone'** a. ruined.

ndomesticate (un-dō-mes'-ti-kāt) v.t. make unfit for domestic life; allow to revert to wild state.—**undomes'ticated** a. untamed; not fond of housework.

ndoubted (un-dout'-ed) a. not doubted; certain; genuine.—**undoubt'able** a. unquestionable.—**undoubt'ably** adv. — **undoubt'edly** adv. without doubt; certainly.

ndress (un-dres') v.t. divest of clothes or covering; remove dressing from wound.—v.i. take off (one's) clothes.—**un'dress** n. and a. informal dress; off-duty military uniform.—**undressed'** a.

ndue (un-dū') a. not in accordance with what is due or proper; immoderate; not befitting occasion.

ndulate (un'-dū-lāt) v.t. move up and down like waves; cause to vibrate;—v.i. move up and down; vibrate; have wavy edge;—a. wavy. —**un'dulant** a. undulating; wavy.—**un'dulately** adv.—**un'dulating** a. wavy; having series of rounded ridges and depressions, as surface of landscape. —**un'dulatingly** adv.—**undula'tion** n. wave; fluctuating motion, as of waves; wave-like contour of stretch of land; series of wavy lines; vibratory motion.—**un'dulatory** a. pert. to undulation; moving like wave; pert. to theory of light which argues that light is transmitted through ether by wave motions.

nduly (un-dū'-li) adv. in undue manner; immoderately; improperly.

ndying (un-dī'-ing) a. not dying; immortal.

nearned (un-ernd') a. not earned by personal labour.—**unearned income**, income derived from sources other than salary, fees, etc.

nearth (un-erth') v.t. dig up; drive as fox, rabbit, etc. from burrow; (Fig.) bring to light.—**unearth'liness** n.—**unearth'ly** a. not of this world; supernatural.

neasy (un-ē'-zi) a. not at ease; worried; uncomfortable.—**uneas'iness** n. restlessness; constraint; anxiety. —**uneas'ily** adv.

neconomic (un-ek-on-om'-ik) a. not economic; not in accordance with principles of economics.—**uneconom'ical** a. not economical; wasteful; thriftless.

unemployed (un-em-ploid') a. not employed; out of work.—**unemploy'able** a. not capable of being employed.—**unemploy'ment** n. state of being unemployed.

unending (un-en'-ding) a. never-ending; infinite; incessant.—**unend'ed** a.—**ingly** adv.

unenlightened (un-en-līt'-nd) a. not enlightened; living in state of intellectual or spiritual darkness.

unequal (un-ē'-kwal) a. not equal; not of the same length, weight, etc.; ill-assorted or ill-balanced.—**une'qualled** a. not matched; peerless.—**une'qually** adv.—**une'qualness** n.

unequivocal (un-ē-kwiv'-ō-kal) a. not equivocal; undoubted; unambiguous; plain.

uneven (un-ē'-vn) a. not even; rough; not of equal length or quality; not divisible by two without remainder; odd.—**une'venly** adv.—**une'venness** n.

unexceptionable (un-ek-sep'-shun-a-bl) a. without exception; irreproachable; perfect.—**unexcep'tional** a. not exceptional; usual.

unexpected (un-eks-pek'-ted) a. not expected; sudden; without warning.

unfadable (un-fā'-da-bl) a. not liable to fade; imperishable.—**unfa'ded** a. not faded; fresh.—**unfa'ding** a. (Fig.) ever-lasting.

unfailing (un-fā'-ling) a. not liable to fail; ever loyal; inexhaustible.—**unfail'ingly** adv.

unfair (un-fār') a. unjust; prejudiced. —**unfair'ly** adv.—**unfair'ness** n.

unfaithful (un-fāth'-fóól) a. not faithful; disloyal; inaccurate or misleading.

unfamiliar (un-fa-mil'-yar) a. not familiar; strange; not experienced in or acquainted with.—**unfamil'iarity** n.—**unfamil'iarly** adv.

unfashionable (un-fash'-un-a-bl) a. not fashionable; dowdy.—**unfash'-ionableness** n.—**unfash'ionably** adv.—**unfash'ioned** a. not moulded or fashioned.

unfathomable (un-fath'-om-a-bl) a. not fathomable; not capable of being plumbed; (Fig.) inexplicable. — **unfath'omableness** n. — **unfath'omably** adv.—**unfath'omed** a. unplumbed; bottomless; not solved.

unfeeling (un-fēl'-ing) a. void of feeling; callous; unsympathetic.—**unfeel'ingly** adv.

unfeigned (un-fānd') a. not feigned; genuine; sincere.—**unfeign'edly** adv. —**unfeign'edness** n.

unfetter (un-fet'-er) v.t. remove fetters from; set free.—**unfett'ered** a.

unfilial (un-fil'-yal) a. not proper in son or daughter; disrespectful.

unfit (un-fit') a. not fit; unqualified; improper; not adapted for;—v.t. disqualify.—**unfit'ly** adv.—**unfit'ness** n.—**unfit'ting** a.—**unfit'tingly** adv.

unflinching (un-flin'-shing) a. not flinching; resolute; steadfast.—**unflin'chingly** adv.

unfold (un-fōld') v.t. open folds of; spread out; (Fig.) disclose;—v.i. expand.—**unfold'er** n.—**unfold'ing** n.

unfortunate (un-for'-tū-net) a. not fortunate; ill-timed; unsuccessful.— n. prostitute.—**unfor'tunately** adv.— **unfor'tunateness** n.

unfrequented (un-frē-kwen'-ted) a. not frequented; seldom visited.— **unfre'quent** a. not frequent; happening seldom.

unfrock (un-frok') v.t. deprive of frock, esp. deprive of status of monk or priest.—**unfrocked'** a.

unfunded (un-fun'-ded) a. not funded; having no permanent funds for payment of interest; floating.— **unfunded debt**, that portion of international debt which represents war debts.

unfurl (un-furl') v.t. loose from furled state, as flag; unfold; expand; —v.i. be spread out.

ungainly (un-gān'-li) a. clumsy; awkward;—adv. in clumsy manner.— **ungain'liness** n.

ungarnished (un-gar'-nisht) a. not garnished; without decoration.

unglaze (un-glāz') v.t. remove glass from.—**unglazed'** a. not fitted with glass; (of pottery) fired without glaze.

ungodly (un-god'-li) a. not godly; profane.—**ungod'liness** n. state of being ungodly; wickedness.

ungovernable (un-guv'-er-na-bl) a. uncontrolled; incapable of restraint. —**ungov'ernableness** n.—**ungov'ernably** adv.—**ungov'erned** a. not governed; unbridled.

ungracious (un-grā'-shus) a. lacking in courtesy; not kindly.—**ungrace'-fully** adv.—**ungrace'fulness** n.—**ungra'-ciously** adv.—**ungrace'ful** a. not graceful; gawky.

ungrudging (un-gruj'-ing) a. not grudging; generous.—**ungrudged'** a. not stinted.—**ungrudg'ingly** adv.

ungual (ung'-gwal) a. having nails, hooves, or claws.—**ung'ulate** a. having hoofs.

unguarded (ungar'-ded) a. not guarded; careless; indiscreet.—**unguar'dedly** adv.

unguent (ung'-gwent) n. ointment. —**ung'uentary** a. pert. to unguents. —**unguen'tous** a. resembling an unguent.—**ung'uinous** a. oily.

unhallowed (un-hal'-ōd) n. not hallowed; profane; wicked.—**unhall'owing** n.

unhand (un-hand') v.t. let go.— **unhand'ily** adv. awkwardly.—**unhand'-**iness n.—**unhand'led** a. not handle— —**unhand'y** a. not handy; incovenient; lacking skill.

unhappy (un-hap'-i) a. not happy miserable; out of place; tactless.— **unhapp'ily** adv.—**unhapp'iness** n.

unhealthy (un-hel'-thi) a. not health or hygienic; habitually weak or il not wholesome.—**unhealth'ful** a.— **unhealth'fully** adv.—**unhealth'ily** ad —**unhealth'iness** n.

unheard (un-herd') a. not heard; no given hearing.—**unheard of**, unpre cedented.

unhesitating (un-hez'-i-tā-ting) (not hesitating; spontaneous; resol ute.—**unhesita'tingly** adv. withou hesitation.

unhinge (un-hinj') v.t. take fron hinges; (Fig.) cause mental in stability.—**unhinged'** a. (of mind unstable; distraught.

unholy (un-hō'-li) a. not holy; pro fane; polluted; (Colloq.) frightful.— **unho'lily** adv.—**unho'liness** n. qualit of being unholy

unhorse (un-hors') v.t. throw fron horse; cause fall from horse.

unhygienic (un-hī-jen'-ik) a. no hygienic; insanitary; unhealthy.

uni-, (ū'-ni) prefix. one or single.

uniaxial (ū-ni-ak'-si-al) a. havin single axis; having one directio along which ray of light can trave without bifurcation.

unicellular (ū-ni-sel'-ū-lar) a. havin single cell; monocellular.

unicorn (ū'-ni-korn) n. fabulou animal with horse's body and singl horn protruding from foreheac team of three horses, with tw abreast, and one in front.

uniform (ū'-ni-form) a. havin always same form; conforming t one pattern; regular; consistent not varying;—n. official dress, etc —**u'niformed** a. wearing uniform.— **uniform'ity** n. conformity to pattern or standard.—**u'niformly** adv. – **u'niformness** n.

unify (ū'-ni-fī) v.t. make into one make uniform.—**u'nifiable** a. capabl of being made one.—**unifica'tion** n state of being made one; weldin together of separate parts.

unilateral (ū-ni-lat'-e-ral) a. one sided; binding one side only, as in party agreement.—**unilateral'ity** n.— **unilat'erally** adv.

unimaginable (un-i-maj'-i-na-bl) a not imaginable; inconceivable.— **unimag'inableness** n.—**unimag'inabl** adv.—**unimag'inative** a. not imagina tive; dull; uninspired.—**unimag'in** atively adv.—**unimag'inativeness** n.

unimpaired (un-im-pārd') a. no impaired; not weakened; undam aged; unspoiled.

unimpeachable (un-im-pē'-cha-bl a. not impeachable; irreproachable blameless.—unimpeachabil'ity, unimpeach'ableness n.—unimpeach'ably adv.—unimpeached' a.

uninformed (un-in-formd') a. having no accurate information; ignorant; not expert.

uninhabitable (un-in-hab'-i-ta-bl) a. not inhabitable; not fit for living in.—uninhabitabil'ity, uninhab'itableness n.—uninhab'ited a. having no inhabitants; desert.

unintelligent (un-in-tel'-i-jent) a. not intelligent; mentally dull.—unintell'igence n.—unintell'igently adv.—unintelligibil'ity n.—unintell'igible a. not intelligible; not capable of being comprehended.—unintell'igibleness n.—unintell'igibly adv.

unintentional (un-in-ten'-shun-al) a. not intentional; accidental; involuntary.—uninten'tionally adv.

uninterested (un-in'-ter-es-ted) a. not interested.—unin'teresting a. not interesting.—unin'terestingly adv.

union (ūn'-yun) n. act of joining two or more things into one; federation; marriage; harmony; combination; trade-union; pipe-connection;—un'ioned a. joined.—un'ionist n. one who supports union.—Union Jack, national flag of United Kingdom, consisting of crosses of St. George, St. Andrew and St. Patrick.

unique (ū-nēk') a. single in kind; having no like or equal; peerless.—unique'ly adv.—unique'ness n.

unisexual (ū-ni-sek'-sū-al) a. of one sex only, as plant; not hermaphrodite or bisexual.

unison (ū'-ni-son) n. harmony; concord; (Mus.) identity of pitch.—in unison, with all voices singing same notes or notes with interval of octave; (Fig.) in agreement.

unit (ū'-nit) n. single thing or person; group regarded as one; standard of measurement; (Math.) least whole number.—u'nitary a. pert. to unit(s); whole.—unit trust, fund, supervised by a trustee, used to buy stocks and shares, individuals sharing in the results in proportion to the number of 'units' they have bought.

Unitarian (ū-ni-tā'-ri-an) n. one who rejects doctrine of Trinity and asserts oneness of God.—Unita'rianism n.

unite (ū-nīt') v.t. join; make into one; form whole; associate; cause to adhere;—v.i. be joined together; grow together; act as one; harmonise.—uni'ted a. joined together; harmonious; unanimous.—uni'tedly adv.—uni'ter n.—u'nity n. state of oneness; agreement; (Math.) any quantity taken as one.—United Nations Organ-isation, organisation of peace-loving states set up after World War 2 with Security Council as chief executive body.—popular abbrev.

UNO.—United States, federal union of states, as U.S.A.

univalve (ū'-ni-valv) a. having one valve;—n. single-celled mollusc.—unival'vular a.

universe (ū'-ni-vers) n. all created things regarded as system or whole world.—univer'sal a. pert.to universe; embracing all created things; worldwide; general (as opp. of particular); total;—n. universal proposition; general concept.— univer'salise v.t. make universal.—universal'ity n.—univer'sally adv.—univer'salness n.

university (ū-ni-ver'-si-ti) n. institution for educating students in higher branches of learning, and having authority to confer degrees; members of university collectively.

univocal (ū-niv'-ō-kal) a. having one meaning only; unequivocal; sure; (Mus.) having unison in sounds;—n. word with one meaning.

unjust (un-just') a. not just; partial; biassed; dishonest.—unjustifi'able a.—unjustifi'ably adv.—unjust'ly adv. unfairly.—unjust'ness n.

unkempt (un-kemt') a. dishevelled; rough.

unkind (un-kīnd') a. lacking in kindness; cruel; callous.—unkind'liness n. lack of kindliness.—unkind'ly a. not kindly; harsh;—adv. cruelly; in manner contrary to nature.—unkind'ness n. lack of kindness.

unknowable (un-nō'-a-bl) a. not capable of being known;—n. that which is beyond man's power to understand; absolute.—unknow'ableness n.—unknow'ably adv.—unknow'ing a. ignorant.—unknow'ingly adv.—unknown' a. incalculable;—n. unknown quantity; part of globe as yet unvisited by man.

unlawful (un-law'-fool) a. not lawful; illicit.—unlaw'fully adv. illegally.—unlaw'fulness n.

unleavened (un-lev'-nd) a. not leavened; made without yeast, as unleavened bread.

unless (un-les') conj. except; if not.

unlettered (un-let'-erd) a. illiterate.

unlicensed (un-lī'-senst) a. not licensed; having no permit to sell certain commodities, as tobacco, wine. etc.

unlike (un-līk') a. dissimilar;—prep. different from;—adv. in different way from.—unlike'lihood, unlike'ness n.—unlike'ly a. improbable;—adv. improbably.—unlike'liness n.

unload (un-lōd') v.t. remove load from; remove charge from, as gun; sell out quickly; (Fig.) unburden, as one's mind;—v.i. discharge cargo.—unload'ed a. not containing charge, as gun; not containing plate or film, as camera.

unlovable (un-luv-a-bl) a. not lovable; disagreeable; unattractive.—

unloved' *a.* not loved.—**unlove'liness** *n.* lack of loveliness; ugliness.—**unlove'ly** *a.* not lovely; repellent.—**unlov'ing** *a.* not loving; cold.

unlucky (un-luk'-i) *a.* not lucky; unfortunate; inauspicious; inopportune.—**unluck'ily** *adv.*

unmake (un-māk') *v.t.* destroy what has been made; annul.—**unmade'** *a.*—**unmak'able** *a.*—**unmak'ing** *n.*

unman (un-man') *v.t.* deprive of manly courage.—**unman'like** *a.* not manlike.—**unman'liness** *n.*—**unman'ly** *a.* cowardly; effeminate.

unmannerly (un-man'-er-li) *a.* not polite; ill-bred.—**unmann'ered** *a.* discourteous.—**unmann'erliness** *n.*

unmarried (un-mar'-id) *a.* not married; single.—**unmarr'iageable** *a.* not fit to marry; under age to marry without parents' consent.—**unmarr'iageableness** *n.*

unmeaning (un-mēn'-ing) *a.* without meaning; unintentional; insignificant.—**unmean'ingly** *adv.*—**unmeant** (un-ment') *a.* not intended.

unmeasured (un-mezh'-ūrd) *a.* not measured; limitless; not stinted.—**unmeas'urable** *a.*—**unmeas'urableness** *n.*—**unmeas'urably** *adv.*

unmentionable (un-men'-shun-a-bl) *a.* not worthy of mention; not fit to be mentioned.—**unmen'tionableness** *n.*

unmindful (un-mīn'-ful) *a.* forgetful; regardless.—**unmind'fully** *adv.*—**unmind'fulness** *n.*

unmistakable (un-mis-tā'-ka-bl) *a.* not mistakable; recognisable; well-defined.—**unmista'kableness** *n.*—**unmista'kably** *adv.*

unmounted (un-moun'-ted) *a.* not mounted; on foot; (of gem) unset; (of picture) not framed or pasted on cardboard.

unmoved (un-mŏŏvd') *a.* not moved; calm; not stirred emotionally.—**unmov'able**, **unmove'able** *a.* incapable of being moved, physically, or emotionally.—**unmov'ably** *adv.*—**unmov'edly** *adv.*—**unmov'ing** *a.*

unmusical (un-mū'-zi-kal) *a.* not musical; discordant; not fond of, or unskilled in, music.

unnatural (un-nat'-ū-ral) *a.* not natural; not in accordance with usual course of events; not composed; abnormal.—**unnat'uralise** *v.t.*—**unnat'uralised** *a.* not naturalised; alien.—**unnat'urally** *adv.*

unnavigable (un-nav'-i-ga-bl) *a.* not navigable.—**unnavigabil'ity** *n.*—**unnav'igated** *a.* not sailed over; uncharted.

unnerve (un-nerv') *v.t.* cause someone to lose nerve; undermine courage of.—**unnerved'** *a.* afraid; deprived of nerve.

Uno (ū'-nō) *n.* a coined word from initial letters of *United Nations Organisation.*

unobtrusive (un-ob-trŏŏ'-siv) *a.* not obtrusive; unassuming.—**unobtrus'ively** *adv.*—**unobtrus'iveness** *n.*

unoccupied (un-ok'-ū-pīd) *a.* not occupied; untenanted; not engaged in work; not under control of troops.

unopposed (un-o-pōzd') *a.* not opposed; having no rival candidate in election.

unorthodox (un-or'-thō-doks) *a.* not orthodox.—**unorth'odoxy** *n.* heresy.

unostentatious (un-os-ten-tā'-shus) *a.* not ostentatious; not showy; modest.—**unostenta'tiously** *adv.* unobtrusively.

unpalatable (un-pal'-a-ta-bl) *a.* not palatable; disagreeable; unpleasant.

unparalleled (un-par'-a-leld) *a.* having no equal; unprecedented.

unparliamentary (un-pár-li-men'-ta-ri) *a.* not in accordance with Parliamentary procedure; not fit for usage in Parliament.—**unparliament'ary language**, abuse.

unperturbed (un-per-turbd') *a.* not perturbed; unruffled.

unpick (un-pik') *v.t.* unfasten; undo stitching of.—**unpicked'** *a.*

unpolished (un-pol'-isht) *a.* not polished; rough; (*Fig.*) uncouth.

unprecedented (un-pres-e-den'-ted) *a.* without precedent; having no earlier example.—**unprec'edently** *adv.*

unpremeditated (un-prē-med'-i-tā-ted) *a.* not premeditated; unplanned; spontaneous.—**unpremed'itable** *a.*—**unpremed'itatedly** *adv.*—**unpremed'itatedness**, **unpremedita'tion** *n.*

unprepossessing (un-prē-pō-zes'-ing) *a.* not prepossessing; not attractive.—**unprepossessed'** *a.* impartial; not prejudiced.

unprintable (un-prin'-ta-bl) *a.* not printable; too shocking to be set down in print.

unproductive (un-prō-duk'-tiv) *a.* not productive; barren; not profitable.—**unprodu'ctively** *adv.*—**unprodu'ctiveness** *n.*

unprofessional (un-prō-fesh'-un-al) *a.* not in accordance with professional etiquette.—**unprofes'sionally** *adv.*

unprofitable (un-prof'-i-ta-bl) *a.* not profitable; disadvantageous.—**unprof'itableness** *n.*—**unprof'itably** *adv.*

unqualified (un-kwol'-i-fīd) *a.* not qualified; not having proper qualifications; not modified; absolute.—**unqual'ifiedness** *n.*

unquestionable (un-kwes'-tyun-a-bl) *a.* not questionable; certain.—**unques'tionabil'ity**, **unques'tionableness** *n.*—**unques'tionably** *adv.*—**unques'tioned** *a.* not questioned; not disputed.—**unques'tioning** *a.* unhesitating.

unravel (un-rav'-el) *v.t.* disentangle; separate; solve, as mystery;—*v.i.* be disentangled.—**unrav'elment** *n.*

unread (un-red') *a.* not perused; (of persons) ignorant.—**unreadable** (unrēd'-ạ-bl) a. illegible; (of books) not attractive as reading matter; dull.—**unread'ableness** n.

unreal (un-rēl') a. not real; insubstantial; illusive.—**unrealis'able** n. not realisable.—**unrealis'ableness** n.—**unrealised'** a. not realised; unfulfilled.—**unreal'ity** n. want of reality.—**unre'ally** adv.

unreasonable (un-rē'-zn-ạ-bl) a. not reasonable; immoderate; (of prices) exorbitant.—**unrea'son** n. want of reason.—**unrea'sonableness** n.—**unrea'sonably** adv.—**unrea'soned** a. not thought out logically.—**unrea'soning** a. irrational.

unrecognised (un-rek'-og-nīzd) a. not recognised; denied due honour.—**unrecogis'able** a. not recognisable.—**is'ably** adv.

unrelated (un-rē-lā'-ted) a. not related; having no apparent connection; diverse.—**unrel'ative** a. not relative.

unrelenting (un-rē-len'-ting) a. adamant; inflexible; merciless.—**unrelen'tingly** adv.

unremitting (un-rē-mit'-ing) a. relaxing; incessant; persistent.—**unremit'ted** a. not remitted.—**unremit'tedly**, **unremit'tingly** adv.—**unremit'tingness** n.

unrest (un-rest') n. want of rest; disquiet; political or social agitation.—**unrest'ful** a.—**unrest'fulness** n.—**unrest'ing** a. not resting.

unrestricted (un-rē-strik'-ted) a. not restricted; decontrolled.—**unrestric'tedly** adv.

unrighteous (un-rī'-tyus) a. not righteous; evil; unjust; contrary to law and equity.—**unright'eously** adv.—**unright'eousness** n.—**unright'ful** a.—**unright'fully** adv.—**fulness** n.

unruffled (un-ruf'-ld) a. not ruffled; placid.—**unruf'fle** v.i. become placid.

unruled (un-rōōld') a. not ruled; ungoverned; (of paper) blank; unrestrained.—**unrul'iness** n. state of being unruly.—**unrul'y** a. lawless; disobedient.

unsavoury (un-sā'-vor-i) a. not savoury; tasteless; (Fig.) disgusting.

unsay (un-sā') v.t. retract.

unscathed (un-skāTHt') a. unharmed.

unscramble (un-skram'-bl) v.t. decode secret message.

unscripted (un-skrip'-tēd) a. not in the script; impromptu.

unscrupulous (un-skrōō'-pū-lus) a. not scrupulous; ruthless; having no moral principles.—**unscru'pulously** adv.—**unscru'pulousness** n.

unseasonable (un-sē-zn-ạ-bl) a. not seasonable; inopportune; abnormal for time of year, as of weather.—**unsea'sonableness** n. — **unsea'sonably** adv.—**unsea'soned** a. not matured; not flavoured with seasoning.

unseat (un-sēt') v.t. throw from horse; deprive of Parliamentary seat.

unseemliness (un-sēm'-li-nes) n. state or quality of being unseemly.—**unseem'ly** a. not seemly; indecorous; unbecoming.

unseen (un-sēn') a. not seen; invisible;—n. an unprepared passage for translation in language examination.

unsettle (un-set'-l) v.t. move or loosen from fixed position; disturb mind; make restless or discontented.—**unset'tled** a. not settled; changeable, as weather; unpaid, as bills; not allocated; not inhabited.—**unsett'ledly** adv.—**unsett'ledness**, **unsett'lement** n.—**unsett'ling** a. disturbing.

unship (un-ship') v.t. remove from ship; unload; remove from place where it is fitted.—**unship'ment** n.

unshod (un-shod') a. barefoot.

unsighted (un-sī'-ted) a. not sighted; not observed; having view obstructed; (of shot) aimed blindly.—**unsight'able** a. invisible.—**unsight'liness** n. ugliness.—**unsight'ly** a. ugly.

unskilful (un-skil'-fōōl) a. not skilful; not expert; awkward.—**unskil'fully** adv.—**unskil'fulness** n. lack of skill or experience.—**unskilled'** a. untrained.

unsociable (un-sō'-shạ-bl) a. not sociable; over-reserved in society; unfriendly. — **unsociabil'ity**, **unso'ciableness** n.—**unso'ciably** adv.—**unso'cial** a. not social.

unsolicited (un-sō-lis-i-ted) a. not solicited; gratuitous.—**unsolic'itous** a. not solicitous.

unsophisticated (uk-sō-fis'-ti-kā-ted) a. not sophisticated; ingenuous; simple; unadulterated.—**unsophis'tic-atedly** adv.—**unsophis'ticatedness**, **unsophistica'tion** n.

unsound (un-sound') a. imperfect; damaged; decayed; (of mind) insane; not based on logical reasoning; fallacious. — **unsound'ly** adv. — **unsound'ness** n.

unspeakable (un-spēk'-ạ-bl) a. beyond utterance or description (in good or bad sense); ineffable.—**unspeak'ably** adv.

unspoiled (un-spoilt') a. not spoiled; unblemished; ingenuous. Also **unspoilt'**.

unsporting (un-spor'-ting) a. (Colloq.) not like sportsman; unfair.—**unsports'manlike** a. not in accordance with rules of fair play.

unstop (un-stop') v.t. open by removing stopper, as bottle; clear away obstruction.—**unstopped'** a. not stopped; having no cork or stopper.

unstuck (un-stuk') a. not glued together.—**to come unstuck** (Colloq.) come to grief.

unsullied (un-sul'-id) a. not sullied; unblemished; not disgraced.

unsung (un-sung') a. not sung; not

honoured in poetry; not praised publicly.

unsupported (un-su-pōr'-ted) a. not supported; without backing.—**unsuppor'table** a. not supportable; intolerable.—**unsuppor'tably** adv.—**unsuppor'tableness** n.

unthinkable (un-thingk'-a-bl) a. not capable of being contemplated; (Colloq.) highly improbable.—**unthink'ing** a. not thinking; heedless.—**unthinking'ly** adv.

until (un-til') prep. till; to; as far as; as late as;—conj. up to the time that.

untimely (un-tīm'-li) a. not timely; inopportune.—**untime'liness** n.

untiring (un-tīr'-ing) a. not tiring; indefatigable.—**untir'able** a. incapable of being tired out.—**untired'** a. untir'ingly adv.

unto (un'-tóó) prep. to.

untouchable (un-tuch'-a-bl) a. incapable of being touched; unfit to be touched; unassailable; belonging to non-caste masses of India;—n. noncaste Indian.—**untouchabil'ity** n.—**untouched'** a. not touched.

untoward (un-tō'-ard) a. awkward; inconvenient; unlucky.

untravelled (un-trav'-eld) a. not having travelled; unexplored; provincially-minded.

untried (un-trīd') a. not experienced; not tested; not having undergone trial by law.

untrue (un-tróó') a. not true; false; disloyal; not conforming to requisite standard. — **untrue'ness** n. — **untru'ly** adv. falsely.—**untruth'** n.—**untruth'ful** a. dishonest; lying.—**untruth'fully** adv.—**untruth'fulness** n.

untutored (un-tū'-terd) a. untaught; ignorant.

unused (un-ūzd') a. not used; not accustomed.—**unu'sual** a. not usual; uncommon; extraordinary; out of the way.—**unu'sually** adv.

unutterable (un-ut'-er-a-bl) a. unspeakable; beyond utterance; thorough-going.—**unutterabil'ity**, unutt'erableness n.—**unutt'erably** adv.—**unutt'ered** a. unspoken.

unvarnished (un-vár'-nisht) a. not varnished; plain; straightforward.

unveil (un-vāl') v.t. remove veil from; perform in public act of uncovering newly erected statue; (Fig.) disclose;—v.i. become unveiled.

unwarrantable (un-wor'-an-ta-bl) a. not justifiable; improper.—**unwarrantabil'ity**, unwarr'antableness n.—unwarr'antably adv.—**unwarr'anted** a. unauthorised; not carrying guarantee.—**unwarr'antedly** adv.

unwept (un-wept') a. not mourned.

unwholesome (un-hōl'-sum) a. not wholesome; unhealthy; morally decadent. — **unwhole'somely** adv. — **unwhole'someness** n.

unwieldy (un-wēl'-di) a. awkward to handle or move; bulky; difficult to manage.—**unwiel'dily** adv.—**unwiel'diness** n.

unwilling (un-wil'-ing) a. not willing; reluctant; disobliging.—**unwilled'** a. spontaneous.—**unwill'ingly** adv.—**unwill'ingness** n.

unwind (un-wīnd') v.t. wind off; loose what has been wound; roll into ball from skein, as wool, silk, etc.;—v.i. become unwound.

unwitting (un-wit'-ing) a. unawares; not knowing.—**unwitt'ingly** adv.

unwonted (un-wŏn' (or won') -ted) a. unaccustomed; unusual.—**unwon'tedly** adv.—**unwon'tedness** n.

unwordly (un-world'-li) a. not worldly; spiritual; not actuated by self-interest.—**unworld'liness** n.

unwritten (un-rit'-n) a. oral; not expressed in writing.

unyielding (un-yēl'-ding) a. not yielding; stubborn; implacable; not flexible. — **unyiel'ding** adv. — **unyiel'dingness** n.

up (up) adv. higher place; aloft; on high; on one's legs; out of bed; above horizon; in progress; in revolt; as far as; of equal merit; thoroughly; (Colloq.) well versed in; competent.

upas (ū'-pas) n. tree of E. Indian islands, yielding sap of deadly poisonous properties; antiar tree.

upbraid (up-brād') v.t. reprove severely; chide;—v.i. voice reproach.—**upbraid'ing** n. reproach;—a. reproachful.

upbringing (up'-bring-ing) n. process of rearing and training child; education.

up-country (up'-kun-tri) adv. inland;—a. away from sea.

upgrade (up-grad') v.t. promote; improve status of.

upheave (up-hēv') v.t. lift up, as heavy weight.—**upheav'al** n. raising up, as of earth's surface, by volcanic force; (Fig.) revolutionary change in ideas, etc.

uphill (up'-hill) a. going up; laborious; difficult;—adv. towards higher level.

uphold (up-hōld') v.t. hold up; sustain; approve; maintain, as verdict in law court.—**uphold'er** n.

upholsterer (up-hōl'-ster-er) n. one who supplies furniture, curtains, carpets, etc.; one who upholsters chairs, etc.—**uphol'ster** v.t. stuff and cover furniture.—**uphol'stery** n. craft of stuffing and covering furniture, etc.; materials used.

upkeep (up'-kēp) n. maintenance; money required for maintenance, as of home.

upland (up'-land) n. high land;—a. pert. to or situated in higher elevations district.—**up'lander** n.

uplift (up-lift') v.t. lift up; draw money out of bank.—**up'lift** n. upheaval; (*Fig.*) emotional or religious stimulus.

up-line (up'-līn) *n.* railway line leading from provinces to main terminus.

upmost (up'-mōst) *a.* uppermost.

upon (up-on') *prep.* on.

upper (up'-ėr) *a.* (comp. of up) higher in place, rank, or dignity; superior. —*superl.* up'permost, up'most.—*n.* upper part of boot or shoe.—**up'per-case** *n.* (*Print.*) case containing capital letters, reference marks, etc. —**up'per-cut** *n.* (*Boxing*) blow struck upwards inside opponent's guard;— —**up'per-hand** *n.* superiority; advantage.—**up'permost** *a.* highest.—**up'pish** *a.* arrogant; affectedly superior. —**up'pishly** *adv.*—**up'pishness** *n.*

uprise (up-rīz') *v.i.* rise up.—**upri'sing** *n.* act of rising; insurrection; revolt.

uproar (up'-rōr) *n.* tumult; violent, noisy disturbance.—**uproar'ious** *a.* making noise and tumult; rowdy.— **uproar'iously** *adv.*—**uproar'iousness** *n.*

upset (up-set') *v.t.* turn upside down; knock over; defeat; (*Fig.*) disturb or distress.—**up'set** *n.* overturn; overthrow; confusion;—*a.* fixed.—**upset price**, lowest price at which goods will be sold.

upshot (up'-shot) *n.* final issue; conclusion.

upside (up'-sīd) *n.* upper side.— **up'side-down** *adv.* with upper side underneath; inverted; in disorder.

upstairs (up-stārz') *adv.* in upper storey.—**up'stairs** *a.* pert. to upper floor.

upstanding (up-stand'-ing) *a.* (of man, etc.) well set-up; erect.

upstart (up'-stárt) *n.* one who has suddenly risen to wealth, power, or honour; parvenu;—*a.* arrogant;— *v.i.* rise suddenly.

upstream (up'-strēm) *adv.* in direction of source (of stream).

upstroke (up'-strōk) *n.* upward line in handwriting; upward stroke.

upsurge (up-surj') *v.i.* surge upwards.—**upsurge** *n.* welling, as of emotion.

upturn (up-turn') *v.t.* turn up.—**up'turn** *n.* disturbance.—**up'turning** *n.*

upward (up'-wḁrd) *a.* directed towards higher place;—*adv.* upwards. —**up'wards, up'wardly** *adv.* towards higher elevation.

uranium (ū-rā'-ni-um) *n.* white radioactive metallic element (symbol U), used in nuclear fission.—**uran'ic** *a.* **u'ranous** *a.*

urban (ur'-bḁn) *a.* pert. to, or living in, city or town.—**urbane'** *a.* refined; suave; courteous.—**urbane'ly** *adv.*— **urban'ity** *n.* politeness.—**urbanise'** *v.t.* make urban; bring town conditions and advantages to rural areas.

urchin (ur'-chin) *n.* hedgehog; sea-urchin; goblin; mischievous child.

ureter (ū-rē'-tėr) *n.* one of two ducts of kidney conveying urine to bladder.—**ure'thra** *n.* duct by which urine passes from bladder.—*pl.* **ure'thrae.—ure'thral** *a.*

urge (urj) *v.t.* press; drive; exhort; solicit earnestly;—*v.i.* press onward; —*n.* act of urging; incentive; irresistible impulse. — **ur'gency** *n.* compelling necessity; importunity. —**ur'gent** *a.* calling for immediate attention.—**ur'gently** *adv.*;—**ur'ger** *n.*

urine (ū'-rin) *n.* yellowish fluid secreted by kidneys, passed through ureters to bladder.—**u'rie** *a.* pert. to or produced from urine.—**u'rinal** *n.* vessel into which urine may be discharged; public lavatory.—**u'rinary** *a.* pert. to urine.—**u'rinate** *v.i.* pass urine.—**urina'tion** *n.*

urn (urn) *n.* vase-shaped vessel of pottery or metal for ashes of dead after cremation; vessel of various forms usually fitted with tap, for liquid in bulk.—**urn'al** *a.*

us (us) *pron.* *pl.* objective form of we.

use (ūz) *v.t.* make use of; employ; consume; practise habitually; accustom; treat;—*v.i.* be accustomed (only in past tense).—**use** (ūs) *n.* act of using or employing for specific purpose; utility; custom.—**u'sable** *a.* fit for use.—**u'sableness** *n.*—**u'sage** *n.* mode of using; treatment; long-established custom. — **u'sance** *n.* usage; usury; usual time allowed for payment of foreign bills of exchange. —**use'ful** *a.* of use; handy; profitable; serviceable; (*Colloq.*) influential.— **use'fully** *adv.*—**use'fulness** *n.*—**use'less** *a.* of no use; inefficient; futile.— **use'lessly** *adv.*—**use'lessness** *n.*—**u'ser** *n.* one who uses anything.

usher (ush'-ėr) *n.* doorkeeper, esp. in court of law; one who conducts wedding guests to seats in church; official who introduces strangers or walks before person of rank; (*Arch.*) assistant-master in school;—*v.t.* introduce; inaugurate; show into room and announce name (of visitor).—**usherette'** *n.* girl employed, as in cinema, to show patrons to seats.—**to usher in**, precede.

usquebaugh (us'-kwe-baw) *n.* whisky.

usual (ūzh-ū-ḁl) *a.* customary; ordinary.—**u'sually** *adv.*—**u'sualness** *n.*

usurp (ū-zurp') *v.t.* take possession of unlawfully or by force.—**usurpa'tion** *n.* act of usurping; violent seizing of power.

usury (ū'-zhū-ri) *n.* orig. business of lending money with interest; charging of exorbitant interest on money lent.—**u'surer** *n.* money-lender, esp. one who charges high rates of interest. —**usu'rious** *a.*—**usu'riously** *adv.*

utensil (ū-ten'-sil) *n.* vessel of any

kind which forms part of everyday domestic equipment.

uterine (ū'-tẽr-in) *a.* pert. to uterus or womb; born of same mother but by different father.

utilise (ū'-ti-līz) *v.t.* make useful; turn to profit.—u'tilisable *a.*—utilisa'tion *n.*—u'tiliser *n.*—util'ity *n.*

utilitarian (ū-til-i-tā'ri-an) *a.* pert. to utility or utilitarianism; of practical use.—Utilita'rian *n.* one who accepts doctrines of Utilitarianism.—Utilita'rianism *n.* doctrine, ultimate aim of all human actions must be 'greatest happiness for greatest number.'

utmost (ut'-mōst) *a.* situated at farthest point or extremity; to highest degree;—*n.* most that can be; greatest possible effort.

utopia (ū-tō'pi-a) *n.* any ideal state, constitution, system, or way of life.—uto'pian *a.* ideally perfect but impracticable; visionary.

utter (ut'-ẽr) *a.* farthest out; extreme; total; unconditional.—utt'erly *adv.*—utt'erness *n.*

utter (ut'-ẽr) *v.t.* speak; disclose; put into circulation.—utt'erable *a.* capable of being uttered or pronounced.—utt'erableness *n.*—utt'erance *n.* act of speaking; manner of delivering speech; pronunciation.—utt'erer *n.*

uttermost (ut'-ẽr-mōst) *a.* farthest out; utmost;—*n.* highest degree

uvula (ū'-vū-la) *n.* fleshy tag suspended from lower border of soft palate.—u'vular *a.*

uxorious (uk-sō'-ri-us) *a.* foolishly or excessively fond of one's wife.—uxo'rial *a.* pert. to wife.—uxo'riously *adv.*—uxo'riousness *n.*

V

vacant (vā'-kant) *a.* empty; void; not occupied; disengaged; unintelligent.—va'cantly *adv.*—va'cancy *n.* emptiness; idleness; listlessness; want of thought; place or post, unfilled.—vacate (va-kāt') *v.t.* leave empty; quit possession of; make void.—vaca'tion *n.* act of vacating; recess; holidays.—vaca'tional *a.*

vaccine (vak'-sin, vak'-sēn) *a.* pert. to, or obtained from, cows;—*n.* virus of cowpox, used in vaccination; any substance used for inoculation against disease.—vac'cinate *v.t.* inoculate with cowpox.—vaccina'tion *n.* act or practice of vaccinating.

vacillate (vas'-i-lāt) *v.i.* move to and fro; waver; be unsteady.—vac'illant, vac'illating *a.*—vac'illatory *a.*—vac'illancy *n.*—vacilla'tion *n.*

vacuous (vak'-ū-us) *a.* empty; vacant; expressionless; unintelligent.—vacuity (va-kū'-i-ti) *n.* emptiness;

empty space; lack of intelligence.—vac'uum *n.* space devoid of al matter; space from which air, o other gas, has been almost wholly removed, as by air-pump.—vac'uumclean'er *n.* apparatus for removing dust by suction.—vac'uum-flask *n* double-walled flask for keeping con tents at temperature at which they were inserted.

vagabond (vag'-a-bond) *a.* wandering;—*n.* wanderer or vagrant, having no settled habitation; idle scamp; rascal.—vag'abondage *n.* state or condition of vagabond.

vagary (va-gā'-ri) *n.* whimsical or freakish notion; unaccountable proceeding; caprice.

vagina (va-jī'-na) *n.* (*Anat.*) canal which joins uterus and external orifice.—vagi'nal *a.*

vagrant (vā'-grant) *a.* wandering from place to place; moving without certain direction; roving;—*n.* idle wanderer; vagabond.

vague (vāg) *a.* uncertain; indefinite; indistinct; imprecise.—vague'ly *adv.*—vague'ness *n.*

vain (vān) *a.* useless; unavailing; fruitless; empty; worthless; unsatisfying; conceited; silly; showy.—vain'ly *adv.*—vanity (van'-i-ti) *n.* empty pleasure; futility; conceit.

vainglory (vān-glō'-ri) *n.* excessive vanity; boastfulness.—vainglo'rious *a.* due to vanity; boastful; vaunting.—vainglo'riously *adv.*

valance (val'-ans) *n.* hanging drapery for window, bed, couch, etc. esp. that for hiding space beneath bed.

vale (vāl) *n.* valley.

valediction (val-e-dik'-shun) *n.* farewell; bidding farewell.—valedic'tory *a.* bidding farewell; suitable for leave-taking.

valence, valency (vā'-lens, vā'-lensi) *n.* (*Chem.*) combining power of element or atom as compared with hydrogen atom.

valentine (val'-en-tīn) *n.* affectionate letter or card sent to one of opposite sex on *St. Valentine's Day*, 14th Feb.; person to whom this is sent.

valerian (val-ēr'-i-an) *n.* flowering herb with strong odour; its root, used as sedative drug.

valet (val'-et, val'-ā) *n.* man-servant who attends on gentleman.

valetudinarian (val-e-tū-di-nā'-ri-an) *a.* sickly; infirm; solicitous about one's own health;—*n.* person of sickly constitution; person disposed to live life of invalid.—valetudina'rianism *n.*—valetu'dinary *a.*

valiant (val'-yant) *a.* brave; heroic; courageous; intrepid.—val'iantly *adv.*—val'iantness *n.*—val'iance *n.* courage.

valid (val'-id) *a.* strong; sound or well-grounded; capable of being justified; (*Law*) legally sound.—

al'idly adv.—val'idate v.t. ratify.—val'idness n.—valid'ity n.

lise (vạ-lēs') n. small travelling-ag.

lley (val'-i) n. low ground between lls; river-basin.

lour (val'-or) n. bravery; prowess war; courage; intrepidity.—al'orous a. brave; fearless.—val'or-usly adv.—val'orousness n.

lue (val'-ū) n. worth; utility; nportance; precise signification; quivalent;—v.t. estimate worth of; old in respect and admiration; rize.—val'uer n.—val'ueless a.—al'uable a. precious; worth good rice; worthy;—n. thing of value enerally (pl.).—val'uableness n.—al'uate v.t. set value on.—valua'tion . value set upon thing, esp. by rofessional valuer.—val'uator n.

lve (valv) n. device for regulat-ng flow (as in tube) so arranged as allow passage in one direction, nd prevent it in other; (Anat.) tructure (as in blood-vessel) which llows flow of fluid in one direction nly; (Radio) device allowing urrent to flow in one direction nly, thermionic tube used as recti-er, etc.; (Mus.) device in certain nstruments (as horn, trumpet, etc.) or changing fundamental tone by efinite interval.—val'vular a.

mp (vamp) n. upper leather of hoe or boot; new patch put on old rticle; (Mus.) improvised accom-animent;—v.t. provide (shoe, etc.) ith new upper leather; patch; Mus.) improvise accompaniment to.

mp (vamp) n. woman who allures nd exploits men; adventuress;—v.t. nd i. allure and exploit.

mpire (vam'-pir) n. (Fig.) one who ves by preying on others; extor-ioner.—vam'pire-bat n. of several pecies of bat of S. America which ucks blood.

an (van) n. covered wagon for oods; carriage attached to train or luggage, guard, etc.

an (van) n. leading division of army r fleet; leaders of movement.—an'guard n. detachment of troops ho march ahead of army.

an (van) n. fan for winnowing rain;—v.t. winnow; test quality of re by washing on shovel.—van'ner n.

anadium (van-ād-ium) n. metallic lement (symbol V).

andal (van'-dạl) n. Germanic ation which ravaged Gaul, Spain, . Africa and Rome about 5th cent. —van'dal n. one who wantonly amages or destroys; barbarian.—an'dalism n.

ane (văn) n. device at top of spire, tc. to show direction of wind; weather-cock; blade of propeller, as vindmill, etc.

vanilla (vạ-nil'-ạ) n. plant of orchid family; long pod of plant, used as flavouring.

vanish (van'-ish) v.i. be lost to view; disappear; (Math.) become zero.—van'isher n.—van'ishing a. disappear-ing.—van'ishingly adv.

vanquish (vang'-kwish) v.t. conquer in battle; defeat in contest.—van'quishable a.—van'quisher n.

vantage (van'-tāj) n. advantage; esp. in vantage-point, position of advan-tage.

vapid (vap'-id) a. having lost its life and spirit; flat; insipid.—vap'idly adv.—vap'idness n.—vapid'ity n.

vapour (vā'-pur) n. light, cloudy substance which impairs clearness of atmosphere, as mist, fog, smoke, etc.; anything unsubstantial;—v.i. pass off in vapour; (Fig.) brag.—va'porise v.t. convert into vapour;—v.i. pass off in vapour.—vaporisa'tion n.—va'poriser n. device for splitting liquid into fine particles.—va'pourish a. full of vapours.—va'porous a. like vapour; unreal; vain.—va'porously adv.—va'porousness n.—va'pourings n. pl. inane talk.—va'poury a.—va'pour-bath n. steam-bath or Turkish bath.

variable (vā'-ri-ạ-bl) a. changeable; capable of being adapted; unsteady or fickle;—n. that which is subject to change.—va'riably adv.—va'riable-ness n.—variabil'ity n.—va'riant a. different; diverse;—n. different form or reading.—va'riance n. difference that produces controversy; state of discord or disagreement.—variation (vā-ri-ā'-shun) n. act of varying; alteration; extent to which thing varies; in magnetism, deviation of magnetic needle from true north; (Mus.) repetition of theme or melody with various embellishments. —at variance, not in harmony.

varicose (var'-i-kōs) a. enlarged or dilated, as veins, esp. in legs.

variegate (vā'-ri-e-gāt) v.t. diversify by patches of different colours; streak, spot, etc.—variega'tion n.

variety (vạ-rī'e-ti) n. state of being varied; diversity; collection of different things; many-sidedness.—vari'ety-show n. mixed entertain-ment, consisting of songs, dances, short sketches, etc.

various (vā'-ri-us) a. different; diverse; manifold; separate; diversi-fied.—va'riously adv.—va'riousness n.

varnish (vár'-nish) n. clear, resinous liquid laid on work to give it gloss; glossy appearance; glaze; (Fig.) out-ward show;—v.t. lay varnish on.

vary (vā'-ri) v.t. change; make differ-ent; modify; diversify;—v.i. alter, or be altered; be different; be at variance; deviate.—va'ried a. vari-ous; diverse.

vas (vas) n. (Anat.) vessel or duct

containing blood, etc.—**vascular** (vas'-kū-lẹr) *a.* (*Anat.*) pert. to vessels or ducts for conveying blood, etc.—**vascular system**, all blood-vessels of body.

vase (vàz, (*U.S.*) vāz) *n.* vessel for flowers or merely for decoration; large sculptured vessel, used as ornament in gardens.

vassal (vas'-ạl) *n.* one who holds land from superior; dependant; bondman or slave.—**vass'alage** *n.* state of such.

vast (vàst) *a.* of great extent; very spacious; very great in numbers or quantity;—**vast'ly** *adv.*—**vast'ness** *n.*

vat (vat) *n.* large vessel, tub, or cistern, generally for holding liquids.

vault (vawlt) *n.* arched roof; apartment covered with vault, esp. subterranean; cellar; sky; anything resembling vault;—*v.t.* cover with arched roof; form like vault.—**vaul'ted** *a.* arched.

vault (vawlt) *v.i.* spring or jump with hands resting on something; leap or curvet, as horse;—*v.t.* spring or jump over;—*n.* such spring.—**vaul'ting-horse** *n.* wooden stand, used by gymnasts for vaulting.

vaunt (vawnt, vånt) *v.i.* brag or boast;—*v.t.* boast of; make vain display of;—*n.* boast.

veal (vēl) *n.* flesh of calf for table.

vector (vek'-tor) *n.* (*Math.*) any quantity requiring direction to be stated as well as magnitude in order to define properly, e.g. velocity; disease-carrying insect;—*v.t.* direct aircraft along correct course.

veer (vēr) *v.t.* and *v.i.* turn; of wind, change direction, esp. clockwise; (*Naut.*) change ship's course.

vegetable (vej'-e-tạ-bl) *a.* having nature of plants;—*n.* plant, esp. plant used as food, e.g. potato, carrot, cabbage.—**vegetarian** (vej-e-tā'-ri-ạn) *n.* one who abstains from animal flesh and lives on vegetables, eggs, milk, etc.;—*a.* pert. to vegetarianism; consisting of vegetables.—**vegeta'rianism** *n.*—**veg'etate** *v.i.* grow as plant does; lead idle, useless life.—**vegeta'tion** *n.* process of vegetating; vegetable growth; plants in general.—**vegetable marrow**, gourd.

vehement (vē'-he-mẹnt) *a.* acting with great force; impetuous; vigorous; passionate.—**ve'hemently** *adv.*—**ve'hemence**, **ve'hemency** *n.* impetuosity; fury; violence; force.

vehicle (vē'-i-kl, vē'-hi-kl) *n.* any means of conveyance (esp. on land) as carriage, cart, etc.; liquid medium in which drugs are taken, or pigments applied.—**vehicular** (vē-hik'-ū-lạr) *a.* Also **vehic'ulatory**.

veil (vāl) *n.* thin, gauzy material worn by women to hide or protect face; covering; disguise;—*v.t.* cover with veil; conceal.—**veiled** *a.* covered;

concealed; disguised.—**veil'ing** *n.* a of covering with veil; material fro which veil is made.—**to take the ve** become a nun.

vein (vān) *n.* each of vessels or tub which receive blood from capillari and return it to heart; any bloo vessel; (*Biol.*) one of small branchi ribs of leaf or of insect's win streak or wave of different colou appearing in wood, marble, etc distinctive tendency; mood or ca of mind;—*v.t.* mark with veins.—**vein'ing** *n.* system of veins; streake surface.—**vein'ous**, **vein'y** *a.*

veld, veldt (felt, velt) *n.* in S. Africa open grass-country.

vellum (vel'-um) *n.* fine parchmer made of calf's-skin.

velocipede (ve-los'-i-pēd) *n.* vehicl propelled by rider, early form o bicycle.

velocity (ve-los'-i-ti) *n.* rate o motion; swiftness; speed; distanc traversed in unit time in give direction.

velours (vẹ-lóòr') *n.* fabric resem bling velvet or plush; hat made o velours. Also **velour'**.

velvet (vel'-vet) *n.* soft material o silk with thick short pile on on side;—*a.* made of velvet; soft an delicate.—**vel'vety** *a.* soft as velvet —**velveteen'** *n.* poor velvet made o cotton, or of silk and cotton mixed

venal (vē'-nạl) *a.* to be obtained fo money; prepared to take bribes mercenary.—**ve'nally** *adv.*—**venal'it** *n.* corruption.

vend (vend) *v.t.* sell.—**ven'dible** *a* saleable.—**ven'dibly** *adv.*—**vendibil'ity ven'dibleness** *n.*—**vending-machine** *n* slot-machine.—**ven'dor** *n.* seller.

vendetta (ven-det'-ạ) *n.* blood-feud bitter feud.

veneer (vẹ-nēr') *n.* thin layer o valuable wood glued to surface o inferior wood; thin coating of fine substance; (*Fig.*) superficial char or polish of manner;—*v.t.* coat o overlay with substance giving super ior surface; (*Fig.*) disguise wit superficial charm.—**vene er'ing** *n.*

venerate (ven'-e-rāt) *v.t.* regard wit reverence.—**ven'erator** *n.*—**venera'tio** *n.* respect mingled with awe worship.—**ven'erable** *a.* deservin respect by reason of age, characte etc.; sacred for religious or historica associations.—**ven'erably** *adv.*

venereal (ve-nē'-re-ạl) *a.* pert. t sexual intercourse.—**venereal disea** *n.* disease arising from sexual inter course with infected person s.—**ve** **ereology** *n.* study of venerea l disease

Venetian (ve-nē'-shạn) *a.* pert. t city of Venice, Italy.—**vene tian blin** blind made of thin, horizont al slip so hung as to overlap when closed

vengeance (ven'-jạns) *n.* infliction o

ain or loss on another in return for
injury or offence.—**venge'ful** a. disosed to revenge; vindictive.—
enge'fully adv.—**venge'fulness** n.

nial (vē'-ni-al) a. excusable; not
mortal (of sin).—**ve'nially** adv.—
e'nialness n.—**venial'ity** n.

nison (ven'-i-zn, ven'-zn) n. flesh
of deer.

nom (ven'-om) n. poison, esp. that
secreted by serpents, bees, etc.;
pite; malice.—**ven'omous** a. poisonous; spiteful; malicious.—**ven'omusly** adv.—**ven'omousness** n.

nt (vent) n. small opening; outlet;
flue or funnel of fireplace; touchole of gun; stop of wind-instrument;
atterance; emission; voice; escape;
anus of certain lower animals;—v.t.
rive outlet to; let escape; utter or
roice; publish.—**to give vent to**, pour
orth; suffer to escape.

ntilate (ven'-ti-lāt) v.t. fan or
winnow; remove foul air and supply
resh air; expose to discussion;
make public.—**ventila'tion** n. replacement of vitiated air by fresh air;
ree exposure to air.—**ven'tilator** n.
ontrivance for keeping air fresh.

ntral (ven'-tral) a. belonging to
selly; abdominal; opp. of *dorsal;*—
s. one of pair of fins on belly of fish.
—**ven'tricle** n. (*Anat.* or *Zool.*) small
cavity in certain organs, esp. one of
hambers of heart from which blood
s forced into arteries.—**ventric'ular** a.

ntriloquism (ven-tril'-o-kwizm) n.
rt of speaking so that words or
sounds seem to come from some
ource other than speaker. Also
entril'oquy.—**ventril'oquist** n.—**ven-ril'oquise** v.i.

nture (ven'-tūr) n. undertaking of
hance or danger; business speculation;—v.t. risk;—v.i. run risk; dare;
ave presumption to.—**ven'turer** n.
—**ven'turous** a. daring; fearless.—
en'turously adv.—**ven'turousness** n.—
en'turesome a.—**vent'uresomely** adv.
—**vent'uresomeness** n.

nue (ven'-ū) n. district in which
ase is tried; meeting-place; scene.

racious (ve-rā'-shus) a. truthful;
rue.—**vera'ciously** adv.—**veracity** (ve-as'-i-ti) n. quality of being truthful;
ruth; correctness.

randa, verandah (ve-ran'-da) n.
ight, open portico or gallery, along
ide of house, with roof supported
on pillars; covered balcony.

rb (verb) n. (*Gram.*) part of speech
which expresses action or state of
being.—**ver'bal** a. pert. to words;
xpressed in words, esp. spoken
words; literal or word for word;
ert. to verb; derived from verb.—
er'bally adv.—**ver'balise** v.t. and v.i.
out into words; turn into verb.—
er'balism n. something expressed
orally; over-attention to use of

words; empty words.—**verbatim** (ver-bā'-tim) a. and adv. word for word.

verbiage (ver'-bi-ej) n. excess of
words; use of many more words
than are necessary; wordiness, often
with little sense.—**verbose** (ver-bōs')
a. prolix; tedious because of excess
of words.—**verbose'ly** adv.—**verbose'-ness, verbosity** (ver-bos'-i-ti) n.

verdant (ver'-dant) a. green or fresh;
flourishing.—**ver'dantly** adv.—**ver'dancy** n. greenness.—**verdure** (ver'-dūr)
n. greenness or freshness; green
vegetation.

verdict (ver'-dikt) n. decision of jury
in trial; decision or judgment.

verdigris (ver'-di-grēs) n. green corrosion on copper; basic acetate of
copper, used as pigment.

verge (verj) n. limit, border, or edge;
brink; grass edging of flower-bed,
avenue, etc.—**ver'ger** n. one who
carries verge or emblem of authority; attendant upon bishop, etc.;
beadle or pew-opener of church.

verge (verj) v.i. tend; slope.

verify (ver'-i-fī) v.t. prove to be true;
confirm truth of; make good.—
ver'ifier n.—**ver'ifiable** a.—**verifiabil'-ity** n.—**verifica'tion** n. act of verifying
or state of being verified; confirmation.—**ver'ily** adv. (*Arch.*) truly.

verisimilar (ver-i-sim'-i-lar) a. having appearance of truth; probable;
likely.—**verisim'ilarly** adv.—**verisimil'-itude** n. appearance of truth;
probability; likelihood.

veritable (ver'-i-ta-bl) a. actual;
true; genuine.—**ver'itably** adv.

verity (ver'-i-ti) n. quality of being
true; truth.

vermi- (ver'-mi) *prefix* fr. L. *vermis,*
worm.—**vermicelli** (ver-mi-sel'-i,
-chel'-i) n. thin form of spaghetti.—
ver'micide n. substance that destroys
worms.—**vermici'dal** a.—**vermic'ular**
a. pert. to worm; like worm in shape
or movement.—**ver'miform** a. having
shape of worm.

vermilion (ver-mil'-yun) n. cinnabar; prepared red sulphide of
mercury; red colour;—v.t. colour
with red.

vermin (ver'-min) n. collectively
noxious or mischievous little animals, birds, or insects, e.g. rats,
worms, lice, etc.; low contemptible
persons.—**ver'minous** a. infested by
vermin; caused by vermin.

vermouth (ver'-mōóth,-mōót) n.
cordial of white wine flavoured with
worm-wood, used as aperitif.

vernacular (ver-nak'-ū-lar) a. belonging to country of one's birth;
native (usu. applied to language or
idiom);—n. native idiom of place;
mother tongue.

vernal (ver'-nal) a. belonging to, or
appearing in, spring; of youth.—
ver'nally adv.—**vernal equinox, equi-**

nox occurring about 21st March.

vernier (ver'-ni-er) n. short, graduated-scale instrument, for measuring fractional parts.

Veronica (ve-ron'-i-ka) n. genus of plants, including speedwell.

versatile (ver'-sa-til) a. having aptitude in many subjects; liable to change; adaptable.—ver'satilely adv.—versatil'ity n.

verse (vers) n. metrical line containing certain number of feet; short division of any composition; stanza; stave; piece of poetry.—versed (verst) a. skilled; experienced (with in); practised.—versify (ver'-si-fi) v.t. turn prose into verse; express in verse.—v.i. make verses.—ver'sifier n.

version (ver'-shun) n. translation; translation into foreign language; account from particular point of view.

versus (ver'-sus) prep. (Law, Games) against.

vertebra (ver'-te-bra) n. small bony segment of spinal column.—pl. ver'tebrae.—ver'tebral a. pert. to vertebrae or spine.—ver'tebrate a. having backbone;—n. vertebrate animal.

vertex (ver'-teks) n. highest point; summit; (Astron.) zenith; (Geom.) angular point of triangle, etc.—pl. vertexes, vertices (ver'-tek-ses, -ti-sēz).—ver'tical a. situated at vertex; directly overhead or in zenith; perpendicular;—n. vertical line.—ver'tically adv.

vertigo (ver'-ti-gō, ver-tī'-gō) n. sensation of whirling or swimming of head, with loss of equilibrium; dizziness; giddiness.—vertiginous (ver-tij'-i-nus) a. revolving; giddy; causing giddiness.—vertig'inously adv.

verve (verv) n. enthusiasm or vigour; energy; spirit.

very (ver'-i) a. true; real; actual; now used chiefly to emphasise word following.—adv. in high degree; extremely.—ver'ilyadv. (Arch.) truly.

vesical (ves'-i-kal) a. (Med.) pert. to bladder.—ves'icant a. tending to raise blisters;—n. blistering application.—ves'icate v.t. raise blisters on.—vesica'tion n. blistering.—ves'icle n. small bladder-like structure; blister.—vesicular (ve-sik'-ū-lar) a. pert. to vesicles.—vesic'ulate, vesic'ulous a.

Vesper (ves'-per) n. evening star, Venus; evening;—a. pert. to evening or vespers.—ves'pers n.pl. sixth canonical hour; evening service.

vessel (ves'-el) n. utensil for holding liquids or solids; ship; (Anat.) tube through which blood or other fluids flow.

vest (vest) n. waistcoat; knitted or woven undergarment; vestment;—v.t. clothe; cover; put in possession; endow; give right of present or

future enjoyment; furnish with authority.—ves'ted a. that cannot be transferred or taken away.—vest ment n. ceremonial or official garment.—ves'ture n. clothing; dress covering.

vestibule (ves'-ti-būl) n. entrance to house; porch; hall nearest to outer door of house.

vestige (ves'-tij) n. orig. footprint; trace or sign; track; mark of something that has been; remains.—vesti'gial a.

vestry (ves'-tri) n. room attached to church for holding ecclesiastical vestments, prayer meetings, etc.; assembly of parishioners to deal with parochial affairs.

vet (vet) n. (Colloq. abbrev.) veterinary surgeon;—v.t. examine or treat animal; (Colloq. Fig.) examine.

vetch (vech) n. plant of bean family for fodder.

veteran (vet'-e-ran) n. person who has served long time, esp. soldier;—a. long exercised in anything.

veterinary (vet'-e-ri-na-ri) a. pert. to healing of diseases of domestic animals.—veterinarian (vet-e-ri-nā'-ri-an) n. one skilled in treating diseases of animals; now veterinary surgeon.

veto (vē'-tō) n. power or right of forbidding.—pl. ve'toes.—v.t. withhold assent to; negative.

vex (veks) v.t. make angry; irritate; grieve; distress.—vexa'tion n.—vexa'tious a. causing vexation; distressing.—vexa'tiously adv.—vexa'tiousness n.

via (vī'-a, vē'-a) prep. by way of.

viable (vī'-a-bl) a. born alive and sufficiently developed to be able to live; capable of growth; development; durable; practicable; effective; lasting.—viabil'ity n.

viaduct (vī'-a-dukt) n. bridge or series of arches for carrying road or railway over valley.

vial (vī'-al) n. small glass bottle; phial.

viand (vī'-and) n. article of food; chiefly pl., food, victuals, provisions.

vibrate (vī-brāt', vī'-brāt) v.t. move to and fro; cause to quiver;—v.i. swing or oscillate; quiver; thrill or throb; of sound, produce quivering effect; sound tremulous.—vibra'tion n.—vibrator (vī-brā'-tor, vī'-brā-tor) n. one who, or that which, causes vibration.—vi'bratory a. causing vibration.—vi'brant a. thrilling; throbbing; sonorous.

vicar (vik'-ar) n. clergyman of parish in which tithes belong to chapter and allows a salary to him.—vic'arage n. residence of vicar.—vicarial (vī-kā'-ri-al) a. pert. to, acting as vicar.—vic'arship n.—vicarious (vī-kā'-ri-us) a. delegated; substituted; done or suffered for another.—vica'riously adv.—vica'riousness n.

ice (vīs) *n.* depravity or immoral conduct; defect in character, etc.; bad habit.—**vicious** (vish'-us) *a.* depraved; wicked; spiteful.—**vic'iously** *adv.*—**vic'iousness** *n.*

ice (vīs) *n.* device for gripping with two jaws that can be brought together by screw.

ice- (vīs) *prefix* in words denoting one who acts in place of another, or one who is second in authority, as *vice-admiral, vice-chairman, vice-chancellor,* etc.

iceroy (vīs'-roi) *n.* governor of country or province; representative of king.

ice versa (vī'-se-ver'-sa) *adv.* order being reversed; other way round.

icinity (vi-sin'-i-ti) *n.* neighbourhood; nearness.

icissitude (vi-sis'-i-tūd) *n.* regular change or succession; alteration; change of circumstances, esp. of fortune;—*pl.* changes is fortune.—**vicissitu'dinary, vicissitu'dinous** *a.*

ictim (vik'-tim) *n.* living being sacrificed in religious ceremony; person who suffers; dupe or prey.—**vic'timise** *v.t.* make victim of.—**victimisa'tion** *n.*

ictor (vik'-tor) *n.* one who defeats enemy in battle; conqueror; winner in contest.—**vic'tory** *n.* defeat of enemy in battle, or of antagonist in contest; triumph.—**victo'rious** *a.* having conquered; triumphant; winning.—**victo'riously** *adv.*—**victo'riousness** *n.*

ictual (vit'-l) *v.t.* supply with provisions;—*v.i.* take in provisions.—**vict'uals** *n.pl.* food.—**victualler** (vit'-el-ler) *n.* one who supplies.

ideotape (vid'-e-ō-tāp) *n.* tape-recording of a television programme.

ie (vī) *v.i.* strive; contend.—*pr.p.* **vy'ing;**—*pa.p.* and *pa.t.* **vied** (vīd).

iew (vū) *n.* sight; inspection by eye or mind; power of seeing; range of sight; what is seen; pictured representation of scene; mental survey; opinion; aim or intention.—*v.t.* see; look at; survey mentally; consider.—**view'er** *n.* one who views; one who receives television programme; device for examining photographic transparencies.— **view'-halloo'** *n.* huntsman's cry on seeing fox break cover.—**view'find'er** *n.* device in camera for showing limits of picture. —**in view of,** having regard to.

igil (vij'-il) *n.* staying awake, either for religious exercises, or to keep watch; watch or watching; in church, eve of feast;—*pl.* nocturnal devotions.—**vig'ilant** *a.* wakeful; watchful; alert; circumspect.—**vig'ilantly** *adv.*— **vig'ilance** *n.* wakefulness; watchfulness.—**vigilan'te** (-ant'-ā) *n.* member of a vigilance committee.

ignette (vēn-yet', vin-yet') *n.* small designs in printing, used as headings or tail-pieces; photograph or portrait with shaded-off background; (*Fig.*) short, neat description in words.

vigour (vig'-or) *n.* active strength; energy; vitality.—**vig'orous** *a.* full of physical or mental strength; powerful.—**vig'orously** *adv.*—**vig'orousness** *n.*

viking (vik'-ing, vī'-king) *n.* Norse sea-rover or pirate in 8th to 10th cents.

vile (vīl) *a.* mean; worthless; base; depraved; (*Colloq.*) shockingly bad. —**vile'ly** *adv.*—**vile'ness** *n.*—**vilify** (vil'-i-fī) *v.t.* speak ill of; try to degrade by slander; defame or traduce.—**vil'ifier** *n.*—**vilifica'tion** *n.*

villa (vil'-a) *n.* suburban house.

village (vil'-āj) *n.* assemblage of houses, smaller than town and larger than hamlet;—*a.* pert. to village; rustic.—**vill'ager** *n.* inhabitant of village.

villain (vil'-an) *n.* wicked or criminal person; rascal; (*Hist.*) feudal serf.—**vill'ainous** *a.* wicked; vile.—**vill'ainously** *adv.*—**vill'ainousness** *n.*—**vill'ainy** *n.* extreme wickedness.

villein (vil'-en) *n.* (*Hist.*) serf:—**vil'lenage** *n.* tenure of lands by menial services; serfdom.

vim (vim) *n.* (*Colloq.*) force; energy.

vincible (vin'-si-bl) *a.* that may be conquered.

vindicate (vin'-di-kāt) *v.t.* justify; maintain as true and correct; clear of suspicion, dishonour, etc.—**vin'dicable** *a.*—**vindicabil'ity** *n.*—**vindica'tion** *n.* justification.—**vin'dicator** *n.*—**vin'dicatory** *a.*

vindictive (vin-dik'-tiv) *a.* vengeful. —**vindic'tively** *adv.*—**vindic'tiveness** *n.*

vine (vīn) *n.* climbing plant that produces grapes; plant which trails or climbs.—**vi'nery** *n.* greenhouse(s) for rearing vines by heat.—**vineyard** (vin'-yard) *n.* plantation of grape-vines.—**vin'iculture** *n.* cultivation of vines.—**vi'nose, vi'nous** *a.* pert. to, or like, wine; due to wine.

vinegar (vin'-e-gar) *n.* acid liquor used as condiment or in pickling.—**vin'egary** *a.* like vinegar; sour.

vingt-et-un (vangt-ā-ung') *n.* card game, pontoon.

vintage (vin'-tāj) *n.* gathering of grapes; wine of particular year;—*a.* characteristic of particular year or period.—**vint'ner** *n.* one who deals in wine.—**vintage wine,** wine made from grapes of particular year.

vinyl (vī'-nil) *n.* organic radical, base of many thermoplastic materials.

viol (vī'-ol) *n.* stringed instrument, ancestor of the violin.—**bass'-vi'ol** *n.* double-bass.—**vi'olist** *n.* one who plays viol.

viola (vē-ō'-la) *n.* instrument larger than violin, but smaller than violoncello.—**violist** (vī-ō'-list) *n.* one who plays viol or viola.

Viola (vī'-ō-lạ) *n.* (*Bot.*) genus of plants including violet and pansy.

violate (vī'-o-lāt) *v.t.* infringe or break promise; treat with disrespect; outrage or rape.—**viola'tion** *n.* transgression; profanation; infringement.—**vi'olator** *n.*

violence (vī'-o-lẹns) *n.* force; intensity; assault.—**vi'olent** *a.* characterised by improper force; forcible; furious; passionate.—**vi'olently** *adv.*

violet (vī'-o-let) *n.* flower of genus Viola, of bluish-purple colour; colour produced by combining blue and red;—*a.* bluish or purple.

violin (vī-o-lin', vī'-o-lin) *n.* modern musical instrument of viol family, with four strings, played with bow; fiddle.—**violin'ist** *n.*

violoncello (vē-o-lon-chel'-ō, vī-o-lon-chel'-ō) *n.* bass violin, much large than violin. Usu. *abbrev.* to '**cello.—violoncell'ist** *n.*

viper (vī'pẹr) *n.* venomous snake; adder; malicious person.—**vi'perish** *a.* like viper; malignant.—**vi'perous** *a.*

virago (vi-rä'-gō) *n.* scolding woman.

virgin (vẹr'-jin) *n.* girl or woman who has not experienced sexual intercourse; maiden;—*a.* without experience of sexual intercourse; chaste; untilled (of land).—**vir'ginal** *a.* pert. to virgin; maidenly; fresh and pure;—*n.* old musical instrument like spinet.—**virgin'ity** *n.*—**the Virgin,** mother of Christ.

virid (vir'-id) *a.* green.—**virides'cent** *a.* turning green; greenish.—**virid'ian** *n.* bluish-green pigment.—**virid'ity, vir'idness** *n.* greenness.

virile (vir'-il or -īl) *a.* pert. to man; masculine; strong; (of style) having vigour.—**viril'ity** *n.* manliness; power of procreation.

virtu (vẹr'-tōō, vẹr-tōō') *n.* objects of art collectively; taste for such.

virtual (vẹr'-tū-ạl) *a.* being in essence or effect, though not in fact; potential.—**vir'tually** *adv.* to all intents and purposes.—**virtual'ity** *n.*

virtue (vẹr'-tū) *n.* moral excellence; merit; good quality; female chastity; power or efficacy.—**vir'tuous** *a.* upright; dutiful; chaste.—**vir'tuously** *adv.*—**vir'tuousness** *n.*

virtuoso (vir-tū-ō'-sō) *n.* highly skilled musician, painter, etc.—*pl.* **virtuo'si, virtuo'sos.** — **virtuos'ity** *n.* great technical skill in fine arts, esp. music.

virulent (vir'-ū-lẹnt) *a.* extremely poisonous; bitter in enmity; malignant; deadly.—**vir'ulently** *adv.*—**vir'ulence** *n.* acrimony; rancour; malignity; bitterness.—**virus** (vī'-rus) *n.* agent causing disease.

visa (vē'-zạ) *n.* official endorsement, as on passport.

visage (viz'-ạj) *n.* face; look or appearance.—**visaged** (viz'ājd) *a.*

vis-a-vis (vēz-ạ-vē') *adv.* face to face;—*n.* person facing another.

viscera (vis'-e-rạ) *n.pl.* internal organs, e.g. intestines; entrails.—**vis'ceral** *a.*—**vis'cerate** *v.t.* disembowel.

viscid (vis'-id) *a.* glutinous; sticky; tenacious.—**viscid'ity** *n.*—**viscose** (vis'-id) *n.* viscid derivative of cellulose, drawn into fibres and used in making artificial silk.—**viscous** (vis'-kus) *a.* glutinous; tenacious.—**viscos'ity** *n.*

viscount (vī'-kount) *n.* (*fem.* **vi'scountess**) degree or title of nobility next below earl.

visible (viz'-i-bl) *a.* perceptible; in view. — **vis'ibly** *adv.* — **visibil'ity** *n.* degree of clarity of atmosphere.

vision (vizh'-un) *n.* act or faculty of seeing external objects; sight; thing seen; phantom; imaginative insight or foresight.—**vis'ionary** *a.* apt to see visions; indulging in fancy or reverie; impractical; existing only in imagination;—*n.* one prone to see visions.

visit (viz'-it) *v.t.* go, or come, to see; (*Bib.*) punish;—*v.i.* be guest;—*n.* sojourn; official or formal inspection.—**vis'itant** *a.* visiting.—*n.* one who visits; migratory bird.—**visita'tion** *n.* formal or official inspection; dispensation of divine favour or anger.—**vis'itor** *n.* one who visits.

visor, vizor (vīz'-ẹr) *n.* front part of helmet which can be lifted to show face; peak of cap.—**vis'ored** *a.* having or wearing visor.

vista (vis'-tạ) *n.* view, esp. distant view, as through avenue of trees.

visual (viz'-, vizh'-ū-ạl) *a.* relating to sight; used in seeing; visible.—**vis'ually** *adv.* by sight.—**vis'ualise** *v.t.* call up mental picture of.—**visualisa'tion** *n.*

vital (vī'-tạl) *a.* necessary to or containing life; very necessary.—**vi'tals** *n.pl.* essential internal organs, as lungs, heart, brain.—**vi'tally** *adv.*—**vi'talise** *v.t.* give life to; lend vigour to.—**vitalisa'tion** *n.*—**vital'ity** *n.* vital force; vigour.—**vital statistics,** figures of births, marriages, death; (*Colloq.*) measurements of female figure.

vitamin (vit'-a-, vī'-ta-min) *n.* chemical substances present in various food-stuffs, and indispensable to health and growth.

vitiate (vish'-i-āt) *v.t.* make vicious, faulty, or impure; debase; impair; invalidate.—**vitia'tion** *n.*

viticulture (vī-ti-kul-tūr) *n.* cultivation of vines.

vitreous (vit'-re-us) *a.* pert. to, or resembling, glass; glassy; derived from glass.—**vit'reousness** *n.*

vitrify (vit'-ri-fī) *v.t.* convert into glass;—*v.i.* be converted into glass.—**vit'rifiable** *a.*—**vitrifica'tion** *n.*

triol (vit'-ri-ol) *n.* sulphuric acid.—**vitriol'ic** *a.* pert. to, resembling, derived from, vitriol; (*Fig.*) caustic.

tuperate (vĭ-tū'-pe-rāt) *v.t.* abuse in words; revile.—**vitu'perative** *a.*—**busive.**—**vitu'peratively** *adv.*—**vitu'erator** *n.*—**vitupera'tion** *n.*

vace (vĕ-vå'-che) *adv.* (*Mus.*) in lively manner.

vacious (vi-, vĭ-vā'-shus) *a.* lively; prightly; animated; having great itality.—**viva'ciously** *adv.*—**vivacity** vi-, vĭ-vas'-i-ti) *n.* liveliness.

va voce (vĭ'-va vŏ'-sē) *adv.* orally; —*a.* oral;—*n.* (*Colloq.*) oral examina-ion.—*abbrev.* vi'va.

vid (viv'-id) *a.* animated; lively; lear; evoking brilliant images; (of olour) bright; glaring.—**viv'idly** *adv.* —**viv'idness** *n.*

vify (viv'-i-fī) *v.t.* endue with life; nimate.—**vivifica'tion** *n.*

viparous (vĭ-vip'-a-rus) *a.* pro-ucing young in living state, nstead of eggs.—**vivip'arously** *adv.*—ivip'arousness, vivipa'rity *n.*

visection (vi-vi-sek'-shun) *n.* dis-ection of, or experimenting on, ive animals for purpose of scientific nvestigations.

xen (vik'-sn) *n.* she-fox; cross bad-empered woman.—**vix'enish** *a.* like fixen; shrewish.

cable (vō'-ka-bl) *n.* word, esp. with ef. to sound rather than meaning; erm; name.

cabulary (vō-kab'-û-la-ri) *n.* list of vords, usu. arranged in alphabetical rder and explained; word-book; tock of words used by language, lass, or individual.

cal (vō'-kal) *a.* pert. to voice or peech; having voice; uttered by oice; (*Phon.*) sounded; having haracter of vowel.—**vo'cally** *adv.*—o'calise *v.t.* make vocal; utter with oice, and not merely with breath; onvert into vowel;—*v.i.* make vocal ounds, as in singing.—**vo'calist** *n.*

cation (vō-kā'-shun) *n.* divine call o religious career; profession, or ccupation.—**voca'tional** *a.*

ciferate (vō-sif'-e-rāt) *v.t.* utter oisily; bawl;—*v.i.* cry with loud oice.—**vocifera'tion** *n.* vehement tterance; outcry.—**vocif'erator** *n.*—ocif'erous *a.* making loud outcry; lamorous.—**vocif'erously** *adv.*

dka (vod'-ka) *n.* alcoholic liquor.

gue (vōg) *n.* prevailing fashion; node; style.

ice (vois) *n.* faculty of uttering udible sounds; sound produced by rgans of respiration; utterance; uality of utterance; expression of eeling or opinion; vote; share in iscussion:—*v.t.* give expression to; nnounce.—**voiced** (voist) *a.* furnish-d with voice or with expression; *Phon.*) uttered with vocal tone.

void (void) *a.* empty; being without; —*n.* empty space;—*v.t.* make vacant; empty out; make invalid.—**void'ness** *n.*—**void'able** *a.*—**void'ance** *n.* act of voiding; state of being void.

voile (voil, vwål) *n.* thin cotton, woollen, or silk material.

volatile (vol'-a-tĭl) *a.* evaporating quickly; (*Fig.*) spirited; lively; fickle; changeable.—**volat'ilise** *v.t.* and *i.* render or become volatile; cause to vapourise.—**volat'ilisable** *a.* volatilisa'tion *n.*—**volatil'ity** *n.*

volcano (vol-kā'-nō) *n.* opening in crust of earth, from which heated solids, liquids, and gases are ejected. —**volcan'ic** *a.*—**volcan'ically** *adv.*

vole (vōl) *n.* mouse-like rodent.

volition (vō-lish'-un) *n.* act of willing or choosing; exercise of will.—**voli'tional** *a.* pert. to volition.

volley (vol'-i) *n.* discharge of many shots or missiles at one time; (*Fig.*) rapid utterance; (*Tennis*) return of ball before it touches ground;—*v.t.* discharge in volley;—*v.i.* fly in volley; sound together; (*Tennis*) return ball before it touches ground.

volt (vōlt) *n.* practical unit of electro-motive force.—**volt'age** *n.* electro-motive force reckoned in volts.—**volt'meter** *n.* instrument used for measuring electromotive force in volts.

volte-face (volt-fas') *n.* turning round; (*Fig.*) sudden and unexpected reversal of opinion.

voluble (vol'-û-bl) *a.* having flowing and rapid utterance; fluent in speech; glib.—**vol'ubly** *adv.*—**vol'uble-ness**, volubil'ity *n.*

volume (vol'-ūm) *n.* book; part of work which is bound; bulk or compass; cubical content; power, fullness, of voice or musical tone.—volumet'ric *a.* pert. to measurement by volume.—**volumet'rically** *adv.*—volum'inous *a.* consisting of many volumes; bulky.—**volum'inousness** *n.* —volumino'sity *n.*

voluntary (vol'-un-ta-ri) *a.* proceed-ing from choice or free will; uncon-strained; spontaneous; subject to will;—*n.* organ solo played during, or after, church service.—**vol'untarily** *adv.*—**vol'untariness** *n.*

volunteer (vol-un-tēr') *n.* one who enters service, esp. military, of own free will;—*a.* entering into service of one's own free will;—*v.t.* bestow voluntarily;—*v.i.* enter into service of one's own free will.

voluptuary (vo-lup'-tū-a-ri) *n.* one addicted to luxurious living; sensual-ist; epicure;—*a.* concerned with, or promoting, sensual pleasure.—**volup'tuous** *a.*—**volup'tuously** *adv.*—**volup'tuousness** *n.*

vomit (vom'-it) *v.t.* eject from stom-ach by mouth; disgorge;—*v.i.* eject contents of stomach by mouth;—*n.* matter ejected from stomach.—**vom'itory** *a.* provoking vomiting;—*n.* emetic.

voodoo (vōō'-dōō) *n.* magical rites among certain Negro races; one who practises such rites;—*a.* belonging to, or connected with voodoo.—**voo'dooism** *n.*

voracious (vo-rā'-shus) *a.* greedy in eating; eager to devour; ravenous.—**vora'ciously** *adv.*—**vora'ciousness** *n.*—**voracity** (vo-ras'-i-ti) *n.* greediness of appetite; ravenousness.

vortex (vor'-teks) *n.* whirling motion of any fluid, forming kind of cavity in centre of circle; whirlpool.—*pl.* **vortices, vortexes** (vor'-ti-sēz, vor'-tek-sez).—**vor'tical** *a.*—**vor'tically** *adv.*

votary (vō'-ta-ri) *a.* consecrated by vow;—*n.* one engaged by vow; one devoted to service, study, etc.—**vo'taress** *n.* (*fem.*).

vote (vōt) *n.* formal expression of wish, choice, or opinion, of individual, or body of persons; expression of will by majority; right to vote; suffrage; what is allowed by vote;—*v.t.* enact, grant, or establish, by vote; declare by general consent;—*v.i.* express one's choice, will, or preference.—**vo'ter** *n.*

votive (vō'-tiv) *a.* offered or consecrated by vow; given in fulfilment of vow.

vouch (vouch) *v.t.* warrant; attest; affirm;—*v.i.* bear witness; be guarantee (for).—**vouch'er** *n.* one who bears witness or attests to anything; paper or document that serves to vouch truth of accounts, or to establish facts; receipt.

vouchsafe (vouch-sāf') *v.t.* condescend to grant or do something;—*v.i.* deign.

vow (vou) *n.* solemn promise made esp. to deity;—*v.t.* consecrate or dedicate by solemn promise; devote;—*v.i.* make vow.

vowel (vou'-el) *n.* any vocal sound produced with least possible friction; letter or character that represents such sound.

voyage (voi'-āj) *n.* journey esp. by sea;—*v.i.* sail or traverse by water.—**voy'ager** *n.* one who makes voyage.

vulcanise (vul'-kan-īz) *v.t.* treat rubber with sulphur at high temperature to increase durability and elasticity.—**vulcanisa'tion** *n.*—**vul'canite** *n.* rubber so hardened.

vulgar (vul'-gar) *a.* of common people; in common use; coarse or offensive; rude;—*n.* common people.—**vul'garly** *adv.*—**vul'garise** *v.t.* make vulgar.—**vulgarisa'tion** *n.*—**vul'garism** *n.* vulgar expression; grossness of manners.—**vulgar'ity, vul'garness** *n.* commonness; lack of refinement in manners, ideas or language.

vulnerable (vul'-ne-ra-bl) *a.* able t be wounded; offering opening t criticism; assailable; in contra bridge, denoting side which has wo first game in rubber and is subje to increased honours and penaltie —**vul'nerableness, vulnerabil'ity** *n.*—**vul'nerably** *adv.*

vulture (vul'-tūr) *n.* large bird prey; rapacious person.—**vul'turin vul'turish, vul'turous** *a.* characterist of vulture; rapacious.

vying (vī'-ing) *pr.p.* of **vie**.

W

wad (wod) *n.* little tuft or bundle soft mass of loose, fibrous substance for stuffing, etc., roll of bank-note —*v.t.* form into wad; line wit wadding; pad;—*pr.p.* **wad'ding.**—*pa.t.* and *pa.p.* **wad'ded.**—**wad'ding** soft material for wads; cotton-woo

waddle (wod'-l) *v.i.* walk like duck —*n.* clumsy, slow, rocking gait.

wade (wād) *v.i.* walk through som thing which impedes movement, a water, mud, etc.;—*v.t.* cross (stream by wading;—*n.* ford.—**wa'der** *n.* on who wades; long-legged bird, e.g stork, heron.—**wa'ders** *n.pl.* hig water-proof boots.

wafer (wā'-fer) *n.* thin biscuit; thi disc of unleavened bread;—*v.t.* sea with wafer.—**wa'fery** *a.*

waffle (wof'-l) *n.* thin cake of batte

waft (waft) *v.t.* impel lightly throug water or air;—*v.i.* float gently;—*n* breath or slight current of air o odour; puff; signal given by hand.

wag (wag) *v.t.* cause to move to an fro;—*v.i.* shake; swing; vibrate.—*pr.p.* **wag'ging.**—*pa.p.* **wagged.**—*n* swinging motion, to and fro.

wag (wag) *n.* droll, witty person.—**wag'gish** *a.* frolicsome; droll.—**wag'gishly** *adv.*

wage (wāj) *v.t.* pledge; venture on carry on;—*n.* payment paid fo work done; hire; reward; pay;—*p* used with *sing.* significance.—**wage** freeze *n.* condition where wages ar not allowed to rise.

wager (wā'-jer) *n.* something stake on issue of future event or of som disputed point; bet; stake; pledge —*v.t.* bet.

waggle (wag'-l) *v.t.* move one wa and other; wag;—*v.i.* reel or mov from side to side.

wagon, waggon (wag'-on) *n.* four wheeled vehicle for carrying heav freight; railway goods truck.—**wag'oner, wagg'oner** *n.* one who drive wagon.—**wagonette', waggonette'** *n* four-wheeled open carriage.

wagtail (wag'-tāl) *n.* bird distin

guished by long tail almost constantly in motion.

vaif (wāf) *n.* homeless person, esp. neglected child; stray article or animal.

vail (wāl) *v.t.* and *v.i.* lament (over); weep; bemoan; cry loudly;—*n.* loud weeping; doleful cry.—**wail′er** *n.*—**wail′ing** *n.* sobbing.—**wail′ingly** *adv.*

vain (wān) *n.* wagon, esp. in farm use.—**wain′-wright** *n.* wagon-wright.

vainscot (wān′-skot) *n.* panelling of wood extending short way from floor to ceiling; skirting-board;—*v.t.* line with wainscoting.—**wain′scoting, wain′scotting** *n.*

vaist (wāst) *n.* part of human body immediately below ribs and above hips; middle part of anything; part of upper deck of ship between quarter-deck and forecastle.—**waist′band** *n.* part of dress or trousers which fits round waist.—**waist′coat** *n.* short sleeveless garment, worn under jacket.—**waist′line** *n.* division between bodice and skirt of dress; girth.

vait (wāt) *v.t.* stay for; attend;—*v.i.* stop until arrival of some person or event; serve at table; attend (on);—*n.* act, period of waiting;—*pl.* itinerant musicians esp. at Christmas.—**wait′er** *n.* one who waits; attendant in place of public entertainment; salver or tray.—**wait′ing** *n.* and *a.*—**wait′ress** *n.* female waiter.—**to wait upon, on,** attend to wants of someone; call upon.

vaive (wāv) *v.t.* give up claim to; forgo.

vake (wāk) *v.t.* rouse from sleep; bring to life again; waken; excite; hold watch over corpse at night;—*v.i.* awaken; watch; be stirred up or roused to action.—*pa.t.* and *pa.p* **waked** or **woke.**—*pr.p.* **wa′king.**—*n.* vigil; act of sitting up overnight with corpse; local festival or holiday.—**wake′ful** *a.* sleepless; watchful; vigilant; wary.—**wake′fully** *adv.*—**wake′fulness** *n.*—**wa′ken** *v.t.* and *v.i.* wake.—**wake′ner** *n.*—**wa′king** *a.* period when one is not asleep.

vake (wāk) *n.* that part of track immediately astern of ship; air-disturbance in rear of aeroplane in flight.—**in the wake of,** following behind; in rear of.

valk (wawk) *v.t.* pass through, along, upon; cause to step slowly; lead, drive, or ride (horse) at slow pace; —*v.i.* go on foot; appear as spectre; move off;—*n.* act of walking; slowest pace of quadruped; characteristic gait or style of walking; avenue set with trees; stroll; distance walked over; sphere of life; conduct.—**walk′er** *n.*—**walk′ing-stick** *n.* stick or cane used in walking.—**walk′-out** *n.* strike.—**walk′-o′ver** *n.* in

sporting contests, event with only one competitor; easy victory.—**to walk on,** take subordinate part in play or film.

wall (wawl) *n.* structure of brick, stone, etc. serving as fence, side of building, etc.; means of defence;—*pl.* fortifications; works for defence; —*v.t.* enclose with wall; block up with wall.—**walled** *a.* provided with walls; fortified.—**wall′flower** *n.* garden plant, with sweet-scented flowers; woman left sitting at dance for lack of partners.

wallaby (wol′-ạ-bi) *n.* small kangaroo.—**wall′abies** *n.pl.* (*Slang*) Australians.

wallet (wol′-et) *n.* pocket-book for letters, bank-notes, etc.; bag, fitted to hold tools.

wallop (wol′-op) *v.t.* beat soundly; flog; whip;—*n.* stroke or blow of hand.—**wall′oping** *n.* thrashing;—*a.* tremendous; big.

wallow (wol′-ō) *v.i.* roll about (in mud, etc.); thrive or revel in filth or gross vice.

walnut (wawl′-nut) *n.* tree producing dark-brown wood of fine texture; fruit of tree, large nut with crinkled shell.

walrus (wol′-rus) *n.* mammal closely related to seal but with down-turned tusks.

waltz (wawlts) *n.* ballroom dance in three-four time; music for this; valse;—*v.i.* dance waltz.—**waltz′er** *n.* —**waltz′ing** *n.*

wan (won) *a.* having sickly hue; pale; bloodless; pallid; cadaverous; ashy; gloomy.—**wan′ly** *adv.*—**wan′ness** *n.*

wand (wond) *n.* long, slender, straight rod; rod used by conjurers or as sign of authority.

wander (won′-der) *v.t.* roam over; confuse purposely;—*v.i.* ramble; go astray; be delirious; err; depart from subject.—**wan′derer** *n.*—**wan′dering** *a.* unsettled;—*n.* journeying here and there, usually in *pl.*— **wan′deringly** *adv.*—**wanderlust** (wänd′-der-lust) *n.* irrepressible urge to travel.

wane (wān) *v.i.* decrease; fail;—*n.* decrease of illuminated part of moon; decline; diminution; decay.

wangle (wang′-gl) *v.t.* wag or dangle; (*Colloq.*) to obtain by deception;—*n.* (*Colloq.*) trickery.

want (wont) *n.* scarcity of what is needed; poverty; feeble-mindedness; —*v.t.* be without; have occasion for; lack; need; require; crave;—*v.i.* be lacking.—**wan′ted** *a.* required; sought after; searched for (by police).—**wan′ting** *a.* absent; feeble-minded; deficient.—*prep.* without; minus.— **wants** *n.pl.* requirements.

wanton (won′-ton) *a.* moving or flying about loosely; playful; dissolute;—*n.* lewd person;—*v.i.* rove and ramble without restraint; frolic; play; revel; grow luxuriantly.—**wan'tonly** *adv.*—**wan'tonness** *n.*

war (wawr) *n.* armed conflict between two (groups of) states; state of opposition or hostility; profession of arms; art of war;—*v.i.* make war; carry on hostilities; contend.—*pr.p.* **war'ring**;—*pa.t.* and *pa.p.* **warred.**—**war'fare** *n.* hostilities.—**war'-head** *n.* explosive cap on missile.—**war'like** *a.* disposed for war; belligerent; hostile.—**war'monger** *n.* one who foments war or strife.—**war'-paint** *n.* special adornments of Red Indians on warpath; (*Slang*) full dress or regalia.—**war'path** *n.* military foray, esp. among Red Indians on scalping expedition.—**civil war**, war between citizens of same country.—**cold war**, state of international hostility short of actual warfare.

warble (wawr'-bl) *v.t.* trill; carol;—*v.i.* sound melodiously;—*n.* carol; song.—**war'bler** *n.* one that warbles; various greenish-brown birds with pleasant trilling song.

ward (wawrd) *v.t.* watch; guard; repel;—*v.i.* keep guard;—*n.* watch; guard; guardianship; pupil; minor; cell; custody; division of city; room for patients in hospital; slot in key; parry.—**ward'en** *n.* formerly governor of district; head of college, corporate body, etc.; civil defence officer; keeper; guardian.—**ward'er** *n.* jailer.—**ward'robe** *n.* cupboard for holding clothes; wearing apparel.—**ward'-room** *n.* mess-room on battleship for senior officers.—**ward'ship** *n.* office of guardian; state of being under guardian.—**ward in Chancery**, minor under protection of Court of Chancery.

ware (wār) *n.* article of merchandise; pottery; usually in combinations as, *earthen-ware,* etc.;—*pl.* goods for sale; commodities; merchandise.—**ware'house** *n.* store-house for goods; large commercial establishment.

warlock (wawr'-lok) *n.* wizard; one in league with evil spirits; sorcerer.

warm (wawrm) *a.* having heat in moderate degree; not cold; hearty; affectionate;—*v.t.* communicate moderate degree of heat to;—*v.i.* become moderately heated; become animated. — **warm'-blood'ed** *a.* of animals with body-temperature above that of their environment; generous.—**warm'-heart'ed** *a.* affectionate; kindly disposed.—**warm'ly** *adv.*—**warm'ness, warmth** *n.* slight heat; cordiality; heartiness.

warn (wawrn) *v.t.* make aware; notify by authority; caution; put on guard.—**war'ner** *n.*—**war'ning** *n.* admonition;—*a.* cautioning.

warp (wawrp) *v.t.* twist permanently out of shape; bend; pervert; draw vessel or heavy object along by means of cable coiled on windlass; stretch into lengths for weaving;—*v.i.* turn, twist, or be twisted;—*n.* distortion of unseasoned timber; system of spun threads extended lengthwise in loom; towing-line.—**warped** *a.* twisted by unequal shrinkage; depraved.—**warp'er** *n.*—**warp'ing** *n.*

warrant (wor'-ant) *v.t.* give power to do (or forbear) with assurance of safety; guarantee to be as represented; vouch for; assure; indemnify against loss;—*n.* instrument giving power to arrest offender; negotiable writing which authorises person to receive something; naval or military writ inferior to commission.—**warr'antable** *a.* justifiable; legitimate.—**warr'antableness** *n.*—**warr'anted** *a.*—**warr'anter, warr'antor** *n.*—**warr'anty** *n.* security; guarantee.—**warrant officer**, officer in Navy and Army intermediate between non-commissioned and commissioned officer.

warren (wor'-en) *n.* enclosure where rabbits breed; overcrowded slum.

warrior (wawr'-i-er) *n.* soldier; fighting man.

wart (wawrt) *n.* small hard excrescence on skin.—**wart'hog** *n.* African mammal of pig family with large warty protuberances on face.—**wart'y** *a.* like or covered with warts.

wary (wā'-ri) *a.* cautious; heedful; careful; prudent.—**wa'rily** *adv.*—**wa'riness** *n.*

wash (wosh) *v.t.* cleanse by ablution; free from dirt with water and soap; tint lightly and thinly; separate, as gold, by action of water;—*v.i.* perform act of ablution; cleanse clothes in water; be washable;—*n.* clothes, etc. washed at one time; liquid applied to surface as lotion or coat of colour; rough water left behind by vessel in motion; marsh or fen, shallow bay; blade of oar.—**wash'able** *a.*—**wash'-board** *n.* skirting board; board with corrugated surface for washing clothes on.—**wash'er** *n.* one who washes; metal disc for distributing pressure from nut or head of bolt; flat ring to make tight joint.—**wash'erman, wash'erwoman** *n.*—**wash'-house, wash'-ba'sin, wash'-bowl, wash'-pot, wash'-tub** *n.* for washing purposes.—**wash'iness** *n.* being weak, or watery.—**wash'ing** *n.* act of one who washes; ablution; clothes washed at one time;—*a.* used in, or intended for, washing.—**wash'-out** (*Colloq.*) *n.* failure.—**washing soda**, decahydrate-sodium carbonate.—**wash'y** *a.* watery; weak; thin; insipid.—**washed out**, exhausted; faded.

wasp (wosp) *n.* stinging insect like

ee; ill-natured, irritable person.— as'pish a. like wasp; irritable.— as'pishly adv.—was'pishness n.— asp'-waist'ed a. having slender aist.

assail (wos'-āl) n. roystering festivity; drinking-bout; festal song; piced ale flavoured with apples, utmegs, sugar, etc.;—v.i. carouse; old wassail.—wass'ailer n.

aste (wāst) v.t. expend uselessly; use extravagantly; squander; lay vaste; spoil;—v.i. wear away by egrees; corrode; decrease;—a. of no worth; desolate; unproductive;—n. ct of wasting; that which is wasted; efuse; uncultivated country; loss; quandering; useless by-product.— vas'tage n. loss by use, leakage, or ecay.—waste'ful a. full of waste; lestructive; prodigal. — waste'fully dv.—waste'fulness n.—waste'-pipe n. lischarge-pipe for used water.— vas'ter n. one who or that which vastes; (Slang) ne'er-do-well; wast-el.—was'trel n. profligate; waif.—to waste away, be in state of decline.— o lay waste, devastate.

atch (woch) n. state of being on ook-out; close observation; watchnan; sentry; portable time-keeper or pocket, wrist, or fob; one of even divisions of working day on hip; sailors on duty at same time; livision of night;—v.t. give heed to; guard; observe closely;—v.i. be vigilant; be on watch; keep guard; pe wakeful; look out (for); wait for).—watch'er n.—watch'ful a. vigilant; cautious—watch'fully adv.— watch'fulness n.—watch'man n. man who guards property.—watch-night ervice, religious service held on New Year's Eve.—watch'word n. password.

ater (waw'-ter) n. transparent, casteless liquid, substance of rain, etc.; body of water; river; lake; sea; saliva; tear; urine; serum; transparency of gem; lustre;—pl. waves; —v.t. soak with water; put water nto; cause animal to drink; irrigate; give cloth wavy appearance;—v.i. shed water; issue as tears; gather saliva in mouth; take in or obtain water.—wa'ter-bail'iff n. one detailed to prevent poaching on preserved stretch of river; water-bailie; custom-house officer.—wa'ter-butt n. large barrel for catching rain-water from roof.—wa'ter-clos'et n. sanitary convenience flushed by water.— wa'ter-col'our n. artist's colour ground up with water or isinglass; painting in this medium.—wa'ter-col'ourist n.—wa'tercourse n. channel worn out by running water.— wa'tered a.—wa'ter-divin'er n. dowser. —wa'terfall n. fall or perpendicular descent of water of river; cascade.—

wa'ter-gauge n. instrument for measuring height of water in boiler, etc. —wa'ter-glass n. mixture of soluble silicates of potash and soda, used in storing eggs or for preserving stonework.—wa'teriness n.—wa'tering-place n. place where water may be obtained; spa; holiday-resort.—wa'terless a.—wa'ter-lil'y n. aquatic plant with large floating leaves.— wa'ter-line n. line on hull of ship to which water reaches.—wa'ter-logged a. of ground, saturated or full of water.—wa'ter-main n. large pipe running under streets, for conveying water.—wa'ter-mark n. in papermaking, faint design stamped in substance of sheet of paper.— wa'ter-po'lo n. ball game played in water.—wa'ter-proof a. impervious to water;—n. cloth or coat rendered water-proof;—v.t. make impervious to water.—wa'ter-shed, wa'ter-part'ing n. elevated line of division in catchment area between two separate river-systems.—wa'ter-spout n. whirl-wind over water, producing vortex connecting sea and cloud, resulting in pillar of water.— wa'ter-tight a. so fitted as to prevent water escaping or entering.—wa'ter-tow'er n. on railways, etc. raised tank to give steady supply of water at suitable pressure.—wa'ter-way n. navigable channel.—wa'ter-wings n. pl. small rubber floats filled with air to support learners at swimming.— wa'tery a.—above water, financially sound; solvent.—high (low) water, highest (lowest) elevation of tide; maximum (minimum) point of success, etc.—mineral water, water impregnated with mineral matter and possessing specific medicinal properties; artificially aerated water. —in hot water, involved in trouble. —in low water, financially embarrassed.—of the first water, of finest quality.

watt (wot) n. unit of power, being current of one ampere produced by electromotive force of one volt.

wattle (wot'-l) n. twig or flexible rod; interwoven twigs; hurdle made of such rods; fleshy excrescence under throat of cock or turkey; species of Australian acacia;—v.t. bind with twigs; plait.—watt'led a.

wave (wāv) n. waving movement of hand; advancing swell on surface of liquid; surge; unevenness; rise of enthusiasm, heat, etc.; undulating form of electro-magnetic oscillation or of travelling light or sound particles;—v.t. raise into inequalities of surface; move to and fro; give shape of waves; brandish; beckon;— v.i. flap; undulate; signal.—wave'band n. range of wavelengths allotted for broadcasting, etc.—waved a. undulating.—**wave frequency,** number of vibrations of wave per second.— **wav′ily** adv.—**wave′let** n. ripple.— **wave′like** a.—**wa′viness** n.—**wa′ving** a. moving to and fro.—**wa′vy** a. undulating; full of waves.

waver (wā′-ver) v.i. move to and fro; fluctuate.—**wa′verer** n.—**wa′vering** n. and a.—**wa′veringly** adv.

wax (waks) n. a yellowish, sticky substance derived from animal and vegetable substances; beeswax; sealing-wax; cerumen, waxy secretion of ear;—v.t. rub or polish with wax.— **wax′en** a. made of or resembling wax; plastic.—**wax′er** n. one who, or that which, waxes.—**wax′iness** n.— **wax′ing** n.—**wax′-light** n. wax candle or taper.—**wax′-pa′per** n. paper coated with wax for air-tight packing.—**wax′work** n. figure modelled in wax.—pl. exhibition of wax figures.—**wax′y** a.

wax (waks) v.i. increase in size.

way (wā) n. street; highway; passage; path; lane; route; progress; distance; method; custom; habit; means; scheme; movement of ship through water; state or condition.— **way′-bill** n. list of passengers or articles carried by vehicle.—**way′-farer** n. wanderer on foot.—**way′faring** a. travelling;—n. journeying.—**way′lay** v.t. wait in ambush for.—pa.t. and pa.p. **way′laid.**—**waylay′er** n.— **way′side** n. border of road or path;— a. adjoining side of road.—**way′ward** a. perverse; wilful.—**way′wardly** adv. —**way′wardness** n.—**ways and means,** methods; resources.—**by the way,** incidentally.—**each way** (lay bet) for win and place.—**right′-of-way** n. right, established by old custom, to use path through private property. —**under way,** of vessel when moving. —**to make way,** step aside.

we (wē) pron. plural form of I.

weak (wēk) a. feeble; delicate; simple; low; thin; watery; diluted. —**weak′en** v.t. make weak;—v.i. become weak or less resolute.— **weak′-head′ed, weak′-mind′ed** a. feeble intelligence; mentally deficient.— **weak′-kneed** a. irresolute.—**weak′ling** n. feeble person, physically or mentally.—**weak′ly** adv.—**weak′ness** n.—**weaker sex,** women.

weal (wēl) n. streak left on flesh by blow of stick or whip; wale.

weal (wēl) n. welfare.—**the common weal,** well-being of community.

weald (wēld) n. woodland; open country.

wealth (welth) n. riches; abundance. —**wealth′iness** n. riches; opulence.— **wealth′y** a.

wean (wēn) v.t. discontinue gradually breast-feeding of infant; detach or alienate.—**wean′ling** n. newly-weaned infant.

weapon (wep′-un, wep′-n) n. instrument to fight with.

wear (wār) v.t. carry clothes, decorations, etc. upon person; consume by use; deteriorate by rubbing;—v.i. hold out; be impaired gradually by use or exposure.—pa.t. **wore.**—pa.p. **worn.**—n. impairment from use; style of dress; fashion; article worn. —**wear′able** a.—**wear′er** n.—**wear′ing** a. intended for wearing; exhausting to mind and body.—**wear and tear,** loss or deterioration due to usage.— **to wear off,** disappear slowly.

weary (wēr′-i) a. tired; bored; tiresome;—v.t. exhaust one's strength or patience;—v.i. become weary; long (for).—pa.t. and pa.p. **wear′ied.** —pr.p. **wear′ying.**—**wear′ily** adv.— **wear′iness** n. fatigue; ennui.—**wear′isome** a. tedious; causing annoyance. —**wear′isomely** adv.—**wear′isomeness** n.

weasel (wē′-zl) n. small, long-bodied carnivore, related to stoat.

weather (weTH′-er) n. combination of all atmospheric phenomena existing at one time in any particular place;—v.t. expose to air; season by exposure to air; sail to windward of; endure;—v.i. deteriorate, owing to atmospheric conditions.—**weath′er-beat′en** a. marked or roughened by continual exposure to weather.— **weath′ercock** n. pivoted vane to indicate direction of wind; one who changes his mind repeatedly.— **weath′er-glass** n. instrument to indicate changes in atmospheric pressure; barometer.—**weath′ering** n. sloping surface on window-sills, etc. to throw off rain-water; process of decomposing of rocks exposed to elements.—**weath′erside** n. side which faces wind.—**weather ship,** one which records meteorological data.— **weath′er-vane** n. weather-cock.—**to keep one's weather eye open,** be on one's guard.—**under the weather,** rather depressed.

weave (wēv) v.t. cross warp by weft on loom; interlace threads, etc.; plait; fabricate, as tale;—pa.t. **wove.** —pa.p. **wov′en.**—n. style of weaving.—**weav′er** n.

web (web) n. that which is woven; weaver's warp; piece of linen cloth of specific size; membrane which unites toes of water-fowls; network spun by spider; anything as plot, intrigue, cunningly woven.—**webbed** a. having toes united by membrane of skin.—**web′bing** n. strong, hemp fabric woven in narrow strips.

wed (wed) v.t. take for husband or wife; marry; join closely;—v.i. contract matrimony.—pr.p. **wed′ding.**—pa.t. and pa.p. **wed′ded** or **wed.**—**wed′ded** a. married; wholly devoted to (art, etc.).—**wed′ding** n. nuptial ceremony; marriage.

wedge (wej) *n.* piece of wood or metal, tapering to thin edge at fore end, used for splitting or rendering rigid two parts of structure; golf-club with exaggerated loft; anything shaped like wedge;—*v.t.* jam; compress; force (in); squeeze (in); fasten with wedge.—**wedged** *a.* wedge-shaped; jammed tight.—**the thin edge of the wedge**, first step or concession which may lead to inordinate demands.

wedlock (wed'-lok) *n.* marriage; married state.

Wednesday (wednz'-dā, wenz'-dā) *n.* fourth day of week.

wee (wē) *a.* small; tiny.

weed (wēd) *n.* plant growing where it is not desired; worthless person or animal; (*Colloq.*) tobacco;—*v.t.* free from weeds.—**weed'-kill'er** *n.* preparation for killing weeds.—**weed'y** *a.* full of weeds; lanky and weakly. —**to weed out**, eliminate.

weed (wēd) *n.* garment; (*Arch.*) mourning garb, as of widow (usu. in *pl.*).

week (wēk) *n.* seven successive days, usually Sunday to Sunday.—**week'-day** *n.* any day of week except Sunday.—**week'-end** *n.* Friday or Saturday to Monday; holiday for this period.—**week'ly** *a.* pert. to week; happening once a week;—*n.* publication issued weekly;—*adv.* once a week.—**Holy Week**, week preceding Easter Sunday.

weep (wēp) *v.i.* grieve for by shedding tears; cry; drip; rain;—*v.t.* lament; bewail.—*pa.t.* and *pa.p.* **wept**.— **weep'er** *n.*—**weep'ing** *a.* of trees whose branches droop, as **weep'ing will'ow**. —**weep'y** *a.* easily made weep.

weevil (wēv'-il) *n.* different kinds of small beetles whose larvae attack plants and stored grain.

weft (weft) *n.* filling thread carried by shuttle under and over warp in loom.

weigh (wā) *v.t.* find weight of; be equivalent to in weight; deliberate or consider carefully; oppress; raise (anchor, etc.);—*v.i.* have weight; be considered as important; bear heavily (on).—**weigh'-bridge** *n.* machine with platform for weighing both vehicle and goods.—**weigh'er** *n.*— **weight** *n.* gravity as property of bodies; heavy mass; object of known mass for weighing; importance; power and influence;—*v.t.* make more heavy. — **weight'ily** *adv.* — **weight'iness** *n.*—**weightlessness** *n.* lack of response to gravity experienced during space-flights. — **weigh'ty** *a.* having great weight; important.— **dead'-weight** *n.* heavy burden.

weir, wear (wēr) *n.* dam in river; fence of stakes set in stream for taking fish.

weird (wērd) *n.* spell or charm; fate; destiny;—*a.* skilled in witchcraft; unearthly; uncanny; supernatural. —**weird'ly** *adv.*—**weird'ness** *n.*

welcome (wel'-kum) *a.* received gladly; causing gladness; free to enjoy or use;—*n.* kind or hearty reception; salutation;—*v.t.* greet with kindness and pleasure.

weld (weld) *v.t.* join heated metal by fusion; unite closely;—*n.* homogeneous joint between two metals.— **wel'der** *n.*

welfare (wel'-fār) *n.* well-doing or well-being; prosperity.

welkin (wel'-kin) *n.* (*Arch.*) sky; vault of heaven.

well (wel) *n.* shaft sunk deep in ground to obtain water or oil; spring; fountain; source; bottom of lift- or elevator-shaft; cavity or pit below ground-level; chamber for catching surplus water or oil;—*v.i.* issue forth in volume, as water.

well (wel) *a.* in good health; fortunate; comfortable; satisfactory; proper;—*adv.* rightly; agreeably; satisfactorily; soundly;—*interj.* exclamation of surprise, interrogation, etc.—**well'-advised** *a.* prudent; sensible.—**well'-appoint'ed** *a.* handsomely equipped.—**well'-be'ing** *n.* welfare.— **well'-bred** *a.* courteous and refined in manners; of good stock.—**well'-nigh** *adv.* nearly; almost.—**well'-off** *a.* rich.—**well'-to-do** *a.* wealthy.—**as well as**, in addition to; besides.

Welsh, Welch (welsh) *a.* relating to Wales or its inhabitants;—*n.* language of Wales, Celtic family of languages; people of Wales. — **Welsh'man, Welsh'woman** *n.*—**Welsh rabbit**, or **rarebit**, savoury consisting of melted cheese on toast.

welsh, welch (welsh) *v.t.* and *v.i.* abscond without paying out on winning bets.—**welsh'er, welch'er** *n.*

welt (welt) *n.* hem round edge or border; narrow strip of leather between upper and sole of shoe; weal;—*v.t.* furnish with welt; flog.— **welt'ed** *a.*—**welt'ing** *n.*

welter (wel'-tẽr) *v.i.* roll about; wallow in slime, blood, etc.;—*n.* confusion; turmoil.

welter (wel'-tẽr) *a.* pert. to heavily-weighted race in horse-racing;—*n.* heavy-weight rider; class where boxers weigh between 135 lb. and 147 lb. (in America 145 lb.).

wen (wen) *n.* small superficial tumour.

wench (wensh) *n.* (*Arch.*) girl; maid; lewd woman;—*v.i.* associate with lewd women.

wend (wend) *v.t.* direct; betake (one's way);—*v.i.* go.

went (went) *pa.t.* of **go**.

were (wer) *pa.t.* plural of **be**.

werewolf, werwolf (wēr'-wòòlf) *n.*

human being who, at will, could take form of wolf while retaining human intelligence.

west (west) *n.* point in heavens where sun sets; one of four cardinal points of compass; region of country lying to west;—*a.* situated in, facing, coming from west;—*adv.* to west.—**wes'tering** *a.* setting in west.—**west'erly** *a.* situated in west; of wind, blowing from west;—*adv.* in west direction;—*n.* wind blowing from west.—**west'ern** *a.* situated in west; coming from west;—*n.* inhabitant of western country or district; film featuring cowboys in Western States of U.S.A.—**wes'terner** *n.* native of west.—**wes'ternmost**, **west'most** *a.* farthest to west.—**west'ward** *a.* and *adv.* towards west. — **west'wards** *adv.* — **West Country**, south-west England.—**to go west** (*Slang*) die; disappear.

wet (wet) *a.* full of moisture; humid; damp; rainy;—*n.* water; moisture; rain;—*v.t.* make wet; moisten;—*pr.p.* wet'ting.—*pa.p.* wet or wet'ted.—**wet'-blan'ket** *n.* kill-joy.—**wet'ness** *n.*—**wet'-nurse** *n.* woman who suckles child of another.

wether (weTH'-ĕr) *n.* castrated ram.

whack (hwak) *v.t.* hit, esp. with stick; beat;—*v.i.* strike with smart blow;—*n.* blow.

whale (hwāl) *n.* large fish-like mammal;—*v.i.* hunt for whales.—**whale'-boat** *n.* long boat with sharp bow at each end.—**whale'-bone** *n.* baleen, elastic, flexible horny product of jaws of baleen-whale.—**whal'er** *n.* man or ship engaged in whaling industry.

wharf (hwawrf) *n.* structure on bank of navigable waters at which vessels can be loaded or unloaded; quay. — *pl.* wharfs, wharves. — *v.t.* moor at, or place on, wharf.—**wharf'age** *n.* charge for use of wharf;—**wharfinger** (hwawr'-fin-jer) *n.* one who owns or has charge of wharf.

what (hwot) *pron.* interrogative pronoun (used elliptically, in exclamation, or adjectively); relative pronoun, meaning that which (used adjectively); such . . . as; whatever;—*adv.* why? in what respect? to what degree?—**whatev'er** *pron.* anything that; all that.—**whatso'ever** *pron.* whatever.

wheat (hwēt) *n.* edible portion of annual corn-grass.—**wheat'en** *a.* made of wheat or wholemeal.

wheatear (hwēt'-ēr) *n.* small passeriform bird.

wheedle (hwē'-dl) *v.t.* cajole; coax.

wheel (hwēl) *n.* circular frame or disc turning on axis; instrument formerly used for punishing criminals; rotation; cycle; steering-wheel; wheeling movement;—*v.t.* convey on wheels; furnish with wheels;—*v.i.* turn on, or as on, axis; change direction by pivoting about end unit, as troops on march; roll forward; revolve.—**wheel'barrow** *n.* conveyance with single wheel and two shafts for pushing.—**wheel'-house** *n.* (*Naut.*) deck-house to shelter steersman.—**wheel'ing** *n.*—**wheel'wright** *n.* one who makes and repairs wheels.

wheeze (hwēz) *v.i.* breathe audibly —*n.* (*Colloq.*) joke.—**wheez'y** *a.*

whelk (hwelk) *n.* spiral-shelled sea-snail.

whelp (hwelp) *n.* young dog or puppy; lion-cub; youth (contemptuously);—*v.i.* and *v.t.* bring forth young.

when (hwen) *adv.* and *conj.* at what time?; at time that; whereas; at which time.—**whence** *adv.* and *conj.* from what place; from what, or which, cause, etc.—**whencesoev'er** *adv.* and *conj.* from what place, source, or cause, soever.—**whence'er** *adv.* and *conj.* at whatever time. Also **whenev'er**.—**whensoev'er** *adv.* and *conj.* whenever.

where (hwār) *adv.* and *conj.* at what place?; at, or to, place in which.—**whereabout'** *adv.* and *conj.* about where; near what or which place?—*n.* place where one is. Also **where'abouts**.—**whereas'** *conj.* considering that.—**whereat'** *adv.* and *conj.* at which; by what.—**whereby'** *adv.* and *conj.* by which; by what.—**where'fore** *adv.* for which reason? why?—*conj.* accordingly.—**wherein'** *adv.* in which; in which, or what, respect, etc.; in what.—**whereof'** *adv.* of which; of what.—**whereon'** *adv.* on which; on what.—**wheresoev'er** *adv.* in, or to, whatever place.—**whereto'** *adv.* to which; to what; to what end. Also **whereun'to**.—**whereupon'** *adv.* in consequence of which.—**wherev'er** *adv.* at whatever place.—**wherewith'** *adv.* with which; with what.—**wherewithal'** *adv.* wherewith.—**the wherewithal** *n.* money; means.

wherry (hwer'-i) *n.* shallow light boat, for fast sailing; half-decked vessel used in fishing.

whet (hwet) *v.t.* sharpen by rubbing; make sharp, keen, or eager; stir up;—*pr.p.* whet'ting.—*pa.t.* and *pa.p.* whet'ted.—**whet'stone** *n.* fine-grained stone used for sharpening cutlery and tools.—**whet'ter** *n.*

whether (hweTH'-ĕr) *pron.* which of two;—*conj.* used to introduce first of two or more alternative clauses, other(s) being connected by *or.*

whey (hwā) *n.* clear liquid left as residue of milk after separation of fat and casein (curd).—**whey'-face** *n.* palefaced person.

which (hwich) *pron.* interrogative, signifying *who*, or *what one*, of number; relative, used of things; also used adjectively.—**whichev'er** pron. whether one or other.

hiff (hwif) n. puff of air, smoke, etc.; odour; smoke;—v.t. throw out in whiffs; blow;—v.i. emit whiffs, as of smoke.

hile (hwīl) n. space of time;—conj. during time when; as long as; whereas;— adv. during which. — whilst conj. while.—**to while away**, pass (time) usually idly.

him (hwim) n. passing fancy; caprice; fad.—**whim'sical** a. capricious; fanciful; fantastical.—whimsical'ity n. fanciful idea.—**whim'sically** adv. — whim'sicalness n. — whim'sy, whim'sey n. caprice; fancy;—a.

himper (hwim'-per) v.i. and v.t. cry, or utter, with low, fretful, broken voice;—n.—whim'perer n.—whim'pering n.

hin (hwin) n. shrub with yellow flowers; gorse; furze.

hine (hwīn) n. drawling; plaintive wail; complaint;—v.i. utter plaintive cry.—whi'ner n.—whi'ning n.

hinny (hwin'-i) v.i. to neigh;—n. sound made by horse.

hip (hwip) v.t. strike with lash; flog; bind ends of rope with twine; snatch or jerk (away); beat into froth, as cream or eggs;—v.t. start suddenly. — pr.p. **whip'ping**. — pa.t. and pa.p. **whipped**.—n. lash attached to handle; coachman; M.P. appointed to ensure fullest possible attendance of members of his party.—**whipcord** n. cord for whiplash; fabric with pronounced warp twill.—**whip'-hand** n. hand which holds whip; mastery, upper hand.—**whip'persnap'per** n. insignificant person; impertinent young fellow.—**whip'ping** n. flogging.—**whip'-round** n. collection on behalf of colleague.

whippet (hwip'-et) n. cross-bred dog of greyhound type, for racing.

whip-poor-will (hwip'-pŏŏr-wil) n. American bird of nightjar family.

whirr (hwir) v.i. dart, fly, or revolve with buzzing or whizzing noise.—pr.p. **whir'ring**.—pa.t. and pa.p. **whirred**.—n. buzzing or whizzing sound.

whirl (hwerl) v.t. turn round rapidly; cause to rotate;—v.i. rotate rapidly; spin;—n. rapid rotation; anything which whirls; bewilderment.—**whirl'igig** n. spinning toy.—whirl'ing n. and a.—whirl'pool n. circular eddy of water.—**whirl'wind** n. forward-moving, funnel-shaped column of air revolving rapidly and spirally round low-pressure core.

whisk (hwisk) n. rapid, sweeping motion; small bunch of feathers, hair, etc. used for brush; instrument for beating eggs, etc.—v.t. sweep, or agitate, with light, rapid motion;—

v.i. move nimbly and speedily.—**whisk'er** n. one who, or that which, whisks; moustache.—pl. hair on man's cheeks; long, stiff hairs at side of mouth of cat or other animal.—whis'kered a.

whisky (hwis'-ki) n. distilled alcoholic liquor made from various grains. Also whisk'ey, esp. Irish.

whisper (hwis'-per) v.t. utter in low, sibilant tone; suggest secretly or furtively;—v.i. speak in whispers, under breath; rustle;—n. low, soft remark; hint; rumour.—whis'perer n.

whist (hwist) n. card game for four players.

whistle (hwis'-l) n. sound made by forcing breath through rounded and nearly closed lips; small musical instrument; form of hooter;—v.i. make such sound;—v.i. and v.t. to render tune by whistling; signal, by whistling.—whist'ler n. one who whistles.

whit (hwit) n. smallest part imaginable; jot.

white (hwīt) a. of colour of snow; light in colour; hoary; pale; pure; clean; bright; spotless; (Colloq.) honest; decent;—n. colour of pure snow; albuminous part of egg; white part of eye-ball;—v.t. whiten.—**white'-ant** n. termite.—**white'bait** n. newly hatched young of sprat, herring, and related fishes.—**white corpuscle**, leucocyte.—**white elephant**, sacred elephant of Siam; gift entailing more bother and expense than it is worth.—**white'-feath'er** n. symbol of cowardice.—**white'-fish** n. non-oily fish, such as whiting, haddock, cod, plaice, etc.—**white flag**, sign of truce or surrender.—**white'-fri'ar** n. mendicant monk, of Carmelite order.—**white'-horse** n. white-crested wave.—**white'-lead** n. basic lead carbonate.—**white lie**, harmless fib.—**whi'ten** v.t. and v.i. make or turn white.—**whit'ener** n.—**whit'ening** n. whiting.—**white'ness** n.—**white paper**, government report on matter recently investigated.—**white slave**, woman or girl enticed away for purposes of prostitution.—**white'throat** n. small bird of warbler family.—**white'wash** n. mixture of whiting, water, and size, for lining walls;—v.t. cover with whitewash; clear reputation of.—**whi'tish** a. somewhat white.

whither (hwiTH'-er) adv. to which, or what, place?—**whithersoev'er** adv. (Arch.) to whatever place.

whiting (hwī-ting) n. edible sea-fish; pulverised chalk, for making whitewash.

whitlow (hwit'-lō) n. suppurating and inflammatory sore affecting finger-nails.

Whitsunday (hwit'-sun-dā) n. seventh Sunday after Easter, festival day of Church, kept in commemoration of descent of Holy Ghost.—**Whit'sun, Whit'suntide, Whit Week,** week containing Whitsunday.

whittle (hwit'-l) *v.t.* and *v.i.* cut off thin slices or shavings with knife; pare away.

whizz, whiz (hwiz) *v.i.* make hissing sound.—*pr.p.* **whiz'zing.**—*pa.t.* and *pa.p.* **whizzed.**—*n.* hissing and humming sound.—**whis'zingly** *adv.*

who (hōō) *pron.* relative or interrogative, referring to persons.—**whoev'er** *pron.* whatever person; any one, without exception.—**whom** *pron.* objective case of who.—**whom'soever** *pron.* objective of who'soever *pron.* any person, without exception.—**whose** *pron.* possessive case of who or which.—**whodunit** (hōō-dun'-it) *n.* (*Colloq.*) detective story.

whole (hōl) *a.* entire; complete; not defective; unimpaired; sound;—*n.* entire thing; aggregate; gross; sum; amount.—**whole'heart'ed** *a.* hearty; sincere.—**whole'-meal** *n.* and *a.* wheaten flour containing also part of husk of grain.—**whole'sale** *n.* sale of goods in bulk to retailers;—*a.* selling or buying in large quantities; extensive; indiscriminate.—**whole'saler** *n.*—**whole'some** *a.* healthy; nourishing.—**whole'someness** *n.*—**whol'ly** *adv.* completely; perfectly.

whoop (hwōōp, hōōp) *n.* loud yell; —*v.i.* utter loud, high-pitched cry.—**whoop'er** *n.* one who whoops; whistling swan.—**whoop'ing, hoop'ing-cough** *n.* infectious disease marked by fits of convulsive coughing.—to make **whoopee** (*Slang*) celebrate uproariously.

whopper (hwop'-er) *n.* anything large; monstrous lie.—**whop'ping** *a.* (*Slang*) very big.

whore (hōr) *n.* prostitute; unchaste woman;—*v.i.* have unlawful sexual intercourse.

whorl (hworl) *n.* spiral turn of univalve shell; ring of leaves, petals, etc.—**whorled** *a.*

whortleberry (hwor'-tl-ber-i) *n.* small shrub, with bluish-black fruit; bilberry.

why (hwī) *adv.* and *conj.* for what reason? on which account? wherefore?—*interj.* expletive to show surprise, indignation, protest.

wick (wik) *n.* cord which draws up oil or wax, in lamp or candle, to be burned.

wicked (wik'-ed) *a.* evil; immoral; mischievous.—**wick'edly** *adv.*—**wick'edness** *n.*

wicker (wik'-er) *n.* twig or osier; wicker-work;—*a.* made of pliant twigs or osiers.—**wick'er-work** *n.* basket-work.

wicket (wik'-et) *n.* small door or gate, adjacent to or let into larger

door; three upright stumps with bails at which bowler aims in cricket; cricket-pitch.—**wick'et-keep'er** *n.* fieldsman who stands immediately behind wicket in cricket.

wide (wīd) *a.* broad; spacious; distant; bulging; missing mark;—*adv.* to distance; far; astray;—*n.* ball bowled out of batsman's reach.—**wide'-awake'** *a.* fully awake —**wide'ly** *adv.*—**wi'den** *v.t.* make wide or wider;—*v.i.* grow wide or wider expand.—**wide'ness** *n.* width.—**wide'-spread** *a.* extending on all sides circulating amongst numerous people.—**width** *n.* wideness; breadth

widgeon, wigeon (wij'-on) *n.* migratory duck.

widow (wid'-ō) *n.* woman who has lost husband by death;—*v.t.* bereave of husband; be widow to.—**wid'ower** *n.* man whose wife is dead.—**wid'owhood** *n.*

wield (wēld) *v.t.* use with full command; swing; handle; manage; control.—**wield'able** *a.*—**wield'er** *n.*—**wield'iness** *n.*—**wiel'dy** *a.* manageable; controllable.

wife (wīf) *n.* married woman; spouse;—*pl.* **wives.**—**wife'less** *a.* without wife; unmarried.—**wife'ly** *a.* as befits wife.

wig (wig) *n.* false covering for head to imitate natural hair.—**wigged** *a.* wearing wig.

wig (wig) *v.t.* (*Colloq.*) scold.—**wig'ging** *n.* scolding; keelhauling.

wiggle (wig'-l) *v.i.* waggle; wriggle; —*n.* wriggling motion.

wigwam (wig'-wam) *n.* Amer.-Ind. hut.

wild (wīld) *a.* living in state of nature; not domesticated; native; desert; savage; annoyed;—*n.* uncultivated, uninhabited region.—**wild'-cat** *n.* undomesticated cat;—*a.* reckless; highly speculative.—**wild'-cat strike,** stoppage of work against official (trade union) advice.—**wild'-fire** *n.* anything which burns rapidly; sheet-lightning.—**wild'-goose-chase** *n.* foolish, futile pursuit.—**wild'ly** *adv.*—**wild'ness** *n.*—to sow wild oats, be given to youthful excesses.

wilderness (wil'-der-nes) *n.* tract of land uncultivated and uninhabited by human beings; desert; state of confusion.

wile (wīl) *n.* trick or stratagem practised for ensnaring or alluring; ruse;—*v.t.* entice; allure.—**wi'liness** *n.* guile; cunning.—**wi'ly** *a.* crafty; artful; sly.

wilful (wil'-fōōl) *a.* obstinate; intentional.—**wil'fully** *adv.*—**wil'fulness** *n.* obstinacy; stubbornness.

will (wil) *n.* power of choosing what one will do; determination; discretion; wish; (*Law*) declaration in writing showing how property is to be disposed by after death;—*v.t.* determine by choice; decree; bequeath;—*v.i.* exercise act of volition; choose; desire; wish;—*v.* used as auxiliary, to denote futurity.—*pa.t.* would.—**will'ing** *a.* favourably inclined; disposed; ready.—**will'ingly** *adv.* readily; gladly.—**will'ingness** *n.* —**will'-pow'er** *n.* strength of will.— **at will**, at pleasure.—**with a will**, zealously.

will-o'-the-wisp (wil'-ō-the-wisp) *n.* ignis fatuus; jack-o'-lantern; flickering, pale-bluish flame seen over marshes; any person or thing of uncertain movements.

willow (wil'-ō) *n.* tree of genus Salix; cricket-bat.—**will'ow-herb** *n.* tall, perennial plant with bunched purple flowers.—**will'ow-war'bler**, -**wren** *n.* species of bird.—**will'ow-weed** *n.* purple loose-strife. — **will'owy** *a.* abounding in willows; pliant; supple and slender.—**weep'ing-will'ow** *n.* waterside tree with pendent twigs.

willy-nilly (wil'-i-nil'-i) *a.* compulsory;—*adv.* willingly or unwillingly.

wilt (wilt) *v.i. and t.* fade; droop; wither *v.t.* depress.

wimple (wim'-pl) *n.* covering for neck, chin and sides of face, still retained by nuns; veil;—*v.i.* ripple.

win (win) *v.t.* gain by success in competition or contest; obtain; attract; reach, after difficulty;—*v.i.* be victorious;—*pr.p.* **win'ning.**— *pa.t.* and *pa.p.* **won.**—*n.* victory; success.—**win'ner** *n.*—**win'ning** *n.* act of gaining;—*pl.* sum won in game or competition;—*a.* attractive; charming.—**win'ningly** *adv.*

wince (wins) *v.i.* shrink or flinch, as from blow or pain;—*n.* act of wincing.—**win'cer** *n.*

wincey, winsey (win'-si) *n.* cotton flannelette.—**win'ceyette** *n.* light, plain cotton fabric.

winch (winsh) *n.* hoisting machine; wheel-crank; windlass.

wind (wind) *n.* air in motion; current of air; breeze; breath; power of respiration; flatulence; idle talk; point of compass;—*pl.* wind-instruments of orchestra;—*v.t.* follow by scent; run, ride, or drive till breathless; rest (horse) that it may recover wind; expose to wind;—*v.t.* (wind) sound by blowing (horn, etc.).—*pa.p.* **wind'ed** or **wound.**—**wind'bag** *n.* leathern bag, part of bagpipe; (*Slang*) empty, pompous talker.— **wind'-cheat'er** *n.* outer garment of light wind-proof fabric.—**wind'fall** *n.* anything blown down by wind, as fruit; unexpected legacy or other gain.—**wind'-flow'er** *n.* wood-anemone.—**wind'-gauge** *n.* anemometer, instrument for measuring force of wind.—**wind'ily** *adv.*—**wind'iness** *n.*— **wind'-in'strument** *n.* musical instrument played by blowing or air-pressure.—**wind'-jamm'er** *n.* (*Colloq.*) merchant sailing ship.—**wind'less** *a.* calm; out of breath.—**wind'mill** *n.* mill worked by action of wind on vanes or sails.—**wind'pipe** *n.* trachea; pipe admitting air to lungs.— **wind'-screen**, -**shield** *n.* protection against wind for driver or pilot.— **wind'-up** *n.* (*Slang*) panicky apprehension.—**wind'ward** *n.* point from which wind blows;—*a.* facing wind; —*adv.* toward wind.—**wind'y** *a.* consisting of, exposed to wind; tempestuous; flatulent; empty; (*Slang*) frightened.—**before the wind**, with wind driving behind.—**in the wind**, afoot; astir; in secret preparation.— **second wind**, restoration of normal breathing.—**to get wind of**, be secretly informed of.—**to raise the wind** (*Slang*) procure money necessary.—**to sail close to the wind**, take risks.

wind (wind) *v.t.* twist round; coil; twine; wrap; make ready for working by tightening spring; meander;—*v.i.* vary from direct course;—*pa.t.* and *pa.p.* **wound.**— **wind'er** *n.* one who, or that which, winds.—**wind'ing** *a.* twisting or bending from direct line; meandering; serpentine;—*n.* turning; twist. —**wind'ing-sheet** *n.* sheet in which corpse is wrapped.—**wind'-up** *n.* closing stages.—**to wind up**, coil up; bring to conclusion; adjust for final settlement affairs of business or society about to be dissolved; excite to high degree.—**wound'-up** *a.* highly excited.

windlass (wind'-las) *n.* form of winch for hoisting or hauling purposes.

window (win'-dō) *n.* opening in wall to admit air and light, usually covered with glass.—**win'dow-dress'ing** *n.* effective arrangement of goods in shop-window.—**win'dow-sill** *n.* flat portion of window-opening on which window rests.

wine (win) *n.* fermented juice of grape; similar liquor made from other fruits;—*v.i.* drink wine.

wing (wing) *n.* organ of flight; one of two feathered fore-limbs of bird; main lifting surface of aeroplane; aerofoil; side portion of building; right or left division of army or fleet; unit of Royal Air Force consisting of two or more squadrons; in football, etc. section of team to right or left of field; mudguard of motor-car; sidepiece;—*pl.* side walls of stage;—*v.t.* furnish with wings; enable to proceed quicker; wound in wing, arm, or shoulder;—*v.i.* soar on wing.—**wing'-comman'der** *n.* Royal Air Force officer corresponding to lieut.-colonel in army. — **winged** *a.*

furnished with wings; wounded in wing.

wink (wingk) v.t. and v.i. close and open eyelids; blink; convey hint by flick of eyelid;—n. act of winking; hint conveyed by winking.—**forty winks**, short nap.—**to wink at**, connive at; affect not to see.

winnow (win'-ō) v.t. separate grain from chaff by means of wind or current of air; fan; separate; sift; sort out.—**winn'owing** a. and n.

winsome (win'-sum) a. cheerful; charming; attractive. — **win'somely** adv.—**win'someness** n.

winter (win'-tẹr) n. fourth season; (Astron.) in northern latitudes, period between winter solstice and vernal equinox (22nd Dec. to 20th-21st March); any dismal, gloomy time;—a. wintry; pert. to winter;—v.t. keep and feed throughout winter;—v.i. pass winter.—**win'ter-gar'den** n. large glass structure with exotic plants, often used for public concerts, etc.—**win'tergreen** n. herb from which is obtained, oil of wintergreen, used for rheumatism.—**win'triness** n.—**win'try**, **win'tery** a. suitable to winter; cold; snowy.

wipe (wīp) v.t. rub lightly, so as to clean or dry; strike off gently; clear away;—n. act of wiping clean; blow.—**wi'per** n. one who, or that which, wipes.—**wi'ping** n. act of wiping.—**to wipe out**, erase; destroy utterly.

wire (wīr) n. metal drawn into form of thread or cord; telegraphy; telegram;—v.t. bind or stiffen with wire; pierce with wire; fence with wire; install with wires for electric circuit; telegraph; snare;—a. formed of wire.—**wired** a.—**wire'-haired** a. (of dogs) with short, wiry hair.—**wire'-pull'er** n. one who exercises influence behind scenes.—**wire'-worm** n. larva of various click-beetles.—**wi'rily** adv.—**wi'riness** n. state of being wiry; toughness of physique.—**wi'ry** a.—**wi'ring** n. system of electric wires forming circuit.—**a live wire**, wire charged with electricity; enterprising person.

wireless (wīr'-les) n. and a. older term for radio.

wisdom (wiz'-dum) n. quality of being wise; knowledge and capacity to make use of it; judgment.—**wis'dom-tooth** n. posterior molar tooth, cut about twentieth year.

-wise (wīz) adv. suffix in way or manner of, arranged alike, as in clockwise, likewise, etc.

wise (wīz) n. way; manner.

wise (wīz) a. enlightened; sagacious; learned; dictated by wisdom.—**wise'-crack** n. concise witty statement;—v.i. utter one.—**wise'ly** adv.—**wise'ness** n.

wiseacre (wī'-zā-kẹr) n. know-all.

wish (wish) v.t. desire; long for request;—v.i. have desire;—n. expression or object of desire; request.—**wish(ing)-bone** n. forked bone of fowl's breast.—**wish'er** n.—**wish'ful** a. eager; desirous; longing.—**wish'fully** adv.—**wish'fulness** n.

wishy-washy (wish'-i-wosh-i) a. thin and weak.

wisp (wisp) n. twisted handful, usually of hay; stray lock of hair.

wistful (wist'-fŏŏl) a. pensive; sadly contemplative; earnestly longing; wishful; eager; thoughtful.—**wist'fully** adv.—**wist'fulness** n.

wit (wit) n. intellect; understanding; humour; pleasantry;—pl. mental faculties;—v.i. know.—**wit'less** a lacking wit or understanding; silly; stupid.—**wit'lessly** adv. in all innocence.—**wit'lessness** n.—**witt'icism** n witty remark.—**witt'ily** adv.—**witt'iness** n.—**witt'ingly** adv. with foreknowledge or design; knowingly.—**witt'y** a. amusing.—**at one's wits' end**, perplexed.—**to wit**, namely.

witch (wich) n. woman who was supposed to practise sorcery; ugly old woman; hag; crone;—v.t. bewitch; enchant.—**witch'craft** n. black art; sorcery.—**witch'-doc'tor** n. among savage tribes, medicine-man.—**witch'ery** n. sorcery.—**witch'-hunt** n. esp. in U.S. search for, and subsequent trial of, political opponents.

witch, wych (wich) n. **witch'-elm**.—**witch'-al'der** n. low shrub with alderlike leaves.—**witch'-ha'zel** n. shrub with yellow flowers and edible seeds; dried bark and leaves of tree, used as astringent.

with (wiTH) prep. in company or possession of; in relation to; against; by means of; denoting association, cause, agency, comparison.

withal (wiTH-awl') adv. with rest; also.

withdraw (wiTH-draw') v.t. take away; recall; retract;—v.i. go away; retire.—pa.t. **withdrew'**.—pa.p. **withdrawn'**.—**withdraw'al** n.

withe (wiTH, with) n. tough, flexible twig, esp. willow, reed, or osier. Also **with**, **wyth**, **with'y**.—**with'y** a. made of withes; flexible and tough.

wither (wiTH-ẹr) v.t. cause to fade and become dry; blight;—v.i. fade; decay. — **with'ering** a. blighting; scorching;—n. process of withering.—**with'eringly** adv. scathingly.

withers (wiTH'-ẹrz) n.pl. ridge between horse's shoulder-blades.

withhold (wiTH-hōld') v.t. hold or keep;—pa.p. **withheld'**.

within (wiTH-in') prep. in inner or interior part of; in compass of;—adv. in inner part; inwardly; at home.

without (wiTH-out') prep. on or at outside of; out of; not within;

yond; out of limits of; all but;—
v. on outside; out of doors;—**conj.**
cept; unless.

thstand (wiTH-stand') v.t. oppose;
and against; resist.—**pa.t.** and
.p. withstood'.—**withstand'er** n. opponent; resister.

tness (wit'-nes) n. testimony; one
ho, or that which, furnishes
vidence or proof; one who has seen
: has knowledge of incident; one
ho attests another person's signa-
ure;—**v.t.** be witness of or to;—**v.i.**
ive evidence.—**wit'ness-box** n. en-
osure where witness stands in
ourt of law.

zard (wiz'-ard) n. sorcerer; magi-
ian; conjurer;—**a.** with magical
owers.—**wiz'ardry** n.

zen, wizened (wiz'-n, wiz'-nd) a.
ried up.

ad (wŏd) n. plant yielding blue
ye.

obble (wob'-l) v.i. rock from side to
ide; be hesitant,—n. rocking, unqual motion.—**wobb'ler,** n.—**wobb'ly**
haky; unsteady. a.

oe, (wō) n. grief; affliction; sorrow;
isery.—**woe'begone** a. sorrowful;
retched.—**woe'ful,** a. sorrowful;
itiful; paltry.—**woe'fully** adv.

old (wōld) n. wood; open tract of
ountry.

olf (woolf) n. carnivorous wild
nimal, allied to dog; cruel person;
Slang) lady-killer. — pl. wolves
wŏŏlvz).—**v.t.** devour ravenously.
-wolf'-cub n. young wolf; junior
ember of Boy Scouts.—**wolf'-
ound** n. dog bred for hunting
rolves.—**wol'fish, wol'vish** a.—**wol'-
ishly** adv.—**wol'fishness** n.—**wolf's'-
ane** n. aconite.—**to keep the wolf from
ne door,** eke out bare existence.

olfram (woolf'-ram) n. mineral,
errous tungstate, chief source of
etal tungsten. Also **wolf'ramite.**

olverine, wolverene (wool-ve-rēn')
. carnivorous mammal inhabiting
rctic region—glutton or carcajou.

oman (woom'-an) n. adult human
emale; women collectively.—**pl.
omen** (wim'-en).—**wom'anhood** n.
dult stage of women.—**wom'anish**
effeminate.—**wom'anishness** n.—
om'ankind, wom'enkind n. female
ex.—**wom'anlike** a.—**wom'anliness** n.
-**wom'anly** a.

omb (wŏŏm) n. female organ of
onception and gestation; uterus;
atrix.

ombat (wom'-bat) n. group of
ustralian and Tasmanian fur-bear-
g, burrowing marsupial animals.

onder (wun'-der) n. surprise;
mazement; prodigy; miracle;—**v.i.**
el wonder; marvel; be doubtful.—
on'derer n.—**won'derful** a. remark-
ble; amazing.—**won'derfully** adv.—
on'derfulness n.—**won'dering** a.—

won'deringly adv. in wondering and
expectant manner.—**won'derland** n.
land of marvels; fairyland.—**won'-
drous** a. wonderful.—**won'drously** adv.

wont (wŏnt) a. accustomed; used;—
n. habit; custom; use;—**v.i.** be accustomed. — **won'ted** a. accustomed;
habitual; usual.—**won'tedness** n.

won't (wŏnt) v.i. contr. of will not.

woo (wŏŏ) v.t. make love to; court.
—**woo'er** n—**woo'ing** n.

wood (wood) n. land with growing
trees close together; copse; grove;
forest; timber; (Colloq. at game of
bowls) bowl.—**wood'-al'cohol** n. methyl alcohol, product of dry distillation
of wood, esp. beech and birch.—
wood'bine, wood'bind n. wild honeysuckle; (U.S.) Virginia creeper.—
wood'chuck n. small N. American
burrowing rodent.—**wood'cock** n.
migrant game-bird of snipe family.
—**wood'craft** n. expert knowledge of
woodland conditions.—**wood'cut** n.
engraving on wood; impression
from such engravings.—**wood'-cut'ter**
n.—**wood'ed** a. covered with trees.—
wood'en a. made of wood; clumsy;
stupid.—**wood'en-head** n. blockhead.
—**wood'enly** adv. stupidly.—**wood'enness** n. wooden quality; stiffness;
stupidity.—**wood'iness** n.—**wood'land**
n. and a. (of) wooded country.—
wood'-louse n. small isopod crustacean, found in damp places.—
wood'man n. forester; woodcutter.—
wood'pecker n. bird which taps and
bores bark of trees with bill.—
wood'-pig'eon n. ring-dove.—**wood-
sorr'el** n. perennial herb with acid
leaves.—**wood'-spir'it** n. methyl alcohol.—**wood'-wind** n. wooden musical
instrument, as flute, oboe, clarinet,
bassoon, etc.—**wood'y** a. abounding
with, consisting of, wood.—**not out of
the wood,** still in jeopardy.

woof (wŏŏf) n. weft; texture.

wool (wool) n. soft, curled hair of
sheep, goat, etc.; yarn or cloth of
this;—**wool'-gath'ering** n. day-dream-
ing.—**wool'len** n. cloth made of
wool;—**pl.** woollen goods;—**a.** made
of, pert. to, wool.—**wool'liness** n.—
wool'ly a. of, or like wool; muddled
and confused.—**wool'-pack** n. pack of
wool weighing 240 lbs.—**wool'sack** n.
sack or bag of wool; seat of Lord
Chancellor in House of Lords, as
Speaker of House.—**wool'sey** n.
material of cotton and wool mixed;
linsey-woolsey.—**dyed in the wool,**
become inherent; out-and-out.

word (werd) n. spoken or written
sign of idea; term; oral expression;
message; password; promise; brief
remark; proverb;—**pl.** speech; wordy
quarrel;—**v.t.** express in words;
phrase;—**v.i.** talk; discourse.—**word'-
ed** a. phrased; expressed.—**word'ily**
adv. pedantically.—**wor'diness** n. ver-

bosity.—**wor'ding** n. precise words used; phraseology.—**word perfect**, able to repeat correctly from memory.—**word'y** a. verbose; prolix.—word for word, literally; verbatim.—by word of mouth, orally.

work (werk) n. exertion of strength; effort directed to end; employment; toil; manual labour; occupation; deed; fabric; book; embroidery; (Phys.) result of force overcoming resistance over definite distance;—pl. structures in engineering; manufacturing establishment; mechanism of watch, etc.; fortifications;—v.i. exert oneself; labour; act; be effective; have influence (on, upon);—v.t. produce by labour; perform.—**work'able** a. capable of being worked.—**work'er** n. one who is employed; one who works conscientiously; sterile member of colony of insects.—**work'house** n. formerly institute for able-bodied paupers.—**work'ing** n. act of labouring or doing something useful; mode of operation; fermentation;—pl. mine as whole, or part of it where work is being carried on;—a. labouring; fermenting.—**work'man** n. one actually engaged in manual labour; craftsman.—**work'manlike** a. befitting skilled workman.—**work'manship** n.—**work-out** n. practice; trial run.—**work'shop** n. place where things are made or repaired.—to **work off**, get rid of gradually.—to **work out**, solve (problem); plan in detail; exhaust (mine, etc.).—to **work up**, excite unduly; study intensively.

world (werld) n. earth and its inhabitants; whole system of things; universe; any planet or star; this life; human race; mankind; great quantity.—**world'liness** n. state of being worldly.—**world'ing** n. one who is absorbed in affairs or pleasures of world.—**world'ly** a. relating to world; engrossed in temporal pursuits; earthly; not spiritual.—**world'ly-wise** a. experienced in ways of people.—**world'wide** a. extending to every corner of globe.—**man (woman) of the world**, one with much wordly experience.—**old'-world** a. old-fashioned; quaint.

worm (wurm) n. small, limbless, invertebrate animal with soft, long, segmented body; spiral thread; metal screw with endless thread to gear with toothed wheel; spiral pipe through which vapour passes in distillation; grovelling, contemptible fellow;—pl. infestation by parasitic worms;—v.t. work (oneself) in insidiously; insinuate oneself;—v.i. work slowly and secretly.—**worm'cast** n. earth voided and thrown up by earthworm.—**worm'y** a. wormlike; abounding with worms.

wormwood (wurm'-wood) n. bitter plant, used in making absinth vermouth, etc.; bitterness.

worn (wörn) pa.p. of wear.—**worn out** a. no longer serviceable; exhausted; tired.

worry (wur'-i) v.t. torment; vex plague; tear with teeth;—v.i. express undue care and anxiety;—n. mental disturbance; trouble; vexation.—**worr'ier** n.—**worr'isome** a. causing trouble, anxiety, or worry.—**worrying** a. vexatious; harassing; exhausting.—**worr'yingly** adv.

worse (wurs) a. bad, ill, evil, in higher degree; in poorer health more sick;—adv. in manner more evil or bad.—**wor'sen** v.t. make worse—v.i. grow worse.—**wor'sening** n.

worship (wur'-ship) n. dignity honour; religious reverence and homage; title of honour and respect in addressing those of high station—v.t. adore; pay divine honours to—v.i. perform religious service attend church.—pr.p. **wor'shipping**—pa.t. and pa.p. **wor'shipped**.—**wor'shipful** a. highly worthy of respect or reverence.—**wor'shipfully** adv.—**wor'shipper** n.

worst (wurst) a. bad or evil in highest degree; of least value or worth;—adv. in most inferior manner or degree;—n. that which is most bad or evil;—v.t. get better of; defeat.

worsted (woost'-ed) n. yarn spun from long-fibred wools, combed or carded; cloth of this yarn;—a. made of worsted.

wort (wurt) n. plant, herb.

wort (wort) n. liquid of mash of malted grain; malt extract used as medium for culture of micro-organisms.

worth (wurth) n. quality of thing which renders it valuable or useful relative excellence of conduct or of character; value, in terms of money merit; virtue; cost;—a. equal in value to; meriting; having wealth to value of.—**worth'ily** adv. in worth; manner; commendably.—**worth'iness** n.—**worth'less** a. of no worth or value; useless; vile.—**worth'lessly** adv—**worth'lessness** n.—**worth'y** a. deserving; meritorious;—n. local celebrity.—pl. **wor'thies**.

would (wood) pa.t. of will.—**would'-be** a. desiring or professing to be;—n. pretender.

wound (wound) pa.t. and pa.p. of wind.

wound (wöönd) n. injury; cut, stab, bruise, or rent; hurt (to feelings) damage;—v.t. hurt by violence hurt feelings of.

wrack (rak) n. sea-weed thrown ashore by waves; shipwreck; ruin Also rack.

wraith (räth) n. apparition of person seen shortly before or after death

rangle (rang'-gl) v.i. dispute angrily; bicker; in universities, maintain or oppose thesis;—n. angry dispute; argument.—**wrang'ler** n. angry disputant; at Cambridge, one placed in first class of Part II of Mathematical Tripos.

rap (rap) v.t. cover by winding or folding something round; roll, wind, or fold together; envelop.—pr.p. wrap'ping.—pa.t. and pa.p. wrapped.—n. loose garment; covering.—wrap'per n.—wrap'ping n. wrapping material.

rath (rāth) n. violent anger; indignation; rage; fury.—wrath'ful a. angry; furious; raging.—wrath'fully adv.—wrath'fulness n.—wrath'ily adv.

reak (rēk) v.t. inflict (vengeance).

reath (rēth) n. garland or crown of flowers, leaves, etc. entwined together; chaplet; ornamental band for head; drift of snow; wisp of smoke.—**wreathe** (rēTH) v.t. surround; form into wreath; wind round; encircle;—v.i. be interwoven or entwined.

reck (rek) n. destruction of vessel; bulk of wrecked ship; remains of anything destroyed; desolation;—v.t. destroy, as vessel; bring ruin upon.—**wreck'age** n. shattered remains.—**wreck'er** n.

ren (ren) n. tiny song-bird.

rench (rensh) v.t. wrest, twist, or force off by violence; wring; sprain; distort;—n. sudden, violent twist; sprain; spanner with adjustable jaws.

rest (rest) v.t. pull or force away by violence; extort; distort;—n. violent pulling or twisting.

restle (res'-l) v.i. contend by grappling and trying to throw another down; struggle; strive (with).—**wrest'ler** n.—**wrest'ling** n. sport in which contestants endeavour to throw each other to ground.

retch (rech) n. miserable creature; one sunk in degradation.—**wretch'ed** a. very miserable; very poor or mean; despicable.—**wretch'edly** adv.—**wretch'edness** n.

rick, rick (rick) v.t. sprain;—n. slight twist or turn.

riggle (rig'-l) v.i. move sinuously, like worm; keep turning in prone position from side to side; squirm;—v.t. cause to wriggle;—n. act of wriggling; wriggling motion.—**wrigg'ler** n. wrigg'ling n.

right (rīt) n. one who fashions articles of wood, metal, etc.; artificer; builder.

ring (ring) v.t. twist and compress; turn and strain with violence; squeeze or press out; pain; distort; extort;—v.i. turn or twist, as with pain; writhe in anguish.—pa.t. and pa.p. wrung.—**wring'er** n. one who wrings; machine for pressing out water from wet clothes, etc.—**wringing wet**, absolutely soaking.

wrinkle (ring'-kl) n. ridge or furrow on surface due to twisting, shrinking, or puckering; crease in skin; fold; corruption;—v.t. contract into wrinkles;—v.i. shrink unevenly.—wrink'ling n.—wrink'ly a.

wrinkle (ring'-kl) n. valuable hint; good tip.

wrist (rist) n. joint connecting forearm and hand; carpus.—wrist'band n. part of shirt sleeve covering wrist; elastic band to give support to injured wrist.

writ (rit) n. that which is written; in law, mandatory precept issued by court; order of Crown calling for election of member to represent constituency in House of Commons.—**Holy Writ**, Scriptures.

write (rīt) v.t. set down or express in letters or words; copy on paper; compose, as book, song, etc.;—v.i. form characters representing sounds or ideas; be occupied in writing; express ideas in words.—pr.p. wri'ting.—pa.t. and pa.p. writ'ten.—**wri'ter** n. one who writes; scribe; clerk; author; law-agent or solicitor.—wri'ter's-cramp n. neurosis of muscles of hand.—wri'ting n. mechanical act of forming characters on paper; anything written;—writ'ten a.—**Writer to the Signet**, in Scotland, solicitor privileged to prepare Crown writs.—**to write off**, cancel, as bad debts.—**write-off** n. (Colloq.) total wreck.—**to write up**, give written commentary on.—**write up** n. flattering commentary.

writhe (rīTH) v.t. twist; turn to and fro;—v.i. roll about (as in pain).

wrong (rong) a. not right; mistaken; bad; evil; immoral; unjust; illegal; improper; unfit;—n. harm; evil; injustice; transgression; error;—adv. not rightly; erroneously;—v.t. treat with injustice; injure; impute evil to unjustly.—**wrong'-do'er** n. one who injures another; one who breaks law; offender; sinner.—wrong'ful a. unjust; unfair; causing wrong.—wrong'fully adv.—wrong'fulness n.—wrong'-head'ed a. obstinate; stubborn.—**wrong'ly** adv.—wrong'ness n.—**in the wrong**, blameworthy; mistaken.

wroth (roth) a. full of wrath; exasperated; angry; indignant.

wrought (rawt) pa.t. and pa.p. of work.—wrought'-i'ron n. purest form of commercial iron, prepared by puddling.—wrought'-up a. excited; frenzied.

wry (rī) a. turned to one side; twisted; distorted; crooked; askew.—wry'ly adv.—wry'neck n. condition in which head leans permanently towards shoulder; bird of woodpecker family which twists and turns its neck.—**wry'-necked** a.—**wry'ness** n.

wynd (wīnd) n. narrow lane or alley.

X

xenomania (zen-ō-mā'-ni-ạ) n. mania for anything foreign or exotic.

xenon (zen'-on) n. non-metallic element belonging to group of rare or inactive gases.

xenophobia (zen-ō-fōb'-i-ạ) n. dislike, hatred, fear of strangers or aliens.

xerography (ze-rog'-ra-fi) n. photographic process using electrically sensitised material instead of normal chemical emulsion.

X-rays (eks'-rāz) n.pl. Röntgen rays, electro-magnetic rays of very short wave-length, able to penetrate matter opaque to light rays and imprint on sensitive photographic plate picture of objects.

xylene (zī'-lēn) n. dimethyl benzene, hydrocarbon derived from coal-tar used medicinally and as solvent for fats.

xyloid (zī'-loid) a. of nature of wood; woody; resembling wood; ligneous.

xylophone (zī'-lō-fōn) n. musical instrument made of blocks of wood, notes being produced by striking blocks with two small hammers.

Y

yacht (yot) n. light sailing or steam vessel, for pleasure or racing;—v.i. sail in yacht.—**yacht'ing** n. art of sailing yacht;—a. pert. to yacht.—**yachts'man** n.—**yachts'manship** n.

Yahoo (ya-hōō') n. in Swift's *Gulliver's Travels*, imaginary manlike animals with bestial habits; brutish person.

yak (yak) n. species of ox found in C. Asia with hump and long hair.

yam (yam) n. tuber of tropical climbing-plant; sweet potato.

yammer (yam'-ẹr) v.i. whine; wail; talk incoherently.

yank (yangk) v.t. and v.i. (*Slang*) jerk; tug; pull quickly;—n. quick tug.

Yankee (yang'-kē) n. (in U.S.A.) citizen of New England, or of Northern States; (in Europe) American;—a. American.—**Yank** n. (*Slang*) Yankee.

yap (yap) v.i. yelp; (*Slang*) chatter incessantly;—n. yelp.—*pr.p.* **yap'ping**.—*pa.p.* and *pa.t.* **yapped**.

yapp (yap) n. style of bookbinding with limp leather projecting beyond edges of book.

yard (yärd) n. standard measure of

length, equal to three feet or thirty-six inches; measuring rod of this length; yard-stick; (*Naut.*) spar set crosswise to mast, for supporting sail.—**yard'-arm** n. either half of ship's yard.

yard (yärd) n. small, enclosed piece of ground near building; enclosure within which work is carried on.—**The Yard**, headquarters of Criminal Investigation Department of London Metropolitan Police.

yarn (yärn) n. spun thread, esp. for knitting or weaving; thread of rope; (*Colloq.*) story; anecdote; chat;—v.i. tell story.

yarrow (yar'-ō) n. plant having strong odour and pungent taste.

yashmak (yash'-mak) n. veil worn by Mohammedan women, covering face from beneath eyes.

yaw (yaw) v.i. of ship or aircraft, fail to keep steady course;—n. act of yawing; temporary deviation from straight course.

yawl (yawl) n. small, two-masted sailing-boat, with smaller mast at stern.

yawn (yawn) v.i. open mouth involuntarily through sleepiness, etc.; gape;—n. involuntary opening of mouth through sleepiness, etc.; gaping.—**yawn'ing** a. gaping.

yaws (yawz) n. tropical disease of skin; (*Med.*) framboesia.

ye (yē) pron. (*Arch.*) nom. plural of you.

yea (yā) interj. (*Arch.*) yes; ay; indeed.

year (yēr) n. time taken by one revolution of earth round sun, i.e. about 365¼ days; twelve months;—pl. age; old age.—**year'ly** a. and adv. happening every year; annual.—**year'ling** n. young animal, esp. horse, in second year;—a. being year old.—**year'-book** n. reference book of facts and statistics published yearly.—**leap'year**, year of 366 days, occurring every fourth year.

yearn (yẹrn) v.i. seek earnestly; feel longing; long for.—**yearn'ing** n. earnest desire;—a.—**yearn'ingly** adv.

yeast (yēst) n. froth that rises on malt liquors during fermentation; micro-organisms causing this fermentation, used, esp. in breadbaking, as agent to raise dough.—**yeast'y** a. frothy; fermenting.—**yeast'iness** n.

yell (yel) v.i. cry out in loud, shrill tone; scream; shriek;—n. loud, shrill cry.—**yell'ing** n.

yellow (yel'-ō) n. primary colour; colour of gold, lemons, buttercups, etc.;—a. of this colour; (*Colloq.*) cowardly; mean; despicable; of newspaper, sensational;—v.t. make yellow;—v.i. become yellow.—**yell'owish, yell'owy** a. somewhat yellow

—yell'owishness n.—yell'owness, n.—yell'ow-fe'ver n. infectious, tropical disease, characterised by yellow skin, vomiting, etc.—yell'ow-hamm'er n. yellow song-bird; yellow-bunting.—yell'ow-jack n. (Colloq.) yellow-fever; yellow flag flown by ships, etc. in quarantine.

'elp (yelp) n. sharp, shrill bark or cry;—v.i. utter such bark or cry.—yelp'er n.

'eoman (yō'-man) n. man owning and farming own land; freeholder; middle-class farmer; member of volunteer force of cavalry; (Navy) petty officer in charge of signals.—pl. yeo'men.—yeo'manly a.—yeo'manry n. yeomen collectively.—Yeomen of the Guard, formerly, corps of veteran soldiers, employed on ceremonial occasions; now warders of Tower of London.—yeoman service, long and faithful service.

es (yes) interj. word expressing affirmation or consent.—yes'-man n. servile supporter.

ester (yes'-ter) a.—yes'terday n. day before to-day;—adv. on day before to-day.—yes'ter-year n. long ago.

et (yet) adv. besides; at same time; still; at present time; now; at last; even; after all;—conj. nevertheless; moreover.—as yet, up to present time.

ew (ū) n. evergreen tree; its wood, formerly used for bows for archers.

iddish (yid'-ish) n. mixture of dialectal German and corrupt Hebrew, spoken by Jews;—a. pert. to or in this language.

ield (yēld) v.t. produce; give in return, esp. for labour, investment, etc.; bring forth; surrender;—v.i. submit; comply; give way; produce;—n. amount produced; return for labour, investment, etc.; profit; crop.—yield'ing a.—yield'ingly adv.

odel (yō'-dl) v.t. and i. sing or warble, with frequent changes from natural voice to falsetto tone;—n. falsetto warbling.—yo'deller, n.

oga (yō'-ga) n. system of Hindu philosophy; strict spiritual discipline practised to gain control over forces of one's own being.—yo'gi n. one who practises yoga.—yo'gism n.

oghourt (yō'-góort) n. cream made from fermented milk.

oke (yōk) n. wooden frame-work fastened over necks of two oxen, etc. to hold them together; anything having shape or use of yoke; separately cut piece of material fitting closely over shoulders; bond or tie; emblem of submission; bondage; dominion; couple of animals working together;—v.t. put yoke on; couple or join; bring into servitude; attach draught animal to vehicle;—v.i. be joined; match with.

yokel (yō'-kl) n. rustic; ploughman.

yolk (yōk) n. yellow part of egg.

yon (yon) a. that; those; yonder;—adv. yonder.—yon'der a. that or those there;—adv. at distance within view.

yore (yōr) n. past; old times.

york (york) v.t. bowl out cricketer with yorker.—york'er n. ball so bowled that it hits ground directly under batter's bat.

you (ū) pron. of second person in nominative or objective case, indicating person or persons addressed; also used indefinitely meaning, one, they, people in general.—your (ūr) a. gen. case of you, meaning of you, pert. to you; generally used as possess. adj. meaning, belonging to you.—yours pron. possessive of you, when used absolutely, without following noun.—yourself pron. your own person or self [often used for emphasis or as reflexive].—pl. yourselves'.

young (yung) a. not far advanced in growth, life, or existence; not yet old; vigorous; immature;—n. offspring of animals.—young'ish a. somewhat young. — young'ster n. young person or animal; lad.—with young, pregnant.

youth (yōoth) n. state of being young; life from childhood to manhood; lad or young man; young persons collectively.—youth'ful a. possessing youth; vigorous.—youth'fully adv.—youth'fulness n.

yowl (youl) v.i. howl;—n. cry of dog.

yule (yōol) n. feast of Christmas.—yule'tide n. season of Christmas.—yule'-log n. log of wood to burn on open hearth at Christmas.

Z

zeal (zēl) n. intense enthusiasm for cause or person; passionate ardour.—zealot (zel'-ot) n. fanatic; enthusiast.—zeal'otry n. fanaticism.—zealous (zel'-us) a. ardent; enthusiastic; earnest.—zeal'ously adv.—zeal'ousness n.

zebra (zē'-bra) n. genus of African quadrupeds of horse-family, with tawny coat striped with black.—zebra crossing, crossing for pedestrians, marked with black and white lines.

zenana (ze-nà'-na) n. women's apartments in Hindu household, equivalent to harem.

zenith (zen'-ith) n. point of heavens directly above observer's head; summit; height of success; acme; climax.—zen'ithal a.

zephyr (zef'-ir) n. west wind; gentle breeze; fine, soft woollen fabric.

Zeppelin (zep'-e-lin) *n.* cigar-shaped long-range dirigible German airship.

zero (zē'-rō) *n.* nought; cipher; neutral fixed point from which graduated scale is measured; (*Fig.*) lowest point.—*pl.* zer'os.—**zero hour**, precise moment at which military offensive, etc. is timed to begin; crucial moment.

zest (zest) *n.* outer peel of orange or lemon; relish; fillip; stimulus; keen pleasure.

zigzag (zig'-zag) *n.* line with short sharp turns;—*a.* forming zig-zag;—*v.i.* form, or move with, short sharp turns.—*pr.p.* zig'zagging.—*pa.p.* zig'-zagged.—*adv.*

zinc (zingk) *n.* bluish-white metallic element (symbol Zn) used in alloys, esp. brass, and for galvanising iron;—*v.t* coat with zinc, galvanise.—*pr.p.* zinck'ing or zinc'ing.—*pa.t.* and *pa.p.* zincked or zinced.—zinc'ic *a.* pert. to zinc.—**zincif'erous, zinckif'-erous** *a.* containing zinc.—zinc'o *n.* (*Abbrev.*) of zincograph line block engraved on zink.—**zincog'rapher** *n.*—zincograph'ic *a.*—zinc'ography *n.* process of engraving on zinc.—zinc'-oid *a.* resembling zinc.—zinc'otype *n.* zincograph.—zinc'ous *a.* pert. to zinc.

zinnia (zin'-i-a) *n.* plants with bright-coloured flowers like aster.

Zion (zī'-on) *n.* hill in Jerusalem; town of Jerusalem; Church of God; heaven.

zip (zip) *n.* whizzing sound, as of bullet in air; (*Slang*) energy;—*v.t.* shut with zipper.—**zip fastener**, device of interlocking, flexible 'teeth' opened and shut by sliding clip. Also **zip'per** *n.*

zircon (zir'-kon) *n.* crystalline silicate of zirconium of which varieties are jacinth, hyacinth, (symbol Zr).—zirco'-nium *n.* metal obtained from zircon, and resembling titanium.

zither (zith'-er) *n.* flat, stringed box-shaped instrument played with plectrum.

zodiac (zō'-di-ak) *n.* (*Astrol.*) imaginary belt in heavens following path of sun, and divided into twelve equal areas, each containing a constellations, each represented by appropriate symbols, called *signs of zodiac*; namely Aries (*Ram*), Taurus (*Bull*), Gemini (*Twins*), Cancer (*Crab*), Leo (*Lion*), Virgo (*Virgin*), Libra (*Balance*), Scorpio (*Scorpion*), Sagittarius (*Archer*), Capricornus (*Goat*), Aquarius (*Water-bearer*), Pisces (*Fishes*).

zoic (zō'-ik) *a.* pert. to, or having, animal life.

zombie (zom'-bi) *n.* African snake deity; reanimated corpse.

zone (zōn) *n.* girdle; climatic or vegetation belt; one of five belts into which earth is divided by latitude lines, as *frigid zone* of Arctic an Antarctic, *torrid zone* between Trop ics of Cancer and Capricorn, *temperate zone* north of Tropic of Cance and south of Tropic of Capricorn;—*v.t.* enclose; divide into zones divide country into regional areas —zo'nal *a.* pert. to or divided int zones.—zoned *a.* having zones.

Zoo (zŏŏ) *n.* (*Colloq.*) Zoologica Gardens.

zoo- (zō'-ō) *prefix* (derived from Greek word zŏŏn, animal) used in compound words.

zoogeny (zō-oj'-en-i) *n.* doctrine o; origin of living creatures. Also **zoog'ony**.—**zoogen'ic** *a.*

zoogeography (zō-ō-jē-og'-ra-fi) *n.* science which treats of regiona distribution of animals in world.— **zoogeog'rapher** *n.*

zoolatry (zō-ol'-a-tri) *n.* animal worship.—zool'ater *n.*—zool'atrous *a.*

zoolite (zō'-ō-līt) *n.* fossil animal. Also **zool'ith**.

zoology (zŏŏ-, zō-ol'-o-ji) *n.* natura history of animals, part of science of biology.—zoolog'ical *a.*—zoolog'ically *adv.*—zool'ogist *n.*

zoom (zŏŏm) *n.*—*v.i.* (of aircraft) turn suddenly upwards at sharp angle.—**zoom lens**, lens of variable focal length.

zoon (zō'-on) *n.* individual animal; complete product of fertilised germ. —*pl.* zo'a, zo'ons.—zo'onic *a.* pert. to animals.

zoonomy (zō-on'-ō-mi) *n.* science which treats of animal life.—zoon'om'ic *a.*—zoon'omist *n.*

zoophagous (zō-of'-a-gus) *a.* feeding on animals; carnivorous.

zoophilist (zō-of'-il-ist) *n.* lover of animals.—zooph'ily *n.*

zoophyte (zō'-ō-fīt) *n.* plant-like animal, such as sponge.

Zoroastrian (zō-rō-as'-tri-an) *n.* follower of Zoroaster;—*a.* pert. to Zoroaster or his religion;—zoroas'-trianism *n.* ancient Persian religious doctrine taught by Zoroaster, principal feature of which is recognition of dual principle of good and evil; religion of Parsees.

Zouave (zŏŏ-äv') *n.* soldier of French light infantry corps, orig. recruited from Algeria.

Zulu (zŏŏ-lŏŏ) *n.* member of Bantu tribe of S. Africa;—*a.* pert. to Zulus or to Zululand.

zygote (zig'-ōt) *n.* product of union of two reproductive cells.

zymosis (zi-mo'-sis) *n.* fermentation. —zymot'ic *a.* pert. to or caused by fermentation; pert. to or causing infectious disease.—zymot'ically *adv.*

COMMON ABBREVIATIONS

A (*Chem.*) argon; adult (motion picture certificate).

A. Academy; America; Associate; Agency.

a. acre; adjective; answer.

A.A. anti-aircraft; Alcoholics Anonymous; Automobile Association.

A.A.A. Amateur Athletic Association; American Automobile Association.

A.B. Able Seaman; Assistance Board.

abbr. abbreviation.

abl. ablative case.

abr. abridged; abridgement.

A.C. Aircraftman; Assistant Commissioner; Athletic Club.

a/c account.

acc. accusative case.

A.C.G.B. Arts Council of Great Britain.

A.C.M. Air Chief-Marshal.

A.D. in the year of the Lord [L. *anno Domini*].

a.d. after date.

A.D.C. aide-de-camp.

add. addendum.

ad infin. to infinity; forever [L. *ad infinitum*].

adj. adjective.

ad lib. at pleasure [L. *ad libitum*].

ad loc. at the place [L. *ad locum*].

A.D.P. automatic data processing.

adv. adverb.

advert., advt. advertisement.

A.E.A. Atomic Energy Authority.

A.E.R.E. Atomic Energy Research Establishment.

aet. aged (so many years) [L. *aetatis*].

A.E.U. Amalgamated Engineering Union.

a.f.c. automatic frequency control.

Ag (*Chem.*) silver [L. *argentum*].

A.H. in the year of the Hegira (Mohammedan calendar, from A.D. 622) [L. *anno Hegirae*].

Air Cdre. Air Commodore.

Al (*Chem.*) aluminium.

Ala. Alabama (U.S.A.).

alt. alternate; altitude; alto.

a.m. before noon (L. *ante meridiem*).

A.M.D.G. for the greater glory of God (L. *ad majorem Dei gloriam*).

amp. ampérage.

Anat. anatomical; anatomy.

anon. anonymous.

Ant. County Antrim (N. Ireland).

ant(on). antonym.

Anthr. anthropology.

A.N.Z.A.C. (*World War I*) Australian and New Zealand Army Corps.

ap. in the works of (an author) [L. *apud* = 'at'].

a-part., α -part. alpha particle.

Apoc. Apocrypha.

app. appendix.

A.R.A. Associate of the Royal Academy.

Arch. archaic; architecture.

Ariz. Arizona (U.S.A.).

Ark. Arkansas (U.S.A.).

A.R.P. air-raid precautions.

A.S. Anglo-Saxon.

Assoc. Associate; Association.

astr(on). astronomer; astronomy.

At.No. atomic number.

A.U. Angström unit.

Au (*Chem.*) gold [L. *aurum*].

A.V. Authorised Version (of the Bible); (*Physics*) atomic volume.

avdp., avoir. avoirdupois.

Ave. Avenue.

A.V.M. Air Vice-Marshal

A.W. atomic weight.

B (*Chem.*) boron.

B. British; black (on lead pencils).

b. book; born; bowled (by); brother.

B.A. Bachelor of Arts [L. *baccalaureus artium*]; British Academy; British Association.

Ba (*Chem.*) barium.

Bart. Baronet.

B.B. Boys' Brigade; double black (on lead pencils).

B.B.C. British Broadcasting Corporation.

B.C. before Christ; British Council; battery commander; bomber command.

B.C.G. Bacillus Calmette-Guérin (anti-T.B. vaccine).

Bde. Brigade.

Bdg. Building.

B.E.A. British European Airways.

B.Ed. Bachelor of Education.

Beds. Bedfordshire.

B.E.F. British Expeditionary Force.

BENELUX Customs, etc. union of Belgium, Holland and Luxembourg.

Berks. Berkshire.

b.f. brought forward; (*Slang*) bloody fool.

Bi (*Chem.*) bismuth.

Bib(l). Bible; biblical.

biog. biography; biographical.

Biol. biology; biological.

bk. book; bank; back.

bl. barrel; bale.

B.M. British Museum; Brigade Major; of blessed memory [L. *beatae memoriae*]; bench mark.

B.M.A. British Medical Association.

B.N.B. British National Bibliography.

B.O. (*Colloq.*) body odour.

B.O.A.C. British Overseas Airways Corporation.

B. of E. Bank of England.

B. of T. Board of Trade.

Bot. botany; botanical.

b.p. birthplace; bills payable; boiling point; below proof.

B.P.C. British Productivity Council.

B.R. British Rail(ways).

Br (*Chem.*) bromine.

Br. brother.

Brig. brigade; Brigadier.

Britt. Omn. of all Britain [L. *Brittanniarum omnium*].

Bros. (*Commer.*) Brothers.

B.S. British Standard.

B.Sc. Bachelor of Science.

B.S.I. British Standards Institution.

B.S.T. British Summer Time.

Bt. Baronet.

B.T.U. Board of Trade Unit.

B.t.u. British thermal unit.

bu. bushel.

Bucks. Buckinghamshire.

C (*Chem.*) carbon.

C. Cape; Catholic; centigrade; Central; Commander; Companion; Conservative; 100 (in Roman numerals).

c. cent; centime; century; chapter; about (L. *circa*].

C.A. Chartered Accountant; Consumers' Association.

C.A.B. Citizens' Advice Bureau.

Cal. California (U.S.A.).

Cambs. Cambridgeshire.

Capt. Captain.

C.A.T. College of Advanced Technology.

C.B.E. Commander of (the Order of) the British Empire.

C.C. County Council; Cricket Club.

cc. cubic centimetre.

C.D. corps diplomatique; Civil Defence; Chancery Division.

Cdr. Commander (Royal Navy).

Cdre. Commodore (Royal Navy).

Ce (*Chem.*) cerium.

cent. hundred (L. *centum*); century.

cert. certificate; certificated; certified; (*Colloq.*) certainty.

cf. compare [L. *confer*].

cg. centigram.

C.G.S. centimetre-gramme-second; Chief of the General Staff.

ch. chapter; chain (measure).

Chem. chemistry; chemical.

Chron. Chronicles (O.T.).

C.I.A. Central Intelligence Agency (U.S.A.).

C.I.D. Council of Industrial Design; Criminal Investigation Department.

Cl (*Chem.*) chlorine.

cl. centilitre; class; clause.

cm. centimetre.

C.N.D. Campaign for Nuclear Disarmament.

C.O. commanding officer; conscientious objector; Crown Office.

Co. company; county.

c/o care of.

C.O.D. cash on delivery.

C. of E. Church of England.

C. of S. Church of Scotland.

Col. Colonel; Colossians (N.T.).

Coll(oq). colloquial.

Colo. Colorado (U.S.A.).

Com. Commander; Commissioner; Committee; Commonwealth; Communist.

Commer. commerce; commercial.

comp. comparative; compound.

conj. conjugation; conjunction.

Conn. Connecticut (U.S.A.).

cont. continued.

Co-op. Co-operative (Society).

Corp. Corporation.

cos. cosine.

cosec. cosecant.

cot. cotangent.

Coy. Company.

Cpl. Corporal.

C.R.C. Civil Rights' Commission (U.S.A.).

C.R.O. cathode ray oscillograph; Commonwealth Relations Office; Criminal Records Office.

C.S.M. Company Sergeant-Major.

Ct. Court.

ct. carat.

Cu (*Chem.*) copper [L. *cuprum*].

cwt. hundredweight.

Cy (*Chem.*) cyanide.

Cym. Welsh (Welsh: *Cymric*).

D. Dame; Democrat; Distinguished; Doctor; Dominus (Lord); Duke; 500 (in Roman numerals).

d. date; daughter; day; deceased; died; departs; diameter; penny [L. *denarius*].

D.A. deposit account; District Attorney.

Dan. Daniel (O.T.).

dat. dative case.

d.B., d.b. decibel.

D.B.E. Dame Commander of (the Order of) the British Empire.

D.C. District of Columbia (U.S.A.); District Court; (*Mus.*) repeat from the beginning [It. *da capo*].

D.D. Doctor of Divinity.

D.D.R. East Germany [Ger. *Deutsche Demokratische Republik*].

D.D.T. dichloro-diphenyl-trichloro-ethane (an insecticide).

decd. (*Law*) deceased.

def. defendant; defender; definition; deficiency; deficit.

Del. Delaware (U.S.A.).

dept. department; deponent.

deriv. derivation.

Deut. Deuteronomy (O.T.).

D.F. Defender of the Faith; direction finder.

D.G. by the grace of God [L. *Dei gratia*]; thanks be to God [L. *Deo gratias*]; Director-General.

dial. dialect.

dim. diminutive; (*Mus.*) diminuendo.

D.Litt. Doctor of Letters.

do. ditto; the same.

D.O.M. to the Best and Greatest God (L. *Deo Optimo Maximo*].

doz. dozen.

D.P.P. Director of Public Prosecutions.

Dr. Doctor; drawer (of a cheque or bill).

dram. pers. characters of the play [L. *dramatis personae*].

D.T.s (*Colloq.*) delirium tremens.

E. Earl; East; England; English.

E.C. East Central; Established Church; Education Committee.

Eccl(es). Ecclesiastes (O.T.).

Econ. Economics.

E.E.C. European Economic Community.

E.F.T.A. European Free Trade Association (between Austria, Denmark, Norway, Portugal, Sweden, Switzerland and the U.K.).

e.g. for example [L. *exempli gratia*].

E.L.D.O. European Launching Development Organisation.

Electr. electricity, electronics.

E.M.U. electromagnetic unit.

Entom. entomology.

Ep. epistle.

Eph. Ephesians (N.T.).

erg. unit of energy [Gk. *ergon* = 'work'].

E.R.N.I.E. Electronic Random Number Indicator Equipment (used for picking winning numbers of Premium Bonds).

E.S.P. extra-sensory perception.

esp. especially.

Esq. esquire.

Est(d). established.

Esth. Esther (O.T.).

E.S.U. electrostatic unit.

et. al. and others [L. *et alia*; *et alii*]; and elsewhere [L. *et alibi*].

etc. and so on [L. *et cetera*].

Ethnol. ethnology.

E.T.U. Electrical Trades Union.

Euratom European Atomic Energy Community.

Ex(od). Exodus (O.T.).

ex. example; exception; export; executive; examined; exchange.

Ez. Ezra (O.T.).

Ezek. Ezekiel (O.T.).

F (*Chem.*) fluorine.

F. Fahrenheit; Father (R.C.); Fellow; French; Friday.

f. farthing; fathom; feminine; filly; foot; franc; (*Mus.*) loudly [It. *forte*]; function; furlong.

F.A. Football Association; Field Artillery; Fine Arts.

F.B.I. Federation of British Industries; Federal Bureau of Investigation (U.S.A.).

F.C. Football Club; Free Church.

F.D. Defender of the Faith [L. *Fidei Defensor*].

Fe (*Chem.*) iron [L. *ferrum*].

fed. federal; federated; federation.

ff. following (pages); (*Mus.*) very loudly [It. *fortissimo*].

Fid. Def. Defender of the Faith [L. *Fidei Defensor*].

fig. figurative; figure.

fin. the end [L. *finis*]; financial.

Fla. Florida (U.S.A.).

Flt.-Lt. Flight-Lieutenant.

FM. Field-Marshal.

F.O. Foreign Office.

Fr. Father; Frau; French; Friday.

fr. fragment; franc; from.

F.R.C.P. Fellow of the Royal College of Physicians.

F.R.C.S. Fellow of the Royal College of Surgeons.

ft. foot; feet; fort.

fur. furlong.

g. gauge; genitive; gramme; gross; guinea.

Ga. Georgia (U.S.A.).

Gal. Galatians (N.T.).

gal. gallon.

G.B. Great Britain.

g.c.f. greatest common factor.

G.C.E. General Certificate of Education.

Gen. Genesis (O.T.); General.

gen. gender; general; genitive.

Ger. German; Germanic.

G.H.I. Good Housekeeping Institute.

G.H.Q. General Headquarters.

G.I. government issue; American (U.S.) private soldier.

Gib. (*Colloq.*) Gibraltar.

Gk. Greek.

Glam. Glamorganshire.

G.L.C. Greater London Council.

Glos. Gloucestershire.

gm. gramme.

G.M.T. Greenwich Mean Time.

G.P. general practitioner.
G.P.I. general paralysis of the insane.
G.P.O. General Post Office.
gr. grain; gross.
Gram(m). grammar; grammatical.
gtd. guaranteed.

H (*Chem.*) hydrogen.
Hab. Habakkuk (O.T.).
Hag. Haggai (O.T.).
h. and c. hot and cold (water).
Hants. Hampshire (England)
H.B. hard black (lead pencil).
H.E. high explosive; His Eminence; His Excellency.
He (*Chem.*) helium.
Heb. Hebrews (N.T.); Hebrew.
Herts. Hertfordshire (England).
H.F. high frequency.
H.G. His (Her) Grace; Home Guard.
Hg (*Chem.*) mercury [L. *hydrargyrum*].
H.H. His (Her) Highness; His Holiness; double hard (lead pencil).
Hib. Hibernian (= 'Irish').
Hil. Hilary (term in legal calendar).
Hist. history; historical.
hl. hectolitre.
H.M. Her (His) Majesty('s).
H.M.S. Her (His) Majesty's Service; Her (His) Majesty's ship.
H.M.S.O. Her (His) Majesty's Stationery Office.
H.O. Head Office; Home Office.
Ho., ho. house.
Hon. Honorary; Honourable.
Hort. horticulture; horticultural.
Hos. Hosea (O.T.).
hp. high pressure; hire purchase; horse power.
H.Q. headquarters.
hr. hour.
H.R.H. His (Her) Highness.
Hunts. Huntingdonshire.
Hydr. hydraulics.
Hyg. hygiene.

I (*Chem.*) iodine.
I. Island; (*Phys.*) moment of inertia.
ib(id). in the same place [L. *ibidem*].
i/c. in charge.
I.(C.)B.M. Intercontinental Ballistic Missile.
Ice. Iceland; Icelandic.
I.C.F.T.U. International Confederation of Free Trade Unions.
id. the same [L. *idem*].
I.D.L. international date line.
i.e. that is; namely [L. *id est*].
ign. unknown [L. *ignotus*].
I.H.S. contracted form of the Greek word for Jesus [IHϹΟΥϹ].
Ill. Illinois (U.S.A.)
ill. illustrated.
I.M.F. International Monetary Fund.
Imp. Emperor; Imperial [L. *impera-*

tor; imperialis].
imp. imperfect; imperative; imprimatur [L. 'let it be printed'].
in. inch; inches.
Inc. Incorporated.
incl. including; inclusive.
incog. unknown [L. *incognito*].
Ind. Indiana (U.S.A.).
ind. index; indicated; indicative; indirect.
indef. indefinite.
inf. below [L. *infra*]; infinitive.
init. at the beginning [L. *initio*].
I.N.R.I. Jesus of Nazareth, King of the Jews [L. *Iesus Nazarenus Rex Iudaeorum*].
Inst. institute.
inst. instant; of the present month
int. interest.
intr. intransitive.
I.o.M. Isle of Man.
I.O.U. I owe you.
I.o.W. Isle of Wight.
I.Q. intelligence quotient.
Ir. Irish.
irreg. irregular.
I.R.A. Irish Republican Army.
Is. Island(s).
Iss. Isaiah (O.T.).
It. Italian.
I.T.A. Independent Television Authority; Initial Teaching Alphabet.
I.T.O. International Trade Organisation.
I.V.S. International Voluntary Service.

J. Judge; Justice; (*Physics*) joule.
Jam. James (N.T.); Jamaica.
Jno. St. John (N.T.).
jnt. joint.
Jo. Joel (O.T.).
joc. jocular(ly).
Josh. Joshua (O.T.).
J.P. Justice of the Peace.
Jr. Junior.
Judg. Judges (O.T.).

K (*Chem.*) potassium [L. *kalium*].
K. King; Knight.
Kan. Kansas (U.S.A.).
K.B.E. Knight Commander of (the Order of) the British Empire.
K.C. King's Counsel.
kc. kilocycle.
K.C.B. Knight Commander of (the Order of) the Bath.
kg. kilogram.
km. kilometre.
K.K.K. Ku Klux Klan.
K.O. (*Boxing*) knock-out.
K.(P.)G.K. Soviet security police [Russian: *Komitet Partiyno-Gosudarstvennogo Kontrolya* = 'Party and State Control Committee'].
Kt. knight.

kw. kilowatt.

Ky. Kentucky (U.S.A.).

L. Lake; Late; Latin; Latitude; Law; Learner (driver); Liberal; Licentiate; London; 50 (in Roman numerals); Labour; (*Nat. Hist.*); Linnaei [L. 'of Linnaeus'].

l. land; left; line; lira.

L.A. Law Agent; Local Authority; Los Angeles.

La. Louisiana (U.S.A.).

Lab. Labour; Labrador.

lab. labial; laboratory.

Lam. Lamentations (O.T.).

Lat. Latin.

lat. latitude.

lb. pound [L. *libra*].

l.b.w. (*Cricket*) leg before wicket.

l.c.m. least common multiple.

Leics. Leicestershire.

Lev. Leviticus (O.T.).

L.F. low frequency.

l.h.d. left-hand drive.

Li (*Chem.*) lithium.

Lib. Library; Liberal.

Lincs. Lincolnshire.

lit. literal; literary; literature; litre.

LL.D. Doctor of Laws (L. *Legum Doctor*].

loc. cit. in the place cited [L. *loco citato*].

log. logarithm.

lon(g). longitude.

L.P. Labour Party; Lord Provost; letters patent; long-playing record.

l.s.d. pounds, shillings, pence.

L.S.E. London School of Economics.

Lt. Lieutenant.

L.T.B. London Transport Board.

Lt.-Cdr. Lieutenant-Commander (R.N.).

Lt.-Col. Lieutenant-Colonel.

Ltd. Limited.

Lt.-Gen. Lieutenant-General.

L.V. luncheon voucher.

L.W. long wave.

L.W.M. low water mark.

LXX Septuagint Version (of the Bible)

M. Majesty; Marshal; Martyr; Master; Median; Medicine; Member; Monday; Monsieur [Fr.]; 1000 (in Roman numerals).

m. married; masculine; mass; mean; medium; meridian; metre; mile; middle; minute; month.

M.A. Master of Arts.

Maj. Major.

Maj.-Gen. Major-General.

Mar. March; marine; maritime.

Mass. Massachusetts (U.S.A.)

Math(s). mathematics.

Matt. Matthew (N.T.).

M.B.E. Member of (the Order of) the British Empire.

M.C.C. Marylebone Cricket Club.

M.D. Doctor of Medicine [L. *Medicinae Doctor*]; mentally deficient.

Md. Maryland (U.S.A.).

M.E. Middle English

Me. Maine (U.S.A.).

Med. medieval; medical; Mediterranean.

Messrs. the plural of **Mr.**

Met. meteorological; Metropolitan.

meth(s). (*Colloq.*) methylated spirits.

Mex. Mexico; Mexican.

mf. (*Mus.*) moderately loud [It. *mezzoforte*].

M.F.H. Master of the Fox Hounds.

Mg (*Chem.*) magnesium.

mg. milligram.

Mgr. Monsignor.

M.I.5 Military Intelligence, Department Five.

Mic. Micah (O.T.)

Mich. Michigan (U.S.A.).

mil. military.

min. minute; minimum.

Minn. Minnesota (U.S.A.).

Miss. Mississippi (U.S.A.).

mm. millimetre.

Mn (*Chem.*) manganese.

M.O. Medical Officer; Money Order Mass Observation.

Mo. Missouri (U.S.A.).

mod. con. modern conveniences.

M.O.H. Medical Officer of Health.

mol. molecule; molecular.

mon. monetary.

Mont. Montana (U.S.A.).

M.P. Member of Parliament; Military Police; Metropolitan Police.

m.p.g. miles per gallon.

m.p.h. miles per hour.

Mr. Mister.

M.R.A. Moral Rearmament.

M.R.C. Medical Research Council.

Mrs. style of married woman.

MS(S). manuscript(s).

Mt. mount; mountain.

M.T.B. Motor Torpedo Boat.

Mus. music; musical; museum.

M.W. medium wave.

N (*Chem.*) nitrogen.

N. North; New; National; Navy; Norse; Nurse.

n. name; noun; neuter; nominative; new; born [L. *natus*].

Na (*Chem.*) sodium [L. *natrium*]

Nah. Nahum (O.T.).

Nat. National; Nathaniel.

Nat. Hist. natural history.

N.A.T.O. North Atlantic Treaty Organisation.

naut. nautical.

nav. naval; navigation.

N.B. to note [L. *nota bene* = 'note well'].

N.C. North Carolina (U.S.A.).

N.C.O. non-commissioned officer.

N. Dak. North Dakota (U.S.A.)

N.E. North East.
Ne (*Chem.*) neon.
Neb. Nebraska (U.S.A.)
N.E.D.C. National Economic Development Council ('Neddy').
neg. negative.
Neh. Nehemiah (O.T.).
neut. neuter; neutral.
Nev. Nevada.
N.H. New Hampshire (U.S.A.).
N.H.S. National Health Service.
Ni (*Chem.*) nickel.
N.I.C. National Incomes Commission ('Nicky').
N.J. New Jersey (U.S.A.).
N.Mex. New Mexico (U.S.A.).
No(s). number(s).
nom. nominative.
Northants. Northamptonshire.
Northumb. Northumberland.
Notts. Nottinghamshire.
N.S.P.C.C. National Society for the Prevention of Cruelty to Children.
N.T. New Testament; National Trust
Num(b). Numbers (O.T.).
N.U.R. National Union of Railwaymen.
N.U.S. National Union of Seamen: National Union of Students.
N.U.T. National Union of Teachers.
N.W. North West.
N.Y. New York (U.S.A.).
N.Z. New Zealand.

O (*Chem.*) oxygen.
o/a on account of.
O.A.P. Old Age Pension.
Ob(ad). Obadiah (O.T.)
O.B.E. Officer of (the Order of) the British Empire.
obj. object; objective.
obs. observation; obsolete.
O.C. officer commanding.
O.E. Old English.
O.E.D. Oxford English Dictionary.
O.F. Old French.
O.G.P.U. now **K.(P.)G.K.**
O.H.M.S. On Her (His) Majesty's Service.
O.K. all correct.
Okla. Oklahoma (U.S.A.).
O.P. opposite prompter; observation post; out of print; over-proof.
op. cit. in the work quoted [L. *opere citato*].
opp. opposite.
ord. ordained; order; ordinary.
Oreg. Oregon (U.S.A.).
O.T. Old Testament.
O.T.C. Officers' Training Corps.
O.U.D.S. Oxford University Dramatic Society.
~on. Oxfordshire; (of) Oxford.
~nce(s).

Public; Party; Press.

p. page; participle; perch; pint; (*Mus.*) soft [It. *piano*]; passive.
p.a. per annum; by the year.
Pa. Pennsylvania (U.S.A.).
part. participle.
P.A.S. public address system.
pass. passive: here and there [L. *passim*].
Pat. patent; patented.
Pat. Off. Patent Office.
P.A.Y.E. Pay (Tax) As You Earn.
Pb (*Chem.*) lead [L. *plumbum*].
P.C. Privy Councillor: police constable; postcard: Parish Council.
pd. paid.
P.E.N. Poets, Playwrights, Essayists, Editors and Novelists (Club).
Pet. Peter (N.T.).
Ph.D. Doctor of Philosophy.
Phil. Philippians (N.T.); philosophy; philology.
Philem. Philemon (N.T.).
Phys. physics.
pl. plural; place.
P.M. Prime Minister.
p.m. afternoon [L. *post meridiem*]; post mortem [L. 'after death'].
P.M.G. Postmaster-General.
P.O. postal order; post office; Petty Officer; Pilot Officer.
P.O.B. post office box.
Pont. Max. the Pope [L. *Pontifex Maximus* = 'greatest bishop'].
pop. popular; population.
poss. possessive; possible.
P.O.W. prisoner of war.
p.p. on behalf of [L. *per procurationem*]; past participle.
pp. pages; (*Mus.*) very softly [It. *pianisssimo*].
pr. per; present; price; pronoun.
pref. preface; preference; prefix.
pres. present.
P.R.O. Public Relations Officer.
Prof. Professor.
pron. pronunciation.
Prov. Proverbs (O.T.); Provençal.
P.S. postscript; Privy Seal.
Ps. Psalms (O.T.).
pseud. pseudonym.
P.T. physical training.
Pt (*Chem.*) platinum.
pt. pint; payment; part
P.T.O. please turn over.
Pub. public.
P.V.C. polyvinyl-chloride (plastic.)

Q. Queen; question; queue.
q. query; question.
Q.A.s (*Colloq.*) Queen Alexandra's nurses.
Q.C. Queen's Counsel.
q.e.d. which was to be proved [L. *quod erat demonstrandum*]
Q.M.G. Quartermaster-General.
qr. quarter.
Q.T. (*Slang*) on the quiet.
qt. quart.

Qu. Queen.

q.v. which see [L. *quod vide*].

R. Queen [L. *rex*; *regina*]; King [L. *rex*]; River; Royal; (*Chem.*) gas constant; Rupee.

r. radius; ratio; recipe; reserve; right; rod; rood; (*Cricket*) runs.

R.A. Royal Academician.

Ra (*Chem.*) radium.

R.A.C. Royal Automobile Club; Royal Armoured Corps.

rad. (*Math.*) root [L. *radix*].

R.A.D.A. Royal Academy of Dramatic Art.

R.A.F. Royal Air Force.

R.C. Roman Catholic; Red Cross.

Rd. Road.

R.E. Royal Engineers.

Rear-Adm. Rear-Admiral.

rec. receipt; received; recent; recipe; record.

ref. reference.

refl. reflexive.

regd. registered.

Regt. regiment.

rel. relative; related; religion.

Rep. representative; Republic(an); repertory; report(er).

res. residence; resigned.

resp. respectively, respondent.

ret(d). retired; returned; retained.

Rev. Reverend.

revs. (*Tech.*) revolutions.

R.F. Royal Fusiliers; French Republic [Fr. *République Française*].

R.H. Royal Highness.

R.I. Rhode Island (U.S.A.)

R.I.B.A. Royal Institute of British Architects.

R.I.P. may he (she) rest in peace [L. *requiescat in pace*].

R.N. Royal Navy.

R.N.V.R. Royal Naval Volunteer Reserve.

r.p.s. revolutions per second.

R.S. Royal Society.

R.S.P.A. Royal Society for the Prevention of Accidents.

R.S.P.C.A. Royal Society for the Prevention of Cruelty to Animals.

R.S.S. Fellow of the Royal Society [L. *Regiae Societatis Socius*].

R.S.V.P. Please reply. [Fr. *Répondez s'il vous plaît*].

R/T. radio-telephony.

Rt. Hon. Right Honourable.

ry. railway.

S (*Chem.*) Sulphur.

S. South; Saint; Society; Sunday; School; Ship.

s. second; shilling; son; singular; substantive.

$ dollar.

S.A. South America; South Africa; Salvation Army; Nazi German storm troops [Ger. *Sturm-Abteilung*]; (*Slang*) sex appeal.

s.a.e. stamped addressed envelope.

Salop. Shropshire.

Sam. Samuel (O.T.).

S.C. South Carolina (U.S.A.).

Sc. science; scientific.

S.Dak. South Dakota (U.S.A.).

S.E.A.T.O. South East Asia Treaty Organisation.

sec. second; secondary; section.

seq. the following [L. *sequens*].

ser. series.

sf. (*Mus.*) with sudden emphasis [It. *sforzando*].

sgd. signed.

Sgt. Sergeant.

S.H.A.P.E. Supreme Headquarters of the Allied Powers in Europe.

sing. singular.

S.J. Society of Jesus.

Skt. Sanskrit.

Slav. Slavonic.

Sn (*Chem.*) tin [L. *stannum*].

Soc. Society; Socialist.

Sol. Solicitor; Song of Solomon (O.T.).

S.O.S. signal of distress.

S.P.C.K. Society for Promoting Christian Knowledge.

Sr (*Chem.*) strontium.

Sr. Sister; Senior.

S.R. self-raising (flour); State Registered (nurse).

S.R.N. State Registered Nurse.

S.S. steamship; Straits Settlements; Nazi German security police [Ger. *Schutz-Staffel* = 'defence corps'].

St. Saint; Strait; Street.

st. stone (weight); stanza.

Staffs. Staffordshire.

S.T.D. (*Telephone*) Subscriber Trunk Dialling.

sub. subaltern; submarine.

subst. substantive; substitute.

suf., suff. suffix.

supp. supplement.

Supt. Superintendent.

S.W. South West.

syn. synonym.

T. Telegraph; Telephone; Time; Transport; Temperature; Territory; Testament; Tuesday.

t. tempo; transitive; troy (weight); time; ton.

T.A. Territorial Army; telegraphic address.

tan. tangent.

taut. tautology.

T.B. tuberculosis; torpedo boat.

Tech. technical; technology.

tel. telegram; telephone.

Telstar television satellite.

temp. temperature; tempo; temporary.

Tenn. Tennessee (U.S.A.).

Ter(r). Terrace; Territory.
Tex. Texas (U.S.A.).
Th. Thomas; Thursday; Theology.
Thess. Thessalonians (N.T.).
Tim. Timothy (N.T.).
Tit. Titus (N.T.).
T.N.T. trinitrotoluene (explosive).
T.T. tuberculin tested; teetotal.
T.U.C. Trades Union Congress.
T.V. television.

U universal (film).
U. University; Union; United; Upper.
U.A.R. United Arab Republic.
U.D.I. unilateral declaration of independence (by Rhodesia in 1965).
U.H.F. ultra high frequency.
U.K. United Kingdom.
ult. in the preceding month [L. *ultimo*].
U.N.(O). United Nations (Organisation).
U.N.E.S.C.O. United Nations Educational, Scientific and Cultural Organisation.
U.N.I.C.E.F. United Nations International Children's Emergency Fund.
Univ. university; universal.
U.P. United Press (news agency).
U.S.A. United States of America
U.S.S.R. Union of Socialist Soviet Republics.
Utd. united.

V. volts; Victoria; victory; 5 (in Roman numerals).
v. against [L. *versus*]; see [L. *vide*]; verb; verse; vice- [L. *vice* = 'in place of']; volume.
Va. Virginia (U.S.A.).
Vat. Vatican
V.C. Victoria Cross.
V.D. venereal disease.
V.E. Victory in Europe.
Vet. veterinary surgeon.
V.H.F. very high frequency.
v.i. intransitive verb.
V.I.P. very important person.
vid. see [L. *vide*].
viz. namely [L. *videlicet*].
voc. vocative.
vol. volume.

vs. against; versus.
V.S.O.P. very special old pale.
Vt. Vermont (U.S.A.).
v.t. transitive verb.
Vul(g). Vulgate.
vv. verses.

W (*Chem.*) tungsten [L. *wolframium*].
W. West; Welsh; Women; (*Electr.*) wattage; (*Tech.*) total load.
w. wicket; wife; wide; width; with; wrong.
War. Warwickshire.
Wash. Washington (U.S.A.).
W.C. West Central; water-closet.
W.C.C. World Council of Churches.
W.H.O. World Health Organisation.
W.I. Women's Institute.
W.R.I. Women's Royal Institute.
Wilts. Wiltshire.
Wing-Cdr. Wing-Commander.
Wis. Wisconsin (U.S.A.)
Worcs. Worcester
W.R.A.C. Women's Royal Army Corps.
W.R.A.F. Women's Royal Air Force.
W.R.N.S. Women's Royal Naval Service.
wt. weight.
W.Va. West Virginia (U.S.A.).
Wyo. Wyoming (U.S.A.).

X. Christ (from Gk. initial X='Ch') 10 (in Roman numerals); cross.
x (*Math.*) unknown quantity.
Xmas Christmas.

yd. yard.
Y.H.A. Youth Hostels Association.
Y.M.C.A. Young Men's Christian Association.
Yorks. Yorkshire.
Y.W.C.A. Young Women's Christian Association.

z. zero; zone; atomic number.
Zech. Zechariah (O.T.).
Zn (*Chem.*) zinc.